Handbook of Research on Human–Computer Interfaces, Developments, and Applications

João Rodrigues
University of Algarve, Portugal

Pedro Cardoso
University of Algarve, Portugal

Jânio Monteiro
University of Algarve, Portugal

Mauro Figueiredo
University of Algarve, Portugal

A volume in the Advances in Human and Social
Aspects of Technology (AHSAT) Book Series

Published in the United States of America by
Information Science Reference (an imprint of IGI Global)
701 E. Chocolate Avenue
Hershey PA, USA 17033
Tel: 717-533-8845
Fax: 717-533-8661
E-mail: cust@igi-global.com
Web site: http://www.igi-global.com

Library of Congress Cataloging-in-Publication Data

Names: Rodrigues, Joao, 1971- editor.
Title: Handbook of research on human-computer interfaces, developments, and
   applications / Joao Rodrigues, Pedro Cardoso, Janio Monteiro, and Mauro
   Figueiredo, editors.
Description: Hershey, PA : Information Science Reference, [2016] | Includes
   bibliographical references and index.
Identifiers: LCCN 2016010958| ISBN 9781522504351 (hardcover) | ISBN
   9781522504368 (ebook)
Subjects: LCSH: User interfaces (Computer systems)--Handbooks, manuals, etc.
Classification: LCC QA76.9.U83 H35 2016 | DDC 005.4/37--dc23 LC record available at https://lccn.loc.gov/2016010958

This book is published in the IGI Global book series Advances in Human and Social Aspects of Technology (AHSAT) (ISSN: 2328-1316; eISSN: 2328-1324)

British Cataloguing in Publication Data
A Cataloguing in Publication record for this book is available from the British Library.

All work contributed to this book is new, previously-unpublished material. The views expressed in this book are those of the authors, but not necessarily of the publisher.

For electronic access to this publication, please contact: eresources@igi-global.com.

Advances in Human and Social Aspects of Technology (AHSAT) Book Series

Ashish Dwivedi
The University of Hull, UK

ISSN: 2328-1316
EISSN: 2328-1324

MISSION

In recent years, the societal impact of technology has been noted as we become increasingly more connected and are presented with more digital tools and devices. With the popularity of digital devices such as cell phones and tablets, it is crucial to consider the implications of our digital dependence and the presence of technology in our everyday lives.

The **Advances in Human and Social Aspects of Technology (AHSAT) Book Series** seeks to explore the ways in which society and human beings have been affected by technology and how the technological revolution has changed the way we conduct our lives as well as our behavior. The AHSAT book series aims to publish the most cutting-edge research on human behavior and interaction with technology and the ways in which the digital age is changing society.

COVERAGE

- Cyber Behavior
- Technology Dependence
- Human-Computer Interaction
- Cyber Bullying
- Technoself
- Philosophy of technology
- ICTs and social change
- Human Development and Technology
- End-User Computing
- Information ethics

IGI Global is currently accepting manuscripts for publication within this series. To submit a proposal for a volume in this series, please contact our Acquisition Editors at Acquisitions@igi-global.com or visit: http://www.igi-global.com/publish/.

Titles in this Series

For a list of additional titles in this series, please visit: www.igi-global.com

Defining Identity and the Changing Scope of Culture in the Digital Age
Alison Novak (Rowan University, USA) and Imaani Jamillah El-Burki (Lehigh University, USA)
Information Science Reference • copyright 2016 • 316pp • H/C (ISBN: 9781522502128) • US $185.00 (our price)

Gender Considerations in Online Consumption Behavior and Internet Use
Rebecca English (Queensland University of Technology, Australia) and Raechel Johns (University of Canberra, Australia)
Information Science Reference • copyright 2016 • 297pp • H/C (ISBN: 9781522500100) • US $165.00 (our price)

Analyzing Digital Discourse and Human Behavior in Modern Virtual Environments
Bobbe Gaines Baggio (American University, USA)
Information Science Reference • copyright 2016 • 320pp • H/C (ISBN: 9781466698994) • US $175.00 (our price)

Overcoming Gender Inequalities through Technology Integration
Joseph Wilson (University of Maiduguri, Nigeria) and Nuhu Diraso Gapsiso (University of Maiduguri, Nigeria)
Information Science Reference • copyright 2016 • 324pp • H/C (ISBN: 9781466697737) • US $185.00 (our price)

Cultural, Behavioral, and Social Considerations in Electronic Collaboration
Ayse Kok (Bogazici University, Turkey) and Hyunkyung Lee (Yonsei University, South Korea)
Business Science Reference • copyright 2016 • 374pp • H/C (ISBN: 9781466695566) • US $205.00 (our price)

Handbook of Research on Cultural and Economic Impacts of the Information Society
P.E. Thomas (Bharathiar University, India) M. Srihari (Bharathiar University, India) and Sandeep Kaur (Bharathiar University, India)
Information Science Reference • copyright 2015 • 618pp • H/C (ISBN: 9781466685987) • US $325.00 (our price)

Human Behavior, Psychology, and Social Interaction in the Digital Era
Anabela Mesquita (CICE – ISCAP/Polytechnic of Porto, Portugal & Algoritmi Centre, Minho University, Portugal) and Chia-Wen Tsai (Ming Chuan University, Taiwan)
Information Science Reference • copyright 2015 • 372pp • H/C (ISBN: 9781466684508) • US $200.00 (our price)

Rethinking Machine Ethics in the Age of Ubiquitous Technology
Jeffrey White (Korean Advanced Institute of Science and Technology, KAIST, South Korea) and Rick Searle (IEET, USA)
Information Science Reference • copyright 2015 • 331pp • H/C (ISBN: 9781466685925) • US $205.00 (our price)

www.igi-global.com

701 E. Chocolate Ave., Hershey, PA 17033
Order online at www.igi-global.com or call 717-533-8845 x100
To place a standing order for titles released in this series, contact: cust@igi-global.com
Mon-Fri 8:00 am - 5:00 pm (est) or fax 24 hours a day 717-533-8661

Editorial Advisory Board

List of Contributors

Table of Contents

Detailed Table of Contents

Progress and technological innovation achieved in recent years, particularly in the area of entertainment and games, have promoted the creation of more natural and intuitive human-computer interfaces. For example, natural interaction devices such as Microsoft Kinect allow users to explore a more expressive way of human-computer communication by recognizing body gestures. In this context, several Supervised Machine Learning techniques have been proposed to recognize gestures. However, scarce research works have focused on a comparative study of the behavior of these techniques. Therefore, this chapter presents an evaluation of 4 Machine Learning techniques by using the Microsoft Research Cambridge (MSRC-12) Kinect gesture dataset, which involves 30 people performing 12 different gestures. Accuracy was evaluated with different techniques obtaining correct-recognition rates close to 100% in some results. Briefly, the experiments performed in this chapter are likely to provide new insights into the application of Machine Learning technique to facilitate the task of gesture recognition.

In human communication, nonverbal information such as gestures and facial expressions often plays a greater role than language, and an increasing number of devices are designed to be intuitively controlled by gestures. However, there are some disadvantages of this intuitive interaction. One of the chief problems is that these devices have difficulty in distinguishing between unconscious and intentional gestures; they tend to respond erroneously to unconscious movements. In this chapter, authors propose a new gesture analysis method based on the dynamic model. They focused on the "exaggerated gestures" that are effectively used in, such as Japanese Kabuki, effectively used in Disney's animation, and tried to identify their common features and effects. They noted the "preparation" or "follow-through" motions just before and after the emphasized actions and each behavior can be quantified by the undershoot and overshoot value of changes in torque. These methods can provide important knowledge for analyzing features and distinguishing intentions when interacting with gestures.

Chapter 3

Beatriz Sousa Santos, Universidade de Aveiro, Portugal
João Cardoso, Universidade de Aveiro, Portugal
Beatriz Quintino Ferreira, Universidade de Aveiro, Portugal
Carlos Ferreira, Universidade de Aveiro, Portugal
Paulo Dias, Universidade de Aveiro, Portugal

Gesture-based 3D interaction has been considered a relevant research topic as it has a natural application in several scenarios. Yet, it presents several challenges due to its novelty and consequential lack of systematic development methodologies, as well as to inherent usability related problems. Moreover, it is not always obvious which are the most adequate and intuitive gestures, and users may use a variety of different gestures to perform similar actions. This chapter describes how spatial freehand gesture based navigation methods were developed to be used in virtual walkthroughs meant to be experienced in large displays using a depth sensor for gesture tracking. Several iterations of design, implementation, user tests, and controlled experiments performed as formative and summative evaluation to improve, validate, and compare the methods are presented and discussed.

Chapter 4

Pedro Cardoso, University of Algarve, Portugal
João Rodrigues, University of Algarve, Portugal
Jânio Monteiro, University of Algarve, Portugal
Luís Sousa, University of Algarve, Portugal

As computing equipment become ubiquitous, a new set of interfacing devices need to be developed and properly adapted to the conditions where this equipment is to be used. Interacting with machines might present difficulties relative to the handiness of common interfacing devices, when wearing certain clothes, doing certain dirty jobs, or when they are used by people with accessibility needs. In the last decades a new set of input devices were made available, including 3D sensors, which allow machine interacting without the need of touching any device. This chapter presents two prototype solutions supported by one of this 3D sensors, the Leap Motion, to manage appliances and other devices in a building and for the picking and loading of vehicles in a warehouse. The first case is contextualized in the area of the IoT and load scheduling of appliances, as a decisive factor in reduction of the buildings' electrical costs. The second case is presented as a solution to integrate the distribution of fresh and frozen goods where workers use thick clothes/gloves to carry out their work.

Accessibility for remote locations could be easily overcome by teleoperation. When manipulating an object at a remote place, it is beneficial if the operator is capable of feeling the force and position information including environmental object impedance for successful remote manipulation. In this chapter, bilateral control, based on acceleration architecture is explained from the basics starting from the human's haptic perception. The sensorless sensing mechanism "Reaction Torque Observer" is applied to the gripper which enables the operator to feel the remote environment while on remote manipulation. "Disturbance Observer" which is a popular control tool used to attain robustness is also successfully adopted for this application. Further, authors introduce force lock during bilateral teleoperation, which facilitate handling delicate objects. Practical as well as experimental results are discussed and the chapter concludes with suggestions for possible future research directions.

A major area of interest within the fields of human-computer interaction (HCI) and human-robot interaction (HRI) is user feedback. Previous work in HCI has investigated the effects of error feedback on task efficiency and error rates, yet, these studies have been mostly restricted to comparisons of inherently different feedback modalities, for example auditory and visual, and as such fail to acknowledge the many possible variations within each of these modalities, some of which being more effective than others. This chapter applies a user-centered approach to investigating feedback modalities for robot teleoperation by naïve users. It identifies the reasons why novice users need feedback when demonstrating novel behaviors to a teleoperated industrial robot and evaluates both various feedback modalities designed to prevent errors and, drawing on document design theory, studies different kinds of visual presentation regarding their effectiveness in the creation of legible error feedback screens.

In the globalized world, possessing good products may not be enough to reach potential clients unless creative marketing strategies are well delineated. In this context, public relations are also important when it comes to capture the client's attention, making the first contact between the clients and the company's products, while being persuasive enough to make them confident that the company has the right products to fit their needs. Three virtual public relations installations were purposed in this chapter, combining technology with a human like public relations ability, capable of interacting with potential clients located in front of the installation, at angles of up to 57° (degrees), 180° and 360°, respectively. From one to several Microsoft Kinects were used to develop the three interaction models, which allows tracking and recognition of users' gestures and positions (heat map), sound sources, voice commands and face and body extraction of the user interacting with the installation.

In this chapter, the authors discuss a unique technology known as the Sixth Sense Technology, highlighting the future opportunities of such technology in integrating the digital world with the real world. Challenges in implementing such technologies are also discussed along with a review of the different possible implementation approaches. This review is performed by exploring the different inventions in areas similar to the Sixth Sense Technology, namely augmented reality (AR), computer vision, image processing, gesture recognition, and artificial intelligence and then categorizing and comparing between them. Lastly, recommendations are discussed for improving such a unique technology that has the potential to create a new trend in human-computer interaction (HCI) in the coming years.

This chapter deals with the topic of Augmented Reality Mirrors (ARMs) – a kind of specular interfaces making use of Augmented Reality technology. The review presented in the chapter first analyses the current setups for the construction of ARMs. Secondly, it presents a study on their potential for inferring in human perception (e.g. behaviour and emotions) and the high interactivity potential and usability they have. In the third place, it shows their use in different areas of knowledge, namely entertainment, edutainment, clothing, arts and medical therapy. Then, the chapter presents a discussion, highlighting the current technological barriers and the need for more research. Finally, future challenges are provided.

Chapter 10

Pilgrimages and travel for other religious reasons are two of the major drivers of human mobility. Information and communication technologies (ICTs) can contribute to sharing knowledge about religious heritage with tourists, residents, and religious communities. ICT innovations that help individuals find information and acquire knowledge about cultural heritage can bring new experiences and sensations to tourists and residents, in general, and to those who have accessibility problems, in particular. These innovations include augmented reality, location-based services, social networks, gamification, and intelligent interfaces. This paper focuses on religious and spiritual routes and itineraries, presenting a religious tourism experience model that allows tourists to acquire additional knowledge about cultural and religious heritage, based on technological architecture using intelligent human-computer interactions displayed on personal mobile devices. This approach expands personal and spiritual experiences when travelers visit religious heritage sites associated with itineraries.

Chapter 11

Context aware systems strive to facilitate better usability through advanced devices, interfaces and systems in day to day activities. These systems offer smart service discovery, delivery and adaptation all based on the current context. A context aware system must gather the context prior to context inference. This gathered context is then stored in a tagged, platform independent format using Extensible Markup Language (XML) or Web Ontology Language (OWL). The hierarchy is enforced for fast lookup and contextual data organization. Researchers have proposed and implemented different contextual data organizations a large number of which has been reviewed in this chapter. The chapter also identifies the tactics of contextual data organizations as evident in the literature. A qualitative comparison of these structures is also carried out to provide reference to future research.

Chapter 12

Muhammad Nazrul Islam, Military Institute of Science and Technology, Bangladesh
Franck Tétard, Uppsala University, Sweden

Interface signs are the communication cues of web interfaces, through which users interact. Examples of interface signs are small images, navigational links, buttons and thumbnails. Although intuitive interface signs are crucial elements of a good user interface (UI), prior research ignored these in UI design and usability evaluation process. This chapter outlines how a design science research (DSR) approach is used to develop a Human-Computer Interaction (HCI) artifact (semiotic framework) for design and evaluation of user-intuitive web interface signs. This chapter describes how the principles and guidelines of DSR approach are adopted, while performing the activities of the DSR process model to construct the artifact.

Chapter 13

Titilola T. Obilade, Virginia Polytechnic Institute and State University, USA

The development of a user-friendly online module depends on the inputs, the processes and the outcomes from the user interface design, the learner interface design and the instructional design. The online module includes the user interface design, the learner interface and the instructional design. This chapter would examine the theories behind these three designs. What guidelines can be garnered from the theories of these three designs? How can these guidelines be used to develop a user-friendly online module? In addition, it would examine their similarities and how they can be used to develop a user-friendly online module. Further, the chapter recommended an alignment of the garnered guidelines from the three designs to explore the plausible reasons for the high attrition rate in Massive Open Online Courses (MOOC).

Chapter 14

Titilola T. Obilade, Virginia Polytechnic Institute and State University, USA

This chapter developed a framework for evaluating e-learning for use in Human Computer Interaction (HCI). A systems approach was used in the study; input, processes and output. It discussed the different assumptions about how people learn; behaviorism, cognitivism and constructivism. Further, it examined the common threads in the definitions of e-learning and the literature on evaluation of e-learning models. Nine categories of evaluation of e-learning were identified but five were reviewed because the remaining four overlapped. Two separate evaluations were reviewed under each category, making a total of ten reviews. The reviews showed that the evaluations were not conducted in the same way even within the same category making comparisons difficult. The framework was developed from the highlights in the review. The developed framework can be used to evaluate different e-learning modules along common lines making it easy to compare evaluations. It is hoped that over the next few years, a consistency in evaluations of e-learning would be achieved for use in HCI.

Vesna K. Spasojević Brkić, University of Belgrade, Serbia
Goran D. Putnik, University of Minho, Portugal
Zorica A. Veljkovic, University of Belgrade, Serbia
Vaibhav Shah, University of Minho, Portugal

Recent economic crisis has shown that classical approach to individual and local product oriented company is not sustainable in modern economic reality. Possible solution lies in high degrees of both specialization and flexibility product oriented small and medium-sized interchangeable production systems. According to that new wave, the main idea is based on exploring and testing of new possible designs and ways of control of human-computer interfaces for remote control of complex distributed manufacturing systems. Herein, the proposed remote system with Wall interface, video beam presentation mode and using group work enables producers in manufacturing sector to offer a product, through outsourcing manufacturing process and system in a global chain, utilizing ubiquitous computing systems and virtual and networked enterprises concepts, for anywhere-anytime control and give benefits to education sector, too, since students can dynamically interact with a real process to get a remote experimental practice, guaranteeing the availability of lab resource.

Luís Sousa, University of Algarve, Portugal
Mauro Figueiredo, University of Algarve, Portugal
Jânio Monteiro, University of Algarve, Portugal
José Bidarra, Universidade Aberta, Portugal
João Rodrigues, University of Algarve, Portugal
Pedro Cardoso, University of Algarve, Portugal

As Human Computer Interaction technologies evolve, they are supporting the generation of innovative solutions in a broad range of domains. Among them, Serious Games are defined as new type of computer game that is capable of stimulating users to learn, by playing and competing against themselves, against other users or against a computer application. While it could be applied to a broad range of fields and ages, these games are becoming especially relevant in educational contexts and for the most recent generation of students that is growing in a new technological environment, very different from the one we had some years ago. However, in order to become fully accepted as a teaching/learning tool in both formal and informal contexts, this technology has still to overcome several challenges. Given these considerations, this chapter makes a state-of-the-art review of several works that were done in this field, followed by the description of two real world projects, helping to understand the applicability of this technology, but also its inherent challenges.

Chapter 17

Assistive environments are primarily designed to support the healthy and independent living of ageing people. Elderly are often perceived as being resistant to technology; in reality, many of them are willing to accept novel digital technologies into their lives, and to take advantage of what technology has to offer. The "not worth it" impression, on the other hand, is more likely to be triggered by unusable interfaces, that prevent the older users from perceiving technology as both usable and useful. This motivates the need of investigating suitable guidelines for the design of user-system interfaces in the field of smart assistive environments, for which elderly are the typical target users. Focusing on two specific physical user-system interfaces, i.e. smart TVs and touchscreen devices, this chapter discusses the requirements that a design for older users has to address. The theoretical discussion is supported by experimental results gained from an Ambient Assisted Living project carried out by the authors, discussed as a use case in the last part of the chapter.

Stroke is the leading cause of disability that influences the quality of people's daily life. As such, an effective method is required for post-stroke rehabilitation. Research has shown that a robot is a good rehabilitation alternative where conventional robotic assistive system is encoded program by the robot expertise. The major drawback of this approach is that the lack of voluntary movement of the patient may affect the proficiency of the recovery process. Ideally, the robotic assistive system should recognize the intended movement and assist the patient to perform and make the training exercises more effective for recovery process. The electromyography based robotics assistive technology would enable the stroke patients to control the robot movement, according to the user's own strength of natural movement. This chapter briefly discusses the establishment of mathematical models based on artificial intelligent techniques that maps the surface electromyography (sEMG) signals to estimated joint torque of elbow for robotic assistive system.

In the 1990s, when immersive Virtual Reality (VR) was first popular, researchers found it to be an effective intervention in reducing acute pain. Since that time, VR technologies have been used for treating acute pain. Although the exact mechanism is unclear, VR is thought to be an especially effective form of pain distraction. While pain-related virtual environments have built upon pain distraction, a handful of researchers have focused on a more difficult challenge: VR for long-term chronic pain. Because the nature of chronic pain is complex, pharmacological analgesics are often insufficient or unsustainable as an ideal long-term treatment. In this chapter, the authors explore how VR can be used as a non-pharmacological adjuvant for chronic pain. Two paradigms for virtual environments built for addressing chronic pain have emerged – Pain Distraction and what we term Pain Self-modulation. We discuss VR's validation for mitigating pain in patients who have acute pain, for those with chronic pain, and for addressing "breakthrough" periods of higher pain in patients with chronic pain.

Chapter 20

Ayşegül Sağkaya Güngör, Işık University, Turkey
Tuğçe Ozansoy Çadırcı, Yıldız Technical University, Turkey
Şirin Gizem Köse, Yıldız Technical University, Turkey

Advergaming serves as a new and valuable form of online advertising, especially for companies that target young consumers. This study examines the impacts of cognitive overload with placement prominence on respondents' brand recall, recognition and brand attitudes. An experiment was conducted on a group of university students with an exposure to an advergame under low and high cognitive load stimulus. Results showed that brands that are placed prominently are better recalled in high cognitive load condition. However, cognitive overload doesn't have any significant effect on the recognition of the main brand in which the advergames is specifically designed. Moreover, there is no difference in recall of subtly placed products in low and high cognitive load conditions. However, there is a significant difference in brand attitude in different cognitive loads. The study both investigated the context of advergames and as well in-game advertising (IGA) situations. The results of the study have both practical and theoretical implications.

Chapter 21

Tiago Cinto, Telecommunications Research and Development Center, Brazil

It is estimated that 15% of the world's population has some sort of physical or sensory disability, according to the World Health Organization (2011). In an era marked by the rising of new technological devices, the inclusion of this public in digital environments still faces many obstacles, what frequently lets it out of this informational society. In this sense, Companhia Energética de Minas Gerais – CEMIG, one of the biggest Brazilian electrical energy utility company, has started to design and deploy a high-tech, user-friendly, inclusive customer service facility aimed at rendering a wide range of services by means of several gadgets such as self-service kiosks, tablets, and interactive panels and tables to help address the digital divide. For doing so, the applications to be developed and run on those devices need to be carefully studied and previously tested in order to meet the needs and expectations of the target audience. This paper describes the process of designing these innovative solutions to meet the demands of this new service channel.

Chapter 22

Massimiliano Zanin, Innaxis Foundation & Research Institute, Spain
David Papo, Universidad Politecnica de Madrid, Spain

The problem of identity assurance, i.e. determining if a claimed identity can be trusted, has been gaining relevance in the last decade, due to the increasing use of on-line services. While this trend can be seen for many biometric sensors, very few studies have considered the use of brain electric signals. This contribution proposes a first solution, based on the reconstruction of motifs (patterns of connectivity between three electroencephalographic sensors) and on the assessment of their stability across different trials for a single subject. Results indicate that, although computationally costly, this approach is promising in terms of the classification scores obtained.

Chapter 23

Fernando C. Monteiro, Polytechnic Institute of Bragança, Portugal
João Ribeiro, Polytechnic Institute of Bragança, Portugal
Ramiro Martins, Polytechnic Institute of Bragança, Portugal

Counting of bacterial colonies on agar plates is a routine practice to get a rough estimate of the number of viable cells in a sample. The number of colonies in a culture is predominantly manually counted to calculate the concentration of bacteria in the original broth; however, manual counting can be tedious, time-consuming and imprecise. Automation of colony counting has been of increasing interest for many decades, and these methods have been shown to be more consistent than manual counting. Significant limitations of many algorithms used in automated systems are their inability to recognize overlapping colonies as distinct and to count colonies on the plate boundary. This study proposes an interactive counting system and a fully automated system using image processing which overcomes these problems. The proposed system is capable to reduce the manpower and time required for counting while taking account colonies both around the central area and boundary areas of the dish. These systems are part of an application to count colonies based in a mobile phone camera.

Foreword

Since the development of the machine designed by Alan Turing to the present day, the human-computer interfaces have been progressing in various fields at the rate of use.

Initially, computers derived from Turing machine (1936), responded to mathematical needs and its applications focused just to the scientific field; and like almost every technological development was promoted to improve the war performance.

In this process, we generally recognize as some of the major milestones the Z1 (1938) by Konrad Zuse, the Harvard Mark I (1944) by Howard H. Aiken team, Colossus (1944) by Tommy Flowers, the ENIAC (1946) from the University of Pennsylvania, the binary EDVAC (1951) conceived by John von Neumann, the IBM 650 of serial production (1953) and the IBM 360 with integrated circuit boards (1964).

It is perhaps from this moment, that together with the development of processors and commercial microprocessors from Intel, advances in software and hardware introduced by Apple, IBM and Microsoft were added, allowing to extend the use of computer professionals in the applied sciences. These developments and massive applications, forced to think and devise better human-computer interfaces. Many of these ideas resulted in progress for the development of ergonomic keyboards, the integration of Mouse and logical software, which have not stopped until today.

However, it is crucial to analyze which other impacts have produced these advances in computers. In the domestic sphere, from the 80s interfaces and digital-logic processing were introduced into our daily lives, digital watches first, then the management of VHS video recorders. Subsequently the TV, audio equipment, mobile and dashboards of vehicles (90s); white line products and the remaining electrical appliances (early 2000s).

All the technical and scientific disciplines and professions from all the areas were progressing with the improvements offered by the development of new human-computer interfaces. At first, it was required hyper-specialization to operate the technologies in each discipline, however, at the present stage of development, each profession can take full advantage (and in an intuitive way) of the most advanced technologies to achieve the highest standards in their discipline work.

All the technical and scientific disciplines and all areas professions were progressing with the improvements were offering the development of new human-computer interfaces. Initially, hyper-specialization required to operate the technologies in each discipline, however at this stage of development, each profession can make the most (and intuitively) most disruptive technologies to achieve the highest standards in their work discipline.

The wealthiest socioeconomic segments of Generation X, were able to experience these advances from the different microcomputers and personal computers: Texas Instruments TI-99/4A (1981), Commodore 64 (1982), Microdigital TK 83 (1982), Sinclair ZX Spectrum (1982), Microdigital TK 85

(1983), IBM Personal Computer XT (1983), IBM Personal Computer / AT (1984), Apple Macintosh 128K (1984), Microdigital TK90X (1985), Commodore 128 (1985), IBM Personal System / 2 (1987), IBM PS / 1 (1990); gradually enjoying improvements in the speed, visual interfaces, the addition of color and sound, Mouse, TrackBall, TouchPad, camera, microphone, the several operational programs (software), among others.

At the present stage of development of human-computer interfaces, issues of the ongoing investigation by the different universities and centers of scientific and technological development show that the challenges are centered on readings and optical projections (2D, 3D and holographic) for its operation, the decoding of gestures, direction and focus of the eyes and various applications of these advances to improve the physical and visual ergonomics, the automation, education, e-government and public and private management.

In order for these progress achieved greater intensity and speed on its development, it is important to systematize the existing information, ideas, research and analysis of results. Other key is to spread the different digital resources to "connect the dots" as Steve P. Jobs (2005) said, to produce innovations, tangible improvements that society can take advantage and enjoy.

This Handbook of Research on Human-Computer Interfaces, Developments, and Applications, represents a commitment of researchers from different universities of the world, who want to improve the relationship between man and machine, looking for more people to use computer technology and thereby achieve greater welfare for the whole of society.

We are pleased to invite you to this exciting challenge, to discover what these researchers are thinking for our future, which successes they have achieved and what their next challenges will be.

We hope that readers can find "new dots" in this valuable compilation of articles, to develop new ideas, designs and innovations, which helps bring further progress in this interdisciplinary field.

Federico Del Giorgio Solfa
National University of La Plata, Argentina

Preface

Definitions of Human Computer Interaction (HCI) are quite easy to find. Most of those definitions state that HCI involves the manage, study, planning, design and uses of the interaction between humans (users) and computers, being often regarded as the intersection of computer science, behavioral sciences, design, media studies, and several other fields of study.

Given the above definition, it is quite easy to recognize that the boundaries of HCI are quite fuzzy. Historically, in a non-exhaustive overview, HCI evolved from a set of switches, to punched cards, keyboards, mouse pointers, etc., to the new platforms and most recent devices. Things are changing fast. The dialogs in the Stanley Kubrick (1968) "2001: A Space Odyssey" movie between the computer HAL 9000 and humans or the library host hologram in the Simon Wells (2002) "Time Machine" movie where the hologram communicates and interacts naturally with a time traveler, were once science fiction, but not anymore.

Currently most computers and mobile devices have the computational capacity and are equipped to mimic humans' skills like sight and hearing. With the appropriate sensors, those machines can even sense taste, smell, touch, balance, acceleration, temperature, etc. On the other hand, those "computer senses" (e.g., touch and gesture) can be used to control machines in a natural and intuitive way. There is an huge amount of sensors that can be used with that purpose, that range from the embedded cameras that exist in many of our devices, touch screens, mobile 3D sensors such as Structure Sensor, the Leap Motion, to the well-known and used Kinetic sensor from Microsoft.

The truth is that, as J. Jack from Microsoft states, HCI is a moving target. We expect the future of HCI to be supported on ubiquitous communication where computers communicate to give universal access to data and computational services, high functional systems where accessing those functionalities is natural, mass availability of computer graphics, high-bandwidth interaction, wide variety of displays (e.g., on large thin flexible/common surfaces), and embedded computation.

This book concentrates on Human Computer Interfaces, focusing mainly on the Interaction, and state of the art applications, research and trends, having in mind three major sub-areas: (a) Gesture interaction, (b) augmented reality, with special attention to applications in education, and (c) Assistive technologies, with a special emphasis in technologies related to navigation and wellness. Many of those sub-areas are crosswise, as the research and applications are being developed for recreation and for professional purposes. The themes will be spread between the different chapters showing that human computer interfaces and interaction is now and in the future one of the major subjects of study in the areas where humans are involved (bottom line: everywhere!). This book shows applications and research that goes from rehabilitation systems, education to holography and gamming. These are very different fields of research but, at the same time, very similar due to the necessity to interface the machine with humans.

The objective of the book is to bring together a comprehensive collection of research trends on HCI and interfaces from a set of international experts on research, design, evaluation, implementation and use of innovative technologies on the field. It is a book for the generic public, from policy makers, academicians, researchers, advanced-level students, technology developers, which are interested in the new trends in HCI and interfaces. We expect that actors in this huge area will find this text useful in furthering their research exposure to pertinent topics in HCI and assisting in furthering their own research efforts in this field.

Chapter 1 presents an evaluation of 4 Machine Learning techniques by using the Microsoft Research Cambridge (MSRC-12) Kinect gesture dataset. Accuracy was evaluated with different techniques obtaining very high correct-recognition rates. The performed experiments are likely to provide new insights into the application of Machine Learning technique to facilitate the task of gesture recognition. In Chapter 2 it is proposed a new analysis method based on the dynamic model which focuses on human communication. The authors selected a dozen of characteristic "exaggerated gestures" that are effectively used in our everyday lives, such as in Japanese Kabuki and Disney animation, and tried to identify their common effects.

In Chapter 3 it is described how spatial freehand gesture based navigation methods were developed to be used in virtual walkthroughs meant to be experienced in large displays using a depth sensor for gesture tracking. Chapter 4 offers two prototype solutions supported by the Leap Motion 3D sensor, to manage appliances and other devices in a building and for the picking and loading of vehicles in a warehouse. The first case is contextualized in the area of the Internet-of-things (IoT) and load scheduling of appliances, as a decisive factor in reduction of the buildings' electrical costs. The second case is presented as a solution to integrate the distribution of fresh and frozen goods where workers use thick clothes/gloves to carry out their work. Chapter 5 describes the implementation of a remote bilateral gripping architecture that enables the operator to feel the remote teleoperation environment, by communicating vivid sensations from the server side to the master side, through sensorless sensing techniques of Disturbance Observer (DOB) and Reaction Torque Observer (RTOB).

Chapter 6 applies a user-centered approach to investigating feedback modalities for robot teleoperation by naive users. In Chapter 7 are presented three virtual public relations installations, including a holographic installation, combining technology with a human like public relations ability, capable of interacting with potential clients located in front of the installations. Following, in Chapter 8 the authors discuss the Sixth Sense Technology, highlighting the future opportunities and challenges in implemented such technology in integrating the digital world with the real world.

Chapter 9 presents current setups for the construction of Augmented Reality Mirrors (ARMs) – a kind of specular interfaces that use of Augmented Reality technology. It also presents a study on their potential for inferring behaviours and emotions in human perception and shows their use in different areas of knowledge, namely entertainment, edutainment, clothing, arts and medical therapy. Chapter 10 presents a religious tourism experience model and methodology for religious and spiritual ways and itineraries development, in a way to get additional knowledge about the cultural, spiritual and religious heritage, in a technological itinerary, through a personal mobile device.

Chapter 11 focus on context aware systems which strive to facilitate better usability through advanced devices, interfaces and systems in day to day activities. These systems offer smart service discovery, delivery and adaptation, all based on the current context. In this sense, the chapter proposes and implements different contextual data organizations, identifying the tactics of contextual data organizations as evident in the literature. A qualitative comparison of these structures is also carried out to provide reference to future research. Following, Chapter 12 outlines how a design science (DSR) research approach is used to develop a Human-Computer Interaction artifact (semiotic framework) for design and evaluation of user-intuitive web interface signs. The chapter describes how the principles and guidelines of DSR approach are adopted, while performing the activities of the DSR process model to construct the artifact.

Chapter 13 examines the theories behind the user interface design, the learner interface design and the instructional design. It also shows guidelines that can be garnered from these designs theories to develop a user-friendly online module and to explore the plausible reasons for the high attrition rate in Massive Open Online Courses (MOOC). Chapter 14 presents the development a framework for evaluating e-learning for use in Human Computer Interaction (HCI). This framework can be used to evaluate different e-learning modules along common lines making it easy to compare evaluations. Making a contribution that over the next few years, a consistency in evaluations of e-learning would be achieved for use in HCI.

Chapter 15 describes the exploration and testing of new possible designs and ways of control of human-computer interfaces for remote control of complex distributed manufacturing systems. It is shown a remote system with Wall interface, video beam presentation mode and using group work to enable producers in manufacturing sector to offer a product, through outsourcing manufacturing process and system in a global chain, utilizing ubiquitous computing systems and virtual and networked enterprises concepts, for anywhere-anytime control. Chapter 16 explores Serious Games as a method of stimulating users to learn, by playing and competing against themselves, against other users or against a computer application. After presenting some developments they present two real world projects, that help the understanding of the applicability of this technology. In Chapter 17, the authors discuss the requirements that assistive environments have to address, when designed for older users. The theoretical discussion is complemented with experimental results gained from an Ambient Assisted Living project carried out by the authors, discussed as a use case.

In Chapter 18, the authors discuss the establishment of a robotic assistive system that can be used in post-stroke rehabilitation. In particular, they present the mathematical models based on artificial intelligent techniques that map the surface electromyography (sEMG) signals to estimate the joint torque of elbow. Using that information the resulting robotic assistive system recognizes the intended movement and assists the patient to perform and make the training exercises more effective. Chapter 19 describes how VR can be used as a non-pharmacological adjuvant for chronic pain. It is also presented two paradigms for virtual environments built for addressing chronic pain that have emerged – Pain Distraction and what we term Pain Self-modulation. Finally, this chapter discusses VR's validation for mitigating pain in patients who have acute pain, for those with chronic pain, and for addressing "breakthrough" periods of higher pain in patients with chronic pain. Following, in Chapter 20 focus its study on advergaming which serves as a new and valuable form of online advertising. The chapter examines the impacts of cognitive overload with placement prominence on respondents' brand recall, recognition and brand attitudes. The investigation both investigated the context of advergames and as well in-game advertising situations, with practical and theoretical implications.

In Chapter 21, the author addresses the design and development of an inclusive customer service facility, capable of supporting users with physical or sensory disabilities, in rendering a wide range of services, by means of several gadgets such as self-service kiosks, tablets, and interactive panels and tables. In Chapter 22, the authors address the challenge of identity assurance, using brain electric signals obtained from electroencephalographic sensors. They propose a first solution, based on the reconstruction of patterns of connectivity between three electroencephalographic sensors (or motifs) and on the assessment of their stability across different trials for a single subject. Chapter 23 presents a fully automated and an interactive semi-automated counting systems using computer vision to count the number of colonies in a Petri dish culture to reduce the time and avoiding inconsistencies that occur in manual counting of bacterial colonies.

João Rodrigues
University of Algarve, Portugal

Pedro Cardoso
University of Algarve, Portugal

Jânio Monteiro
University of Algarve, Portugal

Mauro Figueiredo
University of Algarve, Portugal

Acknowledgment

The authors would like to acknowledge their research centers, LARSyS (Laboratory of Robotics and Engineering System – FCT: UID/EEA/50009/2013), ISR-Lisbon (Institute for Systems and Robotics, CIAC-UAlg (Center for Research in Communication Sciences and Arts), INESC-ID, Lisbon (*Instituto de Engenharia de Sistemas e Computadores, Investigação e Desenvolvimento) and CIMA- UAlg (Center of Marine and Environmental Research*).

We specially would like also to thanks all the colleagues that help in the chapters' revision: Alvaro Soria, António Amaral, António Cunha, Beatriz Sousa Santos, Carlos Calafate, Célia Ramos, Fernando Belfo, Jaime Carvalho Martins, Ku Nurhanim Ku Abdul Rahim, Laercio Cruvinel, Laura Raffaeli, Maria Angeles Cifredo, Marisol Correia, Massimiliano Zanin, Mirian A. Cifredo-Chacón, Muhammad Islam, Nestor Tiglau, Norbert Krügger, Pandian Vasant, Paula Fernandes, R.M. Maheshi Ruwanthika, Susanna Spinsante, Tael Yi, Timothy Ganesan, Toshiya Naka, Tuğçe Ozansoy Çadırcı, Vesna Spasojevic Brkic, Xin Tong, and Zuzana Berger Haladova.

Chapter 1
A Comparative Study of Machine Learning Techniques for Gesture Recognition Using Kinect

Rodrigo Ibañez
ISISTAN (UNICEN-CONICET) Research Institute, Argentina

Alfredo Raul Teyseyre
ISISTAN (UNICEN-CONICET) Research Institute, Argentina

Alvaro Soria
ISISTAN (UNICEN-CONICET) Research Institute, Argentina

Luis Berdun
ISISTAN (UNICEN-CONICET) Research Institute, Argentina

Marcelo Ricardo Campo
ISISTAN (UNICEN-CONICET) Research Institute, Argentina

ABSTRACT

Progress and technological innovation achieved in recent years, particularly in the area of entertainment and games, have promoted the creation of more natural and intuitive human-computer interfaces. For example, natural interaction devices such as Microsoft Kinect allow users to explore a more expressive way of human-computer communication by recognizing body gestures. In this context, several Supervised Machine Learning techniques have been proposed to recognize gestures. However, scarce research works have focused on a comparative study of the behavior of these techniques. Therefore, this chapter presents an evaluation of 4 Machine Learning techniques by using the Microsoft Research Cambridge (MSRC-12) Kinect gesture dataset, which involves 30 people performing 12 different gestures. Accuracy was evaluated with different techniques obtaining correct-recognition rates close to 100% in some results. Briefly, the experiments performed in this chapter are likely to provide new insights into the application of Machine Learning technique to facilitate the task of gesture recognition.

DOI: 10.4018/978-1-5225-0435-1.ch001

INTRODUCTION

Recent progress in entertainment and gaming systems has brought more natural and intuitive human–computer interfaces to our lives. For example, 3D depth cameras, such as Xbox Kinect, enable the recognition of body gestures and allow a more direct and expressive way of interaction. Kinect allows players to control games through full-body movement without using a remote control. Moreover, Kinect has promoted the development of new natural interaction applications to many domains among larger audiences (e.g., art, education and health, among others).

Although Kinect is able to recognize the position of users' joints, developers are still left with the time-consuming and tedious task of recognizing gestures. In this sense, several approaches to recognize gestures easily have been proposed. The first applications were rule-based approaches that relied on a set of parameters and thresholds on body-part locations (e.g., "RightHand.y>Head.y + 0.5") to recognize simple movements. However, this kind of approach has become an error-prone process that requires domain knowledge, experience, and effort to ad hoc define a set of rules or heuristics to recognize human body gestures. Moreover, making rules to recognize complex gestures like a Smash in a tennis game becomes impractical (Ibañez, Soria, Teyseyre, & Campo, 2014).

In order to overcome these problems and provide a more flexible and robust mechanism to perform high-level gesture recognition, other approaches were proposed using Supervised Machine Learning (SML) techniques. These techniques require a set of labeled training gestures to learn and subsequently identify a new gesture as one of the learned gestures. For example, Bhattacharya, Czejdo, and Perez (2012) used Support Vector Machines (SVM) and Decision Trees (DT) for gesture recognition in a military application. Another successful approach is based on the Dynamic Time Warping algorithm (DTW) (Waithayanon & Aporntewan, 2011).

In this context, the aim of this chapter is twofold. First, a brief survey of current efforts on the application of SML techniques for gesture recognition is presented. Second, a comparative analysis of the performance of various state-of-the-art algorithms is performed. In particular, accuracy of well-known techniques used in Natural User Interaction is compared. The techniques involved in this chapter are Dynamic Time Warping (DTW) (Bhattacharya et al., 2012), Procrustes Analysis (Ross, 2004), Hidden Markov Models (Rabiner, 1990) and Naive Bayes (Russell & Norvig, 2009).

The remainder of this chapter is organized as follows. Section 2 presents an overview of related works. Section 3 describes a Machine Learning approach to gesture recognition and a description of the evaluated techniques. Section 4 discusses the experiments and results, along with the benefits and drawbacks of each technique. Finally, Section 5 presents the conclusions and identifies future lines of work.

BACKGROUND

In the literature, there are numerous approaches to gesture recognition from human body movements captured by video cameras. As mention in (Gavrila, 1999), the ability to recognize humans and their activities by vision is crucial for a machine to interact intelligently and effortlessly with a human-inhabited environment. Over the years, there has been strong interest in human movement from a wide variety of disciplines. In psychology, there have been the classic studies on human perception by Johansson (1973) or, in the hand gesture area, how humans use and interpret gestures (McNeill, 1992). In kinesiology the goal has been to develop models of the human body that explain how it works mechanically and how one might increase its movement efficiency (Calvert & Chapman, 1994). Computer graphics has dealt with the synthesis of human movement and some of the issues have been how to specify spatial interactions and high-level tasks for the human models; see (Badler, Phillips, & Webber, 1993; Badler & Smoliar, 1979; Magnenat-Thalmann & Thalmann, 1990). For a review of the state of the art in human movement recognition in general see (Gavrila, 1999; Aggarwal & Cai, 1999; Yu, Cheng, Cheng, & Zhou, 2004; Weinland, Ronfard, & Boyer, 2011; Turaga, Chellappa, Subrahmanian, & Udrea, 2008); for facial expressions see (Mitra, & Acharya, 2007); for hand gestures see (Pavlovic, Sharma, & Huang, 1997; Wachs, Kölsch, Stern, & Edan, 2011).

Despite these meaningful research efforts, accurate recognition of human body movements was found to be significantly difficult and challenging. Therefore, the development of natural interaction interfaces based on video cameras was found to be significantly difficult and therefore used mainly in certain specialized applications (Zhang, 2012). The broad availability of new 3D cameras, like Microsoft Kinect, has significantly changed this situation. This kind of cameras opens up new opportunities to improve recognition. In addition, these cameras promote the development of natural interaction applications in many domains among much larger audiences.

The Kinect Sensor incorporates several advanced sensing hardware. Specifically, it contains Red-Green-Blue camera, a depth sensor, a four-microphone array, and a processing module that provides full–body 3D motion capture, facial recognition, and voice recognition capabilities. This chapter focuses on the vision aspect and gesture recognition, see (Tashev, 2011) work for details on the audio component.

The depth sensor consists of an Infrared (IR) Projector combined with an IR Camera, which is a monochrome complementary metaloxide semiconductor (CMOS) sensor. Although the exact depth-sensing technology is not disclosed, it is based on the structured light principle. The IR projector is an IR laser that passes through a diffraction grating and turns into a set of IR dots, which are seen by the IR camera. Given that the relative geometry between the IR projector and the IR camera are known, as well as the projected IR dot pattern, if the Kinect sensor can match a dot in the projector pattern with a dot observed in an image, the Kinect sensor can reconstruct the dot in 3D by using triangulation.

The Kinect Sensor is able to estimate the position of several body parts. The sensor represents this part using the Kinect Skeletal Tracking (Microsoft, 2015b). In skeletal tracking, a human body is represented by a number of joints representing body parts such as head, neck, shoulders, and arms. Each joint is represented by its 3d Coordinates.

Skeletal Tracking is optimized to recognize users standing or sitting. To be recognized, users simply need to be in front of the sensor, making sure the sensor can see their head and upper body; no specific pose or calibration action needs to be taken for a user to be tracked. For a recent review of Kinect-based computer-vision algorithms and applications the reader can see (Han, Shao, Xu, & Shotton, 2013).

However, the previous information fails to be sufficient to recognize gestures. The Kinect sensor uses the skeletal tracking and calculates the position of 20 body joints in the 3D space. These positions are recalculated 30 times per second and stored in a structure called stick model. A stick model contains the positions (X, Y, Z) of the 20 body joints for a given time. Three different approaches with an increasing level of flexibility and robustness are used to tackle this problem: the Software Development Kit (SDK) stand-alone approach, the rule-based approach, and the supervised Machine Learning approach.

The SDK alone approach provides Application Programming Interfaces (APIs) to enable developers to access sensor data in real time. Some examples of this approach are Microsoft Kinect SDK (Microsoft, 2015a), OpenNI2 SDK (Occipital, 2015) and OpenKinect (OpenKinect, 2015, http://openkinect.org/).

When we work with the Kinect SDK we can access to two different types of datastreams, *Data Stream* and *Recognition Stream*. The *Data Streams* are basically the streams that the sensor can capture with its sensors like Color with the camera, Depth with the IR Emitter & receiver, audio, etc. The *Recognition Streams* are those who rely on the ones below them and process the data, for example if you want to use *FaceTracking* you will need to enable Color, Depth and Skeleton Tracking in order to enable *FaceTracking*.

You can find everything about Kinect SDK in the namespace Microsoft.Kinect (Microsoft, 2015c). In our opinion, the heart of the SDK are the following classes. The Kinect Sensor is represented by the object *KinectSensor,* we can enable Color, Depth, Skeletal for a sensor, change the angle with ElevationAngle, check what it is status, etc. As mentioned, the Sensor has three streams represented by the classes: *ColorImageStream, DepthImageStream* and *SkeletonStream*. These classes provide Frames with the data in it when the *OpenNextFrame* method is called. Although these APIs are considerably complete, they still demand significant efforts from developers to recognize ad-hoc gestures. Developers need to codify all the processes from the raw data obtained from the sensor so as to detect the intended gesture.

The rule-based approach relies on a set of parameters and thresholds on joint location to track movements (Suma, Lange, Rizzo, Krum, & Bolas, 2011; Kistler, Endrass, Damian, Dang, & Andre, 2012; Hachaj & Ogiela, 2013). With this approach, developers can specify a set of rules that describe the gesture, whereas the framework used helps the developer detect this gesture. Gestures are defined in a high level of abstraction; the developer does not have to know the mechanisms of low-level implementation.

For example, FAAST (Suma et al., 2011) supported the creation of gestures by allowing developers to adjust gestures sensibility by means of threshold values (e.g. "RightHand.y>Head.y + 0,5") and then to map these gestures to key and mouse events to control arbitrary applications via full body nature interaction. Another similar example is the FUBI Framework (Kistler et al., 2012), which describes a richer set of gestures by giving more complex configuration options in a XML-based definition language.

However, these approaches demand noticeable efforts from developers to ad hoc define and test a set of rules or heuristics in order to recognize human body gestures. In addition, these approaches failed to consider some aspects, such as different users' heights and positions within the detection field of Kinect, as well as different speeds and level of skills with which users move. Additionally, making rules to recognize complex gestures, such as a Smash in a tennis game, becomes impractical.

The supervised Machine Learning approach provides a more flexible and robust alternative, because it addresses gesture recognition as a classification problem (Weiland, Ronfard, & Boyer, 2011). In this context, a classification problem consists of assigning one label or a class to a gesture in such a way that it is consistent with available data about the problem. For dealing with a classification problem, Machine Learning techniques can be applied. These techniques use a gesture training set, in which each gesture is labeled to generate a classifier. Besides, this classifier evaluates the similarity between a new gesture and each of the trained gestures, resulting in the label of the most similar gesture.

As mentioned before, this work focuses on the supervised Machine Learning approach. Several attempts successfully adapted Machine Learning techniques to gesture recognition using Kinect's skeleton data; these techniques previously have been applied and extensively studied in the computer vision community. For example, Bhattachayra et al. (2012) applied Support Vector Machines (SVM) and Decision Trees (DT) to recognize aircraft gestures used in the Air Force. Similarly, Waithayanon and Aporntewan (2011) successfully applied an algorithm based on Dynamic Time Warping (DTW). In a related work, Fothergil, Mentis, Kohli, and Nowozin (2012) addressed the problem of collecting gesture datasets to improve the accuracy and performance of the gesture recognition system based on Machine Learning algorithms.

In Ibañez et al. (2014), a tool called EasyGR (Easy Gesture Recognition) that helps to reduce the effort involved in gesture recognition development, by using Machine Learning, was presented. EasyGR was evaluated in the development of a seven gesture recognizer, involving 10 developers. Metrics such as time consumed, code size, and the achieved quality of the developed gesture recognizers were compared, with and without the support of EasyGR. The results showed that the EasyGR approach was practical and reduced the effort involved in implementing gesture recognizers with Kinect.

To sum up, current Machine Learning approaches have been developed to solve a problem in a specific domain. However, few works have performed a comparative study that measures the accuracy of these approaches in the same domain. In this chapter, a comparison among four approaches used in Natural User Interaction is performed. To support the evaluation process described in this chapter, the EasyGR framework was used to develop each Machine Learning technique and the Microsoft Research Cambridge-12 (MSRC-12) dataset (Fothergill et al., 2012) was used to test each technique. The achieved results could help Kinect developers make a decision about selecting the most suitable technique to a particular domain and specific gestures.

GESTURE RECOGNITION AS A MACHINE LEARNING PROBLEM

Kinect identifies people inside its detection field, calculates the position of 20 body joints in the 3D space and stores the positions in a structure called stick model. A stick model contains the positions (X,Y,Z) of the 20 body joints for a given time. A sequence of successive stick models in a time interval represents the movement of the body parts. By analyzing these movements, a developer can recognize gestures and provides mechanisms to support natural interaction between humans and computers.

To support natural interaction mechanism, Machine Learning techniques have been analyzed in this chapter. Figure 1 shows a schematic view of a Machine Learning approach to recognize gestures with Kinect.

The Machine Learning approach consists of two phases: training and recognition. The training phase consists on feeding the recognition techniques with several samples of the gestures to be recognized. The phase starts when a person, playing the trainer role, performs movements in front of Kinect and the Kinect *Software Development Kit* (SDK) codifies and stores the movements as sequences of stick models in a gesture-training dataset. This procedure is repeated several times in order to obtain numerous samples of the gestures to be recognized.

Having the training dataset for the intended gestures, the next step of the phase is applying centering and normalizing transformations to each gesture sample so as to improve the recognition accuracy due to differences in body builds and locations within the Kinect detection field of the trainer and end users. The centering transformation moves the gesture sequences to the center of coordinates (0,0,0), whereas the normalizing transformation multiplies all the positions of the body joints by a scale factor based on the distance between the neck and the torso, which is relative to each person (Lai, Konrad, & Ishwar,2012). At this point, the approach trains the Machine Learning techniques and each technique manages the modified training dataset in order to adjust the acceptance threshold for each gesture.

Once the techniques have been trained, the recognition phase starts when a person, playing the user role, performs some of the trained gestures in front of Kinect. Then, the approach tries to recognize the performed gesture as one of the trained ones. To recognize the performed gesture, the approach follows the same steps as the training phase by normalizing and centering the sequence of stick models so as to

Figure 1. Schematic view of a Machine Learning approach to recognize gestures with Kinect

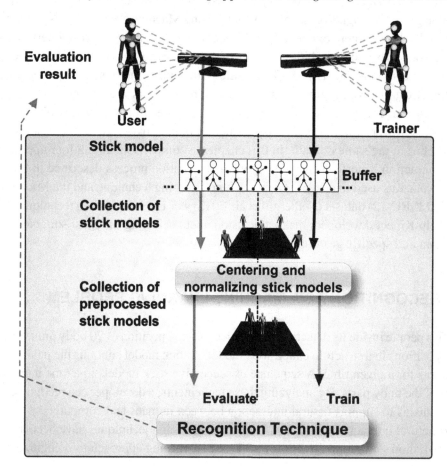

make it invariable to the body build and the position of the user within the detection. Here, instead of training the techniques, the approach evaluates the modified sequence on each of the techniques, compares the sequence of the performed gesture with the set of trained gestures, and presents the recognition result to the user.

It is worth pointing out that the Machine Learning techniques assessed in this chapter have been implemented in a prototype tool that facilitates the incorporation of new techniques and supports different variants of preprocessing capabilities for codifying stick models and comparing gestures. In the next sections, the techniques currently supported by the prototype, which will be used to evaluate their flexibility and viability in gesture recognition, are described.

Machine Learning Techniques to Recognize Gestures

Machine Learning techniques recognize gestures by comparing the trajectories that describe movements of the body joints. Trajectories that represent a gesture are used to compute the acceptance threshold of the gesture. The threshold depends on the Machine Learning technique and represents a value that determines whether a new gesture is similar enough to one of the trained gestures. In this chapter, techniques are grouped according to the way they use the trajectory: techniques that use the trajectory without any transformation and the techniques that applies a transformation to the trajectory before the training process.

To simplify the explanation of each technique, let's suppose that a Smash gesture, which is performed by the right hand, needs to be recognized. A Smash is a powerful downward hit that sends the ball forcefully over the net. Figure 2 shows six frames of a person performing the Smash gesture where each frame contains the stick model of the person which is represented by the 3D position **(x,y,z)** of the 20 body joints. The white joint indicates the position of the right hand in each frame, and the red line indicates the progression of this position in the performance of the Smash. The whole progression of the right hand (i.e., trajectory) is denoted as $T_{rhand}=(x_1,y_1,z_1)...(x_6,y_6,z_6)$. Let's also suppose that the techniques are able to recognize the gesture by analyzing only the trajectory of the right hand. Therefore, a set of training gestures has been stored in the training set and each gesture sample is represented by a sequence of stick models. At this point, the techniques process each trajectory of the right hand in the training set so as to determine the acceptance threshold for the Smash gesture. In particular, these samples should involve trajectories representing not only different ways of performing the same gesture but also different trainers with different body builds since the diversity of samples can improve the accuracy of the recognition techniques.

Figure 2. Sequence of stick models performing the Smash gesture

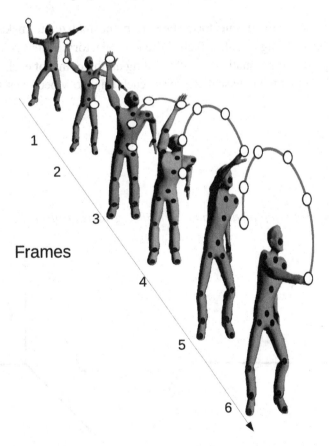

Preprocessing Trajectories

In order to make the trajectories suitable for comparison a preprocessing step is generally applied. This process is useful for improving the accuracy of the recognition by transforming the trajectories to make them invariant to the person's different positions and body builds. That is, the 3D position of the gesture trajectories can significantly vary since the trainers and the users may be in different positions within the Kinect detection field and may also have different body builds.

First, the collections of stick models are moved to the coordinate origin (0, 0, 0) as shown in Figure 3. In order to transform each trajectory, the Centroid is computed using Equation 1 and subtracted from each point of the trajectory using Equation 2, so that the new Centroid of the trajectory becomes the origin. The Centroid is a 3D point that represents the geometric center of the trajectory, and it is calculated by adding all the points of the trajectory and dividing the result by the number of points (i.e., n).

$$Centroid = (\bar{x}, \bar{y}, \bar{z}) = \frac{\sum_{i=1}^{n}(x_i, y_i, z_i)}{n} \tag{1}$$

$$(x_i, y_i, z_i)' = (x_i - \bar{x}, y_i - \bar{y}, z_i - \bar{z}) \tag{2}$$

Finally, at this point, the centered trajectories need to be normalized to make them invariant to the person's body build by calculating a scale s factor of each trajectory, which is a statistical measure of the size of the trajectory, by using Equation 3, and dividing all the points of each trajectory for the scale factor using Equation 4, so that the new scale factor of each trajectory becomes 1.

$$s = \sqrt{\frac{\sum_{i=1}^{n}(x_i, y_i, z_i)'^2}{n}} \tag{3}$$

Figure 3. Process of centering (left picture) and normalizing smash trajectories (right picture)

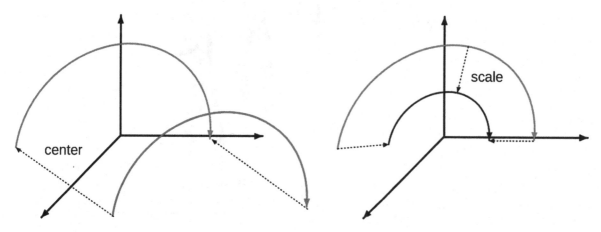

$$\left(x_i, y_i, z_i\right)'' = \left(\frac{x_i'}{s}, \frac{y_i'}{s}, \frac{z_i'}{s}\right) \tag{4}$$

Once all the collections of stick models are centered and normalized, they are ready for the training and recognition process.

Techniques That Are Applied Directly on the Trajectories of the Body Joints

The techniques described in this section are able to train and recognize gestures by directly using the positions of the body joints. The first technique supported is Dynamic Time Warping (DTW) (Salvador & Chan, 2007).

Dynamic Time Warping determines the similarity among gestures by analyzing the time series of the corresponding movements. In the context of gesture recognition, the series are represented by the trajectory points that describe each body joint. DTW optimally aligns the series by iteratively stretching and shrinking the time axis so as to minimize the distance between the series. These series represent the trajectories of the right hand in the previous example, and a distance value that measures the similarity between the trajectories is obtained by applying DTW. For example, Figure 4 shows the alignment of the y coordinate of the right hand between two smash gestures.

The second technique supported is Procrustes Analysis (Ross, 2004). Procrustes Analysis finds the optimal alignment between two shapes, modeled as a finite number of points, by applying a series of mathematical transformations that modify the shapes. In our context, these shapes represent the Smash trajectories, (i.e., the whole trajectory is represented as a static shape). Procrustes Analysis involves three specific transformations: centering, normalizing, and rotating the trajectory. The first two transformations are the same as those applied in the pre-processing step, whereas the last transformation entails rotat-

Figure 4. Time alignment between two smash gestures

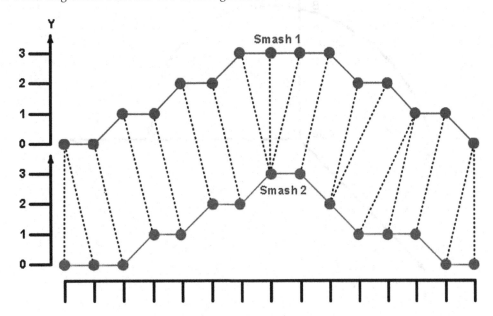

ing the trajectories until the minimum distance among them is obtained (see Figure 5). The minimum distance criterion is the sum of the Euclidean distances between each pair of points of the trajectory. The result of applying Procrustes Analysis is a distance value just like DTW.

Techniques That Requires Preprocessing of Trajectories Before to Be Applied

In this group, two techniques have been included: *Hidden Markov Models (HMM)* (Rabiner, 1990) and *Naïve Bayes* (Russell & Norvig, 2009). Both variants require trajectories to be encoded as finite-state sequences. Therefore, the k-means algorithm is applied to group the points of the Smash trajectories that belong to the same region in k clusters. To group these points, k-means assigns randomly all the points of the trajectories to one of the k clusters and calculates the Centroid of each cluster. The Centroid is a 3D point that represents the geometric center of the trajectory, and it is calculated by summing up all the points of the trajectory and dividing the result by the total number of points. Then, k-means evaluates all the points and reassigns each point to the cluster whose Centroid is nearest to it, according to Euclidean distance between the point and the cluster Centroid. Once all the points have been moved to the corresponding cluster, k-means recalculates the centroid of each cluster and repeats the process until no point movement is required, that is to say, all the points are in the correct cluster. Finally, as each point of the trajectory belongs to one Cluster, we use the identification number of the cluster to encode each training trajectory of the Smash gesture as a numeric sequence, where each number represents a state in which the right hand was located during the Smash performance. For example, Figure 6 shows the points of the smash before and after grouping them by using k-means with four clusters.

Figure 5. Process of rotating smash trajectory

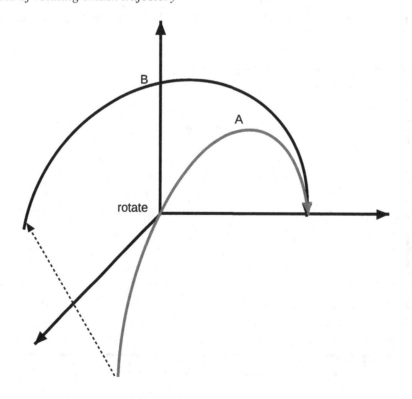

Figure 6. Process of grouping the smash trajectory by k-means

In particular, Naïve Bayes requires one more preprocessing step before being trained. The technique needs to be feed with sequences of the same length; therefore, the preprocessing procedure re-encodes each gesture by using the relative frequency of the numbers in the sequence, that is to say, the procedure counts all the points that belong to the same cluster and divides the result by the total number of points in the sequence. In this way, gestures are encoded as sequences of the same length, representing the number of centroids.

Once the trajectories are expressed as sequences of states and frequencies of states, they are used to feed each of the techniques. *Hidden Markov Models* are used to represent stateless stochastic-processes, but with unknown parameters, i.e., hidden states. Visually a *Hidden Markov Model* is a probabilistic finite-state machine, which is applied to solve three canonical problems: (1) given a trained model, *i.e.*, the states and the probabilities between them, find the probability of generating a specific sequence; (2) given a trained model, find the sequence of hidden states that generated an specific sequence; (3) given a set of sequences, find the transition probabilities between states. In the example, solution (3) is used to train the models, and when a new gesture is performed, the sequence corresponding to the right hand trajectory is evaluated with solution (1).

On the other hand, *Naïve Bayes* is a simple probabilistic classifier based on the Bayes' theorem with strong (naive) independence assumptions. A classifier is used to find a dependent variable or class based on some observed variables. The problem with this definition is that when the number of observed variables increases a model based on probability tables becomes infeasible. Therefore, the Bayes' theorem allows developers to decompose the conditional probability making the problem tractable. In this example, the sequences of relative frequencies are used to compute the variance and the mean assuming a normal distribution, which will be used to recognize new gestures.

Finally, training the techniques on the given training set generates an acceptance threshold for each trained gesture (*i.e.*, the Smash gesture). If the trained technique is DTW or Procrustes Analysis, the threshold indicates a distance, whereas if the trained technique is *Hidden Markov Model* or *Naïve Bayes* the threshold indicates a probability. In the first option, when a user performs a Smash gesture, the evaluation of trajectory of the right hand on the technique must be a distance shorter than the threshold; whereas, in the second option, the evaluation result must be a probability higher than the threshold to recognize the user gesture as a valid Smash gesture.

EXPERIMENTAL RESULTS

This section describes the experiments to assess the accuracy of different gesture-recognition techniques. To test these techniques experiments were conducted using the MSRC-12 dataset (Fothergill et al., 2012), which involves 30 people performing 12 different gestures. The demographics of the participants were

5'0"-6'6" high with an average of 5'8", and aged 22-65 with an average of 31 years of age. In order to pre-process this dataset each gesture instance was individualized and its correctness was checked using the EasyGR tool (Figure 7) (Ibañez et al.,2014). This tool allows non-specialist users to record, edit, and store gestures, enabling these users to easily create a new training set.

Once the dataset was split and its correctness was checked, a cross-validation strategy was applied to estimate the accuracy of the different techniques. In order to build a more realistic experiment, the cross-subject accuracy of the techniques was tested by partitioning the samples into 30 groups, each of which containing the gestures performed by each person. Twenty-nine groups were used for training and one group for testing the technique. The process was repeated 30 times with each of the 30 groups used exactly once as validation data for testing. For each iteration, not only was counted the number of correctly classified gestures, but also a confusion matrix was built to detect possible mislabeled classification of gestures and to perform a more detailed analysis than mere proportion of correct guesses. Finally, all the results from the folds were averaged to produce a single estimation.

Accuracy of the Different Techniques

To determine to what extent the number of different types of gestures used for training influenced the accuracy of the techniques, the number of concurrently recognized gestures was varied among 4 (680 samples), 6 (1020 samples), 8 (1360 samples), 10 (1693 samples) and 12 (2033 samples) different gestures. Particularly, for the techniques that use k-means, the experiments were run using 5 clusters for

Figure 7. EasyGR tool: Recording an smash

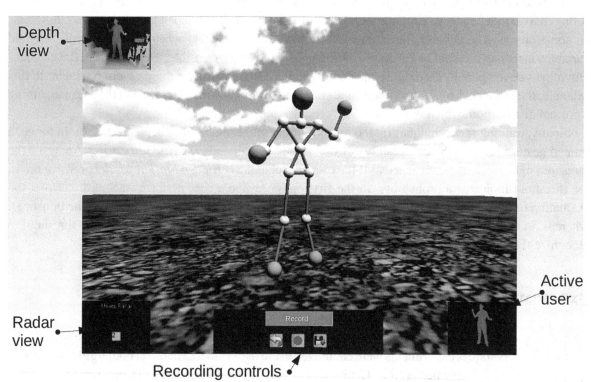

Hidden Markov Models (HMM-5) and 3 clusters for Naïve Bayes (NBA-3) because these number of clusters allow each technique to obtain the best accuracy.

Figure 8 illustrates the experimental results for DTW, Procrustes Analysis (PA), HMM-5, and NBA-3. From the chart, it can be observed that increasing the number of concurrently recognized gestures decreases the techniques' accuracy for almost all techniques. DTW and NBA-3 are the most resistant to this change. For example, DTW decreases the accuracy from 1 to 0.98 when the number of gestures increases from 4 to 12, whereas NBA-3 decreases the accuracy from 0.98 to 0.94 when the number of gestures increases from 4 to 12. On the other hand, HMM-5 and PA are the least resistant. Particularly, HMM-5 decreases the accuracy from 0.96 to 0.85 and PA decreases the accuracy from 0.99 to 0.82, when the number of gestures concurrently recognized increases from 4 to 12.

The confusion matrixes (DTW / Table 1, PA / Table 2, HMM-5 / Table 3 and NBA-3 / Table 4) help to visualize a more detailed analysis of the different techniques: when recognizing 12 different gestures concurrently. A confusion matrix shows how the predictions are made by the technique. In particular, the rows indicate the known type of gesture and the columns indicate the predictions made by the classifier. The value of each element in the matrix is the number of predictions made divided by the total number of tested gestures for each type, thus the sum of all the cell of each row must be 100%. All correct predictions are located along the diagonal of the Table, and the off-diagonal elements show the errors made. Note that the average of the values of the diagonal represents the accuracy of the technique. For most of the gestures, DTW and Naïve Bayes work very well. The classification errors occur if two gestures are too similar to each other. For example, DTW confuses G7 with G2; G7 involves performing a rever-

Figure 8. Graph that compares the number of gesture instances correctly classified for each technique depending on the number of different types of gestures used for training

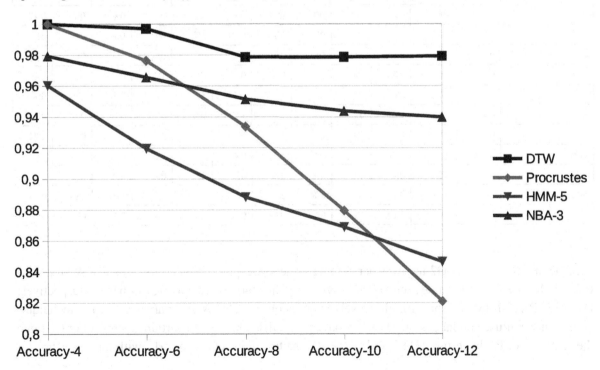

Table 1. Confusion Matrix of DTW for MSRC-12 dataset

	Dynamic Time Warping (precision: 0,98)											
	G1	G2	G3	G4	G5	G6	G7	G8	G9	G10	G11	G12
G1	96%	0%	0%	0%	2%	0%	0%	0%	2%	0%	0%	0%
G2	0%	99%	0%	0%	0%	0%	1%	0%	0%	0%	0%	0%
G3	0%	0%	100%	0%	0%	0%	0%	0%	0%	0%	0%	0%
G4	0%	0%	0%	100%	0%	0%	0%	0%	0%	0%	0%	0%
G5	0%	0%	0%	0%	100%	0%	0%	0%	0%	0%	0%	0%
G6	0%	0%	0%	0%	0%	100%	0%	0%	0%	0%	0%	0%
G7	0%	14%	0%	0%	0%	0%	86%	0%	0%	0%	0%	0%
G8	0%	0%	0%	0%	0%	0%	0%	100%	0%	0%	0%	0%
G9	0%	0%	0%	1%	0%	0%	0%	0%	99%	0%	0%	0%
G10	0%	0%	0%	0%	0%	1%	1%	0%	0%	98%	0%	0%
G11	0%	0%	0%	0%	0%	0%	0%	0%	0%	0%	100%	0%
G12	0%	3%	1%	0%	0%	0%	0%	0%	0%	0%	0%	96%

Table 2. Confusion Matrix of PA for MSRC-12 dataset

	Procrustes Analysis (precision: 0,82)											
	G1	G2	G3	G4	G5	G6	G7	G8	G9	G10	G11	G12
G1	94%	0%	0%	0%	0%	0%	0%	0%	4%	0%	2%	0%
G2	0%	100%	0%	0%	0%	0%	0%	0%	0%	0%	0%	0%
G3	0%	0%	99%	0%	0%	0%	0%	1%	0%	0%	0%	0%
G4	0%	0%	0%	92%	0%	2%	0%	0%	0%	6%	0%	0%
G5	0%	0%	0%	1%	90%	0%	0%	0%	7%	0%	1%	1%
G6	0%	1%	0%	10%	0%	81%	1%	5%	0%	2%	0%	0%
G7	0%	19%	0%	0%	0%	0%	81%	0%	0%	0%	0%	0%
G8	0%	0%	0%	0%	0%	3%	0%	65%	0%	9%	0%	23%
G9	3%	0%	14%	0%	0%	0%	0%	0%	82%	0%	1%	0%
G10	0%	0%	0%	0%	0%	2%	0%	23%	0%	72%	2%	1%
G11	11%	1%	9%	4%	8%	2%	0%	1%	3%	17%	44%	0%
G12	0%	0%	3%	1%	0%	0%	0%	5%	0%	5%	0%	86%

ence flexing the legs, and G2 involves performing a squat. Despite of few confusions, DTW and Naïve Bayes still shows an acceptable accuracy, achieving 98% and 94% correct recognition rates, respectively. However, PA and HMM-5 show a higher level of confusions than DTW and Naïve Bayes. The techniques do not only confuse similar gestures but also have problems to recognize certain gestures. For example, the accuracy of PA in gesture G11 is only 44% and the technique confuses G11 with many gestures.

Table 3. Confusion Matrix of Hidden Markov Models for MSRC-12 dataset

	G1	G2	G3	G4	G5	G6	G7	G8	G9	G10	G11	G12
Hidden Markov Models (precision: 0,847)												
G1	88%	0%	0%	0%	0%	0%	1%	0%	1%	0%	1%	9%
G2	0%	89%	0%	0%	0%	0%	4%	0%	0%	0%	0%	7%
G3	0%	0%	94%	0%	0%	0%	2%	0%	0%	0%	0%	4%
G4	0%	0%	0%	79%	0%	13%	0%	0%	1%	3%	1%	3%
G5	0%	1%	0%	0%	84%	0%	1%	0%	0%	0%	0%	14%
G6	0%	0%	0%	1%	0%	76%	0%	0%	0%	5%	0%	18%
G7	0%	4%	0%	0%	0%	0%	91%	0%	0%	0%	0%	5%
G8	0%	1%	0%	0%	0%	0%	1%	82%	0%	1%	0%	15%
G9	3%	0%	0%	0%	0%	0%	0%	0%	81%	0%	2%	14%
G10	0%	0%	0%	0%	0%	3%	0%	0%	0%	85%	0%	12%
G11	0%	0%	0%	0%	0%	0%	2%	0%	0%	0%	81%	17%
G12	4%	0%	0%	0%	0%	4%	1%	0%	0%	6%	0%	85%

Table 4. Confusion Matrix of Naïve Bayes for MSRC-12 dataset

	G1	G2	G3	G4	G5	G6	G7	G8	G9	G10	G11	G12
Naïve Bayes (precision:0,940)												
G1	97%	0%	0%	0%	1%	0%	0%	0%	1%	0%	1%	0%
G2	0%	92%	0%	0%	0%	1%	7%	0%	0%	0%	0%	0%
G3	0%	0%	99%	0%	0%	0%	0%	1%	0%	0%	0%	0%
G4	0%	0%	0%	89%	0%	5%	1%	0%	0%	4%	1%	0%
G5	0%	0%	0%	0%	99%	0%	1%	0%	0%	0%	0%	0%
G6	0%	0%	0%	5%	0%	90%	0%	1%	0%	4%	0%	0%
G7	0%	1%	1%	0%	0%	0%	98%	0%	0%	0%	0%	0%
G8	0%	0%	0%	0%	0%	0%	0%	98%	0%	2%	0%	0%
G9	0%	0%	0%	0%	1%	0%	0%	0%	95%	3%	1%	0%
G10	0%	0%	0%	1%	7%	1%	4%	2%	1%	84%	0%	0%
G11	0%	0%	0%	0%	0%	0%	1%	0%	4%	0%	95%	0%
G12	0%	0%	1%	0%	0%	1%	0%	1%	0%	6%	0%	91%

Accuracy of the Different Techniques Varying the Number of Samples Used for Training

To determine to what extent the number of samples used for training influenced the techniques' accuracy, the number of samples was varied among 1, 3, 5, and 6 samples by person for each gesture. Figures 9,10,11,12 respectively illustrate the experimental results for DTW, PA, HMM-5 and NBA-3. The

Figure 9. Graph that compares the number of gestures correctly classified for DTW depending on the number of samples and gestures used for training

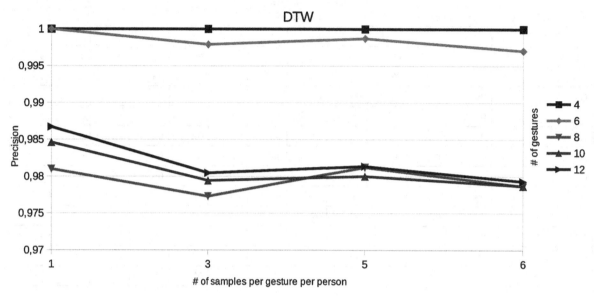

Figure 10. Graph that compares the number of gestures correctly classified for Procrustes Analysis depending on the number of samples and gestures used for training

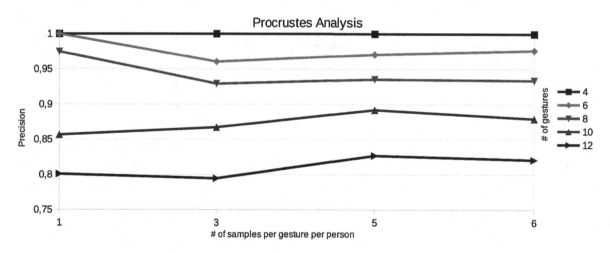

number of samples is listed along the horizontal axis, whereas the technique's accuracy is listed along the vertical axis. From the charts, it can be seen that increasing the number of samples clearly improves the HMM-5's accuracy from 42% to 84.7% and the NBA-3's accuracy from 88% to 94%, whereas the other techniques' accuracy remains nearly invariable.

DTW clearly obtained best recognition rates even with only one sample for person for each gesture. In particular, when the number of samples increases from 1 to 6 samples a minimal reduction in accuracy was observed (0,74%) due to more variations in sample gestures.

Figure 11. Graph that compares the number of gestures correctly classified for HMM-5 depending on the number of samples and gestures used for training

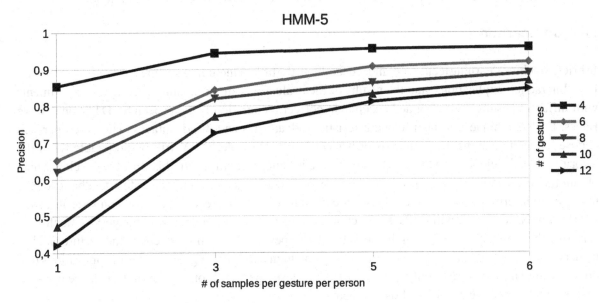

Figure 12. Graph that compares the number of gestures correctly classified for NBA-3 depending on the number of samples and gestures used for training

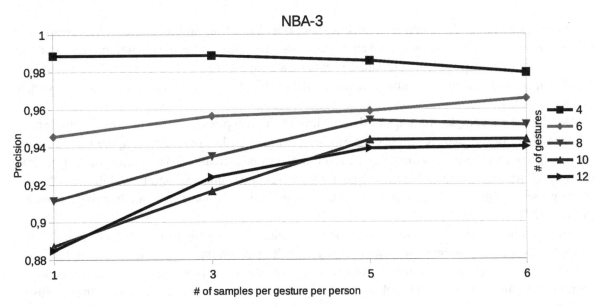

In addition, PA performed very well for a low number of different gestures even for few samples. However, when the number of different gestures increased the accuracy decreased as showed in the previous section.

In particular, HMM-5 was the technique that demanded more samples to improve accuracy. For example, HMM-5 scored the lowest accuracy with one sample, but when the number of samples increased to 6 HMM-5 obtained an accuracy of 84% for all number of gestures.

Finally, NBA-3 is also concerned with the number of samples to improve accuracy but in the same way as HMM-5. Indeed, NBA-3 was able to reach 88% of accuracy with only one sample.

Lesson Learned

In brief, Machine Learning techniques indeed facilitate the task of including gesture recognition in Natural User Interaction applications, and the results of the evaluations are promising. During the experiments with different gestures, we obtained acceptable correct-recognition rates, especially DTW and Naïve Bayes. Each technique has specific characteristics, advantages and disadvantages. The developer will choose the technique that best suits his or her needs. For example, DTW will be preferable when the priority of the developer is to know how the gesture is being recognized. In this way, the developer may obtain the distance from a new-user trajectory to the model trajectory and generate a feedback for the user, i.e., to inform the user how to improve the movement. Instead, techniques based on k-means, such as HMM or Naïve Bayes, will be the better choice if the application needs to vary the gesture fidelity by selecting the number of clusters. In this way, the developer may be willing to reduce the gesture fidelity by decreasing the number of clusters in order to obtain high correct-recognition rates in applications that do not require high gesture fidelity. In such cases, the developer is responsible to find a balance between gesture fidelity and the usability of the application.

FUTURE RESEARCH DIRECTIONS

Recent progress in 3D depth cameras, such as Microsoft Kinect, has promoted the visual analysis of human movements. This low-cost innovative technology has allowed for developing more natural and intuitive interactive applications. The authors' experience aligns with the idea of providing flexible and robust Supervised Machine Learning techniques that enable the design of more intelligent or human-like applications.

Despite the encouraging findings of the viability of these approaches described in the chapter, the following lines of research are still open questions. First, a multi-level game can require that users perform the game gestures more accurate as the levels of the game increases. To be supported by a machine learning approach, developers have to create different sets of gestures that suit user skills at each stage of the game. As future work, it is worth working on alternatives to adapt machine learning techniques to user's skills.

Another line of research worth pursuing is incorporating information of human movements from multiple cameras so as to improve gesture recognition. Relying on one-camera information introduces some limitations such as constrained movements, segmentation or processing speed. These limitations decrease the robustness of the 3D tracking results. To achieve higher precision of 3D tracking, the fusion of multiple cameras tracking information can improve the gesture recognition process. A multi-camera approach can help to disambiguate gestures (movements or body poses) that are ambiguous from the vision of only one camera. Therefore, the challenge here is how to calibrate multiple cameras and fusion multiple-stick models coming from different cameras so that the machine learning techniques can be able to reduce occlusion problems.

A related future research direction is augmenting the capability of the machine learning techniques to be able to discriminate between stand-along gestures and collaboration among people or interactions with objects. For example, a gesture-based application to teach two people how to perform a partner dance such as Tango should be able to determine whether the movements of the partners follow the dance rules in order to help them correct the way they are dancing. Nowadays, the approach presented in this chapter can recognize whether each partner is performing the intended movement in a correct way. However, developers are in charge of providing the specific code for assessing the correct interaction among partners. In this context, further studies on how to combine gestures of two or more partners in one learning model are an interesting line of future work.

CONCLUSION

This chapter presents an analysis of whether the use of Machine Learning techniques is a viable alternative for recognizing gestures with Kinect. Particularly, Dynamic Time Warping, Procrustes Analysis, Naïve Bayes and Hidden Markov Models have been evaluated in recognizing body gestures, based on the positions of the body joint provided by Kinect. The results have showed that DTW (Dynamic Time Warping), HMM (Hidden Markov Models) and Naïve Bayes obtained accuracies of 99,1%, 98,9% and 98,0% respectively, whereas Procrustes Analysis only obtained an accuracy of 81,2%. The results have also showed that DTW and Naïve Bayes were the most resistant-to-change techniques as the number of gesture simultaneously recognized increased, whereas Procrustes Analysis was the most affected achieving an accuracy of 82%. In addition, as the number of samples in the training set increases, the accuracy of all the techniques increases, except for DTW; DTW only required one sample of each gesture to reach its peak. These findings will be useful as a cornerstone for further studies to determine how the machine learning technique can be used to build more intelligent gesture-based applications.

From the experience of the aforementioned learning techniques, the issues that still remain to be further analyzed consist in obtaining the time required for each technique to be trained and be able to recognize a gesture. Additional studies are needed to investigate how the number of gestures to be recognized simultaneously impacts on the time required by a technique to decide whether a gesture is recognized. This way, developers would be able to determine the techniques best suitable to be used in real time. Finally, new experiments with a large and varied number of gestures, and other AI techniques such as Support Vector Machine and Decision Trees, could provide new insights into the application of Machine Learning technique to facilitate gesture recognition.

REFERENCES

Aggarwal, J., & Cai, Q. (1999). Human motion analysis: A review. *Computer Vision and Image Understanding*, *73*(3), 428–440. doi:10.1006/cviu.1998.0744

Badler, N., Phillips, C., & Webber, B. (1993). *Simulating Humans*. Oxford: Oxford Univ. Press.

Badler, N., & Smoliar, S. (1979). Digital representations of human movement. *ACM Computing Surveys*, *11*(1), 19–38. doi:10.1145/356757.356760

Bhattacharya, S., Czejdo, B., & Perez, N. (2012). Gesture classification with machine learning using Kinect sensor data. *Proceedings of the 2012 Third International Conference on Emerging Applications of Information Technology EAIT* (pp. 348-351). doi:10.1109/EAIT.2012.6407958

Calvert, T., & Chapman, A. (1994). Analysis and synthesis of human movement. In T. Young (Ed.), *Handbook of Pattern Recognition and Image Processing: Computer Vision* (pp. 432–474). San Diego: Academic Press.

Fothergill, S., Mentis, H., Kohli, P., & Nowozin, S. (2012). Instructing people for training gestural interactive systems.*Proceedings of the SIGCHI Conference on Human Factors in Computing Systems, CHI '12* (pp. 1737-1746).New York, NY, USA. ACM. doi:10.1145/2207676.2208303

Gavrila, D. M. (1999). The visual analysis of human movement: A survey. *Computer Vision and Image Understanding, 73*(1), 82–98. doi:10.1006/cviu.1998.0716

Hachaj, T., & Ogiela, M. (2013). Computer karate trainer in tasks of personal and homeland security defense. In A. Cuzzocrea, C. Kittl, D. Simos, E. Weippl, L. Xu (Eds.), Security Engineering and Intelligence Informatics, LNCS (Vol. 8128 pp. 430–441). Springer. doi:10.1007/978-3-642-40588-4_30

Han, J., Shao, L., Xu, D., & Shotton, J. (2013). Enhanced computer vision with Microsoft Kinect sensor: A review.. *IEEE Transactions on Cybernetics, 43*(5), 1318–1334. PMID:23807480

Ibañez, R., Soria, A., Teyseyre, A., & Campo, M. (2014). Easy gesture recognition for Kinect. *Advances in Engineering Software, 76*(0), 171–180. doi:10.1016/j.advengsoft.2014.07.005

Johansson, G. (1973) Visual perception of biological motion and a model for its analysis, *Perception Psychophys., 14*(2), 201–211.

Kistler, F., Endrass, B., Damian, I., Dang, C., & André, E. (2012). Natural interaction with culturally adaptive virtual characters. *Journal on Multimodal User Interfaces, 6*(1-2), 39–47. doi:10.1007/s12193-011-0087-z

Lai, K., Konrad, J., & Ishwar, P. (2012). A gesture-driven computer interface using Kinect. *Proceedings of the IEEE Southwest Symposium on Image Analysis and Interpretation (SSIAI)* (pp. 185-188).

Magnenat-Thalmann, N., & Thalmann, D. (1990). Human modeling and animation. In *Computer Animation* (pp. 129–149). Berlin, New York: Springer-Verlag. doi:10.1007/978-4-431-68105-2_10

McNeill, D. (1992). *Hand and Mind—What Gestures Reveal about Thought*. Chicago, London: The University of Chicago Press.

Microsoft. (2015a). Kinect Windows app Development. Retrieved from https://dev.windows.com/en-us/kinect

Microsoft. (2015b). Kinect Skeletal Tracking. Retrieved from https://msdn.microsoft.com/en-us/library/hh973074.aspx

Microsoft. (2015c). Microsoft. Kinect Namespace. Retrieved from https://msdn.microsoft.com/en-us/library/hh855419.aspx

Mitra, S., & Acharya, T. (2007). Gesture recognition: A survey. *IEEE Transactions on Systems, Man, and Cybernetics, Part C: Applications and Reviews, 37*(3), 311–324.

Occipital (2015). OpenNI 2 Downloads and Documentation | The Structure Sensor. Retrieved from http://structure.io/openni

OpenKinect. (2015). Retrieved from http://openkinect.org

Pavlovic, V., Sharma, R., & Huang, T. (1997). Visual interpretation of hand gestures for human-computer interaction: A review. *IEEE Transactions on Pattern Analysis and Machine Intelligence, 19*(7), 677–695. doi:10.1109/34.598226

Rabiner, L. R. (1990). *A tutorial on hidden Markov models and selected applications in speech recognition*. In *Readings in speech recognition* (pp. 267–296). San Francisco, CA, USA: Morgan Kaufmann Publishers Inc. doi:10.1016/B978-0-08-051584-7.50027-9

Ross, A. (2004). *Procrustes analysis (Course report)*. Department of Computer Science and Engineering, University of South Carolina.

Russell, S., & Norvig, P. (2009). Artificial Intelligence: A Modern Approach (3rd ed.). Prentice Hall Press.

Salvador, S., & Chan, P. (2007). Toward accurate dynamic time warping in linear time and space. *Intelligent Data Analysis, 11*(5), 561–580.

Suma, E., Lange, B., Rizzo, A., Krum, D., & Bolas, M. (2011). Faast: The flexible action and articulated skeleton toolkit. *Proceedings of the Virtual Reality Conference* (pp. 247-248). doi:10.1109/VR.2011.5759491

Tashev I. (2011). Recent Advances in Human-Machine Interfaces for Gaming and Entertainment. *Int'l J. Information Technology and Security*, 3(3), 69-76.

Turaga, P., Chellappa, R., Subrahmanian, V. S., & Udrea, O. (2008). Machine recognition of human activities: A survey. *IEEE Transactions on Circuits and Systems for Video Technology, 18*(11), 1473–1488.

Wachs, J. P. J., Kölsch, M., Stern, H., & Edan, Y. (2011). Vision-based hand-gesture applications. *Communications of the ACM, 54*(2), 60–71. doi:10.1145/1897816.1897838 PMID:21984822

Waithayanon, C., & Aporntewan, C. (2011). A motion classifier for Microsoft Kinect. *Proceedings of the 2011 6th International Conference on Computer Sciences and Convergence Information Technology (ICCIT)* (pp. 727-731).

Weinland, D., Ronfard, R., & Boyer, E. (2011). A survey of vision-based methods for action representation, segmentation and recognition. *Computer Vision and Image Understanding, 115*(2), 224–241. doi:10.1016/j.cviu.2010.10.002

Yu, Q., Cheng, H. H., Cheng, W. W., & Zhou, X. (2004). Opencv for interactive open architecture computer vision. *Advances in Engineering Software, 35*(8-9), 527–536. doi:10.1016/j.advengsoft.2004.05.003

Zhang, Z. (2012). *Microsoft Kinect sensor and its effect. Multimedia* (pp. 4–10). IEEE.

KEY TERMS AND DEFINITIONS

Gesture Recognition: A topic in computer science and language technology with the goal of interpreting human gestures via mathematical algorithms.

Kinect: A line of motion sensing input devices by Microsoft for Xbox 360 and Xbox One video game consoles and Windows PCs (codenamed in development as Project Natal).

Machine Learning: A subfield of computer science that evolved from the study of pattern recognition and computational learning theory in artificial intelligence.

Motion Detection: The process of detecting a change in the position of an object relative to its surroundings or a change in the surroundings relative to an object. Motion detection can be achieved by either mechanical or electronic methods.

Pattern Recognition: A branch of machine learning that focuses on the recognition of patterns and regularities in data; in some cases, considered to be nearly synonymous with machine learning.

Skeletal Tracking: A model used to represent the human body as number of joints representing body parts such as head, neck, shoulders, and arms.

Stick Model: The model used by the Kinect Sensor to represent the positions (X, Y, Z) of the 20 body joints for a given time.

Supervised Learning: The machine learning task of inferring a function from labeled training data that consist of a set of training examples.

Chapter 2
Dynamic Motion Analysis of Gesture Interaction

Toshiya Naka
Kyoto University, Japan

Toru Ishida
Kyoto University, Japan

ABSTRACT

In human communication, nonverbal information such as gestures and facial expressions often plays a greater role than language, and an increasing number of devices are designed to be intuitively controlled by gestures. However, there are some disadvantages of this intuitive interaction. One of the chief problems is that these devices have difficulty in distinguishing between unconscious and intentional gestures; they tend to respond erroneously to unconscious movements. In this chapter, authors propose a new gesture analysis method based on the dynamic model. They focused on the "exaggerated gestures" that are effectively used in, such as Japanese Kabuki, effectively used in Disney's animation, and tried to identify their common features and effects. They noted the "preparation" or "follow-through" motions just before and after the emphasized actions and each behavior can be quantified by the undershoot and overshoot value of changes in torque. These methods can provide important knowledge for analyzing features and distinguishing intentions when interacting with gestures.

INTRODUCTION

In face-to-face human communication, nonverbal information such as gestures, eye contact and facial expressions, often plays a greater role than language, and it is well known that gestures serve as a major channel for revealing true feelings within human communication. For instance, Mehrabian (1981) derived the conclusions in his previous researches that about eighty percentage of message was pertaining to feelings and attitudes, and Knapp et al (2013) clarified the effects of gesture, posture, face and eye behavior on human communication and revealed how these nonverbal signals can affect to interact successfully. We frequently use gestures unconsciously, such as waving our hand when we say goodbye and beckoning with the hand when we want someone to come to us. Moreover, in designing the user

DOI: 10.4018/978-1-5225-0435-1.ch002

interface of many types of the latest large screen display and mobile devices, intuitiveness and simplicity are very important factors, and interaction with gestures has been an excellent choice as a method for enabling the easy use of such products. However, there are some disadvantages of this kind of intuitive interaction; one of the chief problems with gesture-based interaction is that these devices find it difficult to distinguish reliably between unconscious and intentional gestures: they tend to respond erroneously to unconscious movements, which impedes successful interaction. The typical reason is that many gestures contain not only movements but also comprise several emotions. Generally, there has been numerous researches of human behaviors in such fields as gesture recognition, for instance Gavrila (1999) summarized the work on the various methodologies for gesture recognition, Baur et al (2015) discussed about the outcome of interpersonal interactions depends not only on the contents that we communicate verbally but also on nonverbal social signals. Bulling et al (2014) provided the hands-on introduction to the field of human activity of recognition, specifically focuses on the activity recognition using on-body inertial sensors. Also the mechanical analysis of human motions has been actively studied in such fields of sports kinematics, Putnam (2003) discussed the segment motion sequences are dependent not only on a knowledge of the joint moments driving the system of linked segments but on the way the segments interact as functions of their motions and orientations, and Hansenab et al (2015) examined the role of rotation axes during an overarm throwing ball task, and found that the minimum inertia axis would be exploited during the throwing phases. Furthermore, in the field of biological cybernetics, Zelic et al (2015) suggested that the speech articulators for syllable uttered, making the speech performance more receptive to environmental forces, resulting in the greater entrainment observed to gesture oscillations.

Additionally, many studies of motion analysis of gesture were designed to examine the human communications. For examples, Cassell et al (1994) proposed an implemented system which automatically generates and animates conversations between multiple human-like agents with appropriate and synchronized speech, intonation, facial expressions and hand gestures, and mentioned that conversation is created by a dialogue planner that produces the text as well as the intonation of the utterances, and Siegman and Feldstein (2014) discussed the role of body movement in communication and action in human interactions. The difficulty of research in this area is that many communication gestures are not simply movements but actually contain several human emotions, so there remain a number of barriers in quantifying such ambiguous human factors.

In this chapter, the author will discuss the importance of nonverbal cues in human communication via the following approach to quantify the function of gesture interactions especially those including emotions, and would like to start the discussion by giving a basic definition of the dynamic model for analyzing the effects of some special "exaggerated gestures" used in contexts such as Japanese *Bunraku* and *Kabuki* (Wood & Hamilton, 2010) and effectively used in dance and *Disney's* animation; see *Disney's* twelve basic principles of animation (Thomas & Ollie, 1997) which are expressing the special emotions (Truong et al. 2015), and try to model their common features as a first approach. Most people frequently accompany these "exaggerated gestures" when wishing to clearly communicate their true message. In the researchers' previous works (Naka et al, 2014), they tried to clarify the dynamic mechanisms of the certain characteristic behaviors and revealed that some special gestures were quantified by the torque values of elements of the human skeletal model. We human tend to apply forces to the required portion of our arms and body for emphasized actions; therefore, it is possible to quantify the dynamic effects in terms of the torque applied to each joint. By selecting hundreds of characteristic gestures and applying them to their proposed model, authors found that it could represent the degree of exaggeration in a quantitative manner, and discovered that their model was applicable to the speaker's emphasized movements in speeches or presentations for attracting the audience's attention (rhetorical emphasis). There was a close correlation between the intended gesture and the applied torques.

In the second half of this chapter, authors will apply their gesture analytical method to specifically identify intentional motion. In these days, it is well known that an increasing number of devices are designed to be controlled by gestures. However, there remain issues with regard to reliably distinguishing between unconscious and intentional gestures. As a solution to this problem, the authors made the following hypothesis that we humans tend to add "preparation" or "follow-through" motions just before and after an "execution" motion (Pyke, 2013) and each behavior will be distinguished by using the undershoot or overshoot value of torque changes with high precision. Then, it is possible to detect the variation in the twisting torque generated at locations such as the shoulder, elbow and wrist joints, and there is a high possibility that a system adopting this method can distinguish between a conscious manipulation and unconscious operation. From some series of experimental results, they revealed that their proposed methods have a potential to solve some important problems facing gesture interaction and to design the best gesture-based interfaces. The next section presents the background about the significance of their researches, gesture recognition technologies and gesture based communication analysis methods.

BACKGROUND

Gesture is a means of nonverbal communication in which visible body actions communicate particular messages or emotional feelings, and it includes movement of the hands, face or other parts of the body. In this chapter, the authors would mainly focus on gestures of full-body motions among such information. One of the goals of gesture analysis is to interpret human motions and even internal intentions via sensing biological information and mathematical algorithms, also to design easy-to-use human interface which allows user interact naturally without any mechanical devices.

With respect to the gesture recognition devices, there are many types of system for any purpose, such as stereoscopic camera, depth camera and gyro sensing which are normally provided with devices having GUIs (graphical user interface). They allow users to perform as such operations as selecting some items on a display or moving the item by intuitively making a hand movement indicating the changes of GUIs. For examples, the PrimeSense (2010) has developed a system that uses an infrared projector, camera and a special microchip to track the movement of objects and individuals in three dimensions, and the Microsoft Kinect (2015) adopted the technology to power its popular Kinect controller for the Xbox 360 game console along with this technology. The Leap Motion (2015) is a device explicitly targeted for hand gesture recognition and provides only a limited set of relevant points and the Google's Soli (2015) is grand new gesture technology which is used radar with a high positional accuracy, and would pick up on slight movements without ever touching the device itself. These gesture input devices are able to provide user to intuitively control the pointer or item on GUI by means of his or her body movement. With regard to these devices, Chen et al (2013) provided a survey of the advantages of depth imagery and the research on the use of depth images for analyzing human. Generally, gesture input devices do not require users to take special training as required in the conventional input devices such as keyboard, and provide an advantageous effect of allowing any user to perform intended operations.

Furthermore, in gesture based interaction, user need to move a pointer according to the hand movement when user extends his or her index finger or select an item indicated by the pointer when such as folds the index finger to fold hand and these operations depend on accurate recognition of the shapes of hands. In the research on these gesture recognition issues, Rautaray & Agrawal (2015) discussed briefly the use of hand gestures as a natural interface in gesture taxonomies, its representations and recognition techniques, software platforms and frameworks, Panwar (2012) presented a real time system for hand gesture recognition on the basis of detection of some meaningful shape based features like orientation, center of mass, status of fingers, thumb in terms of raised or folded fingers of hand and their respective location in image, and Meng et al (2012) proposed a new approach for hand gesture recognition that is accomplished by dominant points based hand finger counting under skin color extraction.

On the other hand, gesture movements may be made unintentionally when users naturally move his or her hands and body in daily life, in other words many gestures contain not only intended movements but also the several unconscious or emotional motions, and it is usually very difficult to distinguish both natural and intentional ones. With respect to the methods for sensing human intentions or emotions via biomedical signs, the fMRI (functional neuroimaging procedure using MRI, 2014) is the most typical technology that measures brain activity by detecting changes associated with blood flow. However, the device is too bulky and less versatility, alternative simple and tiny sensing methods have been proposed in nowadays. For instance, NeuroSky (2011) is a wearable EEG (electroencephalography) biosensor system that detects the brainwave to estimate physiological stress. Q Sensor (Grifantini, 2010) is worn on a wristband and lets user keep track of stress by measuring slight electrical changes in the skin during everyday activities. But as mentioned before, these techniques also have the problems that they are difficult to enable operations using natural and simple body movements and to reliably prevent erroneous operations at the same time. Moreover, they have the basic defects which must be worn on the body, so they are not only cumbersome for the subjects but also having a difficulty to sense the natural emotions. In view of these, this chapter aimed to elucidate the mechanism of motions mathematically and provide the gesture interaction which is capable of controlling using a natural and simple body movement with both reducing erroneous operations and non-invasive simple way.

As the first goal of the research, the authors developed a method to analyze the intentional motion which was captured by the simple and non-invasive sensing methods using the motion capture devices such as Kinect (2105), Prime (PrimeSense, 2014) and VICON (2014). About the gesture analysis methods, many researches are presented such as Kristianslund et al (2012) who quantified the effect of joint moments by calculating the same or different cut-off frequency for the filtering of force and movement data, Georgescu et al (2013) determined the differential contributions of the AON (action observation network) and SNN (social neural network) to the processing of nonverbal behavior as observed in dyadic social interactions, Bronzino and Peterson (2014) provided the comprehensive coverage of physiological systems, biomechanics, bioelectric phenomena and neuroengineering and Robertson et al (2014) presented the new researches detailing advanced analytical tools for investigating human movement.

Unlike these many conventional analysis methods of the emotional motion which were using the biological information and analysis algorithms, the authors focused on the special gestures named "exaggerated gestures" in which the intentional feeling appeared so clearly, and tried to build a common behavior modeling. To deal with the problem, authors put the three hypotheses that 1) the degree of exaggeration will have a high correlation with the relating joints dynamics. In previous studies on the dynamic model, Charlesa et al (2011) provided an experimentally based mathematical model of wrist rotation dynamics in FE (flexion-extension) and RUD (radial-ulnar deviation), and characterized the torques required to overcome the passive mechanical impedance of wrist rotations, Kristianslund et al

(2012) concluded that the force and movement data should be processed with the same filter, and Holle et al (2012) indicated how other aspects of gesture such as emphasis, influence the interpretation of the syntactic relations in a spoken message. However, these conventional models were limited to the specific purpose, and the generic gesture analysis model was not presented.

From the results of preliminary experiments (Naka et al, 2014), then the authors found that these emphasized gestures were frequently used in such as Japanese *Bunraku* and *Kabuki* (Wood & Hamilton, 2010), the special gestures effectively used in dance (Wodehouse & Sheridan, 2014) and *Disney's* animation (Thomas & Ollie, 1997). Further the author made the second hypothesis that 2) these models will have some commonality with some emphasizing actions which used in the speeches or human interactions effectively (rhetorical emphasis). And if the exaggerated gesture is represented by a unified simple model and can be reproduced in accordance with the hypothesis, there will be an important effect in designing the emotional interfaces which is possible to exceed the "uncanny valley". This is Mori's (2015) hypothesis states that as the appearance of a robot is made more human, some observers' emotional response to the robot will become increasingly positive and empathic, until a point is reached beyond which the response quickly becomes that of strong revulsion. However, as the robot's appearance continues to become less distinguishable from that of a being, the emotional response becomes positive once again and approaches human-to-human empathy levels. In other words, user friendly interaction will be able to be reproduced by the well-balanced exaggerated behavior which is conforming to the proposed dynamical model. In the first half of the chapter will be discussed about the dynamic model of the exaggerated gestures in more detail.

In the second half of this chapter, the researchers would like to apply their gesture analysis method to solve the chief problems of gesture-based interaction which is difficult to distinguish between unconscious and intentional gestures; they tend to respond erroneously to unconscious movements. The third hypothesis is put that 3) if some intentions of human will be expressed in such as emphasis operations consciously, they can be measured in the dynamics of behavior. In terms of emotional gesture, there are many researches such as Meijer (1989) pointed out that emotional movement was determined by seven general dimensions: trunk movement, arm movement, vertical direction, sagittal direction, force, velocity and directness and Razuri et al (2015) presented an approach that could predict six basic universal emotions collected by responses linked to human body poses, from a computational perspective. However, these proposals also have the disadvantage of lack of versatility. To solve this problem, authors tried to apply their exaggeration model for identifying unconscious and intentional motions. As they mentioned before, we humans tend to add "preparation" or "follow-through" motions just before or after the intentional ones (Pyke, 2013), and each behavior can be distinguished by using dynamical changes with high precision. From numerous series of experimental results, they confirmed that many systems adopting this method have a high possibility to distinguish between a conscious manipulation and unconscious close-approximation gesture operation.

The advantageous effects of the proposals in this chapter are that these methods are able to analyze human gestures by using dynamic analysis from only a simple and non-invasive motion tracking data, without any ambiguous biological sensing. Moreover, these proposed dynamical model is simple and applicable for not only the general motion analysis but also the wide range of designing the human friendly interactions, such as distinguish between a conscious and unconscious manipulation by applying dynamical exaggeration rules.

DEFINITION OF GESTURE ANALYSIS MODEL

In this section, the author will define the dynamic model and algorithm in order to accurately analyze gestures. As often used in fields such as robotics, human poses and gestures can be expressed by a) the hierarchical structure and b) each parameter of the hierarchical link model shown in Figure 1. Human's body is typically built as a series of nested joints, each of which may have a link associated with it. The joint labelled *humanoid root* is not technically considered a "joint" but is used for positioning the humanoid in space, facing in the +Z direction with +Y up and +X to the humanoid's left (ISO/IE, 2005). In this chapter, the nodes of the fingers are all omitted for simplify a description but they only have to add the fifteen hierarchical figure joints similarly with the body, in the case of analyzing the hands motions.

Dynamic Analysis of Gestures

Once the structure of a human is defined by using this hierarchical model, any gestures can be quantitatively expressed by the rotational angles of time-series around x, y and z axes (local coordinate system) of each joint. Generally, torque τ which is generated at each joint, can be obtained by the motion equation 2-1 using the joint angle θ. This method is termed *kinematics* and has hitherto been used chiefly in the field of robotics. In this equation, θ is each joint's rotational angle as the time-series data set such as $(\theta_1, \theta_2, \cdots \theta_n)$, is the inertia matrix, C is the *Coriolis force*, g is the gravity term and $d\theta/dt$ and $d^2\theta/dt^2$ represent the angular velocity and angular acceleration of each joint, respectively.

$$\tau = M(\theta)\frac{d^2,}{dt^2} + C\left(\theta, \frac{d,}{dt}\right)\frac{d,}{dt} + g(\theta) \tag{2.1}$$

Figure 1. Hierarchical skeletal model and definition of links (H-Anim)

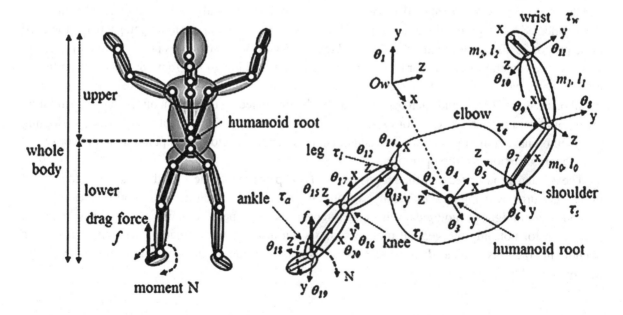

Since this equation is the general formula of the dynamic model, they have to calculate the torque τ using *Lagrange functions* in the following approach (Mochizuki et al, 2000; Naka et al, 2014). In analysis mechanics, *Lagrangian L* of the link structure is defined by equation 2-2, and the equation of motion Q_i is given by the following equation 2-3 using L, when we expressed equation 2-1 of the generalized coordinate system. Using these dynamic equations, they can show the relationship between gestures expressed by θ and the torque variation τ of each joint.

$$L = \sum_{0 < i < n} \{(\textit{Kinetic} \text{ energy of link } i)\text{-}(\textit{Potential} \text{ energy of link } i)\} \tag{2.2}$$

$$Q_i = \frac{d}{dt}\left(\frac{\partial L}{\partial,'_i}\right) - \frac{\partial L}{\partial,_i} \text{ where } i = 0 \sim n \tag{2.3}$$

Furthermore, the equation of motion Q_i can be described by the following non-linear ordinary differential equation 2-4. In this equation, the first term is the angular velocity, the second term shows the *Coriolis* and centrifugal forces, and the third term is gravity. In the case of a rotational movement, Q_i turns into torque τ, which arises at each joint, and T_j shows the conversion matrix which translates into the world coordinate system from the local coordinate of the j-th joint, J_j is the inertia tensor of j-th link and m_i shows the mass of i-th link, g^T is the gravity vector and S_j expresses the position vector at the center of gravity of the j-th link.

$$Q_i = \sum_{j=i}^{n}\sum_{k=0}^{j} trace\left[\frac{\partial T_j}{\partial \theta_k} J_j \frac{\partial T_j}{\partial \theta_i}\right]\frac{d^2,_k}{dt^2} + \sum_{j=i}^{n}\sum_{k=0}^{j}\sum_{l=0}^{j} trace\left[\frac{\partial_2 T_j}{\partial \theta_l \partial \theta_k} J_j \frac{\partial T_j}{\partial \theta_i}\right]\frac{d^2,_k}{dt^2}\frac{d^2,_l}{dt^2}$$

$$-\sum_{j=i}^{n} m_j g^T \frac{\partial T_j}{\partial,_i} S_j \text{ where } i = 0 \sim n \tag{2.4}$$

More generally, humans have to support their upper body and balance their motion with their legs, so it is necessary to consider all the links from the feet to the hands, shown as solid colored links in Figure 1 to accurately analyze gestures. In this case, the feet also need to be regarded as external forces, such as drag and friction forces f and N from the floor as shown figure 2.

$$\tau = J\,_{\ni})^T\begin{pmatrix} f \\ N \end{pmatrix} \tag{2.5}$$

In equation 2-5, f is the drag force acting on the feet, and N represents the moment around the legs. Furthermore, J is the *Jacobian matrix* for θ_i in the general coordinate system. The above equation is the general formula for numerical analysis of gestures. In this chapter, when calculating the inertia tensor J_i, we estimate that each link is approximated with the elliptic cylinder, therefore the density distribution

Figure 2. Model of considering external forces such as drag and friction forces f and N from the floor and approximate each link

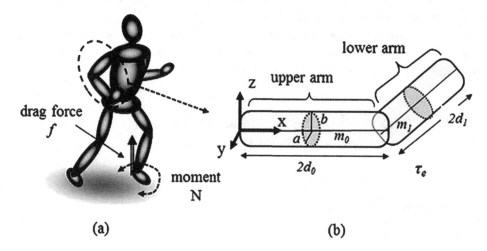

(a)   (b)

inside of each link sets are constant as shown in figure 2 b). Additionally, they estimate that d_{mp} is the minute mass at the point (mass center of gravity at each link is the point x_p, y_p, z_p in the local coordinate system) in the rigid body, then inertia tensor H of the circumference of the center of gravity at each link can be denoted by equation 2-6.

$$H = \begin{bmatrix} I_{xx} & I_{xy} & I_{xz} \\ I_{yx} & I_{yy} & I_{yz} \\ I_{zx} & I_{zy} & I_{zz} \end{bmatrix}$$

(2.6)

Where

$$I_{xx} \int \left(y_p^2 + z_p^2 \right) dm_p, I_{yy} = \int \left(z_p^2 + x_p^2 \right) dm_p, I_{zz} = \int \left(x_p^2 + y_p^2 \right) dm_p,$$
$$I_{xy} = I_{yx} = \int x_p y_p dm_p, \quad I_{yz} = I_{zy} = \int y_p z_p dm_p, \quad I_{zx} = I_{xz} = \int z_p x_p dm_p$$

If they approximate each link such as an elliptic cylinder, the inertia procession J will be given by equation 2-7. In this case, the length of the elliptic cylinder shall be 2d and the center of gravity is at the starting point, and further, the length direction is defined by the x-axis, and the y-axis and z-axis intersect with each other perpendicularly, and their lengths are set to a and b, respectively.

$$J = \begin{bmatrix} d^2m/3 & 0 & 0 & d/2 \\ 0 & a^2m/2 & 0 & 0 \\ 0 & 0 & b^2m/2 & 0 \\ d/2 & 0 & 0 & 1 \end{bmatrix}$$

(2.7)

In addition, in order to accurately determine the degree of emphasis of each motion, they used both the maximum and minimum values of the torque change and total amount of torque values T_{total}, which is integrated in the time period at each motion, and able to distinguish either the intentional or natural actions shown in equation 2-8. In this equation, j shows the number of the main joints that contribute to generate the gesture, and t_s and t_e indicate the start and end times, respectively.

$$T_{total} = \int_{ts}^{te} \sum_{j=1}^{m} \left(\frac{d\ddot{A}_j}{dt} \right)^2 dt \tag{2.8}$$

Exaggerated Gesture Model

Most people accompany verbal information with exaggerated gestures when wishing to clearly communicate their message, and there is the tendency to apply forces to required areas such as the arms and body for these actions. Therefore, the authors believed that it was possible to quantify these effects by the torque and its changes that were applied to each joint. In figure 3, the researchers showed the basic concept of the hand gesture analysis model, in this case depicted by an overhead view of the right hand. When they are instructed to move accurately and quickly to the target position (destination) from the starting point, or when in case of gesture conversation accompanied with exaggeration, the "preparation" and "follow-through" motions are usually added just before or after the start t_s and the target position t_d "execution", and these motions will finally converge with a subtle vibration. In other words, there is a tendency by which the more we try to make our gestures intentional and precise, the more they deviate from unconscious natural motion. So they can quantify these degrees of exaggeration by the maximum and minimum torque values and the total integration within each time period of either preparation T_p or follow-through motions T_f by using equation 2-8.

Figure 3. Typical exaggeration gesture model (e.g., right hand)

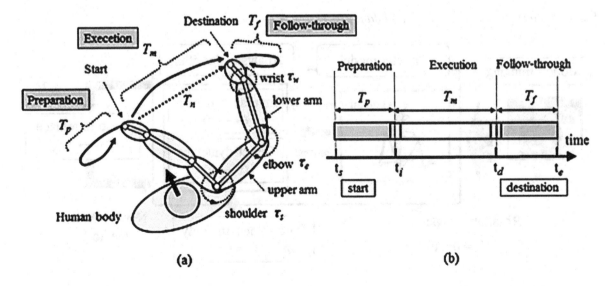

(a)   (b)

EXPERIMENTS AND DISCUSSION

In order to verify the author's hypothesis and the performance of the proposed model, they carried out verification experiments. The block diagram of the gesture assessment system and data processing flow are shown in figure 3. In this system, all gestures are captured by motion tracking and they are changed into time-series-data θ (θ_1, θ_2, $\cdots$ θ_n) of each joint angle. Furthermore, through a process called inverse dynamics, each torque τ that arises at each joint is calculated by using the dynamic analysis algorithm, which was mentioned in the previous section. In our system, it is also possible to reproduce and if necessary compensate for the ideal gestures if we could predict the optimal torque change τ_{new} by using *Newton-Euler method*. They would like to describe this direct dynamics method in more detail later in following sections.

Dynamic Analysis of Gestures

By collecting dozens of exaggerated gestures used in contexts such as Japanese *Bunraku* and *Kabuki*, special gestures effectively used in the dance (Wodehouse & Sheridan, 2014), comic dialogue and *Disney's* animation (Thomas & Ollie, 1997), which are expressing emotions, the author tried to identify common rules of such exaggerated gestures using their assessment system. Some of the typical dynamic analysis results of the exaggerated gesture and torque changes at the main joints are shown in figures 5 and 6. In Figure 5, the left side data indicates the results of the *Kabuki* gesture (Wood & Hamilton, 2010), and τ_{wrist} shows the twisting torque of the wrist joint, $\tau_{shoulder}$ for the shoulder, and τ_{elbow} indicates torque changes at elbow joint of the right arm, respectively. There is a common pattern of additional "preparation" and "follow-through" motions just before and after the "execution" action, and they can be quantified by the undershoot and overshoot values of distorted torque changes such as in shoulder and elbow joints, which are displayed by the gray area in this figure.

In Figure 6, authors showed another type of exaggerated gesture that was used in inspiring speech for attracting audiences' attention. Similarly, in this example, the regions marked in gray indicate the

Figure 4. Gesture analysis system and data processing flow

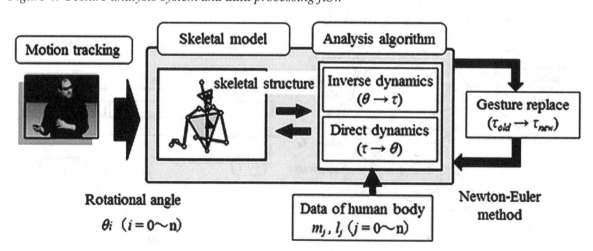

Figure 5. Analysis results of typical exaggerated gestures (e.g., Japanese Kabuki)

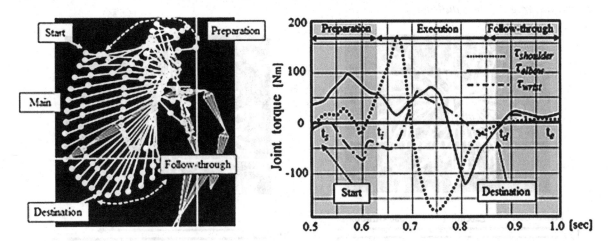

Figure 6. Analysis results of typical exaggerated gestures (e.g., Speech gesture)

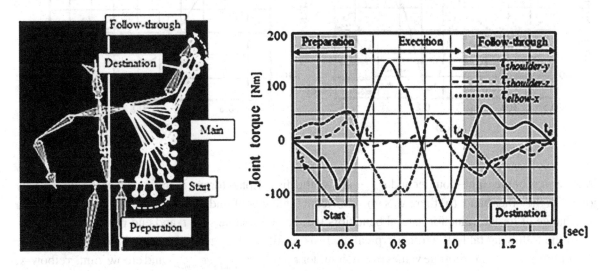

torque change of the "preparation" and "follow-through" motions, and also $\tau_{shoulder-z}$ indicates the twisting torque of outside rotation in z-axis, $\tau_{shoulder-y}$ is the rotation in the y-axis at shoulder joint and $\tau_{el-bowx}$ shows the distortion in the x-axis of elbow. Most of the experimental results of these emotional speech and conversation gestures had the same high correlations between the degree of exaggeration and the torque of the main joints.

In addition, another experimental result for comparison between exaggerated and natural gestures that are more easily understood is shown in Figure 7. In this figure, (a) shows the exaggerated gesture of Japanese comic dialogue that has exactly the same start position t_s and destination t_d, compared with (b) the natural gesture. As it is apparent from this experiment, the undershoot and overshoot in torque changes are measured just before and after the main motion of the exaggerated gesture. Further, in this example, $\tau_{shoulder\_y}$ indicates the twisting torque of the outside rotation in the y-axis, $\tau_{shoulder\_z}$ is the rotation

Figure 7. Comparison of (a) exaggerated gesture and (b) natural motion with same start position and destination (e.g., Comic dialogue)

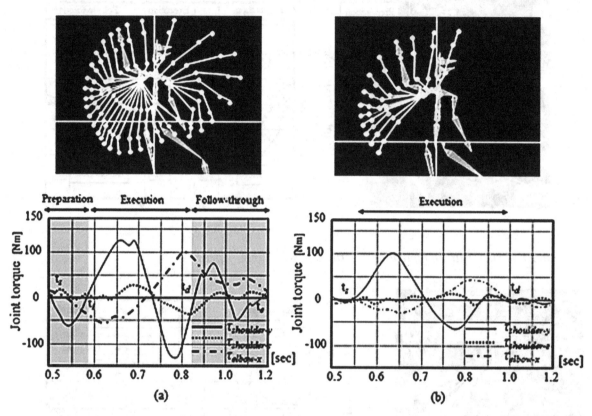

in the z-axis of the right shoulder and τ_{elbow_x} shows the distortional torque in the x-axis of the right elbow joint. On the other hand, (b) there was no significant tendency of undershoot and overshoot observed in the change of torque value for natural behaviors that have the same start t_s and end positions t_d.

In the following table 1, another typical analysis results of exaggerated gestures are listed, with the maximum and minimum torque values of the shoulder $\tau_{shoulder-z}$, $\tau_{shoulder-y}$, $\tau_{shoulder-x}$ and elbow joints τelbow-x, and the total torque ratio T_{main}/T_p of "preparation", T_{main}/T_f of "follow-through" and each "execution"

Table 1. Maximum and Minimum values and total torque ratio

Max /Min [Nm]	$\tau_{shoulder-z}$	$\tau_{shoulder-y}$	$\tau_{shoulder-x}$	$\tau_{elbow-x}$	T_{main}/T_p	T_{main}/T_f
Kabuki	92.5 / -101.4	85.8 / -145.2	25.4 / -71.3	79.3 / -53.7	25.3	29.7
Kabuki	121.8 / -114.7	108.3 / -98.2	31.5 / -70.2	68.9 / -63.8	35.7	30.2
Dance	130.8 / -148.1	165.4 / -169.3	61.2 / -71.4	30.1 / -13.8	43.8	38.2
Comic dialogue	128.9 / -168.3	17.3 / -15.6	101.5 / -54.1	40.1 / -33.2	30.3	20.2
Comic dialogue	97.7 / -106.3	138.3 / -115.6	41.3 / -39.3	20.3 / -19.1	38.7	34.8
Speech	113.3 / -87.4	120.5 / -93.1	33.4 / -21.3	87.9 / -72.3	27.3	29.7
Speech	121.3 / -107.9	33.2 / -52.3	52.5 / -20.0	92.3 / -51.8	22.1	25.9

motion. Furthermore, the significance between T_{main}/T_p versus the total torque of the exaggerated and natural gestures are plotted in figure 8 to clarify the relationship between the degree of emphasis and these values. In this figure, the data shown by circles indicate the ratio T_{main}/T_p of exaggerated gestures and the data shown by triangles show the ratio T_{main}/T_p of natural gestures with the same start position and destination, respectively.

These results reveal a certain correlation between the integrated value of torque within the force interval and torque ratio T_{main}/T_p and T_{main}/T_f. Qualitatively, these ratios represent how much torque is applied to the exaggerated portions within entire motions. In other words, this total torque ratio will be one of the indicators that quantitatively represent the degree of exaggeration. Consequently, it is possible to distinguish between an unconscious and intentional close-approximation motion by using the torque values and the total power ratio. The authors would like to review this issue in greater depth in the latter of this chapter.

Improving the Accuracy of Gesture Analysis

In the researchers' preliminary experiments, they collected about a hundred characteristic gestures made using the whole body, and classified them into five groups (see Appendix), in a way that resembles the plan for comparison with our proposed method (Naka et al, 2015) Figure 9 shows some of the typical analysis results for the joint torque changes. In this figure, (a) shows the exaggerated gestures in the group of Japanese comic dialogue actions, and (b) the upper graph shows the torque changes, but taking into account only the upper body. In comparison with this result, the lower graph shows the body torque that takes into consideration the entire body, that is, with all external forces calculated using equation 2-5. In this typical example, τ_{elbow_x} indicates the twisting torque of the elbow joint, and $\tau_{shoulder\_x}$ shows the twisting torque of the shoulder joint. The entire body needs to be supported with both legs, so we have

Figure 8. Relation between total torque ratios versus torque (right shoulder)

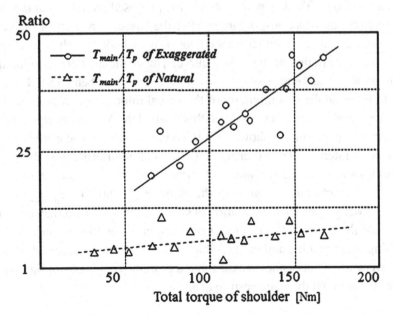

Figure 9. Comparison of joint torque taking the whole body into account (right hand)

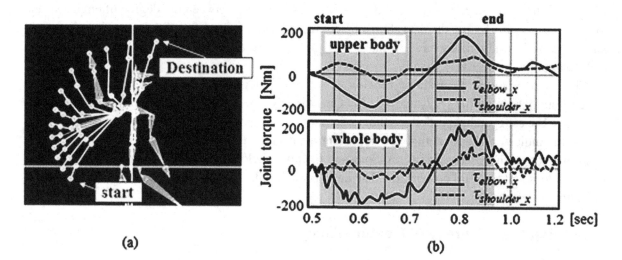

(a)   (b)

to take into account the torque due to torsion *N* and drag force *f* from the floor. These results reflect the high-frequency component that was applied to the torque due to torsion of the main joints. On the other hand, the changes in the extrapolation of torque curves (low frequency) are maintained. These patterns were replicated in the majority of cases within the other five gesture groups (fifty-two gestures in all), which they used in these experiments.

In the researchers next study, they examined the potential for improving the accuracy to identify where there is a transition between ordinary motion and the exaggerated part of the characteristic gestures. In the previous section, authors showed that exaggerated gestures could be quantitatively evaluated by their torque value, and their changes generated at the main joints such as in the gray regions in figures 5 and 6. Expanding this idea, they thought that the start and end points of exaggerated gestures could be accurately determined as follows. The key point noted in the proposed model is that the "preparation" and "follow-through" motions are added just before or after the "execution" part of the gesture mentioned so far. These motions correspond to either undershoot or overshoot, which is just before or after the "execution" motion in the variation of the torque curve. The challenge here is to identify a method of accurately defining the start t_s and end positions t_d of these exaggerated behaviors. The author's response to this problem is to focus on the synchronicity of the verbal information, represented by the voice intensity, with the exaggerated gestures. They named this method the *Non-continuous search* method. The results of our preliminary experiments showed some human motions to be closely and synchronously correlated with the voice intensity. The experimental results of monitoring the relationship between the major torque variations and the voice variation of typical exaggerated gestures are shown in Figure 10. The upper graphs show the changes in torque of the elbow τ_{elbow}, shoulder $\tau_{shoulder}$ and wrist τ_{wrist} joints respectively, and the lower graphs are the variation in sound data with which they are mutually synchronized. These data show the results for exaggerated gestures during an impassioned address by a famous public speaker. Using these results, authors are able to improve the accuracy of identification of the transition point between an ordinary and an exaggerated gesture. This is one of the important problems to be solved in our conventional dynamic gesture analysis.

Figure 10. Typical examples of exaggerated gesture torque (upper) and speech (lower)

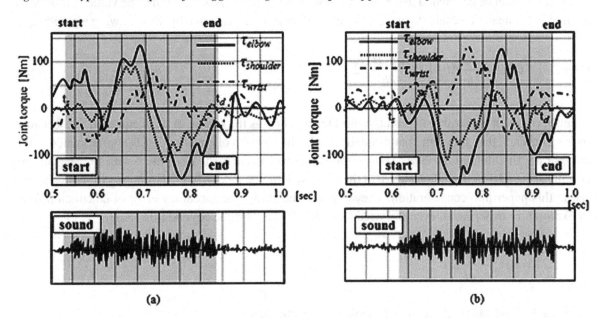

(a)   (b)

Gesture Generation and Compensation by Direct Dynamics

In this section, the author will be making a slight change to the perspective, and would like to discuss the possibility of generating or compensating the ideal motions by *direct dynamics*. This is the confirmation of the second hypothesis as the author has mentioned in "Background", and it is the following; if the exaggerated gesture can be reproduced by ideal conditions, there will be an important effect in designing the emotional interfaces which is possible to exceed the "uncanny valley" (Mori, 2015). In their gesture assessment system shown in figure 4, they mentioned that it is possible to reproduce and compensate for some ideal gestures if we can predict the optimal torque change τ_{new} using the *Newton-Euler method*. In the following, authors will describe the verification experiments and algorithm in more detail. By using the *direct dynamic analysis* method, it is possible to calculate each joint angle θ (θ_1, θ_2, $\cdots$ θ_n) from the amount of change in joint torque τ, which is shown in equation 3-1. When the torque value τ of multiple joints is given, then they can estimate the movements of the link of each joint by using the *Newton-Euler method* as follows. The angular acceleration $d^2\theta / dt^2$ ($d^2\theta_1 / dt^2$, $d^2\theta_2 / dt^2$ ... $d^2\theta_n / dt^2$) that arises at each joint is given by following equation 3-1 from transforming the equation 2-1.

$$\frac{d^2\theta}{dt^2} = M\left(\theta\right)^{-1}\left\{\tau - C\left(\theta, \frac{d\theta}{dt}\right)\frac{d\theta}{dt} - g\left(\theta\right)\right\} \tag{3.1}$$

In case the displacement angle θ (0) and angular acceleration $d^2\theta / dt^2$ (0) of each joint at time $t = 0$ whose start position is determined, and the torque value $\tau(t)$ (which arises at each joint from start time t_s to target time t_d) are given, then they can obtain the numerical solution of θ (t) by defining a suitable value of Δt by solving θ (t) and $d^2\theta / dt^2$ (t) of each time $t = 0, \Delta t, 2\Delta t, 3\Delta t$ ... one by one until the intended time t_e. Both θ (t) and $d^2\theta / dt^2$ (t) at time t are obtained from the value of θ ($t+\Delta t$) in time $t+\Delta t$. Moreover,

$d^2\theta/dt^2$ ($t+\Delta t$) can be calculated using the equation of motion 3-1. Assuming that the value of $d^2\theta/dt^2$ in equation 3-1 is nearly constant, then the time interval [t and $t+\Delta t$] is drawn by the following equation 3-2.

$$\theta\left(t+\Delta t\right)=\theta\left(t\right)+\frac{d\theta}{dt}\Delta t+\left(\Delta t\right)^2\frac{d^2\theta}{dt^2}\bigg/2 \qquad (3.2)$$

Furthermore, it is possible to omit the third term, which is the square of Δt in equation 3-2, because it is insignificant, then they can obtain equation 3-3. The solution of equation 3-3 is approximated to the clause of the first item of the *Euler series expansion* one by one to the last time t_e with Δt. The authors carefully selected the calculation step Δt of the *Newton-Euler method* to 0.0029 by taking the convergence time in this paper into consideration. They checked the convergent accuracy error of calculation from our exploratory experiment, even if it used an insignificant Δt value beyond this value.

$$\theta\left(t+\Delta t\right)=\theta\left(t\right)+\frac{d\theta}{dt}\Delta t \qquad (3.3)$$

Verification of Naturalness of Generated Gestures

In this section, the validity of our proposed *direct dynamic* method is verified by using the twenty-five selected characteristic gestures listed in the Appendix. The authors compared the naturalness of newly generated gestures with each original motion by the following subjective evaluation method. As part of basic experiments, some exaggerated gestures were selectively generated through inverse dynamic calculation from the viewpoint of the difference appears clearly. For these selected gestures, they tried to replace the torque value τ of the natural motion (without exaggeration) by the newly calculated torque value τ_{new} for each gesture, which was classified into groups A to E (listed in the Appendix). Furthermore, they moved from the same start to target position (destination) correctly.

In Figure 11, they show a typical example of (a) a natural gesture without exaggeration and (b) a gesture with exaggeration as a representative case of gesture 18 in group D. Also in figures (c) and (d), the inward and outward rotational swing torque $\tau_{shoulder\_z}$ in the horizontal plane (circumference rotation of z-axis) of the right shoulder is expressed by a solid line, and the external and inner rotation torque (rotation of x-axis) $\tau_{shoulder\_x}$ is shown by a dashed line. Furthermore, a long dashed line shows the inward and outward rotational swing torque $\tau_{shoulder\_z}$ of the left elbow and outward swing and the adduction torque τ_{elbow_y} (rotation around the y-axis) is shown by a small dashed line, respectively. In Figure 12, another typical example of (a) a natural gesture without exaggeration and (b) a gesture with exaggeration as representative cases of an emphasis gesture in speech gesture 21 in group E is shown. In this figure, the inward and outward rotational swing torque $\tau_{shoulder\_z}$ (circumference rotation of z-axis) in the horizontal plane of the right shoulder is expressed by a solid line for both (c) and (d). The external and inner rotation torque (rotation of x-axis) $\tau_{shoulder\_x}$ is showed by a dashed line, and the long dashed line represents the inward and outward rotational swing torque τ_{elbow_z} of the right elbow, and the outward swing and the adduction torque (rotation around y-axis) is τ_{elbow_y}, respectively.

Authors tried to compensate for these behaviors by replacing the torque values of the main link of the natural motion (without exaggeration) with the ideal torque value τ_{new}. Some typical results are shown in the following cases.

Figure 11. (a) Natural gesture (b) Exaggerated gesture and each torque value (Gesture 18 / e.g., comic dialogue)

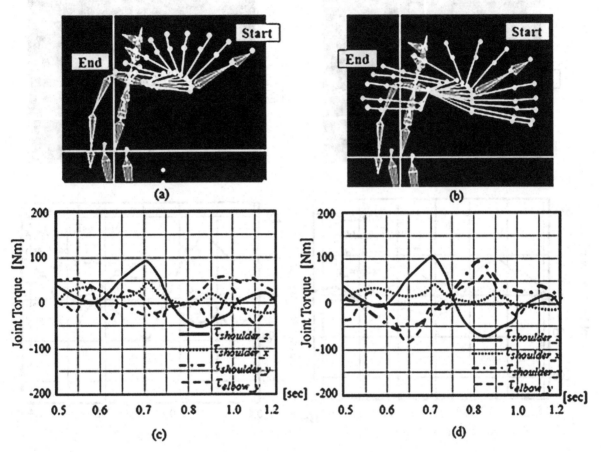

- **Case-1:** For natural gesture 18 in group D, they tried to replace the torque value of the external and inner rotation torque $\tau_{shoulder\_x}$ of the left shoulder with the inward and outward rotational swing torque τ_{elbow_z} of the left elbow, by each exaggerating torque τ_{new}.
- **Case-2:** Same as in case 1 of natural gesture 21 in group E, they replaced the torque value of the external and inner rotation torque $\tau_{shoulder\_z}$ of the right shoulder and inward and outward rotational swing torque τ_{elbow_z} of the right elbow by exaggerating torques τ_{new}.

In both cases, new gestures of each joints angles θ_{new} $(\theta_1, \theta_2, \cdots \theta_n)$ from new torque τ_{new} are given by the above mentioned *direct dynamic* method.

The authors conducted an assessment to verify the reproducibility of natural expressions, which was based on the subjective evaluation of characteristic gestures newly generated by the proposed method. As for the evaluation, they used the *DSCQS* (double stimulus continuous quality scale) method of subjectively comparing the newly generated gestures with the original ones. The flow of evaluation of the *DSCQS* method is as follows. First, they showed evaluators the original exaggerated gesture as the reference for less than ten seconds, and then inserted intervals of about three seconds, after which we showed the newly generated exaggerated gestures for about ten seconds. These trials were carried out in pairs

Figure 12. (a) Natural gesture (b) Exaggerated gesture and each torque value (Gesture 21 / e.g., Speech)

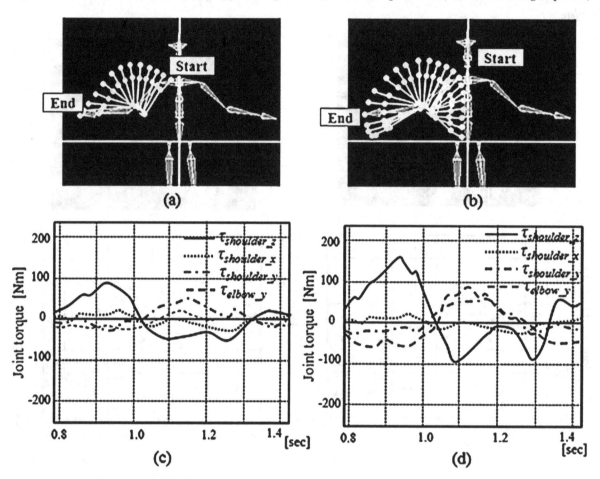

and repeated twice. Each evaluator was requested to perform an evaluation to compare both gestures at the second presentation. In these experiments, the order of presentation was randomly changed without teaching the original gesture (reference). Twelve adults in their twenties (nine men and three women) were selected as evaluators. Each evaluator was asked to mark the subjective evaluation value over each pair of gestures with continuation measures based on the five steps of quality shown in Figure 13. Furthermore, the final score was normalized from 0 to 100 (maximum of measure is one hundred), and the evaluation value of the newly exaggerated gesture from the difference of the reference was expressed in the evaluation difference DE. The average value of ten evaluators was adopted for this DE value as the final evaluation result (the maximum and minimum differences of evaluation results were excluded from each trial). This DE value shows the difference of subjective values of the naturalness of gestures. The more natural impression felt, the smaller the DE vale (near the natural exaggerated gesture). It can be considered an index of natural impression when it has a smaller value.

All evaluation results of the above mentioned *DSCQS* method are shown in table 2. The subjective evaluation values of the original exaggerated gesture which was used as a reference, the value of the newly generated exaggeration and the evaluation difference DE value are listed, respectively. As for the

Figure 13. Measure and value of DSCQS evaluation

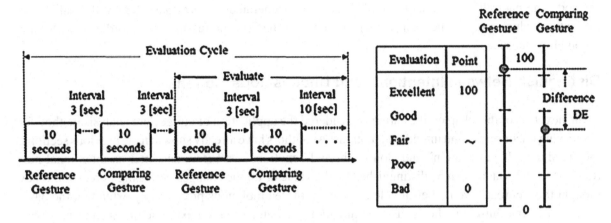

result of Case 1, the average value of the subjectivity evaluation of original exaggerated gesture 18 in group D was 91.0. The average value of the newly generated gesture became 69.8, and the evaluation difference DE became 21.4. On the other hand, as for the result of Case 2, the average value of original gesture 21 in group E was set to 97.3, the average value of the newly generated exaggerated gesture was 80.0 and the evaluation difference DE became 17.3. Furthermore, the total average value of the subjectivity evaluation of original exaggerated gestures ranged from 80.1 to 98.2 for all gestures used in experiments from group A to E, and the average value of the newly generated gesture was 44.3 to 85.7, and each difference DE was set to 35.8 to 12.5. In all categories, the most naturally impressed exaggerated gesture was group E and its subjective value was eighty to ninety percent. The DE value of the newly exaggerated gesture ranged from sixty to seventy percent of near impression for other categories.

From the results of these experiments, the authors concluded that it is possible to obtain the naturally exaggerated gestures by correcting or replacing the torque values of the natural motions with the new

Table 2. Results of subjective evaluation of each exaggerating gestures

		Reference gesture	Generated gesture	DE value
Group A	Gesture 1	90.1	55.0	35.1
	Gesture 3	85.9	55.1	30.8
Group B	Gesture 6	78.3	47.1	31.2
	Gesture 10	80.1	44.3	35.8
Group C	Gesture 11	85.6	51.4	34.2
	Gesture 14	89.3	54.8	34.5
Group D	Gesture 18	91.0	69.6	21.4
	Gesture 19	92.1	64.8	27.3
Group E	Gesture 21	97.3	80.0	17.3
	Gesture 22	98.2	85.7	12.5

torque of the exaggerated gestures. These calculations can be carried out by using the *direct dynamic* method. The naturalness and actuality of those newly generated gestures have achieved a subjective evaluation value of eighty percent or more in terms of natural impression, in accordance with their second hypothesis.

Distinguish Between Intentional and Unconscious Motions

In the next half of this chapter, the authors considered the application of our gesture analysis method for identifying unconscious and intentional motions. As authors have already shown in the previous sections, they tend to add "preparation" and "follow-through" motions just before and after an intentional motion, and each behavior can be distinguished by the value of torque changes with a high precision. They thought this approach would be suitable for solving these ambiguous problems by extending the basic idea. That is the third hypothesis; if some intentions of human will be expressed in such as emphasis operations consciously then they can be measured in the dynamics of behavior.

In the following experiments, subjects were asked to stand in front of a large 100-inch screen and to accurately track the target position from some randomly displayed starting points by using hand gestures only as shown in figure 14 a). When a human subject tried to manipulate the graphical user interface displayed on The screen with greater intentionality (with precision toward the target position), then there was a bigger difference at the start or target position, and this difference appeared as undershoot or overshoot behavior.

Some of the typical experimental results of the torque changes in intentional-gesture analysis are shown in Figure 14. In figure b), $\tau_{shoulder-y}$ shows the twisting torque of the wrist joint in the y-axis and $\tau_{shoulder-z}$ is the z-rotation of shoulder joints. In these experiments, they could observe the same tendency of "preparation" and "follow-through" like behaviors being applied to the intentional motion, and these behaviors could also therefore be quantitatively analyzed by using the undershoot or overshoot value

Figure 14. Typical experimental results of gesture interaction

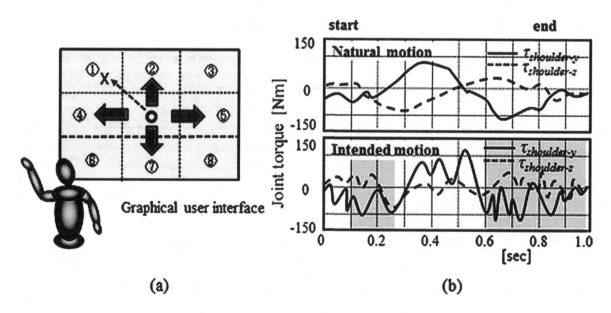

of torque. However, these values of the main joints were not remarkable for such unconscious close-approximation tasks, which were shown in the data at the top of figure 14 b). In order to determine the threshold value T_{total} of these motions that can distinguish either intentional or natural actions, we use the maximum value and amount of change in the torque values shown in equation 2-8.

Application of Proposed Method

In this section, the authors will examine the application named *Lifewall* by using the method proposed in the previous sections. In this application, user stands before a large wall screen (One hundred and fifty inches size) and operates the GUIs using only hand gestures shown in Figure 15. Users can certainly perform the operation by adopting the conscious behavior described in previous section while holding up their left hand. After some exercises, it is possible to operate the GUIs almost as intended with only a light consciousness due to the dynamical determination. Through performance evaluation with various objectives, it was found that subjects felt this kind of gesture operation was very easy to use.

In Figure 15 shows the overall view of their experimental system. In this structure three depth camera sensors (VICON, 2014) are mounted on the top part of the large screen (150 inches size) to be able to capture accurately the motions of user without any occlusion, even if the user moves widely in front of the screen. Subjects were instructed to manipulate the GUIs by using their body gestures standing at the distance of about 1.5 meter from the large screen. In addition to this, in Figure 16 shown the main block diagram of functional structure of the experimental system and the main processing flow of the experimental sequences is the following.

Figure 15. Experimental view of gesture input device

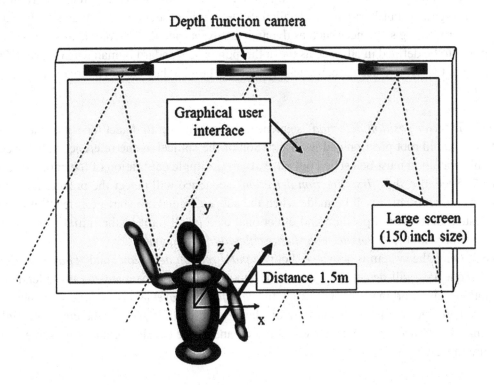

Figure 16. Block diagram of functional structure of experimental sequence

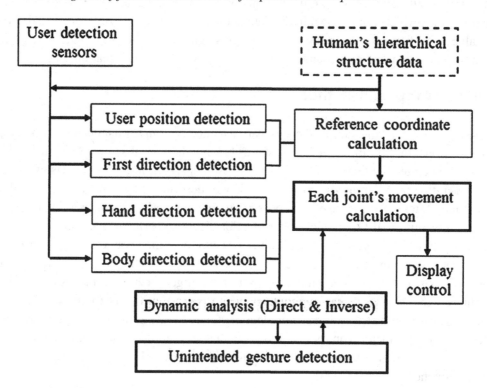

In this system, any gesture of subjects is accurately detected by using the three motion tracking sensors and it is converted into the time series angle data of each joint of the hierarchical structure which was shown in Figure 1. Furthermore, as detailed in the previous sections, a human's body data which necessary for processing sequences such as dynamic analysis (See the "Dynamic analysis of gestures" section), needs to be defined in advance as the anthropometric standard human data (Li, et al, 2015). In this application, the authors used Japanese adult standard human data base. The main processing flows are followings.

Sequence 1: In "*user position detection*" sequence, the system has to detect the set of the coordinates both humanoid root position and its orientation of the subject as the reference value (See Figure 1). This operation must be carried out once after the simple calibration of the entire system.

Sequence 2: Secondly, the "*first direction detection*" sequence will detect the predetermined starting hand movement which will be made when the subject intends to start gestures. Simultaneously, the system detects both position and directional data of all joint as the initial value, working in cooperation with the "*reference coordinate calculation*" sequence.

Sequence 3: Once the system is activated, both "*hand direction detection*" and "*body direction detection*" sequences will detect the subsequent hand and body movements as the intended gesture operations, also working in cooperated with "*each joint's movement calculation*" sequence. In this system, some gesture guide images are displayed on the GUIs such as the cursor or highlighted buttons in conjunction with the movement of a hand, to be capable of checking subjects for their gesture movements.

The most remarkable feature of the proposed approach is that the system has two *"dynamic analysis"* and *"unintended gesture detection"* sequences.

Sequence 4: Unlike other similar systems, *"dynamic analysis"* sequence calculate the dynamic values of each joints which are resulting from the user's movement data, and these calculations are executed in real-time and precisely by using the aforementioned the dynamical algorisms (See the "Dynamic analysis of gestures" section).

Sequence 5: Moreover, as another unique feature *"unintended gesture detection"* sequence is possible to determine between a conscious manipulation and unconscious operation. As the author mentioned in former sections, the basic mechanism is that in accordance with the simple exaggerated gesture model, it could be achieved by detecting the dynamics of the "preparation" or "follow-through" actions in the user operations.

We humans tended to add "preparation" or "follow-through" motions just before or after an intentional motion, the more consciously we behave, the more they are remarkable in these actions. Each behavior can be distinguished by using undershoot or overshoot value of torque changes with high precision. As aforementioned before, it is possible to detect the variation in the twisting torque generated at locations such as the shoulder, elbow and wrist joints. In this sequence, setting each threshold in the twisting torque which acting on the wrist and the elbow and shoulder joints depending on the type of the gesture, and will determine the difference in conscious behavior and unconscious operations by comparison with those target values successively. Consequently, it is possible to control the target system using some natural and simple hand movements in a wide operation range. In figure 17 shows the gesture interaction system named *"LifeWall"* demonstrating.

CONCLUSION

In this chapter, the author discussed the importance of nonverbal cues in human communication to quantify the function of the gesture interactions especially including emotions, and they tried to clarify

Figure 17. Gesture interaction "Lifewall" demonstrations

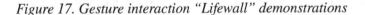

the dynamic mechanisms of the certain characteristic behaviors. The basic idea was that human tended to apply forces to the required portion of their arms and body for emphasized actions; therefore, it was possible to quantify the dynamic effects in terms of the torque applied to the body. And especially, they paid attention to human's special actions named "exaggerated gestures" that were effectively used in our everyday lives or face-to-face conversations, and revealed how to quantitatively analyze the effects and the mechanisms in mathematically.

In the first half of this chapter, the authors proposed a simple "gesture exaggeration" model to analyze the actions and selected hundreds of characteristic gestures which were used frequently and intentionally in such as Japanese *Bunraku* and *Kabuki*, the special gestures effectively used in dance and *Disney's* animation. As the result, they found that it could represent the degree of exaggeration in a quantitative manner by using the simple generic model and there was a high correlation with the torque of torsion. Moreover, the author confirmed that these models has a commonality with some emphasizing actions which were used in the speeches or human interactions effectively (rhetorical emphasis), and there was an important guideline in designing the emotional interfaces by applying the simple and unified model.

In the second half of the chapter, the researchers applied their gesture analysis method to solve one of the chief problems of gesture-based interaction which was difficult to distinguish between unconscious and intentional gestures. They put the hypothesis that if some intentions of human would be expressed in such as emphasis operations unconsciously, they could be measured in the dynamics of behavior. In order to verify the hypothesis, they applied their gesture exaggeration model for identifying unconscious and intentional motions. Generally, we humans tended to add "preparation" or "follow-through" motions just before or after the intentional ones, and each behavior could be distinguished by using dynamical changes with high precision. From numerous series of experimental results, they clarified that many systems which were adopting this method have a high possibility to distinguish between a conscious manipulation and unconscious close-approximation operation. The author's main conclusions are organized as below.

1. Qualitatively, the more the humans want to emphasize their true message, the greater the rate of torque and its value applied to the joints will change additionally. Consequently, the degree of exaggeration of human motion can be quantified by the total value and the extent of changes in torque value that are acting on the major joints of the skeletal structure.

2. We humans tend to add "preparation" or "follow-through" motions just before or after an intentional motion, and each behavior can be distinguished by using an undershoot or overshoot value of torque changes with high precision. The authors proposed gesture exaggeration model was even applicable to the speaker's exaggerated and emphasized movements in the speeches and presentations to attract the audience's attention (rhetorical emphasis). There was a close correlation between intended gestures and the torque applied. On the other hand, the proposed method has the drawbacks that it is widely adaptable for the "exaggerated gestures" which can be modeled for the typical manner, but it has the weakness in applying to the gestures in which the boundary between "exaggeration" and "execution" is unclear motions. In general, these behaviors are hard to distinguish between the intentionally exaggerated and unconscious actions, even if the person judges them. It is left as future challenges.

3. Many systems adopting this method have a high possibility to distinguish between a conscious manipulation and unconscious close-approximation operation. The authors proposed method can provide one of the important knowledge for distinguishing user intentions when interacting with simple operating interfaces using gesture control.

The advantageous effects of these proposals in this chapter are that these methods are able to analyze human gestures by using dynamic analysis from only a simple and non-invasive motion tracking data, without any ambiguous biological sensing method. Moreover, these proposed dynamical model is simple and applicable for not only the general motion analysis but also the wide range of designing the human friendly interactions, such as distinguish between a conscious and unconscious manipulation by applying dynamical exaggeration rules.

FUTURE RESEARCH DIRECTIONS

With regard to the future works, the authors mainly focused on gestures of full-body motions in this chapter. However, the proposed dynamic motion analysis model will be also applicable widely for such as the finger gesture analysis. They are planning to expand the dynamic motion analysis including finger actions by defining the hierarchical structure of hands, such as shown in figure 1. Generally, there are structural differences such that DOF (degree of freedom) of each joint is one or two with exception of the thumb joint, in addition the total amount values of dynamical analysis of fingers are much smaller comparing with body. For these challenges, the authors have to analyze the effects of other than the twisting torques. Furthermore, it is also expected to consider how to improve the SNR for the smaller values of the operating torques. The latest touch devices are equipped with a mechanism for detecting the pressure of fingers (iPhone, 2015) and it's also one of the target application which they have to analyze these mechanisms by using the dynamical analysis (e.g., the correlation between pressure and torque).

ACKNOWLEDGMENT

These researches which were presented in this chapter have been partly supported by Panasonic PK-projects and authors would like to acknowledge for their cooperation, also express the deepest appreciation to Kyoto University for the constructive remarks.

REFERENCES

Baur, T., Mehlmann, G., Damian, I., Lingenfelser, F., Wagner, J., Lugrin, B., & Gebhard, P. (2015). *Context-Aware Automated Analysis and Annotation of Social Human--Agent Interactions. Transactions on Interactive Intelligent Systems, 5(2)*. ACM.

Bronzino, J. D., & Peterson, D. R. (2014). *Biomedical engineering fundamental* (4th ed.). CRC Press.

Bulling, A., Blanke, U., & Schiele, B. (2014). *A tutorial on human activity recognition using body-worn inertial sensors. ACM Computing Surveys, 46(3)*. ACM.

Cassell, J., Pelachaud, C., Badler, N., Steedman, M., Achorn, B., Becket, T., . . . Stone, M. (1994). Animated conversation: rule-based generation of facial expression, gesture & spoken intonation for multiple conversational agents. Proceedings ofACM SIGGRAPH. doi:10.1145/192161.192272

Charlesa, S., & Hogan, N. (2012). *Dynamics of wrist rotations. Journal of biomechanics*. Elsevier B.V.

Chen, L., Wei, H., & Ferryman, J. (2013). A survey of human motion analysis using depth imagery. *Pattern Recognition Letters, 34*(15).

fMRI. (2014). Magnetic Resonance, a critical peer-reviewed introduction; functional MRI. European Magnetic Resonance Forum. Retrieved from http://www.magnetic-resonance.org/ch/11-03.html

Gavrila, D. M. (1999). The visual analysis of human movement: A survey. *Computer Vision and Image Understanding, 73*(1), 82–98. doi:10.1006/cviu.1998.0716

Georgescu, A., Kuzmanovic, B., Santos, N., Tepest, R., Bente, G., Tittgemeyer, M., & Vogeley, K. (2013). *Perceiving nonverbal behavior: Neural correlates of processing movement fluency and contingency in dyadic interactions. Human brain Mapping, 35(4)*. Wiley Periodicals.

Grifantini, K. (2010). Sensor detects emotions through the skin. *MIT Technology Review*. Retrieved from http://www.technologyreview.com/news/421316/sensor-detects-emotions-through-the-skin/

Hansenab, H., Rezzougc, N., Gorcec, P., Ventured, G., & Isableua, B. (2015). *Sequence-dependent rotation axis changes and interaction torque use in overarm throwing. Journal of sports sciences, 34(9)*. Taylor & Francis.

Holle, H., Obermeier, C., Schmidt-Kassow, M., Friederici, A., Ward, J., & Gunter, T. (2012). Gesture Facilitates the Syntactic Analysis of Speech. *Frontiers in Psychology, 3*. doi:10.3389/fpsyg.2012.00074 PMID:22457657

iPhone6s. (2015). Apple Inc., Retrieved from http://www.apple.com/iphone-6s/3d-touch/

ISO IEC 19774. (2005). Specification of Humanoid animation (H-Anim). Retrieved from http://www.web3d.org/documents/specifications/19774/V1.0/index.html

Kinect. (2015). The Microsoft Kinect. Retrieved from https://dev.windows.com/en-us/kinect

Knapp, M., Hall, J., & Horgan, T. (2013). *Nonverbal communication in human interaction* (8th ed.).

Kristianslund, E., Krosshaug, T., & Bogert, A. J. (2012). Effect of low pass filtering on joint moments from inverse dynamics: Implications for injury prevention. *Journal of Biomechanics, 45*(4).

Leap Motion. (2015). Leap Motion. Retrieved from https://www.leapmotion.com/

Li, P., Corner, B., Carson, J., & Paquette, S. (2015). A three-dimensional shape database from a large-scale anthropometric survey.*Proceedings 19th Triennial Congress of the IEA.*

Mehrabian, A. (1981). *Silent messages: Implicit communication of emotions and attitudes* (2nd ed.). Wadsworth.

Meijer, M. (1989). *The contribution of general features of body movement to the attribution of emotions. Journal of Nonverbal behavior, 13(4)*.

Meng, Z., Pan, J., Tseng, K., & Zheng, W. (2012). Dominant points based hand finger counting for recognition under skin color extraction in hand gesture control system.*Proceedings of the 6th International Conference on Genetic and Evolutionary Computing (ICGEC '12)* (pp. 364–367). doi:10.1109/ICGEC.2012.85

Mochizuki, Y., Inokuchi, S., & Omura, K. (2000). Generating artificially mastered motions for an upper limb in baseball pitching from several objective functions. *IEEE Transactions on Systems, Man, and Cybernetics, 30*(3), 373–382. doi:10.1109/3477.846228 PMID:18252371

Mori, M. (2015). The Uncanny Valley. *IEEE*. Retrieved from http://spectrum.ieee.org/automaton/robotics/humanoids/the-uncanny-valley

Naka, T., & Ishida, T. (2014). Proposal of the effective method of generating characteristic gestures in nonverbal communication. *Human computer interaction, LNCS* (Vol. 8511, pp. 102-112).

Naka, T., & Ishida, T. (2015). A proposed dynamical analytic method for characteristic gestures in human communication. HCII, vol8.

NeuroSky. (2011). MindWave. Retrieved from http://neurosky.com/about-neurosky/

OptiTrack. (2014). Prim. Retrieved from http://www.optitrack.com/

Panwar, M. (2012). Hand gesture recognition based on shape parameters. *Proceedings of the International Conference on Computing. Communication and Applications (ICCCA '12)* (pp. 1–6). doi:10.1109/ICCCA.2012.6179213

PrimeSense. (2010). PrimeSense, Retrieved from http://www2.technologyreview.com/tr50/primesense/

Putnam, C. (2003). Sequential motions of body segments in striking and throwing skills: descriptions and explanations. *J. Biomech., 26*(Suppl. 1), 125-135.

Pyke, F. (2013). *Coaching Excellence*. Champaign, Ill: Human Kinetics.

Rautaray, S., & Agrawal, A. (2015). Vision based hand gesture recognition for human computer interaction: A survey. *Artificial Intelligence Review, 43*(1), 1–54. doi:10.1007/s10462-012-9356-9

Razuri, J., Larsson, A., Rahmani, R., Sundgren, D., Bonet, I., & Moran, A. (2015). Recognition of emotions by the emotional feedback through behavioral human poses. *Journal of Computer Science Issues, 12*(1).

Robertson, G., Caldwell, G., Hamill, J., Kamen, G., & Whittlesey, S. (2014). *Research Methods in Biomechanics* (2nd ed.).

Siegman, A., & Feldstein, S. (2014). *Nonverbal behavior and communication* (2nd ed.). Psychology Press.

Soli. (2015). Project Soli. Retrieved from https://www.google.com/atap/project-soli/

Thomas, F., & Ollie, J. (1997). *The Illusion of Life: Disney Animation*. Hyperion.

Truong, A., Boujut, H., & Zaharia, T. (2015). Laban descriptors for gesture recognition and emotional analysis. *The Visual Computer, 32*(1), 83-98.

VICON. (2014). Bonita. Retrieved from http://www.vicon.com/products/camera-systems/bonita

Wodehouse, A., & Sheridan, M. (2014). Exploring emotional response to gesture in product interaction using Laban's movement analysis. *Interaction Studies: Social Behaviour and Communication in Biological and Artificial Systems, 15*(2), 321–342. doi:10.1075/is.15.2.15wod

Wood, B., & Hamilton, T. (2010). Narukami: The Thunder God. *University of Wisconsin Madison*. Retrieved from https://sites.google.com/site/utnarukami/home

Zelic, G., Kim, J., & Davis, C. (2015). Articulatory constraints on spontaneous entrainment between speech and manual gesture. *Human Movement Science*, 42, 232–245. doi:10.1016/j.humov.2015.05.009 PMID:26072361

KEY TERMS AND DEFINITIONS

Dynamic Analysis: Dynamics is a field of applied mathematics concerned with the study of forces and torques and their effect on motion, as opposed to kinematics, which studies the movement of objects without reference to its causes.

Exaggerated Gesture: Exaggeration can be a rhetorical means (rhetorical emphasis) or figure of speech. It may be used to evoke the strong feelings or to create a strong impression of human. In the arts, exaggerations are used to create emphasis or effect, such as Japanese Bunraku, Kabuki, Disney's animation, dances.

Gestures: They include movement of the hands or other parts of the body. They allow individuals to communicate a variety of feelings and thoughts from contempt and hostility to approval and affection, often together with body language in addition to words when they speak.

Nonverbal Communication: Behavior and elements of human communication aside from the words themselves (verbal) that transmit intentions. And it includes such as pitch, speed, tone and volume of voice, gestures and facial expressions, body posture, eye movements and contact, and appearance.

Preparation and Follow-Through: The phases of the movement, in the sport movement especially for ballistic actions such as hitting, throwing and kicking, generally contain three main phases such as preparation, execution and follow-through. The preparation contains all of the movements that prepare an athlete for the performance of the skill, such as the backswing during batting and the run-up in long jumping. The execution is the performance of the actual movement that often includes a point of contact with an object (e.g., bat and ball), the release of an object or a flight phase (e.g., jump and shoot). Finally, the follow-through refers to all of the movements which occur after the execution phase (e.g., pitching, swing and kicking) that to get ready for another movement.

Unconscious: The lack of consciousness or responsiveness to human and other environmental stimuli. In the cognition, it is the processing of perception, memory, learning, thought, and language without being aware of it, and they often respond some erroneously to unconscious movements. We human will realize to have done these actions by unintentionally and mostly semi-automatic, hence it may be better to use the term "subconscious".

APPENDIX

Table 3. Feature of selected exaggeration gestures which was used experiments

		Features of gestures
Group A Japanese *Kabuki*	Gesture 1	Extend the right hand horizontally, bend the left elbow and turn upward: (e.g., "Genroku Mie" in *Kabuki* "Aragoto")
	Gesture 2	Finalize the motion in front of the body while twisting the right hand: (e.g., "Genroku Mie" in *Kabuki* "Shibaraku")
	Gesture 3	Throw a stone with the right hand: (e.g., "Ishinage Mie" in *Kabuki* "Kanjin-Cyoh")
	Gesture 4	Twist the right hand around a sword: (e.g., *Kabuki* "Narukami")
	Gesture 5	Twist the left hand in front of the body: (e.g., "Makugire Mie" in *Kabuki*)
Group B Dance/ Pantomime	Gesture 6	Swing the right hand outwards and carry out a greeting in front of the body. (e.g., Finishing in figure skating)
	Gesture 7	Greeting of finish in ballet
	Gesture 8	Extend both hands for the finale
	Gesture 9	Firmly load the right hand and stop by the side of the body
	Gesture 10	Victory: bring both hands close in front of the body
Group C Animation (e.g., Disney)	Gesture 11	Carry out one accumulation movement and then extend the hand quickly, (e.g., *Walt Disney's Tom & Jerry*)
	Gesture 12	Extend both hands in an exaggerated manner
	Gesture 13	Move slowly and strike your partner with one hand (e.g., Comedy)
	Gesture 14	Move slowly and extend both hands
	Gesture 15	Execute a definite stop and look up with shrugged shoulders
	Gesture 16	Execute a definite stop and throw with the right hand
	Gesture 17	Strikes your partner with the right hand
Group D Comic dialogue	Gesture 18	Transfer your right hand and strike the next partner by being turned towards the front (e.g., *Manzai*)
	Gesture 19	Hit your partner's head with the right hand slowly (e.g., *Manzai*, a form of Japanese entertainment)
	Gesture 20	Turns the right hand and strike in an exaggerated manner
Group E Speech/ Presentation	Gesture 21	Raise your right hand and finger straight (e.g., Speech of B. Obama)
	Gesture 22	Extend and exaggerate, with both hands highly on the body (e.g., Speech of S. Jobs)
	Gesture 23	Bring right hand to the jaw (e.g., Speech of S. Jobs)
	Gesture 24	Extend both hands and close, repeating like a bird (e.g. Speech of S. Jobs)
	Gesture 25	Point and emphasize object with left hand (e.g., Speech of S. Jobs)

Chapter 3
Developing 3D Freehand Gesture-Based Interaction Methods for Virtual Walkthroughs:
Using an Iterative Approach

Beatriz Sousa Santos
Universidade de Aveiro, Portugal

Beatriz Quintino Ferreira
Universidade de Aveiro, Portugal

João Cardoso
Universidade de Aveiro, Portugal

Carlos Ferreira
Universidade de Aveiro, Portugal

Paulo Dias
Universidade de Aveiro, Portugal

ABSTRACT

Gesture-based 3D interaction has been considered a relevant research topic as it has a natural application in several scenarios. Yet, it presents several challenges due to its novelty and consequential lack of systematic development methodologies, as well as to inherent usability related problems. Moreover, it is not always obvious which are the most adequate and intuitive gestures, and users may use a variety of different gestures to perform similar actions. This chapter describes how spatial freehand gesture based navigation methods were developed to be used in virtual walkthroughs meant to be experienced in large displays using a depth sensor for gesture tracking. Several iterations of design, implementation, user tests, and controlled experiments performed as formative and summative evaluation to improve, validate, and compare the methods are presented and discussed.

INTRODUCTION

Gesture-based 3D interaction has been considered a challenging and relevant research topic due to its natural application to gaming, Virtual and Augmented Reality applications (Ni, 2011; Hürst et al., 2013; Billinghurst et al., 2014), and in other scenarios (Garber, 2013), as well as to the prospective alternatives

DOI: 10.4018/978-1-5225-0435-1.ch003

it has brought to the interactivity with the ever more pervasive public large displays (Bowman, 2014). However, this interaction paradigm presents several usability challenges, as the lack of feedback, and problems related to fatigue. Moreover, which are the "best" gestures are not always obvious, and users may use a variety of gestures to perform similar actions (Wobbrock et al., 2009). On the other hand, the relative novelty of these methods results in a lack of systematic methodologies to develop this type of interaction.

We have been developing an interactive system, located at the entrance hall of our Department, including a large public display and a depth sensor, meant to run applications that might support various Department activities, such as providing relevant information to passersby, or experiencing demos and walkthroughs for visitors (Dias et al., 2014). In this scope we have been developing several 3D spatial freehand gesture-based interaction methods envisaging an application in virtual walkthroughs following a user-centered iterative approach. This approach allowed a progressive refinement of the interaction methods based on several rounds of design, implementation and tests with users. According to our experience, performing more than one round of user tests is fundamental as these tests allow the development team better understand the strengths and limitations of both the methods, and also the experimental protocol of the tests in their current versions. Much of this insight is obtained based on observation and feedback from participants. Furthermore, participants often bring a fresh view suggesting improvements that might not occur to the team.

In this chapter we present a brief review concerning the topic of gesture-based 3D interaction.

We focus mainly on the type of gestures used, and describe how we developed and evaluated navigation methods, based on a depth sensor (Kinect) for spatial freehand gesture tracking, to be used in virtual walkthroughs. The results of several rounds of user tests and controlled experiments performed as formative and summative evaluation to improve, validate and compare the methods are presented and discussed, and conclusions are drawn.

BACKGROUND

The use of gestures in human-computer interaction can be traced back to Sketchpad, developed in the sixties by Ivan Sutherland, as it used an early form of stroke-based gestures using a light pen on a display. After this first attempt, gestures have gained popularity as a means of realizing novel interaction methods, and several devices have been developed to support this possibility. Namely, manipulating virtual objects using natural hand gestures in virtual environments was made possible in the eighties through instrumented gloves (Fisher et al., 1986). In the nineties, a vision-based system (Freeman & Weissman, 1995) demonstrated a viable solution for more natural device-free gestural interfaces, and later other approaches have been used, as for instance the ones described in Boussemart et al. (2004), Malik et al. (2005), Karam (2006), and Wachs et al (2011); yet, only the recent advent of affordable depth cameras truly gave an essential momentum to the spatial freehand paradigm of gesture-based user interfaces.

Besides eliminating the need for an input device, spatial freehand gestures have several advantages as an interaction method: they are natural to humans who constantly use them to communicate and control objects in the real world from infancy, and may underpin powerful interactions due to hands' multiple degrees of freedom, promising ease of access and naturalness also due to the absence of constrains imposed by wearable devices (Wachs et al., 2011; Ni, 2011, Ren et al. 2013b; Jankowski & Hachet, 2015).

However, in spite of these advantages, spatial freehand gestures also present some limitations and challenges: gestures may be not easy to remember, long interactions result in fatigue since mid-air interaction with no physical support is tiring, and users may suffer from lack of feedback when using their hands generating frequently cumbersome gestures or feelings. Also, the tracking of hands is still far from error free, as most systems still have difficulties to cope with distance and occlusions issues. These issues may limit the operations the users perform as several hand gestures may be not fully recognized causing frustration. Nonetheless, the low price of this technology made it extremely popular and encouraged its use in numerous solutions, making research on the topic even more pertinent.

While freehand gestures have been used in diverse situations, as computer aided design, medical systems and assistive technologies, computer supported collaborative work systems, mobile, tangible and wearable computing, as well as in entertainment and human-robot interaction, spatial freehand gestures, in particular, have been a major interaction method in virtual reality systems (Ni, 2011). In fact, Karam (2006) identified three types of systems in which gestures have been much used: non-, semi- and fully-immersed interactions, where users interact without being represented in the virtual environment, users are represented by avatars, or as if they are inside the virtual world, respectively. On the other hand, gestures may also be valuable in ubiquitous computing either in implicit or explicit interactions, namely for interaction with large public displays that create the opportunity for passing by users to access and interact with public or private content. In such scenarios, at distance interaction is important and doing it without any input device is most adequate (Vogel & Balakrishnan, 2005; Ni, 2011).

Freehand spatial gestures may be classified in manipulative and semaphoric. According to Quek et al. (2002), manipulative gestures are intended to control some entity by applying "a tight relationship between the actual movements of the gesturing hand/arm with the entity being manipulated", while semaphoric gestures are sets of formalized hand/harm gestures (e.g. to move forward, move backward). Manipulative gestures were first used by Bolt (1980) in the work "Put that there" in association with voice commands. This paradigm has been used to navigate in virtual environments, in direct manipulation interfaces, as well as to control robots; though, many interactive systems employing gestures use a blend of gesture styles, mainly manipulative and semaphoric gestures (Ni, 2011) (Probst et al., 2013). Several authors have explored the use of two-hand gestures in virtual environments for instance dividing navigation and manipulation gestures between the two hands (Balakrishnan & Kurtenbach, 1999), or using gestures to control menu-like widgets in a more generic style of interaction (Boussemart et al., 2004).

According to Karam (2006), semaphoric gestures are practical when distance interaction is of interest as it is the case in ubiquitous computing systems. This type of gestures has been used in smart room applications (Crowley et al., 2000), and interactions with large displays (e.g. Paradiso et al., 2003; von Hardenberg & Berard, 2001; Ren et al., 2013a).

Many input technologies have been used to enable gestures; however, for freehand gestures vision-based input seems an obvious option; a pioneer of this type of solution was Krueger's VIDEOPLACE (Krueger et al., 1985), which used video cameras to detect users' gestures. For long, vision-based technologies have not been effective enough to be usable in daily applications. The overhead and accuracy offered for gesture recognition precluded its widespread usage; nonetheless, there is presently a trend for more perceptual gesture interaction styles based, for instance, on relatively new and inexpensive devices as the Kinect and the Leap, or specifically made solutions as in (Taylor et al., 2014).

Whereas there is still ambiguity in the meaning of the term gesture in interaction, as a wide variety of gesture-based user interfaces do exist, the main motivation for developing them is to obtain more natural interactions; and to attain this goal the principles of interaction design must be followed as in any other type of user interface. Concerning gestures interfaces, Wachs et al. (2011) identify a list of relevant us-ability and technical issues and challenges, due to the lack of universal consensus for gestures-functions associations, and the need to tackle a variety of environments and user appearances. These authors also pinpoint a set of usability requirements such as ubiquity, fast response, feedback, learnability, intuitive-ness, comfort, low cognitive load, number of hands, "come as you are" (e.g. no need to wear any device) and "gesture spotting" (e.g. starting and ending the interaction). Some of these requirements are general, whereas others are more context specific.

While Ni (2011) specifies three components of an interaction framework: input device, interaction techniques, and fundamental design principles and practical design guidelines; according to (Karam, 2006), four fundamental aspects must be considered in the design of gestures sets to be used in gesture interaction systems: application domain, gesture style, enabling technology, and system response.

This chapter is focused on the design, development, use and testing of spatial freehand manipulative and semaphore gestures for virtual walkthroughs to be experienced through a large public display in a vision-based system (more specifically using a depth camera). The hurdles of detecting, tracking and recognizing gestures were tackled by the Kinect SDK, and only a few considerations regarding these issues will be done. Readers are forwarded to the course by LaViola (2014) for a comprehensive survey on gesture recognition and analysis, addressing some of the most recent techniques for real-time recog-nition of 3D gestures.

The input technology used to enable gestures in a system has a direct influence on the usability. Free-hand gestures, unlike many other gesture interaction methods, do not imply any physical contact with any part of the system, which may be viewed as an advantage counterbalancing lower reliability. The output produced by the system as a response to gestures is also relevant in usability. Gesture interaction design should likewise take into account the type of output, which may be visual or audio feedback, or simply the execution of some functionality. As gestures are unconstrained, users should be given feedback help-ing them learn to perform the right gestures (Norman, 2010). This may be done by reflexive feedback (Karam, 2006). Yet, other relevant aspects are the tasks that users have to do using the gestures and the context in which they will perform them. Even though fatigue and sensitiveness to lightning conditions may constitute important issues in the system we developed, the context of use considered (sporadic use of a large public display system for a short period of time) makes spatial freehand gestures a natural choice. In fact, the study performed by Karam and Schraefel (2005) suggests that users are much more tolerant to gesture recognition errors in ubiquitous computing scenarios than in desktop scenarios. This supports the choice of these gestures for the scenario addressed in this work, even if the system setting might induce some recognition errors due to lighting conditions or passing by people, which are virtu-ally impossible to completely overcome.

The aforementioned aspects are in line with the fact that, when developing a system using gestures, the goal should be to develop a more efficient interface for a specific application, and not a generic gesture interface. According to Nielsen et al. (2004), a "human-based approach" to developing such systems is preferable to a "technology-based approach", and should comply with general usability principles. Thus, the gestures should be easy to perform and remember, intuitive, logical (taking into consideration the functionality they trigger), and ergonomic; nevertheless, they should be recognizable by the system unmistakably. A useful approach that has been used to select a set of gestures in several contexts (Nielsen et al., 2004; Höysniemi et al., 2005; Dias et al., 2014) Probst et al (2014) is the Wizard of Oz method, which is most valuable when a relatively complex set of gestures has to be selected, and no clear ideas exist yet on which gestures might be more intuitive. Kühnel et al. (2011) adapted to the development of a gesture-based user interface to a smart-home system a design methodology comprising several user tests.

In our case, previous experience with the system (Dias et al., 2014), and the literature, namely the work of Ren et al. (2013a) proposing a 3D freehand gestural navigation for interactive public displays, provided hints on a set of gestures that might be used as a starting point for a refinement process. This process evolved iteratively based on the analysis of qualitative and quantitative data collected through the observation of users interacting with the system, logging their interaction, and asking for their opinion and suggestions. The results obtained from this analysis were used as formative evaluation to improve alternative interaction methods until they were usable enough to be integrated in our system. According to Ni (2011) the majority of evaluations of freehand gesture systems have been of an exploratory nature used as formative evaluation (Bowman et al., 2005), however, we deem summative evaluation is important to guarantee the methods are usable enough and thus a final user study was performed to compare the alternatives and select the best fit for the virtual walkthrough functionality. Likewise, Hernoux et al. (2015) perform a comparative study, as a summative evaluation, between a novel freehand solution (marker-less and Kinect-based) and a common and functionally equivalent one (data gloves and magnetic sensors) to allow 3D interaction. In this study the users/participants were asked to interact with the Virtual environment through object selection and manipulation, and navigation.

DEVELOPING FREEHAND GESTURE-BASED NAVIGATION METHODS

We have been developing an interactive system located at the entrance hall of our Department which included a large public display and a depth sensor - DETI-Interact (shown in Figure 1), meant to run applications that might support various Department activities, such as providing relevant information to passersby, or making demos and walkthroughs for visitors (Dias et al., 2014). Since the onset, and considering the aims of this system (where the navigation methods were to be integrated), the main rational defined was the utilization of simple and natural freehand gestures, that would neither involve very high concentration nor effort by the user for the execution of the various actions. Moreover, the gestures should also be intuitive, or, at least, easy to learn for the target users. We have been developing an interactive system located at the entrance hall of our Department which included a large public display and a depth sensor - DETI-Interact (shown in Figure 1), meant to run applications that might support various Department activities, such as providing relevant information to passersby, or making demos and walkthroughs for visitors (Dias et al., 2014). Since the onset, and considering the aims of this system (where the navigation methods were to be integrated), the main rational defined was the utilization of simple and natural freehand gestures, that would neither involve very high concentration nor effort by the user for the execution of the various actions. Moreover, the gestures should also be intuitive, or, at least, easy to learn for the target users.

As a first approach, we devised a method using a set of formalized semaphoric gestures performed by the users' dominant hand like controlling a pointer ("Free hand" method). As previously mentioned, semaphoric gestures have been considered practical when distance interaction is of interest as it is the case in ubiquitous computing systems (Karam, 2006), and have been used in interactions with large displays. The set of gestures was selected in order to provide a sense of continuity and consistency relatively to the user interface already in use for the rest of the system (allowing access to useful information to students and visitors through movements of the dominant hand). This method offered a similar interaction to the

Figure 1. DETI-Interact: where the gesture navigation methods are meant to be used

typical mouse-based interface, and thus it was expected to be familiar, have a high guessability (Wobbrock et al., 2005), and be easy to learn. The virtual camera was controlled by the gestures of users' dominant hand (Figure 2a) and the navigation speed giving a step towards or backwards from the Kinect sensor; the bigger the step, the higher the speed of the movement (Dias et al., 2015).

Despite offering coherence with previous applications running on the system, these applications are of a much different nature of the intended virtual walkthroughs, and thus the Free hand method had some potential drawbacks. On the one hand, using a metaphor evoking a "real world" navigation method might be more appropriate; on the other hand, the virtual walkthrough would generally take longer, implying that a more comfortable hand position would be fundamental, as well as that forward and backward steps should be avoided.

Figure 2. Main aspects of the freehand gesture-based navigation methods

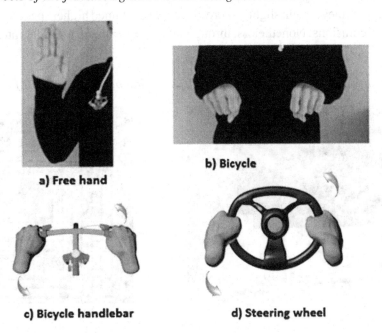

Therefore, inspired by the work of Ren et al. (2013a) that proposed a "flying broomstick" as a metaphor for a navigation method using 3D freehand gestures for virtual tours in a large public display, the "Bicycle" method was devised. This method is based on riding a bicycle, a familiar "real world" metaphor. This is also in line with the fact mentioned in the related work, that many interactive systems employing gestures use a blend of gesture styles, mainly manipulative and semaphoric (Ni, 2011). The gesture set selected to integrate the Bicycle navigation method is mainly composed of manipulative gestures, which are similar to the ones used to control a bicycle, i.e., the user initiates the action by placing both hands alongside with closed fists as if to grab the handlebar of a bicycle (Figure 2b). When the user moves the right hand slightly forward, the camera turns left; while left hand in front and right hand back turns the camera right. The speed control is done by advancing or pulling back both hands in parallel. To increase the range of speed, the user may step forward or backward getting closer or further from the depth sensor, increasing or decreasing the overall speed, respectively (Dias et al., 2015).

After some preliminary tests to fine-tune an experimental protocol to test the null hypothesis that the two methods were equally usable in the intended scenario, Free hand and Bicycle navigation methods were compared through a user study performed by 17 participants. Each participant navigated for 5 minutes in a maze having as goal collecting the maximum number of objects (boxes) spread along the path (Figure 3), after a training period to get acquainted with the system and methods.

A within-subjects experimental design was used having as input variable the navigation method (with two levels, "Bicycle" and "Free hand"), and as output variables user performance and satisfaction. Performance was assessed by the number of boxes gathered, the number of collisions with the walls, and the velocity attained by the participants, similarly to earlier studies concerning navigation (Sousa Santos et al., 2009; Lapointe et al., 2011). Satisfaction was assessed through a post-task questionnaire. Readers are forwarded to (Dias et al., 2015) for details concerning the experiment, data analysis, and discussion of the results. This first study allowed evolving the methods, and fine-tuning the experimental protocol that was later applied to validate and compare forthcoming methods.

The data analysis results suggested that participants performed globally better when navigating using the Free hand method as they caught slightly more objects, and attained higher speeds, with approximately the same number of collisions. Nonetheless, throughout the experiment, a similar interest by the users in

Figure 3. Participant's view with a box to catch (left) and plan of the maze (right)

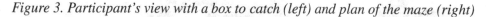

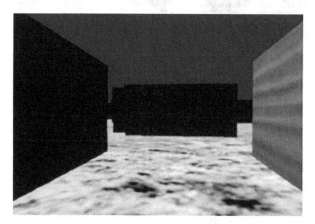

both methods was noticed by the experimenter. While, in fact, the users' performance and satisfaction were better in some of the measured variables with the Free hand, participants considered Bicycle as a suitable and natural method for navigation. Additionally, participants suggested some improvements such as to include the possibility to start/stop the motion by opening the hands, and even proposed other metaphors as controlling a motor boat rudder. In retrospective we understood that the main constraint of the Bicycle method was that users could not stop the interaction efficiently. This may be explained by the "non-parkable" issue (Bowman, 2014), which precludes increasing precision in spatial freehand 3D interfaces. The release of the new Kinect SDK helped solve this significant problem since the gestures could be easily modified to include grabbing to begin any movement. Furthermore, we also realized the affordance provided by the metaphor, a bicycle handlebar, could be visually explored fostering a greater discoverability of possible actions. This characteristic is very relevant since these methods are to be implemented on public displays applications, requiring a self-explanatory user interface, where the visual representation of a bicycle handlebar may indicate passing-by users how to initiate interaction. The issue that a virtual walkthrough in our system could generally take longer than the typical "information grabbing task", together with the observation that users generally navigate at full speed not taking advantage of the speed control, suggested that we could forgo a speed control avoiding wider arm motion. This allowed not only simplifying the interaction method, but also decreasing the risk of fatigue.

Based on the insight obtained from this study, a new method was developed as an evolution of Bicycle. In this new method, "Bicycle handlebar", users can actually perform the grab action activating the navigation motion when they place their hands alongside as if they were to grab the handlebars of a bicycle. Users can easily stop releasing both hands. Similarly, to the previous method, when users position their right hand slightly forward and the left hand back, the virtual camera turns left; left hand front and right hand back turns the camera to the right. A 3D model of a bicycle handlebar and an avatar of the hands (Figure 2c) are shown and rotate accordingly with the users' hands position. This method does not consider any velocity control mechanism, due to the aforementioned reasons.

During the preliminary evaluation of the Bicycle handlebar method, an alternative natural and intuitive metaphor for a navigation method came up. As a result, the "Steering wheel" method was devised. This method evokes a powerful metaphor, intuitive to most users, as it mimics the natural gestures of the users' hands when driving a car by grabbing the steering wheel. Again, the grab event of both hands activates the navigation motion, and by releasing both hands the user stops the motion. In this case users have to position their right hand slightly up and the left hand down, to turn left; alternatively, left hand up, and right hand down, turns right. A 3D model of a steering wheel is shown (Figure 2d) and rotates accordingly to the users' hands position as in the preceding method.

The two last methods only differ in the orientation of gestures that must be performed in order to determine in which direction the view camera will turn. In the Bicycle handlebar method, the hands gestures must be back and forward in relation to the depth sensor, while in Steering wheel the hands gesture must be performed up and down. Nevertheless, both methods foster the discoverability of possible actions through the visual representation of the handlebar or the steering wheel, suggesting inexperienced users how to interact.

These methods were evaluated in our public display system in order to obtain a validation and comparison concerning their usability in the context of virtual walkthroughs.

IMPLEMENTING THE METHODS

Navigation in virtual environments is usually characterized by the manipulation of a virtual camera to an anticipated position. Often, it is done by simulating the humans' head movement in the real world. Our methods use a gaze-directed steering technique, in which the navigation direction is determined by the forward vector of the viewing camera (Bowman et al., 2005) controlled by the users' hands depending on the method used.

In this section a brief overview of the used technologies is done and some implementation details concerning the Bicycle handlebar and the Steering wheel methods are described. Details concerning the implementation of the Freehand and Bicycle methods can be obtained in (Dias et al., 2015).

Technologies Used

The previous iterations of DETI-Interact were fully developed on Windows Presentation Foundation (WPF), which currently does not have support for a native 3D engine. On the other hand, previous works related with this project used diverse development frameworks (XNA and Unity) not supported by WPF, making them impossible to integrate within DETI-Interact. Since the XNA Framework was discontinued by Microsoft, a search for a 3D engine that might be integrated in WPF started by setting the requirements considered to be fundamental for the development of new features for future versions of DETI-Interact:

- Importing models in various formats;
- Assembling a scene with 3D objects;
- Supporting textures;
- Supporting skeletons for the implementation of avatars;
- Continuous development and improvement.

After this search, we concluded that there are not many 3D tools that might be integrated with WPF, and most are open-source and not being developed anymore.

We selected the 3D engines offering most guaranties in terms of continuous development and larger number of features. The selection was narrowed down to two engines: Helix 3D Toolkit2, and NeoAxis 3D Engine3 (http://helixtoolkit.codeplex.com/).

While the Helix Toolkit did not have all the previously selected features (e.g. support for textures and rigged models), and its development seemed stagnant, NeoAxis presented all the features, and had several recently released updates. Hence, our choice was to use NeoAxis as 3D engine (http://www.neoaxis.com/).

The NeoAxis 3D Engine is a free integrated development environment that allows the development of video games, simulators, as well as virtual reality and visualization software. It includes a full set of tools for fast and logical development of 3D projects. It uses C# with the .NET 3.5 framework as programming language and the rendering is done by OGRE (http://www.ogre3d.org/). Using the .NET framework makes it possible to integrate this 3D engine within WPF applications, which was one of our main requirements.

Regarding gesture tracking we used the Kinect SDK. The initial free hand and bicycle methods where developed using the SDK 1.6 that do not provide any grab gestures, whereas the Bicycle handle bar and Steering wheel used the SDK 1.8 that already provides the grab gestures. The sensor used was a Kinect for XBOX.

Algorithms

Algorithm 1 describes how Bicycle handlebar navigation was implemented. The hands position and state are retrieved from the skeleton data provided by the Kinect SDK. Considering the Z components of the hands position (using the reference system depicted in Figure 4) we determine which direction to steer the view camera, by incrementing/ decrementing its horizontal value. NeoAxis was used to control the physics of the scene, enabling the collision detection. Using a collision sphere attached to the camera that encompasses the navigation models (i.e. the Bicycle handlebar and the steering wheel), it was possible to detect the collision between this sphere and the walls of the maze. If no collision is detected, a new position for the camera is calculated by getting its current position and direction using a constant navigation speed factor. On the contrary, if a collision is detected, the camera is reset to a position determined by moving a few units in the opposite direction. The movement stops when the user opens at least one of his/her hands.

As mentioned, in Bicycle handlebar the gesture of the hands must be back and forward in relation to the sensor, while in Steering wheel the hands gestures must be performed up and down. For the Steering wheel method, we follow a similar approach where the Y components of the hands position are analyzed instead of the Z components, as the two methods only differ in the orientation of the gestures that must be performed in order to determine in which direction the view camera will turn.

Figure 4. Reference system used in the navigation methods

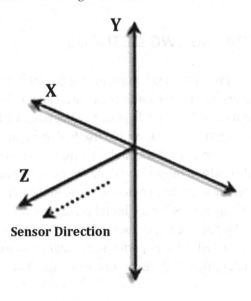

Algorithm 1. Determining the steering direction in Bicycle handlebar

```
input: HandLeft, HandRight
output: CameraDirection.Horizontal, CameraPosition
forall the render tick event do
        if left and right hands grab event then
                if HandLeft.Z - HandRight.Z < threshold then
                        // Turn the camera left
                        CameraDirection.Horizontal + = NavigationRotation;
                else
                        if HandRight.Z - HandLeft.Z < threshold then
                                // Turn the camera right
                                CameraDirection.Horizontal - = NavigationRotation;;
                        end
                end
                if Collision is not detected then
                        // Determine new view position
                        CameraPosition + = CameraDirection * NavigationSpeed;
                else
                        // Reset position
                        CameraPosition - = CameraDirection * NavigationSpeed * 2;
                end
        else
                // Stop motion
        end
end
```

COMPARING AND VALIDATING TWO METHODS

A new study with 53 participants was performed comparing the Bicycle handlebar and the Steering wheel methods. This was a controlled experiment meant to evaluate and compare the usability of the methods in order to assess if any of them or both were adequate to integrate in DETI-Interact; its workflow is represented in Figure 5. In this experiment users would use both navigation methods, navigating twice through the same maze. The experiment started with a short introduction to the project and the description of the methods. The main goal consisted in getting out of the maze in the shortest period of time. The experiment reached the end after the users had navigated through the maze with both methods. Finally, a questionnaire was given to participants. After the initial presentation, each user started the navigation with both methods (Figure 6). During the experiment, the application logged relevant data from the navigation, and the observer monitored the user performance and registered significant information. In what follows a more detailed description of the experiment is presented.

Figure 5. Experiment comparing the Bicycle handlebar and the Steering wheel methods: observer and participant's workflow, navigation methods, and data collected

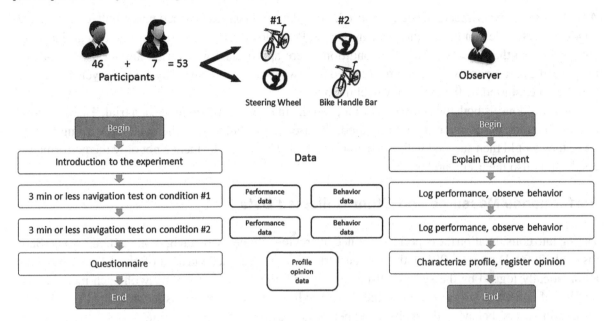

Figure 6. Participants' view during the virtual walkthrough with the Bicycle handlebar (left) and the Steering wheel (right) methods

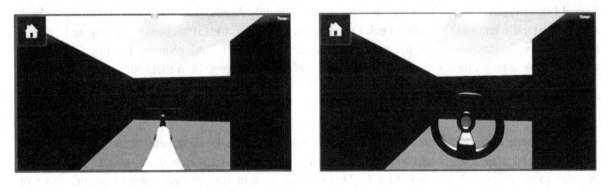

Hypothesis and Variables

The null hypothesis was defined as:

H0: Both navigation methods are equally usable to perform virtual walkthroughs in our system.

After defining the hypothesis, the main variables were identified. The independent variable (or input) was identified as the navigation method (with two levels: Bicycle handlebar, and Steering wheel), and the dependent variables (or output) as the usability of the navigation measured by performance measures (such as distance travelled, time and collisions logged by the system), and the satisfaction, opinion, and preferences of the participants collected from the post-task questionnaire.

Experimental Design

A within-group experimental design was used, i.e., all participants performed under both experimental conditions, Bicycle handlebar, and Steering wheel. Possible effects on the results due to learning were anticipated, so the order in which the conditions were approached was varied among users. For this purpose, the participants were randomly divided into two groups: one started by using Bicycle handlebar and the other started by the Steering wheel method.

This was done as both the starting position, and the maze were the same in each trial. Thus, it would be possible that, while using the first method, the user would fail to find the exit, yet learning how to do it, they would then succeed with the second method. This might influence not only the performance results, but also the users' preferences.

Performance Measures and Other Collected Data

Taking into consideration the experience gained in previous studies with navigation methods (Sousa Santos et al., 2009; Dias et al., 2015), the user performance was recorded via a set of quantitative measures automatically logged by the system: distance travelled, time spent navigating with each method, and number of collisions with the walls of the maze. Additional information was recorded by the observer, concerning users' behavior, difficulties and performance during the experiment.

After performing the navigation with both methods, users were asked to answer a questionnaire with a few questions about their profile (as age, gender, experience with different input devices), as well as about their satisfaction, opinion, and preferences regarding the two methods. The questionnaires used a 5 level Likert-type Scale (1-Strongly Disagree and 5- Strongly Agree) with the same questions for both methods: Handle bar and Steering wheel. Questions were related to if it was easy to navigate (ENa), if the gestures were intuitive (INa), had annoying characteristics (Ach) and, required training (Rtr). Users were also asked about their satisfaction (Sat), and preference between both methods.

Task

With each method, users had to navigate in the virtual maze until they reached the exit, or for a maximum period of 3 minutes. Users were guided by five numbered marks on the floor that represented the path to the exit (as shown in Figure 7). This task was designed to compel users to perform a set of navigation sub-tasks:

- Forward motion;
- Cornering;
- Turning back;
- Navigating onto a specific point;
- Navigating through doorways.

The authors had previously tested the task in order to detect possible issues that might make it too easy or too difficult for the users, such as speed control, maze complexity, door frame size and corridor width. A few adjustments were done empirically.

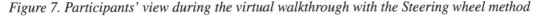

Figure 7. Participants' view during the virtual walkthrough with the Steering wheel method

Participants

The users that most likely would interact with our public display system were targeted: 53 volunteers (8 female and 45 male students aged between 16 and 28) participated in the experiment. Some participants stated that they had already experience with similar devices (e.g. Playstation Move), or had used the current version of DETI-Interact (at the date).

Results

We performed an exploratory data analysis of the logged and recorded data aiming to draw conclusions about the defined hypothesis regarding the two navigation methods.

Table 1 and Figures 8 and 9 show the main results for the performance variables (measured in a ratio scale): distance, time, number of collisions measured with the two navigation methods.

The boxplots of the logged data referring to travelled distance and time are shown in Figure 8. The two methods show similar median values and distributions for these two variables. A t-Student test did not reject the equality hypothesis of travelled distance (p= 0.99), neither a Wilcoxon Matched Pairs test rejected the equality hypothesis of time spent by participants (p=0.58). However, we notice that many participants spent the maximum time given, suggesting that the experiment should have had a longer maximum time.

Table 1. Average and median of the results obtained with the two navigation methods

	Average ± Standard Deviation		Median	
	Bicycle Handlebar	**Steering Wheel**	**Bike Handlebar**	**Steering Wheel**
Distance	282.7 ± 68.0	282.8 ± 81.2	296.7	283.0
Time (s)	147.2 ± 34.5	143.2 ± 37.0	159.0	156.0
Collisions	11.5 ± 8.8	12.0 ± 8.5	10	11

Figure 8. Box plots of navigation test results: distance travelled and time spent with both methods (Bicycle handlebar - BHB, and Steering wheel - SW)

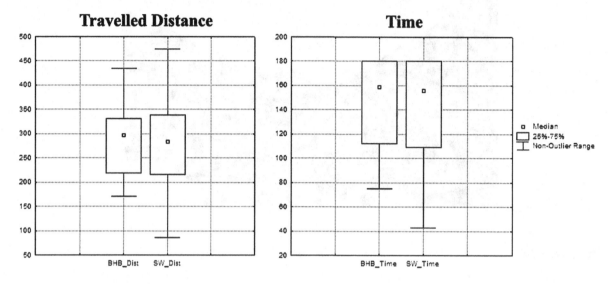

Figure 9. Box plots of navigation test results: number of collisions with both methods (Bicycle handlebar - BHB, and Steering wheel - SW)

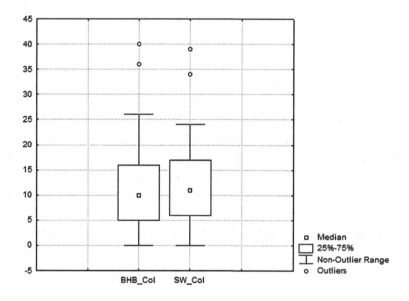

Figure 9 depicts the number of collisions, and shows that participants made slightly more collisions while using the Steering wheel method, when compared with the Bicycle handlebar. This could be due to the size of the model used to represent the steering wheel, which was larger than the bicycle handlebar model. Perhaps the former was occluding to a larger extent the view of the camera, hindering the participant to perform a "clear" turn; however, this difference is not statistically significant (t-Student test p=0.69).

These results show that participants had similar performance while using the two methods, corroborating the stated null hypothesis. Yet, we identified aspects that should be done differently, in future user studies with a similar goal of comparing different methods to interact with our system: participants should be allowed to interact until the goal is attained, rather than defining a maximum navigation time. In fact, defining such boundary may influence the conclusions drawn from the results. In cases when a user spent the 3 minutes navigating it is more difficult to discriminate the performance between the methods, as such user might have needed much more time to exit the maze (due to usability problems) or, could have been very close to reach the exit, and simply was not given enough time.

As mentioned, the post-task questionnaire asked users' opinion concerning easiness of navigation (ENa), gesture intuitiveness (INa), annoying characteristics (Ach), and requiring training (Rtr). Users were also asked about their satisfaction (Sat), and preference between both methods. Figure 10 shows the questionnaire results concerning the ordinal variables INa, ACh, and Sat that were statistically different between the two methods. Wilcoxon Matched Pairs test rejected the equality hypothesis (with $p=0.02$ and $p=0.03$, both < 0.05 for INa and ACh, and $p=0.08 < 0.10$ for Sat), suggesting that participants had different opinions about the methods concerning these variables, which probably is why the Steering wheel method was preferred by more participants (30), than the Bicycle handlebar (18) (the remaining participants did not express any preference). This result is significantly different (as shown by a Binomial test, $p=0.01$).

The previous results show that participants had similar performance while using the two methods corroborating the stated null hypothesis concerning the performance dimension of usability. Hence, the two methods developed to interact and perform virtual walkthroughs in our system seem adequate. However, Steering wheel got better results concerning satisfaction, and was preferred by more participants; this might be due to the current greater evocative power of the steering wheel metaphor when compared to the bicycle handlebar.

CONCLUSION

This chapter describes how spatial freehand gesture based navigation methods were developed to be used in virtual walkthroughs meant to be experienced in large displays. Two methods were developed and performance and satisfaction results from tests with users suggest that both seem adequate to be used as navigation methods in scenarios similar to our system, while one was preferred.

Figure 10. Questionnaire results concerning the variables (from left to right INa, ACh, Sat) significantly different between the methods (Bicycle handlebar-blue; Steering wheel-red)

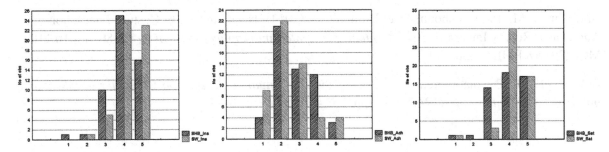

As we have considered that virtual walkthroughs might take longer than the simple "information grabbing tasks" typically performed by our users in the system, the navigation methods used in such walkthroughs must avoid uncomfortable or tiresome positions and motions. However, if these methods are to be integrated in applications meant to be used for much longer than a few minutes, fatigue will definitely become a more relevant usability challenge, still needing to be better tackled.

Using the iterative approach described in this chapter we were able to eventually develop two methods that are usable for our target users and context of use. The followed approach guided us in a situation of scarcity of guidelines, and although it involved several rounds of user evaluation entailing a relatively complex procedure, it provided enlightening insights, and experience that we consider generalizable and that will definitely help in future cases. Moreover, this approach should involve evaluation methods aimed to quantitatively assess some usability dimensions (as times and errors), as well as methods aimed to qualitatively assess other dimensions, more difficult to assess in a quantitative way (as satisfaction). The two methods provide information of a different nature that complements each other.

Despite that the developed methods were devised to be used with a large display, they seem fit enough to be used in walkthroughs in virtual environments experienced with other types of displays, namely head mounted displays or wall projections. In fact, the literature mentions virtual reality applications as a major application scenario for freehand gestures, and thus we consider testing our methods in such situations as a promising line of future work.

We note that the iterative approach undertaken in the design of the navigation methods shows an interesting and clear parallelism to the iterative approaches usually taken while developing interactive software. In particular, in this work we also followed a user-centered approach, with several iterations and evaluations in the end of each round. Thus, we believe that, similarly to the software development cycles, undertaking such an iterative approach to develop spatial freehand navigation methods is advantageous.

ACKNOWLEDGMENT

The authors are grateful to the subjects who participated in the controlled experiment, as well as to all the people that have in anyway contributed to improve this work.

REFERENCES

Balakrishnan, R., & Kurtenbach, G. (1999). Exploring Bimanual Camera Control and Object Manipulation in 3D Graphics Interfaces. *Proceedings of the SIGCHI Conference on Human Factors in Computing Systems: The CHI Is the Limit* (pp. 56–62). doi:10.1145/302979.302991

Billinghurst, M., Piumsomboon, T., & Huidong, B. (2014). Hands in Space- Gesture Interaction with Augmented Reality Interfaces. *IEEE Computer Graphics and Applications, 34*(1), 77–80. doi:10.1109/MCG.2014.8 PMID:24808171

Bolt, R. (1980). Put-that-there. *Proceedings of the 7th annual conference on Computer graphics and interactive techniques - SIGGRAPH '80* (pp. 262–270).

Boussemart, Y., Rioux, F., Rudzicz, F., Wozniewski, M., & Cooperstock, J. R. (2004). A framework for 3D visualisation and manipulation in an immersive space using an untethered bimanual gestural interface.*Proceedings of the ACM symposium on Virtual reality software and technology - VRST '04* (pp. 162–165). doi:10.1145/1077534.1077566

Bowman, D. A. (2014). 3D User Interfaces. In M. Soegaard & R. Friis Dam (Eds.), *The Encyclopedia of Human-Computer Interaction* (Ch. 32, 2nd ed.). Aarhus, Denmark: The Interaction Design Foundation. Retrieved from https://www.interaction-design.org/literature/book/the-encyclopedia-of-human-computer-interaction-2nd-ed/3d-user-interfaces

Bowman, D. A., Kruijff, E., Poupyrev, I., & LaViola, J. (2005). *3D User Interfaces: Theory and Practice*. Addison Wesley.

Crowley, J. L., Coutaz, J., & Bérard, F. (2000). Perceptual user interfaces: Things that see. *Communications of the ACM, 43*(3), 54–64, ff. doi:10.1145/330534.330540

Dias, P., Parracho, J., Cardoso, J., Quintino Ferreira, B., Ferreira, C., & Sousa Santos, B. (2015). Developing and evaluating two gestural-based virtual environment navigation methods for large displays. Proceedings of Human-Computer Interaction (HCI) International 2015, Chapter Distributed, Ambient, and Pervasive Interactions (LNCS) (Vol. 9189, pp. 141-151). Springer. doi:10.1007/978-3-319-20804-6_13

Dias, P., Sousa, T., Parracho, J., Cardoso, I., Monteiro, A., & Sousa Santos, B. (2014). Student Projects Involving Novel Interaction with Large Displays. *IEEE Computer Graphics and Applications, 34*(2), 80–86. doi:10.1109/MCG.2014.35 PMID:24808202

Fisher, S., McGreevy, M., Humphries, J., & Robinett, W. (1986). Virtual Environment Display System. *Proceedings of the 1986 workshop on Interactive 3D graphics I3D '86* (pp. 77–87). doi:10.1145/319120.319127

Freeman, W. T., & Weissman, C. (1995). Television control by hand gestures.*Proceedings of International Workshop on Automatic Face and Gesture Recognition* (pp. 179–183).

Garber, L. (2013). Gestural Technology: Moving Interfaces in a New Direction. *Computer, 46*(10), 22–25. doi:10.1109/MC.2013.352

Hernoux, F., & Christmann, O. (2014). A seamless solution for 3D real-time interaction: Design and evaluation. *Virtual Reality (Waltham Cross), 19*(1), 1–20. doi:10.1007/s10055-014-0255-z

Höysniemi, J., Hämäläinen, P., Turkki, L., & Rouvi, T. (2005). Children's intuitive gestures in vision-based action games. *Communications of the ACM, 48*(1), 44–50. doi:10.1145/1039539.1039568

Hürst, W., & Van Wezel, C. (2013). Gesture-based interaction via finger tracking for mobile augmented reality. *Multimedia Tools and Applications, 62*(1), 233–258. doi:10.1007/s11042-011-0983-y

Jankowski, J., & Hachet, M. (2015). Advances in Interaction with 3D Environments. *Computer Graphics Forum, 34*(1), 152–190. doi:10.1111/cgf.12466

Karam, M. (2006). *A framework for research and design of gesture-based human computer interactions* [Doctoral Dissertation]. University of Southampton.

Karam, M., & Schraefel, M. C. (2005). A study on the use of semaphoric gestures to support secondary task interactions. In *CHI '05 extended abstracts on Human factors in computing systems* (pp. 1961–1964). New York, NY, USA: ACM Press. doi:10.1145/1056808.1057067

Krueger, M. W., Gionfriddo, T., & Hinrichsen, K. (1985). VIDEOPLACE---an artificial reality. *ACM SIGCHI Bulletin, 16*(4), 35–40. doi:10.1145/1165385.317463

Kühnel, C., Westermann, T., Hemmert, F., Kratz, S., Müller, A., & Möller, S. (2011). I'm home: Defining and evaluating a gesture set for smart-home control. *International Journal of Human-Computer Studies, 69*(11), 693–704. doi:10.1016/j.ijhcs.2011.04.005

Lapointe, J., Savard, P., & Vinson, N. G. (2011). A comparative study of four input devices for desktop virtual walkthroughs. *Computers in Human Behavior, 27*(6), 2186–2191. doi:10.1016/j.chb.2011.06.014

LaViola, J., Jr. (2014). An Introduction to 3D Gestural Interfaces. Proceedings of the ACM SIGGRAPH 2014 Courses (pp. 25:1–25:42).

Malik, S., Ranjan, A., & Balakrishnan, R. (2005). Interacting with large displays from a distance with vision-tracked multi-finger gestural input.*Proceedings of the 18th annual ACM Symposium User Interface Software and Technology - UIST '05* (pp. 43-52). doi:10.1145/1095034.1095042

Ni, T. (2011). *A Framework of Freehand Gesture Interaction: Techniques, Guidelines, and Applications* [Doctoral Dissertation]. Virginia Tech. Retrieved from http://scholar.lib.vt.edu/theses/available/etd-09212011-230923/unrestricted/Ni_T_D_2011.pdf)

Nielsen, M., Störring, M., Moeslund, T. B., & Granum, E. (2004). A procedure for developing intuitive and ergonomic gesture interfaces for HCI. In Gesture-Based Communication in Human-Computer Interaction, (LNCS) (Vol. 2915, pp. 409–420). Springer. doi:10.1007/978-3-540-24598-8_38

Norman, D. A., & Nielsen, J. (2010). Gestural Interfaces: A Step Backward In Usability. *Interaction,* 46–49. doi:10.1145/1836216.1836228

Paradiso, J. A. (2003). Tracking Contact and Free Gesture Across Large Interactive Surfaces. *Communications of the ACM, 46*(7), 62–69. doi:10.1145/792704.792731

Probst, K., Lindlbauer, D., & Greindl, P. (2013). Rotating, tilting, bouncing: using an interactive chair to promote activity in office environments. Proceedings of the Extended Abstracts on Human Factors in Computing Systems CHI '13 (pp. 79–84). doi:10.1145/2468356.2468372

Probst, K., Lindlbauer, D., & Haller, M. (2014). A chair as ubiquitous input device: exploring semaphoric chair gestures for focused and peripheral interaction.*Proceedings of the 32nd International Conference on Human Factors in Computing SystemsCHI '14* (pp. 4097–4106). doi:10.1145/2556288.2557051

Quek, F., McNeill, D., Bryll, R., Duncan, S., Ma, X.-F., Kirbas, C., & Ansari, R. et al. (2002). Multimodal human discourse: Gesture and speech. *ACM Transactions on Computer-Human Interaction, 9*(3), 171–193. doi:10.1145/568513.568514

Ren, G., Li, C., O'Neill, E., & Willis, P. (2013a). 3D freehand gestural navigation for interactive public displays. *IEEE Computer Graphics and Applications*, *33*(2), 47–55. doi:10.1109/MCG.2013.15 PMID:24807939

Ren, G., & O'Neill, E. (2013b). 3D selection with freehand gesture. *Computers & Graphics*, *37*(3), 101–120. doi:10.1016/j.cag.2012.12.006

Sousa Santos, B., Dias, P., Pimentel, A., Baggerman, J. W., Ferreira, C., Silva, S., & Madeira, J. (2009). Head-mounted display versus desktop for 3D navigation in virtual reality: A user study. *Multimedia Tools and Applications*, *41*(1), 161–181. doi:10.1007/s11042-008-0223-2

Taylor, S., Keskin, C., Hilliges, O., Izadi, S., & Helmes, J. (2014). Type–Hover–Swipe in 96 Bytes: A Motion Sensing Mechanical Keyboard.*Proceedings of CHI 2014* (pp. 1695–1704).

Vogel, D., & Balakrishnan, R. (2005). Distant freehand pointing and clicking on very large, high resolution displays.*Proceedings of the 18th Annual ACM Symposium on User Interface Software and Technology* (pp. 33–42). doi:10.1145/1095034.1095041

Von Hardenberg, C., & Bérard, F. (2001). Bare-Hand Human-Computer Interaction. *Proceedings of the ACM Workshop on Perceptive User Interfaces* (pp. 113–120).

Wachs, J., Kölsch, M., Stern, H., & Edan, Y. (2011). Vision-Based Hand Gesture Applications. *Communications of the ACM*, *54*(2), 60–71. doi:10.1145/1897816.1897838 PMID:21984822

Wobbrock, J., & Aung, H. (2005). Maximizing the guessability of symbolic input. Proceedings of the Extended Abstracts on Human Factors in Computing Systems CHI'05 (pp. 1869–1872). doi:10.1145/1056808.1057043

Wobbrock, J. O., Morris, M. R., & Wilson, A. D. (2009). User-defined gestures for surface computing. *Proceedings of CHI '09* (pp. 1083-1092).

KEY TERMS AND DEFINITIONS

3D User Interface: A human-computer interface involving 3D interaction, i.e., in which the user performs tasks directly in a 3D spatial context.

Freehand Gesture: A gesture performed in the absence of constraints imposed by wearable devices (as gloves) or handheld tracking devices.

Gesture: A form of non-verbal communication consisting in moving a part of the body (typically a hand or the head) with an underlying meaning.

Manipulative Gesture: A gesture meant to control an entity with the hands by acting directly on it in a real or virtual environment.

Navigation: A fundamental task in 3D environments allowing users to find their way and move around the environment. It presents several challenges as providing spatial awareness, and efficient ways to move between distant places. It includes travel and wayfinding (motor and cognitive components, respectively).

Semaphoric Gesture: A gesture requiring prior knowledge or learning based on a formalized dictionary used to trigger a pre-defined action.

User Study: A type of experimental research method involving users, which may be used to seek insight to guide future efforts to improve existing techniques, methods or products or to show that a theory applies under specific conditions. It should involve quantitative and qualitative methods.

Virtual Walkthrough: A tour allowing users to walk through a specific place (e.g. a virtual museum, virtual library or virtual university campus) without having to travel physically.

Chapter 4
Using a Hands–Free System to Manage Common Devices in Constrained Conditions

Pedro Cardoso
University of Algarve, Portugal

Jânio Monteiro
University of Algarve, Portugal

João Rodrigues
University of Algarve, Portugal

Luís Sousa
University of Algarve, Portugal

ABSTRACT

As computing equipment become ubiquitous, a new set of interfacing devices need to be developed and properly adapted to the conditions where this equipment is to be used. Interacting with machines might present difficulties relative to the handiness of common interfacing devices, when wearing certain clothes, doing certain dirty jobs, or when they are used by people with accessibility needs. In the last decades a new set of input devices were made available, including 3D sensors, which allow machine interacting without the need of touching any device. This chapter presents two prototype solutions supported by one of this 3D sensors, the Leap Motion, to manage appliances and other devices in a building and for the picking and loading of vehicles in a warehouse. The first case is contextualized in the area of the IoT and load scheduling of appliances, as a decisive factor in reduction of the buildings' electrical costs. The second case is presented as a solution to integrate the distribution of fresh and frozen goods where workers use thick clothes/gloves to carry out their work.

INTRODUCTION

Definitions of Human-Computer Interaction (HCI) are easy to find. The majority of those definitions say that Human–computer interaction involves the study, planning, design and uses of the interaction between users and computers. The HCI, term introduced more than three decades ago in works like (Card, Moran, & Newell, 1980; Carlisle, 1976), is often regarded as the intersection of computer science, behavioral sciences, design, media studies, among other fields of study. It is therefore quite easy to recognize that the boundaries of what is HCI are relatively fuzzy, including a wide-range of practice

DOI: 10.4018/978-1-5225-0435-1.ch004

fields. Historically, in a non-exhaustive way, HCI evolved from sets of switches, punched cards, monitors, keyboards, mouse pointers, touch-screens, motion detection devices, to bionic interfaces. HCI is changing fast. Dialogs between the computer HAL 9000 and humans in the 1968 film "2001: A Space Odyssey" (Kubrick, 1968) or the ones with the artificially intelligent, Vox 114, library host hologram in "Time Machine" movie, which communicates and interacts naturally with a time traveler (Wells, 2002), the invasive neural interfaces presented in "The Matrix" (Wachowski & Wachowski, 1999) or many of the interacting technologies presented in "Minority Report" (Spielberg, 2002) were once science fiction, but in the global sense not any more.

The truth is that, as Jonathan Grudin from the Microsoft Corporation claims, HCI is a moving target (Grudin, 2012). The future of HCI is expected to be supported on the ubiquitous and continuous presence of devices where computers communicate to give universal access to data and computational services. The future user expects high functional systems where, among other things, accessing those functionalities is natural, with mass availability of computer graphics, high-bandwidth interaction, and wide variety of displays (e.g., on common surfaces, with flexibility, large and thin).

Most computers and mobile devices have already the computational capacity and are equipped with devices to mimic humans' senses like sight and hearing. With the appropriate sensors other "feelings" can be easily achieved like temperature, taste, smell, touch, balance or measure acceleration (Bhowmik, 2014). The input devices of these computers can be used to control machines in a natural and intuitive way, giving a new dimension to the traditional users' interfaces.

There is an extensive list of works that study "human senses" devices to interact with computers. In Breen et al. (2014) a survey of the key concepts and underlying technologies is presented for voice and language understanding (including voice recognition, hardware optimization, speech synthesis, natural language understanding, etc.). A multimodal human-computer interaction focused on body, gesture, gaze, and affective interaction is presented in (Jaimes & Sebe, 2007). Senses like smell and taste are starting to be more effectively achieved. For instance, in (Villarreal & Gordillo, 2013) the results of a sensor model of aspiration and the design of a smell system device inspired in biological process is presented. In (Halder et al., 2012) the development of a polymer membrane is addressed, based in potentiometric taste sensors with efficient selectivity and sensitivity to mimic the mammalian tongue for measurement of basic tastes like saltiness, sourness, bitterness, sweetness and umami or savory.

Besides the usual keyboards/mouse or touchscreen devices, driven among others by the game industry, one of the more developed type of interactions are the ones based on non-touching gesture recognition. For this purpose, several types of sensors can be used, such as: embedded cameras or mobile 3D sensors, such as the Structure Sensor (Struture sensor, 2015), the Leap Motion (Leap Motion, 2015), the Kinetic (Kinect, 2015) or the zSense (Withana, Peiris, Samarasekara, & Nanayakkara, 2015).

Bearing the previous context in mind, this chapter aims to present a proof-of-concept of two systems, supported on the Leap Motion sensor, which were designed to be used in: (1) programming of home appliances, based on simple monitors spread in the building with the respective Leap Motion sensor. In this case, an architectural plan of the building is used to display the appliances' locations. Then, for each appliance, a programming interface, combined with consumption statistics and information about the equipment is presented, keeping the navigation between the diverse interfaces supported on intuitive swipe gestures. The system is connected to a central energy management system which has the objective of optimizing the energy costs of the building, either by selecting lower tariff rates or by selecting self-production hours to start the appliances. The second example is an application used for the (2) the picking and loading docking area of fresh and frozen goods in a warehouse, where the employees wear gloves/thick clothes or have dirty hands, which make troublesome the use of common interfaces, like a keyboard or a mouse. In particular, it is presented a prototype which makes possible the navigation through a set of menus presenting vehicles' routes information, list of products to be picked from the warehouse and products' loading order into the vehicles.

The remainder of this chapter is organized as follows. The next section presents some background about gesture recognition technologies with more detail on the Leap Motion Sensor. The third section presents details about the implementation of the already introduced prototypes. The last section presents some conclusions over the developed work.

BACKGROUND

A gesture recognition device is an electronic device capable of identifying human gestures. The type of the technologies involved in those devices can be used to categorize them. A recent example is the (1) radar-based sensor developed by Project Soli (ATAP, Google's Advanced Technology and Projects group) which looks for a small, gesture-recognizing, radar-enabled sensor that aims to provide a way for people to interact with their smart-watches without touching their displays (Baldwin, 2015). A second example of technology is supported on the use of (2) wired gloves (Camastra & De Felice, 2013; Tongrod, Kerdcharoen, Watthanawisuth, & Tuantranont, 2010) that detect movements of the hands (e.g., position and rotation) and fingers (e.g., bending) or, in a reverse way, provide kinesthetic communication which recreates the sense of touch by applying forces, vibrations, or motions to the user. One of the firsts commercially available hand-tracking glove-type devices was the (Zimmerman, Lanier, Blanchard, Bryson, & Harvill, 1987) which provides data (to the computer) concerning the fingers' bending, hands' position and orientation, and tactile feedback to the wearer of the glove. Some surveys which include data gloves can be found for instance in (Dipietro, Sabatini, & Dario, 2008; Pantelopoulos & Bourbakis, 2010; Sturman & Zeltzer, 1994). In a third category, (3) depth-aware cameras technologies are included, as the Microsoft Kinect (Kinect, 2015), used for instance in (Alves et al., 2015) to implement the interaction with a virtual public relations avatar or in (Ren, Yuan, Meng, & Zhang, 2013) where it was used to input data to arithmetic computation and to play the rock-paper-scissors game. In (Ren, Yuan, & Zhang, 2011) the authors propose a method called Finger-Earth Mover's Distance that only matches fingers, not the whole hand shape, thus better distinguishing hand gestures. Another depth-aware camera is the Leap Motion sensor which will be analyzed in the next sections. Other technologies like (4) Stereo cameras and (5) 2D cameras technologies were used for instance in the recognition of hand gestures using computational vision in (Li, An, Min, & Hong, 2011; Liu & Kehtarnavaz, 2013; Saleiro et al., 2015; Ushaw, Ziogas, Eyre, & Morgan, 2013). More comprehensive literature reviews on hand tracking and gesture recognition can be found in (Erol, Bebis, Nicolescu, Boyle, & Twombly, 2007; Mitra & Acharya, 2007; Rautaray & Agrawal, 2015; Suarez & Murphy, 2012).

In terms of dedicated devices, many have appeared in the market in the last years, most of the times associated with the gaming industry or inspired by technologies presented in movies, which were science fiction at the time of their shooting. For example the Tobii EyeX (Tobii, 2015), from one of the world leaders in eye tracking, is a device that combine eye tracking with input from traditional controls. It allows navigation using the eyes complemented with keyboards, touchpads or voice command to select an item. The Elliptic Labs sensor (Elliptic-Labs, 2015) is a device that allows the control of the smartphone or tablet without touching it. Ultrasound signals sent from speakers integrated in the smartphones/tablets bounce against the hand and are recorded by microphones, allowing e recognition of the hand gestures. The Airwriting (Lehne, 2015) allows writing without keyboard. The system uses a glove which has acceleration and angular rate sensors (gyroscopes) to detect the movements of the hand and transfer them over a wireless connection to a computer system, offering an interface for wearable computing applications. The eyeSight (Singlecue, 2015) is a touch-free advanced gesture control interface which allows to control almost all of the house's electronics that is Infrared or Wi-Fi controlled (e.g., TVs, projectors, cable and satellite boxes, disc players, and media players). The eyeSight uses gesture recognition technology from movements made in its camera's field of view. A similar product is the Pointgrab software (Pointgrab, 2015) which enables any consumer electronic device including televisions, personal computers, tablets, and smartphones to be operated by gesture control using finger, one hand and two hands shapes and movements, while using a standard camera. The device uses depth information to essentially create a "virtual touch space" right in front of users, so they can point directly at anything on the screen to access it through intuitive actions such as swipe, thumbs up, grab, drag and drop, two hands zoom and rotate to interact with it. The Myo Armband (Myo Armband, 2015), as the name suggests, is an band to be placed in the user's arm, allowing the control of presentation (compatible with some of the major presentations software, e.g., Microsoft PowerPoint, Prezi and Google slides), and media players and related software (e.g., Netflix, Spotify, VLC). The device uses electromyography (EMG) sensors, highly sensitive Inertial Measurement Unit (IMU) sensors containing three-axis gyroscopes, accelerometers and magnetometers to detect the user's movements and gestures. The Microsoft Kinect (Kinect, 2015) is a motion sensor developed for the Xbox 360 and Xbox One, along with the company Prime Sense, allowing players to interact with video games without the need of a control/joystick. The device, among other things, has a RGB camera that allows the facial recognition of the person in front of the console, an infrared depth sensor which allows to scan the 3D around environment, a built-in microphone which in addition to capturing the nearest voices can differentiate the external noise allowing easy voices commands development using the SDK (Software Development Kit), and detects 48 points of articulation of the body. Some examples of use for the Kinect sensor are the interaction with art installations (Alves et al., 2015), in robotics (El-laithy, Huang, & Yeh, 2012), or for head pose classification (Yun, Changrampadi, & Gu, 2014).

Comparisons between the devices and technologies can be found for instance in (Bachmann, Weichert, & Rinkenauer, 2014; Billinghurst, 2013; Cheng, Yang, & Liu, 2015; Marin, Dominio, & Zanuttigh, 2014; Rautaray & Agrawal, 2015).

As mentioned, this document will mainly focus on the Leap Motion (Leap Motion, 2015) controller. The Leap Motion uses optical sensors and infrared light to detect object in front of the sensors (see Figure 1). The device consists of two monochromatic infrared cameras and three infrared LEDs. The location of the cameras and LEDs allows to observe a nearly semi-spherical area (approximately 150 degrees) with an effective range of approximately 25 to 600 millimeters (1 inch to 2 feet) above the device, corresponding to roughly 225.000 cubic centimeters (approximately 8 cubic feet) of interactive 3D space. It tracks infrared light with a wavelength of 850 nanometers, which is outside the visible light spectrum, and is capable of handling up to 200 frames per second using the infrared cameras. The device is connected via a USB port to the computer.

The Leap Motion has an Application Programming Interface (API) capable of detecting multiple hand gestures. The configurations and proper combinations of gestures' detection, allow the recognition of a large set of actions such as a circular movement by a finger, a straight line movement by the hand with fingers extended, a forward tapping movement by a finger/hand, a downward tapping movement

Figure 1. Leap Motion right-handed coordinate system
Adapted from (Leap Motion, 2015)

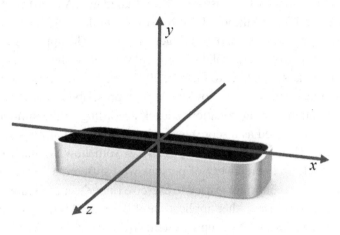

by a finger/hand, or the opening or closing of the hands, done with one or both hands, generally used to implement zoom in or out. Other examples are the movement from side to side with the hand to indicate a swipe gesture or a finger poking forward that can be used to indicate a screen tap gesture. Besides the system's recognition and tracking of hands and fingers it can also recognize and track hand/finger-like tools, such as pencils. The device operates in an intimate proximity with high precision and tracking frame rate, reporting discrete positions, gestures, and motion (Leap developer portal, 2015; Potter, Araullo, & Carter, 2013; Sanders, 2014; Spiegelmock, 2013; Sutton, 2013). The Leap Motion API measures physical quantities, namely: distance (in millimeters), time (in microseconds), speed (in millimeters/second) and angle (in radians). At the time of writing, the API supported several programming languages and platforms as C++, C#, Unity, Objective-C, Java, Python, JavaScript, and Unreal Engine.

The Leap Motion controller senses the space as a 3D space with standard Cartesian coordinate system, also known as right-handed orientation (see Figure 1). The origin of the coordinate system is centered at the top of the device. The x-axis is placed horizontally along the device, with positive values increasing from left to right (staying in front of the device) and the z-axis is placed also on horizontal plane, perpendicular with x-axis with values increasing towards the user (the front side of the device). The y-axis is placed vertically, with positive values increasing upwards. The API presents motion tracking data to the applications as a series of snapshots called frames. Each frame of tracking data contains the measured positions and other information about each entity detected in that snapshot such as hands, fingers, and tools, as well as recognized gestures and factors describing the overall motion in the scene. For instance the Hand class has methods such as palmPosition which returns a vector with the center position of the palm in millimeters from the Leap Motion Controller origin or the palmVelocity which returns a vector with the rate of change of the palm position in millimeters/second. Optional configuration properties allow the gesture detection improvement using "out of the box" gestures examples possible to be retrieved with Leap Motion API. For example, in a circle gesture, where the user can do a circle with a finger, there are two properties selectable: minimum radius and minimum arc (by default, minimum radius is set to 5 mm and minimum arc set to 1.5π radians). For a swipe gesture, there are also two properties selectable, minimum length set by default to 150 mm and minimum velocity set to 1000 mm/s.

The literature has a significant amount of works based on the device in study. For instance, the suitability of the Leap Motion controller for Australian Sign Language (Auslan) recognition is studied in (Potter, Araullo, & Carter, 2013). In Sutton (2013) the use of the Leap Motion is proposed to execute air painting through gesture and movement of the fingers in the air. The application allows to paint with up to ten simultaneous brush strokes controlled by the movement of the fingers and thumbs on both hands. In (Liu, Zhang, Patrick Rau, Choe, & Gulrez, 2015) the authors propose an online interactive system for hand rehabilitation. The system allows doctors to prescribe motion exercises to be imitated by the patients. In return patients get automatic feedback according to the similarity of the requested and performed movements (reflected as a score), engaging a gamming attitude which motivates them in the rehabilitation process (Nap & Diaz-Orueta, 2014). A somehow similar work was proposed in (Khademi et al., 2014) to help in the recovery of persons who suffered a stroke. In this case the hand tracking data of the Leap Motion controller is used to exercise finger's individuation using an adaptation of a Fruit Ninja game. It's easy to find other application of the Leap Motion controllers such as music control (Tubb & Dixon, 2015), contact-free input system (Bachmann, Weichert, & Rinkenauer, 2014), shape modeling (Cui & Sourin, 2014), etc. In the Leap Motion app store ("Leap Motion App Store," 2015) is possible to find hundreds of applications that use the controller divided in several categories, such as: computer controls, creative tools, education, games, music and entertainment, productivity, science and virtual reality.

APPLICATIONS OF THE LEAP MOTION CONTROLLER

This section presents two prototypes that use the Leap Motion, developed for two real scenarios. The first one addresses the control of appliances/smart objects in a smart building targeting energy efficiency. In the second case, the problem of picking and loading of vehicles is addressed for a warehouse, when the workers have difficulties associated with the handling of common input devices such as keyboard and mouse.

Control of Appliances in a Building

We are witnessing an increase in the energy produced by renewable sources, either motivated by the high cost of fossil fuels or by an increment in environmental restrictions. In this scenario, the traditional view of a distribution grid, that uses centralized generators to provide power to consumers, is being replaced by a Smart Grid solution, where renewable energy sources are being integrated into the grid, following a distributed generation schema (Shen, 2012). One major drawbacks of some of these sources, with higher expression in the energy obtained from wind and photovoltaic sources, is that they are many times characterized as intermittent resources since their power varies according to uncontrollable environmental conditions. In such scenario, the introduction of demand side management solution is seen as a desirable strategy to control/reduce the necessity of peak power units.

By creating a new range of appliances that integrate Information Technologies (IT) and the Internet of Things (IoT), users have now the possibility to get information, control or adjust every equipment, machine or lamp in their building (e.g., house, hotel or factory) either automatically, semi-automatically or manually. When combined with an optimization solution this not only allows a maximization of investments made in renewable sources, but also a reduction of consumption costs, resulting from the adjustment of the work periods of electrical devices according to energy tariff rates of distribution system operators (Monteiro, Eduardo, Cardoso, & Semião, 2014).

Users play a key role in such systems. More precisely, the flexibility given by them to the load scheduling of appliances plays a decisive factor in its ability to perform cost reduction. It is therefore important for an optimization system to reflect user comfort levels and to interact with them using easy and intuitive interfaces (Monteiro, Cardoso, Serra, & Fernandes, 2014). In a scenario where many home residences, hotels, factories, etc., are moving from dozens to hundreds, or even thousands of electric devices, the usability and ergonomics of the traditional selection menus and sub-menus using a keyboard/ mouse/ touch screen that should be placed around the building divisions, becomes inappropriate for giving a command, or to query any information from a device. Numerous examples of possible interactions can be mentioned, such as the request about the consumption of a lamp, or a group of lamps represented in a daily graph, or a cycle changing of a machine (e.g., washing or drying), or the selection of the home scenario that requires less consumption during a week day, or even to check all the consumption statistics of an air-conditioning in a specific location on a hotel.

The Leap Motion sensor, due to their reduced size and price, can be integrated in several different locations in the buildings, allowing the replacement of the traditional peripherals/hardware interface. Furthermore, as a hands-free interface, the Leap Motion can provide easy navigation on the home residence/hotel/factory plant, with the real localization of the electric devices shown in any television or screen located anywhere on the building's rooms. Within those plants, the user could navigate from device to device, individually selecting, turning them on/off or requesting information about them. Another major advantage of these hands-free interface is the fact that the interaction can still occur if the user is wearing gloves or has dirty hands (e.g., for instance when cooking or working in a factory).

In this sense, the goal of creating a system capable of energy management is to implement a set of so-called smart objects supported in the concept of the IoT was endeavored. The objective was to have objects that communicate with each other and act based on an optimized control system, allow a better use of the energy produced by renewable energy sources and the consequent reduction of costs, while respecting electrical circuit constraints, user restrictions and correspondent comfort levels (Monteiro, Eduardo, Cardoso, & Semião, 2014). Taking this in mind, a hands-free 3D gesture recognition solution was developed, combining 2D and 3D representations of buildings, objects and menus, supports an intuitive interface between humans and the energy management device, facilitating such interaction in a way that cannot be achieved with other interface paradigms.

In Figure 2 is presented an example of a residential house with three floors that has several controllable objects, presented inside the red rectangles. For instance, in the ground floor the house has a boiler, an air conditioner device, the electrical vehicle charger controller and the electric meter that, besides measuring the consumptions also obtain tariff rates information, used ahead to semi-automatically schedule the house devices and optimize the electrical cost of the building.

One of the objectives during the development of this interface was to define a short number of movements and, at the same time, select the most intuitive ones, namely: the horizontal (left/right or forward/backward) and vertical (upward/downward) swipe gestures. The horizontal swipe gesture was used to navigate between devices, options and menus, while the vertical swipe gestures were used to select and deselect options and menus as we will see next.

The Leap Motion API has the SwipeGesture class which has, among others, the attributes direction, pointable, position, speed, and start_position. The SwipeGesture objects are generated for each swiping finger or tool, which must be enabled in the application. You can set the minimum length and velocity

Figure 2. 2D House model presenting the appliances (inside the red rectangles) and the selected objected (pointed by a green arrow)

required for a movement to be recognized as a swipe with default values equal to 150 mm for the Gesture.Swipe.MinLength and 1000 mm/s for the Gesture.Swipe.MinVelocity configuration parameters. For instance, the correct swipe movement associates a 3D direction vector ranging from -1.0 to +1.0 in each direction, after a gesture is completely recognized, given the minimum length and velocity configurations properties.

The developed interface was designed to react to the six different independent types of swipe gestures. The swipe gestures are "opposite" on pairs, namely:

1. Up/Down swipe, accomplished by a bottom to top or top to bottom gesture (made "along" the y-axis);
2. Forward/Backward swipe, accomplished by a back to front or front to back gesture (made "along" the z-axis); and
3. Left/Right swipe, accomplished by a right to left or left to right gesture (made "along" the x-axis).

For the first case, the up/down swipe, the movement depends mainly on a vertical movement action along the y-axis, e.i., the direction vector, with components (x,y,z), corresponds to an upward direction if $y \approx 1$ (used in the interface as a "deselect" action) and a downward direction if $y \approx -1$ (used as a "select" action). However, since it is almost impossible to do a swipe gesture with a vector direction with components exactly $x = 0, y = \pm 1$ and $z \approx 0$, it was considered a range of values to detect and differentiate between swipes types. Therefore, any swipe direction vector that agrees with the condition $y \in [-1, -0.5[$ and $x, z \in [-0.5, 0.5]$ is considered as a downward swipe. Oppositely, a swipe direction vector that agrees with the condition $y \in]0.5, 1]$ and $x, z \in [-0.5, 0.5]$ is considered as an upward swipe.

Forward/backward swipes are handled in a similar way. In more details, a movement is considered as a forward/backward swipe if the movement is essentially a horizontal movement along the z-axis. Considering this, any swipe direction vector that agrees with the condition $z \in [-1, -0.5[$ and $x, y \in [-0.5, 0.5]$ is considered as a forward swipe. Oppositely, a swipe direction that agrees with the condition $z \in]0.5, 1]$ and $x, y \in [-0.5, 0.5]$ is considered as a backward swipe.

The final case considers a horizontal swipe from right to left or left to right. In these cases, the swipe direction vector agrees with the condition $x \in [-1, -0.5[$ and $y, z \in [-0.5, 0.5]$ or $x \in]0.5, 1]$ and $z \in [-0.5, 0.5]$, respectively. These six presented swipes are mutually independent, i.e., for every type of swipe there is only one possible choice.

Tests made with users have shown that the best configuration to trigger the generation of a SwipeGesture object in any direction were attained when the minimum length and velocity where set to 100 mm and 400mm/s, respectively.

Taking the swipe movements in consideration, the application interaction starts at interface presented in Figure 2. Using left and right swipes it is possible to navigate between the appliances in the current floor of the house. The selected appliance in pointed by a green arrow. Forward swipe will move to appliances in an upper floor, while a backward swipe will move to one in a lower floor. To select an appliance, the user does a down swipe activating the interface presented in Figure 3 (top), which is particular for each kind of appliance. In the dryer machine example, presented in Figure 3, the interface has four sub interfaces, namely: "New Program", "Scheduling", "STATS" and "INFO". The "New Program" interface allows the user to program the appliance according with its needs. In this sense, the user must indicate allowed start and end times. As the names suggest, these times indicate the lower and upper limit for the program to be started. Again, a down swipe will focus on the text boxes and forward/backward swipes are used to set the values (time and date). Left/right swipes will move between the widgets and a down swipe when widget button "Submit" is focused will send the programming request to the optimization system.

The actual start of the program is computed using an algorithm to manage the scheduled loads of the building, optimizing the costs while maintaining the user's restrictions (e.g., the working times).

At this stage, the prototype development has the scheduling of the electric appliances being done by a Genetic Algorithms (GA) (Gendreau & Potvin, 2010; Goldberg, 1989). In a nutshell, the building has an aggregator that receives requests from the building appliances. Those requests contain information about the expected (electrical) load curve and the already mentioned times. The electrical load curve serves to place the starts of the appliances along the day such that the scheduling does not creates overloads, by placing several charges simultaneously and, at the same time, to choose the instant to start the appliances taking into consideration the electrical cost whenever the users has different tariff rates and/or has self-production from renewal sources (e.g., solar panel). The GA process is supported on populations of chromosomes which were encoded as a list of integers (epoch times). Each individual of the population corresponds to the beginning (initial time) of a set of consumer machines program, e.g., $[t_1, t_2, \ldots, t_n]$. This means that the fist appliance will start at time t_1, the second appliance will start at

Figure 3. Appliance interfaces. On top, the interface for the programming of a dryer machine and, on the bottom, the interface showing the schedullng of the dryer machine and other appliances

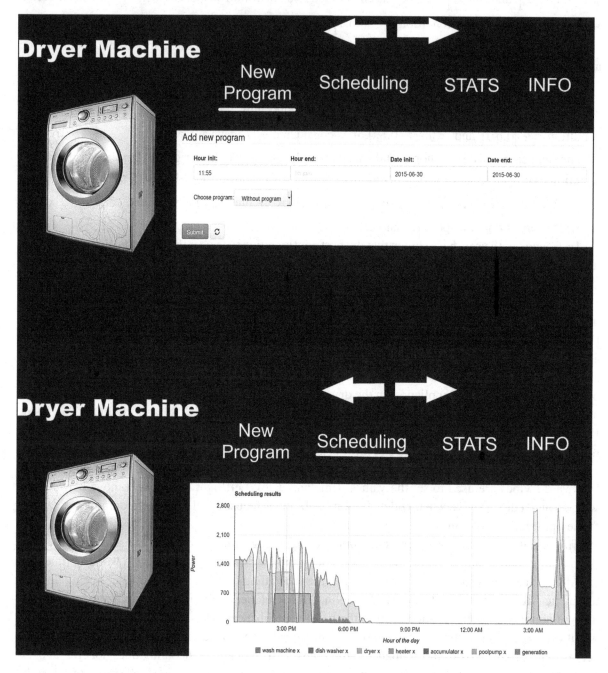

time t_2, and so on. GAs work by combining selection, recombination and mutation operators. The selection operator drives the population toward better solutions by recombining genes of selected parents to produce offspring that will form the next generation. Mutation is used to escape from local minima. In the prototype, the GA was configured with three mutation operators: (1) Swap mutator which exchanges genes in a chromosome, corresponding to swapping the start times between two machines, having the advantage of not "losing the best known spots/times" to place the loads. The second mutator is the (2) Integer Gaussian mutator which uses a random integer number, influenced from a Gaussian distribution with deviation and mean parameters pre-configured, to slightly move the charges around their current position. This mutator also as the effect of not totally "losing the best spots" to place the loads, since in general only slight changes are made to the initial time of the programs. In addition to the previous mutators, it was defined a (3) "Pseudo-Greedy" mutator that uses a roulette to influence the genome by giving better probabilities of moving charges to the lower cost tariff periods or to the predicted cost zero intervals due to renewable power forecast. This "Pseudo-Greedy" mutator is more disruptive than previous ones since the offspring chromosomes can be very different from the parents. Furthermore, a single point crossover was used. The single point crossover gets two parent chromosomes and defines a cutting points. Data beyond that point in either chromosome is swapped between the two parents, producing the offspring. This allow to join the best portions of the individuals to obtain improved ones. An important part is the selection of the parents for the crossover which in our case was the roulette wheel operator. In roulette wheel the parents are selected according to their fitness, i.e., chromosomes with better fitness get a larger chance of being selected. As the operator's name suggests, the process can be figured as a roulette wheel where the slices are bigger or smaller accordingly to the corresponding chromosome fitness function.

To define the quality of the individual it is necessary to define a fitness function which was computed taking into consideration the load curves, set as

$$F = \sum_{t \in T} \alpha(t) C(t) + \beta(t),$$

where T represents a set of time intervals, $C(t)$ translates the cost of energy for interval t,

$$\alpha(t) = \begin{cases} [P(t) - R(t)] \Delta_t & \text{if } P(t) > R(t) \\ 0 & \text{otherwise} \end{cases}$$

and

$$\beta(t) = \begin{cases} \infty & \text{if } P(t) > P_{max} \text{ or } t < t_{min,i} \text{ or } t + w_i > t_{max,i} \\ 0 & \text{otherwise} \end{cases}.$$

In the definition of α and β, $P(t)$ translates the sum of load's power scheduled to work at the time interval t; P_{max} translates the power limit; Δ_t translates the time period discretization window; $t_{min,i}$ i s the instant from which the i-appliance can be programmed to work; $t_{max,i}$ is the instant until which the i-appliance has to finish its program; w_i is the length of the i-appliance's program; and R translates the forecasted generation vector of renewable sources. On other words, α is the power consumed from the electrical provider during the Δ_t period and the definition of β has two objectives: prevention in case of an erroneous prediction of the power generated by renewable resources and ensure that the appliance does its work between $t_{min,i}$ and $t_{max,i}$, i.e., β is a penalty value activated whenever the sum of load's power scheduled to work at the time interval t overcomes the power limit or the users time intervals are not satisfied.

The overall scheduling procedure is a dynamic process, in the sense that an appliance can request a scheduling at any time, and can be summarized in the following steps:

Step 1: Start the aggregator (scheduler).
Step 2: Put the aggregator on wait for a scheduling request.
Step 3: Appliance i is programmed (usually by a human) and sends a scheduling request to the aggregator.
Step 4: The aggregator takes into consideration the appliance characteristics and configuration (e.g., start after $t_{min,i}$, end before $t_{max,i}$, and specific program load curve) and uses the GA to find an optimal starting time for the i-appliance to work. Other appliances, previously scheduled, can be shifted in time.
Step 5: The aggregator informs the appliances about their new scheduling, including the reschedule appliances.
Step 6: Return to Step 2.

An example of the scheduling results can be seen in Figure 3 (bottom), where we can observe that the majority of the appliances/loads where placed during the sun peak and late night. The first case is due to the fact that the house has solar panels and the energy consumed from those panels (self-production) will be considered as having null cost. The second case results from the adopted tariff which is lower in the late night/early morning periods.

The "STATS" and "INFO" menus show statistics about the operation of the appliance and useful appliance information (e.g., brand and location), respectively. To return to the previous interfaces, up swipes are used.

It is important to stress at this time, that not all of the devices/appliances that can be selected in the interface are used in the optimization algorithm. For instance, while the information about lightings (lamps) can be accessed, they weren't scheduled by the optimization algorithm. Regarding the other appliances, such as the pool pump, dish washer, drying machine, etc. all the information and full interaction was made available, including the creation of new programs, scheduled programs and statistics. The enumeration of all the options available is out of the focus of this chapter, nevertheless it is important to mention that the navigation on those options are done only with 6 swipes. As a final remark, the interface was made in Unity 3D (Jackson, 2015; Unity 3D, 2015).

Picking and Loading in a Warehouse

This section presents a part of the studies developed with the objective of building a system to manage and optimize the distribution of fresh and frozen goods by a distribution fleet (Cardoso, Schütz, Mazayev, Ey, & Corrêa, 2015). In short, the system integrates an Enterprise Resource Planning (ERP) software with an optimization system to minimize the costs of the distribution routes. The routing optimization software computes circuits from the depots to the delivery points using cartographic information and takes into consideration multiple objectives to be minimized, namely: the number of vehicles, the total traveled distance and the balance of the vehicle loads (Cardoso, Schütz, Mazayev, & Ey, 2015).

In a sequence line the distribution process can be described as follows (see Figure 4). First a client sends an order with a list of products and quantities to a seller that introduces the data into an ERP. This order is to be delivered in one of the following days. At a convenient moment, the system manager starts the routes optimization procedure by sending a signal to the system which, for modularity convenience, is divided in four main modules: HUB, OPT, DB, and MAPS. The signal triggered by the administrator goes to the HUB module which begins by requesting the new/necessary data from the ERP, e.g., customers' orders, new customers' data (geographical location), list of available vehicles and new products' data. The received data is then stored on the DB module which acts as a local database, avoiding the overload of the ERP with repetitive and intensive data requests.

The MAPS module contains a distance matrix which stores the routes between all possible delivery locations in order to avoid the need for on the fly computations of those routes. In this sense, the insertion of new locations, or an update, on the DB module prompts the MAPS module to update the distance matrix. On other words, the MAPS module maintains a n by n matrix of routes (being n the number of delivery locations), including estimated distances and travel time between locations. Furthermore, the routing directions details between locations are also stored which, in order to help the navigation between customers, can then be latter presented in GPS devices available in the distribution vehicle. The Open Street Maps Routing Machine (OSRM) server (OSRM, 2015) and Google Maps (Google-Maps-API, 2015; Svennerberg, 2010) are the services used to obtain the routing data. The use of the OSRM overcomes the present limit of accesses to Google's API. In both cases, the existing API returns the estimated distance and time, and the directions by a simple call to the corresponding endpoint, provided the location coordinates and configuration parameters. The route´s data is also stored in the DB module, which is supported on a MongoDB database (Chodorow, 2013; MongoDB, 2015), which is a non-relational database (often called NoSQL database). More specifically, MongoDB is a document-oriented database, with high performance and high reliability (Redmond & Wilson, 2012). Other characteristics

Figure 4. Diagram of the flow from the customers to the optimizer and reverse

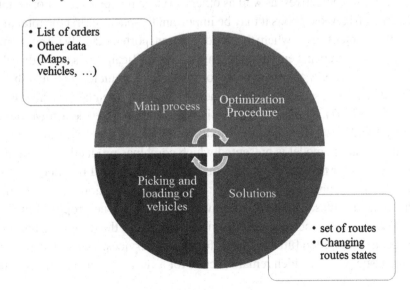

include easy scalability (vertically and horizontally through replication and auto-sharding, respectively) and MapReduce (Miner & Shook, 2012). A MongoDB database is structured as a set of collections which store documents as BSON objects (binary JSON document format) (Bassett, 2015). In each collection, the documents are allowed to have a dynamic schema, i.e., documents in the same collection are not forced to have the same structure. This schema-less property is particularly helpful in certain cases of the problem in study as for instance in the storing of the clients' orders or of the routes. For instance, for the second case, a complete route can be stored in a searchable single document, which in a relational database would probably been stored in a more intricate solution with several "interconnected" entities.

In the presence of the necessary information, the HUB module sends a start signal, with the necessary data, to the actual optimization module, OPT module. The OPT module implements a hybrid algorithm based on the Push Forward Insertion Heuristic (PFIH) (Solomon, 1987) which computes solutions for an adapted Capacitated Vehicle Routing Problem with Time Windows (CVRPTW) (Cardoso, Schütz, Mazayev, & Ey, 2015; Lin, Hu, & Shen, 2010; Reed, Yiannakou, & Evering, 2014; Schulze & Fahle, 1999). A solution for the CVRPTW problem is composed by a set of routes, each one starting at some depot, that visits/delivers goods to each customer once, within given time intervals, and without violating the vehicle's capacities. The problem is intrinsically a multi-objective problem. Two general goals are the minimization of the number of routes, which corresponds to the number vehicles to process the demand, and the total travel distance or time, corresponding to another distribution procedure cost. Other goals may occur in real problems, like the minimization of the difference between the longest and shortest route, or the maximization of the minimum load of the vehicles. The optimization of these last two objectives produces balanced routes in terms of worker effort and vehicle loads. Depending on the problem beneath, other variants of the CVRPTW were introduced in previous works. The number of vehicles, the total travel distance, the makespan, the total waiting time, and the total delay time were considered in (Castro-Gutierrez, Landa-Silva, & Moreno Perez, 2011). The same work addresses real scenarios, where consideration like the traveled distance vs. traveled time are made, unlike the common datasets which consider that an unit of distance (generally computed as Euclidean distances) always corresponds to a time unit, e.g. (Solomon, 1987).

The same constraints and objectives, as well as others, arise in real problems. For instance, in the distribution of frozen and refrigerated goods it may be important to optimize first the total distribution time since, refrigerating the compartments where the goods are transported (usually through the consumption of fuel to keep the dedicated freezing engines working) adds significant costs to the distribution process. A method that minimizes not only the fixed costs for dispatching vehicles, but also the transportation, inventory, energy and penalty costs for violating time-windows is presented in (Chen, Hsueh, & Chang, 2009; Hsu, Hung, & Li, 2007). The same works discuss the time-dependent travel and time-varying temperatures, during the day, which led to the modification of the objective functions as well as the constraints and a mathematical model is presented which combines production scheduling and vehicle routing with time windows for perishable food products. The objective of the model is to maximize the expected total profit of the supplier by optimizing the optimal production quantities, the time to start producing and the vehicle routes. There are some variants like the one proposed in (Pavone, Bisnik, Frazzoli, & Isler, 2009) where a stochastic problem is considered as the designing motion strategies for a team of mobile agents, required to fulfill requests for on-site services. The services are generated by a spatio-temporal stochastic process which remains active for a certain deterministic amount of time, and then expires (describing customer impatience), and are fulfilled when one of the mobile agents visits the location of the request. Please refer to (Eksioglu, Vural, & Reisman, 2009; Pillac, Gendreau, Guéret, & Medaglia, 2013) for a more comprehensive review of applications and solution methods for dynamic vehicle routing problems.

In terms of approaches to solve the CVRPTW, several where made. The use of meta-heuristics is a common solution (Bräysy & Gendreau, 2002; Caric & Gol, 2008; Ghiani, Guerriero, Laporte, & Mus-manno, 2003; Moura, 2008). However, the time required by these methods is a major problem when we take into consideration the premises of answering in near-real with good solutions. Furthermore, many of these meta-heuristics do not scale well, i.e., they solve well small problems but have difficul-ties to handle large data sets. Other solutions include heuristics like the one for the distribution of fresh vegetables presented in (Osvald & Stirn, 2008), in which the perishability represents a critical factor. The problem was formulates as a vehicle routing problem with time windows and time-dependent travel-times and solved using a heuristic approach based on the Tabu Search (Glover & Laguna, 1997) and performance was verified using modified Solomon's problems. A somewhat similar work was pro-posed in (Tarantilis & Kiranoudis, 2002), which deals with distribution problem formulated as an open multi-depot vehicle routing problem encountered by a fresh meat distributor. To solve the problem, a stochastic search meta-heuristic algorithm, termed as the list-based threshold accepting algorithm, was proposed. A generalization of the asymmetric capacitated vehicle routing problem with split delivery was considered in (Ambrosino & Sciomachen, 2006). The solution determines the distribution plan of two types of products, namely: fresh/dry and frozen food. The problem was solved using a mixed-integer programming model, followed by a two-step heuristic procedure. The distribution of fresh vegetables was studied in (Abousaeidi, Fauzi, & Muhamad, 2011). The focus of the document was the delivery of fresh vegetables selecting the best routes particularly for urban areas such as Kuala Lumpur city.

Returning to the OPT module, has already mentioned, the optimization procedure implements a hybrid adapted Push Forward Insertion Heuristic with solution seeding and post-optimization, which can be divided into the following three steps:

Step 1: [Solution seeding] In the first step the optimizer computes a seed partial solution, which takes into consideration the customers' demands and the vehicle capacities to estimate the minimum required number of vehicles. The seed partial solution has a set of routes with the form depot-customer-depot where the customers are chosen iteratively, in the sense that for each route consecutively is chosen the farthest customer (not yet assigned to a route) from all the routed customers. On other words, the first customer to be given a new route is the one farthest away from the depot. The second route will be started with the customer farther away from the depot and the customer in the first route, etc. The idea behind this process comes from the fact that these selected locations are not, in general, satisfied by the same vehicles. The process was computationally validated to enhance the convergence process. Possible bad decisions can be later repaired through post-optimization, namely with the ejection operator (see Step 3).

Step 2: [Complete the seeded routes] The second stage consists in the completion of the seeded routes using the PFIH. The PFIH is a greedy constructive heuristic where the tour-building procedure sequentially inserts customers into the solution. The procedure can be described by the following stages: (A) Let S be the set of routes instantiated in Step 1; (B) If all customers were placed in a route of S, then stop the procedure and return the built solution (S) to Step 3; Otherwise (C) for all non-inserted customers compute their PFIH cost and choose the one with smallest value. The i-customer's cost is given by $-\alpha d\left(i,o\right) + \beta b_i + \lambda\left(b_i - a_i\right)^{-1}$, where i is a client, o is the depot, $d\left(i,o\right)$ is the distance between client i and the depot, $\left[a_i, b_i\right]$ is the client's i time window interval, and $\alpha, \beta,$ and λ are parameters such that $\alpha + \beta + \lambda = 1$. Different $\alpha, \beta,$ and λ allow to give more or less importance to formula parcels, resulting in distinct orderings of the customers, which can prioritize the insertion of customers near the depot, with earlier closing window or with smaller time windows to be inserted first; (D) Try to insert the customer into an existing route, minimizing the traveled distance and taking into consideration the constraints (customer's time windows and vehicle's capacities); (E) If the insertion of customers is impossible without violating the constraints, use the selected customer to start a new route (depot-customer-depot) and add it to S ; (F) Update the distances, delivery times and vehicle capacities. Return to step (B). Using different combinations of $\alpha, \beta,$ and λ will produce a set of solutions which are sent to the next step.

Step 3: [Post optimization] This stage is computed until all routes were closed by the ERP/administrator (which, as we will see next, can close route by route) or all PFIH parameters were tested. The stage starts by getting (and removing) the most promising solution from the ones return from Step 2. Simultaneously, for each ejection rate value a taboo list is started which will contain all computed solutions before applying post-optimization. Then the selected solution is improved by applying: (a) a 2-Opt operator route by route tries to rearrange the sequence by which the customers are visited in order to reduce the route distance/time, maintaining feasibility (Caric & Gol, 2008); (b) a cross route operator similar to the Genetic Algorithms' One Point Crossover operator (Magalhães-Mendes, 2013), i.e., the operator receives two paths as input, and tries to find points where the routes can be crossed, simultaneously improving the total distance without losing feasibility; and (c) a band ejection operator which is a generalization of the radial ejection (Schrimpf, Schneider, Stamm-Wilbrandt, & Dueck, 2000) which selects a route and for each customer located in the route ejects it and a certain number of geographical neighbors which are then reinserted in other routes. The conjunction of the operators helpfully diminishes the total distance and reduce the number of routes present in the original solution.

The first two steps are quite fast and, therefore, it is during the third step that new orders arriving from the HUB module to the OPT module are treated. On other words, the OPT module has two threads: one which is responsible for the continuous communications with the HUB module and whenever new orders arrive they are placed in shared memory with a second thread that implements the previously described optimization process. This optimization thread is implemented such that at the end of each optimization cycle it checks the (threads) shared memory for new orders that will be treated as ejected customers, i.e., it tries to insert them in the existing routes or creates a new route if that is not possible. During the optimization process, solutions that improve previous solutions or possess new orders are sent to the HUB module, which in turn stores them on the local database and resends them to the ERP/administrator for visualization.

The system is dynamic in the sense that it can receive new orders while optimizing and the administrator can block routes during the process. The blocking of routes means a partial block of the solution, which allows to load the vehicles in a phased way. Furthermore, in order to better access the products when making the deliveries to the customers, it is important to load the vehicles in the reverse order of the customers visit, keeping the first products to be delivered near the doors and so forth.

Given the closed routes, the loading order information is sent to the warehouse where the picking and loading of the vehicles is to be made by workers. Problems may arise if for instance the workers can't easily interact with the computers having the orders information. This problem can arise for instance if the worker are wearing thick clothes, gloves or, simply have dirty hand from directly operating products (e.g., clothes to work under negative temperatures or the handling of fresh meat/fish).

An HCI alternative to manage the picking and loading of the products, as the one presented next, may therefore be in asset. The solution is based on a 3D Leap Motion sensor allowing, with simple gestures, to interact with a picking loading of vehicle interface. The main objective was to present a proof-of-concept which led us to devise a simple interface composed by three main interface pages. These pages are associated with the routes, picking and loading actions as explained next.

The application was developed in Unity 3D (Unity 3D, 2015) and starts by opening a page listing the routes (see Figure 5 - top). For each route a set of information is presented, namely:

1. The vehicle license plate and number ID for questions of vehicle identification by the workers; (b) the state of the vehicle, which can be in three conditions, namely: "loaded", "unloaded" or in the process of "picking & loading";
2. The corresponding route represented in a map;
3. The hour that the vehicle should leave the depot (such that the customers' time windows are satisfied) and the estimated arrival time; and
4. The total estimated distance (to fill up the fuel deposit, if necessary).

The vehicles' exit hours are used to sort the loading such that the ones exiting earlier are usually loaded first. Horizontal front/back or back/front swipes (recall the previous section for more details on swipes) are used to navigate through the routes/vehicles. A down swipe selects the vehicle and moves to another interface showing the list of products to be picked from the warehouse (see Figure 5 - middle). To avoid several travels into the warehouse, the products request is grouped such that, if several clients request some specific product then, the person in charge of picking that product will carry all the items in a single trip to the warehouse.

The process is repeated for all products. If the list of products exceeds the available displaying space then the user can navigate up/down in the list by doing front/back swipes. The active product has a larger font and a vertical down/up swipe activates/deactivates a check box, used to register the products already picked. At any time, a horizontal left to right swipe returns to the previous interface. When all products were picked, and are ready to be loaded, a horizontal right to left swipe is used to activate the vehicles' loading page. The loading page presents a list of costumers in the vehicle's loading order, i.e., the first customer in the list is the last to receive the products. As already mentioned, this allows easier access to the products during the delivery process. Horizontal back and front swipes allow the navigation between customers and the corresponding list of products to be loaded (Figure 5 - bottom). Again, a vertical down/up swipe activates/deactivates a check box, used to register the products/customers already loaded. Figure 6 shows an example of a user navigating in the list of products to be picked from the warehouse.

Figure 5. Interface for the picking and loading of vehicles: routes data (top), picking information (middle) and loading order (bottom).

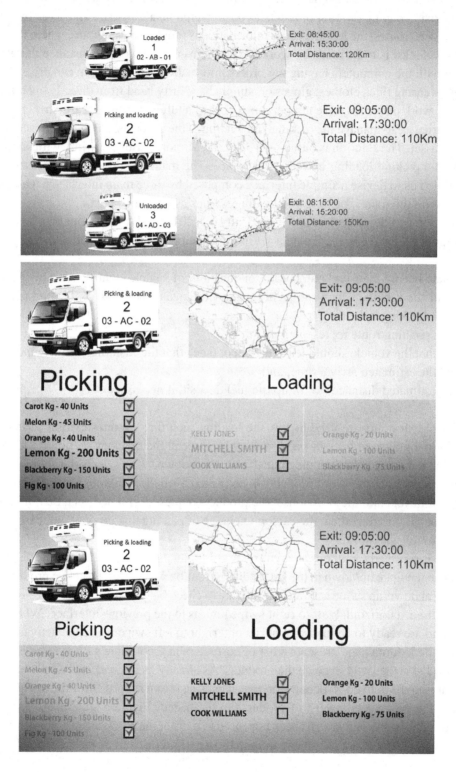

Figure 6. Using Leap Motion to navigate through the picking and loading interface

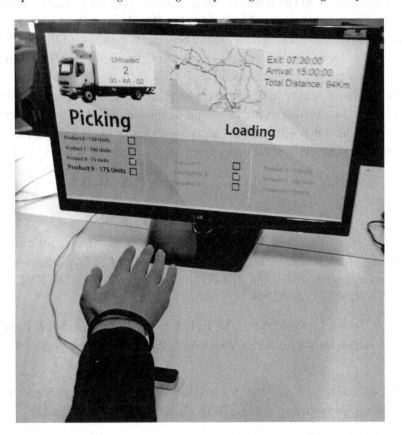

CONCLUSION

This chapter presented two proof-of-concept studies, conducted to implement HCIs supported on the Leap Motion sensor. The resulting solutions are capable of overcoming the difficulties of placing or working with common devices (e.g., mouse or keyboard). The first solution, demonstrated the development of a possible interface to control building appliances in order to optimize electrical costs. The system allows the programming of the building's appliances to work at specific hours or to be (semi-)automatically programmed, according with the electrical tariffs or self-production predictions. Due to the small size of the sensor, it can be placed in a room wall in conjunction with a display, allowing access to the main electrical programming system of the building. In the second case, the proposed system is to be placed in a warehouse's docking area, where workers may wear thick clothes/gloves or have dirty hands. In this case, the system is connected to a vehicle routing solution which defines the loads that each vehicle should carry. The solution presents routes information (e.g., vehicle identification, route duration and navigation instructions) to prioritize the loading of the vehicles. In a second interface, the picking procedure is managed in order to optimize it, which follows the loading of the vehicles in a predefined order, the reverse of the deliveries sequence.

The performed test have shown that the developed interfaces can be useful, but some problems may arise at the beginning since it is necessary some adaptation to the use of the Leap Motion controller.

Nevertheless, the used sensor had fast and accurate gesture tracking, in a small and inexpensive device, which allows it to be combined almost with every display. Possible drawbacks are the supported conditions of operation, including the working temperature between 0° to 45° C (32° to 113° F) or the relative humidity (5% to 85%). Also, bad light conditions, such as bright sunlight or light sources, or reflective surfaces above the sensor are not recommended.

With this work in mind it is easy to devise other applications using approaches similar to the ones proposed in this chapter. Two further examples would be the navigation of a digital cooking book during meals preparation, where it is usual to have dirty hands, or as interfacing devices in places where diseases can be transmitted by the contact with objects (e.g., hospitals, kiosks).

REFERENCES

Abousaeidi, M., Fauzi, R., & Muhamad, R. (2011). Application of geographic information system (GIS) in routing for delivery of fresh vegetables. *Proceeding of the 2011 IEEE Colloquium on Humanities, Science and Engineering* (pp. 551–555). IEEE. http://doi.org/ doi:<ALIGNMENT.qj></ALIGNMENT>10.1109/CHUSER.2011.6163794

Alves, R., Negrier, A., Sousa, L., Rodrigues, J. M. F., Felisberto, P., Gomes, M., & Bica, P. (2015). Interactive 180° Rear Projection Public Relations. *Procedia Computer Science, 51,* 592–601. doi:10.1016/j.procs.2015.05.327

Ambrosino, D., & Sciomachen, A. (2006). A food distribution network problem: A case study. *IMA Journal of Management Mathematics, 18*(1), 33–53. doi:10.1093/imaman/dpl012

Bachmann, D., Weichert, F., & Rinkenauer, G. (2014). Evaluation of the Leap Motion Controller as a New Contact-Free Pointing Device. *Sensors (Basel, Switzerland), 15*(1), 214–233. doi:10.3390/s150100214 PMID:25609043

Baldwin, R. (2015). Google's Project Soli to bring gesture control to wearables. *Engadget.com.* Retrieved from http://www.engadget.com/2015/05/29/atap-project-soli/

Bassett, L. (2015). *Introduction to JavaScript Object Notation: A To-the-Point Guide to JSON* (1st ed.). O'Reilly Media.

Bhowmik, A. K. (Ed.), (2014). *Interactive Displays.* Chichester, UK: John Wiley & Sons, Ltd.; doi:10.1002/9781118706237

Billinghurst, M. (2013). Hands and speech in space. In Proceedings of the 15th ACM on International conference on multimodal interaction - ICMI '13 (pp. 379–380). New York, New York, USA: ACM Press. http://doi.org/ doi:10.1145/2522848.2532202

Bräysy, O., & Gendreau, M. (2002). Tabu Search heuristics for the Vehicle Routing Problem with Time Windows. *Top (Madrid), 10*(2), 211–237. doi:10.1007/BF02579017

Breen, A., Bui, H. H., Crouch, R., Farrell, K., Faubel, F., & Gemello, R. … Mulbregt, P. (2014). Voice in the User Interface. In Interactive Displays (pp. 107–163). Chichester, UK: John Wiley & Sons, Ltd. http://doi.org/ doi:<ALIGNMENT.qj></ALIGNMENT>10.1002/9781118706237.ch3

Camastra, F., & De Felice, D. (2013). LVQ-Based Hand Gesture Recognition Using a Data Glove. In *Neural Nets and Surroundings* (pp. 159–168). doi:10.1007/978-3-642-35467-0_17

Card, S. K., Moran, T. P., & Newell, A. (1980). The keystroke-level model for user performance time with interactive systems. *Communications of the ACM, 23*(7), 396–410. doi:10.1145/358886.358895

Cardoso, P. J. S., Schütz, G., Mazayev, A., & Ey, E. (2015a). Solutions in Under 10 Seconds for Vehicle Routing Problems with Time Windows Using Commodity Computers. In A. Gaspar-Cunha, C. H. Antunes, & C. C. Coello (Eds.), *Evolutionary Multi-Criterion Optimization* (pp. 418–432). Springer International Publishing; doi:10.1007/978-3-319-15892-1_28

Cardoso, P. J. S., Schütz, G., Mazayev, A., Ey, E., & Corrêa, T. (2015b). A Solution for a Real-time Stochastic Capacitated Vehicle Routing Problem with Time Windows. *Procedia Computer Science, 51*, 2227–2236. doi:10.1016/j.procs.2015.05.501

Caric, T., & Gol, H. (2008). Vehicle Routing Problem. (T. Caric & H. Gol, Eds.). InTech. http://doi.org/ doi:<ALIGNMENT.qj></ALIGNMENT>10.5772/64

Carlisle, J. H. (1976, June 07-10). Evaluating the impact of office automation on top management communication. *Proceeding of the National Computer Conference and Exposition AFIPS, 1976* (p. 611). New York, USA: ACM Press. http://doi.org/ doi:10.1145/1499799.1499885

Castro-Gutierrez, J., Landa-Silva, D., & Moreno Perez, J. (2011). Nature of real-world multi-objective vehicle routing with evolutionary algorithms. *Proceeding of the 2011 IEEE International Conference on Systems, Man, and Cybernetics* (pp. 257–264). IEEE. http://doi.org/ doi:10.1109/ICSMC.2011.6083675

Chen, H.-K., Hsueh, C.-F., & Chang, M.-S. (2009). Production scheduling and vehicle routing with time windows for perishable food products. *Computers & Operations Research, 36*(7), 2311–2319. doi:10.1016/j.cor.2008.09.010

Cheng, H., Yang, L., & Liu, Z. (2015). A Survey on 3D Hand Gesture Recognition. *IEEE Transactions on Circuits and Systems for Video Technology*, 1. doi:10.1109/TCSVT.2015.2469551

Chodorow, K. (2013). *MongoDB: The Definitive Guide*. O'Reilly Media.

Cui, J., & Sourin, A. (2014). Feasibility Study on Free Hand Geometric Modelling Using Leap Motion in VRML/X3D. *Proceeding of the 2014 International Conference on Cyberworlds* (pp. 389–392). IEEE. http://doi.org/ doi:10.1109/CW.2014.60

Dipietro, L., Sabatini, A. M., & Dario, P. (2008). A Survey of Glove-Based Systems and Their Applications. *IEEE Transactions on Systems, Man and Cybernetics. Part C, Applications and Reviews, 38*(4), 461–482. doi:10.1109/TSMCC.2008.923862

Eksioglu, B., Vural, A. V., & Reisman, A. (2009). The vehicle routing problem: A taxonomic review. *Computers & Industrial Engineering, 57*(4), 1472–1483. doi:10.1016/j.cie.2009.05.009

El-laithy, R. A., Huang, J., & Yeh, M. (2012). Study on the use of Microsoft Kinect for robotics applications. *Proceedings of the 2012 IEEE/ION Position, Location and Navigation Symposium* (pp. 1280–1288). IEEE. http://doi.org/ doi:10.1109/PLANS.2012.6236985

Elliptic-Labs. (2015). Ultrasound Gesture Recognition. Retrieved from http://www.ellipticlabs.com/

Erol, A., Bebis, G., Nicolescu, M., Boyle, R. D., & Twombly, X. (2007). Vision-based hand pose estimation: A review. *Computer Vision and Image Understanding, 108*(1-2), 52–73. doi:10.1016/j.cviu.2006.10.012

Gendreau, M., & Potvin, J. (2010). Handbook of Meta-heuristics (2nd ed.). Springer + Business Media.

Ghiani, G., Guerriero, F., Laporte, G., & Musmanno, R. (2003). Real-time vehicle routing: Solution concepts, algorithms and parallel computing strategies. *European Journal of Operational Research, 151*(1), 1–11. doi:10.1016/S0377-2217(02)00915-3

Glover, F. W., & Laguna, M. (1997). *Tabu Search*. Springer. doi:10.1007/978-1-4615-6089-0

Goldberg, D. E. (1989). Genetic Algorithms in Search, Optimization and Machine Learning (1st ed.). Boston, MA, USA: Addison-Wesley Longman Publishing Co. Inc. Retrieved from http://portal.acm.org/citation.cfm?id=534133

Google-Maps-API. (2015). Google Maps API. Retrieved from https://developers.google.com/maps/

Grudin, J. (2012). A moving target: The evolution of HCI. In Human-computer interaction handbook: Fundamentals, evolving technologies, and emerging applications (3rd ed., pp. xxvii–lxi).

Halder, A., Mahato, M., Sinha, T., Adhikari, B., Mukherjee, S., & Bhattacharyya, N. (2012). Polymer membrane electrode based potentiometric taste sensor: A new sensor to distinguish five basic tastes. *Proceedings of the International Conference on Sensing Technology ICST* (pp. 785–789). http://doi.org/doi:10.1109/ICSensT.2012.6461784

Hsu, C.-I., Hung, S.-F., & Li, H.-C. (2007). Vehicle routing problem with time-windows for perishable food delivery. *Journal of Food Engineering, 80*(2), 465–475. doi:10.1016/j.jfoodeng.2006.05.029

Jackson, S. (2015). *Unity 3D UI Essentials*. Packt Publishing.

Jaimes, A., & Sebe, N. (2007). Multimodal human-computer interaction: A survey. *Computer Vision and Image Understanding, 108*(1-2), 116–134. doi:10.1016/j.cviu.2006.10.019

Khademi, M., Mousavi Hondori, H., McKenzie, A., Dodakian, L., Lopes, C. V., & Cramer, S. C. (2014). Free-hand interaction with leap motion controller for stroke rehabilitation. *Proceedings of the extended abstracts of the 32nd annual ACM conference on Human factors in computing systems CHI EA '14* (pp. 1663–1668). New York, New York, USA: ACM Press. http://doi.org/doi:10.1145/2559206.2581203

Kinect. (2015). Kinect. Retrieved from https://dev.windows.com/en-us/kinect

Kubrick, S. (1968). 2001: A Space Odyssey. USA, UK: Metro-Goldwyn-Mayer (MGM).

Leap developer portal. (2015). Leap Developer Portal. Retrieved from https://developer.leapmotion.com/documentation/csharp/devguide/Leap_Overview.html

Leap Motion App Store. (2015). Retrieved from https://apps.leapmotion.com/

Lehne, M. (2015). Airwriting. Retrieved from http://www.informatik.kit.edu/english/309_6566.php

Li, X., An, J., Min, J., & Hong, K.-S. (2011). Hand gesture recognition by stereo camera using the thinning method. *Proceeding of the 2011 International Conference on Multimedia Technology* (pp. 3077–3080). IEEE. http://doi.org/ doi:<ALIGNMENT.qj></ALIGNMENT>10.1109/ICMT.2011.6001670

Lin, L., & Hu, J., & Shen, B. (2010). A new hybrid method of Genetic Algorithm, Tabu and Chaotic search for CVRPTW. *Proceeding of the 2010 IEEE International Conference on Intelligent Computing and Intelligent Systems* (pp. 336–340). IEEE. http://doi.org/ doi:10.1109/ICICISYS.2010.5658353

Liu, K., & Kehtarnavaz, N. (2013). Real-time robust vision-based hand gesture recognition using stereo images. *Journal of Real-Time Image Processing*. doi:10.1007/s11554-013-0333-6

Liu, Z., Zhang, Y., Patrick Rau, P.-L., Choe, P., & Gulrez, T. (2015). Leap-Motion Based Online Interactive System for Hand Rehabilitation. In Cross-Cultural Design Applications in Mobile Interaction, Education, Health, Transport and Cultural Heritage, LNCS (Vol. 9181, pp. 338–347). http://doi.org/ doi:10.1007/978-3-319-20934-0_32

Magalhães-Mendes, J. (2013). A Comparative Study of Crossover Operators for Genetic Algorithms to Solve the Job Shop Scheduling Problem. *WSEAS Transactions on Computers*, *12*, 164–173.

Marin, G., Dominio, F., & Zanuttigh, P. (2014). Hand gesture recognition with leap motion and Kinect devices. *Proceedings of the2014 IEEE International Conference on Image Processing (ICIP)* (pp. 1565–1569). IEEE. http://doi.org/ doi:10.1109/ICIP.2014.7025313

Miner, D., & Shook, A. (2012). *MapReduce Design Patterns: Building Effective Algorithms and Analytics for Hadoop and Other Systems* (1st ed.). O'Reilly Media.

Mitra, S., & Acharya, T. (2007). Gesture Recognition: A Survey. *IEEE Transactions on Systems, Man and Cybernetics. Part C, Applications and Reviews*, *37*(3), 311–324. doi:10.1109/TSMCC.2007.893280

Mongo, D. B. (2015). MongoDB. Retrieved from https://www.mongodb.org/

Monteiro, J., Cardoso, P. J. S., Serra, R., & Fernandes, L. (2014a). Evaluation of the Human Factor in the Scheduling of Smart Appliances in Smart Grids. In C. Stephanidis & M. Antona (Eds.), *Universal Access in Human-Computer Interaction. Aging and Assistive Environments* (pp. 537–548). Springer International Publishing; doi:10.1007/978-3-319-07446-7_52

Monteiro, J., Eduardo, J., Cardoso, P. J. S., & Semião, J. (2014b). A distributed load scheduling mechanism for micro grids. *Proceedings of the 2014 IEEE International Conference on Smart Grid Communications (SmartGridComm)* (pp. 278–283). IEEE. http://doi.org/ doi:10.1109/SmartGridComm.2014.7007659

Motion, L. (2015). Leap Motion. Retrieved from https://www.leapmotion.com/

Moura, A. (2008). A Multi-Objective Genetic Algorithm for the Vehicle Routing with Time Windows and Loading Problem. In *Intelligent Decision Support* (pp. 187–201). Wiesbaden: Gabler; doi:10.1007/978-3-8349-9777-7_11

Myo Armband. (2015). Retrieved from https://www.myo.com

Nap, H. H., & Diaz-Orueta, U. (2014). Rehabilitation Gaming. In Gamification for Human Factors Integration (pp. 122–147). IGI Global. http://doi.org/ doi:10.4018/978-1-4666-5071-8.ch008

OSRM. (2015). OSRM: Open Source Routing Machine. Retrieved from http://project-osrm.org/

Osvald, A., & Stirn, L. Z. (2008). A vehicle routing algorithm for the distribution of fresh vegetables and similar perishable food. *Journal of Food Engineering*, *85*(2), 285–295. doi:10.1016/j.jfoodeng.2007.07.008

Pantelopoulos, A., & Bourbakis, N. G. (2010). A Survey on Wearable Sensor-Based Systems for Health Monitoring and Prognosis. *IEEE Transactions on Systems, Man and Cybernetics. Part C, Applications and Reviews*, *40*(1), 1–12. doi:10.1109/TSMCC.2009.2032660

Pavone, M., Bisnik, N., Frazzoli, E., & Isler, V. (2009). A Stochastic and Dynamic Vehicle Routing Problem with Time Windows and Customer Impatience. *Mobile Networks and Applications*, *14*(3), 350–364. doi:10.1007/s11036-008-0101-1

Pillac, V., Gendreau, M., Guéret, C., & Medaglia, A. L. (2013). A review of dynamic vehicle routing problems. *European Journal of Operational Research*, *225*(1), 1–11. doi:10.1016/j.ejor.2012.08.015

Pointgrab. (2015). Retrieved from http://www.pointgrab.com/

Potter, L. E., Araullo, J., & Carter, L. (2013). The Leap Motion controller. *Proceedings of the 25th Australian Computer-Human Interaction Conference on Augmentation, Application, Innovation, Collaboration OzCHI '13* (pp. 175–178). New York, New York, USA: ACM Press. http://doi.org/doi:10.1145/2541016.2541072

Rautaray, S. S., & Agrawal, A. (2015). Vision based hand gesture recognition for human computer interaction: A survey. *Artificial Intelligence Review*, *43*(1), 1–54. doi:10.1007/s10462-012-9356-9

Redmond, E., & Wilson, J. R. (2012). *Seven Databases in Seven Weeks* (1st ed.). Pragmatic Bookshelf.

Reed, M., Yiannakou, A., & Evering, R. (2014). An ant colony algorithm for the multi-compartment vehicle routing problem. *Applied Soft Computing*, *15*, 169–176. doi:10.1016/j.asoc.2013.10.017

Ren, Z., Yuan, J., Meng, J., & Zhang, Z. (2013). Robust Part-Based Hand Gesture Recognition Using Kinect Sensor. *IEEE Transactions on Multimedia*, *15*(5), 1110–1120. doi:10.1109/TMM.2013.2246148

Ren, Z., Yuan, J., & Zhang, Z. (2011). Robust hand gesture recognition based on finger-earth mover's distance with a commodity depth camera. *Proceedings of the 19th ACM international conference on Multimedia - MM '11 (p. 1093)*. New York, New York, USA: ACM Press. http://doi.org/ doi:<ALIGNMENT.qj></ALIGNMENT>10.1145/2072298.2071946

Saleiro, M., Farrajota, M., Terzic, K., Krishna, S., Rodrigues, J. M. F., & du Buf, J. M. H. (2015). Biologically inspired vision for human-robot interaction. In M. Antona & C. Stephanidis (Eds.), Universal Access in Human-Computer Interaction 2015, Part II, LNCS (Vol. 9176 pp. 505–517). Doi:10.1007/978-3-319-20681-3_48

Sanders, B. (2014). *Mastering Leap Motion*. Packt Publishing.

Schrimpf, G., Schneider, J., Stamm-Wilbrandt, H., & Dueck, G. (2000). Record Breaking Optimization Results Using the Ruin and Recreate Principle. *Journal of Computational Physics*, *159*(2), 139–171. doi:10.1006/jcph.1999.6413

Schulze, J., & Fahle, T. (1999). A parallel algorithm for the vehicle routing problem with time window constraints. *Annals of Operations Research, 86*(0), 585–607. doi:10.1023/A:1018948011707

Shen, X. (2012). Empowering the smart grid with wireless technologies[Editor's Note]. *IEEE Network, 26*(3), 2–3. doi:10.1109/MNET.2012.6201208

Singlecue. (2015). eyeSight. Retrieved from http://www.singlecue.com/

Solomon, M. M. (1987). Algorithms for the Vehicle Routing and Scheduling Problems with Time Window Constraints. *Operations Research, 35*(2), 254–265. doi:10.1287/opre.35.2.254

Spiegelmock, M. (2013). *Leap Motion Development Essentials*. Packt Publishing.

Spielberg, S. (2002). Minority Report. USA: 20th Century Fox; DreamWorks Pictures.

Structure sensor. (2015). Retrieved from http://structure.io/

Sturman, D. J., & Zeltzer, D. (1994). A survey of glove-based input. *IEEE Computer Graphics and Applications, 14*(1), 30–39. doi:10.1109/38.250916

Suarez, J., & Murphy, R. R. (2012). Hand gesture recognition with depth images: A review. *Proceedings of the 21st IEEE International Symposium on Robot and Human Interactive Communication IEEE RO-MAN* (pp. 411–417). IEEE. http://doi.org/ doi:10.1109/ROMAN.2012.6343787

Sutton, J. (2013). Air painting with Corel Painter Freestyle and the leap motion controller. Proceedings of the ACM SIGGRAPH 2013 Studio Talks on - SIGGRAPH '13 (p. 1). New York, New York, USA: ACM Press; doi:10.1145/2503673.2503694

Svennerberg, G. (2010). *Beginning Google Maps API 3*. Apress. doi:10.1007/978-1-4302-2803-5

Tarantilis, C. D., & Kiranoudis, C. T. (2002). Distribution of fresh meat. *Journal of Food Engineering, 51*(1), 85–91. doi:10.1016/S0260-8774(01)00040-1

Tobii. (2015). Tobii EyeX. Retrieved from http://www.tobii.com/en/eye-experience/

Tongrod, N., Kerdcharoen, T., Watthanawisuth, N., & Tuantranont, A. (2010). A low-cost data-glove for Human computer interaction based on ink-jet printed sensors and ZigBee networks. *Proceedings of the International Symposium on Wearable Computers ISWC '10* (pp. 1–2). IEEE. http://doi.org/ doi:10.1109/ ISWC.2010.5665850

Tubb, R., & Dixon, S. (2015). An Evaluation of Multidimensional Controllers for Sound Design Tasks. *Proceedings of the 33rd Annual ACM Conference on Human Factors in Computing Systems CHI '15* (pp. 47–56). New York, New York, USA: ACM Press. http://doi.org/ doi:10.1145/2702123.2702499

Unity 3D. (2015). Unity 3D. Retrieved September 1, 2015, from http://unity3d.com/

Ushaw, G., Ziogas, E., Eyre, J., & Morgan, G. (2013). An Efficient Application of Gesture Recognition from a 2D Camera for Rehabilitation of Patients with Impaired Dexterity.*Proceedings of the International Conference on Health Informatics* (pp. 315–318). doi:10.5220/0004190103150318

Villarreal, B. L., & Gordillo, J. L. (2013). Perception Aptitude improvement of an odor sensor: Model for a biologically inspired nose, LNCS (Vol. 7914, pp. 126–135). Doi:10.1007/978-3-642-38989-4_13

Wachowski, A., & Wachowski, L. (1999). *The Matrix*. USA, Australia: Warner Bros.

Wells, S. (2002). *The Time Machine*. USA: Warner Bros.

Withana, A., Peiris, R., Samarasekara, N., & Nanayakkara, S. (2015). zSense: Enabling Shallow Depth Gesture Recognition for Greater Input Expressivity on Smart Wearables. *Proceedings of the 33rd Annual ACM Conference on Human Factors in Computing Systems CHI '15* (pp. 3661–3670). New York, New York, USA: ACM Press. Doi:10.1145/2702123.2702371

Yun, Y., Changrampadi, M. H., & Gu, I. Y. H. (2014). Head pose classification by multi-class Ada-Boost with fusion of RGB and depth images. *Proceedings of the 2014 International Conference on Signal Processing and Integrated Networks (SPIN)* (pp. 174–177). IEEE. http://doi.org/ doi:10.1109/SPIN.2014.6776943

Zimmerman, T. G., Lanier, J., Blanchard, C., Bryson, S., & Harvill, Y. (1987). A hand gesture interface device. *Proceedings of the SIGCHI/GI conference on Human factors in computing systems and graphics interface CHI '87* (pp. 189–192). New York, New York, USA: ACM Press. Doi:10.1145/29933.275628

KEY TERMS AND DEFINITIONS

Gesture Recognition: Computational interpretation of the gestures made by humans. The gestures are in general input commands to the computational system which can be recognize using technologies like accelerometers, gyroscopes, computational vision, or ultrasounds.

Hands-Free Interaction System: System capable of accepting input commands from a user without the need to touch anything.

Human-Computer Interaction: The study of interaction between users and computers, often regarded as the intersection of computer science, behavioral sciences, design and several other fields of study.

Internet-of-Things: Environment where everything on it is provided with a unique identifier and has the ability to transfer data (communicate) over a network. Many times associated with the ability of consumer electronics to communicate and receive orders over a network.

Leap Motion Sensor: Sensor which allows the interaction with digital content in virtual and augmented reality, allowing the tracking of the movement of hands and fingers with very low latency, converting them into 3D input, using a combination of software and hardware.

Load Scheduling: Manual, semi-automatic or automatic procedure used to schedule the electrical loads in infrastructure usually in order to achieve electrical or monetary savings.

Vehicle Routing Problem: A combinatorial optimization and integer programming problem seeking to service a number of customers with a fleet of vehicles. Variants include the need to attaining certain restrictions as vehicles' capacities' and clients' time windows.

Chapter 5
Remote Gripping for Effective Bilateral Teleoperation

A.M. Harsha S. Abeykoon
University of Moratuwa, Sri Lanka

R.M. Maheshi Ruwanthika
University of Moratuwa, Sri Lanka

ABSTRACT

Accessibility for remote locations could be easily overcome by teleoperation. When manipulating an object at a remote place, it is beneficial if the operator is capable of feeling the force and position information including environmental object impedance for successful remote manipulation. In this chapter, bilateral control, based on acceleration architecture is explained from the basics starting from the human's haptic perception. The sensorless sensing mechanism "Reaction Torque Observer" is applied to the gripper which enables the operator to feel the remote environment while on remote manipulation. "Disturbance Observer" which is a popular control tool used to attain robustness is also successfully adopted for this application. Further, authors introduce force lock during bilateral teleoperation, which facilitate handling delicate objects. Practical as well as experimental results are discussed and the chapter concludes with suggestions for possible future research directions.

INTRODUCTION

The prefix *tele* from Greek origin means *at a distance* and teleoperation literally means *operating a machine at a distance*. Teleoperation extends the human capability to manipulate objects remotely by providing the operator with similar conditions as those at the remote location. Most controllers encountered in daily activities are unilateral controllers. As the name implies, communication is performed unilaterally. A simple TV remote controller is an example for a unilateral controller. In a bilateral controller, master (operator) and slave (environment) sides are bilaterally controlled. The intention is to feel the environment at the distance while it is being controlled. Bilateral control system enables the slave side environment to be reflected in the master side and master side operating intention to be reflected in the slave side.

DOI: 10.4018/978-1-5225-0435-1.ch005

Humans have five sensors for vision, smell, sound, taste, and touch. Sound and visual senses of the human can be stored and reproduced in a remote place, but the sense of the nose (smell) and tongue (taste) cannot normally be transmitted or stored via electronic means. Touch, the fifth sense, can be transmitted and reproduced using the bilateral control concept. Target of bilateral control is the transmission of haptic information by electronic means from a remote location. The term *haptic* means the *sense of touch*.

The significant aim in advanced bilateral teleoperation is to achieve high haptic perception and to give the operator the feeling of *telepresence* (as if the operator is physically present at the remote site). For a perfect bilateral teleoperation, both position tracking and force control should be achieved simultaneously. Consider an example where high precision position control should be achieved. The position of a cutting tool should be maintained despite the changes in the material properties and the variations in cutting forces during high precision machining. Similarly, there are applications that need force control. Contact force has to be maintained carefully while handling fragile objects. In such applications, force need to be controlled regardless of the position. Thus, position control and force control have opposing requirements. In this chapter authors introduce acceleration control to achieve position control and force control simultaneously in realizing bilateral teleoperation.

The bilateral control system is a popular and successful concept behind several engineering applications such as mine excavation, space robots, and medical surgeries. Following applications highlight the importance of haptic feedback in teleoperation.

The Da Vinci Surgical system is designed to facilitate complex surgery using a minimally invasive approach. It is controlled by a surgeon from a console. The surgeon performs operation through small incisions. He sits at the console while operating. On patient-side, cart with four interactive robotic arms are controlled from the console. Da Vinci's patient-side cart holds up to three EndoWrist instruments and one 3D camera. Surgeon operates by viewing a magnified 3D HD image of the patient's interior. The surgeon uses controls that work like forceps. As surgeon moves controls, Da Vinci responses in real time, translating hand, wrist and finger movements into smaller, precise movements of EndoWrist instruments at the patient-side cart (Intuitive Surgical Inc, 2015). In this approach there is no haptic feedback to the surgeon from the organs touched through the EndoWrist instruments. The surgeon relies on the vision system and assumes the force applied through EndoWrist instruments on the organ and proceeds the operation. The lack of haptic feedback in Da Vinci Surgical system is a greater risk. If haptic feedback is introduced, the surgeon does not want to rely only on the vision system and it avoids the assumption of force applied through the EndoWrist instruments on organs (Ishii, Katsura, Nishi, & Ohnishi, 2008). With the aging of population, the skill preservation of an expert has been a serious concern especially in fields like handcraft production. The solution of digital skill preservation proposed by Shimono et al (2007) has been developed through nearly a decade and the latest research on motion copying system and haptic database facilitates reliable remote manipulation from another country (Nagata & Katsura, 2015). This is possible to operate few patients at a time by a single expert surgeon (Kebude, Morimitsu, Katsura, & Sabanovic, 2014). This text introduces a successful sensorless haptic feedback method which could be used in minimally invasive surgery in the future.

The sizes of the master and slave manipulators are not always same. Bilateral controlled master-slave manipulator system with different sizes call "scale bilateral control." When the size of the slave becomes very small it is categorized under macro-micro manipulation (Kobayashi, Nakamura, Tatsuno, & Iijima, 1993). In a micro environment, the force acting on the environment and its dimension are small. Therefore, force sensors are readily not available to be used in a constrained space. Takeo and Kosuge (1997) proposed a bilateral scaled tele-operation system without using force sensors in a micro environment. Recently, the research focuses to enhance the quality of haptic information in macro-micro manipulation by introducing advanced filtering methods (Takeya & Katsura, 2015).

In nuclear applications, telerobots are widely used to reach areas where the thermal or radiation environment limits the presence of a human. The TELEMAN research program in 1989, launched by the EU, has succeeded in developing a number of robots for nuclear power plants. Nuclear accident robots are mainly controlled by a remote operator using the vision feedback provided by the camera installed on the robot (AZORobotics, 2013) and it lacks the haptic feedback.

"Hot cell" robots used in handling radioactive material have been developed for almost twenty years. Initially, mechanical master-slave system with telescopic arm was developed in the 1980s. This system is composed of a slave arm in the hot cell which can extend up to 4m, a through-wall tube and a master arm is in the non-radioactive working area. Master and the slave are separated through the wall. Next generation tools use computer-assisted tele-manipulation technology with haptic feedback which allows 150m distance from the hot cell to the operator workstation. The electrical links replace the mechanical links. The master is small compared to the slave arm and respective scale ratios also have introduced. This hot cell robot is introduced to the marketplace recently. The future research is focused on vibration filtering and to attach the slave arm to ceiling of the hot cell or to a mobile gantry to increase the operation field (Djedidi, Selliez-Vandernotte, & Malcolm, 2015). Although hot cell robots are capable of manipulating a wide range of objects with high level of precision, slave arm still lack the gripper lock facility which is discussed in this text.

Sensing remotely is inadequate for object handling in a remote environment; it requires gripping the object without damage. This chapter aims to describe the haptic teleoperation starting from the basics of human sensors and extend the discussion towards history, applications, acceleration control architecture which facilitates simultaneous position tracking and force control, mathematical analysis of bilateral control concept, sensorless sensing mechanisms, force sensing technologies and gripping mechanisms. Further authors introduce a force lock based on sensorless sensing mechanisms. Authors justify the proposed models by presenting the experimental results.

BACKGROUND

Human Sensors

Humans have five sensory organs, namely eye, ear, nose, tongue, and skin. These organs are sensitive to different stimulus from the environment; eyes for light, ears for sound, nose for smell, tongue for taste, and skin for touch. They carry signals to the human brain to gather information and to judge the surrounding.

Figure 1 depicts human sensors and corresponding stimulus. Eye, ear, and nose are sensitive to stimulus at a distance if a suitable medium is present. For example, a human can observe a faraway object in the presence of adequate light, and hear a sound through a suitable medium. To touch an object directly, a human applies a force on the object surface and the reaction coming from the object is sensed to judge the object's texture and hardness. In other words, an action and a reaction are required to feel a touch sense successfully.

Figure 1. Human sensors and stimulus

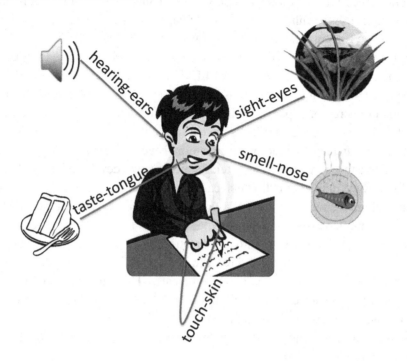

Transmission of Sensation

If someone wishes to store live motion, an eye-like instrument is needed to be invented that enable to store captured motion in a database. It would be available for future generations to playback to extract the recorded motion movements. Similar technique must be practiced for sound. Due to successful efforts of centuries, auditory information recording techniques and static and dynamic visual information recording techniques were invented in early 19th century. Today, audio and video recording, and playback, is extensively used.

With the rapid development of communication technologies, Internet enables worldwide transmission of text documents, sounds, and visual information. Transmission of taste and smell usually involves advance chemical sensors and people do not even attempt to record and transmit taste, and smell, due to its inherited difficulty. Although the human body has a skin to feel the touch, the information acquired through the skin is unique and different from other sensors. To feel the touch sense, a human should act and receive a reaction from the environment.

Transmission of Touch

Some objects could not be manipulated by a bear human hand due to the potential risk of handling as in radioactive materials. If the object is placed faraway, similarly a remote manipulator arm should be used.

If a robot arm is used at the remote end, there should be a technique to transmit operator's intention to the robot arm and to receive the environmental feedback to the operator. If this is successful, humans could manipulate things at a distance while feeling the remote object. Such a solution could be equally useful for outer space explorations, experiments in sea beds, and in telesurgery. This is often referred to as tele haptics and could be used if the remote environment is not easily accessible by the operator due to the difficulties in the distance, or due to the risks associated with working on the environment.

Basic requirements for successful touch sensing can be listed as follows:

- A manipulator should be placed at the remote location where the object needs to be manipulated. Ideally, this manipulator (slave) should work as for the control signals from the operator's (master) end.
- Human operator should have an interface to interact with the remote manipulator. This interface should be capable of recreating the object's feeling to the operator.
- Real time communication should be established between human interface (master) and remote manipulator (slave).
- Human operator and remote object should be present.

The force exerted by master through the interface needs to transmit through the communication channel to the remote manipulator to actuate the slave. Newton's third law is equally valid to feel the touch sense. Therefore, the object's reaction exerted on the remote manipulator should transmit to the human operator through the communication channel and the interface.

Figure 2 illustrates the process of remote touch sensing. When an object is touched, its reaction is felt back in real time. Similarly, the touch sense should be transmitted back in real time. When an object is grasped by fingers, the object's reaction on different fingers from different directions is felt. Successful tele haptic should also have sensations from different directions of the object. This haptic teleoperation (tele haptics) will be elaborated in following sections.

TELEOPERATION

Research on teleoperation has contributed many technical advancements. Application of teleoperation systems can be described in three keywords; they are *distance, accessibility,* and *scale transfer.* The keyword *distance* refers to the applications where teleoperation is used to combat the distance. A simple example would be a remote controller of a television. Second keyword refers to the *accessibility* to the

Figure 2. Process of remote touch sensing

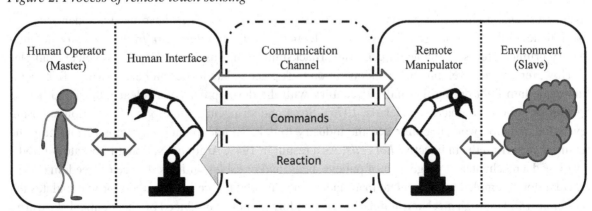

environment that the machine operates. Teleoperation is extensively used in many hazardous environments where human operators are inaccessible. Teleoperation systems used in mines and outer space experiments are two such examples. *Scale transfer* denotes the operator's intention to operate a machine with a scale change from the input to the output. Macro micro manipulations, power assist systems, impedance scaling, power scaling, and position scaling are some of the examples (Abeykoon & Perera, 2014).

Teleoperation usually involves some kind of feedback from the working environment. This may be a simple visual feedback or it can sense through sensors positioned at the work site. It is possible to achieve teleoperation through *unilateral control* or *bilateral control*. Many controllers people encounter in day-to-day lives are unilateral controllers. As the name implies, control signal communication is performed unilaterally from the operator to the actuator, and the operator side is not controlled by the actuator's response. This should not be misunderstood as feedback or open loop applications. A unilateral controller may or may not have a feedback. A simple TV remote controller is an example for a unilateral controller. When an operator presses a channel as his wish, the TV set actuates. Most teleoperation processors are unilateral. The main advantage is its simplicity and they do not require a bilateral approach as for the application.

Bilateral teleoperation extends the human capability to manipulate objects remotely by providing the operator with similar conditions as those at the remote location. This is achieved via installing a similar robot manipulator called the master, at the human's end that provides motion commands to the slave, which is performing the actual task on remote environment (Abeykoon & Ohnishi, 2007). Jelatis (1975) has defined master-slave manipulators as, "general purpose mechanical devices, used by a human operator in a normal environment, to extend his hand and arm manipulative capacity into a more-or-less remote hostile environment with the aid of direct (or indirect) visual observation, with movements characterized by naturalness, to obviate the need for extensive training, to feel, to reflect the elastic characteristics of task objects and forces exerted on them, and compliance to follow task-constrained paths or orientations at substantial misalignments with operator-applied forces."

Transferring tactile sensation from the actuator is not possible with the unilateral control. In bilateral teleoperation (control), communication is performed bilaterally from the master to the slave and vice versa. Therefore, bilateral control is applicable for transferring tactile sensation because bidirectional communication is essential to fulfill the law of action and reaction for touch. A detailed discussion on bilateral control will be presented in the proceeding sections of this chapter.

History of Teleoperation

History of *remote manipulation* dates back to our early ancestors. They have used wooden sticks to manipulate food on an open fire. The roots of teleoperation, *performing work from a distance* is found in very primitive tools, available for centuries. Blacksmiths tongs used in forging is a typical example.

However, major development on teleoperation took place in late forties and early fifties. Teleoperation came into light during the mid-19th century with the development of nuclear industry to handle hazardous radioactive materials (Jelatis, 1975). Strict and stringent regulations on radiation exposure levels for radiation workers compelled the industry to develop teleoperation systems maintaining the required gaps from the radioactive *hot cells*. As a result, in 1949, Argonne National Laboratory (ANL) developed a mechanical arrangement of pulleys, belts, and/or cables with six degree of freedom (DOF) end effector assembled to manipulate materials in the shielded hot-cells. The operator manipulates the master arm and through mechanical links, corresponding motion is produced on the identical slave arm.

With little mental effort, co-ordinated six DOF movements could be used to produce at the end effector movements, one to one kinematic correspondence between master and slave motions. The mechanical master-slave manipulators (MSM) provide inherent force position feedback to the human operator. Such systems have a limited distance range that could successfully transmit the haptic motion intension. Usually pulleys, gears, and arms transmit the motion. In longer distances, haptic sensation is distorted by the device's load itself. Force feedback from slave side to the master side via direct mechanical coupling is known as passive bilateral system (Bicker, Burn, Hu, Pongaen, & Bashir, 2004).

The mechanical MSM's were adequate for a certain range of tasks. Depending on the magnitude of the radioactivity of the material inside the shielded hot cell, length of the separation and wall thickness had to be altered. There was a maximum limit for the separation due to the visibility and for the increased mechanical load. These drawbacks paved the way for electrically linked manipulators. In the next phase, operators drive electric motors via a bank of switches or joysticks to replicate the motion in the remote slave arm while viewing the scene directly through a television screen. The Argonne National Laboratory lately developed a *position symmetric type bilateral control* scheme as presented in Figure 3(a). Here, the position error of master and slave joints controls the slave motor whereas slave and master position error back drives the master (Bicker, Burn, Hu, Pongaen, & Bashir, 2004). The bilateral control scheme was further developed as *force backward type* and *force reflecting type* as shown in Figure 3(b) and Figure 3(c). In force backward type, slave reaction is provided as the feedback to the master operator and the position error of master and slave controls the slave motor. In force reflecting type, position error of master and slave is used to control the slave motor and force error is used to control the master.

In position symmetric type, which is illustrated in Figure 3(a), the control intention is to equalize the positions from the master side to the slave. Force is not controlled. In force backward type shown in Figure 3(b), slave position is controlled from the master position and slave force is copied to the master. In force reflecting type, which is presented in Figure 3(c), researchers have attempted to rectify the

Figure 3. Evolution of bilateral control scheme

(a) Position symmetric type

(b) Force backward type

(c) Force reflecting type

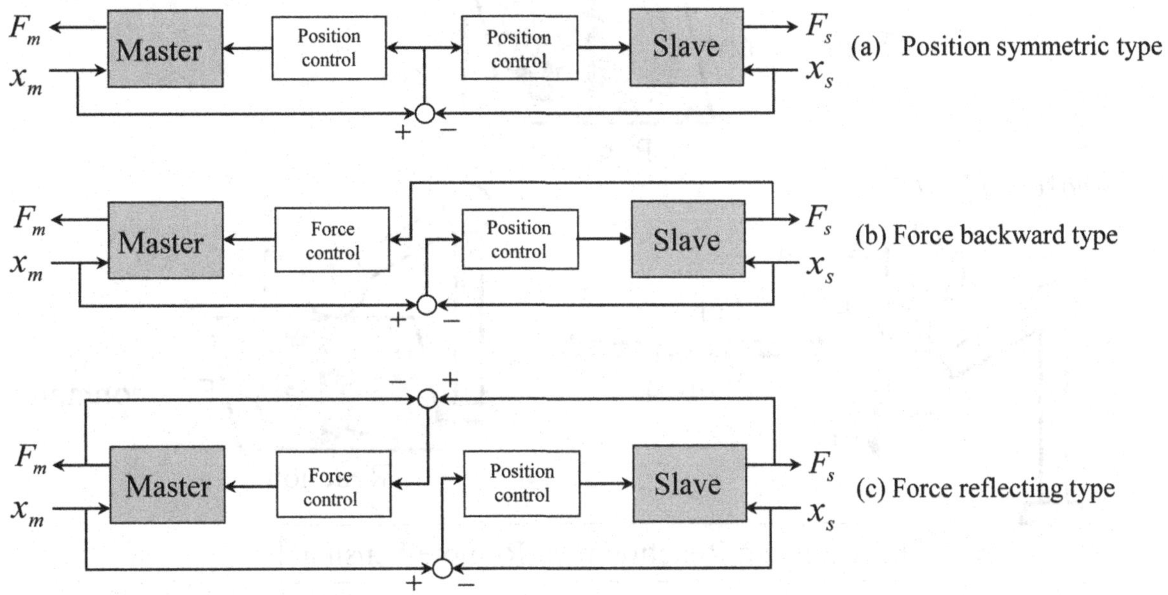

problems identified in the previous architectures. Positions will be copied from the master to the slave while slave force reaction is copied back to the master. Even in this architecture, positions as well as forces are conveyed one way.

Figure 4 illustrates the sketch of a touch sense. If it is to be felt successfully, Equations 1 and 2 should be satisfied. The notations x, F respectively denote position and force. The subscripts m, s represent master and slave.

$$x_m = x_s \tag{1}$$

$$F_m = -F_s \tag{2}$$

None of the above architectures fulfills the requirements of Equations 1 and 2 as both force and position information should be exchanged bilaterally between the master and the slave. In the following section, authors introduce a successful method, which satisfies Equations 1 and 2.

Figure 4. Effective direct and remote touch sense

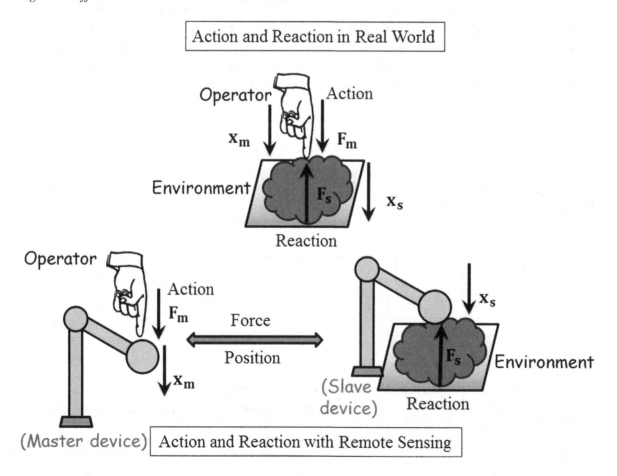

MAIN FOCUS OF THE CHAPTER

Acceleration Control

In a control system, the main target is to maintain the error close to zero despite of the disturbances. According to Salisbury (1980), the opposing requirements in position control and force control may be best understood by looking at the control stiffness given in Equation 3.

$$k = \frac{\partial f}{\partial x} \tag{3}$$

Where, k, f and x respectively denote control stiffness, force and position. In ideal force control, k, control stiffness, should be zero irrespective of the position. Similarly, k should be infinity in ideal position control. In practice, ideal force control or position control cannot be achieved as for the actuator and controller limitations. Therefore, in practice, stiffness k, which is varying from zero to infinity, could be observed.

Modern motion systems should ideally interact with an unknown environment. However, the word *unknown* is a relative expression. Designer's target is to make a manipulator to work in an open space rather than in the limited space. They will contact with various environments and do their tasks, which require an ability to be compliant with the contact environment. Conventional motion control is not always suitable for future applications due to lack of adaptive capability to the environment. A motion controller in an open environment will require various control stiffness for the stable and transparent transition between high stiffness to low stiffness tasks and vice versa, in order to achieve natural behavior in a controlled task. In conventional control, fixed control stiffness is always preferred as for the stability implications.

In ideal bilateral teleoperation, ideal position control ($k = \infty$) and ideal force control ($k = 0$) both should be simultaneously achieved. However, this contradicts with the conventional control theory as force and position are said to be orthogonal and could not be achieved simultaneously.

Rather than having different control stiffnesses in control point of view, it would be more natural to define a common goal for all control tasks. Figure 5 describes the robust acceleration control system. The system controller is given acceleration referance $\ddot{\theta}_{sys}^{ref}$ as the input and external acceleration $\ddot{\theta}^{ext}$ are interfering with the system. The acceleration reference is achieved through a robust position servo controller and it supresses the external acceleration input. Force controller should be implemented to control external acceleration. Therefore, when $\ddot{\theta}_{sys}^{res}$ is commanded to a motor, the position controlling intention ($\ddot{\theta}_{sys}^{ref}$) and its orthoganel force ($\ddot{\theta}^{ext}$) could be controlled symultaniously. This is possible only if the quantities are combined in the acceleration demension as shown in Figure 5. Different control stiffnesses could be achieved by changing the contol gains in force and position control.

The bilateral control concept is based on acceleration architecture, and it is elaborated in the forthcoming section.

Figure 5. Robust acceleration control system

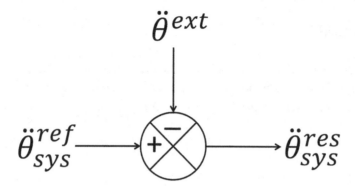

Bilateral Control Concept

Use of a proxy-like robot arm at the remote site extends and leverage operator's skills and decision making abilities. In this section, authors intend to elaborate the design of control structures enabling a human operator to interact with a remote environment through interface devices based on *acceleration architecture*. Its potential enables humans to assemble outer space equipment from earth, heart surgeries through tiny incisions, seabed telemanipulations, network robotics, and to safely handle toxic waste with a haptic feedback.

Main idea of the bilateral control is sensing an environment remotely while controlling the remote manipulator, based on operator's intention. The operator's action is realized by two functionally related systems (actuators). The operator is in contact with one of the actuator (master) and the environment is in contact with another actuator (slave). The operator defines the task to be assigned to the slave actuator by manipulating the master actuator. The slave actuator replicates the operator motion on the remote site. When slave actuator is facilitated with suitable sensors, its interaction with the environment and motion are sensed and transmitted back to the operator through the master actuator. In other words, slave side is controlled through the position and force information from the master side and the master side is controlled by the position and force information from the slave side. Therefore, this system enables the slave side environment to be reflected in the master side and master side operating intention reflected in the slave side.

A key objective of bilateral control is to achieve high transparency. In simple terms, the word *transparency* means, how well the force/ position information of the slave side is transparent at the master side (Yokokohji & Yoshikawa, 1994). In other words, transparency is the match of the impedance perceived by the operator with the environment (Lawrence, 1993).

As for the control theory, it has been pointed out that the bilateral controller cannot achieve transparency and stability simultaneously due to the uncertainty of the system and the environment, which is explained in the acceleration control section. Therefore, a bilateral system should strike a balance between the stability and the transparency (Hashtrudi-Zaad & Salcudean, 2002a, 2002b).

In conventional bilateral control, force sensors assist the detection of force outputs of master and slave. However, force sensors have narrow bandwidth of operation and they cannot be placed easily in the place where the force to be measured. At Ohinishi laboratory of the department of system design engineering, Keio University Japan was able to transmit vivid sensation from the salve side to the master side through sensorless sensing technique of Disturbance Observer (DOB) and Reaction Torque Observer (RTOB) (Murakami, Yu, & Ohnishi, 1993; Ohnishi, Matsui, & Hori, 1994; Katsura, Matsumoto, & Ohnishi, 2007). Therefore, authors used reaction torque observer, which is a variant of the disturbance observer, as the force sensor (Abeykoon & Ohnishi, 2006; Abeykoon & Senevirathne, 2012; Abeykoon & Chinthaka, 2014), for over a decade and results are presented in the subsequent sections.

Bilateral control is a realization of natural law of motion of two objects. However, input from the operator or the environment response consist of elements of disturbance and the force. Therefore, to realize a good bilateral system, good disturbance rejection mechanism should be in action. Robust motion control with bilateral control is achieved through the disturbance observer. Ohnishi et al. (1994) proposed disturbance observer and according to them, a disturbance observer identifies the total mechanical load torque and the effects of parameter changes. Acceleration control plays an important role in realizing this motion control. Disturbance observer is explained in the following section.

Bilateral control structure is derived based on the law of action and reaction. When the operator manipulates the system from the master side, slave side has to be in contact with the environment. However, in applications where master and slave are different, scaling may be used. Bilateral scaling mainly consists of position, force, and impedance scaling methods and sometimes time scaling (Abeykoon & Perera, 2014). Nevertheless, this section will present bilateral control scheme based on acceleration architecture for identical master and slave actuators without scaling.

Considering an ideal bilaterally teleoperated system without scaling, the behavior can be expressed simply as:

- The position response on the master side is produced based on the operator intention and the position response is replicated on the slave side. Positions should be identical despite the dynamic behavior of the manipulated object. Ideally, master should follow the slave position response.
- The force response of the master side is produced based on the operator intention and the force response on the slave side from the environment should be identical in magnitude and opposite in direction despite of the dynamic behavior of the manipulated object; the law of action and reaction should be realized.
- Satisfy both behaviors simultaneously.

Above conditions are mathematically represented as Equations 4 and 5, which are similar to Equations 1 and 2. Same equations are represented with different notations for the easy of explanation of bilateral control architecture based on acceleration control. Assume a single degree of freedom (1 DOF) master and slave translational devices.

$$x_m^{res} - x_s^{res} = 0 \tag{4}$$

$$F_m^{ext} + F_s^{ext} = 0 \tag{5}$$

Here subscripts m, s respectively denote the master and the slave. The superscript res represents response. F_m^{ext} is the action force which is applied to master system by the operator and F_s^{ext} is the reaction force which is applied to slave system from the real environment. Also x denotes position response. Figure 6 depicts the structure and components of a bilateral control for a multi degree of freedom robot manipulators.

Figure 6. Structure and components of bilateral control

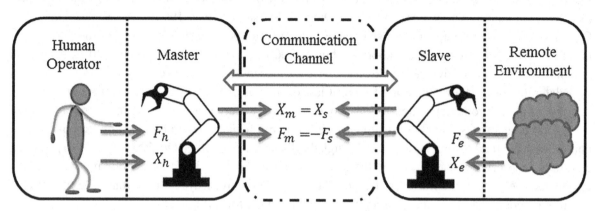

Since bilateral control should attain both ideal position control and ideal force control that are opposite simultaneously, control stiffness should tend to infinity and converges to zero time to time, which is contrary with the control theory. Therefore, bilateral control system with acceleration control is practical for the scenario after converting Equations 4 and 5 to a common dimension, which is acceleration. Therefore, Equation 4 is double differentiated and Equation 6 could be derived. Equation 5 could be transformed to Equation 7 assuming equal inertia/mass in both master and slave sides. $\ddot{x}^f$ denotes the information in acceleration dimension obtained from force information and $\ddot{x}^p$ denotes the information in acceleration dimension obtained from position responses. It could be theoretically and experimentally proved that Equations 6 and 7 could be simultaneously achieved if they are combined in the acceleration dimension. Equation 6, which is derived by the position tracking equation, is called *differential mode* and Equation 7, which is derived by the force equality, is called as *common mode*.

Additionally, the transmission of the force sensation between master and the slave should be performed in rigid hard time for real world haptic teleoperation. Thus, reaction torque observer is used as a force sensor in the bilateral control. It is possible to realize both force control and position control independently and simultaneously to the bilateral control through differential mode and common mode. Additionally, the use of information in acceleration dimensions for bilateral control facilitates easy expandability to the system for multi degree of freedom (Shimono, Katsura, & Ohnishi, 2005).

$$\ddot{x}^p_m - \ddot{x}^p_s = 0 \qquad (6)$$

$$\ddot{x}^f_m + \ddot{x}^f_s = 0 \qquad (7)$$

Control targets in differential and common modes are respectively represented in Equations 8 and 9. Therefore, Equation 8 is known as differential mode and Equation 9 represents force serving based on the acceleration dimension. This is called as the common mode between the master and the slave systems. The subscripts $diff$, com denote differential mode and common mode.

$$\ddot{x}^p_m - \ddot{x}^p_s = \ddot{x}_{diff} \rightarrow 0 \qquad (8)$$

$$\ddot{x}_m^f + \ddot{x}_s^f = \ddot{x}_{com} = 0 \tag{9}$$

Equations 8 and 9 could be represented using a 2nd order Hadamard matrix H_2 and it is represented in Equation 10.

$$\begin{bmatrix} \ddot{x}_{com}^{res} \\ \ddot{x}_{diff}^{res} \end{bmatrix} = \begin{bmatrix} 1 & 1 \\ 1 & -1 \end{bmatrix} \begin{bmatrix} \ddot{x}_m^f & \ddot{x}_m^p \\ \ddot{x}_s^f & \ddot{x}_s^p \end{bmatrix} = H_2 \begin{bmatrix} \ddot{x}_m^f & \ddot{x}_m^p \\ \ddot{x}_s^f & \ddot{x}_s^p \end{bmatrix} \tag{10}$$

Only the diagonal components of the simplified matrix of Equation 10 are considered for further analysis. It gives the sum of force information and the difference in position information. The reference values for master and slave systems in acceleration dimension can be derived as follows. Figure 7 shows the control block satisfying Equation 12.

$$\begin{bmatrix} \ddot{x}_{com}^{res} \\ \ddot{x}_{diff}^{res} \end{bmatrix} = \begin{bmatrix} \ddot{x}_m^f + \ddot{x}_s^f \\ \ddot{x}_m^p - \ddot{x}_s^p \end{bmatrix} \tag{11}$$

$$\begin{bmatrix} \ddot{x}_m^{ref} \\ \ddot{x}_s^{ref} \end{bmatrix} = \begin{bmatrix} -1 & -1 \\ -1 & 1 \end{bmatrix} \begin{bmatrix} \ddot{x}_{com}^{res} \\ \ddot{x}_{diff}^{res} \end{bmatrix} = \begin{bmatrix} -1 & -1 \\ -1 & 1 \end{bmatrix} \begin{bmatrix} \ddot{x}_m^f + \ddot{x}_s^f \\ \ddot{x}_m^p - \ddot{x}_s^p \end{bmatrix} \tag{12}$$

Figure 7. Acceleration based bilateral control

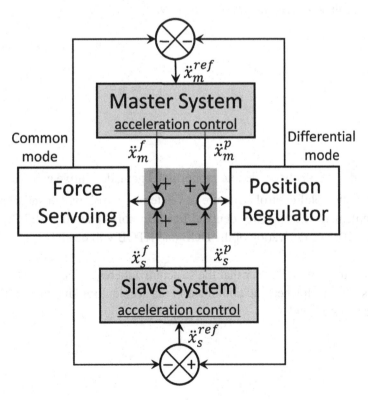

The control goal also can be presented as Equations 13 and 14, without converting to acceleration dimensions.

$$x_{diff} = x_m^{res} - x_s^{res} = 0 \tag{13}$$

$$F_{com}^{ext} = F_m^{ext} + F_s^{ext} = 0 \tag{14}$$

The model transformation can be expressed as Equation 15 using a 2nd order Hadamard matrix H_2.

$$\begin{bmatrix} x_{com} & F_{com} \\ x_{diff} & F_{diff} \end{bmatrix} = \begin{bmatrix} 1 & 1 \\ 1 & -1 \end{bmatrix} \begin{bmatrix} x_m^{res} & F_m^{ext} \\ x_s^{res} & F_s^{ext} \end{bmatrix} \tag{15}$$

In order to achieve Equations 13 and 14, acceleration references $\ddot{x}^{ref}$ can be derived as Equations 16 and 17 according to acceleration control architecture.

$$\ddot{x}_m^{ref} = C_p \left(x_s^{res} - x_m^{res} \right) - C_f \left(F_m^{ext} + F_s^{ext} \right) \tag{16}$$

$$\ddot{x}_s^{ref} = C_p \left(x_m^{res} - x_s^{res} \right) - C_f \left(F_m^{ext} + F_s^{ext} \right) \tag{17}$$

Where C_p and C_f are denoted by Equations 18 and 19.

$$C_P = k_P + k_d s + \frac{k_i}{s} \tag{18}$$

$$C_f = k_f \tag{19}$$

Where, k_p, k_d, k_i and k_f respectively denote proportional gain, derivative gain, integral gain, and force gain. Figure 8 depicts the total control structure of bilateral control, which satisfies Equations 16 and 17. The block is implemented using two identical linear motors. Therefore, RTOB becomes Reaction Force Observer (RFOB). The derivation of the DOB and RTOB will be elaborated in the following section.

As for the control structure, it is clear that the structure adheres to the control Equations 16 and 17. Positions and forces are transformed and combined in the acceleration dimension. DOB and RFOB are used in both master and slave sides.

Figure 8. Bilateral control structure based on DOB and RFOB

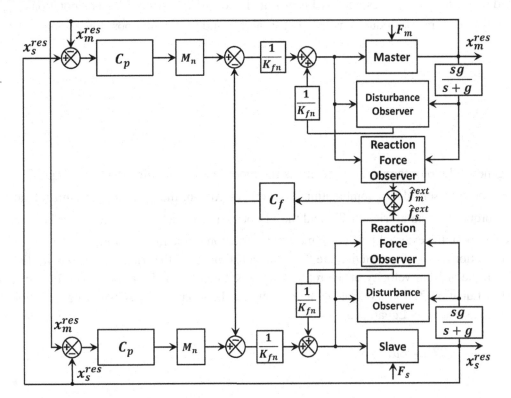

DISTURBANCE OBSERVER

The traditional force sensors, which were implemented to sense the external force, have some inherited drawbacks. The sensor should be installed on the actuator, on the gripper surface, or in an appropriate site. The force sensation is restricted to the position where it is installed. Physical force sensor itself adds inertia or mass to the system, which will not be accounted by the sensor during reaction force estimation. Traditional force sensors lack the ability to detect only the reaction force from the environment. In addition, they have narrow bandwidth and hence the detected force is so dull. Therefore, it is clear that force sensors are not suitable for transmission of vivid force sensation.

The Disturbance Observer (DOB) proposed by Ohnishi et al. (1996) is used mainly in DC motor control applications. DOB's main application is that it could be used to detect unknown disturbances acting on the system. Reaction Torque Observer (RTOB), a varient of the DOB is used to detect the external forces acting on the system. RTOB is capable of obtaining wider bandwidth through shortening the sampling time. Hence, RTOB is suitable for transmission of vivid force sensation. Therefore, RTOB can be represented as an effective technique for the improvement of operationality for bilateral control (Shimono, Katsura, & Ohnishi, 2005).

Let's model the DOB starting from the servo motor. When a DC servo motor with one degree of motion is considered, under an ideal motor driver, the dynamic equation of a servo motor can be represented as in Equation 20 and the generated torque from the motor can be written as Equation 21. The generated motor torque T_m is essentially linear function of motor current I_a^{ref}. The notations K_t, J, θ respectively denote motor torque constant, motor inertia, and the angular position response.

$$J\frac{d\theta}{dt} = T_m - T_l \tag{20}$$

$$T_m = K_t I_a^{ref} \tag{21}$$

The generated motor torque T_m accelerates the motor while providing the load torque T_l. The load torque can be represented as a combination of reaction torque of the external mechanical load T_{ext}, interactive torque T_{int}, static friction T_f, and the viscous friction $B\dot{\theta}$. When the motor is running with zero acceleration, the external load consumes major fraction of the motor torque.

Static friction and viscous friction are the main constituents of the friction. Viscous friction always depends on the angular velocity of the rotor (Huang & Lee, 2008). Therefore, load force can be represented as Equation 22 and motor generated torque can be modified by substituting Equation 22 into Equation 20 as shown in Equation 23.

$$T_l = T_{ext} + T_{int} + (T_f + B\dot{\theta}) \tag{22}$$

$$T_m = J\frac{d\dot{\theta}}{dt} + T_{ext} + T_{int} + (T_f + B\dot{\theta}) \tag{23}$$

Laplace domain equation of Equation 21 is shown in Equation 24 whereas Equation 25 shows Laplace domain representation of Equation 23 after rearranging. The notation s denotes the Laplace operator.

$$T_m(s) = K_t I_a^{ref}(s) \tag{24}$$

$$\dot{\theta}(s) = \frac{T_m(s) - [T_{ext}(s) + T_{int}(s) + T_f(s) + B\dot{\theta}(s)]}{Js} \tag{25}$$

Equations 24 and 25 are used to develop the DC motor model as presented in the control block diagram in Figure 9. For a single servo motor, control system's interactive torque T_{int} can be considered as zero. The addition static friction T_f, viscous friction $B\dot{\theta}$, reaction torque of the external mechanical load T_{ext}, and the interactive torque T_{int} is known as the disturbance torque of a motor (Mizuochi, Tsuji, & Ohnishi, 2006).

The load torque T_l presented in Equation 22 and generated motor torque in Equation 21 simplifies Equation 20 to Equation 26 as shown below.

Figure 9. DC motor model

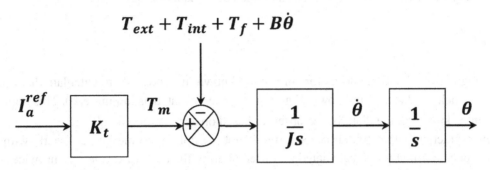

$$J\ddot{\theta} = K_t I_a^{ref} - (T_{ext} + T_{int} + T_f + B\dot{\theta}) \tag{26}$$

Parameters K_t, and J are subjected to variations and estimation errors. Thus, these can be re-written in terms of nominal values and variations. The inertia of the motor J can be altered significantly from its nominal value with the mechanical configuration of the system. It can be represented as Equation 27. The subscript n denotes the nominal values of corresponding parameters.

$$J = J_n + \Delta J \tag{27}$$

Furthermore, due to torque pulsation and the flux distribution variation by the rotor position, or sometimes due to calculation errors, the motor torque constant can be changed from its nominal value and could be represented as Equation 28.

$$K_t = K_{tn} + \Delta K_t \tag{28}$$

By substituting Equations 27 and 28 to Equation 26 and rearranging Equation 29 can be derived.

$$J_n\ddot{\theta} = K_{tn} I_a^{ref} - (T_{int} + T_{ext} + T_f + B\dot{\theta} + \Delta J\ddot{\theta} - \Delta K_t I_a^{ref}) \tag{29}$$

The term within the parenthesis in Equation 29 is called as total disturbance torque to the system T_{dis}.

$$T_{dis} = T_l + \Delta J\ddot{\theta} - \Delta K_t I_a^{ref}$$

$$= T_{int} + T_{ext} + (T_f + B\dot{\theta}) + (J - J_n)\ddot{\theta} + (K_{tn} - K_t)I_a^{ref} \tag{30}$$

Introducing T_{dis} to Equation 29 leads to Equation 31,

$$J_n\ddot{\theta} = K_{tn} I_a^{ref} - T_{dis} \tag{31}$$

By rearranging Equation 31, T_{dis} can be calculated as in Equation 32.

$$T_{dis} = K_{tn} I_a^{ref} - J_n \ddot{\theta}$$

(32)

When angular acceleration and motor current are known, it is possible to calculate the disturbance torque T_{dis}, which is otherwise unknown. Equation 32 is represented as in Figure 10. This implemented arrangement is known as the disturbance observer based on acceleration architecture.

However, practically the angular acceleration is not possible to be measured directly with angular encoders. Hence, normally it is calculated by differentiating the angular displacement twice, which is measured from the encoders. This structure includes a differentiator that may result in high noise. The noise can be suppressed by using a low pass filter at the output of the disturbance torque calculation. If first order low pass filter is used, we can express the estimated disturbance torque $\hat{t}_{dis}$ as in Equation 33. g_{dis} is the cut off frequency of the low pass filter.

$$\hat{t}_{dis} = \frac{g_{dis}}{(s + g_{dis})} \{K_{tn} I_a^{ref} - J_n \ddot{\theta}\}$$

(33)

The modified block diagram after adding low pass filter is presented in Figure 11.

Without using force sensors, disturbance observer observes the disturbance force in the system. A certain time delay is present in this calculation. Therefore, block diagram in Figure 11 can be rearranged as in Figure 12 as a practical way of estimating the disturbance torque, excluding time delay and by eliminating the differentiator. Equation 34 expresses the estimated disturbance torque $\hat{t}_{dis}$ as shown in Figure 12.

$$\hat{t}_{dis} = \frac{g_{dis}}{s + g_{dis}} \left(K_{tn} I_a^{ref} + J_n g_{dis} \dot{\theta}\right) - J_n g_{dis} \dot{\theta}$$

(34)

Figure 10. Disturbance calculation based on acceleration

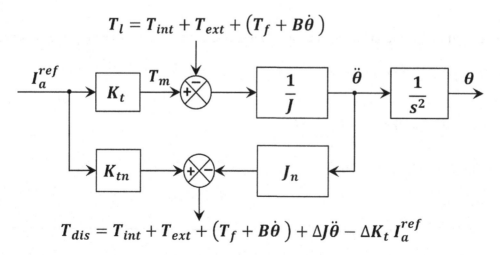

Figure 11. Disturbance observer with low pass filter

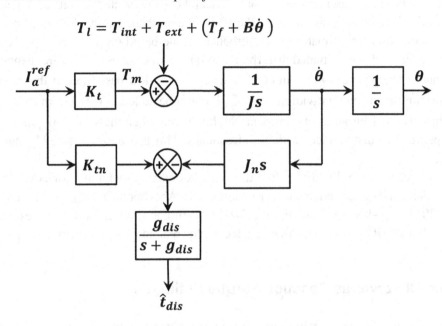

Figure 12. Disturbance observer

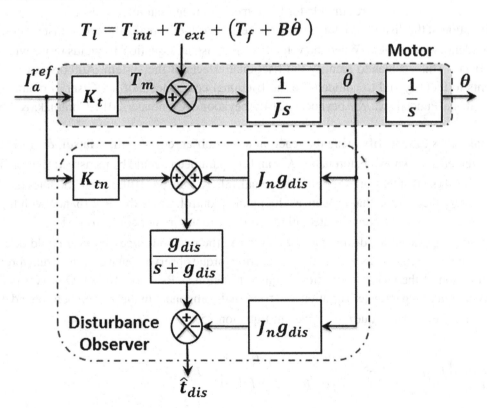

The practical disturbance observer used by many researchers is presented in Figure 12. The disturbance observer is introduced to identify and suppress the effect of disturbance torque for robust motion control.

The disturbance observer estimates the disturbance torque based on the measured current and the acceleration. Feedback of the estimated disturbance torque compensates the low frequency component of the disturbance, which is below the cut off frequency g_{dis} of low pass filter. If the $\hat{t}_{dis}$ is converted back to the current dimension by dividing it by K_t, it could be added to the system to compensate the unknown disturbance. Disturbance observers are highly useful when the system requires higher bandwidth to compensate the disturbances with high frequency. This is usually achieved by having a higher sampling rate.

The authors have successfully applied the disturbance observer technique for position controllers, velocity controllers, and current controllers (Ruwanthika & Abeykoon, 2015; Pillai, Perera, Chinthaka, & Abeykoon, 2014; Abeykoon & Senevirathne, 2012). Disturbance observer not only estimates the disturbance torque but also it could be modified to calculate the reaction torque (external torque) (Abeykoon & Ohnishi, 2008).

Disturbance Observer as Reaction Torque Estimator

In this section, reaction torque estimation is performed by extending the discussion of disturbance observer. Then torque control is presented with the reaction torque estimation and the disturbance observer.

The disturbance observer is capable of providing a much wider bandwidth than force sensors, because it is possible to set the sampling time shorter and it is possible to set the observer a high gain. Therefore, reaction torque observer is more suitable for force measurement than force sensors.

Identification of the disturbance force is not only effective for the realization of robust motion control, but also to identify parameters. When the velocity $\dot{\theta}$ is constant, Equation 13 yields terms with only the friction effects. This enables to identify the frictional effects of the system. Authors have conducted experiments to identify and to compensate the frictional components of a DC servo motor using the DOB (Chinthaka, Punchihewa, & Abeykoon, 2014; Abeykoon & Chinthaka, 2014; Chinthaka & Abeykoon, 2015).

External forces can identify using the reaction torque observer (Ohnishi, Matsui, & Hori, 1994). If frictional elements are known beforehand, K_{tn} and J_n parameters could be measured (Perera, Pillai, & Abeykoon, 2014) so that they are very close to actual values. Low pass filter's gain denotes the sensitivity of the disturbance torque that influences the motion control. Since the disturbance with higher frequency than g_{dis} cannot be compensated, higher order torques are not compensated.

For practical applications, disturbance observer and the reaction force observer could be identical, provided the cut off frequencies are equal. The reaction torque observer behaves as a virtual force sensor. The modification of the DOB for reaction torque estimation as Reaction Torque Observer is achieved by identifying internal parameter variation and frictional component in the system beforehand. Calculation of estimated external torque $\hat{t}_{ext}$ is given in Equation 35.

$$\hat{t}_{ext} = \frac{g_{rec}}{s + g_{rec}}\left(K_{tn}I_a^{ref} + J_n g_{rec}\dot{\theta} - \begin{pmatrix} T_{int} + T_f + B\dot{\theta} + \\ \Delta J\ddot{\theta} + \Delta K_t I_a^{ref} \end{pmatrix}\right) - J_n g_{rec}\dot{\theta} \tag{35}$$

Where g_{rec} denotes the cut-off frequency of RTOB low pass filter. The modified control block diagram of the DOB with the steps to identify the external torque as RTOB is shown in Figure 13. The DOB calculates and estimates reaction torque as quickly as possible by increasing the cutoff frequency within the stable frequency range.

For a single motor control system, T_{int} can be assumed as zero. Figure 14 depicts a torque controller. Torque is calculated from the reaction torque observer. Disturbance observer is used to attain robust motion control.

Torque feedback technology is a basic feature in the real world haptics. Torque feedback control by acceleration is provided in the above figure. Torque feedback control is attained by reaction torque observer loop. DOB promotes the robustness for the external disturbances, I_{dis} is the compensation current for the disturbance, and $\hat{t}_{ext}$ is the external torque calculated by the reaction torque observer.

Results: Bilateral Control

The bilateral teleoperation system is implemented on a one DOF master slave system as illustrated in Figure 15 (Abeykoon & Pillai, 2014).

Figure 13. Reaction Torque Observer

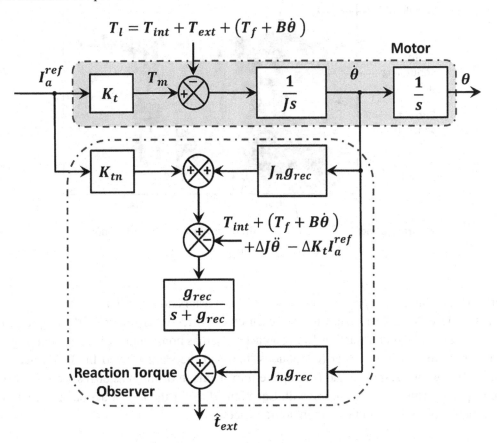

Figure 14. Torque controller based on DOB and RTOB

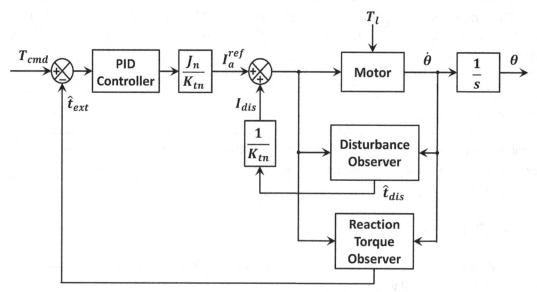

Figure 15. Hardware setup

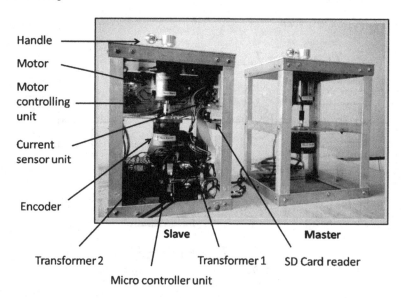

Figure 16 (a) illustrates the position response for both master and slave. The master position response as well as the slave position response follows each other perfectly as shown in the diagram. Position tracking is achieved based on Equation 13 in contact as well as non-contact (free) motion. Figure 16(b) shows the torque response of master (continuous line) and the slave (dotted line), and master torque follows the slave torque response and a complete mirror image of the master response is observed in the slave response. This is in accordance with Equation 14 as for the law of action and reaction. Force servoing is achieved both in contact and in non-contact motion.

Figure 16. (a) Master and slave position responses in bilateral control (b)Torque responses of both master and the slave

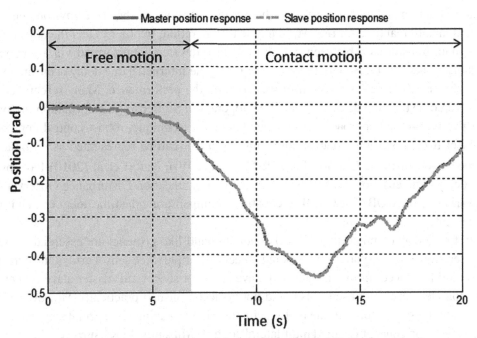

(a) Master and slave position responses in bilateral control

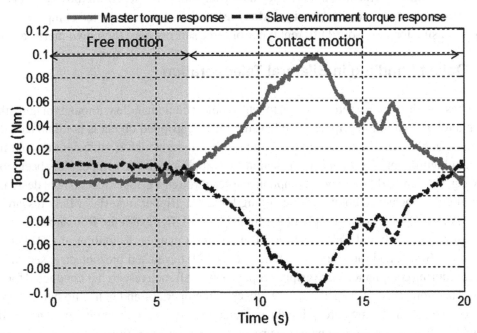

(b) Master and slave torque responses in bilateral control

REAL WORLD HAPTIC SENSATION

Transmission of action and reaction between the master operator and the slave environment should be accomplished in hard real time for real world haptic teleoperation. In order to feel the object, the operator touches, data transmission between master and slave devices is performed via a communication network like Ethernet, Wi-Fi, Bluetooth, or even through the Internet. Time delay occuring in the communication channel deteriorates the control stability and the performance. Many researchers have attempted to overcome the time delay in bilateral teleoperation. Scattering transformation motivated by a concept of passivity-based approach, wave variable control technique, robust control approaches like H_∞, two-layer fuzzy controller concept, and smith predictor can be represented as examples of time delay compensation methods (Natori, Tsuji, & Ohnishi, 2010). Natori et al (2010) have proposed a novel time delay compensation method based on the Communication Disturbance Observer (CDOB), which is a variant of the DOB. The CDOB is capable of compensating the time delay, even it is unknown and time varying.

Not only time delay compensation, but also human hand like grippers are essential for real world haptic teleoperation to sense spatially distributed objects. Multiple force sensor arrays and corresponding actuators should be placed in both master and slave sides for successful master slave bilateral teleoperation. If separate sensors are used, this could not be accomplished practically. However, if RTOB is used, force could be sensed through the motor actuator without having any special sensors. This spatial bilateral teleoperation concept is called multilateral control (Mitsantisuk, Katsura, & Ohishi, 2010; Ishii & Katsura, 2010; Okura & Katsura, 2010). They have transmitted motion from the place of actuation to the remote environment via cable mechanism. Many researchers have conducted compliance force control of grippers using force sensors. Different types of force sensors have their own merits and demerits.

Delicate Object Handling in Bilateral Teleoperation

Each object has a withstandable force limit up to which object could handle without damaging the object. Introducing a force limit to the gripper would ensure that the gripped object is not damaged due to the excessive force applied and is maintaining a static gripped force which is sufficient to hold the object firmly. Throughout the past few decades, research on compliance force grippers has been conducted. Work of Wang and Lan (2014) achieved compliance force through a gripper mechanical design, whereas Becedas et al (2011) achieved compliance gripping force via gripper material. Many researchers used various types of force sensors for compliance gripping control. For example, Romano et al (2011) used pressure sensors, Goldfarb and Celanovic (2000) used strain gauges, Kamali et al (2014) used Force Sensing Resister (FSR), and the work of Lorenz et al (1990) have used piezoelectric sensors for force measurements during compliance force gripper experiments. All such research is conducted for unilateral robot arms. Therefore, there is no grip force feedback to the operator and hence no haptic perception.

Grip force control and haptic perception during teleoperation is important in applications like robot – assisted minimally invasive surgery where a surgeon performs an operation at a distance through instruments inserted into the body through a small incision (Abeykoon & Ohnishi, 2007), in hazardous object handling and pick and place in the industry. Force feedback significantly improves the performance of a robotic surgical system. It is important to maintain compliance force continuously on a slave to protect gripped object and to avoid slipping from gripper arms while providing force feedback to the master operator. Ideally, a force lock should be implemented at the slave gripper. Gupta et al (2006) and Pierce et al (2014) have tested a bilateral gripper, which lacks force-locking feature when handling delicate objects. Those studies achieved gripping force sensing through kinesthetic, tactile sensors and stain gauges.

Force Sensing Technologies for Master Slave Manipulation

The sensing technologies of force and tactile sensing for master slave manipulation are based on the measurement of displacement, current, pressure, resistance, capacitance, piezoelectric voltage, and vibration (Puangmali, Althoefer, Seneviratne, Murphy, & Dasgupta, 2008). Accuracy and the reliability of the force measurement depend on sensor placement. If the force, which is to be measured, is transferred through mechanical links such as links, cables, and gear wheels, it leads error due to friction, backlash, inertia, and gravity effects. Thus, the force measurement should be conducted at the closest place where it is generated.

The force sensors based on displacement such as potentiometers, encoders, Linear Variable Differential Transformers (LVDT), and accelerometers detect distance or its derivatives. Force is usually detected using strain gauges attached to the motion joints. Force is calculated as part of the manufacturer's calibration. The friction at joints and backlash in drive mechanisms introduce errors to force measurements. Force or torque estimation based on current and acceleration could be calculated using the RTOB, as previously explained. For accurate measurements of external forces, the RTOB should be properly calibrated using correct parameters such as motor torque constant, friction elements, and inertia. In pressure-based sensors, force is measured through measuring the reaction of pneumatic or hydraulic pressure. This method also induces errors for the force measurement due to backlash of the driving mechanisms and frictions at the joints of measurement. Tactile sensors based on piezoelectric materials could be utilized at the expense of limited force range and displacement (Puangmali, Althoefer, Seneviratne, Murphy, & Dasgupta, 2008). Although flexible gripper based on inflatable rubber pockets driven by a pneumatic actuator could grasp up to 20 kg, it has the disadvantage of using the air compressor.

Force Feedback Gripper for Bilateral Teleoperation

Authors propose a system with force lock on the slave side to protect the object from excessive force applied through the master. When the force limit is attained, it will be notified to the master operator in terms of a small vibration. Slave object is preserved as the gripper maintained the specified maximum force. After engaging the force lock, master operator is feeling as if he is pressing a spring. This feeling is generated using a virtual spring controller placed on the master side. The lock will be released when the operator intends to release the object. The operator could modify the lock release condition. Master and slave follow bilateral control when it is not running in force lock mode. The proposed system is experimented in a single degree of freedom bilateral hardware system, which consists of identical two rotary motors and therefore torque lock is applied instead of the force lock. Thus, the main phases available during the force lock gripper operation could be listed as follows:

- Bilateral control
- Vibration notification
- Torque control at the slave side/ Spring sensation at the master side
- Release condition

Modeling is described in following paragraphs and the results are presented at the end of this section for the proposed torque feedback bilateral gripper.

The torque controller protects the gripped object from the excessive torque imposed by the master operator. The operator should initially specify the torque limit of the object. As for simulation purposes, the reaction of the environmental object F can be modeled as acceleration force, with mass M, damping force with damping coefficient B, and spring force with spring coefficient k as in Equation 36. θ denotes the angular displacement.

$$F = M\ddot{\theta} + B\dot{\theta} + k\theta \tag{36}$$

The master and the slave follow bilateral control until slave environment reaction reaches the specified torque limit of the object. The torque controller is activated when the reaction torque from the slave environment is equal or exceeds the specified torque limit. Thus, slave manipulator is locked at that maximum torque limit until the master operator satisfies the object release conditions. In this phase, the master and the slave no longer follow the bilateral control equations. The control block diagram of the slave is similar to Figure 14. The operator defines torque limit $T_{\lim it}$ as for the object's specification is considered as the reference torque. The estimated reaction torque from the slave environment via the RTOB of slave actuator $\hat{t}_{ext}$ is taken as the feedback. The torque error T_{err} in Equation 37 is fed to the PID controller and the output of the PID controller provides current reference I_a^{ref} to the slave motor. The disturbances are also estimated via DOB and compensating current I_{dis} is fed to the slave motor current input.

$$T_{err} = T_{\lim it} - \hat{t}_{ext} \tag{37}$$

By the time of torque lock activation, the objective Equations 4 and 5 of bilateral control are violated because slave torque is locked at the predefined torque limit $T_{\lim it}$. Therefore, master operator feels the loss of reaction torque coming from the slave environment as a sudden torque reduction causing a forward position step, which is undesirable although it provides a torque limit achievement notification. Therefore, a virtual spring controller is introduced on to the master manipulator. The block diagram of spring controller where master operator experiences position step due to loss of slave environment is depicted in Figure 17(a). Magnitude of the position step can reduce by increasing the spring constant of the virtual spring. This position step is undesirable in practical applications as it generates an impulsive reaction to the master operator. Hence, for practical application, block diagram of Figure 17(a) is modified as shown in Figure 17(b) to facilitate the sense of continuous torque increasing to the operator if he further presses his lever towards torque increasing direction.

This will not have any effect on the gripped object on the slave. The spring torque T_{sp} is produced as in Equation 38 around the equilibrium position θ_{eq}^s, which may change if the object impedance changes during the locked operation.

$$T_{sp} = k_{sp}(\theta_{eq}^s - \theta_m) \tag{38}$$

Figure 17. (a) Spring controller with loss of reaction torque notification (b) Spring controller with the sense of continuous torque increasing

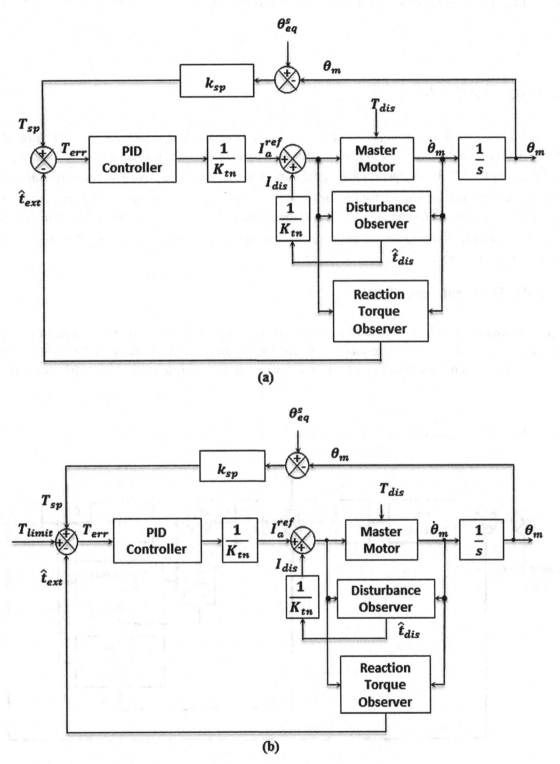

The notation k_{sp} denotes virtual spring coefficient. Reference torque T_{ref} for both scenarios in Figure 17 (a) and (b) are presented as Equations 39 and 40 respectively.

$$T_{ref} = k_{sp}(\theta^s_{eq} - \theta_m) \tag{39}$$

$$T_{ref} = T_{\lim it} + k_{sp}(\theta^s_{eq} - \theta_m) \tag{40}$$

The intention of virtual spring controller is to equalize the positions in lock mode. A vibration alert generates on the master operator side to notify the torque limit attainment on the slave side. This is available only for 500 ms. A square wave signal is incorporated on to the slave equilibrium position θ^s_{eq}, which is copied from the slave position during torque lock is active. It is used as the reference to the master position controller. Here also predefined torque limit $T_{\lim it}$ is given as the feedback to the master operator to avoid the operator feeling the sudden loss of reaction. Figure 18 presents the control block diagram of the vibrator.

Results: Bilateral Force Lock

Figures 19 and 20 provide the torque lock results. The limit of 0.10 Nm is used as the torque limit of the slave environmental object. The results are obtained using an Aluminium block as the slave environmental object. The locked object at the torque limit is released when the conditions

Figure 18. Block diagram of vibration signal generator

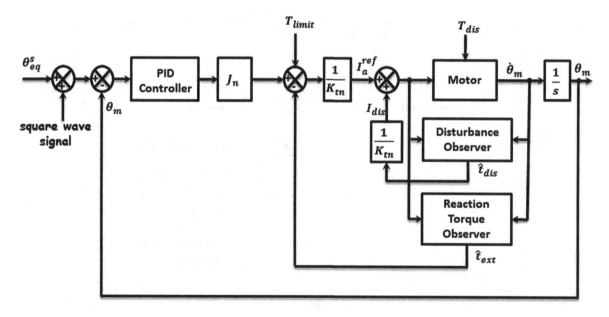

$(x_{eq}^s - x_m < 0) \& (\hat{t}_{ext,m} < T_{\lim it})$ are satisfied as for the master operator's intention. Figure 19 presents the force applied by the master operator and the response from the slave environmental object. Near 19th second, the reaction torque from the slave environment reaches the torque limit and hence activated the torque lock. The torque remains constant in the slave side until 36th second on which the master operator satisfies the release condition. During torque lock, master operator is free to increase his holding torque with virtual spring. The vibration notification is presented at the time of engaging the lock. The vibration or virtual spring effect has not affected the torque lock on the slave side. The shaded areas in following figures represent bilateral control in action before the torque lock engages and after the torque lock releases.

Figure 20 provides the master and slave position response corresponding to Figure 19. Both master and slave follow same positions as for the bilateral control theory during the first 19s. When the torque lock is active, slave actuator maintains a constant position where master position changes with the master operator's holding torque variations. Here, the vibration notification is visualized. When the master operator satisfies the release condition, again master and slave follow each other obeying the bilateral control.

Figure 21 represents torque variations and position responses on the same figure for the comparison. The slave torque response is invertedly plotted as for the sign convention.

Figure 19. Master and slave torque responses in bilateral gripper

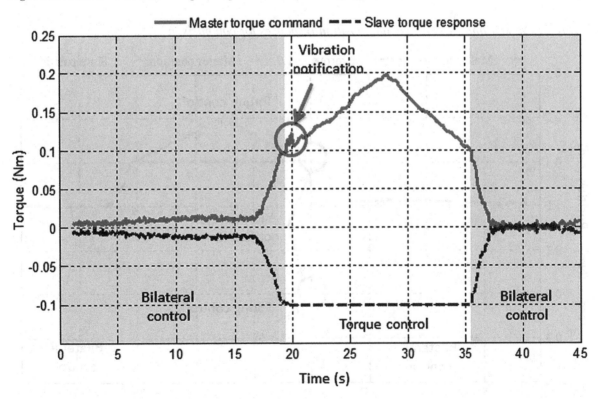

Figure 20. Master and slave position responses in bilateral gripper

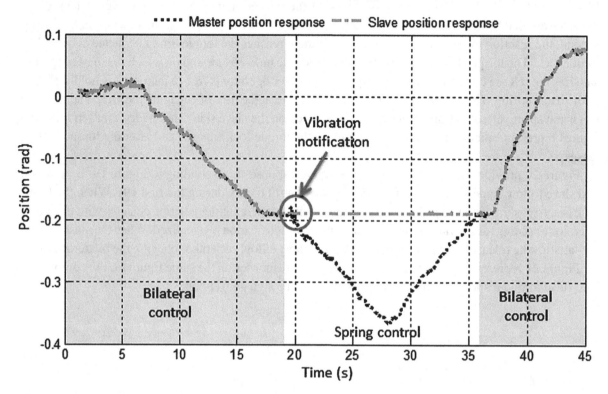

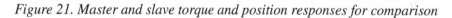

Figure 21. Master and slave torque and position responses for comparison

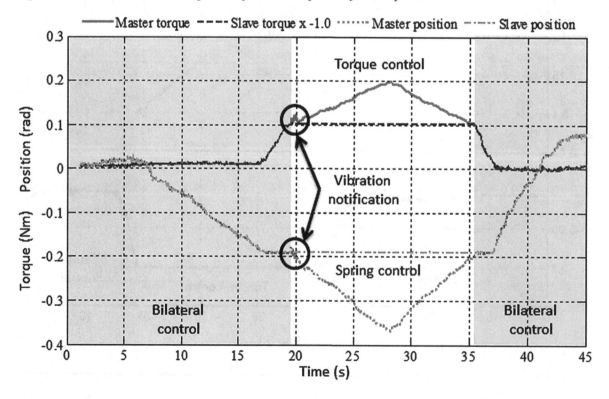

FUTURE RESEARCH DIRECTIONS

Since distances between the operator and the environment vary from few meters to two countries, it is important to have reaction torque as well as the positions to be exchanged in the real time. Fast and reliable communication methods are preferred to achieve good transparency and operationality in bilateral teleoperation. Bilateral control systems have severe stability consequences if time delay varies significantly. Many researchers have used the smith predictor, CDOB, etc. to compensate time delay (Natori, Tsuji, & Ohnishi, 2010). The complex manipulators with several DOFs require large quantity of data to transmit bilaterally in rigid hard time. Compression and decompression of motion data is a possible future study area.

When a human hand touches an object, the force is applied through the phalanges from proper orientation of interphalangeal joints and sense is felt through fingertips. Fingertip can identify force, frequency, texture, temperature, and object material with experience. Object dimension is decided from the final finger orientation. Human hand consists of 14 interphalangeal joints and all or few of them will be used when an object is being grasped. Human like hand design for remote manipulation with force feedback is a challenge because it should be able to acquire the torque generated from 14 interphalangeal joints separately to communicate between master and the slave. Using 14 actuators (motors) might end up with a bulky hand. The available designs of human like hand mostly used as a prosthetic hand use thread and mechanical links to operate interphalangeal joints. Therefore, such systems are incapable to differentiate torque generated by every joint and fail to sense the reaction from the grasped object (steepergroup, 2015). Future research should be extended to human like hand design with individual actuators for 14 interphalangeal joints with compact, flexible, and force feedback capability.

Research of bilateral control could extend to operator wearable gloves, which is capable of sensing the reaction from remote human like hand. Similarly, the force/ position response from the wearable glove should be transmitted to remote replica of the human hand. In most applications, force sensor is installed at the fingertip and actuation is performed at a different location. However, with the DOB, force sensing and actuation are accomplished at the same location. Therefore, human-like hand implementation with DOB will be an interesting study area in the future.

This chapter discussed DOB and RTOB based force estimation and successful bilateral teleoperation. When a human touches an object, it could be identified using different properties of the material such as object impedance, texture, temperature, and material. Therefore, a single sensor must be developed that can integrate all sensory features, just like in a human fingertip. To convey the dimension and the spatial impedance, multilateral control should be further developed.

CONCLUSION

Rapid development of the computing and communication technologies has led to faster real time bilateral transmission of motion data. DOB and RTOB were presented to be used as a control technique to achieve robustness in motion controllers. The concepts of DOB and RTOB were presented in detail such that it could be applied for a similar application. RTOB could be effectively used in haptic teleoperation as a force/torque sensor. Vivid torque sensing could be achieved using the DOB and RTOB combination in both master and slave sides.

With fast communication and wider bandwidth, a vivid sensation could be transmitted from one point to another point in real time. It is vital to limit the force acting on the slave object if it is a delicate object. In such a situation, the proposed force lock could be effectively used. The proposed force lock undergoes several states like bilateral control, force control, spring control, etc resulting step changes during state transition. The step changes usually cause system instability. During active force lock the system violates the basic equations of the bilateral control. Therefore, the proposed system is designed to retain the stability during state transition. Commercially available Da Vinci surgical system lacks the haptic feedback to the surgeon. If DOB and RTOB are successfully implemented on to the EndoWrist instruments, haptic feedback could be successfully transmitted to the surgeon without force sensors. The proposed force lock could be successfully implemented to applications like tele-surgery where the gripped organs needed to be handled with care.

Tele-manipulators with haptic feedback for hot cell operation in nuclear power plants are recently introduced to the commercial market. It still lacks the force lock on the gripper. The complexity and the functionality to mimic the human-like hand using DOB and RTOB are yet to be realized.

REFERENCES

Abeykoon, A. M. H. S., & Chinthaka, M. K. C. D. (2014). Position based static friction estimation for DC motors using disturbance observer.*Proceedings of 2014 7th International Conference on Information and Automation for Sustainability (ICIAfS)* (pp. 1-6). Colombo: IEEE.

Abeykoon, A. M. H. S., & Ohnishi, K. (2006). Realization of virtual slave model of a forceps robot using bilateral control.*Proceedings of 32nd Annual Conference on IEEE Industrial Electronics* (pp. 4468-4473). IEEE. doi:10.1109/IECON.2006.348100

Abeykoon, A. M. H. S., & Ohnishi, K. (2007). Virtual tool for bilaterally controlled forceps robot-for minimally invasive surgery. *Transaction on International Journal of Medical Robotics and Computer Assisted Surgery*, 3(3), 271–280. doi:10.1002/rcs.147 PMID:17729375

Abeykoon, A. M. H. S., & Ohnishi, K. (2008). Improvement of tactile sensation of a bilateral forceps robot by a switching virtual model. *Transactions on Advanced Robotics*, 8(8), 789–806. doi:10.1163/156855308X314506

Abeykoon, A. M. H. S., & Perera, G. V. A. G. A. (2014). Review on bilateral teleoperation with force, position, power and impedance scaling.*Proceedings of 2014 7th International Conference on Information and Automation for Sustainability* (pp. 1-7). Colombo: IEEE.

Abeykoon, A. M. H. S., & Pillai, M. B. (2014, September). RTOS based embedded controller implementation of a bilateral control system. *Journal of the National Science Foundation of Sri Lanka*, 3(42), 217–228.

Abeykoon, A. M. H. S., & Senevirathne, H. R. (2012). Disturbance observer based current controller for a brushed DC motor.*Proceedings of 2012 IEEE 6th International Conference on Information and Automation for Sustainability* (pp. 47-52). IEEE. doi:10.1109/ICIAFS.2012.6419881

AZORobotics. (2013, June 11). *Applications of Robots to Clean Nuclear Power Plants*. Retrieved from http://www.azorobotics.com/Article.aspx?ArticleID=102

Becedas, J., Payo, I., & Feliu, V. (2011). Two-flexible-fingers gripper force feedback control system for its application as end effector on a 6-DOF manipulator. *IEEE Transactions on Robotics, 27*(3), 599–615. doi:10.1109/TRO.2011.2132850

Bicker, R., Burn, K., Hu, Z., Pongaen, W., & Bashir, A. (2004). The early development of remote tele-manipulation systems. In M. Ceccarelli (Ed.), *Proceedings of the International Symposium on History of Machines and Mechanisms HMM '04* (pp. 391–404).

Chinthaka, M. K. C. D., & Abeykoon, A. M. H. S. (2015, May). Friction compensation of DC motors for precise motion control using disturbance observer. *ECTI Transactions on Computer And Information Technology, 9*, 66–74.

Chinthaka, M. K. C. D., Punchihewa, R. U. G., & Abeykoon, A. M. H. S. (2014). Disturbance observer based friction compensator for a DC motor. *Proceedings of 2014 11th International Conference on Electrical Engineering/Electronics, Computer, Telecommunications and Information Technology (ECTI-CON)* (pp. 1-6). IEEE. doi:10.1109/ECTICon.2014.6839747

Djedidi, A., Selliez-Vandernotte, C., & Malcolm, F. (2015, January 7). Hot cell robot. *Nuclear Engineering International*. Retrieved from http://www.neimagazine.com/features/featurehot-cell-robot-4483658/

Goldfarb, M., & Celanovic, N. (2000, September). A flexure-based gripper for small-scale manipulation. *Robotica, 17*(2), 181–187.

Gupta, G. S., Mukhopadhyay, S. C., Messom, C. H., & Demidenko, S. N. (2006). Master–slave control of a teleoperated anthropomorphic robotic arm with gripping force sensing. *IEEE Transactions on Instrumentation and Measurement, 55*(6), 2136–2145. doi:10.1109/TIM.2006.884393

Hashtrudi-Zaad, K., & Salcudean, S. E. (2002a). Bilateral parallel force/position teleoperation control. *Journal of Robotic Systems, 19*(4), 155–167. doi:10.1002/rob.10030

Hashtrudi-Zaad, K., & Salcudean, S. E. (2002b). Transparency in time-delayed systems and the effect of local force feedback for transparent teleoperation. *IEEE Transactions on Robotics and Automation, 8*(1), 108–114. doi:10.1109/70.988981

Huang, G., & Lee, S. (2008). PC-based PID speed control in DC motor. *Proceedings of the International Conference on Audio, Language and Image Processing* (pp. 400-407). IEEE.

Intuitive Surgical, Inc. (2015). *da Vinci Surgery: The da Vinci Surgical System*. Retrieved from http://www.davincisurgery.com/da-vinci-surgery/da-vinci-surgical-system/

Ishii, E., Katsura, S., Nishi, H., & Ohnishi, K. (2008, November). Development of multi-degree-of-freedom bilateral forceps robot system using FPGA. *Electronics and Communications in Japan, 91*(6), 23–33. doi:10.1002/ecj.10118

Ishii, T., & Katsura, S. (2010). Articulated multilateral control for haptic broadcasting system. *Proceedings of 36th Annual Conference on IEEE Industrial Electronics Society* (pp. 1872-1877). IEEE. doi:10.1109/IECON.2010.5675383

Jelatis, D. G. (1975). Characteristics and evaluation of "Master-slave Manipulators". In T. B. Sheridan (Ed.), *Performance Evaluation of Programmable Robots and Manipulators* (pp. 141–146). Annapolis, Maryland: National Bureau of Standards (U.S.).

Kamali, M., Moosavian, S. A. A., & Cheraghpour, F. (2014). Improving grasp capabilities of KNTU hand using position & force sensors.*Proceedings of 22nd Iranian Conference on Electrical Engineering* (pp. 1278-1283). IEEE. doi:10.1109/IranianCEE.2014.6999731

Katsura, S., Matsumoto, Y., & Ohnishi, K. (2007, February). Modeling of force sensing and validation of disturbance observer forforce control. *IEEE Transactions on Industrial Electronics, 54*(1), 530–538. doi:10.1109/TIE.2006.885459

Kebude, D., Morimitsu, H., Katsura, S., & Sabanovic, A. (2014). Multilateral control-based motion copying system for haptic training.*Proceedings of 2014 IEEE 23rd International Symposium on Industrial Electronics* (pp. 2250 - 2255). IEEE. doi:10.1109/ISIE.2014.6864968

Kobayashi, H., Nakamura, H., Tatsuno, J., & Iijima, S. (1993). Micro-macro tele-manipulation system. *Proceedings of 2nd IEEE International Workshop on Robot and Human Communication* (pp. 165 - 170). IEEE.

Lawrence, D. A. (1993, October). Stability and transparency in bilateral teleoperation. *IEEE Transactions on Robotics and Automation, 9*(5), 624–637. doi:10.1109/70.258054

Lorenz, R. D., Meyer, K. M., & De Riet, D. M. V. (1990). A novel, compliant, four degree-of-freedom, robotic fingertip sensor. *IEEE Transactions on Industry Applications, 26*(4), 613–619. doi:10.1109/28.55983

Mitsantisuk, C., Katsura, S., & Ohishi, K. (2010, April). Force control of human–robot interaction using twin direct-drive motor system based on modal space design. *IEEE Transactions on Industrial Electronics, 57*(4), 1383–1392. doi:10.1109/TIE.2009.2030218

Mizuochi, M., Tsuji, T., & Ohnishi, K. (2006). Improvement of disturbance suppression based on disturbance observer.*Proceedings of 9th IEEE International Workshop on Advanced Motion Control* (pp. 229-234). IEEE. doi:10.1109/AMC.2006.1631663

Murakami, T., Yu, F., & Ohnishi, K. (1993, April). Torque sensorless control in multidegree-of-freedom manipulator. *IEEE Transactions on Industrial Electronics, 40*(2), 259–265. doi:10.1109/41.222648

Nagata, K., & Katsura, S. (2015). Synchronism evaluation of multi-DOF motion-copying system for motion training.*Proceedings of 2015 IEEE International Conference on Mechatronics* (pp. 500-505). IEEE. doi:10.1109/ICMECH.2015.7084027

Natori, K., Tsuji, T., & Ohnishi, K. (2010, March). Time-delay compensation by communication disturbance observer for bilateral teleoperation under time-varying delay. *IEEE Transactions on Industrial Electronics, 57*(3), 1050-1062.

Ohnishi, K., Matsui, N., & Hori, Y. (1994, August). Estimation, identification, and sensorless control in motion control system. *Proceedings of the IEEE, 82*(8), 1253–1265. doi:10.1109/5.301687

Ohnishi, K., Shibata, M., & Murakami, T. (1996, March). Motion control for advanced mechatronics. *IEEE/ASME Transactions on Mechatronics, 1*(1), 56–67. doi:10.1109/3516.491410

Okura, T., & Katsura, S. (2010). Analysis of system connection in multilateral control system considering number of subsystems.*Proceedings of 36th Annual Conference on IEEE Industrial Electronics Society* (pp. 1234-1239). IEEE. doi:10.1109/IECON.2010.5675546

Perera, G. V. A. G. A., Pillai, M. B., & Abeykoon, A. M. H. S. (2014). DC motor inertia estimation for robust bilateral control.*Proceedings of 7th International Conference on Information and Automation for Sustainability* (pp. 1-7). Colombo: IEEE.

Pierce, R. M., Fedalei, E. A., & Kuchenbecker, K. J. (2014). A wearable device for controlling a robot gripper with fingertip contact, pressure, vibrotactile, and grip force feedback.*Proceedings of IEEE Haptics Symposium* (pp. 19-25). doi:10.1109/HAPTICS.2014.6775428

Pillai, M. B., Perera, G. V. A. G. A., Chinthaka, M. K. C. D., & Abeykoon, A. M. H. S. (2014, July). Analysis of a DC motor based velocity controller using disturbance observer. *Indian Journal of Social Research*, 5, 1–7.

Puangmali, P., Althoefer, K., Seneviratne, L. D., Murphy, D., & Dasgupta, P. (2008, April). State of the art in force and tactile sensing for minimally invasive surgery. *IEEE Sensors Journal*, 8(4), 371–381. doi:10.1109/JSEN.2008.917481

Romano, J. M., Hsiao, K., Niemeyer, G., Chitta, S., & Kuchenbecker, K. J. (2011). Human-inspired robotic grasp control with tactile sensing. *IEEE Transactions on Robotics*, 27(6), 1067–1079. doi:10.1109/TRO.2011.2162271

Ruwanthika, R. M. M., & Abeykoon, A. M. H. S. (2015). 3D environmental force: position impedance variation for different motion parameters.*Proceedings of Moratuwa Engineering Research Conference (MERCon)* (pp. 112-117). IEEE. doi:10.1109/MERCon.2015.7112330

Salisbury, J. K. (1980). Active stiffness control of a manipulator in Cartesian coordinates.*Proceedings of 19th IEEE Conference on Decision and Control including the Symposium on Adaptive Processes* (pp. 95-100). IEEE. doi:10.1109/CDC.1980.272026

Shimono, T., Katsura, S., & Ohnishi, K. (2005). Improvement of operationality for bilateral control based on nominal mass design in disturbance observer.*Proceedings of 31st Annual Conference of IEEE Industrial Electronics Society* (6-10). IEEE. doi:10.1109/IECON.2005.1569217

Shimono, T., Katsura, S., & Ohnishi, K. (2007, April). Abstraction and reproduction of force sensation from real environment by bilateral control. *IEEE Transactions on Industrial Electronics*, 54(2), 907–918. doi:10.1109/TIE.2007.892744

steepergroup. (2015). *bebionic*. Retrieved from http://bebionic.com/

Sumiyoshi, Y., & Ohnishi, K. (2004). The transformation of modified 4-channel architecture.*Proceedings of the 8th IEEE International Workshop on Advanced Motion Control* (pp. 211-216). IEEE.

Takeo, K., & Kosuge, K. (1997). Implementation of the micro-macro teleoperation system without using slave-side force sensors.*Proceedings of 1997 IEEE International Conference on Robotics and Automation*. (vol. 2, pp. 1600 - 1605). IEEE. doi:10.1109/ROBOT.1997.614369

Takeya, M., & Katsura, S. (2015). Modal-space filtering by expectation value extraction for high-scaling bilateral control. *IEEJ Journal of Industry Applications, 4*(6), 681–687. doi:10.1541/ieejjia.4.681

Wang, J.Y., & Lan, C.C. (2014). A constant force compliant gripper for handling objects of various sizes. *ASME Transaction of Journal of Mechanical Design, 136*(7).

Yokokohji, Y., & Yoshikawa, T. (1994, October). Bilateral control of master-slave manipulators for ideal kinesthetic coupling-formulation and experiment. *IEEE Transactions on Robotics and Automation, 10*(5), 605–620. doi:10.1109/70.326566 PMID:11539289

KEY TERMS AND DEFINITIONS

Bilateral Teleoperation: Operating a machine at a distance while exchanging the action and reaction information between the master and the slave bidirectionaly in real time via a communication channel.

Control Stiffness: The change in the force per arbitrary small change in the displacement.

Disturbance Observer (DOB): An observer use to attain robust operation which is immune to the system disturbances.

Force Lock: A gripper locking mechanism which is activated after satisfying the assigned force limit and maintains the constant force until object release logic is true.

Haptic: the sense of touch.

Master: The operator issuing the commands through a human machine interface to control the remote machine/manipulator.

Reaction Torque Observer (RTOB): A modified version of disturbance observer to estimate reaction torque/force exerted by external environment on the motor if frictional elements and parameter variations are known beforehand.

Slave: The machine/manipulator following the command signal issued from the remote location.

Teleoperation: Operating a machine at a distance.

Chapter 6
Multimodal Feedback in Human–Robot Interaction:
An HCI-Informed Comparison of Feedback Modalities

Maria Vanessa aus der Wieschen
University of Southern Denmark, Denmark

Kamil Kukliński
Białystok University of Technology, Poland

Kerstin Fischer
University of Southern Denmark, Denmark

Lars Christian Jensen
University of Southern Denmark, Denmark

Thiusius Rajeeth Savarimuthu
University of Southern Denmark, Denmark

ABSTRACT

A major area of interest within the fields of human-computer interaction (HCI) and human-robot interaction (HRI) is user feedback. Previous work in HCI has investigated the effects of error feedback on task efficiency and error rates, yet, these studies have been mostly restricted to comparisons of inherently different feedback modalities, for example auditory and visual, and as such fail to acknowledge the many possible variations within each of these modalities, some of which being more effective than others. This chapter applies a user-centered approach to investigating feedback modalities for robot teleoperation by naïve users. It identifies the reasons why novice users need feedback when demonstrating novel behaviors to a teleoperated industrial robot and evaluates both various feedback modalities designed to prevent errors and, drawing on document design theory, studies different kinds of visual presentation regarding their effectiveness in the creation of legible error feedback screens.

INTRODUCTION

Industrial robots are increasingly recognized as a time- and cost-efficient alternative or assistance to human labor, with the number of robots installed in industrial settings growing constantly. The statistical department of the International Federation of Robotics (2014) estimates the amount of industrial robots sold in 2013 to be around 168,000. However, adjusting these industrial robots to novel behaviors

DOI: 10.4018/978-1-5225-0435-1.ch006

is usually a time-consuming and also expensive task carried out by programmers (Chernova & Thomaz, 2014); consequently, much recent work focuses on learning from demonstration, where the robot acquires novel tasks from the demonstration by people other than programmers (e.g. Muxfeldt, Kluth, & Kubus, 2014) – if however naïve users demonstrate tasks to a robot, the interface needs to be intuitive and user-friendly and has to ensure that the number of errors remains low. Thus, users need feedback when demonstrating novel tasks to the robot.

Research on feedback has been mostly restricted to comparisons of inherently different feedback modalities, for example auditory and visual. These studies fail to acknowledge that there are endless varieties of each of these modalities, of which some might be more effective than others. Auditory feedback, for instance, can be realized as verbal messages, earcons, and auditory icons (Nam & Kim, 2010). However, there are several teleoperation modalities that require the human user to be physically near the robot (Kirstein, 2014) such as the case with the MARVIN platform (Savarimuthu et al., 2013), the robotic platform that is studied in the present paper. Researchers in this field seem to focus mostly on user safety issues in these forms of teleoperation, while paying far too little attention to intuitive interaction.

Based on aus der Wieschen (2015), this chapter examines different types of error feedback for human-robot interaction, arguing that error feedback is a crucial factor in designing intuitive human-robot interaction between naïve users and industrial robots. The major objectives of this chapter are to determine the problems novice users may cause for the robot platform under consideration and to examine how feedback can help users solve these problems on their own. Furthermore, this chapter develops design guidelines for the design of error feedback screens. In particular, this research seeks to address three questions:

1. Which errors occur when naïve users teleoperate the MARVIN platform?
2. How can feedback prevent these errors or help users to resolve them?
3. Which factors influence the legibility of feedback screens?

Both qualitative and quantitative research methods were adopted to provide answers to these questions. This paper comprises four studies, of which three were conducted as user tests in a lab setting, and one in form of a survey. The baseline study identifies the most common problems that occur in human-robot interaction with an industrial assembly robot and asks when and why naïve users wish for feedback. The second lab study presents novice users with three feedback modalities that the users in the baseline study requested. As one of the three modalities – visual feedback – proved to be very inefficient (even though previous research has reported on the efficiency of visual feedback), a survey was conducted in order to find out which factors influence the legibility of error feedback screens. The most legible feedback screens were then tested in the same lab setting to validate the survey results.

BACKGROUND

Learning from Demonstration (LfD)

When robots were initially introduced to industrial contexts, only two approaches to robot teaching were known: robot programing and reinforcement learning (Bakker & Kuniyoshi, 1996). Both approaches have their disadvantages when applied in practice: Robot programing implies complicated programing of complex behaviors while reinforcement learning does not provide enough information for the robot to learn complex tasks (Bakker & Kuniyoshi, 1996). Inspired by the biological idea of imitation, where it is an effective way of transmitting knowledge used by humans and animals, LfD was introduced as a natural and intuitive way to teach robots (Demiris & Hayes, 2002; Bakker & Kuniyoshi, 1996). Bakker and Kuniyoshi (1996, p.3) defined imitation as something that "[...] takes place when an agent learns a behavior from observing the execution of that behavior by a teacher" which can be applied to humans and animals, as well as robots that are built to behave human-like.

The main goal of LfD is to have lay users program a robot by demonstrating a task. Programing becomes an interactive activity between the user and the robot and to make this interaction effective, efficient and user-friendly, an intuitive user interface that allows users to operate, and consequently, teach the robot a task without being an expert in robotics or robot programing is required (Friedrich, Dillmann, & Rogalla, 1999). This lack of expertise, however, has been shown to cause problems in HRI. For instance, Marhenke, Fischer, and Savarimuthu (2014) have shown that errors occur when the expectations of naïve users are not fulfilled. Their research found that users expect teleoperated robot arms to behave similar to their own arms. When the robot in their study reacted to the users' controls with delay, i.e. did not immediately stop moving when the users stopped moving their arm, it led to problems that not only potentially damage the robot, but also make learning from demonstration less robust.

ERRORS IN LEARNING FROM DEMONSTRATION

This section describes the baseline study which investigated the possible problems that can occur when naïve users use an industrial robot and explore when and why these users need feedback.

The Robot

The robot platform used for the studies in this chapter is the MARVIN platform (Savarimuthu, et al., 2013), located in a laboratory at the University of Southern Denmark in Odense. The robot, which can learn by demonstration how to perform assembly tasks, has two Universal Robot UR5 robot manipulator arms, of which the users in our studies control one in order to teleoperate the robot. The robot arm is controlled by means of a Schunk Force-Torque sensor on the tool center point (TCP) of the robot arm, which is used to measure the forces and torques acting on the robot TCP during user interaction. The two control modes are a data glove and a control peg (in later studies replaced by a novel teleoperation device), both used in combination with a dead man's switch. Both of the control modes consist of teleoperation devices that are used to control the robot movements. The first control mode uses a data glove equipped with a magnetic tracking sensor placed in the middle of the outer part of the hand that tracks the user's movements (see figure 1). A second sensor is placed in the index finger of the glove, allowing the user to open and close the gripper when closing their hand. The second control mode, the control peg is equipped with the same magnetic sensor that tracks the user's movements. The technical details for the peg are described in Kukliński et al (2014). It resembles the square peg of the Cranfield Benchmark (see figure 1), an assembly set (Collins, Palmer & Rathrnill, 1985) and is to be held in the hand. Unlike the data glove, the control peg is not equipped with a second sensor that allows the user to open and close the gripper. Consequently, the grasping needs to be executed by the robot supervisor, who can also change in between three different grasp modes on behalf of the user. Both control modes require the so-called dead man's switch, which needs to be pressed in order to send a signal to

Figure 1. User demonstrating a peg-in-hole task using a data glove

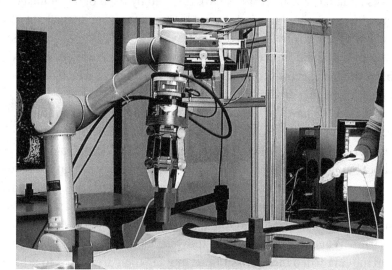

the computer and thus the robot. It is to be held in the opposite hand of the control peg or glove and can be used as a safety measure: Whenever the user lets go of the switch, the robot will stop. As outlined in Marhenke, Fischer, and Savarimuthu (2014) however, the dead man's switch reacts with a slight delay.

Method

The Users

The 33 participants in this study were students and staff from the technical faculty at the University of Southern Denmark. The fields of study or work of most participants are technical, sometimes even related to robotics, which arguable makes them resemble real users. Moreover, the demographic survey found that many users play video games on a regular basis, which is at least similar to teleoperating a robot in a virtual environment. As one of the goals was to investigate the usability of the MARVIN platform for novice users, a requirement in participant selection was that they had no prior experience with the MARVIN platform, which none of them had. Three facilitators worked together observing, asking questions, reminding users to think aloud, and taking notes. A robot operator was present at all times to ensure user safety and solve technical issues.

The Task

As the participants never worked with MARVIN before and only learned about its abilities from a short video user guide, a simple assembly task using objects from the Cranfield set for them to perform was predefined. In any other case, it would have been useful to allow the users to select the task they want to do, as this might reveal use scenarios that designers did not anticipate (Buur & Binder, 2006). The users are asked to perform an assembly task using objects from the Cranfield set.

Procedure

The users were first shown a 10-minute introduction video, in which they learned about the robot's abilities, as well as about possible problems and their resolution. They were then led to the MARVIN platform, with which they had to solve a simple assembly task. While performing the task, users were encouraged to "think aloud" (Van Someren, Barnard, & Sandberg, 1994), Moreover, users were interviewed about their experience with the robot during and after the task performance. After the interaction, users were presented with things to think with alongside the interview, in order to generate ideas for possible feedback modalities and for a more intuitive control device. For this, the facilitators used objects such as toys and a handheld gaming device.

Think-Aloud Method

Users were asked to "think aloud" (Van Someren, Barnard, & Sandberg, 1994) while demonstrating a simple assembly task to the robot, under the pretense that they have to inform the robot expert about their current and planned actions and the behavior of the robot. That is, they were asked to share any thoughts and feelings they had with the experiment facilitators and the robot expert. The role of the facilitators was then to be listeners, and to encourage the users to continue verbalizing their thoughts. A clear advantage of this method is that it reveals underlying cognitive processes, which the user might not be aware of and thus could not have reported in an interview (Rubin & Chisnell, 2008). A weak point of the think aloud method is that users are not used to verbalize their thoughts for other people to hear, as such, it might make the user feel uncomfortable (Rubin & Chisnell, 2008).

User Experience Interviews

To counter this drawback, users were also interviewed about their experience with the robot during and after the task performance. The facilitators followed Goodwin's (2009) suggestions on how to facilitate interviews with the goal to understand the users. As the facilitators each only tried out the robot for a few minutes prior the experiments, they were not able to predict what kind of problems and topics could arise. Hence, they did not follow a prepared interview script, rather, their questions emerged spontaneously through the observation and ad hoc interpretation of the users' behavior and thought-aloud utterances. The facilitators were novice robot users themselves, and as such they were naturally curious and genuinely interested in the users' experiences. This, in combination with the similar demographic background with the users, as well as the facilitators positioning themselves as fellow non-experts (as opposed to the PhD student) made it easier for them to create rapport with the users and to engage in a natural conversation with them. Usually one would think that a group of three facilitators would seem overwhelming to the participant, however, the study finds that the users enjoyed the company of them and perceived the facilitators as people who are there to help them. However, the facilitators did not directly answer questions of the users or help them unless absolutely necessary. Bernsen and Dybkjær (2009) suggest facilitators only help their users unless the users feel very bad, for example if they feel bad about having caused a problem, or there is a technical problem that requires the experimenters to step in. Likewise, questions should only be answered when they do not reveal any information that might influence the performance of the user (Bernsen & Dybkjær, 2009).

Things to Think With

Moreover, the users were presented with things to think with alongside the interview, in order to generate ideas for possible feedback modalities and for a more intuitive control device. As the facilitators had almost no knowledge about the possible problems related to robot teleoperation prior to conducting the user studies, and therefore found themselves unable to build prototypes of a feedback device or a new control device, they used objects such as toys and a handheld gaming device in the place of actual prototypes. Brandt (2007) investigated in what way differences in the level of detail of a 3D prototype have an influence on the feedback from the users. She states that one of the major advantages of tangible mock-ups is that they address several perceptual motor skills and senses of the user, which in turn encourages the user to reflect and comment on their multi-sensory experience with the mock-up. Brandt found that while low-fidelity mock-ups evoke a broad variety of reactions and comments from the users, high-fidelity prototypes lead users to focus on details. In that sense, using these toys and other objects the facilitators found in the lab promised to help the researchers create general design ideas, rather than suggestions for fine details, which would only be relevant in the later stages of the iterative design process.

Results

Problems Caused by the Users

It was distinguished between problems leading to security stops and problems making a restart of the system necessary. Security stops are initiated by the MARVIN platform in order to prevent a situation that would make a complete restart necessary. A security stop stops all movement and prevents the user from manipulating the robot any further. It is then up to the robot expert on the computer to end the security stop and hand over the control to the user again. If the robot expert foresees that the user might cause further damage by trying to resolve the situation, he can choose to reset the robot to the start position before letting the user control the robot again. Restarts are necessary when the system was unable to initiate a security stop in time, when the robot was damaged badly, or due to unknown technical issues.

In our study with 33 participants, eight users caused security stops, seven users forced the system to restart, and an additional three users caused both security stops and system restarts. The reasons for security stops were a) too much pressure (7 times), b) the arm being in a position where the position of the robot joints cannot be configured anymore, i.e. singularity (3 times), and c) self-collision (2 times). The MARVIN platform had to be restarted after a security stop either because users brought the arm into a bad position (singularity or twisted arm, 9 times) or pushed so hard into the table with the robot that the finger covers fell off (3 times).

Reasons Why Naïve Users Cause Problems

These problems occurred partly due to a lack of knowledge; for example, users are generally unaware how to determine when the force threshold limit is exceeded and do not realize that they cannot directly manipulate any part of the arm separately except for the gripper. Other reasons are technical, such as the delay of the dead man's button and the high sensitivity of the controllers. Interestingly, users often did not even know that they caused problems and were surprised about the security stops.

Lay Users Do Not Understand Complex Principles of Robotics

In robot teleoperation, the robot is controlled by means of a preset control point within the tool center in the robot arm. In the baseline study, the control peg and the data glove function as controllers. These are equipped with a sensor. When the controllers are moved and the dead man's button is pushed, the controller's movements are tracked. The robot will then imitate these movements with the reference point in the gripper, while the remaining joints of the arm will adapt their positions in correspondence with the gripper's position (Liljekrans, 2012). That is, it is not directly possible for the user to control any other part of the robot but the TCP of the gripper. If a user wishes to move a certain part of the arm, for example to bend the elbow in order to resolve singularity, the user has to change the position of the gripper in such a way that the rest of the arm adapting to the new position of the gripper will bend, resulting in resolved singularity. The MARVIN user is thus expected to understand that the only one reference point at a time he/she has control over is located in or very close to the gripper. This concept was not explained to the novice users participating in our studies. The facilitators asked 12 out of 16 users to tell them or point to the part of the robot arm they thought they controlled. As the reference point in this study was located in the center of the gripper, this was the correct answer. However, only 3 out of 12 noticed that the reference point was in the gripper. Arguably close enough, one user thought it was in the fingers. The majority, 7 out of 12, believed they had direct control over all parts of the robot. One participant falsely located the reference point in the part between elbow and wrist.

Dead Man's Switch Reacts with a Delay

The robot is only supposed to move when and for as long as the dead man's button is pushed in. However, there is a slight delay of between 33 milliseconds to 1 second during which the robot continues to move after the dead man's button has been let go. That is, even if users notice a problem, such as too much pressure or singularity being about to happen, and wishes to stop moving the robot in order to prevent the problem, the problem might still happen, as the user cannot calculate the distance the robot will continue to move during the delay. Marhenke, Fischer, and Savarimuthu (2014) found that since teleoperation is so intuitive, users expect the robot movements to be a translation of their own movements. Therefore, users do not expect the robot to continue moving after they themselves stopped moving.

Users furthermore make large movements. Even though in the introduction video users were specifically told not to make large movements, this was still a major cause of the problems mentioned above.

Sensitivity is Too High

The researchers asked users how they felt about the speed and sensitivity of the robot. The users found the speed to be good. Moreover, in a recent study on reasons for singularity in teleoperation of the MARVIN platform, Marhenke, Fischer, and Savarimuthu (2014) did not find speed to be a cause of problems. On the other hand, many users complained about the high sensitivity.

Users Do Not Know How Far They May Push into the Foam

Users were instructed that they may not push "too far" into the foam, yet, users were quite clueless about how to interpret this message from the instruction video. Users are unable to see when exactly the force threshold limit is exceeded.

Implications for Feedback Design

Our baseline study showed that users want feedback mainly for two reasons: to inform them about the current state of the robot and to warn the users of any problems likely to happen in the near future. Information of the current state relevant to the user could be: current problems (such as too much pressure, singularity, twisted arm, and self-collision), security stops, the currently selected grasp mode, and the current position of the peg/separator in relation to their desired position in the faceplate. As problems such as singularity and self-collision may be predictable to a certain degree, users could be warned in advance, thus preventing the problems from happening. However, as such prediction models cannot actually predict the future with full certainty, one would have to develop a threshold for the probability of a given problem to happen. Warning the users too early could lead to fatigue or the users not taking the warning seriously anymore, while warning the users too late could mean that the problem cannot be avoided anymore.

The baseline study furthermore set out to gather information both on the users' preferences for the size and shape of a feedback screen or any other device with feedback, and on the users' ideas for possible abilities and design features. Regarding the shape, size, and feel of the feedback object, users were handed them everyday objects such as pens, packs of sugar and plastic bottles. These are to resemble a low-fidelity prototype. As far as the functions and features of the new feedback object are concerned, the facilitators handed users, for instance, a Nintendo DS handheld game console as a high-fidelity prototype for inspiration. The objects were handed to users only if it seemed appropriate as part of the dialogue between user and facilitators.

The study found that handing the users objects of strikingly different materials enabled the users to describe their ideas better. Users liked being able to use these objects to give examples when describing abstract concepts, such as softness. Providing the users with tangible examples, eliminated the time-consuming process of the users having to think up their own examples.

Users were told that the researchers are thinking about building a controller with inbuilt feedback screen similar to the Nintendo DS, but did not know what exactly the many buttons, the touch-pen and the two screens should be used for. While many users did not think they would like a feedback screen before, after given the Nintendo DS they came up with several ideas.

Users suggested three feedback modalities: audible feedback, tactile feedback, and visual feedback. The next section sets out to describe these modalities in detail.

USER-CENTERED EXPLORATION OF FEEDBACK MODALITIES

Previous Work on Feedback

Affirmative Feedback and Error Feedback

Sun, Ren, and Cao (2011) distinguish between affirmative feedback and error feedback in HCI. Affirmative feedback is feedback given to users to affirm them that they are not making an error at the moment or to guide users, for example in simulated environments. Affirmative feedback has been shown to be especially helpful for visually impaired or the elderly. At the same time, Sun, Ren, and Cao (2011) identify three disadvantages of affirmative feedback when given to users who do not have the same needs as the groups mentioned above. One of them is that constant feedback annoys people when they are performing correctly. Another reason is that constant tactile and auditory feedback cause fatigue and may lower the user's responsiveness to feedback. Moreover, constant vibrotactile feedback may be a hindrance to performing tasks that require motor skills, as the vibration might lower the accuracy of the movements. As opposed to affirmative feedback, error feedback is only given to users when there is an error or an error is likely. As such, it informs the user that there is an error and asks them to correct it.

Visual Feedback

The literature distinguishes between two kinds of visual feedback in teleoperation, visual feedback and additional visual feedback. By visual feedback, researchers refer to what the human operator sees at all times when teleoperating the robot. As teleoperation can take place either physically close or remote to the robot, this visual feedback is either the actual robot in the environment the user shares with it, or a representation thereof on a screen. This representation can be actual video footage of the robot and its environment or a computer-generated 2D or 3D simulation. As an addition to the visual feedback described above, there can be other types of visual feedback. Some researchers only consider these additional kinds of feedback to be visual feedback, while interactions with only the feedback described above are referred to as interactions without any feedback by them. There is a variety of additional visual feedback used in human-robot interaction. The possibilities for displaying additional visual information in screen-based teleoperation are principally open-ended. Clock displays, for instance, are used to facilitate temporal awareness (Glas, Kanda, Ishiguro, & Hagita, 2012). In targeting tasks, a cross hair as well as numerical information of the targets position can be laid over the video image a user sees (Hoff, Gatrell, & Spofford, 1991). On the other hand, additional visual feedback for industrial robots that is manifested in the real world remains as yet largely unexplored. Previous findings on the different error feedback modalities are summarized in tables 1-4.

Table 1. Overview of relevant literature on visual feedback

Visual Feedback – Point of View, System Responsiveness, and Fidelity of Visual Representation	
point of view: field of view, camera perspective	• wider field of view leads to increased efficiency and lower error rates (Pazuchanics, 2006) • in operation of uninhabited ground vehicles, providing users with a third person camera perspective can make up for deficiencies in first person view (Pazuchanics, 2006)
system responsiveness: frame rates, temporal delay	• higher frame rates result in better task timing and fewer errors (Massimino & Sheridan, 1994), especially with inexperienced users (Liu, Tharp, French, Lai & Stark, 1993) • -increased latency (time between event happening and event being visually perceivable by user) leads to slower movements and thus increases the time to task completion (Mateo, Gilkey & Cowgill, 2007)
fidelity of visual representation: depth cues, levels of environmental detail	• stereoscopic displays increase efficiency and decrease error rates (Park & Woldstad, 2000) and improve spatial judgement (Yeh & Silverstein, 1992) as compared to monoscopic displays • low environmental detail reduces decision time and increases efficiency, but may increase error rates (Sellner, Hiatt, Simmons & Singh, 2006)

Table 2. Overview of relevant literature on auditory feedback

Auditory Feedback (Nam & Kim, 2010)	
verbal messages	two kinds: concatenation (recordings of real human voices), and synthesis-by-rule (computer-generated sounds imitating human speech)
earcons	musical sounds, cannot be intuitively interpreted by users, but meaning can be learned (Blattner, Sumikawa & Greenberg, 1989)
auditory icons	every day sounds that metaphorically draw connection between an action on computer and a similar action in real life

Table 3. Overview of relevant literature on haptic feedback

Haptic Feedback	
kinesthetic vs. tactile feedback	• suited for conveying different information: tactile feedback can inform users of changes in state, e.g. from the robot moving freely to the robot hitting something, kinesthetic feedback can inform about intensity of force (Nitsch & Färber, 2013) • -while users preferred vibrotactile force feedback and thought it worked better than haptic force feedback, vibrotactile feedback neither led to reduced applied forces nor to improved task timing or lower error rates. Haptic force feedback significantly lowered the amount of pressure in surface contact (Radi et al, 2010)

Table 4. Overview of relevant literature on multimodal feedback

Multimodal Feedback		
Sun, Ren and Cao (2011)	• no feedback • auditory only • vibrotactile only • visual only • auditory + vibrotactile • auditory + visual • vibrotactile + visual • auditory, visual + vibrotactile	• task completion time: no significant differences • task performance: vibrotactile feedback most accurate, combination of visual and audible feedback least accurate • user preference: users preferred combination of visual and audible feedback even though it led to least accurate task performance; users disliked vibrotactile feedback, even though it led to most accurate task performance; combination of auditory and vibrotactile feedback is confusing
Diaz et al (2006)	• visual • visual + auditory • visual + haptic • visual + auditory + haptic	• best performance: haptic feedback and combination of haptic feedback and auditory feedback • addition of auditory feedback makes both visual and haptic feedback more effective, but increases task completion time
Burke et al (2006)	• meta literature review comparing 43 studies	• effects of additional auditory and tactile feedback depend on the types and amount of tasks to be performed as well as the workload they require from the user • both auditory-visual and tactile-visual feedback are more effective than visual feedback alone, as they reduce the cognitive load of the user • auditory-visual feedback is especially helpful in single tasks with normal workload, while tactile-visual feedback helps users perform better in settings where multiple tasks need to be performed and there is high workload
Richard et al (1996)	• only graphic feedback of the virtual world • graphic feedback of the virtual world plus LEDs as visual feedback for grasping forces • graphic feedback of the virtual world plus auditory force feedback • graphic feedback of the virtual world plus haptic force feedback • graphic feedback of the virtual world, haptic force feedback plus visual feedback, and • graphic feedback of the virtual world, haptic force feedback and auditory force feedback.	• addition of one feedback modality (haptic, visual or auditory) feedback improves the task performance as compared to no force feedback • haptic feedback provided the strongest results • - combinations of haptic and visual as well as haptic and auditory feedback together improved the task performance even more, with the combination of haptic and auditory force feedback leading to the best task performance

Multisensory Feedback

Teleoperation is a task that inherently demands much visual attention of the user. Studies on multimodal feedback investigate in what way feedback modalities such as auditory, tactile and visual feedback can help decrease the cognitive workload of the user and lead to improved task times and fewer errors. While some researchers do not consider it to be a type of visual feedback, in most of the reviewed studies what the robot operator sees, that is, the actual robot or a video- or computer-generated representation thereof on a screen, is considered visual feedback. To them, the addition of another feedback modality, such as auditory, tactile or visual (different from the one described above), means that the user is provided with multisensory feedback. Researchers who do not define the visual representation of the robot as visual feedback, refer to this feedback condition as "no feedback." Table 4 summarizes previous findings on multimodal feedback.

The results of previous research together suggest that combinations of feedback modalities are more promising than visual, tactile or auditory only. However, given that participants saw an introductory video describing the kinds of possible errors and how to resolve them before they entered the experiments, it was also possible that all they needed to know was that an error was about to occur, and thus that audible and vibrotactile feedback were totally sufficient. Furthermore, what exactly the visual feedback should show is still open.

Design of the Feedback Modalities

Based on the ideas generated in the baseline study and based on the results from previous work, three feedback modalities for the MARVIN platform were designed and implemented: audible feedback, vibrotactile feedback in the control device, and two types of error screens. Feedback is given to users immediately when the force measured in the gripper exceeds the threshold limit and until the force is acceptable again.

Visual Feedback

Two versions of visual feedback were created, which were labeled abstract and concrete visual feedback. One of the major differences between the two versions lays in the fidelity of the visual representations; while the "abstract" visual feedback only presents a 3-dimensional vector arrow representing the direction and magnitude of force as measured by the force-torque sensor, the "concrete" visual feedback presents the user with an overview of the entire workstation from a 3rd person camera perspective and a wide field of view. As the literature has shown advantages and drawbacks for both abstract and concrete feedback, these two versions were created to find out which one works best in our scenario.

Abstract Visual Feedback

The abstract visual feedback was created with and is displayed in real time in RobWork, a collection of C++ libraries for simulation and control of robot systems (Ellekilde & Jorgensen, 2010). RobWork is used for research and education as well as for practical robot applications and is a robots library developed by the CARO group. The real time images are presented on a large screen on the other side of the workspace, facing the user. The RobWork user menu is visible at all times. The actual feedback takes up the rest of the space on the screen. When the force measured in the gripper is not larger than the threshold limit, a gradient light blue background image is visible. As soon as and for as long as the limit is exceeded, a red, three-dimensional vector appears, starting approximately in the center of the space reserved for the actual visual feedback image. The vector represents the direction of the force in a three-dimensional space and its length is proportional to the magnitude of the force (see figure 2 and Figure 3).

Figure 2. Abstract visual feedback showing the direction and magnitude of the force

Figure 3. Affirmative feedback: no problem

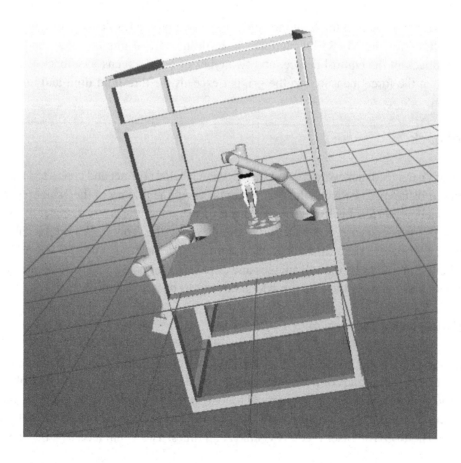

Concrete Visual Feedback

Like the abstract visual feedback, the concrete visual feedback is generated by RobWork and shown on a large screen in the same location. At all times, a gray 3D simulation model of the entire workstation is shown. Moreover, the locations of two items of the Cranfield set – the faceplate and the currently manipulated peg/separator – are tracked and these objects are visualized in gray as well. The visualization is not a static image; rather, it is a direct real time representation of the workstation and Cranfield objects and their position in space. There is a grid visible on the xy-plane. When the force limit is not exceeded, there is the same gradient blue background as in the abstract visual feedback modality (figure 4). While the force exceeds the threshold limit, the background color alternates between red and blue. Moreover, the color of the faceplate as well as of the tracked peg/separator changes to red.

Vibrotactile Feedback

Vibration is built into the handheld teleoperation device. This feedback is given to the user with a constant strength while the force threshold limit is exceeded. This is again triggered by the force measurement in the force-torque sensor mounted on the robot arm. The researchers' intention was to compare both kinesthetic and tactile feedback, but as teleoperation concerns movement in a 6-dimensional space, feedback is not readily available, limiting them to tactile feedback. As previous research has shown that vibrotactile feedback is better suited to inform users of changes in state (e.g. from no error to error) than to inform the users what exactly the nature of the problem is, the authors tried to counter this drawback by having the users watch an instructional video before the task in which they learned how to identify and resolve the most common problems.

Figure 4. Error feedback: force threshold exceeded

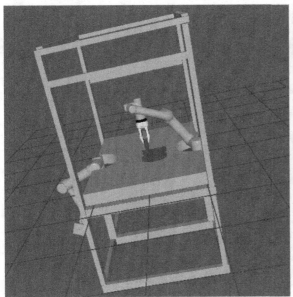

Auditory Feedback

For the audible feedback the researchers selected a buzzer earcon found on a sound compilation CD (alarme.wav, 1995). The sound file is two seconds long and played repeatedly for the duration of the force threshold limit being exceeded. As opposed to verbal messages and auditory icons, earcons are not intuitively interpretable by the users; however, like the vibrotactile feedback, they do alert the users of a change in state, which the users then can investigate using what they have learnt in the introduction video.

These four feedback modalities were tested on users in a second study, which is described in the next section.

Experimental Tests of the Feedback Modalities

The above mentioned modalities were tested in a study under the same conditions as in the baseline study (with 28 new participants) and found that both auditory and vibrotactile feedback are efficient in informing users that there is a problem, but neither communicate what exactly the problem is, nor what the suggested resolution strategy for the user to take is. The visual feedback on the other hand, was not only very ineffective in getting the users' attention, but was also not understood by the novice users. More worryingly, it increased the task completion time (see Figure 5). It was concluded that a combination of auditory or visual feedback as attention getters with legible feedback as information on the nature and solution of the problem is desirable. That is, given the results from previous work regarding the effectiveness of visual feedback, it was concluded that the kind of visual information displayed must have a considerable impact on the usefulness of the feedback given. The reseachers therefore turned to research in document design in order to inform the creation of different possible feedback screens. Subsequently, a survey with 200 participants that investigated the role of text-image relationships on the legibility of error feedback screens was conducted.

Figure 5. Task completion times with audible, vibrotactile, abstract visual and concrete visual feedback

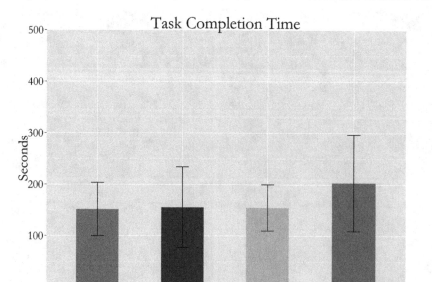

DESIGNING VISUAL FEEDBACK SCREENS

Shneiderman (1998) identifies eight principles for effective user interface design in HCI, of which most can be applied to HRI feedback screen design. The principles relevant for our design are: maintenance of consistency, provision and facilitation of straightforward means of error recovery, giving the user a sense of being in complete control, and avoiding to overload the user's short-term memory.

Relationships between Text and Image in the Feedback Screens

Based on the five text-image relationships Schriver (1997) identified, feedback screens for each of the four main problems was created. All of them consist in both text and image. Some feedback screens are animations of up to three screens, while others are just a single screen. Below is a general description of the feedback screens and their connection to Schriver's text-image relationships (see also Table 5).

- **Redundant:** The relationship of text and image is redundant, if text and image present the same or very similar ideas. An advantage of using this relationship in designing feedback for novice users is that in presenting information to these users in two modes can help them understand it better. Expert users, on the other hand, might not welcome redundancy as much, as they are not struggling to understand the information and therefore do not need it presented two or more times. The redundant visual feedback screen presents both the problem and the solution. It consists in two screens, the first one showing the problem in both text and image, the second one showing the solution in both text and image (see Figure 8 and Figure 9).
- **Complementary A:** In a complementary text-image relationship, text and image present different content, and both text and image need to be understood in order to understand the main idea. This screen informs the user about the correct resolution strategy in text, while the problem is presented in the image on the same screen.

Table 5. Overview of information presented in the nine feedback modalities

		Information in Text	Information in Image
redundant (*animated*)	screen 1	problem	problem
	screen 2	resolution	resolution
complementary A		resolution	problem
complementary B		problem	resolution
supplementary A		problem & resolution	resolution
supplementary B (*animated*)	screen 1	problem	problem
	screen 2	problem	resolution
juxtapositional A		resolution	problem
juxtapositional B (*animated*)	screen 1	problem	resolution
	screen 2	problem	resolved problem
stage-setting A		("Warning!")	problem
stage-setting B		problem & resolution	(warning triangle)

- **Complementary B:** Here, the text expresses the problem, while the image suggests the solution.
- **Supplementary A:** Like in the complementary text-image relationship, text and image in a supplementary relationship present different content. However, one mode (text or image) presents the main idea, while the other mode only reinforces the dominant one or explains how the dominant mode is to be interpreted. In this feedback screen, the textual information is designed to be more dominant than the information found in the image. Therefore, the text states both the problem and the resolution strategy. The image supports the text by being a visual representation of the resolution.
- **Supplementary B:** Contrary to the other feedback with a supplementary text-image relationship, most information is carried in the image here. This visual feedback combines two screens in a combination. Both screens have the same text supporting the images, namely stating the problem. The images contain information on both the problem and the solution.
- **Juxtapositional A:** In a juxtapositional text-image relationship, text and image present different, often clashing contents, and only together make up the main idea. In the feedback screens based on this relationship, image and text contain opposing content. While the text presents the solution, the image is a visualization of the problem.
- **Juxtapositional B:** Again, opposing content is presented in text and image. There are two screens. On both of them, the text states the problem. The first image is an instruction on how to resolve the problem stated in the text, the second one is an image of the resolved situation.
- **Stage-Setting A:** In this text-image relationship, text and image present different content as well. One mode (text or image) sets the stage for the theme or ideas presented in the other mode. The text in this feedback screen sets the stage for the illustration. For all four problems here, the text is "Warning!". The image then contains an illustration of the respective problem.
- **Stage-Setting B:** this feedback screen the image sets the stage for the text. Like in the other feedback with a stage-setting text-image relationship, the stage-setter – this time the image – is realized as the same image for all four problems, namely a warning triangle. The text contains information on both the nature of the problem and the suggested resolution strategy.

Text

The text of the feedback screens is short, and exclamation marks aid in making the statements appear as important imperative messages. The language is plain, with the exception of technical expressions such as "singularity," which even inexperienced users should be familiar with after having watched the introductory video. Within each of the four problems, there is exactly one expression for each of the two text information categories problem and resolution. This makes it easier for the user to recognize the text in a very short amount of time.

The text is black, in order to create a high contrast in combination with the white background, thus aiding legibility. The typeface is 48-point Myriad Pro Regular. On-screen documents should be designed using large point-sizes. Moreover, as the screen in the laboratory setup is about two meters away from the users, the point-size has to be large in order to be comfortably legible. Myriad Pro is a sans serif face, thereby possessing the quality of being highly legible, especially in short sentences in on-screen documents (Schriver, 1997).

Images

For the sake of simplicity, images are mostly composed of simple geometrical shapes and do not have shadows or other 3D effects added to them. All images are similar to each other to ensure consistency.

There are two versions of each of these feedback screens, one in colors similar to the colors found in the MARVIN workstation, the other one mainly in black and white. Both versions have details in red and green.

Additional RobWork Feedback Screen

A third feedback screen, which is a combination of the abstract visual and the concrete visual feedback screen, was designed. The 3D simulation of the MARVIN platform is portrayed in gray on a light blue background like in the concrete visual feedback from study 2. However, in contrast to the screen from the previous study, the background does not change color. When the force threshold limit is exceeded, a red force vector like the one from the abstract visual feedback screen is visible, starting at the point in the gripper where the force-torque sensor is located. Additionally, the tracked peg held by the gripper as well as the faceplate change their color from gray to red when the force threshold limit is exceeded (see Figure 7).

The influence of text-image relationships on lay users' ability to recognize problems and their solutions in feedback screens was tested in a survey. The most legible screens were then tested for their efficiency in another lab experiment

TESTING THE LEGIBILITY OF VISUAL FEEDBACK SCREENS

The legibility of feedback screens based on the nine text-image relationships described above was tested with a survey.

This online survey with 200 participants is mainly concerned with the legibility of the feedback screens. The authors consider a feedback screen to be legible and effective, if users are able to find out which problem there is and what the solution to this problem is. Two questions emerge from these criteria:

Figure 6. Example of "redundant" feedback – text and image present the same information

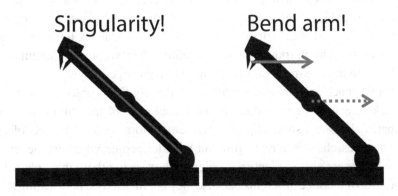

Figure 7. Additional RobWork feedback screen: a combination of the abstract and concrete feedback screens from the previous study

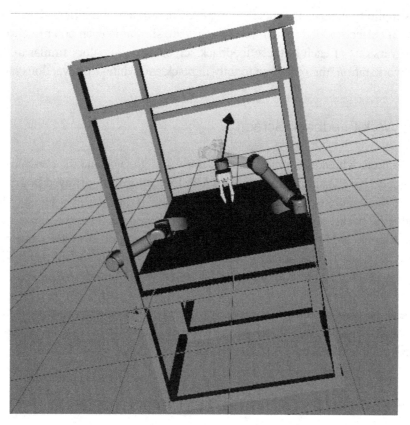

1.   Do users identify the problem correctly?
2.   Do users find the correct solution to the problem?

Survey Design

After being asked about their age, education, experience with robots, video game playing habits and interest in technology, the survey participants get an introduction to the context of the survey. There is an introductory text as well as a short video. The introductory text explains learning by demonstration in lay terminology, and states that the survey is concerned with feedback to prevent problems in robot learning by demonstration. The introduction video explains how to prevent singularity, pressure, and self-collision, and how to resolve those problems should they happen anyway.

Users see eleven feedback screens and are asked to identify the problem as well as the resolution. Each of the feedback screens is presented on an individual page of the survey, together with the two questions. Participants also see a short clip of a problem, before each of the sets of feedback screens and questions, as the researchers wanted to find out whether people who have never worked with the MARVIN platform before are able to identify problems when seeing them in a video. The second study found that users often do not notice problems because they are focused on performing their task and their visual attention is directed at the gripper or any object inside the gripper. The survey-takers are able to focus their visual attention to any part of the robot that is shown in the video. Moreover, they have the option to watch the video several times. The researchers wanted to find out if the four problems this study is concerned with could actually be identified by novice users, as a negative answer to this question would all the more underline that feedback is crucial in human-robot systems operated by naïve users. The problem in the videos is the same problem that is being presented in the respective corresponding feedback screen. The videos are short clips of up to ten seconds length taken from footage of real users from the lab studies, except one video of over-rotation, which was recorded by the CARO group for the purpose of this study, as the researchers did not have a second video of over-rotation. There are two different videos of over-rotation, two different videos of singularity, two different videos of self-collision, and five different videos of the force threshold limit being exceeded. The feedback screens and questions presented after each of the eleven videos are the same in both versions of the survey and presented in the same order. After each video, before the feedback screen and the two questions about the feedback screen, users are asked to explain what happened in the video.

Participants are randomly assigned to one of nine conditions. The condition determines on which text-image relationship the feedback screens the participant is going to see are based. All users see the three RobWork feedback screens, as well as eight of the redesigned feedback screens. All eight screens are based on the same text-image relationship. Half of them are in color, the other half is in black and white with red and green details. The problems singularity, over-rotation and self-collision are each portrayed two times, one time in black and white and one time in color. Too much pressure is presented a total of five times, two times with a redesigned feedback screen like the other three problems, and three times with the three RobWork feedback screens. The order in which the feedback screens are presented is the same for all participants.

Data Analysis

Any answer that describes the problem correctly counts as a correct answer, regardless of the wording the participant chooses. For example, both "singularity" and "the arm is fully stretched" are classified as correct problems. The same rule applies to the resolution strategies. Moreover, "resetting the robot" is always counted as an acceptable solution as well. While in a real work setting it would be very time consuming to reset the robot to the start position whenever a problem occurred or is about to happen, it is an adequate resolution strategy in our lab experiments according to experts on the MARVIN platform.

Answers such as "the robot is not handled carefully" are considered partially correct answers, as the participant acknowledges that there is a problem, but fails to identify the actual problem. An example for a partially correct solution is "the human has to solve the problem." While this is true, the participant does not describe what exactly the human has to do.

Results

Our results suggest that feedback screens based on some text-image relationships are more legible than those based on others (see Figure 8). The study found that 'stage-setting B' and 'redundant' feedback screens are the most legible (with 'stage-setting B' being the most legible), as they helped the participants identify both the problems and the results best. Feedback screens based on some other text-image relationships are either misleading as to what the problem and solution is or whether there even is a

Figure 8. The feedback screens based on nine text-image relationships differ in legibility

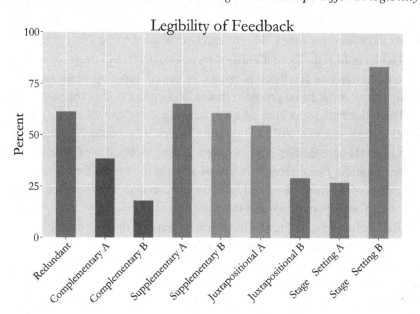

problem or a solution. The results propose that information presented in text might be more legible to novice users than information in images. Thus, feedback screens should provide information about both the problem and the solution in text, and additional images may show the problem, the solution or both. Moreover, this study shows that the legibility of a feedback screen is dependent on the users' knowledge and preconceptions of the robot. Feedback screens of problems that users can understand by using common sense and relating concepts to common situations in the real world (e.g. exceeding the force threshold) are generally more legible than feedback screens of problems that require advanced or expert knowledge of robotics (e.g. singularity) to be classified as a problem.

The percentage of problems that users identified correctly in our feedback screens (57.5%) is about five times as high as the percentage of problems that users identified correctly in the videos the saw. The percentage of misunderstood problems in the videos and in the feedback screens are nearly the same. Users do not know what problem there is on the feedback screen about six times more often than they do not know what problem is shown in the video. Most users thought there is no problem at all in the video (71,8%), while the amount of unnoticed problems in the feedback screens is much smaller (11,7%). As a result, the problems in the videos are most often not noticed, while the problems on the feedback screen are noticed and identified correctly nearly two thirds of the times. Too much pressure was more visible in the videos (21.6%) than other problems. Over-rotation was identified the least (6.1%). The videos about self-collision were the most misleading (28.7%), while the problem in the over-rotation videos was not mistaken for another problem very often (5.4%). The amount of videos seen by users that stated they do not know what the problem is, is not very high. Still, only in half as many instances of singularity videos as of too much pressure videos did the users not know what the problem actually was. Throughout all problem videos, most of the times users thought there was no problem at all. This was most obvious in the over-rotation videos (86.4%). The videos with the least unnoticed problems as compared to videos of other problems are the self-collision videos (60%). These results both stress the importance of feedback, and the need for feedback that clearly communicates what the problem and its solution is.

LIFE TEST OF VISUAL FEEDBACK MODALITIES

Lab Study

Two types of feedback screens are tested in the same lab setting that the authors used for the previously described studies (see also aus der Wieschen, Fischer, & Krüger, 2015). One is stage-setting B, the highest-scoring text-image relationship according to the survey, and the other is redundant. Although redundant feedback only was the third-highest scoring feedback, it was chosen because the literature finds one of the key strengths of redundant text-image relationships to be that it is suitable for communicating difficult information to novices (Schriver, 1997). The study uses a between-subject design with 45 participants in three conditions, who either did not receive any feedback at all while performing the task, were given a combination of vibrotactile (for attention-getting) and stage-setting visual feedback (for further information), or were provided with a combination of vibrotactile and redundant visual feedback. Due to technical problems with the data logging, the researchers lost the data from four of the participants from the second condition and three from the third.

The researchers developed an automatic pre-warn system for avoiding the dangerous situations described above. In particular, to measure the pressure acting perpendicularly on the end effector, the researchers use the force-torque sensor which is mounted between the end effector and universal robot. When the predefined threshold of force measured by force-torque is exceeded, vibrotactile feedback information warning about too much pressure is displayed to alert the user. Similarly, the singularity warning was used when the value of second joint angle was approaching zero. Furthermore, the over-rotation warning was displayed when the value of the last joint angle was approaching the minimum or maximum. As self-collision is hard to detect, there is no automated solution how to warn about it, and thus this problem was disregarded in the following.

Four measures were automatically logged:

1. The length of the demonstration path by tracking position information,
2. The amount of time for which the teleoperation controller was actively used,
3. The time it took to complete the entire task including breaks, and
4. Errors, i.e. all instances of the threshold limit being exceeded, over-rotation, and singularity.

Robust learning from demonstration, with direct trajectories and little to no noise to generalize over, requires these measures to be as low as possible.

Results

Length of Demonstration Path (in Meter)

Results show an increase in performance when participants get redundant visual feedback (M=4.14, SD=0.93) compared to stage setting feedback (M=5.89, SD=1.93) (see Figure 9). This effect is statistical significant using an independent samples t-test, t(9.2)=2.39, p=0.04.

Figure 9. Stage-setting B feedback screens lead to longer demonstration paths

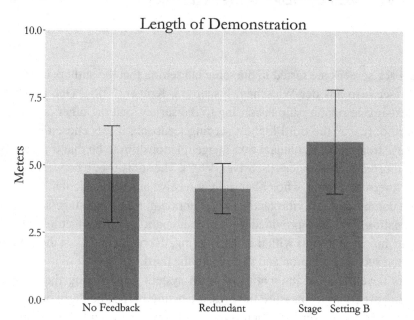

Total Task Timing (in seconds)

Redundant feedback was found to decrease total task time (M=266.89, SD=75.31) compared to stage-setting feedback (M=389.56, SD=242.55) (see Figure 10). This effect is not statistically significant (t(7.9)=1.39, p=0.20); however, this might be due to the large interpersonal differences within the stage-setting feedback condition.

Figure 10. For task timing, no statistically significant differences between redundant and stage setting feedback was found

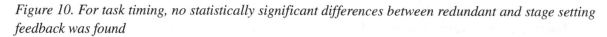

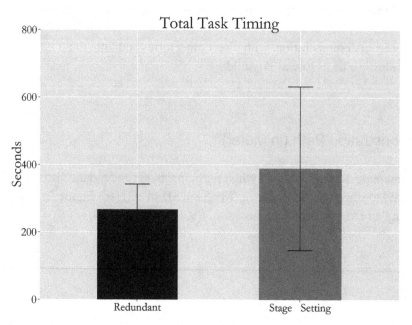

Number of Errors

Participants made most errors in the stage-setting feedback condition (M=7.50, SD=5.45), compared to the redundant feedback condition (M=3.33, SD=1.83) (see Figure 11). This difference in marginally significant, using an independent samples t-test, $t(8.1)=2.09$, $p=0.07$.

What is interesting here is that even though 'stage-setting B' feedback was shown to be the most efficient in the survey with 200 participants, in this experiment it led to the longest demonstration path, longest task completion time, and highest error rate, i.e. the quality of the demonstration data was not improved by the feedback provided. Future studies should investigate how reliable certain research methods, such as surveys, are at predicting the quality of feedback screens.

SOLUTIONS AND RECOMMENDATIONS

The evidence from this chapter suggests that error feedback is crucial in robot teleoperation by novice users. Feedback should not only warn the user of a problem, but also inform them of the nature of it and suggest a resolution strategy. The study supports the idea to use either auditory or vibrotactile feedback as an attention getter to warn the user, and error feedback screens to inform the user both about the problem and about the solution. The survey resulted in several design guidelines: both problem and solution should be explained in text and 2D illustrations are more legible than 3D illustrations. The results show that problems that users can relate to in their own world, such as too much pressure, are most easy to identify, while problems that require knowledge of robot kinematics, such as singularity, are hard to understand and identify for users. Furthermore, the present study shows that HRI designers not only have to consider which type of feedback modality to use, but most importantly that even subtle changes made within one modality can lead to significant differences in legibility.

Figure 11. Users made least errors in the redundant feedback condition

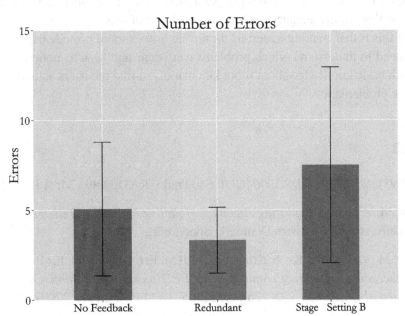

FUTURE RESEARCH DIRECTIONS

Future work should set out to create a framework for the description of the individual qualities and applications of different feedback modalities. User studies with different tasks would have to be conducted in order to be able to create generalizable results that include possible influencing factors such as time pressure, experience and cognitive load, and modeling these and their relationship with other modalities.

CONCLUSION

This chapter investigated why naïve robot users need feedback, what the strengths and weaknesses of the different feedback modalities are, and which factors influence the legibility of feedback. The studies found that lay users need feedback because they have expectations about how the robot works that do not match with the robot's actual functionality. Accordingly, it was established that the main functions of error feedback should be not only to notify the user of a problem, but also to communicate what exactly the problem is and to facilitate resolution strategies. The results from the experiments showed that no single feedback modality on its own is capable of fulfilling these three requirements. While vibration and sound feedback showed to be efficient at alerting the user, they were unable to inform the user about the nature and solution of the problem. For visual feedback the opposite was true. Therefore, it was concluded that a combination of either audible or tactile with visual feedback would be ideal. In order to make the visual feedback even more efficient, the researchers drew on document design theory to investigate how to create legible feedback. The authors found that specific combinations of texts and images helped users identify problems and their solutions better than others. In specific, feedback screens that are based on a redundant text-image relationship seem to help novice users understand what the problem and its solution is. The evidence from this study suggests that the legibility of a feedback screen is dependent on the users' knowledge and preconceptions of the robot. Feedback screens of problems that users can understand by using common sense and relating concepts to common situations in the real world, such as applying too much pressure with the robot gripper a surface, are generally more legible than feedback screens of problems that require advanced or expert knowledge of robotics to be classified as a problem. An implication of this is that training materials for novice users should provide users with not only the knowledge they need to understand which problems can occur and how to notice, prevent and solve them, but also with basic knowledge about robot kinematics, so that the users actually understand why these problems are problematic.

REFERENCES

[alarme.wav]. (1995). *MAX SOUNDS 5000* [CD]. São Paulo: RÁDIO 89 FM, A RÁDIO ROCK.

aus der Wieschen, M. V. (2015). *Exploring Feedback Modalities for Robot Teleoperation* [Unpublished master's thesis]. University of Southern Denmark, Sonderborg.

aus der Wieschen, M. V., Fischer, K., & Krüger, N. (2015). Error Feedback for Robust Learning from Demonstration.*Proceedings of the Tenth Annual ACM/IEEE International Conference on Human-Robot Interaction Extended Abstracts* (pp. 225-226). ACM. doi:10.1145/2701973.2702724

Bakker, P., & Kuniyoshi, Y. (1996). Robot see, robot do: An overview of robot imitation. *Proceedings of the AISB96 Workshop on Learning in Robots and Animals* (pp. 3-11).

Bernsen, N. O., & Dybkjær, L. (2009). *Multimodal Usability*. London: Springer.

Blattner, M. M., Sumikawa, D. A., & Greenberg, R. M. (1989). Earcon and icons: Their structure and common design principles. *Human-Computer Interaction, 4*(1), 11–44. doi:10.1207/s15327051hci0401_1

Brandt, E. (2007). How tangible mock-ups support design collaboration. *Knowledge, Technology & Policy, 20*(3), 179–192. doi:10.1007/s12130-007-9021-9

Burke, J. L., Prewett, M. S., Gray, A. A., Yang, L., Stilson, F. R., & Redden, E. (2006). Comparing the effects of visual-auditory and visual-tactile feedback on user performance: a meta-analysis.*Proceedings of the 8th international conference on Multimodal interfaces* (pp. 108-117). doi:10.1145/1180995.1181017

Buur, J., & Binder, T. (2006). *User Centred Product Design. MCI*. University of Southern Denmark.

Chernova, S., & Thomaz, A. (2014). *Robot Learning from Human Teachers*. Morgan & Claypool Publishers.

Collins, K., Palmer, A., & Rathrnill, K. (1985). The Development of a European Benchmark for the Comparison of Assembly Robot Programming Systems. In R. K. (Ed.), Robot technology and Applications (pp. 187-199). Berlin: Springer. doi:10.1007/978-3-662-02440-9_18

Demiris, J., & Hayes, G. (2002). f 3 Imitation as a Dual-Route Process Featuring Predictive and Learning Components; 4 Biologically Plausible Computational Model. In *Imitation in animals and artifacts* (p. 327).

Díaz, I., Hernantes, J., Mansa, I., Lozano, A., Borro, D., Gil, J. J., & Sánchez, E. (2006). Influence of multisensory feedback on haptic accessibility tasks. *Virtual Reality (Waltham Cross), 10*(10), 31–40. doi:10.1007/s10055-006-0028-4

Ellekilde, L. P., & Jorgensen, J. A. (2010, June). Robwork: A flexible toolbox for robotics research and education. *Proceedings of the 2010 41st International Symposium on and 2010 6th German Conference on Robotics (ROBOTIK)* (pp. 1-7). VDE.

Friedrich, H., Dillmann, R., & Rogalla, O. (1999). Interactive robot programming based on human demonstration and advice. In *Sensor Based Intelligent Robots* (pp. 96–119). Springer Berlin Heidelberg. doi:10.1007/10705474_6

Glas, D., Kanda, T., Ishiguro, H., & Hagita, N. (2012, July). Temporal Awareness in Teleoperation of Conversational Robots. *IEEE Transactions on Systems, Man, and Cybernetics. Part A, Systems and Humans, 42*(4), 905–912. doi:10.1109/TSMCA.2011.2181162

Goodwin, K. (2009). Understanding potential users and customers. In K. Goodwin (Ed.), Designing for the Digital Age: Creating Human-Centered Products and Services (pp. 112-153). John Wiley & Sons.

Hoff, W. A., Gatrell, L. B., & Spofford, J. R. (1991). Machine-vision-based teleoperation aid. *Telematics and Informatics, 8*(4), 403–423. doi:10.1016/S0736-5853(05)80062-0

IFR statistical department. (2014, February 20). *All-time-high for industrial robots in 2013*. Retrieved from worldrobotics.org: http://www.worldrobotics.org/index.php?id=home&news_id=272

Kirstein, F. (2014). *Comparing Control Modalities for Robot Learning from Demonstration* [Unpublished MA thesis]. Sønderborg: University of Southern Denmark.

Kukliński, K., Fischer, K., Marhenke, I., Kirstein, F., aus der Wieschen, M. V., Sølvason, D., & Savarimuthu, T. R. (2014). Teleoperation for learning by demonstration: Data glove versus object manipulation for intuitive robot control. *Proceedings of the 6thInternational Congress on Ultra Modern Telecommunications and Control Systems and Workshops* (pp. 346-351).

Liljekrans, D. (2012). *Investigating peg-in-hole strategies through teleoperation* [MSc thesis]. University of Southern Denmark, Odense.

Liu, A., Tharp, G., French, L., Lai, S., & Stark, L. (1993, October). Some of what one needs to know about using head-mounted displays to improve teleoperator performance. *IEEE Transactions on Robotics and Automation*, *9*(5), 638–648. doi:10.1109/70.258055

Marhenke, I., Fischer, K., & Savarimuthu, T. R. (2014). Reasons for Singularity in Robot Teleoperation. *Proceedings of the 2014 ACM/IEEE international conference on Human-robot interaction* (pp. 242-243). ACM. doi:10.1145/2559636.2559828

Massimino, M. J., & Sheridan, T. B. (1994, March). Teleoperator Performance with Varying Force and Visual Feedback. *Human Factors: The Journal of the Human Factors and Ergonomics Society*, *36*(1), 145-157.

Mateo, J. C., Gilkey, R. H., & Cowgill, J. L. (2007, October). Effect of Variable Visual-Feedback Delay on Movement Time. *Proceedings of the Human Factors and Ergonomics Society Annual Meeting* (pp. 1373-1377).

Muxfeldt, A., Kluth, J. H., & Kubus, D. (2014).Kinesthetic Teaching in Assembly Operations – A User Study. In D. Brugali et al. (Eds.), Proceedings of the SIMPA 2014, LNAI (Vol. 8810, pp. 533-544).

Nam, Y., & Kim, J. (2010). A semiotic analysis of sounds in personal computers: Toward a semiotic model for human-computer interaction. Semiotica, 182(1/4), 269-284.

Nitsch, V., & Färber, B. (2013, October-December). A Meta-Analysis of the Effects of Haptic Interfaces on Task Performance with Teleoperation Systems. *IEEE Transactions on Haptics*, *6*(4), 387–398. doi:10.1109/TOH.2012.62 PMID:24808391

Park, S., & Woldstad, J. (2000). Multiple two-dimensional displays as an alternative to three-dimensional displays in telerobotic tasks. *Human Factors*, *42*(4), 592–603. doi:10.1518/001872000779698060 PMID:11324852

Pazuchanics, S. L. (2006, October). The Effects of Camera Perspective and Field of View on Performance in Teleoperated Navigation.*Proceedings of the Human Factors and Ergonomics Society Annual Meeting* (pp. 1528-1532). doi:10.1177/154193120605001603

Radi, M., Reiter, A., Zaidan, S., Nitsch, V., Färber, B., & Reinhart, G. (2010). Telepresence in Industrial Applications: Implementation Issues for Assembly Tasks. *Presence (Cambridge, Mass.)*, *19*(5), 415–429. doi:10.1162/pres_a_00009

Richard, P., Birebent, G., Coiffet, P., Burdea, G., Gomez, D., & Lagrana, N. (1996). Effect of frame rate and force feedback on virtual object manipulation. *Presence (Cambridge, Mass.), 5*(1), 95–108. doi:10.1162/pres.1996.5.1.95

Rubin, J., & Chisnell, D. (2008). *Handbook of Usability Testing–How to Plan, Design, and Conduct Effective Tests.* Indianapolis, IN: Wiley.

Savarimuthu, T. R., Liljekrans, D., Ellekilde, L.-P., Ude, A., Nemec, B., & Krüger, N. (2013). Analysis of human Peg-in-Hole Executions in a Robotic Embodiment using uncertain Grasps. *Proceedings of the 9th International Workshop on Motion and Control, RoMoCo 2013.* doi:10.1109/RoMoCo.2013.6614614

Schriver, K. (1997). *Dynamics in Document Design.* New York: Wiley.

Sellner, B. P., Hiatt, L. M., Simmons, R., & Singh, S. (2006, March). Attaining situational awareness for sliding autonomy. *Proceedings of the 1st ACM SIGCHI/SIGART conference on Human-robot interaction HRI '06* (pp. 80-87).

Shneiderman, B. (1998). Designing the User Interface: Strategies for Effective Human-Computer Interaction (3rd ed.). Reading, MA: Addison-Wesley.

Sun, M., Ren, X., & Cao, X. (2011). Effects of Multimodal Error Feedback on Human Performance in Steering Tasks. *Information and Media Technologies, 6*(1), 193–201.

Van Someren, M. V., Barnard, Y. F., & Sandberg, J. A. (1994). *The think aloud method: A practical guide to modelling cognitive processes.* London: Academic Press.

Yeh, Y.-Y., & Silverstein, L. D. (1992, October). Spatial Judgments with Monoscopic and Stereoscopic Presentation of Perspective Displays. *Human Factors: The Journal of the Human Factors and Ergonomics Society, 34*(5), 583-600.

KEY TERMS AND DEFINITIONS

Affirmative Feedback: A constant feedback given to users as long as there is no problem.

Document Design: The study of creating documents that meet the readers' needs.

Error Feedback: Feedback given to users when there is a problem.

Feedback Modality: Classifies feedback by which sensory modality it addresses, i.e. auditory, visual, tactile, or olfactory.

Learning by Demonstration: A machine learning from a human or another machine how to perform an action, by the teacher simply demonstrating the task.

Multimodal Feedback: A combination of two or more feedback modalities.

Text-Image Relationship: The way texts and images can be combined.

User-Centered Design: An iterative design approach that considers the users' needs at every stage.

Chapter 7
PRHOLO:
360° Interactive Public Relations

João Rodrigues
University of Algarve, Portugal

Ricardo Alves
University of Algarve, Portugal

Luís Sousa
University of Algarve, Portugal

Aldric Negrier
University of Algarve, Portugal

Jânio Monteiro
University of Algarve, Portugal

Pedro Cardoso
University of Algarve, Portugal

Paulo Felisberto
University of Algarve, Portugal

Mauro Figueiredo
University of Algarve, Portugal

Bruno Mendes da Silva
University of Algarve, Portugal

Roberto Lam
University of Algarve, Portugal

Jaime Carvalho Martins
University of Algarve, Portugal

Miguel Gomes
SPIC - Creative Solutions, Portugal

Paulo Bica
SPIC - Creative Solutions, Portugal

ABSTRACT

In the globalized world, possessing good products may not be enough to reach potential clients unless creative marketing strategies are well delineated. In this context, public relations are also important when it comes to capture the client's attention, making the first contact between the clients and the company's products, while being persuasive enough to make them confident that the company has the right products to fit their needs. Three virtual public relations installations were purposed in this chapter, combining technology with a human like public relations ability, capable of interacting with potential clients located in front of the installation, at angles of up to 57° (degrees), 180° and 360°, respectively. From one to several Microsoft Kinects were used to develop the three interaction models, which allows tracking and recognition of users' gestures and positions (heat map), sound sources, voice commands and face and body extraction of the user interacting with the installation.

DOI: 10.4018/978-1-5225-0435-1.ch007

INTRODUCTION

Customer acquisition is the most, or at least one of the most important parts of any company's marketing strategies. Today, the first contact with any company is probably the company's website, which should do its best to contain all the necessary information so that the customer can resolve unanswered questions. However, a website is one medium that in many cases may not be enough to capture the clients' attention and answer all their questions.

A Public Relation (PR) or a salesperson are normally responsible for the first personal contact with potential clients, helping the establishment of links between the customers' demand and the company's offers. New customers are most of the time unaware of all the details surrounding a company's products and services, and in an initial stage, have many unanswered questions. Many times, companies having several exhibitions, conferences, events, etc., need a number of human PRs, that is either not available or that they do not want or like to move or allocate. In such cases they might prefer a high tech creative digital PR to represent the company.

A real size human PR can be digitally represented using avatars or videos of a prerecorded person. There are several technics for projecting these digital representations, where three of the most common are: (a) Frontal projection, which is the most common technique used. The drawback of this technique is that the user in some situations can conceal the projection with his/her presence in front of the installation. (b) Rear projection, which usually uses an ultra-short throw projector, with the projection being made from the back of the projected area onto a retention film. The main advantages of this technique are to allow the projector to be hidden from the users that are in front of the display area, and of course, the lack of occlusion on the projection, which could occur due to the user's presence. (c) Holographic representation, which are alternative technique that uses a holographic images of the digital representation of the PR person. One of the techniques used to create this holographic representation is the Pepper's Ghost (see e.g., Figueiredo, Cardoso, Gonçalves, & Rodrigues, 2014). The main drawback of this technique is the requirement of a large space, while the advantage being the most likeness to capturing a client's attention due to its attractiveness and novelty.

In this Chapter three PR installations are presented. All these installations allow the interaction with a user, supporting several features like the track and recognizing of gestures, users' positions (heat map), sound sources, voice commands, and the extraction of the face and body of the user which is interacting with the installation. The first two installations are of real size persons (avatar or video), with the first using a holographic representation and the second a rear projection representation. The third is a prototype installation, combining a holographic representation of an object or face, with a screen where a menu is displayed. The area for the users' interaction with the PR changes in each of the three installations reaching, respectively, 57° (degrees), 180° and 360° in front of the installation.

The main contribution of this chapter is the development of a model that is capable of tracking users' sounds, position, and gestures inside the working range of the Microsoft Kinect sensors (Kinect, 2014) used in the installations. By installing several Microsoft Kinect sensors, all users are tracked on-the-fly, and the one closest to the installation is chosen to interact with it, by using the most appropriate sensor (depending on the installation). If no user is detected by the installation, the sensors search for a sound source, and when the location is fixed to the emitting sound source, the best-located sensor initiates voice command detection of small sentences or words.

A database is used to store the interactions, tracking data, user's extracted information (e.g., biometric information), allowing posterior statistical analysis, such as user's actions, favorite menus, etc. Currently, natural interaction (NI) is widely used for many different applications, but none of them have all the characteristics mentioned above.

The structure of the chapter is as follows: the present section introduces the subject and chapter goals. In the "Contextualization" section, the state of the art and the contextualization of the installations are presented. Section "Frontal Holographic Installation" presents the first of the three installations, which is a full sized holographic human PR installation, with all the necessary modules to support the interactions. Section "180° Rear Projection Installation" explains the advances between the frontal installation and the 180° installation, including the introduction of the rear projection. In Section "360° Interactive Public Relations" is again shown the advances from the 180° installation to a 360° Interactive PR. The final section summarizes the discussion, results and conclusion from all the installations.

CONTEXTUALIZATION

In the Time Machine movie (2002), directed by Simon Wells, the library scene features a hologram that hosts, communicates and interacts naturally with a time traveler. Amazingly, a product of this kind, operating in its fullness, does not yet exist, while the technology needed to develop it already does (Figueiredo et al., 2014). On the other hand, as mentioned in the introduction section, the markets are increasingly demanding these kind of products.

Holography is a technique for recording interference patterns of light that can generate or display images in three dimensions (António, Herrera, & Enriquez, 2013; Mihaylova, 2013). One of the most common technique to generate so called "holograms" is the Pepper's Ghost (Sprott, 2006), due to John Henry Pepper that popularized the effect. The Pepper's Ghost is an illusion technique used in theatre and in some magic tricks. In its basics, it is a combination of lighting techniques and a large piece of glass, forming a 45° angle with the audience, that present a combination of light passing through from behind the glass and light reflecting of the glass at a 90° angle from the line of sight of the viewers. The so-called "hologram" is actually an object or image hidden from the audience and reflected on a foil/glass. The best effect is achieved when using a dark background. An example applied to the theatre, illustrating the entire length technique, can be found in (Rennie, 2014). Another example is the D'Strict 3D Sensing Hologram Installation product (D'Strict, 2014), incorporating a hologram and a monitor in a small box, allowing interaction through gestures.

At the commercial level there are already some systems featuring, in some extend, the installations presented in this chapter, many of them reported on web sites, like Flyaway (Flyaway, 2015), where it is possible to find a Christie Digital film presenting a music concert by two hologram Musicians (based on Pepper's Ghost technique). This product consists on a projection system that lies between the stage and the audience and projects the characters to the stage, followed by a reflection through a mirror system, similar to the solution presented in Dimensional (2015). Another similar example, now at the level of airports, shows a hologram with human dimensions AVA (Advanced Virtual Avatar), used as a PR (AVA, 2015). However, none of the presented products follows the movement of the interlocutor (user) or allows the interaction with the hologram through its movements.

As already mentioned, the D'Strict has the "3D Sensing Hologram Installation" product (D'Strict, 2014), which includes a hologram and a small display box, where the gesture interaction is possible. However, the hologram is only visible frontally and dimensions are limited, roughly to 1.0 × 0.5 m (meters). The Active8-3D (2015) presents both medium and large holographic systems, where the holograms are only visible in front of the installation, with a limited interactivity, e.g., it uses a control to interact with the hologram. The same company introduced the 3D-holopyramid, an approach to the 360° hologram, but of reduced dimensions, with images ranging from 45 × 25 cm (centimeters) to 90 × 68 cm. The system does not allow interactivity and features angles where the hologram is not seen, losing the effect of a realistic 360° installation.

Also within the 360° projection there is the Litefast Magic Displays (Litefast, 2013). Although not visible when active, there is a mechanical system rotating at high speeds in a cylinder, limiting the product in terms of maintenance and particularly limiting the development of a full size PR. Also, no interactivity is present by the system. The Vizoo (2015), with its Cheoptics360 product, also presents a 360° and frontal solutions. In the 360° product, the object is projected onto a form of "Pyramid", implying again blind spots on the hologram (where you do not see the hologram correctly), with the product not presenting any interactivity. Paradigm (Rearpro, 2015) has a high number of products, several supporting interactivity. However, none of the solutions resembles the PRHOLO (PRHOLO-Holographic Public Relations) project desired effect, presented in this chapter, although the company is designated as one of the world's leaders in gesture-based systems and multi-touch interactivity. Canadian startup H+ Technology created a see-through tabletop box called Holus, presenting a tiny 3D digital world you can interact with (Holus, 2015), but is still a prototype under financing in Kickstarter.

There are also several solutions that use interactive systems with tables and screens. For instance, Vertigo (2015) has several solutions with a high level of interactivity. Other companies present solutions that incorporate some of features explained above. Examples are: Globalzepp (2015), Holodisplay (2015), AVconcepts (2015), Eonreality (2015), Xstage (2015), Holomedia (2015) and the Musion (2015) that present a set of solutions of holograms projected on various surfaces with various shapes and sizes, including 360°. It is possible to continue enumerating more examples of installations and companies that present products similar to the ones included in this chapter, but most of them are based on frontal holograms (Pepper's Ghost technique) or use the pyramid technique and none of those systems presents all the features developed in the installation introduced in this document.

While the Pepper's Ghost is one of the most commonly used techniques, there is also another technique that was proposed in 1908, by Professor Gabriel M. Lippmann from the French Academy of Sciences. It is based on a series of lenses placed on the surface of an image that creates a sense of depth called "La Photographie Integral" (Lippmann, 1908). This technique relies on recording of a full parallax image (including all the directions) using a spherical lens structure, known as fly's-eye lens, with both used to either capture or to represent pictures. The screen used was basically constituted by a large number of small convex lenses. In 1920, several scientists, including Herbert Ives, tried to simplify the solution proposed by Lippmann, introducing the sheet of lenticular lens solution. Each of these sheets are comprised of an array of fine, spherical lenses designed such that, when seeing from different angles, different pixels are displayed in a given image. To this end, on the opposite face of the sheet, which in use is rather flat, is placed an image specially constructed to fit the desired prospects. One of the first uses of these solutions, called lenticular printing, is widely known in the form of cards or other form of advertising in which, depending on the user's position, different images appear. Starting from the original solution, this technology has been used more recently to create 3D images on a flat screen.

The holodeck (Verge, 2015), a solution proposed by Microsoft, reuses the concept of "lenticular lens" to get a sense of depth and 3D. For this, multiple images are sent separated by a few degrees, allowing the reception of a "different image" in each eye. If different images are positioned according with the user's point of view then the holographic effect is obtained. Another example can be found in (Dick, Almeida, Soares, & Nunes, 2011).

There are still other solutions in research, such as TeleHuman (Kim, Bolton, Girouard, Cooperstock, & Vertegaal, 2012), which is a 3D videoconferencing system that supports 360° motion parallax, where a viewer moves around the cylinder and the projection follows him (Telehuman, 2013). However, this system has limitations when viewed by two or more observers, with one observer seeing the figure (avatar or video) and the remaining seeing the inverse of the picture or a "hole". In addition, the system does not follow the user who is interacting with the hologram. There are also mechanic systems, as the 360° system from the University of California (Jones, McDowall, Yamada, Bolas, & Debevec, 2007). Microsoft presents Vermeer (Butler et al., 2011), a display allowing visualization of 360° and interaction by touching on the display without the need of glasses or other instrumentation. However due to the small size and state of research, it seems that for now it is not applicable in real situations. Other applications are, for example, holographic desks for handling objects (Hilliges, Kim, Izadi, Weiss, & Wilson, 2012), and approaches that use computer graphics with interaction with holograms (Bimber, Zeidler, Rundhoefer, Wetzstein, & Moehring, 2005). More solutions exists, see e.g., the works of Lim and Kim (2014), Noor and Aras (2015), and Yamaguchi (2015).

In terms of user interaction, it can be done by using several different types of sensors and cameras. Usually it uses three-dimensional (3D) sensors, such as the Asus Xtion (Asus, 2014), the Microsoft Kinect (Kinect, 2014), or the Structure Sensor (Structure, 2014). All those sensors are very popular due to their hands free capability for controlling devices and graphical user interfaces, while tracking users' skeletons, recognizing joints and gestures of one or several users. Not all 3D sensors have this capability. The Leap Motion (Leap, 2014) sensor is also a 3D sensor, but it has only the capability to track hands and gestures (with finer details than the mentioned above). All these capabilities allow for what is now called natural interaction.

From the sensors mentioned above, the Microsoft's Kinect is one of the most famous 3D sensor on the market, popularized by the video gaming industry. In addition, this sensor is used in many applications, for example: in robotics (El-laithy, Huang, & Yeh, 2012), for head pose classification (Yun, Changrampadi, & Gu, 2014), enabling interaction with art installations (Alves et al., 2014; Weiss, Frid, Malin, & Ladijenski, 2015), applied in assistive technologies, such as enhancing visual performance skills on older adults (Chiang, Tsai, & Chen, 2012) or for the operation of wheelchairs (Kondori, Yousefi, Liu, & Li, 2014). More applications can be found, e.g., in (Cruz, Lucio, & Velho, 2012; Fong, Zhuang, Fister, & Fister, 2013; Kamizono, Abe, Baba, Takano, & Murakami, 2014; Cippitelli, Gasparrini, Gambi, & Spinsante, 2014; Rahman, Poon, Amin, & Yan, 2015; Gasparrini, Cippitelli, Spinsante, & Gambi, 2015). Interaction can also be achieved using other 3D sensors, like the Leap Motion, where the interaction with holograms for teaching technical drawings can be applied (Figueiredo et al., 2014). For the installations presented in this chapter up to eight Kinects were used.

FRONTAL HOLOGRAPHIC INSTALLATION

As mentioned briefly in the Introduction section, the frontal Public Relation installation consists of a human size holographic PR for an industrial (commercial) installation. The hologram can be represented by an avatar or a video from a real human PR, both allowing visualization of different contents (text, image, video, maps, etc.). The interactivity is achieved using a single Kinect sensor and based in very intuitive gestures. All interactions are recorded, creating and returning to the company key statistics about their main products, based on the attention given to each presented content, users' actions, favorite menus, viewing direction, face and body extraction, etc. (Alves et al., 2015a).

The holographic frontal installation uses the Pepper's Ghost technique for the hologram projection. As mentioned in the Contextualization section, this technique uses either a glass or a transparent acrylic, or also, for better results, a Mylar film in a 45° angle over the projected image, and the resulting holographic image appears in a 90° angle from the line of sight of the installation user/viewer. Figure 1 top row-left shows the illustration of this technique. More details on how to create the full sized holographic installation is out of the focus of this chapter, nevertheless, for more information about scaled installations see the works of Figueiredo et al. (2014) and Alves et al. (2015a). Also in Fig. 1, in the middle is represented the position of the Kinect (necessary for the interaction) as well as the area it covers in front of the installation. On the second row-right is the illustration of the frontal installation.

Two main modules constitute the fontal installation: (a) Users Data Module, responsible for manipulating and handling the data received from the Kinect Sensor, creating statistics, reading gestures, head direction, body and face extraction, sound and RFID information. (b) Database and Interface Module, responsible for storing information gathered from the previous module, as well as the application configuration settings and interface options. In addition, it is responsible for displaying and processing the visual information, such as the virtual characters and menus. The following subsections will cover these modules in more detail.

Figure 1. Frontal installation, from top to bottom, left to right. Illustration of the holographic scheme using Pepper's Ghost technique. Representation of the position of the Kinect (necessary for the interaction, heat map, etc.) as well as the area it cover in from of the installation. Gestures representation ("pose" and "swipe"). The swipe gesture illustration. Example of a heat map and the user being mapped to matrix M. The illustration of the frontal installation. An illustration of a user looking to his right, center and left. Finally, the face and body extraction

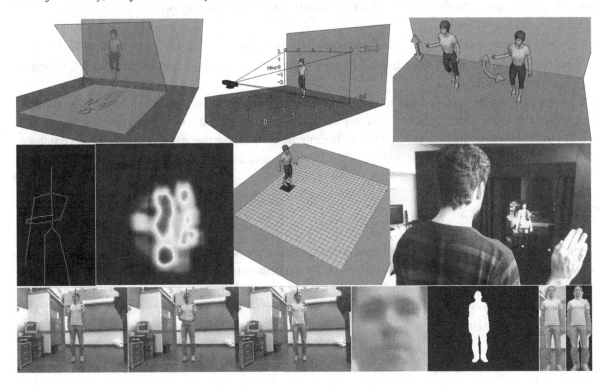

Users Data Module

All the data from the Kinect sensor (Kinect, not Kinect 2) is handled and manipulated by the Users Data Module. For more details about Kinect, and how to program it see, e.g., Miles (2012). The sensor records sound using a four-microphone array, color (RGB), depth frames and the skeleton: 25 joints of 2 users and can track up to 6 individual users. The Kinect covers a space from about 0.8 m to 4 m, with 43° vertical by 57° horizontal field of view; as described in (Kinect, 2014; KinectSpec, 2014). All this data is handled and manipulated in 5 main phases: (a) Spatial information, (b) gestures recognition, (c) heat map, (d) user head direction, (e) body and face extraction, (f) sound extraction and (g) RFID module.

It is also important to stress that the initial implementation and tests of the user data modules were conducted with male subjects around 23 years old. Nevertheless, all the parameters presented in the phases described below were tested with male and female users, from 12 to 50 years, with heights from 1.40 to 1.90 meters. Interaction (user data module) tests are presented in (Alves et al., 2015c), which shows tests results for the 360° holographic installation (see below), which integrates results from the user data modules for all the installations presented here. No tests were done with elder persons or persons with any kind of motor deficiency.

Spatial Information

The frontal installation uses a single Kinect sensor ($i = 1$) in the top or bottom of the installation (in Figure 1 second row right, the sensor is near the floor). The user's spatial information (x, y, z) regarding theirs joints and their global position (P), are queued in two FIFO (First In, First Out) lists, one being used for the current detected users (Pc_i), and the other for the lost users (Pl_i). Every time new information is available, given by the Kinect sensor, three different scenarios may occur:

1. The *detection of a new user* is automatically added to the end of the current users list (Pc_i), as well as the information regarding all its joints, the time of entry (t) and an internal ID, which is incremented afterwards.
2. If the *detected new user already exists*, then the new information is stored with the previous information onto the current users list as well as the time of entry of the new information.
3. In the case where the *user is lost*, then all information regarding that user is updated to the database (see below, Section Database and Interface Module), and the user is added to the lost users list and removed from the current users list.

Gestures Recognition

The users can interact with the installation using gestures (Alves et al., 2015a; 2015b). The gestures are used as an input for the hands free system. After experimenting with several different gestures, the "swipe gesture" and the "pose gesture" were chosen because of their intuitive nature. Figure 1, first row right illustrates the two gestures, in the most left side the "pose", and on the most right the "swipe". The implementation consists in:

1. The *pose gesture* can be detected using a vector defined by the arm, $\vec{V_a}$, calculated by subtracting the *hand* (right/left) position (P_h), from the *elbow* (right/left) position (P_e), and using the user's body vector $\vec{V_b}$, that is calculated by subtracting the *shoulder center* position (P_{sc}), from the *spine* position (P_s) (Kinect, 2014). In order to validate a menu pose gesture, the following conditions have to be met:

    a. The user is considered doing the gesture only if the distance between the *elbow* and the Kinect must be approximately the same as the *hand* and the Kinect, $|z_h - z_e| \geq 0.6d(P_h, P_e)$, where d is the Euclidean distance, and z_h and z_e are the *z-axis* coordinates of the *hand* and *elbow* respectively. Also, of course, the user needs to be facing the Kinect.

    b. Plus, the angle between $\vec{V_a}$ and $\vec{V_b}$ has to be between $20° \leq \theta \leq 160°$, with
    $$\theta = \mathrm{acos}\left(\left(\vec{V_b}.\vec{V_a}\right) / \left(\left\|\vec{V_b}\right\|\left\|\vec{V_a}\right\|\right)\right).$$

    c. To increase the reliability of the pose gesture it is verified if at least 85% out of the previous detections made in the past 1 s (second) are according to the above conditions. If the user is performing the pose gesture, it is considered:

        i.   up, if the angle θ is less than 90°;
        ii. down, otherwise.

2. The *swipe gesture* requires a minimum swipe speed velocity of $v_s = 200$ cm/s and a minimum swipe distance of $d_s = 30$ cm. These values were empirically chosen, after experimenting with different users. By analyzing only user information acquired from current instance t to $t - \Delta t_s$, with Δt_s a time window computed using $\Delta t_s = d_s / v_s$, a swipe was made if in any other sub-interval Δt_k (defined [t, $t - \Delta t_s$]), with k the latest instance of Δt_k, all *hand* positions (h) have the same signal along the whole interval Δt_k. The hand positions are computed using the current hand position subtracted by its previous hand position, taking only into account the x component for the horizontal swipe, or the y component for the vertical swipe ($|\sum_{j=k-\Delta t_k}^{k-1} \mathrm{sgn}\,(h_{j+1,\{x,y\}} - h_{j,\{x,y\}})| = k - 1$), and if the total distance travelled, taking only into account the x/y component respectively for the horizontal and vertical swipe, between the first and the last point of that sequence is greater or equals to $d_s \geq |h_{k,\{x,y\}} - h_{k-\Delta t_k,\{x,y\}}|$.

Figure 1, second row left illustrates a horizontal swipe movement, and in the same row right the user is doing a pose gesture.

Heat Map

The heat map (Alves et al., 2015a) can be useful for obtain statistics about the most active locations of a user or a group of users. The users' global position (P) returned by Kinect, represents the distance in each axis between the Kinect and the user, with the x and z axis constituting the horizontal and vertical distance respectively, as shown in Fig. 1 top row middle. As mentioned before, it is assumed that the physical limits of the Kinect is 4 m in length and in width (Kinect, 2014; KinectSpec, 2014). A matrix M with size of $N \times N$ can be created, with $N = 26\,\mathrm{px}$ (pixels), dividing the region in squares of approximately $4 / N \times 4 / N$ m, where each square has the area of approximately 0.024 m² (see Fig. 1, second row and third column). A user position detected from Kinect on instance t is mapped to matrix M using $(x_t, \ y_t) = (-x_{k_t} \times (N / 4) + N / 2, z_{kt} \times (N / 4))$, with x_k and z_k the coordinates obtained from Kinect. Starting with M equal to the null matrix, every detection made at instance t increments the mapped entry value, as well as its 8 neighbours: $M \left(x_t + i, \ y_t + j\right) = M \left(x_{t-1} + i, \ y_{t-1} + j\right) + 1$, with $i, j = \{-1, 0, 1\}$. After this step, the matrix M holds estimated values for the positions of a user, or group of users. The matrix is then normalized and converted to a color map using JET color map. Figure 1, second row and column shows the heat map of a single user during the interaction with the installation for a period of more or less 15 minutes.

User's Head Direction

One of the installations' goals is to know whether the user is watching or not to it. In other words, an objective is to estimate the time spent by the user in interactive activities with the installation (e.g., doing gestures, reading the available information, and/or seeing images/videos). Due to the Kinect color resolution, getting the precise point the user is looking at, i.e., "eye-tracking" (Martins, Rodrigues, & Martins, 2015), is quite difficult and imprecise.

For that reason, the computation of where the user's head is facing to was implemented as an alternative. That estimation was achieved employing reference points (Alves et al., 2015a). First, the position of the user's eyes was obtained using the Kinects SDK, see Figure 1 bottom left (read dots). Those eyes' positions are then combined with the *shoulders'* (*S*) positions (left, center and right), marked with black dots (on the shoulders) in the same figure. Using the coordinates of this set of points, a vector $\vec{V}_s = \left(x_{Sl} - x_{Sr}, y_{Sl} - y_{Sr}\right)$ is obtained as well as its normal vector $\vec{V}' = \left(-V_{Sy}, V_{Sx}\right)$. Vector $\vec{V}_s$ defines the direction containing both shoulders' points and, in order to compute it, the positions of the *left shoulder* (*l*) and the *right shoulder* (*r*) are used, i.e., $\vec{S}_{l/r} = \left(x_{S_l/S_r}, y_{S_l/S_r}\right)$. In the same figure, the sketched vertical (or almost vertical) blue line corresponds to the "application" $\vec{V}'$ to the *shoulders' center* position (Kinect, 2014). Three different scenarios can happen, i.e., a user can have:

1. An eye on each side of the blue line (Figure 1 bottom left-center), meaning that the user is looking to the front.
2. Both eyes can be placed on the left side of the blue line (Figure 1 bottom left-left), thus the user is looking to the right.
3. Alternatively, the user can have both eyes placed on the right side of the blue line, (Figure 1 bottom left-right), determining that the user is looking left.

Depending on the user's position, extreme left and right directions where excluded and a timer was implemented in order to count the time a user spent looking at each direction.

Body and Face Extraction

One of the features of the installation allows face or body "selfies" which, for instance, can be used for "promotional gifts" or, under the user request, to be inserted in a social network. The face extraction is done directly by Kinect SDK (Kinect, 2014), see Figure 1 bottom row, 4th column. However, the full body photo is not directly achieved from the SDK, which is done as explained next.

Every time a new depth frame from the sensor is available, the first three bits represent which user that pixel belong to, from 1 to 6, with 0 representing the background. For each user a Boolean mask is constructed (Figure 1 bottom row, 5th column) and the contours are smoothed using a Gaussian filter ($\sigma = 2$). The next step determines the highest and lowest coordinates values, $x_{min/max}$ and $y_{min/max}$, of the Boolean mask, which are used to crop the color image and optionally applying the Boolean mask itself. The illustration of the resulting images is shown in Figure 1 bottom row, from the 5th to the 7th column.

Sound Extraction

Each Kinect is equipped with a built-in microphone array, composed of 4 microphones that enable sound extraction. With this setup the microphone array is capable of sound source location formally entitled beam forming, that is, the capacity of calculating differences between captured audio streams and estimating the sound source direction. For each Kinect, the audio beam angle range, covers 100° in front of itself, 50° from the center to each side (Kinect, 2014). The beam angle can be one of 11 different values, an integer multiple of 10 ranging from -50 to 50 including 0. Each of this values represent sound source directions, for each sound source located. In addition, the Kinect SDK also estimates a confidence level (Kinect, 2014) of that estimation, with values ranging from 0.0 to 1.0, where 0.0 represents no confidence and 1.0 maximum confidence. The Kinect SDK supports speech recognition in several languages, allowing the detection of words or sentences captured by the microphone array.

The installation saves the direction from where the sound appears, but more importantly, the system has a list of "keywords" and "key-phrases" (saved in a GRXML file) that when identified and confirmed (using the available functions in Kinect SDK) trigger a response using a stored answer, which uses an implemented text-to-speech functionality or, optionally, a ".wav" pre-recorder sentence. The keywords can also trigger actions similar to the gesture interaction.

In general, if during 30 s (configurable) there are no gesture, or user detected, but there are sounds which do not produce recognized words, then the installation returns an audio personalized message to call the attention to itself.

RFID Module

The RFID module was developed to allow Radio-Frequency Identification (RFID) interaction between the installation (RFID's passive reader) and users badges (RFID's passive tags), in the form of ID cards. An RFID receiver module (RFID, 2014) is attached to the installation and connected to the on-board computer. A user can pass his/her badge in front the installation's RFID receiver module to interact with the installation.

This interaction can be materialized in several different ways, e.g., to welcome guests in a special event by a vocal and a visual greeting from the installation. For instance, the guests' names can be previously stored in a database (see next section) and, when the RFID matches the ID from the RFID card, the system uses text-to-speech to greet the guest. This application is an integral part of the system as a hole, and can be activated and deactivated whenever necessary.

Database and Interface Module

In this section, the main features of the database will be will briefly explained. The database is supported on a relational database management system, namely MySQL. There are two types of information stored in the database module:

1. Statistics and
2. Menus and configurations, i.e., information for and from the interface module.

For the first case, statistics, the information stored in the database is been discussed along the chapter, i.e., the module stores the acquired data from all of the installation's inputs devices (e.g., user's ID, number of users, time present in front of the installation, time interacting with the installation and with each menu, time spend looking into the installation, user(s) positions, gestures, interactions, visualizations, and biometry).

For the second case, menus and configurations, the interface module is responsible for reading the information stored in the database and then uses it to generate graphical user interface layouts, and responses to the users' inputs. The layouts can be generated by the application supported on

1. Menu title contents which serve as links to other menus,
2. By fitting small text descriptions, or
3. Images, video and other media content, with the respective descriptions, in order to give the user a more appealing explanation.

Besides the contents, other configuration are also stored in the database, e.g., the orientation of the layouts with options like diagonal or vertical. An option for displaying only video or images is available. This data (layout and configurations data) is loaded from the database when the application starts. The use of the database provides easier modification, updates and synchronization between multiples installation.

In terms of the Interface Module, user's inputs generate responses from the PR avatar or video. For example, if a new user starts interacting with the installation, the video/avatar waves their hand (or any other predefined movement) and shows the user's photo on the display. In another example, if the user selects a menu option then avatar/video triggers the menu change by "touching" the menu.

It is important to reinforce, that all interaction data is saved on the database, such as the time spent interacting with menus, requests of content provided by the installation, etc. Finally, it is also important to recall that the installation presented in Figure 1 second row right is an holographic representation, in this case of an avatar of a lady, with 1.70 m height.

180° REAR PROJECTION INSTALLATION

In this section the modifications done to the frontal installation to cope with a set of Kinects will be explained. The system is illustrated using a rear projection installation, although the software development and interaction is exactly the same using a full human size rear projection or a holographic installation.

Two main problems were detected in some situations when using the previous installation (Frontal Holographic Installation), namely:

1. It occupies a considerable space to project a real size person, and
2. The interaction can only occur when the user is in front of the installation (due to the Kinect limitations).

Also the price of the installation is of some concern.

The first problem (as well as the installation price) can be solved by using a rear projection installation instead of a holographic installation. Although the rear projection installation is less impactful than the holographic one, this is an option that each company can take.

The second problem can easily be solved by making use of four Kinect sensors instead of using a single one. The use of four Kinetics, organized in a way that optimizes overlapping areas from their neighbor sensors (see Figure 2 first row left), allows to capture a 180° field of view. Figure 2 first row right shows a snapshot of real time data streaming obtained from the Kinects' system, with the RGB information in the top, the depth information (the whiter the closest to the Kinect sensor) in the middle, and the skeletons (in green) at the bottom. In the top of each image is shown the number of frames per second (fps) that each Kinect is acquiring at the moment.

Now, the application is composed by 3 modules (Alves et al., 2015b):

1. Users' Data Module, similar to the one in the frontal installation, is responsible for manipulating and handling data received from each of the Kinect Sensors (creating statistics, reading gestures and sounds, etc.);
2. Global Management Module (new module), responsible for converting the users' spatial information, obtained from each individual sensor, to a global reference system and disambiguate users that are detected by multiple Kinects; and
3. Database and Interface Module (similar to the frontal installation), responsible for storing information gathered from the set of sensors as well as the global information (retrieved by the Global Management Module).

Similar to the frontal installation, the Database and Interface Module has also at is charge the application's configuration settings and interface options, and is responsible for displaying and processing the visual information (texts and menus).

To implement the present solution, three physical properties are needed from the Kinects' system:

1. The Kinects relative position $C_i(x, y, z)$ in a global reference (red dot in Fig. 2 second row left), where $i = 0..3$ represents the Kinect index,
2. Their horizontal rotation β_i, and
3. Their vertical angle ϕ_i. Parameter β_i and ϕ_i represent the frontal directions of each sensor.

The Kinects SDK has built in methods for retrieving the vertical angle. In order to determine the Kinect's position, C_i, the horizontal angle they are facing has to be calculated first. As already mentioned, the installation captures a 180° angle, visible in Figure 2 second row left, where the intersection angle (α) between Kinects' views can be obtained by solving equation $180 = 4 \times \lambda - 3 \times \alpha$, where $\lambda = 57°$ is the Kinect's horizontal field of view angle (Kinect, 2014), which gives $\alpha = 16°$. The horizontal angles β_i can be calculated, starting with the Kinect on the right and counter-clockwise (Figure 2 second

Figure 2. 180° installation. From left to right, and top to bottom: the physical installation layout. Real time data streaming from 4 Kinects: RGB, depth and skeletons. 180° Kinect coordinate system, the physical coordinates and angles relative to each Kinects. A real time sound source beams example from all 4 Kinects, in a polar plot. A map of 4 users in front of the installation and the respective heat map from the previous users (5 minutes) represented on a JET color map. Finally, examples of the installation working

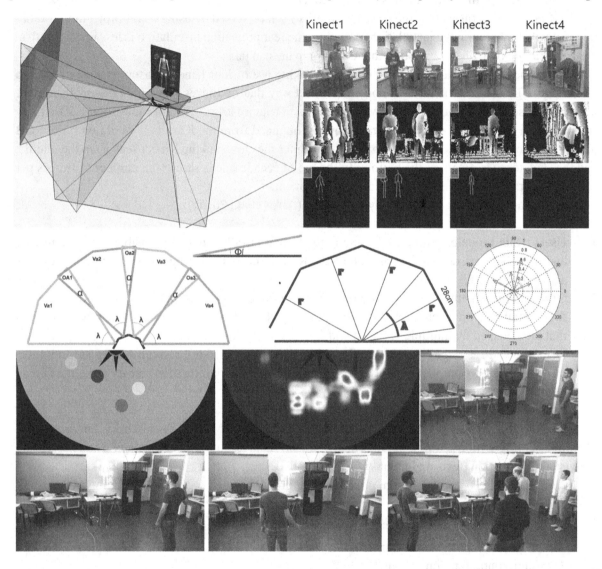

row left): $\beta_0 = \lambda / 2 = 28.5°$ and $\beta_l = \beta_{l-1} + \lambda - \alpha$, with $l = 1..\,3$ returning $\beta_1 = 69.5°$, $\beta_2 = 110.5°$ and $\beta_3 = 151.5°$.

Positions C_i would ideally be the same for all Kinects, but because the Kinect's width is $w_{KS} = 28$ cm (Kinect, 2014) this is not physically possible. Therefore, the Kinect sensors need to be distanced from the center point by a distance r in the direction of the angle they are facing (Fig. 2 second row middle). The distance can be calculated using $r = w_{KS} / \left(2 \times \tan\left((\beta_1 - \beta_0) / 2\right)\right)$, resulting in $r \approx 36$

cm. Position C_i can be calculated using $C_i(x,y,z) = (r \times \cos(\beta_i), 0, r \times \sin(\beta_i))$, thus $C_0(x,y,z) \approx (32,0,17)$ cm, $C_1(x,y,z) \approx (12,0,34)$ cm, $C_2(x,y,z) \approx (-12,0,34)$ cm and $C_3(x,y,z) \approx (-32,0,17)$ cm. With all C_i values and r calculated for the positioning of the sensors, it is now possible to program the components of the NI model.

Global Management Module

The Global Management Module, as the name refers, is responsible of managing users, sounds detected by the Kinects, selecting the user that is interacting (gesture/sound) with the installation, creating a global reference, and solving inconsistencies when two Kinects detect the same user because of the overlapping areas on their field of view. Working similar as the Users Data Module, the Global Management consists of two FIFO lists: one containing the current detected users Gc and the other for lost users Gl.

Global Reference Conversion

Once the update of all the Users Data Modules are done, users from Pc_i, their values are transformed to a global reference and positioned onto an array of potential users, Uc. The coordinates returned by the Kinect are converted from the coordinates shown in Figure 1 top middle, to a global reference, that can be seen in Figure 2, third row left. In the figure aforementioned, the lighter area represents the interaction zone that starts from the center of the Kinect group, having a 4-meter radius.

On the same image, each user is represented by a circle, occupying approximately 50 cm. The conversion of the Kinects coordinates to a global reference system, where the x axis grows from left to right, the y axis grows from up to down, and the z axis is the depth distance, is necessary for the Kinects physical layouts, as well as the distances between each other and their rotation in the horizontal plane (β_i) and vertical plane (ϕ_i).

For each Kinect sensor a coordinate unitary vector is determined for each axis: $\vec{V_a}$ representing the vector of the axis the Kinect is facing, $\vec{V_b}$ representing the axis with an horizontal 90° to $\vec{V_a}$ and $\vec{V_c}$ representing the third axis with 90° to both $\vec{V_a}$ and $\vec{V_b}$ pointing upwards in relation to Kinect. The three vectors can be computed as

$$\vec{V_a}(x,y,z) = (\cos(\beta_i) \times \sin(\pi/2 + \phi_i), \cos(\pi/2 + \phi_i), \sin(\beta_i) \times \sin(\pi/2 + \phi_i)),$$

$$\vec{V_b}(x,y,z) = (\cos(\beta_i + \pi/2) \times \sin(\pi/2 + \phi_i), \cos(\pi/2 + \phi_i), \sin(\beta_i + \pi/2) \times \sin(\pi/2 + \phi_i)),$$

and

$$\vec{V_c}(x,y,z) = (\cos(\beta_i) \times \sin(\phi_i), \cos(\phi_i), \sin(\beta_i) \times \sin(\phi_i)).$$

The Kinect SDK returns a user's joint positions, $\dot{J}$, in meters. The new position in the global reference, Ig, can now be calculated, in meters, by $Ig = \left(J_x \times \overrightarrow{V_a} + J_y \times \overrightarrow{V_c} + J_z \times \overrightarrow{V_a} + C_i \right) / 100$ m. Jg represents the conversion of any joint or a user's global position from any sensor to the global reference system. By using this transformation, we denote Pg as the global position of the user and, finally, all users are mapped onto the same global reference system, see Fig. 2 third row left (Alves et al., 2015b).

Detecting the Same User in Multiple Kinects

In a multiple Kinect configuration, the field of view of a Kinect overlaps the ones of the neighbor Kinects and vice versa (Figure 2 top left), which led to the implementation of a method to determine if the same user is being detected by two neighbor Kinects.

The method compares the users on Uc with each other to find if they might be the same user, using the following cumulative criteria:

1. The Euclidean distance between the global positions of the two compared users (for instance Pg_1 and Pg_2) is less than 50 cm and the two users were detected by different Kinects
2. Given the last $T = 5$ skeletons information, the global position variation on all axis are similar, i.e., $(| Pg_{1/2,x}\left(\delta\right) - Pg_{1/2,x}\left(\delta - 1\right) |< 15\,\text{cm}) \wedge$ $(| Pg_{1/2,y}\left(\delta\right) - Pg_{1/2,y}\left(\delta - 1\right) |< 15\,\text{cm}) \wedge$ $(| Pg_{1/2,z}\left(\delta\right) - Pg_{1/2,z}\left(\delta - 1\right) |< 15\,\text{cm})$, with $\delta = \left\{ t,\ldots, t - T \right\}$ (then it is assumed that both users are in fact the same user).

If the relation between the users was found, the newest user will be forced to change his/her internal ID to the internal ID of the oldest detected user. If the two users have the same internal ID, then they are automatically associated as being the same user, meaning that the association was already established in a previous situation. In any of the cases, the closest user to its Kinect will be marked and added to the end of the Gc list, with the other removed from that list.

The threshold values mentioned in this subsection were determined empirically. Nevertheless, the above mentioned 50 cm were considered as the minimum space that a user/person occupies and the 15 cm, which is roughly 1/3 of that length, was considered the minimum value an user can slightly move but still be in the same place/be the same person (we can call it "personal space").

Updating, Adding and Removing Users

Upon completing the previous step, the marked users will be added to the current users' list, Gc, where a detected user can be either completely new in the list, or can be already an existing user of Gc, but with new information. The users marked as new (are stored in Uc, being represented by u_l, with l ranging from 0 to the size of array Uc), are compared to each user already on Gc (where the user is gc_j, with j ranging from 0 to size of list Gc). If both users u_l and gc_j have the same internal ID, then the user gc_j will be updated with the last skeleton (global reference) of the user u_l. On the other hand, if user u_l does not have the same ID with any user of G_c then u_l is a new user and will be inserted at the end of the list Gc.

An occlusion detection method was developed in order to recover lost users, necessary because sometimes users can block the Kinect's view. A verification in the lost users list Gl for Δt seconds is made when a new user is detected. For all of the last positions of all lost users (k) for the previous Δt seconds, Gl_k, the current position of a detected user (u), Gu_c, is considered to belong to a previous user if the Euclidean distance $d_{i,u}$ between Gl_i and Gc_u is less than 50 cm. The closest distance d is chosen if more than one lost uses is closer than 50 cm to the position P_u, recovering all information to the current users list Gc (empirically it was used $\Delta t = 5$ s).

The user that will be selected to interact with the installation is the one in the Gc list that is close to the installation, and maintains this status until he leaves the 180° space analyzed by the system. However, if the user leaves the space or does not have any type of movement during 30 seconds then the selected user will correspond to the next element in the Gc list that is close to the installation.

180° Heat Map

As mentioned in the Heat Map in the frontal installation section, the users' heat map is one of the most important features, being very useful to obtain statistics about the installation surroundings, including most active locations (and the times spent on those locations) of a group of users or a single user. The heat map is calculated by using the user's global position (Pg). Furthermore, the heat map region has approximately 8 × 4 meters, given by the physical range limits of the Kinects (a little bellow 4 meters; (Kinect, 2014)). To be more precise, it is approximately a semi-circle with a 4 m radius and center in the middle of the Kinect sensor group (see Figure 2 third row right).

As in the frontal installation, the heat map is transformed now into a *HM* matrix with a $2N \times N$ size, creating a new map divided by small squares of approximately $(4/N) \times (4/N)$ m. Also similar to the frontal installation, the value of *N* was 26 px, resulting in a 0.024m^2 square area. The remaining process is exactly equal to the one done for the heat map in the frontal installation. Figure 2 third row middle shows the heat map where several users (4) are moving during 5 minutes in front of the installation.

Sound

The installation is capable of detecting sound source angles and interact with users even if they are not present in from of it. As mentioned before, the Kinect sensor is capable of speech recognition, however in a 4 Kinect configuration (180° installation), where 16 microphones are present (4 × 4), the Kinect that is most frontal do the sound source location must be selected to handle the speech recognition.

As mentioned, the Kinect has the capability of detecting the sound source location within a 100° angle. In a 4 Kinect configuration, where the sensors are positioned side by side and misaligned from each other, the total aggregated audio source range is calculated by summing the 100° angle from each Kinect minus the 3 overlapping areas (O_a), that exist due to the adjacent positioning of the multiple Kinect's close to each other. The total audio source range of this 4 Kinects configuration is given by S_d $\approx 223°$ ($S_d = 4 \times 100° - 3 \times O_a$), that is greater than the field of view of 180°.

Because of the wide angle of the audio range obtained from 4 Kinects, a transformation was applied to all individual audio beam angles, converting the 223° range into a 180° range, $\varphi_t = \varphi_o \times 180 / S_d$, where φ_t represents the transformed angle and φ_o the original audio beam angles. By doing this transformation, the resulting location of the sound source will become distorted from the real sound source location (i.e. captured), nevertheless, since the objective is just to select witch Kinect will be responsible for handling speech recognition this small distortion will not influence the selection. An alternative solution would be to clip all sound information from the audio source inside the range $[-(S_d - 180)/2, 0]$ and $[180, 180 + (S_d - 180)/2]$ degrees. To determine which Kinect will handle speech recognition when a user is interacting with the system using their voice or when environmental sound is detected, the following algorithm is applied:

1. Read the sound beam and confidence levels from all 4 Kinects microphones.
2. For each Kinect sum and store the result of the audio beam angles multiplied by the respective confidence levels.
3. For filtering isolated sounds and noise, step ii) is repeated several times (10 times).
4. After step iii) is done it is determined which of the sums has the greatest value.
5. If there is a tie or a close tie (between 5% of the highest value), the selection is done by selecting the value that has the sound beam closest to 0° (corresponding to the most frontal sound relative to the middle of the Kinect).
6. The Kinect associated to the maximum computed value will be chosen to process the speech recognition.

Figure 2 second row right displays a polar plot containing real time sound source beams from 4 Kinects. In this case the selected Kinect was the second from the right.

In terms of speech recognition, the process is similar to the frontal installation, after the selection of the active sensor. The Kinect captures sounds from the users words and sentences and compares them with the ones stored on the speech SDK, and then detects with a degree of certainty if the word is valid or not. If a keyword is detected and confirmed the application triggers a response using a pre-stored answer (using text-to-speech) using a synthesized voice or a pre-recorded voice. Actions can also be triggered by keywords similar to the gesture interaction (the same as the frontal installation). When the installation does not detect sound for 30 seconds, it emits a pre-recorded message through its speakers to call attention to itself (this is only done if no user is interacting with the installation).

Database and Interface Module

This module is exactly the same as the frontal installation. Figure 2 second row right and bottom row shows the prototype installation with several users interacting whit it.

360° INTERACTIVE HOLOGRAPHIC PUBLIC RELATIONS

The 360° holographic installation, is very similar in terms of development to the 180°. The main differences are: (a) is also a holographic installation (as the frontal installation), with a holographic projection that can, in this case, be seen from a 360° degree walk. (b) The interaction can be done by 4 or 8 Kinect sensors, which are put in a "circular" (hexagonal) disposition, where the center is the hologram.

In terms of the holographic installation, it continues to use the Pepper's Ghost technique, but now, the area of projection is divided in 8 slices, i.e., the holographic display is composed by an 8 sided prism made from acrylic. A short throw projector projects the image onto a special acrylic in a rear projection way, which is then reflected by an 8 sided prism, giving the ("illusion" of a) hologram fluting inside of the 8 prism structure. Each volume to be holographic projected object is also divided in 8 views. Each view will be projected in each slice of the holographic projection. Figure 3 first and second rows left, shows the representation of the installation, with the field of view of each Kinect sensor, bottom two rows show the installation working. More details about the technique of projection is out of the focus of this Chapter (Alves et al., 2015c).

In term of interaction (b) the installation can use from 4 to 8 Kinects. Figure 3 first row center, shows the RGB, depth and skeletons from the 8 installation Kinects. In the case of 4 Kinects they are organized in a cross "+" while in the case of 8 Kinects they are placed forming an octagon around the installation, as shown in see Fig. 3, first and second row left, where the blue field of views represents the 4 Kinects and the blue plus the red the 8 Kinects. As already mentioned, in this installation, each Kinect sensor is positioned in a hexagonal way, side by side from each other, at the same distance to the center of the installation. Being $r1$ ($r1 = 60$ cm, for the present installation) the distance from the center of the hexagon where the holographic projection is shown to the Kinect. Each Kinect is positioned perpendicular to the line where the distance $r1$ is calculated, being their lines drawn with a 45° angle from each other (or 90° angle in the case of using only 4 Kinects); see Figure 3 second row and column.

Regarding the configuration of the 4 Kinects, four zones were considered. Each of these zones have a 33° angle that is not covered by the interaction ("dead zones"), i.e., as already mentioned, each Kinect can cover around a radius of 4 meters in front of it, with a 57° horizontal field of view (thus four Kinects can cover $4 \times 57° = 228°$). The uncovered angle is 132°, which divided by 4 parts results in a 33° angle (see Figure 3 third row and column). In the case of using 8 Kinects there is an overlap angle between to neighbor Kinects of 12°. Again, this angle can be obtained by multiplying the number of Kinect by their field of view ($4 \times 57° = 456°$), subtracting 360° and dividing the total overlap area by 8 (($456°-360°$) / $8 = 12°$), see Fig. 3 second row right and third row left. The Kinect position C_i, for $i = 1..4$ and $i = 1..8$ (4 and 8 Kinects), can be calculated using $C_i\left(x, y, z\right)$ as shown in the 180° installation, but now using $r1$ and the angles mentioned above (see also Figure 3 second row right). In the following sections the differences between the 180° and 360° installation will be described in terms of interaction.

The application was developed as in the 180° installation, with three modules that have the same functionalities, namely: (a) Users Data Module, (b) Global Management Module and (c) Database and Interface Module. The first one is exactly the same as shown before. The other two modules are similar, nevertheless some differences exist.

Global Management Module

The 360° Global Management Module, as the 180°, is responsible of managing the users, the sound detected by each Kinect, selecting the user that is interacting with the installation, creating a global reference, and solving inconsistencies when 2 side-by-side Kinects (in the case of the 8 Kinects configuration) detect the same user due to the overlapping areas on their field of view.

Figure 3. 360° holographic installation. From Left to right, and top to bottom: The holographic representation of the installation with the 8 field of views of the Kinects sensors; RGB, depth and skeleton for each of the 8 sensors; Real time sound sources beams example, from the 8 Kinects configuration, in a polar plot; A second view of the holographic installation; the 360° Kinect coordinate system; the physical coordinates and angles relative to each Kinect; A map of users in front of the installation and the respective heat map represented on a JET color map for the 8 and 4 Kinects configuration; And examples of the installation working

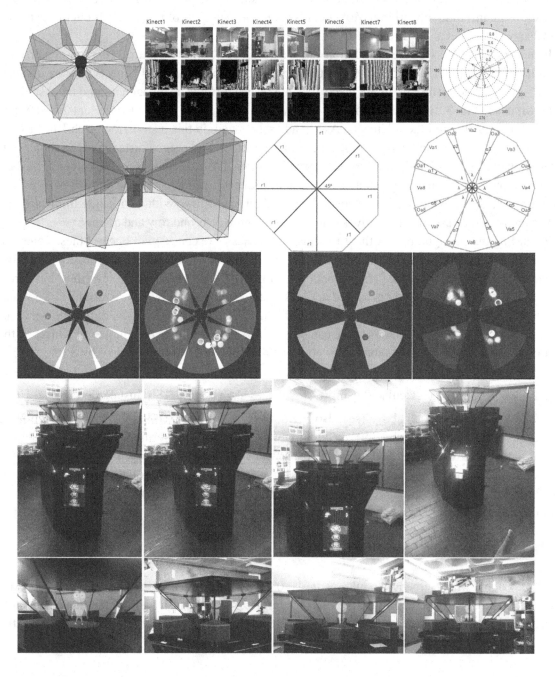

Detecting, Updating, Adding and Removing Users

The process of detecting, updating, adding and removing users applies the same methods as the 180° installation: making use of two global FIFO lists, one for the current users Gc and other for the lost users Gl. Users are added or removed based on the separated FIFO lists of each Kinect Pc_i (current users) and Pl_i (lost users). However, the problem where adjacent Kinects detect two users only persists on the 8 Kinects configuration, since the 4 Kinects configuration has no overlapping areas. Therefore, the algorithm presented in Section "Detecting the Same User in Multiple Kinects" is applied to the 8 Kinect configuration, where the Gc and Gl FIFO lists will have the exact same users as the union of the Pc_i and Pl_i lists. In the case of the 4 Kinects configuration it is not possible to determine (with the algorithms shown in this Chapter) if a user/person is moving from one Kinect field of view to other Kinect field of view.

To solve this problem a solution was implemented that allows a user to leave the area of interaction with the installation and return to it a few minutes or hours later, and still be recognized as the same user. For details about this implementation, see the work of Alves et al. (2015c).

Sound

As mentioned, in a 4 Kinect configuration there are a total of 4 microphone arrays composed by and aggregate of 16 microphones. As stated before, each Kinect can capture 100° degrees of audio in front of it, resulting in 400° of audio source location. The 100° range from each Kinect was firstly normalized to a 90° range. This transformation allows a 360° audio source location. In the 8 Kinect configuration there are a total of 8 microphone arrays composed by and aggregate of 32 microphones, resulting in 800° of audio source location, and the normalization has done to 45°. This transformation also allows a 360° audio source location instead of the 800°. The above distortions does not significantly change the audio source locations, because the final resulting audio source location is extrapolated using the distorted audio source locations from several Kinects. The implemented algorithm for beam audio source was the same as 180° installation. Figure 3 first row right represents the real time audio beam angle sources captured and transformed in a polar plot. In this case, the Kinect sensor selected to do the sound functions, such as speech recognition, was the one corresponding to the longest vector (Kinect number 2, in the example).

360° Heat Map

In this installation the heat map has the shape of a ring, with the inner radius, of the inside circle, approximately equal to 0.6 m, and the outer radius approximately equal to 4.6 meters (both counting from the central point/middle of the 360° installation). The computation and update of the heat map is done as presented for the 180° installation. The second and fourth columns of Figure 3 third row shows, for a group of 4 persons moving around the installation for about 5 minutes, the heat maps represented as JET color map for the 360° installation with 8 and 4 Kinects, respectively. In this case, it was verified that in both configurations some persons were quite static in several locations, creating the red circular blogs presented in the images.

Database and Interface Module

This module is exactly the same as the one for the frontal and the 180° installations. The last two rows of Figure 3 show the prototype installation. Nevertheless, in this installation, due to its specification, the menu is presented in a LED screen (see also the illustration shown in Figure 3 second row left). Alternatively, 8 LED screens could be used with the menus duplicated in each screen, one for each view of the hologram which is located in the top of the installation. This allows the hologram (mainly with an avatar representation) to follow the user when he is moving inside the interaction region (see Fig. 3, bottom row). The hologram will always be with its frontal representation turned to the field of view of the selected user, even when the user is not gesturally interacting with the installation, but continues moving inside the interaction region, or giving voice commands/demands, and the installation (hologram) is responding to him/her.

Another implemented functionality turns the frontal view of the hologram to the biggest sound source when no user is present, followed by a sound calling the attention of a possible future user to the installation.

CONCLUSION

In this chapter, three interactive complementary installations were presented, based on a model for natural interaction. A hologram (avatar or video) replaces a public relations person, establishing the first contact between a company and a potential client. The installations are capable of recognizing sound sources and voice commands while interacting with sound and gestures.

The fully customizable nature of the application is a major asset. The application is also capable of extracting statistics about the user's gestures and positions at any instance of time, the most requested contents, as well as the time spent by users in each of the contents. The installation works in a frontal (57°), 180° and 360° interaction environment. When a user is interacting with the installation, the gesture commands are obtained tracking his joints. Two main gestures were considered: (a) the swipe gestures and (b) pose gesture. Swipe gestures recognition can fail when the user does it with lack of speed or extend (distance). As for the pose gesture, it allows users' easy navigation through the menus. There were no noticeable failures in its recognition, except to the lack of speed or extend (distance), as previously.

Results regarding the recognition of multiple detections of a user have also shown good outcomes, even in complex environments, with errors susceptible of occurring in two situations.

1. In the case of the 180° installation and the 360° installation with 8 Kinect sensors, the users' tracking can fail if they abruptly change their positions (e.g., run) or are not facing the center of the installation. These errors result mainly from the small overlap area of the two neighbor Kinects. The possible incapability of tracing abrupt changes of position is due to one of the limitations of Kinect sensors, which does not detect well users when they are sideways to it. On the other hand, results on recovering users were satisfactory. If a Kinect is obstructed and a user does not move, then it works as expected, as long as the obstruction doesn't take too long. However, if the user moves to a different location, the results have shown not to be so reliable. In addition, if another user switches position with the obstructed user, then he/she will be recognized as the user that switched places with.

2. The second pitfall occurs in the case of the 360° installation with 4 Kinects, where it is not possible (at the moment) to track a user that "moves" from one Kinect to another. In these cases, the user is lost and a new user is created as he/she switch between Kinect areas.

Current work focuses in the solving of the above problem (Alves et al., 2015c), by improving obstruction and overlap difficulties, as well as users leaving the installation and returning back a few minutes/hours later. To achieve this last feature, biometric information, such as distance between joints, color descriptors in each joint, and face recognition (when possible), is being used. Future work includes the prediction of user movements to increase certainty about the user position inside the interaction region.

ACKNOWLEDGMENT

This work was supported by projects PRHOLO QREN I&DT, nr. 33845 and FCT, LARSyS (UID/EEA/50009/2013) and CIAC (PEstOE/ EAT/UI4019/2013). We also thank our project leader SPIC - Creative Solutions [www.spic.pt].

REFERENCES

Active8-3D (2015). 3D holographic projection displays. Retrieved from http://www.activ8-3d.co.uk/

Alves, R., Madeira, M., Ferrer, J., Costa, S., Lopes, D., Silva, B. M., . . . Rodrigues, J. (2014). Fátima revisited: an interactive installation. *Proceedings of the SGEM2014 Conference on Arts, Performing Arts, Architecture & Design SGEM '14* (pp. 141-148).

Alves, R., Negrier, A., Sousa, L., Rodrigues, J. M. F., Felisberto, P., Gomes, M., & Bica, P. (2015b). Interactive 180° Rear projection public relations. *Procedia Computer Science, 51*(0), 592–601. doi:10.1016/j.procs.2015.05.327

Alves, R., Sousa, L., Negrier, A., Rodrigues, J. M. F., Cardoso, P. J. S., Monteiro, J., . . . Bica, P. (2015a). PRHOLO: Interactive holographic public relations. *Proceedings of the3rd International Conference on Advances in Computing, Communication and Information Technology* (pp. 124-128). doi:10.15224/978-1-63248-061-3-74

Alves, R., Sousa, L., Negrier, A., Rodrigues, J.M.F., Monteiro, J., Cardoso, P., Felisberto, P., Gomes, M., & Bica, P. (2015c). 360° Public relations, an interactive installation. *The Visual Computer.*

António, S., Herrera, R., & Enriquez, E. (2013). Projection's panel of models for touch screen. *International Journal of Innovative Research in Computer and Communication Engineering, 1*(9), 2057–2064.

Asus. (2014). Asus Xtion pro. Retrieved from http://goo.gl/HxQcli

AVA. (2015). AVA advanced virtual assistant. Retrieved from http://airportone.com/airportvirtualassistancesystem.htm

AVconcepts. (2015). Retrieved from http://www.avconcepts.com/

Bimber, O., Zeidler, T., Rundhoefer, A., Wetzstein, G. & Moehring, M. (2005). Interacting with augmented holograms, In SPIE, Practical Holography XIX: Materials and Applications, 41-54.

Butler, A., Hilliges, O., Izadi, S., Hodges, S., Molyneaux, D., Kim, D., & Kong, D. (2011). Vermeer: direct interaction with a 360° viewable 3D display. *Proceedings of the24th Annual ACM Symposium on User Interface Software and Technology* (pp. 569-576). doi:10.1145/2047196.2047271

Chiang, I., Tsai, J. C., & Chen, S. T. (2012). Using Xbox 360 Kinect games on enhancing visual performance skills on institutionalized older adults with wheelchairs. Proceedings of the IEEE 4th International Conference on Digital Game and Intelligent Toy Enhanced Learning (DIGITEL) (pp. 263-267).

Cippitelli, E., Gasparrini, S., Gambi, E., & Spinsante, S. (2014). Depth stream compression for enhanced real time fall detection by multiple sensors. *Proceedings of the IEEE Fourth International Conference on Consumer Electronics, Berlin (ICCE-Berlin)* (pp. 29-30). doi:10.1109/ICCE-Berlin.2014.7034215

Cruz, L., Lucio, D., & Velho, L. (2012). Kinect and RGDB images: Challenges and applications. *Proceedings of the Conference on Graphics, Patterns and Images Tutorials (SIBGRAPI-T)* (pp. 36-49).

D'Strict. (2014). 3D sensing holographic installation. Retrieved from http://global.dstrict.com/projects/j4.php

Dick, J., Almeida, H., Soares, L. D., & Nunes, P. (2011) 3D Holoscopic video coding using MVC, In *IEEE International Conference on Computer as a Tool (EUROCON)*, 1-4. doi:10.1109/EUROCON.2011.5929394

El-laithy, R. A., Huang, J., & Yeh, M. (2012). Study on the use of Microsoft Kinect for robotics applications. Proceedings of the IEEE Position Location and Navigation Symposium (PLANS) (pp. 1280-1288). doi:10.1109/PLANS.2012.6236985

Eonreality (2015) Eonreality. Retrieved June 30, 2015, from http://eonreality.com/

Eyeliner 3D. (2015). Dimensional studios, musion setup: How it works. Retrieved from http://www.eyeliner3d.com/musion_eyeliner_setup_video.html

Figueiredo, M. J., Cardoso, P. J., Gonçalves, C. D., & Rodrigues, J. M. (2014). Augmented reality and holograms for the visualization of mechanical engineering parts. *Proceedings of theIEEE 18th International Conference on Information Visualisation* (pp. 368-373). doi:10.1109/IV.2014.17

Flyway. (2015). 3D holographic projection – the future of advertising? Retrieved from http://flyawaysimulation.com/news/3630/3d-holographic-projection-future-of-advertising/

Fong, S., Zhuang, Y., Fister, I., & Fister, I. Jr. (2013). A biometric authentication model using hand gesture images. *Biomedical Engineering Online, 12*(1), 111. doi:10.1186/1475-925X-12-111 PMID:24172288

Gasparrini, S., Cippitelli, E., Spinsante, S., & Gambi, E. (2015) Depth Cameras in AAL Environments: Technology and Realworld Applications. In L.B. Theng (Ed.), Assistive Technologies for Physical and Cognitive Disabilities (Ch. 2). Hershey, PA, USA: IGI Global. doi:10.4018/9781466673731

Globalzepp. (2015). Retrieved from http://www.globalzepp.com/

Hilliges, O., Kim, D., Izadi, S., Weiss, M., & Wilson, A. D. (2012). HoloDesk: Direct 3D interactions with a situated see-through display. *Proceedings of theSIGCHI Annual Conference on Human factors in computing systems* (pp. 2421 – 2430). doi:10.1145/2207676.2208405

Holodisplay. (2015). Retrieved from http://www.holodisplays.com/

Holomedia. (2015). 3D live interactive holographic. Retrieved from http://www.holomedia.co.uk/

Holus (2015) Holus: The interactive tabletop holographic display. Retrieved from http://www.digital-trends.com/cool-tech/holus-tabletop-hologram-kickstarter/

Jones, A., McDowall, I., Yamada, H., Bolas, M., & Debevec, P. (2007). Rendering for an interactive 360° light field display. In ACM SIGGRAPH 2007. doi:10.1145/1275808.1276427

Kamizono, T., Abe, H., Baba, K. I., Takano, S., & Murakami, K. (2014). Towards activity recognition of learners by Kinect. *Proceedings of the3rd International Conference on Advanced Applied Informatics* (pp. 177-180). doi:10.1109/IIAI-AAI.2014.45

Kim, K., Bolton, J., Girouard, A., Cooperstock, J., & Vertegaal, R. (2012) TeleHuman: effects of 3D perspective on gaze and pose estimation with a life-size cylindrical telepresence pod. *Proceedings of theSIGCHI Conference on Human Factors in Computing Systems (CHI '12)* (pp. 2531-2540). doi:10.1145/2207676.2208640

KinectSpec. (2015). Kinect for Windows sensor components and specifications. Retrieved from https://msdn.microsoft.com/pt-pt/library/jj131033.aspx

Kondori, F., Yousefi, S., Liu, L., & Li, H. (2014). Head operated electric wheelchair. *Proceedings of theIEEE Southwest Symposium on Image Analysis and Interpretation (SSIAI)* (pp. 53-56).

Leap. (2014). Leap motion. Retrieved from https://www.leapmotion.com/

Lim, S., & Kim, S. (2014). Holographic projection system with 3D spatial interaction. Proceedings of the 5th International Conference on Advanced Data and Information Engineering (DaEng-2013) (pp. 409-416). doi:10.1007/978-981-4585-18-7_46

Lippmann, M. (1908). La photographie integral. *Compt. Rend. Acad. Sci., 146,* 446.

Litefast. (2013) Litefast MAGIC displays. Retrieved from http://www.litefast-display.com/products/litefast-products/litefast-magic/litefast-magic.html

Martins, J. M. S., Rodrigues, J. M. F., & Martins, J. C. (2015). Low-cost natural interface based on head movements. *Proceedings of the6th International Conference on Software Development and Technologies for Enhancing,* Fraunhofer FIT, Sankt Augustin, Germany. doi:10.1016/j.procs.2015.09.275

Microsoft. (2014). Kinect for Windows. Retrieved from http://goo.gl/fGZT8X

Mihaylova, E. (Ed.). (2013). *Holography - Basic Principles and Contemporary Applications.* InTech. doi:10.5772/46111

Miles, R. (2012). *Start here! Learn the Kinect API.* Pearson Education.

Musion. (2015). Retrieved from http://www.musion.co.uk/

Noor, A. K., & Aras, R. (2015). Potential of multimodal and multiuser interaction with virtual holography. *Advances in Engineering Software, 81*, 1–6. doi:10.1016/j.advengsoft.2014.10.004

Rahman, M. M., Poon, B., Amin, M. A., & Yan, H. (2015). Support system using Microsoft Kinect and mobile phone for daily activity of visually impaired. In Transactions on Engineering Technologies (pp. 425-440). doi:10.1007/978-94-017-9588-3_32

Rearpro. (2015). Paradigm audio visual. Retrieved from http://www.rearpro.com/

Rennie, J. (2014). The Tupac hologram, virtual Ebert, and digital immortality. Retrieved from http://www.smartplanet.com/blog/thesavvy-scientist/the-tupac-hologram-virtual-ebert-anddigital-immortality/454

RFID. (2014). RFID Reader ID-12LA (125 kHz). Retrieved from https://www.sparkfun.com/products/11827

Sprott, J. C. (2006). Physics demonstrations: A sourcebook for teachers of physics. Univ of Wisconsin Press.

Structure. (2014). Structure sensor. Retrieved from http://structure.io/

Telehuman. (2013). Telehuman. Retrieved from http://www.hml.queensu.ca/telehuman

Verge. (2015). To build a holodeck: an exclusive look at Microsoft's Edison lab. Retrieved from http://www.theverge.com/2011/12/28/2665794/microsoft-edison-lab-holodeck-tour

Vertigo. (2013). Retrieved from http://www.vertigo-systems.com/

Vizoo. (2015). Vizoo, cheoptics. Retrieved from http://www.vizoo.com/flash/

Weiss, C. M., Frid, A., Malin, M., & Ladijenski, V. (2015). Generating 3D CAD art from human gestures using Kinect depth sensor. *Computer-Aided Design and Applications, 12*(5), 608-616.

Xstage. (2015). Retrieved from http://www.xstage.de/

Yamaguchi, M. (2015). Holographic 3D touch sensing display. In *Digital Holography and Three-Dimensional Imaging, DM3A-1*. Optical Society of America. doi:10.1364/DH.2015.DM3A.1

Yun, Y., Changrampadi, M. H., & Gu, I. Y. (2014). Head pose classification by multi-class AdaBoost with fusion of RGB and depth images. *Proceedings of theInternational Conference on Signal Processing and Integrated Networks* (pp. 174-177). doi:10.1109/SPIN.2014.6776943

KEY TERMS AND DEFINITIONS

3D Interaction: A form of human-computer interaction where users are able to move and perform interaction in a three-dimensional space.

Computer Vision: A scientific discipline concerned with the theory behind artificial systems that extract information from images. The image data can take many forms, such as video sequences, views from multiple cameras, or multi-dimensional data (including 3D data). As a technological discipline, computer vision seeks to apply its theories and models to the construction of systems based on (computer) vision.

Gesture Recognition: A topic in computer science and language technology with the goal of interpreting human gestures via mathematical algorithms, in the present case based on computer vision algorithms.

Hologram: A photographic recording of a light field, rather than of an image formed by a lens, and it is used to display a fully three-dimensional image of the holographed subject, which is seen without the aid of any intermediate optics.

Human-Computer Interaction: Also called human-machine interaction, is a researcher field related to the design and use of computer technology, focusing particularly on the interfaces between people (users) and computers; it can both observe the ways in which humans interact with computers as well as design technologies that let humans interact with computers in novel ways.

Interfaces: A shared boundary across which two separate components of a computer system, the exchange can be between software, computer hardware, peripheral devices, humans and combinations of these.

Natural Interaction: The common denomination used by designers and developers of human-computer interfaces to refer to a user interface that is effectively invisible, and remains invisible as the user continuously learns increasingly complex interactions.

Rear Projection: A projection technique where the projector is placed behind the screen, shooting straight towards the audience.

Chapter 8
Sixth Sense Technology:
Exploring Future Opportunities in Human Computer Interaction

Zeenat S. AlKassim
United Arab Emirates University, UAE

Nader Mohamed
United Arab Emirates University, UAE

ABSTRACT

In this chapter, the authors discuss a unique technology known as the Sixth Sense Technology, high-lighting the future opportunities of such technology in integrating the digital world with the real world. Challenges in implementing such technologies are also discussed along with a review of the different possible implementation approaches. This review is performed by exploring the different inventions in areas similar to the Sixth Sense Technology, namely augmented reality (AR), computer vision, image processing, gesture recognition, and artificial intelligence and then categorizing and comparing between them. Lastly, recommendations are discussed for improving such a unique technology that has the po-tential to create a new trend in human-computer interaction (HCI) in the coming years.

INTRODUCTION

Technology has invaded human life tremendously. Gone are the days when kids asked for dolls and cars. These days even toddlers spend hours playing on electronic devices. This trend should not be seen as only a negative. This invasion of technology has its positive side as well. There is no doubt that technological inventions have simplified and improved the quality of people's lives. It has shortened distances, brought people together and simplified tasks. This should be the main objective of inventions and research. They need to be exploited to serve humans in the best possible way. One such technology, unique in its kind, is the so-called Sixth Sense Technology. This technology, though not widely known, has the potential to create a revolution on this planet as it changes the way people and machines interact, thus providing a better and more natural interaction (Gupta & Shahid, 2011; Poongodi, 2012). However, this technol-

DOI: 10.4018/978-1-5225-0435-1.ch008

ogy did not make it to the market as a final product like many other technologies. The world has seen a number of inventions released into the market in the last two decades (Streitz, Tandler, Müller-Tomfelde & Konomi, 2001). Thus, some questions are raised. What are the reasons that Sixth Sense Technology has not been released to the masses yet? Does it lack sponsors? Or is it that this technology is not up to the level of competition compared to other inventions? Or maybe it did not grab the attention of society yet? These questions will be answered at the end of this chapter after discussing the technology.

This chapter will discuss the Sixth Sense Technology, along with the opportunities of such technology and challenges limiting its implementation in real life. Most importantly, it also discusses other trending and competing technologies in the field of Human Computer Interaction. When discussing those technologies, a comparison will be made from which one can get an idea of the different possible implementation approaches of the Sixth Sense Technology. Furthermore, recommendations will be offered for implementing Sixth Sense Technology components and more doors for future research work in the field of HCI will be opened or further exploration.

BACKGROUND

Reviews on the Sixth Sense Technology were mostly positive upon its introduction in media. Arora (2012) described the Sixth Sense Technology as that which upon emergence into market may lead to evolvement of new devices and hence new markets. It could be a big help to people with special needs or could help control machineries in industries, as suggested by the author. However, the author concludes that security threats and other issues are yet to be considered when releasing this technology. In a different review, the authors suggested combining the concepts of Augmented Reality and Sixth Sense in order to come up with new and better gadgets that allow humans to be machine-free (Raghupatruni, Nasam & Lingam, 2013). As they mentioned in their paper, "With the advent of sixth sense technology, if it can have its roots into all the fields we can expect things to happen in a much better way" (p. 39). They explain in details the implementation steps of Sixth Sense Technology in schools and show how time spent in performing tasks is reduced significantly in places like exams and libraries. On the other hand, they explain how some issues are to be tackled with like cost and security threats when implementing this new technology in public places. Singh (2015) conducted his dissertation work on Sixth Sense Technology. In his work, he brought into light the different uses of this technology. It is unique, as mentioned by the author, in the fact that a Sixth Sense Device allows computing and task performing on any nearby surface. However, he also brought into light the challenges that stand as a wall blocking the full implementation of the discussed technology, like security and health concerns, and hardware improvement of the Sixth Sense device. Overall, though many researchers who found the technology of Sixth Sense it to be promising, they suggested further improvements and the addressing of its shortcomings before implementation in real life.

OPPORTUNITIES OF SIXTH SENSE TECHNOLOGY

What Is It?

Sixth Sense Technology, or Sixth Sense, is a concept or an implementation idea introduced by its inventor, Pranav Mistry, in Tedx Talks a couple of years ago. As Mistry and Maes (2009) mentioned, it is a technology designed to bridge the gap between the physical and digital worlds in a very unique and new way. This bridging is intelligently done, to the point that people are able to live their lives normally and interact with physical objects displaying digital information, as if they are in a digital world. Because of this, the technology was named Sixth Sense due to the extraordinary abilities that a person can perform while wearing the device, as if exhibiting an extra sixth sense in addition to the five human senses of hearing, seeing, touching, smelling, and tasting. The technology was presented in the form of a prototype built by Mistry and his team members at the Massachusetts Institute of Technology (MIT) labs. What is more interesting is that new technological ideas usually come at the cost of simplicity. However, the prototype built by Mistry and his team provides a new concept and is simple to set up. It comprises only five modules as depicted in Figure 1, namely a camera, projector, mirror, colored markers, and computing device. The Sixth Sense prototype was built using computer vision and image processing algorithms. All modules are combined to form a wearable device, as shown in Figure 1. So how does it work? The camera plays the role of the user's eyes and sends captured images of the front view to the computing device, which processes and displays results back through the projector onto the object in front of the

Figure 1. Sixth Sense Technology Prototype
(Mistry, 2009)

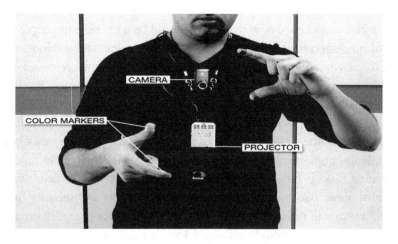

Figure 2. Drawing on wall through hand movements
(Mistry, 2009)

user. The mirror helps to project at a good angle that is visible to the person, while colored markers help in the detection and tracking of the person's hands. This quite simple construction of a working device can perform and simplify many tasks for humans. A person can draw on walls with hand gestures, check the time by gesturing a circle on the hand, view a flight status update on a flight ticket, or use the palm of the hand to dial a number, and much more as shown in Figures 2 through 5. An infinite number of applications can be designed utilizing the concept of Sixth Sense technology.

Figure 3. Using hand to dial phone number
(Mistry, 2009)

Figure 4. Viewing live flight updates on a ticket
(Mistry, 2009)

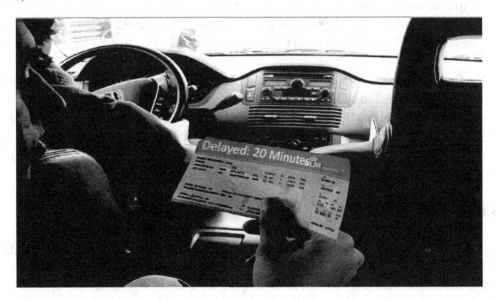

Figure 5. Displaying a real watch on wrist
(Mistry, 2009)

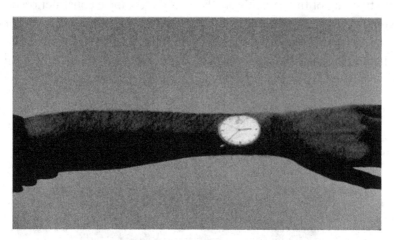

- **Applications of Sixth Sense:** a wide variety of applications of Sixth Sense in different fields exist, including the medical, manufacturing, visualization, path planning, entertainment, and military fields. With this device, a person can accomplish the following:

  - Take a camera snapshot using a simple hand gesture right at the moment with no delays.
  - Check the weather forecast on a newspaper with live blowing winds displayed on the paper.
  - Check Amazon reviews of a book that is displayed digitally on it before buying it.
  - Watch live videos on a piece of paper or live news on a newspaper.
  - View a map on the wall where the user can control the map using zoom and gestures.
  - Sort, resize, and organize phone pictures displayed on the wall with hand gestures.
  - View and recognize people through digital information that is retrieved from the web and displayed on their bodies, which works by face recognition.
  - Understand foreign languages when travelling through instant Google translation.
  - Travel to any destination through GPS service.

As such, Mistry might have been right in calling the device a *Wear Ur World* (WUW). When Mistry's prototype was introduced at Tedx Talks, the crowds were amazed at this technology (literally stood and gave Mistry a round of applause!) that is believed to have put new definitions in the field of human-computer interaction (HCI). It has come up with a somewhat unique way of combining the digital and physical worlds together during a time when the field of augmented reality (AR) is flourishing with researchers who are trying to generate new ideas and inventions.

Why Is It the Focus of this Chapter?

So why is there an interest in such a technology? As is clear, Sixth Sense has many opportunities when implemented as a final device (Rao, 2010). It introduces a new technique of interaction with machines, a natural one, unlike some other inventions. It is a new approach in artificial intelligence. Humans normally communicate through hand movements. With Sixth Sense, communication is still done through hand movements. According to Tomi Ahonen, who is the most influential expert in mobile devices as listed by Forbes in the year 2012 and the most published author in the mobile industry, AR is expected to be the eighth mass media in the coming years (Grier, Thiruvengada, Ellis, Havig, Hale, & Hollands, 2012). He disclosed his predictions during Tedx Talks in 2012 (Grier et al, 2012). Companies are investing in AR every day to come up with new devices in the market. As such, Sixth Sense, which can be categorized under AR, has the potential to lead the technological world in all fields of education, recreation, health, and so on. As proposed by Gupta and Sharma (2012), a virtual classroom using Sixth Sense Technology is an example of implementing Sixth Sense in real life. According to the authors, this will revolutionize the educational system since intangible digital information will be transformed into tangible information where students and teachers can interact with this digital information through hand gestures. These classrooms will include the zoom in and zoom out feature, which helps students focus on certain parts when reading books, the hand calculator, which eradicates the need for students to bring calculators, and many other implementations along with a shift from smart boards that require computers or projectors to smart boards that work with hand gestures only, without the need for projectors and other equipment.

- **Applications of Sixth Sense in Virtual Classrooms:** This implies a drastic shift from the traditional educational system to a fun and interactive educational system as per the education sector.

    - Information will be easily available to students with a quick hand gesture without the need for browsing the Internet on computers.
    - There will be no need to carry calculators to school and college.
    - Calculations will be easily done using the palm as a calculator.
    - Paper notes will be replaced by digital notes that are more interactive and easy to use.
    - Pictures of the outside can be easily taken and viewed in class by the instructor using simple hand gestures.
    - Emails can be viewed by simply making an '@' hand gesture.
    - Students will be kept up-to-date in terms of useful information available on the Internet.
    - E-books will be used in class, and forgetting books at home will not be a problem.
    - Smart classrooms will be built with no projectors or smart boards or marker pens, but with just one Sixth Sense Technology device in each class that does all functions.

Thus, the authors have shown how Sixth Sense could change the educational system to a better and more interactive one. In fact, this is one among other possible implementations of this technology in different sectors to create a better and productive environment. Sixth Sense Technology can also be integrated with other technologies and enhanced in terms of features. It supports multi-touch and multi-user interactions. It can be made small and lightweight and can include all features like Bluetooth, GPS, camera, Wi-Fi, microphone, speakers, and touch pad. This integration can open doors for this invention in the market. It can also be designed to recognize commands using speech or a simple head tilt, and respond accordingly. Furthermore, it can be designed to work on several platforms (like Google Glass), such as iPhone and Android. As per production, Sixth Sense Technology can be implemented using minimum hardware components. It requires only five main parts and integration between them. The device can be used even in the dark due to the built-in projector or laser light. It is an all-in-one device that is easy to carry. Most importantly, Sixth Sense implementation can be perceived by many as a step forward towards developing new methods of human-computer interaction.

As such, many papers were published suggested ideas for the implementation of the Sixth Sense Technology. Nadiger and Bhat (2013) proposed combining Sixth Sense Technology with holography to create a new system that will revolutionize the world, as they mention. Holographic projectors will enable viewing 3D pictures or videos without the use of 3D glasses. The authors propose these two technologies together will be able to create the virtual presence of a human being. This will simplify communication, as they predict. The Sixth Sense Technology will map human movements to a computer, and the holographic projector will take this digital component and convert it into holograms at the other end. The hardware requirements for this approach are the same as those used by Pranav Mistry in his Sixth Sense device, namely sensors, tracking device, camera, mirror, projector, microphone, and a portable computing device as well as a holographic projector that takes inputs specified by a computer and projects 3D holograms. The paper describes in detail how this integrated system will work. First, human movements are mapped onto a digital surface, which is done by a Sixth Sense device. The mouse rollers are connected to a human hand instead, and the computer can detect the hand movements, just like detecting a mouse, using the X and Y axes. This method was done by Pranav Mistry. However, the Nadiger and Bhat want to develop this approach further by having the computer detect the entire body movements, instead of hands only, by placing sensors (vision sensors like charge-coupled device (CCD) cameras to get visual input) on the human body. The movement of the sensors can be tracked on the computer. Finally, the holographic projector, which is connected to the same mapping device, will produce 3D projections of the body movements.

Agrawal and Gupta (2012) have proposed using Sixth Sense Technology to build a mouse movement system using the finger. With this method, a user's hand acts as a mouse. The project in their paper was built similar to that of Pranav Mistry, using the same five main components, namely camera, colored markers, laptop, projector, and a mirror. First, a user with colored markers on his/her finger tips makes a hand gesture. The camera is used to capture live video. This video is sent to the laptop. Inside the laptop is a MATLAB code that does the main processing. This captured video is divided into images, which are processed and sent to the projector. Finally, the mirror reflects the projected image in front of the user. Using this method, a user's hand acts as a mouse. Using hand gestures, different tasks can be done, such as capturing images, browsing the Internet, and more. All the working code has been built with MATLAB using the image processing toolbox. The code has been built in such a way that it recognizes red, green, and yellow marker colors only. This application was confined to the computer screen. The group could successfully implement the Sixth Sense Technology using simple components and spend around $150 on the project. These papers might be a proof of the efficiency and usability of the Sixth Sense Technology, as well as its simplicity and flexibility.

CHALLENGES OF SIXTH SENSE TECHNOLOGY

Where Is It Today?

In spite of the many opportunities of the Sixth Sense Technology discussed in the previous section, Sixth Sense still remains an idea that has not been implemented in real life. It was only developed into a prototype by Pranav Mistry and his work team and presented to the world in 2009. Even during presentation, there were no live demos of the possible applications of the device despite the presenter wearing the device. All possible applications were recorded previously in a video. This raises questions of whether implementing such a technology into a customer end device is possible or not.

Although the world was fascinated with this idea that they found is unique and creative, and in spite of this idea winning many awards, it has not been sponsored by any party to build the prototype further into a finished product. Why? This is because there are a couple of challenges, mainly technical, that limit the implementation of the Sixth Sense. These challenges are same as the ones faced when trying to implement AR in real life. The main challenge is the wide existing gap between fast emerging innovative ideas and the comparatively slow advancement in technology. Sixth Sense Technology, similar to augmented reality, requires advanced software and hardware. Many of those requirements, unfortunately, cannot be met yet. Sixth Sense Technology requires that a single device can recognize different objects in front of the user, perform processing, and output relevant information back onto the objects. This requires a lot of processing. Unfortunately, this implies that hardware limitations are hindering the production of Sixth Sense Technology devices.

It is also interesting to note that although the open source has been given for free to the public by Mistry in 2013 after the Sixth Sense idea has grabbed the interest and attention of hundreds of producers and computer enthusiasts, the code could not be run by the majority (if any) of the people who downloaded the code. Pranav Mistry has confessed that his team was trying to remove the dependency on Microsoft code libraries (Mistry, 2009). Thus, there were some software challenges that have also prevented improving the Sixth Sense prototype further into a final product to be used by consumers. The building of the Sixth Sense concept into a product requires accuracy in object recognition and good calibration of the different components with the user. Possible errors common in AR, such as registration and sensing errors, must be solved when designing the all-in-one device. Software challenges include those in computer vision. A Sixth Sense device responds to the user based on hand commands; thus, advanced image processing is required in order to be able to detect, track, and correctly classify different hand gestures. A common challenge in hand detection and tracking algorithms is how to distinguish between the user's hands and the surrounding environment. Sixth Sense Technology works by detecting and tracking the user hands against any environmental background. It is also preferred that the device works in multi-vendor environments. This will allow the mobile phone to act as the processing unit, whether it is iOS, Android, Windows, or any other programming platform. Thus, the real life implementation of Sixth Sense Technology requires dramatic advances in technology, both hardware and software, many of which have not been achieved until recently.

There are other concerns as well regarding the implementation of such a technology that can retrieve and display digital information continuously. Security and privacy are two big concerns. Through Sixth Sense, a person could obtain information about a total stranger in public due to the face recognition ability of the device; therefore, privacy of strangers may be invaded. The quick access of the device to the web and social networks might increase the risks of hacking of people's accounts. Most importantly, Sixth Sense Technology works by continuous capturing of images or live videos of nearby objects. This raises many concerns of the usage of such technology in the public. This is inferred from the case of Google Glass. The production of Google Glass and release into market was seen by many to be a violation of people's privacy. As such, Google Glass, called 'Glasshole' instead, was banned in many public places (Gibbs, 2014). This privacy concern of the Sixth Sense device must be addressed prior to release of such technology to the public.

In addition, safety and health concerns cannot be neglected as well. The brightness of the projector built into the Sixth Sense device should not affect a user's eyes. Google Glass was banned during vehicle driving in some places (Scheck, 2014). Sixth Sense might also raise similar issues, though it is important to point out that Sixth Sense Technology does not project digital information on top of the user's view space, as is the case with Google Glass. Sixth Sense devices project onto objects in front of the user, thus distractions are believed to be non-invasive. Social acceptance of wearing such devices in the public might take time. Though such devices are no doubt desirable, over reliance might not be beneficial. Such devices tend to drag users away from real life. However, a good point to note is that Sixth Sense may seem to bridge the real and digital world in a quite natural way, since the digital information can be viewed by all people and is not restricted to only the user's sight. Nevertheless, though Sixth Sense may have great potential to revolutionize HCI, the extent to which it will be integrated into human life must be defined (Chopra & Narang, n.d.). For instance, it seems difficult to decide the extent to which this technology should be implemented in educational systems. While it will introduce a new educational environment with lots of advantages, as discussed by Gupta and Sharma (2012), challenges in controlling virtual classes exist, such as controlling cheating during exam invigilation. Such extremely life changing technology requires the acceptance of teachers and students and that they become comfortable with it. To make Sixth Sense into a great technological idea, efforts are required to develop an acceptable design. This is because lessons were learnt from the release of other technologies in the market. Google Glass was criticized by many for its shape, appearance, and impracticality for people wearing eye glasses (Porges, 2015). Furthermore, with no physical surface to touch, Sixth Sense Technology should provide a natural feeling for users and make them feel comfortable when interacting with the device, just like when using physical objects.

- **Challenges of Sixth Sense Technology:** The factors hindering the further production and release of the Sixth Sense devices are summarized as follows:
  - Hardware limitations
  - Software limitations
  - Privacy issues
  - Security concerns
  - Health issues
  - Social acceptance
  - Practicality in real life
  - Acceptable design

SIXTH SENSE TECHNOLOGY: OPPORTUNITIES VS. CHALLENGES

So far, discussion of both opportunities as well as challenges of Sixth Sense Technology has been explained, thus a list of the advantages and disadvantages of this technology can be made. Every innovative idea, as is the case of the Sixth Sense, has its pros and cons. Table 1 illustrates the pros and cons of Sixth Sense.

Being inspired by the paper of Karahanna, Straub and Chervany (1999), and the framework developed by Ammenwerth, Iller and Mahler (2006), an IT adoption model was developed. However, this model is derived from the Probability and Impact Matrix (PIM) from the book about project management of Meredith and Mantel (2011). Table 1 represents the pros and cons of the Sixth Sense. Each pro/con is given a score that equals *probability×impact*. Probability represents the possibility of the feature occurring

Table 1. Pros and cons of sixth sense technology

	Features	Pro/Con	Score	Level
1	Introduces a new method of interaction with objects, a natural one with hand movements that humans are already familiar with.	Pro	0.6×0.6=0.36	HIGH
2	SS requires on-time fast processing, large memory to store digital information of every object, accurate collaboration between the hardware components; these are difficult to achieve.	Con	0.7×0.7=0.49	HIGH
3	Being categorized under AR, it is a promising technology; AR is growing rapidly and expected to become next mass media as discussed earlier; investment in SS expected to be profitable.	Pro	0.8×0.5=0.40	HIGH/ MEDIUM
4	Prone to errors in hand gesture and object recognition algorithms.	Con	0.3×0.6=0.18	MEDIUM
5	SS provides numerous applications in different fields like education, recreation, health; not confined to one industry.	Pro	0.7×0.4=0.28	MEDIUM
6	SS converts intangible digital information to tangible ones, leading to more interaction with the digital world.	Pro	0.7×0.4=0.28	MEDIUM
7	SS provides quick access to information; saves time.	Pro	0.8×0.9=0.72	HIGH
8	Does not require a specific hardware projection surface; any surface can serve the purpose, even walls; hence practical invention.	Pro	0.6×0.6=0.36	HIGH
9	Has tendency to replace physical devices; an example is hand palm replacing a physical calculator.	Pro	0.9×0.4=0.36	MEDIUM
10	Privacy issues arise; like capturing images and retrieving information of people in public.	Con	0.6×0.8=0.24	HIGH
11	Security issues are difficult to tackle, especially that a SS device accesses the Internet and retrieves information frequently.	Con	0.5×0.6=0.30	MEDIUM/ HIGH
12	Safety and health issues need to be addressed; like exposure of users' eyes to projection light for long and using the SS device while performing critical jobs.	Con	0.4×0.4=0.16	LOW
13	SS is flexible and allows room for further improvement and addition of features; can support multi-platforms, or accept both hand gestures and sound recognition.	Pro	0.4×0.7=0.28	MEDIUM
14	SS introduces a new living style, that might be difficult to accept for many people.	Con	0.3×0.3=0.09	LOW
15	The integration of digital world into the real life might drag people away from the real life.	Con	0.2×0.6=0.12	MEDIUM
16	The hardware is easy to build, with only five basic parts connected together.	Pro	0.8×0.8=0.64	HIGH
17	Due to projection, a SS device can be used in dark surroundings as well.	Pro	0.7×0.3=0.21	MEDIUM
18	Interacting through hand gestures for long might be uncomfortable, leading to hand strain commonly known as gorilla-arm effect (Hincapié-Ramos, Guo, Moghadasian, & Irani, 2014).	Con	0.5×0.5=0.25	MEDIUM
19	More chances of social acceptance, since digital information appears to all people, not confined to only user's sight.	Pro	0.5×0.5=0.25	MEDIUM
20	SS devices need to be made small in size and easy to wear; unlike the prototype developed by Mistry. Use of color markers is not practical.	Con	0.8×0.5=0.40	HIGH/ MEDIUM

(values between 0-1). Impact represents the impact of the feature after occurring, whether it is negative or positive. The values of these two factors were predicted by the authors based on the technological advances, trends, and challenges as well as the impacts of some recent technological developments. For instance, the feature number 16 is given high values for both *probability* (Since the hardware being easy to build is a fact) and *impact* (the hardware being easy to be build is important in implementation). Lastly, the scores are given HIGH (red quadrant), MEDIUM (yellow quadrants) or LOW (green quadrant), or a combination based on the quadrant the score falls into, on the designed matrix. The IT adoption model for the Sixth Sense Technology, similar to the PIM chart (Meredith & Mantel, 2011), has been developed as in Figure 6. The circles represent the pros while the squares represent the cons of SS, as discussed in Table 1.

This built IT model works by studying each quadrant. The red quadrant (HIGH scores) represent those features of the technology that are sure to happen and greatly affect the technology implementation. Thus, if majority are pros, the technology is assumed to be well adopted on implementation and release in the market. However, if majority are cons in the red quadrant, then it is assumed that difficulties will hinder the success of the technology upon release. In case of the Sixth Sense Technology, its pros are dominant in the red quadrant. Hence, chances of adoption of SS technology when released are high.

IMPLEMENTATION OF SIXTH SENSE TECHNOLOGY

Recent and Rising Technologies Similar to Sixth Sense

Sixth Sense Technology, as discussed, has created a new definition for HCI. It can be fair to say that it has potential, is unique in idea, and is quite easy to use. Also, it has the potential to succeed in the mar-

Figure 6. IT adoption model of Sixth Sense Technology
(Source: Authors)

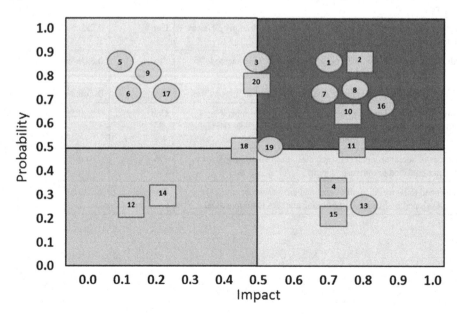

ket, as concluded from the IT model of Figure 6. However, it still remains a concept that has not been implemented as a final product due to many challenges that were also explored in the previous sections. Exploring other technological inventions and ideas in fields similar to Sixth Sense will help establish a blueprint for the successful implementation of Sixth Sense. These similar fields include AR, computer vision, HCI, artificial intelligence, image processing, and gesture recognition.

Augmented reality, similar to Sixth Sense Technology, brings the real and virtual worlds together. It has a long history and has been known since the 1960s. Augmented reality may involve senses like hearing, touching, and smelling. A large variety of different categories exist under AR based on factors as discussed by Van Krevelen and Poelman (2010). Under AR, there is a visual display that can be either video see-through, optical see-through, or projective as well as an audio display. There are also different display positions, such as head-worn, handheld, or spatial. Users may interact with AR devices visually, through gesture recognition, through audio and speech recognition, through text input, or through a hybrid method. In general, AR requires sophisticated hardware and software, similar to Sixth Sense. As such, there are many limitations of AR, namely in portability, calibration, depth perception, over-reliance, and social acceptance. Accurate positioning in some applications and accurate timing in other applications are difficult to achieve. Synchronization remains a hindrance to the vast implementation of AR today. The two common problems when designing AR systems are registration and sensing errors. These are reasons that most AR implementation is limited to smartphones and tablet apps where accuracy is not a critical issue. Improvements in processing speeds of hardware and software are still needed and under research. Another negative point regarding AR is lack of standards in multi-vendor environments. According to Percivall (2011), "There are no standards for AR APIs or data. Thus, developers must rewrite their AR applications for each OS and device platform they want to address. The lack of standards also affects interoperability, such as using AR data from one platform with applications written for another." (IEEE Computer, 2009, p. 2).

However, despite these challenges in implementation, AR has been long introduced to the mainstream, and there is a wide range of applications, including medical, manufacturing, visualization, path planning, entertainment, and military, as explored by Azuma (1997). There are many opportunities for AR to grow. Perhaps, it has grown tremendously in the past few years, and many applications have been designed in this AR Researchers are still going on to explore new implementations of AR. A number of mobile apps have also been developed. A recent three-phase study was conducted in the U.K. in 2013 to demonstrate applications of AR and how this enhances engineering projects. It concluded that AR enhances processes, business value, and the exchange of information and that the construction process has been made easier and faster through the implementation of AR (Fletcher, 2013). In Figure 7, the use of AR is illustrated. Engineers view a real city plan model along with virtual buildings with the help of AR eye worn devices. This eliminates the need to construct real building models to view city planning.

Google Glass became a hot topic right from its introduction in the market in 2013. The invention of Google Glass (Figure 8) attracted news headlines and social media everywhere. It can be considered a measure of success for AR technology. Google Glass can be classified as an AR technology, basically belonging to HUD (head-up displays). It is a huge leap in terms of AR and artificial intelligence as well as HCI. The main goal of the Glass Project was to save time, as per Starner (2013) who is the technical manager of the Google Glass Project and a professor at Georgia Institute of Technology. The device is small and lightweight and includes all features, such as Bluetooth, GPS, camera, Wi-Fi, microphone, speakers, and touch pad. It recognizes commands by speech or just a head tilt and responds accordingly. Unlike AR, Google Glass was designed to work on other platforms, such as the iPhone as well. Upon

Figure 7. Part (a) and (b) illustrate AR in Architectural and Civil Engineering
(Van Krevelen & Poelman, 2010)

(a)   (b)

release, dissatisfaction spread regarding the cost and appearance of the Glasses. While attempts were made to reduce cost and improve the design of the Glasses, another and bigger concern was privacy (Gibbs, 2014). These privacy concerns are similar to those concerning Sixth Sense, that a person could take picture or record another person without permission in public. Overall, Google Glass received positive reviews from many users, but wasn't that hit expected by Google. This might be because it is fair to say that this project was more of a prototype than a finished product. As such, production of Google Glass stopped in 2015 and has not continued further as announced by the company (Porges, 2015).

Virtual laser keyboards work similarly to Sixth Sense Technology. Figure 9 shows the laser keyboard developed by Celluon that is available in the market. Laser keyboards constitute three main modules that are very similar to the modules constituting Sixth Sense, namely the sensing, illuminating, and projecting module (Alkassim, 2012; Fornari, 2012). First, the illuminating module directs a laser beam in front of the user. When the user presses a key, the user's fingers hit the laser beam, which in turn is reflected into the webcam camera. Then, the sensing module, which consists of the webcam camera, captures images and processing is performed to detect keystrokes. The projecting module consists of a projector that projects a keyboard image in front of the user. The laser keyboard was already built by the Celluon Company using their 'patented' technology as described in their YouTube video published on October 2013. It has also been available for sale online. In comparison to the typical physical keyboards, laser keyboards have many positive points that might make them a winner in this contest, such

Figure 8. Google Glass
(Miller, 2013)

Figure 9. Virtual Laser Keyboard
(Fornari, 2012)

as being simple in implementation as well as cheap, easy to carry, and invulnerable to wear and tear (Ferson, 2013). Laser keyboards are a good example of how virtual technologies can surpass physical implementation in many devices.

The Kinect Sign Language Translator, depicted in Figure 10, is a prototype designed by Microsoft Research Asia in collaboration with the Chinese Academy of Sciences and Beijing Union University (Chai et al., 2013). It is principally a system that translates sign language to written Mandarin language and Mandarin spoken language to sign language. This project was meant to bridge the gap between sign language users and verbal language users. The prototype was built using gesture recognition through Microsoft Kinect Technology. The Kinect technology is the same as that used in gaming consoles. Thus, this system works on advanced sensors and software technology. Interestingly, this prototype represents one of the applications of Sixth Sense Technology that could be implemented.

FreeGlass is a wearable hands-free 3D gesture-sensing Digital Eye Glass system built by a group at the University of Toronto (Lo et. al, 2013). This device, shown in Figure 11, has many features similar to the Sixth Sense Technology, in the fact that it connects a virtual world with our real world. In general, this device recognizes the user's simple hand gestures, interprets them, and produces results accordingly, making the user capable of interacting with the virtual features imposed on the surrounding environment. It comprises a 3D camera ASUS Xtion (Prime Sense) and a head-worn display, such as Epson Moverio BT-100, which is connected to a wearable computer like ODROID-X2, which is capable of providing self-gesture AR applications. The ASUS Xtion consists of 3D sensors and is a Prime Sense based range camera that uses an infrared projector and infrared camera for depth map determining. Epson Moverio BT-100 displays the results. Finally, the processing is done by ODRIOD-X2. The 3D camera they use, Prime Sense 3D, can calculate the distances of the objects from the user by means of a depth map. Since

Figure 10. Kinect Sign Language Translator
(Chai et al., 2013)

the background is constantly moving, the camera uses depth information to perform close range hand detection and segmentation and to discriminate between foreground (one's own head) and the surrounding background. The 3D hand gesture recognition consists of two parts, hand detection and gesture recognition. The gesture recognition consists of two stages, segmentation and classification. In segmentation, the camera provides two image types, principally the infrared image (greyscale) and computed depth map. From these two images, the binary image is formed, which provides the final image mask for hand extraction. In the classification stage, two types of hand gestures exist, which are point up and point angled. The images are fed into the neural network and this neural network outputs the probability of each gesture. Regression algorithms are also used. Training is done for variations in hand gestures. This device has many applications, such as providing an AR interface with real physical objects.

Figure 11. FreeGlass, a hands-free 3D gesture-sensing Digital Eye Glass system
(Lo et. al, 2013)

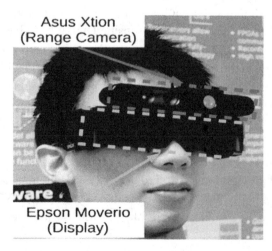

This FreeGlass includes the reality window manager (RMW), where users drag around an augmented window that is capable of features, such as conference calling, browsing web pages, and GPS maps; it also allows specifying objects of interest within the window and scanning quick response (QR) codes. A lot of effort has been put into this device by the team in terms of processing and the results produced are quite satisfactory and incredible. However, many issues are yet to be addressed if the prototype is adapted as a finished product, mainly synchronization and hand recognition. Objects with high brightness intensity in the surroundings hinder the hand recognition process. The chances of inaccurate hand detection are high. As such, this project is an example of the tedious task of combining the virtual and real worlds in an effective manner.

Another approach of combining the virtual and real worlds is through handheld devices. The AR software on handheld mobile devices is improving drastically every year and gaining more popularity. Figure 12 illustrates how an AR app helps in virtually viewing magnetic field lines around a magnet picture. According to Gervautz and Schmalstieg (2012), the first form of AR was in head-mounted displays (HMDs), which displays computer-generated images digitally through a digital video camera and image compositing or optically through mirror see-through displays, which combine onto the real world and allow the user to interact hands free. However, the HMDs have not been so successful due to a lack of devices that are simultaneously attractive, lightweight, and inexpensive. This prompted the popularization of AR software on handheld mobile devices. Several techniques for tracking include fiducial markers, natural feature tracking, global localization systems, and on-the-fly reconstruction, as discussed by Gervautz and Schmalstieg (2012). In terms of interacting with AR programs through the mobile screen, techniques include embodied interaction, tangible interaction, ray picking, and the layered pie menu. The most challenging issue of AR software is tracking and localization by the camera. Another issue of AR apps is visualization. The virtual objects imposed on the real environment should look as real as possible. This depends on factors like rendering, registration (correct position of virtual object with the surrounding), occlusion (correct placing of virtual objects relative to depth), and shadows (virtual objects casting shadows depending on surrounding light intensity). By applying such techniques to Sixth Sense devices, experiencing a virtual world in the real physical world will be implemented more efficiently. A number of AR apps are out in the market and can be used efficiently by users.

Figure 12. Viewing virtual magnetic field lines through an AR app
(Gervautz & Schmalstieg, 2012)

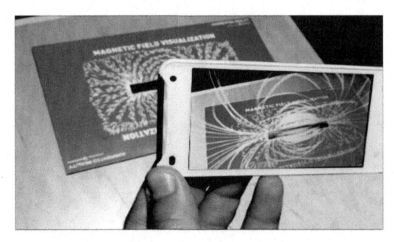

Similar inventions have been released into the market in the recent years, as AR has become a good market in which to invest. However, do all inventions perform a good job of connecting the virtual and real worlds together? Sony's SmartEyeGlass, expected to be released in 2015, is a HUD, that is very similar to Google Glass, as depicted in Figure 13. It is also a good example of how AR could be integrated into real life. It connects to the mobile phone and allows the display of AR apps in front of the user's eyes in the view space (Sony Cooperation, 2015). It even detects head tilts and responds accordingly. Thus, precision and accuracy in detection of head orientation are important. However, though it sounds a promising invention, it is still more of a prototype than a finished product. Those SmartEyeGlass devices work differently in comparison to SS devices. They work within the vicinity user's eyesight, unlike SS that recognizes objects in front of the user. SmartEyeGlass, at least until now, is confined to certain applications. Additionally, makes the user an eyeglass person, unlike Sixth Sense that communicates with digital data through hand gestures. Moreover, those smart eyeglasses by Sony will be subject to the same challenges of Google Glass and Sixth Sense, like safety and security. These prototypes raise questions of the efficiency of HUDs.

Other wearable projects that have been released recently include smart watches like the Apple Watch and SAMSUNG's Wrist Watch. The AR experience in these devices is absent (SAMSUNG, 2015). They perform limited functions like listening to a book or displaying the heart beat rate. However, if the AR experience is added, will the hand wearable perform better than head wearable? One can assume that it is difficult to experience the virtual world through small screens like wrist watches. Moreover, the limitations of the AR handheld devices explored previously also apply to such wrist watches.

Oculus Rift, a finished and incredible Virtual Reality product, unlike the previously discussed prototypes, is to be released in 2016. The prototype is depicted in Figure 14. The Rift provides a great and unique experience, similar to the AR experience in that users experience new worlds that are an extension in case of AR or complete different versions in case of VR to the real world, in the gaming industry. It includes accurate head and positioning tracking (Oculus, 2013). The Rift covers the user's eyes entirely and hence might be thought to create isolation of gamers from the real surrounding world. Other issues are also a concern, such as social acceptance, over-reliance, and health, which make Oculus Rift in a critical phase of a 'yes' or 'no' into the market, just like the Sixth Sense.

Figure 13. SONY's SmartEyeglass
(Claydon, 2015)

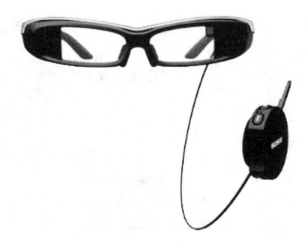

Figure 14. Oculus Rift
(Miller, 2015)

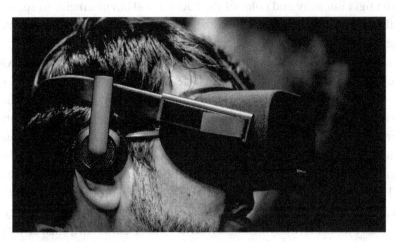

- **Innovative Ideas Similar to Sixth Sense Technology:** Following are the discussed innovative ideas:
  - Google Glass
  - Virtual Laser Keyboard
  - 3D Hands Free Gesture-Sensing FreeGlass
  - Kinect Sign Language Translator
  - AR Wearable Devices
  - AR Handheld Devices
  - Sony's SmartEyeGlass
  - SAMSUNG's Wrist Watch
  - Oculus Rift

SOLUTIONS AND RECOMMENDATIONS

Different Implementation Approaches

Based on the before discussion of the different inventions/prototypes in the world of HCI, a division is possible based on the method of interaction with the device and the placement of the device with respect to the user's body.

The first category is Category A. The approach under this category is that approach implemented by Mistry when developing the Sixth Sense Technology prototype with five main components, which are projector, mirror, camera, portable processing device (like a mobile phone), and colored markers (Mistry, 2009). The device works by camera capture, followed by the processing and display of results of objects in the user's sight. It is worn on the chest. The approach by Mistry in Sixth Sense has a major disadvantage, which is the use of colored markers. The use of color markers for the camera to detect finger movements is impractical. In addition, the size of the prototype is big for a portable device. Moreover, this approach works by projection of the virtual world onto objects. Projection, in general, tends to be affected by the light intensity and color of the background environment. In spite of the limitations of the prototype, the concept of Sixth Sense is somewhat unique because it introduces a natural way of interacting with nearby objects through hand gesture recognition. This natural interaction with machines and the smooth merging of the virtual and real worlds can be regarded as a twist in AR and HCI.

The next, Category B, is the approach of virtual laser keyboards. This approach is very similar to Category A in the fact that it works by image capture, then processing and display. The four main modules for building virtual laser keyboards are the projecting (projector), processing (mobile or computer), illuminating (laser), and sensing (camera) (Alkassim, 2012). However, it has been categorized in a different group due to the fact that devices here are not wearable, unlike Category A. Projection happens from the device in front of the user. Moreover, the use of laser is necessary for Infrared reflection and finger detection. This is unlike Category A, which implements colored markers instead of a laser.

The next categorization is Category C. It constitutes devices that are worn over the eyes. This category includes Google Glass, FreeGlass, Sony's SmartEyeGlass, and Oculus Rift, each of which was discussed in previous sections. However, differences do exist. Category C displays more advancement in software and hardware set-up. These devices can detect head position and head movements. They display digital information in front of the user's eyes. Digital information is projected in front of the user's eyes on the top side. Companies like Google and Sony have definitely excelled over other competitors because the developers were successful in reducing the size of the device. Category C does not require a surface for projection, unlike categories A and B. Further, hand gestures are not used much. An exception is the 3D camera selfgesture sensing, FreeGlass, that was built by a group at the University of Toronto. It is worn over the eyes but depends on hand gesture recognition (Lo et. al, 2013). The Oculus Rift is a bit different in that it isolates users from the surrounding world (Virtual Reality) and is so far restricted to the gaming industry (Oculus, 2013).

Category D is confined to approaches that limit the experience of AR to a small screen. Examples of this approach are the handheld devices with AR apps and wrist-worn devices like smart watches. Here, the connection to the virtual world is only limited to the screen of the handheld device or the wrist watch. Thus, implementation through handheld device screens does not give the same natural feeling as in Sixth Sense or Oculus Rift or Google Glass. Moreover, this approach depends entirely, in terms of hardware requirements, on the handheld device. As such, a lot of hardware requirements are needed for the handheld devices to be able to support a variety of applications. The different categories are summarized in Table 2. It should be noted that this categorization is an updated version to the one presented by AlKassim and Mohamed (2014).

Table 2. Categorizing the different implementation approaches

Criteria	Category A	Category B	Category C	Category D
Method of Interaction	Hand Gesture by Colored Markers	Finger Movement using Projected Laser	Head tracking, Sound Recognition	Object Recognition, Touch Sensing
Position	Chest-worn	Non-wearable device	Eye-worn	Handheld/Wrist-worn
Example	Sixth Sense Technology	Virtual Laser Keyboards	• Google Glasses • FreeGlass • Sony's SmartEyeGlass • Oculus Rift	• AR mobile apps on handheld devices • Smart wrist watches

Comparing the Implementation Approaches

Exploring other technologies can help form a list of reasons that the Sixth Sense Technology has not been developed further and released to the public, in spite of its potential as a new innovative idea and unique approach. The four categories formed in the previously can be compared to generate the pros and cons of each category.

Category A presents a natural method of interaction, using hands, with the virtual information displayed in front of the user. Virtual projection happens on the objects in front of the user. There is no eye strain, as might be possible in the eye-worn devices in Category C. However, there is a possibility of hand strain, commonly known as gorilla-arm effect (Hincapié-Ramos et. al, 2014). In addition, projection is noticeable by all the people around. Thus, it does not isolate a person in his/her own virtual world. However, as mentioned in the previous section, a prototype falling under this category was designed by Mistry and worked by placing colored markers on the user's fingers. This use of colored markers on top of the user's fingers sounds impractical. Further, the size of the prototype was quite large, and the projection does not work well in bright surroundings. The Sixth Sense prototype, in general requires improvement in terms of both software and hardware, and a surface or wall is required to project the images or videos in front of the user. This is unlike Category C, where no projection surface is required.

There has been a considerable increase in the number of eye-worn AR gadgets released into the market. In addition to the ones discussed previously, there are also Samsung Gear VR, Razer OSVR, Archos VR Headset, Microsoft HoloLens, HTC Vive, and Panasonic VR goggles (Betters, 2015). Those eye-worn devices, falling under Category C, have been successfully built into devices that are closer to finished products than mere prototypes. They present sophisticated software implementation. However, certain issues of such new inventions are prominent; for instance, concerns of isolation from the real world exist. As mentioned, Google Glasses were banned in some places while driving (Scheck, 2014). Category C does not seem to represent a natural method of interaction in comparison to Category A.

Category B was implemented as a finished product by several companies, one of which is Celluon's laser keyboard. This category is similar to the Sixth Sense Technology of Category A, except that it replaces the colored markers in Sixth Sense with laser technology. Thus, in this regard, this approach is more practical in comparison to Category A since users need not carry the laser module. It is built-in inside the device itself. Any surface could be used for projection, even a user's hands. However, this approach suffers from difficulty in detecting keystrokes under a highly bright environment, colored surfaces, or rough surfaces. In addition, in spite of the portability and advantage of such keyboards in terms of wear and tear, none of the companies succeeded in reaching the typing speeds and accuracy of physical keyboards as per the reviews of users, leading to their widespread doom in the market (Ferson, 2013).

Category D, as discussed previously, limits the AR experience to the device screen. Many apps are being developed to work through mobile devices. Though these apps impose a virtual world into real life, this bridging between the two worlds is only confined to the device screen. As such, whatever be the number of AR apps developed by developers, some might find this approach in general unable to surpass other approaches. The other approaches in Category A, B, and C provide a more interactive virtual world experience. Thus, Category D is the least favorable approach. In spite of this, investment in AR apps is growing and is an active and successful market.

Thus, as can be seen, each category has its pros and cons. These are summarized in Table 3. As inferred, Sixth Sense Technology in Category A seems to provide a natural way of experiencing a virtual world while interacting with real objects. It can be applied to many life activities and is not confined to certain industries. It seems to have potentials to compete with other innovative ideas in the market. However, the prototype designed was quite poor and couldn't display all the possible implementations of the technology and thus requires further improvements. Controversially, a number of eye-worn technologies of Category C have been released into the market with more advanced prototypes (they cannot be called finished products yet, as indicated by the developers themselves), in spite the fact that the AR experience provided by them is confined to the user's view point in front of the eyes. On a different scale is Category D, where the AR experience is limited to a small screen of handheld devices, which rely on how much improvement can be made in the hardware of those devices. Thus, it is fair to say that Sixth Sense Technology of Category A might surpass other categories in terms of concept, creativity, and virtual world experience. However, Google Glass and similar projects in Category A surpass other categories in terms of hardware and software implementation. Nevertheless, it is interesting to note that while Google Glass and Sony's SmartEyeGlass were sponsored and developed by companies, the Sixth Sense prototype was built by an MIT media lab team using Microsoft core libraries. If Sixth Sense is implemented by huge sponsors as well, the resulting device will surely be fascinating as well.

FUTURE RESEARCH DIRECTIONS

With the categorization and comparison of different technologies in similar fields as Sixth Sense Technology, insight can be garnered from the implementation requirements of such technology so that it can be produced as a finished product and be made available to the public for revolutionizing the world of HCI.

Sixth Sense Technology requires fast computing devices to be able to recognize objects or people in front of users, retrieve information about them from the web, and project digital data. Hand gestures are also recognized and processed to understand what the user intends to do. These devices are wearable by the user, and must be small and compact, unlike the chest-worn prototype presented by Mistry, to ensure ease of use throughout the day. The dependence on colored markers on top of the user's fingers for accurate hand gesture recognition, in the Sixth Sense prototype of Mistry (2009) and Agrawal and Gupta (2012), is impractical, and more efficient methods of hand gesture recognition are required.

Table 3. Comparing the different implementation approaches

	Category A	**Category B**	**Category C**	**Category D**
Pros	• natural interaction • simple implementation/working	• simple implementation/working • use of laser more practical than colored markers • lightweight	• small size • no projection surface required • no colored markers required • no problem with bright environment	• rising technology • easier to develop AR apps than a complete device
Cons	• use of colored markers is impractical • bulky size • projection surface needed • performance affected by light and moving background	• performance affected by surrounding bright light	• social acceptance and over-reliance • isolation from real life	• limited AR experience • hardware limitations of handheld devices

There are many hand movement detection algorithms that work without the need to wear colored markers. An example is the Kinect sensor implemented by Chai et al. (2013) in their project, the Kinect Sign Language Translator. In terms of software development, extremely accurate positioning and accurate timing are required. These software requirements might be difficult to achieve. Synchronization might remain a hindrance to the vast implementation of Sixth Sense in life activities. This is inferred from the synchronization challenges in other AR devices. Thus, there are hardware and software requirements for Sixth Sense that cannot be met by the currently available technologies yet.

Most importantly, this innovative and unique HCI approach requires sponsoring and support by large companies, like other projects, such as Oculus Rift. To reach the public for widespread use of Sixth Sense, it must be financially affordable. This is to avoid the inconvenience that took place upon the release of Google Glass and its limited availability to most people.

To integrate Sixth Sense Technology into daily life activities, the device must be comfortable and of acceptable appearance and design. These lessons are learned from other innovations that reached the market and were not successful because of discomfort and bad design. For instance, the virtual laser keyboard developed by Alkassim (2012) works properly by implementing a unique implementation approach of mostly image processing, and is a good substitute for physical keyboards. However, the size of the prototype is too big and impractical for real life implementation. The brightness of the projecting module of Sixth Sense can also be controlled, altering from high under a bright environment to low in dark environments. This is to avoid health issues. Health issues are common in eye-worn devices in terms of eye strain due to nearby projection.

Sixth Sense Technology can also support many features to simplify life activities and can be made comfortable for people with special needs. A complaints regarding Google Glass include that they do not consider hearing impaired people.

Most importantly, the technology needs social acceptance. This is possible when the extent to which this technology will be integrated in human lives is defined. For instance, in educational systems, Sixth Sense can be implemented in such a way that students integrate digital information into real life but would not be distracted into a virtual world away from the real life. Therefore, the opportunities of Sixth Sense Technology and uniqueness of this innovative technology should be recognized. With this recognition, efforts must be made to implement this technology as a final product by keeping in mind the challenges that stand as hindrance in developing such technologies. Finally, the result will be the availability of such technology to the public and a new era in HCI, similar to that of the release of touch screens (Myers, 1998) and AR apps into the market.

There is no doubt that such wearable inventions are strongly coming in the market. Google Glass has not died yet. Google Glass is expected to be back in the market with updated and improved features, in what is called Google Glass 2.0 and Google Glass EE (Enterprise Edition) (Page, 2014). It is believed that these features will include improvements in both software and hardware performance of the Glass. This shows that though the release of Google Glass Explorer Edition, was met with a number of negative reviews as discussed before, it formed a good start for the production of other improved versions expected to be released soon in or after 2015. Google Glass, with its limited applications, was greatly successful in the enterprise market. An example is Augmedix that was used in the healthcare sector to automatically record videos hands-free in hospitals (Shakil, Tran, & Dehy, 2014). As such, Google Glass and such wearable devices like Sixth Sense might most probably be a huge success in the business market.

A scenario of implementation of Sixth Sense Technology is that of virtual classrooms, as explained by Gupta and Sharma (2012). The educational system can be made more interactive and informative, with an ability to quickly browse the Internet for more information. For instance, in libraries, students can view reviews on books with the help of SS devices before borrowing books. Classrooms can become more entertaining if students can view videos displayed on top of textbook images. This can be so called as 'interactive' textbooks. SS devices can decrease the bag loads for students and teachers when going to schools/colleges, as many devices can be replaced like calculators and notepads. SS devices can make students calculate on their hand palms instead, and can also make students use white plain papers to display digital books. Sixth Sense can also revolutionize airports and make travelling more interactive. Passengers can view any delays in the flight time or change of gate numbers digitally on their flight ticket. SS devices can scan the flight ticket, retrieve information from the airport operation control center regarding any changes, and display the information back onto the printed flight tickets. In this way, the emerging of 'interactive' airports will be possible. Similarly, many fields can be improved with the implementation of the SS technology.

Considering the implementation requirements of the Sixth Sense Technology, it is worthy to discuss the recent advancements in science and technology. Similar to how a number of innovative gadgets were introduced lately into the market, a lot of advancements have been made in hardware and software. In terms of processing, the speed of processors has been improving since the past few decades. Intel is commonly known for the production of the fastest processors, like Core i7 and Core i5. Parallel computing and multi-threading (commonly called hyper-threading technology, HT) have been a focus for many researchers to come up with fast processors (Tian et. al, 2003). These are essential for a quick detecting and responding SS device. Another improvement in hardware is in batteries. Smart devices are limited by their period of duration without being powered. Long lasting batteries are required when a lot of processing is performed, as in the SS technology. Lithium-ion batteries deteriorate with aging. Hence, there have been a number of attempts to come up with more efficient long-lasting batteries. Examples are the solid state batteries and triple capacity batteries developed by MIT scientists, and aluminium graphite batteries developed by Stanford University scientists (Edwards, 2015). The former Nano 'yolk' triple batteries developed at MIT can charge full in only 6 minutes and are inexpensive in production. Similarly, other promising battery inventions are being produced and tested. Regarding the huge data storage requirements of SS technology, cloud storage and similar technologies can help store large amounts of data and make the data accessible/available at the same time. In terms of software, object recognition and hand gesture recognition are crucial for the working of SS devices. Recently, many algorithms are being designed in these fields. There are a number of different types of hand gesture recognition algorithms, like the template-matching, appearance-based, skeletal-based and the 3D (Pavlovic, Sharma & Huang, 1997). No algorithm has proved to be more successful over the other algorithms. Every approach has its pros and cons. However, there are many products in the market that proved efficiency in hand, body and face movements recognition. A common example is the Kinect sensor by Microsoft and ASUS Xtion Pro. Accurate detection and tracking of hand gestures need to be achieved. Machine learning like the involvement of trained Artificial Neural Networks (ANN) and Support Vector Machines (SVM), has proved efficient in object and hand detection. These methods have been implemented in papers reviewed by Suarez and Murphy (2012). Hence, with these advancements in science and technology, the release of the sixth sense technology into the market is possible in the near future. Even if Sixth Sense Technology is implemented in certain industries or in small-scale due to technical limitations, this will serve as a good start for future large-sale implementation and further advancements in a world of six senses.

CONCLUSION

This chapter discusses the trending technologies in the current century in the areas of computer vision, virtual reality, AR, artificial intelligence, and HCI. More specifically, it reviews a technology called Sixth Sense that has been named this due to its ability to provide a feeling of possessing a sixth sense in addition to the five human senses. It bridges the gap between the real and virtual worlds in a natural interactive manner and could have many applications if released in the market. The first Sixth Sense prototype was developed by Pranav Mistry, introduced on Tedx Talks in 2009 to the public, and the open source code was available online in 2013 to the people. However, since then, there have not been any improvements or efforts in providing this technology to society. This is due to the many challenges that are faced, some of which are common challenges regarding AR and similar innovations. As such, those innovations were reviewed and categorized according to certain defined criteria. A comparison has been made between the different categories as well as the advantages and disadvantages of each category. This review into those innovative devices will help explore the different possible implementation approaches of the Sixth Sense Technology. This review will also help avoid mistakes when developing Sixth Sense into a finished product by learning from the mistakes and issues faced by other inventions. Finally, future recommendations are discussed regarding providing this technology to the people. One important conclusion drawn from all the innovative ideas is that no overall idea stands out. Each idea is strong in some aspects, while weak in other aspects. Further, while different new innovative ideas are always introduced, the advancement in the technical world improves gradually. This non-parallel development pace of the two makes it difficult to implement many innovative ideas. As such, many software and hardware requirements are not yet met. This is similar in the case of the Sixth Sense Technology. This might explain why it has not been implemented as a final product. However, there is no doubt that the Sixth Sense Technology, when implemented, will introduce a new era in HCI; that of natural interaction with digital objects by simple hand gestures and of close interaction with the virtual world while living in the real world.

Thus, it is fair to say that Sixth Sense Technology has the potential to revolutionize the IT industry. At this point, the questions raised in the beginning of this discussion can be answered. What are the reasons that Sixth Sense Technology has not been released to the public yet? Several challenges exist that are predominantly technical, which makes it difficult to implement Sixth Sense Technology on a large scale in today's life. However, there are advancements in science and technology, which allow small scale implementation of the experience of Sixth Sense. Does it lack sponsors? Yes, it does. Sixth Sense Technology was presented as a prototype built by an MIT lab team. Projects like Google Glass and Oculus Rift could reach the market since these innovative ideas were supported. Is the problem that this technology is not up to the level of the competition compared to other inventions, or that it does not attain the attention of the public? The answer is definitely no. Sixth Sense Technology is a new interactive innovation with a unique concept of naturally living a virtual world imposed on the real world. It attracted public attention when presented in 2012 and has the potential to become a big hit in the market upon release.

REFERENCES

Agrawal, P., & Gupta, K. (2012). Mouse Movement Through Finger by Image Grabbing using Sixth Sense Technology. *International Journal of Engineering Science and Advanced Technology*.

AlKassim, Z. (2012). Virtual laser keyboards: A giant leap towards human-computer interaction. *Proceedings of the 2012 International Conference on Computer Systems and Industrial Informatics (ICCSII)* (pp. 1-5). IEEE. doi:10.1109/ICCSII.2012.6454614

AlKassim, Z., & Mohamed, N. (2014). Sixth sense technology: Comparisons and future predictions. *Proceedings of the 2014 10th International Conference on Innovations in Information Technology (INNOVATIONS)* (pp. 122-127). IEEE.

Ammenwerth, E., Iller, C., & Mahler, C. (2006). IT-adoption and the interaction of task, technology and individuals: A fit framework and a case study. *BMC Medical Informatics and Decision Making*, 6(1), 3. doi:10.1186/1472-6947-6-3 PMID:16401336

Arora, M. (2012). Basic Principles of Sixth Sense Technology. *VRSD International Journal Of Computer Science and Information Technology, VSRD-IJCSIT*, 2(8), 687–693.

Azuma, R. T. (1997). A survey of augmented reality. *Presence (Cambridge, Mass.)*, 6(4), 355–385. doi:10.1162/pres.1997.6.4.355

Betters, E. (2015). Virtual Reality: The VR headsets to buy in 2015, whatever your budget. Retrieved from http://www.pocket-lint.com/news/132945-virtual-reality-the-vr-headsets-to-buy-in-2015-whatever-your-budget

Chai, X., Li, G., Lin, Y., Xu, Z., Tang, Y., Chen, X., & Zhou, M. (2013). Sign language recognition and translation with Kinect. *Proceedings of theIEEE Conf. on AFGR*.

Chopra, A., & Narang, N. (2014). The Sixth Sense Technology and Its Various Security Threats. *International Journal of Information & Computation Technology*, 4(7), 663-670.

Claydon, M. (2015). Alternative realities: from augmented reality to mobile mixed reality.

Edwards, L. (2015). Future batteries, coming soon: charge in seconds, last months and power over the air. *Pocket Lint.com*. Retrieved from http://www.pocket-lint.com/news/130380-future-batteries-coming-soon-charge-in-seconds-last-months-and-power-over-the-air

Ferson, P. (2013). Review: Celluon Magic Cube laser keyboard. *Neowin.net*. Retrieved from http://www.neowin.net/news/review-celluon-magic-cube-laser-keyboard

Fletcher, S. (2013). Opportunities in Augmented Reality for Engineers. *Geodatapoint.com*. Retrieved from http://geodatapoint.com/articles/view/opportunities_in_augmented_reality_for_construction_operations_processes

Fornari, F. (2012). The future of human-computer interaction: overview of input devices.

Gervautz, M., & Schmalstieg, D. (2012). Anywhere interfaces using handheld augmented reality. *Computer*, 45(7), 26–31. doi:10.1109/MC.2012.72

Gibbs, S. (2014, February 19). Google Glass advice: how to avoid being a glasshole. *The Guardian, Technology.*

Grier, R. A., Thiruvengada, H., Ellis, S. R., Havig, P., Hale, K. S., & Hollands, J. G. (2012). Augmented Reality–Implications toward Virtual Reality, Human Perception and Performance.*Proceedings of the Human Factors and Ergonomics Society Annual Meeting,*56(1), 1351-1355. SAGE Publications. doi:10.1177/1071181312561388

Gupta, A. K., & Shahid, M. (2011). The Sixth Sense Technology.*Proceedings of the 5th National Conference; INDIACom-2011 Computing For Nation Development* (pp. 10-11).

Gupta, M., & Sharma, S. (2012). *Virtual Class room using six sense Technology. IOSR Journal of Computer Engineering* (Vol. 6). IOSRJCE.

Hincapié-Ramos, J. D., Guo, X., Moghadasian, P., & Irani, P. (2014). Consumed Endurance: A metric to quantify arm fatigue of mid-air interactions.*Proceedings of the 32nd annual ACM conference on Human factors in computing systems* (pp. 1063-1072). ACM. doi:10.1145/2556288.2557130

Karahanna, E., Straub, D. W., & Chervany, N. L. (1999). Information technology adoption across time: A cross-sectional comparison of pre-adoption and post-adoption beliefs. *Management Information Systems Quarterly, 23*(2), 183–213. doi:10.2307/249751

Lo, R., Chen, A., Rampersad, V., Huang, J., Wu, H., & Mann, S. (2013). Augmediated reality system based on 3D camera selfgesture sensing. *Proceedings of the 2013 IEEE International Symposium on Technology and Society (ISTAS)* (pp. 20-31). IEEE.

Meredith, J. R., & Mantel, S. J. Jr. (2011). *Project management: a managerial approach.* John Wiley & Sons.

Miller, C. C. (2013). Google searches for style. *The New York Times. Retrieved, 5.*

Miller, J. (2015). What it's like to use the Oculus Rift and Touch you'll buy in 2016: Diving ever deeper into another world. Retrieved from http://www.cnet.com/products/oculus-rift/

Mistry, P. (2009). SixthSense. Fluid Interfaces Group, MIT Media Lab. Retrieved from http://www.pranavmistry.com/projects/sixthsense/

Mistry, P., & Maes, P. (2009). SixthSense: a wearable gestural interface. Proceedings of the ACM SIGGRAPH ASIA 2009 Sketches (p. 11). ACM.

Myers, B. A. (1998). A brief history of human-computer interaction technology. *interactions, 5*(2), 44-54.

Nadiger, N., & Bhat, A. (2013). Sense, H. P. U. S. Applications (IJEBEA). Retrieved from www.iasir.net

Oculus, V. R. (2013). *Oculus Rift: Next-Gen Virtual Reality.* Oculus VR.

Page, C. (2014). Intel-powered Google Glass 2 set to shake up the enterprise in 2015. *The Inquirer.* Retrieved from http://www.theinquirer.net/inquirer/news/2384204/intel-powered-google-glass-2-set-to-shake-up-the-enterprise-in-2015

Pavlovic, V., Sharma, R., & Huang, T. (1997, July). Visual interpretation of hand gestures for human-computer interaction: A review. *IEEE Transactions on Pattern Analysis and Machine Intelligence*, *19*(7), 677–695. doi:10.1109/34.598226

Percivall, G. (2011). Increasing Market Opportunities for Augmented Reality Through Collaborative Development of Open Standards. *Position Paper for the International AR Standards Meeting*.

Poongodi, M (2012). Sixth Sense Technology. *Int. J. EnCoTe*, 102, 09 – 20.

Porges, S. (2015). The Problems With Google Glass: A Eulogy. *Forbes*. Retrieved from http://www.forbes.com/sites/sethporges/2015/01/16/the-problems-with-google-glass-a-eulogy/

Raghupatruni, S., Nasam, N., & Lingam, K. (2013). Sixth Sense Enabled Campus-Possibilities and Challenges. *International Journal of Computers and Applications*, *75*(8).

Rao, S. (2010). Sixth sense technology. *Proceedings of the 2010 International Conference on Communication and Computational Intelligence INCOCCI* (pp. 336-339). IEEE.

Samsung. (2015). Wearable Tech. Retrieved from http://www.samsung.com/us/mobile/wearable-tech

Scheck, A. (2014). Special report: Seeing the (google) glass as half full. *Emergency Medicine News*, *36*(2), 20–21. doi:10.1097/01.EEM.0000443910.87918.22

Shakil, I., Tran, P., & Dehy, R. (2014). *U.S. Patent Application 14/167,353*.

Singh, K. J. (2015). Sixth Sense Technology and Its New Applications. *International Journal of Emerging Research in Management and Technology, 4*.

Sony Cooperation. (2015). SmartEyeglass. Retrieved from https://developer.sony.com/devices/mobile-accessories/smarteyeglass/

Starner, T. (2013). Project Glass: An Extension of the Self. In *Pervasive Computing* (pp. 1536-1268).

Streitz, N. A., Tandler, P., Müller-Tomfelde, C., & Konomi, S. I. (2001). Roomware: Towards the Next Generation of Human-Computer: Interaction based on an Integrated Design of Real and Virtual Worlds. In Human-Computer Interaction in the New Millennium (pp. 551-576). Addison Wesley.

Suarez, J., & Murphy, R. R. (2012, September). Hand gesture recognition with depth images: A review. Proceedings of the RO-MAN, 2012 IEEE (pp. 411-417). IEEE. doi:10.1109/ROMAN.2012.6343787

Tian, X., Chen, Y. K., Girkar, M., Ge, S., Lienhart, R., & Shah, S. (2003, April). Exploring the use of hyper-threading technology for multimedia applications with Intel® OpenMP compiler. In *Proceedings of the InternationalParallel and Distributed Processing Symposium '03*. IEEE. doi:10.1109/IPDPS.2003.1213118

Van Krevelen, D. W. F., & Poelman, R. (2010). A survey of augmented reality technologies, applications and limitations. *International Journal of Virtual Reality*, *9*(2), 1.

KEY TERMS AND DEFINITIONS

Augmented Reality: The technology of viewing of virtual elements overlaid on the real world with the help of computer processing.

Embodied Interaction: A technique by which users interact with virtual objects through touching the device screen.

Fiducial Markers: Certain patterns designed on objects, like black and white bar codes, that help in object detection or tracking.

Global Localization Systems: A method of determining the position relative to a large environment constructed by 3D.

Layered Pie Menu: The method where moving towards or away from the object opens up several menus from which to select.

Natural Feature Tracking: A tracking technique that works by determining the pose relative to a known surface in the surrounding environment.

On-the-Fly Reconstruction: A method of regenerating a new physical environment, like viewing a virtual sofa in a physical living room.

Ray Picking: The technique of selecting an object in the surroundings by casting a virtual ray on it through the mobile screen.

Registration: A measure of how the virtual world is integrated onto the real world.

Tangible Interaction: A method by which the physical object itself is moved.

216

Chapter 9
Interacting with Augmented Reality Mirrors

Cristina Portalés
Universitat de València, Spain

Sergio Casas
Universitat de València, Spain

Jesús Gimeno
Universitat de València, Spain

Ricardo Olanda
Universitat de València, Spain

Francisco Giner
Universidad Politécnica de Valencia, Spain

ABSTRACT

This chapter deals with the topic of Augmented Reality Mirrors (ARMs) – a kind of specular interfaces making use of Augmented Reality technology. The review presented in the chapter first analyses the current setups for the construction of ARMs. Secondly, it presents a study on their potential for inferring in human perception (e.g. behaviour and emotions) and the high interactivity potential and usability they have. In the third place, it shows their use in different areas of knowledge, namely entertainment, edutainment, clothing, arts and medical therapy. Then, the chapter presents a discussion, highlighting the current technological barriers and the need for more research. Finally, future challenges are provided.

INTRODUCTION

Rochat and Zahavi (2011) define mirrors as "peculiar objects associated with peculiar, uncanny experiences": Compared to other objects, mirrors are uncanny at a basic physical and experiential level. The natural attraction that mirrors have for human beings may be explained by cognition and neurological factors, and many studies have been carried out related to visual perception in mirrors (Dieguez, Scherer, & Blanke, 2011; Duñabeitia, Molinaro, & Carreiras, 2011; Jones, Collis, Watson, Foster, & Fraser, 1994; Sambo & Forster, 2011; Savardi, Bianchi, & Bertamini, 2010). Indeed, they are a source of visual enhancement as well as illusory perception. Physically, mirrors are a particular kind of surface in the environment, typically flat and polished. Any surface in the environment reflects light, but a perfectly flat and polished mirror reflects close to a 100%, depending on how it is manufactured. In simple physical terms, mirrors are obstacles to light with the particular property of abruptly inverting its direction in space while maintaining its structure, hence the structure of the optic array that we perceive.

DOI: 10.4018/978-1-5225-0435-1.ch009

Unlike regular mirrors, augmented reality mirrors (ARMs) can virtually change the image of the scene reflected in the mirror by means of the augmented reality (AR) technology. Overall, the AR systems are those that simultaneously (Azuma, 1997): 1) combine real and virtual objects; 2) are interactive in real time and 3) are registered in 3D. Therefore, to be considered as an ARM these characteristics have to be fulfilled. In this regard, there exist other computer-based mirror setups where image processing is applied but e.g. there isn't any kind of 3D registration, such as in (Cheng et al., 2008; Fujinami, Kawsar, & Nakajima, 2005; Jun-Ren, Chien-Lin, Jin-Kun, Jar-Ferr, & Chung-Hsien, 2008; Kim, Lee, & Kim, 2004; Morimoto, 2001; Poh, McDuff, & Picard, 2011; Shahid, Krahmer, Swerts, Melder, & Neerincx, 2009; Ushida, Tanaka, Naemura, & Harashima, 2002). These works are usually referred as digital or interactive mirrors, being ARMs a special and/or an extended case of them. – In order to highlight that an ARM follows the Azuma's definition, in some parts of the text we use the term 'pure' ARM.

The term 'AR' was first coined by Caudell and Mizell (1992) to describe a digital display used by aircraft electricians that blended virtual graphics onto a physical reality. At that time, the definition of the AR technology was linked to head-mounted displays (HMDs), as being the unique displays using this technology (Figure 1 left). It is afterwards when AR applications were related to other kind of displays, and thus the definition of AR was extended and unlinked to the display technology. However, it is not until the beginning of the new century that AR applications can be found in which a change of paradigm was introduced by changing the spatial positioning of the camera and introducing the user(s) as a part of the augmented scenario, so that ARMs were born (Figure 1 right).

Since then, the research community and also some industries have invested in the design and construction of ARMs for different purposes. Given the increasing number of such mirrors and the different features they consider, a well-established taxonomy of ARMs is needed. In this regards, it is one of the aims of this chapter to establish a taxonomy that serves as a reliable classification of these mirrors, to what both technological and user-related issues have to be taken into account. Besides, and in order to establish the features of the taxonomy, it is also one of the aims of this chapter to provide a deep review of the state of the art in ARMs, considering the different application areas, highlighting the specific characteristics of such mirrors and giving a comparative study.

In the following sections, the technology beyond the design of ARMs and their implications related to perception and human factors are reviewed. Afterwards, the different areas of application where ARMs play an important role are introduced, focusing on the great benefits and potential of this technology.

Figure 1. Change of paradigm (example of vision-based ARM)

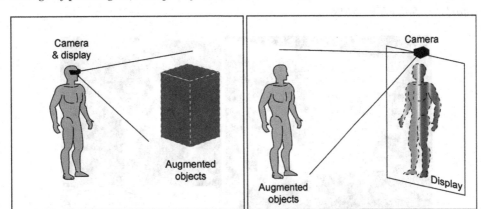

Based on these issues, a comparative table of the different state of the art ARMs is given and discussed, by following the proposed taxonomy. Finally, our insights on future directions and conclusions are reported.

CONCEPT AND DESIGN OF AUGMENTED REALITY MIRRORS

The design of ARMs is mainly comprised of two parts:

1. The tracking technology or inputs, i.e. the kind of sensor(s) that track the positioning of users and/ or objects in real time to allow the 3D registration of the real and virtual worlds; and
2. The display technology or outputs, i.e. the approach to visually merge and visualize virtual and real information.

Tracking Technology / Inputs

Different kind of sensors are used to obtain 3D registration in AR applications, such as mechanical, optical (e.g. RGB or IR cameras), acoustic or inertial sensors (Portalés Ricart, 2009, pp. 121-146). Nowadays, tracking is mostly achieved with vision-based approaches by using optical sensors, and there exist different software solutions that allow the creation of augmented reality applications, such as ARToolKit (ARToolKit community, 2015; HITLab, 2003), where special makers are used to provide user interaction. Moreover, the development of new approaches and the evolution of the computer vision technology allows the registration to be achieved with natural feature tracking techniques with sufficient accuracy. In this sense, the use of additional devices and/or objects is not required, and therefore users do not need to carry any kind of device that may hinder the sense of immersion, while the interaction can be produced with e.g. gestures.

Through Figure 2 and Figure 3 left an example of the evolution of tracking technology is shown for different versions of the Pictogram Room (Casas, Herrera, Coma, & Fernández, 2012; Herrera, Jordan, & Gimeno, 2006; Salve TV, 2008), an ARM for the treatment of Autism Spectrum Disorders (ASD). In Figure 2. left, the user (head and hands) and objects of the environment are tracked with infrared technology (version released in 2006). In Figure 2. right, both users and objects are tracked with AR markers

Figure 2. Images of the Pictogram Room, where: left, IR-based tracking (Herrera et al., 2006); right ARToolKit markers (Salve TV, 2008)

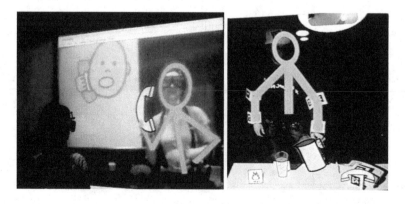

Figure 3. Examples of the construction of ARMs, where: left, a video-based ARM with back-projection onto a projection screen, from the Pictogram Room (Casas et al., 2012); right, an optical-based ARM with a half-silvered mirror and a back projection (from the user perspective the virtual character matches his image; from the camera perspective, it does not)

and making use of the ARToolKit library (version released in 2008). In Figure 3. left, a Kinect sensor (Microsoft, 2015) is used to track the full movements of a user (version released in 2012). Differently from the first and second cases, in the last case the user is not required to wear any kind of artefacts, thus resulting in a more natural interaction.

Display Technology / Outputs

Regarding the display technology, there can be found two different paradigms for building ARMs: the first uses live video stream to render the real scene whereas the second uses a half-silvered or semi-transparent mirror. From now on, we will refer to the first design concept as video-based ARMs, and the second as optical-based ARMs. This design concept is aligned with that of the AR technology (e.g. optical vs. video see-through HMDs) (Bimber & Raskar, 2005, pp 71-72).

In video-based ARMs, synthetic and real objects are computationally merged together and the scene is usually rendered on a PC screen or back-projected onto a projection screen (Figure 3. left). Several examples of video-based ARMs can be found. For instance, in Rahman et al. (2010), a mirror system, to display representations of users with virtual makeup features, was presented. The system consisted of a PC screen, a webcam, an IR camera and RFID technology. Additionally, two IR emitters were fitted in the user's ear-pins in order to determine the approximate distance of the user to the screen. The user was able to view the possible outcomes of different makeup applications in the digital mirror. It also incorporated 3D face reconstruction, IR-based face tracking and OpenGL content to deliver an augmented made-up face. In Straka et al. (2011), an ARM that renders the user image from different angles was introduced. To that end, the user body was spatially (3D) reconstructed. The mirror consisted of a monitor and a set of eight cameras situated in a room forming a circle, with the user situated at its center.

On the other hand, in optical-based ARMs, virtual and real objects are optically merged (Figure 3 right). The virtual objects appear to the back of the reflected image in a half-silvered or semi-transparent mirror, as they are rendered in a LCD monitor that is situated to the back of the mirror or back-projected to the mirror. For instance, an optical-based ARM was introduced in Alhamid et al. (2012) to facilitate and enhance the user's awareness of various physiological functions using biomedical sensors in real time. The system was composed of a mirror, a small projector and a camera. Additionally, it was equipped with biofeedback sensors, a pressure pad, a decision support agent, and a set of response interfaces. Users could use their fingers to navigate through the biofeedback information that was collected and displayed onto the mirror in real time. Proximity sensors located along the edge of the mirror were used to measure the position of fingers and pass this information to the computer to control the mouse movement and actions.

Some works dealing with a comparative study of optical vs. video-based displays are found in (Azuma, 1997; Bimber & Raskar, 2005, pp. 71-92; Rolland, Holloway, & Fuchs, 1994). Although none of these works relates to the special case of ARMs, some of the reported characteristics can be extrapolated for ARMs (e.g. resolution). In the following lines, some of these issues and others are briefly reported:

- **Resolution:** In the video-based ARMs the resolution of the real and synthetic worlds is restricted by the imaging sensors and the display technology. On the other hand, in the case of the optical-based ARMs the real world is seen by the naked eye and thus it has a greater resolution than the synthetic world.
- **Field of view (FOV):** In the case of video-based technology, the acquired image of the real world is restricted by the FOV of the camera(s), which is usually different from the human FOV; in optical-based technology such restriction is not present.
- **Eye-to-Eye:** In optical-based ARMs the image that users perceive from themselves is that of a regular mirror, and thus eye-to-eye visual interaction is direct, natural. On the contrary, this is not possible with the video-based case – though approximate solutions can be found by eye tracking and image interpolation –, as the image of the user is retrieved by a camera (or cameras) fixed at a certain location.
- **Depth:** In optical-based ARMs, the virtual image is rendered at some (often fixed) distance, while the user itself and other real objects are at varying distances. Therefore, if the virtual and real distances are not matched for the particular objects that the user is looking at, the users perceive wrong relative depths, and thus the augmented scene is not properly visualized. Additionally, the real objects are perceived stereoscopically and thus it is required to perform eye tracking to adapt the virtual objects to the user point of view, as in e.g. (Jae Seok, Gi Sook, Tae Hwan, & Soon Ki, 2014), so the rendered image is only correctly placed for a single user. An example of this is depicted in Figure 3. right, where a wrong registration of virtual and real worlds is perceived from a third person point of view. On the other hand, in the video-based case both real and virtual worlds are displayed in the same plane and there is no need to retrieve eye tracking, while the virtual and real objects appear optically correct for the user and other viewers. However, neither the virtual nor the real world is seen stereoscopically in this case.
- **Occlusions:** In video-based displays, the occlusion of overlapping virtual and real objects is computationally solved, and usually a depth image is used to calculate the relative depths between them. On the other hand, occlusion is a difficult issue to solve in optical-based displays, and some authors propose different solutions as e.g. adding a light-blocking device in the form of an LCD panel underneath the semi-transparent mirror (Mulder, 2006).

- **Qualitative Aspects:** Qualitative aspects of the displayed augmented scene include e.g. the shape of the objects, their colour, brightness, contrast, shading, texture, and level of detail. As in video-based ARMs both the virtual and the real environments are digitalized and computationally blended, both virtual and real worlds may have similar qualitative aspects, and thus the augmented scene can bring more sense of realism than in optical-based ARMs. For instance, in the video-based case, it is easier to match the brightness of the real and virtual worlds and synthetic shadows can be easier to create on the real objects.

PERCEPTUAL AND HUMAN FACTORS ISSUES

ARMs are interactive per se, as they are based on AR technology. Additionally, they are highly intuitive, as usually interaction is provided by means of natural movements of users when they look the reflected image of themselves through the mirrors. In the following lines some issues related to perception and human factors are reviewed, namely augmentation, number of users, stimuli and level of interaction.

Augmentation (User-Centered vs. Non-Centered)

In ARMs, the synthetic objects augmenting the real world can be related to the user himself or to other objects in the environment. The former case can be referred as user-centered augmentation, while the latter case is non-centered.

In user-centered augmentation, the image that users perceive of themselves is virtually modified. An example if this is the Augmented User by Giner Martínez and Portalés Ricart (2005a, 2005b), which proposed a game of changing personalities/identities by means of users being augmented themselves with virtual content. To the best of our knowledge, this work can claim to be the first attempt to build a user-centered ARM interface, and it can be considered as the predecessor of other AR applications and research works proposing an identity change by the use of ARMs, as in e.g. (Castro & McDonald, 2012; Maister, Slater, Sanchez-Vives, & Tsakiris, 2015; Mayans Martorell, 2012a). In the initial arrangement, the mirror showed users being converted in the Mr. and Mrs. Potato characters (Figure 4 left), as it was built for two users interacting simultaneously. Other versions of the Augmented User showed users being transformed into the famous film characters Jack Lemmon and Walther Matthau (Figure 4 right) or Stan Laurel and Oliver Hardy, and also by changing the faces of the two users that were interacting. Later, the authors introduced a multi-mirror setup (with three ARMs), where users experimented an identity transformation by moving from one mirror to the others. The outcomes of the research highlighted the fact that the users experimenting different identities through the user-centered ARM, reacted with a change in their own behavior. For instance, when being transformed into the cartoon characters of Mr. and Mrs. Potato, a kind of funny game was established between the two users, provoking laughs and fun; on the other hand, when being transformed into famous characters, users tried to imitate them, including their tone of voice and the way they moved or acted.

On the other hand, in non-centered applications the focus can be placed on either adding virtual content to the environment, or adding virtual content to objects in the environment (augmenting objects). In these cases, as the augmentation is external to the users, the attention is placed in the augmented objects and usually a task has to be performed by using them in a certain way (recall Figure 2).

Figure 4. Users interacting with the Augmented User ARM (Giner Martínez & Portalés Ricart, 2005a, 2005b)

Number of Users (Single User vs. Multiuser)

A further classification can be given based on the number of people interacting simultaneously. Therefore, we can differentiate between single user and multiuser applications.

Single user applications deal only with one user and are usually related with user-centered AR scenarios. Optical-based ARMs are of such kind, as the displayed virtual environment is adapted to the user point of view. Also, some video-based ARMs can be found that restrict the interaction to a single user, such as in Hilsmann and Eisert (2009). Typical examples of this kind of applications are those related with the clothing or cosmetic industries, where users can change the clothes they wear or can test different types of makeup. It must be also considered as single user applications those that only allow one user interacting with the system, even though there may be more users viewing the ARM. An example of this can be found in Martinez Plasencia et al. (2014), where one user is handling an augmented interface while other people in the showroom are visualizing the augmented scene.

On the other hand, multiuser ARMs allow the interaction of more than one user simultaneously. It can be distinguished the case in which users do actions in an independent way, without interfering with the actions performed by others users, such as in (Giner Martínez & Portalés Ricart, 2005b, 2007), and the case in which several users can carry out a task collaboratively, either in one or in both of the real and virtual worlds, as for instance in (Portalés & Perales, 2009; Portalés Ricart, Perales Cejudo, & Cheok, 2007).

Stimuli (Visual, Sonic, Haptic and Multimodal)

Visual stimuli are predominant in augmented reality applications, and thus also in ARMs. Nevertheless, other stimuli can be considered as part of the augmented scenario, such as sonic and tangible stimuli. In some cases, the tangible elements can be further augmented with virtual contents, such as in Herrera et al. (2006). In other cases, they can be the interface to interact with the virtual contents, such as in Rahman et al. (2010). On the other hand, sonic stimuli can be generated in real time by the computer or can refer to pre-recorded audio which is triggered by user actions, e.g. (Portalés Ricart et al., 2007). It can be also the case that the sound produced by the user(s) is collected with microphones and serves as the interaction element of the augmented scene, as in (Portalés & Perales, 2009).

Level of Interaction (Low vs. High)

By the use of ARMs, a new kind of interaction is proposed: users interact with the augmented world, where they form an active part, as their reflected image (or their augmented image) is the central part of the created environment. In this way, interaction appears as more natural and intuitive.

Some ARM applications provide merely augmentation to some kind of objects (or the user himself), while others additionally allow the interaction of users with the augmented content. According to these definitions, the level of interaction can be referred as low or high, respectively. Examples of ARMs providing low level interaction can be found in e.g. (Eisert, Fechteler, & Rurainsky, 2008; Pereira, Silva, & Alves, 2011; Vera, Gimeno, Coma, & Fernández, 2011). Examples of a high level interaction are e.g. (Hilsmann & Eisert, 2009; Portalés Ricart et al., 2007).

AREAS OF APPLICATION

Entertainment, Education and Edutainment

Many researchers have reported that AR has an immense potential to enhance users' learning and teaching experiences in different areas including e.g. science, environmental science, microbiology or biomedicine and that it can support and enhance a variety of pedagogical approaches, such as constructivist learning, situated learning, game-based learning and enquiry-based learning (Bower, Howe, McCredie, Robinson, & Grover, 2014). Many of the developed AR applications in the area of education have a fun and/or gaming component. In the same way, many of the developed AR applications for the entertainment field have a learning component, and thus usually the term of edutainment (education and entertainment) is usually preferred.

Many examples can be found in the research community showing the benefits of ARMs in these fields. For instance, the Augmented Teaching application by Giner Martínez and Portalés Ricart (2007) is a video-based ARM that follows the concept of the Augmented User, but introduces some changes in order to be applied for the edutainment sector. Basically, in this application more users were allowed to interact simultaneously in a single mirror and the physical markers are simplified in order to be carried out easier by children. Through a new kind of AR-theatre setup, it was proposed that an audience located at the other side of a projection screen could see the augmented reality scenario with the augmented actors.

A different mirror setup was proposed in Portalés Ricart (2007a, 2007b) and Portalés Ricart et al. (2007), consisting of a kind of augmented toy-house built with LEGO blocks. Differently from most of the ARM applications, the mirror-like screen was intended to render the augmented image of some physical dolls that acted as avatars of the users, rather than the users themselves. The application was designed to explore coexistence and multicultural factors through gaming, with the use of a video-based ARM displayed on a PC screen. The augmented scenario was built with the MXR ToolKit library (Mixed Reality Lab, 2006) and it consisted on a coexistence game for children, which had to deal with different social, cultural and pedagogical issues to interact with a partner. In the proposed augmented environment, tangible, visual and auditory stimuli were present.

After the availability of the Kinect sensor for PC in 2011, many applications made use of this technology. For instance, in Vera et al. (2011) a virtual character controlled by an actor is presented. The

Figure 5. Users interacting with the ARM in (Portalés Ricart, 2007b)

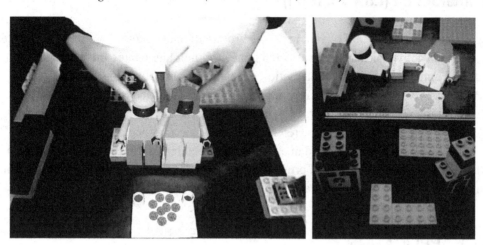

character talks with an audience through an ARM. The proposed system was composed of two scenarios: the control scenario, where the movements of the actor were tracked with a Kinect sensor; and the augmented scenario, where the audience could interact with the avatar and other virtual objects. The actor was further allowed to choose the avatar facial expression by using a WiiMote control. The audience could talk with the avatar or walk around him and the virtual objects while they could see themselves through the ARM. Another example is presented in Li and Fu (2012), where an optical-based ARM was built to show an application called Air Drum, where a user standing in front of the mirror was able to control and play a set of virtual drums. The movements of the user and thus the interaction was acquired with a Kinect sensor.

Parallel to the available works in the research community, there exist commercial solutions making use of ARMs or interactive mirrors, specially related to the entertainment industry. A good example is the EyeToy Play (Playstation, 2003), a video game for PlayStation 2 first released in 2003. In this platform different actions are triggered by moving one's body, which is captured by the integrated camera – the EyeToy. The software recognizes pixel changes in the video image (2D registration) and compares the proximity of the change to other game objects to play the game. Its second version, the EyeToy Play 2 (Playstation, 2004) released in 2004, uses the image acquired by the camera to render the players on a television screen, allowing them to interact with different virtual objects that are present on the augmented environment.

More recently, commercial applications for the Xbox 360 equipped with a Kinect sensor also make use of ARMs. For instance, the game Fantastic Pets puts players on-screen where their movements and voice commands allow them to play side-by-side with a pet of their own creation. Players start with four domestic animals that can be morphed into imaginative creations from mystical unicorns to ferocious dragons. Kinect for Xbox 360 technology enables players to step inside the world and onto the screen where they can play and care for their pets (IGN, 2010). Another example is the game Kinect Party (Lynch, 2012) which provides eighteen different modes that incorporate features of the Kinect motion-sensing and camera system. The game can support the tracking of up to six players that can select any one of the eighteen modes, or opt to have the game randomly select the modes and cycle through them every few minutes.

Clothing, Cosmetic and Optical Retail

During the last years, different ARM solutions have been introduced in the clothing, cosmetic and optical retail sectors. While customers are shopping, mirrors are used to see how they look like with the products before buying them, and they can be replaced by their corresponding virtual ones when ARMs are used. In Robina Town Center (2012), ARMs are installed in real shops, therefore customers can try many different clothes and accessories very fast without search them in the shop. Commercial applications like the one shown in Zugara (2015) provide virtual clothes and accessories, so users can try them on and shop from home. Both ARMs (at shop or at home) have in common that the user is not limited by the physical elements which can be found or carried while shopping, and all the articles are available in every size to try them on.

Pachoulakis and Kapetanakis (2012) perform a review of virtual fitting rooms that include ARMs. In the one hand, this report highlights the importance of the "fun factor" because it attracts possible customers. In the other hand, it reviews the different kind of motion capture technologies and 3D visualization techniques, which enable the simulation of realistic clothes based on the user's movement and morphology.

Most of the ARMs in clothing, cosmetic and optical retail are video-based. A camera is used to capture the image of the user, from which its position and movements are acquired, which is finally augmented and displayed in a monitor or big screen. Planar fiducial markers are used in Imagine That (2015a) to show rigid clothes over the customer. In Pereira et al. (2011) user's face and hands are recognized without markers, and the user movement is computed using inverse kinematics. With the aim to improve the mixture between the real user and the virtual clothes, different approaches can be found. Imagine That (2015b) implements 3D deformable clothes so the apparel looks more realistic. Fitnect Interactive (2014) uses RGB-D cameras to improve the 3D registration between the customer and realistic 3D clothes. In this case the real size of the clothes can be used because RGB-D cameras calculate the real volume of the user in metric units. In Hilsmann and Eisert (2009) the real customer clothes can be modified in color and texture using a 3D reconstruction vision-based algorithm. In this case, virtual clothes keep the illumination and shape from the real ones so the registration with the user is very realistic. However, only a few parameters can be modified. In Straka et al. (2011) a free view-point ARM is presented using 8 RGB-D cameras around the user. The customer can change the view to see how he looks like from every angle wearing the virtual clothes. An example of an optical-based ARM for the clothing sector is the Virtual Dressing developed by Magic Mirror (2014), which has been exhibit e.g. at the PARCO Millenia Walk mall (TIC Singapore, 2013) and provides different apps: wear and compare, virtual dressing, play and win, photo booth and advertising. In Anthony (2011) a magic bathroom mirror is presented, which is an optical-based ARM that uses Kinect technology to provide human-computer interaction. Additional interaction is provided through objects (skin care products, prescriptions) with RFID tags that are recognized by the system.

Although full body ARMs are mostly used in virtual fitting rooms, other kinds of mirrors are simulated with ARMs. In Eisert et al. (2008) a small ARM is used in order to create a virtual mirror for the real-time visualization of customized sport shoes. In this case, the ARM is similar to the one used when trying on new shoes in a shop. Both feet tracking is implemented using the silhouette extracted from the camera image. Very realistic 3D models are used, which can be personalized at runtime. In Difei et al. (2014) and in Yuan et al. (2011) an upper part mirror is simulated to try on glasses in real time without markers. A video-based ARM is used in order to create a very realistic mixture of the glasses on the head of the customer, including occlusions between real and virtual information. When mobile devices are used as visualization devices, the ARM is similar to a hand mirror. In Total Immersion (2014) a commercial application for selling glasses is shown, where customers can try on every model using their tablet or mobile device. L'Oréal (2015) and EZface (2015) present hand-held ARMs too, where users can try different pre-designed make ups. In these cases, users can share their results in social networks, so the ARMs may attract many potential customers and not only the one trying on the products.

Museums and Artistic Exhibitions

The use of AR through the artistic community is extended, some of them making use of ARMs. Because of the illusions that such mirrors introduce, they are an appeal to deal with perception issues, also questioning user identities, which has been the motive of different artistic pieces in the last years. For instance, in Un∞ three different identity changes are proposed through three different augmented mirrors, each of them dealing with different aspects related to human perception (Figure 6): the emotional mirror, referred to the psychological identity, the true I against the apparent one, the one that is shown to others; the stereotype mirror, referred to the physical identity, the physical I pretended or invented, designed to the personal pleasure and for the others; and the multicultural mirror, referred to the social identity, i.e. a sum of identities (Martínez De Pisón et al., 2006; Portalés Ricart, 2009). The setup is composed of three aligned video-based ARMs with back projection. Each mirror allows simultaneous interaction with two users, where each one wears a set of AR-based markers on its head and a pair of markers on its hands.

Other artistic exhibitions make use of facial recognition to propose an identity change, following the Augmented User metaphor by literally changing the image of the users for faces of other individuals and/or adding synthetic objects in the augmented mirror. For instance, in Faces by Castro and McDonald (2012), people virtually exchange their face. The installation uses the idea of wanting a new identity:

Figure 6. Image of the artistic piece Un∞ at the Centro Párraga (Murcia, Spain)

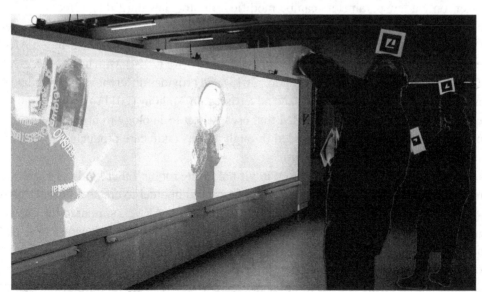

when the subject is placed by the first time in front of the mirror, he sees his face unchanged, but after closing their eyes to make a wish and open them again, find they have a new one. Users get a mixture of fear, surprise and fun experience. The Augmented User Interface by Mayans Martorell (2012a, 2012b) is composed of a set of artistic trials programmed in Processing, and through the app, the viewer can have access to different artistic applications where the alteration and perception of their own identity is questioned. In both cases, the setup is composed of a video-based ARM displayed on a screen.

A different kind of concept is proposed in AR-Jazz, which is an artistic piece to visualize sound and movements in live jazz performances through a video-based ARM (Portalés & Perales, 2009). The augmented scenario is built by using the MaxMSP software (Cycling, 2015), and both the musicians and the audience are able to see the musicians on the stage and a 3D shape representing the sound. In this context, the musicians mainly interact with the 3D shape, which is displayed in the ARM, through the sound produced by their instruments. An additional interpreter (one of the musicians, a singer or a dancer), wears an inertial motion unit, to additionally interact with the mirror by means of his movements.

Another mirror arrangement and artistic concept is given in Portalés et al. (2010), where the augmented users are inserted into lineal video sketches, also displayed in a video-based ARM. The motivation of this piece departs from the idea that "history" is usually seen as too-boring to learn by young people, and thus it tries to show some historical moments in a fashion way. This application is achieved by combining two technologies: the first one is a cinema filming with authors that interpret a sketch; the second part concerns the AR and it is managed with the ARToolKit library. In this mirror, users see themselves virtually transformed in one of the actors thanks to the Augmented User metaphor, being augmented with some kind of 3D shapes. To increase engagement, actors at the video sketches do talk to the user, looking to where he/she is located. Both technologies are visually integrated within a combination of spatial aligned projections.

Another interesting video-based ARM for museums is introduced in Gimeno et al. (2011) (Figure 7). The system consists of two projection screens that mix the exhibition environment with multimedia and virtual 3D objects that visitors can manipulate through a combination of AR markers and a Kinect sensor. At the exhibition environment, the users are able to walk through a map of the Valencia region,

Figure 7. Image of the ARM presented (Gimeno et al., 2011)

which contains a total of 70 hot points that refer to different heritage sites of interest. User interaction with the hot spots allow them to virtually visit the sites within an augmented environment. A work in a similar line, but using a map of Slovakia, is presented in Haladová et al. (2014).

Medical Therapy

Medicine has been traditionally one of the first and main application areas of AR (Azuma, 1997). As computers have gradually invaded our societies, the application of IT solutions to medical procedures has become increasingly common. IT applications in medicine include computer vision and imaging (Doi, 2007), robotics (Taylor & Stoianovici, 2003), database and information systems (Müller, Michoux, Bandon, & Geissbuhler, 2004), VR (Krijn, Emmelkamp, Olafsson, & Biemond, 2004; Malloy & Milling, 2010; Rose, Brooks, & Rizzo, 2005) and AR (Tang, Kwoh, Teo, Sing, & Ling, 1998), to name a few.

Since the first X-Ray images were taken in 1896, a great deal of effort was driven to create devices that allowed physicians to see inside the human body. After Computer Tomography (CT) was invented in the 1970s, and MRI became available in the 1980s (Sielhorst, Feuerstein, & Navab, 2008), research for innovative medical imaging procedures focused on the development of AR tools that allowed physicians to obtain more information about the patient's body in real-time. In this regard, some of the research focused on the X-Ray paradigm to obtain see-through images of the body without having to perform surgical incisions (or making small ones) in the patient's body. Augmentation techniques are especially important in micro-surgery where minimum invasive techniques are required (being spine and brain surgery the main reference in micro-surgery). The smaller the incision the less the surgeon is able to actually see. Thus, the use of AR is fully justified in order to enhance the view of the surgeon. Examples of this ideas can be seen in (Birkfellner et al., 2002; Fuchs et al., 1998; Marescaux, Rubino, Arenas, Mutter, & Soler). A short review can be looked up in Shuhaiber (2004).

Although Computer Aided Surgery (CAS) and image-based diagnostic have been the traditional areas where AR has been applied, AR and ARM systems are being deployed also for therapy improvement.

On the other hand, mirrors have been traditionally used in medical therapy for a long time. The uses of mirrors in therapy include pain relief, rehabilitation and treatment of anxiety disorders, among others. One of the most common uses of mirror therapy (MT) is the treatment of phantom limb pain (PLP). Several works have studied the use of mirror therapy for PLP (Chimes, Bernstein, Cortazzo, & Huber, 2009) and the use of MT has proven to be effective (Chan et al., 2007) in the treatment of this condition, although the amount of pain relief obtained is controversial.

MT in rehabilitation includes treatment of patients with cerebral palsy (Feltham, Ledebt, Deconinck, & Savelsbergh, 2010), recovery from hemiparesis (Altschuler et al., 1999; Dohle et al., 2009; Stevens & Stoykov, 2003) and motor rehabilitation after a stroke (Thieme, Mehrholz, Pohl, Behrens, & Dohle, 2012; Yavuzer et al., 2008), to mention just a few. Another use of MT includes the treatment of anxiety disorders, such as anorexia nervosa (Key et al., 2002) or body dysmorphic disorder (Windheim, Veale, & Anson, 2011), and other rarer conditions such as mirror agnosia, mirrored-self misidentification or asomatognosia (Connors & Coltheart, 2011; Fotopoulou et al., 2011; Paysant, Beis, Le Chapelain, & André, 2004).

Although the use of mirrors can be helpful for the treatment of several conditions, illness and disorders, the reflection (even if we can distort the image by the use of optical mechanisms) of just a real depiction of the human body, constrains its use to a few applications. Moreover, some of the uses of mirrors in therapy are limited by the physical space and vision angle that the specific set-up offers.

In contrast, the combination of mirrors or mirror-like perspectives with the use of the AR paradigm can bring a whole new set of applications and therapies, and can enhance and improve the traditional uses of MT, overcoming most of its limitations. Thus, although surgery and image-based diagnostic have been the traditional areas of AR application, the use of AR (with or without mirrors) for therapy is being explored in the last years. AR allows treating other disorders such as phobias (C. Botella, Bretón-López, Quero, Baños, & García-Palacios, 2010; C. M. Botella et al., 2005; Juan et al., 2005) or cognitive problems (Richard, Billaudeau, Richard, & Gaudin, 2007) that will be harder to treat using a mirror. AR is being used also for the treatment of PLP, as in (Carrino et al., 2014), for cerebral palsy rehabilitation (Correa, Ficheman, do Nascimento, & De Deus Lopes, 2009) or for the treatment of motor impairment (Alamri, Jongeun, & El Saddik, 2010; Burke et al., 2010).

Although some ARM works can be found in other related medical fields, such as anatomy education (Blum, Kleeberger, Bichlmeier, & Navab, 2012), it is harder to find ARM systems for medical therapy use. There are some works, such as (Desmond, O'Neill, Paor, McDarby, & MacLachlan, 2006; Regenbrecht, Franz, McGregor, Dixon, & Hoermann, 2011; Trojan et al., 2014), although they are not pure ARM systems but adaptations of the mirror therapy. They make use of the mirror paradigm but in a first-person fashion instead of allowing the users to see a reflected image of themselves. Also, the VirHab system introduced by Feintuch et al. (2009), targeted at treating pain and impairment of upper extremities, is based on video processing rather than providing a 3D registration of virtual and real objects, so it cannot be considered a pure ARM.

The potential of ARM systems is not being fully exploited, probably because not all the medical therapies require a mirror image, and simpler AR systems are sufficient in most cases, or maybe because the shortcomings of current technology prevent to achieve better results. One of the most interesting uses of ARM technology for medical therapy can be found in the Pictogram Room (Casas et al., 2012; Herrera et al., 2006; Salve TV, 2008). This is a video-based augmented mirror application that was designed to help people with ASD. Its goal is to help them overcome the difficulties they have in understanding body language, body awareness, imitation or joint attention. These critical skills can be addressed in an entertaining way, so that children with ASD can learn while they play (see Figure 8).

Figure 8. Dealing with autism with the ARM developed in Casas et al. (2012), where: in the left image a trainer and a user with ASD are interacting with one of the applications, showing only virtual avatars; in the right image, a user with ASD is interacting with the ARM-like application. Note that for the purpose of the current book chapter, actors with non-ASD have been used in the production of the images

DISCUSSION AND FUTURE RESEARCH DIRECTIONS

ARMs are interesting from a conceptual point of view, as they can bring new ways of interaction and perception through an augmented self-observation.

Given the increasing number of ARM works, and the many directions that they follow (video-based vs. optical-based, different tracking systems, different levels of interactions and stimuli, etc.) a well-established taxonomy of the different ARM systems is needed, which shall include both technological and user-related issues. In this regards, we have proposed a taxonomy considering, as the technology, the inputs (tracking) and outputs (displays) and, as user-related issues, the augmentation, number of users, stimuli and level of interaction. The classification in these items has not been arbitrarily established, but is a reflection of the differential features of the state of the art in ARMs, which has also been provided after an exhaustive literature review. In Table 1 a summary of the proposed taxonomy is given, were the reviewed ARMs are classified, also addressing the area of application for what they have been constructed. It has to be highlighted that the works included in this table are those that follow the Azuma's definition of Augmented Reality, and thus can be considered as pure ARMs. Although an intensive search has been done on different editorial portals, we acknowledge that maybe some existing works have not been included due to the huge amount of research work on the topic of Augmented Reality and also due to the lack of indexing, access and/or visibility of some publications.

Table 1. Classification of ARMs (only pure ARMs are here addressed and thus other digital and/or interactive mirrors are not included)

Reference	Tracking	Display	Augmentation	Users	Stimuli	Level of interaction	Area of application
(Giner Martínez & Portalés Ricart, 2005a, 2005b)	Vision-based (markers)	Video-based (projector)	User-centered	Multiuser	Visual	Low	Entertainment
(Herrera et al., 2006)	IR	Video-based (projector)	User-centered	Single user	Visual Haptic	Low	Medical therapy
(Martínez De Pisón et al., 2006)	Vision-based (markers)	Video-based (projector)	User-centered	Multiuser	Visual	Low	Artistic exhibitions
(Giner Martínez & Portalés Ricart, 2007)	Vision-based (markers)	Video-based (projector)	User-centered	Multiuser	Visual	Low	Edutainment
(Portalés Ricart et al., 2007)	Vision-based (markers)	Video-based (screen)	User-centered (avatar) & non-centered	Multiuser	Visual Sonic Haptic	High	Edutainment
(Eisert et al., 2008)	Natural features & single camera	Video-based (screen)	User-centered	Single user	Visual	Low	Clothing
(Salve TV, 2008)	Vision-based (markers)	Video-based (projector)	User-centered	Single user	Visual Haptic	Low	Medical therapy
(Hilsmann & Eisert, 2009)	Vision-based (markers)	Video-based (screen)	User-centered	Single user	Visual	High	Clothing
(Portalés & Perales, 2009)	Inertial sensor & microphone	Video-based (projector)	Non-centered	Multiuser	Visual Sonic	High	Artistic exhibitions
(Sato, Kitahara, & Ohta, 2009)	Vision-based (markers) & 2 video cameras	Optical-based (screen)	User-centered & non-centered	Single user	Visual tangible (no augmented)	High	Multipurpose

continued on following page

Table 1. Continued

Reference	Tracking	Display	Augmentation	Users	Stimuli	Level of interaction	Area of application
(Portalés et al., 2010)	Vision-based (markers)	Video-based (projector)	User-centered	Single user	Visual Sonic Tangible (augmented)	Low	Museum
(Rahman et al., 2010)	IR & RFID	Video-based (screen)	User-centered	Single user	Visual tangible (no augmented)	High	Cosmetic
(Anthony, 2011)	Depth (Kinect)	Optical-based (screen)	User-centered & non-centered	Single user	Visual	High	Multipurpose (shopping, social media)
(Gimeno et al., 2011)	Vision-based (markers) & Depth (Kinect)	Video-based (projector)	User-centered & non-centered	Multiuser	Visual Sonic Tangible (augmented)	High	Museum
(Pereira et al., 2011)	Vision-based (markers & natural features)	Video-based (screen)	User-centered	Single user	Visual	Low	Multipurpose
(Straka et al., 2011)	Vision-based(hand gestures) & Multicamera capture system	Video-based (projector)	User-centered	Single user	Visual	Low	Multipurpose
(Vera et al., 2011)	Depth (Kinect)	Video-based (projector)	Non user-centered	Multiuser	Visual Sonic	Low	Edutainment
(Yuan et al., 2011)	Vision-based (face tracking)	Video-based (screen)	User-centered	Single user	Visual	Low	Optical retail
(Alhamid et al., 2012)	Vision-based (facial recognition) & biomedical sensors	Optical-based (projector)	User-centered	Single user	Visual Sonic Tangible (no augmented)	High	Medical therapy
(Blum et al., 2012)	Depth (Kinect)	Video-based (screen)	User-centered	Single user	Visual	High	Education
(Casas et al., 2012)	Vision-based (body shape) & Depth (Kinect)	Video-based (projector)	User-centered	Multiuser	Visual Sonic	High	Medical therapy
(Castro & McDonald, 2012)	Vision-based (facial recognition)	Video-based (screen)	User-centered	Single user	Visual	Low	Artistic exhibitions
(W. H. A. Li & Fu, 2012)	Depth (Kinect)	Optical-based (projector)	Non user-centered	Single user	Visual Sonic Tangible (no augmented)	High	Edutainment
(Mayans Martorell, 2012a)	Vision-based (face tracking)	Video-based (screen)	User-centered	Single user	Visual	High	Multipurpose
(Pachoulakis & Kapetanakis, 2012)	Depth (Kinect & Asus Xtion)	Video-based (screen)	User-centered	Single user	Visual	High	Clothing
(Robina Town Center, 2012)	Depth (Kinect)	Video-based (screen)	User-centered	Single user	Visual	Low	Clothing
(TIC Singapore, 2013)	Depth (Kinect)	Video-based (screen)	User-centered	Single user	Visual	Low	Clothing
(Difei et al., 2014)	Vision-based (face tracking)	Video-based (mobile)	User-centered	Single user	Visual	Low	Optical retail

continued on following page

Table 1. Continued

Reference	Tracking	Display	Augmen-tation	Users	Stimuli	Level of interaction	Area of application
(Fitnect Interactive, 2014)	Depth (Kinect)	Video-based (screen)	User-centered	Single user	Visual	High	Clothing
(Jae Seok et al., 2014)	Depth (Kinect)	Optical-based (screen)	Non user-centered	Single user	Visual	Low	Multipurpose
(Magic Mirror, 2014)	Depth (Kinect)	Optical-based (screen)	User-centered	Single user	Visual	Low	Clothing
(Martinez Plasencia et al., 2014)	Depth & leap motion	Optical-based (screen and projector)	User-centered & non-centered	Single user	Visual	High	Museum
(Total Immersion, 2014)	Vision-based (face tracking)	Video-based (mobile)	User-centered	Single user	Visual	Low	Optical retail
(EZface, 2015)	Vision-based (face tracking)	Video-based (mobile)	User-centered	Single user	Visual	Low	Cosmetic
(Imagine That, 2015a)	Vision-based (markers)	Video-based (screen)	User-centered	Single user	Visual	Low	Clothing
(Imagine That, 2015b)	Vision-based (natural features)	Video-based (screen)	User-centered	Single user	Visual	Low	Clothing
(L'Oréal, 2015)	Vision-based (face tracking)	Video-based (mobile)	User-centered	Single user	Visual	Low	Cosmetic
(Zugara, 2015)	Vision-based (markers)	Video-based (screen)	User-centered	Single user	Visual	Low	Clothing

The table provides a good indicator on the past and current trends in the development, interaction issues and fields of application of ARMs. For instance, regarding to the tracking technology, it can be seen how, from the early ARMs, a shift from marker-based to natural feature tracking has been produced. This is aligned with the evolution of the AR tracking technologies and sensors, where the Kinect sensor has had great impact in the construction of ARMs since its appearance on the market. On the other hand, regarding to the display technology, it can be seen that most of the ARMs are video-based rather than optical-based. This fact may be explained because of the simpler construction, data blending and occlusion solving of the formers. It can also be seen that the projector and screen solutions are predominant over the mobile solutions. This can be explained due to the fact that the reduced dimensions of mobile technologies do not allow the visualization of greater parts of the body, and thus it is only preferred in the optical retail and cosmetic-related applications where only the user's face is of interest. While clear preferences and/or temporal tendencies can be seen regarding to the technology used in ARMs, a different scenario is seen in human-related factors. Generally speaking, the kinds of featured issues (e.g. single vs. multiuser augmentation) are independent of the year of construction of the mirror and of the area of application. This can be explained because these factors are user-related – and thus remain constant through the years (e.g. visual human perception) – rather than being technologically dependent.

Through the different analysis of the reported examples in different areas such as edutainment, arts or even retail industries, we can state that ARMs allow the creation of environments of play and fun by enhancing the image that users perceive of themselves and/or their surrounding objects, to what users are easily engaged. Additionally, there are some evidences that self-observation in such displays can influence the behaviours and emotional states of users (Giner Martínez & Portalés Ricart, 2005a; Maister et al.,

2015; Melder et al., 2007), also being applicable in psychological therapy (Casas et al., 2012; Herrera et al., 2006; Salve TV, 2008). In this regard, rehabilitation with the use of augmented reality systems and games are demonstrating great potential as innovative adjunctive therapies for health professionals in their treatment of several conditions. Many of these works are recent, and some other are currently being developed. Nevertheless, the potential of ARMs for therapy use has not been deeply explored yet, and different uses of ARM for therapy and medical diagnosis are expected and welcome. For instance, ARM technology could be used to facilitate doctor-patient communication, so that patients can use an ARM (showing, for instance, the internal parts of the body on top of their reflected image) to better explain symptoms and signal their pain with higher precision.

Though the potential of ARMs is high, there still exists the need to invest in their design, construction and performance, especially in order to allow more reliable visual depictions leading to a deeper sense of immersion. Attending to both display paradigms of building ARMs, it can be summarized that the main shortcomings of the current technology in video-based ARMs is the lack of a correct geometrical perspective due to the spatial positioning of the camera that does not allow eye-to-eye contact and the fact that the scene is not seen stereoscopically; on the other hand, the main shortcoming of optical-based ARMs is the lack of a correct blending of the real and virtual objects because the proportion of reflection of the half silvered mirrors hinder efficient occlusions of real and virtual objects and because there is a lack of a correct depth perception as the virtual objects are displayed on a single plane while the image reflected on the mirror is perceived stereoscopically. Therefore, we believe that research on new optical arrangements, components and materials is needed.

In this regards, there are some evidences that the technology involved in ARMs will present some improvements in the upcoming years. Though still not used in the current ARMs, the research community is already working on different technologies to computationally materialize objects, such as changing surfaces, levitating objects or 3D holography. This could be of interest for optical-based ARMs as, computationally materialize the virtual contents rather than projecting them to the back of the mirror, would solve the incorrect depth perception. For instance, in Follmer et al. (2013) a work on changing surfaces through user interaction is presented. Other works on levitating objects within e.g. acoustic fields can be found in Foresti et al. (2013) and Suthar et al. (2014), and some authors have worked in projecting images on levitated particles in the 3D space (Ochiai, 2014; Ochiai, Hoshi & Rekimoto, 2014). 3D holography is also a promising alternative. In Li et al. (2015) full-colour 3D holographic virtual objects are generated by using a graphene-based material, which is visible from a wide angle with the naked eye. By computationally materializing the virtual content, the next generation of optical-based ARM would enable multiuser interaction, as the virtual and real contents would appear correctly registered from different points of view. However, in this setups the need of solving occlusion effectively would remain as an open issue, and thus they should be combined with other approaches.

On the other hand, challenging future directions following a video-based approach may try to solve the lack of eye-to-eye interaction by locating the camera(s) beneath the screen. To that end, the optical paths of the captured and the rendered image have to be separated, what could be done by considering different spectral bands, e.g. with the use of multi- or hyper-spectral systems (Kang, Tang, Xiang & Huang, 2015; Goel et al., 2015). Besides, the lack of stereoscopy of both virtual and real worlds could be solved by the consideration of autostereoscopic displays (Urey, Chellappan, Erden & Surman, 2011). Nevertheless, it seems cumbersome to combine both setups with the current technology.

CONCLUSION

In this chapter the state of the art of ARMs have been given, also proposing a new taxonomy which is summarized in Table 1. The accurate description and classification of the existing ARM systems is one of the main contributions of this chapter, but not the only one. To perform this classification, we have first created a very comprehensive review list of state-of-the-art ARM research works, listing them by application area. We have also analysed carefully the different properties of the different ARMs (tracking system, display type, level of interaction, number of users, etc.). This study allows us to define, in an accurate way, the ARM paradigm and clarify which AR applications with mirrors can be considered "pure ARMs". This is something that, to our knowledge, has not been done before for this kind of AR applications.

As a broad conclusion regarding this analysis of the different ARM technologies, we can conclude that video-based ARMs are usually preferred over optical-based ARMs, as the majority of ARM systems are video-based. This is because of its simpler construction compared to the optical-based ones. However, optical-based ARMs represent best the ARM paradigm, and it is a matter of time that they be the preferred ARM technology. Tracking technology is also biased towards depth and vision-based (markerless) tracking, because they allow a more natural interaction and the maturity of the current technologies allows real-time applications.

While on the technological side we have observed clear tendencies on the construction of ARMs according to their year of construction and application area, user-related features are independent of those factors. Besides, user-centered and single user ARM applications are also the most common choice for ARMs.

In addition, through the different sections of the chapter, the many benefits that ARMs can bring in different areas of knowledge and for the industry are also reported. Nowadays, ARMs can be found in the cosmetic industry, museums and the edutainment field, among others, showing prominent benefits. These systems are highly interactive and intuitive, and allow the realization of engaging augmented environments. Indeed, mirrors have a natural attraction for human beings, which may be explained by cognition and neurological factors and thus the addition of the Augmented Reality technology to regular mirrors can open new avenues in research and industrial applications.

As we can see, ARM is a very promising technology. However, the immaturity of the current display technology in ARMs (video- and optical-based), may have a negative impact in different perception and human-related issues and, thus, it may hinder their extended use and deeper research in certain areas such as medical therapy. Maybe, once the research community achieves a qualitative improvement of the current technology, the great potential that ARMs have beyond providing play and fun can be strengthened.

REFERENCES

Alamri, A., Jongeun, C., & El Saddik, A. (2010). AR-REHAB: An Augmented Reality Framework for Poststroke-Patient Rehabilitation. *IEEE Transactions on Instrumentation and Measurement*, *59*(10), 2554–2563. doi:10.1109/tim.2010.2057750

Alhamid, M. F., Eid, M., & El Saddik, A. (2012, May 18-19). A multi-modal intelligent system for biofeedback interactions. *Paper presented at the 2012 IEEE International Symposium on Medical Measurements and Applications Proceedings (MeMeA).*

Altschuler, E. L., Wisdom, S. B., Stone, L., Foster, C., Galasko, D., Llewellyn, D. M. E., & Ramachandran, V. S. (1999). Rehabilitation of hemiparesis after stroke with a mirror. *Lancet, 353*(9169), 2035–2036. doi:10.1016/S0140-6736(99)00920-4 PMID:10376620

Anthony, S. (2011). The New York Times' magic mirror will bring shopping to the bathroom. *Extremetech.com*. Retrieved from http://www.extremetech.com/computing/94751-the-new-york-times-magic-mirror-will-bring-shopping-to-the-bathroom

ARToolKit community. (2015). ARToolKit - Innovation Through Community Retrieved from http://artoolkit.org/

Azuma, R. T. (1997). A Survey of Augmented Reality. *Presence (Cambridge, Mass.), 6*(4), 355–385. doi:10.1162/pres.1997.6.4.355

Bimber, O., & Raskar, R. (2005). *Spatial Augmented Reality: Merging Real and Virtual Worlds.*

Birkfellner, W., Figl, M., Huber, K., Watzinger, F., Wanschitz, F., Hummel, J., & Bergmann, H. et al. (2002). A head-mounted operating binocular for augmented reality visualization in medicine--design and initial evaluation.[Evaluation Studies Research Support, Non-U S Gov't]. *IEEE Transactions on Medical Imaging, 21*(8), 991–997. doi:10.1109/TMI.2002.803099 PMID:12472271

Blum, T., Kleeberger, V., Bichlmeier, C., & Navab, N. (2012). mirracle: An augmented reality magic mirror system for anatomy education. *Proceedings of the 2012 Virtual Reality conference*. Retrieved from http://doi.ieeecomputersociety.org/10.1109/VR.2012.6180909Doi: 10.1109/VR.2012.6180909

Botella, C., Bretón-López, J., Quero, S., Baños, R., & García-Palacios, A. (2010). Treating Cockroach Phobia with Augmented Reality. *Behavior Therapy, 41*(3), 401–413. doi:10.1016/j.beth.2009.07.002 PMID:20569788

Botella, C. M., Juan, M. C., Banos, R. M., Alcaniz, M., Guillen, V., & Rey, B. (2005). Mixing realities? An application of augmented reality for the treatment of cockroach phobia.[Case Reports]. *Cyberpsychology & Behavior, 8*(2), 162–171. doi:10.1089/cpb.2005.8.162 PMID:15938656

Bower, M., Howe, C., McCredie, N., Robinson, A., & Grover, D. (2014). Augmented Reality in education – cases, places and potentials. *Educational Media International, 51*(1), 1–15. doi:10.1080/09523987.2014.889400

Burke, J. W., McNeill, M. D. J., Charles, D. K., Morrow, P. J., Crosbie, J. H., & McDonough, S. M. (2010, March 25-26). Augmented Reality Games for Upper-Limb Stroke Rehabilitation. *Paper presented at the 2010 Second International Conference on Games and Virtual Worlds for Serious Applications (VS-GAMES).*

Carrino, F., Rizzotti, D., Gheorghe, C., Kabasu Bakajika, P., Francescotti-Paquier, F., & Mugellini, E. (2014). Augmented Reality Treatment for Phantom Limb Pain. In R. Shumaker & S. Lackey (Eds.), *Virtual, Augmented and Mixed Reality. Applications of Virtual and Augmented Reality, LNCS* (Vol. 8526, pp. 248–257). Springer International Publishing. doi:10.1007/978-3-319-07464-1_23

Casas, X., Herrera, G., Coma, I., & Fernández, M. (2012). A Kinect-based augmented reality system for individuals with autism spectrum disorders. *Paper presented at the Computer Graphics Theory and Applications*, Rome, Italy.

Castro, A., & McDonald, K. (2012). Faces - 2012 Retrieved from http://arturocastro.net/work/faces.html

Caudell, T. P., & Mizell, D. W. (1992, January 7-10). Augmented reality: an application of heads-up display technology to manual manufacturing processes. *Paper presented at theTwenty-Fifth Hawaii International Conference onSystem Sciences.* doi:10.1109/HICSS.1992.183317

Chan, B. L., Witt, R., Charrow, A. P., Magee, A., Howard, R., Pasquina, P. F., & Tsao, J. W. et al. (2007). Mirror Therapy for Phantom Limb Pain. *The New England Journal of Medicine*, *357*(21), 2206–2207. doi:10.1056/NEJMc071927 PMID:18032777

Cheng, C.-M., Chung, M.-F., Yu, M.-Y., Ouhyoung, M., Chu, H.-H., & Chuang, Y.-Y. (2008). Chromirror: a real-time interactive mirror for chromatic and color-harmonic dressing. *Paper presented at theCHI '08 Extended Abstracts on Human Factors in Computing Systems*, Florence, Italy. doi:10.1145/1358628.1358762

Chimes, G. P., Bernstein, C. D., Cortazzo, M. H., & Huber, L. M. (2009). Poster presentation. *PM & R*, *1*(9Suppl.), S220. doi:10.1016/j.pmrj.2009.08.290

Connors, M. H., & Coltheart, M. (2011). On the behaviour of senile dementia patients vis-à-vis the mirror: Ajuriaguerra, Strejilevitch and Tissot (1963). *Neuropsychologia*, *49*(7), 1679–1692. doi:10.1016/j.neuropsychologia.2011.02.041 PMID:21356221

Correa, A. G. D., Ficheman, I. K., do Nascimento, M., & De Deus Lopes, R. (2009, 15-17 July 2009). Computer Assisted Music Therapy: A Case Study of an Augmented Reality Musical System for Children with Cerebral Palsy Rehabilitation. *Paper presented at the Ninth IEEE International Conference on Advanced Learning Technologies ICALT '09.*

Cycling. (2015). Cycling '74 MAX. Retrieved from https://cycling74.com/

Desmond, D. M., O'Neill, K., Paor, A. D., McDarby, G., & MacLachlan, M. (2006). Augmenting the Reality of Phantom Limbs: Three Case Studies Using an Augmented Mirror Box Procedure. *Journal of Prosthetics and Orthotics*, *18*(3), 74–79. doi:10.1097/00008526-200607000-00005

Dieguez, S., Scherer, J., & Blanke, O. (2011). My face through the looking-glass: The effect of mirror reversal on reflection size estimation. *Consciousness and Cognition*, *20*(4), 1452–1459. doi:10.1016/j.concog.2011.06.003 PMID:21723147

Difei, T., Juyong, Z., Ketan, T., Lingfeng, X., & Lu, F. (2014, 14-18 July 2014). *Making 3D Eyeglasses Try-on practical. Paper presented at the 2014 IEEE International Conference on Multimedia and Expo Workshops (ICMEW).*

Dohle, C., Pullen, J., Nakaten, A., Kust, J., Rietz, C., & Karbe, H. (2009). Mirror therapy promotes recovery from severe hemiparesis: A randomized controlled trial. *Neurorehabilitation and Neural Repair*, *23*(3), 209–217. doi:10.1177/1545968308324786 PMID:19074686

Doi, K. (2007). Computer-Aided Diagnosis in Medical Imaging: Historical Review, Current Status and Future Potential. *Computerized medical imaging and graphics: the official journal of the Computerized Medical Imaging Society, 31*(4-5), 198-211. doi:10.1016/j.compmedimag.2007.02.002

Duñabeitia, J. A., Molinaro, N., & Carreiras, M. (2011). Through the looking-glass: Mirror reading. *NeuroImage, 54*(4), 3004–3009. doi:10.1016/j.neuroimage.2010.10.079 PMID:21056672

Eisert, P., Fechteler, P., & Rurainsky, J. (2008, June 23-28). 3-D Tracking of shoes for Virtual Mirror applications. *Paper presented at the IEEE Conference on Computer Vision and Pattern Recognition CVPR '08.*

EZface. (2015). The new era of virtual tester technology Retrieved from http://www.ezface.com/products/#try-it-on

Feintuch, U., Tuchner, M., Lorber-Haddad, A., Meiner, Z., & Shiri, S. (2009, June 29-July 2). *VirHab - A virtual reality system for treatment of chronic pain and disability.* Paper presented at the Virtual Rehabilitation International Conference, 2009. doi:10.1109/ICVR.2009.5174210

Feltham, M. G., Ledebt, A., Deconinck, F. J. A., & Savelsbergh, G. J. P. (2010). Mirror visual feedback induces lower neuromuscular activity in children with spastic hemiparetic cerebral palsy. *Research in Developmental Disabilities, 31*(6), 1525–1535. doi:10.1016/j.ridd.2010.06.004 PMID:20591615

Fitnect Interactive. (2014). Fitnect. Virtual mirror, shopping window, virtual store, and much more. Retrieved from http://www.fitnect.hu/

Follmer, S., Leithinger, D., Olwal, A., Hogge, A., & Ishii, H. (2013). inFORM: dynamic physical affordances and constraints through shape and object actuation. *Paper presented at the26th annual ACM symposium on User interface software and technology*, St. Andrews, Scotland, United Kingdom. doi:10.1145/2501988.2502032

Foresti, D., Nabavi, M., Klingauf, M., Ferrari, A., & Poulikakos, D. (2013). Acoustophoretic contactless transport and handling of matter in air. *Proceedings of the National Academy of Sciences of the United States of America, 110*(31), 12549–12554. doi:10.1073/pnas.1301860110 PMID:23858454

Fotopoulou, A., Jenkinson, P. M., Tsakiris, M., Haggard, P., Rudd, A., & Kopelman, M. D. (2011). Mirror-view reverses somatoparaphrenia: Dissociation between first- and third-person perspectives on body ownership. *Neuropsychologia, 49*(14), 3946–3955. doi:10.1016/j.neuropsychologia.2011.10.011 PMID:22023911

Fuchs, H., Livingston, M., Raskar, R., Colucci, D. n., Keller, K., State, A., . . . Meyer, A. (1998). Augmented reality visualization for laparoscopic surgery. In W. Wells, A. Colchester & S. Delp (Eds.), Medical Image Computing and Computer-Assisted Intervention MICCAI'98 (Vol. 1496, pp. 934-943): Springer Berlin Heidelberg. doi:10.1007/BFb0056282

Fujinami, K., Kawsar, F., & Nakajima, T. (2005). AwareMirror: a personalized display using a mirror. *Paper presented at theProceedings of the Third international conference on Pervasive Computing*, Munich, Germany. doi:10.1007/11428572_19

Gimeno, J., Olanda, R., Martinez, B., & Sanchez, F. M. (2011). Multiuser augmented reality system for indoor exhibitions. *Paper presented at the Proceedings of the 13th IFIP TC 13 international conference on Human-computer interaction*, Lisbon, Portugal, 4. doi:10.1007/978-3-642-23768-3_86

Giner Martínez, F., & Portalés Ricart, C. (2005a, 3-7 October). The Augmented User: A Wearable Augmented Reality Interface. *Paper presented at theInternational Conference on Virtual Systems and Multimedia (VSMM'05)*, Ghent, Belgium.

Giner Martínez, F., & Portalés Ricart, C. (2005b). El Túnel Mágico. *Paper presented at the Nuevos materiales y tecnologías para el arte*, Madrid, Spain.

Giner Martínez, F., & Portalés Ricart, C. (2007). Augmented teaching. *Paper presented at the International Technology, Education and Development Conference (INTED'07)*, Valencia, Spain.

Goel, M., Whitmire, E., Mariakakis, A., Saponas, T. S., Joshi, N., Morris, D., . . . Patel, S. N. (2015). HyperCam: hyperspectral imaging for ubiquitous computing applications. *Paper presented at the2015 ACM International Joint Conference on Pervasive and Ubiquitous Computing*, Osaka, Japan. doi:10.1145/2750858.2804282

Hadalová, Z., & Samuelčík, M. Varhaníková (2014, December). Augmented Map Presentation of Cultural Heritage Sites. *Paper presented at theInternational Conference on Current Issues of Science and Research in the Global World*, Vienna, Austria (pp. 345-349).

Herrera, G., Jordan, R., & Gimeno, J. (2006). Exploring the advantages of Augmented Reality for Intervention in Autism Spectrum Disorders. *Paper presented at theSecond World Autism Congress*, Cape Town, South Africa.

Hilsmann, A., & Eisert, P. (2009). Tracking and Retexturing Cloth for Real-Time Virtual Clothing Applications. *Paper presented at theProceedings of the 4th International Conference on Computer Vision/ Computer Graphics Collaboration Techniques*, Rocquencourt, France. doi:10.1007/978-3-642-01811-4_9

HITLab. (2003). ARToolKit Retrieved from http://www.hitl.washington.edu/artoolkit/

IGN. (2010). THQ announces Fantastic Pets, first augmented reality title on Kinect for XBox 360. Retrieved from http://www.ign.com/articles/2010/10/21/thq-announces-fantastic-pets-first-augmented-reality-title-on-kinect-for-xbox-360

Imagine That. (2015a). 2D Fitting Room Retrieved from http://www.imaginethattechnologies.com/default.asp?mn=1.27

Imagine That. (2015b). 3D Fitting Room Retrieved from http://www.imaginethattechnologies.com/default.asp?mn=1.26

Jae Seok, J., Gi Sook, J., Tae Hwan, L., & Soon Ki, J. (2014). Two-Phase Calibration for a Mirror Metaphor Augmented Reality System. *Proceedings of the IEEE, 102*(2), 196–203. doi:10.1109/JPROC.2013.2294253

Jones, B., Collis, K., Watson, J., Foster, K., & Fraser, S. (1994). Images in mirrors: Recollections, alternative explanations and modes of cognitive functioning. *Research in Science Education, 24*(1), 191–200. doi:10.1007/BF02356344

Juan, M. C., Alcaniz, M., Monserrat, C., Botella, C., Banos, R. M., & Guerrero, B. (2005). Using Augmented Reality to Treat Phobias. *IEEE Computer Graphics and Applications, 25*(6), 31–37. doi:10.1109/MCG.2005.143 PMID:16315475

Jun-Ren, D., Chien-Lin, H., Jin-Kun, L., Jar-Ferr, Y., & Chung-Hsien, W. (2008). Interactive multimedia mirror system design. *IEEE Transactions on Consumer Electronics, 54*(3), 972–980. doi:10.1109/tce.2008.4637575

Kang, L., Tang, X.-z., Xiang, Y.-h., & Huang, Y.-s. (2015). *Research progress and perspective of hyperspectral image projectors.* Paper presented at the Proc. SPIE 9522, Selected Papers from Conferences of the Photoelectronic Technology Committee of the Chinese Society of Astronautics 2014, Part II.

Key, A., George, C. L., Beattie, D., Stammers, K., Lacey, H., & Waller, G. (2002). Body image treatment within an inpatient program for anorexia nervosa: The role of mirror exposure in the desensitization process.[Clinical Trial Controlled Clinical Trial]. *International Journal of Eating Disorders, 31*(2), 185–190. doi:10.1002/eat.10027 PMID:11920979

Kim, I.-J., Lee, H. J., & Kim, H.-G. (2004). Magic mirror: a new VR platform design and its applications. *Paper presented at the2004 ACM SIGCHI International Conference on Advances in computer entertainment technology*, Singapore. doi:10.1145/1067343.1067394

Krijn, M., Emmelkamp, P. M. G., Olafsson, R. P., & Biemond, R. (2004). Virtual reality exposure therapy of anxiety disorders: A review. *Clinical Psychology Review, 24*(3), 259–281. doi:10.1016/j.cpr.2004.04.001 PMID:15245832

L'Oréal. (2015). Makeup Genius. Introducing the first ever virtual makeup tester. Retrieved from http://www.lorealparisusa.com/en/brands/makeup/makeup-genius-virtual-makeup-tool.aspx

Li, W. H. A., & Fu, H. (2012). Augmented reflection of reality. *Paper presented at theACM SIGGRAPH 2012 Emerging Technologies*, Los Angeles, California, USA. doi:10.1145/2343456.2343459

Li, X., Ren, H., Chen, X., Liu, J., Li, Q., Li, C., & Gu, M. et al. (2015). Athermally photoreduced graphene oxides for three-dimensional holographic images. *Nature Communications, 6*. doi:10.1038/ncomms7984 PMID:25901676

Lynch, C. (2012). Kinect Party review. More fun from the fun kings Retrieved from http://www.ign.com/articles/2012/12/21/kinect-party-review

Magic Mirror. (2014). World market leader for interactive digital signage Retrieved from http://www.magicmirror.me/

Maister, L., Slater, M., Sanchez-Vives, M. V., & Tsakiris, M. (2015). Changing bodies changes minds: Owning another body affects social cognition. *Trends in Cognitive Sciences, 19*(1), 6–12. doi:10.1016/j.tics.2014.11.001 PMID:25524273

Malloy, K. M., & Milling, L. S. (2010). The effectiveness of virtual reality distraction for pain reduction: A systematic review. *Clinical Psychology Review, 30*(8), 1011–1018. doi:10.1016/j.cpr.2010.07.001 PMID:20691523

Marescaux, J., Rubino, F., Arenas, M., Mutter, D., & Soler, L. (2004, November10). Augmented-reality-assisted laparoscopic adrenalectomy. *Journal of the American Medical Association, 292*(18), 2214–2215. PMID:15536106

Martínez De Pisón, M. J., Sanmartín, F., Carbonell, A., Furió, D., Cuesta, S., Rodríguez, L., . . . Piqueras, D. (2006). *Especulaciones a un tiempo.*

Martinez Plasencia, D., Berthaut, F., Karnik, A., & Subramanian, S. (2014). *Through the combining glass.* Paper presented at the Proceedings of the 27th annual ACM symposium on User interface software and technology, Honolulu, Hawaii, USA.

Mayans Martorell, J. (2012a). *Augmented User Interface.* Master, Universidad Politécnica de Valencia, Valencia. Retrieved from https://riunet.upv.es/handle/10251/27578

Mayans Martorell, J. (2012b). Augmented User Interface - Artistic Essays. Retrieved from https://www.youtube.com/watch?v=aWVPZAFSidk

Melder, W. A., Truong, K. P., Uyl, M. D., Leeuwen, D. A. V., Neerincx, M. A., Loos, L. R., & Plum, B. S. (2007). Affective multimodal mirror: sensing and eliciting laughter. *Paper presented at theinternational workshop on Human-centeredmultimedia*, Augsburg, Bavaria, Germany. doi:10.1145/1290128.1290134

Microsoft. (2015). Meet Kinect. Retrieved from https://www.microsoft.com/en-us/kinectforwindows/meetkinect/default.aspx

Mixed Reality Lab. (2006). Software. MXR ToolKit Retrieved from http://mixedrealitylab.org/projects/software/

Morimoto, C. H. (2001). *Interactive Digital Mirror.* Retrieved from http://doi.ieeecomputersociety.org/10.1109/SIBGRAPI.2001.963060 doi:10.1109/SIBGRAPI.2001.963060

Mulder, J. D. (2006). Occlusion in Mirror-Based Co-Located Augmented Reality Systems. *Presence (Cambridge, Mass.), 15*(1), 93–107. doi:10.1162/pres.2006.15.1.93

Müller, H., Michoux, N., Bandon, D., & Geissbuhler, A. (2004). A review of content-based image retrieval systems in medical applications—clinical benefits and future directions. *International Journal of Medical Informatics, 73*(1), 1–23. doi:10.1016/j.ijmedinf.2003.11.024 PMID:15036075

Ochiai, Y. (2014). Pixie Dust: Graphic generated by Levitated and Animated Objects in Computational Acoustic-Potential Field Retrieved from http://96ochiai.ws/PixieDust/

Ochiai, Y., Hoshi, T., & Rekimoto, J. (2014). Pixie dust: Graphics generated by levitated and animated objects in computational acoustic-potential field. *ACM Transactions on Graphics, 33*(4), 1–13. doi:10.1145/2601097.2601118

Pachoulakis, I., & Kapetanakis, K. (2012). Augmented Reality Platforms for Virtual Fitting Rooms. *The International Journal of Multimedia & Its Applications, 4*(4), 35–46. doi:10.5121/ijma.2012.4404

Paysant, J., Beis, J. M., Le Chapelain, L., & André, J. M. (2004). Mirror asomatognosia in right lesions stroke victims. *Neuropsychologia, 42*(7), 920–925. doi:10.1016/j.neuropsychologia.2003.12.001 PMID:14998706

Pereira, F., Silva, C., & Alves, M. (2011). Virtual Fitting Room Augmented Reality Techniques for e-Commerce. In M. Cruz-Cunha, J. Varajão, P. Powell, & R. Martinho (Eds.), *ENTERprise Information Systems* (Vol. 220, pp. 62–71). Springer Berlin Heidelberg. doi:10.1007/978-3-642-24355-4_7

Playstation. (2003). EyeToy: Play, from http://es.playstation.com/ps2/games/detail/item42149/EyeToy-Play/

Playstation. (2004). EyeToy Play 2 Retrieved from http://es.playstation.com/ps2/games/detail/item42521/EyeToy-Play-2/

Poh, M.-Z., McDuff, D., & Picard, R. (2011). A medical mirror for non-contact health monitoring. *Paper presented at theACM SIGGRAPH 2011 Emerging Technologies*, Vancouver, British Columbia, Canada. doi:10.1145/2048259.2048261

Portalés, C., & Perales, C. D. (2009). Sound and Movement Visualization in the AR-Jazz Scenario. *Paper presented at theInternational Conference on Entertainment Computing (ICEC)*. doi:10.1007/978-3-642-04052-8_15

Portalés, C., Viñals, M. J., Alonso-Monasterio, P., & Morant, M. (2010). AR-Immersive Cinema at the Aula Natura Visitors Center. *IEEE MultiMedia*, *17*(4), 8–15. doi:10.1109/MMUL.2010.72

Portalés Ricart, C. (2007a). Live LEGO House: A Mixed Reality Game for the Edutainment. *Scottish Online Journal of E-Learning*, *1*(1), 19–28.

Portalés Ricart, C. (2007b). Live LEGO House: an interactive space to explore coexistence through gaming. *Paper presented at the International Technology,Education and Development Conference (INTED'07)*, Valencia (Spain).

Portalés Ricart, C. (2009). *Entornos multimedia de realidad aumentada en el campo del arte* [Doctoral Thesis]. Universidad Politécnica de Valencia, Valencia.

Portalés Ricart, C., Perales Cejudo, C. D., & Cheok, A. (2007). Exploring Social, Cultural and Pedagogical Issues in AR-Gaming Through The Live LEGO House. *Paper presented at theACM SIGCHI International Conference on Advances in Computer Entertainment Technology*, Salzburg, Austria. doi:10.1145/1255047.1255103

Rahman, A. S. M. M., Tran, T. T., Hossain, S. K. A., & El Saddik, A. (2010, October 17-20). Augmented Rendering of Makeup Features in a Smart Interactive Mirror System for Decision Support in Cosmetic Products Selection. *Paper presented at the 2010 IEEE/ACM 14th International Symposium on Distributed Simulation and Real Time Applications (DS-RT)*.

Regenbrecht, H. T., Franz, E. A., McGregor, G., Dixon, B. G., & Hoermann, S. (2011). Beyond the Looking Glass: Fooling the Brain with the Augmented Mirror Box. *Presence (Cambridge, Mass.)*, *20*(6), 559–576. doi:10.1162/PRES_a_00082

Richard, E., Billaudeau, V., Richard, P., & Gaudin, G. (2007, September 27-29). *Augmented Reality for Rehabilitation of Cognitive Disabled Children: A Preliminary Study*. Paper presented at the Virtual Rehabilitation, 2007.

Robina Town Center. (2012). Virtual change room. Retrieved from https://www.youtube.com/watch?v=Zmw6xMtEqro

Rochat, P., & Zahavi, D. (2011). The uncanny mirror: A re-framing of mirror self-experience. *Consciousness and Cognition*, *20*(2), 204–213. doi:10.1016/j.concog.2010.06.007 PMID:20889353

Rolland, J. P., Holloway, R. L., & Fuchs, H. (1994). A comparison of optical and video see-through head-mounted displays. *Paper presented at the SPIE - Telemanipulator and Telepresence Technologies.*

Rose, F. D., Brooks, B. M., & Rizzo, A. A. (2005). Virtual reality in brain damage rehabilitation. *Cyberpsychology & Behavior*, *8*(3), 241–262. doi:10.1089/cpb.2005.8.241 PMID:15971974

Salve TV. (2008). Open night lab Retrieved from http://www.salve-tv.net/web/de/webtv/webtv.php?VideoSuche=open+night+lab&RubrikSuche=0&autoplay=false&area=

Sambo, C. F., & Forster, B. (2011). When far is near: ERP correlates of crossmodal spatial interactions between tactile and mirror-reflected visual stimuli. *Neuroscience Letters*, *500*(1), 10–15. doi:10.1016/j.neulet.2011.05.233 PMID:21683122

Sato, H., Kitahara, I., & Ohta, Y. (2009). MR-Mirror: A Complex of Real and Virtual Mirrors. *Paper presented at the 3rd International Conference on Virtual and Mixed Reality: Held as Part of HCI International 2009*, San Diego, CA, USA. doi:10.1007/978-3-642-02771-0_54

Savardi, U., Bianchi, I., & Bertamini, M. (2010). Naïve predictions of motion and orientation in mirrors: From what we see to what we expect reflections to do. *Acta Psychologica*, *134*(1), 1–15. doi:10.1016/j.actpsy.2009.11.008 PMID:20015479

Shahid, S., Krahmer, E., Swerts, M., Melder, W. A., & Neerincx, M. A. (2009). Exploring social and temporal dimensions of emotion induction using an adaptive affective mirror. *Paper presented at theCHI '09 Extended Abstracts on Human Factors in Computing Systems*, Boston, MA, USA. doi:10.1145/1520340.1520562

Shuhaiber, J. H. (2004). Augmented reality in surgery. *Archives of Surgery (Chicago, Ill.)*, *139*(2), 170–174. doi:10.1001/archsurg.139.2.170 PMID:14769575

Sielhorst, T., Feuerstein, M., & Navab, N. (2008). Advanced Medical Displays: A Literature Review of Augmented Reality. *Display Technology. Journalism*, *4*(4), 451–467. doi:10.1109/jdt.2008.2001575

Singapore, T. I. C. (2013). 3D Augmented Reality Virtual Fitting Room Retrieved from https://www.youtube.com/watch?v=gz5ynrfJSDM

Stevens, J. A., & Stoykov, M. E. P. (2003). Using Motor Imagery in the Rehabilitation of Hemiparesis 1. *Archives of Physical Medicine and Rehabilitation*, *84*(7), 1090–1092. doi:10.1016/S0003-9993(03)00042-X PMID:12881842

Straka, M., Hauswiesner, S., Rüther, M., & Bischof, H. (2011). A Free-Viewpoint Virtual Mirror with Marker-Less User Interaction. In A. Heyden & F. Kahl (Eds.), *Image Analysis* (Vol. 6688, pp. 635–645). Springer Berlin Heidelberg. doi:10.1007/978-3-642-21227-7_59

Suthar, K., Benmore, C. J., Den Hartog, P., Tamalonis, A., & Weber, R. (2014, 3-6 Sept. 2014). Levitating water droplets formed by mist particles in an acoustic field. *Paper presented at the 2014 IEEE International Ultrasonics Symposium (IUS).*

Sutherland, I. E. (1965). The Ultimate Display. *Paper presented at theCongress of the Internation Federation of Information Processing (IFIP).*

Tang, S. L., Kwoh, C. K., Teo, M. Y., Sing, N. W., & Ling, K. V. (1998). Augmented reality systems for medical applications. *IEEE Engineering in Medicine and Biology Magazine, 17*(3), 49–58. doi:10.1109/51.677169 PMID:9604701

Taylor, R. H., & Stoianovici, D. (2003). Medical robotics in computer-integrated surgery. *IEEE Transactions on Robotics and Automation, 19*(5), 765–781. doi:10.1109/tra.2003.817058

Thieme, H., Mehrholz, J., Pohl, M., Behrens, J., & Dohle, C. (2012). Mirror therapy for improving motor function after stroke. *Cochrane Database of Systematic Reviews, 14*(3). doi:10.1002/14651858. CD008449.pub2 PMID:22419334

Total Immersion. (2014). TryLive for eyewear. Next generation virtual try-on and fitting solutions for the eyewear and eyecare industry Retrieved from http://www.trylive.com/solutions/trylive-eyewear-virtual-mirror/overview

Trojan, J., Diers, M., Fuchs, X., Bach, F., Bekrater-Bodmann, R., Foell, J., & Flor, H. et al. (2014). An augmented reality home-training system based on the mirror training and imagery approach. *Behavior Research Methods, 46*(3), 634–640. doi:10.3758/s13428-013-0412-4 PMID:24338625

Urey, H., Chellappan, K. V., Erden, E., & Surman, P. (2011). State of the Art in Stereoscopic and Autostereoscopic Displays. *Proceedings of the IEEE, 99*(4), 540–555. doi:10.1109/JPROC.2010.2098351

Ushida, K., Tanaka, Y., Naemura, T., & Harashima, H. (2002). i-mirror: An Interaction/Information Environment Based on a Mirror Metaphor Aiming to Install into Our Life Space. *Paper presented at theInternational Conference on Artificial Reality and Telexistence (ICAT),* Tokyo Japan.

Vera, L., Gimeno, J., Coma, I., & Fernández, M. (2011). Augmented Mirror: Interactive Augmented Reality System Based on Kinect. In P. Campos, N. Graham, J. Jorge, N. Nunes, P. Palanque, & M. Winckler (Eds.), *Human-Computer Interaction – INTERACT 2011* (Vol. 6949, pp. 483–486). Springer Berlin Heidelberg. doi:10.1007/978-3-642-23768-3_63

Windheim, K., Veale, D., & Anson, M. (2011). Mirror gazing in body dysmorphic disorder and healthy controls: Effects of duration of gazing. *Behaviour Research and Therapy, 49*(9), 555–564. doi:10.1016/j. brat.2011.05.003 PMID:21726855

Yavuzer, G., Selles, R., Sezer, N., Sutbeyaz, S., Bussmann, J. B., Koseoglu, F., & Stam, H. J. et al. (2008). Mirror therapy improves hand function in subacute stroke: A randomized controlled trial.[Randomized Controlled Trial]. *Archives of Physical Medicine and Rehabilitation, 89*(3), 393–398. doi:10.1016/j. apmr.2007.08.162 PMID:18295613

Yuan, M., Khan, I. R., Farbiz, F., Niswar, A., & Huang, Z. (2011). A mixed reality system for virtual glasses try-on. *Paper presented at the10th International Conference on Virtual Reality Continuum and Its Applications in Industry*, Hong Kong, China. doi:10.1145/2087756.2087816

Zugara. (2015). The Webcam Social Shopper (WSS) Retrieved from http://zugara.com/virtual-dressing-room-technology/webcam-social-shopper

KEY TERMS AND DEFINITIONS

Autostereoscopic Display: Devices displaying stereoscopic images without the use of special headgear or glasses on the part of the viewer.

Eye-to-Eye Interaction: Regarding to ARMs, to have direct visual contact with the own reflected eyes on the mirror surface.

Half-Silvered Mirror: A half reflecting, half pass-through mirror.

Image Blending: Mixing two images. The output image is a combination of the corresponding pixel values of the input images.

Taxonomy: The practice and science of classifying things or concepts, including the principles that underlie such classification.

User Engagement: An assessment of an individual's response to some type of technology.

Uncanny: Something that is so remarkable that it is beyond what is natural.

Chapter 10
Augmented Reality for Smart Tourism in Religious Heritage Itineraries:
Tourism Experiences in the Technological Age

Célia M.Q. Ramos
University of Algarve, Portugal

Cláudia Henriques
University of Algarve, Portugal

Robert Lanquar
La Rochelle Business School, France

ABSTRACT

Pilgrimages and travel for other religious reasons are two of the major drivers of human mobility. Information and communication technologies (ICTs) can contribute to sharing knowledge about religious heritage with tourists, residents, and religious communities. ICT innovations that help individuals find information and acquire knowledge about cultural heritage can bring new experiences and sensations to tourists and residents, in general, and to those who have accessibility problems, in particular. These innovations include augmented reality, location-based services, social networks, gamification, and intelligent interfaces. This paper focuses on religious and spiritual routes and itineraries, presenting a religious tourism experience model that allows tourists to acquire additional knowledge about cultural and religious heritage, based on technological architecture using intelligent human-computer interactions displayed on personal mobile devices. This approach expands personal and spiritual experiences when travelers visit religious heritage sites associated with itineraries.

DOI: 10.4018/978-1-5225-0435-1.ch010

INTRODUCTION

Due to the expansion of leisure time and paid vacations, religious tourism has increased exponentially over the last 70 years. Currently, people are not interested in only passively visiting sites and monuments. Tourists ask for more responsiveness and shared personal and spiritual experiences of this heritage. In this context, information and communication technologies (ICTs) can contribute to deepening and intensifying tourists' knowledge about tangible and intangible, as well as religious and spiritual, heritage, bringing these visitors closer to the values of the host community while they participate in learning processes.

Any technological innovation that helps individuals to find information during the process of selecting a product or service has an impact on tourist behavior. The acquisition of knowledge about religious heritage by tourists, residents, and, in particular, those who have accessibility challenges (i.e., physical and mental disabilities) requires specific innovations in order to offer new experiences and sensations. One solution is augmented reality (AR) based on locations, social networks, and intelligent human-computer interfaces, as well as usability and accessibility concepts, which integrate user-centered functionalities.

These technologies, when associated with a religious itinerary such pilgrimages or religious routes, can enhance the personal and spiritual experiences of tourists, residents, and religious communities, while contributing to preserving heritage sites. Tourism combined with AR can provide alternative ways to access threatened places that lessen the negative impacts of tourism by reducing visitor overcrowding.

In this context, the present chapter proposes a framework for the development of a technological architecture for mobile devices that integrates different user-centered technologies, including AR functionalities, to be used by tourists visiting regions that provide personal and spiritual experiences associated with itineraries. In order to achieve this objective, the authors start by describing the contributions that ICT makes to religious tourism, adding value to religious tourism experiences through AR techniques associated with location systems and mobile devices. These allow the development of services that present each region's religious practices, taking into consideration religious itineraries in innovative ways that contribute to creating an updated model of religious tourism experiences.

The next section presents the framework of this religious tourism experience model (RTEM), including all the technologies that contribute to creating smart environments and facilitating the development and definition of the methodology needed to build the technological architecture associated with the proposed religious tourism model. This technological architecture consists of an intelligent application applied to religious tourism by creating technology-based religious itineraries that tell stories and cultivate and disseminate tourist information about heritage through mobile technology.

The last section suggests future directions in research and ways that the proposed technological model can be improved. Finally, some conclusions are presented about the RTEM and technological architecture presented in this chapter.

TOURISM AND TOURISM EXPERIENCES IN THE TECHNOLOGICAL AGE

The rise of the economy of experiences (Pine & Gilmore, 1999, 2011) has led to the definition of the concept of "tourist experience," which combines tourists' actions with a set of memories and emotions related to the places visited (Noy, 2007). These are influenced by the tourists, scenes (i.e., destinations), and residents (Cutler & Carmichael, 2010).

According Pine and Gilmore (1999, p. 12), a tourist experience can be defined as a "set of activities in which individuals engage on personal terms." For Oh et al. (2007, p. 120), who analyzed this concept from the consumers' perspective, a tourist experience is something "pleasant, engaging, and memorable."

Each tourist experience is lived through subjectively by each individual who engages with heritage on physical, emotional, spiritual, and intellectual levels (Tung & Ritchie, 2011, p. 1371), which allow each tourist to build his or her own travel experiences (Wickens, 2002). Consequently, each tourist experience is able to satisfy a "wide range of personal needs ranging from pleasure to a search for meaning" (Li, 2000, p. 865). A tourist experience is characterized by subjectivity, as it involves an individual tourist, particular moment, and existential context or situation (Borrie & Roggenbuck, 2001; Carry, 2004; Cohen, 1979).

A tourism experience can be seen as a global consumption experience of a destination (Agapito, Valle, & Mendes, 2014). Tourist experiences (see Figure 1) join the "education," "entertainment," "aesthetic," and "escapist" dimensions (Pine & Guilmore, 1999) and have the ability to satisfy a "wide range of personal needs" (Li, 2000, p. 865) associated with spaces, places, and landscapes (Seamon, 1979; Tuan, 1993). Therefore, providing these experiences needs to be regarded as a series of steps, namely, 1) thematization, 2) the use of senses and suggestions, 3) remarkable elements, and 4) memorable events or places.

To be "memorable," experiences must be associated with a theme, stimulation of the senses, spatiality, positivity, and a structured souvenir mix. As such, the creation of experiences must be based on a narrowing of the gap between production and consumption, bearing in mind the concept of "prosumer"— consumers involved in, and committed to, the production of experiences (Richards & Wilson, 2006). With regard to cultural creative tourism experiences associated with given themes, this needs to be understood in the context of different levels of depth of experience, as well as different types of tourists (Richards & Wilson, 2006).

Figure 1. The experience realm
Source: Adapted from Pine and Guilmore, 1999, p. 30

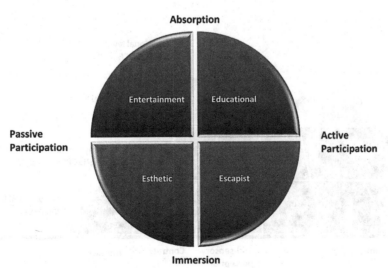

According to Ooi (2005, p. 51), "the tourism industry is in the business of selling experiences." The cited authors defined three characteristics of tourism experiences. First, tourists have different social and cultural backgrounds, which means that a single product needs to interest all customers with different levels of education. Second, multi-faceted offers mean that tourists can appreciate a product even if they do not have the same backgrounds. Last, existential experiences make it possible for tourism products to facilitate only pleasurable experiences, taking into consideration tourists' psychological and cognitive functions.

To analyze these three characteristics of tourism experiences in the context of a "theory of tourism experiences," Ooi (2005) developed an approach constituted of six perspectives. These include cognitive psychology, to investigate how tourists' perceptions affect their experiences; benefits obtained, to analyze how to improve tourists' well-being and their knowledge about places and cultures; and depth of experimental engagement, to study how experiences emotionally affect tourists. These perspectives also comprise phenomenology, to learn how experiences allow tourists to gather more reflexive and intimate information; relationships between tourists and residents, to examine how tourists' experiences are similar to those of the local population; and personal interpretations and relationships with products, to evaluate if engaging experiences depend on the degree of tourist interaction with products.

More recently, the concept of "the experience pyramid" appeared, which considers two perspectives (Lapland Centre of Expertise for the Experience Industry [LEO], 2009): meaningfulness criteria and levels of experience as shown in the following list and Figure 2 below:

Figure 2. The experience pyramid
Source: Adapted from LEO, 2009, p. 12

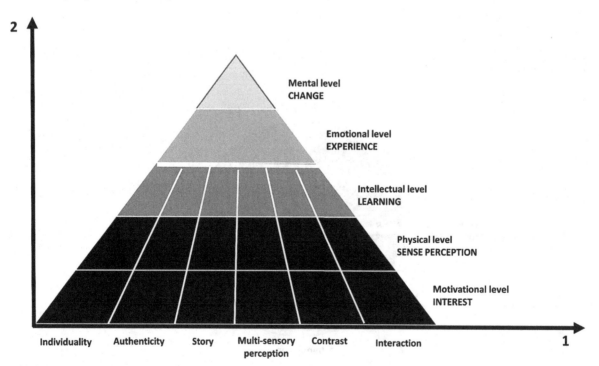

1. Meaningfulness Criteria:
    a. **Individuality:** the only one of its kind, customizability and possibility of varying the service.
    b. **Authenticity:** credibility, realism, common world, visual harmony, and culturally aesthetic sustainability.
    c. **Story:** the significance and theme of the product, the reason for choosing the product, and storyline and dramaturgy.
    d. **Multi-Sensory Perception:** harmony of various sensory stimuli including smell, touch, taste, sight, and hearing.
    e. **Contrast:** the opportunity to escape from ordinary, everyday roles and obligations, which can mean an experience is exotic for one person and plain and ordinary for another.
    f. **Interaction:** the product's interactions with the customer and interactions between other customers, staff, environments, and friends.
2. Levels of Experience:
    a. **Motivation Level:** individuality, authenticity, story, multi-sensory perception, contrast, and interactions.
    b. **Physical level:** individuality, authenticity, story, multi-sensory perception, contrast, and interactions.
    c. **Intellectual level:** individuality, authenticity, story, multi-sensory perception, contrast, and interactions.
    d. **Emotional Level:** a multi-sensory, individual, and comprehensive emotional experience that has personal significance.
    e. **Mental Level:** an experience of personal development and personal change that can be monitored and analyzed.

The theme "culture" has gained increasing importance, particularly through increased recognition of the symbiotic relationship between culture and economy from the 80s onward. According to the United Nation Educational, Scientific and Cultural Organization (UNESCO) (2009), the following are regarded as cultural domains: "cultural and natural heritage" (i.e., museums, archaeological and historical places, cultural landscapes, and natural heritage), "performance and celebration" (i.e., performing arts, music, festivals, fairs, and feasts), "visual arts and crafts" (i.e., fine arts, photography, and crafts), 'books and press' (i.e., books, newspaper, magazine, other printed matter, libraries, and book fairs), "audio-visual and interactive media," and "design and creative services." At the same time, UNESCO identifies "related domains," such as "tourism" (i.e., charter travel and tourist services, hospitality, and accommodations) and "sports and recreation" (i.e., sports, physical fitness and well-being, amusement and theme parks, and gambling).

The definition of cultural tourism is challenging (Richards, 2005), and it is mainly based on the conjunction of two complex concepts. The European Association for Tourism and Leisure Education developed under the Cultural Tourism Research Project—and strongly inspired by the Irish Tourist Board (1988)—uses a conceptual approach that defines cultural tourism as the movement of people to visit cultural attractions outside their usual place of residence, with the purpose of acquiring new information and experiences to satisfy their cultural requirements (Richards, 2005). According to Richards (2005), the attractions that tend to draw mainly cultural tourists are, among others, museums and archaeological sites; architecture (i.e., ruins, buildings and cities); arts, sculpture, crafts, art galleries, and artistic festivals and events; music and dance; drama (i.e., theatre and film); literary and linguistic studies; and religious festivals and pilgrimages. For each group of attractions, Csapó (2012) proposed a classification of the main forms of cultural tourism, which relate to specific cultural features: heritage tourism, cultural thematic routes, cultural city tourism or cultural tours, traditions or ethnic tourism, event and festival tourism, religious tourism or pilgrimage routes, and creative culture or creative tourism.

The World Religious Travel Association (2008) reported that a progressively important segment of cultural tourism relates to "faith travel." "Faith travel" is motivated by religious or spiritual reasons or associated with religious heritage. Previously a largely domestic phenomenon, religious tourism has turned into a major international commercial service. Travel agencies offer an extensive portfolio of multifaith journey packages to ancient places of worship, sacred destinations and pilgrimage sites associated with mainstream faiths. Globalization transformed religious tourism into a marketable economic product for different markets (i.e., spirituality, physical and mental health, leisure activities, culture, city breaks, and short stays) because religion has an enormous influence on the daily life of many people (Lanquar, 2014; UNWTO, 2008).

For the United Nations World Tourism Organization (2011, pp. XV–XVI) the involvement of local communities is as important as discerning visitors in protecting and preserving religious cultural sites, events, and pilgrimages that form the basis of religious tourism. Good governance guarantees the long-term future of these "products," which should not be viewed merely as a source to generate revenue but also as services in which the participation and interest of communities are vitally important.

Religious tourism also can be defined "as travel with the core motive of experiencing religious forms, or the products they induce, like art, culture, traditions, and architecture" (Strategic Initiatives & Government Advisory [SIGA], 2012, p. 2). It is a form of tourism in which believers travel individually or in groups as pilgrims, missionaries, or pleasure seekers (Petroman et al., 2011). In addition to the motivation of experiencing religious activities, religious tourists intend to visit religious sites and locations with or without religious motivations (i.e., for the architectural and cultural importance of these sites) and pilgrimage routes (Csapó, 2012).

The emergence of increasingly well-travelled and experienced tourists and pronounced globalization has provoked new patterns of consumption and behavior (Ramos, Rodrigues, & Rodrigues, 2015). These tourists travel in search of tourism experiences that contribute to their personal enrichment (Crompton & McKay, 1997), and they, therefore, are especially receptive to following proposed routes including creative options and amenable to engaging in co-creation activities (Binkhorst, 2007). These factors have motivated the development of new strategies in marketing (Ramos et al., 2015), in which tourist experiences are seen as consumer experiences (Mossberg, 2007; Moutinho, 1987; Swarbrooke & Horner, 1999; Woodside, Crouch & Ritchie, 2000).

Tourists are consumers who consume or experience every moment during visits (Mossberg, 2007), and the marketing significance of tourist activities lies in these tourists' consumption (Quan & Wang, 2004). Physical and social environments influence tourists' experiences while traveling, as do other consumers (Mossberg, 2007). At the same time, the tourism industry must offer opportunities for participation or involvement that fulfil tourists' needs at that particular time (Andersson, 2007).

The integration of ICTs has particularly benefited the facilitation of experiences and enhanced tourism experiences (Neuhofer & Buhalis, 2012, 2013). According to Neuhofer, Buhalis, and Ladkin (2013), two of the most significant advances in the area of experiences are the increasing levels of co-creation and the integration of ICTs.

Neuhofer and Buhalis (2013, p. 2) reported that ICTs "can thus be created in multiple experience spaces, on multiple levels of engagement and social circles of interaction, leading to more meaningful experiences and added value for the tourist." At the same time, ICTs potentiate strategic differentiation and competitive advantage by empowering customer co-creation, engagement, and personalization.

According to Neuhofer (2013, p. 3), "technologies accompany tourists in all stages, from the pre- to the during—and post-stages of travel." In reference to cultural tourism or, more specifically, religious tourism, technology has led to the prevalence of bottom-up models in planning processes, enabling interactive, incremental, and inclusive practices (Rheingold as cited in Garau, 2014, p. 238).

The integration of ICT into religious tourism is widely used for religious purposes, mainly via the Internet. Many religious leaders agree that ICT allows the dissemination of religious messages while reducing costs, expanding markets from regional to global, and providing 24-hour advertising and pilgrimage services (Draganić & Rajević, 2011).

As discussed earlier, the integration of ICT into tourism can create environments that enable tourists' involvement in order to enhance their travel experiences, add value, and even encourage ICT use in other tourism products. In addition, it allows the dissemination of information through immediate access to texts and documents that add cultural information. The interactive nature of this new medium facilitates dynamic forms of learning and contributes to increasing knowledge.

In the case of religious tourism, new technologies also enhance dialogue and co-creation activities among travelers from different cultures and religions, contributing to personal enrichment and expanding tourists' experiences. For tourist destinations, ICTs enhance the development of new strategies to increase innovation and differentiation in the supply of tourist services.

In this context, the present study sought to investigate what types of technologies can be used to enhance tourism experiences and, in particular, how they can be applied in religious tourism and the construction of a religious tourist experimentation model. In order to achieve this objective, the authors identified several practices associated with tourism experiences, such as genius loci (Favre-Brun, Jacquemin, & Caye, 2012), the work of Garau (2014), and the Melaka (Aziz & Siang, 2014) and Cluny experiences (Metaio, 2015), in which ICT has contributed to innovation in the tourism sector.

For example, the Cluny program is one of the first AR initiatives developed for a religious site (Metaio, 2015; Père & Faucher, 2007). Cluny was the largest church in Christendom until the construction of the Basilica of Saint Peter in Rome. The site visited today by tourists represents only 10 percent of what it was until the French Revolution dismantled the Order of Cluny and transformed the Maior Ecclesia, the abbey church, into a stone quarry. From 2006 to 2007, the Cluny digital project recreated the destroyed former abbey in a virtual reality corresponding to the structure of Cluny III, which was built at the end of the eleventh century by the monk Gunzo. This is how the project got the name of "Gunzo Project." To celebrate the eleven hundredth anniversary of the Foundation of the Order of Cluny, in 2010, several communities, associations, and research centers brought together engineers, art historians, archaeologists, and geographers, who decided to use AR to render the former abbey as realistically as possible. The Gunzo Project, therefore, was a consortium of researchers focused on using new imaging technologies to enhance knowledge about, and experiences of, the Cluny religious heritage.

In another example associated with tourism and experiences in the technological age and considered a best practice, in July 2015, UNESCO (2015) decided to include the four Saint James's Ways of northern Spain on the World Heritage List—a decision made during the thirty-ninth session of the World Heritage Committee of UNESCO, on 8 July, in Bonn, Germany. Part of the Saint James's Way that crosses France (i.e., El Camino Francès) had already been in this category since 1993. The pilgrimage routes are El Camino Primitivo, which begins in Oviedo; the Coastal Way, 936 kilometers long; the Vasco-Rioja Way, which starts at Irun; and the Way of Liebana, which connects El Camino with the Monastery of Santo

Toribio. For these Saint James's Ways, 2015 was quite important, with a vast diffusion of AR in the main halting places. To ensure the routes' inclusion on UNESCO's list, the autonomous community of Galicia, among other places, provided subventions to local software companies to develop AR projects for the different pilgrimage roads. These initiatives have increased and potentiated experiences associated with heritage sites, enhancing cultural knowledge acquisition and bringing added value to tourism destinations while, in turn, these AR projects have enriched religious heritage itineraries and tourism experiences.

Each technological innovation that helps in the search for tourism information and product selection processes has an impact on tourist behavior (Buhalis & Law, 2008; Pendrana, 2014). Overall, tourism is characterized by a high degree of innovation over time (Hjalager, 2010).

For innovation to take place, Engelberger (1982) suggested that there must be three conditions: consumer need, appropriate technology, and organizations' financial interest. Kalmanek (2012) further argued that successful innovation requires three essential elements: consumer need, technology know-how or knowledge, and a favorable economic situation. In addition, for religious tourism experiences to be innovative, they need to pay attention to three elements—people, technology, and business—as these apply to religious tourism. To achieve the goal of creating new experiences in this area, it is important to develop innovative religious tourism experiences (Henriques, Ramos, & Rodrigues, 2014).

Figure 3 represents the interactions between the various elements that are pertinent to innovation processes. Innovation is created in the area where the three elements overlap in the diagram, in order to meet consumer needs (e.g., tourists), taking into account the existing knowledge (e.g., technology) and the relationship between culture and economics (e.g., organizations).

Figure 3. Religious tourism experience
Source: Author's elaboration.

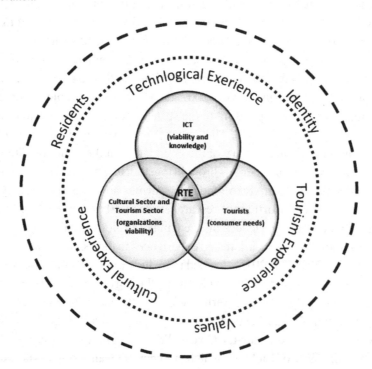

Regarding the consumer element, it is important to consider tourists and the local population in order to add value to tourists' experiences through the acquisition of cultural knowledge by both residents and tourists. In the technology element, it is necessary to investigate the entire range of technology that can be integrated into technological architecture in order to develop a religious tourist experience model. The organization element promotes the sharing with, and dissemination of, knowledge about religious heritage to tourists and residents, with the objective of increasing the number of visitors and acquisition of knowledge about tangible and intangible heritage.

Tourists' behavior, interests, and motivations need to be researched in primary and secondary sources, with the goal of collecting and selecting information that meets tourists' expectations, to add value and enable co-creation of content (Neuhofer, Buhalis, & Ladkin, 2013). The promotion of cultural and religious heritage can thus be shared, and the knowledge acquired can be presented through technological devices to the right people with the right content at the best time and in the right context (Burke & Hiltbrand, 2011). Disclosure of information can be done through brochures, suggestions of thematic itineraries, or shared documents on mobile devices.

Tourist behavior has undergone changes over time, especially in how tourists easily adopt new technologies, even as the tourism industry has incorporated technological innovations. Tourists are increasingly comfortable with technology, using mobile devices, sharing their experiences through social networks—including recommender systems; enjoying services based on their location; looking for new experiences; seeking to experience heritage and culture; and wanting to feel and live new experiences. This allows tourism destinations to encourage visits to their valued and well-known heritage sites, and, at the same time, travelers enhance their tourist experiences while adding value to their journey and increasing their knowledge.

When knowledge related to tangible and intangible heritage is shared with, and disseminated to, people, in general, and tourists and residents, in particular, for those who have accessibility problems, in order to create new products for tourists who are more technologically experienced and looking for new experiences and sensations. This can be applied to religious and cultural tourism by creating technological religious routes that tell stories, cultivate tourists' interest, and publicize heritage through mobile technology. Emerging technologies increase the potential attractiveness of tourist destinations, allowing the creation of new strategies and innovation in terms of products or services. Therefore, in the present study, innovation appears at the junction of these three elements in order to satisfy tourists and residents' need to share and gain knowledge about heritage using technology—all of which is made possible by the RTEM proposed below.

FRAMEWORK OF THE RTEM

When identifying the technologies that can be relevant to developing an RTEM, as discussed above, those designated "smart technology" need to be considered. According to Neuhofer et al.'s (2015, p. 243) work, this term implies this technology is "intelligent and smart," and it has several functionalities that can be adapted to various circumstances, persons, or places. Smart technology, therefore, potentiates new opportunities for the creation of tourism experiences (Buhalis & Amaranggana, 2013; Neuhofer et al., 2015; Tussyadiah & Fesenmaier, 2009; Wang, Park, & Fesenmaier, 2012), enabling contemporary experience creation (Gretzel & Jamal, 2009) through the use of integrated technologies in mobile devices. This includes AR (Bower, Howe, McCredie, Robinson, & Grover, 2014; Buhalis & Amaranggana, 2013; Chen, 2014; Garau, 2014; Yovcheva, Buhalis, Gatzidis, & van Elzakker, 2014), location-based systems (Gavalas et al., 2014; Pendrana, 2014; Yovcheva et al., 2014), social networks (Munar & Jacobsen, 2013), user-centered design (Bower et al., 2014; Chen, 2014; Gavalas et al., 2014; Yovcheva et al., 2014), gamification (Buhalis & Amaranggana, 2013; Fino, Martín-Gutiérrez, Fernández, & Davara, 2013; Mortara et al., 2014; Xu, 2011; Xu, Weber, & Buhalis, 2013), recommendation systems (Fesenmaier, Wöber, & Werthner, 2006; Gavalas et al., 2014), mobile technologies (Gavalas et al., 2014), and Internet-based technologies, among others.

The connections between these kinds of technologies have led to increased and strengthened collaboration, interaction, and co-creation between tourism consumers so that these consumers now play an important role in the tourism industry (Buhalis & Law, 2008). Consumers are more personally engaged (Pine & Gilmore, 1999), and these technologies enable the creation of intelligent systems for tourists (Gretzel, 2011), which present relevant information to tourists in the proper time, context, and place (Burke & Hiltbrand, 2011).

SMART TECHNOLOGY IN THE PROPOSED RTEM

Smart technology helps tourists in their decision-making processes about heritage sites they are visiting, involving travelers in choices and turning visitors into destination or product agents when they recommend destinations to friends and share their tourism experiences in social networks. If this is complemented with gamification features integrated into the development of smart, user-centered interfaces and based on usability and accessibility rules, this technology increases consumer loyalty to destinations or products (Xu et al., 2013).

Figure 4 displays a model for creating innovative, personalized experiences with the three elements presented earlier—people, organizations, and technology—in this case associated with the creation of innovative tourism experiences. In this context, the element of people refers to tourists and their travel needs, which are associated with the organization element. The organization element represents all tourism companies, which each include departments and employees who facilitate access to tourism

Figure 4. Smart technology for personalized experiences
Source: Adapted from Neuhofer et al., 2015, p. 251

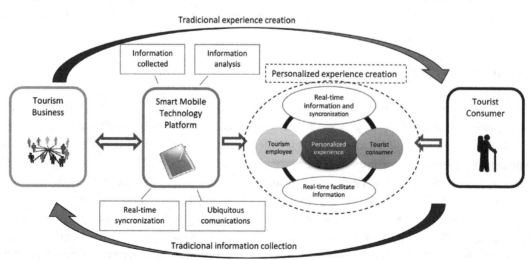

products and services in destinations. The last element, technology, is designated as "smart mobile technology platform."

This technological platform (see Figure 4) requires information aggregation, ubiquitous connections, and real time synchronization. These aspects facilitate the creation of personalized experiences mainly when tourism consumers encounter tourism employees who can satisfy tourists' consumption needs and meet these consumers' expectations of their visit.

In the RTEM, mobile technology is the most important element, as it gives tourists access to information anytime and anywhere, through such items as smartphones, tablets, or other mobile devices (Gavalas et al., 2014). Each mobile device should include a location-based system, which can be Wi-Fi, Bluetooth, or near field communication (NFC), permitting communication over short distances by radio-frequency identification (RFID). Quick response (QR) code readers are also useful, as each point of interest (POI) can have a QR code that provides access to contextual and multimedia information. In addition, concepts associated with design interaction should be considered in the development of intelligent user-centered computer interfaces, including rules associated with accessibility, usability, and intuitive functionality.

Mobile devices have fostered the emergence of a new information culture, which helps to promote tourism and publicize potential resources. Travelers have more information that is more comprehensible and easy to interpret because it allows interaction with virtual information as an additional environment (Garau, 2014). Tourism destinations thus have more ways to differentiate their cultural offer according to their target audience. The local community, as a private and economic sector, can use the Internet and mobile devices, including sales and marketing channels, to publicize events, the nearest restaurants, and other tourist services that complement travel itineraries.

These devices have capabilities that enable the development of applications through which overlaying layers of information content onto the real world is possible. This content can come in different formats—audio, image, and video—and can help to provide details and to publicize the most complete representation of tourist facilities connected to cultural and religious heritage sites. For example, maps can be added with the location of features associated with the same religious period, integrating virtual elements that identify other POIs that complement particular thematic routes. For the local community, in addition to the economic component, these devices present educational possibilities that allow residents to publicize more fully their private religious and heritage resources, which adds value to their own experiences of local heritage.

This capacity to overlay layers onto the real world is possible with the aid of AR techniques, which permit a better understanding of reality (Dunleavy & Dede, 2014; Garau, 2014). According with Dadwal and Hassan (2015), AR can help travelers to find a particular monument or restaurant and locals to create virtual brochures and create virtual experiences associated with tourism attractions, whether monuments or restaurants. Tourists can also have access to additional services to increase the value associated with their tourism experiences, taking into account specific situations and contexts.

In addition, AR technology allows quantitative expansion of perceptions of heritage and increases the level of qualitative attraction to the same, enhancing the increased emotional involvement of travelers and resulting in more interactions by providing additional information and fun with multimedia resources. These transform heritage into more tangible, concrete, relevant, and useful tourism products (Dadwal & Hassan, 2015) and construct images that appeal to the five senses (i.e., sound, location (e.g., global positioning system [GPS]), touch, smell and visual effects) and that are integrated into an interactive real world that increases travelers and consumers' satisfaction (Barreda, Bilgihan, Nusair, & Okumus, 2015).

Customer satisfaction has an impact on visitors' loyalty and confidence. In addition, effective communication and information exchange enable organizations to know their clients better, and, consequently, offer products suited to their characteristics and preferences. Providers can understand the factors that influence decisions to purchase or use services or products (Jung, Chung, & Leue, 2015; Park & Kim, 2014; Xu et al., 2013). Regarding processes of making purchase decisions and the inclusion of consumer behavior models, it is also important to analyze the stages of these processes (Schiffman & Kanuk, 2009, as cited in Dadwal & Hassan, 2015), as well as the dynamics of environments in which tourism activities take place (Burke & Hiltbrand, 2011).

When tourism experiences provided by AR are applied to marketing, they allow the creation of attractive, interactive experiences, in which it is possible to obtain virtual rewards affecting visitors' reality. The two main positive impacts of these rewards are that consumers view advertising—and not making zapping—and that the rewards help increase conversion rates (Dadwal & Hassan, 2015).

To be successful, the implementation of AR associated with marketing depends on consumers' adoption and dissemination of information through their mobile devices, in order to influence their behavior. The Technological Acceptance Model (TAM) proposed by Davis (1989) is considered one of the most influential models in information systems research related to the acceptance and use of technology by users. This model identifies if the "perception of being easy to use" and "perception of … usefulness" has influenced changes in consumer behavior in the adoption of technology (Dadwal & Hassan, 2015).

The TAM has been used as the basis for other models, namely, Bandura's social cognitive theory and the Theory of Planned Behavior, in regard to the adoption of new technologies. However, other factors need to be addressed, such as motive and interest, which influence consumers' purchasing decisions, change the future of organizations, and enhance retention and customer attraction. These improve consumers' relationships with products and increase customer lifetime value (Dadwal & Hassan, 2015), as considered in the proposed experience model (LEO, 2009; Pine & Gilmore, 1999).

Dadwal and Hassan (2015) reported that AR and gaming are trendy phenomena associated with marketing. Xu et al. (2013) also observed that gamification is a trend, which can be applied in tourism in many ways, to stimulate motivation and behavioral change. Blohm and Leimeister (2013, p. 276) argued that "gamification is a persuasive technology that attempts to influence user behavior by activating individual motives" since it increases user satisfaction, conveyance of optimism, and facilitation of social interaction, as well as providing meaning while supporting learning processes. Gamification also can be applied in marketing to improve customer loyalty and brand image.

Gamification is a term that appeared for the first time in 2008 (Deterding, Dixon, Khaled, & Nacke, 2011), and it refers to the use of game design elements and game thinking in non-gaming contexts (Deterding et al., 2011). This concept is seen as an innovative transformation in business, encouraging consumer engagement while increasing brand perception (Xu et al., 2013).

According to Zichermann and Cunningham (2011, p. XIV), gamification can be defined as "the process of game thinking and game mechanics to engage users and solve problems," which consists of a set of tools and techniques based on games to shape consumers' behavior toward products, processes, and platforms. This then generates economic and social value for companies, beyond just technology producers. For Prince (2013, p. 163), "Foursquare is perhaps the most successful and well-known gamified application." It considers social networks based on location, for example, interactions between a user and a cafeteria can mean the former receives free coffee as a reward.

Sigala (2015) found that gamification has a high potential in marketing, since this industry is characterized by a certain degree of persuasion, motivation, and manipulation. In addition, the cited author argued that this approach will be the next generation of marketing that will revolutionize human-computer interactions and user experiences by motivating consumers through games that have an impact on their behavior.

According to Sigala (2015), despite the extensive potential that gamification has for tourism, there is a large gap in the literature of studies that analyze the impact of gamification on travelers' experiences and behavior and take into account the use of technology. The cited author also confirmed that research is needed on the domain experiences of gamification across websites, based on the argument that this can inform professionals about how gamification applications involve consumers.

For the RTEM proposed in this paper, gamification was considered relevant when taking into account the importance of engaging and retaining tourists, to help raise awareness of brands and destinations and to enable the sharing of user experiences. In parallel, this approach offers an outlet for cultural consciousness, historical reconstruction, and awareness of intangible heritage (e.g., customs and traditions) and material associated with religion.

In terms of business strategy, gamification services increase the need for new business models and value creation networks, but these models are still unclear about how these services should be applied (Blohm & Leimeister, 2013) because these models must take into account value creation and customer engagement and enhance user experiences, in addition to gamification. These new business models, besides gamification and AR, are associated with the use of intelligent environments. They incorporate the opportunities social media present to innovate in the ways human resources are managed and consumer behavior can be changed, in accordance with how positive emotional feedback is applied (Blohm & Leimeister, 2013).

Social media can be defined as "internet-based applications that carry consumer-generated content" (Barreda et al., 2015; Sigala, 2015; Xiang & Gretzel, 2010), which represent a popular source of information and include media impressions created by consumers about their experiences. Moreover, these are archived or shared online for easy access by other impressionable consumers (Xiang & Gretzel, 2010). These applications enable interaction, communication, collaboration, and the creation of user content in several types of social media, such as social networks, blogs and micro-blogs, virtual worlds, and collaborative projects like Wikipedia.

User-generated content plays a critical role in communities and has a widely acknowledged importance in all fields and in tourism, in particular (Akehurst, 2009). This content's positive effects have recognized repercussions on intangible matters, such as the image of, or information on, specific products or services (Milano, Baggio, & Piattelli, 2011), appealing to customers' interest and promoting online participation. Social media applications and other technologies allow tourists increasingly to digitize and share online knowledge and information, as well as emotions and experiential moments, enhancing human-computer interactions (Munar & Jacobsen, 2013).

Over the years, it has been found that more and more tourists are a part of the process of creating "collective intelligence" (Xiang & Gretzel, 2010), which challenges the established marketing practices of many tourism businesses and destinations while building consumer-brand relationships (Davis, Piven, & Breazeale, 2014; Park & Kim, 2014). "Collective intelligence" (Xiang & Gretzel, 2010), "business intelligence" (Burke & Hiltbrand, 2011), "intelligent environments" (Blohm & Leimeister, 2013), "smart user-centered interfaces" (Xu et al., 2013), "recommender systems" (Gavalas et al., 2014; Staab et al.,

2002), and "smart technology" (Neuhofer et al., 2015) are terms used for information systems developed to achieve the objective of identifying and selecting customer preferences. These systems can be classified according to target applications, use of knowledge, ways recommendations are formulated, and algorithm implementation (Gavalas et al., 2014).

These systems are considered a means of reducing information overload and offering travel recommendations to tourists, which creates a "collective intelligence" on the web that can transform established marketing practices and be relevant to many business, in general, and to tourism, in particular. The trustworthiness of online travelers, together with the collaborative intelligence associated with marketing, can create "marketing intelligence" (Xiang & Gretzel, 2010). According to Xiang and Gretzel (2010) online reviews related to tourism in social media already are having an impact on travel decision making, as this type of social media content is transforming travel experiences.

Once the structure and representation of online tourism is understood, the tourism industry must design effective tourism information systems that permit the implementation of successful marketing campaigns. The restructuring of the travel information industry is essential to informing better tourism marketing practices, which encompass communication, promotion, product distribution, management, and research associated with marketing intelligence (Xiang & Gretzel, 2010).

To enhance the competitiveness of tourist destinations, the right information should be given to the appropriate tourists at the right time and in the right contexts, in order to increase their involvement and motivate them to increase the value of their experiences and, consequently, their satisfaction. Burke and Hiltbrand (2011, pp. 9–10) stated that "business intelligence is part of the digital experience … [to] learn … how to engage users and revolutionize the user experience through the application of game mechanics … to drive behaviors based on business requirements" that afford valuable information about the consumer's decisions and behavior.

In this context, to achieve the previously mentioned research objective, it is necessary to consider the use of information systems integrated with business intelligence tools, taking into consideration the information lifecycle (Burke & Hiltbrand, 2011). This includes:

1. Ensuring information quality,
2. Continuously increasing information,
3. Disseminating appropriate information to decision makers to support travelers' decision-making processes,
4. Customizing tourists' experiences, and
5. Interacting with information to provide key measures of sustainability—key performance indicators.

This allows providers to analyze tourism businesses' success and consumer behavior in a way that increases consumer engagement while providing new tourism experiences.

To create intelligent environments for tourists, recommender systems need to include a smart, user-centered interface that integrates usability and accessibility features to support surplus learning and tourist behaviors. This needs to take into consideration that interaction and interface design can affect tourists' decision-making process (Staab et al., 2002).

These kinds of systems should be personalized, adaptive, and anticipatory, as well as integrating contextual information. They need to be available for everybody, anywhere, and at any time. Personalization is the most important key to engaging consumers and providing exceptionally valuable experiences. From the moment that personalization was first considered by the tourist industry, the consumers' expectations of their tourism experiences increased significantly (Buhalis & Amaranggana, 2013). Personalization can be considered to be a process of collecting personal information about the needs and preferences of customers with the goal of creating offers and information that perfectly fit customers' needs. Consequently, tourism service providers are starting to meet this expectation in order to be able to provide the right offer at exactly the right time (Buhalis & Amaranggana, 2013). Staab et al. (2002, p. 54) defined these systems as "the convergence of ubiquitous computing and communication and intelligent user-friendly interfaces."

In the conceptualization of intelligent user interfaces, different designs can mean different decision strategies and can influence users' emotions, level of involvement, and the quality of their experiences (Staab et al., 2002). In this context, to develop an environment of Human-Computer Interaction, it is necessary to use a design that permits providers to solve business problems and engage users through meaningful, valuable experiences, incorporating content that fits customers' interests and needs and motivates them to interact more fully.

Within tourism, the design of interfaces becomes even more challenging (Yovcheva et al., 2014, p. 24), since this implies the need to overcome problems, including overlap of annotations, overly small size of annotations, distance-based filtering of annotations that leads to errors, linear layout and movement of annotations that creates confusion, and, finally, any application that does not load properly. For user-centered interfaces, the complexity greatly increases, as the information has to be different from tourist to tourist and needs to be tailored to match tourists' location (Pendrana, 2014). At the same time, users can interact with real and virtual objects or display three-dimensional simulations in real time or with audio files, to understand what they are visiting and seeing.

Location-based systems should include all services linked to, and associated with, locations, such as amenities or attractions, and require a robust technological architecture, since databases need to work asynchronously and non-asynchronously, with collaborative capabilities (Pendrana, 2014). These databases must be robust—with great storage capacities—and capable of storing virtual objects associated with assets and with those loaded by tourists on social networks when tourists visit POIs (Bower et al., 2014).

Other technology to be included is GPS and location-based systems, such as NFC, that can be integrated into several mobile devices (Buhalis & Law, 2008) and that permit users to communicate across short distances by RFID. Image recognition software, speakers, and sound systems (Bower et al., 2014) are also necessary to make interactions between tourists and POIs possible, via an intelligent human-computer interface.

To engage customers and define these intelligent interfaces, the concepts of gamification presented above which are considered a part of social gaming, need to be included. This can be described as a new business model (Buhalis & Law, 2008) that uses the resources made available by social media, enables interactions between different consumers in different scenarios, and includes the concepts of emotions, bugs, predictions, and learning (Camerer, 2003), which were associated with an experience economy by LEO (2009) and Pine and Guilmore (1999).

To create an RTEM it is necessary to include all the technologies presented above, as well as the connectivity and ubiquitous access provided by the Internet. These combine in a technological architecture associated with applications that contribute added value and offer new smart tourism experiences whenever residents or travelers visit heritage sites.

DEVELOPMENT OF THE PROPOSED RTEM

The above described combination of culture, religion, and tourism has promoted an increasing number of potential religious travelers. The digital age, in turn, has reinforced the need to establish dynamic relationships between tourism, religion, culture, and technology in order to satisfy the interests of residents, tourists, and religious communities, for the purpose of disseminating information related to tangible and intangible assets, such as access to texts and documents. ICTs, by their intrinsic nature, have become excellent partners of the tourism industry in recent decades, yet few products currently exist that make the link between religious tourism and regional cultural and heritage.

Technological solutions to fill this gap need to consist of intelligent applications applied to religious tourism, creating technological virtual religious itineraries that tell a story and cultivate an understanding of tourism heritage and disseminate this through mobile technology. These applications should integrate the technologies discussed above and be solutions characterized by a human-computer interface developed in accordance with user-centered design methodologies. These last include accessibility and usability concepts that can engage—and expand tourism experiences for—tourists, residents, and religious communities.

Figure 5 presents the proposed experience model of religious tourism based on current technological trends that link one user to all users and all of these to each one. The model can create a smart technology platform to engage players (e.g., tourists), maintaining and communicating effectively the information associated with tangible and intangible cultural heritage, in this case, mainly religious culture. This model seeks to engage travelers with cultural content, including historical reconstructions and raising awareness of heritage and culture.

As shown in Figure 5, the model's center represents the environment provided by the proposed RTEM, which allows tourism consumers to enjoy religious tourism experiences via several technologies that are integrated and linked in one technological platform. The technologies in Figure 5 and discussed above indicate six important features of the technology defined as relevant to the model:

1. **Mobile Devices:** These permit ubiquitous consumer communication and allow users to have access to information based on their location.
2. **AR:** This allows a better understanding of the real world and permits the integration of virtual elements that complement religious resources, while tourists participate in games that offer opportunities to engage consumers and facilitate the acquisition of knowledge about heritage.
3. **Gamification:** Gaming mechanics solve problems, making it possible to measure and evaluate the reputation or performance of a product or destination, which facilitates positive changes in consumer behavior in terms of loyalty and engagement created by access to rewards, such as privileged information or access to places.
4. **Social Media:** With the user-generated content and sharing tools associated with gamification, this has become a tool used to define new business models strategically.
5. **Business Intelligence:** Tools can be used to analyze the information collected in social gaming associated with AR and to enhance the discovery of new consumption patterns of tourists and residents, allowing the monitoring and evaluation of tourism behaviors.
6. **Intelligent Interfaces (Human-Computer Interaction):** These are the key to increasing the value of religious tourism experiences since interfaces offer personalized information according to consumer preferences, age, and segment, which is made possible by other technologies listed above: AR, gamification, social media, and business intelligence.

Figure 5. RTEM technology framework
Source: Author's elaboration

The development of an application based on this RTEM would enable tourists, through personal mobile devices, to get additional data on the cultural, spiritual, and religious heritage of a region or destination. The mobile device projects a factual environment that allows the recapture of local background on tourism and religious heritage, enhancing tourists' affective involvement with the displayed heritage and facilitating their personal and spiritual experiences.

METHODOLOGY USED TO DEVELOP THE RTEM

The methodology needed to develop the RTEM can be divided into two phases: 1) planning and definition of content associated with cultural and religious heritage and 2) planning and implementation of the RTEM:

1. **First Phase:** Developing the information about places that should be shared with the public can be divided into three steps:
    a. Researching primary sources.
    b. Researching secondary sources.
    c. Defining and structuring the contents to be shared and disseminated based on the RTEM, to facilitate the dissemination and acquisition of knowledge about religious heritage (all sources are examined to define a list of POIs to be included in technological routes; for each POI, information is collected, organized, and structured to describe the POI and present it to the public).
2. **Second Phase:** Implementing the RTEM can be structured into three steps:
    a. Analyzing the technologies that can be included in the model.
    b. Designing the religious tourism experience technological architecture.
    c. Implementing the religious tourism experience applications.

When analyzing the technologies to be considered in the model, it is important to consider all the emergent technology discussed earlier and identified in Figure 5, which can contribute to developing smart tourism experiences associated with religious heritage and which can be combined in technological architecture applications.

Figure 6 shows the structures of the religious tourism experience technological architecture model that can be developed for the RTEM, which is prepared to receive and transmit information in real time to synchronized databases. In the model below, information communication is ubiquitous, allowing travelers to access personalized information. In situations in which this is not possible, the application also allows users to download information beforehand (i.e., non-synchronized data). Communication is two-way: to the travelers, sending contextualized information and connected to their profiles, and to databases, storing user-created content, such as videos or photos that tourists upload to social networks, and tracking users' visits to heritage sites and their gamification results. All the information is stored in databases, collected from several sources, and analyzed by appropriate tools to achieve insights into the resulting tourism business intelligence, such as new trends and consumer behaviors. Travelers can have access to the technological architecture via applications developed for mobile devices, which include a location-based system characterized by human-computer interaction. User design concepts can be applied to define the intelligent interface, which can be developed with functionalities associated with users' interests and profiles. For example, if the traveler is a child and he or she wants to learn about a POI, this user needs to have access to different information designed differently as compared with that offered his or her parents. Functionalities should be adequate for the user's age. For example, the parents may prefer to read original documents that tell the POI's history while their child prefers to watch a video, which is more appealing and requires more engagement, thus contributing to expanding their individual tourism experiences.

The application environment provided by the religious tourism experience technological architecture model presented in Figure 6 focuses on one POI, which could be a religious or cultural heritage asset such as a statue, a restaurant, or a museum. Each POI is integrated in its own technological itinerary, defined by a theme, religious event, or a gaming itinerary to obtain rewards.

Figure 6. RTEM technological architecture
Source: Author's elaboration

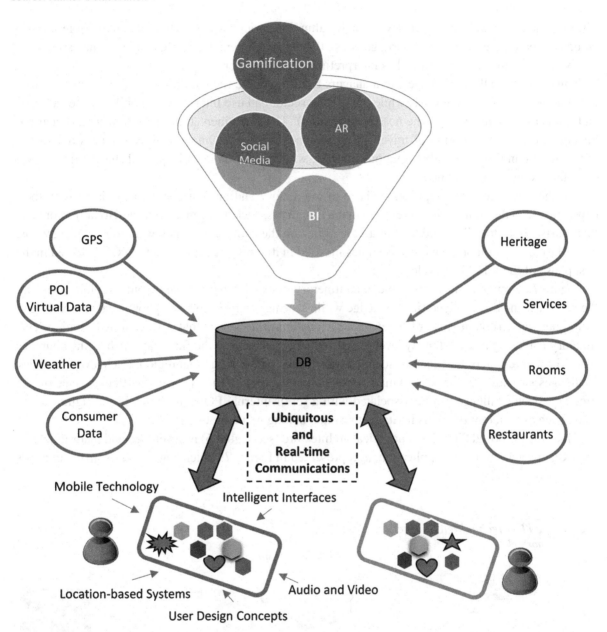

The proposed tourism religious experience application enables travelers to acquire new knowledge and to participate through user-generated content about the same POI, in which users write commentaries about the POI or another tourism site or share their photos and videos with friends on social networks. Taking into account all the concepts presented in the section above, RTEM, and corresponding technological architecture, the next step is to implement all the functionalities associated with the model.

IMPLEMENTATION OF THE RTEM

The proposed AR applications can develop new cultural experiences since AR tools can promote tourism while enhancing the potential of heritage sites. Tourists can interact with POIs and, at the same time, receive clearer information that makes interpreting the sites easier.

This approach allows heritage site managers to differentiate the cultural supply according to their target audience and communities, while the private sector can use Internet and mobile devices as sales and marketing channels (e.g., the nearest restaurant). The implementation of these technological applications creates a new kind of traveler who searches for new technological experiences associated with tourism, in this case within religious tourism, while acquiring knowledge and sharing their travel experiences through social networks.

For these travelers, the applications have to tell a story and present content associated with their experiences, so the solution is to create thematic itineraries, such as a game connected to faith moments that tourists have to follow and visit in all the points on their itinerary if they want to receive rewards. These last are a result of the game mechanics inserted in itineraries centered on the POIs selected in the first phase of the RTEM's development.

Figure 7 below presents an example of an itinerary in which tourists have to tour a region to visit all the churches and acquire specific knowledge while sharing their reviews and photos and responding to some questions to obtain a reward, for example, a free dinner at an event that will occur in the region. This itinerary is like a game with many levels, represented by a circle on the first map, such as the churches that exist in a region or the places associated with a saint who lived in that region. Each level has many challenges, as shown in the second map, for example, visiting all the POIs in a particular place on the itinerary. Each challenge can be associated with a set of internal POIs, as shown in the figure on the right, such as different religious heritage items that belong to a famous church.

Thus, the proposed RTEM technological architecture (see Figure 6) is developed and materialized in an AR gamification mobile application, as represented in Figure 7, which engages consumers, expands

Figure 7. RTEM technological itinerary
Source: Author's elaboration

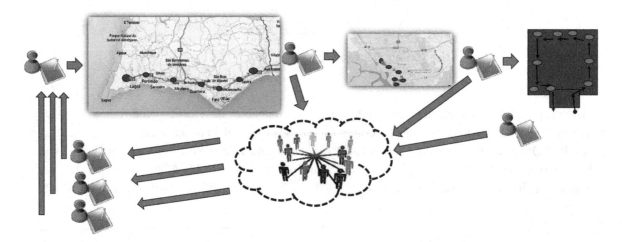

tourism experiences, and presents technological innovations that match the individual tourist's motivations. Meanwhile, it allows the development of sustainability indicators using business intelligence tools.

SUGGESTIONS FOR FUTURE RESEARCH

The development of the proposed RTEM presents some challenges and limitations that need to be overcome: privacy concerns of tourists, selection of the right databases, and economic interests. The first problem is related to the acquisition of data by third parties through social media and gamification, which has to be overcome with the implementation of rules related to privacy of information.

The second challenge has to do with the size of databases, as this aspect enables the management, storage, processing, and dissemination of information, which increases exponentially when data collection occurs at high speeds in association with attractions, accessibility, amenities, and ancillary services—representing a large volume of data that increases every day. The final issue is related to the need to establish public-private partnerships that are essential when developing technological solutions with the characteristics listed above.

Each of these challenges is associated with an element considered essential for innovation, and, as such, each problem has to be overcome in order to mitigate any inconvenience to individual consumers, in particular, and to contribute to the joint creation of innovative solutions that meet the interests of all.

Looking ahead, the authors of this paper intend to include in the technological architecture model presented in Figure 6 features that include the concepts of encoding and communicating between objects via the Internet (i.e., the Internet of Things), which enables participation in integrated networks in the areas of knowledge and intelligent systems. Another goal is to integrate the model into the development of innovative urban solutions that seek to structure the offer and its valuation, to maximize the participation of companies and cities with the inclusion of cloud computing technologies, the Internet of Things, user-centered services, and stakeholder engagement (i.e., smart cities).

CONCLUSION

Tourism experiences can combine activities related to entertainment, education, aestheticism, and escapism, which allow tourists to create a set of memories and emotions related to the places they visit. These activities can contribute to tourism experiences at different levels or can be associated with different types of meaning that, when combined, can transform a trip into something memorable.

Cultural tourism has attracted tourists seeking to satisfy their need to acquire knowledge and new experiences, in which pilgrims and religiously motivated travel are extremely important factors in human mobility. Tourists today are more widely traveled and experienced, traveling with the goal of having new tourism experiences that add fresh travel-related value. These tourists are receptive to co-creation activities and easily accept new technologies, which can potentiate multiple creative tourist experiences and help tourism organizations to acquire knowledge about consumer behavior.

The acquisition of cultural knowledge about religious heritage can increase the numbers of visitors, and technological solutions that enhance religious tourism experiences can create a new kind of tourism—technological tourism—which offers new experiences through new technological features associated with religious places. To create technological religious tourism experiences, tourism managers need to structure the process into two phases: defining content to share and developing technological solutions.

The content associated with the most pertinent POIs in each region has to be researched in primary and secondary sources, followed by the definition of the content and information structure of what will be presented to visitors. Technological solutions should consider functionalities that can adapt to different situations, individuals, and places. These solutions need to integrate mobile devices, AR, gamification, social networks, location-based systems, and user-centered design to create applications characterized by an intelligent human-computer interface.

Ubiquitous communication via mobile devices provides access to information anytime and anywhere. In turn, AR is essential to integrating elements that add additional information to religious resources, and, when associated with gamification, AR presents opportunities to engage consumers while facilitating their acquisition of knowledge about heritage sites and contributing to the measurement and evaluation of tourism businesses' sustainability.

User-generated content and shared consumer commentaries provided in social networks, when integrated with business intelligence tools on a strategic level, permit the definition of new business models and enhance the discovery of tourists and residents' new consumption patterns. To engage consumers more fully, the proposed application should have an intelligent human-computer interface that shows personalized information matching the visitors' profiles. The application has to tell a story that leads tourists along a certain route in a religious itinerary, just as a game might do, creating an affective involvement with the targeted heritage and enhancing tourists' personal and religious experiences.

The applications associated with the proposed religious tourism experiences model encourage the development of a new type of tourism beyond sun and sand— "technological tourism." This tourism's consumers are more technologically savvy, enjoying access to information and culture on a less seasonal basis and looking for new experiences and entertainment value.

The most important innovation in this model is the integration of ICTs, tourism businesses, residents, tourists, and cultural and religious heritage into a single technological solution that meets the needs of religious tourism consumers, creating economic value for tourism organizations while adding value to tourists' experiences. The most valuable conclusion is that holistic applications can provide not only better travel experiences but also solutions to World Heritage Sites threatened by overcrowding, offering an alternative form of access to heritage sites and objects that lessens the impact of visitors but, at the same time, heightens their overall travel experience.

ACKNOWLEDGMENT

This work was supported by CEFAGE (PEst-C/EGE/UI4007/2013).

REFERENCES

Agapito, D., Valle, P., & Mendes, J. (2014). The sensory dimension of tourist experiences: Capturing meaningful sensory-based themes in Southwest Portugal. *Tourism Management*, *42*, 224–237. doi:10.1016/j.tourman.2013.11.011

Akehurst, G. (2009). User generated content: The use of blogs for tourism organizations and tourism consumers. *Service Business*, *3*(1), 51–61. doi:10.1007/s11628-008-0054-2

Andersson, T. (2007). The Tourist in the Experience Economy. *Scandinavian Journal of Hospitality and Tourism*, *7*(1), 46–58. doi:10.1080/15022250701224035

Aziz, K. A., & Siang, T. G. (2014). Virtual Reality and Augmented Reality Combination as a Holistic Application for Heritage Preservation in the UNESCO World Heritage Site of Melaka. *International Journal of Social Science and Humanity*, *4*(5), 333–338. doi:10.7763/IJSSH.2014.V4.374

Barreda, A. A., Bilgihan, A., Nusair, K., & Okumus, F. (2015). Generating brand awareness in Online Social Networks. *Computers in Human Behavior*, *50*, 600–609. doi:10.1016/j.chb.2015.03.023

Binkhorst, E. (2007). Creativity in Tourism Experience- a closer look at sitges. In G. Richards & J. Wilson (Eds.), *Tourism, Creativity and Development* (pp. 125–145). London: Routledge.

Blohm, I., & Leimeister, J. M. (2013). Gamification. *Business & Information Systems Engineering*, *5*(4), 275–278. doi:10.1007/s12599-013-0273-5

Borrie, W., & Roggenbuck, J. (2001). The Dynamic, Emergent, and Multi-phasic Nature of on-site Wilderness Experiences. *Journal of Leisure Research*, *33*(2), 202.

Bower, M., Howe, C., McCredie, N., Robinson, A., & Grover, D. (2014). Augmented Reality in education–cases, places and potentials. *Educational Media International*, *51*(1), 1–15. doi:10.1080/09523987.2014.889400

Buhalis, D., & Amaranggana, A. (2013). Smart tourism destinations. In Z. Xiang & L. Tussyadiah (Eds.), *Information and Communication Technologies in Tourism 2014* (pp. 553–564). Springer International Publishing. doi:10.1007/978-3-319-03973-2_40

Buhalis, D., & Law, R. (2008). Progress in information technology and tourism management. 20 years on and 10 years after the internet. The state of etourism research. *Tourism Management*, *29*(4), 609–623. doi:10.1016/j.tourman.2008.01.005

Burke, M., & Hiltbrand, T. (2011). How gamification will change business intelligence. *Business Intelligence Journal*, *16*(2), 8–16.

Camerer, C. (2003). *Behavioral game theory: Experiments in strategic interaction*. Princeton, NJ: Princeton University Press.

Cary, S. (2004). The tourist moment. *Annals of Tourism Research*, *31*(1), 61–77. doi:10.1016/j.annals.2003.03.001

Chen, W. (2014). Historical Oslo on a handheld device–a mobile augmented reality application. *Procedia Computer Science*, *35*, 979–985. doi:10.1016/j.procs.2014.08.180

Cohen, E. (1979). A Phenomenology of Tourist Type. *Sociology*, *13*(2), 179–201. doi:10.1177/003803857901300203

Crompton, J. L., & McKay, S. L. (1997). Motives of visitors attending festival events. *Annals of Tourism Research*, *24*(2), 425–439. doi:10.1016/S0160-7383(97)80010-2

Csapó, J. (2012). The role and importance of cultural tourism in modern tourism industry. In M. Kasimoglu (Ed.), *Strategies for Tourism Industry - Micro and Macro Perspectives* (pp. 201–232). Rijeka, Croatia: InTech Open Access Publisher. doi:10.5772/38693

Cutler, S. Q., & Carmichael, B. A. (2010). The Dimensions of the Tourist Experience, The Tourism and Leisure Experience Consumer and Managerial Perspectives. In M. Morgan, P. Lugosi, & J. R. Brant Ritchie (Eds.), *Aspects of Tourism* (pp. 3–26). Toronto: Channel View Publications.

Dadwal, S. S., & Hassan, A. (2015). The augmented reality marketing-a merger of marketing and technology in tourism. In N. Ray (Ed.), *Emerging Innovative Marketing Strategies in the Tourism Industry* (pp. 78–96). Hershey, PA: IGI Global. doi:10.4018/978-1-4666-8699-1.ch005

Davis, F. D. (1989). Perceived usefulness, perceived ease of use, and user acceptance of information technology. *Management Information Systems Quarterly*, *13*(3), 319–340. doi:10.2307/249008

Davis, R., Piven, I., & Breazeale, M. (2014). Conceptualizing the brand in social media community: The five sources model. *Journal of Retailing and Consumer Services*, *21*(4), 468–481. doi:10.1016/j.jretconser.2014.03.006

Deterding, S., Dixon, D., Khaled, R., & Nacke, L. (2011). From game design elements to gamefulness: defining gamification.*Proceedings of the 15th International Academic MindTrek Conference: Envisioning Future Media Environments* (pp. 9-15). New York, NY: ACM. doi:10.1145/2181037.2181040

Draganić, T., & Rajević, D. (2011). Impact of IT and other technologies to Religious Tourism. *International Journal of Economics and Law*, *1*(2), 31–40.

Dunleavy, M., & Dede, C. (2014). Augmented reality teaching and learning. In *Handbook of research on educational communications and technology* (pp. 735–745). New York, NY: Springer New York. doi:10.1007/978-1-4614-3185-5_59

Engelberger, J. F. (1982). Robotics in practice: Future capabilities. *Electronic Servicing & Technology magazine*.

Favre-Brun, A., Jacquemin, C., & Caye, V. (2012). Revealing the "spirit of the place": Genius Loci, a spatial augmented reality performance based on 3D data and historical hypotheses. *Proceedings of the 18th International Conference on Virtual Systems and Multimedia (VSMM)* (pp. 103-108). Milan: IEEE.

Fesenmaier, D. R., Wöber, K. W., & Werthner, H. (Eds.). (2006). *Destination recommendation systems: Behavioral foundations and applications.* Cambridge: CAB International. doi:10.1079/9780851990231.0000

Fino, E. R., Martín-Gutiérrez, J., Fernández, M. D. M., & Davara, E. A. (2013). Interactive Tourist Guide: Connecting Web 2.0, Augmented Reality and QR Codes. *Procedia Computer Science*, *25*, 338–344. doi:10.1016/j.procs.2013.11.040

Garau, C. (2014). From Territory to smartphone: Smart Fruition of Cultural Heritage for Dinamic Tourism Development. *Planning Practice and Research*, *29*(3), 238–255. doi:10.1080/02697459.2014.929837

Gavalas, D., Konstantopoulos, C., Mastakas, K., & Pantziou, G. (2014). Mobile recommender systems in tourism. *Journal of Network and Computer Applications*, *39*, 319–333. doi:10.1016/j.jnca.2013.04.006

Gretzel, U. (2011). Intelligent systems in tourism: A social science perspective. *Annals of Tourism Research*, *38*(3), 757–779. doi:10.1016/j.annals.2011.04.014

Gretzel, U., & Jamal, T. (2009). Conceptualizing the creative tourist class: Technology, mobility, and tourism experiences. *Tourism Analysis, 14*(4), 471–481. doi:10.3727/108354209X12596287114219

Henriques, C., Ramos, C., & Rodrigues, J. M. F. (2014). Realidade Aumentada Aplicada a Valorização do Turística do Património Religioso no Algarve. *Proceedings of Management Studies International Conference -TMS ALGARVE 2014* (p. 106). Olhão: Portugal.

Hjalager, A. M. (2010). A review of innovation research in tourism. *Tourism Management, 31*(1), 1–12. doi:10.1016/j.tourman.2009.08.012

Jung, T., Chung, N., & Leue, M. C. (2015). The determinants of recommendations to use augmented reality technologies: The case of a Korean theme park. *Tourism Management, 49*, 75–86. doi:10.1016/j.tourman.2015.02.013

Kalmanek, C. (2012). The essential elements of successful innovation. *Computer Communication Review, 42*(2), 105–109. doi:10.1145/2185376.2185393

Lanquar, R. (2014). *Mondialisation et tourisme religieux. Vietnam Institute of Culture and Arts Studies (VICAS)*. Vietnam: Novembre, Nguyen Luong Bang.

LEO. (2009). The Experience Pyramid. *Lapland Center of Expertise for the Experience Industry*. Retrieved from http://reiselivsnytt-utmark.sfskog.no/upload/Audny%20Chris%20%C3%98iamo-Holsen%20 foredrag.pdf

Li, Y. (2000). Geographical consciousness and tourism experience. *Annals of Tourism Research, 27*(4), 863–883. doi:10.1016/S0160-7383(99)00112-7

Metaio (2015). Augmented Reality Museum Experience. *Metaio AR*. Retrieved from https://www.youtube.com/watch?v=RxSb4tjdTPk

Milano, R., Baggio, R., & Piattelli, R. (2011, January). The effects of online social media on tourism websites. In Information and Communication technologies in tourism 2011 (pp. 471-483). doi:10.1007/978-3-7091-0503-0_38

Mortara, M., Catalano, C. E., Bellotti, F., Fiucci, G., Houry-Panchetti, M., & Petridis, P. (2014). Learning cultural heritage by serious games. *Journal of Cultural Heritage, 15*(3), 318–325. doi:10.1016/j.culher.2013.04.004

Mossberg, L. (2007). A Marketing Approach to the Tourist Experience. *Scandinavian Journal of Hospitality and Tourism, 7*(1), 59–74. doi:10.1080/15022250701231915

Moutinho, L. (1987). Consumer behaviour in tourism. *European Journal of Marketing, 11*(10), 5–44. doi:10.1108/EUM0000000004718

Munar, A. M., & Jacobsen, J. K. S. (2013). Trust and involvement in tourism social media and web-based travel information sources. *Scandinavian Journal of Hospitality and Tourism, 13*(1), 1–19. doi:10.1080/15022250.2013.764511

Neuhofer, B. (2013). Experiences are co-created and technology –enhanced. *eTourismLab, Bournemouth University*. Retrieved from http://blogs.bournemouth.ac.uk/etourismlab/tag/experience-economy

Neuhofer, B., & Buhalis, D. (2012, June). Understanding and managing technology-enabled enhanced tourist experiences. *Proceedings of the 2nd Conference on Advances in Hospitality and Tourism Marketing & Management*, Corfu, Greece.

Neuhofer, B., & Buhalis, D. (2013). Technology Enhanced Tourist experiences: a holistic exploration of how technology can enhanced tourist experiences. *eTourismLab, Bournemouth University*. Retrieved from http://blogs.bournemouth.ac.uk/etourismlab/tag/experience-economy

Neuhofer, B., Buhalis, D., & Ladkin, A. (2013). A Typology of Technology-Enhanced Tourism Experiences. *International Journal of Tourism Research*, *16*(4), 340–350. doi:10.1002/jtr.1958

Neuhofer, B., Buhalis, D., & Ladkin, A. (2015). Smart technologies for personalized experiences: A case study in the hospitality domain. *Electronic Markets*, *25*(3), 243–254. doi:10.1007/s12525-015-0182-1

Noy, C. (2007). The poetics of tourist experience: An autoethnography of a family trip to Elliot. *Journal of Tourism and Cultural Change*, *5*(3), 141–157. doi:10.2167/jtcc085.0

Oh, H., Fiore, A. M., & Jeoung, M. (2007). Measuring Experience Economy Concepts: Tourism Applications. *Journal of Travel Research*, *46*(2), 119–132. doi:10.1177/0047287507304039

Ooi, C. (2005). A theory of tourism experiences: The management of attention. In T. O'Dell & P. Billing (Eds.), *Experiencescapes: Tourism, Culture, and Economy* (pp. 51–69). Copenhagen: Copenhagen Business School Press.

Park, H., & Kim, Y. K. (2014). The role of social network websites in the consumer–brand relationship. *Journal of Retailing and Consumer Services*, *21*(4), 460–467. doi:10.1016/j.jretconser.2014.03.011

Pendrana, M. (2014). Location-based services and tourism: Possible implications for destination. *Current Issues in Tourism*, *17*(9), 753–762. doi:10.1080/13683500.2013.868411

Père, C., & Faucher, S. (2007). Cluny: de la gestion de données à la réalité augmentée. In Actes du colloque Virtual Retrospect (pp. 61-67). Bordeaux, France: Archéovision.

Petroman, I., Petroman, C., Buzatu, C., Marin, D., Dumitrescu, A., Statie, C., & Rus, I. (2011). A Religious and Ethnic Tourism Profile of Europe. *Scientific Papers Animal Science and Biotechnologies*, *44*(2), 490–493.

Pine, J., & Gilmore, J. (1999). *The experience economy*. Boston: Harvard Business School Press.

Pine, J., & Gilmore, J. (2011). *The Experience Economy*. Boston: Harvard Business Press.

Prince, J. D. (2013). Gamification. *Journal of Electronic Resources in Medical Libraries*, *10*(3), 162–169. doi:10.1080/15424065.2013.820539

Quan, S., & Wang, N. (2004). Towards a structural model of the tourist experience: An illustration from food experiences in tourism. *Tourism Management*, *25*(3), 297–305. doi:10.1016/S0261-5177(03)00130-4

Ramos, C. M. Q., Rodrigues, P. M. M., & Rodrigues, J. M. F. (2015). Opportunities, emerging features and trends in electronic distribution in tourism. *International Journal of Information Systems and Social Change*, *6*(4), 17–32. doi:10.4018/IJISSC.2015100102

Richards, G. (2005). *Cultural tourism in Europe*. Wallingford, UK: ATLAS.

Richards, G., & Wilson, J. (2006). Developing creativity in tourist experiences: A solution to the serial reproduction of culture? *Tourism Management, 27*(6), 1408–1441. doi:10.1016/j.tourman.2005.06.002

Seamon, D. (1979). *A geography of the lifeworld: Movement, rest, and encounter*. London: Croom Helm.

SIGA. (2012). Diverse Beliefs: Tourism of Faith Religious tourism gains ground. Strategic Initiatives & Government Advisory (SIGA) Team. New Delhi: Yes Bank-FICCI. Retrieved from http://www.ficci.com/spdocument/20207/Diverse-Beliefs-Tourism-of-Faith.pdf

Sigala, M. (2015). The application and impact of gamification funware on trip planning and experiences: The case of TripAdvisor's funware. *Electronic Markets, 25*(3), 189–209. doi:10.1007/s12525-014-0179-1

Staab, S., Werthner, H., Ricci, F., Zipf, A., Gretzel, U., Fesenmaier, D. R., & Knoblock, C. (2002). Intelligent systems for tourism. *IEEE Intelligent Systems, 17*(6), 53–64. doi:10.1109/MIS.2002.1134362

Swarbrooke, J., & Horner, S. (1999). *Consumer Behaviour in Tourism*. Oxford: Butterworth-Heinemann.

Tuan, Y. (1993). *Passing strange and wonderful: aesthetics, nature, and culture*. Washington: Island Press.

Tung, V. W. S., & Ritchie, J. R. (2011). Exploring the essence of memorable tourism experiences. *Annals of Tourism Research, 38*(4), 1367–1386. doi:10.1016/j.annals.2011.03.009

Tussyadiah, I. P., & Fesenmaier, D. R. (2009). Mediating the tourist experiences: Access to places via shared videos. *Annals of Tourism Research, 36*(1), 24–40. doi:10.1016/j.annals.2008.10.001

UNESCO. (2009). *The 2009 UNESCO Framework for Cultural Statistics (FCS)*. UNESCO Institute for Statistics.

UNESCO. (2015). *Routes of Santiago de Compostela: Camino Francés and Routes of Northern Spain*. Retrieved from http://whc.unesco.org/en/list/669/

UNWTO. (2008). *International Conference on Tourism, Religions and Dialogue of Cultures Cordoba, Spain, October 2007*. Madrid, Spain: World Tourism Organization. Retrieved from http://pub.unwto.org/WebRoot/Store/Shops/Infoshop/4947/9D4A/39D1/F45C/D0A6/C0A8/0164/81C3/081216_turismo_religioso_cordoba_excerpt.pdf

UNWTO. (2011). Religious Tourism in Asia and the Pacific. Madrid, Spain: World Tourism Organization. Retrieved from http://publications.unwto.org/sites/all/files/pdf/110325_religious_tourism_excerpt.pdf

Wang, D., Park, S., & Fesenmaier, D. R. (2012). The role of smartphones in mediating the touristic experience. *Journal of Travel Research, 51*(4), 371–387. doi:10.1177/0047287511426341

Wickens, E. (2002). The sacred and the profane: A tourist typology. *Annals of Tourism Research, 29*(3), 834–851. doi:10.1016/S0160-7383(01)00088-3

Woodside, A., Crouch, G., & Ritchie, J. R. (2000). *Consumer Psychology of Tourism, Hospitality and Leisure*. Wallingford, Oxon: CABI Publishing.

WRTA. (2008). Religious Tourism Cultural Diversity. *World Religious Travel Association (WRTA)*. Retrieved from http://www.multifaiths.com/faith-communities/religious-tourism

Xiang, Z., & Gretzel, U. (2010). Role of social media in online travel information search. *Tourism Management, 31*(2), 179–188. doi:10.1016/j.tourman.2009.02.016

Xu, F., Weber, J., & Buhalis, D. (2013). Gamification in tourism. In *Information and Communication Technologies in Tourism 2014* (pp. 525–537). New York, NY: Springer International Publishing. doi:10.1007/978-3-319-03973-2_38

Xu, Y. (2011). *Literature review on web application gamification and analytics* (pp. 11–05). Honolulu, HI.

Yovcheva, Z., Buhalis, D., Gatzidis, C., & van Elzakker, C. P. (2014). Empirical Evaluation of Smartphone Augmented Reality Browsers in an Urban Tourism Destination Context. *International Journal of Mobile Human Computer Interaction, 6*(2), 10–31. doi:10.4018/ijmhci.2014040102

Zichermann, G., & Cunningham, C. (2011). *Gamification by design: Implementing game mechanics in web and mobile apps*. Sebastopol, CA: O'Reilly Media, Inc.

KEY TERMS AND DEFINITIONS

Augmented Reality: This facilitates a better understanding of the real world and permits the integration of virtual elements that help to complement real resources.

Business Intelligence: This results from information systems that combine data with analytical tools in order to provide information relevant to decision making, while seeking to improve the quality and availability of this information to decision makers.

Consumer Behavior: This is the focus of studies of consumers and the processes they employ to choose, use (i.e., consume), and dispose of products and services.

Cultural Heritage: This comprises physical artifacts and intangible attributes of a place or society that are inherited from past generations. Tangible heritage includes buildings, monuments, landscapes, books, works of art, and artifacts. Intangible heritage includes folklore, traditions, language, and knowledge.

Gamification: Gaming mechanics can be used to solve problems in nongaming environments, such as in a business, making it possible to measure and evaluate the reputation or performance consumers associate with products and destinations.

Intelligent Interface: This is any human-computer interface that can predict what users want to do and present information based on this prediction. The key idea is that this interface is more intuitive and helpful in a way that presents information to users in an appropriate context that is more adequate to their needs.

Social Media: These aggregates of online communications channels can be considered tools that can be used to define new business models strategically, taking into consideration analyses of community user-generated content and information shared with other members of these online communities.

Tourism Experience: This is a set of activities in which individuals engage on their personal terms, such as pleasant and memorable places, allowing each tourist to build his or her own travel experiences so that these satisfy a wide range of personal needs, from pleasure to a search for meaning.

Chapter 11
Organizing Contextual Data in Context Aware Systems:
A Review

Umar Mahmud
Foundation University Islamabad (FUI), Pakistan

ABSTRACT

Context aware systems strive to facilitate better usability through advanced devices, interfaces and systems in day to day activities. These systems offer smart service discovery, delivery and adaptation all based on the current context. A context aware system must gather the context prior to context inference. This gathered context is then stored in a tagged, platform independent format using Extensible Markup Language (XML) or Web Ontology Language (OWL). The hierarchy is enforced for fast lookup and contextual data organization. Researchers have proposed and implemented different contextual data organizations a large number of which has been reviewed in this chapter. The chapter also identifies the tactics of contextual data organizations as evident in the literature. A qualitative comparison of these structures is also carried out to provide reference to future research.

INTRODUCTION

Context aware systems aim at smart service discovery, delivery and adaptation based on a person or a group's context. The context is considered as the set of attributes that describe an activity among participant persons and applications (Mahmud & Malik, 2014; Mahmud, 2015). The context requires a four stage process where in the contextual data is gathered, is represented and stored, is subsequently recognized and activity identified using machine learning techniques and finally the services are adjusted based on the recognition outcome (Mahmud & Javed, 2014). The complete system is set within the physical bounds of the environment that encompasses sensors, users and services. Context Aware Systems constitute mobile platforms and facilitate mobile computing (Musumba & Nyongesa, 2013; Hong, Suh, & Kim, 2009; Kiani, Anjum, Knappmeyer, Bessis, & Antonopoulos, 2013).

DOI: 10.4018/978-1-5225-0435-1.ch011

The context is gathered from the sensors present on the environment. This context can also be acquired through user devices as well as interaction with the users present in the environment. Gathering the context requires a representation technique that maintains the diverse data acquired from the environment thus conforming to heterogeneity across multiple platforms. The collected data is consistently represented and stored in the system. Two research questions are highlighted in context gathering phase. First: What is the suitable technique for context data representation? And second: How is the data organized? Feng et al have raised the question of organization of contextual data as well. (Feng, Apers, & Jonker, 2004). The theme of this chapter is the organization of contextual data and the survey of published evidences.

HCI is the branch of computer science that strives to improve the interactions between humans and machines. It is a cross discipline encompassing computer science, cognition and psychology. HCI includes smart interfaces that recognize gestures to control applications (Schmidt, Context-Awareness, Context-Aware User Interfaces, and Implicit Interaction, 2014). HCI bridges the gap between human factors and the computing world to provide better interfaces based on the user's preference, mood and state. User preferences are observed by monitoring the user's activity (Malik, Mahmud, & Javed, 2009). The early computers could only be used by trained professionals who used keyboards and stared at black screens with white text all day.

Software Requirements Engineering (SRE) is the study of the end user to gather refined software requirements (Sommerville, 2015). The user being naïve is unable to explicitly provide requirements in a design and development friendly manner. Observing the users facilitates design and development with reduced risk in a Software Development Life Cycle (SDLC). SRE focuses on the daily activities and interaction of a user with his machine. With the advent of HCI the usage has become global where old and young both can use computing devices easily (Carroll, 2014). The core concept of HCI is increase in usability. Usability being a nonfunctional requirement as part of SDLC has now evolved into enhanced experience, entertaining, ease of learning with ease of using developer tools, gesture and mood recognition and context awareness (Dix, Finlay, Abowd, & Beale, 2003).

The actions performed by humans consciously or unconsciously follow some context. This context is acquired explicitly through sensors present in the environment or implicitly deduced though simple cognition mechanisms, traditionally (Grudin, 2001). The HCI aspect allows us to improve the usability of applications through which we can provide better, effective and efficient services. A simple application that switches the orientation of a tablet based on the holding style of the user is an example of context awareness in HCI (Schmidt, 2014).

This chapter serves as a probe into the context awareness research work and enlists the evidences of proposed organizations of contextual data. The list is not exhaustive and is populated using common keyword like "context-awareness", "context-aware systems", "context structure", "context organization", "context gathering and acquisition", "context aware applications", "contextual data", "context organization", "context structure" and "context representation", etc. The search is carried out for published works as research papers in conferences and journals.

Researchers working on contextual data organization have proposed different context structures based on their approach and focus. These structures can be categorized into loose tactics which is presented in this chapter. The characteristics of contextual data are also outlined and a comparison of published contextual organizations is also presented.

CONTEXT ORGANIZATION AND CONTEXT REPRESENTATION

Context gathering and representation has two distinct components: Context Representation and Context Organization. The representation of contextual data is concerned with *how the storage system is developed* while the organization is concerned with *how the data is structured.*

Gathering the contextual data and its subsequent storage is the first task in a context aware system (Strang & Linnhoff-Popien, 2004). Contextual data is viewed as an attribute-value pair at this level. The attributes correspond to the properties as acquired through the sensors and the device. The values of these properties describe a distinct context situation.

The contextual data is gathered from the sensors present in the environment as well as through the user devices. The gathered data is raw, acquired through wireless or wired links and may require post-processing to remove noise. The contextual data is dynamic and corresponds to the mobility of the nodes in the smart space. This data can also be used to deduce more information based on the supporting axioms. Contextual data is also found in both atomic and composite forms (Sheng, et al., 2009).

Characteristics of Contextual Data

The characteristics of contextual data outline comprehensiveness and flexibility (Goslar & Schill, 2005; Nykänen & Rodriguez, 2014; Strang & Linnhoff-Popien, 2004; Malik, Mahmud, & Javed, 2007; Bolchini, Curino, Quintarelli, Schreiber, & Tanca, 2007; Loke, 2006; Raychoudhury, Cao, Kumar, & Zhang, 2013). These properties also include the issues that must be considered while creating a contextual data store.

- **Easy Access:** The contextual data must so be organized so as to provide easy access for updating and recovery. Tree based structures provide efficient retrieval and storage in the form of a hierarchy.
- **Context Sharing and Interoperability:** The contextual data is acquired through different sensors present in the environment installed on heterogeneous platforms. Some sensors maybe shared among different participants. Similarly, different participants may have the same context. McAvory has proposed a sensor ontology that describes the sensor information using XML (McAvoy, Chen, & Donnelly, 2012). To share the contextual data among sensors and participants as well as among several participants, the model should mask the underlying heterogeneity of the distributed system as well as provide a mechanism that provides predicted information in the event of missing or imperfect contextual data (Mahmud, Iltaf, & Kamran, 2007).
- **Equality and Similarity:** It is possible that two contexts have the same value for all attributes. This leads us to identify both as equal contexts. Meanwhile, two distinct contexts maybe interpreted as belonging to the same context with a degree of similarity. The degree of similarity can be measured mathematically using distance measures. The degree identifies the closeness of different context descriptions measured at perhaps different times. Different contexts organized by different systems can be similar if they describe the same situation.
- **Uncertainty and Freshness:** The system must identify latest values from earlier ones as provided by the sensors in terms of freshness. This can be achieved be keeping timestamps. This also helps in categorizing long-term and short-term contexts. Due to the noisy nature of the sensors and the

underlying network, a degree of certainty must be present with each value. The uncertainty only helps in the decision making process as it gives the confidence on the outcome produced by the system.

- **Type of Context Information:** The context includes all information that can be acquired through sensors or deduced within the bounds of the environment. A context is composed of several contextual data types that further describe an aspect of the context. Knappmeyer et al list a number of contextual data types (Knappmeyer, Kiani, Reetz, Baker, & Tonjes, 2013). These include Spatial Context: describing the location attributes, Temporal Context: describing the time related attributes, Device Context: describing user's interaction devices, Network and Communication Context: describing network attributes, Environmental Context: describing environment attributes, Individuality and User Profile Context: Describing habits and preferences of the user, Activity Context: describing activities, Mental Context: describing user intentions and emotions and Interaction Context: describing social and community interactions. This list is not exhaustive and can include more contextual data types. Agrawala discovers that the feature sin a context model should include location, time and interaction history, subject of the context and user profiles (Agrawala, 2013).

Tactics of Context Structure

Context data is gathered from the sensor present in the environment as well as the devices. This data is stored in a flat storage structure as attribute-value pairs. The storage structure is then structured to provide hierarchy for fast access. This hierarchy also provides a manageable organization of the contextual data.

Among the evidences of context organization in literature, different tactics of context organization exists (Mahmud, Farooq, Javed, & Malik, 2012; Mahmud, Iltaf, & Kamran, 2007; Truong & Dustdar, 2009). These tactics are observed both implicitly and explicitly in literature. Different researchers have implemented different context structures for different problems within the confines of context awareness. To provide a review of different structures it is more appropriate to logically group them as tactics of context organization on the basis of similarities as well as the theme of organization as followed by the researchers. Bunningen et al outlines that context can be organized either at conceptual level or at operational level (van Bunningen, Feng, & Apers, 2005). The conceptual organization focuses on semantics and relations the operational level focuses on acquisition and modelling as reported by Perera et al (Perera, Zaslavsky, Christen, & Georgakopoulos, 2014).

This chapter considers the basis of these tactics as the presence or absence of contextual data types at Level 1 of the hierarchy. The contextual data types are the entities present in the context hierarchy and include User information, Activity information, Rules and Policies, Quality attributes and Community information. These tactics are discussed as follows and are shown in Figure 1.

EVENT CENTRIC STRUCTURE (ES)

The ES views the contextual data as a description of a distinct event. Different values of the contextual attribute set can correspond to the same event and each distinct event is labelled as an activity. This separates activity from time and space of context (Grudin, 2001). The task of a context aware system here is to classify current context as an activity (Mahmud & Javed, 2012), (Schmidt, Beigl, & Gellersen,

Figure 1. Tactics of context structure

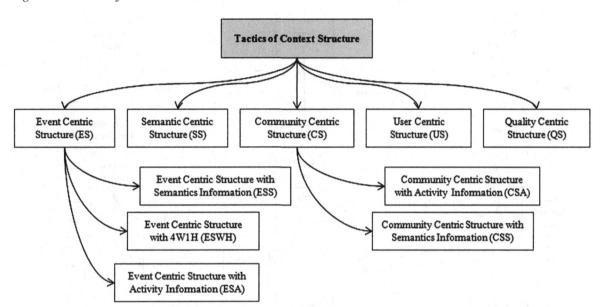

1999). Zhu identifies that a context includes many features or properties e.g., time, location and preferences stored as attribute-value pairs. These features can be given a label of activity or event (Zhu, et al., 2012). Structurally the event information is not stored as a Level 1 contextual data type in the hierarchy. There are cases where the event or activity is stored as a Level 2 contextual data type. This value is populated after classification of the situation. Figure 2 shows the research work carried out by different authors as ES.

Among the different organizations the earliest is the structure as proposed by Schilit and Theimer who distinguishes among Device context: of all the devices, User context: of the user and users' preferences and Physical context: of the environment (Schilit & Theimer, 1994). The Environment is shared by the devices and the users. The users' devices are considered as part of the device context. Together the user, the devices and the environment constitute the activity.

Chen and Kotz extended Schilit and Theimer's work by introducing time as a contextual data type (Chen & Kotz, 2000). Accordingly, the context includes Computing Context: pertaining to computing artefacts, User Context: pertaining to the user, Physical Context: pertaining to the environment and Time Context: pertaining to time of day, date and season. This work gave importance to time in addition to location. The presence of time imposed dynamism on the contextual data and demanded separation of dynamic and static contextual data types (Mahmud, Farooq, Javed, & Malik, 2012).

Brown et al proposed the context structure as composed of Location: information of the space, User: information of the user and Time and Environment: information of the sensors (Brown, Bovey, & Chen, 1997). Time and environment include information gathered through sensors less the space related information. The whole context describes a distinct activity.

Dey and Abowd consider context as a set of Primary information and Secondary information (Dey A. K., 2001; Dey & Abowd, 1999). The Primary involves spatial, behavioural and temporal data while all other data is Secondary. The spatial, behavioural and temporal information is maintained as a Level 2 structure rooted at Primary context.

Figure 2. Event centric structures (ES)

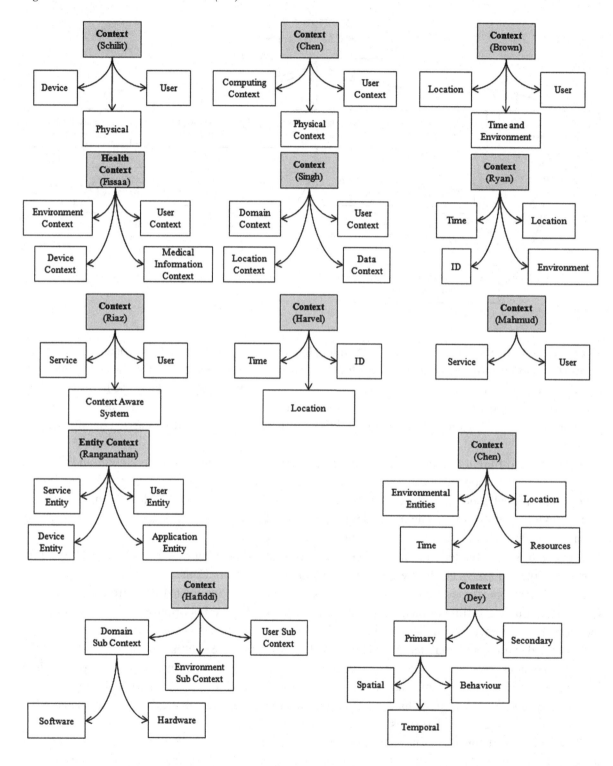

Singh et al organizes context as Domain Context: that describes the domain knowledge, Location Context: the spatial information, Data Context: information regarding data sets and User Context: information about the user (Singh, Vajirkar, & Lee, 2003).

Ryan et al presents an activity based structure as part of Mobile Computing Fieldwork Environment (MCFE) (Ryan, Pascoe, & Morse, 1997). This work is similar to e-Notes. The structure is composed of Location: concerned with spatial attributes, Environment: concerned with surroundings, ID: concerned with user identification and Time: concerned with temporal attributes.

Riaz et al considers context to be composed of Services context, the User context and the Context aware system's context (Riaz, Kiani, Lee, Han, & Lee, 2005). In this case the context aware system is considered as a distinct entity that provides services to the users on the basis of user's context, and hence has its own context. This work is similar to Dix et al's work where the context aware system is considered a separate entity (Dix, et al., 2000).

Hafiddi et al organizes context as:

- **User Sub Context:** containing features describing the user,
- **Environment Sub Context:** containing features describing the environment and
- **Device Sub Context:** containing features describing the devices (Hafiddi, Baidouri, Nassar, & Kriouile, 2012).

The Device Sub Context is further organized into

- **Software Category:** information about software parameters and
- **Hardware Category:** information about hardware parameters.

This organization distinguishes among the user and the user's device. All the services are part of the user devices.

An improvement over the structure proposed by Riaz et al is given by Mahmud et al where the context aware system is considered as a service present in the environment. The structure thus reduces to Users' Context: all information about the user, and the Services' Context: all information about the services present in the environment as well as the devices carried by the user (Mahmud, Farooq, Javed, & Malik, 2012; Mahmud, Iltaf, & Kamran, 2007). This system is designed to arbitrate and deliver better services to the user.

Fissaa et al has identified a generic theme to represent context and applied it on the e-Health Domain (Fissaa, Guermah, Hafiddi, Nassar, & Kriouile, 2014). The context is specifically the Health Context which is structured as Environment Context: describing location, date and time, User Context: describing blood group and age: Device Context: describing medical sensors and Medical Information Context: describing medical history and current status.

Ranganathan et al has proposed that context be viewed as an entity (Ranganathan, McGrath, Campbell, & Mickunas, 2003). The context entity is a super class of all entities in the system. The Sub contexts are Service Entity: those that provide a service, Application Entity: all applications in the environment, User Entity: all users in the environment and Devices Entity: all devices in the environment. This model is part of the GAIA system (Ranganathan & Campbell, 2008).

Chen and Nugent propose an ontological model for context which represents the activity (Chen & Nugent, 2009). The structure composes of Environment Entities: within which activity occurs, Time: during which activity occurs, Location: where the activity occurs and Resources: utilized by the activity.

Harvel et al views the context as an event modelled using a hypercube (Harvel, et al., 2004). The context structure is along the cardinal axes of the cube and includes Location: pertaining to spatial information, Identity: pertaining to the user and Time, pertaining to temporal information. The principal planes are then composed of combinations of the principal axes. This system is successfully implemented for digital portrait images that require location, time and identification information only.

Event Centric Structure with Activity Information (ESA)

There is a possibility that the user activity can be modelled as a sub-layer to user context thus making it a Level 2 contextual data type. In this case the user activity is either identified through user interaction or is classified post acquisition. The presence of distinct activity information contradicts the ES but is acceptable following the strict rules for ES which consider all that do not have activity information as a Level 1 contextual data type. Figure 3 shows the ESA structure.

Li et al structure context as Domain Specific context and Upper Level context. The Domain Specific includes the domain related contextual information. The Upper Level includes the high level situation and is composed of Environment: surrounding information, Person: the user, Activity: the ongoing activities, Location: spatial and Time: temporal (Li, Fang, & Xiong, 2008). In this mechanism the activity information is modelled as a Level 2 contextual data type of the Upper Level context.

Figure 3. Event centric structure with activity information (ESA)

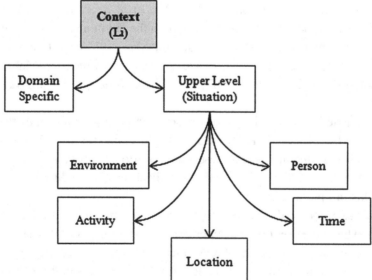

Event Centric Structure with 4W1H (ESWH)

Another approach describes the context as an event using 4W1H. This approach identifies the Who, What, Where, When and How of a context. This approach is of interest since it structures the context as a core set of interrogative statements. Figure 4 shows ESWH structures.

Castelli and Zambonelli provide a 4W approach for context data representation. The contextual structure is composed of Who: the user, What: the task, When: temporal and Where: spatial information (Castelli & Zambonelli, 2009). This approach has been used by Mahmud et al for context aware service delivery (Mahmud, Iltaf, Rehman, & Kamran, 2007; Mahmud, 2012).

Figure 4. Event Centric Structures with 4W1H (ESWH)

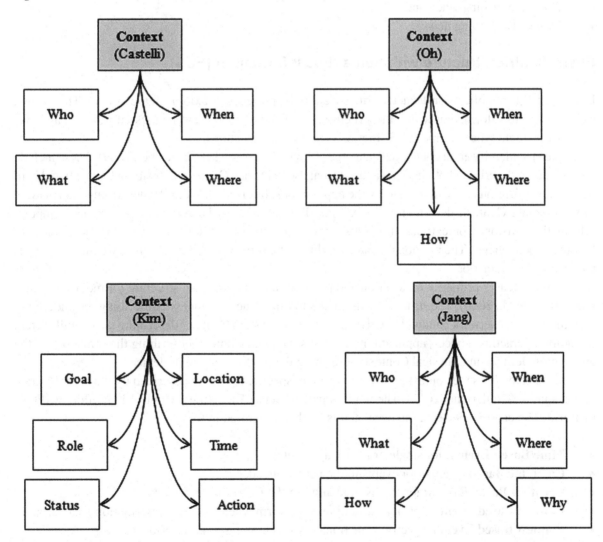

Same has been implemented by Oh et al as part of ubiController project (Oh, Yoon, & Woo, 2006). Oh et al introduces the contextual data type 'How' in addition to 4W approach thus making it 4W1H. The how identifies in what manner the activity will take place.

Kim et al and Jang and Woo working separately describe Context as 5W1H i.e., Why, Who, What, When, Where and How (Kim, Son, & Baik, 2012; Jang & Woo, 2006). The presence of Why highlights the need of the interaction by highlighting the semantics. The specific model as recommended by Kim et al includes:

- **Goal:** Describing why,
- **Role:** Describing who,
- **Status:** Describing what,
- **Location:** Describing where
- **Time:** Describing when and
- **Action:** Describing how.

Event Centric Structure with Semantics Information (ESS)

Logic, semantics, policies or deduction rules lead to the presence of axioms in the system. The context can include this information within the structure. The ES that includes semantics information as Level 1 contextual data type is termed ESS. Figure 5 shows ESS structures.

Soylu et al identify eight contextual data types (Soylu, Causmaecker, & Desmet, 2009). These include User Context: describing both internal and external users, Device Context: describing both soft and hard devices, Application Context: describing the applications, Information Context: describing information, Environmental Context: describing physical and digital artefacts, Time context: describing temporal information, History Context: describing history of interactions and Relational Context: describing relational dependencies. The relational context includes the semantics while the history context includes the history of interactions.

Dix et al focuses primarily on location and proposes a contextual data structure for mobile environments (Dix, et al., 2000). The structure is divided into Infrastructure Context: describing the underlying system including network bandwidth and display system, System Context: describing the overall system including interacting devices, applications and users, Domain Context: describing the semantics of the application domain and Physical Context: describing the physical nature of devices and sensors.

Beltran et al views the context as an event or more specifically a rule described by the user (Beltran, Arabshian, & Schulzrinne, 2011). The work is part of Sense Everything, Control Everything (SECE) platform. The context viewed as an event and is further structured in to:

- **Time Based Events:** for single or recurring events,
- **Calendar Based Events:** for events in the user's calendar,
- **Location Based Events:** for events in locality of the user or users friends,
- **Context Based Events:** specify the actions to perform when a context information changes and
- **Request Based Events:** specify the actions to execute in response to prior requests.

The Context Based Events include rules and axioms that label this structure as ESS.

Figure 5. Event centric structures with semantics information (ESS)

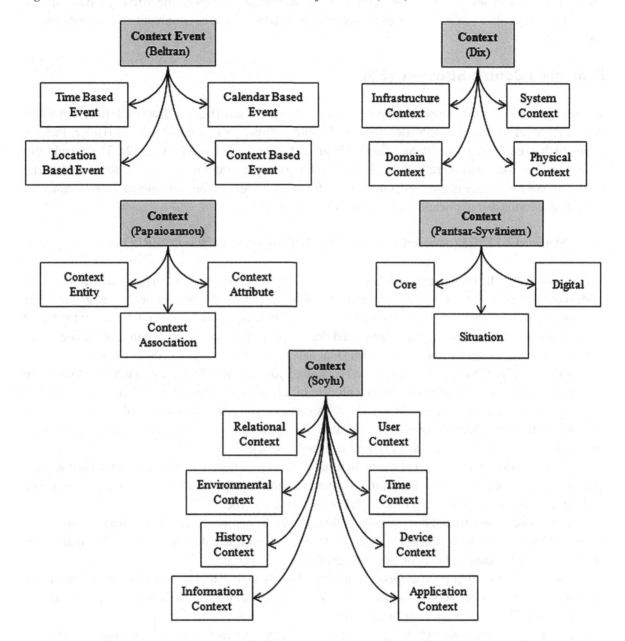

Papaioannou et al describes an entity-attribute-value structure required for context inference (Papaioannou, et al., 2014). The structure includes Context Entity: describing items in the environment, Context Attribute: describing properties of the items and Context Association: describing the relationship among entities and attributes as values. Context Association includes the semantics of the entities present in the environment.

Pantsar-Syväniem et al describes three progressive levels of context (Pantsar-Syväniem, Simula, & Ovaska, 2010). The Core context is the physical level context pertaining to the external state of the environment. The Digital context is the mid-level context and is domain specific. This provides a context derivability mechanism. The Situation context maintains information about the activity. This organization is process-centric where in the Core context is gathered from the environment and Digital context is deduced.

Semantics Centric Structure (SS)

The sensors present in the environment provide raw contextual data. This raw data needs to be converted to a meaningful form using deduction thus establishing semantics of context entities (Hofer, Pichler, Leonhartsberger, Altmann, & Werner, 2002; Mahmud, Farooq, Javed, & Malik, 2012). The meaningful form cannot be measured directly through sensors. For example, state of a service is dependent on the availability of the service queue. A deduction rule for service state can be constructed through conjunctions, disjunctions and implications as shown in Equation 1.

$$(queueState==FULL)\&\&(networkQueueState!=EMPTY)\rightarrow serviceState=OVERLOAD \tag{1}$$

Logic demands the presence of deduction rules in the system. These rules can be used to derive composite context or could be viewed as policies that highlight relations among entities. Similarly, policies are required that define the system constraints. These axioms and policies can either be kept external to the contextual data repository and rules fired during context acquisition. Structurally the logical or semantics or policy context is a Level 1 contextual data type. Figure 6 shows SS structures.

Gellersen et al reports on two products the Technology for Enabling Awareness (TEA) and MediaCup and proposes that the context awareness is a process of labelling situation as described by multi sensor data (Gellersen, Beigl, & Schmidt, 2000). The context is a fact that describes temporal-spatial situations as acquired through logical and physical contextual data types. The context is thus composed of Physical: physically measurable attributes and Logical: deduced attributes.

Hofer et al follows Gellersen et al's approach and identifies context to be Physical: which is measureable and Logical: which is derivable (Hofer, Pichler, Leonhartsberger, Altmann, & Werner, 2002). The derivable contextual data type is a meaningful contextual data type.

The composite contextual data type is derivable and can be composed of other composite types. According to Sheng et al context can be classified as Atomic: having unit value and Composite: combination of atomic and composite values (Sheng, et al., 2009).

Roussaki et al divides context as Geographical: pertaining to time and space and Logical: everything else including rules (Roussaki, Strimpakou, Pils, Kalatzis, & Liampotis, 2010; Roussaki, Kalatzis, Liampotis, Kosmides, Anagnostou, & Sykas, 2015).

Badii et al describes context as Device: of a data source, Semantic: high level context including location, environment and entity, and Application: where reasoning can be inserted (Badii, Crouch, & Lallah, 2010). The reasoning is used for context inference.

Salvi et al proposes the presence of relationship between two contexts in addition to atomic and composite contextual data types (Salvi, Ottaviano, Peinado, & Arredondo, 2009). The structure is composed of Atomic Data: which is the basic data unit having a single value, Context Data: which is the compound derivable context and Relationship: which is the relation among contexts. The model is similar to relational database.

Vajirkar et al proposes a data mining based context framework in an e-health application that combines generic context and domain specific context (Vajirkar, Singh, & Lee, 2003). The structure is composed

Figure 6. Semantics centric structures (SS)

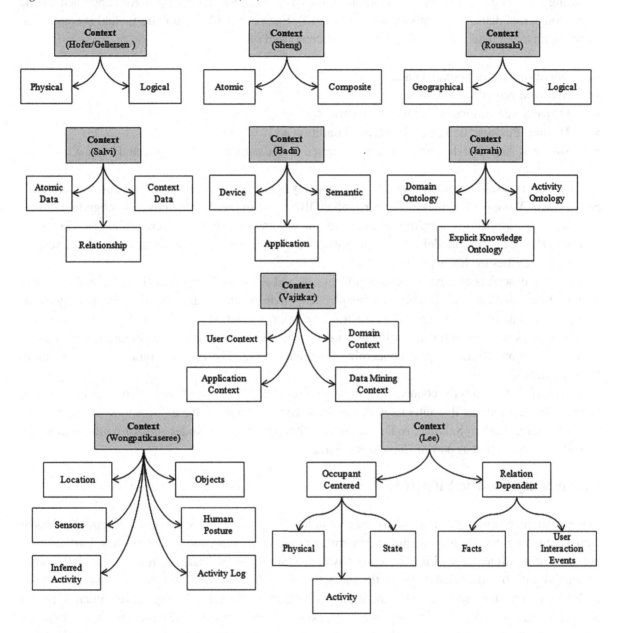

of User Context: information about the user and the user history, Application Context: information of the application requirements of conference and network, Domain Context: information of the patient and its location and Data Mining Context: describing data queries and deductions. The application deduces the unknown attributes that are part of the data mining context by asking queries.

Jarrahi and Kangavari present a Knowledge Flow Management System (KFMS) that models the flow of information from the source to destination while providing improvements in quality (Jarrahi & Kangavari, 2012). The context structure is implemented using ontology and is composed of Domain Ontology: models the concepts and relations, Activity Ontology: models atomic activities and Explicit Knowledge Ontology: models the similar activities as described by the task.

Wongpatikaseree et al proposes an Ontology Based Activity Recognition (OBAR) approach having a rich contextual data (Wongpatikaseree, et al., 2012). Each context has a unique ID and is acquired at a certain time and date. Specifically, a context is composed of:

- **Location:** refers to spatial data,
- **Sensors:** provide sensor data,
- **Objects:** the entities within the environment,
- **Human Posture:** describes the human condition and
- **Inferred Activity:** describes the activity based on the activity of the object and location.

The human posture is used to increase the accuracy of the recognition process within a smart home environment. Wongpatikaseree et al further applies OBAR on Context Aware Activity Recognition Engine (CARE) when applied in e-Health Domain as an improvement (Wongpatikaseree, Kim, Makino, Lim, & Tan, 2013). The main model remains the same and is a logical system with the addition of Activity Log: that describes the history of the patient.

Lee et al describes context as Occupant Centered and Relation Dependent (Lee, Choi, & Elmasri, 2009). Occupant Centered Context includes physical environment around the user, the activity of the user and the state of the user while the Relation Dependency Context includes the facts of the environment as well as the information about the user interaction events. This scheme separates the information of the environment from the facts concerning the environment. The facts are represented as relations among entities.

Cioara et al structures the context as Context Resource: the generator of context for example sensors, Actors: physical entities that interact with the resources and Policies: the axioms that are used by the actors (Cioara, Anghel, Salomie, & Dinsoreanu, 2009). The Actor includes semantic information and considers environment as part of Context Resource.

Community Centric Structure (CS)

The environment of a context aware system includes many artefacts including computing devices as well as human users. Humans within an environment are viewed as cooperating entities. Furthermore, presence of multiple users within the same physical area of interest leads to group and social context. The activity is now identified based on the sub activities of the group e.g., a quiz in a class room where multiple students take an exam while multiple invigilators monitor it. The high level situation is thus dependent on the social context. The social context can also include relationships among entities and can also involve information mined from social networks. The context structure is considered a CS if community or social contextual data type is present in Level 1. Figure 7 shows CS structures.

Petrelli et al models context while considering the social information within a context aware museum guide application (Petrelli, Not, Zancanaro, Strapparava, & Stock, 2001). The structure is composed of Material Context: consisting of physical and available resources and Social Contexts: consisting of the communal and personal traits of a user.

Suganuma et al structures context as *User Context*, concerned with personal traits and devices and *Social Context,* concerned with persons and their traits bounded by the environment (Suganuma, Yamanaka, Tokairin, Takahashi, & Shiratori, 2008). The environmental attributes and the services present in the environment are considered as part of social context.

Figure 7. Community centric structures (CS)

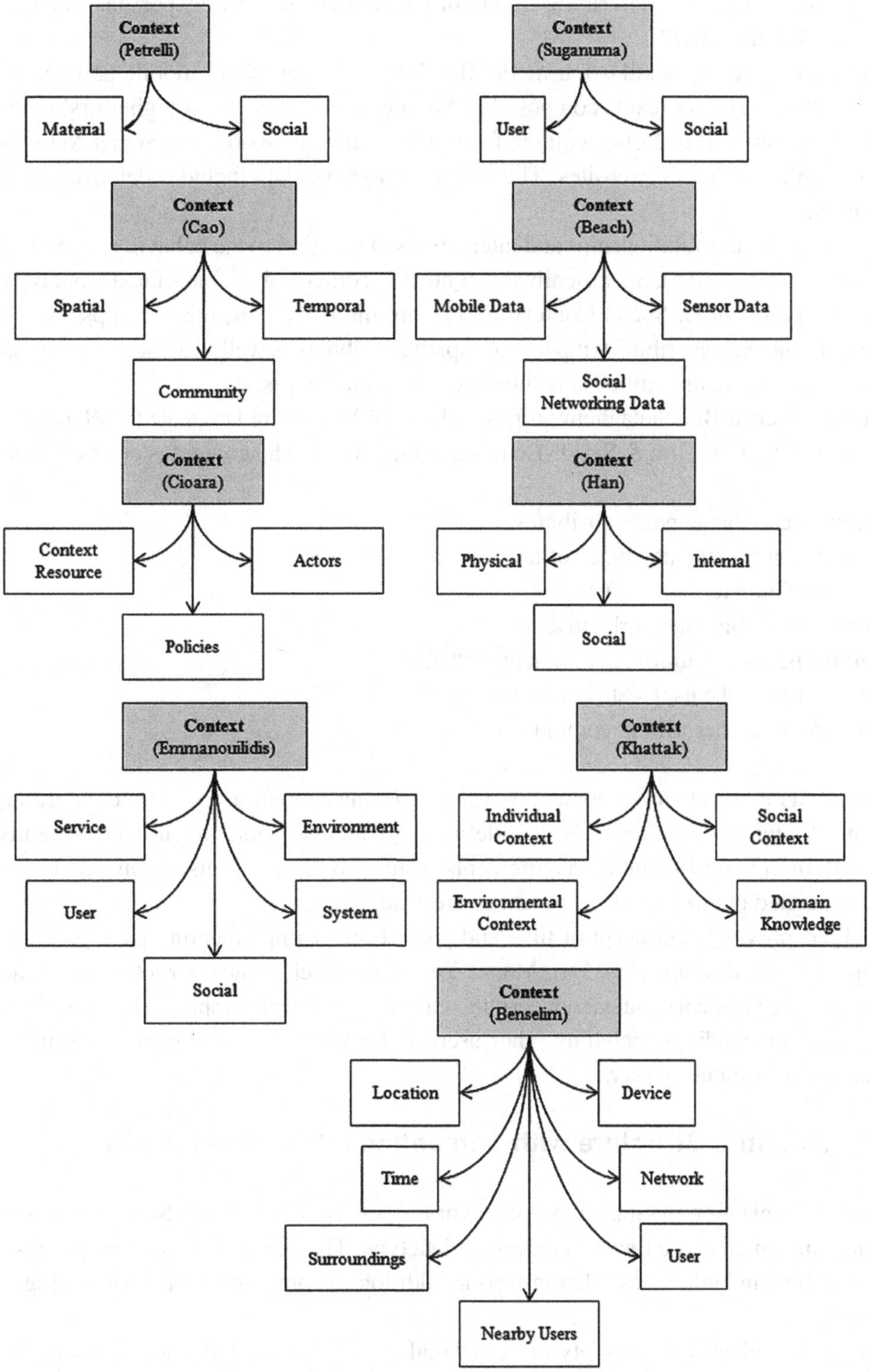

Cao et al structures context as Spatial Context: describing location, Temporal Context: describing time and Community Context: describing community including user, nearby persons and services (Cao, Klamma, Hou, & Jarke, 2008).

Beach et al presents a SocialFusion model that integrates data from mobile and social resources (Beach, et al., 2010). The context is composed of Mobile Data: acquired through users' mobile devices and includes location, Sensor Data: acquired from static sensor networks and Social Networking Data: acquired through online social websites. The social networking data includes data from users' friends and community.

Khattak et al considers relationships and interactions in addition to the behaviour as part of the social context (Khattak, et al., 2014). Specifically the context is composed of: Individual Context: describing the user and its preferences, Social Context: describing the behaviour, relationships and interactions, Environmental Context: describing temporal and spatial attributes as well as devices and Domain Knowledge: describing the domain entities in addition to rules and axioms.

Benselim and Seridi-Bouchelaghem propose a Unified Modelling language (UML) based approach for context structure (Benselim & Seridi-Bouchelaghem, 2013). The context is composed of:

- **Location:** describing spatial attributes,
- **Device:** describing the attributes of user devices,
- **Time:** describing temporal attributes,
- **Network:** describing network attributes,
- **Surroundings:** describing environmental attributes,
- **User:** describing the user's attributes and
- **Nearby Persons:** describing community attributes.

Emmanouilidis et al organizes context as User: defining human users, Service: defining services Environment: defining environment, Social, defining social characteristics in a collaborative activity and System: defining non-functional requirements (Emmanouilidis, Koutsiamanis, & Tasidou, 2013). This works is carried out to provide a context aware guidance service.

Han et al has provided a concept of time and prediction by implementing past, present and future contexts within a social setup (Han, Jyri, Ma, & Yu, 2008). Each context structure in a time has three components that are Physical Context: concerning real world physical computing entities, Social context: including social surroundings including other users and Internal Context: concerning user emotions, thoughts and tasks as input by user.

Community Centric Structure with Semantics Information (CSS)

In this context organization the logical, semantic or relation information is also maintained in addition to community information as a Level 1 contextual data type. This structure is primarily focused on community information and maintains relationships in addition to community information. Figure 8 shows CSS structures.

Siebra et al has identified a variety of contextual items (Siebra, Salgado, Tedesco, & Brézillon, 2005). The Task context is the information of scheduled tasks. Individual context and Group context holds information about the user and the community similar to Petrelli et al (Petrelli, Not, Zancanaro, Strapparava, & Stock, 2001). Interaction and planning context holds data about the relationships between

Figure 8. Community centric structure with semantics information (CSS)

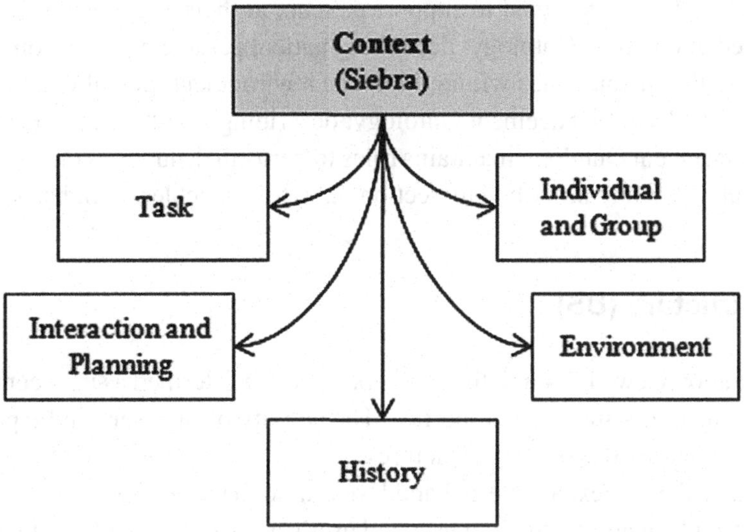

users and their tasks. Environment context includes the environment information. Finally, the History context holds information about past interactions.

Community Centric Structure with Activity Information (CSA)

In this context organization the activities of individuals and groups is also maintained in addition to community information as a Level 1 contextual data type. Figure 9 shows CSA structures.

Lewis et al developed a Group Context Model focusing on the community and presents a data model (Lewis, Novakouski, & Sánchez, 2012). The context is composed of People: describing individuals, organizations and groups, Objects: describing devices and equipment, Places: describing location, Activities: describing the behaviour and status of users and Events: describing change.

Figure 9. Community centric structures with activity information (CSA)

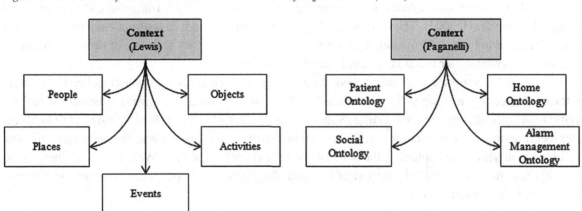

Paganelli et al outlines a context model for a home-based assistance program (Paganelli, Spinicci, & Giuli, 2008). The system is designed to support patients in their tasks as part of e-Health domain. The model is divided into Patient Ontology: describing patient parameters, location and activity, Home Ontology: describing the surroundings within the home environment, Social Ontology: describing the network resources and Alarm Management Ontology: describing rule-based policies for alarm triggering. The Alarm Management Ontology maintains rules to perform deductions on logical contextual data similar to Hofer et al's structure described in Section 3.2 (Hofer, Pichler, Leonhartsberger, Altmann, & Werner, 2002).

User Centric Structure (US)

The context organization viewed through the user's perspective is termed as user centric structure. This mechanism models the user's state and properties. The activity of the user can be present as a Level 1 contextual data type. Figure 10 shows US structures.

Gwizdka structures the context as Internal and External to the user (Gwizdka, 2000). This approach is user-centric and all information regarding user and user's devices is considered internal. The environment and the services are external to the user.

Feng et al constructs context as an n-dimensional space having n-attributes (Feng, Apers, & Jonker, 2004). The context is structured into *User-Centric Context*, describing behaviour, profile and emotional and physiological state of the user and *Environmental Context*, describing physical, social and computational entities. This structure includes the user's activity as a Level 2 contextual data type.

Yamabe et al follows a similar approach at around the same time when Feng et al published his work. This approach models activity as a Level 2 contextual data type. The work is carried out for CITRON project (Yamabe, Takagi, & Nakajima, 2005). The Context structure includes User Context: spatial, behavioural, emotional and physical information of the user, Environment Context: air and sound information and Muffin: state of the device. Muffin is a prototype device capable of contextual data acquisition.

Bhattacharyya et al has proposed a structure for a context aware patient monitoring application (Bhattacharyya, Saravanagru, & Thangavelu, 2011). The context is structured as composed of Human Factors that are related to Users and their Activities and Physical Environment that is related to Location and Environmental Condition. The Environmental Conditions include light, pressure, temperature and heart rate of the patient, all of which are gathered through sensors. The activity of the users is modelled using the similar approach of Feng et al.

Chen et al describes the context using ontology as part of the CoBrA framework (Chen, Finin, & Joshi, Ubicomp 2003, 2003). The CoBrA-ONT includes Place Related: describing environment, Agent Related: describing user information, Agent Activity: describing activity and state of the user and Agent Location: describing user location (Chen, Finin, & Joshi, 2003).

Simons and Wirtz present a context modelling profile that structures the context as Person: relating to the user, Meeting: relating to the user's meeting, Time Slot: relating to temporal information and Activity: relating to the state of the meeting (Simons & Wirtz, 2007). This system is designed to facilitate user meetings through context awareness. The system also maintains privacy and restriction information.

Löwe et al views the context as the state of the user (Löwe, Mandl, & Weber, 2012). The context includes *Location* or spatial information of the user, *Identification* or information about the user and *Activity* or behaviour of the user.

Figure 10. User centric structures (US)

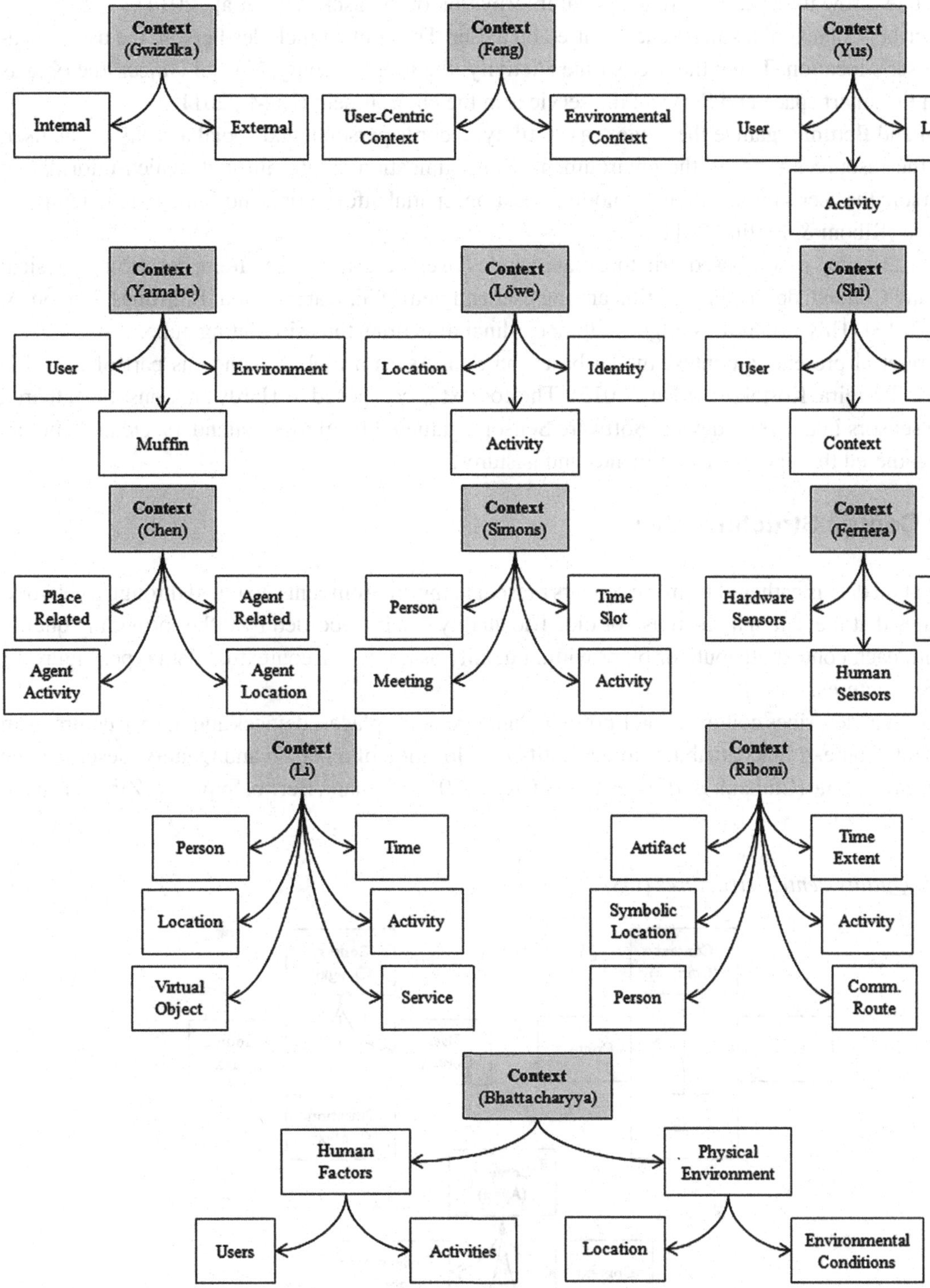

Yus et al describes semantics of context that includes User: information of the user, Activity: behaviour and state of the user and Location: spatial information of the user (Yus, et al., 2014).

Li describes context of a smart space centred on a user. The context includes Person: the user, Location: the user's location, Time: the user's time, Activity: the user's activity, Virtual Object: the objects present in the smart space and Service: the services in the environment (Li M., 2011).

Riboni and Bettini organize the context as Activity: records personal and social activity of the user, Artifact: the resources used by the environment, Communication Route: through which information flows, Person: the user's information, Symbolic Location: spatial information and Time Extent: temporal information (Riboni & Bettini, 2011).

Shi et al describes a cube based structure that includes User: describing user, Item: describing physical artefacts and Context: describing relation among user and item (Shi, Karatzoglou, Baltrunas, Larson, & Hanjalic, 2014). This structure is aligned along cardinal directions thus simulating cube.

Ferriera et al presents a context model based on Sensors on a mobile device as part of AWARE framework (Ferreira, Kostakos, & Dey, 2015). The context is composed of Hardware Sensors: gathered hardware sensors in a mobile device, Software Sensors: gathered from logs, calendars, etc and Human Sensors: gathered through voice commands and gestures.

Quality Centric Structure (QS)

The contextual data is gathered from the sensors present in the environment separated through a network. This implies that the data may be noisy or old. The quality can be recorded by either providing quality values with each context attribute or by providing quality as a Level 1 contextual data type. Figure 11 shows QS structures.

Chihani et al describes context as an Entity: includes persons, places, devices and infrastructure in an environment, Context: links attributes to the Entity e.g., location of a person and Quality: describes the value of each attribute (Chihani, Bertin, Jeanne, & Crespi, 2011; Chihani, Bertin, Suprapto, Zimmermann,

Figure 11. Quality centric structures (QS)

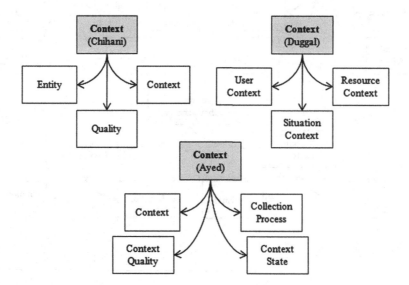

& Crespi, 2012). The quality contextual data type enforces a concept of Quality of Context (QoC) which assigns a value to a contextual data for better activity recognition and subsequent service adaptation.

Duggal et al describes context as User Context: information regarding a user including social and activity information, Situation Context: information including spatial and temporal information and Resource Context: information including parameters for quality of contextual data (Duggal, Misra, & Srinivasaraghavan, 2012).

Ayed et al provides UML stereotypes to support context properties in a UML Class Diagram (Ayed & Berbers, 2006; Ayed, Delanote, & Berbers, 2007). Specifically, the context is composed of Context: describing type including location, network and preferences, Collection Process, describing temporal including event based or period based occurrences, Context Quality: describing quality attributes that must be satisfied and Context State: describing status that can alter an application.

Comparisons of Different Organizations

Context has been organized in various ways conforming to different situations. Among all contextual organizations the attribute-value pairs remains generally the same but have been organized differently at Level 1 as discussed in Section 4. Furthermore, the out-degree of the root node is different. Table 1 shows the comparison of the different contextual organizations. It is not easy to provide a common yard-stick to compare among different structures or organizations. In this chapter a qualitative comparison is made through the presence of context data types at Level 1 of the context structure. These context data

Table 1. Comparison of different contextual organizations

Author(s)	Tactics of Context Organization	Out-Degree at Root Context	Distinct Contexts at Level 1					
			Activity/ Event	Semantics/ Logic/ Policy	Social/ Community	User	Environment	Quality
Schilit and Theimer (Schilit & Theimer, 1994)	ES	3				✓	✓	
Chen and Kotz (Chen & Kotz, 2000)		3				✓	✓	
Brown et al (Brown, Bovey, & Chen, 1997)		3				✓	✓	
Fissaa et al (Fissaa, Guermah, Hafiddi, Nassar, & Kriouile, 2014)		4				✓	✓	
Singh et al (Singh, Vajirkar, & Lee, 2003)		4				✓		
Ryan et al (Ryan, Pascoe, & Morse, 1997)		4				✓	✓	
Riaz et al (Riaz, Kiani, Lee, Han, & Lee, 2005)		3				✓		
Harvel et al (Harvel, et al., 2004)		3				✓		
Mahmud et al (Mahmud, Iltaf, Rehman, & Kamran, 2007)		2				✓		
Ranganathan et al (Ranganathan, McGrath, Campbell, & Mickunas, 2003)		4				✓		
Chen and Nugent (Chen & Nugent, 2009)		4					✓	
Hafiddi et al (Hafiddi, Baidouri, Nassar, & Kriouile, 2012)		4				✓	✓	
Dey (Dey, 2001)		2						

continued on following page

Table 1. Continued

Author(s)	Tactics of Context Organization	Out-Degree at Root Context	Distinct Contexts at Level 1					
			Activity/ Event	Semantics/ Logic/ Policy	Social/ Community	User	Environment	Quality
Li et al (Li, Fang, & Xiong, 2008)	ESA	2						
Castelli and Zambonelli (Castelli & Zambonelli, 2009)	ESWH	4				✓		
Oh et al (Oh, Yoon, & Woo, 2006)		4				✓		
Kim et al (Kim, Son, & Baik, 2012)		6	✓			✓		
Jang and Woo (Jang & Woo, 2006)		6	✓			✓		
Beltran et al (Beltran, Arabshian, & Schulzrinne, 2011)	ESS	4	✓					
Dix et al (Dix, et al., 2000)		4					✓	
Papaioannou et al (Papaioannou, et al., 2014)		3		✓				
Pantsar-Syväniem et al (Pantsar-Syväniem, Simula, & Ovaska, 2010)		3	✓					
Soylu et al (Soylu, Causmaecker, & Desmet, 2009)		8		✓		✓	✓	
Hofer et al (Hofer, Pichler, Leonhartsberger, Altmann, & Werner, 2002)	SS	2		✓				
Gellersen et al (Gellersen, Beigl, & Schmidt, 2000)		2		✓				
Sheng et al (Sheng, et al., 2009)		2		✓				
Roussaki et al (Roussaki, Strimpakou, Pils, Kalatzis, & Liampotis, 2010)		2		✓				
Salvi et al (Salvi, Ottaviano, Peinado, & Arredondo, 2009)		2		✓				
Badii et al (Badii, Crouch, & Lallah, 2010)		2		✓				
Jarrahi et al (Jarrahi & Kangavari, 2012)		3	✓	✓				
Vajirkar et al (Vajirkar, Singh, & Lee, 2003)		4		✓		✓	✓	
Wongapatikaseree et al (Wongpatikaseree, Kim, Makino, Lim, & Tan, 2013)		6	✓	✓				
Lee et al (Lee, Choi, & Elmasri, 2009)		2		✓				
Petrelli et al (Petrelli, Not, Zancanaro, Strapparava, & Stock, 2001)	CS	2			✓			
Suganuma et al (Suganuma, Yamanaka, Tokairin, Takahashi, & Shiratori, 2008)		2			✓	✓		
Cao et al (Cao, Klamma, Hou, & Jarke, 2008)		3			✓			
Beach et al (Beach, et al., 2010)		3			✓			
Cioara et al (Cioara, Anghel, Salomie, & Dinsoreanu, 2009)		3	✓		✓			
Han et al (Han, Jyri, Ma, & Yu, 2008)		3			✓		✓	
Emmanouilidis et al (Emmanouilidis, Koutsiamanis, & Tasidou, 2013)		5			✓	✓	✓	
Khattak et al (Khattak, et al., 2014)		4			✓	✓	✓	
Benselim et al (Benselim & Seridi-Bouchelaghem, 2013)		7			✓	✓	✓	

continued on following page

Table 1. Continued

Author(s)	Tactics of Context Organization	Out-Degree at Root Context	Distinct Contexts at Level 1					
			Activity/ Event	Semantics/ Logic/ Policy	Social/ Community	User	Environment	Quality
Siebra et al (Siebra, Salgado, Tedesco, & Brézillon, 2005)	CSS	5	✓	✓	✓	✓	✓	
Lewis et al (Lewis, Novakouski, & Sánchez, 2012)	CSA	5	✓		✓			
Paganelli et al (Paganelli, Spinicci, & Giuli, 2008)		4			✓		✓	
Gwizdka (Gwizdka, 2000)	US	2				✓		
Feng et al (Feng, Apers, & Jonker, 2004)		2				✓	✓	
Yus et al (Yus, et al., 2014)		3	✓			✓		
Yamabe et al (Yamabe, Takagi, & Nakajima, 2005)		3				✓	✓	
Löwe et al (Löwe, Mandl, & Weber, 2012)		3	✓			✓		
Shi et al (Shi, Karatzoglou, Baltrunas, Larson, & Hanjalic, 2014)		3				✓		
Chen et al (Chen, Finin, & Joshi, Ubicomp 2003, 2003)		4	✓			✓	✓	
Simons and Wirtz (Simons & Wirtz, 2007)		4	✓			✓		
Ferreira et al (Ferreira, Kostakos, & Dey, 2015)		3				✓		
Li (Li M., 2011)		3	✓			✓	✓	
Riboni and Bettini (Riboni & Bettini, 2011)		6	✓			✓		
Bhattacharyya et al (Bhattacharyya, Saravanagru, & Thangavelu, 2011)		2	✓			✓		
Chihani et al (Chihani, Bertin, Jeanne, & Crespi, 2011)	QS	3						✓
Duggal et al (Duggal, Misra, & Srinivasaraghavan, 2012)		3	✓			✓		✓
Ayed et al (Ayed, Delanote, & Berbers, 2007)		4	✓					✓

types include Activity, Semantics, Community, User, Environment and Quality information. Another comparison is made on the basis of out-degree of the root contextual data structure. The comparison table shows that the information of User and The Environment is the preferred choice of many researchers as a Level 1 contextual data type. Similarly, the number of contextual data types at Level 1 is kept higher to include more types at higher levels.

CONCLUSION

Context aware systems have opened the road to advancements in smart service adaptation and user facilitation in day to day tasks. A context aware system is composed of context gathering phase, context representation phase, context inference phase and context adaptation phase. The context gathering phase acquires contextual data from the environment and stores it. Storage is carried out using xml and owl based techniques but requires a contextual structure to provide hierarchy. This structure is the focus of this chapter.

This chapter provides a review of contemporary contextual data structures as found in the literature. Among different tactics the researchers have provided event centric, semantics centric, community centric, user centric and quality centric approaches. A list of evidences is presented in this chapter and a qualitative comparison drawn to facilitate further researchers.

The consequence of this research is to identify which context inference mechanism is suitable for which tactics of contextual data storage. The method would be to test different algorithms for inference on different organizations to measure the effectiveness of storage. Furthermore, the branching factor as well as the depth of the context storage structure also affects the performance of context retrieval.

REFERENCES

Agrawala, A. K. (2013, January). CMSC 818G class Information-Centric Design of Context-Aware Systems: Retrieved from http://www.cs.umd.edu/class/spring2013/cmsc818b/_professor.html

Ayed, D., Delanote, D., & Berbers, Y. (2007). MDD Approach for the Development of Context-Aware Applications. *Proceedings of the6th International and Interdisciplinary Conference (CONTEXT 2007)* (pp. 15-28). Roskilde, Denmark: Springer. doi:10.1007/978-3-540-74255-5_2

Badii, A., Crouch, M., & Lallah, C. (2010). A Context-Awareness Framework for Intelligent Networked Embedded Systems. *Proceedings of theThird International Conference on Advances in Human-Oriented and Personalized Mechanisms, Technologies and Services* (pp. 105-110). Reading, UK: IEEE. doi:10.1109/CENTRIC.2010.29

Beach, A., Gartrell, M., Xing, X., Han, R., Lv, Q., Mishra, S., & Seada, K. (2010). Fusing Mobile, Sensor, and Social Data To Fully Enable Context-Aware Computing. *Proceedings of the Eleventh Workshop on Mobile Computing Systems & Application (HotMobile '10)* (pp. 60-65). Annapolis, Maryland: ACM. doi:10.1145/1734583.1734599

Beltran, V., Arabshian, K., & Schulzrinne, H. (2011). Ontology-based User-defined Rules and Context-aware Service Composition System. *Proceedings of the 8th international conference on The Semantic Web* (pp. 139-155). Heraklion, Greece: ACM.

Benselim, M. S., & Seridi-Bouchelaghem, H. (2013, February). Extending UML Class Diagram Notation for the Development of Context-aware Applications. *Journal of Emerging Technologies in Web Intelligence*, 5(1), 35–44. doi:10.4304/jetwi.5.1.35-44

Bhattacharyya, S., Saravanagru, R. K., & Thangavelu, A. (2011, May). Context Aware Healthcare Application. *International Journal of Computers and Applications*, 22(3), 7–12.

Bolchini, C., Curino, C. A., Quintarelli, E., Schreiber, F. A., & Tanca, L. (2007, December). A Data-oriented Survey of Context Models. *ACM SIGMOD*, 36(4), 19–26. doi:10.1145/1361348.1361353

Brown, P. J., Bovey, J. D., & Chen, X. (1997). Context-aware applications: From the laboratory to the marketplace. *IEEE Personal Communications*, 4(5), 58–64. doi:10.1109/98.626984

Cao, Y., Klamma, R., Hou, M., & Jarke, M. (2008). Follow Me, Follow You - Spatiotemporal Community Context Modeling and Adaptation for Mobile Information Systems. *9th International Conference on Mobile Data Management* (pp. 108-115). Beijing: ACM. doi:10.1109/MDM.2008.30

Carroll, J. M. (2014). Human Computer Interaction - brief intro. In M. Soegaard & R. F. Dam (Eds.), *The Encyclopedia of Human-Computer Interaction* (2nd ed.). Aarhus, Denmark: The Interaction Design Foundation.

Castelli, G., & Zambonelli, F. (2009). Contextual Data Management and Retrieval: A Self-Organized Approach. *Proceedings of the IEEE/WIC/ACM International Joint Conferences on Web Intelligence and Intelligent Agent Technologies WI-IAT '09* (pp. 535-538). Milan, Italy: IEEE.

Chen, G., & Kotz, D. (2000). A Survey of Context-Aware Mobile Computing Research. Dartmouth College, Hanover, New Hampshire. Retrieved from http://www.cs.dartmouth.edu/reports/TR2000-381.pdf

Chen, H., Finin, T., & Joshi, A. (2003). An Intelligent Broker for Context-Aware Systems (CoBrA). *Proceedings of the Fifth International Conference on Ubiquitous Computing Ubicomp '03* (pp. 183-184). Seattle: ACM.

Chen, H., Finin, T., & Joshi, A. (2003). An Ontology for Context-Aware Pervasive Computing Environments. *The Knowledge Engineering Review, 18*(3), 197–207. doi:10.1017/S0269888904000025

Chen, L., & Nugent, C. (2009). Ontology-based Activity Recognition in Intelligent Pervasive Environments. *International Journal of Web Information Systems, 5*(4), 410–430. doi:10.1108/17440080911006199

Chihani, B., Bertin, E., Jeanne, F., & Crespi, N. (2011). Context-aware systems: a case study. *Proceedings of the International Conference on Digital Information and Communication Technology and its Applications (DICTAP '11)* (pp. 718-732). Dijon, France: Springer. doi:10.1007/978-3-642-22027-2_60

Cioara, T., Anghel, I., Salomie, I., & Dinsoreanu, M. (2009, June1). A generic context model enhanced with self-configuring features. *Journal of Digital Information Management, 7*(3), 159–166.

Dey, A. K. (2001). Understanding and using context. *Personal and Ubiquitous Computing, 5*(1), 4–7. doi:10.1007/s007790170019

Dix, A., Finlay, J. E., Abowd, G. D., & Beale, R. (2003). Human-Computer Interaction (3 ed.). Prentice-Hall.

Dix, A., Rodden, T., Davies, N., Trevor, J., Friday, A., & Palfreyman, K. (2000). Exploiting space and location as a design framework for interactive mobile systems. *ACM Transactions on Computer-Human Interaction, 7*(3), 285–321. doi:10.1145/355324.355325

Duggal, A., Misra, M., & Srinivasaraghavan, R. (2012). Categorising Context and Using Short Term Contextual Information to Obtain Long Term Context. *Proceedings of the 11th International Conference on Trust, Security and Privacy in Computing and Communications* (pp. 1771 - 1776). Liverpool, UK: IEEE. doi:10.1109/TrustCom.2012.2

Emmanouilidis, C., Koutsiamanis, R.-A., & Tasidou, A. (2013, January). Mobile guides: Taxonomy of architectures, context awareness, technologies and applications. *Journal of Network and Computer Applications, 36*(1), 103–125. doi:10.1016/j.jnca.2012.04.007

Feng, L., Apers, P. M., & Jonker, W. (2004). Towards Context-Aware Data Management for Ambient Intelligence. *Database and expert systems applications, LNCS* (Vol. 3180, pp. 422-431). Retrieved from http://link.springer.com/chapter/10.1007%2F978-3-540-30075-5_41

Ferreira, D., Kostakos, V., & Dey, A. K. (2015). AWARE: Mobile context instrumentation framework. *Frontiers in ICT, 2*(6), 1–9.

Fissaa, T., Guermah, H., Hafiddi, H., Nassar, M., & Kriouile, A. (2014). Towards an Ontology Based Architecture for Context-Aware Services Composition. *Proceedings of the2014 International Conference on Multimedia Computing and Systems (ICMCS)* (pp. 990-995). Marrakech: IEEE. doi:10.1109/ICMCS.2014.6911303

Gellersen, H.-W., Beigl, M., & Schmidt, A. (2000). Sensor-based Context-Awareness for Situated Computing.*Proceedings of Workshop on Software Engineering for Wearable and Pervasive Computing,* (pp. 77-83). Limerick, Ireland.

Goslar, K., & Schill, A. (2005). Modeling Contextual Information using Active Data Structures. *Lecture Notes in Computer Science, 3268*, 325–334. doi:10.1007/978-3-540-30192-9_32

Grudin, J. (2001). Desituating Action: Digital Representation of Context. *Human-Computer Interaction, 16*(2), 269–286. doi:10.1207/S15327051HCI16234_10

Gwizdka, J. (2000). What's in the context? *Proceedings of theACMSIGCHI Conference on Human Factors in Computing Systems (CHI '00)* (pp. 1-6). The Hague, Netherlands: ACM.

Hafiddi, H., Baidouri, H., Nassar, M., & Kriouile, A. (2012, September). Context-Awareness for Service Oriented Systems. *International Journal of Computer Science Issues, 9*(5).

Han, L., Jyri, S., Ma, J., & Yu, K. (2008). Research on Context-Aware Mobile Computing. *Proceedings of the22nd International Conference on Advanced Information Networking and Applications* (pp. 24-30). Okinawa: IEEE.

Harvel, L., Liu, L., Abowd, G. D., Lim, Y.-X., Scheibe, C., & Chatham, C. (2004). Context Cube: Flexible and Effective Manipulation of Sensed Context Data. *Lecture Notes in Computer Science, 3001*, 51–68. doi:10.1007/978-3-540-24646-6_4

Hofer, T., Pichler, M., Leonhartsberger, G., Altmann, J., & Werner, R. (2002). Context-Awareness on Mobile Devices – The Hydrogen Approach.*Proceedings of the 36th Annual Hawaii International Conference on System Sciences* (pp. 292-302). Hawaii: IEEE.

Hong, J.-y., Suh, E.-, & Kim, S.-J. (2009). Context-aware systems: A literature review and classification. *Expert Systems with Applications, 36*(4), 8509–8522. doi:10.1016/j.eswa.2008.10.071

Jang, S., & Woo, W. (2006). 5W1H: Unified User-Centric Context (White Paper). *GIST U-VR Lab.,* South Korea.

Jarrahi, A., & Kangavari, M. R. (2012). An Architecture for Context-Aware Knowledge Flow Management Systems. *International Journal of Computer Science Issues, 9*(2), 40–51.

Khattak, A. M., Akbar, N., Aazam, M., Ali, T., Khan, A. M., Jeon, S., & Lee, S. et al. (2014). Context Representation and Fusion: Advancements and Opportunities. *Sensors (Basel, Switzerland)*, *14*(6), 9628–9668. doi:10.3390/s140609628 PMID:24887042

Kiani, S. L., Anjum, A., Knappmeyer, M., Bessis, N., & Antonopoulos, N. (2013). Federated broker system for pervasive context provisioning. *Journal of Systems and Software*, *86*(4), 1107–1123. doi:10.1016/j. jss.2012.11.050

Kim, J.-D. K., Son, J., & Baik, D.-K. (2012). CA5W1H Onto: Ontological Context-Aware Model Based on 5W1H. *International Journal of Distributed Sensor Networks*, *2012*, 1–11. doi:10.1155/2012/247346

Knappmeyer, M., Kiani, S. L., Reetz, E. S., Baker, N., & Tonjes, R. (2013). Survey of Context Provisioning Middleware. *IEEE Communications Surveys and Tutorials*, *15*(3), 1492–1519. doi:10.1109/ SURV.2013.010413.00207

Lee, H., Choi, J. S., & Elmasri, R. (2009). A classification and modeling of the quality of contextual information in smart spaces. *Proceedings of theIEEE International Conference on Pervasive Computing and Communications* (pp. 1-5). Galveston, TX, USA: IEEE. doi:10.1109/PERCOM.2009.4912889

Lewis, G., Novakouski, M., & Sánchez, E. (2012). A Reference Architecture for Group-Context-Aware Mobile Applications. *Proceedings of theFourth International Conference on Mobile Computing, Applications and Services (MobiCASE 20120* (pp. 44-63). Seattle, WA: EAI.

Li, M. (2011). Ontology-based context information modeling for smart space. *Proceedings of the10th IEEE International Conference on Cognitive Informatics & Cognitive Computing (ICCI*CC)* (pp. 278-283). Banff, AB: IEEE. doi:10.1109/COGINF.2011.6016153

Li, Y., Fang, J., & Xiong, J. (2008). A Context-Aware Services Mash-Up System. *Proceedings of the Seventh International Conference on Grid and Cooperative Computing* (pp. 707-712). Shenzhen: IEEE. doi:10.1109/GCC.2008.62

Loke, S. W. (2006, April). Context-aware artifacts: Two development approaches. *IEEE Pervasive Computing / IEEE Computer Society [and] IEEE Communications Society*, *5*(2), 48–53. doi:10.1109/ MPRV.2006.27

Löwe, R., Mandl, P., & Weber, M. (2012). Context Directory: A context-aware service for mobile context-aware computing applications by the example of Google Android. *Proceedings of the2012 IEEE International Conference on Pervasive Computing and Communications Workshops (PERCOM Workshops)* (pp. 76-81). Lugano: IEEE. doi:10.1109/PerComW.2012.6197616

Mahmud, U. (2015). UML based Model of a Context Aware System.[IJAPUC]. *International Journal of Advanced Pervasive and Ubiquitous Computing*, *7*(1), 1–16. doi:10.4018/IJAPUC.2015010101

Mahmud, U., Farooq, U., Javed, M. Y., & Malik, N. A. (2012, March). Representing and Organizing Contextual Data in Context Aware Environments. *Journal of Computing*, *4*(3), 61–67.

Mahmud, U., Iltaf, N., & Kamran, F. (2007). Context Congregator: Gathering Contextual Information in CAPP. Proceedings of the 5th Frontiers of Information Technology FIT '07 (pp. 134–141). Islamabad, Pakistan: COMSATS.

Mahmud, U., Iltaf, N., Rehman, A., & Kamran, F. (2007). Context-Aware Paradigm for a Pervasive Computing Environment (CAPP). Proceedings of the WWW\Internet 2007 (pp. 337–346). Portugal: Villa Real.

Mahmud, U., & Javed, M. Y. (2012, July). Context Inference Engine (CiE): Inferring Context. *International Journal of Advanced Pervasive and Ubiquitous Computing, 4*(3), 13–41. doi:10.4018/japuc.2012070102

Mahmud, U., & Javed, M. Y. (2014). Context Inference Engine (CiE): Classifying Activity of Context using Minkowski Distance and Standard Deviation-Based Ranks. In Systems and Software Development, Modeling, and Analysis: New Perspectives and Methodologies (pp. 65-112). IGI Global.

Mahmud, U., & Malik, N. A. (2014). Flow and Threat Modelling of a Context Aware System. *International Journal of Advanced Pervasive and Ubiquitous Computing, 6*(2), 58–70. doi:10.4018/ijapuc.2014040105

Malik, N. A., Mahmud, U., & Javed, M. Y. (2007). Future challenges in context aware computing. Proceedings of the WWW/Internet '07 (pp. 306-310).

Malik, N. A., Mahmud, U., & Javed, M. Y. (2009, August). Estimating User Preferences by Managing Contextual History in Context Aware Systems. *Journal of Software, 6*(4), 571–576.

McAvoy, L. M., Chen, L., & Donnelly, M. (2012). An Ontology-based Context Management System for Smart Environments. *Proceedings of theSixth International Conference on Mobile Ubiquitous Computing, Systems, Services and Technologies, UBICOMM 2012* (pp. 18-23). Barcelona, Spain: IARIA.

Musumba, G. W., & Nyongesa, H. O. (2013). Context awareness in mobile computing: A review. *International Journal of Machine Learning and Applications, 2*(1), 1–10. doi:10.4102/ijmla.v2i1.5

Nykänen, O. A., & Rodriguez, A. R. (2014). Problems in Context-Aware Semantic Computing. *International Journal of Interactive Mobile Technologies, 8*(3), 32–39. doi:10.3991/ijim.v8i3.3870

Oh, Y., Yoon, H., & Woo, W. (2006). Simulating Context-Aware Systems based on Personal Devices. *Proceedings of the4th International Symposium on Ubiquitous Virtual Reality (ISUVR 2006)*, (pp. 49-52). Daejeon, Korea.

Paganelli, F., Spinicci, E., & Giuli, D. (2008). ERMHAN: A Context-Aware Service Platform to Support Continuous Care Networks for Home-Based Assistance. *International Journal of Telemedicine and Applications, 2008*, 1–13. http://www.hindawi.com/journals/ijta/2008/867639/. doi:10.1155/2008/867639 PMID:18695739

Pantsar-Syväniem, S., Simula, K., & Ovaska, E. (2010). Context-awareness in smart spaces. *Proceedings of theIEEE Symposium on Computers and Communications (ISCC)* (pp. 1023-1028). Riccione, Italy: IEEE. doi:10.1109/ISCC.2010.5546630

Papaioannou, I., Kalatzis, N., Roussaki, I., Liampotis, N., Kosmides, P., & Anagnostou, M. (2014). Multi-user context inference based on neural networks. *Proceedings of the2014 IEEE International Conference on Pervasive Computing and Communications Workshops (PERCOM Workshops)* (pp. 466-471). Budapest: IEEE. doi:10.1109/PerComW.2014.6815251

Perera, C., Zaslavsky, A., Christen, P., & Georgakopoulos, D. (2014). Context Aware Computing for The Internet of Things: A Survey. *IEEE Communications Surveys and Tutorials*, *16*(1), 414–454. doi:10.1109/SURV.2013.042313.00197

Petrelli, D., Not, E., Zancanaro, M., Strapparava, C., & Stock, O. (2001). Modelling and adapting to context. *Personal and Ubiquitous Computing*, *5*(1), 20–24. doi:10.1007/s007790170023

Ranganathan, A., & Campbell, R. H. (2008). Provably Correct Pervasive Computing Environments. *Proceedings of the 2008 Sixth Annual IEEE Conference on Pervasive Computing and Communications (PERCOM '08)*. Washington DC, USA: IEEE Computer Society. doi:10.1109/PERCOM.2008.116

Ranganathan, A., McGrath, R. E., Campbell, R. H., & Mickunas, M. D. (2003). Use of Ontologies in a Pervasive Computing Environment. *The Knowledge Engineering Review*, *18*(3), 209–220. doi:10.1017/S0269888904000037

Raychoudhury, V., Cao, J., Kumar, M., & Zhang, D. (2013, April). Middleware for pervasive computing: A survey. *Pervasive and Mobile Computing*, *9*(2), 177–200. doi:10.1016/j.pmcj.2012.08.006

Riaz, M., Kiani, S. L., Lee, S., Han, S.-M., & Lee, Y.-K. (2005). Service Delivery in Context Aware Environments: Lookup and Access Control Issues. *Proceedings of the 11th IEEE International Conference on Embeded and Real-Time Computing Systems and Applications* (pp. 455-458). IEEE. doi:10.1109/RTCSA.2005.94

Riboni, D., & Bettini, C. (2011, March). COSAR: Hybrid reasoning for context-aware activity recognition. *Personal and Ubiquitous Computing*, *15*(3), 271–289. doi:10.1007/s00779-010-0331-7

Roussaki, I., Strimpakou, M., Pils, C., Kalatzis, N., & Liampotis, N. (2010). Optimizing context data dissemination and storage in distributed pervasive computing systems. *Journal of Pervasive and Mobile Computing*, *6*(2), 218-238.

Ryan, N., Pascoe, J., & Morse, D. (1997). Enhanced Reality Fieldwork: the Context Aware Archaeological Assistant. *Computer Applications in Archaeology*. Retrieved from https://www.cs.kent.ac.uk/pubs/1998/616/content.html

Salvi, D., Ottaviano, M., Peinado, I., & Arredondo, M. T. (2009). An Architecture for Data Collection and Processing in Context-Aware Applications. *Proceedings of the 3rd International Conference on Ambient Intelligence* (pp. 252-255). Salzburg, Austria: Springer.

Schilit, B. N., & Theimer, M. M. (1994). Disseminating active map infrastructure to mobile host. *IEEE Network*, *8*(5), 22–32. doi:10.1109/65.313011

Schmidt, A. (2014). Context-Awareness, Context-Aware User Interfaces, and Implicit Interaction. In M. Soegaard & R. F. Dam (Eds.), *The Encyclopedia of Human-Computer Interaction* (2nd ed.). Aarhus, Denmark: The Interaction Design Foundation.

Schmidt, A., Beigl, M., & Gellersen, H.-W. (1999). There is more to context than location. *Computers & Graphics*, *23*(6), 893–901. doi:10.1016/S0097-8493(99)00120-X

Sheng, Q. Z., Pohlenz, S., Jian, Y., Wong, H. S., Ngu, A. H., & Maamar, Z. (2009). ContextServ: A platform for rapid and flexible development of context-aware Web services. *Proceedings of the IEEE 31st International Conference on Software Engineering* (pp. 619-622). Vancouver: IEEE.

Shi, Y., Karatzoglou, A., Baltrunas, L., Larson, M., & Hanjalic, A. (2014). CARS2: Learning Context-aware Representations for Context-aware Recommendations. *Proceedings of the 23rd ACM International Conference on Conference on Information and Knowledge Management (CIKM 14)* (pp. 291-300). Shanghai: ACM.

Siebra, S. A., Salgado, A. C., Tedesco, P. A., & Brézillon, P. (2005). A Learning Interaction Memory using Contextual Information. *Proceedings of the CEUR Workshop*. Retrieved from: http://www.cin. ufpe.br/~mbjn/D1.pdf

Simons, C., & Wirtz, G. (2007). Modeling context in mobile distributed systems with the UML. *Journal of Visual Languages and Computing, 18*(4), 420–439. doi:10.1016/j.jvlc.2007.07.001

Singh, S., Vajirkar, P., & Lee, Y. (2003). Context-Based Data Mining Using Ontologies.Conceptual Modeling – ER 2003, LNCS (Vol. 2813, pp. 405–418).

Sommerville, I. (2015). *Software Engineering* (10th ed.). USA: Pearson Education.

Soylu, A., Causmaecker, P. D., & Desmet, P. (2009). Context and Adaptivity in Pervasive Computing Environments: Links with Software Engineering and Ontological Engineering. *Journal of Software, 4*(9), 992–1013. doi:10.4304/jsw.4.9.992-1013

Strang, T., & Linnhoff-Popien, C. (2004). A Context Modelling Survey. *Proceedings of theFirst International Workshop on Advanced Context Modelling, Reasoning and Management (Ubicomp 2004)*. Nottingham, England: ACM.

Suganuma, T., Yamanaka, K., Tokairin, Y., Takahashi, H., & Shiratori, N. (2008). A Ubiquitous Supervisory System Based on Social Context Awareness. *Proceedings of the 22nd International Conference on Advanced Information Networking and Applications* (pp. 370-377). GinoWan, Okinawa, Japan: IEEE. doi:10.1109/AINA.2008.123

Truong, H.-L., & Dustdar, S. (2009). A Survey on Context-aware Web Service Systems. *International Journal of Web Information Systems, 5*(1), 5–31. doi:10.1108/17440080910947295

Vajirkar, P., Singh, S., & Lee, Y. (2003). Context-Aware Data Mining Framework for Wireless Medical Application. *Lecture Notes in Computer Science, 2736*, 381–391. doi:10.1007/978-3-540-45227-0_38

van Bunningen, A. H., Feng, L., & Apers, P. M. (2005). Context for ubiquitous data management. *Proceedings of theInternational Workshop on Ubiquitous Data Management (UDM 2005)* (pp. 17-24). Tokyo, Japan: IEEE. doi:10.1109/UDM.2005.7

Wongpatikaseree, K., Ikeda, M., Buranarach, M., Supnithi, T., Lim, A. O., & Tan, Y. (2012). Activity Recognition using Context-Aware Infrastructure Ontology in Smart Home Domain. *Proceedings of the2012 Seventh International Conference on Knowledge, Information and Creativity Support Systems (KICSS)* (pp. 50-57). Melbourne: IEEE. doi:10.1109/KICSS.2012.26

Wongpatikaseree, K., Kim, J., Makino, Y., Lim, A. O., & Tan, Y. (2013). Architecture for Organizing Context-Aware Data in Smart Home for Activity Recognition System. InDistributed, Ambient, and Pervasive Interactions, LNCS (Vol. *8028*, pp. 173–182). doi:10.1007/978-3-642-39351-8_20

Yamabe, T., Takagi, A., & Nakajima, T. (2005). Citron: A Context Information Acquisition Framework for Personal Devices. *Proceedings of the11th IEEE International Conference on Embedded and Real-Time Computing Systems and Applications (RTCSA' 05)* (pp. 489-495). Hong Kong, China: IEEE. doi:10.1109/RTCSA.2005.32

Yus, R., Pappachan, P., Das, P. K., Finin, T., Joshi, A., & Mena, E. (2014). Semantics for Privacy and Shared Context. *Proceedings of theInternational Semantic Web Conference (ISWC 2014)* (pp. 1-11). Trantino, Italy: Elsevier.

Zhu, H., Chen, E., Yu, K., Cao, H., Xiong, H., & Tian, J. (2012). Mining Personal Context-Aware Preferences for Mobile Users. *Proceedings of the 2012 IEEE 12th International Conference on Data Mining (ICDM)* (pp. 1212-1217). Brussels: IEEE.

KEY TERMS AND DEFINITIONS

Context: Context includes all attributes belonging to humans, machines, devices and the surroundings that describe a distinct situation or activity. The context is gathered through sensors that are part of the environment and the devices carried by the humans.

Context Awareness: The ability of a computer system to recognize the context and subsequently adapt the services for improved user experience.

Contextual Data: The values of different attributes of a context.

Context Inference: Inferring the activity or situation of a context through machine learning or rule based engines.

Context Organization or Context Structure: The hierarchy in the context representation for fast search.

Context Representation: The mechanism of representing contextual data in machine readable as well as human understandable form.

Human Computer Interaction (HCI): The study of how humans interact with computer based systems. This includes computers as well as hand held devices. The aim of HCI is to provide better and human centred interfaces.

Service: An application present in the environment that provides some functionality. It is typically implemented as a Service Oriented Architecture (SOA).

Situation or Activity: The human understandable stereotype of a distinct context e.g., driving, lecturing etc.

Chapter 12
Using a Design Science Research Approach to Develop a HCI Artifact for Designing Web Interfaces:
A Case Study

Muhammad Nazrul Islam
Military Institute of Science and Technology, Bangladesh

Franck Tétard
Uppsala University, Sweden

ABSTRACT

Interface signs are the communication cues of web interfaces, through which users interact. Examples of interface signs are small images, navigational links, buttons and thumbnails. Although intuitive interface signs are crucial elements of a good user interface (UI), prior research ignored these in UI design and usability evaluation process. This chapter outlines how a design science research (DSR) approach is used to develop a Human-Computer Interaction (HCI) artifact (semiotic framework) for design and evaluation of user-intuitive web interface signs. This chapter describes how the principles and guidelines of DSR approach are adopted, while performing the activities of the DSR process model to construct the artifact.

INTRODUCTION

Interface signs are the key elements of web user interfaces (UI). These signs act as the communication artifacts between the users and designers/systems (see figure 1). Examples of interface signs are navigational links, thumbnails, small images, command buttons, symbols, icons, and the like. Interaction between users and web systems is mediated via web interfaces, and in particular interface signs since the content and functions of web systems are directed primarily through interface signs. Thus, at the low level, end users are required to interpret the 'interface signs' of user interfaces to understand the system's logic and

DOI: 10.4018/978-1-5225-0435-1.ch012

to perform tasks (Derboven et al., 2003). Thus, designing user-intuitive interface signs and evaluating the intuitiveness of interface signs become essential in the UI design and usability evaluation process (De Souza, 2005; Islam, 2013; Islam & Tetard, 2013). Consequently, Bolchini et al. (2009) suggested 'interface signs' as one of the major dimensions of web UI design and usability evaluation. However, very few studies explicitly focused on interface signs in UI design and evaluation (Speroni et al., 2006).

Web user interfaces basically consist of a large number of interface signs. 'Sign' is the central notion of semiotic theories; the key criteria to consider something as a sign are that:

1. A sign should have some meaning, and
2. A sign should be interpreted (Peirce, 1931-58).

This means that it is the designer's task to make any interface sign of a web UI meaningful, and to ensure that end-users can interpret the meaning of the interface sign correctly. Interface designers should encode the referential content or objects as an 'interface sign'. In that way, end-users can correctly decode the sign and understand its referential meaning. However, there is no one-to-one connection between an object and a sign (see Figure 2). Users may interpret a given sign in a number of different ways, while different signs may have the same meaning. So, some signs are easy to interpret, while others may not. As a consequence, end-users may perform a specific task appropriately when their interpretation matches the referential object (or meaning) of the interface signs, as encoded by designers. It is therefore utmost important to understand why and how some signs are more intuitive than others. In order to achieve this, we have developed the Semiotic Interface sign Design and Evaluation (SIDE) framework to design and evaluate web interface signs to make them intuitive for end users and to improve overall we usability (Islam, 2014).

Figure 1. Snapshot of Bikroy.com homepage shows some interface signs marked by ovals (retrieved from www.bikroy.com/en in November, 2015)

Figure 2. Different user interprets (a) a sign referring to different object/meaning, and (b) different signs referring to the same object/meaning

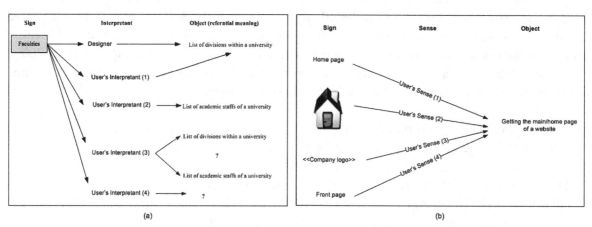

Design science is described as an innovative problem solving activity (Venable, 2006), and focuses on how to develop artifacts having desired properties (Carlsson, 2005). In other words, DSR focuses on the creation of innovative IT-artifacts to solve real-world problems. DSR thus provides new knowledge, technical capabilities, practices, and products through the design of innovative artifacts and the evaluation of performance of these artifacts (Hevner et al, 2004; March & storey, 2008; Vaishnavi & Kuechler, 2004).

The present research develops the SIDE framework as a Human-Computer Interaction (HCI) artifact in order to design and evaluate web interface signs. Therefore, the methodology followed in the research is based on the DSR approach. In this chapter, a design science - oriented research design in HCI is presented to show how a DSR approach is well suited to develop a HCI artifact (the SIDE framework) for designing and evaluations of interface signs. The chapter describes how authors developed their research design based on design science principles, practice rules and procedures.

This chapter is organized as follows. The DSR methodology and the related HCI work that follows DSR method are briefly presented in the following section. After that, an overview of the SIDE framework is presented. Next, we explain how a DSR methodology is followed to develop the SIDE framework, followed by a discussion and conclusions in the final section.

BACKGROUND

Design Science Research (DSR) Methodology

Design science research (DSR) is one of the most widely used research approaches in engineering, computer science, and information systems research. Design science research, as conceptualized by Simon (1996), focuses on the creation of innovative IT-artifacts to solve real-world problems. Hevner & Chatterjee (2010) define DSR as follows: "Design science research is a research paradigm in which a designer answers questions relevant to human problems via the creation of innovation artifacts, thereby contributing new knowledge to the body of scientific evidence. The designed artifacts are both useful and fundamental in understanding that problem". DSR thus provides new knowledge through the design of innovative artifacts and the evaluation of performance of these artifacts (Vaishnavi and Kuechler, 2004; Hevner et al., 2004; March & Storey, 2008). In a broader sense, the definition of an artifact includes any designed object that provides a solution to an understood research problem (Peffers et al., 2007).

Simon (1996) highlights the differences between natural science and design science. Natural science research is concerned with *how things are* while the design science research are concerned with *how things ought to be* to attain the objectives or goals. March and Smith (1995) describe two fundamental processes of design science, that includes 'build' and 'evaluate', and four types of products, that includes constructs, models, methods, and instantiations. However, the artifacts that a DSR can include are (a) constructs–conceptual vocabulary of a domain in which problems and solutions are defined and communicated; (b) models–which represent a real world situation by means of constructs; (c) methods–which define a set of steps to solve problems; (d) instantiations–which operationalize the constructs, methods, or models in working systems; (e) new theories; (f) social innovations; (g) new properties of technical, social or informational resources; and (h) new design and developments models (March & Smith, 1995; Gregor 2002; March & Storey, 2008; Ellis & Levy 2010).

The concept of design science further developed by a number of authors, including Peffers et al (2007), Archer (1984), Takeda et al. (1990), Vaishnavi and Kuechler (2004), Hevner et al. (2004), and Nunamaker et al (1990). Hevner et al. (2004) claim that design activities are central to the information systems (IS) discipline and present a conceptual framework for understanding, executing, and evaluating IS research combining behavioural science and design science paradigms. However, Peffers et al. (2007) synthesized the process elements proposed by other IS scholars, and found that the scholars to a large extent agree on common process elements. As a result of their synthesis, Peffers et al. (2007) proposed a process model that consists of six activities that include:

1. Problem identification and motivation,
2. Definition of solution objectives,
3. Design and development,
4. Demonstration,
5. Evaluation, and
6. Communication.

A distinguishing feature of their DSR process model is that research can get initiated at almost any step, such as problem-centered initiation (refers to starting research with activity *a*), objective-centered solution (refers to starting research with activity *b*), design and development centered initiation (refers to starting research with activity *c*), and client/context initiation (refers to starting research with activity *d*).

DSR Method in HCI

Human-Computer Interaction (HCI) is a discipline primarily focusing on design, evaluation, and implementation of interactive systems. The ACM special interest group of CHI defines HCI as "a discipline concerned with the design, evaluation, and implementation of interactive computing systems for human use and with the study of major phenomena surrounding them" (ACM SIGCHI, 1992). In fact, HCI studies how a computer system is designed more practically, more easily, and more intuitively; and it also studies how users interact with such computer systems (Fetaji et al., 2007).

Though DSR gained wide recognition and acceptance as a formal research approach in many disciplines including information systems, but the DSR method is much abundant in HCI (Adikari et al, 2009). According to Adikari et al. (2009), design science research is also appropriate for HCI. Only a few studies have been conducted in HCI that explicitly used the DSR approach to produce an IT artifact. For example, in Adikari et al. (2009), a design science approach is used to integrate User-Centered Design (UCD) perspective into Agile Requirements Engineering to improve design quality of software systems. Another study (Adikari, 2006), test the impact of usability modelling and user modelling in software requirements specifications following a design science research approach to produce usable human computer systems.

Therefore, the chapter shows a how a HCI artifact is produced and evaluated following a DSR research approach, as well as highlights the benefits experienced of using the DSR method in HCI research.

THE SIDE FRAMEWORK: A HCI ARTIFACT

The SIDE framework (see Figure 3) is based on research and empirical data collected over a period of three years (2011-2013). The main goal of the SIDE framework is to provide support for designing and evaluating user-intuitive interface signs to improve web usability. The SIDE framework is thus created for

1.   Designing the interface signs to be intuitive for end users;
2.   Assessing the intuitiveness of interface signs to end users;
3.   Finding problems with interface signs;
4.   Providing possible design solutions to improve the intuitiveness of interface signs; and
5.   Integrating semiotic features into usability evaluation processes to improve system usability.

The SIDE framework includes (a) a set of determinants (themes) and attributes (sub-themes) of interface signs, and (b) a set of semiotic heuristics for interface sign design and evaluation (see Table 1).
The SIDE framework includes the following five semiotic layers:

1.   The Syntactic level comprises the features of interface sign presentation,
2.   The Pragmatic level deals with the relation of interface signs to their interpretation or use,
3.   The Social level deals with the meaning of the interface sign in terms of its social consequences,
4.   The Environment level deals with the users' presupposed knowledge or ontology to interpret the meaning of interface sign,
5.   The Semantic level is the meaning of the sign. Each layer subsequently is defined by determinants and determinants in turn have attributes.

Each level subsequently defines determinants and the determinants have attribute(s); for example, interactivity, color, clarity and readability, presentation, context, and consistency are the determinants of syntactic level; sign color, color lightness, and color contrast are the attributes of color (a determinant) (see the Figure 3).

Figure 3. The SIDE framework: levels, determinants, and attributes

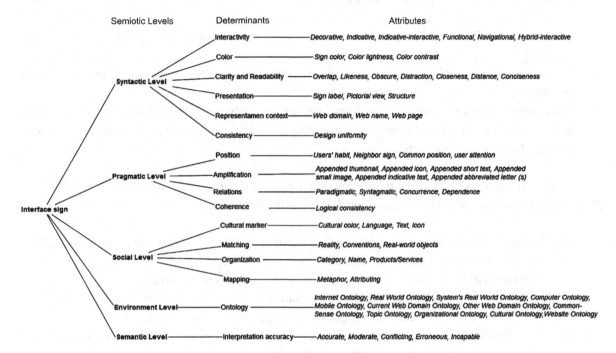

Table 1. Proposed semiotic heuristics (only the condensed set of heuristics are presented here, full set of heuristics are available in (Islam & Bouwman, 2015a))

Levels	Semiotic Heuristics
Syntactic	• Present clearly the purpose of interactivity • Make effective use of color to design an interface sign • Make the representation readable and clearly noticeable • Make a sign presentation clear and concise • Create the representation context appropriately • Follow a consistent interface sign design strategy
Pragmatic	• Place the interface sign at the proper position in a UI • Make effective use of amplification features in interface sign design • Create good relations among the interface signs of a UI • Retain logical coherence in interface sign design
Social	• Design interface signs to be culturally sensitive or reactive, when necessary • Match with the reality, conventions, or real-world objects • Make effective use of organizational features in interface sign design • Map with metaphorical and attributing properties
Environment	• Model the profiles of the focused end-users • Make effective use of ontological guidelines in interface sign design
Semantic	• Design an interface sign to get its accurate meaning by the end users

The framework also includes three processes:

1. **Interpretative Process:** The process of interpreting interface signs to capture their referential meaning.
2. **Generative Process:** The process of designing the interface sign that encodes the referential content or meaning.
3. **Evaluative Processes**: The process of investigating or analyzing interface signs to assess the intuitiveness for end-users, to identify design problems and to recommend possible design solutions in order to improve intuitiveness.

The SIDE framework is discussed more comprehensively in (Islam, 2014; Islam & Bouwman, 2015a; 2015b). In this chapter, we brief discussed each level of the framework:

- **The Syntactic Level:** This level comprises the features of interface sign presentation. The following determinants of the syntactic level are derived:
  - **Interactivity:** Interface signs carry six kinds of proposed interactivity:
    - *Decorative: (*Not clickable and uses mainly for a decorative or aesthetic purpose
    - *Indicative:* Not clickable and provides suggestions or hints in the UI
    - *Indicative-Interactive:* One can interact with this kind of sign only for understanding some indication or hints, not for performing a task
    - *Functional:* Clickable and performs a task
    - *Navigational:* Clickable and goes through to further details of information
    - *Hybrid-Interactive:* combines the properties of other attributes of interactivity, e.g., combines the indicative-interactive, functional, and navigational attributes.
  - **Color:** This determinant is concerned with the color used (*sign color*), the *lightness* of the color, and the *contrast* of the color.
  - **Clarity and Readability:** This determinant does not directly impact the participants' interpretations of interface signs, but indirectly helps to interpret them appropriately. This determinant includes the following attributes:
    - *Overlap*: The sign's texts that are merged by overlapping a few letters
    - *Likeness:* The signs' labels that are too similar to other signs
    - *Obscure:* Signs that are unclear, hidden, and difficult to understand
    - *Distract:* Signs that might be properly understandable by the end user, but are less important than what their appearance make out to be
    - *Closeness:* Signs that are placed too close to another sign
    - *Distance:* Refers to the use of noticeable distance between related interface signs
    - *Conciseness:* The use of short and effective text as a sign label.
  - **Presentational Aspects:** The presentational aspects of an interface sign on the syntactic level is concerned with the *labels* of the interface sign, what the sign looks like (*pictorial view*), and the *structure* of the interface sign such as the layout, shape, size, font size, etc.
  - **Context:** This determinant on the syntactic level is concerned with the name of the web domain, the name of the website or web application (*web name*), and the *webpage* that holds the interface sign

- ○ **Consistency:** This determinant is concerned with consistent design (*design uniformity*) that should be followed when designing interface signs for a particular web application. The uniform design strategy for a website helped participants to develop their thinking process to interpret the meaning of the interface sign.
- **The Pragmatic Level:** The pragmatic level deals with the relation of interface signs to their interpretation or use. The following determinants of the syntactic level are derived:
  - ○ **Position:** Interface sign location on the pragmatic level is concerned with three main attributes:
    - ▪ *Users' Habits:* Refers to how users interact with interface signs at a particular position in an UI
    - ▪ *Neighbor Signs:* Refer to the surrounding or close by signs
    - ▪ *User Attention:* Refers to placing an interface sign at a particular position in a UI to get users attention
    - ▪ *Common Positions:* Refers to particular positions for interface signs.
  - ○ **Amplification**: This determinant on the pragmatic level is concerned with the following attributes:
    - ▪ *Appended Thumbnail:* Meaningful thumbnail appended with an interface sign
    - ▪ *Appended Icon:* Meaningful icon appended with an interface sign
    - ▪ *Appended Small Image:* Meaningful small images appended with an interface sign
    - ▪ *Appended Short Text*: Short text appended with an interface sign that provides hints for the meaning of the sign
    - ▪ *Appended Indicative Text*: Meaningful small text appended with an iconic interface sign
    - ▪ *Appended Abbreviated Letter(s):* Common abbreviated letter(s) appended with a linguistic sign, e.g., 'e' for electronic, 'I' for internet, 'web' for internet or online, etc..

These attributes are individually not enough to express the meaning of an interface sign properly, but they impact the perceived meaning, complexity, and confidence when appended with other interface signs.

- **Relations**: The relations on the pragmatic level refer to the associations between interface signs in a UI. This determinant concerned four types of relations:
  - ○ *Paradigmatic:* Relations that hold among interface signs of the same paradigm
  - ○ *Syntagmatic:* Refers to a relation among interface signs that makes a sequential order within the signs or combines them with a sequential order
  - ○ *Concurrence:* A few thematic or functional relations exist together among the interface signs in a UI
  - ○ *Dependence:* The meaning of the interface sign depends on another sign or is controlled by another sign in a UI
- **Coherence:** This determinant is concerned with the quality of being logical in interface sign design (*logical consistency*). The *logical consistency* refers to how well the meaning of the interface sign is logically related with real-world facts.
  - ○ **The Social Level:** The social level deals with the meaning of the interface sign in terms of its social consequences. The following determinants of the syntactic level are derived:

- **Cultural Marker**: The cultural marker on the social level is concerned with the sign *color* and its cultural consequences, the *language* of the sign label, the *text* of the sign and its cultural consequences, and the *iconic* interfaces for a particular cultural context.
- **Matching**: This determinant is concerned with *reality* (the interface sign represents or follows some underlying reality), *conventions* (the sign is designed following the conventions of interface signs), and *real-world objects* (the interface sign corresponds or matches with a real-world object).
- **Organization**: This determinant refers to the owner or interlocutor of a website that is concerned with an organization's *category*, an organization's *name*, and an organization's *products or services*.
- **Mapping**: This determinant is concerned with *metaphors* that resemble users' real-world experiences more realistically in order to enhance interpretation accuracy, and *attributing* that refers to the use of parts in interface sign design; participants interpreted the meaning of the (whole) interface sign properly when they determined its parts and understood the meaning of the parts.
  - **The Environment Level:** The environment level deals with the environmental or surrounding factors that are collectively capable of affecting the users' behavior. The level builds on the users' *presupposed knowledge* or *ontology*. The environment level represents the users' knowledge and memory, and an association of users' interpretations of interface signs with the referential meanings of the signs, because the users' memory and knowledge form the basis to understand the meaning of a sign in a semiosis process. The determinant 'ontology' for this level is derived.
- **Ontology:** The term 'ontology' is defined as the set of concepts and skills that a user should have to understand the referential meaning of an interface sign (Bolchini et al. 2009; Speroni 2006). Thus the ontology is important for interpreting the meaning of a sign accurately. The studies found a set of ontologies to interpret the meaning of the interface signs, for example, *Internet Ontology* (concept related to the web, web surfing, world of web, etc., e.g., the 'Logout' sign), *Current Web Domain Ontology* (the knowledge of web interface signs which is specific enough for the current web domain, e.g., the 'Spam' sign in the email application domain).
  - **The Semantic Level:** The semantic level is the meaning of the sign and the relationships of the interface sign, the referential meaning of interface signs from a designer perspective, and the referential meaning of interface signs from a user perspective. The determinant that is derived for this level is the 'interpretation accuracy'.
- **Interpretation Accuracy:** This determinant refers to the accuracy level of users' interpretations of interface signs with respect to the designers' intended or assigned meaning of the signs. The accuracy level of users' interpretations of interface signs falls into five categories:
  - *Accurate:* A user's interpretation completely matches the designer's assigned meaning
  - *Moderate:* The user interprets more than one distinct meaning or object, one of which was the correct one and the probability to obtain the right object at the first attempt may be less than for the accurate interpretation
  - *Conflicting:* The user interprets more than one distinct object from the interface signs and is confused about choosing the right object that will match the designer's assigned meaning or object
  - *Erroneous:* A user's interpretation matches a completely different object than the designer's assigned meaning
  - *Incapable:* The user was not able to interpret the interface sign at all.

USING THE DSR METHODOLOGY TO DEVELOP THE SIDE FRAMEWORK

The DSR methodology includes three elements for design science research (Peffers et al, 2007) that are followed throughout:

1. Principles that defined the design science research.
2. Practice rules for design science research.
3. A process model for conducting the design science research. Next, we discuss how we followed the key elements of DSR methodology to propose the SIDE framework, an HCI artifact for user-interface design and evaluation.

Principles of DSR

Design science research is fundamentally a problem-solving process (Hevner & Chatterjee, 2010). DSR creates and evaluates IT artifacts intended to solve an understood research problem and follows a rigorous process to create the artifacts. To develop the SIDE framework, our research process follows the principles of DSR in the following ways:

1. **Creates an Artifact to Solve Identified Problems:** This research *creates* an artifact (i.e., the SIDE framework) intended to *solve* an identified research problem (i.e., to provide semiotic means to design and evaluate user-intuitive interface signs for improving system usability). The SIDE framework is used for designing and evaluating the web interface signs so that they are intuitive for end-users, which in turn improves web usability. Thus, the artifact has a profound impact on the interface design and evaluation. As well, it improves the ease-of-use or usability of web systems.
2. **Follows a Rigorous Process:** To make this design research rigorous, a set of empirical studies are carried out following the activities of the DSR process model described by Peffers et al. (2007) and the DSR guidelines described by Hevner et al. (2004) in creating the SIDE framework. The DSR guidelines, DSR process models and the studies are discussed in the following sections.
3. **Evaluates the Created Artifact:** The SIDE framework is evaluated to assess its quality and applicability. The performance of the SIDE framework is measured when the framework is applied to design and evaluate interface signs. A subjective assessment is carried out to assess the contributions of the SIDE framework from the evaluators' perspective.

Practice Rules for DSR

Hevner et al. (2004) provide seven guidelines to carry out DSR that constitute characteristics of good design science research (Peffers et al., 2007). Here we present how this research follows the guidelines of DSR discussed by Hevner et al. (2004).

1. **Design as an Artifact:** The SIDE framework is created as an artifact for designing and evaluating the web interface signs to improve system usability.
2. **Problem Relevance:** The research problems, identified through a systematic review and an empirical study, are relevant to the design of user-intuitive web interface signs. Users interact with web applications by means of interface signs. Users' inaccurate interpretation of the meaning of

interface signs and users' difficulties in interpreting the meaning of interface signs lead users to create usability problem(s) and to perform their task with low performance and low satisfaction; this in turn impacts the ease-of-use or usability of web systems. A solution to these problems will definitely provide knowledge and understanding that enable UI practitioners to apply the solution effectively and efficiently in designing and evaluating web user interfaces. Hevner et al. (2004) stated that the relevance of any DSR effort is with respect to a constituent community; for example, practitioners who design, implement, and evaluate the information systems are members of a constituent community for IS researchers. UI practitioners focus on the design, development, and evaluation of information systems in order to improve the ease-of-use or usability of information systems, and thus can be considered as members of the constituent IS community. The research problems thus are relevant for information systems research; more explicitly related to the design and evaluation of user interfaces of web information systems.

3. **Design Evaluation:** The utility, quality, and efficacy of the SIDE framework are demonstrated via empirical studies. The research evaluates the performance (e.g., thoroughness, validity, effectiveness, efficiency, etc.) of the SIDE framework, and assesses the contributions of the SIDE framework from the evaluators' perspective.

4. **Research Contribution:** The contributions of the research are the SIDE framework as a designed artifact, the evaluation results of the SIDE framework in terms of performance measurement, and the contributions' assessment. The artifact incorporated a set of determinants, attributes, and heuristics to design and evaluate web interface signs. In the evaluation, this research also shows how the framework can be used to design and evaluate web user interfaces. These contributions advance practitioners' understanding of how best to design and evaluate web user interfaces from a semiotic perspective in order to improve web usability.

5. **Research Rigor:** The research carries out a systematic literature review and six empirical studies (studies are discussed in (Islam, 2014)). The studies are carried out following the DSR process activities described by Peffers et al. (2007). Empirical studies are conducted both to create the artifact (the SIDE framework) and to evaluate the artifact.

6. **Design as a Search Process** : Iteration is a central property of design science research (Hevner et al, 2004). A number of studies that are carried out continuously sought to find the semiotic features or instruments (i.e., determinants, attributes, and/or semiotic heuristics/ guidelines for user-intuitive interface sign design and evaluation) and to evaluate the derived semiotic instruments to observe their impact. These iteratively occurred over a period of 36 months. The resultant set of semiotic instruments is triangulated to different semiotic levels to propose the SIDE framework. Again, a study is carried out to assess the quality and applicability of the SIDE framework. The results of this evaluation study are used to refine and update the SIDE framework. Thus, the research is iterative.

7. **Communication of Research:** The outcomes of the research are presented in different forums or conferences related to (a) information systems (e.g., IRIS 2011, MCIS 2011, and MCIS 2012); (b) human-computer interaction (e.g., IHCI 2012 and HCII 2013); and (c) semiotic in informatics (e.g., ICISO 2011 and ICISO 2014). A total of 17 papers are published based on the research in international conferences, seminars, and journals, and as a book chapter and technical reports. The framework is also communicated to practitioners in an evaluation study.

Figure 4. The DSR methodology process for this research

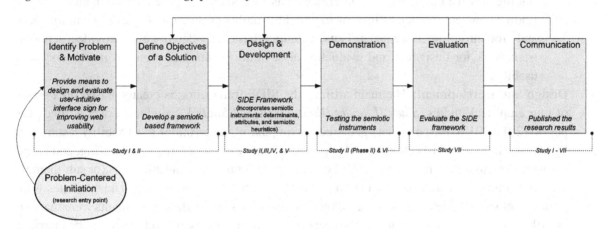

Procedures for DSR

A systematic literature review and six empirical studies are carried out in this research. A brief overview of these studies is presented in Islam's (2014) dissertation. The activities of the DSR process model (Peffers et al., 2007) were followed to design and conduct these studies (see Figure 4).

1. **Problem Identification and Motivation:** Our research specifies research problems and justifies the need and the value of a solution through the *Study I* and *Study II (Phase I)*. *Study I* is carried out to understand the current status (i.e., research strengths, gaps, and opportunities for further research) of semiotic research in UI design and evaluation. In *Study II (Phase I)*, a usability test (UT) is carried out followed by a sign test (a test to find the users' interpretation accuracy of the meaning of interface signs) to observe how users perform tasks in the UT when their interpretation accuracy with task-related signs is not accurate. This study shows that users interpret the meaning of interface signs accurately when the signs are intuitive for them; user performance is high when their interpretation accuracy with task-related signs is accurate, and users' interpretation accuracy of interface signs impacts the overall web usability. The studies find that further research is needed to investigate and find the fundamental issues related to the design and evaluation of user-intuitive interface signs from a semiotic perspective in order to improve web usability. Thus, the research identifies the research problems and justifies the solutions with two studies.

2. **Define Objectives of a Solution:** *Study II* (Phase II) shows that considering semiotic perception in designing interface signs improves the users' interpretation accuracy of the meaning of interface signs, and also improves the intuitiveness of interface signs. Thus, *Study I* and *Study II* show that semiotic has a significant role in the design and evaluation of web interface signs. Based on the results of these studies, the objective of this research is defined as: *to find semiotic means to provide valuable insights for designing and evaluating user-intuitive web interface signs in order to improve web usability.* The major challenges to accomplish this objective include:

    a. finding the factors in the design of user-intuitive interface signs,
    b. finding what kind of presupposed knowledge users have to interpret the meaning of interface signs,

    c.   finding how the intuitiveness of interface signs for end users can be evaluated, and

    d.   finding how semiotic can be integrated into the usability evaluation to assess the intuitiveness and problems of interface signs. Thus, a solution has been offered, i.e. to provide a semiotic framework for designing and evaluating user-intuitive interface signs to improve system usability.

3.   **Design and Development:** The main artifact, the SIDE framework, is created based on a series of four empirical studies (*Study II, Study III, Study IV,* and *Study V*) conducted over a three year period (2011-2013). Based on data gathered making use of observations in a usability testing lab, by analytical (expert) inspections, and by structured and semi-structured interviewing, and based on the data analyses from the four studies, determinants (or themes) and attributes (or sub-themes) for a user-intuitive design and evaluation of interface signs were formulated. The attributes were grouped into a set of determinants, based on their features. Finally, the determinants were mapped onto the five semiotic layers matching the properties of determinants to develop a Semiotic Interface sign Design and Evaluation (SIDE) framework. For example, the attributes of *sign color, color lightness* and *color contrast* are assigned to the determinant 'Color', while 'Color' matches with the syntactic level (see Figure 3).

4.   **Demonstration:** A number of semiotic features or instruments (i.e., determinants, attributes, heuristics) identified preliminary from *Study II (phase I), Study III,* and *Study IV* are demonstrated to assess the effectiveness and usefulness of these instruments. For example, the semiotic instruments found from *Study II (phase I)* are used to redesign a number of signs in *Study II(Phase II)*, and the users' interpretation accuracy and the intuitiveness of interface signs improved for the redesigned signs are observed. *Study VI* demonstrates the ways semiotic can be integrated into usability testing to improve the system usability. Thus this research tests the effectiveness of semiotic instruments for improving the system usability through *Study II (phase II)* and *Study VI.*

5.   **Evaluation:** An empirical study is conducted (*Study VII*) to evaluate the SIDE framework to assess and measure how well the artifact supports a solution (e.g., improve the interface signs' intuitiveness, evaluate the intuitiveness of interface signs, and recommend design solution for the problematic signs). In this study, the performance of the SIDE framework for evaluating the interface signs (i.e., to evaluate the intuitiveness of interface signs and to find the problems of designing interface signs intuitive for end-user) is evaluated. The metrics used to evaluate the performance of the SIDE framework are thoroughness, validity, effectiveness, efficiency, reliability, learnability, appropriateness, and accuracy. A subjective assessment is also carried out to assess the valuable insights and important characteristics of the SIDE framework from the evaluators' perspective. The outcomes of this evaluation are used to refine and update the SIDE framework.

6.   **Communication:** The present research resulted on articles in academic journals, academic conference proceedings and as a book chapter and technical reports. The results are published at different points of research progress in order to update or refine the research objectives, to identify the appropriate semiotic features or instruments to develop the SIDE framework, and to design the research studies.

DISCUSSION AND CONCLUSION

Though a few models and approaches have been proposed to conduct research in HCI, but current thinking on a "design science" for HCI is in flux (Prestopnik, 2013). According to Prestopnik (2013), "to think formally about design science is to think formally about the very nature of scholarship in HCI". Therefore, this paper through a case study outlines how a DSR approach is used to develop an HCI artifact for web interface design. The DSR methods and guidelines originally proposed for the information system research are adopted here to build an HCI artifact. By adopting the DSR method in our HCI research project (a doctoral research project (Islam, 2014)), we experienced the following benefits:

1. **Where to Start and What's Next:** The DSR process activities guide us on what we have to do next at any stages of our research progress. The DSR method also provides an insightful guideline to understand the research entry point to initiate a research project, for example, 'problem-centered initiation' was the research entry point for our research project (see Figure 4). Because, from the literature review (*Study I*), we found that semiotic means are not available in the existing literatures, while it was required for UI practitioners to design and evaluate web interface signs to make them intuitive for end-users.

2. **How to Maintain Research Rigor:** The DSR process helps us to maintain research rigor at each and every stage of development of the artifact (i.e., the SIDE framework) and evaluation of the artifact. DSR suggests us to do the iterations to distill the preliminary findings, i.e., the components (attributes and determinants) of the SIDE framework, prior to produce the final artifact and its evaluation. The method also guided us to assess the quality and applicability of the proposed artifact in order to refine and update the proposed artifact.

3. **Push to Publish and Communicate:** The DSR process itself pushes us to communicate our findings at different stages of research progress with the experts, other researcher, and practitioners. Our research thus benefited from feedback obtained continuously from HCI professionals, researchers, and students. This feedback supported us to update and refine the study design, data analysis approach and the study outcomes.

4. **Provide Fundamental Insights to Create the Artifact:** The literature on HCI research methods mostly helped us to design the user studies and laboratory experiments and to collect and analyse the study data. It was a challenge for us to find a suitable research approach to develop a HCI artifact for interface design based on multiple studies. DSR approach provided us upper level directions and inner understanding to conduct this research project properly. In our case, DSR acts as a guide to improve our confidence on research progress and outcomes, to maintain research rigor, and to distill each component (determinant and attribute of user intuitive interface signs) of the SIDE framework during the development process before going to the actual validation stage.

The paper presents how a HCI artifact is developed for designing and evaluating interface signs to make them intuitive for end-users following the DSR methods in detail. The paper also discusses our experiences of using the DSR approach in HCI research. We hope that this paper will provide a vibrant suggestion on how a DSR method can be used in HCI research.

REFERENCES

ACM SIGCHI. (2009). Curricula for Human-Computer Interaction. Retrieved from http://www.sigchi.org/resources/education/cdg/

Adikari, S., McDonald, C., & Collings, P. (2006). A design science approach to an HCI research project. *Proceedings of the OZCHI '06* (pp. 429–432). doi:10.1145/1228175.1228265

Adikari, S., McDonald, C., & Collings, P. (2009). Little Design Up-Front: A Design Science Approach to Integrating Usability into Agile Requirements Engineering.*Proceedings of the HCI International '09* (pp. 549-558). doi:10.1007/978-3-642-02574-7_62

Archer, L. B. (1984). Systematic method for designers. In N. Cross (Ed.), *Developments in Design Methodology* (pp. 57–82). London: John Wiley.

Bolchini, D., Chatterji, R., & Speroni, M. (2009). Developing heuristics for the semiotics inspection of websites. *Proceedings of the SIGDOC '09* (pp. 67–72). doi:10.1145/1621995.1622009

Carlsson, S. A. (2005). Developing Information systems design knowledge: A critical realist perspective. *The Electronic Journal of Business Research Methodology*, *3*(2), 93–102.

De Souze, C. S. (2005). *The Semiotic Engineering of Human-Computer Interaction*. Cambridge: MIT Press.

Derboven, J., Geerts, D., & Grooff, D. D. (2013). Researching user interpretation beyond designer intentions.*Proceedings of the extended Abstracts CHI '13* (pp. 367-372). ACM Press.

Ellis, T. J., & Levy, Y. (2010). A guide for novice researchers: Design and development research methods. *Proceedings of Informing Science & IT Educational Conference (InSITE)*. Retrieved from http://citeseerx.ist.psu.edu/viewdoc/download?doi=10.1.1.170.2962&rep=rep1&type=pdf

Fetaji, M., Loskoska, S., Fetaji, B., & Ebibi, M. (2007). Investigating Human Computer Interaction Issues in Designing Efficient Virtual Learning Environments.*Proceedings of the 3rd Balkan Conference in Informatics BCI '07*, Sofia, Bulgaria.

Gregor, S. (2002). *A theory of theories in information systems. In Information Systems Foundations* (pp. 1–20). Building the Theoretical Base.

Hevner, A., & Chatterjee, S. (2010). Design Science Research in Information Systems. In *Design Research in Information Systems* (pp. 9–22). Springer. doi:10.1007/978-1-4419-5653-8_2

Hevner, A. R., March, S. T., Park, J., & Ram, S. (2004). Design science in information systems research. *Management Information Systems Quarterly*, *28*(1), 75–105.

Islam, M. N. (2013). A Systematic Literature Review of Semiotic Perception in User Interfaces. *Journal of Systems and Information Technology*, *15*(1), 45–64. doi:10.1108/13287261311322585

Islam, M. N. (2014). *Design and Evaluation of Web Interface Signs to Improve Web Usability: A Semiotic Framework* [PhD Thesis]. Åbo Akademi University, Finland.

Islam, M. N., & Bouwman, H. (2015a). An Assessment of a Semiotics Framework for Evaluation of User-Intuitive Web Interface Signs. *Universal Access to the Information Society Journal*, *14*(4), 563–582. doi:10.1007/s10209-015-0403-6

Islam, M. N., & Bouwman, H. (2015b). Towards User-Intuitive Web User Interface sign Design and Evaluation: A Semiotic Framework. *International Journal of Human-Computer Studies, 86*, 121–137. doi:10.1016/j.ijhcs.2015.10.003

Islam, M. N., & Tétard, F. (2013). Integrating Semiotics Perception in Usability Testing to Improve Usability Evaluation. In M. Garcia-Ruiz (Eds.) Cases on Usability Engineering: Design and Development of Digital Products (pp. 145-169). Hershey, PA, USA: IGI Global. doi:10.4018/978-1-4666-4046-7.ch007

March, S. T., & Smith, G. F. (1995). Design and natural science research on information technology. *Decision Support Systems, 15*(4), 251–266. doi:10.1016/0167-9236(94)00041-2

March, S. T., & Storey, V. C. (2008). Design science in the information systems discipline: An introduction to the special issue on design science research. *Management Information Systems Quarterly, 32*(4), 725–730.

Nunamaker, J. F. Jr, & Chen, M. (1990). Systems development in information systems research.*Proceedings of the Twenty-Third Annual Hawaii International Conference on System sciences* (Vol. 3, pp. 631–640). doi:10.1109/HICSS.1990.205401

Peffers, K., Tuunanen, T., Rothenberger, M. A., & Chatterjee, S. (2007). A design science research methodology for information systems research. *Journal of Management Information Systems, 24*(3), 45–77. doi:10.2753/MIS0742-1222240302

Peirce, C. S. (1931-58). *Collected Writings*. In C. Hartshorne, P. Weiss, & A. Burks (Eds.). *Harvard University Press*.

Prestopnik, N. (2013). *Design Science in human-computer interaction: a model and three examples* [PhD Dissertation]. Syracuse University, Syracuse, NY.

Simon, H. A. (1996). *The Sciences of the Artificial* (3rd ed.). Cambridge, MA: MIT Press.

Speroni, M., Bolchini, D., & Paolini, P. (2006). Interfaces: "Do Users Understand Them?" *Proceedings of the Museums and the Web '06*. Retrieved from http://www.archimuse.com/mw2006/papers

Takeda, H., Veerkamp, P., & Yoshikawa, H. (1990). Modeling design process. *AI Magazine, 11*(4), 37.

Vaishnavi, V., & Kuechler, W. (2004). Design research in information systems. Retrieved from http://www.citeulike.org/group/4795/article/6505471

Venable, J. R. (2006). The Role of Theory and Theorising in Design Science Research.*Proceedings of the First International Conference on Design Science Research in Information Systems and Technology*, Claremont, California, USA (pp.1-18).

KEY TERMS AND DEFINITIONS

Design Science Research: Design science research is a research method for performing research in Information Systems (IS). It involves the design of innovative artifacts to improve and understand the behavior of aspects of Information Systems.

Research Methods: The process used to collect information and data for the purpose of making business decisions. It is often necessary to include a consideration of the concepts and theories which underlie the methods. The methodology may include surveys, design science research, experiment, etc.

Semiotics: The central concept of semiotics is the concept of 'sign.' Semiotics is concerned with sign, signification, and signifying systems. In other words, semiotics is defined as the study of signs and its process of signification.

Sign: Anything like a sound, a word, an image, etc. can be defined as a sign if it refers to some object rather than itself. For instance, the word 'ENTRY' on a door outside a hall room provides an indication to use that door to in the hall room. In this case, we may treat the word 'ENTRY' as a sign.

Usability: Usability is defined as the effectiveness, efficiency and satisfaction with which specified users achieve specified goals in particular environments. Effectiveness is the accuracy and completeness with which specified users can achieve specified goals in particular environments. Efficiency is the resources expended in relation to the accuracy and completeness of goals achieved. Satisfaction is the comfort and acceptability of the work system to its users and other people affected by its use.

Usability Evaluation: Assessing the *usability* of a product with the purpose of identifying *usability* problems and/or obtaining *usability* measures. In usability evaluation, usability of a system is evaluated with respect to criteria such as effectiveness, efficiency and satisfaction of intended users.

User Interface Design: UI design is the design of user interfaces for machines, web and software, with the focus on maximizing the overall usability and user experiences.

Web Interface Sign: Web user interface encompass a number of navigational links, command buttons, images, symbols, logos, etc. These have a referential or intended meaning that refers to another object. Therefore, these user interface elements are defined as interface signs. For instance, the interface sign 'Admission' in a university website stands for providing admission related information for prospective students.

Chapter 13

Implications of Similarities in Instructional Design, Learner Interface Design and User Interface Design in Designing a User-Friendly Online Module

Titilola T. Obilade
Virginia Polytechnic Institute and State University, USA

ABSTRACT

The development of a user-friendly online module depends on the inputs, the processes and the outcomes from the user interface design, the learner interface design and the instructional design. The online module includes the user interface design, the learner interface and the instructional design. This chapter would examine the theories behind these three designs. What guidelines can be garnered from the theories of these three designs? How can these guidelines be used to develop a user-friendly online module? In addition, it would examine their similarities and how they can be used to develop a user-friendly online module. Further, the chapter recommended an alignment of the garnered guidelines from the three designs to explore the plausible reasons for the high attrition rate in Massive Open Online Courses (MOOC).

INTRODUCTION

Many online modules exist and it is not all these websites that are user-friendly. Online modules are platforms that allow communication between the learner and the module. Usually, when the learner is at the computer, the designer is not going to be present. Whether the use of a website is for learning or for purchasing goods; the website needs to be user-friendly. This chapter would examine the theories in user interface design, learner interface design and instructional design. Further, it would garner guidelines from their theories. In addition, it would examine how the similarities in these three designs can be used in developing a user-friendly online module.

DOI: 10.4018/978-1-5225-0435-1.ch013

USER INTERFACE

User interface design began with the design of software systems like Microsoft Disk Operating System (MS DOS), MS Windows, Windows 95, Macintosh Operating System (Mac OS and later with the development of application software like word processors, spread sheets and graphic designs (Jones & Farquahar, 1997). There are many definitions of user interface.

"User interface is the communication medium between the user and the technology or machine" (Vrasidas, 2011, p.228). It is through the user interface that humans can talk to the computer (Galitz, 2002, Chap. 2). It is the human end of the computer (Beynon-Davies, 1993, Chap. 19). A user interface is the software and hardware of the computer that allows the user to interact with the information from the computer (Mandel, 1997, Chap. 2).

Human-computer interface and human-human interface are synonyms for the user interface (Marcus, 2002). A user interface has input and output devices. These input devices include the mouse, the finger (for touch screen), keyboard and the voice for voice recognition (Galitz, 2002, Chap.2). The screen display is an output device. A user interface is the channel of communication that occurs between the user and the computer.

Computer based instruction was initially limited to text on the computer screen that was controlled by the keystroke from the keyboard. After the introduction of the graphical user interface, instructional delivery through the computer became revamped (Jones, 1995). User interfaces should be unobtrusive in their function by allowing the user to work seamlessly with the technology (Galitz, 2002, Chap.2; Vrasidas, 2011). The user interface is made up of windows, controls, menus, buttons, metaphors, online help and documentation.

The user interface is not the Hyper Text Markup Language (HTML) code (Vrasidas, 2011). It also includes non-traditional components like trackers, 3 D pointing devices and whole hand held devices (Bowman, Kruijff, LaViola & Poupyrev, 2001). User interfaces with assistive technologies have additional icons that would indicate the type of assistive technology on the user interface (see Figure 1). The mouse pointer enhancements are an assistive technology device for the user interface.

Figure 1. The four red lines on the computer screen enclose the cursor so that users with visual challenges can quickly locate the cursor (The red lines would appear as grey in a black and white image)

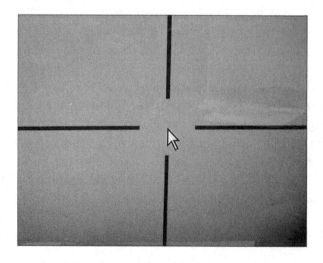

The user interface includes the software, hardware, tutorials and the manuals that come with the software and hardware (Mandel, 1997, Chap. 2). There are two main types of user interfaces; the Graphical User Interface (GUI) and the Web User Interface (see Figures 2 and 3).

Figure 2. Screen shot of graphical user interface

Figure 3. Screen shot of web user interface

The GUI is the "graphical representation of, and interaction with, programs, data, and objects on the computer screen" (Mandel, 1977 p.160). They usually have icons, menus and pointers. The web interface is the design of the information being presented (Galitz, 2002, Chap.2). User interface designs are used as game-based learning by integrating software applications in the learner interface (Liang, Lee & Chou, 2010).

At the onset, the purpose of creating the web interface design was to give information. The HTML used was directed at technical people and not at the general population. Therefore, the general user has problems with the web interface today (Galitz, 2002, Chap. 2). This can be an explanation to why some web sites are not user friendly.

The World Wide Web (WWW) is an open system because beyond the page that the designer has designed for the user, the user can link to other sites not created by the designer (Jones & Farquhar, 1997). Ritchie and Hoffman (1997) pointed out that a World Wide Web page with links to other sites is not an instructional page but it becomes an instructional web based lesson when it incorporates the principles of instructional design. Educational software is a closed system because the information provided in the software is finite. It is the designer that has the control in closed systems (Jones & Farquhar, 1977).

Models of User Interface

There are different models of user interface. The models have functional variations. This chapter would discuss four models of user interface.

1. Goals, Operators, Methods and Selection Rules Model (GOMS)

The goals, operators, methods and selection rules model (GOMS) and the keystroke-level model were proposed by Card, Moran and Newell in 1980 (John, 2003; John & Kieras, 1995; Shneiderman, 1998). The GOMS was developed using text editing applications but it can be applied to other task domains (John & Kieras, 1995).

The general goal can be to write a paper and one of the several sub goals would be to edit the manuscript. The goal is what the user wants to do. The operators are the motor and the perceptual actions that take place to achieve the goal. They are controlled by the software that the user is using. The operator could be a command like delete but on a graphical user interface, it could be any of the menu selections on the computer. It could also be a gazed-based user interface (Stellmach & Dachselt, 2012). The operator could also be a gestural interface (Lü, & Li, 2011; Rautaray, Kumar & Agrawal, 2012). Figure 4 shows different hand motions in front of a gestural interface.

The methods are the processes used in navigating the operators and sub goals to achieve the overall goal. The selection is the different combinations of selections and operators through which the overall

Figure 4. Gestural user interface

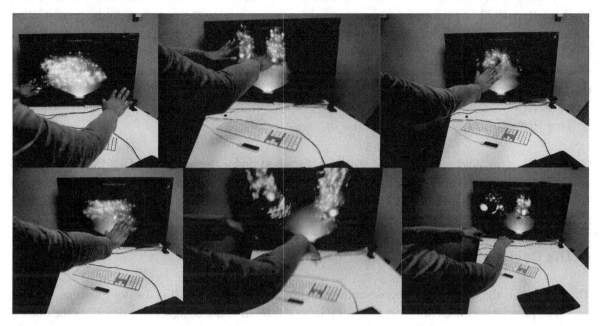

goals can be achieved. As an example, in writing a paper using a word processor, the user would need to use different applications like editing, pasting and deleting functions.

Hennicker and Koch (2001) proposed a user interface model that would use a conceptual, navigation and presentation design. Mandel (1997) described the user interface model as the user's model, the programmer's model and the designer's model. He further makes an analogy of a house being built; the architect designs the house like the designer, the builder builds or develops the house from the architect's design like the programmer and the user is the person or people that would be living in the house like the end user.

2. The User's Model

The user's model would reflect on the user. A user's model for a child may show playful icons with cartoon characters but an adult user's model would not show cartoon icons. Regardless of the user, certain information must be extracted from the users. The designer must analyze the user. Are they novice or expert users (Shneiderman, 1998)? The designer must survey and interview potential users (Mandel, 1997). S/he should visit the work sites of the prospective users and get feedback from the users. The designers can videotape users at work (Galitz, 2002). Further, psychological characteristics of the user must be added.

These characteristics include the attitude, motivation, patience, expectations, stress level and cognitive style of the users (Galitz, 2002). In addition, the physical characteristics of the user would determine the design. These physical characteristics include the age, gender, left or right-handedness and disabilities of hearing, vision or a motor handicap. Hennicker and Koch (2001) proposed visual modeling and storyboarding by user interface designers.

The designers should also do a usability testing (Mandel, 1997). The term usability was first used by Bennett in 1979 and the definition rests on the effective use of the computer by humans (Galitz, 2002). Nielsen (1993) defined usability as a property of a user interface with attributes of learnability, efficiency, memorability, errors and satisfaction. He argues against such terms as user-friendly or user-centered design because a computer is made to serve the human and different users have different needs on the computer.

3. The Programmer's Model

Going back to the analogy of a house that was discussed under the section of GOMS, the programmer is like the house builder (Shneiderman, 1998). S/he writes the codes or the program. Johnson and Henderson (2002) suggest that before programmers begin to draw dialog boxes, they should start with a conceptual model of the design.

4. The Designer's Model

The designer is the intermediary between the programmer and the user. It is the designer that sees the user. The programmer does not meet the user (Galitz, 2002). It is the designer that describes the objects that the user works with. In addition, the designer describes how these objects are presented to the user and the interaction of the user with them (Mandel, 1997, Chap.3).

Some Theories of User Interface Design

There are several theories that are used in user interface. Some of these are Fitt's law, cognitive information processing, perception, vision research, minimalism and color theory. Shneiderman (1998, Chap. 2) asserted that there were thousands of theories existing on user interfaces. These theories can be divided into two categories (MacKenzie, 2003; Shneiderman, 1998, Chap. 9). They can be explanatory or predictive. The explanatory theories explain concepts of designs and observable behaviors. The predictive theories relate to the execution time or error rates of tasks performed.

Fitts' Law (MacKenzie, 2003; Shneiderman, 1998, Chap. 9) is used in the design of pointing devices. Fitts' Law predicts the time it would take for the cursor to move a certain distance from the moment the pointing device is activated. It is dependent on the distance the hand has to move from the pointing object to the target object. The predictions from Fitts' Law are dependent on whether the movement is vertical or horizontal. Further, the predictions are dependent on the arm position, the device grasp and the shape of the target (Shneiderman & Plaisant, 2010, Chap.8).

The cognitive information processing model of acquiring knowledge, retrieving information, organization and prior experience are used in designing software (MacKenzie, 2003; Mandel, 1997, Chap. 4). It explains how information is stored and retrieved. In addition to using the cognitive information processing system, design principles are based on human perception (Ware, 2003). It is through perception theory that designers can determine how many pixels can be conveniently displayed on a phone screen (Ware, 2003).

The vision research theory is used in the design of 3-dimensional user interfaces (Ware, 2003). Ware (2003) introduced the term, information psychophysics which is how humans see information patterns when the patterns are expressed through light, color and simple patterns. Color theory suggests an appropriate choice of color in the design. It is through the knowledge of color theory that Liquid Crystal Display (LCD) monitors and Cathode Ray Tubes (CTR) produce mixtures of three colors (Ware, 2003).

However, color theory is separate from the culture that some groups attach to color. In some parts of Asia, the red color symbolizes good fortune while in Europe, it symbolizes danger (Ware, 2003). Ware (2003) argued that affordance theory could not be strictly used in the design of user interfaces because by the Gibsonian definition, affordances referred to the physical properties of the object.

However, by more recent definitions of affordance, it does not have to be a physical characteristic that can be touched (Obilade, 2015). There are different types of affordance like technological affordance, educational affordance and perceived affordance (Obilade, 2015). These newer definitions of affordance give room for the user to intuitively know how to use the product without engaging any frustrations from his/her inability to make the product perform what it is intended to do (Obilade, 2015). A perceived affordance gives clues on how to use the product (see Figures 5 and 6).

On minimalism, Johnson (2010) wrote, "Minimize the amount of prose text in a user interface; don't present users with long blocks of prose text to read" (Johnson, 2010, p. 50). In addition, Wroblewski (2011) noted that "When it comes to mobile forms, be brutally efficient and trim, trim, trim" (Wroblewski, 2011, p. 103). " One of the biggest challenges of designing interfaces for complex systems is figuring out which aspects the users don't need to deal with and reducing their visibility (or leaving them out altogether)" (Garrett, 2011, p.114).

Apart from the use of theory and principles in designing a user interface, designers use specific guidelines for the design of the information on the display screen. (Beynon-Davies, 1993, Chap.19; MacKenzie, 2003; Shneiderman, 1998, Chap. 9) These principles include choice of fonts, typeface, color, audio and consistency in the terminology (Obilade, 2016). If the same image would be displayed on a mobile phone and on a PC, determine the number of pixels that can be conveniently displayed on

Figure 5. The push sign on the glass door is a perceived affordance. It gives a clue on how to open the door.

Figure 6. The pull sign on the glass door is a perceived affordance. It gives a clue on how to open the door.

each device (Obilade, 2016). Referring to pixels on a mobile phone, Wrobleski (2011) wrote, "Pixel density impacts how physically big or small elements appear on a screen. A higher pixel density means each pixel is physically smaller" (Wroblewski, 2011. p.110).

User-Friendly Guidelines from Theories of User-Interface Design

1. State clear goals for the user-interface.
2. Define the sub-goals.
3. Define the motor and perceptual actions that must take place to achieve the goal.
4. Make the user-interface reflect the persona of the user.
5. Know the physical characteristics of the user including his/her left/right handedness.
6. Know the motivation, attitudes, patience, expectations, stress level and cognitive style of the user.
7. Conduct a usability testing.
8. Define the time it would take for the cursor to move from the time the pointing device is activated. This is important in gestural and gaze-based user interfaces.
9. If the same image would be displayed on a mobile phone and on a PC, determine the number of pixels that can be conveniently displayed on each device.
10. Avoid color combinations that color blind people would not be able to see. Red and green color combinations are not seen by people who are color blind.
11. Choose appropriate typeface, font and color.
12. Apply the principles of affordance.
13. Apply minimalism.

LEARNER INTERFACE

Moore (1989) classified the various interactions in distance learning into three categories. These interactions were learner-content, learner-instructor and learner-learner. Following these categorizations, Hillman, Willis and Gunawardena (1994) introduced the learner interface interaction as the interaction between the learners and the technology used to deliver the instruction. The learner interface became the fourth category in the various interactions in distance learning. It is the point of interaction "…between the learner and his or her content, instructor and fellow learners" (Hillman et al., 1994, p.32).

The learner interface is the medium through which the learner makes a point of contact with the content, the other learners and the instructor. It is through technology that the learner makes contact with the other interfaces. Lucas (1991) pointed out that the visual design of the learner interface affects the motivation of the learner.

The learner should be presented with visual hierarchies (Krug, 2014). Krug (2014) wrote, "… make sure that the appearance of the things on the page-all of the visual cues-accurately portray the relationships between the things on the page: which things are similar, and which things are part of other things" (p.33). The visual design of the learner interface includes the graphical elements of an interface, the layout of the screen, and the images used to represent commands on the screen (Lucas, 1991).

Consistency in the text, consistency of the fonts and consistency in the icon would keep the learner focused on the learning material and keep him/her from wondering what inconsistent icons mean (Lucas, 1991 & Galitz, 2002, Chap. 8). Headers should be placed consistently on the same spot on every page (Lucas, 1991). Designers should avoid the use of scrolling to the next page. Rather, they should have an icon that changes the pages (Galitz, 2002, Chap. 8). The design of the learner interface should make recovery from errors easy (Johnson, 2010; Krug, 2014; Wroblewski, 2011). "Minimizing the amount of navigation options on mobile screens helps to prevent errors as well" (Wroblewski, 2011, p. 65).

Some Theories of Learner Interface Design

The principles and guidelines from theories in learner interface must be applied to develop a user-friendly learner interface. Gnanam, Srinath and Sivhakumaar (2011) asserted that the learner interface consisted of cognitivist, constructivist and collaborative theory or a mixture of the three theories. Jones, Farquhar and Surry (1995) proposed the use of cognitive strategies in computer-based instruction.

These cognitive strategies are the methods through which information is stored, comprehended and retrieved from memory. They include methods like organization of learning material and use of schemas. Jones et al. (1995) proposed the use of metacognitive theories in the design of interfaces for computer-based instruction. The learner selects the most appropriate strategy for the particular learning problem. The learner controls the cognitive process through strategy selection. S/he monitors cognitive processes through goal setting and goal checking. The learner is able to change the cognitive strategy to another cognitive strategy if the one being used does not work.

The learner interface was successfully used as a constructivist educational tool in designing web-based video games that taught geography and physical sciences at the grade level (Vichido, Estrada & Sanchez, 2003). They (Vichido et al., 2003) collected demographic data, data on experiences and interests of students before designing the learner interface for the students. In addition, the learners were given a pretest before exposing them to the concepts through video gaming. The results of the study showed that the students who learned the concepts of geography and the physical sciences through gaming scored higher than on the pretest.

Ortiz, Ayala and Osorio (2003) used a group-based zone of proximal development to develop a learner interface for computer supported collaborative learning (CSCL). They gathered information about learners and about what the designers believed about the learners. The information gathered from both learners and designers was used to develop the learner interface. They also had to get information on the various topics that those in the learning group were going to learn. Finally, Ortiz et al. (2003) used the knowledge from the group's zone of proximal development to develop the interface.

User-Friendly Guidelines from Theories of Learner Interface Design

1. Determine how the learner interface can motivate the learners.
2. Keep the visual design of the learner interface simple.
3. Be consistent in the use of texts, fonts and icons.
4. Place headers in the same spot on every page.
5. State unambiguous goals and set sub goals.
6. Determine what the designer believes about the learners.
7. Determine what the learners know about the lesson content before designing the module.
8. Use visual hierarchies.
9. Determine the learners' zones of proximal development.

INSTRUCTIONAL DESIGN

Instructional design is synonymous to instructional systems development (Molenda, 1997). Instructional system design is not instructional theory (Merrill, 1977). "Instructional design (ID) theory is a set of prescriptions for determining appropriate instructional strategies to enable learners to acquire instructional goals. ID theory is prescription based and is founded in learning theory and related disciplines" (Merrill, 1977, p. 381). It is a prescriptive theory because the theories predict the learning outcomes (Tennyson & Schott, 1977).

The instructional design for the learning outcome is developed based on the instructional theory (Tennyson & Schott, 1977). Instructional theory describes how the instructional design works and why it works while instructional design describes what to do through a series of systematically designed steps. It usually begins with a needs assessment. There are several models. Basically, instructional design can be divided into analysis, design, development, implementation and evaluation (ADDIE) (Merrill 1997; Molenda, 1997).

Instructional design has its origins in systems engineering and behaviorist psychology (Molenda, 1997). The early models of instructional design used engineering concepts and terminologies like feedback, input, output, channel and lead time (Molenda, 1977).

At the end of World War II, psychologists were invited by the Military to design and develop military training materials. They focused research on designing instruction specific to the learning outcome and developed a systems approach to analyze performances.

Skinner's work on programmed instruction was developed further by Gagné, Glaser and Pask (Tennyson & Schott, 1977). These psychologists were employed by the military to design programmed instruction. After the development of Gagné's theory in the early sixties, instructional design moved towards a cognitive approach. Gagné's theory described how to achieve learning outcomes through segmented steps. In addition, Ausubel's theory of advance organizers and Vygostky's theory of zone of proximal development contributed to the shift from behaviorist to the cognitivist approach (Tennyson & Schott, 1977).

Andrews and Goodson (2011) reviewed 40 models of instructional design after identifying more than 60 models of instructional design. The results from their study were first published in 1980 (Andrews & Goodson, 1980) but the results are still relevant today. They found that most of the models were either based on theoretical or on empirical origins. Some models were also based on the users' past experience.

Some Theories of Instructional Design

Instructional design is developed through use of learning theories and theories of instruction (Tennyson & Elmore, 1977). These learning theories are embedded in cognitive roots. Schema theory, advance organizers, assimilation theory and discovery learning are all learning theories. The theories of instruction include elaboration theory, the Minnesota Adaptive Instructional System, knowledge representation and integrated instructional strategies.

Schema Theory

The term *schema* was first used by Bartlett in 1932 (Tennyson & Elmore, 1977). "For this combined standard, against which all subsequent changes of posture are measured before they enter consciousness, we propose the word *schema*" (Bartlett, 1932, p.199). Bartlett conducted his experiments by reading ghost stories from a North American folk-tale to participants and asking them to recall the stories (Bartlett, 1932).

The participants in his experiment did not come from the culture from which the ghost stories were taken from. He noticed that different participants relayed the stories by omitting parts that did not fit into their repertoire of ghost stories regardless of how many times the stories were retold.

The participants also added parts that were not in the story to fit into their existing repertoire. He postulated that learners were able to recall material if they had a schema organized in their memory (Kintsch, 1997). Ausubel added that the interpretation of what the learner made of his /her schema was a cognitive process. Ausubel described the schemata as several slots inside the memory. These slots are filled with related information in an organized way by the learner for easy recall. However, when the learner does not store the information in an organized way, recall would be difficult or impossible (Obilade, 2016; Tennyson & Elmore, 1977).

Agatha Christie's detective protagonist, Miss Marple was describing schema when she said:

Has it ever occurred to you ... how much we go by what is called, I believe, the context? There is a place in Dartmoor called Grey Wethers. If you were talking to a farmer there and mentioned Grey Wethers, he would probably conclude that you were speaking of these stone circles, yet it might be possible that you might be speaking of the atmosphere; and in the same way, if you were meaning the stone circles, an outsider, hearing a fragment of the conversation, might think you meant the weather. So when we repeat a conversation, we don't as a rule, repeat the actual words; we put in some other words that seem to us to mean exactly the same thing. (Christie, 1985, pp. 82-83)

Advance Organizers

Advance organizers are closely related to schema theory. Advance organizers help the learner to build a conceptual framework provided the material to be learnt has a structure (Ausubel, 1960; Tennyson & Elmore, 1977). They cannot be used to learn new material like the Greek alphabet because the Greek alphabet cannot be broken into structure (Tennyson & Elmore, 1977).

Assimilation Theory

Ausubel postulated that if the material to be learnt is connected to what the learner already knows, it makes meaningful learning for the learner. Assimilation theory works well for conceptual ideas but it does not work for learning technical details (Tennyson & Elmore, 1977). The presentation of advance organizers of concepts and lessons that have structure at the beginning of the lesson would increase the assimilation of the new material because the new material can find a structure to anchor on.

Discovery Learning

Jerome Bruner's work and Gestalt psychology contributed to the development of discovery learning (Einsiedler, 1977). Discovery learning allows the learners to discover through inquiry under the guidance of a teacher and the learning material (Hammer, 1997).

Supporters of discovery learning are opposed to putting specific learning objectives in a lesson plan (Andrews & Goodson, 2011). Discovery learning is not always welcome by teachers who want to teach by the rule (Hammer, 1997; Tennyson & Elmore, 1997). Skeptics of discovery learning propose that discovery learning should be guided discovery and not just pure discovery (Mayer, 2004). Discovery learning is the practice of social constructivism or cognitive constructivism (Mayer, 2004).

User-Friendly Guidelines from Theories of Instructional Design

1. Conduct a needs assessment.
2. Use a design, development, implementation and evaluation method.
3. Determine the learning theories you would use in the lesson content.
4. Determine the model of instructional design that you would use (see Figure 7).

Figure 7 is the Dick and Carey model. The Dick and Carey instructional design model is one of the several models of instructional design.

Adapted from "A Model For The Systematic Design of Instruction," by W. Dick, In R. Tennyson, F. Schott, N. Seel, & S. Dijkstra (Eds.), *Instructional Design: International Perspectives Volume 1: Theory, Research and Models,* 1997, p. 365. Mahwah, New Jersey: Lawrence Erlbaum Associates.

Similarities in User Interface Design, Learner Interface Design and Instructional Design

In order to design a successful web site or develop a user-friendly online module, the three types of designs being examined in this chapter must consider the characteristics of the learner. The characteristics of the

Figure 7. The Dick and Carey model

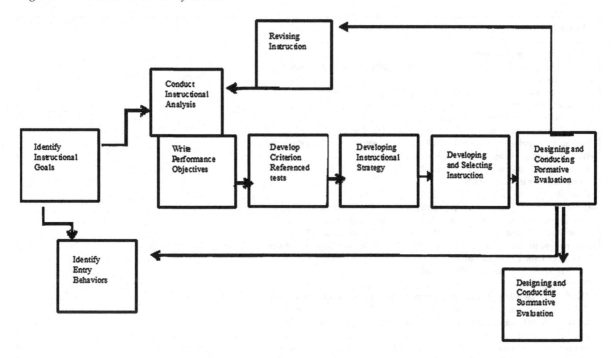

learner would be the age, sex, culture, entry-level competencies of the user, the right/left handedness of the user, the stress level, the patience, the motivating factors and other relevant information that can impact the learning process. The psychological attributes of the intended user must also be considered. There are similarities in the three designs (see Table 1).

Figure 8. illustrates the similarities in the designing of user and learner interfaces. The major steps of planning, designing, analyzing, testing and refining are the steps of instructional design in Figure 8. The steps in testing and refining would reflect the implementation and evaluation in the ADDIE model in instructional design.

Table 1 shows the similarities in the user interface, learner interface and instructional design. These similarities occur in the three designs already discussed in this chapter. The designer must know the attributes of the user or learner in all of the three designs. The designer must gather information about the tasks to be performed in all the three designs. The environment in which the design would be used must be analyzed in all the three designs. The three designs require collaboration from different experts. The three designs require feedback and evaluation of their processes.

Analogy of User Interface, Learner Interface and Instructional Design to a Car

A lot of processes are involved before a car gets to the user. In this chapter, I have decided to use a car for simplicity. The driver is the user or learner. However, before purchasing the car, the user interface designer similar to the manufacturers would have determined the characteristics of the driver including policies that might affect the driver's experience. The instructional designer would have put the instructions on how to navigate the car in such a way that the driver would have an accident free driving experience. The learner interface would be the interactions the user (or driver) has with other road users.

Table 1. Similarities

1 Learner Attributes (Mandel, 1997, p. 256) -Specifying the target audience -Identifying the age bracket, user demographics, skills, knowledge background **2. Objectives** - State objectives of the design (Dick,1997, p.364) **3.Perform User Analysis** (Dick, 1997, p. 365, Mandel, 1997, p. 256) -Procedure-based task analysis and cognitive-based task analysis -This analysis includes questions like; what steps are taken to perform the task? -What information is needed to complete the tasks? -How frequently do users perform the task? **4. Gather User Requirements** (Dick, 1997, p. 365, Mandel, 1997, p. 256) -Gathering of user requirements and analysis would answer questions like: -How much are users and managers willing to pay for the product? -What should the interface feel like, what affordances would be used? -Information for user requirements is gathered through focus groups, structured interviews, and user surveys. **5. Analyze User Environment** (Dick, 1997, p. 365, Mandel, 1997, p. 257) -Where do the users perform their tasks? -The designers would gather information on where the users would use the design. -Will it be used on a mobile phone? Will it be used at home or in the office? -What are the affordances in the physical environment? Light, noise and space. -The types of computers, Mac or PC. -Human factors, ergonomics and physical considerations; keyboard affordances, Users with special needs. **6. Match Requirements to User Tasks** (Dick, 1997, p. 365, Mandel, 1997, p. 257) -Avoid excessive cognitive load -If the feature is not necessary and is above what the users need, the designer should not include it. Apply minimalism. **7. Feedback** (Dick, 1997, p. 365, Mandel, 1997, p. 259) -The designer should always go back to the user analysis phase and determine if the learner characteristics, the environment or other requirements have changed during the design and development process. **8. Evaluation** (Dick, 1997, p. 365, Mandel, 1997, p. 259) -The designer should evaluate the design **9. Theory** -All the designs are based on one or more theories. **10. Collaboration** -There is collaboration of experts from different fields. **11. History** -The three designs were developed in response to post World War II.

The Massive Open Online Courses (MOOC) Experience

Massive Open Online Courses became popular after Stanford University began its MOOC in 2011. In the Stanford experience, one-sixth of the students completed the course (Rodriguez, 2012). Twenty thousand students had completed the course from over 190 countries (Rodriguez, 2012). Similar platforms to the MOOC are Coursera, EdX and Udacity.

The interest in MOOC is on the rise because it has been successfully used in many universities and is a welcome reduction in tuition costs. However, research has also shown that MOOC is facing many challenges. It has a low course completion rate, a high degree of student attrition, poor student engagement and poor student motivation (Gašević, Kovanović, Joksimović & Siemens, 2014; Jordan, 2014; Jordan, 2015a; Jordan, 2015b; Koller, Ng, Do, & Chen, 2013; Xiong et al., 2015). A review of research

Figure 8. Alignments of user interface, learner interface and instructional design

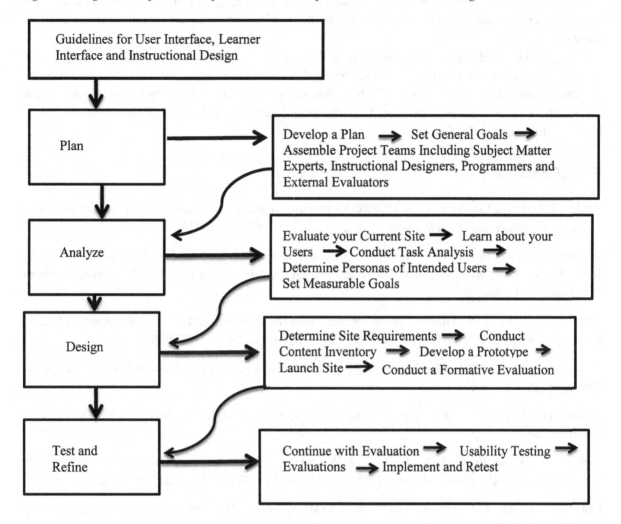

conducted on MOOC showed that lack of motivation of learners was responsible for a high attrition rate. Studies have shown that even though an average of 43,000 students enrolls in MOOC only 6.5% complete the courses (Jordan, 2014).

Currently, there are several studies going on to explore the possible reasons for the low attrition rates. In sync with the ongoing studies, this chapter would recommend an exploration of the three designs examined in this chapter and alignment of the guidelines identified to developing a successful MOOC with less attrition.

CONCLUSION

The purpose of this chapter was to determine the implications of the similarities in user interface design, learner interface design and instructional design in developing a user-friendly online module. It examined the processes and similarities in the three designs that could be used in developing a user-friendly online module. The results of the review showed that the knowledge of learner attributes, the environment and performance user analysis contribute to the development of a user friendly-website in all the three designs studied.

User-friendly guidelines were garnered from the theories in each of the three designs; instructional design, learner interface design and user interface design. There were similarities in the learner attributes, objectives, task analysis, evaluation and in the collaboration of experts. Further, the chapter recommended an alignment of the garnered guidelines from the three designs to explore the plausible reasons for the high attrition rate in MOOC.

REFERENCES

Andrews, D. H., & Goodson, L. A. (1980). A comparative analysis of models of instructional design. *Journal of Instructional Development, 3*(4), 2–16. doi:10.1007/BF02904348

Andrews, D. H., & Goodson, L. A. (2011). A comparative analysis of models of instructional design. In G. Anglin (Ed.), *Instructional technology: Past, present, and future* (pp. 205–225). Santa Barbara, CA: Libraries Unlimited.

Ausubel, D. P. (1960). The use of advance organizers in the learning and retention of meaningful verbal material. *Journal of Educational Psychology, 51*(5), 267–272. doi:10.1037/h0046669

Bartlett, F. C. (1932). *Remembering: A study in experimental and social psychology London*. Cambridge University Press.

Beynon-Davies, P. (1993). *Information systems development. Houndsmills*. Basingstoke: The Macmillan Press Ltd.

Bowman, D. A., Kruijff, E., LaViola, J. J. Jr, & Poupyrev, I. (2001). An introduction to 3-D user interface design. *Presence (Cambridge, Mass.), 10*(1), 96–108. doi:10.1162/105474601750182342

Christie, A. (1985). The thumbmark of St. Peter. In *Miss. Marple: The complete short stories* (pp. 72–86). New York: G. P. Putnam's Sons.

Dick, W. (1997). A model for the systematic design of instruction. In R. Tennyson, F. Schott, N. Seel, & S. Dijkstra (Eds.), Instructional design: International perspectives (Vol. 1: Theory, research and models, pp. 361-369). Mahwah, New Jersey: Lawrence Erlbaum Associates.

Einsiedler, W. (1997). Research on instructional methods: An European perspective. In R. Tennyson, F. Schott, N. Seel, & S. Dijkstra (Eds.), Instructional design: International perspectives (Vol. 1: Theory, research and models, pp. 1-16). Mahwah, New Jersey: Lawrence Erlbaum Associates.

Galitz, W. O. (2002). *The essential guide to user interface design: An introduction to GUI design principles and techniques*. New York: John Wiley & Sons.

Garrett, J. J. (2011). *The elements of user experience: user-centered design for the web and beyond*. Berkeley, CA: New Riders.

Gašević, D., Kovanović, V., Joksimović, S., & Siemens, G. (2014). Where is Research on Massive Open Online Courses Headed? A Data Analysis of the MOOC Research Initiative. *The International Review of Research in Open and Distant Learning, 15*(5).

Gnanam, S. P., Srinath, M. V., & Sivhakumaar, V. P. (2011). Emerging web instructional design model for developing web based learning resources. *European Journal of Scientific Research*, *56*(4), 548–555.

Hammer, D. (1997). Discovery learning and discovery teaching. *Cognition and Instruction*, *15*(4), 485–529. doi:10.1207/s1532690xci1504_2

Hennicker, R., & Noch, N. (2001). Modeling the user interface of web applications with UML. In A. Evans, R. France, A. Moreira, & B. Rumpe (Eds.), Proceedings of the Practical UML-Based Rigorous Development Methods- Countering or Integrating the Extremists, Workshop of the Puml-Group Held Together with UML 2001 (Vol. P-07, pp. 158–172). Toronto, Canada. Retrieved from http://subs.emis.de/LNI/Proceedings/ Proceedings07 /ModeltheUseInterf_12.pdf

Hillman, D. C., Willis, D. J., & Gunawardena, C. N. (1994). Learner-Interface interactions in distance education: An extension of contemporary models and strategies for practitioners. *American Journal of Distance Education*, *8*(2), 30–42. doi:10.1080/08923649409526853

John, B. E. (2003). Information processing and skilled behavior. In J. Carroll (Ed.), *HCI model, theories and frameworks: Towards a multidisciplinary science* (pp. 55–101). San Francisco, CA: Morgan Kaufmann. doi:10.1016/B978-155860808-5/50004-6

John, B. E., & Kieras, D. E. (1995). The GOMS family of user interface analysis techniques: Comparison and contrast. *ACM Transactions on Computer-Human Interaction*, *3*(4), 320–351. doi:10.1145/235833.236054

Johnson, J. (2010). *Designing with the mind in mind: simple guide to understanding user interface design rules*. CA: Morgan Kaufmann.

Johnson, J., & Henderson, A. (2002). Conceptual models: Begin by designing what to design. *Interaction*, *9*(1), 25–32. doi:10.1145/503355.503366

Jones, M. G. (1995). Visuals for information access: A new philosophy for screen and interface design. In D. Beauchamp, R. Braden, & R. Griffen (Eds.), *Imagery and visual literacy* (pp. 264–272). International Visual Literacy Association.

Jones, M. G., & Farquhar, J. D. (1997). User interface design for web-based instruction. In B. Khan (Ed.), *Web-based instruction* (pp. 239–254). Englewood Cliffs, NJ: Educational Technology.

Jones, M. G., Farquhar, J. D., & Surry, D. W. (1995). Using metacognitive theories to design user interfaces for computer based learning. *Educational Technology*, *35*(4), 12–22.

Jordan, K. (2014). Initial trends in enrolment and completion of massive open online courses. *International Review of Research in Open and Distance Learning*, *15*(1), 133–160.

Jordan, K. (2015a). Massive Open Online Course Completion Rates Revisited: Assessment, Length And Attrition. *International Review of Research in Open and Distance Learning*, *16*(3), 341–358.

Jordan, K. (2015b). MOOC completion rates: The data. Retrieved from http://www.katyjordan.com/MOOCproject.html

Kintsch, W. (1997). Introduction. In F. C. Bartlett (Ed.), *Remembering: A study in experimental and social psychology* (pp. xi–xvi). London: Cambridge University Press.

Koller, D., Ng, A., Do, C., & Chen, Z. (2013). Retention and intention in massive open online courses: In depth. *EDUCAUSE Review*, *48*(3), 62–63.

Krug, S. (2014). *Don't make me think, revisited: A common sense approach to web usability*. California: Pearson Education.

Liang, C., Lee, Y.-Z., & Chou, W.-S. (2010). The design considerations for game-based learning. *Educational Technology*, *50*(2), 25–28.

Lü, H., & Li, Y. (2011, May 7-12). Gesture avatar: A technique for operating mobile user interfaces using gestures. In D. Tan, S. Amershi, B. Begole, W. Kellogg, & M. Tungare (Eds.), *Proceedings of the International Conference on Human Factors in Computing Systems CHI '11*, Vancouver, BC, Canada. ACM.

Lucas, L. (1991). Visually designing the computer-learner interface. *Educational Technology*, *31*(7), 56–58.

MacKenzie, S. (2003). Motor behavior models for human-computer interaction. In J. Carroll (Ed.), *HCI model, theories and frameworks: Towards a multidisciplinary science* (pp. 27–54). San Francisco, CA: Morgan Kaufmann; doi:10.1016/B978-155860808-5/50003-4

Mandel, T. (1997). *The elements of user interface design*. New York: John Wiley & Sons.

Marcus, A. (2002). Dare we define user-interface design? *Interaction*, *9*(5), 19–24. doi:10.1145/566981.566992

Mayer, R. E. (2004). Should there be a three-strikes rule against pure discovery learning? *The American Psychologist*, *59*(1), 14–19. doi:10.1037/0003-066X.59.1.14 PMID:14736316

Merrill, M. D. (1997). Instructional transaction theory: An instructional design model based on knowledge objects. In R. Tennyson, F. Schott, N. Seel, & S. Dijkstra (Eds.), Instructional design: International perspectives (Vol. 1: Theory, research and models, pp. 381-394). Mahwah, New Jersey: Lawrence Erlbaum Associates.

Molenda, M. (1997). Historical and philosophical foundations of instructional design: A north American view. In R. Tennyson, F. Schott, N. Seel, & S. Dijkstra (Eds.), Instructional design: International perspectives (Vol. 1: Theory, research and models, pp. 41-53). Mahwah, New Jersey: Lawrence Erlbaum Associates.

Moore, M. G. (1989). Editorial: Three types of interaction. *American Journal of Distance Education*, *3*(2), 1–7. doi:10.1080/08923648909526659

Nielsen, J. (1993). *Usability engineering*. London: Academic Press.

Obilade, T. T. (2015). Affordances then and now: Implications for designing instruction. *Distance Learning*, *12*(3), 9–16.

Obilade, T. T. (2016). *Make Me See it: Pedagogical Strategies of Visual Literacy*. Oklahoma: Tate Publishing.

Ortiz, M., Ayala, G., & Osorio, M. (2003). Formalizing the learner model for CSCL environments. In E. Chávez, J. Favela, M. Mejía, & A. Oliart (Eds.), *Proceedings of theFourth Mexican International Conference on Computer Science* (pp. 151-158). doi:10.1109/ENC.2003.1232889

Rautaray, S., Kumar, A., & Agrawal, A. S. (2012). Perception and machine intelligence human computer interaction with hand gestures in virtual environment. *Perception and machine Intelligence, LNCS* (Vol. *7143*, pp. 106–113). doi:10.1007/978-3-642-27387-2_14

Ritchie, D. C., & Hoffman, B. (1997). Incorporating instructional design principles with the world wide web. In B. Khan (Ed.), *Web-based instruction* (pp. 135–158). Englewood Cliffs, NJ: Educational Technology Publications.

Rodriguez, C. O. (2012). MOOCs and the AI-Stanford like Courses: Two successful and distinct course formats for massive open online courses. *European Journal of Open, Distance, and E-Learning*.

Shneiderman, B. (1998). *Designing the interface: Strategies for effective human-computer interaction*. Reading, MA: Addison-Wesley.

Shneiderman, B., & Plaisant, C. (2010). *Designing the interface: Strategies for effective human-computer interaction*. Reading, MA: Addison-Wesley.

Stellmach, S., & Dachselt, R. (2012). Designing gaze-based user interfaces for steering in virtual environments. *Paper Presented at the Proceedings of the Symposium on Eye Tracking Research and Applications*, Santa Barbara, California. Retrieved from http://luxator.cs.uni-magdeburg.de/uise/Forschung/Publikationen/2012-ETRA-GazeNavGUIs.pdf

Tennyson, R. D., & Elmore, R. L. (1997). Learning theory foundations for instructional design. In R. Tennyson, F. Schott, N. Seel, & S. Dijkstra (Eds.), Instructional design: international perspectives (Vol. 1: Theory, research and models, pp. 55-78). Mahwah, New Jersey: Lawrence Erlbaum Associates.

Tennyson, R. D., & Schott, F. (1997). Instructional design theory, research, and models. In R. Tennyson, F. Schott, N. Seel, & S. Dijkstra (Eds.), Instructional design: International perspectives (Vol. 1: Theory, research and models, pp. 1-16). Mahwah, New Jersey: Lawrence Erlbaum Associates.

Vichido, C., Estrad, M., & Sanchez, A. (2003). A constructivist educational tool: Software architecture for web-based video games. In E. Chávez, J. Favela, M. Mejía, & A. Oliart (Eds.), *Proceedings of the Fourth Mexican International Conference on Computer Science* (pp. 144-150). doi:10.1109/ENC.2003.1232888

Vrasidas, C. (2011). Human-Computer interaction and usability of online learning environments. In G. Anglin (Ed.), *Instructional technology: past, present, and future* (pp. 227–235). Santa Barbara, CA: Libraries Unlimited.

Ware, C. (2003). Design as applied perception. In J. Carroll (Ed.), *HCI model, theories and frameworks: Towards a multidisciplinary science* (pp. 11–26). San Francisco, CA: Morgan Kaufmann. doi:10.1016/B978-155860808-5/50002-2

Wroblewski, L. (2011). Mobile first. New York, NY: A Book Apart.

Xiong, Y., Li, H., Kornhaber, M. L., Suen, H. K., Pursel, B., & Goins, D. D. (2015). Examining the relations among student motivation, engagement, and retention in a MOOC: A structural equation modeling approach. *Global Education Review*, 2(3), 23–33.

Chapter 14
HCI and E-Learning:
Developing a Framework for Evaluating E-Learning

Titilola T. Obilade
Virginia Polytechnic Institute and State University, USA

ABSTRACT

This chapter developed a framework for evaluating e-learning for use in Human Computer Interaction (HCI). A systems approach was used in the study; input, processes and output. It discussed the different assumptions about how people learn; behaviorism, cognitivism and constructivism. Further, it examined the common threads in the definitions of e-learning and the literature on evaluation of e-learning models. Nine categories of evaluation of e-learning were identified but five were reviewed because the remaining four overlapped. Two separate evaluations were reviewed under each category, making a total of ten reviews. The reviews showed that the evaluations were not conducted in the same way even within the same category making comparisons difficult. The framework was developed from the highlights in the review. The developed framework can be used to evaluate different e-learning modules along common lines making it easy to compare evaluations. It is hoped that over the next few years, a consistency in evaluations of e-learning would be achieved for use in HCI.

INTRODUCTION

This chapter would develop a framework for evaluating e-learning for use in Human Computer Interaction (HCI). Before an evaluation can be done, there must be an input, some processes and an output. How do we know that the output is actually the desired outcome? How do we know if the process we are using is actually the correct process? If the process is correct, can the input be wrong?

This chapter will attempt to answer some of these questions by developing a framework for evaluating e-learning. However, before examining different models of e-learning, the inputs, processes and the outputs in Human Computer Interaction will be examined (see Figure 1). The HCI process takes place in a system.

DOI: 10.4018/978-1-5225-0435-1.ch014

Figure 1. Input, process and output in a system

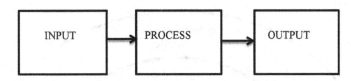

A system is a set of objects together with relationships between the objects and between their attributes. (Hall and Fagan, 1956)

---we propose that a system be taken as a nested network, with the underlying structure of a nested graph. (Harary and Batell, 1981)

Miller (1956) described a system as an entity that has common properties, constraints and the parts within the system are dependent on parts within and outside the system. The common thread in the three definitions is the inter and intra connections of all the parts.

In systems theory, the system consists of the inputs, the processes, the outputs and the feedback (Richey, 1986). The interactions in the system could be the processes, the constraints, the instructions and the feedback (Miller, 1965; Richey; 1986). The feedback can be negative or positive. The negative feedback does not connote a bad process. The negative feedback is what keeps the system the same. As illustrated in Figure 2, the information from A goes back into A through channel B so that the system remains the same. This is a negative feedback. When the inputs from A keep increasing in steady amounts, this is a positive feedback. "Positive feedback alters variables and destroys their steady state" (Miller, 1965 p. 35).

A system can also be affected by the supra system. The supra system has control over the system. The environment can be the immediate environment or the total environment (Miller, 1965). The immediate environment includes the system without the supra system. The total environment includes the immediate environment and the supra system. An example of a system is a university. The university makes use of an e-learning platform. Inside the system, there are subsystems. Each subsystem carries out similar functions. In each system, there is an echelon of processes that are arranged in hierarchy.

Figure 2. Illustration of a feedback system

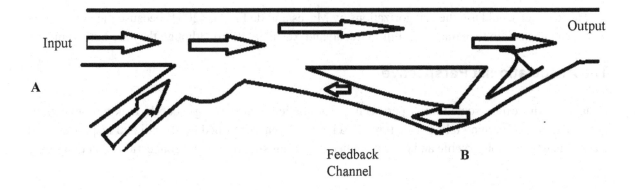

Figure 3. Illustration of systems in e-learning

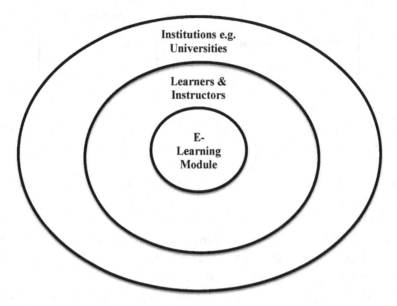

Systems contain levels of different functions. The e-learning model/module is affected by learners' and instructors' interactions. Similarly, the policies of the institutions would affect how the learners and instructors interact with the system.

The goals or learning outcomes in human computer interaction depend on the learning theory or the objectives. The objectives would be the input. In using a general systems theory to evaluate e-learning, the framework must align with the inputs, processes and outputs.

Assumptions about How People Learn

Collins, Greeno and Resnick (1996) grouped these assumptions into three groups; empiricist, rationalist and pragmatist-sociohistoric. Mayes and de Freitas (2004) grouped these assumptions into:

1. Associationist/ empiricist or learning as activity
2. Cognitive perspective or learning as achieving understanding and
3. Situative perspective or learning as social practice (constructivism).

This chapter would use the categorizations by Mayes and de Freitas (2004) because theirs is a more recent categorization than that of Collins, Greeno and Resnick (1996) although they are both similar.

The Associationist Perspective

Behaviorists have the associationists' perspective. They believe that learning occurs by making connections in the activities. Learning takes place through a behavior that is learned by stimuli and responses. The learned behavior is observable and is now applied to similar situations. The connections that determine the behavior can be strengthened or weakened. The associationist perspective is used in programmed instruction.

The Cognitivist /Rationalist Perspective

Collins, Greeno and Resnick (1986) identified three traditions to be the cognitive vies; Gestalt psychology, constructivism and symbolic information processing. The Gestalt psychology stresses on the insight in learning and perception. Some researchers classify the symbolic information processing as associationist because symbolic information processing operates through networks. The two separate views of seeing the symbolic information processing as behaviorist on one hand and as cognitive on another hand shows that these classifications are not absolute. The boundaries are fluid.

Further, learning through the symbolic processing system is based on the acquisition of schemas. The developments of schemas ultimately lead to automacity. Metacognitive models, mental models, problem solving problems and general competencies for thinking come under symbolic information processing (Mayes & de Freitas, 2004).

The Situative Perspective

Learning is acquired through interaction with members of a community of learners. The members of the community become active participants in the community and they learn through their interaction in the community of practice. The situative perspective pays attention to procedures and completion of tasks. It views acquisition of knowledge through different levels of participation in the community of practice. As the learner moves from one level of practice to a higher level, the learner's responsibility increases.

Application of the Systems Theory to Human Computer Interaction

Using the systems theory, a comprehensive analysis can be done to determine if the theory or objectives applied to e-learning matches the pedagogy. Instructional tutoring systems and e- training models can be evaluated on a systems approach. For this chapter, e-learning model and e-learning module are used interchangeably and refer to an e-learning platform like a learning management system or an e-learning course that can be a class lesson or a training course.

Summary of Associationist, Cognitivist and Situative Perspective

The associationist perspective is akin to the behaviorist approach that observes the activities of the outcomes for the learners. The cognitivist perspective analyses the processes and relies on schema formation. The cognitivist and associationist perspective can take place with one learner or a group of learners. The situative perspective cannot take place with one learner. The learner must be in a community of learners. Learning becomes a social interaction in the situative perspective. As some members of the community of practice leave at graduation, a new set of learners join. They move along different trajectories (Driscoll, 2000). A comprehensive evaluation of e-learning models or modules can be conducted by applying the systems theory.

Evaluation of E-Learning Models

An evaluation of e-learning models in a standard, measurable way will determine if the consumers of e-learning are getting the desired results. There are many models of e-learning and each one claims to be better than the previous ones. It is imperative that there should be a consistent, uniform method of evaluating all the existing models of e-learning. In the literature, there is so much diversity in the descriptors of e-learning that using descriptors like online-learning, distance education, distance-learning, e-learning, mobile-learning, web based learning on search databases would bring up millions of results. The diversity of results cuts across all disciplines.

METHOD OF SELECTING RESEARCH ARTICLES

The databases of research publications in PsycINFO, ERIC, Google Scholar, Summons and EBSCO Host were surveyed for peer-reviewed articles on evaluation of e-learning models. The reference lists of relevant articles were also surveyed to broaden the search base for articles relevant to the search. The search words used were e-learning, evaluation, model of e-learning, distant learning, online learning, web- based learning and distance education. There was no custom range for the years in which the articles were selected. Only articles that were relevant to the search were selected.

Grouping the different types of evaluation methods used in evaluating e-learning into categories would help in developing a framework for evaluating e-learning models or modules. Attwell (2006) categorized the evaluation of e-learning into nine groups. These were case studies of specific e-training programs, comparison with traditional learning, tools and instruments for evaluating e-learning, meta-analysis of data on the effectiveness of e-learning, benchmarking models, return on investment reports, product evaluation, performance evaluation and handbooks for the evaluation of e-learning.

For brevity, this chapter used five categories; benchmarking models, return on investment reports, product evaluation, performance evaluation and handbooks for the evaluation of e-learning as some of the categories used by Attwell (2006) overlapped. In addition, under each category two evaluations for e-learning were examined for use of theory.

If theory was not used, the criterion that was used was explored. Further, the variations and similarities in the evaluations for each category were examined. The objectives in the evaluations for e-learning were also examined. The highlights from each category were extracted. At the end of the chapter, a framework was developed using the highlights from each category. The developed framework can be used to evaluate any e-learning module.

E-Learning

Although there are many definitions of e-learning, a common thread in the plethora of definitions is the use of technology to learn. Some authors have tried to separate e-learning from distance education by affirming that e-learning is strictly through the internet and distance education can be through hard copies (Ruhe & Zumbo, 2009).

E-learning attracts a lot of research and development and funding (Attwell, 2006). Researchers have focused on different parts of e-learning. Some evaluated only the inputs. Others focused on processes and some evaluated the learning outcomes (Attwell, 2006; García, & Jorge 2006; Kathawala & Wilgen,

2004; Masoumi & Lindstrom, 2012; Mayes & de Freitas, 2004). According to Ibis Capital (2013), Europe has over 3000 plus e-learning companies. The e-learning market is the fastest growing market in education and made a revenue of 91 billion dollars in 2012. Internet use has tremendously expanded to 2.4 billion users from the year 2000. Forty percent of the global 500 Fortune companies use e-learning to train their employees. Considering the statistics on the trends on the use of the internet and e-learning, it is obvious that there is no shortage of e-learning.

Evaluation

Evaluation is a systematic investigation to determine the merit and worth of a set of activities (Ruhe & Zumbo, 2009). The etymology of the word evaluation is from the French word "évaluer to find the value of, from é-out (see ex-) + valuer (see value)" Online Etymology Dictionary (n.d). Evaluation means to find the value out of something. It is the means by which evidence is gathered and interpreted to determine how well the instructional product or system performs (Gagne, Briggs & Wager, 1992).

Evaluation became important in the 1920's when the government wanted to measure the cost effectiveness of its health and educational programs (Owston, 2008). Evaluation started as far back as the Chinese and Egyptian empires when their ministers were evaluated Scriven (1991). When evaluation is conducted in education on a variety of events and groups of students, teachers and administrators, it is an educational evaluation (Gagne, Briggs & Wager, 1992).

Scriven (1974) proposed the goal free evaluation in which the evaluator is not restricted to the stated objectives but can evaluate any of the outcomes. According to Scriven (1974) an educational program or product can be evaluated as follows; need, market, performance in field trials, consumer performance, performance comparison, performance long term, performance side effects, performance process, performance causation, performance statistical significance, performance educational significance, costs and cost effectiveness and extended support.

Stufflebeam's (1974) educational evaluation methods were goal based. His model was based on context, input, process and product, the CIPP model. The context assesses the needs. The input would assess the strategies put in place in the educational program for cost-effectiveness. The processes are the documentations and program activities. The product would be the impact of the educational program which could be the intended and unintended outcomes (Owston, 2008; Ruhe & Zumbo, 2009). The evaluation methods proposed by Scrivens (1974) and Stufflebeam (1974) are still in use today but cannot address all the needs of e-learning.

Another commonly used model is the Kirkpatrick model which was developed in 1959 (Kirkpatrick, 2006a). Some researchers feel that these models are antiquated and cannot be used for the evaluation of e-learning (Galloway, 2005; Hamtini, 2008; Peak & Berge, 2006) while some feel it can still be used (Horton, 2006).

Gaps and Highlights in the Literature

The highlights in the literature show that e-learning has come to stay. The gaps reveal that literature that claim to conduct evaluation of e-learning, evaluate the technology attached to the e-learning and not the pedagogy. A lot of research has focused on software used for e-learning or on the learning platforms. While they are important, the focus should not shift entirely to the technologies and ignore the pedagogy. Some evaluations focus on the performance scores of students that use the software and not on the pedagogy that was used in the e-learning software (Davies & Graff, 2005; Hannafin & Foshay, 2008).

Further, when the company manufacturing or marketing the software sponsors the research the results seem to extol the software or the company (Young, 2002). Another gap is that there are several models of evaluation and they do not always measure the same things. In the same evaluation model, methodologies are not consistent. Some evaluations were done without any stated theory. Also, it appears that the discipline of the evaluators imparts the evaluation. Instructional designers tend to state the theory when they evaluate e-learning.

However, evaluation done by some other disciplines just delve into the software and the theory is missing. Further, some definitions like E-learning Platforms, Learning Systems and Learning Management Systems used in the papers were not consistent (Attwell, 2006; Ćukušić, Alfirević, Granić & Garača, 2010; Garcia & Jorge, 2006) but had similar meanings.

Categorizations of Evaluations used for E-Learning

There are many categories of evaluation models (Kifer, 1995; Ruhe & Zumbo, 2009). However, there is scant literature on the categorization of evaluations used for e-learning. The evaluation of e-learning project (Attwell, 2006) categorized the evaluation of e-learning into nine. Some of the nine categories used by Attwell (2006) overlap and this chapter used only five categories for brevity. The five categories examined in this chapter are the benchmarking model, the return on investment report, product evaluation, performance evaluation and the hand book of evaluation.

OUTLINES FOR REMAINING CHAPTER

1. Benchmarking model
2. Return on Investment (ROI)
3. Product evaluation
4. Performance evaluation
5. Handbook for evaluation of e-learning
6. Summary table from chapter findings
7. Overall summary of the categories of evaluation of e-learning
8. Steps taken in this chapter to develop a framework
9. Framework for evaluating e-learning model
10. Conclusion

BENCHMARKING MODELS

"The process of comparing one's business processes and performance metrics to industry bests and/or best practices from other industries. Dimensions typically measured are quality, time, and cost. Improvements from learning mean doing things better, faster, and cheaper" (Scepanovic, Devedžić & Kraljevski, 2011). Benchmarking became a popular evaluation tool of e-learning in 2005 (Scepanovic, Devedžić & Kraljevski, 2011).

There are usually a set of criteria against which e-learning is evaluated. Benchmarking models are not consistent in their choice of criteria and lack theoretical foundations. Even within the same country the criteria for the benchmarking models are not the same and so it is difficult to compare results. Some of the benchmarking models were started as projects and lacked continuity because the projects were no longer funded (Scepanovic, Devedžić & Kraljevski, 2011). When most of these models were evaluated, persons vested in the program evaluated them and the results usually extolled the values of the model (Legon & Runyon 2007; Shattuck, 2007).

In this chapter, Quality Matters (Quality Matters, 2013) and the E-learning Maturity Model (Marshall, 2005a) were selected as two examples of benchmarking models because both models were used in tertiary institutions in two separate continents. Quality Matters was developed in the United States and it has been used in the United States. The E-learning Maturity Model was developed in New Zealand and has been used in New Zealand (Marshall, 2005a, 2005b).

Quality Matters is a popular benchmarking model tool in the United States and is used by most universities and technical colleges, (Shattuck, 2007). The Quality Matters benchmark tool includes verbs in the criteria that make the objectives ambiguous. Some objectives like "encourage student cooperation", "let students know what to expect", "encourage faculty-student contact" and "interaction" are ambiguous and give room to multiple interpretations. The Quality Matters benchmark tool focuses on the online course.

The emphasis is on the course subject being taught. As part of the benchmark, there must be an expert in the subject being taught online. It does not emphasize the pedagogy. It does not identify technological variables, or learner variables that would affect the online course. It does not emphasize the environmental variables. The model was developed based on criteria from eleven national standards across the country. Quality Matters is not based on a theoretical model. Quality Matters model proponents admit that the tool is based on rubrics, which can change when literature reviews reflect new evidence.

The E-learning Maturity Model Evaluation was developed by Marshall and Mitchell (Marshall, 2005a) and has been used to assess the e-learning programs in the tertiary institutions in New Zealand. The model only looks at the process in training of instructors that teach online and the readiness of institutions to maintain the e-learning programs. The developers admit that the model is not interested in pedagogy and it is not interested in evaluating the technology (Marshall & Mitchell, 2002). Its emphasis was to determine whether the various tertiary institutions were able to provide high quality e-learning that was sustainable. It emphasizes the process of the design of the e-learning and determines if it meets the needs of students, instructors and staff of the institutions. Marshall and Mitchell (2002) developed the e-learning maturity model from the Seven Principles of Chickering and Gamson and the benchmarks developed by the Institute of Higher Education (Marshall, 2005a). They also adapted the capability maturity model (Marshall & Mitchell, 2002).

Table 1. Highlights from benchmarking model

• Uses selected criteria
• Can be based on rubrics
• Objectives may not be stated clearly
• Not based on any theory
• Learning outcomes not stated clearly
• Usually measures quality, time, and cost
• Measures processes

Summary on Benchmarking Models

A review of benchmarking models has shown that studies done using the benchmarking model did not examine the same criteria. The two benchmarking models examined did not include pedagogy. The e-learning maturity model focuses on the training of the online instructors and on the maturity of the institutions to maintain e-learning. They were more concerned about the ability of the institution to offer e-learning programs.

The criteria used by Quality Matters included examination of the course content by a committee that included an expert in the field and if the committee did not approve, the course content was taken back and reviewed a second time. It did not include clear objectives and it did not include clear learning outcomes. In addition, the developers admit that the criteria can change when they see a need to change that may arise from a literature review. Although both models are not based on any theory, many schools of higher learning appear to have been using the models successfully. Further, the seven principles that were used in the development of the e-learning maturity model made use of theory.

RETURN ON INVESTMENT REPORT (ROI)

Return on Investment (ROI), strictly speaking, is an accounting-based method of comparing the costs and benefits of a product, program or service by converting all tangible costs and benefits to financial measures. It can be used, however, to include intangible costs and benefits, particularly as the concept is applied to public expenditures for education and training (Barker, 2005, p. 3).

Most business companies use ROI reports to check if the money spent on the e-training programs of their employees is profitable. Measuring ROI can be difficult because there are soft and hard costs involved (Gale, 2002). The hard costs are the documentation of the e-learning. If the training could have taken the employees a day out of work if they did a face-to-face training as opposed to an e-learning training that they would complete in a few hours, the company would find it cost effective to do the e-training (Gale, 2002). In ROI analysis, attempts must be made to convert all the documentation into monetary values.

Return on investment models vary depending on who is carrying out the research. The objective of a vendor-based model is different from the objective of an academic based model because they both have different goals. The vendor that would use the vendor-based model wants to increase sales and the academician would use the model for publication. There are different formulae for calculating ROI depending on the type of program

For one-time programs
Program Benefits / Costs X 100 = ROI (expressed as a percentage)
For prepared programs
Total cost of design, development, duplication, delivery and support
(divided by) the number of students over the life of the course
For a range of results
ROI = (value of benefits - cost of training) / cost of training. (Barker, 2005, p. 13)

In conducting an ROI on e-learning, many models can be used including the Kirkpatrick model. This may be because the model was developed as far back as 1959 (Kirkpatrick, 2006a) and major companies have been training their employees using this model even before e-learning began. Donald Kirkpatrick's model was developed from his work on his dissertation.

The following description of the Kirkpatrick model is from Kirkpatrick's book on evaluating training programs. The Kirkpatrick model is a four level approach to evaluation of training programs. It has been used in technical and managerial sectors (Kirkpatrick, 2006 b).

The first level or level one is also called reaction. This is usually a survey of the participants of the training program to the training. Questions are asked about the content, the instruction and the overall. A question on content could be: The skills taught in this class are relevant to my personal development with options varying from disagree strongly to agree strongly. Kirkpatrick also calls the first level a customer satisfaction survey (Kirkpatrick, 2006b). He points out that even though the trainees are not paying for the training, they are nonetheless customers and their satisfaction or dissatisfaction can make or break the training program.

The second level is learning. According to Kirkpatrick, learning has occurred if there has been a change in attitude, if there has been an increase in knowledge or if there has been an improvement of skills.

The third level is behavior. In Kirkpatrick's model, behavior is the change that occurs as a result of attending the training program. Kirkpatrick's identifies four conditions that must be present for a desired behavior; 1.) The person must have a desire to change 2.) The person must know what to do and how to do it. 3.) The person must work in the right climate and 4.) The person must be rewarded for changing.

Kirkpatrick identifies five types of climate that may enable or disable the behavior that was achieved at the training. In a preventing climate, the trainee is prevented from performing the new behavior learnt at the training. In a discouraging climate, the trainee is discouraged from performing the new behavior that was learnt at the training. In a neutral climate, the training is not prevented or discouraged from performing the new behavior. The reception of the boss to the new skills is one of indifference but may slide into a discouraging climate or even a preventing climate if the behavior negatively interferes with the job.

An encouraging climate encourages the trainee's new behavior and a requiring climate requires the trainee to inform the supervisor of the new skills and in some instances, a contract may be signed between the trainee and the boss for the boss to see that the new behavior learnt are transferred to the job.

The fourth level is also called the results. This is the outcome of the training. It could be measurable in monetary values and it may not be measured in monetary values. A training to effect a change in attitude to minorities may be measured in non-monetary values as increased motivation.

Two case studies were selected as examples for ROI. Young's (2002) article was selected even though it was as far back as 2002 because it pointed out biases in reporting and e-learning was just beginning to take off in 2002. In this chapter, Young's article was compared with Nathan's (2009). Young (2002) conducted an ROI on top-level management executives on their attitudes to e-training and on the justification of e-learning to the employees. In 2000, Young's (2002) company had also conducted a similar study on top level managers but the literature did not indicate if it was the same set of participants. Computer aided telephone interviewing tool was used.

Young's (2002) article did not discuss the use of theory but mentioned the name of the company as the first to conduct such a study in that area. The interviews were all conducted over the telephone. Only the top management personnel were interviewed. The learners or trainees were not interviewed. The results were based on perception and attitudinal questions to determine if e-learning had an impact on their organization and if they would continue to use e-learning. There were no questions on learner variables, technology variables or pedagogy variables. There was no use of theory. Young (2002) presented the results using bar charts and it was easy to see the responses of the respondents.

Although the title of Young's (2002) article was, "Is e-learning making ROI?" the study was based on perceptions and attitudes of top-level managers to e-learning and not entirely on ROI. Also, Young (2002) was the vice president of the software company that was instituting e-learning programs in the companies tested thereby creating a source of bias in reporting.

The second case study is an ROI on an online course (Nathan, 2009). In this study, Nathan (2009) discussed the theory he was going to use. A modified Kirkpatrick model was used. The modified Kirkpatrick model had additional levels instead of the four levels that the Kirkpatrick model has. The fourth and fifth levels were combined to determine the business impact of the online lesson. The design objectives were matched to every level of the model. The data collected from the evaluation of levels one and levels two were converted to monetary values. The benefits were calculated in dollar amounts and tables were used to illustrate the conversion. Nathan (2009) described the processes.

Summary on ROI

Most training organizations usually evaluate using ROI. Return on investments is an evaluation tool that usually surmises the results in monetary value. Mathematical calculation exists for calculating ROI. However, it does not have to be in monetary value alone. It can be examined in terms of the attitudinal views as was done by Young (Young, 2002). He looked at the ROI from the attitudinal responses of the top management personnel. Young's (2002) reporting could be seen as biased because he was the vice president of the company that was supplying the software for e-learning.

Kirkpatrick's model is still being used by organizations to evaluate e-learning even though the model existed before e-training began. Nathan's (2009) ROI study was based on the Kirkpatrick model and he matched the theory to the objectives of his evaluation. It was not all aspects of his evaluation that was converted to monetary values but he was able to match most of the aspects of evaluation to monetary value.

PRODUCT EVALUATION

Patton (1997) p. 23 suggests that before an evaluation must be conducted, evaluation must be defined because it is on the functionality of that definition that the evaluator would be conducting the evaluation. In product evaluation the evaluator should be able to answer the question, "what are the cost, benefits, and market for a specific product?" (Patton, 1997) p. 194

The first product evaluation that would be discussed is the evaluation of nine open source-learning platforms that were evaluated to determine the most adaptable learning platform to the user (Graf &

Table 2. Highlights from ROI

- Accounting based method of comparing cost and benefits
- Theory used
- Can also be used to compare intangible cost
- Attempts to convert documentation into monetary value
- Goals of ROI vary depending on the purpose of the evaluator
- Can measure attitudinal change
- Can measure the input, process or output

List, 2005). The second product that would be examined would be the evaluation of computer-based instruction (CBI) software on a high school's high stake's test (Hannafin & Foshay, 2008).

Graf and List (2005) used a qualitative weight and sum approach (QWS) to evaluate the nine open learning platforms. Graf and List (2005) explained how the QWS approach was used to evaluate software. The QWS uses weights that are measured according to a range of criteria from not valuable to essential. In between, the values are marginally valuable, valuable, very valuable, extremely valuable and essential is the highest value.

Each of these values is represented by a symbol. The software product is now weighted according to the symbols. The software product that has the highest number of weights would be the most adaptable. If Moodle has nine values for extremely valuable while the other platforms have three values for valuable, then Moodle would be judged the most adaptable. Graf and List (2005) initially started with 36 open source-learning platforms and eventually streamlined to nine open source-learning platforms.

They tested the nine learning platforms using a questionnaire and the questions covered eight categories, which were divided into sub categories. These categories covered areas of usability, adaptability, communication tools, learning objects, management of user data, administration, course management and technical aspects.

After the platforms were ranked according to the highest number of weights, Moodle scored the highest and Sakai scored the lowest. The research was funded by the Austrian Ministry of Education and not by any of the open source-learning platforms so the results would not have been influenced by any of the software companies.

Graf and List (2005) did not define terms like open source-learning and they did not define-learning platforms. They defined adaptability and explained the criteria used to rank the-learning platforms. However, Graf and List (2005) did not describe the users that filled the questionnaires in order to rate them. They also used variables in the sub categories but these variables were not identified.

Hannafin and Foshay (2008) compared the performance scores from using a CBI product that helped high school students to master competency in Mathematics to the performance scores obtained from using a traditional method of teaching Mathematics. The results showed that the students that used the CBI product outperformed the students that studied using traditional methods. The evaluation was conducted in a high school where the 10th grade students had failed the competency exam for Mathematics.

The CBI product used was Plato Learning Systems. In addition to using Plato, the school also employed other methods to help the failing students including one on one tutoring, community volunteers and parental assistance. The evaluation focused only on the effectiveness of the Plato Learning System. The evaluation did not account for the contribution of the one on one help or on the impact of the help by volunteers and parents to the students' success. Students that failed or marginally passed the 8th grade Massachusetts Comprehensive Assessment System (MCAS) were enrolled in the Plato Learning System in preparation for their 10th grade MCAS. The MCAS was taken in 8th and 10th grades.

The study evaluated the scores of students who had gone through the Plato Learning System for Mathematics in 10th grade and compared it with their scores when they were in 8th grade and had only traditional methods of learning Mathematics. The variables tested were the data from the Plato Learning Systems and the MCAS scores. Hannafin and Foshay (2008) did correlation analysis on the MCAS scores of the students while they were in 8th grade and when they were in the 10th grade and had taken the Plato Learning System modules for Mathematics. The correlations showed that the MCAS scores improved after taking the Plato Learning System.

In addition, the Mathematics instructor in charge of the Plato Learning System in the school was interviewed and the interview was reported qualitatively. Hannafin and Foshay (2008) also pointed the limitations in their studies that the students were not only helped by the CBI program but that they were helped by volunteers, students helping fellow students and the instructor helping students. Further, the teachers had to take staff development courses. In the study, Hannafin and Foshay (2008) explained that the Plato Learning System was based on cognitive theories of learning where the student masters a module before moving on to the next module.

Summary on Product Evaluation

While both articles examined did a product evaluation, they evaluated different aspect of the product. Graf and List (2005) used a software product to evaluate nine open source learning systems. The criteria chosen were subjective. Values used in the criteria were marginally, valuable, valuable, very valuable, extremely valuable and essential. A qualitative weight and sum approach was the software being used as an evaluation tool. Graf and List (2005) did not identify the variables that were used. They pointed out that there was no bias in their reporting because none of the open source learning systems sponsored the evaluations.

Hannafin and Foshay (2008) looked at only the output from the product, i.e the performance scores. Admittedly, they did not look at other variables that could have contributed to the improved performance of the students. The teachers took staff development courses. The students had help from volunteers, fellow students and other support network before their grades improved but these variables were not factored into the evaluation.

PERFORMANCE EVALUATION

Scriven (1991) differentiated between performance evaluation and product evaluation because performance evaluation is usually absorbed under product evaluation. Performance evaluation is the measurement of a particular achievement through its output or through its processes (Scriven, 1991). Patton (1997) also agreed that before an evaluation begins, the evaluator must define evaluation because it would be this definition that would drive the approach of the evaluation.

Davies and Graff (2005) evaluated the performances of undergraduate students who participated in on line discussions and compared it with the performances of undergraduate students who participated less frequently in online discussions by following the students' grades for up to a year. The second study

Table 3. Highlights from product evaluation

• Evaluation must be defined before evaluating the product
• Can be used to evaluate software used in learning
• Criteria can be developed to rank the product being evaluated
• Processes of the product that include usability and adaptability can be evaluated
• Output of the product like scores can be evaluated
• Can make use of theories of learning
• Interactions included use of volunteers

that would be examined was by Ćukušić et al. (2010). This was an empirical study that looked at the performances of the e-learning process across 14 schools in Europe.

Davies and Graff (2005) did not give a theory of their research. Although their results showed that the students who participated more in online discussions performed better than students who participated less frequently, they concluded that the evaluations did not prove that the online discussions improved the grade performances of the students because it was not statistically significant. Davies and Graff (2005) asserted that the quality of the on line interaction was not measured but it was the number of times the students accessed Blackboard that was counted. However, they presented both sides of the literature that supported on line-learning discussions and improved student performance and online-learning discussions without a change in grade performances of students. They followed part time and full time students for a year and followed their grade results.

The students were all enrolled in the same school and used the Blackboard. The Blackboard had four sections; communication, main content, group areas and student. The students were able to communicate through the Blackboard using the group areas and the student areas. Davies and Graff (2005) combined the number of times that students communicated through the group area and through the students' areas and plotted these variables against their grade performances.

Their analysis showed that the students who scored the highest grades were the ones who interacted most on the Blackboard. The students who scored the lowest grades were the ones who interacted least on the Blackboard. Their results were not statistically significant. It is only after reading the introduction and the discussion section that their hypothesis becomes clear. They also stated their variables.

The purpose of the study by Ćukušić et al. (2010) was to evaluate the e-learning platform process from planning, implementing to learning outcomes using the Unified E-Learning Environment for School Project (UNITE) as a model. Further, the study was to determine if there were any relationships between the implementation of the model and the subject of learning.

According to Ćukušić et al. (2010), previous studies looked at a part of the e-learning model. They declared that previous studies had looked at processes, implementation, learning outcomes and inputs as separate entities but their own study was the first to look at the entire e-learning process from planning to learning outcomes and to establish a link between the planning and the-learning outcomes.

Ćukušić et al. (2010) described many variables like the educational context of the learners, identification of learners' needs, learners' technological skills and learning styles. The educational context of the learners was where the e-learning would take place. Most of the literature on evaluation of e-learning models examined for this chapter did not describe the variables that were important to the learners.

Ćukušić et al. (2010) mentioned models that would be familiar to European researchers and may not be familiar to American researchers. They used terms that were probably commonly used in the European context. They used terms like e-learning scenario to describe the planning stage of the e-learning platform. They also used the word assessment to mean evaluation. They discussed the theory of the input, process and outcomes in e-learning.

Ćukušić et al. (2010) stated their research hypotheses. They also evaluated the e-learning model using two questionnaires that were sent out to 15 teachers across 14 schools in the European block. There were 56 close-ended questions that were sent by email. The questions were divided into sections that covered planning, controlling, implementing and evaluation. Controlling the e-learning process included analyzing the data and identifying methods of evaluation. Ćukušić et al. (2010) concluded that there was a positive relationship between the systematic planning of the different aspects of the e-learning process and the e-learning performance.

Table 4. Highlights from performance evaluation

- Outputs like achievement scores are measured
- Inputs like attendance can be measured
- Inputs like learning style can affect performance
- Processes like the interactions learners make with the e-learning platform can be measured

Summary on Performance Evaluation

Davies and Graff (2005) conducted their evaluation by comparing the performances of students who engaged frequently in online discussion with those that engaged less frequently in online discussions. They only looked at the performance scores of the students. Although, students who spent the longest time in online discussions scored higher than those who spent the least amount of time in online discussions, their results were not statistically significant. They admitted that their study did not examine the quality of the online discussions.

Ćukušić et al. (2010) evaluated the entire e-learning platform from planning, to implementation to outcomes and concluded that the e-learning platforms gave a better outcome when it was planned. However, they concluded that there was no link between the planning of the different aspects of the e-learning process and the subject content. They identified many variables in their evaluation. They identified learners' needs, learners' technological needs and learners' learning systems. They did not follow their respondents for a year like Davies and Graff (2005).

HANDBOOKS FOR THE EVALUATION OF E-LEARNING

The handbooks that would be mentioned in this chapter are the evaluation cookbook (Harvey, 1998) and the Kellogg evaluation handbook (Kellogg, 2010). These two books were written with the inputs of several technocrats in evaluation. The Kellogg evaluation handbook was specifically written for the evaluation of Kellogg programs.

The evaluation cookbook was developed by the Learning Technology Dissemination Initiative (Harvey, 1998). It has been used as a reference material by many authors in Europe (Attwell, 2006; Michaelson, Helliar, Power & Sinclair, 2001). It gives practical guidelines on evaluation.

The Kellogg's evaluation handbook is used to evaluate programs sponsored by the Organization ("Evaluating The Kellogg Project," n.d.; Kellogg, 2004). In one of their programs, the W.K. Kellogg Foundation provided Internet access, email account, web page, networking and training to neighborhoods around Trinity College. Computer classes and use of on-site computers were also provided (Sirbirsky, 2002).

The project participants were surveyed as part of the evaluation of the effectiveness of the technology in improving communication. One hundred and seventeen participants were contacted but only 71 responded. The participants included administrators, a church treasurer, volunteers and the director of a youth organization. The evaluation report did not indicate how long the organization had provided the technology service but from the questionnaire, it could be inferred that the service had been provided within one year (Sirbirsky, 2002).

The participants were contacted by email. The participants were asked to respond to open-ended questions on whether or not the provision of the technology had met the needs of their organization. Close-ended questions on their knowledge and attitude to the technology provided were also asked. The results showed that the Kellogg's sponsored program had met the participants' expectations and also indicated that it needed improvement in the area of technical assistance (Sirbirsky, 2002).

Another evaluation conducted on a program sponsored by Kellogg's was the Community Learning Initiative courses (Sirbirsky, 2001). The Community Learning Initiative courses were incorporated into student classes and primarily focused on engaging students in service learning and research. A total of 305 students and 13 faculties were evaluated. The faculties were those that incorporated Community Learning Initiative courses into their own courses. The Community Learning Initiative courses also included fieldwork. The courses were offered in spring 1999 and in fall 2000. Sixteen Community Learning Initiative courses were offered in spring 1999 and in fall 2000. The evaluation report (Sirbirsky, 2001) did not state if any of the courses were online and if the questionnaires were online.

Importantly, the evaluation measured the academic impact of the Community Learning Initiative courses on students and examined faculties' attitudes in incorporating Community Learning Initiative courses in their own courses. Some of the questions were open-ended. The results from the students' responses showed that they felt the Community Learning Initiative was a positive experience. The faculties agreed that the Community Learning Initiative courses contributed to the students' learning.

As a basis for comparing, attempts were made to get information from websites of other food companies to determine if they had handbooks on evaluation and how evaluations of their sponsored programs on technology were conducted. The search did not yield enough detailed information to be included in this chapter.

Summary on the Handbooks for the Evaluation of E-Learning

The two handbooks for the evaluation of e-learning mentioned in this chapter were the evaluation cook book and the Kellogg evaluation handbook. Several experts in evaluation contributed to the writing of both handbooks. This section examined the evaluation of two projects sponsored by the W.K. Kellogg Foundation. One project was the provision of technology to the community. The participants were surveyed using email and the responses showed that the provision had improved communication.

Table 5. Highlights from handbooks for the evaluation of e-learning

• Inputs come from evaluation technocrats
• The Evaluation Cookbook was a sponsored project of the Learning Technology Dissemination Initiative and is used as a reference book. It contains different evaluation methods and guidelines.
• Some handbooks of evaluation were developed specifically for a company's product.
• W.K. Kellogg Foundation has an Evaluation Handbook devoted to evaluating projects sponsored by the organization
• One of the evaluations (Sirbirsky, 2002) conducted on a program by Kellogg's had diverse group of participants unlike other evaluation methods previously discussed in this chapter.
• The two evaluations conducted on the projects sponsored by the Kellogg Foundation evaluated the outputs from the program by surveying the attitude of the participants.
• While it would have been good to compare how another food company evaluated their technology sponsored programs, the available information from websites of other food companies was not sufficient to be included in this chapter.

The second project was the inclusion of a course on services and student engagement in their regular courses. The report on the second project did not indicate if any of the courses were online or if the questionnaires were delivered online. The results showed that the participants had a positive attitude to the project.

SUMMARY TABLE FROM CHAPTER FINDINGS

The table below shows a quick summary of the findings from the five categories of evaluations examined in this chapter. The ✓ means that the element identified was used in the evaluation e.g. use of theory was used in at least one of the evaluations under benchmarking. X means that the element was not used for the evaluation e.g. monetary value was not measured in the evaluations that used benchmarking. The elements are use of theory, criteria, rubrics, monetary value, achievement/performance scores, usability, attitude change, interaction with learners/with e-learning platform and attendance.

Overall Summary of the Categories of Evaluations of E-Learning

This chapter was on the evaluation of e-learning. Although there are many definitions of evaluation, the meaning has not changed over the years. It is only that more definitions have been added. Many of the definitions of evaluation were as far back as the 1950's (Kirkpatrick, 2006a) and 1970's (Scriven, 1974; Stufflebeam, 1974) but the definitions are still as valid today as they were then. Similarly, there are many definitions of e-learning. The commonality in the definitions of e- learning is that it is an electronic means of learning.

Within the same categories of evaluations of e-learning, the evaluations done were not done the same way. This was the pattern for all the articles on evaluation that was reviewed. Some evaluations examined the output (Davies & Graff, 2005; Hannafin & Foshay, 2008) while some evaluated the processes alone (Graf & List, 2005) and some evaluated the inputs, the implementation and the learning outcomes

Table 6. Summary table from chapter findings

Elements	Benchmarking	ROI	Product Evaluation	Performance Evaluation	Handbook
Use of Theory	x	✓	✓	✓	x
Criteria	✓	x	✓	x	x
Rubrics	✓	x	x	x	x
Monetary Value	x	✓	x	x	x
Achievement / Performance Scores	x	✓	✓	✓	x
Usability	x	x	✓	✓	✓
Attitude Change	x	✓	x	x	✓
Interaction with learners/ with e-learning platform	x	x	✓	✓	✓
Attendance	x	x	✓	✓	x

altogether (Ćukušić et al., 2010). Some evaluations looked at learner variables (Ćukušić et al., 2010) and some looked at attitudinal variables (Young, 2002).

The criteria used in some evaluations were given a monetary value because the e-learning was seen as an investment by the company (Nathan, 2009). This was usually the case in ROI evaluations although Young (2002) conducted an ROI based on an attitudinal survey. The criteria in some evaluations were given a weighted value (Graf & List, 2005; Marshall, 2005a; Shattuck, 2007). Some of the criteria had ambiguous statements compounded by the use of non-specific verbs (Shattuck, 2007).

Few of the articles brought congruence between the domain of theory and the e-learning outcomes (Ćukušić et al. 2010; Nathan, 2009; Marshall, 2005). Several of the articles examined did not explain their use of theory. Proponents of some models admitted that they did not base their models on theory (Marshall, 2005a; Shattuck, 2007). However, a closer look at their models showed that they had adapted models from other domains that were based on theory.

An evaluation that was sponsored by the software company that owned the software that was being evaluated reported with a bias (Young, 2002). Young (2002) interviewed the top management personnel and did not interview the employees that actually took part in the e-training.

The Kirkpatrick model was commonly used by companies that wanted to evaluate their training programs (Nathan, 2009). This could be because the Kirkpatrick model has been around since 1959 (Kirkpatrick, 2006a) and many of the companies that were using the model had been using it as far back as 1959 before e-learning was birthed. Some companies modified the model before using it but it was still basically a Kirkpatrick model (Nathan, 2009).

This chapter reviewed several articles published in European countries and in the United States of America and did not see any that described the systems theory even though, in their evaluation, they were using the systems theory. A British article described the activity theory and it had similarities to the systems theory, only the name appeared to be different (Mayes & de Freitas, 2004). Articles from Europe also used assessment to mean evaluation (Attwell, 2006).

This chapter has been able to point out the differences and similarities in the patterns of evaluations of e-learning. These differences make it difficult to compare evaluations across and within categories. Perhaps, over the next few years, a consistency can be achieved.

STEPS TAKEN IN THIS CHAPTER TO DEVELOP A FRAMEWORK

Step 1

Identify the categories of methods used to evaluate e-learning;

- Benchmarking
- ROI
- Product Evaluation
- Performance Evaluation
- Handbook on Evaluation

Step 2

Examine two e-learning models/modules under each category and compare along lines of similarities if they have any. Itemize all the similarities and use them as elements in the summary table.

Step 3

Match the elements to input, processes and output (Box 1.)

Box 1.

Elements	Input/Processes/Output
Use of Theory	Input
Criteria	Input, Processes, Output
Rubrics	Input, Processes, Output
Monetary Value	Output
Achievement/Performance Scores	Output
Attitude Change	Output
Interaction with learners, e-learning platform	Process
Attendance	Process, Output
Usability	Input/Process

Framework for Evaluating E-Learning Models

After examining two evaluations that were done in each of the five categories, this chapter pulled out the common threads from the highlights. These common threads were then aligned into tables (see Tables 8 & 9) to develop a framework for evaluating E-learning models.

Table 7. Steps for evaluating e-learning model

Step 1 Select any e-learning module/platform e.g. Learning Management System
Step 2 Determine the tasks that can be done by the e-learning module. For example; if the e-learning module was not developed from any theory than you cannot examine along the line of a theory. Similarly, if the e-learning module was not developed from a criterion, you cannot examine along the lines of criteria.
Step 3 Determine if you want to evaluate the input, processes or output from the e-learning module.
Step 4 Go to the task table in Table 9 and select the tasks that can be evaluated for the e-learning module.

Table 8. Framework/task table for evaluating e-learning models. Model and Module are used interchangeably.

Select one e-learning module. Examine the tasks and parts of the system in the modules.	
Tasks	**Part of the System**
Examine Objectives in the Evaluation of E-Learning	Input/Output
Examine how the E-Learning Model was Developed	Input
Examine Criteria if Used	Input/Process/Output
Examine Variations if any in the Models Examined	Input/Process/Output
Examine Similarities if any in the Models Examined	Input/Process/Output
Examine Theory used if any	Input
Examine Attitudes of Participants	Output
Examine Behavior Change	Output
Usability of the Technology	Input/Process

Table 9. Examples of Inputs, Processes and Outputs. The lists in the table are not exhaustive.

Inputs can be educational level of learners, usability of e-learning module or the technology used.
Processes can be attendance of learners over the e-learning module, interaction with other learners and instructors over the e-learning module, training of instructors on the e-learning module.
Outputs can be performance scores, documentation converted to monetary value, benefits, or attitude change.

CONCLUSION

This chapter started with a discussion of the input, process and output in a HCI system. Next, it addressed the different assumptions about how people learn; behaviorism, cognitivism and constructivism. Further, it examined the literature on evaluation of e-learning models, the common threads in the definitions of e-learning, the definitions of evaluation and the historical background of evaluation.

In addition, it discussed the gaps and highlights in the literature. It described the evaluations of e-learning under five categories. Two evaluations were reviewed under each category meaning a total of ten evaluations were examined altogether. Subsequently, a framework for evaluating e-learning was developed using the highlights from the review and matching them with inputs, processes and outputs. The developed framework can be used to evaluate different e-learning modules along common lines making it easy to compare evaluations. It is hoped that over the next few years, a consistency in evaluations would be achieved for use in HCI.

REFERENCES

Attwell, G. (Ed.). (2006). Evaluating e-learning a guide to the evaluation of e-learning: Evaluate Europe Handbook Series, (2), 1-46.

Barker, K. C. (2005). Linking adult literacy and e-learning a national study conducted for abc Canada literacy foundation 2005. Retrieved from http://www.futured.com /ReturnonInvestmentineLearning-aGuide.pdf.pdf

Carter, I., Leslie, D., & Kwan, D. (2012). Applying universal instructional design to course websites by using course evaluations. *Collected Essays on Learning and Teaching, 5*(21), 119–125.

Collins, A., Greeno, J., & Resnick, L. (1992). *Cognition and learning. B. Berliner & R. Calfee, Handbook of Educational Psychology*. New York: Simon & Shuster MacMillan.

Ćukušić, M., Alfirević, N., Granić, A., & Garača, Ž. (2010). E-learning process management and the e-learning performance: Results of a European empirical study. *Computers & Education, 55*(2), 554–565. doi:10.1016/j.compedu.2010.02.017

Davies, J., & Graff, M. (2005). Performance in e-learning: Online participation and student grades. *British Journal of Educational Technology, 36*(4), 657–663. doi:10.1111/j.1467-8535.2005.00542.x

Driscoll, M. P. (2000). *Psychology of learning for instruction*. Boston: Allyn and Bacon.

Evaluating the Kellogg Project. (n. d.). retrieved from http://www.trincoll.edu/orgs/planning/Kellogg/

Evaluation. (n. d). Online Etymology Dictionary. Retrieved from http://www.etymonline.com/index. php?term=evaluation

Gagne, R. M., Briggs, L. J., & Wager, W. W. (1992). *Principles of Instructional design*. TX: Harcourt Brace Jovanovich.

Gale, S. F. (2002). Measuring the roi of e-learning. *Workforce*, *81*(8), 74.

Galloway, D. L. (2005). Evaluating distance delivery and e-learning: Is kirkpatrick's model relevant? *Performance Improvement*, *44*(4), 21–27. doi:10.1002/pfi.4140440407

García, F. B., & Jorge, A. H. (2006). Evaluating e-learning platforms through SCORM specifications. *Proceedings of theIADIS Virtual Multi Conference on Computer Science and Information Systems*.

Graf, S., & List, B. (2005). An evaluation of open source e-learning platforms stressing adaptation issues. *Proceedings of 5th IEEE International Conference on Advanced Learning Technologies Computer Society*, Kaohsiung, Taiwan. (pp. 163-165). Retrieved from https://www.campussource.de/aktuelles/docs/icalt2005.pdf

Hall, A. D., & Fagen, R. E. (1956). Definition of system. *General Systems*, *1*(1), 18–28.

Hamtini, T. M. (2008). Evaluating e-learning programs: An adaptation of Kirkpatrick's model to accommodate e-learning environments. *Journal of Computer Science*, *4*(8), 693–698. doi:10.3844/jcssp.2008.693.698

Hannafin, R., & Foshay, W. (2008). Computer-based instruction's (cbi) rediscovered role in k-12: An evaluation case study of one high school's use of CBI to improve pass rates on high-stakes tests. *Educational Technology Research and Development*, *56*(2), 147–160. doi:10.1007/s11423-006-9007-4

Harary, F., & Batell, M. F. (1981). What is a system? *Social Networks*, *3*(1), 29–40. Retrieved from http://deepblue.lib.umich.edu/bitstream/handle/2027.42/24489/0000765.pdf?sequence=1 doi:10.1016/0378-8733(81)90003-4

Harvey, J. (Ed.), (1998). Evaluation cook book. Retrieved from http://www.icbl.hw.ac.uk/ltdi/cookbook/cookbook.pdf

Horton, W. (2006). So how is e-learning different? In D. L. Kirkpatrick & J. D. Kirkpatrick (Eds.), *Evaluating e programs* (pp. 95–113). San Francisco: Berrett-Koehler.

Ibis Capital. (2013). Global e-learning investment review. Retrieved from http://www.ibiscapital. co.uk/media/16158/IBIS%20Capital%20-%20e-Learning%20Flyer.pdf

Kathawala, Y., & Wilgen, A. (2004). E-learning: Evaluation from an organization's perspective. *Training & Management Development Methods*, *18*(4), 501–513.

Kellogg (2010). W.K. Kellogg foundation evaluation handbook. Retrieved from http://www.wkkf.org/knowledge-center/resources/2010/w-k-kellogg-foundation-evaluation-handbook.aspx

Kifer, E. (1995). Evaluation: a general view. In G. J. Anglin (Ed.), Instructional Technology: past, present, and future (pp. 384-392). Englewood, Colarado: Libraries Unlimited.

Kirkpatrick, D. L. (2006a). Preface. In D. L. Kirkpatrick & J. D. Kirkpatrick (Eds.), *Evaluating training programs: the four levels* (pp. xv–xvii). San Francisco: Berrett-Koehler.

Kirkpatrick, D. L. (2006b). The four levels: an overview. In D. L. Kirkpatrick & J. D. Kirkpatrick (Eds.), *Evaluating training programs: the four levels* (pp. xv–xvii). San Francisco: Berrett-Koehler.

Legon, R., & Runyon, J. (2007). Research on the impact of the quality matters course review process. *Paper presented at the 23rd Annual Conference on Distance Teaching & Learning.*

Marshall, S. (2005a). Report on the e-learning maturity model evaluation of the New Zealand tertiary sector. Retrieved from http://www.utdc.vuw.ac.nz/research/emm/documents/SectorReport.pdf

Marshall, S. (2005b). Determination of New Zealand tertiary institution e-learning capability: An application of an e-learning maturity model. *Journal of Distance-learning, 9*(1), 58–63.

Marshall, S., & Mitchell, G. (2002). An e-learning maturity model. *Paper presented at the 19th Annual Conference of the Australian Society for Computers in Learning in Tertiary Education*, Auckland, New Zealand.

Masoumi, D., & Lindstrom, B. (2012). Quality in e-learning: A framework for promoting and assuring quality in virtual institutions. *Journal of Computer Assisted Learning, 28*(1), 27–41. doi:10.1111/j.1365-2729.2011.00440.x

Mayes, T., & De Freitas, S. (2004). JISC e-Learning Models desk study, Stage 2: Review of e-learning theories, frameworks and models Retrieved from http://www.jisc.ac.uk/uploaded_documents/Stage%20 2%20Learning%20Models%20(Version%201).pdf

Michaelson, R., Helliar, C., Power, D., & Sinclair, D. (2001). Evaluating FINESSE: A case-study in group-based CAL. *Computers & Education, 37*(1), 67–80. doi:10.1016/S0360-1315(01)00035-5

Miller, G. A. (1956). The magical number seven, plus or minus two: Some limits on our capacity for processing information. *Psychological Review, 63*(2), 81–97. doi:10.1037/h0043158 PMID:13310704

Miller, J. G. (1965). Living systems: Basic concepts. *Behavioral Science, 10*(3), 193–237. doi:10.1002/bs.3830100302 PMID:5318173

Nathan, E. P. (2009). Determining the roi of an online english as a second language program. *Performance Improvement, 48*(6), 39–48. doi:10.1002/pfi.20085

Owston, R. (2008). Models and methods for evaluation. In Handbook of research on educational communications and technology (pp. 605-617).

Patton, M. Q. (1997). *Utilization –focused evaluation: the new century text.* California: Sage.

Peak, D., & Berge, Z. L. (2006). Evaluation and elearning. *Turkish online journal of distance education, 7*(1), 124-131.

Quality Matters. (2013). *Higher education program.* Retrieved from https://www.Quality matters.org/ higher-education-program

Richey, R. (1986). Theoretical bases of instructional design: systems and communications. In R. Richey (Ed.), *The theoretical and conceptual bases of instructional design* (pp. 33–56). London: Nichols.

Ruhe, V., & Zumbo, B. D. (2009). *Evaluation in distance education and e-learning: The unfolding model: NewYork.* Guilford Press.

Scepanovic, S., Devedžić, V., & Kraljevski, I. (2011). E-learning benchmarking: A review of approaches, models and tools in higher education. Proceedings of the ICERI '11 (pp. 3064-3073).

Scriven, M. (1974). Pros and cons about goal free evaluation. In W. J. Popham (Ed.), *Evaluation in education: current applications* (pp. 34–67). California: McCutchan.

Scriven, M. (1991). *Evaluation thesaurus.* California: Sage.

Shattuck, K. (2007). Quality matters: Collaborative program planning at a state level. *Online Journal of Distance Learning Administration*, *10*(3). Retrieved from http://www.westga.edu/~distance/ojdla/fall103/shattuck103.htm

Sirbirsky, D. (2001). Student perception of community learning initiative courses. Retrieved from http://www.trincoll.edu/orgs/planning/Kellogg/Reports/Student%20Perception%20of%20Community%20Learning%20Courses.pdf

Sirbirsky, D. (2002). Smart neighborhood Trinfo Café web survey 2002. Retrieved from http://www.trincoll.edu/orgs/planning/Kellogg/Reports/Smart%20Neighborhood%20Web%20Survey%20Report.pdf

Stufflebeam, D.L. (1974). Evaluation according to Daniel L. Stufflebeam. In W.J. Popham (Ed.), *Evaluation in education: current applications* (pp. 116-143). California, USA: McCutchan.

Young, K. (2002). Is e-learning delivering roi? *Industrial and Commercial Training*, *34*(2), 54–61. doi:10.1108/00197850210417537

Chapter 15

Interface for Distributed Remote User Controlled Manufacturing
Manufacturing and Education Sectors Led View

Vesna K. Spasojević Brkić
University of Belgrade, Serbia

Zorica A. Veljkovic
University of Belgrade, Serbia

Goran D. Putnik
University of Minho, Portugal

Vaibhav Shah
University of Minho, Portugal

ABSTRACT

Recent economic crisis has shown that classical approach to individual and local product oriented company is not sustainable in modern economic reality. Possible solution lies in high degrees of both specialization and flexibility product oriented small and medium-sized interchangeable production systems. According to that new wave, the main idea is based on exploring and testing of new possible designs and ways of control of human-computer interfaces for remote control of complex distributed manufacturing systems. Herein, the proposed remote system with Wall interface, video beam presentation mode and using group work enables producers in manufacturing sector to offer a product, through outsourcing manufacturing process and system in a global chain, utilizing ubiquitous computing systems and virtual and networked enterprises concepts, for anywhere-anytime control and give benefits to education sector, too, since students can dynamically interact with a real process to get a remote experimental practice, guaranteeing the availability of lab resource.

INTRODUCTION

In order to remain competitive in a growing global marketplace, product manufacturers today are forced to find new solutions to satisfy their customers. Recent economic crisis has shown that classical approach to individual and local product oriented company is not sustainable in modern economic reality (Falkenberg et al., 1998). The solution for the process of globalization and free movement of goods between the

DOI: 10.4018/978-1-5225-0435-1.ch015

markets of countries around the world lies in high degrees of both specialization and flexibility product oriented small and medium-sized interchangeable production systems.

Those systems must be successfully merged and their work well synchronized with the lowest possible costs. More than 5 million manufacturing and construction enterprises operating in Europe (99.6%) are SMEs (Gagliardi et al., 2012), while more than 80% of them in the manufacturing sector are micro industrial companies with less than 10 employees, with employment of 39% European workforce employment (Gagliardi et al., 2012). Those small companies do not have resources for large marketing activities and it results with a low usage of their production capacities. On the other hand, the Standish Group Int.`s report (Eveleens & Verhoef, 2009; Rubinstein, 2007) for IT projects success rate has shown less than 40% rate, with the conclusion that human factors issues and other soft factors that dominate over technical factors have not been resolved to the present day. The most recent way in the transition of small and medium enterprises (SMEs) manufacturing companies, with the objective to sustain competitive advantage on market is to shift to third generation ubiquitous manufacturing (Dubey, Gunasekaran & Chakrabarty, 2015).

According to this new type of solutions, the main idea herein is based on exploring and testing of new possible designs and ways of control of human-computer interfaces for remote control of complex distributed manufacturing systems, such as the one given by Putnik, Shah, Castro and Cunha (2011). In those systems that enable manufacturing of a product, each component of the outsourced manufacturing process is with a system that can be remotely controlled in decentralized manufacturing process. In that way, integration of resources and stakeholders in a global chain that utilizes ubiquitous computing systems and virtual and networked enterprises concepts for anywhere-anytime control is possible and highly efficient.

Within this new framework of the remote control presented in (Putnik et al., 2011), user interfaces represent "multiple channels" for human-computer interaction (Shah, Putnik & Castro, 2012) that give possibilities for effective and efficient employment and higher production capacities usage. The key components for remote control functionality are:

1. Control panel for remote machine controls (e.g. to move axes, start/stop spindle, upload and run a machine program etc.).
2. Communications controls.
3. Panel to see absolute and relative positions of each axis, i.e. the feed-back information from the machine movements.
4. Video frame to get live video feeds from the machines.

This innovation can also be used as 'Distributed and Remote Lab' that enables paradigm shift to interdisciplinary, real-world problem solving in engineering education with the main goal to emphasize the importance of practical experiences in the development of competences in the fields of Industrial and Manufacturing Engineering.

PROBLEM BACKGROUND

This part emphases the theoretical explanation of the problem, and outlines statistical methodology that was used in analysis of experimental data.

Theoretical Background on Interfaces

In contemporary manufacturing system operation effective human communication is vital (De Moor & Weigand, 2007), although literature focuses on integration of recent technologies with manufacturing systems rather than to soft factors issues (Dubey et al., 2015; Slater, 2004). Barnum (2010) also points out that today the focus must be on the user, not on the product. Accordingly, it should be noted that new communication channels, as very important ones, are described in detail in Shah et al. (2012), emphasizing the importance of the multiplex (multi-channel) communication system, giving special attention to human operator and remote cell.

The developed "client" user interface for the distributed manufacturing system subjected here belongs to the Ubiquitous Manufacturing System Demonstrator, and is described in detail in Spasojević-Brkić et al. (2013) and Putnik et al. (2011). According to Slater (2004) and Holzinger (2005) human-computer interaction (HCI) issues imply that usability must be considered before prototyping takes place and user interface design should be more properly called user interface development, analogous to software development. As noticed by Streitz, Tandler, Müller-Tomfelde and Konomi (2001), contemporary user interfaces should be designed both for single-user and multi-user applications that support collaborative work, while its'size could be from very small (palm size) to very large (wall size). Today even traditional HCI is transformed to human-information interaction (Streitz et al., 2001).

Accordingly, the examination of distributed remote user controlled manufacturing system herein includes two distinct types (versions) of user interface developed at the University of Minho, Guimaraes, Portugal: 1) Window and 2) Wall Interface. In Window user interface type the live video feed from the remote cell is shown inside a window panel on the interface, while Wall interface version presents the live cell video feedback in the whole background of the user interface. The remote user or the "client" operates on a remote cell while simultaneously receiving live video feedback as well as CNC machine status feedbacks, as shown in Figure 1 (Spasojević-Brkić et al., 2013; Putnik et al., 2011; Hornbæk, 2006). For both versions of user interfaces two types of display were used: computer desktop screen and video beam mode of presentation (smartphones' version is still under development). The choice of those two types of displays enables to compare standard remote operating mode (desktop display) with a real-time life-size live picture of the remote cell like being close to the cell physically (video beam display), since previous research by Hou, Nam, Peng and Lee (2012), in the field of games playing, has shown that participants experienced a greater sense of physical and self-presence in front of larger screen. Testing was conducted in the laboratory at the Faculty of Mechanical Engineering in Belgrade, Serbia. The referred two-way multiplex communication (Shah et al., 2012) is tested both working individually and in small collaborative group consisting of two persons. Previously developed Roomware (i-Land) (Nacenta, Aliakseyeu, Subramanian & Gutwin, 2005) also supports both individual and group work.

Experimentation phase included 68 students (individuals) from the Faculty of Mechanical Engineering, Belgrade University, Serbia that operated machines in the laboratory at Universidade Minho, Guimarães, Portugal. The students` task was to remotely control the cell, i.e., CNC machine as shown in Figure 1, namely, to connect to the remote cell, start a CNC machine, upload a g-code CNC program to conduct operations on the machine, remotely use the emergency stop button, move axes, assess the status of the machine and real-time positions of the axes. The main goal of the experiment was to evaluate measures of distributed remote user controlled manufacturing system in order to decide which type of interface (Wall or Window), mode of presentation (Desktop or Video beam) and type of work (individual or group) gives better results when working in different environments.

Figure 1. (a) Wall Interface; (b) Window Interface
(Spasojević-Brkić et al., 2013)

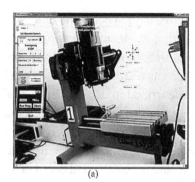
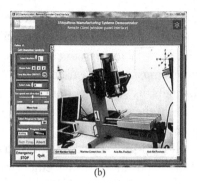

(a)   (b)

Evaluation of the parameters of efficiency, effectiveness and satisfaction of respondents is implemented as follows. During the experiments the percentage of accuracy, percentage of task completion, task execution time and number of mistakes made by the user were measured. After the task was completed, a survey using the questionnaire with the Likert scale from 1 to 5 was conducted, with the emphasis on satisfaction with the interface, comparison of obtained information's and difficulties of control during operating CNC machine, such as realistic display of the environment, consistency of object behavior, user representation and smoothness of display of changes in motions. According to the recommendations of the (Payne, 2014), 25 to 50% of the questions in the questionnaire were recorded (set in the opposite direction in relation to other issues). Evaluation included comparisons of interfaces regardless of and including displays types, modes of presentation and individual or group work and also using all combinations of examined parameters.

Many authors (Spasojević-Brkić, Putnik, Veljković, Shah, & Castro, 2014; McLellan, 2004; Mikropoulos, 2006; Mikropoulos & Strouboulis, 2004; Slater, 2004), find immersion (the objective and measurable property of the system or environment that leads to a sense of presence) and presence (as the subjective sense of being in a place), as critical features distinguishing virtual environments from other types of computer applications. Dalgarno and Lee (2010) find that the representational fidelity, along with the types of interactivity available within the environment, lead to a high degree of immersion and consequently to a strong sense of presence. Representational fidelity and learner interaction are very important characteristics of distributed and remote environment, so representational fidelity measures that are empirically explored in this survey and defined in (Spasojević-Brkić et al., 2014; Dalgarno & Lee, 2010), are: a) Realistic display of the environment, b) Smooth display of view changes and object motion, c) Consistency of object behavior and d) User representation.

Theoretical Outlines for Used Statistical Methods

Statistical method used for data analysis includes - descriptive statistics, *z*- tests, *p*-tests, regression analysis, U* Mann Whitney test, Spearman correlation coefficients (Montgomery & Runger, 2010) and index of interdependence.

Descriptive statistics is used with the aim to determine further statistical methods for data analysis. Measured parameters were: number of measurements, mean, median, standard deviation, coefficient of variation (%) and Kolmogorov test for normality (if needed). Therefore, in case of normality of distributed data parametric methods were used, such as z-test for comparisons, regression analysis, with the coefficient of correlation.

In case of nonparametric data U* Mann Whitney tests were used for comparisons, or Spearman correlation coefficient, for nonparametric regression analysis. For comparisons of categorical data the proportion tests was used (Montgomery & Runger, 2010).

Assessment criteria for the of impact of parameters are based on p-value, according to the following criteria:

$p>0.05$ non significance, marked as n.s. and with =

$p<0.05$ some significance exists, marked with *, and with > $\qquad$ (1)

$p<0.01$ strong significance exists, marked with ** and with >>

$p<0.001$ absolute significance exists, marked with *** and with >>>

In case of simple linear regression, the criteria for correlations are based on the following:

$|r| \in [0.5; 0.7)$ no correlation, marked as n.s.

$|r| \in [0.5; 0.7)$ weak correlation, marked as * $\qquad$ (2)

$|r| \in [0.7; 0.9)$ strong correlation, marked as **

$|r| \in [0.9; 1]$ absolute correlation, marked as ***.

Furthermore, for detailed comparisons of data obtained for multiple (groups) parameters, interdependence coefficients were developed to compare obtained data for individuals and groups.

Index of Interdependence

Index of interdependence is created to compare the results of correlation relationships for examined measures between Wall and Window interfaces with the desktop and video beam presentation, for the experiments conducted with a single user or for group users. It is not related to correlation coefficient of covariates, and therefore the term interdependence is used.

Definition

Index of interdependence is a measure of the number and strength of correlations for observed measures, regardless of the type of correlation, based on p-values for nonparametric testing (Equation 1) or values of criteria for correlation strength (Equation 2) for parametric testing, depending of the used method.

Therefore let:

N - number of measures,

n_m - number of possible correlations for measure m with other measures, $m = 1...N$,

$w_1 = 1, w_2 = 2, w_3 = 3$ weights of correlation relationship depending of p-value or correlation coefficient, i.e.

$w_1 = 1$ for $p_1 = 0.05$ or $|r| \in [0.5; 0.7]$,

$w_2 = 2$ for $p_1 = 0.01$ or $|r| \in [0.7; 0.9]$, $\qquad\qquad (3)$

$w_1 = 3$ for $p_1 = 0.001$ or $|r| \in [0.9; 0.1]$.

If $n_{ji}, i = 1...m, j = 1, 2, 3$ is the number of measurements in correlation with measurement i, following the Equations 2 and 3 weight for observed measurement is:

$$w_i = \sum_{i=1}^{3} n_{ij} w_i, \qquad\qquad (4)$$

with

$$w_{mi} = n_i \cdot w_3, i = 1...N \qquad\qquad (5)$$

where w_{m_i} is maximum weight for individual measurements, and m_i is the number of correlations for individual observed parameters.

Therefore, using Equation 4, maximum weight is:

$$w = \sum_{i=1}^{m} w_i \qquad\qquad (6)$$

where m is number of correlations for all observed parameter relationships.

Then, following Equations 4 and 5, index of interdependence can be expressed as

$$C_{mi} = w_i / w_{m_i}, i = 1,...,m_i \qquad\qquad (7)$$

Therefore, using Equation 7, overall index of interdependence is equal

$$C_m = \sum_{i=1}^{m} C_{mi}, i = 1,..,m \qquad\qquad (8)$$

where m is number of correlations for the all observed parameter relationships.

ANALYSIS OF GENERAL DATA FOR PARTICIPANTS

This section describes and analyzes general data of individual/single and group participants obtained in conducted experiments.

Descriptive Statistics

For 68 individuals, as well as for 34 groups who participated in the experiment descriptive data for their basic characteristics are shown in Tables 1 and 2, for individual and group work. It can be seen that individual participants were all together on average, had 23.074 years, with average grade during the studies 8.265 (on scale from 6 to 10), with computer literacy of 3.985 (on the scale from 1 to 5), capability of knowledge transfer 3.588 (on scale from 1 to 5) and with desire to learn new software 4 (on scale from 1 to 5). Group participants had similar values of measured parameters.

Additional comparisons include examining gender of the participants, which indicates that the number of male participants is significantly higher than the number of female participants (at $p<0.001$) as it is shown in Table 3. Also, as to homogeneity of the groups, there is no significant difference between homogeneous (same gender) and non-homogeneous groups (mixed gender), as shown in Table 4.

Table 1. Descriptive statistics for basic characteristic of single participants

Measured Parameter - Individuals	N	Mean	Med	SD	c_v (%)	Kolm	p-value	par. type
age	68	23.074	23.00	2.949	12.78			param.
grade point average with scale 6-10 (*GPA*)	68	8.265	8.00	0.745	9.02			param.
computer literacy	68	3.985	4.00	0.782	19.63			param.
capability of knowledge transfer	68	3.588	4.00	0.738	20.56	0.205	$p < 0.01$	non. param.
desirability for learning new software	68	4.000	4.00	0.712	17.81			param.

Legend: Med - median, SD - standard deviation, c_v - coefficient of variation, par. type - type of parameter Normal or Non-normal distributed i.e. parameter or nonparametric tests, Kolm - results for Kolmogorov normality test, p-val. - p - value of test

Table 2. Descriptive statistics for basic characteristic of single and group participants

Measured Parameter - Groups	N	Mean	Med	SD	c_v (%)	Kolm	p-val.	par. type
age	34	23.162	23.00	2.295	9.91			param.
grade point average with scale 6-10 (*GPA*)	34	8.265	8.00	0.593	7.18	0.290	$p <0.05$	non. param.
computer literacy	34	3.985	4.00	0.621	15.59			param.
capability of knowledge transfer	34	3.588	3.50	0.529	14.74			param.
desirability for learning new software	34	4.000	4.00	0.536	13.41			param.

Legend: Med - median, SD - standard deviation, c_v - coefficient of variation, par. type - type of parameter Normal or Non-normal distributed i.e. parameter or nonparametric tests, Kolm - results for Kolmogorov normality test, p-val. - p - value of test

Table 3. Comparison between the number of male and female participants

			p -value	Significance
number of male	>>>	number of female	0	p < 0.001

Table 4. Comparison between the number of homogeneous and non-homogeneous groups

			p -value	Significance
number of homogeneous groups	=	number of non-homogeneous group	0.0867	n.s.

ANALYSIS OF DATA FOR INTERFACE USABILITY MEASURES

Regarding usability measures for both individual and group participation in the experiments, in the first step descriptive statistics for the examined parameters was conducted, followed by hypothesis testing for individuals and groups, with an analysis of the number of mistakes. Final examination of interface usability measures includes comparison between individual and group work parameters.

Descriptive Analysis of Interface Usability Measures

Descriptive analysis parameters such as percentage of task completion (*PTE*), percentage of accuracy (*POA*) and task execution time (*TET*), both in the Wall and Window environment and on desktop and Video beam, are used to measure interface usability, as presented in Tables 5 and 6 for individual and group work.

Table 5. Descriptive statistics for respective parameters of interface usability for single work

Measured Parameters Individual Work	N	Mean	Med	SD	cv (%)	Kolm	p-value	par. type
PTE S WA	68	4.529	5.0	0.701	15.48	0.381	p < 0.01	non. param.
PTE S WI	68	4.515	5.0	0.743	16.46	0.390	p < 0.01	non. param.
POA S WA	68	4.559	5.0	0.678	14.86	0.390	p < 0.01	non. param.
POA S WI	68	4.559	5.0	0.608	13.34	0.384	p < 0.01	non. param.
TET S WA D	68	2.735	3.0	0.785	28.68	0.252	p < 0.01	non. param.
TET S WA V	68	2.941	3.0	0.689	23.41	0.289	p < 0.01	non. param.
TET S WI D	68	2.559	2.0	0.699	27.33	0.317	p < 0.01	non. param.
TET S WI V	68	2.750	3.0	0.699	25.42	0.257	p < 0.01	non. param.
TET S WA	136	2.838	3.0	0.743	26.16	0.259	p < 0.01	non. param.
TET S WI	136	2.654	3.0	0.703	26.49	0.280	p < 0.01	non. param.
TET S D	136	2.647	3.0	0.746	28.17	0.285	p < 0.01	non. param.
TET S V	136	2.846	3.0	0.698	24.53	0.271	p < 0.01	non. param.

Legend: PTE - percentage of task completion, POA - percentage of accuracy, TET - task execution time, WA - Wall interface, WI - Window interface, D - desktop display, V - video beam display, S - single (individual) work, Med - median, SD - standard deviation, c_v - coefficient of variation, par. type - type of parameter Normal or Non-normal distributed i.e. parameter or nonparametric tests, Kolm - results for Kolmogorov normality test, p-val. - p - value of test

Table 6. Descriptive statistics for respective parameters of interface usability for group work

Measured Parameters Group Work	N	Mean	Med	SD	cv (%)	Kolm	p-value	par. type
PTE G WA	34	4.529	4.500	0.563	12.44	0.239	$p < 0.05$	non. param.
PTE G WI	34	4.515	4.750	0.597	13.21	0.292	$p < 0.05$	non. param.
POA G WA	34	4.559	4.500	0.574	12.60	0.253	$p < 0.05$	non. param.
POA G WI	34	4.559	4.500	0.489	10.72	0.258	$p < 0.05$	non. param.
TET G WA D	34	2.353	2.000	0.485	20.62	0.414	$p < 0.05$	non. param.
TET G WA V	34	2.706	3.000	0.676	24.96	0.264	$p < 0.05$	non. param.
TET G WI D	32	2.344	2.000	0.653	27.86	0.451	$p < 0.05$	non. param.
TET G WI V	34	2.471	2.000	0.563	22.80	0.357	$p < 0.05$	non. param.
TET G WA	68	2.529	2.000	0.610	24.12	0.337	$p < 0.05$	non. param.
TET G WI	66	2.409	2.000	0.607	25.20	0.401	$p < 0.05$	non. param.
TET G D	66	2.348	2.000	0.568	24.19	0.427	$p < 0.05$	non. param.
TET G V	68	2.588	3.000	0.629	24.29	0.311	$p < 0.05$	non. param.

Legend: PTE - percentage of task completion, POA - percentage of accuracy, TET - task execution time, WA - Wall interface, WI - Window interface, D - desktop display, V - video beam display, G - group work, Med - median, SD - standard deviation, c_v - coefficient of variation, par. type - type of parameter Normal or Non-normal distributed i.e. parameter or nonparametric tests, Kolm - results for Kolmogorov normality test, p-val. - p - value of test

Statistical Tests for Usability Measures

Comparisons between percentage of task completion and percentage of accuracy (Table 7) indicate that percentage of task completion is slightly greater in groups when Wall interface is used. Furthermore, percentage of accuracy is significantly greater for single individuals working with Wall interface.

Test results for task execution time (Table 8) indicate slightly higher values when Wall interface is used in individual work than in groups, in cases when desktop display is used, while desktop when working in groups behaves poorly (les well) than video beam. In case of Window interface, video beam display has slightly higher values for individual work than for groups, as well as in overall interface examination. All tests indicate differences at $p<0.05$ significance level.

Table 7. Test results for interface usability measures

			p-value	significance
PTE S WA	=	PTE S WI		*n.s.*
PTE G WA	=	PTE G WI		*n.s.*
PTE S WA	<	PTE G WA	0.026	$p<0.05$
PTE S WI	=	PTE G WI		n.s.
POA S WA	>>	POA S WI	0.008	$p < 0.01$
POA G WA	=	POA G WA		*n.s.*
POA S WA	=	POA G WA		*n.s.*
POA S WI	=	POA G WI		*n.s.*

Legend: PTE - percentage of task completion, WA - Wall interface, WI - Window interface, D - desktop display, V - video beam display, S - single (individual) work, G - group work

Table 8. Test results for Task execution time (TET)

			p-value	significance
TET S WA D	=	*TET S WA V*		*n.s.*
TET G WA D	>	*TET G WA V*	0.0159	*p*<0.05
TET S WA D	>	*TET G WA D*	0.0107	*p*<0.05
TET S WA V	=	*TET G WA V*		*n.s.*
TET S WA	=	*TET G WA*		*n.s.*
TET S WI D	=	*TET S WI V*		*n.s.*
TET G WI D	=	*TET G WI V*		*n.s.*
TET S WI D	=	*TET G WI D*		*n.s.*
TET S WI V	>	*TET G WI V*	0.0457	*p*<0.05
TET S WI	=	*TET G WI*		*n.s.*
TET S D	=	*TET G D*		*n.s.*
TET S V	>	*TET G V*	0.0110	*p*<0.05

Legend: TET - task execution time, WA - Wall interface, WI - Window interface, D - desktop display, V - video beam display, S - single (individual) work, G - group work

Analysis of the Number of Mistakes in Experiments

For an analysis of the number of mistakes (*NM*) made by experiment participants, *p*-test for proportion is used. The number of correct experiments was compared with the number of experiments with error (Table 9). The number of correct experiments is far more greater for individual work, regardless of the type of interface or type of display, with all its combinations, at significance level $p<0.001$.

In the team work experiments (working in groups), the number of correct experiments is far more larger irrespective of using Wall type of interface or of the type of display compared to single usage, or the in combination of Wall interface and video beam display ($p<0.001$). In other cases of combinations of the type of interface and mode of display, the number of correct experiments is significantly greater than the number of mistakes ($p<0.01$) (Table 7).

ANALYSIS OF REPRESENTATIONAL FIDELITY MEASURES

Data analysis for representational fidelity measures was conducted for both single and group work, with comparison between them. Measured parameters included learning preferences, realistic display of the environment, consistency of object motion, consistency of object behavior, and user representation. Analysis of data was conducted in three phases - descriptive statistics, hypothesis testing for individual parameters and regression analysis with index of interdependence between measured data with the aim of comparing them.

Descriptive Statistics for Fidelity Measures

All measures that describe representational fidelity parameters for individual and group work are presented in Tables 10 and 11, together with determined statistical method that is used.

Table 9. Comparisons between the number of mistakes (NM) in experiments

			p-value	significance
NM S WA D 0	>>>	NM S WA D N	0	$p < 0.001$
NM G WA D 0	>>	NM G WA D N	0.0012	$p < 0.01$
NM S WA D N	=	NM G WA D N		n.s
NM S WA V 0	>>>	NM S WA V N	0	$p < 0.001$
NM G WA V 0	>>>	NM G WA V N	0	$p < 0.001$
NM S WA 0	>>>	NM S WA N	0	$p < 0.001$
NM G WA 0	>>>	NM G WA N	0	$p < 0.001$
NM S WA V N	=	NM G WA V N		n.s
NM S WA N	=	NM G WA N		n.s
NM S WI D 0	>>>	NM S WI D N	0	$p < 0.001$
NM G WI D 0	>>	NM G WI D N	0.0012	$p < 0.01$
NM S WI D N	=	NM G WI D N		n.s
NM S WI V 0	>>>	NM S WI V N	0	$p < 0.001$
NM G WI V 0	>>	NM G WI V N	0.0012	$p < 0.01$
NM S WI 0	>>>	NM S WI N	0	$p < 0.001$
NM G WI 0	>>>	NM G WI N	0	$p < 0.001$
NM S WI V N	=	NM G WI V N		n.s
NM S WI N	=	NM G WI N		n.s
NM S D 0	>>>	NM S D N	0	$p < 0.001$
NM G D 0	>>>	NM G D N	0	$p < 0.001$
NM S D N	=	NM G D N		n.s
NM S V 0	>>>	NM S V N	0	$p < 0.001$
NM G V 0	>>>	NM G V N	0	$p < 0.001$
NM S V N	=	NM G V N		n.s

Legend: NM - the number of mistakes in experiments, WA - Wall interface, WI - Window interface, D - desktop display, V - video beam display, S - single (individual) work, G - group work

Testing Representational Fidelity Measures

Hypothesis testing is conducted for both interface types (Wall and Window), types of work (individual and group), and display types (if needed).

Participants slightly prefer working in groups than individually (Table 12).

Analysis of realistic display of the environment indicates that it is not influenced by the type of interface or type of display, as well as their combinations, in experiments with a single participant (Table 13). For group participation, experiments Wall interface has significantly more realistic display of the environment than Window (p<0.01), while desktop is far better than video beam display (p<0.001). Those differences are not viable in combinations for the types of interfaces and displays. Comparisons of realistic display of environment for individual and group work show no difference, i.e., it is not influenced by the type of interface or display.

Table 10. Descriptive statistics for representational fidelity measures for individual work

Measured Parameter Individual Work	N	Mean	Med	SD	c_v (%)	Kolm	p-val.	par. type
Gla s	68	4.368	5.0	1.145	26.21	0.386	$p < 0.01$	non. param.
SLA S	68	1.882	1.0	1.333	70.82			non. param.
RDE S WA D	68	3.956	4.0	0.905	22.88			param.
RDE S WA V	68	4.088	4.0	0.926	22.65			param.
RDE S WI D	68	3.882	4.0	0.923	23.77			param.
RDE S WI V	68	3.897	4.0	0.917	23.52			param.
RDE S WA	136	4.022	4.0	0.915	22.74			param.
RDE S WI	136	3.890	4.0	0.916	23.56			param.
RDE S D	136	3.919	4.0	0.911	23.25			param.
RDE S V	136	3.993	4.0	0.923	23.12			param.
SDM S WA D	68	4.074	4.0	1.041	25.56			param.
SDM S WA V	68	4.074	4.0	1.041	25.56			param.
SDM S WI D	68	4.059	4.0	1.063	26.20			param.
SDM S WI V	68	4.029	4.0	0.962	23.86			param.
SDM S WA	136	4.074	4.0	1.037	25.46	0.248	$p < 0.01$	non. param.
SDM S WI	136	4.044	4.0	1.010	24.98			param.
SDM S D	136	4.066	4.0	1.048	25.79	0.262	$p < 0.01$	non. param.
SDM S V	136	4.051	4.0	0.999	24.65			param.
COB S WA D	68	4.221	4.0	0.844	19.99	0.263	$p < 0.01$	non. param.
COB S WA V	68	4.250	4.0	0.853	20.07	0.296	$p < 0.01$	non. param.
COB S WI D	68	4.147	4.0	0.902	21.75			param.
COB S WI V	68	4.279	4.0	0.844	19.72	0.274	$p < 0.01$	non. param.
COB S WA	136	4.235	4.0	0.845	19.96	0.280	$p < 0.01$	non. param.
COB S WI	136	4.213	4.0	0.873	20.71	0.265	$p < 0.01$	non. param.
COB S D	136	4.184	4.0	0.871	20.82	0.259	$p < 0.01$	non. param.
COB S V	136	4.265	4.0	0.845	19.82	0.286	$p < 0.01$	non. param.
URE S WA D	68	4.265	4.5	0.857	20.10			param.
URE S WA V	68	4.309	4.0	0.738	17.13	0.281	$p < 0.01$	non. param.
URE S WI D	68	4.176	4.0	0.929	22.25			param.
URE S WI V	68	4.221	4.0	0.844	19.99	0.278	$p < 0.01$	non. param.
URE S WA	136	4.287	4.0	0.797	18.60	0.292	$p < 0.01$	non. param.
URE S WI	136	4.199	4.0	0.885	21.07	0.281	$p < 0.01$	non. param.
URE S D	136	4.221	4.0	0.892	21.13	0.294	$p < 0.01$	non. param.
URE S V	136	4.265	4.0	0.791	18.55	0.280	$p < 0.01$	non. param.

Legend: GLA - group learning preferences, SLA - individual learning preferences, RDE - realistic display of the environment, SDM - consistency of object motion, COB - consistency of object behavior, URE - user representation, WA - Wall interface, WI - Window interface, D - desktop display, V - video beam display, S - single (individual) work, G - group work, Med - median, SD - standard deviation, c_v - coefficient of variation, par. type - type of parameter Normal or Non-normal distributed i.e. parameter or nonparametric tests, Kolm - results for Kolmogorov normality test, p-val. - p - value of test

Table 11. Descriptive statistics for representational fidelity measures for group work

Measured Parameter Group Work	N	Mean	Med	SD	c_v (%)	Kolm	p-val.	par. type
GLA G	34	4.368	5.0	1.110	25.41	0.312	$p < 0.05$	non. param.
SLA G	34	1.882	1.5	1.213	64.42			non. param.
RDE G WA D	34	3.956	4.0	0.762	19.27			param.
RDE G WA V	34	4.088	4.0	0.691	16.89			param.
RDE G WI D	34	3.882	4.0	0.749	19.30	0.239	$p < 0.05$	non. param.
RDE G WI V	34	3.897	4.0	0.705	18.08			param.
RDE G WA	68	4.022	4.0	0.725	18.03	0.186	$p < 0.05$	non. param.
RDE G WI	68	3.890	4.0	0.722	18.56	0.193	$p < 0.05$	non. param.
RDE G D	68	3.919	4.0	0.751	19.17	0.219	$p < 0.05$	non. param.
RDE G V	68	3.993	4.0	0.699	17.51			param.
SDM G WA D	34	4.074	4.5	0.863	21.18			param.
SDM G WA V	34	4.074	4.5	0.889	21.82			param.
SDM G WI D	34	4.059	4.0	0.911	22.44			param.
SDM G WI V	34	4.029	4.3	0.825	20.48			param.
SDM G WA	68	4.074	4.5	0.869	21.34	0.218	$p < 0.05$	non. param.
SDM G WI	68	4.044	4.0	0.863	21.33	0.187	$p < 0.05$	param.
SDM G D	68	4.066	4.3	0.881	21.66	0.189	$p < 0.05$	non. param.
SDM G V	68	4.051	4.5	0.851	21.02	0.216	$p < 0.05$	non. param.
COB G WA D	34	4.221	4.5	0.676	16.02	0.248	$p < 0.05$	non. param.
COB G WA V	34	4.250	4.5	0.643	15.12			param.
COB G WI D	34	4.147	4.3	0.702	16.93			param.
COB G WI V	34	4.279	4.5	0.630	14.72			param.
COB G WA	68	4.235	4.5	0.655	15.46	0.216	$p < 0.05$	non. param.
COB G WI	68	4.213	4.5	0.665	15.79	0.196	$p < 0.05$	non. param.
COB G D	68	4.184	4.5	0.685	16.38	0.222	$p < 0.05$	non. param.
COB G V	68	4.265	4.5	0.632	14.81	0.189	$p < 0.05$	non. param.
URE G WA D	34	4.265	4.5	0.688	16.13			param.
URE G WA V	34	4.309	4.5	0.551	12.78	0.312	$p < 0.05$	non. param.
URE G WI D	34	4.176	4.5	0.777	18.61			param.
URE G WI V	34	4.235	4.5	0.666	15.71	0.243	$p < 0.05$	non. param.
URE G WA	68	4.287	4.5	0.619	14.44	0.267	$p < 0.05$	non. param.
URE G WI	68	4.206	4.5	0.719	17.09	0.232	$p < 0.05$	non. param.
URE G D	68	4.221	4.5	0.730	17.29	0.223	$p < 0.05$	non. param.
URE G V	68	4.272	4.5	0.607	14.22	0.279	$p < 0.05$	non. param.

Legend: GLA - group learning preferences, SLA - individual learning preferences, RDE - realistic display of the environment, SDM - consistency of object motion, COB - consistency of object behavior, URE - user representation, WA - Wall interface, WI - Window interface, D - desktop display, V - video beam display, S - single (individual) work, G - group work, Med - median, SD - standard deviation, c_v - coefficient of variation, par. type - type of parameter Normal of Non-normal distributed i.e. parameter or nonparametric tests, Kolm - results for Kolmogorov normality test, p-val. - p - value of test

Table 12. Comparison between participants preferences for individual and group work

			p -value	significance
GLA S	>	SLA S	0.02	p<0.05
GLA G	=	SLA G		n.s.
GLA S	=	GLA G		n.s.
SLA S	=	SLA G		n.s.

Legend: GLA - group learning preferences, SLA - individual learning preferences, WA - Wall interface, WI - Window interface, D - desktop display, V - video beam display, S - single (individual) work, G - group work

Table 13. Comparisons for realistic display of the environment (RDE)

			p-value	significance
RDE S WA D	=	RDE S WI D		n.s.
RDE G WA D	=	RDE G WI D		n.s.
RDE S WA D	=	RDE G WA D		n.s.
RDE S WA V	=	RDE S WI V		n.s.
RDE G WA V	=	RDE G WI V		n.s.
RDE S WA D	=	RDE S WA V		n.s.
RDE G WA D	=	RDE G WA V		n.s.
RDE S WA V	=	RDE G WA V		n.s.
RDE S WI D	=	RDE S WI V		n.s.
RDE G WI D	=	RDE G WI V		n.s.
RDE S WI D	=	RDE G WI D		n.s.
RDE S WA	=	RDE S WI		n.s.
RDE G WA	>>	RDE G WI	0.004	p < 0.01
RDE S WI V	=	RDE G WI V		n.s.
RDE S WA	=	RDE G WA		n.s.
RDE S WI	=	RDE G WI		n.s.
RDE S D	=	RDE S V		n.s.
RDE G D	>>>	RDE G V	0	p < 0.001
RDE S D	=	RDE G D		n.s.
RDE S V	=	RDE G V		n.s.

Legend: RDE - realistic display of the environment, URE - user representation, WA - Wall interface, WI - Window interface, D - desktop display, V - video beam display, S - single (individual) work, G - group work

Single participants' tests for consistency of object motion (Table 14) lead to the conclusion that Wall interface shows far better results than the Window ($p<0.001$). In contrast working in group consistency of object motion is far better for Window than for Wall interface ($p<0.001$). Further more, consistency of object motions where interfaces are compared regarding the type of work (individual or group) no differences are indicated, as a consequence of weaker strength of nonparametric testing. For group work desktop display behaves slightly better than video beam ($p<0.05$).

Table 14. Tests for consistency of object motions

			p -value	significance
SDM S WA D	=	SDM S WI D		n.s.
SDM G WA D	=	SDM G WI D		n.s.
SDM S WA D	=	SDM G WA D		n.s.
SDM S WA V	=	SDM S WI V		n.s.
SDM G WA V	=	SDM G WI V		n.s.
SDM S WA D	=	SDM S WA V		n.s.
SDM G WA D	=	SDM G WA V		n.s.
SDM S WA V	=	SDM G WA V		n.s.
SDM S WI D	=	SDM S WI V		n.s.
SDM G WI D	=	SDM G WI V		n.s.
SDM S WI D	=	SDM G WI D		n.s.
SDM S WA	>>>	SDM S WI	0	p < 0.001
SDM G WA	<<<	SDM G WI	0	p < 0.001
SDM S WI V	=	SDM G WI V		n.s.
SDM S WA	=	SDM G WA		n.s.
SDM S WI	=	SDM G WI		n.s.
SDM S D	=	SDM S V		n.s.
SDM G D	>	SDM G V	0.025	p <0.05
SDM S D	=	SDM G D		n.s.
SDM S V	=	SDM G V		n.s.

Legend: SDM - consistency of object motion, WA - Wall interface, WI - Window interface, D - desktop display, V - video beam display, S - single (individual) work, G - group work

Consistency of object behavior is far better (significantly better) when Wall interface is used than Window interface, when desktop display is used ($p<0.001$ for single work and $p<0.01$ for group work), without differences for the type of work (Table 15).

Use of desktop instead of video beam display for tracking consistency of object behavior (Table 15) is far better for single users ($p<0.001$) and slightly better for group users ($p<0.05$). Furthermore, for single user's desktop display is far better solution than video beam when Window interface is used for tracking object behavior ($p<0.001$).

Group work shows no differences. For both single and group work, consistency of object behavior is far better for Wall than for Window interface ($p<0.001$). Also, use of desktop display is far better for tracking consistency of object behavior for single users ($p<0.001$), and significantly better for group users with regard to video beam display ($p<0.01$). The type of work doesn't influence the consistency of object behavior, depending of interface or display (Table 15).

User representation and smoothness of display of changes in motion (Table 16) test for single participants indicates that Wall has far better characteristic than Window interface. The same conclusion can be drawn for the use of desktop display compared to video beam ($p<0.001$). Only non- significant results are for use of Wall and Window display on desktop display.

Table 15. Tests for consistency of object behavior (COB)

			p -value	significance
COB S WA D	>>>	*COB S WI D*	0	$p < 0.001$
COB G WA D	>>	*COB G WI D*	0.0018	$p < 0.01$
COB S WA D	=	*COB G WA D*		*n.s.*
COB S WA V	>>>	*COB S WI V*	0	$p < 0.001$
COB G WA V	=	*COB G WI V*		*n.s.*
COB S WA D	>>>	*COB S WA V*	0	$p < 0.001$
COB G WA D	>	*COB G WA V*	0.047	$p < 0.05$
COB S WA V	=	*COB G WA V*		*n.s.*
COB S WI D	>>>	*COB S WI V*	0	$p < 0.001$
COB G WI D	=	*COB G WI V*		*n.s.*
COB S WI D	=	*COB G WI D*		*n.s.*
COB S WA	>>>	*COB S WI*	0	$p < 0.001$
COB G WA	>>>	*COB G WI*	0	$p < 0.001$
COB S WI V	=	*COB G WI V*		*n.s.*
COB S WA	=	*COB G WA*		*n.s.*
COB S WI	=	*COB G WI*		*n.s.*
COB S D	>>>	*COB S V*	0	$p < 0.001$
COB G D	>>	*COB G V*	0.0015	$p < 0.01$
COB S D	=	*COB G D*		*n.s.*
COB S V	=	*COB G V*		*n.s.*

Legend: COB - consistency of object behavior, WA - Wall interface, WI - Window interface, D - desktop display, V - video beam display, S - single (individual) work, G - group work

For the case of experiments in group usage of Wall interface (Table 16), it behaves far better than Window ($p<0.001$), as well as desktop display compared to video beam. There is also a significant advantage for Wall over Window interface, when video beam is used, as well as desktop display for both Wall and Window interface ($p<0.01$).

The type of work doesn't influence user representation and smoothness of display of changes in motion depending of interface or display (Table 16).

Correlations for Representational Fidelity Measures

Further analysis includes correlation analysis based on Spearman correlations or on correlation coefficient, depending of the type of variables. Correlations are conducted for all representational fidelity measures regarding the interface in use, for single and group experiments.

Additional comparisons between interfaces were conducted using the index of interdependence. Those comparisons include single participants, group participants and comparison between interfaces regarding the type of work.

Table 16. Tests for user representation and smoothness of display of changes in motion (URE)

			p -value	significance
URE S WA D	=	*URE S WI D*		*n.s.*
URE G WA D	=	*URE G WI D*		*n.s.*
URE S WA D	=	*URE G WA D*		*n.s.*
URE S WA V	>>>	*URE S WI V*	0	$p < 0.001$
URE G WA V	>>	*URE G WI V*	0.005	$p < 0.01$
URE S WA D	>>>	*URE S WA V*	0	$p < 0.001$
URE G WA D	>>	*URE G WA V*	0.006	$p < 0.01$
URE S WA V	=	*URE G WA V*		*n.s.*
URE S WI D	>>>	*URE S WI V*	0	$p < 0.001$
URE G WI D	>>	*URE G WI V*	0.003	$p < 0.01$
URE S WI D	=	*URE G WI D*		*n.s.*
URE S WA	>>>	*URE S WI*	0	$p < 0.001$
URE G WA	>>>	*URE G WI*	0	$p < 0.001$
URE S WI V	=	*URE G WI V*		*n.s.*
URE S WA	=	*URE G WA*		*n.s.*
URE S WI	=	*URE G WI*		*n.s.*
URE S D	>>>	*URE S V*	0	$p < 0.001$
URE G D	>>>	*URE G V*	0	$p < 0.001$
URE S D	=	*URE G D*		*n.s.*
URE S V	=	*URE G V*		*n.s.*

Legend: URE - user representation, WA - Wall interface, WI - Window interface, D - desktop display, V - video beam display, S - single (individual) work, G - group work

In Tables 17, 18, 19 and 20 correlation relations between representational fidelity measures for Wall and Window interface, and for single and group participation in experiments are shown. Tables also include weights for all observed representational fidelity measurements (w_i), with their maximum weights (w_{mi}) and their index of interdependences (C_{mi}). Tables also present overall index of interdependence, for all representational fidelity measures for the type of interface and the type of work.

Comparison of representational fidelity measures between Wall and Window interfaces was conducted graphically using index of interdependence. Smaller index of interdependence indicates a larger independency of the measure.

Comparison of indexes between interdependence for between Wall and Window interfaces for a single participant is shown in Figure 2. It is obvious that critical representational fidelity measure, especially for Wall interface is the consistency of object behavior with $C_{mi} = 0.6$ for both types of display (desktop and video beam). For Window interface high index ($C_{mi} = 0.6$) is for the consistency of object behavior with video beam display, as well as for the user representation and smoothness of display of changes in motion, and also for video beam display. The smallest index of interdependence is for learning affinity. The *Cmi* is obtained using Equation 7.

Table 17. Correlations for representational fidelity measures for wall interface and a single user

WALL INDIVIDUAL WORK	GLA S	SLA S	RDE S WA D	RDE S WA V	SDM S WA D	SDM S WA V	COB S WA D	COB S WA V	URE S WA D	URE S WA V	w_i	w_{mi}	C_{mi}
GLA S	X	*	n.s.	n.s.	n.s.	n.s.	n.s.	n.s.	n.s.	n.s.	1	27	0.037
SLA S	*	X	*	*	n.s.	n.s.	n.s.	n.s.	n.s.	n.s.	3	27	0.111
RDE S WA D	n.s.	*	X	X	**	X	***	X	n.s.	X	6	15	0.400
RDE S WA V	n.s.	*	X	X	X	n.s.	X	***	X	***	4	15	0.267
SDM S WA D	n.s.	n.s.	**	X	X	X	***	X	n.s.	X	5	15	0.333
SDM S WA V	n.s.	n.s.	X	n.s.	X	X	X	***	X	**	5	15	0.333
COB S WA D	n.s.	n.s.	***	X	***	X	X	X	***	X	9	15	0.600
COB S WA V	n.s.	n.s.	X	***	X	***	X	X	X	***	9	15	0.600
URE S WA D	n.s.	n.s.	n.s.	X	n.s.	X	***	X	X	X	3	15	0.200
URE S WA V	n.s.	n.s.	X	***	X	**	X	***	X	X	7	15	0.467
												Cm	3.348

Legend: GLA - group learning preferences, SLA - individual learning preferences, RDE - realistic display of the environment, SDM - consistency of object motion, COB - consistency of object behavior, URE - user representation, WA - Wall interface, D - desktop display, V - video beam display, S - single (individual) work, w_i - weight for observed measurement, W_{m_i} - maximum weight for individual measurements, C_{m_i} - index of interdependence for measured parameter m_i of i parameters, C_m - overall index of interdependence

Table 18. Correlations for representational fidelity measures for window interface and a single user

WINDOW INDIVIDUAL WORK	GLA S	SLA S	RDE S WI D	RDE S WI V	SDM S WI D	SDM S WI V	COB S WI D	COB S WI V	URE S WI D	URE S WI V	w_i	w_{mi}	C_{mi}
GLA S	X	*	n.s.	n.s.	n.s.	n.s.	n.s.	n.s.	n.s.	n.s.	1	27	0.037
SLA S	*	X	n.s.	n.s.	n.s.	n.s.	n.s.	n.s.	n.s.	n.s.	1	27	0.037
RDE S WI D	n.s.	n.s.	X	X	*	X	n.s.	X	n.s.	X	1	15	0.067
RDE S WI V	n.s.	n.s.	X	X	X	*	X	***	X	***	7	15	0.467
SDM S WI D	n.s.	n.s.	*	X	X	X	*	X	n.s.	X	2	15	0.133
SDM S WI V	n.s.	n.s.	X	*	X	X	X	***	X	***	7	15	0.467
COB S WI D	n.s.	n.s.	n.s.	X	*	X	X	X	*	X	2	15	0.133
COB S WI V	n.s.	n.s.	X	***	X	***	X	X	X	***	9	15	0.600
URE S WI D	n.s.	n.s.	n.s.	X	n.s.	X	*	X	X	X	1	15	0.067
URE S WI V	n.s.	n.s.	X	***	X	***	X	***	X	X	9	15	0.600
												Cm	2.607

Legend: GLA - group learning preferences, SLA - individual learning preferences, RDE - realistic display of the environment, SDM - consistency of object motion, COB - consistency of object behavior, URE - user representation, WI - Window interface, D - desktop display, V - video beam display, S - single (individual) work, w_i - weight for observed measurement, W_{m_i} - maximum weight for individual measurements, C_{m_i} - index of interdependence for measured parameter m_i of i parameters, C_m - overall index of interdependence

Table 19. Correlations for representational fidelity measures for wall interface and group work

WALL GROUP WORK	GLA G	SLA G	RDE G WA D	RDE G WA V	SDM G WA D	SDM G WA V	COB G WA D	COB G WA V	URE G WA D	URE G WA V	w_i	w_{mi}	C_{mi}
GLA G	X	n.s.	n.s.	n.s.	n.s.	n.s.	n.s.	n.s.	n.s.	n.s.	0	27	0.000
SLA G	n.s.	X	n.s.	n.s.	n.s.	n.s.	n.s.	n.s.	n.s.	n.s.	0	27	0.000
RDE G WA D	n.s.	n.s.	X	X	**	X	*	X	n.s.	X	3	15	0.200
RDE G WA V	n.s.	n.s.	X	X	X	*	X	***	X	n.s.	4	15	0.267
SDM G WA D	n.s.	n.s.	**	X	X	X	*	X	n.s.	X	3	15	0.200
SDM G WA V	n.s.	n.s.	X	*	X	X	X	***	X	*	5	15	0.333
COB G WA D	n.s.	n.s.	*	X	*	X	X	X	***	X	5	15	0.333
COB G WA V	n.s.	n.s.	X	***	X	***	X	X	X	***	9	15	0.600
URE G WA D	n.s.	n.s.	n.s.	X	n.s.	X	***	X	X	X	3	15	0.200
URE G WA V	n.s.	n.s.	X	n.s.	X	*	X	***	X	X	4	15	0.267
												Cm	2.400

Legend: GLA - group learning preferences, SLA - individual learning preferences, RDE - realistic display of the environment, SDM - consistency of object motion, COB - consistency of object behavior, URE - user representation, WA - Wall interface, D - desktop display, V - video beam display, G - group work, w_i - weight for observed measurement, W_{m_i} - maximum weight for individual measurements, C_{m_i} - index of interdependence for measured parameter m_i of i parameters, C_m - overall index of interdependence

Table 20. Correlations for representational fidelity measures for window interface and group work

WINDOW GROUP WORK	GLA G	SLA G	RDE G WI D	RDE G WI V	SDM G WI D	SDM G WI V	COB G WI D	COB G WI V	URE G WI D	URE G WI V	w_i	w_{mi}	C_{mi}
GLA G	X	n.s.	n.s.	n.s.	n.s.	n.s.	n.s.	n.s.	n.s.	n.s.	0	27	0.000
SLA G	n.s.	X	n.s.	n.s.	n.s.	n.s.	n.s.	n.s.	n.s.	n.s.	0	27	0.000
RDE G WI D	n.s.	n.s.	X	X	***	X	***	X	***	X	9	15	0.600
RDE G WI V	n.s.	n.s.	X	X	X	*	X	**	X	*	4	15	0.267
SDM G WI D	n.s.	n.s.	***	X	X	X	*	X	**	X	3	15	0.200
SDM G WI V	n.s.	n.s.	X	*	X	X	X	*	X	n.s.	2	15	0.133
COB G WI D	n.s.	n.s.	***	X	*	X	X	X	*	X	5	15	0.333
COB G WI V	n.s.	n.s.	X	**	X	*	X	X	X	*	4	15	0.267
URE G WI D	n.s.	n.s.	***	X	**	X	*	X	X	X	6	15	0.400
URE G WI V	n.s.	n.s.	X	*	X	n.s.	X	*	X	X	2	15	0.133
												Cm	2.333

Legend: GLA - group learning preferences, SLA - individual learning preferences, RDE - realistic display of the environment, SDM - consistency of object motion, COB - consistency of object behavior, URE - user representation, WI - Window interface, D - desktop display, V - video beam display, G - group work, w_i - weight for observed measurement, w_{m_i} - maximum weight for individual measurements, C_{m_i} - index of interdependence for measured parameter m_i of i parameters, C_m - overall index of interdependence

Figure 2. Comparisons of Indexes of interdependence between wall and window interfaces for single work

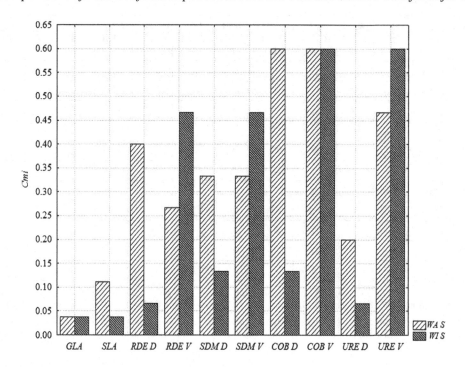

Regarding the correlations between representational fidelity measures for group work, and comparing the interfaces (Figure 3), a high value of indexes of interdependence (Equation 7) have consistency of object behavior for Wall interface with video beam display and realistic display of the environment with video beam display for Window interface (0.6). Minimum indexes (0.0), for both interfaces, are for learning affinity, both in group and individual work.

Comparison of correlations for representational fidelity measures and Wall interface between individual and group work is shown in Figure 4. For individual work, high indexes of interdependence (Equation 7) are for the consistency of object behavior, regardless of the type of display (0.6). Also indexes are high for user representation and smoothness of display of changes in motion when video beam display was used (0.467) and for realistic display of the environment with desktop display (0.4). For the case of group work, high indexes of interdependence for Wall interface are only for the consistency of object behavior, with Window display (0.6).

For individual work, the smallest correlation, expressed by index of interdependence using Equation 7, is for group learning affinity (0.037), while learning affinities for groups do not exist.

Comparison of correlations for representational fidelity measures and Window interface between individual and group work is shown in Figure 5. For individual work, high indexes of interdependence (Equation 7) are for the consistency of object behavior, the user representation and smoothness of display of changes in motion with video beam display (0.6), while in group work such a value of index has realistic display of the environment, when desktop is used. High indexes in individual work are also for realistic display of the environment and for consistency of object motion, both with video beam display (0.467).

For individual work, the smallest measure of correlation is for single and group learning affinity (0.037), while learning affinities for groups do not exist.

Figure 3. Comparisons of Indexes of interdependence between wall and window interfaces for group work

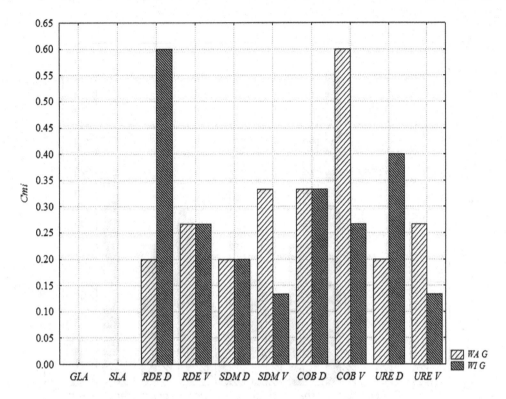

Figure 4. Comparisons of Indexes of interdependence for wall interface between individual and group work

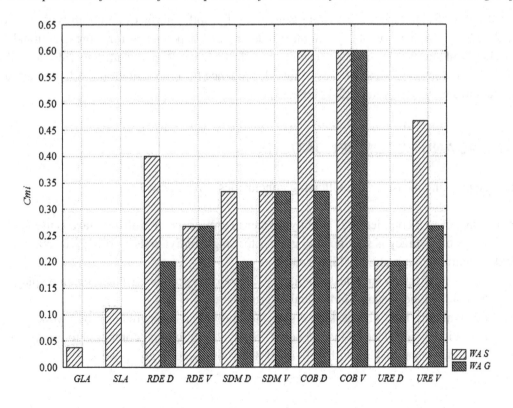

Figure 5. Comparisons of Indexes of interdependence for window interface between individual and group work

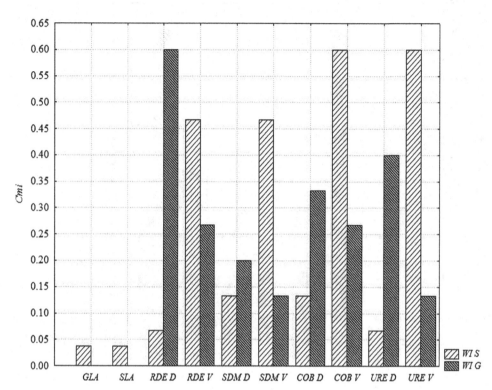

Overall index of interdependence, using Equation 8 for both interfaces and both types of work are presented in Figure 6. It is visible that highest index of interdependence for representational fidelity measures has Wall interface for individual work - 3.35, followed by Window interface, also for individual work (2.61). For work in groups, indexes of interdependence for representational fidelity measures are smaller and have very close values (2.4 and 2.33).

SOLUTIONS AND RECOMMENDATIONS

For interface usability measures the following conclusions can be drawn:

- Percentage of task completion is slightly greater in groups when Wall interface is used.
- Percentage of accuracy is significantly greater for single individuals working with Wall interface.
- Task execution time is slightly higher in cases:
  - For Wall interface with desktop display, for work in groups for video beam display, regardless of the type of work (individual or group);
  - For Wall interface with desktop display, for individual compared to group work;
  - For Window interface and video beam display, for individual compared to group work;
  - For video beam display with individual work compared to group work.

Figure 6. Overall indexes of interdependence for wall and window interfaces and single and group work

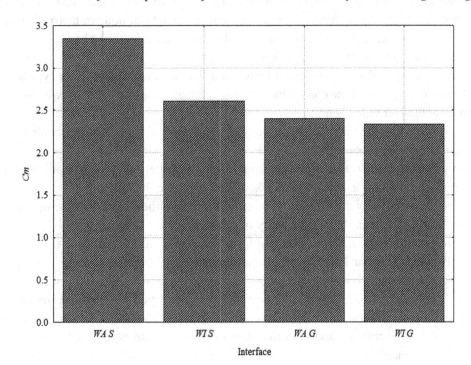

- The number of mistakes for Wall interface is far smaller ($p<0.001$) than those for correct experiments for overall interface and for video beam display regardless of the type of work (individual or group), as well as for individual work with desktop display. In cases of group work with desktop display, the number of correct experiments is significantly greater than the number of mistakes ($p<0.01$);
- The number of mistakes for Window interface is far smaller for individual work regardless of the display, and overall regardless of the type of work (individual or group) with $p<0.001$. In case of group work the number of correct experiments is significantly greater in cases of desktop and video beam display ($p<0.01$);
- In case of displays for both types of work (individual or group) the number of correctly conducted experiments is far greater than the number of mistakes ($p<0.001$);
- The number of mistakes is lower in group work using Wall type of interface regardless of the type of display compared to single usage.
- Regarding learning preferences there no difference in opinions between individual participants and group work, but there is a slight group learning preference for participants.
- For group participation experiments Wall interface has significantly more realistic display of the environment than Window ($p<0.01$), while desktop is far better than video beam display ($p<0.001$).
- Consistency of object motion shows that:
  - For single work Wall interface shows far better results than the Window;
  - When working in group the consistency of object motion is far better for Window than for Wall interface;

- Comparison between interfaces in terms of the type of work (individual or group) doesn't indicate differences, as a consequence of weaker strength of nonparametric testing;
- For group work, desktop display behaves slightly better than video beam.
- Consistency of object behavior shows that:
  - For single work Wall display is far better than Window, regardless of the type of display;
  - Also, for single work the consistency of object behavior is much better expressed on desktop display than on video beam;
  - For group work the tracking consistency of object behavior is much better for Wall interface than for Window interface;
  - Group work s shows that use of desktop display is better than video beam, with far greater influence of better desktop display when Wall interface is used;
  - Type of work (individual or group) does not influence the use of the type of interface or the type of display, regarding consistency of object behavior.
- User representation and smoothness of display of changes in motion indicate that:
  - Wall interface is far better for use than Window interface regardless of the type of work (single or group);
  - Desktop display is also far more convenient for user representation and smoothness of display of object motions than video beam for both types of work (individually or in group)
  - For user representation and smoothness of display of changes in motion the type of work is of no influence.
- Comparison of correlation measures for representational fidelity measures shows that
  - Indexes of interdependence for a single participant indicate a high value (a large number of correlations) for Wall interface in cases of the consistency of object behavior (0.6), regardless of the type of display, with the smallest index of interdependence for learning affinities in groups (0.037);
  - Window interface for single work has the largest indexes *Cmi* in cases of the consistency of object behavior and user representation and smoothness of display of changes in motion, when video beam display was used;
  - Indexes of interdependence for group work indicate high values for the consistency of object behavior for Wall, and realistic display of the environment for Window interface, with video beam display in both cases (0.06);
  - Correlations for learning affinity in individuals or groups does not exist, regardless of the interface, when data for groups are examined;
  - Comparing correlations of representational fidelity measures for individual and group work for Wall interface show more measures with high indexes of interdependence for individual work, such as consistency of object behavior (0.6) regardless of the type of display, compared with same measure for group work, where index is 0.6 only if video beam is used. Also, indexes for user representation and smoothness of display of changes in motion using video beam display and realistic display of the environment for desktop display exceed 0.4 for individual work;
  - Correlations for Window interface for individual and group work indicate greater indexes of interdependence for single work than for groups. That means that high indexes (0.6) exist for two measures, representational fidelity for individual work (consistency of object behavior and user representation and smoothness of display of changes in motion when video beam

was used), and realistic display of the environment and consistency of object motion, both with video beam display (0.467). For the case of group work, realistic display of the environment, when desktop is used has index of 0.6;

◦ For individual work the smallest indexes are for learning affinities, while for group work they do not exist;

◦ Comparisons of overall index of interdependence show that the highest value has Wall interface for a single user, while for group work indexes are smaller and almost equal for Wall and Window interface.

FUTURE RESEARCH DIRECTIONS

Intensive competition in the global economy widens the implementation of web-based collaboration platforms and forces research in the field of personalized interaction between clients and producers, through opening new future research directions. In the future, it is expected broad application of herein proposed remote system with Wall interface, video beam presentation mode and using group work in the future and as a logical consequence answers to the following questions:

• The impact of proposed solutions on theory development.
• The impact of proposed solutions on organizational performance improvement.
• The impact of proposed solutions on sustainable business development.
• The impact of proposed solutions on educational systems development.

CONCLUSION

In order to remain competitive in a growing global marketplace, product manufacturers should apply new designs and ways of control of human-computer interfaces for remote control of complex distributed manufacturing systems. Therefore, the focus must be placed on the user and human communication, rather than only the product. The examination of distributed remote user controlled manufacturing system developed in Portugal is tested by Serbian students, as future users of new production paradigm. According to that, the same concept can be used as `Distributed and Remote Lab`, where students use real-world problem solving techniques in engineering education. The following conclusions appear.

Statistically significant results show that despite the fact that the participants are more accustomed to work in Window type of interface surrounding, which is reflected in their conducting of the tasks faster, with less mental effort, other measures of satisfaction and efficiency suggest that for remote collaborative control of production systems Wall type of interface taking into account all examined measures behaves better (easier for work, offering smaller information delay and greater representational fidelity). Percentage of task completed is equal for Wall and Window interfaces, while the accuracy of task is significantly better for Wall compared to Window interface. Time of task execution, when working both individually or in group, is longer when desktop is used compared to video beam. When working in group, work time is shorter than the time when working individually.

Finally, statistical tests show that the best result can be obtained when working in group on Wall interface with usage of video beam mode of presentation, as shown in Figure 7. Also, for group work, indexes of interdependence for representational fidelity measures are smaller and have very close values for both Wall and Window interfaces.

Figure 7. Wall Interface, video beam presentation mode, working in group

Accordingly, the proposed remote system with Wall interface, video beam presentation mode and using group work enables producers in manufacturing sector to offer a product, through outsourcing manufacturing process and system in a global chain, utilizing ubiquitous computing systems and virtual and networked enterprises concepts, for anywhere-anytime control and give benefits to education sector, too, since students can dynamically interact with a real process to get a remote experimental practice, guaranteeing the availability of lab resource. Accordingly, successful applications could be expected in both manufacturing and education sectors in the future.

Nomenclature

Abbreviations, used in the experiments and in their analysis are presented in Table 21.

Table 21. Nomenclature for presented chapter

General	
WA	Wall interface
WI	Window interface
D	desktop display
V	video beam display
S	Individual (individual work)
G	Group (group work)
Statistical	
N	number of measurements
Mean	mean of sample

continued on following page

Table 21. Continued

General	
Med	median
SD	standard deviation
cv(%)	coefficient of variation
Kolm	value of Kolmogorov statistics
p-value	p value of test
n.s.	non-significant measure
r	correlation coefficient parametric or Spearman
n_m	number of possible correlations for measure m with other measures
m	denominator of measure
w_i	weights of correlation relationships
w_{mi}	maximum weight for individual measurements
w	maximal weight
C_{mi}	index of interdependence
C_m	overall index of interdependence
z	test for standard normal distribution
U*	Mann - Witney nonparametric test
param.	parametric measure
non. param.	nonparametric measure
Parameters for Interface Usability Measures	
POA	Percentage of accuracy
PTE	Percentage of task completion
TET	Task execution time
NM	Number of mistakes
Parameters for Fidelity Measures	
GLA	Learning preferences in group
SLA	Individual learning preferences
RDE	Realistic display of environment
SDM	Consistency of object motion
COB	Consistency of object behavior
URE	User representation and smoothness of display of changes in motion

REFERENCES

Barnum, C. M. (2010). *Usability testing essentials: ready, set... test!* Elsevier.

Dalgarno, B., & Lee, M. J. (2010). What are the learning affordances of 3-D virtual environments? *British Journal of Educational Technology*, *41*(1), 10–32. doi:10.1111/j.1467-8535.2009.01038.x

De Moor, A., & Weigand, H. (2007). Formalizing the evolution of virtual communities. *Information Systems, 32*(2), 223–247. doi:10.1016/j.is.2005.09.002

Dubey, R., Gunasekaran, A., & Chakrabarty, A. (2015). Ubiquitous manufacturing: overview, framework and further research directions. *International Journal of Computer Integrated Manufacturing,.*

Eveleens, J. L., & Verhoef, C. (2009). Quantifying IT forecast quality. *Science of Computer Programming, 74*(11), 934–988. doi:10.1016/j.scico.2009.09.005

Falkenberg, E. D., Hesse, W., Lindgreen, P., Nilsson, B. E., Oei, J. H., Rolland, C., . . . Voss, K. (1998, October). A framework of information systems concepts. Proceedings of IFIP WG (Vol. 8).

Gagliardi, D., Muller, P., Glossop, E., Caliandro, C., Fritsch, M., Brtkova, G., ... & Ramlogan, R. (2012). A recovery on The horizon. *Annual report on European SMEs, 2013.*

Holzinger, A. (2005). Usability engineering methods for software developers. *Communications of the ACM, 48*(1), 71–74. doi:10.1145/1039539.1039541

Hornbæk, K. (2006). Current practice in measuring usability: Challenges to usability studies and research. *International Journal of Human-Computer Studies, 64*(2), 79–102. doi:10.1016/j.ijhcs.2005.06.002

Hou, J., Nam, Y., Peng, W., & Lee, K. M. (2012). Effects of screen size, viewing angle, and players' immersion tendencies on game experience. *Computers in Human Behavior, 28*(2), 617–623. doi:10.1016/j.chb.2011.11.007

McLellan, H. (2004). Virtual realities. In Handbook of research for educational communications and technology, (2nd ed., pp. 457-487).

Mikropoulos, T. A. (2006). Presence: A unique characteristic in educational virtual environments. *Virtual Reality (Waltham Cross), 10*(3-4), 197–206. doi:10.1007/s10055-006-0039-1

Mikropoulos, T. A., & Strouboulis, V. (2004). Factors that influence presence in educational virtual environments. *Cyberpsychology & Behavior, 7*(5), 582–591. doi:10.1089/cpb.2004.7.582 PMID:15667053

Montgomery, D. C., & Runger, G. C. (2010). *Applied statistics and probability for engineers.* John Wiley & Sons.

Nacenta, M. A., Aliakseyeu, D., Subramanian, S., & Gutwin, C. (2005). A comparison of techniques for multi-display reaching.*Proceedings of the SIGCHI conference on Human factors in computing systems* (pp. 371-380). ACM. doi:10.1145/1054972.1055024

Payne, S. L. B. (2014). *The Art of Asking Questions: Studies in Public Opinion, 3* (Vol. 3). Princeton University Press.

Putnik, G. D., Shah, V., Castro, H., & Cunha, M. M. (2011). The Functionality of Remote Controlling in Ubiquitous Manufacturing Systems Demonstrator for I* PROMS 'efm' Showcase. *Tekhné-Revista de Estudos Politécnicos/Polytechnical Studies Review, 9*(15), 169-189.

Rubinstein, D. (2007). Standish group report: There's less development chaos today. *Software Development Times, 1.*

Shah, V., Putnik, G. D., & Castro, H. (2012). Prototype Multiplex Communication System for Remote Control of Machine Tools. In Virtual and Networked Organizations, Emergent Technologies and Tools (pp. 241-252). Springer Berlin Heidelberg. doi:10.1007/978-3-642-31800-9_25

Slater, M. (2004). How colorful was your day? Why questionnaires cannot assess presence in virtual environments. *Presence (Cambridge, Mass.)*, *13*(4), 484–493. doi:10.1162/1054746041944849

Spasojević-Brkić, V., Putnik, G., Shah, V., Castro, H., & Veljković, Z. (2013). Human-computer interactions and user interfaces for remote control of manufacturing systems. *FME Transactions*, *41*(3), 250–255.

Spasojević-Brkić, V., Putnik, G., Veljković, Z., Shah, V., & Castro, H. (2014). Representational fidelity in distributed and remote lab environment. *FME Transactions*, *42*(3), 243–248. doi:10.5937/fmet1403243s

Spasojević-Brkić, V. K., & Punik, G. (2013). User evaluation of the interfaces for the remote control of manufacturing systems. *Serbian Journal of Management*, *8*(2), 201–212. doi:10.5937/sjm8-4281

Streitz, N. A., Tandler, P., Müller-Tomfelde, C., & Konomi, S. I. (2001). Roomware: Towards the Next Generation of Human-Computer Interaction based on an Integrated Design of Real and Virtual Worlds. In Human-Computer Interaction in the New Millenium (pp. 551-576). Addison Wesley.

KEY TERMS AND DEFINITIONS

Distributed Manufacturing Systems: Manufacturing system that consists of decentralized manufacturing practices located in different geographical areas and coordinated using information technology.

Index of Interdependence: Index of interdependence is a measure of the number and strength of correlations for observed measures, regardless of the type of correlation, based on p-values for nonparametric testing or values of criteria for correlation strength for parametric testing, depending of the used method.

Interface Usability Measures: Interface usability measures herein describe the extent to which an interface for distributed remote control of manufacturing system achieves specified goals as context dependent tool shaped by the interaction between tools, problems and people.

Remote Control of Manufacturing Systems: Control of machine from a distance by visual control of data and production, using user interfaces as a "channels" for human-computer interaction.

Representational Fidelity Measures: Representational fidelity measures describe the fidelity of the representation important for interactivity available within the environment.

Type of Display: Refers to desktop and video beam display modes for manufacturing control.

Type of Work: Individual or group work used for manufacturing control of distributed remote user controlled manufacturing system.

Wall Interface: Wall interface shows the live video feed from the remote cell on wall panel on the interface, and the human "client" operator is watching the remote cell through on wall while controlling the remote CNC machine(s).

Window Interface: Window interface shows the live video feed from the remote cell inside a window panel on the interface, and the human "client" operator is watching the remote cell through a window while controlling the remote CNC machine(s).

Chapter 16
Developments of Serious Games in Education

Luís Sousa
University of Algarve, Portugal

José Bidarra
Universidade Aberta, Portugal

Mauro Figueiredo
University of Algarve, Portugal

João Rodrigues
University of Algarve, Portugal

Jânio Monteiro
University of Algarve, Portugal

Pedro Cardoso
University of Algarve, Portugal

ABSTRACT

As Human Computer Interaction technologies evolve, they are supporting the generation of innovative solutions in a broad range of domains. Among them, Serious Games are defined as new type of computer game that is capable of stimulating users to learn, by playing and competing against themselves, against other users or against a computer application. While it could be applied to a broad range of fields and ages, these games are becoming especially relevant in educational contexts and for the most recent generation of students that is growing in a new technological environment, very different from the one we had some years ago. However, in order to become fully accepted as a teaching/learning tool in both formal and informal contexts, this technology has still to overcome several challenges. Given these considerations, this chapter makes a state-of-the-art review of several works that were done in this field, followed by the description of two real world projects, helping to understand the applicability of this technology, but also its inherent challenges.

INTRODUCTION

The term "serious games" refers to the use of computer games for training and education with a purpose that extends beyond pure entertainment. They have been gaining popularity for some time now, to deal with real world problems by modeling and simulating them. While being used in a broad range of applications, including Military Training (Numrich, 2008), Humanitarian and Environmental Games, Health (Macedonia, 2009; Blackman, 2005; Sawyer, 2008) or Political Games (Democracy 2, 2015; President Forever, 2015) they perform an important role in education, branded as Educational Games (von Wangenheim & Shull, 2009; Mayo, 2007; Kelly et al., 2007; Zyda, 2007; Westera, Nadolski, Hummel

DOI: 10.4018/978-1-5225-0435-1.ch016

& Wopereis, 2008). Moreover, they are starting to be applied to other innovative fields. For instance, they are seen as a way of instructing and motivating citizens to participate in energy management, as in the game 2020 Energy (2015).

But how do we broadly define "game"? Klopfer (2008) defines it as goal-oriented activity, based on specific rules that players perceive as enjoyable. In terms of Serious Games, Zyda (2007) define them as "a mental contest, played with a computer in accordance with specific rules, that uses entertainment to further government or corporate training, education, health, public policy, and strategic communication objectives." In this definition the term entertainment may collide with the concept of a serious game. However, considering that "ludic" is not usually a priority in most activities of the educational context, a game may be the motivating factor that is needed in many learning resources.

In education, the research in innovative ICT solutions for Human Computer Interaction extends far beyond the conventional inclusion of multimedia contents, to include and recognize the role of new learning experiences. In this field, ludic learning models can cover various scientific fields, not only in formal educational contexts, but also in informal ones.

However, in order to become fully accepted as a teaching/learning tool in both formal and informal contexts, game technology has to overcome some challenges. One of the main issues is how to measure their actual learning effects. In this field some studies (Backlund & Hendrix, 2013) while evaluating the effectiveness of game-based learning concluded that, among the several studies analyzed, serious games had shown a positive effect on learning. The results of such studies are important to overcome a second difficulty related with the acceptance of these teaching tools by teachers, students and parents allowing it to be integrated in the curricula.

Given these considerations, in this chapter we analyze and describe current developments in serious games, with a special focus in education. This includes a state-of-the-art review of serious games applications, together with the description of two implementations aimed to help illustrate their applicability in real world scenarios. In one of these implementations we describe a solution that integrates the structure of a simple game in the last generation of ebooks. The idea is to create an electronic book that enables dynamic integration of text with images, audio, video and animations, but that may be used as a game. As serious games can be used in informal contexts, in the second implementation, we describe a solution that uses 3D electronic sensors in a wearable device (glove) to create a game capable of teaching sign language alphabet to any person who wants to learn it.

BACKGROUND

So far. serious Games have been used in several educational contexts that include natural sciences (Liu, Tan & Chu, 2009; Wang, 2008), mathematics (Chow, Woodford, & Maes, 2011; Kablan, 2010; Ke & Grabowski, 2007; Ke, 2008; Kordaki, 2011; Liao, Chen, Cheng, Chen & Chan, 2011; Main & O'Rourke, 2011; Panoutsopoulos, H. & Sampson, 2012; Sung, Chang, & Lee, 2008; Rosas et al., 2003; Wilson et al., 2006), problem solving (Huang, Yeh, Li & Chang, 2010; Yang, 2012), computing (Papastergiou, 2009; Sindre, Natvig & Jahre, 2009), software development (Gresse von Wangenheim, Thiry, & Kochanski, 2009), language learning (Connolly, Stansfield & Hainey, 2011), geography (Asaolu, 2012; Tüzün, Yılmaz-Soylu, Karakuş, İnal & Kızılkaya, 2009; Virvou, Katsionis & Manos, 2005), history (Huizenga, Admiraal, Akkerman & ten Dam, 2009; Kennedy-Clark & Thompson, 2011) and health (Tüzün, 2007;

Gomoll, O'Toole, Czarnecki & Warner, 2007; Gomoll, Pappas, Forsythe & Warner, 2008; Qin, Chui, Pang, Choi & Heng, 2010).

In terms of the natural sciences, serious games have been used in both outdoor and indoor education scenarios. As described by Liu, Tan and Chu (2009), by using mobile communication and wireless technologies, students can now move to any place, allowing scientific experimentation, augmented reality, image collection, resource sharing, and communication with colleagues. However, this solution can also be applied to more formal contexts, as described by Wang (2008), where Web-based quiz-games were developed for elementary school classes. Globally, the results of these studies have demonstrated an increase in the motivation and learning outcomes of students.

Mathematics is another of the application fields that have seen a large number of research studies and developments focusing in serious games. However, the effectiveness of these games is still far from reaching the desirable goals. As stated by Backlund and Hendrix (2013) the effect of serious games in mathematics varies significantly, with only nearly half of the studies demonstrating a positive result in the learning outcome.

Another important field of research concerns problem solving, with several projects trying to create serious games for this purpose. For instance, Huang, Yeh, Li and Chang (2010) developed a game called Idea Storming Cube (ISC), which aims to engage students in divergent thinking, applied to debris flow problems. According to Yang (2012) there is a quantitative improvement in problem-solving and learning motivation due to the introduction of digital game based learning, suggesting it can be exploited as a useful and productive tool to support students in effective learning while enhancing the classroom atmosphere.

In terms of computing and software development serious games are also becoming very popular with several studies giving positive results. For instance, in Papastergiou (2009), the author assessed the effectiveness and motivational appeal of a computer game for learning computer memory concepts in a high school Computer Science curriculum. Their results show that the gaming approach was at the same time more effective in promoting students' knowledge of computer memory concepts and more motivational than the non-gaming approach.

However, in this field the results of some studies are not as positive. In Sindre, Natvig, and Jahre (2009), a question/answer-based computer game called Age of Computers was introduced to replace traditional weekly paper exercises in a Computer Fundamentals' course at the university level. Their results have shown that with equal time being spent on the various learning activities, the effect of playing the game was not better than the other activities. According to Gresse von Wangenheim, Thiry, and Kochanski (2009) the results of an explorative study that investigates the learning effectiveness of a game prototype on software measurement was not very successful. While the results of the study reveal that the participants consider the content and structure of the game appropriate, no indication of a significant difference on learning effectiveness was shown.

In terms of language learning, serious games have the potential to increase the ability to listen, talk, read and write. This requires the creation of games that combine audio, video, driven by the language. In this area, Piirainen–Marsh and Tainio (2009) addressed additional language learning from the participation in the social activity of collaborative game-play. They describe how players engaged with the language resources offered by the game during collaborative play. Following a different perspective, Connolly, Stansfield, and Hainey (2011) describe the educational value of Alternate Reality Games (ARGs), for the teaching of modern European languages. ARGs are a form of narrative that often involves multiple media and gaming elements to tell a story that could be affected by the actions of the participant. The results of this study have shown that in general student attitudes towards the ARG were very positive, with the majority of students agreeing that they would be willing to play the game over a prolonged period of time as part of a foreign language course. In addition, through using the ARG, students believed they obtained skills relating to cooperation, collaboration and teamwork.

Geography is another field that has already seen the implementation of educational games. For instance, Asaolu (2012) experimented with the Lainos World software. The effect of this software on students' geographical knowledge was analyzed using online surveys, yielding a positive result. Tüzün, Yılmaz-Soylu, Karakuş, İnal, and Kızılkaya (2009) designed and developed a three-dimensional educational computer game for the learning about geography by primary school students. While testing it, they have verified that students demonstrated higher intrinsic motivations and lower extrinsic motivations learning within the game-based environment. Virvou, Katsionis, and Manos (2005) conducted an evaluation study on a virtual reality educational game that they had developed for teaching geography. While the results were positive, they revealed that students who were poor performers had benefited the most from the game environment, whereas the subgroup of good students had benefited the least from the game environment.

In terms of the istory subject, Huizenga, Admiraal, Akkerman, and ten Dam (2009) tested the effects of a game for the first year of secondary education, and evaluated student's achievements concerning the historical knowledge of medieval Amsterdam. Their results have shown that those pupils who played the game gained significantly more knowledge about medieval Amsterdam than those pupils who received regular instruction, while no significant differences were found with respect to motivation for History or the Middle Ages. Kennedy-Clark, and Thompson (2011) present the results of a study in which university students were asked to collaboratively solve inquiry-based problems related to historical disease epidemics using game-based learning. Their results indicated that students attended to visual information with more specificity than text-based information when using a virtual environment.

In terms of health, serious games have the potential to be used for behavior change, as is described by Munguba, Valdes, and da Silva (2008) where they were used a game as therapy for nutrition education, in a program for obese children. In another example, games were used for first aid classes in secondary school contexts as described by Tüzün (2007). In healthcare serious games have been used to teach surgery at medical university level, as described by Qin, Chui, Pang, Choi, and Heng (2010), supporting a reduction in the training costs, as well as in the associated risk for patients.

Still in the field of health, one important application of serious games lies in rehabilitation, which occurs after a disease or traumatic incident. In these scenarios, as stated by Rego, Moreira, and Reis (2010), the introduction of games has the potential to contribute to an increase in the motivation during rehabilitation sessions, which is a major problem in therapy due to the repetitive nature of such exercises.

In all the above-mentioned fields, the introduction of serious games in education creates new learning possibilities that were not available a few years ago. For each of them several technologies may be involved, targeting the development of learner skills and/or knowledge acquisition. To illustrate some of these solutions, in the next section we describe the implementation process and resulting structure of two projects that were undertaken to increase the game-like nature of real world learning applications.

APPLICATIONS OF SERIOUS GAMES IN EDUCATION

In this section two topics of serious games in education are explored. We start by describing the research involved in the implementation of a gamified book that merges an ebook with a game. Afterwards we showcase another concept that considers human 3D gesture recognition, using sensors, to support the creation of a learning tool that can be used by anyone who wants to learn sign language alphabets.

Development of Gamified Books

With the emergence of distributed learning technologies, students can now learn in a more informal setting using mobile devices, without being confined to a room full of computers. Furthermore, teachers and educators have emphasized the importance and need for "authentic learning activities", where students can work with real world problems (Brown, Collins, & Duguid, 1989). Therefore, the development of educational activities for students, that combine learning resources from the real world with those from the digital world, has become an important and challenging research topic. This may be accomplished, for example, through the use of mobile communication and wireless technologies, which can be moved to any place, allowing for scientific experimentation, augmented reality, image collection, resource sharing, and communication with colleagues.

The current context of mobility offers the possibility of integrating the typical structure of a game in a new type of electronic book - the gamebook (g-book) - to be used in tablets. The concept is, in essence, an interactive ebook, which enables the integration of text with images, audio, video and animations. There are clear pedagogical benefits in the development of an innovation that combines a book with a game with potential in various learning contexts (formal, informal or non-formal).

The mobile learning concept is part of a societal model that assumes digital skills as a valid stance. We refer, in particular, the ability to:

1. Analyze and produce digital information where and when the user wants,
2. Make decisions in the context of an information society,
3. Apply creative skills and innovation (technological and methodological),
4. Engage in collaborative work and
5. Master an operational knowledge about digital media and global communications.

In this context, this sub-section describes the creation of a gamebook that may be effective in various learning situations. Ongoing research involves the evaluation of three major components, clearly distinguishable:

1. Assess the potential of the current ebook technology,
2. Study the role of narratives in games, and
3. Determine the potential of gamebooks for certain educational applications.

Given these considerations in the following we explore the integration of the structure of a simple game in the last generation of ebooks. The idea is to create an electronic book that not only enables the dynamic integration of text with images, audio, video and animations, but also that may be used as a game, aligning ebooks with two learning scenarios: mobile learning and educational games.

Furthermore, it makes sense to consider the integration of mobile and educational games in a system managed by students, allowing them to set personal goals, manage content and communicate with each other. In practice, these Personal Learning Environments (PLEs) are made up of several components, which may include social networks, virtual worlds and authoring software, interconnecting various learning resources suitable to the pedagogical contexts and skills to be acquired by each learner. In this sense, due to their characteristics and potential for interactivity, ebooks (or gamebooks) can be a valued part of these PLEs.

Ebook Formats

At the most basic level, the ebook is an electronic book that can have a simple format, such as a text in PDF. However, there are currently more advanced standards, such as EPUB3 (universal) or iBooks 2 (Apple), that can integrate multimedia components. Ideally, an ebook should have sufficient quality for current devices with their high-resolution displays, and be compatible with a wide variety of reader apps, and if necessary allowing the conversion to other formats. In fact, however, there are more than a dozen formats not compatible with each other, and sometimes they do not adapt to higher resolution screens.

Over the years, teachers have often used multimedia encyclopedias and textbooks, on CD, DVD, or available online. But more recently a new generation of electronic books has emerged, that can offer more interactive and dynamic learning experiences. Students of the "PlayStation generation" tend to respond better to this dynamic and interactive content, with the ability to display not only text but also other media with hypertext links, search facilities, and connection to online databases. One benefit of these ebooks for students is for example the possibility of being able to select any word that they do not understand and find immediately its definition.

Another potential use refers to the capability to simultaneously have several students accessing the same book and thus share learning experiences. More specifically, they can communicate and share files, having opportunities to communicate in the context of group work, even if accessing from different locations. The ebook can also contain tests, allowing students to make their self-assessment.

An economic advantage refers to financial aspects; currently the cost of textbooks represents a high expense for students and their families. The introduction of electronic books contributes to reducing these costs effectively. Furthermore, it is also expected the emergence of cheaper mobile devices, which is happening in countries such as China and India. Altogether, the widespread use of ebooks will also benefit the environment by reducing paper consumption, bearing in mind that a device may store thousands of ebooks.

On a less positive note, despite huge advances with the technology, many applications used to read ebooks do not have really useful features such as the ability to highlight, mark text, bookmark or write notes. These are apparently trivial matters, but they are important for a student. In a paper book the student usually highlights the most important parts and adds annotations in the margins. In this way, when he reads the book again, he will focus mainly in these parts.

Although there are several standards for ebooks, not all reading applications and mobile devices use the same. Thus, to reach a wide audience, it is necessary to adopt some of the most commonly used formats for reading electronic books, for example, Adobe PDF in computers, Mobi for the Amazon Kindle, EPUB for the Barnes & Noble Nook, and iBook for Apple's iPad. The Portable Document Format (PDF) is the most popular format for creating digital books and can be read by the free Adobe Reader installed on most computers. It is an open standard that enables the creation of ebooks with support to the use of sound, images, video, notes and bookmarks. Its main advantage is to keep the layout of the printed book within original quality on any device. However, this benefit is a major disadvantage on mobile devices. The text is difficult to handle in a PDF file, when we visualize a page on a mobile device such as a smartphone, the characters become too small forcing the user to increase or decrease size in order to view the contents of the page. In other ebook formats, such as EPUB and iBook, there are no physical constraints to a fixed style and everything scales.

EPUB is a format based on open specifications, primarily written in XML and XHTML. The EPUB format is supported by a wide range of devices and platforms, including Android devices, Nook, iPhone, iPad, iPod, MobiPocket, Adobe Digital Editions, FBReader, Stanza, Sony Reader, and many other readers and applications. Of the most popular devices, the only one that does not support EPUB is the first Amazon Kindle. The EPUB specification is an open standard, allowing the creation of ebooks with sound, images and video (in its newest specification - EPUB3). This specification introduces innovative features to address structure limitations, such as: precise layouts specialized for comic books, support for MathML, support for multimedia, and introduction of notes.

The Amazon Kindle is an electronic book reader very popular in the US. Early versions used the Kindle proprietary format AZW. This is basically the Mobipocket format based on the Open eBook standard using XHTML. This specification supports images, notes and bookmarks. In late 2011, Amazon started selling the Kindle Fire along with the new file format Kindle Format 8 (KF8), which supports a subset of the features of HTML5 and CSS3. This is also a proprietary specification and expands the functionality of the earlier versions of the Kindle, in order for the Kindle Fire to support sound and video.

Ebook Authoring Tools

There are several ecosystems and tools that can be used to create ebooks and distribute them for personal computers and mobile devices. The simplest way to create digital books, for multiple mobile platforms, is to start with PDF or RTF files and use applications, like Calibre, that converts PDF files in multiple formats such as EPUB, or MOBI for the Kindle, among others. Calibre is a free application that runs on Windows, Mac OS X and Linux.

There are other free or open applications that support the creation of electronic books. For example, the application eCub allows the creation of simple books in EPUB or MobiPocket, from text files or XHTML. However, eCub is very limited, with no WYSIWYG capabilities. It is suitable for the production of simple ebooks with front and back pages with an image, index, a title page and it can convert content to a sound file (WAV or MP3). The eCub is free and is available for Windows, Mac OS X, Linux, FreeBSD and Solaris.

Booktype is an open platform, available since 2012, which allows editing and writing of ebooks for different platforms by exporting in PDF, EPUB, MOBI, ODT and HTML. This application also exports the ebook directly to Amazon, Barnes & Noble and iBookstore online stores, as well as to online printing sites. Digital books written with this application are immediately available in any of these platforms. When writing the ebook, the author does not need to worry about formatting, since it will automatically be formatted to work in these different platforms. Booktype also provides a set of collaborative tools for reviewers, editors, translators, designers, and authors, enabling the different participants to work collaborative in the production of an ebook. Some of the features offered by this platform include: intuitive drag-and-drop tools, chat, messages, adding images and text formatting. Booktype also maintains a history of all changes, which allows the author to compare different editions and return to a previous edition. It is even possible to use snippets (pieces of computer code). One of the disadvantages of this platform is the need for installing on a server and accessing via web browser, which requires some additional expertise.

The Firedocs eLML editor can also be used to create ebooks (Weibel et al., 2009). The eLML framework (eLesson Markup Language) is an XML platform for creating online classes using XML. It exports produced materials in SCORM, HTML, PDF and EPUB format. The main objective is to ensure that classes are modeled according to the ECLASS reference, which defines five distinct sections: Entry, Clarify, Look, Act, Self-assess, Summary. Current implementation only supports JPG, PNG, GIF and SVG images. It does not allow Java scripts and forms, so some of the functionalities as the glossary, references to labels and self-assessment tests are not available in the EPUB format.

Sigil is an open WYSIWYG editor used by Google to create ebooks following the EPUB2 specification for Windows, OS X and Linux. This application imports, creates and edits XHTML documents and exports them into EPUB2 documents. Ebooks created with Sigil may contain text, pictures and links, but this standard does not support video or sound. It also provides multiple views of the work: book, code and a split mode. In the book view, it allows content edition in WYSIWYG mode.

Finally, we should mention the electronic books created in the iBook format from Apple. These ebooks are created with a free application - the iBooks Author tool. The format is proprietary, although based on the EPUB standard specification, with some differences in the CSS3 tags. This tool makes the process of creating ebooks very easy, by presenting a very complete set of integrated features, including: sound, image, video, dictionary, text underline, annotations, text-to-speech conversion, navigation and many widgets to enhance the interactive experience. The introduction of widgets in the iBook is an enriching experience for readers of an electronic book. iBook Author offers seven types of pre-defined widgets:

1. Photo gallery,
2. Video or audio media file,
3. Review questions,
4. Slide show;
5. Interactive tagged images, to give detailed information on specific parts of an image or graph,
6. 3D models, and
7. Objects created in HTML.

The ease of creating widgets allows users to add any object to an interactive iBook, and there are many possibilities, from calculators, puzzles, maps, YouTube videos, among many others. Table 1 summarizes the characteristics of the authoring applications surveyed.

Development of a Game-Book Prototype

This section outlines the implementation of a novel concept, the *gamebook* (or g-book) with a story that can be read sequentially or not. The main difference refers to the ability to choose different paths to the main characters or the unfolding of the history, as happens in games. The reader/player makes choices that affect how the story unfolds and his decisions have a significant impact on events and the final outcome.

Some choices may be as simple as turning right or left at the end of a road. Others may be much more difficult, requiring decisions about facts or occurrences, such as, problems arising in natural disasters, environmental pollution and climate change. In a particular story the student may be the main character - the hero of the story - or simply manipulate variables with consequences at the strategic level. Thus, not only decisions change the story, but also the sequence of choices can change the ending.

Table 1. Summary of free ebook authoring tools

Content	eCub	Booktype	Firedocs	Sigil	iBooks Author
Photos	√	√	√	√	√
Graphics					√
Sound					√
Videos					√
Hyperlinks	√	√	√	√	√
Animation					√
Search					√
Dictionary					√
Underline					√
Markers					√
Notes					√
Digital Speech					√
Collaboration		Messages			
Tests and self assessment					√
Widgets / programs / *apps*					√

A gamebook may follow typical genres and formats of electronic games, such as puzzle, RPG, adventure, strategy, among others, where the reader will face threats, adversaries, and discover the truth behind an intricate story. Ultimately, the objective of this project is to create a didactic narrative built on situations capable of providing expectation, suspense, challenge and other positive emotions. Based on the latter, it is theoretically possible to engage students in the study of a particular subject matter, and get more results in terms of attention, retention and understanding. In fact, the possibility and value of integrating game play in learning practices is indicated clearly by several researchers, who recognize its potential in making learning more meaningful and in assimilating new subject matter (Prensky, 2001; Gee, 2003; Kirriemur & McFarlane, 2004; Johnson, 2005).

The ongoing research involves three strategic components, clearly distinguishable:

1. Establish the potential of the technology: the most common formats and authoring tools that allow the creation of gamebooks that are effective in learning;
2. Identify the role of narratives and games: what kinds of narrative and game genres can be recreated as gamebooks for learning, and what learning activities can be prepared based on this typology.
3. Demonstrate real educational applications: according to a specific level of education, what pedagogical models can better integrate gamebooks, and in which subject areas are most effective.

After starting exploring the Apple iBook format (Bidarra *et al.*, 2012), essentially due to the vast potential for multimedia authoring with the iBooks Author tool, we built a model of a dynamic book considering all the multimedia features and widgets available. However, this was merely an interactive e-book, since using the features available we could not implement the desired g-book. Another question was that in this case the e-book becomes available only for the iOS mobile devices.

We also tested the EPUB3 standard with the creation of a dynamic book about a beautiful lagoon with a diversified fauna and flora in the middle of Portugal (Óbidos) (Bidarra, Figueiredo & Natálio, 2014). In the project we tried many different widgets and scripts that somehow emulated the effects achieved with the Apple format iBooks. Still, this implementation was not implemented like a g-book as we desired.

Since we were not able to implement the desired g-book with the traditional ebook authoring tools described previously, we decided to explore the Unity3D platform (Unity, 2015). Unity3D is a game development tool. It is an integrated authoring tool for creating video games or other interactive content such as architectural visualizations or real-time 3D animations. Unity's development environment runs on Microsoft Windows and Mac OS X, and the applications it produces can be run on Windows, Mac, Xbox 360, PlayStation 3, Wii, iPad, iPhone, as well as Android mobile devices. It can also run the developed prototype in a web browser using the Unity web player plugin, supported on Mac and Windows.

Supported by the Unity3D platform, we developed a novel educational g-book prototype for the curriculum of "Environmental Studies", fit for the children in the 4th grade program, with the title "Adventures in the Guadiana River" (Figure 1).

In addition to a story that can be followed by reading the text, consisting of a trip along the Guadiana River, there are several devices that make the development of the narrative more memorable. First of all, a basic text adapted to the target audience was illustrated with appealing images and galleries on various aspects of the river, emphasizing its environmental context. To ensure the engagement of readers, the narrative requires the fulfilment of certain tasks that are supported by interactive activities, in particular, the inclusion of thematic videos and their exploitation through multiple-choice questions (Figure 2).

The ultimate goal was to allow students the possibility to choose different paths to the unfolding of the story. The prototype already has a narrative based on a journey of discovery, with various unexpected situations to maintain interest. For now, the implemented g-book allows the student to progress to the next chapter of the book if the student answers half of the questions of a quiz correctly (Figure 3).

Figure 1. The "Adventures in the Guadiana River" g-book prototype developed with Unity3D

CAPÍTULO 1

O Rio Guadiana

O rio Guadiana nasce em Espanha (na lagoa de Regedoura).
Passa no Alentejo e vem desaguar no Algarve, junto à cidade de Vila Real de Santo António.

2

Figure 2. Quiz developed with Unity3D

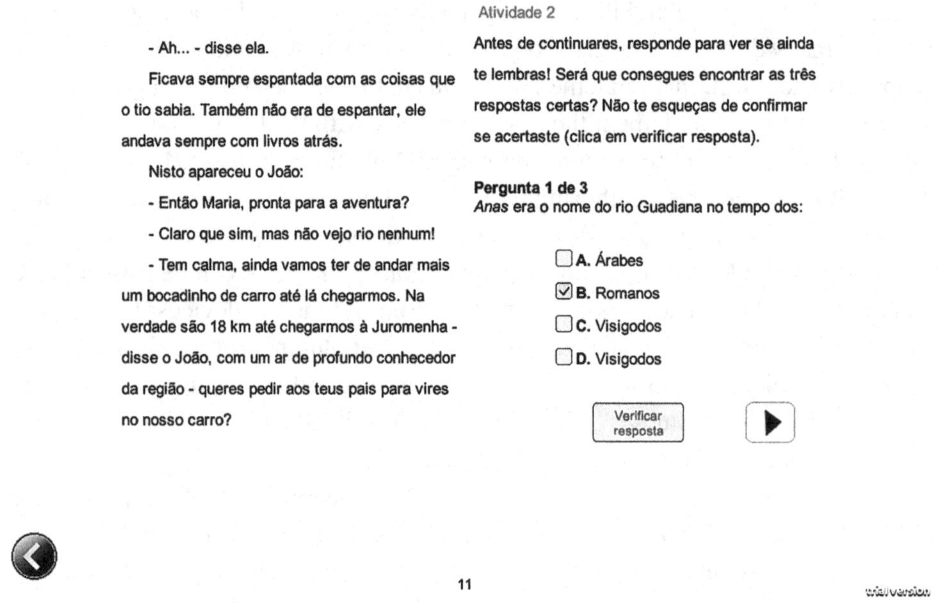

Atividade 2

- Ah... - disse ela.

Ficava sempre espantada com as coisas que o tio sabia. Também não era de espantar, ele andava sempre com livros atrás.

Nisto apareceu o João:

- Então Maria, pronta para a aventura?

- Claro que sim, mas não vejo rio nenhum!

- Tem calma, ainda vamos ter de andar mais um bocadinho de carro até lá chegarmos. Na verdade são 18 km até chegarmos à Juromenha - disse o João, com um ar de profundo conhecedor da região - queres pedir aos teus pais para vires no nosso carro?

Antes de continuares, responde para ver se ainda te lembras! Será que consegues encontrar as três respostas certas? Não te esqueças de confirmar se acertaste (clica em verificar resposta).

Pergunta 1 de 3
Anas era o nome do rio Guadiana no tempo dos:

☐ **A.** Árabes
☑ **B.** Romanos
☐ **C.** Visigodos
☐ **D.** Visigodos

Verificar resposta ▶

11

Figure 3. Scores enable the progress throughout the book

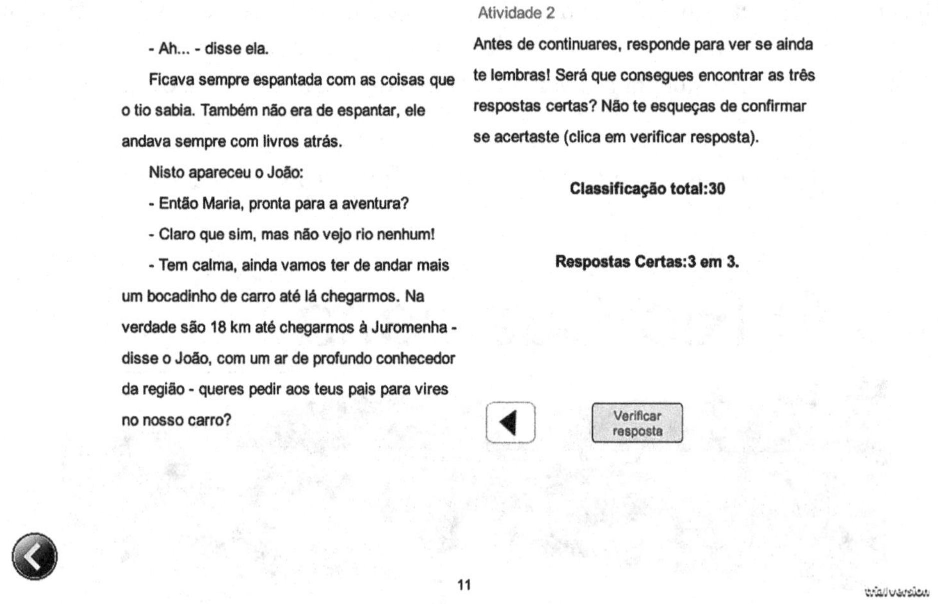

Atividade 2

- Ah... - disse ela.

Ficava sempre espantada com as coisas que o tio sabia. Também não era de espantar, ele andava sempre com livros atrás.

Nisto apareceu o João:

- Então Maria, pronta para a aventura?

- Claro que sim, mas não vejo rio nenhum!

- Tem calma, ainda vamos ter de andar mais um bocadinho de carro até lá chegarmos. Na verdade são 18 km até chegarmos à Juromenha - disse o João, com um ar de profundo conhecedor da região - queres pedir aos teus pais para vires no nosso carro?

Antes de continuares, responde para ver se ainda te lembras! Será que consegues encontrar as três respostas certas? Não te esqueças de confirmar se acertaste (clica em verificar resposta).

Classificação total:30

Respostas Certas:3 em 3.

◀ Verificar resposta

11

Development of a Serious Game for the Learning of Sign Language Alphabet

In this section we describe the implementation of a Serious Game that was created to help people in the process of learning a sign language. To do it, both, a computer game and a hardware device, called GyroGlove, were implemented. When interacting with the computer, the user is asked to represent alphabet letters by replicating the hand and fingers' positions, which are obtained using the GyroGlove module. The GyroGlove then sends that information to the computer using a wireless interface, which interprets the letter that is being done by the user and scores it.

In the following, we start by describing the implementation of the GyroGlove and afterwards the game that results from the combination of both modules.

Implementation of the Gyroglove

Currently, there are several sensors that are able to track and recognize body gestures such as Kinect (Microsoft, 2015), Leap Motion (Leap Motion, 2015), Structure Sensor (Occipital, 2015), Asus Xtion (Xtion, 2015), among others. All these sensors have a great importance to the industry of gaming and user-machine interaction tools. These sensors when complemented with appropriate software have the ability to detect the body posture and/or the user's hand, and accurately replicate that structure on a 3D mesh, to detect gestures.

All these sensors are based on color cameras (RGB) and/or depth (using infrared) and therefore have problems of spatial limitations, i.e. the user has to be located near the device, in the area where these cameras are oriented to, otherwise, they do not work properly. In addition to spatial limitations, in most cases, these devices do not work when they are close to an infrared source, for example on sunlight, or in a room with fluorescent lamps.

In order to overcome these limitations, in this subsection we adopt a different solution, based on a new tracking and gesture recognition system, supported by Inertial Measurement Units (IMUs) that detect the 3D rotation of the hand and fingers of a user. Afterwards, based on this system, a Serious Game for the learning of sign language gestures will be presented.

Inertial Measurement Unit

An Inertial Measurement Unit sensor is an electronic device capable of measuring various types of inertial forces. Depending on the composition of the entire device, it can be formed by several independent sensors comprising an gyroscope, an accelerometer, a magnetometer and, less commonly, an altitude sensor (using atmospheric pressure). In this work we opted to use an IMU in the electronic glove that contains both, an accelerometer and a gyroscope. The results of each of them are mapped to three axes, thus for each IMU sensor a total of 6 degrees of freedom will be obtained.

The accelerometer, such as its name suggests, measures the acceleration (m/s^2) applied to the device in relation to a specified axis. When stationary, i.e. static, the accelerometer only measures the gravitational force of the Earth (9.8 m/s^2) in the downward axis. Its exact value depends on the location and elevation where the device is placed. The accelerometer can measure static (gravity) or dynamic forces. One of its most common applications, on mobile phones and tablets, is the tilt-sensing. By measuring the force of gravity in all three axes, it is possible to know the direction of the device in relation to the gravity of the earth and so automatically rotate the screen to the user's benefit.

The costs of accelerometers depend on their capabilities, among which the most important ones are:

1. The maximum range;
2. Accuracy;
3. Number of measurement axes.

In terms of maximum range, it is measured in G-forces, with 1.0 G indicating an acceleration of 9.8 m/s^2. Typically, accelerations range from ±2 G to ±250 G, for the majority of available accelerometers.

In terms of accuracy, the higher the range of these values, the lower will be its accuracy, due to high granularity. The data obtained by the accelerometer are usually composed of integers of 16 bits, in 2's complement (from -32768 to + 32767). So, if a wide-ranging is used, i.e. ±16 G or more, a lower precision will be available.

Accelerometers can measure acceleration in one axis, or up to three axes. Although accelerometers are fairly accurate for long periods of time, they are unstable in short time, i.e. measured values are quite granular in short periods of time. When an accelerometer is placed in a device that moves or shakes significantly, is not possible to measure accurately all the acceleration data. These electronic components are rather more reliable when there are fewer changes in acceleration over time (measuring static forces).

The gyroscope is a sensor capable of measuring the angular speed, i.e. the speed at which an object rotates on a given axis. It is used when we need to know the direction of a moving object. The angular velocity is measured in degrees per second (%/s).

Such as the accelerometer, the gyroscope has also some intrinsic characteristics, which include:

1. The maximum range;
2. Its Accuracy;
3. Number of measurement axes.

The maximum range is measured in degrees per second, and usually has a value that ranges between $\pm\frac{30°}{s}$ and $\pm\frac{2000°}{s}$. If a too low range is chosen, the device can be quite accurate but cannot exceed its maximum angular velocity. On the other hand, if the maximum value is too high, the accuracy is reduced. Thus it is necessary to adjust this value according to the desired application. Like the accelerometer, there are gyroscopes able to measure the angular speed using one, or up to three axes. While the gyroscopes are very accurate in measuring angular velocity, they suffer from drift problems when measuring low constant angular velocities, even when immobilized. This problem is due to intrinsic errors and noise production phase, with different drift values for each module. Unlike the accelerometer, the gyroscopes are very accurate in short periods of time, and inaccurate otherwise (due to the drift problems). Thus they can be combined, thus complementing each other.

GyroGlove Background

The glove developed in this work, called GyroGlove (GyG) uses several MPU-6000 sensors, that combine both and Inertial Measurement Unit with a Magnetic Pickup (MPU). As shown in Figure 4 (InvenSense, 2015) a central controller module is used to program and configure all the IMU sensors and to serve as interface between the glove and the computer. Each sensor has an accelerometer and a gyroscope. Both 3-axes are programmable with a maximum configurable range of ±2 G, ±4 G, ±8 G, ±16 G and $\pm\dfrac{250°}{s}$, $\pm\dfrac{500°}{s}$, $\pm\dfrac{1000°}{s}$, $\pm\dfrac{2000°}{s}$ respectively. As the sensors are placed in the hand and in the user's fingers, high values of G-forces or high angular velocities are not expected to occur. Thus to keep the values as much accurate as possible, a maximum range of ±2G and $\pm\dfrac{500°}{s}$, were respectively used for the accelerometer and gyroscope.

The sensors are strategically placed on the glove, in order to be able of extracting the three-dimensional rotation of each finger and also of the hand. To do it, sensors were positioned in the most critical and important locations of the hand, trying to minimize the number of sensors, without limiting the capturing capability of the device, when measuring the rotations of the whole hand.

The anatomical names of the hand bones, that were considered more important to capture the gesture, were the distal, intermediate and proximal phalanges (see Figure 5, left). Considering the above observations, it was decided to use eleven sensors on these locations, enabling the data retrieval of all the rotational data of the fingers and hand. Except for the thumb, in all the other fingers the distal bones are very short, making it very uncommon to fold this finger's part without moving its adjacent. Thus in all the fingers we decided to put two sensors. In the thumb, we decided to place them in the Distal Phalange and Proximal phalanges. In all the other fingers they were placed in the intermediate and proximal phalanges (see Figure 5, right). The last sensor (i.e. number 11) was placed on top of the hand, next to the main module, to extract the overall orientation of the hand. This latter sensor is the basis for the correlation of all the other sensors, as will be explained later. For easier identification, all modules were numbered from 1 to 11, as shown in (see Figure 5, right).

These sensors are integrated with a DMP (Digital Motion Processor) system that is used to process complex algorithms of a 6-axes motion fusion. These algorithms are proprietary, registered by InvenSense and the mode of operation is not of public knowledge.

Figure 4. MPU-6000 sensor module

Figure 5. Left: anatomic names of bones in hand. Right: location and number identification of the sensors and main module

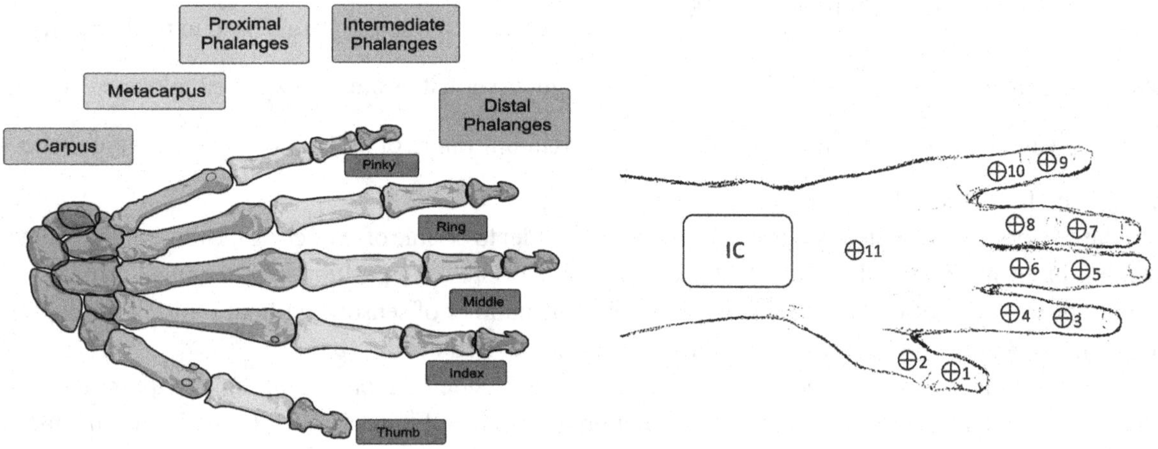

The computation supported by these algorithms, in the IMU modules, is useful for four reasons:

1. Support a reduction and even elimination of the problems associated with the inaccuracies of accelerometers and gyroscopes.
2. It is time saving for post-processing on the controller module or PC.
3. It eliminates the problems/limitations associated with the Euler angles.
4. They process angles in the form of quaternions.

In order to eliminate or reduce the problems of inaccuracies of the sensors, digital filters can be used. The accelerometer is very accurate over long periods of time but is inaccurate for short periods. The gyroscope is just the opposite. Thus, a very easy way to reduce both problems is to join the data from the two sensors, using a complementary filter. This filter combines in a single equation, a low pass filter for the gyroscope and a high pass filter for the accelerometer. Being C, the complement value which can range from 0.0 to 1.0 and dt the sample time, the final angle of each axis (An^t_{axis}) is computed using its previous value (An^{t-1}_{axis}) through $An^t_{axis} = C(An^{t-1}_{axis} + Ga^t_{axis} \times dt) + (1 - C)Aa^t_{axis}$. In this equation, the value of Ga^t_{axis} represents the raw angle computed around each axis, which is obtained from the gyroscope data using $Ga^t_{axis} = \dfrac{Gd_{axis}}{G_{sen}}$. In this later expression, Gd_{axis} represents the raw data around each axis of the gyroscope and G_{sens} the gyroscope sensitivity, which is calculated using $G_{sens} = \dfrac{2^{16}}{G_{range}} = 131.072$, with $G_{range} = 500$ (which represents the range chosen for the gyroscope).

Regarding Aa^t_{axis}, it represents the raw accelerometer angle, that can be calculated around each axis (Aa_x and Aa_y) using $Aa_x = \tan^{-1}\dfrac{Ad_y}{Ad_z} * \dfrac{180}{\pi}$ and $Aa_y = \tan^{-1}\dfrac{Ad_x}{Ad_z} *180 / \text{À}$.

The angle around the z-axis cannot be calculated the same way as the y and x-axes, because the accelerometer computations rely on gravity, that points in the Z direction (i.e. in the z-axis). This is a phenomenon known as Gimbal Lock, a problem/limitation that occurs when working with Euler angles.

This means that the angle around the z-axis (An_z) can only be calculated with the gyroscope, therefore, this angle will suffer from a small drift along time.

The complementary filter algorithm has a simple implementation, is fast and enough efficient. For best results one may employ the Kalman filter (Ristic, Arulampalam, & Gordon, 2004). Though more complex and computationally expensive, it is more efficient. This algorithm relies on all observed values over a predetermined time and estimates the future state of the system based on the previous states.

Despite regarding filters as a good way to obtain a better reliability of the orientation of the sensor over both short and long time periods, their implementation, especially the Kalman filter, may require excessive computational capability, typically unavailable in a simple micro-controller.

Using Euler angles, also induces a negative effect, a problematic phenomenon, known as Gimbal Lock, with a loss of a degree of freedom on a 3-axes system. Gimbal Lock is a mathematical problem associated with Euler angles, impossible to solve. Without introducing too much detail into this phenomenon, this is a real problem that many 3D programs such as games and animation editors try to solve. While Euler angles are the easiest way to get the orientation of the sensor, which are easy to understand and implement, they have limitations and therefore must be avoided.

At this level, the DMP system is of the highest importance. This proprietary system uses the quaternary system, that does not suffer from the same problem as the Euler angles. The quaternion is an alternative way to represent an angle on a 3D space and is represented by $Q = q_w + q_x i + q_y j + q_z k$, where q_x , q_y and q_z translate the values of the position direction vectors and q_w the rotation about this axis, formed by the direction vector. Alternatively, the quaternion Q can also be expressed in a matrix form by:

$$Q = \begin{bmatrix} 1 - 2q_y^2 - 2q_z^2 & 2(q_x q_y - q_z q_w) & 2(q_x q_z - q_y q_w) \\ 2(q_x q_y - q_z q_w) & 1 - 2q_x^2 - 2q_z^2 & 2(q_y q_z - q_x q_w) \\ 2(q_x q_z - q_y q_w) & 2(q_y q_z - q_x q_w) & 1 - 2q_x^2 - 2q_y^2 \end{bmatrix}$$

Hardware

The hardware component of the GyroGlove consists of three major blocks, comprising:

1. Eleven MPU-6000 sensors;
2. Main controller module;
3. Receiver module connected to the PC.

Each IMU sensor has a size of 17 x 23 mm (see Figure 4). The main controller acts as the intermediary interface between the sensors and the application on the PC. It is responsible for programming and configuring all the sensors and to send the data via Bluetooth to the receiver on the PC. It consists of:

1. A Microcontroller, ATMega Atmel 328p (Atmel, 2015), with a 8MHz oscillator.
2. A USB to/from UART converter (FT232RL) that converts the Micro USB port data to the microcontroller and vice versa.

3. One Battery Charger LiPo (MCP73831).
4. A voltage supervisor circuit (BD523G).
5. A LED that emits a warning (to the user) if the battery is low.
6. A Voltage Regulator (TPS13733), that regulates the 5V tension from the USB or battery voltage to the main 3.3V of the circuit.
7. A charge distributor (LTC4413) that provides an automatic way of selecting the power source. When only the battery is connected, only this power source is used in the circuit. When the USB is connected, it becomes the main source power, regardless of how many sources are connected (USB and / or battery).
8. A Bluetooth Module (HC-06).

The receiver is a Bluetooth module similar to that used in the controller, but with the ability to be used as a master device, i.e. it has the initiative to bind to other Bluetooth modules. Similar to the controller circuit, the circuit of the receiver has:

1. A USB to/from UART converter (FT232RL) that converts the USB Micro port data to Bluetooth;
2. A Bluetooth Module.

All modules, PCB controller and receiver, were produced by handmade methods and its description is out of the scope of this article. In figure 6, on the left, the final result of the PCBs are shown and on the right the entire system is shown attached to the glove.

Figure 6. PCB prototypes on left. Assembled prototype glove on the right.

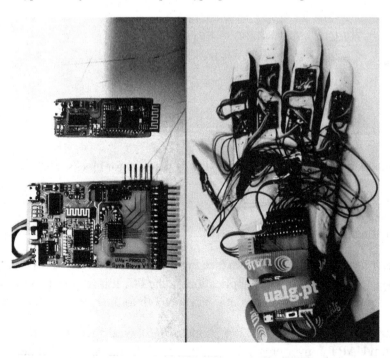

Interface between the GyroGlove and PC Application

The transmission of data to the PC has to be done quickly, to avoid delays between finger's rotations and their representation in the screen (lag). For this reason, as represented in Figure 7, the microcontroller and Bluetooth modules are programmed to use a 115200 bps transmission rate. This is the maximum possible rate allowed by the devices. The limitation is due to the fact that the oscillator (8 MHz) on the micro-controller does not allow higher speeds. For the same reason, the interface between the micro-controller and the sensors communicates at a top speed of 2 MHz SPI. The maximum frequency of the ATMega328P on the SPI interface is 1/4 of the oscillator frequency. These transmission speeds allow the system to update all data on the PC at a frequency of 33.3 Hz, confirmed by various tests.

Similarly to the Game-Book described in the previous section, the PC version of the developed application for the PC was made using Unity3D (Unity, 2015) which, by processing angles in the quaternions form, constitutes an ideal tool to work directly with the data obtained from the IMU sensors. The communication between the PC and the glove is made using an ASCII character oriented data packet, with the format shown in Table 2.

The packet starts with the ASCII character $, followed by the quaternion data X, Y, Z and W. This data is transmitted using four 16-bit fields (i.e. each one with two 8 bit parts, represented by (X_m, X_l), (Y_m, Y_l), (Z_m, Z_l), and (W_m, W_l), where m and l respectively represent the most and less significant parts). They are followed by the index/number of the associated sensor i (as identified in Figure 5 right). Finally, CR and LF respectively represent the Carriage Return and Line Feed codes, signaling the end of the packet.

Figure 7. Communications scheme between the GyroGlove and PC

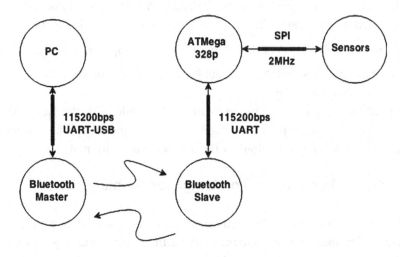

Table 2. Structure of the transmitted packet between the GyroGlove and PC

1 Byte	1 Byte	1 Byte	1 Byte	1 Byte	1 Byte	1 Byte	1 Byte	1 Byte	1 Byte	1 Byte	1 Byte
$	X_m	X_l	Y_m	Y_l	Z_m	Z_l	W_m	W_l	i	CR	LF
	X		Y		Z		W				

The DMP system can compute the exact rotation of each sensor by itself but needs an initial and self-controlled set up configuration. This auto-configuration aims to reduce and possibly eliminate the drift problem caused by the gyroscope, as previously presented. Thus, after the power up of the system, all the sensors enter into an auto-configuration phase that can last between 10 and 20 seconds. When finished, all sensors will be stable, but before that, the extracted rotational data is not usable since it suffers from extreme drift, even if stabilized in the correct orientation.

Afterwards to correct the offset problem it is necessary to know, a priori the state of the rotation of all the sensors, i.e. to position all sensors in a known orientation. Given Q quaternion with an unknown direction, applying $K = Q^{-1} \times Q$, we obtain a quaternion with no rotation, stabilized. In an application on the PC where there are objects that replicate the users' hand orientation, an initialization is required to associate both. Thus, in a process guided by the application, the user places his hand with a certain orientation, before powering up the system. Being i the sensor number and $t1$ the time in which the initial configuration is finished, all rotations of the sensors in time $t1$ are stored in the quaternion U_{it1}. For all subsequent time instants, the user's hand rotation is obtained using $K_i[t] = U_{it1}^{-1} \times S_i[t]$, where $S_i[t]$ represent the data from the sensors, after the initial setup configuration (after $t1$). If the user's hand is not placed with all the sensors stabilized, $K_i[t]$ must be obtained from $K_i[t] = \left(U_{it1}^{-1} \times D_i\right)^{-1} \times S_i[t]$ with D_i being the quaternion with the offset rotation of each sensor that we had before powering up the system.

Thus, at startup, the user should keep his hand as straight as possible on a table or horizontal plane during initial setup configuration. Afterwards $K_i[t] = U_{it1}^{-1} \times S_i[t]$ is applied, avoiding the offset rotations of the sensors, with the exception of the ones positioned on the thumb. In fact, as can be easily seen from Figure 6, right side, when the hand is positioned horizontally on a table, all sensors are straight (without rotation), with the exception of the two sensors in the thumb. In this particular case, it is necessary to estimate the associated rotation of these two sensors and apply $K_i[t] = \left(U_{it1}^{-1} \times D_i\right)^{-1} \times S_i[t]$ to each of them. In this particular case, we opted to apply an initial rotation of $-45°$ to both x and y axis. These values were obtained empirically.

For testing and calibrating purposes, an application was made with the Unity 3D software. This application replicates the position of the user's hand, using a 3D model of a human hand, as shown on figure 8. Examples of four different situations of the user's hand position are shown.

Learning Application of Portuguese Sign Language Alphabet

After testing the GyroGlove with the application described in the last section, a game was developed to help and encourage the learning of a sign language using the GyroGlove. Gestural language is known to be difficult to learn and thus a game intended to help in its learning process could be considered an advantage.

As the GyroGlove only allows the detection of the rotations of all fingers and hand, it cannot be used to learn sign language words, phrases or sentences, but only the sign language alphabet where each letter possess a direct relationship with the hand position and fingers.

Figure 8. Four examples of the user's hand replication on a human 3D model. From left to right and top to bottom. Hand tilted to the left, hand closed, hand straight with index finger pointing.

As the GyroGlove system was developed in Portugal, an alphabet of the Portuguese Sign Language (PSL) was used as the first sign language that this system can recognize. The hand's position of the PSL can be seen in Figure 9, that contains both, the sign language of the alphabet and of the numbers.

Recognition of Sign Language

In order to recognize each of the hand's positions shown in Figure 9, it is necessary to compare all the rotations of the sensors with all rotations associated with a particular letter of the alphabet.

Instead of comparing the quaternion of each sensor, a comparison is made between the quaternion of each two adjacent sensors, pre-defined, as well as the relation of the hand sensor quaternion (number 11 on the glove) with the vertical axis. This last one is used to determine the overall direction of the hand (face up, or down, left etc.).

There are 11 distinct relations identified by R_j (with j ranging from 1 to 11). To determine the relations between each other, it is necessary to compute the angle between each rotation, between all sets of two sensors.

As illustrated by Table 3 and Figure 10, each sensor is associated with another one. For example, sensor n° 8 (Ring Proximal finger) is related to sensor n° 7 and n° 11, which in the following will be identified as relation R_8 and R_7 respectively.

Figure 9. Portuguese Sign Language Alphabet
Adapted from (Vivendo em Silêncio, 2015)

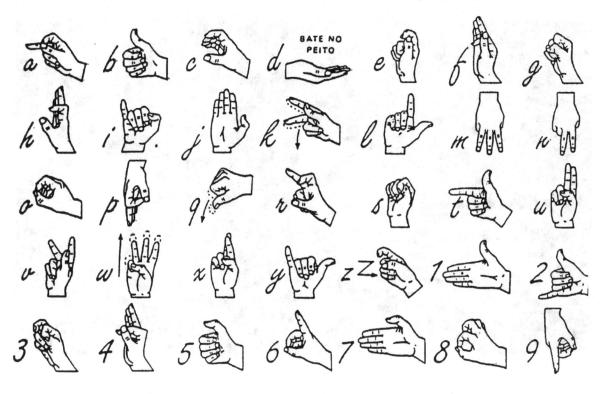

Figure 10. Association between adjacent sensors and vertical axis

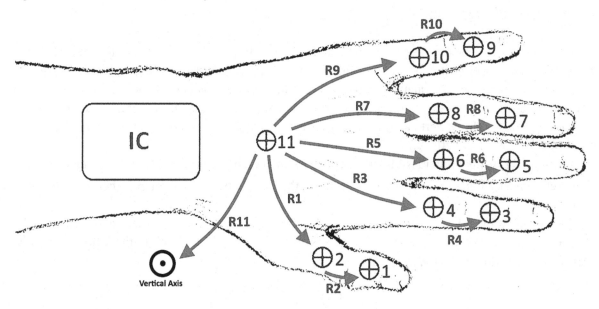

Table 3. Association between sensors for gesture recognition

Sensor	Relation with Sensor ID nº x (R_x)
ID: 1 – Thumb Distal	2 (R_2)
ID: 2 – Thumb Intermediate	1 (R_2) 11 (R_1)
ID: 3 – Index Intermediate	4 (R_4)
ID: 4 – Index Proximal	3 (R_4) 11 (R_3)
ID: 5 – Middle Intermediate	6 (R_6)
ID: 6 – Middle Proximal	5 (R_6) 11 (R_5)
ID: 7 – Ring Intermediate	8 (R_8)
ID: 8 – Ring Proximal	7 (R_8) 11 (R_7)
ID: 9 – Pinky Intermediate	10 (R_{10})
ID: 10 – Pinky Proximal	9 (R_{10}) 11 (R_9)
ID: 11 – Hand	2 (R_3) 4 (R_3) 6 (R_5) 8 (R_7) 10 (R_9) Vertical Vector (R_{11})

As a quaternion defines a rotation and not a vector in space, it is necessary to apply the rotation of each quaternion to a known vector $\vec{V}_{front} = (0,0,1)$. Applying $\vec{V}_i = K_i \times \vec{V}_{front}$, results in $\vec{V}_i$, which is a vector with the rotation of K_i (raw quaternion data obtained from the sensors).

After obtaining $\vec{V}_i$, the vector defining the orientation in 3D space of each sensor, it is necessary to calculate the absolute, shorter angle between each two orientation vectors. This angle is computed using the relation between each sensor pair, applying $A_j = \left| \arccos \dfrac{\vec{V}_n . \vec{V}_m}{\left\| \vec{V}_n \right\| . \left\| \vec{V}_m \right\|} \times \dfrac{180}{\pi} \right|$ for each set of two sensors (shown in Table 3 and Figure 10). A_j represents the angle in degrees formed between each set of sensors n and m (with $n, m = \{1, \dots, 11\}$) and also between the main hand sensor (sensor nº11) and the vertical vector $\vec{V}_{up} = (0,1,0)$. Angles A_j can range from $0°$ o $180°$.

To identify the hand's position, it is firstly necessary to record these positions, calculating the angles between each sensor A_j and its reference. To do it, for each letter of the alphabet, $l = \{a, \dots, z\}$, both the maximum angle $S_{max_{j,l}} = \max\limits_{t-\Delta_{sample} \leq w \leq 0} A_j[w]$ and minimum angle $S_{min_{j,l}} = \min\limits_{t-\Delta_{sample} \leq w \leq 0} A_j[w]$ are computed. In order to be validated, the hand's position needs to hold a certain association with a letter for Δ_{sample} seconds.

Whenever new hand data is available, in K_i, all current vector angles, A_j, are calculated. Then for each letter l and during a minimum period of time ($\Delta ts = 1s$, defined empirically) it is verified if every angle falls between $S_{min_{j,l}}$ and $S_{max_{j,l}}$. In order to allow an adjustment of the detection sensitivity a margin value was introduced. Thus, after analyzing all the data A_j a positive gesture detection is considered if $S_{min_{j,l}} - \Delta_m \leq A_j \leq S_{max_{j,l}} + \Delta_m$ is verified during a Δts period of time (Δ_m set to 20).

Implemented Game for the Learning of Sign Language Alphabets

Figure 11 presents the Serious Game that was developed for the learning of the sign language alphabet. The interface consists of 4 parts: (1) the letter and hand's position of the corresponding image, (2) a visual input of the hand's position replicated in a 3D human model, (3) a scoring system and (4) a level bar to indicate how close the user is standing next to the goal.

When the users play with the application, random letters are dynamically shown. The user then has to replicate the image shown in the right side. Eventually when he is well succeeded, the system scores the associated result, according with the time spent to do the associated letter and the correctness of the hand's position.

CONCLUSION

In this chapter we made a review of the current trends and developments in Serious Games, with a special focus in Education. The details of two real implementations help illustrate the technologies that could be involved in the creation of these games and its applicability to very distinct and innovative fields.

In the first of these examples we showcase the educational g-book prototype for the curriculum of "Environmental Studies", created for children in a 4th grade program. This g-book concept has the potential to challenge students to become actively involved in the educational process, as it allows students to try different routes and distinguish what is important from what is secondary, enabling them to create and

Figure 11. Game for learning stimulation of alphabet sign language. The user is encouraged to replicate the hand position.

annotate material from various sources, while also encourages the exploration of new issues. These are, however, aspects that need to be investigated and validated by future research in the educational context.

In the second example a serious game was developed for learning the sign language alphabet, combining hardware and software. The game prototype was tested, demonstrating a high level of accuracy in the recognition of the letters inserted by users.

FUTURE RESEARCH DIRECTIONS

There is an enormous potential in integrating games with the solutions that already support collaboration and interactivity, not only to make them become more engaging, but also behavior-changing. Serious Games can be used to help people think differently, in a more integrated, holistic way, as required in complex solutions.

In order to achieve it, more research needs to be done into how Serious Games can develop better students and professionals, make teams more productive and make applications become more collaborative.

The solutions presented in this chapter highlight the potential of Serious Games, in education. In future these solutions need to be tested, to verify their effectiveness.

REFERENCES

2020 Energy. (2015). Retrieved from http://www.2020energy.eu/game

Asaolu, O. S. (2012). International Evaluation of a Localized Geography Educational Software. *African Journal of Computing & ICT*, *5*(4).

Atmel. (2015). *Atmel.* Retrieved from www.atmel.com/devices/atmega328p.aspx

Backlund, P., & Hendrix, M. (2013, September). Educational games - Are they worth the effort? A literature survey of the effectiveness of serious games. *Proceedings of the 2013 5th International Conference on Games and Virtual Worlds for Serious Applications (VS-GAMES).*

Bidarra, J., Figueiredo, M. J. G., & Natálio, C. (2014, November 13-14). Designing eBook Interaction for Mobile and Contextual Learning. *Proc. of 2014 International Conference on Interactive Mobile Communication Technologies and Learning*, Thessaloniki, Greece (pp. 11-19). doi:10.1109/IMCTL.2014.7011095

Bidarra, J., Figueiredo, M. J. G., Valadas, S., & Vilhena, C. (2012, November 8-9). O gamebook como modelo pedagógico: desenvolvimento de um livro interativo para a plataforma iPad. *Proc. of 6th International Conference on Digital Arts*, Faro, Portugal (pp. 373-376).

Blackman, S. (2005, February). Serious games ... and less! *Computer Graphics*, *39*(1), 12–16. doi:10.1145/1057792.1057802

Brown, J. S., Collins, A., & Duguid, P. (1989). Situated cognition and the culture. *Educational Researcher*, *18*(1), 32–42. doi:10.3102/0013189X018001032

Chow, A. F., Woodford, K. C., & Maes, J. (2011). Deal or No Deal: Using games to improve student learning, retention and decision-making. *International Journal of Mathematical Education in Science and Technology*, *42*(2), 259–264. doi:10.1080/0020739X.2010.519796

Connolly, T. M., Stansfield, M., & Hainey, T. (2011). An alternate reality game for language learning: ARGuing for multilingual motivation. *Computers & Education*, *57*(1), 1389–1415. doi:10.1016/j.compedu.2011.01.009

Gee, J. P. (2003). *What video games have to teach us about learning and literacy*. New York: Palgrave Macmillan.

Gomoll, A. H., O'Toole, R. V., Czarnecki, J., & Warner, J. J. (2007). Surgical experience correlates with performance on a virtual reality simulator for shoulder arthroscopy. *The American Journal of Sports Medicine*, *35*(6), 883–888. doi:10.1177/0363546506296521 PMID:17261572

Gomoll, A. H., Pappas, G., Forsythe, B., & Warner, J. J. (2008). Individual Skill Progression on a Virtual Reality Simulator for Shoulder Arthroscopy A 3-Year Follow-up Study. *The American Journal of Sports Medicine*, *36*(6), 1139–1142. doi:10.1177/0363546508314406 PMID:18326032

Gresse von Wangenheim, C., Thiry, M., & Kochanski, D. (2009). Empirical evaluation of an educational game on software measurement. *Empirical Software Engineering*, *14*(4), 418–452. doi:10.1007/s10664-008-9092-6

Huang, C.-C., Yeh, T.-K., Li, T.-Y., & Chang, C.-Y. (2010). The idea storming cube: Evaluating the effects of using game and computer agent to support divergent thinking. *Journal of Educational Technology & Society*, *13*(4), 180–191.

Huizenga, J., Admiraal, W., Akkerman, S., & ten Dam, G. (2009). Mobile game-based learning in secondary education: Engagement, motivation and learning in a mobile city game. *Journal of Computer Assisted Learning*, *25*(4), 332–344. doi:10.1111/j.1365-2729.2009.00316.x

InvenSense. (2015). Invensense. Retrieved from www.invensense.com

Johnson, S. (2005). *Everything bad is good for you: How today's popular culture is actually making us smarter*. New York: Riverhead Books.

Kablan, Z. (2010). The Effect of Using Exercise-Based Computer Games during the Process of Learning on Academic Achievement among Education Majors. *Educational Sciences: Theory and Practice*, *10*(1), 351–364.

Ke, F. (2008). Computer games application within alternative classroom goal structures: Cognitive, metacognitive, and affective evaluation. *Educational Technology Research and Development*, *56*(5), 539–556. doi:10.1007/s11423-008-9086-5

Ke, F., & Grabowski, B. (2007). Gameplaying for maths learning: Cooperative or not? *British Journal of Educational Technology*, *38*(2), 249–259. doi:10.1111/j.1467-8535.2006.00593.x

Kelly, H., Howell, K., Glinert, E., Holding, L., Swain, C., Burrowbridge, A., & Roper, M. (2007). How to Build Serious Games. *Communications of the ACM*, *50*(7), 44–49. doi:10.1145/1272516.1272538

Kennedy-Clark, S., & Thompson, K. (2011). What Do Students Learn When Collaboratively Using A Computer Game in the Study of Historical Disease Epidemics, and Why? *Games and Culture, 6*(6), 513–537. doi:10.1177/1555412011431361

Kirriemur, J., & McFarlane, A. (2004). *Literature review in games and learning. NESTA Futurelab Series*. Bristol: NESTA Futurelab.

Klopfer, E. (2008). *Augmented Learning*. Cambridge, Massachusetts: The MIT Press. doi:10.7551/mitpress/9780262113151.001.0001

Kordaki, M. (2011). A computer card game for the learning of basic aspects of the binary system in primary education: Design and pilot evaluation. *Education and Information Technologies, 16*(4), 395–421. doi:10.1007/s10639-010-9136-6

Leap Motion. (2015). Leap Motion Sensor. Retrieved from www.leapmotion.com

Liao, C. C. Y., Chen, Z.-H., Cheng, H. N. H., Chen, F.-C., & Chan, T.-W. (2011). My-Mini-Pet: A handheld pet-nurturing game to engage students in arithmetic practices. *Journal of Computer Assisted Learning, 27*(1), 76–89. doi:10.1111/j.1365-2729.2010.00367.x

Liu, T.-Y., Tan, T.-H., & Chu, Y.-L. (2009). Outdoor natural science learning with an RFID-supported immersive ubiquitous learning environment. *Journal of Educational Technology & Society, 12*(4), 161–175.

Macedonia, M. (2009). Virtual worlds: A new reality for treating posttraumatic stress disorder. *IEEE Computer Graphics and Applications, 29*(1), 86–88. doi:10.1109/MCG.2009.18 PMID:19363961

Main, S., & O'Rourke, J. (2011). New Directions for Traditional Lessons: Can Handheld Game Consoles Enhance Mental Mathematics Skills? *Australian Journal of Teacher Education, 36*(2), 4. doi:10.14221/ajte.2011v36n2.4

Mayo, M. (2007). Games for Science and Engineering Education. *Communications of the ACM, 50*(7), 31–35. doi:10.1145/1272516.1272536

Microsoft. (2015). Kinect for windows. Retrieved from www.microsoft.com/en-us/kinectforwindows

Munguba, M. C., Valdes, M. T. M., & da Silva, C. A. B. (2008). The application of an occupational therapy nutrition education programme for children who are obese. *Occupational Therapy International, 15*(1), 56–70. doi:10.1002/oti.244 PMID:18288771

Numrich, S. K. (2008). Culture, models, and games: Incorporating warfare's human dimension. *IEEE Intelligent Systems, 23*(4), 58–61. doi:10.1109/MIS.2008.63

Occipital (2015). Structure sensor. Retrieved from www.structure.io

Panoutsopoulos, H., & Sampson, D. G. (2012). A Study on Exploiting Commercial Digital Games into School Context. *Journal of Educational Technology & Society, 15*(1), 15–27.

Papastergiou, M. (2009). Digital Game-Based Learning in high school Computer Science education: Impact on educational effectiveness and student motivation. *Computers & Education, 52*(1), 1–12. doi:10.1016/j.compedu.2008.06.004

Piirainen–Marsh, A., & Tainio, L. (2009). Collaborative Game-play as a Site for Participation and Situated Learning of a Second Language. *Scandinavian Journal of Educational Research, 53*(2), 167–183. doi:10.1080/00313830902757584

Positech Games.(2015). *Democracy 2* [Game]. Retrieved from http://positech.co.uk/democracy2/

Prensky, M. (2001). *Digital game-based learning*. New York: McGraw Hill.

President Forever. (2015). Retrieved from http://270soft.com/us-election-games/president-election-game-2016/

Qin, J., Chui, Y.-P., Pang, W.-M., Choi, K.-S., & Heng, P.-A. (2010). Learning blood management in orthopedic surgery through gameplay. *IEEE Computer Graphics and Applications, 30*(2), 45–57. doi:10.1109/MCG.2009.83 PMID:20650710

Rego, P., Moreira, P. M., & Reis, L. P. (2010, June). Serious games for rehabilitation: A survey and a classification towards a taxonomy. *Proceedings of the 5th Iberian Conference on Information Systems and Technologies (CISTI)* (pp. 1-6).

Ristic, B., Arulampalam, S., and Gordon, N. (2004). Beyond the Kalman filter: Particle filters for tracking applications (Vol. 685). Boston: Artech house.

Rosas, R., Nussbaum, M., Cumsille, P., Marianov, V., Correa, M., Flores, P., & López, V. et al. (2003). Beyond Nintendo: Design and assessment of educational video games for first and second grade students. *Computers & Education, 40*(1), 71–94. doi:10.1016/S0360-1315(02)00099-4

Sawyer, B. (2008). From cells to cell processors: The integration of health and video games. *IEEE Computer Graphics and Applications, 28*(6), 83–85. doi:10.1109/MCG.2008.114 PMID:19004688

Sindre, G., Natvig, L., & Jahre, M. (2009). Experimental validation of the learning effect for a pedagogical game on computer fundamentals. *IEEE Transactions on Education, 52*(1), 10–18. doi:10.1109/TE.2007.914944

Squire, K., & Jenkins, H. (2003). Harnessing the power of games in education. *Insight (American Society of Ophthalmic Registered Nurses), 3*(1), 7–33.

Sung, Y.-T., Chang, K.-E., & Lee, M.-D. (2008). Designing multimedia games for young children's taxonomic concept development. *Computers & Education, 50*(3), 1037–1051. doi:10.1016/j.compedu.2006.07.011

Tüzün, H. (2007). Blending video games with learning: Issues and challenges with classroom implementations in the Turkish context. *British Journal of Educational Technology, 38*(3), 465–477. doi:10.1111/j.1467-8535.2007.00710.x

Tüzün, H., Yılmaz-Soylu, M., Karakuş, T., İnal, Y., & Kızılkaya, G. (2009). The effects of computer games on primary school students' achievement and motivation in geography learning'. *Computers & Education, 52*(1), 68–77. doi:10.1016/j.compedu.2008.06.008

Unity. (2015). Unity 3D. Retrieved from https://unity3d.com

Virvou, M., Katsionis, G., & Manos, K. (2005). Combining software games with education: Evaluation of its educational effectiveness'. *Journal of Educational Technology & Society*, *8*, 54–65.

Vivendo em Silêncio. (2015). Dactiologia Portuguesa. Retrieved from https://vivendoemsilencio.files. wordpress.com/2010/07/dactl-lgp.jpg

von Wangenheim, C. G., & Shull, F. (2009). To game or not to game? *IEEE Software*, *26*(2), 92–94. doi:10.1109/MS.2009.54

Wang, T.-H. (2008). Web-based quiz-game-like formative assessment: Development and evaluation. *Computers & Education*, *51*(3), 1247–1263. doi:10.1016/j.compedu.2007.11.011

Weibel, R., Bleisch, S., Nebiker, S., Fisler, J., Grossmann, T., Niederhuber, M., & Hurni, L. et al. (2009). Achieving more sustainable elearning programs for GIScience. *Geomatica*, *63*, 109–118.

Westera, W., Nadolski, R. J., Hummel, H. G. K., & Wopereis, I. G. J. H. (2008). Serious Games for higher education: A framework for reducing design complexity. *Computer Assisted Learning*, *24*(5), 420–432. doi:10.1111/j.1365-2729.2008.00279.x

Wilson, A., Dehaene, S., Pinel, P., Revkin, S., Cohen, L., & Cohen, D. (2006). Principles underlying the design of "The Number Race", an adaptive computer game for remediation of dyscalculia'. *Behavioral and Brain Functions*, *2*(1), 1–14. doi:10.1186/1744-9081-2-1 PMID:16734905

Xtion. (2015). Asus Xtion Pro Live. Retrieved from www.asus.com/Multimedia/Xtion_PRO_LIVE

Yang, Y.-T. C. (2012). Building virtual cities, inspiring intelligent citizens: Digital games for developing students' problem solving and learning motivation. *Computers & Education*, *59*(2), 365–377. doi:10.1016/j.compedu.2012.01.012

Zyda, M. (2007). Creating a Science of Games: Introduction. *Communications of the ACM*, *50*(7), 26–29. doi:10.1145/1272516.1272535

KEY TERMS AND DEFINITIONS

Augmented Reality: Real time integration between digital information, with live video and the user's environment.

Body Gesture Sensors: A sensor that is used to acquire the position of body gestures.

eBook: An electronic book that integrates text, images or video.

Educational Game: A computer game used for education purposes.

Gamified Books: An electronic book that integrates text, images or video, with a computer game.

Inertial Measurement Unit (IMU) Sensor: An electronic device capable of measuring various types of inertial forces.

Sign Language Alphabet Learning: The process of learning a visually perceived language that is based on a naturally evolved system of articulated hand gestures which translate alphabet letters.

Chapter 17

User Interfaces in Smart Assistive Environments:
Requirements, Devices, Applications

Laura Raffaeli
Università Politecnica delle Marche, Italy

Ennio Gambi
Università Politecnica delle Marche, Italy

Laura Montanini
Università Politecnica delle Marche, Italy

Susanna Spinsante
Università Politecnica delle Marche, Italy

ABSTRACT

Assistive environments are primarily designed to support the healthy and independent living of ageing people. Elderly are often perceived as being resistant to technology; in reality, many of them are willing to accept novel digital technologies into their lives, and to take advantage of what technology has to offer. The "not worth it" impression, on the other hand, is more likely to be triggered by unusable interfaces, that prevent the older users from perceiving technology as both usable and useful. This motivates the need of investigating suitable guidelines for the design of user-system interfaces in the field of smart assistive environments, for which elderly are the typical target users. Focusing on two specific physical user-system interfaces, i.e. smart TVs and touchscreen devices, this chapter discusses the requirements that a design for older users has to address. The theoretical discussion is supported by experimental results gained from an Ambient Assisted Living project carried out by the authors, discussed as a use case in the last part of the chapter.

INTRODUCTION

Within the wide field of Human-Computer Interfaces (HCI), this chapter is going to discuss the specific and peculiar aspects related to the interaction between users and a "smart assistive environment".

Population ageing is taking place in nearly all the countries of the world. Ageing results from decreasing mortality, and, especially in developed countries, from declining fertility. This process leads to a relative reduction in the proportion of children, and to an increase in the share of people in the main working ages and of older persons in the population. The global share of older people (aged 60 years or

DOI: 10.4018/978-1-5225-0435-1.ch017

over) increased from 9.2% in 1990, to 11.7% in 2013, and will continue to grow as a proportion of the world population, reaching 21.1% by 2050 (United Nations, 2013).

Ageing has profound consequences on a broad range of economic, political and social processes. First and foremost is the increasing priority to promoting the wellbeing of the older people, in most countries of the world. Indeed, already in 2002, the Madrid International Plan of Action (MIPAA), adopted at the Second World Assembly on Ageing, emphasized that older persons should be able to participate in, and benefit equitably, from the fruits of development to advance their health and wellbeing, and that societies should provide enabling environments for them to do so (United Nations, 2002).

The need of sustaining the relevant part of population represented by older adults, from a social and an economical point of view, asks for new approaches: a market segment including people aged 50 and older emerges, the so-called gray market or silver market, challenging companies and societies (Kohlbacher & Herstatt, 2011) with new requests and needs. Within this market, an important role is expected to be played by assistive technologies, to help ageing people maintaining their ability in performing the activities of daily living (ADLs) and, therefore, their independence (Memon, Wagner, Pedersen, Beevi, & Hansen, 2014).

However, in order to make the new technologies really useful for this purpose, it is necessary to first analyze the requirements of the users. Specifically, interaction modalities and interfaces should be properly designed to encourage the older user to approach new technologies, and to stimulate user's wish to benefit from the available tools.

Among the possible tools for user interaction, two categories of devices, touchscreen devices and smart TVs, are addressed in this chapter, discussing their main features, advantages and disadvantages, and the related usability issues. These devices are the ones selected for the use case proposed by the authors. The research project fits in the field of Ambient Assisted Living (AAL), and proposes an architecture for assistive environments, in which interaction is managed by means of multimodal interfaces suitable also for the elderly. The target platform consists of an integrated architecture offering several services, aimed at improving the quality of life, supporting independent and active ageing of subjects living at home alone.

BACKGROUND

Assistive technologies have the potential to play a key role to help ageing people performing their daily activities at home, and thus maintaining their independence. This is a relevant issue, as globally, 40% of older persons aged 60 years or over live independently, that is to say, alone or with their spouse only. Independent living is far more common in the developed countries, where about three quarters of older persons live independently, compared with only a quarter in developing countries, and one eighth in the least developed countries. As countries develop and their populations continue to age, living alone or with a spouse only will likely become much more common among older people in the future.

As a result of the increase in life expectancy, however, the need to create a protected and safe environment that allows the elderly people to best use their motor and cognitive skills is becoming gradually more obvious.

As already stated, from the technology point of view, AAL and Ambient Intelligence (AI) will support new generations of older adults, for longer and improved quality living. Several public institutions, at a national and wider level, are carrying on specific initiatives to promote the flourishing of new actors in the silver market, to create sustainable economic systems able to offer AAL products, services and solutions, to face the emerging needs, such as the European Ambient Assisted Living Joint Programme (AAL Joint Programme, 2014).

The real benefits of new technologies, however, rely on the impact of ageing on the technology access. Czaja (2005) argues that, to ensure that older people are able to successfully use the new solutions, it is necessary to identify the problems that may be encountered and consequently provide an efficient design of the system. As for any device or product that aims to be brought to the market, the design of the user-device interaction plays a fundamental role. This is further emphasized when dealing with solutions targeting older users or consumers, due to their specific requirements, needs, and habits. Comorbidity that typically affects elderly patients as a result of the natural ageing process, or physical impairments (motor, visual, hearing, and so on), may generate a number of physical and/or cognitive limitations that can possibly prevent older users from efficiently performing some basic operations, which are common and natural when interacting with technological platforms.

Important elements to evaluate, when selecting the methods to interface the system, especially in an AAL context, are the acceptance of new devices by the users and their willingness to use them. Older adults could have difficulty in learning to use new technologies, or simply reject the idea of introducing new equipment in their home environment and change their habits.

The challenge is therefore to develop systems, devices and interfaces that older people can use easily, intuitively and independently in their home environment, without having to face the difficulties of learning the smart home systems, and without feeling forced to change their lifestyles. Elderly people have a multitude of devices available to approach the technology, thus a fundamental point is the choice of the most suitable tools of interaction, depending on the application and the target users.

Several studies have analyzed the relationship between older people and technology. Positive results were detected in the interaction with everyday devices, such as television or microwave ovens (Coleman, Gibson, Hanson, Bobrowicz, & Mckay, 2010), but not with more sophisticated devices. In general, older people have positive attitudes towards products and technologies they really need (Fisk, Rogers, Charness, Czaja, & Sharit, 2009). A further investigation, carried out by Morris, Goodman, and Brading (2007) about the use of computers and the Internet by older users, supports this view, showing that the most common reason for not wanting to learn using the computer is that they are simply not interested. That is, normally, the elderly do not want to make the effort to learn to use a new technology if it is not strictly necessary. The objective is, therefore, to realize a system which is user-friendly, as intuitive as possible, and that delivers a real benefit in older people's lives. This concept is considered as a key point also in a document delivered by the AAL Association (Nedopil, Schauber, & Glende, 2013), in which some general advices for the design of products and services for seniors are summarized:

- **Provide Additional Value:** Seniors' decisions to use a specific product or technology depend on the associated perceived future advantages (Melenhorst, Rogers & Bouwhuis, 2006), such as safety or comfort. It is recommend to clarify how users can benefit from the solution actually delivered to him.
- **Provide Adaptable Support:** According to Lawton (1999), technical solutions are successful only if they address individual abilities very precisely. The individual activation of modular components that can be used for different services, allows easy, inexpensive adaptability and extension.

- **Keep it Simple:** The design of clear menus and structures, and the provision of essential functions, reduce the complexity of learning and using the technological tool. On the other hand, attractive design is appealing also to older people.
- **Enable a Joyful Experience:** In order to encourage the users to use AAL solutions, it is useful to provide an enjoyable experience (Ryu, Kim, & Lee, 2009), also because emotionally positive experiences become more important as people grow older.

Other aspects to consider in the design phase of interfaces for AAL systems are the security and privacy issues.

To provide an adequate response to users' needs, AAL systems typically rely on the collection of big amounts of personal data, from which relevant knowledge on the user's habits is originated. Such a process is critical and necessary to enable the automatic detection of anomalous events, and a prompt reaction to them, according to the level of risk and danger estimated. Collecting and processing of personal data, like health-related data, or data about the person's habits and preferences, like those collected by environmental sensors, raise serious issues about privacy protection. National legal frameworks, which define comprehensive requirements for data privacy, apply to AAL systems too. Adherence to such requirements needs new organizational and technical solutions, if compared to conventional IT security tools, due to specific constraints. As a matter of fact, most of the devices (sensors, actuators) integrated in AAL platforms are significantly limited (with respect to common PC platforms) in terms of processing resources, power availability, and transmission capacity. They must devote the available energy and computation capabilities to the execution of core functionalities; as a consequence, supporting security and authentication-related tasks becomes a quite challenging issue (Trappe, Howard, & Moore, 2015).

Despite the design challenges, however, both security and privacy aspects play an important role in the successful adoption of assistive technologies in the home environment. The user's perception of security, strongly depends on his/her conditions (e.g. health, level of autonomy and independence): as reported by Wilkowska and Ziefle (2012), healthy adults require, and insist on, the highest security and privacy standards, compared with the ailing elderly.

Focusing on HCI, the main issue is the prevention of unauthorized users from accessing the information and interfacing with the system. In fact, if a malicious user is able to gain access to the assistive technologies, he might be able not only to collect sensitive information on user habits, but also to interfere practically, by sending commands to the assisted environment through actuators. This represents a clear and considerable threat for the elderly that would be exposed to significant risks, getting damages instead of benefit from the technology. Therefore, the capability to implement data protection and user authentication in the communication between system and interfaces is another important aspect in the choice and design of the interfaces.

SYSTEM USER INTERFACES

The following sub-sections focus on the two interface devices employed in the assistive environment described by the authors: smart TV and touchscreen devices.

Technology offers a great variety of different tools to enable HCI, however, some of them seems to be not suitable, such as the computer. It is generally considered as a complex device to use for elderly and the interaction by means of the mouse is difficult, because it requires precise movements of the wrist (Chaparro et al., 2000).

Alternatively, Holzinger (2003) states that the touchscreen is one of the most natural technologies. As for elderly, one of the problems is the dimension of items such as buttons and text, however this feature can be controlled via software.

The TV, on the other hand, is one of the most familiar home equipment, and this can help to overcome the fear about technology and the unwillingness to interact with it.

Smart TV

Smart TVs, with respect to traditional TVs, incorporate additional features by combining broadcasting and Internet, and change the usual idea of interaction, by allowing the active participation of users. These tools provide applications, video contents, multimedia, convergence or intelligent services, as well as evolve into a device that serves as a digital hub for households.

The TV is one of the most common home appliances, and the commercial spreading of smart TVs is increasing. According to market forecasts, they will account for 73% of global flat screen TV shipments by 2017, up from just 33% in 2013 (Business Insider, 2014).

Among the several devices supporting user driven interaction, the employment of the smart TV in an assisted environment is motivated by the usually limited experience of elderly with personal computers or portable devices and the need for simplified and intuitive controllers.

In fact, even if nowadays the technology is offering numerous applications, aiming to facilitate the daily life, elder people remain technology-fearful. They often believe that HCI is complex and that they lack both knowledge and the required experience. However, most elder people would benefit from the use of typical Internet Technologies, like video-conference, news reading, or message exchange with both relatives, friends, and social or health services.

The use of the smart TV does not require specific technical skills, and the interaction is simple, familiar, and intuitive. Thanks to these features, it is expected that the learning process will be very short and, thus, will be taken up positively by the users.

Despite the widespread of smart TVs, there is no industry standard, so each vendor offers various services and applications on different platforms. This causes additional costs and work to develop, because for any application or service, it is required to build a different version for each platform.

The platform selected in the project discussed by the authors mainly includes a specific operating system, which manages the several modules needed to carry out the basic functions related to the TV set and to enable the execution of interactive applications. Developers can create their personalised applications by downloading the Software Development Kit (SDK) on the PC. Several functionalities can be implemented, also thanks to the specific Application Programming Interface (API) provided by the manufacturer. These include, for example, the possibility to let the smart TV communicate with other devices connected to the same home network, or to save configuration data in an internal file of the TV. Once the development of an application is completed, it may be automatically retrieved and downloaded on the smart TV by means of a web server, for the normal execution.

The security problems for smart TVs are still an open issue of current great interest. In fact, smart TVs use the same operating systems and software stacks as regular PCs, so they are vulnerable to similar software-based attacks, but security updates are provided much less frequently. Therefore, these devices introduce new risks to users' security and privacy because they are becoming a valuable target for criminals. According to Michele and Karpow (2014), this is due to the following reasons: smart TVs are becoming increasingly widespread; the use of standard libraries with known vulnerabilities makes it easier for attackers to develop exploits and malwares; smart TVs with built-in cameras and microphones are placed in sensitive environments, such as private houses, but also conference rooms. Availability of powerful hardware and fast Internet connections further increases their attractiveness. The target features of attackers are for example the apps, the web browser, the media player, and the voice commands.

Until recently, manufacturers did not worry about the security problems and users were often not aware of them. Now they are making some progress toward the analysis of the countermeasures to be adopted to prevent attacks. Besides the application of security features to new products, it is important that the devices support software updates, in order to maintain the same level of security each time new vulnerabilities are discovered.

Referring to the user interaction, the fundamental tool to interact with the smart TV is the remote control. On one hand, this brings a number of advantages, due to the ease of use and the familiarity for all categories of users. On the other hand, the remote control is not very functional when dealing with operations that require many steps, such as text input or browsing the available contents. For this reason it is better to limit transitions from one page to another, to avoid the need of moving backward and forward among pages, and, at the same time, try to make the navigation through the contents easy and intuitive. Another trick is to limit the use of the remote control to the arrows keys and Enter/Return keys.

Finally, for smart TV equipment supporting voice recognition, it is possible to define a set of custom commands and associate them to the corresponding browsing or control functions. People with motor difficulties could exploit this facility.

Touchscreen Devices

Touchscreen technology is currently very popular in the market. Touchscreen devices are characterized by very different screen shapes and sizes, such as tablet, smartphones and fixed touchscreens.

Typically, they have the advantage of being intuitive to use, computationally powerful, personal, provided with high-resolution screens, rich of sensors (e.g. cameras, accelerometers and GPS) and wireless interfaces (e.g. Near Field Communication (NFC), WiFi, Bluetooth), and mostly portable.

However, each device has distinct features and offers specific advantages, so it is important to choose the right one according to the user's needs. Fixed touchscreens, due to large size, are particularly suitable for visually impaired subjects, but cannot be moved easily. Conversely, smartphones have very small dimensions and consequently great portability. However, they are not appropriate for users with visual problems or poor motor skills. Tablets, instead, ensure mobility and acceptable screen size, thus featuring a good compromise among the other devices.

As Greenstein and Arnaud (1998) state, the most obvious advantage of touchscreen technology is that the input is also the output device. This is a great benefit for the elderly, since they normally suffer from age-related attentional decline. Moreover, such a technology does not require an advanced mental model, so it is considered an easier approach than classical HCI, based on separate input and output devices, such as mouse and keyboard. Bhalla and Bhalla (2010) discuss the advantages and disadvantages of using touchscreens over other pointing devices, as summarized in Table I.

Table 1. Advantages and disadvantages in using touchscreens over other pointing device According to Bhalla and Bhalla (2010)

Advantages	Disadvantages
• Touching a visual display of choices requires little thinking and is easy to learn. • Touchscreens are the fastest pointing devices. • Touchscreens have easier hand-eye coordination than mice or keyboards. • No extra work space is required as with other pointing devices. • Touchscreens are durable in public access and in high volume usage.	• User's hand may obscure the screen. • Screens need to be installed at a lower position and tilted to reduce arm fatigue. • Some reduction in image brightness may occur. • They cost more than alternative devices. • Screens get very dirty. • These devices require massive computing power which leads to slow devices and low battery life. • Touchscreen devices usually have no additional keys: when an application crashes, you can't get to the main menu as the whole screen becomes unresponsive.

Among them, the first advantage, i.e. ease to learn and requiring little thinking, is probably the most important and the one which enabled the widespread use of touchscreen devices. Although very useful and widely adopted by the young, such a technology may be inadequate for older adults (Cullen, Dolphin, Delaney, & Fitzpatrick, 2008). Indeed, unlike the interaction based on the remote control of the smart TV, to which elderly users are already accustomed, touch devices are, in most cases, a new technology, never used before.

Burkhard and Koch (2012) show that, among 30 interviewed elderly subjects, the majority expressed the acceptance of using touch, preferring, however, large screen sizes and lightweight tablet. Another study, conducted by Mohadisdudis and Ali (2014), reports on the barriers to smartphone usage among the elderly. In such a survey 21 subjects aged 60 and above were interviewed in order to collect information about their demographics, experiences and perceived barriers in using smartphones.

Although the objective of that paper is not to identify usability problems, but rather to understand why the elderly prefer to use mobile phones less advanced than smartphones, however some interesting considerations can be inferred.

Firstly, the respondents tend to use the mobile device only for calls and they are not interested or able to carry out more advanced features. For example, not all the interviewees were able to read or write text. One of the reasons is the visual impairment, which is a factor of great importance, especially considering that in a smartphone the font size is significantly reduced compared to other devices. Laziness, lack of interest or knowledge, and mild cognitive impairments are additional barriers to their use.

Some of the respondents defined the smartphone "unnecessary", while others indicated that having a mobile device able to call makes them feel safe, allowing to reach their families. From these statements, it can be seen that the introduction of a new device, never used before, such as a touchscreen device, can be accepted by the elderly only if it provides real benefits and suits their physical and cognitive skills, as mentioned in the "Background" Section. For this reasons, interaction via touch devices, despite being a new technology, fits well as an interface to the smart home or assistive environment. In fact, it is easier to use than other pointing methods and it may bring significant benefit to the lives of the elderly, allowing them to control and monitor the entire house through a few simple gestures, and making them feel safe and at ease.

Nevertheless, the touchscreen interface design requires particular attention because it has to adapt to the particular needs of older users. Consequently, during the design phase of the user interface, usability and acceptability criteria must be considered.

USABILITY

In the design phase of a multimedia consumer product, it is necessary to consider issues related to usability, defined by ISO 9241 (ISO, 1998) as: "The effectiveness, efficiency and satisfaction with which specified users achieve specified goals in particular environments", meaning (W3C Consortium):

- **Effectiveness:** The accuracy and completeness with which users can achieve specified goals in particular environments.
- **Efficiency:** The resources expended in relation to the accuracy and completeness of goals achieved.
- **Satisfaction:** The comfort and acceptability of the work system to its users and other people affected by its use.

In this context, we talk about usability referring to satisfactory interaction for the user, both in terms of efficiency and comfort. Therefore, the targets addressed by usability rely in saving the user's cognitive effort, offering products that are easy to understand, learn, use and remember, and that avoid errors or make them recoverable. These features can be accounted for in the following aspects:

- **Information Architecture:** It represents an information map enabling users to find their route towards the knowledge (Resmini & Rosati, 2012). Users, however, become aware of the information architecture of a system only when it is not clear; on the contrary, if not noticed, it means that the information architecture fits perfectly with the users' concept map: so the information is well structured.
- **Interface Design:** It has to take into account not only aesthetic issues, but also the graphic rules of usability and readability derived from perceptual and cognitive sciences.

Referring to the design of graphic interfaces, Nielsen (2005) stated the main guidelines to consider in order to provide a tool for interaction that is easy to use and which has a good impact on users, also at the first sight. They include:

- **Visibility of System Status:** The system should always keep users informed about what is going on, through appropriate feedback within reasonable time.
- **Match between System and the Real World:** The system should speak the users' language, with words, phrases and concepts familiar to the user, rather than system-oriented terms. Follow real-world conventions, making information appear in a natural and logical order.
- **User Control and Freedom:** Users often choose system functions by mistake and need a clearly marked "emergency exit" to leave the unwanted state without having to go through an extended dialogue. Support undo and redo.
- **Consistency and Standards:** Users should not have to wonder whether different words, situations, or actions mean the same thing. Follow platform conventions.

- **Error Prevention:** Even better than good error messages is a careful design, which prevents a problem from occurring in the first place. Either eliminate error-prone conditions or check for them and present users with a confirmation option before they commit to the action.

- **Recognition Rather than Recall:** Minimize the user's memory load by making objects, actions, and options visible. The user should not have to remember information from one part of the dialogue to another. Instructions for use of the system should be visible or easily retrievable whenever appropriate.

- **Flexibility and Efficiency of Use:** Accelerators (unseen by the novice user) may often speed up the interaction for the expert user such that the system can cater to both inexperienced and experienced users. Allow users to tailor frequent actions.

- **Aesthetic and Minimalist Design:** Dialogues should not contain information which is irrelevant or rarely needed. Every extra unit of information in a dialogue competes with the relevant units of information and diminishes their relative visibility.

- **Help Users Recognize, Diagnose, and Recover from Errors:** Error messages should be expressed in a plain language (no codes), precisely indicate the problem, and constructively suggest a solution.

- **Help and Documentation:** Even though it is better if the system can be used without documentation, it may be necessary to provide help and documentation. Any such information should be easy to search, focused on the user's task, list concrete steps to be carried out, and not be too large.

These general principles are not defined specifically for the elderly: the adoption of new technologies in the AAL field, instead, requires their adaptation to the peculiarity and needs of older adults (Rashidi & Mihailidis, 2013; Castilla et al., 2013). Czaja (2005) states that, according to data gathered, older people are not resistant toward the use of computers, but their receptivity depends on several factors such as ease of use, available support, and training. Technology is continuously evolving and it is important that elderly start interacting with high tech devices, so that they will be able to gradually accomplish more difficult tasks and benefit from an increasing number of services. Moreover, if the interaction is frequent, first it could become a new daily habit and secondly people won't forget what they have learnt. To ensure that people of all ages benefit from the technology, the main steps to follow are: understand the obstacles, improve the design to cope with the difficulties and plan how to teach people in a suitable way. Finally, in the design of technology, it is necessary to consider both changes in cognitive abilities and decline in audition, visual and motor skills due to ageing. In the first case, some studies suggest to adopt a practical training rather than a conceptual one, to reach a better result from the learning process. Reduced motor skills, on the other hand, make it difficult to use common input devices such as mouse or keyboards, while visual impairments require for example a larger size of elements on the screen.

In the following table (Nedopil, Schauber, & Glende, 2013), a sum up of guidelines referred to elderly users' main requirements is provided.

These guidelines, as well as Nielsen's principles, are not defined for a specific type of interface, while in the following sub-sections the usability issues will be discussed by separating the different methods. In our case, users interact with the system by means of applications running on smart TVs, and portable touchscreen devices.

Smart TV

Guidelines are considered to be the best resource that designers and developers can use to ensure that their products are usable. Because of this, manufacturers devise their own set of usability, user experience and user interface guidelines. Referring to the smart TV, for example, Samsung suggests the Principles for Designing Applications for Samsung Smart TV (Samsung Dev. Forum). The key factors that must be respected when designing a user experience suitable for TV applications mainly concern:

- **Simplicity:** The layout of the application should be user-friendly. Applications should not require a separate guide or a manual.
- **Clarity:** If navigation is ambiguous, users will feel confused and insecure. Users should always know exactly "where" they are within an application.
- **Consistency:** The screen layout should be maintained among the pages of the same application. It is recommended to keep it consistent overall with all of the necessary basic navigation features such as four-directional navigation, going into levels, or returning to the previous screen on the content list.
- **Feedback:** The application should provide a feedback on user's actions. For example, when an item is selected, it should be displayed with a different look to identify the change of status. Or when the time required to load data exceeds a certain period, a loading animation must be displayed to provide visual confirmation that the screen will soon change according to user's request.
- **Aesthetic Considerations:** Applications designed specifically for use on a TV must pay particular attention to the associated TV-specific design factors such as colour, resolution, and screen composition.
- **User Control:** Move, Return, Enter, and other basic navigation functions should be clear. The movements that occur on the screen have to be in the direction expected by the user, and an intuitive layout must be provided accordingly.

Touchscreen Portable Devices

As for Samsung TV applications, even for Android-based touchscreen portable devices the Android User Experience Team developed some basic design principles (Android Dev.). The main guidelines that need to be taken into account in the realization of our applications are:

- **Design Different Interfaces Depending on the Screen Size:** For example, tablets and smartphones have different features and advantages, and require proper design.
- **Use Simple and Clear Graphic Elements:** They have influence on the effectiveness and the quality of interaction. Associating a text label to each button or icon can help to specify its meaning.
- **Large Target Elements:** The size of the target elements has a great influence on the accuracy of the interaction. Specifically, according to Parhi, Karlson, and Bederson (2006), buttons should be at least 9.2 mm wide.
- **Confirmation of Target Capture:** It is useful to provide a visual or audible feedback once the target has been captured, in order to communicate to the user the success of the operation.
- **Indicate the Position of the Page:** While browsing, the user should always be able to know where he is. moreover, it is preferable to avoid deep navigation hierarchies that could cause user confusion and disorientation.

USE CASES

Related Works

Numerous projects can be found in the literature referred to systems in the AAL field, employing different methods for the interaction. Grguric, Mosmondor, Kusek, Stocklow, and Salvi (2013), for example, cite some projects that employ graphical interfaces in platforms for AAL services. For these solutions, a good user interaction design is fundamental, as confirmed by several studies showing that the users' acceptance strongly influences the success of technological innovations. However, they also propose to apply a gesture-based approach to an existing AAL platform. The introduction of an alternative mean of interaction enables to broaden the user's possibilities and to enrich the interaction experience.

Another gesture-based approach for the interaction with smart environment has been proposed by Kühnel et al. (2011). In such a case, three-dimensional gesture is exploited, using a smartphone as an input device: movements and rotations of the device correspond to different commands to be sent to the smart home. However, this solution does not seem very adequate to elderly subjects, due to their poor motor skills and the need to memorize the different gestures. On the other hand, voice commands represent an interaction system already known and much more natural. In this case, a major disadvantage is the sensitivity of the system to noisy environments, for example in the presence of a blaring television. Nevertheless, Portet, Vacher, Golanski, Roux, and Meillon (2013) design and evaluate a voice interface for the smart home, conducting a thorough analysis on the acceptability of this kind of interaction by the elderly subjects. The authors state that voice interfaces are highly preferred by users, compared with tactile systems, since they do not have to be physically available in the place where the command is sent. However, in recent years, thanks to the characteristics of portability of some touch devices, this problem is on the way to be overcome.

In what concerns the specific types of application, several projects have been proposed that focus on the matter of social interaction for the elderly, addressing the issue of the user interaction in different ways.

Alaoui and Lewkowicz (2013), for example, describe an AAL European project for the design of an application for social interaction for elderly people. They choose to develop the application over a smart TV platform because of the familiarity of almost everyone with this device, aiming at encouraging its usage, and thus helping the users to avoid social isolation and improve relationships.

Pires et al. (2012), instead, present an application that allows elderly and mobility impaired people to interact with audio-visual Internet-based communication services, both by means of a touchscreen computer and a smartphone. In this project, the key point is the multimodality. The first device supports speech, touch and keyboard/mouse interaction as input modalities, while output is displayed on the GUI or through speech synthesis. The second one supports speech interaction and touch, and simple gesture (e.g. tilt rotations of the device) can be used to scroll up or down on a list. User's feedback is provided through a vibration. After the users' evaluations, they concluded that the use of Natural User Interfaces (NUIs) together with multimodal interaction, allows an easier use of complex technological devices and services.

Description of Authors' Proposal

The project developed by the authors deals with assistant technologies for residential autonomy in the silver age. It covers several aspects of the home living, such as independent living, home security, health monitoring and environmental control (De Santis et al., 2015).

The equipment used includes sensors and actuators, electro-medical devices, network and gateway devices, servers and user interfaces.

The envisioned system architecture is composed by several domains, or subsystems:

1. Domotic System
2. Behavior Detection
3. Telemedicine
4. System-User Interface

Each subsystem includes a set of sensors generating data with specific features, all managed by means of server applications that provide a unique integrated platform for data processing. Depending on the usage and on the functionalities to implement, in some cases data can be stored locally and the processing operation is performed by the local server, while in other cases the local server collects all the data received from a specific type of sensor, and sends the remote server an aggregated information, properly processed. The system comprises a wide range of heterogeneous sensors that differ according to type, transmission method, network technology (i.e. Controller Area Network (CAN) bus, Ethernet, Wi-Fi, Wireless SubGHz).

Along the different communication links, proper privacy and identity protection policies shall be ensured. Several standards have been proposed to support end-to-end (E2E) security and key establishment, like Datagram Transport Layer Security (Tschofenig & Fossati, 2013), Internet Key Exchange (IKEv2) scheme (Kaufman, 2005), and HIP-DEX (Moskowitz, 2014; Nie, Vaha-Herttua, Aura, & Gurtov, 2011) protocols. An interesting approach to further improve these standards has been suggested in Saied and Olivereau (2012) and Saied, Olivereau, Zeghlache, and Laurent (2014). In these papers, a proxy-based solution is proposed for delegating the heavy cryptographic operations from a constrained device to less constrained nodes in its neighborhood. In both Saied and Olivereau (2012) and Saied, Olivereau, Zeghlache, and Laurent (2014), only one set of intermediary proxies are used in the key establishment protocols. This approach is generalized in Porambage, Braeken, Kumar, Gurtov, and Ylianttila (2015), where two different sets of proxies are used, corresponding to two constrained end nodes.

Despite efficient security mechanisms have not been implemented yet in the system proposed by the authors, it is an important point that is expected to face in the near future.

Domotic System

The home automation infrastructure for the domotic system is based on a two-layer architecture:

- **CAN Bus Level:** To connect and enable the management of sensors and actuators.
- **Ethernet Level:** To support the interconnection among CAN and IP-based networks.

Sensors include PIRs (Passive Infra-Red), magnetic sensors applied on doors and windows, gas, smoke and water leaks sensors, and possibly other alarm sensors. Each sensor is connected to a home automation node for data acquisition and transmission toward a gateway device, that performs the interconnection between the two architectural levels. On the other hand, actuators enable control for lights, windows and doors opening and closing. When controlling the actuators from a user interface, the command is transferred over the Ethernet network, it reaches the proper gateway and is forwarded to the selected node. The architecture of the home automation system is pictorially represented in Figure 1.

Figure 1. Representation of the home automation system architecture. some gateways are equipped with a radiofrequency interface (Sub-GHz frequency ranges). Examples of wireless nodes are the magnetic sensors placed on windows and on the refrigerator door. Each gateway is assigned its IP address and each node connected to it has its own identifier (ID): this way, the IP address-ID pair identifies a unique device.

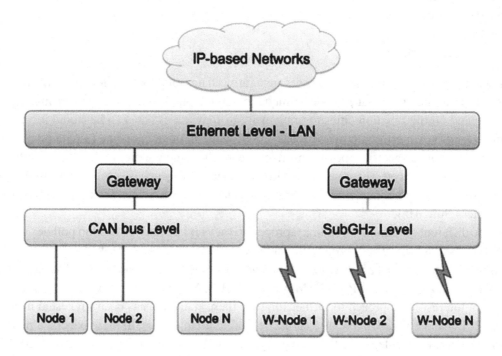

The network dedicated to power load detection and monitoring is part of the home automation system and it consists of a set of meter nodes that provide essentially two functions: to send information about the power consumption to the server, and to enable/disable a load when receiving the proper command. Meter nodes can be connected to a single load or to a master switch. In the proposed set-up, both configurations are employed, in order to monitor the power consumption of the whole supply line and to control some selected loads. The operating principle is the same as for the other CAN devices the home automation is equipped with. For the monitoring function, the power meter measures the consumption at predefined intervals and sends this information to the server. Referring to the load control, it is possible to configure up to three thresholds: if the power absorption exceeds one of these values for a certain time interval, the node can send a notice to the server or directly disable the corresponding load.

Telemedicine

The devices involved in the telemedicine subsystem are a set of electro-medical devices, and a platform that automatically transmits the collected measures through the local gateway. The medical devices are a scale, a blood pressure meter and an oximeter, and they support Bluetooth technology. After each measurement, the values are sent via Bluetooth to the gateway, which forwards them over the IP network to a remote platform so that the doctor/caregiver can monitor the patient's health condition anytime. The platform chosen, and the associated biomedical devices, have been certified as medical equipment, so that the expected requirements for a telemedicine system have been satisfied.

Behaviour Detection

The objective of this sub-system is to detect and evaluate some features in the user's behaviour. This analysis includes several activities and requires data collection from a wide range of devices. For example, an integrated smart shoe, whose insole is equipped with force sensing resistors, allows posture and balance evaluation. Moreover, pressure sensors are placed on the bed and on the sofa, for the localization and the evaluation of the level of activity of a person.

Finally, a set of wearable sensors (e.g. accelerometers, gyroscopes, temperature sensors) measures the user's parameters, that are collected by a central node named Body Sensor Network Concentrator (BSNC).

Data originated from each set of sensors are collected by the corresponding coordinator node and forwarded to the server, where they are processed by specific applications, to infer the desired information.

System-User Interfaces

User interfaces essentially enable both input and output functions, e.g. to send commands to the domotic system and to visualize user's medical parameters. Multimodal interaction by means of touchscreen portable devices and Smart TVs has the objective to better fulfil the needs and capabilities of the users.

Irrespective of the interface device, the data flow is bidirectional and involves mostly the local Wi-Fi and Ethernet networks. Communication between the interface physical devices and the other system devices does not take place directly. Each request passes through the server that manages it and addresses the proper device.

Results: Test and Validation

The assistive home technology described in the previous section is already available as a Proof of Concept (PoC), as depicted in Figure 2. Some aspects, such as infrastructures and data acquisition are more consolidate; others should be improved and more widely investigated, implementing, for example, machine learning algorithms for behaviour prediction based on the data collected by the platform.

The system is able to acquire data from sensors and send such information to the local server in real time. First implementations of the user interfaces are already available, both for the smart TV (as depicted in Figure 3) and for the touchscreen devices (as depicted in Figure 4).

These applications allow to check the status of the lights and turn them on or off, to activate scenarios and open or close blinds and windows. Through specific services, the user can obtain the values of the measurements obtained from biomedical devices and visualize them on the screens. Monitoring functionalities are also available for checking the status of the environmental sensors and of the activities carried out by the user. Monitoring the power consumption of the electric loads is clear and immediate thanks to proper graphic representations.

According with the criteria mentioned in the Usability section, graphics chosen are very simple and easily understandable, there are no animations and each page is provided with a help button.

The features are identified by both text and icons, in order to promote the content recognition rather than the memorisation. Icons exploit commonly used symbols, and the majority of them is black, providing a strong contrast to the light background and avoiding to confuse the user. Colours are exploited rarely to provide additional information (for example, a yellow light bulb indicates the light is on, while

Figure 2. Demo environment set up in the telecommunications lab

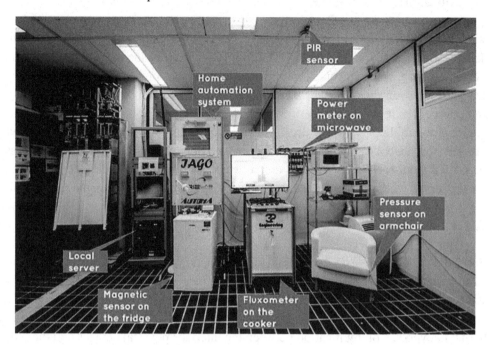

Figure 3. Main menu of the smart TV application
(Icons from "icons8.com")

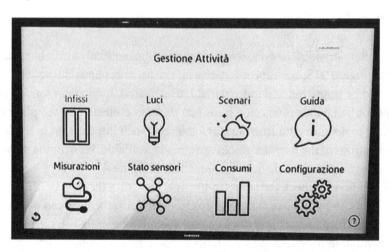

the colourless bulb icon indicates it is off). Also the text is black on the light background, it uses a clear and large font, to facilitate the reading even to people with visual difficulties, as suggested in Table 2. The graphic style chosen is the same for both interfaces, ensuring coherence among the various parts of the same application, and between the two different ones. Drop-down menus, although widely used in mobile interfaces to save space, have not been adopted in this case, as they make it difficult to identify immediately all features. In addition, to encourage the elderly who exhibit concentration and cognitive impairments, different information are never provided in parallel.

Figure 4. Application running on the tablet: sub-menu for lights and loads control
(Icons from "icons8.com")

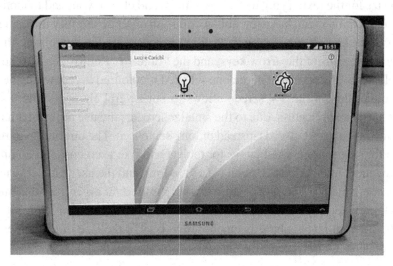

Table 2. Interfaces design recommendations for elderly users, derived from accessibility guidelines

Supported Dimension	Recommendation
Vision	- Offer an adaptable display size with a minimum font of 12 to 14 point - Keep high the contrast between the background and text or buttons - Items can be grouped by colour or, alternatively, by means of size, volume and texture
Hearing	- Use low-range to mid-range frequencies and pulses of sound rather than sustained frequencies - Consider potential background noise - Consider interactions with hearing aids - Avoid computer-generated voices - Use natural speech rhythm, stress and intonation
Mobility	- Allow sufficient time for inputs - Reduce to a minimum motor input for users with motor control problems - Offer auditory, visual or sensory feedback to confirm a motor input - Reduce the number of targets, increase their size and keep sufficient space between them - Use static menus instead of dropdowns
Cognition	- Provide only task-relevant information - Present information in small, screen-sized chunks - Do not provide parallel information at the same time - Indicate the user's current position within the information space - Apply strategies to reduce the users' working memory (e.g. by presenting all available functions instead of showing them only on request) - Use commonly used symbols that are intuitive and known from real life

Several checks have been made to detect conditions that may cause errors. For example, when receiving a response from the server, the applications first verify that data are not null and in the expected format. Then, if everything is correct, it is possible to go on with the processing, otherwise an error notification is provided to the user. This operation avoids a possible application crash due to the processing of an incorrect or unexpected data format.

During navigation the user should always know where he is; for this reason, each page has a showy title that defines its content.

As for the Smart TV, the application developers have properly organized the contents within the pages and set a quite big size for the text, trying to create a simple and clear layout and to facilitate the reading.

Moreover, the application menu has a few sub-sections, in order to simplify the navigation among the contents by means of the keys of the remote control. As suggested in the guidelines, the application can almost be controlled by means of the arrow keys, and the "Enter" / "Return" keys. When the user moves among the menu elements, the text label of the one selected is coloured in red, while the others are black.

While the big dimension of the TV screen allows to put several elements into a single page, conversely, in the touchscreen application, due to the smaller screens, the use of the text has been limited to the minimum, preferring to use keywords instead of long sentences. The buttons are large sufficiently, at least 9.2 mm wide for smartphones, and larger for tablets and fixed screens, and complex control techniques have been avoided. Interactions do not have a time limit and the user can perform them easily and without haste. The confirmation of target capture is a very important aspect, for this purpose, the visual and audio feedback provided natively by the operating system has been exploited. Moreover, as shown in Figures 5 and 6, different layouts have been chosen to best fit the size of the screen: the application can automatically understand the size of the screen and choose the proper layout.

Figure 5. Screenshot of the user interface that monitors the state of some sensors: layout for smartphones (Icons from "icons8.com")

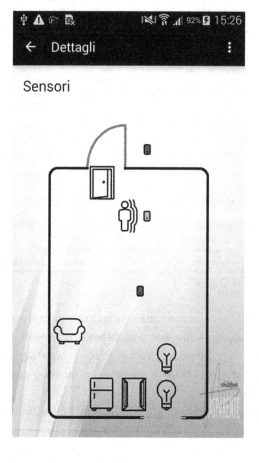

Figure 6. Screenshot of the user interface that monitors the state of some sensors: layout for tablets and fixed screens
(Icons from "icons8.com")

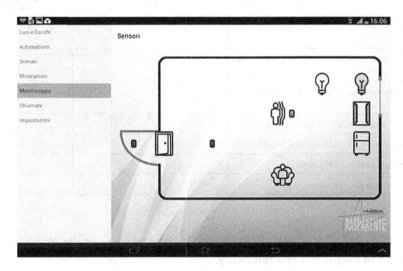

Once the development phase was concluded, a verification of the functions, usability, reliability and effectiveness of the user interface prototypes has been performed.

The system has been tested in the Laboratory by people not involved in the project: it works correctly in all the different conditions of use. As for the interaction, they were able to effectively use the application and browse the available functionalities. Moreover, in order to assess the usability of the interfaces, an evaluation form has been produced, addressed to persons who do not know the project. The short questionnaire, in addition to the indication of suggestions and problems, consists of five key points the user is requested to evaluate: look and feel, intuitive operation, efficiency, easy detection of features and navigation, user feedback. It also requests a personal opinion about the level of usability of the application when used by elderly people.

The survey has been conducted in the Telecommunications Laboratory on 15 users among students and technical staff, who rated the application and provided some useful suggestions to improve it.

Although the tests were not carried out by individuals with characteristics similar to those of the target users, since they are typically young volunteers, they still provide an initial positive response from people not involved into the project, considering the first impressions and getting tips for the improvements.

The results can be considered very good, as the average score is between 7.6 and 9.2 for all the five main features (see Table 3), and few marginal problems have been reported, that however do not affect the correct operation of the application. Also regarding the estimated acceptability and usability by older users, the opinion of respondents gives a positive outcome, with scores ranging from 7.2 to 8.

FUTURE RESEARCH DIRECTIONS

The continuous evolution and development of technology give rise to new devices appearing in people's daily life, and, according to each single user's experiences and background, different amount of time may be needed to get accustomed to them. When dealing with solutions designed for older people, it is

Table 3. Key points of the evaluation form and corresponding scores

Evaluated Aspects	Rate on the Prototype for Smart TVs	Rate on the Prototype for Touchscreen Devices
Look and feel: clarity, first impact, coherence among the different sections	9.2	8.7
Intuitive operation: easy to use and learn how to interact with the application	9	8.4
Immediate detection of features, ease of navigation through the contents	8.9	8.8
Efficiency: level of user control, ability of reaching the goals	9.2	8.7
Feedback on user's decisions, notifications, error handling	8.2	7.6
Estimated usability by disabled or elderly users	7.7	7.2
Estimated acceptability and impact on users	8	7.5

well-known that the requested learning effort should be reduced at a minimum, and properly balanced by a clear perception of usefulness and reliability.

The research progresses in the field of smart assistive environments are moving towards the target of ever less obtrusive technologies, embedded in traditional environments, that shall require no or very limited user interaction. According to this trend, it is foreseen that the devices and technologies able to support natural interaction, such as the one based on gesture or voice recognition, will see increasing adoption, together with properly designed applications. In this perspective, the smart TV device discussed in this chapter as a possible physical mean of user interaction in assisted living environments, is expected to be widely adopted, thanks to the capability of natively supporting both voice and gesture recognition. For sure, further developments shall be targeted to increase the range of commands and instructions the device is able to take as input, and to improve the responsiveness of the devices, for example by means of software interfaces to mimic a human interaction.

The positive feedback collected by several research projects about the adoption of touchscreen devices in human-system interaction, provides a solid foundation on which further research efforts and developments may be built. In this context, a very critical role is played by the software applications providing the functionalities of the touchscreen interface. A huge amount of literature exists, supporting the so-called user-centered design (UCD) approach, according to which the final user of the envisioned interface shall be involved since the very initial steps of the design, by the adoption of suitable protocols for the collection of unstructured user requirements and their translation into technical guidelines.

The UCD process addresses the whole design and development life-cycle, while focusing on gaining a deep understanding of who will be using the product. UCD is based upon an explicit understanding of users, tasks, and environments; it is driven and refined by user-centered evaluation, and addresses the whole user experience (UX).

The adoption of the UCD methodology in the field of elderly-oriented technologies and interfaces poses specific issues, and requires to clearly identify users' needs and expectations, typically by resorting to a multi-disciplinary team. In particular, gaining adequate knowledge and understanding of older adults' UX may be challenging, as the notion of experience is inherent to everyone's existence as a human being (Roto, Law, Vermeeren, & Hoonhout, 2011). Experience, in general, covers everything personally encountered, undergone, or lived through; UX differs from 'experiences in a general sense', in that it explicitly refers to the experience(s) derived from using, interacting with, or being confronted passively with systems (a general term used to denote products, services, and artefacts, that a person can interact with, through a user interface). Future research directions shall be targeted to exploring the UX concept referred to older adults, paying attention to specific interaction events, which may have an impact on the user's emotion, and focusing on how a single person experiences the encounter with a system from moment to moment (e.g., measuring emotions at various moments in time, to uncover which elements in an interaction may induce which emotions). Better understanding of these complex issues could even lead to the design of new devices, better responding to older users' expectations, capabilities, and emotional approach.

CONCLUSION

This chapter discussed the issues related to HCI in specific scenarios like Assisted Living Environments, where technology aims to address specific needs and requirements exhibited by elderly people, typically affected by physical or cognitive impairments, of different nature.

Older people are frequently perceived and portrayed as being resistant to technology; in reality, many of them are willing to accept novel digital technologies into their lives, and to take advantage of what technology has to offer. Understanding new technologies makes older adults feel connected to others, and to the world in general. Technology rejection is usually due to a missing perception of the potential benefits attainable from its usage, not necessarily because it is too difficult or time-consuming to learn. On the other hand, an unusable and bad designed interface often causes a "not worth it" impression. Therefore, the ultimate objective is to design tools, applications, and services, both usable and useful. The chapter focused on two classes of devices usually selected as system interfaces within AAL platforms, i.e. smart TVs and touchscreen devices, by discussing the technological and usability issues related to their use. The specificity of the target users addressed by assistive technology makes it necessary to review and properly elaborate on guidelines applied to the design of suitable user interfaces, from the identification of the user's requirements, to the selection of the physical devices featuring the requested characteristics, up to the design of the software applications to execute.

The discussion on design principles for user-system interfaces based on smart TVs and touchscreen devices has been supported and validated by the experimental results of an AAL project carried out by the authors, and by the experience gained during its development. Guidelines and recommendations about user interfaces specifically designed for Ambient Assisted Living applications have been proposed for possible adoption in a user-oriented design approach.

REFERENCES

Alaoui, M., & Lewkowicz, M. (2013). A livingLab approach to involve elderly in the design of smart TV applications offering communication services. In Online Communities and Social Computing (pp. 325–334). Springer Berlin Heidelberg. Retrieved from http://www.aal-europe.eu/ doi:10.1007/978-3-642-39371-6_37

Android Developers. (n. d.). *Android Design Principles*. Retrieved from http://developer.android.com/design/get-started/principles.html

Bhalla, M. R., & Bhalla, A. V. (2010). Comparative study of various touchscreen technologies. *International Journal of Computers and Applications*, *6*(8), 12–18. doi:10.5120/1097-1433

Burkhard, M., & Koch, M. (2012). *Evaluating Touchscreen Interfaces of Tablet Computers for Elderly People* (pp. 53–59). Mensch & Computer Workshopband.

Business Insider. (2014). *Smart TVs are on pace to take over the entire TV market*. Retrieved from http://www.businessinsider.com/smart-tvs-are-on-pace-to-take-over-the-entire-tv-market-2014-7#ixzz3fwn3kdUm

Castilla, D., Garcia-Palacios, A., Breton-Lopez, J., Miralles, I., Baños, R. M., Etchemendy, E., & Botella, C. et al. (2013). Process of design and usability evaluation of a telepsychology web and virtual reality system for the elderly: Butler. *International Journal of Human-Computer Studies*, *71*(3), 350–362. doi:10.1016/j.ijhcs.2012.10.017

Chaparro, A., Rogers, M., Fernandez, J., Bohan, M., Choi, S., & Stumpfhauser, L. (2000). Range of motion of the wrist: Implications for designing computer input devices for the elderly. *Disability and Rehabilitation*, *22*(13-14), 633–637. doi:10.1080/09638280050138313 PMID:11052213

Coleman, G. W., Gibson, L., Hanson, V. L., Bobrowicz, A., & Mckay, A. (2010, August). Engaging the disengaged: how do we design technology for digitally excluded older adults?*Proceedings of the 8th ACM Conference on Designing Interactive Systems* (pp. 175-178). ACM. doi:10.1145/1858171.1858202

Cullen, K., Dolphin, C., Delaney, S., & Fitzpatrick, M. (2008). Survey of older people and ICTS in Ireland. *Age Action*, 27. Retrieved from http://www.ageaction.ie/userfiles/.../survey-of-older-people-andicts-in-ireland.pdf

Czaja, S. J. (2005). The impact of aging on access to technology. In: *Accessibility and computing*, SIGACCESS Newsletter, 83, 711. Retrieved from http://www.sigaccess.org/wp-content/uploads/formidable/sep05_all.pdf

De Santis, A., Gambi, E., Montanini, L., Pelliccioni, G., Raffaeli, L., Rascioni, G., & Spinsante, S. (2015, May). Smart Homes for Independent and Active Ageing: Outcomes from the TRASPARENTE Project. *Paper presented at the 2015 Italian Forum on Ambient Assisted Living*, Lecco, Italy.

Fisk, A., Rogers, W. A., Charness, N., Czaja, S. J., & Sharit, J. (2009). *Designing for Older Adults: Principles and Creative Human Factors Approaches* (2nd ed.). New York: CRC Press. doi:10.1201/9781420080681

Greenstein, J. S., & Arnaut, L. Y. (1988). Input Devices. In Handbook of Human-Computer Interaction (pp. 495-519). North Holland: Amsterdam.

Grguric, A., Mosmondor, M., Kusek, M., Stocklow, C., & Salvi, D. (2013, June). Introducing gesture interaction in the Ambient Assisted Living platform universal. *Proceedings of the 2013 12th International Conference on Telecommunications (ConTEL)* (pp. 215-222). IEEE.

Holzinger, A. (2003). Finger instead of mouse: touch screens as a means of enhancing universal access. *Proceedings of User interfaces for all 7th international conference on Universal access: theoretical perspectives, practice, and experience* ERCIM '02, Berlin, Heidelberg (pp. 387–3970. Springer-Verlag. doi:10.1007/3-540-36572-9_30

Hummen, R., & Moskowitz, R. (2014). *HIP Diet EXchange*. DEX.

International Standards Organization. (1998). *ISO 9241 Part 11 – Guidance on usability*. Retrieved from https://www.iso.org/obp/ui/#iso:std:iso:9241:-11:ed-1:v1:en

Kaufman, C. (2005). Internet key exchange (IKEv2) protocol.

Kohlbacher, F., & Herstatt, C. (Eds.). (2010). *The silver market phenomenon: Marketing and innovation in the aging society*. Springer Science & Business Media.

Kühnel, C., Westermann, T., Hemmert, F., Kratz, S., Müller, A., & Möller, S. (2011). I'm home: Defining and evaluating a gesture set for smart-home control. *International Journal of Human-Computer Studies*, *69*(11), 693–704. doi:10.1016/j.ijhcs.2011.04.005

Lawton, M. P. (1999). Environmental taxonomy: Generalizations from research with older adults. In S. L. Friedman & T. D. Wachs (Eds.), *Measuring environment across the life span* (pp. 91–124). Washington, DC: American Psychology Association. doi:10.1037/10317-004

Melenhorst, A. S., Rogers, W. A., & Bouwhuis, D. G. (2006, March). Older adults' motivated choice for technological innovation: Evidence for benefit-driven selectivity. *Psychology and Aging*, *21*(1), 190–195. doi:10.1037/0882-7974.21.1.190 PMID:16594804

Memon, M., Wagner, S., Pedersen, C. F., Beevi, F. H. A., & Hansen, F. O. (2014). Ambient assisted living healthcare frameworks, platforms, standards, and quality attributes. *Sensors (Basel, Switzerland)*, *14*(3), 4312–4341. doi:10.3390/s140304312 PMID:24599192

Michele, B., & Karpow, A. (2014). Watch and be watched: Compromising all smart tv generations. *Proceedings of the 2014 IEEE 11th Consumer Communications and Networking Conference (CCNC)* (pp. 351-356). IEEE. doi:10.1109/CCNC.2014.6866594

Mohadisdudis, H. M., & Ali, N. M. (2014, September). A study of smartphone usage and barriers among the elderly. *Proceedings of the 2014 3rd International Conference on User Science and Engineering (i-USEr)* (pp. 109-114). IEEE. doi:10.1109/IUSER.2014.7002686

Morris, A., Goodman, J., & Brading, H. (2007). Internet use and non-use: Views of older users. *Universal Access in the Information Society*, *6*(1), 43–57. doi:10.1007/s10209-006-0057-5

Nedopil, C., Schauber, C., & Glende, S. (2013). *Knowledge base – AAL stakeholders and their requirements*. AAL Association.

Nie, P., Vähä-Herttua, J., Aura, T., & Gurtov, A. (2011, October). Performance analysis of HIP diet exchange for WSN security establishment. *Proceedings of the 7th ACM symposium on QoS and security for wireless and mobile networks* (pp. 51-56). ACM. doi:10.1145/2069105.2069114

Nielsen, J. (1995). *10 usability heuristics for user interface design.* Retrieved from http://www.nngroup. com/articles/ten-usabilityheuristics/

Parhi, P., Karlson, A. K., & Bederson, B. B. (2006, September). Target size study for one-handed thumb use on small touchscreen devices.*Proceedings of the 8th conference on Human-computer interaction with mobile devices and services* (pp. 203-210). ACM. doi:10.1145/1152215.1152260

Pires, C. G., Pinto, F. M., Teixeira, V. D., Freitas, J., & Dias, M. S. (2012). Living Home Center - A personal assistant with multimodal interaction for elderly and mobility impaired e-inclusion.*Proc. of PROPOR.* Coimbra.

Porambage, P., Braeken, A., Kumar, P., Gurtov, A., & Ylianttila, M. (2015, June). Proxy-based end-to-end key establishment protocol for the Internet of Things. *Proceedings of the 2015 IEEE International Conference onCommunication Workshop* (ICCW) (pp. 2677-2682). doi:10.1109/ICCW.2015.7247583

Portet, F., Vacher, M., Golanski, C., Roux, C., & Meillon, B. (2013). Design and evaluation of a smart home voice interface for the elderly: Acceptability and objection aspects. *Personal and Ubiquitous Computing, 17*(1), 127–144. doi:10.1007/s00779-011-0470-5

Rashidi, P., & Mihailidis, A. (2013). A survey on ambient-assisted living tools for older adults. *Biomedical and Health Informatics. IEEE Journal of, 17*(3), 579–590.

Resmini, A., & Rosati, L. (2012). A brief history of information architecture. *Journal of Information Architecture, 3*(2).

Roto, V., Law, E., Vermeeren, A. P. O. S., & Hoonhout, J. (2011). User experience white paper. Bringing clarity to the concept of user experience. Result from Dagstuhl Seminar on Demarcating User Experience 2010.

Ryu, M.-H., Kim, S., & Euehun Lee, E. (2009, May). Understanding the factors affecting online elderly user's participation in video UCC services. *Computers in Human Behavior, 25*(3), 619–632. doi:10.1016/j. chb.2008.08.013

Saied, Y. B., & Olivereau, A. (2012, June). D-HIP: A distributed key exchange scheme for HIP-based Internet of Things. *Proceedings of the 2012IEEE International Symposium on aWorld of Wireless, Mobile and Multimedia Networks* (WoWMoM) (pp. 1-7). IEEE. doi:10.1109/WoWMoM.2012.6263785

Saied, Y. B., Olivereau, A., Zeghlache, D., & Laurent, M. (2014). Lightweight collaborative key establishment scheme for the Internet of Things. *Computer Networks, 64,* 273–295. doi:10.1016/j.comnet.2014.02.001

Samsung Developers Forum. (2014). *Principles for Designing Applications for Samsung Smart TV.* Retrieved from http://www.samsungdforum.com/UxGuide/2014/01_principles_for_designing_applications_for_samsung_smart_tv.html

Trappe, W., Howard, R., & Moore, R. (2015). Low-energy security: Limits and opportunities in the internet of things. *Security Privacy, IEEE, 13*(1), 14–21. doi:10.1109/MSP.2015.7

Tschofenig, H., & Fossati, T. (2014). A TLS/DTLS 1.2 Profile for the Internet of Things.

United Nations. (2002, April 8-12). Report of the Second World Assembly on Ageing. Madrid, 2002.

United Nations, Department of Economic and Social Affairs, Population Division. (2013). World Population Ageing 2013, ST/ESA/SER.A/348.

Wilkowska, W., & Ziefle, M. (2012). Privacy and data security in E-health: Requirements from the users perspective. *Health Informatics Journal*, *18*(3), 191–201. doi:10.1177/1460458212442933 PMID:23011814

Wood, E., Willoughby, T., Rushing, A., Bechtel, L., & Gilbert, J. (2005). Use of Computer Input Devices by Older Adults. *Journal of Applied Gerontology*, *24*(5), 419–438. doi:10.1177/0733464805278378

World Wide Web Consortium. (n. d.). Retrieved from http://www.w3.org/2002/Talks/0104-usability-process/slide3-0.html

KEY TERMS AND DEFINITIONS

Acceptability: Refers to the quality of being acceptable, of meeting someone's needs adequately.

Actuator: A mechanical device for moving or controlling something.

Assistive Technologies: Information Technology (IT) products and services developed specifically to be accessible by elderly, by people with disabilities or with chronic diseases, to help to compensate for functional limitation and increase or maintain their functional abilities.

Domotic System: Set of technological components capable of performing functions that can be partially autonomous, programmed by the user, or even completely autonomous.

Electro-Medical Device: Electronic instrument or equipment used for medical purposes and health care.

Interface: Component that mediates the relationship between two entities. For example, a user interface is a point of interaction between the user and the machine.

Sensor: A device that detects or senses a physical stimulus (as heat, light, sound, pressure, magnetism, etc.) and transmits a resulting impulse.

Telemedicine: The set of medical and IT techniques enabling the remote care of a patient, or to provide health services remotely.

Chapter 18
Robotic Assistive System:
Development of a Model based on Artificial Intelligent Technique

Ku Nurhanim Ku Abdul Rahim
Universiti Technologi Petronas, Malaysia

P. Vasant
Universiti Technologi Petronas, Malaysia

I. Elamvazuthi
Universiti Technologi Petronas, Malaysia

T. Ganesan
Universiti Technologi Petronas, Malaysia

ABSTRACT

Stroke is the leading cause of disability that influences the quality of people's daily life. As such, an effective method is required for post-stroke rehabilitation. Research has shown that a robot is a good rehabilitation alternative where conventional robotic assistive system is encoded program by the robot expertise. The major drawback of this approach is that the lack of voluntary movement of the patient may affect the proficiency of the recovery process. Ideally, the robotic assistive system should recognize the intended movement and assist the patient to perform and make the training exercises more effective for recovery process. The electromyography based robotics assistive technology would enable the stroke patients to control the robot movement, according to the user's own strength of natural movement. This chapter briefly discusses the establishment of mathematical models based on artificial intelligent techniques that maps the surface electromyography (sEMG) signals to estimated joint torque of elbow for robotic assistive system.

INTRODUCTION

Stroke is a serious global health problem which ranks as the second or third cause of death and disability of patients in many countries (Langhorne, Bernhardt & Kwakkel, 2011). Each year, about 795,000 people in America suffer from stroke. Amongst these stroke cases, relatively 610,000 people are suffered the first stroke attack and 185,000 people are suffered the recurrent stroke and from the statistics also show that 36.9% is the relative rate of stroke death from 1999 until 2009 (Go et al., 2013). In United Kingdom, approximately 152,000 stroke cases appear, and in China 1.3 million people have strokes each year with 75% of them live with varying degrees of disabilities.

DOI: 10.4018/978-1-5225-0435-1.ch018

A survey conducted by National Stroke Association of Malaysia (NASAM) shows that out of more than 50,000 cases of stroke reported each year in Malaysia, about four hundred stroke survivors attend daily therapy session at various rehabilitation centres throughout Malaysia. Also, the Ministry of Health reported in 2011, that with advance observant of medical care, it has successfully prevented 12-15% of death due to stroke cases per year. It is a common practice to discharge stroke patients early from the hospital and refer them to the therapist as hospital outpatients for rehabilitation training care. However, local hospitals are unable to provide good rehabilitation treatment for outpatients due to the lack of professional therapists (Nordin, Aziz, Alkaff, Sulong & Aljunid, 2012).

In other parts of the world, robotic assistive system has been introduced to maintain the consistency of rehabilitation training. With this, the human therapist is able to observe more than one patient at a time, make clinical decisions and monitor the progress of each patient (Mazzoleni, Darion, Carrozza & Guglielmelli, 2010). In addition, robotic assistive system supports intensive, repetitive and task oriented training and safety in consonant with motor re-learning program compared to conventional rehabilitation approaches which involves therapists (Harwin, Parton & Edgerton, 2006). The robotic assistive systems are designed for upper limb robots and gait rehabilitation, and offer two modes of operation namely passive and active motion. During passive motion, the system guides the patient limb movement while the patient stays in rest condition. Active motion consists of two types of motion; active-assisted motion and active resisted motion. In active-assisted motion, the system acts as an assistance, providing the external force for the patient to complete the task movement, whereas, in active-resisted motion, the patient completes the task with opposing forces (Tong & Hu, 2008).

Hemiparesis/Hemiplegia is the most common stroke that contribute to the lack of gait performance (Flansjer, Holmback, Downham, Parlten & Lexell, 2005), weakness of specific muscles, reduced mobility, loss of inter-joint coordination and sensation, and abnormal postural adjustment (Cirtea & Levin, 2000). From clinically aspect, repetitive rehabilitation training has proven best method for motor control recovery with intensive training sessions. In conventional therapy, the repetitive task of rehabilitation is time consuming and labor intensive for both the patients and therapists (Hidler, Nichols, Pelliccio & Brady, 2005). Since last decade, several studies on the use of robotic assistive system have increased for rehabilitation of post stroke patients. The utilization of robotic assistive system can easily determine repetitive and task oriented training exercise, better control of introduced force and reproduction of precise force in cyclic movement. Robotic assistive system is also more robust during therapy sessions (Kreb, 2006).

The surface electromyography (sEMG) signals provide measurement of the muscle contraction using the electrode sensor placed on the surface skin. Robotic assistive system utilizes sEMG signals as a trigger input for the system (Krebs et al., 2003) and act as proportional myoelectric control for upper limb exoskeleton (Song, Tong, Hu & Li, 2008) and lower limb exoskeleton (Hayashi, Kawamoto & Sankai, 2008; Ferris, Czerniecki & Hannaford, 2005; Kang, Ryu, Kim, Mun, 2004). The sEMG signals are then converted as estimated joint torque by mapping them with joint torque estimation models. Different approaches of joint torque estimation models have been done by researches such as the Hill Based model, Artificial Neural Network (ANN) and mathematical models (Rosen, Fuchs & Arcan, 1999; Wang & Buchanan, 2002; Song & Tong, 2005; Park, Kwon & Lee, 2009; Parasuraman, Arif, Jauw, 2010; Ullah & Kim, 2009; Arif, Parasuraman & Jauw, 2010). However, the Hill Based Muscle Model has complex architecture that needs to be solved with different set of differential models. The ANN model is only effective within the data learning set. Other types of data need to be trained to obtain good results. The aim of this research is to development an artificial intelligent technique with mathematical models that convert the 'surface electromyography' (sEMG) signals to 'estimated joint torque' of elbow flexion for robotic assistive system. The estimated joint torque would be obtained by optimizing the parameters of the mathematical model to the closest value of actual torque. Artificial intelligence algorithms are used to optimize the internal parameters of the mathematical model to find the best fit mathematical model and minimize the error between estimated joint torque and actual joint torque. As the findings of this work is to investigate the most optimal mathematical models of sEMG signals for joint torque estimation based on intelligent algorithms.

BACKGROUND

Patients after stroke mostly undergo an intensive rehabilitation training to re- learn a motor skill of functional movement activities, to improve the muscle strength (Masiero et al., 2009) and body balance (Koceska & Koceska, 2013). In conventional therapy, the repetitive task of rehabilitation is time consuming and labour intensive for both the patients and therapists. Specifically, for gait rehabilitation, it requires more than one therapist at one session of training to assist lower limb function to perform exercise (Hidler, Nichols, Pellicio & Brady, 2005). Performing such rehabilitation training causes burdensome for therapist even with excellent skills to maintain the quality of training to fully assist the patient. As a result, limited amount and less quality of rehabilitation is received by patients (Meinders, Gitter & Czernieki, 1998; Ferris, Sawaicki & Domingo, 2005; Cooper et. al, 2008; Senanayake & Senanayake, 2009). Usually, tools such as elastic band, rope, dumbbell and others rehabilitation tools have been used to carry out range of motion and strength exercises of rehabilitation training (Akdogan & Demir, 2006). Since last decade, several studies on the use of robotic assistive system have increased for rehabilitation of post stroke patients. The utilization of robotic assistive system can easily determine repetitive and task oriented training exercise, better control of introducing force and reproduction of precise force in cyclic movement. The robotic assistive system is also more robust during therapy sessions (Kreb, 2006).

Robotic assistive system is an important device to assist the disabled patients who have suffered from stroke. Robotic assistive system can be divided into upper and lower limb robots as shown in Figure 1.

Figure 1. Robotic assistive system

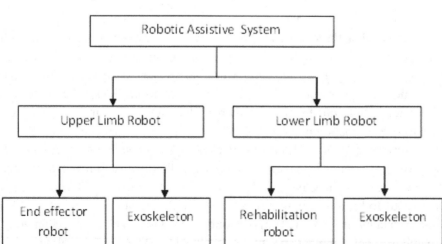

The upper limb robot includes arm, elbow and hand, whereas, the lower limb robot includes hip, knee and ankle. The upper limb robot is classified into two types: end effector robot and exoskeleton. End effector type refers to devices that interact with the patient at the end of the robot arm. These robot arms are designed to be adaptable with different body size. Exoskeleton type can be reassembled as human joint anatomy and apply torque to specific joints. This type of device is allowed a larger space with several degrees of freedom to control the orientation of the arm (Loureiro, Harwin, Nagai & Johnson, 2011). The lower limb robot is divided into two categories; rehabilitation robot and exoskeleton. Rehabilitation Robot is designed to administer training exercises for patients who suffer from Stroke, Cerebral Palsy or Parkinson Disease. This device is divided into two sub-categories: treadmill-based rehabilitation robot and over-ground based rehabilitation robot. Rehabilitation robots are automated gait devices that are invented from the view of the clinician to help patient to walk and to replace the role of therapist. Exoskeleton of lower limb robot has two sub-categories: performance–augmenting exoskeleton and mobile medical exoskeleton. Mobile medical exoskeleton is used as an assistive rehabilitation device. This exoskeleton requires the patient to balance body themselves, unlike rehabilitation robot designed with body weight support system which help to support patient body weight (Low, 2011) Performance-augmenting robot increases the performance for an able-bodied wearer that allows to carry heavy load for disaster relief workers, wildfire fighters and helping soldier (Dollar & Herr, 2008).

There are various types of Robotic assistive system for upper and lower limb functions. Several systems such as LOKOMAT, MIT-MANUS (Hogan, Krebs, Sharon & Charnnarong, 1995), ARMin (Nef et al., 2006) and Hybrid Assisted Limb (HAL) Type-C (Sankai, 2010) have been developed, gone into clinical trials and have been used for rehabilitation training at hospitals. Robotic assistive system can be more precise when the movement of the robot could be adjusted according to the ability level of the user based on sEMG signals. sEMG signals measure the muscle activities according to comfort level of user during the task movement. The advantages of sEMG signals for robotic assistive system are sEMG signals are relatively attached to the desired movement of the user. User intended movement can be deliberated by measuring muscle activities. sEMG signals are measured while the user performed the task movement. None additional physical/metal load necessary needed. sEMG signals emerge approximately (20ms-80ms) based on the muscles before the muscles contract. Fast processing time is required to assist the intended motion for the robotic assistive system. The EMG signals are converted into estimated joint torque using several models. Nevertheless, these sEMG signals should be able to convert into the estimated joint torque values using joint torques estimation model. From the related work, it can be seen that different joint torques estimation models have been applied. Several researchers have carried out research on EMG signal estimation joint torques mapping with Hill- Based Muscle Model, Artificial Neural Network (Rosen et al., 1999) and Mathematical Model (Parasuraman et al., 2010; Ullah & Kim, 2009; Arif et al., 2010). Hill Based Muscle Model is a classical model which is related to anatomy/ physiology of human. This model calculates the muscle force/torque with established relationship of force length and force velocity. The internal parameter of this model is optimized by machine learning technique (Rosen et al., 1999). However, Hill Base Muscle model predictive power is affected by its global nature. Artificial Neural Network model is a black box model can depend on large number of input without any relationship of muscle. It is capable to represent specific physiology task by the operator but it is limited within the learning set only. Another drawback of this model is that it needs to provide training for data of different tasks and also modification of the neural network architecture to enhance the quality of findings (Rosen et al., 1999; Wang & Buchanan, 2002; Song & Tong, 2005; Park et al., 2009). However, to overcome the current problems, through a suitable mathematical model can be analyzed using regression method (Chen, Ding, Zhao & Han, 2011). Researches have utilized mathematical models by optimizing the unknown internal parameter using, Genetic Algorithm (Arif et al, 2010) Simulated Annealing (Parasuraman et al., 2010) and Levenberg Marquardt (Ullah & Kim, 2009) for elbow flexion movement.

Artificial intelligent techniques such as particle swarm optimization, genetic algorithm and simulated annealing are being used in other engineering applications. Nejad & Salajegheh (2013), have discussed the routing optimization for a rescue robot for genetic algorithm and simulated annealing. The results show the shortest path and time are achieved by genetic algorithm that produces the optimum path for 6 different test environment. The results from genetic algorithm have shown that the search solution with the number of target points of paths increased consistently compared to simulated annealing. Orchard & Clark (2004), have studied on genetic algorithm and simulated annealing to optimize antenna design. The overall results show that genetic algorithm provides better optimization in term of cost function except for element 12 and 17 of yagi antenna. Genetic algorithm, works well up to tested problem 2.43×10^{12}. Simulated annealing performed poorly in test case antenna of run time, the best and the worst performance within 5%. It worked well in testing, problem until $1,19 \times 10^{12}$ only. The research by Louis, Chen Pullammanappallil (1999), involves seismic velocity inversion using genetic algorithm and simulated annealing algorithms. BASIN model calculates error which 10 random seed, with genetic algorithm optimization produces smaller error than $0.0068 \mathrm{sec}^2$ and average velocity model error 0.63km/sec which proves a better velocity model than simulated annealing. Although the simulated annealing geological model is an acceptable model by the expert, but, it takes much convergence time than genetic algorithm.

In research work by Singh and Gupta (2013), particle swarm optimization and genetic algorithm algorithms are obtained for weight optimization of composite leaf spring. The results from particle swarm optimization outperformed simulated annealing for design values of leaf led parameter in term of breadth, thickness, maximum bending stress, maximum deflection and estimated mass. The weight saving by particle swarm optimization archived 85.05% compared to simulated annealing 78.84%. Ethni et al. (2009) have done a research on induction motor fault identification using particle swarm optimization and simulated annealing. The findings demonstrated particle swarm optimization produced a success rate of 90% when developing induction motor winding fault. This shows particle swarm optimization is robust and suitable for nonlinear multivariable type problems. Jeevandam and Thanusneddi (2009), implemented particle swarm optimization and simulated annealing algorithm for power system stabilizer for multi-machine system. The results indicate that particle swarm optimization produces better and optimal tuning parameter of the power system stabilizer compared to simulated annealing where both algorithms use optimized objective function for various conditions for five different systems. This research work has proven that simulated annealing produced high settling time, high peak amplitude and high computational time compares to particle swarm optimization.

Azarkish, Farahat, Masoud and Sarvari (2012), have studied on geometry design of longitudinal fin using genetic algorithm and particle swarm optimization. Both algorithms are suitable to find the temperature distribution of range T=500k to T= 300k in the inverse design of convective-radiative fin profile. The results indicated that particle swarm optimization produced better performance because the convergence decreases by four times and the population decreases by three times compared to genetic algorithm. Mandal, Kar, Mandal & Ghosal (2011), used genetic algorithm and particle swarm optimization for finite impulse response (FIR) high pass filter design. The results showed that particle swarm optimization yielded was the best optimized parameter of high pass filter order of 30 to 40. Particle swarm optimization produced sharp transition band responses, better consistency, higher stop band attenuation and a small ripple compared to genetic algorithm. Genetic algorithm produced the suboptimal higher error and slower convergence time compared to particle swarm optimization. Sivandam & Deepa (2009), implemented particle swarm optimization and genetic algorithm for lower order system modelling application. Both algorithms showed the unit step response of lower order system close to ideal for higher order system. In terms of computational time, particle swarm optimization produced faster, which 15s less than genetic algorithm. Genetic algorithm showed that execution time and errors of the objective function of lower order system were higher compared to particle swarm optimization.

MAIN FOCUS OF THE CHAPTER

The chapter focuses investigate the most optimal mathematical models to convert sEMG signal into estimated joint torque.

Overall Research Methodology

From Figure 2, it can be seen that the sEMG signals are initially obtained through signal acquisition from bicep brachii muscles for elbow flexion. These signals are then converted into estimated joint torque based on mathematical models that are optimized using genetic algorithm and particle swarm optimization. The actual joint torque is obtained from dynamic modeling. Then, the estimated joint torque is compared with the actual joint torque. A correlation analysis is carried out on the mapping of these two

Figure 2. Overall research methodology

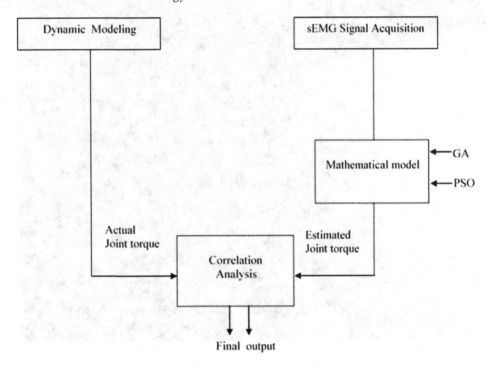

joint torques using performance measurement indices such as Pearson Correlation (*R*) and Coefficient of Determination (R^2).

This research concentrated on elbow movements. Therefore, the muscles associated with them would be described. Bicep Brachii is the primary muscle between elbow and ulna joint. Research shows that Bicep Brachii muscle is active during flexion of the supination forearm under all conditions during static and dynamic contraction. Brachialis is the other muscle where the sole function is for the elbow flexion task. However, this muscle is categorized as deep muscle where it is partially covered by biceps. In addition, Brachioradialis muscle is effective when the forearm is flexing actively at any rotational position. Joint range of motion for elbow flexion / extension are from 0° to 140°.

Experimental Work

The surface electromyography (sEMG) signal acquisition was recorded with sampling frequency 1kHz using surface wireless-trigno sensor system from Delsys Inc. Boston, M.A, USA. Two channel electrodes are placed on biceps brachii muscle as shown in Figure 3. The experiments were carried four males and one female healthy subject. The experiment was conducted after obtaining approval from the Ethics Committee of University and the subject. The movement task involved was elbow flexion of 90 degrees with and without load.

It can be seen that the top arrow on the wireless- trignor sensor should be aligned parallel to muscle fibre to acquire the maximum signal. This sensor should be placed at the centroid of the muscle to avoid

Figure 3. Delsys wireless sensor placed on bicep brachii muscles

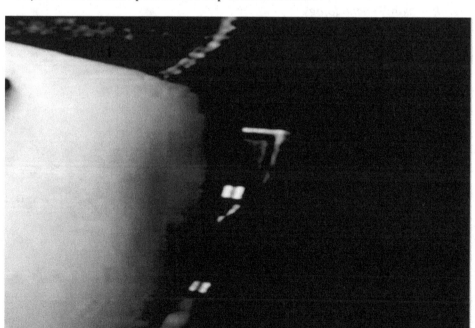

the tendon insertion. Sensor contact will intersect the muscle action potential with maximum sensitivity to measure the muscle activities. This sensor must be avoided from placing on or near the tendon of the muscle because the muscle fibres become thinner and less in number when approaches tendon, and this would result in reduced amplitude of sEMG signals. Sensor placement also should not put on the motor point of the muscle because it introduces minimal electrical current that causes a perceptible twitch at surface muscle. The position of the sensor should not the outside edge of muscles which will make the sensor detecting crosstalk signal from adjacent muscles.

sEMG Signal Processing

The signals are then processed using the EMGWorks Analysis ver. 4.07 software (Delsys Inc, 2014). The signal processing of sEMG signals is as following step:

1. **Raw Signal:** The raw sEMG signals are acquired from wireless-trigno sensor sensor electrode. The range of raw sEMG signal amplitude is $0V_{rms}$ to $15mV_{rms}$ or $\pm5Vp\text{-}p$. Raw sEMG signals cannot be used directly because it contains noise. There are some factors of noise from various sources such:
    a. **Motion Artifact:** Motion artifact noise is generated between the interface of detection sensor and surface skin. This electrical signal noise has an energy frequency from 0Hz to 20Hz.
    b. **Ambient Noise:** This type of noise originally generates from electromagnetic device, especially from the dominant component of AC power source with frequency 50Hz or 60Hz.
    c. **Inherent Noise:** All electronic components for detection and recording sEMG signal equipment generate electrical noise. However, this noise can be reduced by obtaining intelligent circuit design with high quality electronics component.
    d. **Inherent Stability of the Signal:** sEMG signal amplitude is affected by quasi-random nature of firing rate of the motor unit between the range frequency 0Hz to 20Hz.
2. **Filtering:** Bandpass filter of the 4th order Butterworth filter is applied to remove the noise. The cutoff frequency has been set at 20Hz and 400Hz.
3. **Feature Extraction:** Root mean square (RMS) has been used for feature extraction as shown in Equation (1).

$$RMS = \sqrt{\frac{1}{N}\sum_{n-1}^{N} x_n^2} \tag{1}$$

where,

x = sEMG data

N = number of samples

4. **Muscle Activation:** This function uses a threshold value that can be set by the user to determine the active muscle region. The lowest value from sEMG signals are considered as noise level and the active region of muscle which have RMS sEMG signal values that are greater than the noise level value.

DYNAMIC MODELING

The Actual Joint Torque is Obtained from the Dynamic Modeling

Dynamic modeling involves the following steps:

1. **Marker Tracking:** Modelling the elbow flexion movement of static and dynamic motion was recorded by using six cameras on Qualisys Tracking Markers System Inc., Goternborg, Sweden. Markerpoints were placed on the lower arm and hand.
2. **Modelling of Biomechanical Data:** The static and dynamic motion data are modelled into body segment parameters using 3D-Visual C-Motion Inc. software to obtain the actual torque in the form of signals. These signals are processed similar to the sEMG signals.

Joint Torque Estimation Model

The mathematical models used in this research involve Equations (2) to (10) since these equations are best suited for regression analysis. The Equations (2) to (6) are chosen based on previous research (Arif, Parasuraman & Jauw, 2010).and Equation (7) to (10) based on earlier research (Ullah & Kim, 2009).

$$MM_{(1)} = x_1 \cdot u_i + x_2 \cdot u_i^{\frac{1}{2}} \tag{2}$$

$$MM_{(2)} = x_1 \cdot u_i^{x_2} \tag{3}$$

$$MM_{(3)} = x_1 \cdot e^{\left(\frac{x_2}{u_i}\right)} \tag{4}$$

$$MM_{(4)} = x_1 \cdot u_i^{x_2} + x_3 \cdot u_i^{x_4} \tag{5}$$

$$MM_{(5)} = x_1 \cdot u_i^4 + x_2 \cdot u_i^3 + x_3 \cdot u_i^2 + x_4 \cdot u_i^1 + x_5 \cdot u_i^0 \tag{6}$$

$$MM_{(6)} = x_1 + x_2 \cdot \sqrt{u_i} \tag{7}$$

$$MM_{(7)} = u_i^{x_1} \cdot e^{\left(x_2 - x_3 \cdot u_i\right)} \tag{8}$$

$$MM_{(8)} = x_1 + x_2 \cdot \cos\left(u_i\right) + x_3 \cdot \sin\left(u_i\right) \tag{9}$$

$$MM_{(9)} = x_1 + x_2 \cdot \sin\left(u_i\right) \tag{10}$$

where,

$MM_{(1)}$ to $MM_{(9)}$ = mathematical model for estimated joint torque

u_i = processed sEMG data sample

x_i = where, i= (1, 2, 3..) as random value parameter associated

with selected mathematical model.

Fitness Function

A fitness function is used to minimize the errors in order to determine the optimal convergence. The fitness function given in Equation (11) is used to evaluate the performance of each selected mathematical model given in Equations (2) to (10). In addition, the fitness function helps in determining the final optimal value in the GA and PSO algorithms.

$$SSE = \sum_{i=1}^{n} \left(T_{act(i)} - MM_{(y)(i)}\right)^2 \tag{11}$$

where,

i = data sample

SSE = sum of squared error as fitness function

$T_{act(i)}$ = actual joint torque

$MM_{(y)(i)}$ = estimated joint torque using mathematical model, $y = 1,2,3...$

Implementation of Algorithms

The sEMG signals are converted into estimated joint torque using a mathematical model that is optimized using genetic algorithm and particle swarm optimization algorithms. The genetic algorithm and particle swarm optimization are implemented using C language of Bloodshed Dev C++ version 4.9.9.2 .

Genetic Algorithm

The genetic algorithm flowchart is shown in Figure 4 and parameters setting of genetic algorithm are provided in Table 1.

Figure 4. Flowchart of genetic algorithm

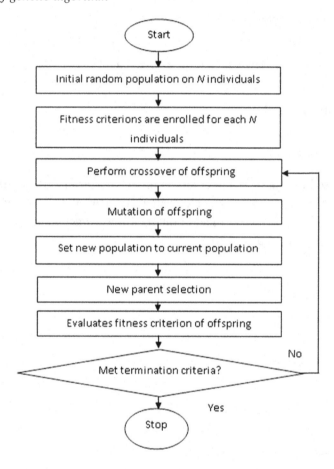

Table 1. Genetic Algorithm parameter setting

Parameter	Values
Length of individual string	6 bits
No. of individual in population	6
Initial string of individuals	Random
Bit type of individual string	Real-coded
Type of crossover	N-point
Crossover probability rate	0.5
Type of mutation	N-bit flip
Mutation probability rate	0.166
Selection type	Roulette Wheel

The following steps would be executed based on Figure 4:

Step 1: Initialize N individuals for random chromosome in the population.
Step 2: Assign fitness conditions for each N individuals in the population.
Step 3: Perform crossover from current population and create offspring for the next generation.
Step 4: Mutate the offspring of this generation.
Step 5: Roulette wheel selection chooses the parent population to create next generation.
Step 6: New population of N individuals is selected.
Step 7: Replace new population with the current population.
Step 8: Evaluates the fitness of each offspring in the generation.
Step 9: If the termination criteria are met stop iteration else got to step 3.

Particle Swarm Optimization

The particle swarm optimization flowchart is shown in Figure 5 and parameters setting of particle swarm optimization are provided in Table 2.

Figure 5. Flowchart of particle swarm optimization

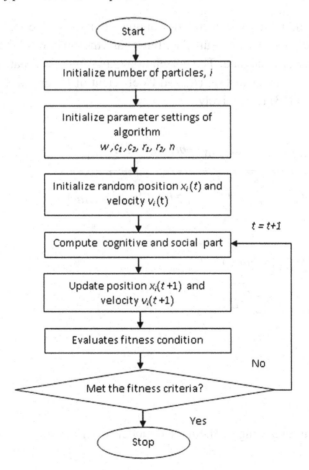

Table 2. Particle Swarm Optimization Algorithm parameter setting

Parameter	Values
Initial parameter (w, c_1, c_2, r_1, r_2)	(1,1.2,0.5,0.5,0.5)
No. of particles	6
Initial social influence $(s_1, s_2, s_3, s_4, s_5, s_6)$	(1.1,1.05,1.033,1.025,1.02,1.017)
Initial personal influence $(p_1, p_2, p_3, p_4, p_5, p_6)$	(3,4,5,6,7,8)

The following steps would be executed based on Figure 5:

Step 1: Initialize number of particles, i and parameter setting w, c_1, c_2, r_1, r_2, n.
Step 2: Initialize randomly position $x_i(t)$ and velocity $v_i(t)$ of the particles.
Step 3: Compute cognitive part and social part of the particles.
Step 4: Next iteration update position and velocity of the particles
Step 5: Evaluates the fitness of each particle of the swarm.
Step 6: If the fitness criteria are met and $t < T_{max}$ stop iteration else got to step 3; where t is swarm iteration and T_{max}, maximum proceed iteration.

Performance Measurement

The performance measurement is based on correlation analysis that uses 'Coefficient of Determination', (R^2) and 'Pearson Correlation', (R). They measure the strength and the direction of the relationship between two variables by determining optimal data. The correlation between the estimated joint torque and the actual joint torque using Pearson Correlation (R) and Coefficient of Determination (R^2) are expressed in equation (12) and equation (13) respectively:

$$R = \frac{\sum_{i=1}^{n}(T_{act(i)} - mean\_T_{act(i)})(MM_{(y)(i)} - mean\_MM_{(y)(i)})}{\sqrt{\sum_{i=1}^{n}(T_{act(i)} - mean\_T_{act(i)})^2 \sum_{i=1}^{n}(MM_{(y)(i)} - mean\_MM_{(y)(i)})^2}} \tag{12}$$

$$R^2 = \frac{\sum_{i=1}^{n}\left(MM_{(y)(i)} - mean\_T_{act(i)}\right)^2}{\sum_{i=1}^{n}\left(T_{act(i)} - MM_{(y)(i)}\right)^2 + \sum_{i=1}^{n}\left(MM_{(y)(i)} - mean\_T_{act(i)}\right)^2} \tag{13}$$

where,

i = data sample

$MM_{(y)(i)}$ = estimated joint torque using mathematical model, $y = 1,2,3\ldots\ldots$

$T_{act(1)}$ = actual joint torque

$mean\_T_{act(i)}$ = mean of actual joint torque

$mean\_MM_{(y)(i)}$ = mean of estimated joint torque

RESULT AND DISCUSSION

The result of sEMG signal optimization using mathematical $MM_{(1)}$ to $MM_{(9)}$. The unknown random parameters of each mathematical model are optimized using genetic algorithm and particle swarm optimization are shown this section.

Optimization of Mathematical Model Using Genetic Algorithm of Elbow Flexion of 90° without an External Load

Figure 6 shows an example graph of joint torques elbow flexion 90° for $MM_{(7)}$ without an external load by using genetic algorithm. This graph illustrates the comparison of estimated joint torque with genetic algorithm optimization and actual joint torque.

Figure 6. Joint torques of elbow flexion 90° without an external load for $MM_{(7)}$ using GA

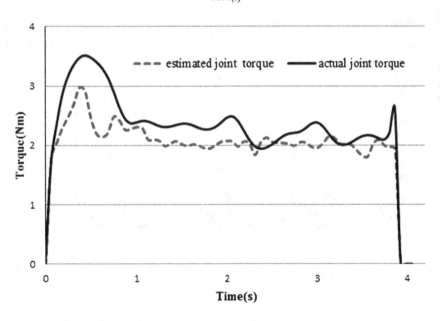

Table 3 and Figure 7 indicate the results coefficient of determination (R^2) for each mathematical model of all subjects optimizations of genetic algorithm for elbow flexion 90° without external between estimated joint torque and actual joint torque.

Table 4 and Figure 8 show the results of the Pearson Correlation (R) for each mathematical model of all subjects optimizations of genetic algorithm for elbow flexion 90° without external between estimated joint torque and actual joint torque.

Table 3 and Figure 7 show the results of R^2 and Table 4 and Figure 8 indicate the findings of R for elbow flexion 90° without an external load by using genetic algorithm. As shown in Figure 7 and 8, it can be seen that the mathematical models of $MM_{(5)}$, $MM_{(8)}$ and $MM_{(9)}$ obtained the lowest average value with R^2 is 0.62 ± 0.06 and R is 0.78 ± 0.04. It can be observed that the average value of all subjects for $MM_{(1)}$, $MM_{(2)}$, $MM_{(3)}$, $MM_{(4)}$, $MM_{(6)}$ and $MM_{(7)}$ of R^2 is more than 0.8 and R is more than 0.9. The $MM_{(7)}$ is shown the optimal mathematical model compared to $MM_{(1)}$, $MM_{(2)}$, $MM_{(3)}$, $MM_{(4)}$, and $MM_{(6)}$. The $MM_{(7)}$ has the highest average value of all subjects for R^2 and R where the average value of R^2 is 0.86 ± 0.02 and the average value of R is 0.93 ± 0.01.

Figure 7. Error bar each mathematical model of R^2 for elbow flexion of 90° without an external load of GA

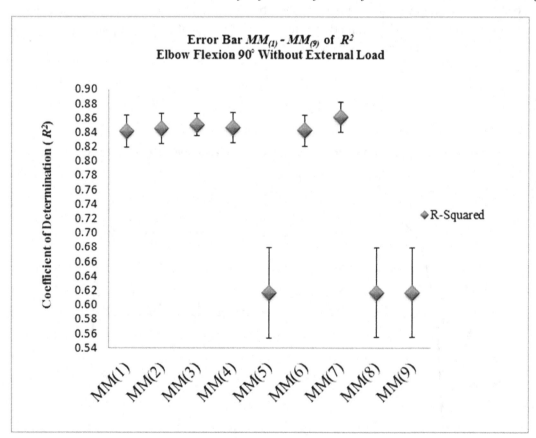

Table 3. Summarised of results of coefficient of determination (R^2) for elbow flexion of 90° without an external load of GA

MODEL	Coefficient of Determination (R^2)						
	S1	S2	S3	S4	S5	Average	Standard deviation
$MM_{(1)}$	0.83	0.85	0.87	0.85	0.81	0.84	0.02
$MM_{(2)}$	0.84	0.86	0.84	0.81	0.87	0.84	0.02
$MM_{(3)}$	0.86	0.87	0.85	0.83	0.86	0.85	0.02
$MM_{(4)}$	0.85	0.86	0.84	0.81	0.87	0.85	0.02
$MM_{(5)}$	0.57	0.56	0.67	0.70	0.59	0.62	0.06
$MM_{(6)}$	0.84	0.85	0.87	0.85	0.81	0.84	0.02
$MM_{(7)}$	0.86	0.89	0.86	0.83	0.87	0.86	0.02
$MM_{(8)}$	0.57	0.56	0.67	0.70	0.59	0.62	0.06
$MM_{(9)}$	0.57	0.56	0.67	0.70	0.59	0.62	0.06

Figure 8. Error bar each mathematical model of R for elbow flexion of 90° without an external load of GA

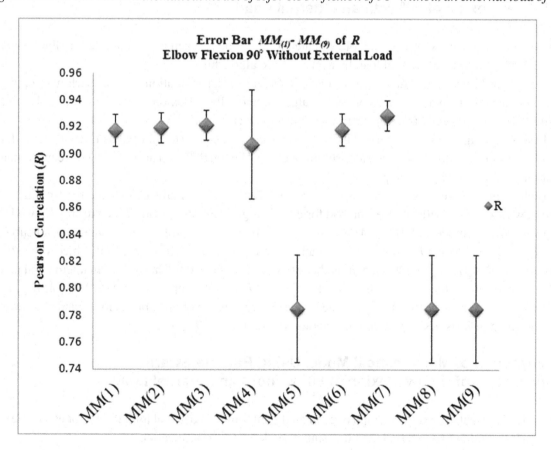

Table 4. Summarised of results of Pearson Correlation (R) for elbow flexion of 90° without an external load of GA

MODEL	Pearson Correlation (R)						Standard deviation
	S1	S2	S3	S4	S5	Average	
$MM_{(1)}$	0.91	0.92	0.93	0.92	0.90	0.92	0.01
$MM_{(2)}$	0.92	0.92	0.92	0.90	0.93	0.92	0.01
$MM_{(3)}$	0.92	0.93	0.92	0.90	0.93	0.92	0.01
$MM_{(4)}$	0.92	0.93	0.92	0.83	0.93	0.91	0.04
$MM_{(5)}$	0.76	0.75	0.82	0.83	0.76	0.78	0.04
$MM_{(6)}$	0.91	0.92	0.93	0.92	0.90	0.92	0.01
$MM_{(7)}$	0.93	0.94	0.93	0.91	0.93	0.93	0.01
$MM_{(8)}$	0.76	0.75	0.82	0.83	0.77	0.78	0.04
$MM_{(9)}$	0.76	0.75	0.82	0.83	0.77	0.78	0.04

Optimization of Mathematical Model Using Genetic Algorithm of Elbow Flexion of 90° with an External Load

Figure 9 illustrates an example graph of estimated joint torque and actual joint torque for elbow flexion 90° of $MM_{(7)}$ without an external load by using genetic algorithm.

Table 5 and Figure 10 indicate the results coefficient of determination (R^2) for each mathematical model of all subjects' optimizations of genetic algorithm for elbow flexion 90° with an external between estimated joint torque and actual joint torque with an external load..

Table 6 and Figure 11 show the results of the Pearson Correlation (R) for each mathematical model of all subjects optimizations of genetic algorithm for elbow flexion 90° with an external between estimated joint torque and actual joint torque.

Table 5 and Figure 10 show the results of R^2 and Table 6 and Figure 11 indicate the findings of R for elbow flexion 90° with an external load for genetic algorithm optimization. The results showed that the mathematical models of $MM_{(5)}$, $MM_{(8)}$ and $MM_{(9)}$, obtained the lowest average value for all subjects with R^2 is 0.66±0.06 and R is 0.81±0.03. It can be seen that the average value of all subjects for $MM_{(1)}$, $MM_{(2)}$, $MM_{(3)}$, $MM_{(4)}$, $MM_{(6)}$ and $MM_{(7)}$ of R^2 is above 0.8 and R is above 0.9. The optimal mathematical model is $MM_{(7)}$ according to the average value for all subjects of R^2 and R compared to $MM_{(1)}$, $MM_{(2)}$, $MM_{(3)}$, $MM_{(4)}$ and $MM_{(6)}$. It can be seen that $MM_{(7)}$ has the highest average value of all subjects for R^2 and R where the average value of R^2 is 0.87±0.03 and the average value of R is 0.93±0.02.

Optimization of Mathematical Model Using Particle Swarm Optimization of Elbow Flexion of 90° without an External Load

Figure 12 represents an example graph of estimated joint torque and actual joint torque for elbow flexion 90° of $MM_{(7)}$ without an external load by using particle swarm optimization.

Figure 9. Joint torques of elbow flexion 90° with an external load for $MM_{(7)}$ using GA

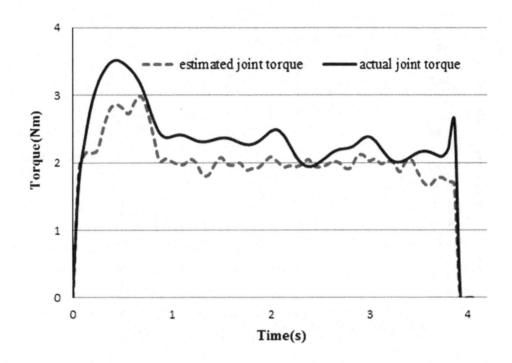

Estimated Joint torque Vs. Actual Joint Torque Elbow Flexion 90° With External Load for $MM_{(7)}$

Table 5. Summarised results of Coefficient of Determination (R^2) for elbow flexion of 90° with an external load of GA

MODEL	Coefficient of Determination (R^2)						
	S1	S2	S3	S4	S5	Average	Standard deviation
$MM_{(1)}$	0.87	0.85	0.83	0.85	0.83	0.85	0.02
$MM_{(2)}$	0.90	0.86	0.86	0.82	0.84	0.86	0.03
$MM_{(3)}$	0.87	0.84	0.82	0.80	0.82	0.83	0.03
$MM_{(4)}$	0.90	0.87	0.86	0.80	0.85	0.86	0.03
$MM_{(5)}$	0.65	0.62	0.63	0.75	0.63	0.66	0.06
$MM_{(6)}$	0.88	0.85	0.83	0.85	0.83	0.85	0.02
$MM_{(7)}$	0.91	0.89	0.87	0.83	0.86	0.87	0.03
$MM_{(8)}$	0.65	0.62	0.63	0.75	0.63	0.66	0.06
$MM_{(9)}$	0.65	0.62	0.63	0.75	0.63	0.66	0.06

Figure 10. Error bar each mathematical model of R^2 for elbow flexion of 90° with an external load of GA

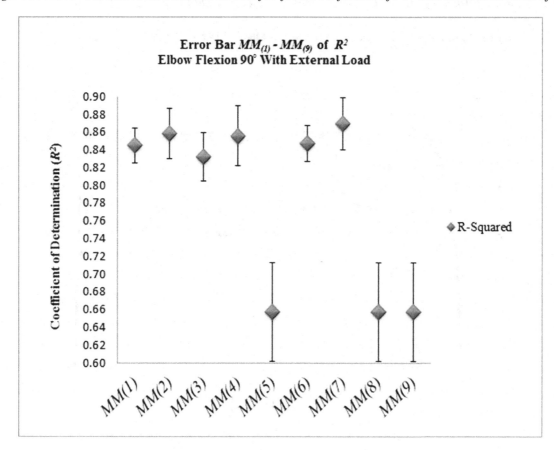

Table 6. Summary of results of Pearson Correlation (R) for elbow flexion of 90° with an external load of GA

MODEL	Pearson Correlation (R)						
	S1	S2	S3	S4	S5	Average	Standard deviation
$MM_{(1)}$	0.93	0.92	0.91	0.92	0.91	0.92	0.01
$MM_{(2)}$	0.95	0.93	0.93	0.92	0.92	0.93	0.01
$MM_{(3)}$	0.94	0.92	0.91	0.90	0.90	0.91	0.01
$MM_{(4)}$	0.95	0.93	0.93	0.90	0.92	0.93	0.02
$MM_{(5)}$	0.81	0.79	0.79	0.87	0.80	0.81	0.03
$MM_{(6)}$	0.94	0.92	0.91	0.92	0.91	0.92	0.01
$MM_{(7)}$	0.95	0.94	0.93	0.91	0.93	0.93	0.02
$MM_{(8)}$	0.81	0.79	0.79	0.87	0.80	0.81	0.03
$MM_{(9)}$	0.81	0.79	0.79	0.87	0.80	0.81	0.03

Figure 11. Error bar each mathematical model of R for elbow flexion of 90° with an external load of GA

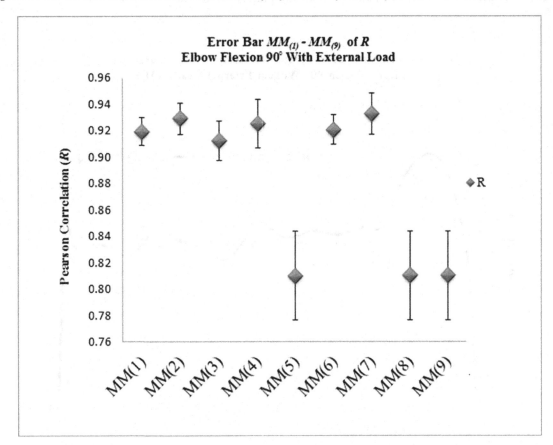

Table 7 and Figure 13 indicate the results coefficient of determination (R^2) for each mathematical model of all subjects' optimizations of particle swarm optimization for elbow flexion 90° without an external between estimated joint torque and actual joint torque.

Table 8 and Figure 14 denote the results of the Pearson Correlation (R) for each mathematical model of all subjects' optimizations of particle swarm optimization for elbow flexion 90° without an external load between estimated joint torque and actual joint torque.

Table 7 and Figure 13 represent the results of R^2 and Table 10 and Figure 14 illustrate optimizations of particle swarm optimization for elbow flexion 90° without an external load. The results denote that mathematical models of $MM_{(5)}$, $MM_{(8)}$ and $MM_{(9)}$ give the lowest average value of R^2 is 0.62 ± 0.06 and lowest average value of R is 0.78 ± 0.04 for all subjects. The average value of all subjects for $MM_{(1)}$, $MM_{(2)}, MM_{(3)}, MM_{(4)}, MM_{(6)}$ and $MM_{(7)}$ of R^2 is above 0.8 and R is above 0.9. It can be seen that $MM_{(2)}$ and $MM_{(7)}$ have the highest average values of all subjects for R^2 and R associated to $MM_{(1)}$, $MM_{(3)}, MM_{(4)}$, and $MM_{(6)}$. It can be observed that the optimal mathematical model are $MM_{(2)}$, and $MM_{(7)}$. The results show that the average value of R^2 is 0.87 ± 0.03 and the average value of R is 0.93 ± 0.01 for $MM_{(2)}$, the average value of R^2 is 0.87 ± 0.02 and the average value of R is 0.93 ± 0.01 for . $MM_{(7)}$.

Figure 12. Joint torques of elbow flexion 90° without an external load for $MM_{(7)}$ using PSO.

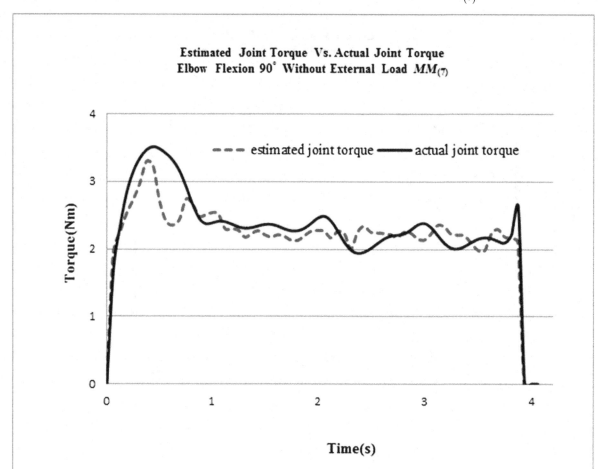

Table 7. Summarised result of Coefficient of Determination (R^2) for elbow flexion of 90° without an external load of PSO

MODEL	Coefficient of Determination (R^2)						
	S1	S2	S3	S4	S5	Average	Standard deviation
$MM_{(1)}$	0.83	0.85	0.87	0.85	0.87	0.85	0.01
$MM_{(2)}$	0.87	0.90	0.88	0.83	0.87	0.87	0.03
$MM_{(3)}$	0.86	0.89	0.81	0.82	0.85	0.85	0.03
$MM_{(4)}$	0.81	0.82	0.85	0.84	0.87	0.84	0.03
$MM_{(5)}$	0.57	0.56	0.67	0.70	0.59	0.62	0.06
$MM_{(6)}$	0.84	0.85	0.87	0.85	0.81	0.84	0.02
$MM_{(7)}$	0.86	0.90	0.88	0.85	0.86	0.87	0.02
$MM_{(8)}$	0.57	0.56	0.67	0.70	0.59	0.62	0.06
$MM_{(9)}$	0.57	0.56	0.67	0.70	0.59	0.62	0.06

Figure 13. Error bar each mathematical model of R^2 for elbow flexion of 90° without an external load of PSO

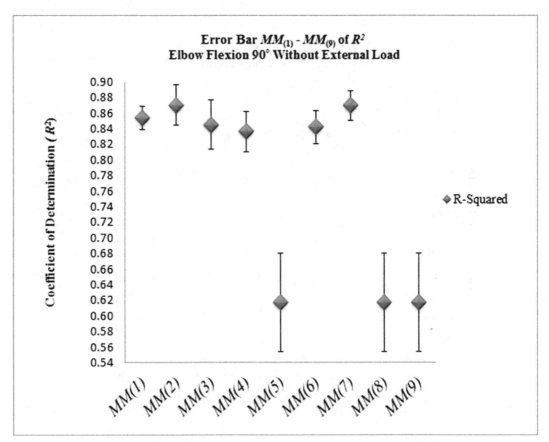

Table 8. Summarised result of Pearson Correlation (R) for elbow flexion of 90° without an external load of PSO

MODEL	Pearson Correlation (R)						
	S1	S2	S3	S4	S5	Average	Standard deviation
$MM_{(1)}$	0.91	0.92	0.93	0.92	0.93	0.92	0.01
$MM_{(2)}$	0.93	0.95	0.94	0.91	0.93	0.93	0.01
$MM_{(3)}$	0.93	0.94	0.90	0.91	0.92	0.92	0.02
$MM_{(4)}$	0.90	0.90	0.92	0.91	0.93	0.91	0.01
$MM_{(5)}$	0.76	0.75	0.82	0.83	0.77	0.78	0.04
$MM_{(6)}$	0.91	0.92	0.93	0.92	0.90	0.92	0.01
$MM_{(7)}$	0.93	0.95	0.94	0.92	0.93	0.93	0.01
$MM_{(8)}$	0.76	0.75	0.82	0.83	0.77	0.78	0.04
$MM_{(9)}$	0.76	0.75	0.82	0.83	0.77	0.78	0.04

Figure 14. Error bar each mathematical model of R for elbow flexion of 90° without an external load of PSO

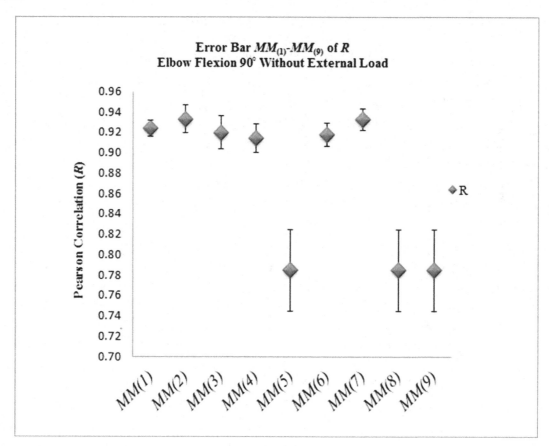

Optimization of Mathematical Model Using Particle Swarm Optimization of Elbow Flexion of 90° with an External Load

Figure 15 denotes an example graph of estimated joint torque and actual joint torque for elbow flexion 90° of $MM_{(7)}$ with an external load by using particle swarm optimization.

Table 9 and Figure 16 show the results coefficient of determination (R^2) for each mathematical model of all subjects' optimizations of particle swarm optimization for elbow flexion 90° with an external between estimated joint torque and actual joint torque.

Table 10 and Figure 17 denote the results of the Pearson Correlation (R) for each mathematical model of all subjects optimizations of particle swarm optimization for elbow flexion 90° with an external between estimated joint torque and actual joint torque.

Table 9 and Figure 16, Table 10 and Figure 17 represent the optimizations of particle swarm optimization for elbow flexion 90° with an external load R^2 and R. The findings represent the average value for all subjects for R is above 0.9 and R^2 is above 0.8 for $MM_{(1)}$, $MM_{(2)}$, $MM_{(3)}$, $MM_{(4)}$, $MM_{(6)}$ and $MM_{(7)}$. It can be seen that the optimal mathematical model are $MM_{(2)}$ and $MM_{(7)}$ where both mathematical model indicate highest average value for all subjects of R^2 and R compared to $MM_{(1)}$, $MM_{(3)}$, $MM_{(4)}$, and $MM_{(6)}$. It can be observed that for $MM_{(2)}$, the average value of R^2 is 0.87±0.02 and the average value of R is

Figure 15. Joint torques of elbow flexion 90° with an external load for $MM_{(7)}$ using PSO.

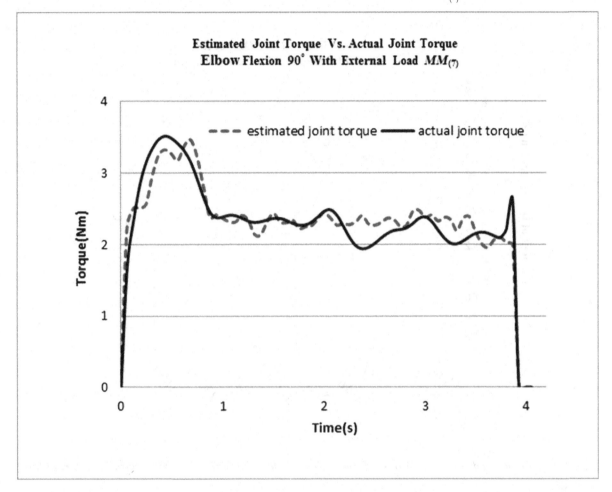

Table 9. Summarised result of Coefficient of Determination (R^2) for elbow flexion of 90° with an external load of PSO

MODEL	Coefficient of Determination (R^2)						
	S1	S2	S3	S4	S5	Average	Standard deviation
$MM_{(1)}$	0.88	0.85	0.83	0.85	0.83	0.85	0.02
$MM_{(2)}$	0.90	0.87	0.86	0.85	0.85	0.87	0.02
$MM_{(3)}$	0.82	0.84	0.85	0.81	0.80	0.83	0.02
$MM_{(4)}$	0.85	0.83	0.82	0.85	0.82	0.84	0.02
$MM_{(5)}$	0.65	0.62	0.63	0.75	0.63	0.66	0.06
$MM_{(6)}$	0.88	0.85	0.83	0.85	0.83	0.85	0.02
$MM_{(7)}$	0.91	0.89	0.87	0.84	0.85	0.87	0.03
$MM_{(8)}$	0.65	0.62	0.63	0.75	0.63	0.66	0.06
$MM_{(9)}$	0.65	0.62	0.63	0.75	0.63	0.66	0.06

Figure 16. Error bar each mathematical model of R^2 for elbow flexion of 90° with an external load of PSO

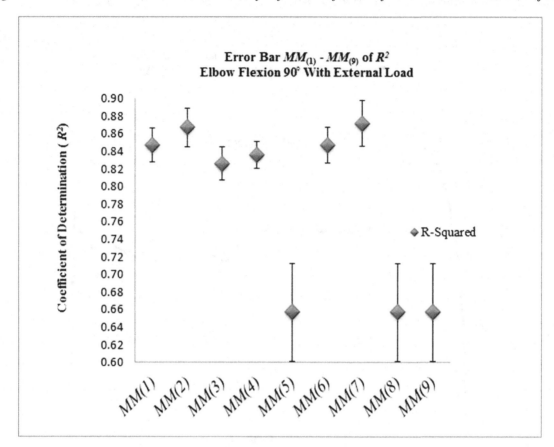

Table 10. Summarised result of Pearson Correlation (R) for elbow flexion of 90° with an external load of PSO

MODEL	Pearson Correlation (R)						
	S1	S2	S3	S4	S5	Average	Standard deviation
$MM_{(1)}$	0.94	0.92	0.91	0.92	0.91	0.92	0.01
$MM_{(2)}$	0.95	0.93	0.93	0.92	0.92	0.93	0.01
$MM_{(3)}$	0.91	0.92	0.92	0.90	0.90	0.91	0.01
$MM_{(4)}$	0.92	0.91	0.91	0.92	0.91	0.91	0.01
$MM_{(5)}$	0.81	0.79	0.79	0.87	0.80	0.81	0.03
$MM_{(6)}$	0.94	0.92	0.91	0.92	0.91	0.92	0.01
$MM_{(7)}$	0.95	0.94	0.93	0.92	0.92	0.93	0.01
$MM_{(8)}$	0.81	0.79	0.79	0.87	0.80	0.81	0.03
$MM_{(9)}$	0.81	0.79	0.79	0.87	0.80	0.81	0.03

Figure 17. Error bar each mathematical model of R for elbow flexion of 90° with an external load of PSO

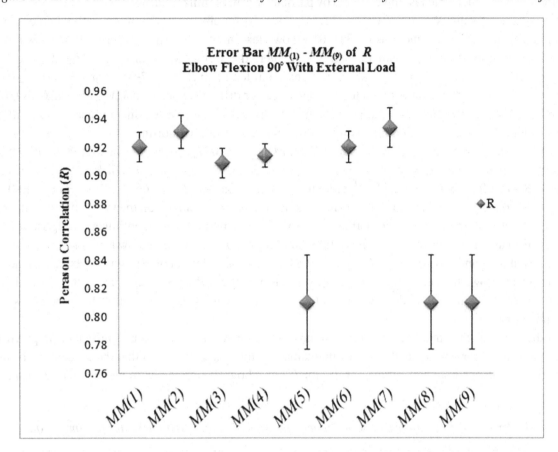

0.93±0.01, and for $MM_{(7)}$, it is found that the average value of R^2 is 0.87±0.03 and the average value of R is 0.93±0.01. Mathematical model of $MM_{(5)}$, $MM_{(8)}$, $MM_{(9)}$ are determined as the lowest average value of R^2 with 0.66±0.06 and the lowest average value of R is 0.81±0.03.

DISCUSSIONS

The overall results of the movement for elbow flexion of 90° without an external load and elbow flexion of 90° with an external load, it is found that the average value of R^2 is more than 0.8, and average value of R is more than 0.9 for $MM_{(1)}$, $MM_{(2)}$, $MM_{(3)}$, $MM_{(4)}$, $MM_{(6)}$, $MM_{(7)}$ by using genetic algorithm and particle swarm optimization algorithm. The optimal mathematical model is obtained by the highest correlation of R^2 and R between estimated joint torque and the actual joint torque for the results which are obtained for both genetic algorithm and particle swarm optimization algorithm. It should be noted that the fitness value was used to obtain the convergence only. However, the best mathematical model was chosen based on R^2.

It can be observed that the optimal mathematical model is $MM_{(7)}$ where the average value R^2 is 0.86±0.02 and R is 0.93±0.01 for elbow flexion 90° without an external load, and R^2 is 0.87±0.03 and R is 0.93±0.02 elbow flexion 90° with an external load are based on genetic algorithm. The optimal mathematical model which is implemented by particle swarm optimization algorithm is $MM_{(7)}$ where the average value of value R^2 is 0.87 ± 0.02 and R is 0.93 ± 0.01 for elbow flexion of 90° without an external load and R^2 is 0.87 ± 0.03 and R is 0.93 ± 0.01 elbow flexion of 90° with an external load. It is found that $MM_{(2)}$ is also an optimal mathematical model where the average value of R^2 is 0.87 ± 0.03 and R is 0.93 ± 0.01 for elbow flexion of 90° without an external load and R^2 is 0.87 ± 0.02 and R is 0.93 ± 0.01 elbow flexion of 90° with an external load. Since the error difference between $MM_{(2)}$ and $MM_{(7)}$ is 0.01, therefore, $MM_{(7)}$ is chosen as the optimal mathematical model for particle swarm optimization algorithm. This is done to make a direct comparison with genetic optimization algorithm.

The worst fit mathematical models are $MM_{(5)}$, $MM_{(8)}$ and $MM_{(9)}$ for elbow flexion 90° without an external load and elbow flexion of 90° with an external load. The average value of R^2 is 0.62 ± 0.02 and R is 0.78 ± 0.02 for elbow flexion of 90° without an external load and R^2 is 0.66 ± 0.60 and R is 0.81 ± 0.03 elbow flexion of 90° with an external load is by using genetic algorithm for all the worst fit mathematical models. Each of the worst fit for the mathematical execution of particle swarm optimization algorithm has obtained an average value of R^2, which is 0.62 ± 0.06 and R is 0.78 ± 0.04 for elbow flexion of 90° without an external load and R^2 is 0.66 ± 0.06 and R is 0.81 ± 0.03 elbow flexion of 90° with an external load.

Table 11 shows the performance comparison in terms of R^2, R, execution time for the optimal and the worst fit mathematical models are based on optimization using genetic algorithm and particle swarm optimization.

Table 11 indicates that the percentage improvement of R^2 and R are not significant compared to both algorithms for optimal and worst fit mathematical models. It is shown that the percentage of improvement between both algorithms is 1.2% for R^2 for elbow flexion 90° without an external load and

Table 11. Performance comparison between genetic algorithm and particle swarm optimization

Optimal					
Task movement	Mathematical model	Measurement Performance	GA	PSO	% Improvement
Elbow flexion 90° without external load	$MM_{(7)}$	R^2	0.86	0.87	1.2%
		R	0.93	0.93	0%
		Execution time(s)	30.846	6.3778	**79%**
Elbow flexion 90° with external load	$MM_{(7)}$	R^2	0.87	0.87	0%
		R	0.93	0.93	0%
		Execution time(s)	218.9642	5.7676	**97%**
Worst Fit					
Task movement	Mathematical model	Measurement Performance	GA	PSO	% Improvement
Elbow flexion 90° without external load	$MM_{(5)}$,	R^2	0.62	0.62	0%
		R	0.78	0.78	0%
		Execution time(s)	58.1766	2.5808	**95.6%**
Elbow flexion 90° with external load	$MM_{(5)}$,	R^2	0.66	0.66	0%
		R	0.81	0.81	0%
		Execution time(s)	11.29	2.0918	**81%**

0% for R^2 of 90° of elbow flexion with an external load, and 0% for R for all the task movement for optimal mathematical model. The percentage of improvement for the worst fit mathematical model is 0% for R^2 of 90° of elbow flexion with and without an external load, 2.9% and 0% for R for all the task movements. In terms of execution time, PSO has produced the highest percentage of improvement with 79% for elbow flexion of 90° without an external load and 97% for elbow flexion 90° with an external load for optimal mathematical model as compared to GA. For worst fit mathematical model, PSO also produced the highest percentage of improvement as compared to GA with 95.6% for elbow flexion of 90° without an external load and 81% for elbow flexion of 90° with an external load. The results for R and R^2 are achieved based on five different subjects (four male and one female) for the elbow flexion.

It can be seen that the results conform to the results that is obtained by, (Arief et al., 2010) using Genetic Algorithm (GA) and (Parasuraman et. al, 2010) by using the Simulated Annealing algorithm (SA) to optimise the sEMG signals as to estimate the joint torque using the mathematical models. It shows that the genetic algorithm and particle swarm optimization have an improved result of 12% for R of 90° of elbow flexion without load, and 14.8% for R of 90° of elbow flexion with external load as compared to other researchers' work, (Arief et al., 2010), (Parasuraman et al., 2010). Nevertheless, it can be inferred that the use of GA and PSO have produced comparable performance. As stated in Table 11, PSO algorithm produced the fastest computational time in this research. PSO algorithm is also reported as the fastest computational time as compared to GA in other works for the geometry optimization design of the longitudinal fin (Mandal et al., 2011), for a high pass filter design (Sivandam et al., 2009) and lower order modelling of control system design engineering (Ethni et al., 2009). Hence, overall, PSO is considered to have produced the best results. The above comparison is made to justify the results which are obtained by using the proposed method, although a direct comparison could not be carried out.

The conventional robotic assistive system is pre-programmed based on human motion and the patient's movement exercises would follow the motion movement that has been set. The major drawback of this approach is that the lack of voluntary movement of the patient may affect the proficiency of the recovery process. Ideally, the robotic assistive system should recognize the intended movement and assist the patient to perform and make the training exercises more effectively. The main idea here is that the robotics assistive system should recognize the intended movement without any additional input device to communicate with the system. This is the main reason why sEMG signals are obtained during the muscle contraction while the user is doing the task training. The sEMG signals are then converted as estimated joint torque by using joint torque estimation models. Different methods of joint torque estimation models have been done by other researchers such as the Hill Based model (Song & Tong, 2005), (Wang & Buchanan, 2002), (Rosen et al., 1999). Artificial Neural Network (ANN) (Park et al., 2009), (Wang &Buchanan, 2002), (Rosen et al., 1999) and Mathematical Models ((Arief et al., 2010), (Parasuraman et al., 2010), (Song & Tong, 2005). However, the Hill Based Muscle Model has complex architecture that needs to be solved with different set of differential models. The ANN model is only produce good results within training data set. Others data set need to be trained to get the accurate results. The mathematical models have used different optimization techniques such as Genetic Algorithm (GA) and Simulated Annealing (SA). However, the performance is below 0.9 according to Pearson Correlation(R) index from previous research work. In this research work, further investigation have done on sEMG signal convert to estimated torque by implementing the mathematical models with genetic algorithm and particle swarm optimization technique. The findings of this research found that both algorithms have shown the results mathematical model $MM_{(1)}$, $MM_{(2)}$, $MM_{(3)}$, $MM_{(4)}$, $MM_{(6)}$, $MM_{(7)}$ are above 0.9 refer to Pearson correlation Index. Although both algorithms show comparable results, particle swarm optimization has shown faster convergence time compared to genetic algorithm. Amongst these mathematical models, $MM_{(7)}$ has shown the best optimal mathematical model based on Coefficient of Determination (R^2) index performance.

FUTURE RESEARCH DIRECTIONS

Further work of sEMG signal optimization using mathematical models could be explored using other algorithms such as differential evolution, harmony search to obtain better accuracy output of estimated joint torque. Besides that, other movement task on upper and lower limb such as open and close hand, climbing stairs, knee flexion/extension movement could be investigated to obtain sEMG signal for estimated torque. This is important in development of robotic assistive device designed agreeing to natural human muscle strength from measurement of muscle activities of sEMG signal.

CONCLUSION

This research has contributed to the establishment of a suitable mathematical model as the joint torque estimation model based on surface electromyography (sEMG) signals using the genetic algorithm and particle swarm optimization. It can be seen that, the best mathematical models for elbow flexion with and without load are $MM_{(2)}$ and $MM_{(7)}$ and worst mathematical model $MM_{(5)}$, $MM_{(8)}$, $MM_{(9)}$. Statistical analysis was done based on the consistency average value of R and R^2 on all subjects to conform the estimated joint torque to the nearest value to actual joint torque. The finding showed that the mathematical model could be an alternative model for joint torque estimation of sEMG signals robotic assistive system. It is believed that this finding would play as an important role in future development of the robotic assistive system for various applications.

ACKNOWLEDGMENT

The authors would like to thank Ministry of Education (MOE), Malaysia for sponsoring this project under the PRGS Grant (0153AB-I31) & MyBrain Scheme, and Universiti Teknologi PETRONAS (UTP) for supporting this project.

REFERENCES

Akdogan, E., & Demir, M. H. (2012). Rehabilitation technologies: Biomechanics point of view. In A Roadmap of Biomedical Engineers and Milestone (pp. 1-36).

Arif, W. O., Parasuraman, S., & Jauw, V. L. (2010). Robot-assisted stoke rehabilitation: Estimation of muscle force/joint torque from EMG using GA. *Proceedings of theIEEE EMBS Conference on Biomed. Eng. & Science* (pp. 341-347).

Azarkish, H., Faraha, S., Masoud, S., & Sarvari, H. (2012). Comparing the performance of the particle swarm optimization and the genetic algorithm on the geometry design of longitudinal fin. *Inter. J. Of Mech, & Aerospace Engineering*, *6*(1), 262–26.

Cirtea, M. C., & Levin, M. F. (2000). Compensatory strategy for reaching stroke. *Brain*, *123*(5), 940–953. doi:10.1093/brain/123.5.940 PMID:10775539

Chen, L., & Ding, Q., Zhao & X., Han, J., (2011). Hierarchical projected regression for torque of elbow joint using EMG signals. *Proceedings of the5th International Conference on Bioinformatics and Biomedicals Eng.* (pp. 1-5). doi:10.1109/icbbe.2011.5780183

Cooper, R. A., Dieranno, B. E., Brewer, B., LoPresti, E., Ding, D., Simpson, R., & Wang, H. et al. (2008). A perspective on intelligent devices and environments in medical rehabilitation. *Journal of Med. Eng & Physics*, *30*(10), 1387–1398. doi:10.1016/j.medengphy.2008.09.003 PMID:18993108

Dollar, A. M., & Herr, H. (2008). Lower extremity exoskeletons and active orthoses: Challenges and state of art. *IEEE Transactions on Robotics*, *24*(1), 144–158. doi:10.1109/TRO.2008.915453

Ethni, S. A., Zahawi, B., Gaouris, D., & Acarnley, P. P. (2009). Comparison of particle swarm optimization and simulated annealing algorithms for induction motor fault identification. *Proceedings of the* 7th *IEEE Inter. Conference on Industrial Informatics 2009* (pp. 470-474).

Ferris, D. P., Czerniecki, J. M., & Hannaford, B. (2005). An ankle -foot orthosis powered by artificial pneumatic muscles. *Journal of Applied Biomechanics*, *21*(2), 189–197. PMID:16082019

Ferris, D.P., Sawaicki, G.S., & Domingo, A., (2005). Powered lower limb orthoses for gait rehabilitation. *For Spinal Cord Injury Rehabil.*, *11(2)*, 34-49.

Flansjer, U. B., Holmback, A. M., Downham, D., Parlten, C., & Lexell, J. (2005). Realibility of gait performance test in men and women with hemiparesis after stroke. *Rehabil. Medicine*, *37*(2), 75–82. doi:10.1080/16501970410017215

Go, A. S., Mozaffarian, D., Roger, V. L., Benjamin, E. J., Berry, J. D., Borden, W. B., & Turner, M. B. et al. (2013). Heart Disease and Stroke Statistics--2013 Update: A Report From the American Heart Association. *Circulation*, *127*(1), 143–152. doi:10.1161/CIR.0b013e318282ab8f

Harwin, W.S., Patton, L. & Edgerton, V.R., (2006). Challenges and opportunities for robot-mediated neurorehabilitation. *Proceedings of IEEE '06*, *94(9)*, 1717-1726.

Hayashi, T., Kawamoto, H., & Sankai, Y. (2008). Control method of robot suit HAL working as operator's muscle using biological and dynamical information. *Proceedings of the IEEE Inter. on Conference Robots and Sys.* (pp. 3063-3068).

Hidler, J., Nichols, D., Pelliccio, M., & Brady, K. (2005). Advances in the understanding and treatment of stroke impairment using robotic device. *Topics in Stroke Rehabilitation*, *12*(2), 22–35. doi:10.1310/RYT5-62N4-CTVX-8JTE PMID:15940582

Hogan, N., Krebs, H. I., Sharon, A., & Charnnarong, J. (1995, November). Interactive robot therapist. US patent 5, 466, 213.

Jeevandam, A., & Thanusneddi, K. G. (2009). Robust design of decentrialized power system stabilizers using metaheuristics optimization techniques for multimachine system. *Serbian J. Of Electrical Eng.*, *6*(1), 89–103. doi:10.2298/SJEE0901089J

Kang, S. J., Ryu, J. C., Kim, K. H., & Mun, M. S. (2004). A real -time control of powered gait orthosis by biosignal.*Proc. Of the 11th World Congress of The Inter. Society for Prosthetics and Orthosis, Hong Kong*.

Kreb, H. I. (2006). An overview of rehabilitation robotics technologies. *Proceedings of theAmerican Spinal Injury Association Symposium.*

Krebs, H. I., Palazzolo, J. J., Dipietro, L., Ferraro, M., Krol, J., Rannekleiv, K., & Hogan, N. et al. (2003). N. Rehabilitation robotics: Performance-based progressive robot-assisted therapy. *Autonomous Robots*, *15*(1), 7–20. doi:10.1023/A:1024494031121

Koceska, N., & Koceski, S. (2013). Review: Robot device for gait rehabilitation. *International Journal of Computers and Applications*, *62*(13), 1–8. doi:10.5120/10137-4279

Langhorne, P., Bernhardt, J., & Kwakkel, G. (2011). Series stroke rehabilitation. *Lancet*, *377*(9778), 1695–1702. doi:10.1016/S0140-6736(11)60325-5 PMID:21571152

Loureiro, R. C. V., Harwin, W. S., Nagai, K., & Johnson, M. (2011). Special review issue: Advances in upper limb stroke rehabilitation: a technology push. *Medical & Biological Engineering & Computing*, *49*(10), 1103–1118. doi:10.1007/s11517-011-0797-0 PMID:21773806

Louis, S. J., Chen, Q., & Pullammanappallil, S. (1999). Seismic velocity inversion with genetic algorithm. *Proc. of the Congress on Evolutionary Computation* (p. 2).

Low, K. H. (2011, August 3-5). Robot-assisted gait rehabilitation: from exoskeleton to gait systems. *Defence Science Research Conference&Expo, Singapore* (pp. 1-10). doi:10.1109/DSR.2011.6026886

Mandal, S., Kar, R., Mandal, D., & Ghosal, D. (2011). Swarm Intelligence based optimal linear phase FIR high pass filter design using particle swarm optimization with constriction factor and inertia weight approach. *World Academy Of Science, Eng. & Tech.*, *5*(8), 1156–1162.

Masiero, S., Carraro, E., Ferraro, C., Gallina, P., Rossi, A., & Rossati, G. (2009). Special Report: Upper limb rehabilitation robotics after stroke: A perspective from the university of Padua, Italy. *Journal of Rehabilitation Medicine*, *41*(12), 981–985. doi:10.2340/16501977-0404 PMID:19841828

Mazzoleni, S., Darion, P., Carrozza, M. C., & Guglielmelli, E. (2010). Application of robotics and me-chatronics systems to neurorehabilitation. Intech.

Meinders, M., Gitter, A., & Czernieki, J. M. (1998). The role of ankle plantar flexor muscle work during walking.*Scandinavian Journal ofRehabilitation Medicine, 30*(1), 39–46. doi:10.1080/003655098444309 PMID:9526753

Ministry of health Malaysia. (2014). Health Facts 2010. Retrieved from www.moh.gov.my

Nef, T., Mihelj, M., Colombo, G., & Riener, R. (2006). ARMin robot for rehabilitation of the upper extremities. *Proceedings of theIEEE Inter. Conference on Robotics and Automation, Orlando* (pp. 3152–3157). doi:10.1109/ROBOT.2006.1642181

Nordin, N. A. M., Aziz, N. A., Alkaff, S. E., Sulong, S., & Aljunid, S. (2012). Rehabilitation for patients after stroke in a tertiary hospital: It is early and intensive enough? *International Journal of Therapy and Rehabilitation, 19*(11), 603–611. doi:10.12968/ijtr.2012.19.11.603

Nejad, S. K., & Salajegheh, S. (2013). A Routing optimization approach for rescue robots based on evolutionary algorithm. *Switzerland Research Park Journal, 102*, 470–494.

Orchard, B., & Clark, A. R. (2004). Optimizing algorithms for antenna design. In *The Transaction of SA Institute Elec. Engineer* (pp. 279-289).

Parasuraman, S., Arif, W. O., & Jauw, V. L. (2010). Robot assisted stroke rehabilitation: Joint torque/ force conversion from EMG using SA Process. In H. Liu, . . . (Eds.), Proceedings of ICIRA 2010 (pp. 612–623). doi:10.1007/978-3-642-16587-0_56

Park, W., Kwon, S. C., Lee, H. D., & Kim, J. (2009). Thumb-tip force estimation from sEMG and musculoskeletal for real-time trigger prosthesis. *Proceedings of the IEEE 11th Inter. Conference on Rehabil. Robotics*, Kyoto (pp. 305-310).

Rosen, J., Fuchs, M. B., & Arcan, M. (1999). Performances of Hill type and neural network muscle models-toward a myosignal-based exoskeleton. *Computers and Biomedical Research, an International Journal, 32*(5), 415–439. doi:10.1006/cbmr.1999.1524 PMID:10529300

Sankai, Y. (2010). HAL-Hybrid Assistive limb based on Cybernetics. In *Robotic Research*. Springer.

Senanayake, C., & Senanayake, S. M. N. A. (2009). *Theraputic rehabilitation robotics for lower extremity: a review*. Proc. of World Academy Of Science Eng. & Tech.

Singh, S. J., & Gupta, M. (2013). Comparison of particle swarm optimization & simulated annealing for weight optimization of composite leaf spring. *Inter. J. Of Computational Eng. & Management, 16*(4), 14–24.

Sivandam, S. N., & Deepa, S. N. (2009). A comparative study using genetic algorithm and particle swarm optimization for lower order system modeling. *Inter. J. Of The Computer. The Internet & Management, 17*(3), 1–10.

Song, R., Tong, K. Y., Hu, X., & Li, L. (2008). Assistive control system using continuous myoelectric signal in a robot -aided arm training for patients after stroke. *IEEE TRANS. on Neural Sys. &. Rehabil. Eng, 16*(4), 371–379.

Song, R., & Tong, K. Y. (2005). Using recurrent artificial neural network model to estimate voluntary torque in dynamic situations. *J. of Medical & Bio. Eng. & Comput, 43*(4), 473–480.

Tong, R. K., & Hu, X. (2008). Service Robotics: Robot- assisted training for stroke rehabilitation. InTech.

Ullah, K., & Kim, J. H. (2009). A mathematical model for mapping EMG signal to joint torque for the human elbow joint using nonlinear regression. *Proc. 4th Int. Conf. On Autonomous Robots &Agents-* Wellington pp.103-108.

Wang, L., & Buchanan, T. S. (2002). Prediction of joint moment using of neural network of muscle activation from EMG signal. *IEEE Transactions on Neural Systems and Rehabilitation Engineering, 10*(1), 30–34. doi:10.1109/TNSRE.2002.1021584 PMID:12173737

ADDITIONAL READING

Bamajian, J. V., & Deluca, C. J. (1985). *Introduction Muscle Live. 5ᵗʰ Edi.* MD: Williams and Wilkins Baltimore.

De luca, C.J. (1997). The use of surface eletromyography in biomechanics. *J. of Applied Science, 13,* 135-163.

Gamet, D., & Fokapu, O. (2008). *Electromyography. Encyclopedia of Bio-Materials and Biomedical Eng.* Information Healthcare USA.

Hamilton, N., Weimar, W., & Luttgen, K. 2008. Ch.6. The upper extremity, the elbow, forearm, wrist, and hand. In Kinesiology Scientific Basis of Human Motion (11th ed., pp. 124-152). McGraw Hill Edu.

Haupt, R. L., & Haupt, S. E. (2004). *Introduction to optimization. Practical Genetic Algorithm 2ⁿᵈ Edi.* Wiley Interscience Publishing.

Hogan, N., & Mann, R. W. (1980). Myoelectric signal processing optimal estimation applied electromyography -Part I: Derivation of the optimal myoprocesso. *IEEE Transactions on Bio-Medical Engineering, 27*(7), 382–395. doi:10.1109/TBME.1980.326652 PMID:7409804

Montgomery, D.C., Perk, E.A., & Vining, G.G. (2006). Polynomial Regression Model. In *Introduction to Linear Regression Analysis* (Ch.7, pp. 213-214). John Wiley Sons Inc.

Motulsky, H.J., & Ransnas, L.A. (1987). Fitting curves to data using nonlinear regression: a practical and nonmathematical review. *FASEB Journal, 1*(5), 365-374.

Catalog Of Curves for Curve Fitting. (n. d.). *Ministry Of Forest Research Program OF British Columbia.*

Pandy, M. G., Merritt, J. S., & Barr, R.E. (2009). Biomechanics of the musculoskeletal system, Biomedical system analysis. In M. Kutz (Ed.), Biomed. Eng. & Design Handbook (Vol.1 Fundamentals, Ch. 7, 2nd ed.). Singapore: McGraw Hill.

Tassinary, L. G., & Caciopo, J. T. (2000). *The skelemotor system: Surface electromyo-graphy.* In J.T. Caciopo, & G. Bernston (Eds.), Handbook of Physiology (2nd ed.). Cambridge University Press.

Travis, W., Beck, T., & Housh, J. (2008). Use of electromyography in studying human movement. In Y. Hong, & R. Barlett (Eds.), Handbook of Biomechanics & Human Movement Science (Ch. 15, pp. 214-227).

KEY TERMS AND DEFINITIONS

Human Motion Tracking: Recording action of human movement by using either non-visual or visual tracking system.

Proportional Myoelectric Control: Control system utilizes a microcontroller or computer that inputs electromyography (EMG) signals from sensors on upper limb or lower limb to activates the actuator on robotic assistive device.

Surface Electromyography: (sEMG): Signal of muscle activity that measures the electrical impulse manifestation of the neuromuscular activity during muscle contraction.

Chapter 19

Immersive Virtual Reality as a Non–Pharmacological Analgesic for Pain Management:
Pain Distraction and Pain Self–modulation

Diane Gromala
Simon Fraser University, Canada

Chris Shaw
Simon Fraser University, Canada

Xin Tong
Simon Fraser University, Canada

Weina Jin
Simon Fraser University, Canada

ABSTRACT

In the 1990s, when immersive Virtual Reality (VR) was first popular, researchers found it to be an effective intervention in reducing acute pain. Since that time, VR technologies have been used for treating acute pain. Although the exact mechanism is unclear, VR is thought to be an especially effective form of pain distraction. While pain-related virtual environments have built upon pain distraction, a handful of researchers have focused on a more difficult challenge: VR for long-term chronic pain. Because the nature of chronic pain is complex, pharmacological analgesics are often insufficient or unsustainable as an ideal long-term treatment. In this chapter, the authors explore how VR can be used as a non-pharmacological adjuvant for chronic pain. Two paradigms for virtual environments built for addressing chronic pain have emerged – Pain Distraction and what we term Pain Self-modulation. We discuss VR's validation for mitigating pain in patients who have acute pain, for those with chronic pain, and for addressing "breakthrough" periods of higher pain in patients with chronic pain.

INTRODUCTION

Chronic pain (CP) is defined as pain that lasts more than 6 months and persists beyond the healing of its putative cause (Gatchel, Peng, Peters, Fuchs, & Turk, 2007). An estimated 20% of people in North America and 15-20% in industrialized nations (Benjamin, Morris, McBeth, Macfarlane, & Silman, 2000) suffer from CP. As a serious health problem, CP is under-recognized by policymakers (Breivik,

DOI: 10.4018/978-1-5225-0435-1.ch019

Eisenberg, O'Brien, 2013) and is inadequately managed by the healthcare system. In recent years, because of the relative ineffectiveness and potential addictive tendency of pharmaceutical treatments such as opioid analgesics, non-pharmacologic interventions have become a vital part of CP management, as they address the affective, cognitive, behavioral and socio-cultural dimensions of pain. The enormous physical, mental and economic burden that CP imposes on individuals and society demands the need for novel technologies to augment non-pharmaceutical, self-management based interventions.

In recent decades, innovative technologies are being designed and developed to assist individual healthcare, especially for the management of chronic conditions, such as Virtual Reality (VR), wearable computing, immersive 3-Dimensional (3D) sound, and serious games. Among these, immersive VR, which during its emergence was solely recognized for its entertainment value, has become more popular and widely accepted as a non-pharmacological analgesic in medical settings. VR is defined as an artificial environment that is created with computer graphic software and presented to the user in such a way that the user suspends disbelief and accepts it as a real environment.

One of VR's best-known applications in medical field is pain management, especially to attenuate acute pain that occurs during medical procedures. In a number of research projects, VR has been considered successful as a method for distracting patients and reducing their perceived bodily pain, as well as managing emotional disorders, such as overcoming anxiety (Gold, Kant, Kim, & Rizzo, 2005). VR has been applied to help patients with acute pain from dental procedures (Bidarra et al., 2013), cancer-related treatment (Schneider & Workman, 1999), and burn patient wound debridement (Hoffman et al., 2008).

Besides acute pain, there are also studies that suggest CP patients can also benefit from VR applications (Shahrbanian, Ma, Korner-Bitensky, & Simmonds, 2009). CP patients, although requiring long-term pain reduction strategies, also suffer from shorter-term spikes in pain intensity. However, it is not yet known if the analgesic effects of VR persist beyond the VR sessions. Few VEs and VR games have been developed for or researched with CP patients (Li, Montano, Chen, & Gold, 2011).

In this chapter, we will first depict the medical problem and the existing non-technological and technological solutions for health-related Human Computer Interaction (HCI) design. Then we mainly discuss two design paradigms of VR systems for pain management: pain distraction & pain self-modulation. For pain distraction, we created a VR game Mobius Floe (MF). It steers patients' attention outward to reduce pain and anxiety. Our Virtual Meditative Walk (VMW) system is designed to help patient focus inward with pain self-modulation training. It is an immersive VE that incorporates biofeedback sensors and stereoscopic sound. We discuss each VR system, including the supporting medical theory, the design and development approaches we took, and our user testing with patients. Design guidelines that arose from our practice are also offered for the two VR systems. The most crucial point – how to understand the experience of CP patients and communicate such experience – is outlined and discussed in order to inspire more designers and researchers are interested in designing systems for Chronic Pain patients.

RELATED WORK

Chronic Pain and Related Medical Conditions

Pain is the feeling, or the perception, of irritating, sore, stinging, aching, throbbing, miserable, or unbearable sensations arising from a part of the body (Mark F. Bear, Barry W. Connors, Michael A. Paradiso. Neuroscience: Exploring the Brain, 3rd Edi. Wolters Kluwer; Feb. 7 2006). It is an essential human experience that warns us of impending injury, infection or damage. As the underlying damage heals, harmful stimuli disappear and the pain generally dissipates; this form of pain is often termed acute pain. In contrast, CP is pain that remains despite the fact that the injury has healed. It is a subjective perception that results from a dynamic interaction among physiological, psychological, and social factors (Gatchel, 2007).

Chronic pain is associated with many medical conditions. It can be a symptom or caused by a series of disease conditions, for instance, post-trauma/injury or infection, cancer, rheumatoid arthritis, fibromyalgia, and so on. It evolves different parts of the body: migraine, neck pain, low back pain, knee pain, ankle pain, and so on. It also leads to somatic and mental disorders: sequelae such as insomnia, anxiety, depression, decreasing mobility and increasing social isolation (Gatchel et al., 2007). Because of its correlation with a variety of medical conditions, CP defies easy categorization (Bowker & Star, 2000); although it leads to disability, it is not categorized as a disability per se.

The American Academy of Pain Management reported that 43% of all adult Americans had CP in the past 12 months (Tsang et al., 2008), which prevalence is far greater than these of heart disease, diabetes, and cancer combined. CP can affect people of all ages, genders and races, and contributes greatly to the rates of morbidity, mortality, and disability. The tremendous human suffering from CP markedly decreases individuals' Quality of Life (QoL), work and family functioning. Patients admitted to a multidisciplinary pain center in Norway reported health-related QoL as poor as that reported from dying cancer patients (Fredheim et al., 2008). Besides, CP patients are at increased risk of mental disorders, such as depression and anxiety (Benjamin et al., 2000).

The expenditure on CP is enormous. According to the Institute of Medicine's conservative estimate, its economic cost in the US is $560–635 billion annually, which is around 4% of the US Gross Domestic Product (GDP) (Institute of Medicine (US) Committee on Advancing Pain Research, Care, and Education, 2011). These costs are reported to exceed those estimated for heart disease, cancer and diabetes. Other studies showed CP took up 3% of GDP in Ireland and 10% of GDP Sweden (Breivik et al., 2013).

Difficulties of Chronic Pain Treatment

Chronic or long-term pain is one of numerous chronic conditions, one that potentially poses one of the greatest difficulties because it is a relatively recently recognized concept (Tunstall-Pedoe, 2006). Acute pain is the kind of pain we are most familiar with and dealing with, but not CP. Moreover, the public is rarely as aware of this condition compared to other chronic diseases such as diabetes, heart disease, cancers and so on (Chaiamnuay, Darmawan, Muirden, & Assawatanabodee, 1998). The public and healthcare professionals who are not familiar with CP tend to doubt what patients describe, leading to stigmatization of patients as lazy, drug-seeking hypochondriacs or malingerers (Epping-Jordan, Pruitt, Bengoa, & Wagner, 2004). This, in turn prevents patients from being properly diagnosed and from finding adequate treatment (Borsook & Kalso, 2013).

For CP, usually the cause and cure are unknown (Borsook & Kalso, 2013). There is no objective examination such as X-Ray or blood test for diagnosis. Thus, the complexity of CP condition involves neurobiological, psychological and social dimensions, and as such, no universal treatment exists (Fishbain, Cole, Lewis, Rosomoff, & Rosomoff, 2008). Since complete and sustained recovery from CP is rare, the goal of CP management is to relieve pain, improve function and increase wellbeing.

For pain management, the first-line treatment is pharmacological agents, such as opioid analgesics or non-steroidal anti-inflammatory drugs. Pain medications are one of the most prescribed drugs in physician's offices and emergency rooms. Despite their frequent use, pain medications do not achieve satisfactory effectiveness. For example, the average long-term pain reduction rate for opioid analgesics is approximately 32% (Turk, 2002). An epidemiological study showed opioid usage was significantly associated with reporting of moderate/severe or very severe pain, poor self-rated health, not being engaged in employment, higher use of the health care system, and a negative influence on quality of life (Eriksen, Sjøgren, Bruera, Ekholm, & Rasmussen, 2006). The pharmaceutical treatment only addresses the neurobiological aspects of the comprehensive condition, while ignoring psychological and social factors of CP. Moreover, for chronic patients who usually need long-term treatment, opioid analgesics can have serious risks, including drug dependence, addiction (Jamison et al., 2010), abuse and overdose (Portenoy, 1996). These issues, along with the growth in pain medication prescription, have become a prominent health issue among families and society.

Non-Pharmaceutical Interventions for Chronic Pain

Non-pharmacological treatment, together with pharmacological treatment, are part of a comprehensive CP management approach, as World Health Organization (WHO)'s pain guideline suggests (WHO Guidelines on the Pharmacological Treatment of Persisting Pain in Children with Medical Illnesses, 2012). Non-pharmacologic approaches include behavioral, cognitive and physical therapies (Chang, Fillingim, Hurley, & Schmidt, 2015). These strategies usually have little or no side effects, and when properly used, can reduce the use of pain medication.

Non-pharmacological strategies tackle the complex CP problem in psychological and social aspects. Unlike pharmacological treatment where patients passively take medications, the non-pharmacological interventions require patients to actively participate in the pain management process. The ultimate participation of patients in the pain care is self-management—that is, the individual's ability to manage the symptoms, treatment, physical and social consequences and lifestyle changes inherent in living with a chronic condition (Barlow, Wright, Sheasby, Turner, & Hainsworth, 2002). As suggested by Institute of Medicine, support of patient self-management is a key component of effective chronic illness care and improved outcomes (Institute of Medicine US Committee on Advancing Pain Research, 2011). After all, for most CP individuals, pain care happens at home, at work or in the community outside any healthcare settings.

This shifts pain management paradigms from pharmaceutical therapy to multimodal therapy, which is constituted of pharmaceutical and non-pharmaceutical therapy. To move from physician-centric to patient-centric self-management pain care requires novel technologies to augment evidence-based non-pharmacological interventions that integrate self-management approaches.

For technology innovation in healthcare, finding an easy solution from scratch is rare. A fast design approach is to inspect existing non-technology medical interventions and design technology based on them. Several existing non-pharmacological interventions that could be employed and enhanced by VR technology to relieve pain include are Mindfulness-Based Stress Reduction (MBSR), biofeedback and distraction. MBSR and biofeedback are skillful techniques for CP patients, while distraction is mostly used for acute pain alleviation.

MBSR is a standardized meditation program created in 1979 from the effort to integrate Buddhist mindfulness meditation with contemporary clinical and psychological practice (Chiesa & Serretti, 2009). Through a combination of mindfulness meditation, body awareness, and yoga, MBSR enables patients to regulate their mental state and reduce stress. Studies showed MBSR is effective at reducing pain ratings, pain sensitivity and anxiety scores when compared with baseline testing and other cognitive manipulations (Zeidan, Gordon, Merchant, & Goolkasian, 2010). However, to acquire the skillful MBSR technique, individuals need to receive long and persistent training, which may potentially be addressed by HCI technology.

Biofeedback is a treatment technique which enables a person, with the help of electronic equipment, to learn to control otherwise involuntary bodily functions (Bray, 1998). It utilizes multiple sensors to collect real-time physiological data from a patient, such as brainwave, heart and respiratory rate, skin temperature and electrical activity, and muscle tone. These data are then processed by computer and encoded as visual or audio stimuli to be received by the patient. Such an output-input feedback loop enables patients to be more aware of the involuntary physiological process in their body, and thus to train their brain to manipulate them at will. In many types of CP, the biofeedback intervention has shown to be effective in reducing perceived pain (Newton-John, Spence, & Schotte, 1995), (Jensen et al., 2013), (Weeks, Whitney, Tindall, & Carter, 2015). By employing VR as the output device in the biofeedback loop, the immersive, undisrupted virtual space may enhance this technique, and patients can adapt to the control of their inner organs, and learn to truly relax their mind, body and emotions much more easily.

Distraction is one of the most commonly-used and highly endorsed strategies for controlling pain. It keeps the attention away from pain by engaging in other thoughts or activities (Johnson, 2005). The underlying neural mechanism of distraction analgesia can be explained by several theories: Gate Control Theory proposed by Melzack and Wall, and Multiple Resources Theory by Wickens (Wickens, 2008). In previous studies, some of the effective distractors include: listening to music, watching television, reading books, dreaming and playing video games. The VR researches mentioned above which have pain-attenuating effects are based on cognitive distraction analgesia.

Innovative Self-Management Healthcare Technology and Systems for Chronic Conditions

Traditional health care services and systems are in transition towards self-care management to meet escalating demand (MacKichan, Paterson, Henley, & Britten, 2011) for medical and health care support for people with chronic illness. Even where specialized treatment for CP exist -- usually in multidisciplinary pain treatment centers -- patients endure long waits, ranging, for example, from 1 to 6 years in Canada. Given this context, it perhaps comes as no surprise that among groups of patients who are considered to be "at risk," CP patients are more "successful" in dying when they attempt suicide than any other group.

The emerging field of HCI is using interactive technologies to promote self-healthcare and self-management for patients, including VR, Wearable Computing Technologies, Immersive 3D Soundscapes, Serious Games and so forth. These self-management technologies provide more potential and possibilities for chronic patients to build a more personalized care system that gives patients and users more choices and responsibility to be involved in self-management of long-term conditions. The idea and technology system of self-management is a milestone, turning patients from a passive attitude to a more proactive role in individual care. In the research of Torsi et al. (Torsi, Nasr, Wright, Mawson, & Mountain, 2009), they describe how self-management generally starts with a positive change in body functions and symptoms, and actuates the body through activities that help patients to better manage their illness by means of providing various types of knowledge and solutions.

Technologies for Pain

The field of HCI tackles the pain problem mainly from two aspects: short-term pain distraction, and long-term pain management and functional rehabilitation.

For acute pain or short-term pain reduction, innovative technologies are developed to help patients who undergo painful medical procedures in clinical settings. Bucolo, et al. designed a tangible augmented reality device to alleviate anxiety and pain in pediatric burns patients (Bucolo, Mott, & Kimble, 2006). A prospective randomized controlled trial involving fifty pediatric patients showed that the augmented reality group recorded lower pain scores throughout the burn dressings changes compared to control group patients. Fassbender, et al. developed a low-cost 3 projector display system for pain reduction in hospital settings. As a substitute for head-mounted display for pain distraction, this may provide an alternative way for patients to immerse in the restorative virtual environments (Fassbender & de Souza, 2012).

For chronic pain or long-term pain management, the major work focuses on rehabilitation systems for CP. Several games address this rehabilitation exercises, such as in (Correa-Agudelo, Hernandez, Ferrin, & Gomez, 2015; Gotsis et al., 2013). Although interactive rehabilitative technologies may be efficacious for many chronic conditions, Chronic Pain is a special case, as it is more complex since it is closely associated with emotion, such as fear of motion, low confidence, and avoidance behavior. Therefore, Olugbade et al. developed an automated system that recognizes pain-related expressions from body movement (Olugbade, Aung, Bianchi-Berthouze, Marquardt, & Williams, 2014). Besides rehabilitative needs, researchers also address the other needs for CP patients. David et al. did a field study with 20 older CP patients, and developed a digital communicating picture frame to support the communication needs (David, Benjamin, Baecker, Gromala, & Birnholtz, 2011). Hourcade et al. aim to help children with chronic headaches communicate with health care providers about their headaches through a zoomable multi-touch app (Hourcade, Driessnack, & Huebner, 2012).

Virtual Reality Technologies and Chronic Pain

Virtual Reality (VR) is a system that transports users into a Virtual Environment (VE). VR generates an immersive experience through a combination of Head-Mounted Displays (HMD) or stereoscopic displays, headphones with sound/music and noise reduction, and devices for manipulation/navigation of the VE like a rumble pad, joystick or another (Li et al., 2011).

VR treatments for the reduction of acute pain have seen promising results in multiple studies. Hoffman et al. convincingly demonstrated that immersive VR is very effective to attract people's attention into computer generated virtual places (Borsook & Kalso, 2013) so that it can be used as the powerful pain control technique and tool for patients to manage and alleviate their pain (Tunstall-Pedoe, 2006). A VE titled SnowWorld, which draws patient's attention away from their embodied experience of pain and toward the virtual 3D environment was used to curb the wound care pain of U.S. soldiers injured with significant burns at the U.S. Army Institute of Surgical Research (USAISR). SnowWorld featured a snowy landscape where the patient could throw snowballs and be hit by snowballs in the virtual space. This experience combined with analgesic medications served to improve the soldier's pain experiences in regards to "time spent thinking about pain" and experienced "pain unpleasantness", both of which declined significantly with the introduction of VR to their standard wound care routine (Maani et al., 2008).

Hoffman et al. reported significantly reduced levels of pain in dental patients undergoing scaling and root planing in those who were immersed in cognitive distraction via a VR simulation over patients who were asked to watch a movie and those who had no distraction present during their procedures (Hoffman et al., 2001). Their results imply that immersive VR applications may serve as an effective non-pharmacologic analgesic which could to be used in tandem with existing prescribed pain medications for dental pain; this conclusion by extension may also be applicable to other pain demographics, especially considering the surrounding literature. For example, in a randomized control trial study by Das et al., a VR game was added to the procedural care schedule of children with acute burn injuries. The introduction of VR to their normally prescribed pharmacological analgesics decreased the average of the children's self-reported Faces Scale pain ratings from 4.1 (SD 2.9) to 1.3 (SD 1.8) (Das, Grimmer, Sparnon, McRae, & Thomas, 2005). Studies show that VR is an ideal training method and is as effective as opioids for reducing pain.

While there is evidence supporting VR's effectiveness in managing acute pain, little is known about the use of VR for CP and/or for long-term pain rehabilitation. Only a few studies have investigated VR for CP management and the data are preliminary. Sato et al. investigated the use of VR for treating complex regional pain syndrome in adults (Sato et al., 2010). In this pilot study, a VR mirror visual feedback system was created and applied to the treatment of complex regional pain syndrome in five adult patients (46–74 years old). This study demonstrates how VR could be applied for the treatment of CP. Sarig-Bahat et al. investigated VR's ability to treat chronic neck pain with 67 patients. The researchers used a VE that encouraged patients to increase their range of motion by 'spraying' flies with a virtual spray canister. However, in their results, investigators found that a single session of VR resulted in increased cervical range of motion and decreased neck pain (Sarig-Bahat, Weiss, & Laufer, 2010).

In this book chapter, we introduce the main two strategies we have used to help patients better self-manage their pain in VR: pain distraction and pain self-modulation. Pain distraction theory for CP patients is built upon its success for acute pain patients. Pain self-modulation approach is based on prior work of Shaw et al. (Shaw, Gromala, & Song), from which we learned how biofeedback could be incorporated into a VR environment and the approaches to transforming bio-data to physiological states so that it could be therapeutic for patients.

PAIN SELF-MODULATION AND PAIN DISTRACTION

This section describes two types of VR paradigms used in VR systems for CP patients – Pain Self-modulation & Pain Distraction. In this section we also discuss the technical and theoretical inspirations behind the design of Virtual Meditative Walk (VMW) and Mobius Floe (MF). The inspirations for the particular projects are diverse in nature. The attention of patients when managing their pain is driving to focus inward in VMW and outward in MF. Those two paradigms are the main design mechanisms used in most of the VR projects for both acute and CP managements.

Focus OUTWARD: Pain Distraction and Mobius Floe

Mobius Floe is an immersive VR game designed as a tool to help chronic and acute pain patients lower their pain and anxiety. MF draws the attention away from patients' embodied experience of pain and toward the virtual three-dimensional environment and its current happenings. Patients are immersed in a virtual wintry setting where they move through snowy paths and trails while experiencing action-packed encounters. Patients are presented with a world so captivating that it enables them to feel the sense of embodiment, as if they are inside and part of the world itself. The game also includes many tasks that stimulate the patients' working memory and seeks their constant attention, thus drawing the patients' attention away from their physical pain into another embodied state.

Mobius Floe aims to learn from the game design literature and to improve upon previous attempts such as SnowWorld's pain distraction VR by extending the software's ability to evoke a sense of immersion and cognitively distract users more reliably. Most importantly, to incorporate the pain distraction strategy for chronic conditions and test how effective such VR technology systems could be for CP patients. MF focuses the patient away from their bodily awareness by continuously engaging activities, which help reduce the intensity of perceived pain. User testing of our current designs with acute and CP patients in a qualitative fashion will be critically important to evaluate the effectiveness of MF for purposes of perceived pain reduction, and to determine if any effects persist beyond the VR experience itself.

Pain Management Theory: Pain Cognitive Distraction and Gate Control Theory

Pain Gate Control Theory

Pain perception varies across different individuals according to their mood, emotional condition and prior experience, even if the pain is caused by similar physical stimuli and results in a similar degree of damage. In 1965, Ronald Melzack and Patrick Wall outlined a scientific theory about psychological influence on pain perception; the 'gate control theory' (Melzack & Wall, 1965). According to the gate control theory, pain signals are not free to reach the brain as soon as they are generated at the injured tissues or sites. They need to encounter certain 'neurological gates' at the spinal cord level and these gates determine whether the pain signals should reach the brain or not. In other words, pain is perceived when the gate gives way to the pain signals and it is less intense or not at all perceived when the signal gate closes.

Cognitive Distraction as the Pain Management Strategy

Attentional state is possibly the most commonly studied psychological variable that modifies pain perception (Villemure & Bushnell, 2002). The influential gate control and neuromatrix theories of pain both state that to attend to pain is one way of increasing the experience of pain. Therefore, diverting attention away from pain is a key to manage it. Individuals are less likely to notice pain when they are distracted by cognitively demanding tasks. In their review, Fernandez and Turk found imagery methods to be the most effective distractions and pain-acknowledging distraction techniques least effective. The greater the attentional capacity a distraction demands, the more effective it is at reducing perceived pain, consistent with theories regarding attention as a limited pool of information processing resource.

Given that an individuals' attentional capacity is finite, a distracting task that requires a great deal of the person's attentional resources should leave little attentional capacity available for processing painful stimuli. Moreover, multiple resource theories suggest that attentional resources within different sensory systems function relatively independently; an activity that involves one sensory modality may not deplete the attentional resources in another sensory modality. Thus, a highly engaging and interactive distraction activity that involves multiple sensory systems are likely to be more effective than a more passive distractor, or even a distractor that involves only one or two sensory systems.

MF aims to learn from previous VRs like SnowWorld and improve upon them. By extending the software's ability and implement more engaging game components with pain metaphors, MF could become more immersive and cognitively distractive for pain management. It also incorporates techniques from cognitive sciences by introducing n-back and attention switching tasks, which function together to provide cognitive load to the players in the form of tasks that are presented to them throughout the length of the game, providing continuous action and constantly capturing their attention to keep their minds occupied. For example, Neuron Tree characters will attack the players when they are within proximity, while secondary tree characters that look like environmental trees will start moving and surprising the player when they are within proximity as well (Figure 2). This will require the players to switch their attention between their tasks and the environment in order to look out for other potential harm. Further into the game, players are prompted to complete an n-back memory task where they have to remember the order of the objects lined up in front of them. As they continue further down the guided path, they are then presented with the opportunity to receive a bonus item when they complete the puzzle in the correct order. As we aim to provide pain distraction for as long as possible in one sitting, one of the methods we employed to fulfill this goal is through a procedurally-generated landscape. This ensures that the game does not end before the player has received as much of the pain distraction as they need. Since landscape tiles are constantly being randomly plotted in front of the current tile that the player is on, players might find it harder to anticipate what is coming up next. This enables a different experience each time a patient plays the game and therefore renews their interest in proceeding through the game.

Sense of Immersion and Embodiment in VR: Designing for Immersion

To deliver a sense of visual immersion, VR display VEs to users with a head-mounted display. Head tracking allows a user to interact with and actively view the environment in 360 degrees. Therefore, the

Figure 1. The snowy world in Mobius Floe: HMD view

Figure 2. The neuron tree in MF

images that the user sees are directly affected by the position of their head movement. Another way VR is reactive is through the manipulation of the environment, usually through a mouse or keyboard. These advanced systems allow users to interact on many levels with the VE, exploiting many of their senses, and encouraging them to become immersed in the world they are experiencing.

Immersion relates to how present the user feels in the world and how real the environment seems. When immersion is strong, much of the user's attention is focused in the VE leaving little of it to notice other things such as pain.

MF enables patients' attention to be drawn away from their embodied experience of pain and towards the virtual space and its current happenings. A patient is able to look around the game world using the Oculus Rift HMD, or with a mouse if preferred, as they are guided through the environment. Patients are presented with a world so captivating that it enables them to feel the sense of embodiment, as if they are inside or part of the world itself. This is achieved by employing three types of digital immersion: Sensory, Challenge-based, and Imaginary (Ermi, 2005).

In MF, sensory immersion is achieved through realistic visual environments and ambient sounds to help draw players into the virtual space, and head-mounted displays and headphones also occlude distractions from the physical world. Challenge based immersion take form as playful or threatening interactive and reactive characters scattered throughout the environment to keep the players on their toes and constantly focused in the game. Finally, a storyline ties all the elements in the game together, making them relevant and coherent. Players can also experience greater depth of immersion when they can identify themselves with the character or role they are playing in the game world, enabling them to become more emotionally involved as described in A Grounded Investigation of Game Immersion (Brown & Cairns, 2004).

Virtual Reality System Design: Pain Metaphors and Pain Toolkits in Mobius Floe

Immersive Background: A Journey through the Snowy World

Players are immersed in a virtual wintry setting where they glide through snowy paths and trails while experiencing action-packed encounters. The journey takes the player from a cozy cabin (Figure 1), out to a snowy landscape, and up a perilous mountain while constantly facing them with barriers and enemies that they have to fight to get through.

Neuron Trees

After completing the training inside the cabin, the player will then explore the outside environment on a pre-defined rail. The patient will soon find themselves being approached by monsters that appear to be half neuron, half tree (Figure 2). The Neuron Trees signify the neurological systems in the human body that are causing the pain experience.

Neuron Trees have menacing expressions and require sedation for the player to escape successfully. They chase the player and will damage the player's Health Points (HP) on contact. Neuron Trees also serve as a key mode of cognitive distraction as they coerce the player into taking defensive actions against them in a strategic and time sensitive manner. They appear in multiple areas throughout the player's path in different numbers, positioning, and even ambush methods.

The Otters

Sea otters (Figure 3) also wander the game space and are able to be interacted with by the player. The otters were implemented into this environment to represent help and concern from the players' family and friends. Unlike Neuron Trees, they are friendly entities in the game, and are always approaching the player on sight. The patient can hurl sea urchins at the otters the same way they fire analgesics to the neuron trees. Otters that receive sea urchins will drop bonus items such as health packs.

Projectiles

There are three types of projectiles that players could choose as to throw at characters: sea urchins, morphine, and gabapentin. Patients are able to calm the neuron trees down by firing abstract analgesics at them with a mouse click. Each projectile has its own functionality, all of which are described for the player inside the tutorial cabin. Sea urchins are treats for sea otter characters should the player choose to receive help from them. Overuse of drugs towards the Neuron Trees however results in negative consequences, some of which manifest as detrimental behaviors in the Neuron Trees, while others affect

Figure 3. The sea otter in MF

the visual rendering of the virtual space in a negative way. For example, overuse of morphine slows the neuron trees down considerably, but they become more aggressive once the effect wears off.

The depictions of drugs and their effects in the VEs can represent pain patients' affective experience by translating the effects of each analgesic into gameplay, including the consequences of overuse. Administering drugs to the neuron trees stimulates the working memory of the pain patients, and at the same time implies that the patient's sensation of bodily pain is being ceased by their active participation in the meantime.

Health Points

The Health Point (HP) mechanics associates the player with the gameplay experience and how well they are performing in the game. Simultaneously, it acts as a motivator to keep the player focused on their tasks. The HP is visually depicted as a red icicle, as seen in multiple figures in the top left space of the screen. Players are able to collect health packs as bonus items when completing certain tasks.

Head-Mounted Displays

Nechvatal in his paper in *Leonardo* speculates on what would be required from a philosophical perspective of the truest digital immersion, whereby the technology used would have to immerse us in such a manner as to render itself invisible during use. The ontological separation between one's body and one's presence in the virtual space would be resolved and the participant's sense of presence and self-awareness would be truly immersed within the VR.

Current HMDs for use with VR software are looking extremely promising for immersive experiences and are improving at a rapid pace. The use of HMDs or other VR viewers is critical to the pain distraction intent underlying the design of MF, and can of course be used for other purposes aligned with participant immersion for future research projects. The Oculus Rift produced by Oculus VR® is a well-known HMD which is scheduled to be available to consumers in summer 2015, and has been available for use to researchers and developers for several years. A key critique of the device thus far has been resolution, which has been somewhat resolved in the Oculus DK2 (also known as Crystal Cove), which has a resolution of 960 x 1080p per eye.

Discussions: Design Challenge, Opportunities, and Implications

Mobius Floe is an immersive VR game designed as a tool to help chronic and acute pain patients lower their pain and anxiety. The n-back tasks discussed in the previous section, sea otters and neuron trees will be in the proximity of the player at the same time, encouraging attentional switching and dual-task paradigms. The player must switch their attention between the neuron trees' location, the n-back task memorization, their health points, and the otters, fully engaging their cognitive load. For example, the players may find themselves fending off neuron trees, trying to memorize the n-back task hint and trying to feed the otters simultaneously.

In the future work of MF, we will conduct focus groups with both acute and CP patients. We will focus primarily on how patients evaluate the pain experience metaphors implemented. By situating MF within health and serious game research, specifically on pain distraction, its game design metaphors and novel approach will provide more insights and inspirations for other researchers and game designers.

Focus INWARD: Pain Self-Modulation and the Virtual Meditative Walk

This section outlines a novel approach constructed for managing CP using VR, biofeedback technology and the MBSR technique. The results of this research suggest that learning MBSR while immersed in a VE can lead to further decreases in perceived pain in contrast to learning MBSR without VR.

Pain Management Theory: Pain Self-Modulation and MBSR Meditation

The system incorporates biofeedback sensors, an immersive VE, and stereoscopic sound titled the Virtual Meditative Walk (VMW). It was designed to enable CP patients to learn Mindfulness-based stress reduction (MBSR), a form of meditation. By providing real-time visual and sonic feedback, VMW enables patients to learn how to manage their pain. A proof-of-concept user study was conducted to investigate the effectiveness of the VR system with CP patients in clinical settings. Results show that the VMW was more effective in reducing perceived pain compared to the non-VR control condition.

We employ VR technologies for pain mitigation and management by controlling changes in 3D visual & sonic elements based on MBSR and biofeedback data in real-time to support their learning of mindfulness meditation techniques. MBSR, a form of mindfulness meditation, is a technique that takes time and effort to learn. Initially, it requires a focus on one's internal states, rather than on the external world.

VMW incorporates a unique VE with biofeedback and meditation, and addresses CP patients' specific embodied conditions and bodily awareness. We take into consideration their proprioceptive and interoceptive senses, which strongly shape human movement, interaction and experience, and bring embodied states - and how they are affected or transformed- into conscious awareness by mapping the changes in one's embodied states (through biofeedback mechanisms) onto changes in visual and sonic qualities of VR environment. Doctors recommend biofeedback and MSBR for self-managing CP. But it takes a lot of effort to learn, and to practice every day. Our studies suggest that VR can help because it gives users immediate feedback. That way, users could have a better sense of whether their efforts are actually producing any changes in the stress levels. We believe that six sessions using VR will accelerate learning.

Virtual Reality System Design: Decisions on Developing the Virtual Meditative Walk

Immersive Background: A Trail in the Forest

MBSR, a form of mindfulness meditation, is a technique that takes time and effort to learn. Initially, it requires a focus on one's internal states, rather than on the world. The design of the VMW provides a peaceful, non-distracting and safe environment for users to immerse themselves in as they learn to achieve a stable meditative practice as they learn to control (or exert agency over) the physiological aspects that are necessary to achieve the positive effects of MBSR.

The VMW is a VE where participants immersed in the VR find themselves "walking" in a beautiful forest composed primarily of a deciduous forest and undergrowth. The surrounding area is relatively mountainous, reminiscent of the trails found along the northwest coast of North America. The camera slowly moves along a worn dirt pathway, as if the user is walking. This allows patients to explore the forest without requiring physical distractions or attention in order to achieve further passage (Figure 4).

Figure 4. Trail design in the Virtual Meditative Walk VR environment

Interactive Feedback Loop: The Fog and Galvanic Skin Response (GSR) Sensor

The GSR sensors continuously track the patient's changing arousal levels, and in turn modify the VMW's weather. The light fog in the forest, for example, recedes as a patient's GSR levels start to stabilize in favor of a mindful state. Alternatively, the fog thickens and draws closer when the patient's arousal levels increase. This serves as seamless visual feedback for patients immersed in the VMW. Figure 5 and 6 show how the VE changes according to variable changes in the patients' biofeedback data.

Figure 5. As patients stay in painful and stressful state, the environment will become foggy

Figure 6. As patients approach an inferred meditative state, the fog begins to dissipate and sounds become more audible and spatial

During meditation sessions, we monitored GSR levels of patients and used this data to control the dynamics of the VE in real-time. This real-time biofeedback system allowed patients to see their progress as they performed mindfulness and encouraged them to pursue the practice. During a session, the patient saw a foggy forest, with the fog representing the patient's GSR level. As the stress level went down, the fog faded away, and this indicated that the patient was in a meditative state. The fog indicated the cause and effect mechanism of biofeedback in the VE. Based on one of our former studies, the fog animation was designed with abstraction in mind. The fog aimed to distribute the attention of the user while showing the changes of GSR in real-time.

User Testing with Chronic Pain Patients

To evaluate the effectiveness of VMW and learn patients' experience inside the VE, we then conducted a user study with CP patients in the clinical settings.

Study Intent

This proof-of-concept study was designed to determine if a VE, combined with MBSR training and biofeedback, helps pain patients better manage their long-term CP, given the limitations of VR pain distraction. Will patients feel better using the VMW to learn MBSR, compared to patients who learn MBSR without immersive VR? If such a VR intervention is able to reduce perceived pain levels among CP patients in a clinical setting, it may be possible that the long-term benefits for patients learning MBSR to better manage their long-term persistent pain could be significantly improved.

Our focus groups and participatory design sessions made it clear that the use of VR itself may impose limitations that require greater investigation. For example, we found that some patients cannot sit for more than 20 minutes, that others cannot tolerate the weight or pressure of a HMD like the Oculus Rift, and that the planned use of a treadmill was too problematic to use in this initial stage. And so the study not only served as a proof-of-concept experiment, but it provided us further insight into how future studies can be better designed to accommodate customized patient needs.

Participants

It is crucial to understand that CP is a dysfunction of the pain response system. As such, categorization is often deemed to be counterproductive, since it draws researchers back into habitual ways of confusing the pain system dysfunction with acute pain the latter of which may have resulted from injury or infection. Where subcategories are used by a subset of health professionals and researchers focus on CP, they are more often categories of neuropathic, nociceptive and idiopathic pain. Also, while patients may cite the source of pain was mostly from their lower back, legs, hips, neck, and shoulders, all have more than one source of pain. More importantly, based on our prior publications in ACM fields, stating " which" category almost always derails the paper because readers return to thinking that CP is acute pain, that it can be cured and that they know what the CP condition is. Therefore, in this study, patients of various types of pain were included from a clinic rather then selecting certain patients.

Initially, the study included twenty participants. However, because seven participants refused to fill out the pain assessment forms, their data was excluded. The participants who were included comprised thirteen patients from the Greater Vancouver area, ranging from 35 to 55 years of age (mean = 49, SD = 8.2); each had a diagnosis of CP.

Procedure

Six participants (3 male, 3 female) were randomly assigned to the control group, and the other seven (3 male, 4 female) were assigned to the VR group. The experimenter introduced each participant to the study, and then attached the GSR sensors. Participants in the control group were required to listen to

Figure 7. A participant in the VMW study using the DeepStream stereoscopic viewer

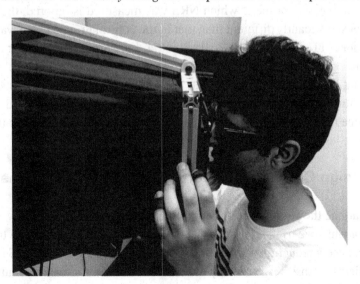

the MBSR training audio track. Participants in the VR group listened to the same MBSR training audio track while immersed in the VMW. Firsthand Technology's DeepStream VR viewer was used. Patients in both groups participated in the MBSR training for twelve minutes.

Apparatus and Instruments

The construction of the physical setup for the VMW required the use of the DeepStream VR viewer, which was installed in a room in a pain clinic for the study. The DeepStream is a stereoscopic VR viewer compatible with PC or Mac computers; it is mounted on a movable arm to ensure flexibility and to maximize patient comfort. The DeepStream rests directly in front of the participant's eyes and does not grip the head, unlike HMDs such as the Oculus Rift, which may cause unnecessary discomfort or pain with this particular participant demographic. The GSR sensors, which are small clips, were gently put onto two of the patient's fingertips; none of the participants reported discomfort from their use.

A simple statistical analysis was conducted before and after the study session in order to compare perceived reported pain levels. Study investigators used an 11-point Numerical Rating Scale (NRS) in which patients self-report their pain levels between the numerical values 0 and 10; 10 equates to the worst pain possible and 0 equates to no pain felt. The NRS instrument was chosen because of its simplicity of understanding and ease of use, and because the investigators wanted to avoid distressing the pain patients with complex and lengthy questionnaires. Prior experience taught us that these participants, who may already be feeling some discomfort, end studies prematurely when confronted with the same lengthy questionnaires that they are compelled to fill out for most of their clinical visits.

Results and Analysis

In this study, time and condition were two independent variables. Time was a within-subjects factor as every participant measured before and after their MBSR experience. The study used a between-subjects design; a participant either belonged to the VR group or to the control group. Therefore, a two-way mixed ANOVA was run to analyze the collected data. We found a significant main effect of Time, $F(1, 11) = 10.44$, $p < .01$, $r = .61$. The main effect of Condition was not significant, $F(1, 11) = 1.53$, $p > .05$, $r = .25$. This indicated that when the time at which NRS was measured is ignored, the initial pain level in the VR group was not significantly different than that in the control group. There was a significant Time x Condition interaction, $F(1, 11) = 8.16$, $p < .05$, $r = .54$, indicating that the changes in the pain level in the VR group were significantly different compared to the change in the control group. Specifically, there was a significant drop in NRS ratings in the VR group, $t(6) = 2.86$, $p < .05$, $r = .57$, but a very weak drop in the control group, $t(5) = 1.24$, $p > .05$, $r = .26$. These findings indicate that the VMW (VR paired with biofeedback for MBSR training) was significantly more effective than MBSR alone at reducing reported pain levels among participants.

Discussions: Design Challenge, Opportunities, and Implications

It is promising to examine the pain reduction reported by participants in the VMW study, as the impact the VR had on CP patients occurred after such a short amount of time. Compared to the control group, the VR group experienced a reduction of pain, on average, equaling 2.6 on the NRS scale. One must also consider that the patients themselves were only immersed in the VR for twelve minutes, which is a short

Figure 8. VR and Control Groups NRS Rating LS mean value before and after experiment

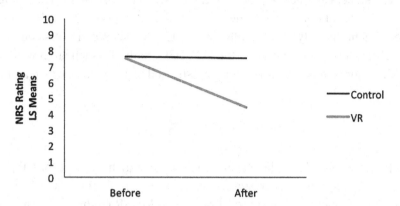

amount of time for an MBSR session. Future studies with longer immersion times and a focus on how long the analgesic effect may linger after the meditative session is the natural next step in continuing this line of inquiry. The introduction of more detailed reporting methods of perceived pain, such as the use of the McGill Pain Questionnaire, could also yield new insights into the details surrounding perceived reported pain after the VR intervention. This will require greater effort put towards the understanding of pain patient experience within the context of the clinic to ensure their comfort and stamina are not negatively impacted.

In the medical field, the gold standard of "clinical trial"(medical jargon of "user study") is randomized control trial (RCT), where the subjects are randomly allocated to the intervention or control group. RCT is the most rigorous method of determining whether a cause-effect relationship exists between intervention and outcome. In our study design, the randomization principle is used to minimize the systematic error despite the small sample size. With a control group, the study sample size doubles. It is usually difficult for HCI technological study to meet the strict requirements of RCT. In this study, 20 patients had been recruited originally. However, it was conducted in a clinical setting, so some patients were not able to finish the study or the questionnaire because of the physical pain or treatment they had. Admittedly, the sample size – 13 participants – is one of the limitations of this study. However, in HCI community, it is also a sample size that is convincing enough for collecting evidence. Another difficulty is the blind testing, because it is often impossible to blind the participant (and researcher) in an intervention study which involves interaction with computer technology. The same scenario also appears in surgical research. Although it is sometimes possible to use a sham treatment as a control (e.g. Fake needles in an acupuncture study), it is somewhat more difficult in the context of VR.

Although the single trial outlined does not speak to the effectiveness of potential long-term capabilities for VR CP management, the VMW enables CP patients to consider that their pain experiences could be further managed through MBSR practiced over the long-term. By multiple training sessions and regularized practice, patients can learn to more easily situate the psychophysical mediation of their internal experiences into everyday life. The pain reduction reported by the NRS data is an early step in proving that VR and biofeedback systems may be an effective first step in promoting this behavioral change.

The VMW was designed using a cross-platform game engine that enables researchers or patients to run the VMW on a wide variety of devices, including handheld phones and tablets. These could enable patients to enhance their MBSR skills in a more easily accessible manner outside of clinical settings. This would also allow researchers and health practitioners to extend the use of VR technology from research and clinical settings to patient homes. To achieve this goal, a key approach would be to migrate the current VE to devices patients already own. Smaller, portable stereoscopic viewers could also be used with mobile devices such as Google Cardboard or the FOV2GO, both of which are low-budget stereoscopic viewing devices; this approach is currently being investigated by the study investigators for future work.

CONCLUSION

Our immersive VR research explores the design space for pain management for CP patients. Pain self-modulation and pain distraction mechanisms were utilized in designing the VE, combining general non-pharmacological pain management approaches, such as MBSR meditation, games, and biofeedback technologies. Preliminary research results validated that both pain management strategies could function effectively on reducing the pain and stress levels of CP patients. In the next phase, we will be working on conducting studies with CP patients, and gather their feedback for polishing our VR design.

Chronic pain is a chronic condition; self-managing it reduces its negative effects, stays degeneration, and improves QoL. The research described in this chapter is our first phase towards studying how effective and efficient VR pain self-management may be when combined with biofeedback and MSBR for CP patients. Our prior research strongly suggested that it was effective in reducing stress among healthy users, particularly those who had not meditated before. Subsequently, as preparation for building a VE specific to their needs and requirements, we conducted numerous studies to ascertain problems specific to CP patients: QoL, habits using technology, specific/variable problems and sequelae, sonic preferences/sensitivities, attitudes toward meditation practices, and what visuals they imagined when they try meditation and/or visualizing techniques to reduce their pain levels.

In clinical settings, we taught participants to learn MSBR in the study using our VR system. We also imported VMW to mobile terminals as a software application for on-going reinforcement and to capture adherence to regular MBSR practice. Therefore, in our next phase, we plan to strengthen patients' self-care and management skills:

1. Through VR by providing six VR sessions in the doctors' clinic;
2. Providing a mobile app and training so they could keep learning self-management in the same, albeit non-immersive, context, and tracking their data for self-comparison.

This chapter discussed the difficulties CP patients are dealing with and summarized our practices and experience working on designing and developing healthcare system for CP patients, conducting experiments and studies with them. Our self-care technology systems are introduced from three perspectives: problem faced, approaches taken, and study outcomes; we introduced the design space with various types of technologies. Challenges and opportunities are explored in this chapter; design guidelines and principles that summarized from our experience and practice are also offered. By offering our design problem and resolutions for each problem with various technologies, we illustrated how to better understand CP patients and communicate with them so that we could be ready to face them in the design, development and testing procedures. It is significant to understand patients' mental and physical needs: during the focus group or user testing process, which would allow researchers to further help CP patients living with long-term pain and designing self-care technologies.

FUTURE WORK

While treatment of severe CP solely by pharmacological approaches is limited and problematic, there are alternatives and adjuvant approaches that help patients manage their long-term pain and reduce its intensity. Medical applications of VR have begun to emerge over the past decade, including rehabilitation, surgical simulators, and telepresence surgery. These works indicate that VR has been effective for treating acute pain; however, such VEs present limitations for managing CP. Most of the studies have been done in clinical settings and most VR environments are not specifically designed for a longer term, whereas managing CP is a complex long process. Therefore, in the future research, how VR can approach patients in a long-term scale and how different types of VEs can take effect should be focused and investigated. Furthermore, although it has been learned that pain can be cognitively distracted, how effective each environment, game components and cognitive task can function for CP patients has not been well understood. Therefore, the immersion of VEs, cognitive task, and gaming elements should be in the research agenda.

REFERENCES

Barlow, J., Wright, C., Sheasby, J., Turner, A., & Hainsworth, J. (2002). Self-management approaches for people with chronic conditions: A review. *Patient Education and Counseling*, *48*(2), 177–187. doi:10.1016/S0738-3991(02)00032-0 PMID:12401421

Benjamin, S., Morris, S., McBeth, J., Macfarlane, G. J., & Silman, A. J. (2000). The association between chronic widespread pain and mental disorder: A population-based study. *Arthritis and Rheumatism*, *43*(3), 561–567. doi:10.1002/1529-0131(200003)43:3<561::AID-ANR12>3.0.CO;2-O PMID:10728749

Bidarra, R., Gambon, D., Kooij, R., Nagel, D., Schutjes, M., & Tziouvara, I. (2013). Gaming at the dentist's – serious game design for pain and discomfort distraction. In B. Schouten, S. Fedtke, T. Bekker, M. Schijven, & A. Gekker (Eds.), *Games for Health* (pp. 207–215). Springer Fachmedien Wiesbaden.

Borsook, D., & Kalso, E. (2013). Transforming pain medicine: Adapting to science and society. *European Journal of Pain (London, England)*, *17*(8), 1109–1125.

Bowker, G. C., & Star, S. L. (2000). *Sorting Things Out: Classification and Its Consequences*. MIT Press.

Bray, D. (1998). Biofeedback. *Complementary Therapies in Nursing & Midwifery*, *4*(1), 22–24. doi:10.1016/S1353-6117(98)80009-7 PMID:9677930

Breivik, H., Eisenberg, E., & O'Brien, T. (2013). The individual and societal burden of chronic pain in Europe: The case for strategic prioritisation and action to improve knowledge and availability of appropriate care. *BMC Public Health*, *13*(1), 1229. doi:10.1186/1471-2458-13-1229 PMID:24365383

Brown, E., & Cairns, P. (2004). A Grounded Investigation of Game Immersion. Proceedings of the CHI '04 Extended Abstracts on Human Factors in Computing Systems (pp. 1297–1300). New York, NY, USA: ACM.

Chaiamnuay, P., Darmawan, J., Muirden, K. D., & Assawatanabodee, P. (1998). Epidemiology of rheumatic disease in rural Thailand: A WHO-ILAR COPCORD study. Community Oriented Programme for the Control of Rheumatic Disease. *The Journal of Rheumatology*, *25*(7), 1382–1387. PMID:9676773

Chang, K.-L., Fillingim, R., Hurley, R. W., & Schmidt, S. (2015). Chronic pain management: Nonpharmacological therapies for chronic pain. *FP Essentials*, *432*, 21–26. PMID:25970869

Chiesa, A., & Serretti, A. (2009). Mindfulness-based stress reduction for stress management in healthy people: A review and meta-analysis. *Journal of Alternative and Complementary Medicine (New York, N.Y.)*, *15*(5), 593–600. doi:10.1089/acm.2008.0495 PMID:19432513

Epping-Jordan, J., Pruitt, S., Bengoa, R., & Wagner, E. (2004). Improving the quality of health care for chronic conditions. *Quality & Safety in Health Care*, *13*(4), 299–305. doi:10.1136/qshc.2004.010744 PMID:15289634

Eriksen, J., Sjøgren, P., Bruera, E., Ekholm, O., & Rasmussen, N. K. (2006). Critical issues on opioids in chronic non-cancer pain: An epidemiological study. *Pain*, *125*(1-2), 172–179. doi:10.1016/j.pain.2006.06.009 PMID:16842922

Ermi, L. (2005). Fundamental Components of the Gameplay Experience: Analysing Immersion.

Fishbain, D. A., Cole, B., Lewis, J., Rosomoff, H. L., & Rosomoff, R. S. (2008). What percentage of chronic nonmalignant pain patients exposed to chronic opioid analgesic therapy develop abuse/addiction and/or aberrant drug-related behaviors? A structured evidence-based review. *Pain Medicine (Malden, Mass.)*, *9*(4), 444–459. doi:10.1111/j.1526-4637.2007.00370.x PMID:18489635

Fredheim, O. M. S., Kaasa, S., Fayers, P., Saltnes, T., Jordhøy, M., & Borchgrevink, P. C. (2008). Chronic non-malignant pain patients report as poor health-related quality of life as palliative cancer patients. *Acta Anaesthesiologica Scandinavica*, *52*(1), 143–148. doi:10.1111/j.1399-6576.2007.01524.x PMID:18005378

Gatchel, R. J., Peng, Y. B., Peters, M. L., Fuchs, P. N., & Turk, D. C. (2007). The biopsychosocial approach to chronic pain: Scientific advances and future directions. *Psychological Bulletin*, *133*(4), 581–624. doi:10.1037/0033-2909.133.4.581 PMID:17592957

Gold, J. I., Kant, A. J., Kim, S. H., & Rizzo, A. (2005). Virtual anesthesia: The use of virtual reality for pain distraction during acute medical interventions. *Seminars in Anesthesia, Perioperative Medicine and Pain*, *24*(4), 203–210. doi:10.1053/j.sane.2005.10.005

Hoffman, H. G., Patterson, D. R., Seibel, E., Soltani, M., Jewett-Leahy, L., & Sharar, S. R. (2008). Virtual reality pain control during burn wound debridement in the hydrotank. *The Clinical Journal of Pain*, *24*(4), 299–304. doi:10.1097/AJP.0b013e318164d2cc PMID:18427228

Institute of Medicine (US) Committee on Advancing Pain Research. (2011). Care of People with Pain.

Institute of Medicine (US) Committee on Advancing Pain Research, Care, and Education. (2011). *Relieving Pain in America: A Blueprint for Transforming Prevention, Care, Education, and Research*. Washington (DC): National Academies Press (US).

Jamison, R. N., Ross, E. L., Michna, E., Chen, L. Q., Holcomb, C., & Wasan, A. D. (2010). Substance misuse treatment for high-risk chronic pain patients on opioid therapy: A randomized trial. *Pain, 150*(3), 390–400. doi:10.1016/j.pain.2010.02.033 PMID:20334973

Jensen, M. P., Gertz, K. J., Kupper, A. E., Braden, A. L., Howe, J. D., Hakimian, S., & Sherlin, L. H. (2013). Steps toward developing an EEG biofeedback treatment for chronic pain. *Applied Psychophysiology and Biofeedback, 38*(2), 101–108. doi:10.1007/s10484-013-9214-9 PMID:23532434

Johnson, M. H. (2005). How does distraction work in the management of pain? *Current Pain and Headache Reports, 9*(2), 90–95. doi:10.1007/s11916-005-0044-1 PMID:15745617

Li, A., Montano, Z., Chen, V. J., & Gold, J. I. (2011). Virtual reality and pain management: Current trends and future directions. *Pain Management, 1*(2), 147–157. doi:10.2217/pmt.10.15 PMID:21779307

MacKichan, F., Paterson, C., Henley, W. E., & Britten, N. (2011). Self-care in people with long term health problems: A community based survey. *BMC Family Practice, 12*(1), 53. doi:10.1186/1471-2296-12-53 PMID:21689455

Melzack, R., & Wall, P. D. (1965). Pain mechanisms: A new theory. *Science, 150*(3699), 971–979. doi:10.1126/science.150.3699.971 PMID:5320816

Newton-John, T. R. O., Spence, S. H., & Schotte, D. (1995). Cognitive-Behavioural Therapy versus EMG Biofeedback in the treatment of chronic low back pain. *Behaviour Research and Therapy, 33*(6), 691–697. doi:10.1016/0005-7967(95)00008-L PMID:7654161

Portenoy, R. K. (1996). Opioid therapy for chronic nonmalignant pain: A review of the critical issues. *Journal of Pain and Symptom Management, 11*(4), 203–217. doi:10.1016/0885-3924(95)00187-5 PMID:8869456

Sarig-Bahat, H., Weiss, P. L. T., & Laufer, Y. (2010). Neck pain assessment in a virtual environment. *Spine, 35*(4), E105–E112. doi:10.1097/BRS.0b013e3181b79358 PMID:20110842

Sato, K., Fukumori, S., Matsusaki, T., Maruo, T., Ishikawa, S., Nishie, H., & Morita, K. et al. (2010). Nonimmersive virtual reality mirror visual feedback therapy and its application for the treatment of complex regional pain syndrome: An open-label pilot study. *Pain Medicine (Malden, Mass.), 11*(4), 622–629. doi:10.1111/j.1526-4637.2010.00819.x PMID:20202141

Schneider, S. M., & Workman, M. L. (1999). Effects of virtual reality on symptom distress in children receiving chemotherapy. *Cyberpsychology & Behavior: The Impact of the Internet. Multimedia and Virtual Reality on Behavior and Society, 2*(2), 125–134.

Shahrbanian, S., Ma, X., Korner-Bitensky, N., & Simmonds, M. J. (2009). Scientific evidence for the effectiveness of virtual reality for pain reduction in adults with acute or chronic pain. *Studies in Health Technology and Informatics, 144*, 40–43. PMID:19592727

Shaw, C., Gromala, D., & Song, M. (n.d.). The Meditation Chamber: Towards Self-Modulation. *Proceedings of ENACTIVE/07.*

Torsi, S., Nasr, N., Wright, P. C., Mawson, S. J., & Mountain, G. A. (2009). User-centered Design for Supporting the Self-management of Chronic Illnesses: An Interdisciplinary Approach. In *Proceedings of the 2Nd International Conference on PErvasive Technologies Related to Assistive Environments* (pp. 43:1–43:4). New York, NY, USA: ACM.

Tsang, A., Von, , Korff, M., Lee, S., Alonso, J., Karam, E., & Angermeyer, M. C. (2008). Common chronic pain conditions in developed and developing countries: Gender and age differences and comorbidity with depression-anxiety disorders. *The Journal of Pain: Official Journal of the American Pain Society*, *9*(10), 883–891. doi:10.1016/j.jpain.2008.05.005 PMID:18602869

Tunstall-Pedoe, H. (2006). Preventing Chronic Diseases. A Vital Investment: WHO Global Report.: World Health Organization Geneva.

Turk, D. C. (2002). Clinical effectiveness and cost-effectiveness of treatments for patients with chronic pain. *The Clinical Journal of Pain*, *18*(6), 355–365. doi:10.1097/00002508-200211000-00003 PMID:12441829

Villemure, C., & Bushnell, M. C. (2002). Cognitive modulation of pain: How do attention and emotion influence pain processing? *Pain*, *95*(3), 195–199. doi:10.1016/S0304-3959(02)00007-6 PMID:11839418

Weeks, D. L., Whitney, A. A., Tindall, A. G., & Carter, G. T. (2015). Pilot Randomized Trial Comparing Intersession Scheduling of Biofeedback Results to Individuals with Chronic Pain: Influence on Psychologic Function and Pain Intensity. *American Journal of Physical Medicine & Rehabilitation / Association of Academic Physiatrists*.

WHO Guidelines on the Pharmacological Treatment of Persisting Pain in Children with Medical Illnesses. (2012). Geneva: World Health Organization.

Wickens, C. D. (2008). Multiple resources and mental workload. *Human Factors*, *50*(3), 449–455. doi:10.1518/001872008X288394 PMID:18689052

Zeidan, F., Gordon, N. S., Merchant, J., & Goolkasian, P. (2010). The effects of brief mindfulness meditation training on experimentally induced pain. *The Journal of Pain: Official Journal of the American Pain Society*, *11*(3), 199–209. doi:10.1016/j.jpain.2009.07.015 PMID:19853530

Chapter 20
Advergaming – How Does Cognitive Overload Effect Brand Recall?
Differences between In–Game Advertising (IGA) and Advergames

Ayşegül Sağkaya Güngör
Işık University, Turkey

Tuğçe Ozansoy Çadırcı
Yıldız Technical University, Turkey

Şirin Gizem Köse
Yıldız Technical University, Turkey

ABSTRACT

Advergaming serves as a new and valuable form of online advertising, especially for companies that target young consumers. This study examines the impacts of cognitive overload with placement prominence on respondents' brand recall, recognition and brand attitudes. An experiment was conducted on a group of university students with an exposure to an advergame under low and high cognitive load stimulus. Results showed that brands that are placed prominently are better recalled in high cognitive load condition. However, cognitive overload doesn't have any significant effect on the recognition of the main brand in which the advergames is specifically designed. Moreover, there is no difference in recall of subtly placed products in low and high cognitive load conditions. However, there is a significant difference in brand attitude in different cognitive loads. The study both investigated the context of advergames and as well in-game advertising (IGA) situations. The results of the study have both practical and theoretical implications.

DOI: 10.4018/978-1-5225-0435-1.ch020

INTRODUCTION

Traditional advertising media are being replaced by new ways to communicate with the customers, and many companies are on game now. Consumers are engaged in a media that is focused on entertainment and this new form of advertising strategy is called branded entertainment. As a new form of branded entertainment (Wise, Bolls, Kim, Venkataraman & Meyer, 2008) advergaming can be defined as placing advertising messages, logos, and trade characters within games (Mallinckrodt & Mizerski, 2007). By the use of advergames, the companies can deliver their advertising messages through video games (Hernandez & Chapa, 2010). On the other hand, in game advertising (IGA), which is usually confused with advergames, is defined as inclusion of products within a digital game (Terlutter & Capella, 2013). There is a difference between advergames and IGA (Winkler & Buckner, 2006). In advergames the products or brands are given a prominent role within the online video game and they have an essential role in gaming experience (Hofmeister-Toth & Nagy, 2011). Most of the time advergames are made available to the consumers via websites and they are mostly free of charge (Grossman, 2005). On the other hand, IGA is the application of the product placement in advergames or in any other type of digital games, e.g. video games. They are sponsored paid placements in which the payment is done to the owner of the advergame. The difference between the general advergame environment and IGA can be seen in Figure 1 and 2.

The most challenging issue in the design of advergames is not knowing under which conditions advergames can be effective on consumer perceptions (Redondo, 2012). Therefore, understanding the effects of external stimuli like cognitive load on brand recognition and brand recall will provide important evidence about the issue. As brand placements in games have an interactive nature, playing advergames triggers cognitively involving experiences (Cauberghe & DePelsmacker, 2010). The cognitive resources that are available to the audience during message processing situations are called *cognitive load* (Grigorovici &

Figure 1. The advergame environment in Magnum Advergame

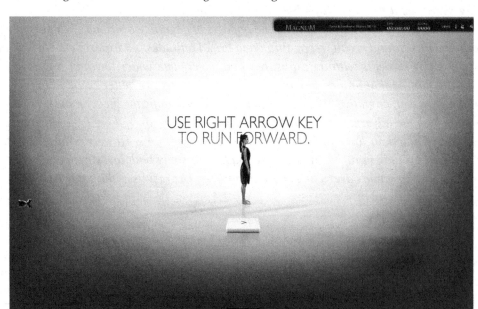

Figure 2. Example of IGA in Magnum Advergame

Constantin, 2004). This study aims to define the possible effects of cognitive load on brand recall for both the main brands and the placed brands in advergames during game play experience.

Advergaming is a technique that offers extensive exposure to branded content. Besides its promotional benefits, the literature on consumer memory on advergames is limited (Hernandez & Minor, 2011). This study aims to investigate a cause-effect relationship between cognitive load and brand recall in the context of an advergame. Also, testing the effectiveness of advergames in terms of brand recognition and brand attitude are considered as fundamental issues and measures (An & Stern, 2011).

In this study an experimental design was used with the manipulation of cognitive load during gameplay. The subjects in the experiment group were given cognitive load objects during the game, and a recall test – which involves exposing to a stimulus – will be used to measure the brand recognition (main brand), brand recall (IGA brands) and brand attitude (main brand) of the subjects. The authors believe that this study will provide useful insights for both academicians and practitioners.

BACKGROUND

Advergames serve as a new medium especially in markets for younger audiences as they use internet and mobile technologies constantly and have a tendency to engage in online and interactive gaming (Santos, Gonzalo & Gisbert, 2007). Placing advertising messages in different media is not a new strategy. Before advergames, advertisers were still placing their advertising messages in movies, television programs and video games. This form of a hybrid advertising strategy is called *product placement*. An early definition of product placement by Balasubramanian (1994) is "a paid product message aimed at influencing audiences via the planned and unobtrusive entry of a branded product into a television program (movie or a video game)." Product placements are a good strategy to prevent the avoidance of the audience towards advertising messages. In the video game industry, the product placement strategies are mostly called "in-game advertising (IGA)".

As the integration between product placement and media has evolved; a new form of promotional content called *branded entertainment* has emerged. Branded entertainment is defined by Hudson and Hudson (2006) as "the integration of advertising into the entertainment content; whereby brands are embedded into storylines of a movie, television program or other entertainment medium." A new and growing form of branded entertainment is advergames. "Advergame" is a term that combines the words "advertising" and "video game" (Grossman, 2005). Advergames present a developing field within the online electronic games industry and are used to promote specific products and/or brands (Dahl, Eagle & Báez, 2009). With the interactivity (Lee, Park & Wise, 2014), entertainment (Martí-Parreño, Aldás-Manzano, Currás-Pérez & Sánchez-García, 2013) and with their viral component, advergames act as an important source in shaping consumers' attitudes towards the brands they promote (Alina, 2013).

Previously academics and practitioners have defined advergames as a special form of IGA. The reason behind this conceptualization is most of the time the design and attributes around the main brand being promoted within the game evokes prominent product placement in video games. What is more, both IGA and advergames make use of the entertainment media. According to Winkler and Buckner (2006) there are differences between advergames and IGA. With IGA companies are basically buying space for their advertisements in games and within an advergame or any online game (An & Kang, 2014). Generally multiple brands are placed and promoted in video games (Yang, Roskos-Ewoldsen, Dinu & Arpen, 2006). On the other hand, an advergame is a digital game that is designed around a brand (Wise et al., 2008). To summarize, in IGA, a number of brands and products are embedded within the game; but in advergame, the game is specifically designed and created to promote a particular brand and the brand becomes the part of the entertainment that is created by the game (Terlutter & Capella, 2013; Winkler & Buckner, 2006).

Placement Prominence and Its Relation to Audience Responses in IGA and Advergames

The way of the placement occurs in a digital game may be critical in terms of achieving the desired brand awareness, attitude or purchase intentions. Placement prominence can be defined as "the extent to which the placement possesses characteristics designed to make the brand/product central focus of audience attention" (Gupta & Lord, 1998). IGA can be integrated into the game play in two ways: prominently or subtly (Terlutter & Capella, 2013). In prominent placement, the brand is visually and verbally placed with a longer duration and they are integrated with the storyline or the content (Gupta & Lord, 1998; Lee & Faber, 2007). In subtle placements brands are only visually made available to the audience without any integration with the medium (Gupta & Lord, 1998; Van Reijmersdal, Rozendaal & Buijzen, 2012).

Product placements can be used to achieve different cognitive, affective and conative responses like, increased brand awareness, brand recall and recognition, and to create desired changes in brand attitude and purchase intentions (Cholinski, 2012; Williams, Petrosky, Hernandez & Page, 2011). There is an expected difference between prominent and subtle placements in terms of audiences' cognitive and affective responses. Most of the research on product placement considers the way the brands are placed in a medium to be associated with cognitive responses like brand recall and recognition (Gunawardena & Waiguny, 2014; Van Reijmersdal et al., 2012). Prominently placed brands are expected to be easily recalled and recognized (Gupta & Lord 1998; Lee & Faber 2007; Van Reijmersdal et al., 2012). The reason behind the higher levels of recall is associated with the high level of integration of the placement and the game (Chaney Lin & Chaney, 2004; Peters & Leshner, 2013). In a gaming environment, the audience is highly focused and shows interest to the content. As a result, they process the environment more attentively (Cauberghe & DePelsmacker, 2010). When the product is not prominently placed, the expected level of recognition is lower (Lee & Faber, 2007). Like cognitive responses, affective responses like brand attitude are also expected to be different based on the placement prominence. There are conflicting opinions in literature in terms of these outcomes. Some studies suggest that prominent placements are expected to create a more negative affective response, as they are more visible to the audience and such placements are evaluated as intrusive (Kinard & Hatman, 2013; Shiv, Edell & Payne, 1997; Van Reijmersdal, 2009; Hernandez, Chapa, Minor, Maldonado & Barranzuella, 2004). Some other findings state that the placement of products in video games and advergames, when compared with other media like movies or television shows, receive a more positive attitude from the audience (Bellman, Kemp, Haddad & Varan, 2014; Williams, et al., 2011). In other studies, it is suggested that as the advertising messages in a gaming environment are presented differently than other media, the players would ignore or not notice the persuasive elements embedded within the game (Raney, Arpan, Pashupati & Brill, 2003). The same situation also applies to advergaming environment.

As advergames become a more popular medium more research has been conducted on understanding and examining the possible outcomes of advergames. As in IGA, advergames also used to achieve certain results. Previous research concerning advergames, like studies on IGA, has focused on affective responses (Hernandez et al., 2004; Winkler & Buckner, 2006) and cognitive responses (Nelson, 2002; Gross, 2010; Hernandez & Minor, 2011; Lai & Huang, 2011; Cauberghe & DePelsmacker, 2010; Lee & Faber, 2007; Peters & Leshner 2013). Glass (2007) suggested that advergames present more favorable outcomes than IGA in non-branded games. Expected changes in attitudes and perceptions are created differently in an advergame due to their certain attributes like interactivity they provide (Kleeberger & Hummel, 2002).

Brands are embedded into an advergame in different ways. The first approach is the passive form of placement, which basically refers to the IGA applications. However, a distinct feature that advergames present is placing the brand as a major part of the game and allowing the gamers to interact with these placements. This type of product placement is an active form of placement (Nelson, 2002; Lee et al., 2014). Advergames are mostly used to create and enhance product awareness with engaging the gamer with the product or brand that is being promoted (Tina & Buckner, 2006). Previous research on the possible effects of interactivity suggest that as brands are associated with the gaming environment combined with a certain level of interactivity, gamers feel higher levels of involvement with the brand (Nelson, 2002) and also they create more positive attitudes towards the brand and the advergame (Goh & Ping, 2014; Sukoco & Wu, 2011; Hernandez, 2011). With their interactivity feature advergames enhance the value of brand advertisements, as they create control and communication between the medium and player (Ghirvu, 2011).

Another important feature of advergames is their entertainment aspect (Martì-Parreño et al., 2013). Entertainment received by playing an advergame induces a better gaming experience and this good experience results in higher levels of brand recall and positive attitude (Adis & Jun, 2013; Vermeir, Kazakova, Tessitore, Cauberghe & Slabbink, 2014). The interactivity and enjoyment provided by advergames makes them stronger than typical product placements and IGA (Cauberghe & DePelsmacker, 2010).

When compared to other forms and media used in typical product placements advergames also hold the difference in terms of duration and exposure. Unlike movies and television programs, gamers playing an advergame can be exposed to the advertising messages for longer periods and more than once (Waiguny, Nelson & Terlutter, 2012).

Cognitive Load and Multitasking Effects

Cognitive load theory, originated in the 1980s, is an instructional theory based on knowledge of human cognition (Sweller, Ayres & Kalyuga, 2011). Since its inception, it has used aspects of human cognitive architecture to generate experimental, instructional effects. As it was put by Kahneman (1973), and developed in the cognitive psychology, limited cognitive capacity theory posits that human attention and cognitive capacity is limited at any given time. Thus, the allocation of limited cognitive capacity influences the processing and outcomes of stimuli we encounter (Kahneman, 1973). In more detail, in the theory, it is stated that "one's total attention capacity can be split into primary tasks and secondary tasks" (Kahneman, 1973; Lynch & Srull, 1982). The former is the spare capacity that has the second priority.

There are some conditions that cognitive resources are depleted and less capacity is left for further processing of information. Some examples of those conditions are; (1) high involvement (Klimmt & Vorderer, 2003), (2) multi-tasking (Paas, Renkl & Sweller, 2003; Sukoco & Wu, 2011), (3) presence of redundant information (Sweller, 2011; Moore & Rideout, 2007)

Klimmt and Vorderer (2003) differentiated between two levels of *involvement*; low and high. Following their argument, a highly involving environment consumes more of users' cognitive resources, leaving less capacity for processing further messages. According to Lewis and Porter (2010) video game environments, which are very similar to online games, entail high cognitive load conditions because of users' high involvement.

Another cognitive source depleting condition is *multi-tasking*. According to the cognitive load theory, participants seem to experience a cognitive overload when they are exposed to multi tasks at a given time. Having done two tasks simultaneously reduces their capacity to process information. Human cognitive architecture meets the requirement for high-element interactivity by its combination of working and long-term memory (Paas, et.al., 2003). Working memory, in which all conscious cognitive processing occurs, can handle only a very limited number— possibly no more than two—of interacting elements (Paas, et.al., 2003).

The third condition is the *presence of redundant information*. Redundant information is defined as any unnecessary information. Processing unnecessary information imposes an extraneous cognitive load (Sweller, 2011). Especially when the participants process the message, which mostly evokes their affective responses, their cognitive response could be reduced (Sukoco & Wu, 2011).

The advergames are presented in an environment that requires high engagement of the game player. In the study by Huh, Suzuki-Lambrecht, Lueck & Gross (2015), derived from the existing literature, some important characteristics of advergames offer explanations for advergames' diminished cognitive effects compared to those of other media: (1) the higher interactivity of game play demanding more cognitive resources than viewing noninteractive media; (2) no fixed content structure or story line in advergames, demanding greater cognitive efforts from the game player to understand and learn the content; and (3) the multimodal, entertaining, and immersive nature of advergames diverting consumer attention from processing and remembering information (Buijzen, Van Reijmersdal & Owen, 2010; Nelson & Waiguny, 2012; Panic, Cauberghe & DePelsmacker, 2013; Verhellen, Oates, DePlasmacker & Dens, 2014; Waiguny, Nelson & Terlutter, 2014; Waiguny & Terlutter, 2011). Following limited cognitive capacity theory (Kahneman, 1973; Lang, 2000), it can be assumed that the more cognitive capacity devoted to achieve goals of the game, the less will remain to process in game advertisements.

The Moderating Impact of Placement Prominence on Cognitive Load

Stated by the cognitive overload studies, the split of information processing between different tasks creates an increased cognitive load while the tasks are competing for the attention (Rosen, 2008; Lee & Shen, 2009; Hernandez, 2011). Visual stimuli further increase the load as the player's eyes switch between the different tasks (Brasel & Gips, 2011). As a result, stated by Hembrooke and Gay (2003), "due to higher cognitive load and divided attention, recall and recognition of specific content is often reduced."

Although the previous discussion leads to the tentative assumption that when the cognitive load is high, the recall and recognition of the brands tend to be low, brand placement and cognitive load may interact in their effects on cognitive and affective outcomes. A study by Lee and Faber (2007) has demonstrated the effect of placement prominence on brand memory and attitudes in traditional brand placements. The majority of the previous research in traditional media found a positive relationship between placement prominence and cognitive variables as brand recall and recognition (Clark & Pavio, 1991; Brennan & Babin, 2004). Brennan and Babin (2004) found that visually prominent brands have the highest amount of recognition.

Inferring from the literature, it is argued that even with an increasing cognitive load, prominent placements are more effective than subtle placements. In high cognitive load condition, since there is limited capacity for the working memory, highly visible brands have a higher chance to be recognized by the player, thus the memory. As verified by Gunawardena and Waiguny (2014)*subtle placements within the peripheral area of the movie will give rise to a greater decrease in recall and recognition than the prominent placements*. On the other hand, subtle placement is not easy to discover in natural setting. Increasing the cognitive load on player will probably result in no change in cognitive responses in subtle placement condition. Combining the literature on cognitive load theory and placement prominence, the following hypothesis are proposed as the basis of the study:

H1: In prominent brand placement, high cognitive load results in a higher brand recall than low cognitive load condition.

H2: In subtle brand placement, there is no significant difference in brand recall between high cognitive load and low cognitive load condition.

H3: In high cognitive load condition, the recognition of the brand that the advergame is specifically designed will be higher, compared to low cognitive load condition.

Although, researchers have found that prominent placements generate higher brand recall and recognition than subtle placements (Gupta & Lord, 1998; Schneider & Cornwell 2002; Van Reijmersdal, 2009), some researchers argue that better recall does not necessarily improve attitude. There is evidence in the literature about the changes of brand attitude with the cognitive load. Yoon, Choi and Song (2011) demonstrated that, in movies, under conditions of high cognitive load, the player's attitude towards a brand is more favorable. Therefore, the following is hypothesized:

H4: In high cognitive load condition, brand attitude is more positive than low cognitive load condition.

MAIN FOCUS OF THE CHAPTER

Issues, Controversies, Problems

Throughout the theoretical background section, it was stated that the cognitive overload is a working memory depleting process (Klimmt & Vorderer, 2003; Paas et.al., 2003; Sukoco & Wu, 2011; Sweller, 2011; Moore & Rideout, 2007). At a condition of overload, attention is directed primarily to the main task; in our case it is game play. All the remaining tasks are regarded as secondary thus has the second priority. In such a condition, it is expected that in game advertising is considered as the secondary, since the main task is to play the game in given directions. However, the question remains how the loaded working memory is influenced with an addition of new a condition, which is placement prominence. Reviewing the literature, it was found that on traditional settings, especially prominent placement has considerable impact on brand recognition and recall (Clark & Pavio, 1991; Brennan & Babin, 2004; Gunawardena & Waiguny 2014).

According to researchers, better recall does not necessarily improve attitude (Yoon, Choi & Song, 2011). Therefore, another question is the effect of cognitive overload on brand attitude toward the brand that the advergame is specifically designed for.

One another problem in the product placement literature is, advergames and IGA are mostly used interchangeably. However, they are two distinct terms. The main difference between these two concepts is the placement of the brand within the game. In the study, IGA and advergame are treated as two different concepts. The effectiveness of each is measured in terms of brand recall and recognition in the presence of cognitive overload.

To summarize, main focus of the study is to investigate the differences in terms of brand recall and recognition between subtle and prominent placements in a cognitive overload condition. Additionally, the effect of cognitive overload on brand attitude is studied.

The Study

To investigate the proposed hypotheses, a 2 (cognitive load (CL): high vs low load) by 2 (brand placement (BP): subtle vs prominent placement) experiment was conducted. Experiment was designed with a web-based casual online advergame to obtain a natural setting to ensure external validity. That's because this type of casual games is usually played during leisure times.

The Method

Experimental Stimuli

It was decided to use an existing advergame. Although it is not possible to control all influencing factors, the advantage is; since participants are really playing the game, it adds real realism to the experiment (Waiguny, Nelson & Marko, 2013). After reviewing several advergames (e.g. Lego Speed Champions, Lego Star Wars, NASCAR - Hungry for Speed, T. Rowe&Price's and Disney's The Great Piggy Bank

Adventure, MINI Maps: Google Maps Racing Advergame etc.), Magnum was selected for the experiment. It was available online at http://pleasurehunt.mymagnum.com/. The reasons for selecting Magnum were:

1. It was very easy to understand and play, does not require any skill.
2. There was a very easy challenge, which was collecting points by picking up small Magnum ice creams. At the same time, challenge inserted a cognitive load to the participant which was considered as the low-load condition.
3. It had 6 different in game advertised brands, 3 of them were prominent placements, and 3 of them were subtle placements – these placements were determined with a pretest which was described below.

Subtle and prominent placements were determined based on the definition by Gupta and Lord (1998). In line with the definition of prominence, the brands were highly visible and the game character was in interaction with the brands. On the other hand, subtly placed brands were not very easy to perceive, although the brand name appeared on the screen. At the same time the interaction of the game character with the products was not much apparent contrary to the prominent placement. Still in order to be sure that the brands were perceived as subtly or prominently placed, a pretest with 10 respondents was conducted. After playing the game for 10 minutes -it is the duration of the real experiment- participants received a list of 6 brands, and asked whether they saw them in the game. The result revealed that 3 prominently placed brands (Samsung, Dove and Urbanears) had a mean score of M=3.49 (sd = 0.59), and 3 subtly placed brands (YouTube, Saab and Spotify) had a mean score of M=2.91 (sd = 0.67). When two means were compared t(9)=6.12, p<0.000, it was concluded that the placement prominence was successful.

Manipulation

In the study there were two levels of cognitive load; high and low. Advergames intrinsically insert cognitive load to the player (Huh, et.al, 2015; Mayer & Moreno, 2003). So, the advergame itself with no additional condition is considered as the low level cognitive load. Brünken, Plass and Leutner (2003) suggested the feasibility of the dual-task approach as a viable alternative to the most commonly used measure of cognitive load. In the study by Beilock and Ramirez (2011) students are forced to a secondary task as to memorize either two (low load) or six (high load) letters, to be loaded cognitively, as they solved math problems. Research has shown that remembering numbers can effectively manipulate cognitive load (Macrae, Hewstone, & Griffiths, 1993; Shiv, Britton, & Payne, 2004). Derived from the literature, to obtain high cognitive load condition, participants were asked to remember a 7-digit number while playing the advergame. This method was also applied by Lee and Shen (2009). Participants were instructed that they would be asked to write down the number later. So, a dual task approach was achieved.

Procedure

The experiment was conducted in a computer laboratory. Participants were seated in front of a computer screen and told that the game they would play was about an interactive lecture. Participants were assigned randomly to one of the 2 conditions (high or low cognitive load). There were two experimental sessions, one with high load condition and other with low load condition. Each experimental session was about 15 minutes. After they had been informed about the game, they were required to play the game for 10 minutes without any interaction with each other. There was always an instructor present throughout the experiment. After 10 minutes of game play, they were asked to fill an online questionnaire that measured average weekly internet use, gaming experience, gaming time, telepresence experience during play, brand recognition, brand recall and brand attitude.

Preliminary Analysis

Sample

100 students from several management courses were participated in exchange for an extra course credit. 54 of the respondents were subjected to secondary task while playing the game, keeping the 7-digit number in mind, by definition, considered as the high cognitive load condition. The remaining 46 were left to play the game only, considered as low cognitive load condition.

Sample consisted of 58 females (58%) and 42 males (42%). Average age was 22. Average weekly Internet use was more than 4 hours, gaming experience was 2.9 years and respondents were playing games more than 4 hours per week on average.

Since subjects' gaming experience and their frequency of game play can affect brand recall (BRc), brand recognition (BRg) and brand attitude (Bra), prior to the analysis, it was required to be sure that groups were not different in terms of average weekly internet use, gaming experience and gaming time. To investigate similarities/differences between groups Pearson chi-square test was applied. According to the results, it was concluded that, the subjects in each group had the same characteristics in terms of their average weekly internet use (χ^2 =4.19, df=3, p=0.241), gaming experience (χ^2 =6.758, df=3, p=0.080) and frequency of game play (χ^2 =0.125, df=2, p=0.939).

Covariate

Because the experiment was held on a natural setting by asking the participants to play an existing online game; telepresence, which is known from existing advergames studies to influence BRg, BRc (e.g. Hernandez, 2011; Vermeir et.al., 2014) and BRa (Hernandez, 2011), was included as covariate in the analysis.

Novak, Hoffman, and Yung (2000) define telepresence as an antecedent of flow. It is defined as a feeling of being part of the environment created by the medium (Hoffman & Novak, 1996). In the study by Vermeir et.al (2014); it is stated that *telepresence is a constituent element of flow that affects in-game advertising outcomes* (Grigorovici & Constantin, 2004; Nelson, Yaros & Keum, 2006). In brief, telepresence is the feeling of being present in a particular situation. Telepresence increases as consumers engage with a medium that is highly interactive and vivid (Suh & Chang, 2006). In other words telepresence is related to the interactivity and vividness components of a technology (Steuer, 1992; Suh & Chang, 2006), and they both need to be present for the audience to feel a certain level of telepresence (Klein, 2003; Suh & Chang, 2006). In an advergame setting due to the certain characteristics of advergames like entertainment and interactivity, the gaming experience is expected to create a certain level of telepresense (Bellman et al., 2014; Klein, 2003). Cauberghe, Geuens, and De Pelsmacker (2011) suggest that the positive effects of brand attitude would increase the telepresence feeling of gamers. Previous studies state that in situations where consumers feel a certain level of telepresence in computer-mediated environments they tend to create a stronger belief towards products being promoted (Kim & Biocca, 1997; Klein, 2003; Suh & Chang, 2006). Telepresence also plays an important role in processing information in a gaming environment. In higher levels of telepresence, felt by the gamers, their attention is highly allocated to game play and they tend to become more attentive to the information provided to them during game play (Besharat, Kumar, Lax & Rydzik, 2013).

Telepresence in online advergames is thought to occur when players mentally become a part of the game and forget about the real world. Thus, none of the groups in the study should go thorough more intense telepresence experience than the other. Telepresence during game play was measured using the scale adopted from Refiana, Mizerski, and Murphy (2005) consisting of 6 items measured on 5-point Likert scale (totally disagree to totally agree).

In another analysis, it was checked whether there were differences between the groups in terms of the telepresence experience. Telepresence of 6 items were calculated (α =0.917, M=3.36, sd=0.037). The mean score implies that the telepresence experience was only at an average level. At the same time, a one-way ANOVA between groups yielded no significant differences (F=0.302, p=0.585).

Dependent Measures

The dependent variables consisted of cognitive constructs for brand recognition (BRg), brand recall (BRc) and brand attitude (BRa). BRg was assessed by asking two questions: (1) Did you recognize that the game that you just played is designed for a specific brand? Yes/no. (2) Could you write down the brand that the game is designed for? Open-ended question with an empty text box under. To measure BRc, respondents were given the 6 brand names present in the game (Dove, YouTube, Spotify, Saab, Urbanears, Samsung). They were asked whether they could remember having seen them in the game. Each brand name had an option to be answered as either I saw or I didn't see. Another dependent measure, BRa, was measured by a scale adopted from Batra and Ahtola (1991). Respondents were asked to indicate their degree of agreement about Magnum brand on how good, valuable, useful, wise and joyful the Magnum brand is. Responses were measured on 5-point Likert scale (totally disagree to totally agree).

Findings

Brand Recall (BRc)

As proposed in Hypothesis 1, we assume that the effect of cognitive load on brand recall for prominent placements would be higher in a high cognitive load situation. First, BRc for the prominently placed brands were calculated. The results indicated that prominent placements received a 64.7% recall (M=4.0867; sd =0.39). To test the hypothesis, we calculated a single factorial ANCOVA with cognitive load as the independent and BRc for prominent placement (BRc_p) as the dependent variable. Telepresence experience during game play served as a covariate. As expected there was a main effect of cognitive load on BRc_p (BRc_p in high cognitive load condition; M=4.27, sd=0.39 versus BRc_p in low cognitive load condition; M=3.87; sd=0.70) in which the difference was significant (F=6.165, p= 0.017). As the results of the ANCOVA yielded a significant difference based on the degree of cognitive load our data succeeded in supporting hypothesis 1 (H1).

Next as theory on IGA suggests that there is either low or no difference in terms of BRc for subtle placements, we hypothesized that there will be no difference in terms of BRc for either high or low cognitive load conditions. Before testing the hypothesis BRc for the subtly placed brands were calculated. The results indicated that subtle placements received a 48.7% recall (M=3.501; sd = 0.64). To test the second hypothesis a second ANCOVA test was conducted using BRc for subtly placed brands (BRc$_s$) as the dependent, cognitive load as the independent variables, and again telepresence served as the covariate. As expected there was no main effect of cognitive load on BRc$_s$ (BRc$_s$ in high cognitive load condition; M=3.53; sd=0.72 versus BRc$_p$ in low cognitive load condition; M=3.49; sd=0.72) in which the difference between two means was not significant (F=0.12, p= 0.912). Although there is a slight difference in terms of means for high and low cognitive situations, the F-test wasn't able to create statistically significant results. The results were consistent with the hypothesis 2 that was proposed. Consequently, hypothesis 2 (H2) was also supported. Another important finding according to the results is that percentage of BRc for prominently placed brands (68.7%) are relatively higher than percentage of subtly placed brands (48.7%).

The results for BRc also support the findings of previous studies about IGA in which relative differences were found according to placement prominence (Nelson, 2002; Cauberghe & DePelsmacker, 2010; Gunawardena & Waiguny, 2014). The difference between BRc for prominent and subtle placements is summarized in Figure 3.

Brand Recognition (BRg)

Hypothesis 3 investigates the effects of cognitive load on brand recognition (BRg) for the brand that the advergame was specifically designed for. The hypothesis proposed that in terms of high cognitive load the brand recognition will be higher compared to low cognitive load condition. To test the hypothesis BRg was used as the dependent and cognitive load as the independent variables, and telepresence was used as the covariate. Almost all of the subjects recognize the brand correctly with a percentage of 94%. A single-factorial ANCOVA was calculated which revealed cognitive load condition did not have any effect on brand recognition (BRg in high cognitive load condition; M=1.93; sd=0.27 versus BRg in low cognitive load condition, M=1.96; sd=0.21; F=0.116; p=0.735). Although there was a slight decrease in recognition when high cognitive load condition was introduced; results of the F-test were not statistically significant. As a result, the third hypothesis (H3) of the study was not supported.

Figure 3. Effects of cognitive load on BRc for prominent and subtle placements for IGA

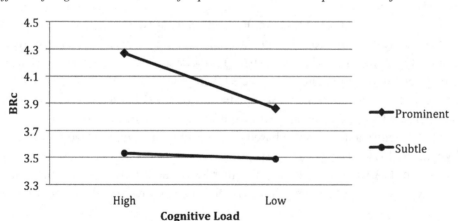

Figure 4. Effect of cognitive load on BRg for the main brand that the advergame is specifically designed for

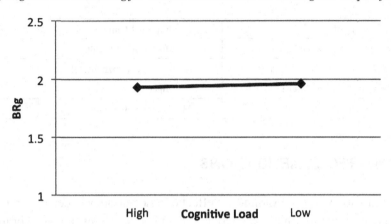

Brand Attitude (BRa)

An analysis of covariance (ANCOVA) was carried out to test the fourth hypothesis of the study. The last hypothesis of the study suggests that in a high cognitive load situation the BRa for the brand that the advergame was specifically designed for will be more positive than low cognitive load condition. To test the hypothesis, we used cognitive load as the independent variable and BRa as the dependent variable. Same as the other hypothesis' tests, telepresence was used as the covariate. As expected the BRa was more positive in a high level of cognitive load (BRa in high cognitive load condition; M =17.41; sd=2.96 versus BRa in low cognitive load condition M= 15.72; sd=2.34). The results of the ANCOVA have yielded a significant effect between the dependent and independent variables (F=4.466, p=0.028). According to the results hypothesis 4 (H4) was supported.

The findings of the study and the results of the hypotheses are summarized in Table 1.

Figure 5. Effect of cognitive load on BRa for the main brand that the advergame is specifically designed for

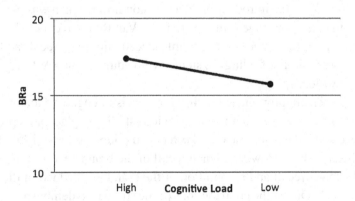

Table 1. Findings of the study

	Hypothesis	Expected Outcome	Result
H1	Prominent placement x high cognitive load	Higher Brand Recall	Supported
H2	Subtle placement x cognitive load	No difference in Brand Recall	Supported
H3	High cognitive load during game play	Higher Brand Recall	Rejected
H4	High cognitive load during game play	More positive Brand Attitude	Supported

SOLUTIONS AND RECOMMENDATIONS

The primary aim of this study was to examine the effect of association between different degrees of cognitive load and brand prominence on players' cognitive and affective responses to brands advertised in digital games and to the main brand. The study indicates that in high and low cognitive load conditions, placement prominence affects the brand recall of IGA, while brand recognition of the main brand is not affected. Moreover, level of cognitive load affects brand attitude toward the main brand.

The sample chosen for this study consists of university students, which is in line with previous research concerning advergames (Cauberghe & DePelsmacker, 2010; Gross, 2010; Okazaki & Yagüe, 2012; Paisley, 2013). The reason behind the use of university students as sample units is their engagement and interest in playing online games. Young players are the main target for branded entertainment.

Cognitive Load and Brand Prominence

One of the findings of the study is; prominently placed brands are better recalled in the presence of high cognitive load than low cognitive load.

According to the cognitive load theory, there is limited cognitive capacity of the human beings, and tasks are allocated based on the given priorities (Kahneman, 1973). After the primary tasks occupy the cognitive capacity, secondary tasks are taken into consideration (Lee & Shen, 2009; Hernandez, 2011). If the primary task has already depleted the capacity, no cognition left for the secondary task. In such a case, the findings of the previous studies suggested a reduced brand recall and recognition of specific content (Hembrook & Gay, 2003). Furthermore, according to Mayer and Moreno (2003), people in multimedia environments experience cognitive overload when dealing with the complexity of both text and pictorial presentations. With the introduction of a new condition, which was placement prominence, in this study, however, the results changed. In the study by Van Reijmersdal et al. (2012), it was found that brand prominence within the game positively influenced children's recall and recognition of the advertised brand. There were similar findings in studies with adults (Gupta & Lord, 1998; Lee & Faber, 2007; Yang & Roskos-Ewoldsen, 2007).

To our knowledge, placement prominence in different levels of cognitive load is investigated for the first time. The findings of the study are in line with previous studies in placement prominence: the more prominently a brand is placed; the better the brand is recalled (Gupta & Lord, 1998; Lee & Faber, 2007; Yang & Roskos-Ewoldsen, 2007). However, when recall of the brand becomes the secondary task, the expectation is toward a lower recall and recognition of the brands embedded in the game (Hembrooke & Gay, 2003), which is IGA. One of the contributions of the study is to demonstrate the ability of placement prominence to reverse the case. If the brand is placed prominently, especially in high cognitive load condition, it is better recalled. It can be explained by the way the placed brands are treated within the game. Interaction of the game character with prominently placed brands is most probably the main reason for that they were recalled better although the player is cognitively loaded. Interactive characteristics of the gaming environment may have taken the attention to the prominently placed brands, while the player is in active use of the brand.

Another explanation could be the secondary task's demand for more cognitive capacity. With an aroused cognitive capacity, players may be more careful about the gaming environment since they are trying to achieve a goal. While they are competing in the game, the brands, which were highly visible and have an interaction with the character that the player is directing, take their attention. On the other hand, since subtle placements are not easy to discover, degree of cognitive load does not make any difference for cognitive variables on players. In any way, examining the mean scores, it can be concluded that in any level of cognitive load, subtle placements are recalled better than average, but not as high as prominent placements.

Brand Recognition

This study showed no impact of cognitive overload on recognition of Magnum brand, which is called the 'main brand' that the advergame was specifically designed for. Regardless of the degree of cognitive load, players recognized the Magnum brand. It is the result of the finding that, there was no significant difference in high and low cognitive load conditions on brand recognition of Magnum.

The result showed the effectiveness of the advergames on cognitive variable, which is the recognition of the main brand. 94% of the respondents recognized the brand correctly. This finding also supported to previous finding of prominent placement. Since throughout the game, the game character is in interaction with the main brand, the result is not a surprise. The advergame is designed in such a way that Magnum brand was in the central focus of player's attention. It can be said that it is the most prominently placed brand in the advergame.

Result on brand recognition supports the idea of the effectiveness of the advergames.

Brand Attitude

Brand attitude is an affective variable that was found to be influenced by the level of cognitive load in the study. Cognitive load leads to affective processing, in which brand recognition is not influenced but attitudes are.

Previous studies found a positive relationship between the association of a brand with an enjoyable experience and brand attitude. The interaction was suggested through spill-over effect (Grigorovici & Constantin 2004; Raney et al., 2003). Spill-over suggests that the effects of an appreciated context, such as interaction with the game, carry over the embedded commercial messages (Van Reijmersdal et al., 2012). Thus, the commercial message benefits from the positive feelings associated with the context.

In our condition, as the level of cognitive load on player was increased, the attitude toward the main brand became more positive. It may be due to the challenging nature of the advergame. The affective response of the player through the main brand becomes more positive, as the cognitive resources are used effectively. This is in line with the previous findings, as Yoon et al. (2011) demonstrated, in traditional marketing, under conditions of higher cognitive load, the viewer's attitude towards a placed brand, which is IGA, is more favorable. Another explanation could be the transfer of entertaining and positive experience to the brand.

The contribution of this study to the literature is providing the evidence for under high cognitive load the attitude toward not only the placed brands but also the main brand of the advergame is more positive in digital games.

Managerial Implications

The findings of the study lead to a number of managerial implications for advertising professionals. Advergames are designed specifically to promote a brand. In advergames, there may be advertisements of other brands, which are called IGA. Advergames and branded environments can be valuable vehicles for delivering brand related messages to especially younger audiences. They provide a certain amount of control for both advertisers and game developers.

The first implication for the professionals is the proven effectiveness of advergames both for the main brand and embedded brands. Although this study specifically designed to investigate the effect of cognitive load, the findings showed that whether in the presence or absence of the cognitive load, embedded brands are recalled by more than fifty per cent of the players, main brand is recognized by the majority of the players (94%), and brand attitude is positive toward main brand. All those findings have proven the success of the new form of branded entertainment.

Going for the details, the placement prominence of a brand in an advergame does influence the advertising effects in terms of brand recall, main brands' recognition and brand attitude, especially in the different levels of cognitive load. This finding is also supported by previous research concerning advergames (Cauberghe & DePelsmacker, 2010)

Cognitive overload is usually created in the advergames by giving multiple instructions to the player or giving a time limit to play the game. It is recommended to the practitioners, even in the game conditions that created cognitive load on player, prominently placed brand that is embedded in the game in an interactive way will be recalled by the young targets. What is more, if there is multi-tasking, the brands will be better recalled, most probably because of aroused attention of the player. On the other hand, trying to embed the brands in the game invisibly, and in a way that is hard to discover will result in low recall rates both in high and low cognitive load conditions.

According to the results, practitioners should not be concerned about the possible negative effects of cognitive overload on brand recognition. Cognitive overload had no effect on recognition of the main brand in either degree; i.e. high or low.

It is among the results that, as players enjoy the game, those positive attitudes are transferred to the brand evaluation. Thus, selecting the target gamers carefully becomes the main issue. For example, in a study a by Ozansoy Çadırcı, Sağkaya Güngör and Köse (2015), the gamers were divided into six different segments in which dormant gamers have the most positive attitude toward IGA. The results of this study, together with the literature (e.g. Wise, et.al), imply that carefully selecting the target players should be the main concern of advergamers, so that they should enjoy the game first. Besides entertainment factor, the relevance between the brand and the game is also an important aspect that affects consumer attitudes.

Advergames are designed to be entertaining and this study verified that advertisers are successfully creating favorable affective and cognitive responses with the new form of branded entertainment.

FUTURE RESEARCH DIRECTIONS

Advergames are rather a new, but highly effective marketing concept targeting young consumers. There are many different subjects that they can be studied. This study examines the effect of cognitive load on cognitive and affective responses to advergaming content. Besides contributions to marketing literature this study also has limitations, which provide further opportunities for future research. The first limitation of the study can be considered as the way the cognitive load was manipulated. Cognitive load was manipulated by forcing subjects to remember a seven-digit number. Another way to manipulate the cognitive load could be inherent to the game, such as giving multiple tasks that should be completed in the game. As a result, it can be assumed that for different manipulations of cognitive load the results may differ. Future research may discover various effects of cognitive load on brand recall and recognition. Also the setting and the nature of the sample also cause some limitations. University students were selected as subjects for an extra course credit. As the students were offered an extra credit they might have acted more cautious during the experiment. Applying an experiment for a larger group and with a real life setting, i.e. without any incentives, may provide further information. In this study telepresence was used as the covariate. Using different variables like game involvement, brand familiarity or general attitude towards advergames might yield further interaction effects. Another area of study could be comparing the effectiveness of IGA with the effectiveness of advergames. They can be compared in different mediums, e.g. tablets, mobile devices etc., which is another area for future research.

CONCLUSION

In conclusion we have identified the possible interaction effects of cognitive load on brand recall, brand recognition and brand attitude in an advergaming context. It was investigated that recall of the prominently placed brands differs in high and low cognitive load conditions. Also the results of the study revealed that for different levels of cognitive load there are differences between subtle and prominent placements. The effect of cognitive load on prominently placed brands is higher than its effect on subtly placed brands. This study demonstrates that the recognition of the main brand in an advergame is not affected by cognitive conditions. This finding suggests an important assumption on the effectiveness and success of advergaming content. When the audience interacts with the product or the brand, their recognition and recall of the brand cannot be negatively affected by external stimuli. Cognitive load also have a positive effect on brand attitude. The results of the study demonstrate the importance and effectiveness of advergames as a communication tool for both cognitive and affective responses.

REFERENCES

Adis, A. A. A., & Jun, K. H. (2013). Antecedents of brand recall and brand attitude towards purchase intention in advergames. *European Journal of Business and Management*, 5(18), 58–67.

Alina, G. (2013). Factors responsible for consumer's attitude towards advergames. *Annals of Faculty of Economics*, 1(1), 1733–1742.

An, S., & Kang, H. (2014). Advertising or games? Advergames on the internet gaming sites targeting children. *International Journal of Advertising, 33*(3), 509–532. doi:10.2501/IJA-33-3-509-532

An, S., & Stern, S. (2011). Mitigating the effects of advergames on children. *Journal of Advertising, 40*(1), 43–56. doi:10.2753/JOA0091-3367400103

Balasubramanian, S. K. (1994). Beyond advertising and publicity: Hybrid messages and public policy issues. *Journal of Advertising, 23*(4), 29–46. doi:10.1080/00913367.1943.10673457

Batra, R., & Ahtola, O. T. (1991). Measuring the hedonic and utilitarian sources of consumer attitudes. *Marketing Letters, 2*(2), 159–170. doi:10.1007/BF00436035

Beilock, S. L., & Ramirez, G. (2011). 5 On the interplay of emotion and cognitive control: Implications for enhancing academic achievement. *Psychology of Learning and Motivation-Advances in Research and Theory, 55*, 137–169. doi:10.1016/B978-0-12-387691-1.00005-3

Bellman, S., Kemp, A., Haddad, H., & Varan, D. (2014). The effectiveness of advergames compared to television commercials and interactive commercials featuring advergames. *Computers in Human Behavior, 32*, 276–283. doi:10.1016/j.chb.2013.12.013

Besharat, A., Kumar, A., Lax, J. R., & Rydzik, E. J. (2013). Leveraging virtual attribute experience in video games to improve brand recall and learning. *Journal of Advertising, 42*(2-3), 170–182. doi:10.1080/00913367.2013.774593

Brasel, S. A., & Gips, J. (2011). Media multitasking behavior: Concurrent television and computer usage. *Cyberpsychology, Behavior, and Social Networking, 14*(9), 527–534. doi:10.1089/cyber.2010.0350

Brennan, I., & Babin, L. A. (2004). Brand placement recognition: The influence of presentation mode and brand familiarity. *Journal of Promotion Management, 10*(1–2), 185–202. doi:10.1300/J057v10n01_13

Brünken, R., Plass, J. L., & Leutner, D. (2003). Direct measurement of cognitive load in multimedia learning. *Educational Psychologist, 38*(1), 53–61. doi:10.1207/S15326985EP3801_7

Buijzen, M., Van Reijmersdal, E. A., & Owen, L. H. (2010). Introducing the PCMC model: An investigative framework for young people's processing of commercial media content. *Communication Theory, 20*(4), 427–450. doi:10.1111/j.1468-2885.2010.01370.x

Cauberghe, V., & DePelsmacker, P. (2010). Advergames. *Journal of Advertising, 39*(1), 5–18. doi:10.2753/JOA0091-3367390101

Cauberghe, V., Geuens, M., & De Pelsmacker, P. (2011). Context effects of TV programme-induced interactivity and telepresence on advertising responses. *International Journal of Advertising, 30*(4), 641–663. doi:10.2501/IJA-30-4-641-663

Chaney, I. M., Lin, K. H., & Chaney, J. (2004). The effect of billboards within the gaming environment. *Journal of Interactive Advertising, 5*(1), 37–45. doi:10.1080/15252019.2004.10722092

Cholinski, A. (2012). The effectiveness of product placement: A field quasi-experiment. *International Journal of Marketing Studies, 4*(5), 14. doi:10.5539/ijms.v4n5p14

Clark, J. M., & Paivio, A. (1991). Dual coding theory and education. *Educational Psychology Review*, *3*(3), 149–210. doi:10.1007/BF01320076

Dahl, S., Eagle, L., & Báez, C. (2009). Analyzing advergames: Active diversions or actually deception. An exploratory study of online advergames content. *Young Consumers*, *10*(1), 46–59. doi:10.1108/17473610910940783

Ghirvu, A. (2011). Advergames: marketing advantages and risks involved. *Marketing from Information to Decision*, 4, 174-183.

Glass, Z. (2007). The effectiveness of product placement in video games. *Journal of Interactive Advertising*, *8*(1), 23–32. doi:10.1080/15252019.2007.10722134

Goh, K. Y., & Ping, J. W. (2014). Engaging Consumers with Advergames: An Experimental Evaluation of Interactivity, Fit and Expectancy. *Journal of the Association for Information Systems*, *15*(7), 388–421.

Grigorovici, D. M., & Constantin, C. D. (2004). Experiencing interactive advertising beyond rich media: Impacts of ad type and presence on brand effectiveness in 3D gaming immersive virtual environments. *Journal of Interactive Advertising*, *5*(1), 22–36. doi:10.1080/15252019.2004.10722091

Gross, M. L. (2010). Advergames and the effects of game-product congruity. *Computers in Human Behavior*, *26*(6), 1259–1265. doi:10.1016/j.chb.2010.03.034

Grossman, S. (2005). "Grand Theft Oreo": The Constitutionality of Advergame Regulation. *The Yale Law Journal*, 2005, 227–236.

Gunawardena, T., & Waiguny, M. K. (2014). So many things to do! How multitasking affects memory and attitude for product and brand placements. *Australasian Marketing Journal*, *22*(4), 288–295. doi:10.1016/j.ausmj.2014.09.001

Gupta, P. B., & Lord, K. R. (1998). Product placement in movies: The effect of prominence and mode on audience recall. *Journal of Current Issues and Research in Advertising*, *20*(1), 47–59. doi:10.1080/10641734.1998.10505076

Hembrooke, H., & Gay, G. (2003). The laptop and the lecture: The effects of multitasking in learning environments. *Journal of Computing in Higher Education*, *15*(1), 46–64. doi:10.1007/BF02940852

Hernandez, M. D. (2011). A model of flow experience as determinant of positive attitudes toward online advergames. *Journal of Promotion Management*, *17*(3), 315–326. doi:10.1080/10496491.2011.596761

Hernandez, M. D., & Chapa, S. (2010). Adolescents, advergames and snack foods: Effects of positive affect and experience on memory and choice. *Journal of Marketing Communications*, *16*(1-2), 59–68. doi:10.1080/13527260903342761

Hernandez, M. D., Chapa, S., Minor, M. S., Maldonado, C., & Barranzuela, F. (2004). Hispanic attitudes toward advergames: A proposed model of their antecedents. *Journal of Interactive Advertising*, *5*(1), 74–83. doi:10.1080/15252019.2004.10722095

Hernandez, M. D., & Minor, M. S. (2011). Investigating the effect of arousal on brand memory in advergames: Comparing qualitative and quantitative approaches. *Qualitative Market Research: An International Journal, 14*(2), 207–217. doi:10.1108/13522751111120701

Hoffman, D. L., & Novak, T. P. (1996). Marketing in hypermedia computer-mediated environments: Conceptual foundations. *Journal of Marketing, 60*(3), 50–68. doi:10.2307/1251841

Hofmeister-Tóth, Á., & Nagy, P. (2011). The content analysis of advergames in Hungary. *Qualitative Market Research: An International Journal, 14*(3), 289–303. doi:10.1108/13522751111137514

Hudson, S., & Hudson, D. (2006). Branded entertainment: A new advertising technique or product placement in disguise? *Journal of Marketing Management, 22*(5-6), 489–504. doi:10.1362/026725706777978703

Huh, J., Suzuki-Lambrecht, Y., Lueck, J., & Gross, M. (2015). Presentation Matters: Comparison of Cognitive Effects of DTC Prescription Drug Advergames, Websites, and Print Ads. *Journal of Advertising*.

Kahneman, D. (1973). *Attention and effort* (p. 246). Englewood Cliffs, NJ: Prentice-Hall.

Kim, T., & Biocca, F. (1997). Telepresence via television: Two dimensions of telepresence may have different connections to memory and persuasion. *Journal of Computer-Mediated Communication, 3*(2).

Kinard, B. R., & Hartman, K. B. (2013). Are you entertained? The impact of brand integration and brand experience in television-related advergames. *Journal of Advertising, 42*(2-3), 196–203. doi:10.1080/00913367.2013.775794

Kleeberger, J., & Hummel, J. (2002). *Online-gaming as a marketing and sales catalyst*. Switzerland: Department of Media and Communication, University of St. Gallen.

Klein, L. R. (2003). Creating virtual product experiences: The role of telepresence. *Journal of Interactive Marketing, 17*(1), 41–55. doi:10.1002/dir.10046

Klimmt, C., & Vorderer, P. (2003). Media psychology "is not yet there": Introducing theories on media entertainment to the presence debate. *Presence (Cambridge, Mass.), 12*(4), 346–359. doi:10.1162/105474603322391596

Lai, M., & Huang, Y. S. (2011). Can learning theoretical approaches illuminate the ways in which advertising games effect attitude, recall, and purchase intention. *International Journal of Electronic Business Management, 9*(4), 368.

Lang, A. (2000). The limited capacity model of motivated mediated message processing. *Journal of Communication, 50*(1), 46–70. doi:10.1111/j.1460-2466.2000.tb02833.x

Lee, J., Park, H., & Wise, K. (2014). Brand interactivity and its effects on the outcomes of advergame play. *New Media & Society, 16*(8), 1268–1286. doi:10.1177/1461444813504267

Lee, M., & Faber, R. J. (2007). Effects of product placement in on-line games on brand memory: A perspective of the limited-capacity model of attention. *Journal of Advertising, 36*(4), 75–90. doi:10.2753/JOA0091-3367360406

Lee, S. Y., & Shen, F. (2009). Joint Advertising and Brand Congruity: Effects on Memory and Attitudes. *Journal of Promotion Management, 15*(4), 448–498. doi:10.1080/10496490903276874

Lewis, B., & Porter, L. (2010). In-game advertising effects: Examining player perceptions of advertising schema congruity in a massively multiplayer online role-playing game. *Journal of Interactive Advertising*, *10*(2), 46–60. doi:10.1080/15252019.2010.10722169

Lynch, J. G. Jr, & Srull, T. K. (1982). Memory and attentional factors in consumer choice: Concepts and research methods. *The Journal of Consumer Research*, *9*(1), 18–37. doi:10.1086/208893

Macrae, C. N., Hewstone, M., & Griffiths, R. J. (1993). Processing load and memory for stereotype-based information. *European Journal of Social Psychology*, *23*(1), 77–87. doi:10.1002/ejsp.2420230107

Mallinckrodt, V., & Mizerski, D. (2007). The effects of playing an advergame on young children's perceptions, preferences, and requests. *Journal of Advertising*, *36*(2), 87–100. doi:10.2753/JOA0091-3367360206

Martí-Parreño, J., Aldás-Manzano, J., Currás-Pérez, R., & Sánchez-García, I. (2013). Factors contributing brand attitude in advergames: Entertainment and irritation. *Journal of Brand Management*, *20*(5), 374–388. doi:10.1057/bm.2012.22

Mayer, R. E., & Moreno, R. (2003). Nine ways to reduce cognitive load in multimedia learning. *Educational Psychologist*, *38*(1), 43–52. doi:10.1207/S15326985EP3801_6

Moore, E. S., & Rideout, V. J. (2007). The online marketing of food to children: Is it just fun and games? *Journal of Public Policy & Marketing*, *26*(2), 202–220. doi:10.1509/jppm.26.2.202

Nelson, M. R. (2002). Recall of brand placements in computer/video games. *Journal of Advertising Research*, *42*(2), 80–92. doi:10.2501/JAR-42-2-80-92

Nelson, M. R., & Waiguny, M. K. (2012). Psychological Processing of In-Game Advertising and Advergaming: Branded Entertainment or Entertaining Persuasion? In *Psychology of entertainment media: Blurring the lines between Entertainment and persuasion* (pp. 93-146).

Nelson, M. R., Yaros, R. A., & Keum, H. (2006). Examining the influence of telepresence on spectator and player processing of real and fictitious brands in a computer game. *Journal of Advertising*, *35*(4), 87–99. doi:10.2753/JOA0091-3367350406

Novak, T. P., Hoffman, D. L., & Yung, Y. F. (2000). Measuring the customer experience in online environments: A structural modeling approach. *Marketing Science*, *19*(1), 22–42. doi:10.1287/mksc.19.1.22.15184

Okazaki, S., & Yagüe, M. J. (2012). Responses to an advergaming campaign on a mobile social networking site: An initial research report. *Computers in Human Behavior*, *28*(1), 78–86. doi:10.1016/j.chb.2011.08.013

Ozansoy Çadırcı, T., Sağkaya Güngör, A., & Köse, Ş. G. (2015). Segmenting the gamers to understand the effectiveness of the in game advertisement.*Proceedings of 1st Annual International Conference on Social Sciences (AICSS)* (Vol. 1, pp. 435-448), İstanbul, Turkey: Yildiz Technical University.

Paas, F., Renkl, A., & Sweller, J. (2003). Cognitive load theory and instructional design: Recent developments. *Educational Psychologist*, *38*(1), 1–4. doi:10.1207/S15326985EP3801_1

Paisley, V. (2013, December). Gamification of tertiary courses: An exploratory study of learning and engagement.*Proceedings of the 30th ASCILITE Conference* (pp. 671-675).

Panic, K., Cauberghe, V., & DePelsmacker, P. (2013). Comparing TV ads and advergames targeting children: The impact of persuasion knowledge on behavioral responses. *Journal of Advertising*, *42*(2-3), 264–273. doi:10.1080/00913367.2013.774605

Peters, S., & Leshner, G. (2013). Get in the game: The effects of game-product congruity and product placement proximity on game players' processing of brands embedded in advergames. *Journal of Advertising*, *42*(2-3), 113–130. doi:10.1080/00913367.2013.774584

Raney, A. A., Arpan, L. M., Pashupati, K., & Brill, D. A. (2003). At the movies, on the web: An investigation of the effects of entertaining and interactive web content on site and brand evaluations. *Journal of Interactive Marketing*, *17*(4), 38–53. doi:10.1002/dir.10064

Redondo, I. (2012). The effectiveness of casual advergames on adolescents' brand attitudes. *European Journal of Marketing*, *46*(11/12), 1671–1688. doi:10.1108/03090561211260031

Refiana, L., Mizerski, D., & Murphy, J. (2005) Measuring the state of flow in playing online Games. In S. Purchase (Ed.), *Proceedings of ANZMAC 2005 Conference, Marketing Research and Research Methodologies (Quantitative)* (pp. 108-113). Freemantle, Australia: School of Business, University of Western Australia.

Rosen, C. (2008). The myth of multitasking. *New Atlantis (Washington, D.C.)*, (Spring): 105–110.

Santos, E., Gonzalo, R., & Gisbert, F. (2007). Advergames: Overview. *International Journal Information Technologies and Knowledge*, *1*, 203–208.

Schneider, L. P., & Cornwell, B. T. (2002). Cashing in on crashes via brand placement in computer games: The effects of experience and flow on memory. *International Journal of Advertising*, *24*(3), 321–343.

Shiv, B., Britton, J. A. E., & Payne, J. W. (2004). Does elaboration increase or decrease the effectiveness of negatively versus positively framed messages? *The Journal of Consumer Research*, *31*(1), 199–208. doi:10.1086/383435

Shiv, B., Edell, J. A., & Payne, J. W. (1997). Factors affecting the impact of negatively and positively framed ad messages. *The Journal of Consumer Research*, *24*(3), 285–294. doi:10.1086/209510

Steuer, J. (1992). Defining virtual reality: Dimensions determining telepresence. *Journal of Communication*, *42*(4), 33–56. doi:10.1111/j.1460-2466.1992.tb00812.x

Suh, K. S., & Chang, S. (2006). User interfaces and consumer perceptions of online stores: The role of telepresence. *Behaviour & Information Technology*, *25*(2), 99–113. doi:10.1080/01449290500330398

Sukoco, B. M., & Wu, W. Y. (2011). The effects of advergames on consumer telepresence and attitudes: A comparison of products with search and experience attributes. *Expert Systems with Applications*, *38*(6), 7396–7406. doi:10.1016/j.eswa.2010.12.085

Sweller, J. (2011). *The Psychology of Learning and Motivation: Cognition in Education* (B. H. Ross & J. P. Mestre, Eds., Vol. 55). London, UK: Academic Press, Elsevier.

Sweller, J., Ayres, P., & Kalyuga, S. (2011). *Cognitive load theory*. New York: Springer. doi:10.1007/978-1-4419-8126-4

Terlutter, R., & Capella, M. L. (2013). The gamification of advertising: Analysis and research directions of in-game advertising, advergames, and advertising in social network games. *Journal of Advertising*, *42*(2-3), 95–112. doi:10.1080/00913367.2013.774610

Tina, W., & Buckner, K. (2006). Receptiveness of gamers to embedded brand messages in advergames: Attitudes towards product placement. *Journal of Interactive Advertising*, *7*(1), 3–32. doi:10.1080/1525 2019.2006.10722123

Van Reijmersdal, E. (2009). Brand placement prominence: Good for memory! Bad for attitudes? *Journal of Advertising Research*, *49*(2), 151–153. doi:10.2501/S0021849909090199

Van Reijmersdal, E. A., Rozendaal, E., & Buijzen, M. (2012). Effects of prominence, involvement, and persuasion knowledge on children's cognitive and affective responses to advergames. *Journal of Interactive Marketing*, *26*(1), 33–42. doi:10.1016/j.intmar.2011.04.005

Verhellen, Y., Oates, C., De Pelsmacker, P., & Dens, N. (2014). Children's Responses to Traditional Versus Hybrid Advertising Formats: The Moderating Role of Persuasion Knowledge. *Journal of Consumer Policy*, *37*(2), 235–255.

Vermeir, I., Kazakova, S., Tessitore, T., Cauberghe, V., & Slabbinck, H. (2014). Impact of flow on recognition of and attitudes towards in-game brand placements: Brand congruence and placement prominence as moderators. *International Journal of Advertising*, *33*(4), 785–810. doi:10.2501/IJA-33-4-785-810

Waiguny, M. K., Nelson, M. R., & Marko, B. (2013). How advergame content influences explicit and implicit brand attitudes: When violence spills over. *Journal of Advertising*, *42*(2-3), 155–169. doi:10.1 080/00913367.2013.774590

Waiguny, M. K., Nelson, M. R., & Terlutter, R. (2012). Entertainment matters! The relationship between challenge and persuasiveness of an advergame for children. *Journal of Marketing Communications*, *18*(1), 69–89. doi:10.1080/13527266.2011.620766

Waiguny, M. K., & Terlutter, R. (2011). Differences in children's processing of advergames and TV commercials. In *Advances in Advertising Research* (Vol. 2, pp. 35–51). Gabler. doi:10.1007/978-3-8349-6854-8_3

Williams, K., Petrosky, A., Hernandez, E., & Page, R. (2011). Product placement effectiveness: Revisited and renewed. *Journal of Management and Marketing Research*, *7*(1), 1–24.

Winkler, T., & Buckner, K. (2006). Receptiveness of gamers to embedded brand messages in advergames: Attitudes towards product placement. *Journal of Interactive Advertising*, *7*(1), 3–32. doi:10.1080/1525 2019.2006.10722123

Wise, K., Bolls, P. D., Kim, H., Venkataraman, A., & Meyer, R. (2008). Enjoyment of advergames and brand attitudes: The impact of thematic relevance. *Journal of Interactive Advertising*, *9*(1), 27–36. doi: 10.1080/15252019.2008.10722145

Yang, M., & Roskos-Ewoldsen, D. R. (2007). The effectiveness of bran placements in the movies: Level of placements, explicit and implicit memory, and brand choice behavior. *Journal of Communication*, *57*(3), 469–489. doi:10.1111/j.1460-2466.2007.00353.x

Yang, M. H., Roskos-Ewoldsen, D. R., Dinu, L., & Arpan, L. M. (2006). The effectiveness of 'in-game' advertising: Comparing college students' explicit and implicit memory for brand names. *Journal of Advertising*, *35*(4), 143–152. doi:10.2753/JOA0091-3367350410

Yoon, S., Choi, Y. K., & Song, S. (2011). When intrusive can be likable. *Journal of Advertising*, *40*(2), 63–76. doi:10.2753/JOA0091-3367400205

KEY TERMS AND DEFINITIONS

Advergames: Mostly Internet-based video games which promote a certain brand, company or product.

Brand Recall: Brand recall is a component of brand awareness. The term refers to the ability of consumers remembering a certain brand name after the exposure of a promotional content.

Brand Recognition: Brand recognition is another component of brand awareness; which refers to the ability of consumers to recognize a certain brand over other ones in a marketplace.

Branded Entertainment: Branded entertainment is a new form of advertising. The term basically refers to the act of integrating an advertising message or a brand with other entertainment content with the use of media like TV shows, movies or video games (Also known as *Branded Content*).

Cognitive Load: Refers to the total amount of mental activity and allocation to a certain task or tasks simultaneously with the task at hand.

In-Game Advertising: Refers to the practice of placing product or inserting advertising content in video games.

Product Placement: Product placement is the inclusion of a branded product in different media like movies, TV programs or video games.

Chapter 21
Towards an Inclusive Walk-in Customer Service Facility

Tiago Cinto
Telecommunications Research and Development Center, Brazil

ABSTRACT

It is estimated that 15% of the world's population has some sort of physical or sensory disability, according to the World Health Organization (2011). In an era marked by the rising of new technological devices, the inclusion of this public in digital environments still faces many obstacles, what frequently lets it out of this informational society. In this sense, Companhia Energética de Minas Gerais – CEMIG, one of the biggest Brazilian electrical energy utility company, has started to design and deploy a high-tech, user-friendly, inclusive customer service facility aimed at rendering a wide range of services by means of several gadgets such as self-service kiosks, tablets, and interactive panels and tables to help address the digital divide. For doing so, the applications to be developed and run on those devices need to be carefully studied and previously tested in order to meet the needs and expectations of the target audience. This paper describes the process of designing these innovative solutions to meet the demands of this new service channel.

INTRODUCTION

Currently, with the increasing growth of Information and Communication Technologies (ICTs), more and more people have access to technologies. This access, however, is not always done the right way. People with disabilities – approximately 15% of the world population (World Health Organization (2011)) – for instance, still face many obstacles to use technological devices, what excludes them from this growing informational society.

In Brazil, approximately 24% of the adult population (ranging between 14 to 64 years old) has at least one of the following disabilities: visual, hearing, mental, or motor (IBGE, 2010). Among the elderly (over 65 years old), this percentage reaches more than 67% of individuals (IBGE, 2010). These numbers, however, do not include illiterate or semiliterate people who are unable to read contents presented by electronic devices, as well as the visually impaired. In 2000, more than fourteen percent of the adult population had some sort of disability (IBGE, 2010), which represents a considerable growth in ten years. In Minas Gerais, the second most populous state of Brazil, for instance, data indicate a growth

DOI: 10.4018/978-1-5225-0435-1.ch021

rate of 5.08 per year of the handicapped population between 2000 and 2010, which grew from 2,667,714 to 4,432,186 individuals most recently (Baptista & Rigotti, 2013). Considering these numbers one can see the importance of using the so-called socially aware design, in other words, the design concerned not only in creating systems that make sense for the whole population, but also aware with the human development of this population (Baranauskas, 2009). The ethics code of the Association for Computing Machinery – ACM (1992) argues that:

In a fair society, all individuals would have equal opportunity to participate in, or benefit from, the use of computer resources regardless of race, sex, religion, age, disability, national origin or other such similar factor.

In this sense, it is important to emphasize the need of designing products that satisfactorily meet the population in its great diversity. This positively contributes to the integration of all social profiles in this growing digital society. Furthermore, according to Shneiderman (2000):

Accommodating a broader spectrum of usage situations forces researchers to consider a wider range of designs and often leads to innovations that benefit all users.

In the theory of action, Norman (1988) defines the so-called gulfs of interaction (depths of interaction), in other words, hypothetical use scenarios that hold off expectations of users and designers. In this sense, Norman emphasizes the need of shortening these gulfs by approximating systems to users' cognitive load, building interfaces that meet expectations of both parts.

In this context and considering the scenario previously described concerning the technological growth, it is possible to think about creating solutions that meet the population in its great diversity, by shortening gulfs previously commented, which makes applications more friendly and accessible. Therefore, it was proposed by CEMIG (Minas Gerais Electric Utility Company) in partnership with CPqD (Telecommunications Research and Development Center), a project to conceive innovative solutions to serve its consumers (an inclusive walk-in customer service facility), including elderly, semiliterate, with disabilities (visual, hearing or motor impaired), or with some temporary mobility restriction. The major goal of this project is to create a walk-in facility that enables customers of all profiles to autonomously interact with devices and request services related to electrical energy with little or no assistance. This is expected to be done with the help of multimodal technological devices such as self-service kiosks, interactive tables, and tablets using specially built inclusive apps to satisfy users' needs.

Self-service kiosks can be described as convenient solutions that provide services for different types of contexts such as malls, banks, and airports. Many of them, however, are not accessible for all users. For instance, most of the kiosks are not accessible for blind people since they are solely based on a touch screen panel without audible feedback. The hearing impaired who can communicate only through sign language is also usually excluded from most of these machines.

Creating solutions for this vast diversity of people with different abilities and needs is a challenge for designers. It is hard to precisely tell the current demands of each group of users (blind, deaf, elderly, etc.) without consulting them. Several works have tried to address most of accessibility problems; however, most of them only treat one or at most two users' concerns (Sandnes et al., 2012; Hagen & Sandnes, 2010). Their contributions represent, nevertheless, a huge step towards more accessible solutions.

Accordingly, one can say that this project innovates by considering a large variety of users' profiles at the same time. In this sense, this paper aims to describe the characteristics, process and methodologies involved with the designing and deployment of the accessible apps, from participative workshops to collect users' feedback to the interaction model carefully developed and evaluated with the target public.

Currently, no self-service kiosk of any electric utility company provides accessibility for user diversity in Brazil. Therefore, apps' specific goals are;

- Streamline user service processes, making them easier to be used by several users' profiles.
- Provide accessibility in interaction with touch screen displays. General self-service kiosks offer a limited number of services.
- Promote autonomy so that users can operate devices without aid of other people, except in cases that human intervention is needed such as documents approval.
- Explore the multisensory natural experience (tact, audition and vision) of users, as well as provide redundancy of information, combining audio, text and, movie (if necessary) responses.
- Allow context retrieval so that users do not have to repeat information when interacting with different self-service kiosks.
- Provide an intelligent system which reacts to the user's actions.
- Improve accessibility for the deaf through an avatar to perform sign language.
- Improve accessibility for people with several degrees of visual impairment, elderly and people with low literacy skills through a feature similar to a screen reader.
- Assist users by means of a contextual help system.
- Enrich communication meaning by means of appropriate iconography, allowing the recognition of services and options even for users with low literacy.

Objectives

This work aims to introduce the designing process used to design and deploy the inclusive solutions to meet demands from the new service channel being built for consumers of CEMIG. Services will be offered in an automated way by this walk-in facility, in other words, through self-service kiosks and other technological devices. In this sense, the interaction model of the applications should allow autonomous and effective use for everyone, including people with or without disabilities (hearing, visual, or motor impaired), elderly, illiterate or semiliterate, experts or not with technological devices. In addition, self-service kiosks will also be equipped with touchscreen devices, directional sound, thermal printers and other accessibility features to help users requesting desired services.

Creating solutions for a wide variety of profiles with different skills and needs represents a challenge for designers of systems and computer scientists. It's risky to precisely define what are the demands of each group of users without involving representatives of these groups. Even professionals with years of experience in usability and accessibility need to confirm their hypotheses. In order to ensure the creation of solutions that make sense for the whole population, it is worth emphasizing the need of methods that put designers close to users, in other words:

An important first step is to define the purpose of the kiosk, the user population who it is intended to serve, and their task goals [...] It is also important to understand the characteristics of the user population and the kinds of environment (physical and organizational) that the system will be located in, so that the design can reflect them [...] Discussion groups, interviews and user-based tests should also be carried out to get user reactions to the concept behind the kiosk and to test prototype versions of it at different stages of the development process (Maguire, 1999).

In this sense, some of the design practices and the artifacts of Organizational Semiotics used in this project will be further commented in next sessions of this work.

BACKGROUND

Usability and Accessibility

Usability can be defined as a quality attribute used to measure the quality of UIs (Nielsen, 1993). Usability aspects include efficiency of use, memorability, learnability, errors, and satisfaction.

Efficiency refers to the users' proficiency level in using and learning a system for the first time.

Memorability evaluates how occasionally users can remember how to use a system without having to start from scratch each time. Regarding this, when it comes to interfaces, Nielsen (2014) states that it is always better to promote recognition over remembering:

Showing users things they can recognize improves usability over needing to recall items from scratch because the extra context helps users retrieve information from memory.

Errors can be defined as problems that occur when tasks are being performed. In such situations, applications must deal well with incorrect behaviors, helping users recover from errors.

Finally, satisfaction is the aspect that identifies the level of user satisfaction when interacting with applications and accomplishing tasks, which means that systems are supposed to be enjoyable for users to interact with.

In what regards accessibility (W3C, 2005), it refers to the tools and features that make a system accessible to every user, including people with special needs.

W3C (2005) states that creating accessible tools means to help people overcome access barriers regardless of their profile/background. It also points out that assistive tools are good not only for people with permanent disabilities, but also for the public at large, such as people experiencing temporary impairment (i.e., mobility impairment requiring the use of crutches, canes or walkers).

Both usability and accessibility are essentially user-centered concerns. The former addresses the ease of use of a system while the latter how it can be accessed by several user profiles. That is to say, because a specific software is user-friendly does not necessarily mean it is suitable to people with disabilities.

As for the inclusive walk-in facility to be deployed, all interactive devices complies with usability and accessibility requirements, in order to effectively meet the needs and expectations of the target audience. Besides, the following concepts of Universal Design (The Center for Universal Design, 1997) are also guiding the design process:

- Equitable use: design for people with diverse abilities;
- Flexibility in use: multi-profile suitability;

- Simple and intuitive use: make an interaction easy to understand, regardless of the user' experience (ICTs);
- Perceptible information: effectively communicate necessary information to users;
- Tolerance for error: reduced error hazard during interaction;
- Low physical effort: design for comfortable use and minimum fatigue;
- Size and space for approach and use: design for appropriate use regardless of user's body size, mobility, and so on.

Participative Design

Participative design aims at actively involving all stakeholders (i.e., developers, end users, partners, etc.) in a product's design, allowing the creation of solutions that meet all needs (Spinuzzi, 2004).

This practice first appeared in Scandinavia in the 70s motivated by a Marxist commitment of democratically empowering workers, generating agreements between trade unions and factories that allowed workers to deliberate about new technologies in the workplace. In the past, workers were forced to accept products disregarding their real needs, which often negatively affected their working routine (Spinuzzi, 2004).

In participative design activities, all participants are required to interact with designers, researchers and developers and may be involved from the initial design stage (i.e., problem definition and exploration) to the last phases, engaging in collaborative development and validation of prototypes and solutions (Spinuzzi, 2004).

Participative design workshops may contribute to the improvement of people's quality of work, providing them with more autonomy to handle tools, processes, concepts, and to perform tasks more efficiently (Spinuzzi, 2004).

One of the key points of the participative design approach is said to be the collaborative work (Spinuzzi, 2004). In this sense, the more heterogeneous the group of end users is the more reliable and comprehensive the results obtained tend to be (regarding data, suggestions and feedback collected). Considering such a very broad and heterogeneous target for this project the workshop brought together perspectives of multi-profile end users. In the literature, authors have carried out researches embracing multiple user profiles, as Cober, Au and Son (2012) and Potter, Korte and Nielsen (2011) who focused on a more specific audience: respectively, blind adults and deaf children. The case study reported next intended to reach the project's widely ranged target audience so that the principles of Usability, Accessibility, and Universal Design (1997) could be comprehensively applied along interface development stage. These activities will be described later in this work.

Organizational Semiotics

In Semiotics theory (Peirce, 1990) sign is everything that represents meaning to people, that is, creates in their minds a concept equivalent to what it represents. During the cognitive process, signs are used by people as a way to assist in the process of understanding concepts. Organizational Semiotics (OS), one of the branches of Semiotics theory, in turn, sees informational systems as organizations formed by social models previously established of beliefs, behaviors, values and perceptions (Stamper, 1993). In this sense, Stamper argues that the design of technologies should start by understanding how people make use of signs in their daily lives.

Cultural conventions, that is, how people work, are classified into three layers, defined as informal, formal and technical (Hall, 1959). Given this classification, Stamper (1993) proposed the Semiotic Onion representation to aid the understanding of how a layer is contained inside the other. The innermost layer is represented by the technical, followed by formal and informal, respectively, as can be seen in Figure 1. Therefore, Organizational Semiotics proposes that the development of systems should start by the informal layer, through the analysis of beliefs, cultures, and behaviors observed in everyday life. Formal layer, in turn, represents the formalization of the procedures observed in the informal layer.

The artifacts of Organizational Semiotics and Semiotic Onion were used to guide the design process of the inclusive apps since they can be considered excellent tools to assist development focused on digital inclusion. In this sense, representatives of the target audience from a wide range of profiles could actively and effectively contribute during the whole project, including those with or without disabilities, elderlies or semiliterate, experts or novices with digital technology. Since the beginning the concern was not only to create systems that could make sense for the population, but also to create solutions that could bring contributions to the human development of this population, in other words, the socially aware design (Baranauskas, 2009).

Semiotic Onion

The Semiotic Onion proposed by Stamper (1993) was adapted for the context of this work and was used to guide the design and development of prototypes, more specifically guiding the inclusive participative workshops carried out. In this sense, one can say that three inclusive participative workshops were carried out to explore each one of the onion's layers, as can be seen by Figure 1.

Figure 1. Semiotic onion

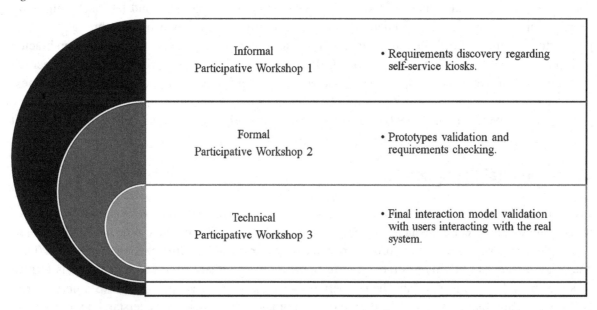

As shown by Figure 1, informal layer contains the culture and values of society, that is, it represents users as people with opinions and needs. In this sense, the first inclusive workshop aimed to integrate participants representing the target audience to researchers for the first time. One can also say that this workshop highlighted the human value of technological aspects at the same time it identified the main abilities and difficulties of participants regarding several services used in their daily lives.

Onion's formal layer, in turn, represents everyday behavior of people in the form of rules and standards, in other words, it is a formalization of reality. This formalization may occur in the form of standards, requirements, or other types of clarifications (i.e., the specification of interaction model), containing the guidelines that determine how users interact with systems. Therefore, the second participative workshop aimed to confirm requirements initially collected in the first workshop held, raise new requirements and collect data, through the interaction of users with a prototype built for the self-service cabin. Data obtained in this workshop was important to confirm assumptions to design interaction model and for the system development as a whole.

Finally, onion's technical layer represents the system itself. Thus, the third workshop is going to be planned for checking system use in real scenarios, in other words, it will evaluate the proposed interaction model in practice.

Related Work

Several researchers in literature have tried to address the problem of designing applications for such a diversified public (Sandnes et al., 2012; Hagen & Sandnes, 2010; Maguire, 1999; Piccolo et al., 2010; Filgueiras et al., 2008).

One interesting work found during the literature review was authored by Maguire (1999), who focused on propose a comprehensive set of guidelines for inclusive self-service kiosks considering the general public, the elderly, and people with motor impairments. Briefly, guidelines proposed concern several UI aspects such as physical access, motivation of use, security, privacy, help, language, structure and navigation, input types (keyboard, touchscreen, or speech (if necessary)), output types (images, colors, graphs, feedback, etc), among others. These guidelines were extensively used during the designing process or to support expert evaluations carried out before placing applications to be tested under workshops.

Numbers previously mentioned in Introduction shows the relevance of designing public technology that is accessible and easy to use. In order to provide technology that can be used by anyone it is worth emphasizing the need of applications that can run with only few adaptations from one profile of user to another (Universal Design). In this sense, a more concrete proposal comes from Hagen and Sandnes (2010) and Sandnes et al. (2012) that created a self-service kiosk prototype that is able to make minor adjustments in its interface to accommodate people with some degree of visual impairment or with different heights. Therefore, one can say that the font size is augmented whenever a user gets his face too close from the screen. Furthermore, the interface is also able to change its height according to the user's height (perceived by a webcam). This prototype, however, was not tested in practice.

Another solution for the blind was proposed by Piccolo et al. (2010). In this case, the application was not only tested with real users but is also being used by the general public since it is available in the Play Store. The authors proposed an interaction model in which blind users can interact with the main features of a smartphone with touchscreen. The navigation is based on few fixed gestures and regions on the screen. Each region represents a function or an application installed in the smartphone (callings, text messages, calendar, among others). Even though the solution was initially designed only for the blind, researchers of this project believe it can be adapted to be used on larger touchscreen and by other users' profiles, which will be further explained in next session of this chapter.

UNIVERSAL DESIGN FOR TOUCHSCREEN

Self-service kiosks will make use of multimodal inclusive apps to provide several services commonly requested in other service channels of the company. In this sense, users will be able to request their bills duplicate, inform bills payment, or update their contacts, for instance, with little or no aid from human facilitators. In order to automate these services, the project has been making extensive use of the results from the workshops planned for each layer represented in the Semiotic Onion previously described. In addition, it has also been supported by two other successful platforms to promote user inclusion, CPqD Alcance and STID (Telecommunications Services for Social Inclusion).

CPqD Alcance (Piccolo, Menezes, & Buccolo, 2009) is a mobile technology for the blind that enables its audience to control various features of their smartphones, such as sending and receiving text messages, making and receiving calls, adjusting system settings, among others. To this end, several gestures were created and validated to make the interaction possible with this public. In addition to gestures, instructions are given by audio to guide users, with the help of a text-to-speech system.

STID (Filgueiras, Martins, Correa, & Osorio, 2008), in turn, makes use of iconic intuitive user interfaces and simplicity to allow access of elderly users and semiliterate to the services of e-government. In this case, the system makes use of personas and pictures to ease concepts understanding, as well as avoids using long pieces of text. In addition, an avatar that interprets Brazilian sign language is also provided to ensure the use of those who are deaf.

Aiming to create an ideal solution, both platforms described have been unified to the requirements raised by the workshops to suit users' diversity, including blind, elderly, deaf, or even those with low levels of literacy. Therefore, the interaction model created for this project unifies the intuitiveness of pictographic interfaces from STID with gesture and voice-based navigation from CPqD Alcance, while also offering other resources to further promote the inclusion of the user community, such as the avatar to interpret Brazilian sign language as support to the hearing impaired.

INCLUSIVE PARTICIPATIVE WORKSHOPS

Altogether, three participative workshops were planned for the project regarding each aspect of the aforementioned onion's layer. This section describes the methodology used for each workshop, as well as main results and impressions obtained.

Participative Workshop 1: Informal Layer

The Participative Design practice chosen for this workshop (Figure 2) was based in the Storytelling activity (Muller, 1997), in which participants share their experiences of success or failure regarding the use of digital technologies.

Figure 2. Participative workshop 1

The practice of Storytelling embraced for this workshop has taken into account the challenge of allowing different people with different disabilities to participate and to communicate with each other in the same activity. Altogether, twelve people were invited and successfully participated: two of them were totally blind, one partially blind, two elderly, one deaf, five literate and one semiliterate.

For this practice participants were invited to reflect on their positive and negative experiences regarding digital technologies, more specifically related to the use of self-service kiosks. Instead of sharing the experiences with the whole group, participants were asked to get together in smaller groups to discuss the experiences and prepare a presentation for only one experience. In this sense, participants ended up creating three distinct groups without having bias in the profiles.

In order to report the experiences of failure or success in the use of self-service kiosks each group was requested to prepare thematic presentations involving 3 distinct aspects: oral, visual and tactile.

The oral presentation involved an oral narrative containing enough detail so that all participants could understand the information, including people with visual impairment. Therefore, it was suggested that this narrative did not make use of any visual artifact (orally described).

The visual presentation could take the form of a poster, containing written information, drawings or other representations at participants' discretion. Similarly, to the oral presentation, this poster should be drawn so that everyone could understand the information, even deaf people, for instance.

Finally, the tactile presentation was more flexible than both previously mentioned since it allowed groups to choose how they would like to represent the experience, provided that they used tactile cues and elements.

In order to ease the creation of presentations some basic office materials and other relevant elements were provided, such as crayons, modeling clays, colored pens and tapes, and box cards.

All presentations should not only to report the story, but also to propose improvements suggestions (for stories of success) or solutions (for failure stories).

In addition to the inclusive scope of this workshop, some participants were also asked to make use of some artifacts to simulate temporary disabilities (i.e., blind or deaf), which comprised eye patches or headphones, for instance. In this sense, during presentations some people were chosen to act as having temporary disabilities. This action aimed to foster the awareness to prepare complete materials so that everyone could understand. It can be said that temporary disabilities are usually experienced by people without disabilities as for the case of trying to see the smartphone screen under high incidence of light, for instance.

After presentations a final discussion was carried out in which participants were able to share their views and comment or give suggestions to other groups.

Results and Discussion

One story presented by participants comprised use reports of the Brazilian voting machine. Group 1 participants (one blind, one partially visual impaired, and two literate people) argued that, despite this equipment theoretically had been designed to meet the population in its diversity, it lacks many aspects that could make it more accessible to voters. By presenting its tactile proposal of voting machine (made with the help of box cards and colored pens), the group criticized the lack of audible feedback to direct users who are blind. In other words, despite currently available keyboards have representations in Braille, it is difficult to confirm the chosen candidate since there is only one piece of visual feedback (composed of the candidate's photo), probably to assist people with low levels of literacy. This problem requires that blind users need to "trust" their choices. A possible improvement suggestion was given by the inclusion of headsets instead of speakers to solve this problem and ensure privacy when voting.

Group 2 (composed of two blind, one elderly, and one literate individual) has chosen to present reports of success or failure involving the use of bank ATMs (automated teller machines). Altogether, two elements were created for tactile presentation (using box cards, modeling clays, and colored pens): the current version of ATMs, containing problems identified by the group, and a possible optimized version, with improvements and suggestions for these problems. For the current version of the ATM, the main criticism involved the misuse of brightness and contrast for the screen, which frequently damages its visibility. The optimized version, in turn, made extensive use of large and embossed numbers, created using high contrast of colors, which does not hinder sight of who interact with it.

Finally, Group 3 (composed of one deaf participant, one elderly, and two literate) has chosen to emphasize problems of parking payment terminals in malls. It was reported that the main problem concerns the keyboard that is positioned far from the screen. This negatively affects information viewing and typing. In addition, in order to notify that users must type their credit/debit card passwords, terminals often display a virtual keyboard representation on their screens, which conveys that it is a touchscreen keyboard when in fact it is not, leading to the error of trying to enter data in the "fake" keyboard.

After presentations a final discussion was carried out. At that time, several people complained that affordable solutions only exist to fulfill legal requirements or are frequently created in a wrong manner, as for the cases involving unnecessary tortuous paths employed by tactile floors often reported by blind participants, for instance.

Partially visual impaired participants, in turn, showed its dissatisfaction when using technological devices in general. Most of these devices are designed for blind or people without visual impairment and barely consider the needs of individuals with only some degree of blindness, which need to interact as if they were totally blind even though they have some sight and want to use it.

One of the elderly reported never to be able to use self-service kiosks and need to ask for help from family due to the complexity employed by these devices.

Finally, participants without disabilities also shared their views on the use of self-service terminals and, in general, frequently criticized the usability of these devices by making interaction difficult even for them who are used to technological devices.

After analyzing data collected in the workshop, some important points mentioned by participants could be consolidated, which served as guidelines for prototyping and deploying solutions, such as intuitive interfaces, simplicity, privacy interaction by audio and screen, suitable brightness, affordable and redundant feedback, multimodal interaction, among others.

Participative Workshop 2: Formal Layer

After the first workshop held, whose main goal was to understand the needs and difficulties of the target audience, each service offered by the facility has started to be prototyped and deployed. When some prototypes were already considerably mature, a new workshop was carried out involving aspects of the second onion's layer. Therefore, Participative Workshop 2 (Figure 3) aimed to evaluate the interaction model proposed through the use of some prototypes by the target audience. In this sense, participants had to interact with the prototype to request passwords and the prototype to request bills duplicate.

The biggest challenge for the project's self-service kiosks is to present an affordable interaction to anyone regardless of the level of literacy or other skills or difficulties. Screen panels of kiosks are touchscreen and this further extends the challenges of creating a universal interaction, since touches on the screen can be extremely complex for users with visual impairments.

Altogether, fifteen participants successfully attended this workshop, again with diversified profiles (two individuals were deaf, three were blind, two were elderly, one was semiliterate, and seven were literate. Each participant individually interacted with the prototypes in a laboratory equipped for such practice. Concerning tasks proposed, first of all, each one of them should have requested its password and then go to the next kiosk for requesting its bill duplicate, without intervention of researchers.

For this practice, users' responses were collected in three distinct levels: visceral (related to the more spontaneous and immediate reactions from users), behavioral (related to the usability during interaction), and reflective (referred to the users' opinion about the system after interaction) (Norman, 2004). For visceral response, video records of users' facial expressions were made during each session of interaction. Recording equipment was located behind false mirrors, making users feel more comfortable during interactions, without even realizing they were being recorded. Behavioral response, in turn, was recorded and analyzed by means of screen-capture software, which registered every touch on the screen made towards achieving planned tasks. Finally, for the reflective level, after interacting with prototypes, participants were requested to answer the pictographic questionnaire Self-Assessment Manikin – SAM (Bradley & Lang, 1994), whose goal is to raise users' opinion regarding the control, motivation and use satisfaction provided by the prototype.

Figure 3. Participative workshop 2

Results and Discussion

Considering results collected for the visceral level, facial expressions usually related doubts or with the feeling that something is not right were noted in some participants, particularly when using the proposed virtual keyboard. To provide an example of an item that caused several doubts one can cite the key "Next field", designed to change focus to the next form field (when there was a need to fill out forms with several fields. This key was often confused with the "Next" button located on the lower right corner of screens, responsible for advancing steps of interaction (based on a step-by-step dialog). This case was not the only problem observed since expressions of doubt have been frequently identified and used to confirm changes in interface requirements. On the other hand, expressions considered to be positive, such as smiles, provided clues to users' satisfaction. Neutral moments could also be noticed. Finally, adverse reactions such as irritation could not be perceived during interactions.

In order to assess responses in the behavioral level records made by screen capture during interactions of each participant with prototypes were analyzed. These records and screenshots taken allowed to measure interaction times for each participant.

On average, as can be seen in Figure 4, elderly participants took 8 minutes and 27 seconds to get their bills. Blind participants took 12 minutes and 23 seconds. The semiliterate individual, in turn, took 12 minutes and 52 seconds. Literate participants took 3 minutes and 11 seconds. Finally, all participants achieved an average time of 7 minutes and 8 seconds. These times complies with at least two physical agencies informed by the company.

For the reflective level, participants ' responses were analyzed by means of SAM questionnaire as previously mentioned. In this sense, positive, negative, and neutral values were assigned for each one of the nine points that compose the questionnaire scale. Therefore, the first three scale points received a positive value, three in the middle, neutral, and the rest of them, negative.

For the analysis of satisfaction data collected with SAM (Table 1), 12 positive and 2 neutral markings were obtained. Motivational dimension, in turn, positively scored 11 times and 3 times for neutrality. Finally, considering the last dimension of SAM, the domain, 9 positive markings were obtained and 4 for neutrality. These results indicate that participants were satisfied and motivated to use the fictional

Figure 4. Average interaction time

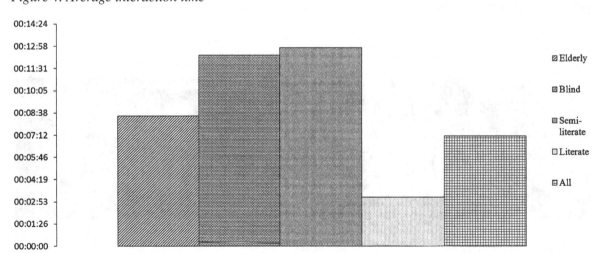

Table 1. SAM results

SAM Dimension								
Satisfaction			Motivation			Domain		
Positive	Neutral	Negative	Positive	Neutral	Negative	Positive	Neutral	Negative
12	2	0	11	3	0	9	4	1

prototype to request bills duplicate, even with some problems as described earlier. Moreover, these results are also in line with results of visceral and behavioral levels.

Finally, it is worth emphasizing that laboratory tests may not reflect the real system use, in other words, this scenario will be evaluated in the Participative Workshop 3 after the deployment of the physical facility, specifically during the assisted use period. Still, these activities were important to evaluate the main features of the interaction model and to show improvement possibilities.

Iconography Workshop

At the same time to prototypes evaluation, an iconography workshop has been carried out. As each participant individually interacted with prototypes, the others could participate in two stimulating activities to help designing icons of the system (Cinto et al., 2015).

For the context of this inclusive facility the design of icons was first based on short stories regarding everyday life of the target audience, in other words, short descriptions that best represented the button action with which the icon was bound. In this sense, one can take as an example the service "compensation for damages", which aims to allow the compensation for damages caused in any electrical household appliance. Thus, a possible representative scenario would be given by: *Scenario representing some burned appliance, containing visual clues of electrical damage with the picture of cash close. This appliance should preferably be a TV given the high percentage of Brazilian homes that have this type of equipment.*

However, proposed scenarios might not be the ideal. Therefore, some studies were carried out to validate them, as stated by Maguire (1999). In this sense, it was possible to verify whether users' expectations could be met with the help of the scenarios proposed. The use of this approach also allowed getting a valuable feedback from the target audience in order to improve the signs of iconography. Altogether, three different studies were carried out with regards to iconography:

- **Study I:** This study happened along with the Participative Workshop 2, whose aim was to measure the intelligibility of icons proposed by comparing them to the set of icons currently being used by the company in other service channels such as Web.
- **Study II:** This activity also happened along with the Participative Workshop 2, whose aim was to carry out a collaborative design activity among participants to build several service icons.
- **Study III:** Extension of Study I containing more participants, however, it was remotely carried out. It did not happen along with the second workshop, however, it was inside its context.

Study I

In what regards Study I, one can say that it comprised two questionnaires composed of icons with its respective labels close and unsorted (one questionnaire for icons proposed and the other for icons currently being used in other service channels). Participants should have analyzed images and linked them to their respective labels. The aim of this experiment was to determine which of the iconographic sets was more intelligible for users.

As the amount of participants in Participative Workshop 2 was not very large, all of them were asked to answer both questionnaires. In pilot studies that led up this workshop it was found that the exposure to one questionnaire prior to the other might influence the next questionnaire to be answered. In this sense, in order to prevent bias in results one can say that an alternate strategy for questionnaires presentation was adopted, that is, half of respondents started the survey with icons proposed and only answered the other proposal after finishing the first questionnaire and vice-versa. Moreover, no proposal was labeled "new" or "current" in order to make participants did not even notice which proposal was being considered.

For Study I and Study III an amount of fifteen icons was evaluated. In this sense, each icon represented a distinct electrical energy service such as "request bill duplicates," "start electrical service," "restart electrical service," and so on.

In Study I, participants were organized by means of a semicircle, as shown by Figure 5. Each participant received a clipboard to place under questionnaire sheets and some pens. In addition, they were asked to try to individually answer questionnaires and not to worry for those icons they could not perceive the meaning.

Study II

Study II consisted of a practice of collaborative design in which participants could exercise their creativity in a relaxed dynamic that produced insights for helping to improve icons designed. In this activity, participants were arranged in three tables preserving some level of profile diversity: Group 1 (two elderlies, one visually impaired, one deaf, and one young participant), Group 2 (One blind participant, one elderly, and three young participants), Group 3 (One blind participant, one deaf, and three young individuals).

Support materials (pictures) representing the electric energy context (trees, lamps, electrical poles, personas, attendants, and so on) were made available to help participants engage and interact with iconic representations, as shown in Figure 5. In addition, they were offered blunt scissors, crayons, pencils

Figure 5. Iconography workshop

and pens, glue, paper and Scotch tape. They were also asked to provide a drawing or a text with their interpretation/understanding of each concept.

Each group was requested to discuss and draw scenes that best represented the proposed themes. Therefore, three rounds of discussion were carried out involving the services: "start electrical service", "restart electrical service", and "provisional connection for events". The choice of the first two services was motivated by the feedback from the previous icon evaluation activity, where some of the icons proposed by the designers proved to be difficult to grasp.

The three discussion rounds took around an hour, each one taking about twenty minutes to be accomplished. This maximum duration was respected to avoid the workshop to become tedious for the participants.

The design of visual representations for the proposed themes was considered to be successful, as it could be seen in drawings of Group 1. It depicted an everyday life story in richness of details and colors, told by participants (anecdote) who made extensive use of available support materials

Group 2 relied on a minimalist design to graphically represent the "start electric service" concept as only two representations were drawn: a plus sign (+) and an image of a power meter (they were inspired by one of the pictures made available). It is worth mentioning that the group used different colors to distinguish elements.

Still regarding the "start electrical service" concept, Group 3 used a similar approach as that of Group 2: they drew a lamp and a plus sign (+) to represent the icon. This choice might be related to groups containing more digitally literate young individuals.

It was possible to observe an unusual pattern of icon designing. Though the groups were formed to gather different profiles, specific profiles seem to have influenced results. Group 3, for example, was formed mainly of three young digitally literate participants, and tended to draw icons by replicating those used in computer interfaces, with small dimensions and few details, and adding elements such as the plus sign (+), arrows (→), and so on. The same pattern was observed in icons created by Group 2, in which young participants were the majority. On the other hand, participants of Group 1 relied on stories to represent the services, possibly due to their age and less familiarity with computer interfaces which explains a strong tendency to produce richly detailed, colorful icons.

This pattern was observed throughout the following activities and it is worth mentioning that regardless of the prevailing profile, all members of the three groups showed a strong commitment to the objective and continued participation in discussions, in a very collaborative way. Participants with disabilities were also able to contribute with ideas and suggestions, assisted by other members of the group. As none of the visually impaired participants was blind from birth, their previous visual experience may have influenced their contributions.

Some noteworthy facts about the workshop involving physically impaired participants were the statement made by one of the blind participants, who expressed his profound gratitude for being invited to join the workshop and for the opportunity to help people to see the world from a blind person's perspective. Another remarkable fact was that one of the deaf participants drew a picture of a mobile phone to represent the icon for "start electric service". Such misunderstanding occurred because the Brazilian Portuguese for "start (electrical) service" ("ligação nova") may be interpreted as "new call" (telephone call) and lead those who are not familiar with the general context of the solution to several mistakes. The same deaf participant also mentioned spontaneously that the (electrical) service "change contact number" concept (presented in the intelligibility study) might be confusing as well. The literature recommends the use of familiar terminology in system designing (Ávila & Costa, 2009; Piccolo et al., 2010).

An alternative approach would be to rename some of the services, bringing them closer in meaning to what customers expect to find.

As mentioned, the intelligibility study preceding the participative workshop aimed at validating some icons designed under the premise of being based on representations of the everyday life of users. An effort was made to represent things participants were used to in order to leverage icons understanding, according to the literature and confirmed by the results of the participative activities, which used icons designed under this principle. Users with little experience with ICTs may rely on previously experienced situations related to the service request through a non-high-tech (traditional) customer service facility. This is especially true in the case of elderly or non-literate users, or even for people not familiar with the language or the context used by the solution.

According to Ávila and Costa (2009) and Piccolo et al. (2010) and results from the participative study, iconographic representations for the elderly, non-literate, and low-literate users must consider everyday situations people can relate to. Younger users with higher level of digital literacy, however, seemed to be more comfortable with minimalistic icons, as those used in ordinary computer interfaces.

Study III

Finally, given the need to expand Study I of intelligibility in order to achieve greater reliability for data analysis, a more comfortable approach for participants was embraced, in other words, questionnaires could remotely be answered, what ended up being featured as the Study III.

For the creation of the online survey forms used in this practice Google Docs was chosen. Altogether, as in Study I, there were two different questionnaires, one for each proposal to be evaluated. As opposed to what happened in Study I when participants had to answer both questionnaires, now individuals had to answer only one instrument. This strategy aimed to reduce the influence that a collection might have on another.

When it comes to sample definition, it was used an internal e-mail list of the CPqD to identify candidates. To this end, 200 employees were randomly selected to receive questionnaires. Individuals were then randomly divided into two groups of 100 people each. Each group received the questionnaire of only one set of icons.

Invitation to participate in the study was sent in September 2014. Forms were made available during one week. At the end of this period 88 answers were sent, 44 for each questionnaire (some answers were randomly discarded in order to get equal amount between sets). The average response time designed for both questionnaires was 10 minutes in order not to discourage invited participants.

After analyzing the results from the three iconic studies, the final versions of icons could be drawn (Figure 6). It can be stated that most of the iconic elements proposed (over 70%) obtained rather good results with respect to intelligibility compared to the icons that were already being used by the company. For those that had some issues with respect to how easy they were to understand, the design activity carried out in Study II provided inputs for corrections and improvements.

Participative Workshop 3: Technical Layer

The onion's technical layer represents the system itself. Once applications are still under development, as soon as deployment finishes, the third workshop planned will be made possible. This workshop is

Figure 6. Iconography results

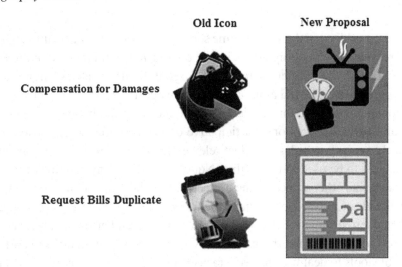

going to validate the proposed interaction model in real situations of use, as well as is going to finish the cycle of workshops to assist the designing and deployment of the solutions.

For doing so, an activity called assisted operation will be carried out. In this sense, consumers of any profile as described earlier will be able to use touchscreen terminals and other gadgets available and answer use satisfaction surveys. These surveys will be answered through the inclusive apps, since they are being developed to collect data after each interaction that finishes.

FUTURE RESEARCH DIRECTIONS

Many directions for further research can arise from this research.

First, although these studies tried to address most of the profile's concerns regarding accessibility, a small number of people participated in the studies, especially in what regards Participative Workshop 1. In this sense, since the more individuals participate in a research study the stronger tend to be the results, it would be rather interesting to have more representatives of the profiles interacting with assistive apps and providing feedback.

Second, although these studies researched the abilities of a small amount of people, results would certainly be improved by also researching the social impacts of assistive technologies of this type with a broader audience.

Finally, inclusive apps were built based solely on the workshops carried out. Carrying out studies of such type can sometimes be expensive depending on the amount of individuals considered. An approach that certainly would reduce costs is the use of guidelines. Although guidelines are largely spread in literature to date, most of times they only consider usability or accessibility for ordinary ways of interaction. Touchscreen devices are still in strong need for collections of this type of rules.

CONCLUSION

Fifteen percent of the world's population has some sort of disability (World Health Organization, 2011). Even with the increasing growth of digital society, the inclusion of this public in digital environments still faces many obstacles, which often increases the digital divide. The challenging inclusive walk-in customer facility proposed by CEMIG aims at allowing any customer to request electrical services with little or no help from human facilitators. As icons can be the key point behind the understanding of service concepts or unusual system options, participative design activities were carried out involving the target audience of the project, in order to collect relevant feedbacks for the development of multimodal applications for devices to be used in the facility. Not only iconography activities were carried out, but also workshops to evaluate other aspects of the project. Altogether, three main workshops were planned; two of them were already performed, obtaining rather good results considering users' feedback regarding applications built and tested. Improvements have been proposed and also validated, and all errors could be identified and solved. In this sense, the artifacts of Organizational Semiotics and Participative Design proved to be valuable tools to deal with projects focused on digital inclusion. It's worth mentioning that without them the project may not have opportunity to obtain feedback from users the way it had, since this can be considered the key concept behind the success of this type of projects. Both applications and physical facility are already under development with a completion forecast dated for 2016. It is expected to create an accessible environment in which consumers of any profile can request services without assistance, a great potential that is corroborated by the promising results obtained with the studies and workshops presented in this chapter.

ACKNOWLEDGMENT

This work was funded by ANEEL's (Brazilian Agency of Electric Energy) R&D program. The authors gratefully acknowledge CEMIG and the colleagues that made the workshop and studies feasible.

REFERENCES

ACM. (1992). *ACM code of ethic and professional conduct*. Retrieved from http://www.acm.org/about/code-of-ethics

Ávila, I. M. A., & Costa, R. G. (2009). Ícones como facilitadores da interação de usuários iletrados com interfaces computacionais. *Cadernos CPqD Tecnologia, 5*(2), 15–36.

Baptista, E. A., & Rigotti, J. I. R. (2013). *A população deficiente no estado de Minas Gerais: uma análise exploratória a partir dos censos demográficos de 2000 a 2010. CEDPLAR/UFMG – TD 487(2013)*. Belo Horizonte, MG: FACE/UFMG.

Baranauskas, M. C. C. (2009) Socially aware computing.*Proceedings of the VI International Conference on Engineering and Computer Education* (pp. 1-5).

Cinto, T., Ávila, I. M. A., & de Souza, F. (2015). Inclusive Participatory Workshop: Accessible Iconography Design. *International Journal of Digital Information and Wireless Communication*, *5*(3), 158–164. doi:10.17781/P001676

Cober, R., Au, O., & Son, J. J. (2012). Using a participatory approach to design a technology-enhanced museum tour for visitors who are blind.*Proceedings of the 2012 iConference*, New York (pp. 592-594). doi:10.1145/2132176.2132301

Filgueiras, L., Martins, S., Correa, D., & Osorio, A. (2008). Personas para caracterização da experiência de uso de tecnologia pela população digitalmente excluída. *Usabilidade, Acessibilidade e Inteligibilidade Aplicadas em Interfaces para Analfabetos, Idosos e Pessoas com Deficiência*, 15-23.

Hagen, S., & Sandnes, F. E. (2010). Toward accessible self-service kiosks through intelligent user interfaces. *Personal and Ubiquitous Computing*, *14*(8), 715–721. doi:10.1007/s00779-010-0286-8

Hall, E. T. (1973). *The silent language*. Anchor Books.

IBGE. (2010). *Censo demográfico 2010: Características gerais da população, religião e pessoas com deficiência*. Retrieved from ftp://ftp.ibge.gov.br/Censos/Censo_Demografico_2010/Caracteristicas_Gerais_Religiao_Deficiencia/caracteristicas_religiao_deficiencia.pdf

Maguire, M. C. (1999). A review of user-interface design guidelines for public information kiosk systems. *International Journal of Human-Computer Interaction Studies*, *50*(3), 263–286.

Muller, M. J., Haslwanter, J. H., & Dayton, T. (1997). Participatory practices in the software lifecycle. In M. Helander, T. K. Landauer, & P. Prabhu (Eds.), *Handbook of Human-Computer Interaction* (2nd ed.). New York: Elsevier Science Inc. doi:10.1016/B978-044481862-1.50077-7

Nielsen, J. (1993). *Usability engineering*. Boston: Academic Press.

Nielsen, J. (2014) Memory recognition and recall in user interface. *Nielsen Norman Group Usability Report*. Retrieved from http://www.nngroup.com/articles/recognition-andrecall/

Norman, D. (1988). *The design of everyday things*. New York: Basic Books.

Peirce, C. S. (1990). *Semiótica – Coleção estudos* (2nd ed.). Perspectiva Publisher.

Piccolo, L. S. G., Menezes, E. M., & Buccolo, B. C. (2011). Developing an accessible interaction model for touch screen mobile devices: preliminary results.*Proceedings of the 10th Brazilian Symposium on Human Factors in Computer Systems* (pp. 257-260).

Piccolo, L.S.G., Schimidt, C.P., Osório, A.F.S., Duarte, R.E., Ávila, I.M.A., Tambascia, C.A., Carvalho, R.F., Aureliano, M.G., & Rolim, L.A.G. (2010). Modelo de interação inclusivo para interface de governo eletrônico. CPqD Foundation.

Potter, L. E., Korte, J., & Nielsen, S. (2011). Seek and sign: An early experience of the joys and challenges of software design with young deaf children.*Proceedings of the 23rd Australian Computer-Human Interaction Conference* (pp. 257-260), New York. doi:10.1145/2071536.2071577

Sandnes, F. E., Tan, T. B., Johansen, A., Sulic, E., Vesterhus, E., & Iversen, E. R. (2012). Making touch-based kiosks accessible to blind users through simple gestures. *Universal Access in the Information Society*, *11*(4), 421–431. doi:10.1007/s10209-011-0258-4

Shneiderman, B. (2000). Universal usability: Pushing human-computer interaction research to empower every citizen. *Communications of the ACM*, *43*(5), 84–91. doi:10.1145/332833.332843

Spinuzzi, C. (2004). The methodology of participatory design. *Technical Communication (Washington)*, *52*(2), 163–174.

Stamper, R. (1993). A semiotic theory of information and information systems/applied semiotics. In *International seminars on the teaching of computing science* (pp. 1-36). Newcastle: Newcastle University.

The Center for Universal Design. (1997). *Universal Design*. Retrieved from http://www.ncsu.edu/ncsu/design/cud/pubs_p/docs/poster.pdf

W3C. (2005). Introduction to web accessibility. Retrieved from http://www.w3.org/WAI/intro/accessibility.php

WHO. (2011). *World report on disability*. Retrieved from http://www.who.int/disabilities/world_report/2011/report.pdf

KEY TERMS AND DEFINITIONS

ACM: Association for Computer Machinery.
ANEEL: Brazilian Agency of Electric Energy.
ATM: Automated Teller Machine.
CEMIG: Minas Gerais Electric Utility Company.
CPQD: Telecommunications Research and Development Center.
IBGE: Brazilian Institute of Geography and Statistics.
ICT: Information and Communication Technologies.
OS: Organizational Semiotics.
SAM: Self-Assessment Manikin (questionnaire).
STID: Telecommunications Services for Social Inclusion.
UI: User Interface.
WHO: World Health Organization.

Chapter 22
Identity Assurance through EEG Recordings

Massimiliano Zanin
Innaxis Foundation & Research Institute, Spain

David Papo
Universidad Politecnica de Madrid, Spain

ABSTRACT

The problem of identity assurance, i.e. determining if a claimed identity can be trusted, has been gaining relevance in the last decade, due to the increasing use of on-line services. While this trend can be seen for many biometric sensors, very few studies have considered the use of brain electric signals. This contribution proposes a first solution, based on the reconstruction of motifs (patterns of connectivity between three electroencephalographic sensors) and on the assessment of their stability across different trials for a single subject. Results indicate that, although computationally costly, this approach is promising in terms of the classification scores obtained.

INTRODUCTION

Identity assurance, *i.e.* the problem of determining if a claim of a particular identity can be trusted to actually be the claimant's identity, has grown in importance in last years, especially with the increasing use of on-line services. Traditionally, this task has been performed through "something you know", as for instance a secret password (Burr, Dodson & Polk, 2004). Due to the easiness in stealing such kind of information, it has been expanded to "something you have", that is, relying on something the user has, *e.g.* a mobile phone, for a "two-factor" authentication. The final frontiers are called "something you are", and is based on something intrinsic to the principal being authenticated. While this last option is the most secure of the three, as for instance it is relatively difficult to steal a fingerprint, it is still not widespread due to several problems: its complexity, the cost of associated measurement sensors, and the fact that not all people can interact with biometric devices (as some people do not have fingers or eyes).

Here we explore the use of brain dynamics to authenticate a person's identity. This approach is based on the idea that, even if a given cognitive task is executed similarly by different subjects, each subject

DOI: 10.4018/978-1-5225-0435-1.ch022

displays some variability, which can be used as a univocal identifier. Because altering our brain activity on a very short time and spatial scale is an arduous task, it is impossible to impersonate another subject. This chapter first introduces the basics of functional brain networks, *i.e.* how the brain activity during the execution of a cognitive task can be mapped into a graph-like structure. The mathematical method for authentication is then discussed, and tested with a set of real brain recordings. Finally, some future lines of works are discussed, and conclusions are drawn.

BACKGROUND

The idea that the brain activity can be described through the electric (and magnetic) field it generates during a task is not new, and was proposed back in 1875 (Swartz, 1988). Electrophysiological techniques such as the ElectroEncephaloGraph (EEG) measure the voltage fluctuations generated by the ionic current within the neurons. More recently, it was recognized that coordination, e.g. synchronization, between electrical activity at different brain regions represent a basic modus operandi of brain information transfer and processing. However, only over the last fifteen years have such structures of interactions been described as networks, thanks to the raising field of complex networks analysis (Albert & Barabasi, 2002; Boccaletti, Latora, Moreno, Chavez & Hwang, 2006).

Network theory is a statistical mechanics understanding of an old branch of pure mathematics: graph theory. In order to represent a system by means of a network, all unnecessary details are deleted, to extract only its constituent parts and their interactions; these are then respectively represented by nodes and links. The structure created by such interactions is then called the network *topology*. Most social, biological, and technological networks (including, of course, the brain) display substantial non-trivial topological properties, *i.e.* patterns of connection between their elements are neither purely regular nor purely random (Costa *et al.*, 2011). These properties can be thought of as features describing the network's structure. The topological properties of a network can directly or indirectly be retrieved from the so-called *adjacency matrix*, which represents which nodes are connected to which other nodes in a network (Costa, Rodrigues, Travieso & Villas Boas, 2007).

The brain can be represented by at least two conceptually different types of networks. The first is obtained by mapping the physical connections between neurons or groups of them, thus representing their wiring diagram: this anatomical pattern of connectivity is called the *connectome* (Sporns, Tononi & Kötter, 2005). A second type of description, which will be used in this Chapter, disregards physical connections, and tries to determine if two regions are "functionally connected", i.e. they are interacting in a given task to perform a function. These *functional networks* are obtained by (*i*) recording the brain activity, for instance by means of an EEG, at different locations; (*ii*) calculatating some form of synchronization between the dynamics of pairs of regions (*e.g.* linear correlation, or more complex causality measures); (*iii*) creating a link between the corresponding nodes when the detected synchronization is statistically significant. A complete discussion of the use of functional networks, and of their pros and cons, can be found in (Bullmore & Sporns, 2009; Papo, Zanin, Pineda-Pardo, Boccaletti & Buldú, 2014).

Following the progressive decrease in their cost and complexity, EEG devices have increasingly been used in HMI applications (McFarland, Krusienski, Sarnacki & Wolpaw, 2008; Iturrate, Antelis, Kübler & Minguez, 2009). There is nevertheless one application for which they have largely been neglected: identity assurance, *i.e.* verifying the identity of the user of an information system. Even if very few examples of

EEG analysis for identity assurance can be found (Gelb & Clark, 2013; Sabarigiri & Suganyadevi, 2014), they are still at a theoretical level, *i.e.* no actual real-world applications have been presented.

REPRESENTING BRAIN ACTIVITY THROUGH MOTIF DYNAMICS

Motifs have been identified as a powerful tool to understand the structure of complex networks at the micro- and meso-scales, *i.e.* focusing on structures created by few (between three and five) nodes. Motifs are defined as patterns of connectivity involving a small number of nodes, usually three, occurring with a significantly higher frequency than expected in randomized networks (Milo *et al.*, 2002; Alon, 2007).

When analyzing the dynamical response of the human brain to given stimuli, for instance during the execution of a cognitive or motor task, it is clear that some general pattern should emerge; for instance, a perceptual task involving the identification of objects will start with a signal from the occipital region, where an abstract representation of the object is created, which will then propagate to the frontal cortex, performing some higher computation. On the other hand, subject-specific connectivity patterns, past experience and knowledge concur in modulating large-scale activity at shorter time scales. It may thus be expected that the small-scale brain dynamics associated with a specific task may be subject-specific, and that may be used as an instrument to ascertain the identity of an individual.

It has recently been proposed that the dynamics of motifs appearing in EEG recordings can be characterized using Information Theory tools, and specifically through symbolic analysis (Zanin & Papo, 2014). The different steps of the process, as depicted in Figure 1, are described as follows:

1. *Division of EEG time series into non-overlapping windows.* The raw time series, as yielded by an EEG machine, are divided into small non-overlapping windows of length τ. As these small time series are analyzed independently, τ represents the time scale at which some target dynamics is expected to emerge – or, in other words, the expected significant cognitive time scale.

2. *Synchronization estimation.* The degree of synchronization, or "shared dynamics", is calculated between all pairs of nodes, *i.e.* of EEG sensors. The presence of synchronization between two brain regions has been associated with information sharing and processing phenomena between them, and alterations of this common dynamics has been related to pathological conditions, including epilepsy and Alzheimer's disease (Bullmore & Sporns, 2009). Depending on the expected characteristic of the synchronization, several metrics can be used: from simple Pearson's linear correlation, up to causality metrics like Granger Causality and Transfer Entropy (Granger, 1988; Schreiber, 2000).

3. *Motif extraction.* As previously introduced, motifs are specific connectivity patterns appearing between a small number of nodes. For the sake of simplicity, here only three-nodes motifs are considered, as depicted in Figure 1. To build motifs, all possible triplets of nodes are considered. A link is established between pairs of nodes when the detected synchronization between the corresponding time series is greater than a threshold ρ. Notice that, as links can either be or not be expressed, a triplet of nodes can be associated with $2^3 = 8$ different motifs (ranging from a totally disconnected graph, up to a completely connected one). As depicted in Figure 1, the resulting motif should be calculated for every possible triplet of nodes (*i.e.* sensors), and for each time window.

4. *Creation of symbolic time series.* Motifs are graphs composed of three nodes, and thus fully described by an adjacency matrix A of size 3 x 3. As the evolution of A cannot be easily analyzed, a new time series is created for each triplet of nodes, in which a symbol is associated with the appearance of specific motifs – for instance, the symbol "0" is introduced whenever a fully disconnected motif is encountered, "8" when the three nodes form a triangle, and so forth.

5. *Symbolic entropy estimation.* Once a symbolic time series is extracted for each triplet of nodes, its variability can be estimated through different Information Theory metrics. A good candidate is the Shannon entropy of the symbols succession, given by:

$$E = -\sum_i p_i \log_2 p_i$$

p_i being the probability of appearance of the *i*-th symbol.

The entropy E thus represents the variability in the motifs within each triplet of sensors. Therefore, $E = 0$ implies that only one motif can appear, as in the case of extremely high (low) values of ρ, which

Figure 1. Representation of the process for analyzing EEG time series by symbolic entropy estimation. (Top) Original time series, which are divided into non-overlapping windows of size τ. (Center) Motif extraction, by calculating the synchronization between pairs of time series within each window. (Bottom) Association of a symbol (number) to each motif.
Adapted from (Zanin & Papo, 2014).

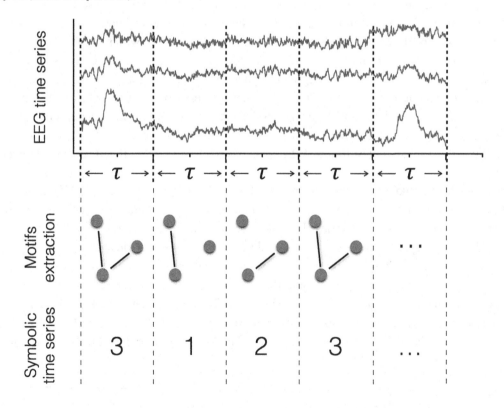

always result in a completely disconnected (completely connected) motif. On the other hand, high entropy should be expected between those extrema, indicating a rich repertoire of neural dynamics. By fixing τ, it is possible to find the value of ρ that maximizes the entropy of the motifs appearing within each triplet of nodes.

The complete analysis process thus starts from a set of n time series, representing the brain activity of a single subject; and yields a vector $P = \left[\rho_{1,1,1}, \rho_{1,1,2}, \ldots, \rho_{n,n,n} \right]$ representing the set of thresholds optimizing the representation of the dynamics of the same individual. Notice that in a 60 channel EEG montage, P will be composed of $60^3 = 216.000$ elements.

TOWARDS AN IDENTITY ASSURANCE PROTOCOL

The process described in the previous section provides an easy way for comparing different EEG recordings, and establishing whether they belong to the same individual. Specifically, two vectors **P** are expected to have similar values if they correspond to recordings of the same individual, provided a similar task was executed in both cases. This Section presents the numerical results obtained from a large data set of EEG recordings, and discusses ways of improving the efficiency and precision of the process.

Data Set Description and Preparation

Validation of the proposed identity assurance method has been carried out with the EEG data set (Zhang, Begleiter, Porjesz, Wang & Litke, 1995) available through the UCI machine learning repository (Bay, Kibler, Pazzani & Smyth, 2000). It consists of 60-second measurements from 60 electrodes placed on the subject's scalp, and sampled at 256 Hz. In each trial, subjects were exposed to an image, representing objects chosen from the Snodgrass and Vanderwart (1980) picture set. A total of 39 subjects and 32 trials per subject were selected from control subjects.

From each trial, a vector of thresholds P was extracted, following the previously described entropy maximization strategy. τ was fixed to 8. This value is low enough to ensure that all fast dynamics are described, while maintaining an acceptable computational cost. The synchronization between the different brain regions was calculated through the absolute value of the Pearson's correlation coefficient.

Method Evaluation

A first evaluation of the method efficiency in discriminating between different subjects is performed on a pair-wise basis. The objective is to confirm that the heterogeneity of P vectors for a given subject is lower than the one observed between vectors corresponding to different people.

Denoting by P_i^j the i-th trial of the j-th subject, the coherence between two vectors can be assessed through a Pearson's linear correlation between the corresponding elements:

$$c_{(i,j),(k,h)} = \left| \rho \left(P_i^j, P_k^h \right) \right|$$

Notice that here ρ represents the correlation coefficient. Two subjects can then be correctly discriminated if their internal coherence (between two trials of the same subject) is higher than the external one (between trials of different individuals):

$$\sum_{j_1,j_2} c_{(i,j_1),(i,j_2)} > \sum_{j_1,j_2} c_{(i,j_1),(k,j_2)}.$$

Figure 2. a represents the difference between internal (dark blue) and external (light blue) coherence between the first four subjects. Additionally, Figure 2. b represents the difference between internal and external coherence for all pairs of subjects; and Figure 2. c the absolute value of the logarithm of the p-value of a Kolmogorov–Smirnov statistical test evaluating the hypothesis that the two distributions (internal and external c) are different. It can be appreciated that, in most cases, the internal and external c distributions are strongly different, suggesting that an identity assurance algorithman be constructed from the **P** vectors.

A full pairwise classification has been carried out on the c values, using a Support Vector Machine model (Noble, 2006) with a Leave One Out cross-validation procedure (Friedman, Hastie & Tibshirani, 2001). For all pairs of subjects i and k, all except one c values have been used to train the model, which was then used to classify the last c (i.e. to assess whether the c corresponded to an internal or external coherence, and therefore if the associated subject was i or j). Figure 3 reports the average classification score for each subject. The global average, 90.99%, indicates that the proposed approach classifies subjects quite accurately.

While relevant from a theoretical point of view, the previously described classification task does not correspond to a real application. The usual problem in an identity assurance context entails assigning an identity to a new EEG recording entering the system; in other words, the classification should not be done between two subjects, but for all subjects present in the system. A complete classification has then been performed, again using a SVM and a LOO cross-validation procedure, in which each trial was classified against all 39 subjects comprising the data set. The classification score, average for each subject, is presented in Figure 4. The average classification score is, in this case, quite lower (63.32%);

Figure 2. Pair-wise classification. (Center) Difference between internal and external coherence for all pairs of subjects (a zoom for the first four of them is presented on the Left panel). (Right) p-value of the K-S test.

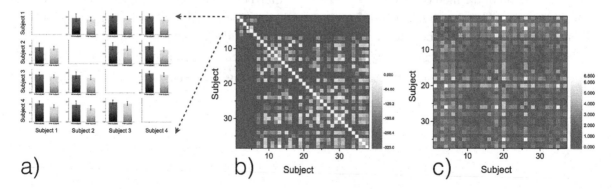

Figure 3. Average pair-wise classification score

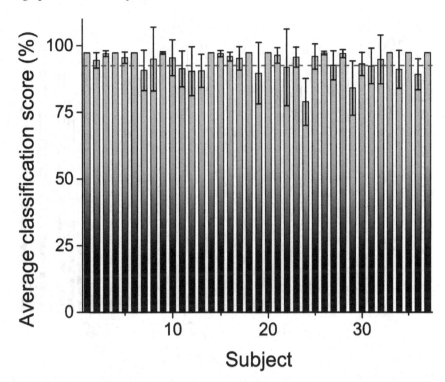

nevertheless, it is still higher than the value expected in a random classification, *i.e.* 2.56%, indicating that this method is capable of extracting meaningful information about the identity of a person.

Figure 4 also highlights an interesting fact, *i.e.* the intrinsic heterogeneity between subjects. Some of them present a unique dynamic, leading to a perfect classification and identification (see, for instance, subjects 1, 4 and 7); on the other hand, some of them cannot be identified by the algorithm (subjects 24).

Reducing the Computational Cost

Although the previously described results confirm that EEG data can be used to perform an identity assurance task in theory, there are several issues that need to be solved before the proposed method can be implemented in a real operational environment. The first is represented by the high computational cost: each time a new trial is introduced in the system, the entropy of every triplet of sensors has to be maximized, which implies a computational cost of the order of $O(n^3)$ – n being the number of nodes or sensors. Using a standard processor, this is equivalent to 30 minutes of computation per subject. Even in a cloud environment with 100 computers working in parallel, the process still requires tens of seconds for a single identification – a delay that may be unacceptable in many applications.

It is thus essential to reduce the computational cost of each analysis. As the cost is a function of the number of triplets of sensors to be analyzed, this can be achieved by reducing its number, *i.e.* by discarding those triplets that codify no useful information – a process known as feature selection (Friedman, Hastie & Tibshirani, 2001) in the data mining field.

Figure 4. Average classification score in a one vs. all scenario

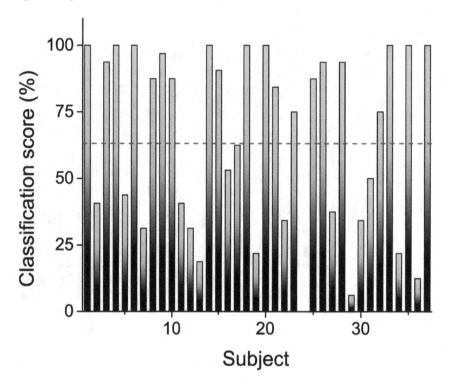

As a first approximation, a random selection process is here considered: a given number of sensor triplets are chosen at random, the resulting classification score calculated, and then averaged over multiple realizations. Figure 5 Left presents the results, in terms of mean and standard deviation of the score, as a function of the number of triplets considered. With around 2000 triplets, the classification score is still quite high (above 90%, with less than 0.1% standard deviation), while the computational cost is drastically reduced (around 2 minutes in a standard processor).

Figure 5. Classification scores in alternative scenarios. (Left) Score as a function of the number of triplets of sensors included in the analysis. (Center) Score as a function of the number of trials available for each subject. (Right) Score when multiple trials are considered at the same time.

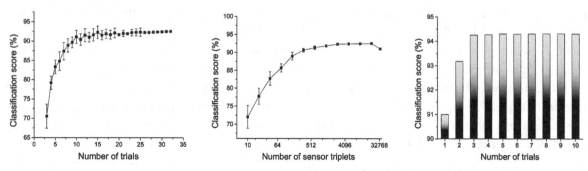

Sensitivity to the Data Set Size

The second problem one ought to analyze is the sensitivity of the proposed method to the initial data set size. The previously described results were based on the use of the complete data set, consisting of 32 trials per subject (expect for the subject being classified, for whom one trial is used in the evaluation). Nevertheless, real-world implementations may be associated with more complicated situations, with a different number of trials per subject. Furthermore, even if a minimum number of trials per subject is required at the system setup, this number may be constrained by the associated initial costs.

Figure 5 Center shows the average classification score (and standard deviation, top and bottom whiskers) as a function of the number of trials initially available – trials were selected at random, the same number for all subjects. A lower bound can be set to 10, below which the method has not enough information to perform a good classification.

Use of Multiple Recordings

A final point that should be discussed is the possibility of improving the classification score by using multiple trials in each analysis. It is in principle possible that some trials are not correctly classified because of some errors or artifacts in the associated signal – for instance, a wrong sensors setup, which may distort the EEG signal. In those situations, the classification score should increase if multiple trials of the same subject are used at the same time, thus diluting the negative effects of a problematic trial.

Suppose the subject i is compared against subject k, by using at the same time a number n of trials; following the previous definition, the two subjects can be discriminated if the average internal coherence is higher than the external one:

$$\frac{1}{n} \sum_{j_1 \in J, j_2 \neq j_1} c_{(i,j_1),(i,j_2)} > \frac{1}{n} \sum_{j_1 \in J, j_2 \neq j_1} c_{(i,j_1),(k,j_2)}$$

In the previous equation, J represents the set of n trials used to define the identity of the i-th subject.

Figure 5 Right depicts the evolution of the average classification score, as a function of the number of averaged trials n – the trials used in each identity evaluation have been chosen at random. It is interesting to notice that using multiple trials increases the score up to a 94%; at the same time, including more than four trials has no effect, indicating that the classification error is not just the result of problems in the EEG signals.

CONCLUSION

This contribution discusses the use of human brain dynamics during a cognitive task in the identity assurance problem, *i.e.* ensuring the identity of a user and avoiding unauthorized accesses to a system. More specifically, brain dynamics is analyzed by means of an information theoretical analysis of the evolution of functional motifs, micro-scale structures created by the correlated dynamics observed within triplets of nodes. When the correlation thresholds are varied in order to maximize the entropy of the dynamics, or in other words its variability, such thresholds strongly correlate for different trials of the same subjects. This correlation can then be used in an identity assurance task, in which the identity of a subject is compared against a set of authorized users.

The main advantage of this approach is the security level it guarantees. Following NIST definition (Burr, Dodson & Polk, 2004), using EEG recordings for ensuring identity would be one of the strongest authentication factors, falling in the "something you are" category. As some aspects of brain dynamics are not under strict voluntary control, particularly at very small spatial and temporal scales, attacks would be very complex: a false EEG signal should be fed into the recording device, synthetized and synchronized in real-time with the inputs associated to the cognitive task.

On the negative side, some aspects of the proposed approach still limit its applicability in a real-world operational environment. First of all, recording brain dynamics requires a technical equipment that, while not expensive, is far from being common. Second, the computational cost required to extract motifs dynamics is significant, implying a long waiting time until the authorization is granted, or the deployment of large-scale computational infrastructures (*e.g.* a cloud-based environment). Both problems are expected to be increasingly less relevant in the future. Furthermore, even under the present conditions, it is possible to find situations in which such limitations are acceptable: for instance, the physical protection of high-value infrastructures, like bank vaults or military installations.

Finally, the relatively low classification score obtained in a global classification task (see Figure 4) implies that the proposed method cannot be used as a primary (*i.e.* stand-alone) identity assurance mechanism. Nevertheless, the method seems promising, and it may be used in conjunction with standard ones (*e.g.* iris or fingerprint recognition) to provide an additional level of security.

REFERENCES

Albert, R., & Barabási, A. L. (2002). Statistical mechanics of complex networks. *Reviews of Modern Physics*, *74*(1), 47–97. doi:10.1103/RevModPhys.74.47

Alon, U. (2007). Network motifs: Theory and experimental approaches. *Nature Reviews. Genetics*, *8*(6), 450–461. doi:10.1038/nrg2102 PMID:17510665

Bay, S. D., Kibler, D., Pazzani, M. J., & Smyth, P. (2000). The UCI KDD archive of large data sets for data mining research and experimentation. *ACM SIGKDD Explorations Newsletter*, *2*(2), 81–85. doi:10.1145/380995.381030

Boccaletti, S., Latora, V., Moreno, Y., Chavez, M., & Hwang, D. U. (2006). Complex networks: Structure and dynamics. *Physics Reports*, *424*(4), 175–308. doi:10.1016/j.physrep.2005.10.009

Bullmore, E., & Sporns, O. (2009). Complex brain networks: Graph theoretical analysis of structural and functional systems. *Nature Reviews. Neuroscience*, *10*(3), 186–198. doi:10.1038/nrn2575 PMID:19190637

Burr, W. E., Dodson, D. F., & Polk, W. T. (2004). *Electronic authentication guideline* (pp. 800–863). US Department of Commerce, Technology Administration, National Institute of Standards and Technology.

Costa, L. D. F., Oliveira Jr, O. N., Travieso, G., Rodrigues, F. A., Villas Boas, P. R., & Antiqueira, L. et al.. (2011). Analyzing and modeling real-world phenomena with complex networks: A survey of applications. *Advances in Physics*, *60*(3), 329–412. doi:10.1080/00018732.2011.572452

Costa, L. D. F., Rodrigues, F. A., Travieso, G., & Villas Boas, P. R. (2007). Characterization of complex networks: A survey of measurements. *Advances in Physics*, *56*(1), 167–242. doi:10.1080/00018730601170527

Friedman, J., Hastie, T., & Tibshirani, R. (2001). The elements of statistical learning. Springer, Berlin: Springer series in statistics.

Gelb, A., & Clark, J. (2013). Identification for development: the biometrics revolution. *Center for Global Development Working Paper 315.*

Granger, C. W. (1988). Some recent development in a concept of causality. *Journal of Econometrics, 39*(1), 199–211. doi:10.1016/0304-4076(88)90045-0

Iturrate, I., Antelis, J. M., Kübler, A., & Minguez, J. (2009). A noninvasive brain-actuated wheelchair based on a P300 neurophysiological protocol and automated navigation. *IEEE Transactions on Robotics, 25*(3), 614–627.

McFarland, D. J., Krusienski, D. J., Sarnacki, W. A., & Wolpaw, J. R. (2008). Emulation of computer mouse control with a noninvasive brain–computer interface. *Journal of Neural Engineering, 5*(2), 101–110. doi:10.1088/1741-2560/5/2/001 PMID:18367779

Milo, R., Shen-Orr, S., Itzkovitz, S., Kashtan, N., Chklovskii, D., & Alon, U. (2002). Network motifs: Simple building blocks of complex networks. *Science, 298*(5594), 824–827. doi:10.1126/science.298.5594.824 PMID:12399590

Noble, W. S. (2006). What is a support vector machine? *Nature Biotechnology, 24*(12), 1565–1567. doi:10.1038/nbt1206-1565 PMID:17160063

Papo, D., Zanin, M., Pineda-Pardo, J. A., Boccaletti, S., & Buldú, J. M. (2014). Functional brain networks: Great expectations, hard times and the big leap forward. *Philosophical Transactions of the Royal Society of London. Series B, Biological Sciences.* PMID:25180303

Sabarigiri, B., & Suganyadevi, D. (2014). The possibilities of establishing an innovative approach with biometrics using the brain signals and iris features. *Research Journal of Recent Sciences.*

Schreiber, T. (2000). Measuring information transfer. *Physical Review Letters, 85*(2), 461–464. doi:10.1103/PhysRevLett.85.461 PMID:10991308

Snodgrass, J. G., & Vanderwart, M. (1980). A standardized set of 260 pictures: Norms for name agreement, image agreement, familiarity, and visual complexity. *Journal of Experimental Psychology. Human Learning and Memory, 6*(2), 174–215. doi:10.1037/0278-7393.6.2.174 PMID:7373248

Sporns, O., Tononi, G., & Kötter, R. (2005). The human connectome: A structural description of the human brain. *PLoS Computational Biology, 1*(4), e42. doi:10.1371/journal.pcbi.0010042 PMID:16201007

Swartz, B. E. (1998). The advantages of digital over analog recording techniques. *Electroencephalography and Clinical Neurophysiology, 106*(2), 113–117. doi:10.1016/S0013-4694(97)00113-2 PMID:9741771

Zanin, M., & Papo, D. (2014). Characterizing Motif Dynamics of Electric Brain Activity Using Symbolic Analysis. *Entropy, 16*(11), 5654–5667. doi:10.3390/e16115654

Zhang, X. L., Begleiter, H., Porjesz, B., Wang, W., & Litke, A. (1995). Event related potentials during object recognition tasks. *Brain Research Bulletin, 38*(6), 531–538. doi:10.1016/0361-9230(95)02023-5 PMID:8590074

Chapter 23

Interactive/Automated Method to Count Bacterial Colonies

Fernando C. Monteiro
Polytechnic Institute of Bragança, Portugal

João Ribeiro
Polytechnic Institute of Bragança, Portugal

Ramiro Martins
Polytechnic Institute of Bragança, Portugal

ABSTRACT

Counting of bacterial colonies on agar plates is a routine practice to get a rough estimate of the number of viable cells in a sample. The number of colonies in a culture is predominantly manually counted to calculate the concentration of bacteria in the original broth; however, manual counting can be tedious, time-consuming and imprecise. Automation of colony counting has been of increasing interest for many decades, and these methods have been shown to be more consistent than manual counting. Significant limitations of many algorithms used in automated systems are their inability to recognize overlapping colonies as distinct and to count colonies on the plate boundary. This study proposes an interactive counting system and a fully automated system using image processing which overcomes these problems. The proposed system is capable to reduce the manpower and time required for counting while taking account colonies both around the central area and boundary areas of the dish. These systems are part of an application to count colonies based in a mobile phone camera.

INTRODUCTION

Bacterial colony is a group of bacteria growing on a plate that is derived from one original starting cell. An agar plate is a sterile Petri dish that contains a growth medium (typically agar plus nutrients) used to culture microorganisms. The growth and maintenance of bacteria on agar plates (Petri dishes) has been a common practice in microbiology.

DOI: 10.4018/978-1-5225-0435-1.ch023

Individual microorganisms placed on the plate will grow into individual colonies, each a clone genetically identical to the individual ancestor organism. Thus, the plate can be used either to estimate the concentration of organisms in a liquid culture or a suitable dilution of that culture, using a colony counter, or to generate genetically pure cultures from a mixed culture of genetically different organisms.

The Colony Forming Unit (CFU) assay is universally recognized as the gold standard method for measuring the effect of radiation on cell viability, environmental control, food and beverage safety assessment and clinical laboratory exams. A significant example is the monitoring or quality control of drinking water, where bacteria such as *Escherichia coli*, *Enterococcus*, *Cryptosporidium* and faecal coliforms are the main indicator of microbiological water quality for human consumption (EPA, 2006). The culturing process starts by inoculating the strain to be examined on the agar, thus a suspension of the strain is spread over the agar surface. After inoculation, bacterial cultures are incubated to reproduce good conditions for pathogens bacteria growth. Figure 1 shows a Petri dish with several *Escherichia coli* colonies.

The number of colonies in a culture is usually counted manually to calculate the concentration of bacteria based on the assumption that each colony has raised from one single bacterium (colony forming unit, CFU). Bacterial colony counting process is usually performed by well-trained technicians manually. However, there might exist hundreds of colonies in a traditional 100mm Petri dish as shown in Figure 1. Thus, this process is time-consuming (sometimes, the human who counts the colonies need to realize the procedure during many hours or even days), tedious (it is a monotonous procedure) and error prone (with the fatigue, the human being has more tendency to fail the evaluation). The obtained counting results depend on the human conducting the count. This variability is one of the sources of error in the

Figure 1. Escherichia coli bacterial colonies in a Petri dish

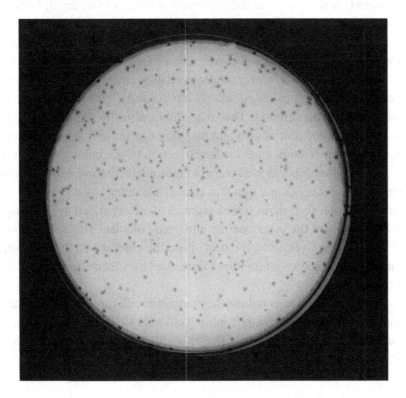

colony counting process that, along with methodological differences between different laboratories or even within a laboratory, can result in considerable fluctuations in results (Bewes, Suchowerska, & Mckenzie, 2008). Due to this, for cultures with high density of colonies, manual counting mostly uses estimation methods, making an extrapolation from a small section of the Petri dish. Automating the detection, counting and analysis of CFU offers significant benefits to eliminate the risk of subjectivity, bias and human error, increasing speed and accuracy, and delivering unprecedented data archiving and retrieval capabilities.

Commercial products exist to facilitate accurate colony counting, ranging from manual counting aids (e.g., counting pens) to all-in-one platforms including image acquisition, processing, and analysis. However, fully automated counting systems also capable of batch processing multiple images at once can be prohibitively expensive for small labs and large facilities may necessitate multiple counting instruments posing a significant budgetary challenge to many laboratories (Putman & Burton, 2005). Yet, with the development of document scanners, mobile phones and digital cameras alternatives to commercial products has been proposed showing that it is not necessary to use costly hardware and imaging system to easily collect the images of bacterial colonies.

Most automatic counting systems, existing on the literature; perform adequately when the colonies are well spaced, large, and circular in shape and with good contrast from the background. When these assumptions are violated, most automatic colony analysis systems can rapidly lose reliability, accuracy and utility. These obstacles include the need to handle confluent growth or growth of colonies that touch or overlap other colonies; the identification of each colony as a unit in spite of differing shapes, sizes, textures, colours and light intensities; the exclusion of colonies around the periphery of the plate reducing statistical accuracy.

To address the above problems, the goal of this study is to design and implement a cost-effective, software-centred system that accepts general digital camera images as its input, for detecting as well as enumerating bacterial colonies in a fully automatic manner. An interactive semi-automatic system is also proposed to overcome any error from the fully automatic system. The proposed systems are capable to reduce the manpower and time required for counting colonies while producing correct colony counting.

In this study, 21 images obtained from a public available database and 5 images obtained with a mobile phone were used. The pre-processing allows the construction of an image only with the Petri dish, removing noise and the background. This step allows also, the separation of the image in two parts, one of them containing the central area and the other one the rim area, and prepares them to the segmentation stage. The segmentation enables the extraction of the colonies from the central area as the rim area. This segmentation is performed using a bottom-hat filtering in both the central area as in the rim area. Information about major and minor axis length, eccentricity and areas from the objects are also used in the rim area. After that, the colonies segmented are separated in two images. One of them containing the unit colonies and the other one the clustered colonies. This separation is performed by the eccentricity of the objects. To finalize, the user chose the counting method. To separate and count the clustered colonies, the automatic system uses a watershed transformation and the interactive system uses the clicks of the user.

The proposed systems are capable to reduce the manpower and time required for counting colonies. The proposed automatic system has difficulty counting colonies in the area of the rim, causing it to have a significant number of non-colonies counted. The interactive method, correct all the problems of the automatic method, producing results similar to the manual count.

BACKGROUND

In different fields of microbiology, immunology and cellular biology, counting colonies of cells growing on agar plates is routine. Manual colony counter usually uses an instrument to count colonies of bacteria or other microorganisms growing on an agar plate. Early counters were merely lighted surfaces on which the plate was placed, with the colonies marked off with a felt-tipped pen on the outer surface of the plate while the operator kept the count manually. More recent counters attempt to count the colonies electronically, by identifying individual areas of dark and light according to automatic or user-set thresholds, and counting the resulting contrasting spots. However, everyone who has already counted colonies knows that this is hard work which takes a lot of time.

Many groups have thought about an improvement of the counting system and the cited publications certainly won't cover all attempts, but no method has achieved a widespread use at all.

The colony counting can occur using different approaches, which could be divided into direct and indirect methods. An indirect method is the traditional plate count method, often preferred because it is cheap. Some technologies can be used for quantification the microbial growth, such as membrane filtration, ATP bioluminescence, direct epi-fluorescent filter microscopy, spiral plating and membrane laser scanning fluorescence cytometry (Uppal & Goyal, 2012). It should not be forgotten that the automatic counting methodology will be only an asset, if it provides good correlation with the results that would be given by a human specialist.

The development of automated counting methods should take into account potential sources of conflict: confluent growth, colonies that touch or overlap the surrounding, and be able to identify and count as being of a different group each colony according the shape, size, texture, colour or light intensity. In addition, such methods must be capable of rejecting common artefacts such as imperfections in the agar, dust and edges of Petri dishes. This tool must be designed to deliver a high degree of accuracy in the count, and it is required reliability and reproducibility.

The previously developed automated colony counting methods relied on various image processing/ analysis techniques for automated detection and counting of colonies on agar media. Corkidi at al. (1998) presented a method that counts bacterial colonies exploring the properties of the surface of microbial colonies. The colonies found in Petri dishes are illuminated so those properties are highlighted. A multi-level threshold algorithm is used to separate and count colonies. This technique does not count colonies on the dish boundary. Marotz et al. (2001) proposed a computer system to detect the microbial colonies in agar Petri dishes with a pre-processing stage composed by the detection of the counting region, image scaling and thresholding. The recognition system is composed by parameter calculation, application of fuzzy logic to determine the local maxima and a measure of goodness to select pixels as potential objects centres, which are used in the final counting. Barber et al. (2001) presented a technique for counting the number of cell colonies when subjected to a certain dose of radiation. The proposed method uses a modified Hough transform, and was designed in order to deal properly with merged or nebulae colonies, which had not been achieved by any other method until then. The results were compared to the counts made by four human experts, and they came to the conclusion that the performances are statistically identical. Dahle at al. (2004) employed a flatbed scanner to count colonies in 12 Petri dishes at a time. After staining, the Petri dishes were put on the specially designed racks used to fix the dishes in the same position from experiment to experiment and decrease shading. Zhang and Chen (2007) presented an automatic colony counter for bacterial colony enumeration without any human intervention. Although it has high accuracy in images with coloured colonies, it has problems with those with transparent media. Niyazi et al. (2007) developed the Clono-Counter, which uses three parameters, namely grey level, maximum area of one colony, and grey level distribution within the colony, for colony counting. Users need to have some experience to find suitable parameters, but some guidelines are provided to speed up the process. Clarke at al. (2010) proposed a low-cost, high-throughput colony counting system consisting of colony counting software and a consumer-grade digital camera or document scanner. The software NICE (NIST's Integrated Colony Enumerator) reads standard image formats, and therefore may be used in conjunction with many imaging systems. Brugger et al. (2012) used a Bayes classifier that is applied to count the final number of bacterial colonies. This step is necessary as some of the colonies are concatenated to form larger groups. Geometric properties such as ratio between major and minor axis of the group are used to verify the number of colonies contained in the group. The colonies that touch the agar boundary were removed. The results were highly correlated with the ones obtained from manual counting. The OpenCFU program created by Geissmann (2013) provides control over the processing parameters and can be used to count cell colonies and other circular objects. Ferrari and Signoroni (2010) proposed an image analysis system capable to address the complex problem of different bacteria species identification on cultured agar plates. Their solution is based on a modular segmentation/classification pipeline where a chain of supervised classification stages provides solutions to a series of nested task issues, from foreground separation toward isolated colony detection and classification. Chiang et al. (2015) proposed a fully automated counting system using image processing methods. To accurately estimate the number of viable bacteria in a known volume of suspension, colonies distributing over the whole surface area of a plate, including the central and rim areas of a Petri dish are taken into account.

Although the majority of these automatic counting approaches produce acceptable performance results, none of them allows an interactive correction of the obtained counting result.

EXPERIMENTAL PROCEDURE

Bacteria growth is an orderly increase in the quantity of cellular constituents. It depends upon the ability of the cell to form new protoplasm from nutrients available in the environment. In most bacteria, growth involves increase in cell mass and number of ribosome, duplication of the bacterial chromosome, synthesis of new cell walls and plasma membrane, partitioning of the two chromosomes, septum formation, and cell division. In the laboratory, bacteria are usually grown using solid or liquid media. Solid growth media such as agar plates are used to isolate pure cultures of a bacterial strain. So, bacterial colony is a group of bacteria growing on a plate that is derived from one original starting cell. All of the bacterial cells in one colony are clones of that original cell since the bacteria reproduce through binary fission.

In this study, were used 21 images obtained from a public available database and 5 images obtained with a mobile phone. As in (Chiang, Tseg, He, & Li, 2015) it was used *Escherichia coli* as microorganism and the spread technique for culture the bacteria colonies. To obtain a single strain of bacteria the broth was first smeared onto a Petri dish. After a period of culturing when the colonies could be observed visually, the target strain was selected and placed in a test tube with nutrients for culturing. The broth was then diluted to a ratio of 1:9. Following repeated dilution, 1 ml of the broth was extracted and smeared with a sterilized spreader on a Petri dish, which was placed within an incubator and cultured for 10 to 15 hours at 37 degrees Celsius.

Image Acquisition

Chiang et al. (2015) used an image capture system to obtain the culture photos (Figure 2). In order to accentuate the region of interest and provide adequate contrast between the colonies and the background, the plate was illuminated from below by a LED panel light, in order to obtain uniform illumination and thin shape. Platform 1 was then used to fix the position of the plate. Since the plate is covered with a lid with a diameter slightly bigger than that of the plate, to take the image inside the plate, platform 2 with the same diameter as the bottom plate was placed just above the lid to exclude the image of the lid.

The main purpose of the design of this apparatus is to obtain the images inside the periphery of the plate, including the edge of periphery. Finally, external light was blocked with the cover, and a CCD camera with 1.3 million effective pixels (1280 (H) × 1024 (V)) was used to capture the images (Chiang et al., 2015).

Figure 2. Image capture system used
Chiang et al. (2015)

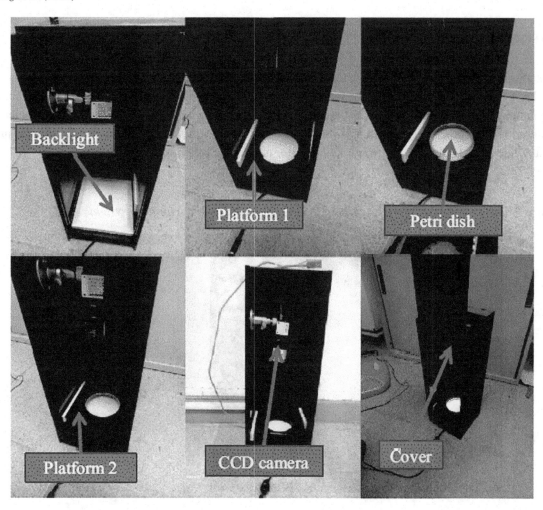

Graphical User Interface

To facilitate the interaction between the human user and the proposed colony counting system, a Graphical user interface (GUI) was created as shown in Figure 3. This GUI is created through the Graphical User Interface Development Environment (GUIDE). This is a development tool for graphical interfaces available from Matlab. The main objective of this was to create software that could be used by everyone, being computer vision expertise or not. This GUI contains a *load* button, to open the image file, two buttons to choose the counting mode, automatic and semi-automatic methods, a text box with the number of counted colonies and a *close* button to finish the application.

Other colony counter systems available from literature such as NICE or OpenCFU have a parameters adjustment step which, although presented as an advantage, could be problematic to be used by humans that do not have knowledge in computer vision. If the user presses the "Automatic" button he will get a fully automated counting and if he presses the "Interactive" button, then he will get a semi-automatic counting which needs human interaction over the colonies that were not counted in the previous stage. The counting result is shown in a text box.

AUTOMATIC COLONY COUNTER

When human operators examine a bacteria colony image, they gradually identify objects from the image. First, the dish region, which is the largest object in the image, is identified. Second, within the dish region, one starts to identify colonies based on some criteria such as colour and shape. If colonies are clustered together, the operator will try to separate the clustered colonies based on their best visual judgment. Once all colonies are identified, the operator counts the total number of colonies.

Figure 3. Graphical user interface created for the proposed colony counting system

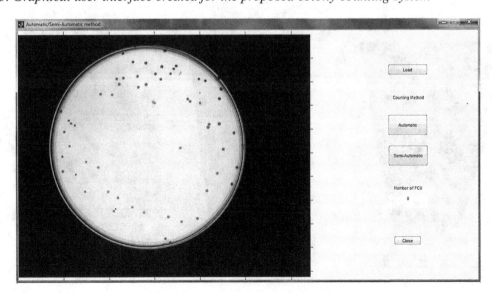

This section introduces procedures used in the colony counting automatic system which includes segmentation of the dish region from background, identifying colonies from central and boundary areas, separating clustered colonies, and reporting colony counts.

Colony Detection

Segmentation distinguishes foreground objects from the background. The role of segmentation is not to lose growth material. Although apparently simple (due to the uniformity of the agar) this task has to face with the contrast between the colonies and the agar and with the light reflexes, especially in the boundary of the dish. In background extraction, the image is segmented into background and Petri dish region. After that, the dish region is also divided into central area and boundary area.

Petri Dish Segmentation

Background intensity variation is an important issue in these cases, especially those with white colonies grown on clear medium where we need to put the dish on a darker surface to enhance the contrast. Otherwise, the colonies cannot be easily seen, even by trained eyes.

To divide the images of Petri dishes into two parts, the images need to be extracted from the background. The process started by filtering the greyscale image with the median filter in order to remove noise and then the magnitude of the gradient was used in a thresholding process to isolate the dish area. By filling the holes surrounded by the most significant connected components, the region inside the border can be retrieved, as shown in Figure 4(b). This image is used as a mask image to enable the extraction of the Petri dish image from the background. The result is shown in Figure 4(c).

Petri dish area is then divided into two parts: the central area of the Petri dish and the boundary area.

Central Area Detection

The greyscale image in Figure 4(c) shows that the Petri dish boundary is darker than the central area.

Thresholding can thus be used for the partition of the central area and boundary area. In this technique, after we define a thresholding level, manual or automatic, the pixels with a low value than this level are classified as background and the pixels with a higher value are classified as objects. Figure 5(a)

Figure 4. (a) Greyscale image of Figure 1; (b) mask of dish area obtained after hole-filling; (c) image of Petri dish extracted from background obtained as a product of (b) and (a)

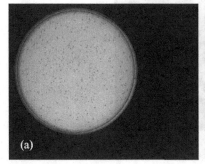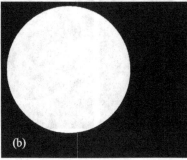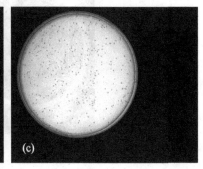

shows the thresholding results of Figure 4(c) followed by morphological open filter in order to remove thin structures. The morphological functions affect the shape of particles on an individual basis using a structuring element. Morphological operations prepare particles in the image for quantitative analysis such as finding the area, perimeter, or orientation. To restore the removed colonies in the central area, holes surrounded by foreground pixels are filled, as shown in Figure 5(b). This mask is used to extract the central region from the Petri dish area as shown in Figure 5(c).

Boundary Area Detection

With the locations of the central area, segmentation of the boundary area can be performed by subtracting the central area mask (Figure 4(b) from the Petri dish area mask (Figure 5(b)). The results are shown in Figure 6(a). This mask is used to extract the boundary region from the Petri dish area as shown in Figure 6(b).

Figure 5. (a) Thresholding result of Figure 4(c); (b) mask of central area obtained after hole-filling; (c) image of central area obtained as a product of (b) and Figure 4(c)

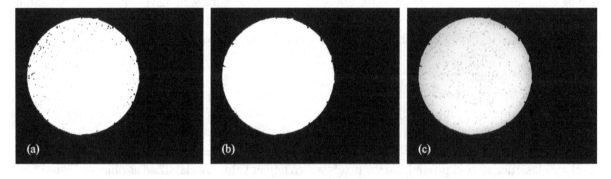

Figure 6. (a) Boundary area mask; (b) image of boundary area obtained as a product of (a) and Figure 4(c)

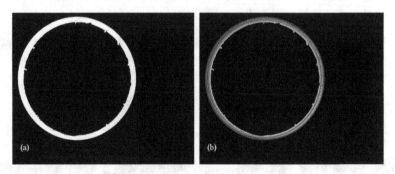

Colony Extraction AND Counting

Colony Detection in the Central Area

The morphological *bottom-hat* filtering is employed to correct the effects of non-uniform illumination. This filter uses a circle structuring element with a radius larger than the colonies' median area (15 pixels) to remove the colonies from the image by a morphological *closing* operation, as shown in Figure 7(a), and then subtracts this image from Figure 5(c). The resulting image shows the components removed in the *closing* operation (the colonies), as shown in Figure 9(b). The colonies in the central area are the extracted by a threshold binarization, as shown in Figure 7(c).

To derive a suitable threshold value for segmentation, only pixels in the central area are considered for histogram statistics. After the segmentation step, segments may contain isolate colonies but also fragments of colonies, cluster of homogeneous or heterogeneous colonies, writings (especially for transparent agars), dirt and scratches on the agar surface. A first problem is therefore to distinguish what is interesting for us from what is not related to the bacterial growth. This has been addressed within a first binary classification stage, where the objective is to keep only segments related to bacterial growth. Very

Figure 7. (a) Result close operation with radius of 15 in Figure 5(c); (b) result of bottom-hat filtering; (c) thresholding results of (b) with the elimination of very small regions

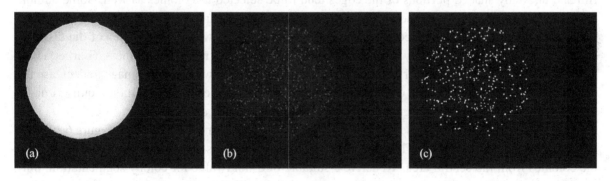

Figure 8. (a) Results of bottom-hat filtering of Figure 6(b). Thresholding result of (a); (c) rim elimination result determined by using length/width ratio of 4 and eccentricity lower than 0.8.

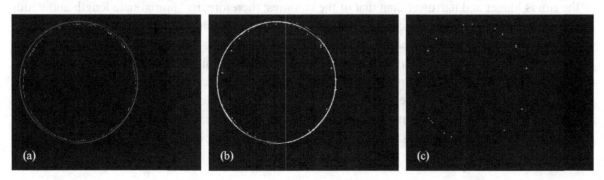

Figure 9. (a) Total number of objects detected in central and boundary areas of the Petri dish; (b) objects classified as 'isolated colonies'; (c) objects classified as 'clustered colonies'

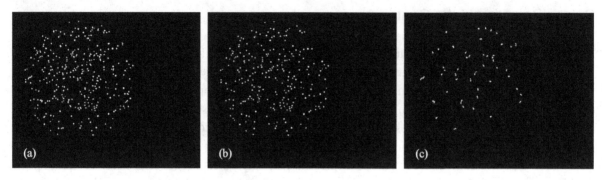

small non-colony objects were then eliminated by a morphological *opening* operation with a structuring element of 20% of the colonies' median area dimension.

Colony Detection in the Boundary Area

Colonies that grow around the edge of dishes are difficult to count because the dish edge has usually similar colour as that of colonies. Thus, when colonies are separated by grey level thresholding, the dish rim and unevenly shaded portions of the edges tend to be selected as colonies as well. Some authors have solved this problem by excluding this area from image processing (Corkidi, et al., 1998; Brugger, et al., 2012). However, since the colonies were distributed over the whole surface area of the dish, excluding colonies around periphery of the dish may reduce statistical representativeness. (Barber, et al., 2001) partially solved the boundary problem by dividing the image with a blank image to decrease the contrast of the edge and used fish eye optics to acquire images. However, this solution requires images to coincide perfectly, and the image division is also computationally demanding.

To extract the colonies from the rim area, the *bottom-hat* transform was applied to Figure 6(b), with the result shown in Figure 8(a). This method is similar to the one used previously in the extraction of the colonies from the central area. To derive a suitable threshold value for colony segmentation, only pixels in the rim area are considered for histogram statistics. The histogram of the resulting non-zero pixels is then used to calculate the threshold using Otsu's method. The thresholding result is shown in Figure 8(b), from which both the rim and colonies are extracted. As shown in Figure 8(b), the image of the rim is longer and narrower than that of the colonies; therefore, its approximate length and width circularly and radically along the centre of the dish are used for elimination.

The length of the component along the arc is approximated by its major axis length, and the width of the component perpendicular to the arc is approximated as the minor axis length. Since a group of more than four colonies rarely forms along the direction of the arc, components in Figure 8(b) with arc lengths greater than four times the width of the minor axis length are regarded as a portion of the rim and eliminated. Portions of the rim not satisfying this criterion remain. To remove these portions, the eccentricity of each component is taken as the threshold. Any component with an eccentricity higher than 0.8 is eliminated. The results are shown in Figure 8(c).

Clustered Colonies Separation

Figure 9 (a) shows the sum of the colonies detected in central area and the colonies detected in boundary area of the Petri dish. Ideally, an isolated foreground object from the detection step corresponds to one colony. However, such an object may correspond to more than one colony because several colonies may aggregate together to form a larger cluster. Hence, to obtain an accurate colony count, those clustered colonies need to be separated. During the classification process, a filter based on morphological processing is applied to classify the components as 'isolated colony' or 'clustered colonies' as shown in Figure 9(b) and Figure 9(c). In this process each component is assessed by a particle filter that takes into account relationships between variables such as area, perimeter, eccentricity and solidity in order to determine whether or not a region is likely to be a valid individual colony.

The currently used assumption is that a single colony is approximately a round shape such that the ratio of its minor and major axis lengths is close to 1. In other words, the greater the deviation of the axial ratio is from 1, the higher the possibility that the object contains more than one colony. On the basis of this assumption, a cut-off value on the ratio of 0.7 was used in order to obtain the 'multiple colonies' candidate objects. Solidity gives the proportion of the pixels in the convex hull that are also in the region where the convex hull specifies the smallest convex polygon that can contain the region. A solidity value lower than 0.95 was used to indicate a clustered colony.

Individual colonies (Figure 9(b)) are accepted for counting whilst the objects identified as clustered colonies (Figure 9(c)) need to be separated. Brugger, et al. (2012) used a Bayes classifier to count clustered colonies. They used properties such as ratio between major and minor axis to determine how many colonies are in the group. In this study, on the basis of morphological features, the distance transform and the watershed algorithm are used to divide the merged colonies. To illustrate the concept, we demonstrate the application of watershed algorithm in Figure 10 over one of the clustered colonies of Figure 9(c).

In this study, it was used the watershed transform based in the immersion approach where the landscape is sequentially flooded from bottom to top. When we sink the whole surface slowly into a lake, water leaks through the holes placed in the gradient minima, rising uniformly and globally across the image, proceeding to fill each catchment basin. In order to avoid water coming from different holes, virtual dams are built at places where the water coming from two different minima would merge. When the image

Figure 10. (a) Enlarged example of clustered colony; (b) Clustered colonies separated in the watershed operation

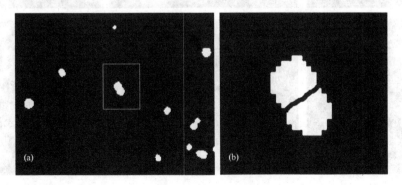

surface is completely flooded the virtual dams or watershed lines separate the catchment basins from one another and correspond to the boundaries of the regions. The watershed operation computes a label matrix identifying the watershed regions of the input matrix, which can have any dimension. The elements obtained are integer values greater than or equal to 0. The elements labelled with 0 do not belong to a unique watershed region. These are called watershed pixels. The elements labelled with 1 belong to the first watershed region, the elements labelled 2 belong to the second watershed region, and so on. After the clustered colonies have been properly split and identified their number is then added to the number of isolated colonies, yielding the total number of colonies in the Petri dish, as shown in Figure 11.

We can see that there are some colonies that were miss-classified from the automatic counter, reducing the performance of the approach. When the user only wants an approximated counting of the colonies

Figure 11. (a) Original image; (b) Petri dish mask; (c) detected Petri dish; (d) detected central area; (e) colonies detected in central area; (f) detected boundary area; (g) thresholded boundary area; (h) colonies detected in boundary area; (i) colonies after clustered separation

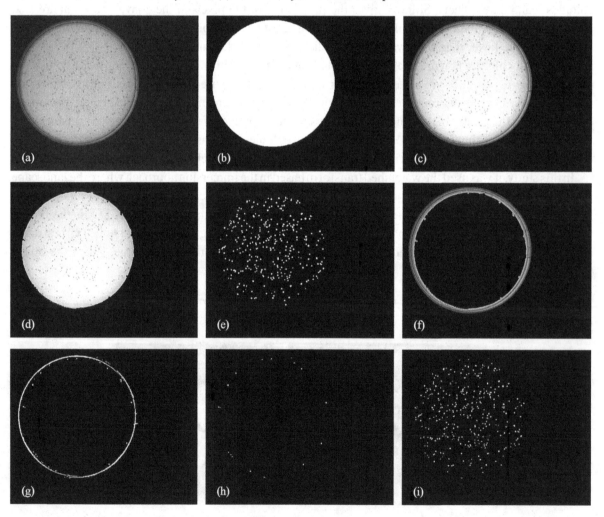

in the Petri dish, the automatic system could be a good approach with a computation time of seconds. However, when the counting results must have to be as correct as possible, we need another methodology to do that, as the one presented in the next section.

INTERACTIVE COLONY COUNTER

For most microbiologists (Geissmann, 2013), a moderate average deviation from colony counter systems (lower than 20%) could often be negligible compared to noise generated by the variety of experimental factors used in the Petri dish cultures. Rather than trying to provide a perfect similarity to human counts, the automatic methods based on digital image processing proposed in the literature usually focus on reducing the involved human labour. However, the final result produced by these methods does not allows for corrections.

Bacteria colony classification is indeed a complicated task even for well-trained human operators, thus a small effort to help correcting the final colony enumeration is required from the user in this interactive colony counter system to allow the identification of missing colony detection. This is done by a process in which the user is asked to select the non-marked colonies resulting from a previous semi-automatic colony detection process.

The semi-automatic stage follows the methodology used in the automatic method described in previous sections from Petri dish segmentation to colony detection in boundary area. This stage counts the colonies and marks them with a green colour, as shown in Figure 12(a). The colonies that are not detected by automatic method are left without any identification. The used conditions to classify an object as a colony are: eccentricity lower than 0.5 and an area up to 1.5 the mean area of all the detected objects.

The interactive stage allows the user to manually mark the non-coloured colonies by clicking the mouse over the colonies. The marks are identified with yellow points in order to indicate that the colony has already been counted, as shown in Figure 12(b). The system also allows the user to delete the previous marked colonies by pressing the *backspace* or the *delete* key from the keyboard. The number of user ticks is then added to the number of isolated colonies previously counted yielding the total number of colonies in the Petri dish.

We can observe from Figure 12(a) that isolated colonies are correctly identified, however, clustered colonies and colonies in the boundary Petri dish are not fully identified. These problems are overcome in Figure 12(b) by user interaction, even in boundary dish area.

Figure 12. (a) Result from automatic colony counter; (b) colony classification by user intervention

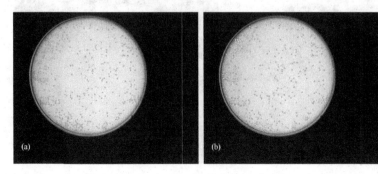

This interactive method provides a colony counting approach that is faster and less tedious than full manually counting approach and simultaneously providing a higher accuracy than the fully automated methods.

EXPERIMENTAL RESULTS AND DISCUSSION

To evaluate the performance of the proposed methods, 26 images of *Escherichia coli* colonies in Petri dishes were selected for the experiments. The spread plate technique with agar was employed for the culturing of bacterial colonies. Five images were collected with a 5-megapixel mobile phone camera without any special apparatus and the other 21, available from (Chiang, et al., 2015), were acquired with a special apparatus in order to accentuate the dish area and to provide adequate contrast between the colonies and the background. In this system the plate was illuminated from below by a LED panel light due to its uniform illumination and thin shape.

Figure 13 (a) shows *Escherichia coli* colonies on a Petri dish obtained with a mobile phone and Figure 13(b) shows images obtained with the system described in (Chiang, et al., 2015).

A user-friendly graphical user interface (GUI) that implements the image processing methods described in the previous section has been developed. When the user opens the image file and choose the automatic counting mode, the program will automatically run without any user intervention.

In order to facilitate any comparison by other authors we decided to present only the evaluation results for the 21 images from (Chiang, et al., 2015). The evaluation results for the mobile phone acquired images are similar with these ones. To evaluate the performance of the proposed methods, the colonies were counted by the fully automatic and the interactive methods and also manually counted by five biomedical engineers. The counting range for the number of colonies counted manually was from 29 to 687 and the range for the fully automated system was from 24 to 591.

The results obtained were compared with state-of-the-art automatic counting systems available from the literature – NICE (Clarke, et al., 2010) and OpenCFU method (Geissmann, 2013). These approaches require the user intervention to manually select the region of interest and several thresholds prior to the automated process. This could be a problem when the users are not expertise in computer vision.

Figure 13. Escherichia coli colonies on a Petri dish. (a) images obtained with a 5-megapixel mobile phone; (b) images available from (Chiang, et al., 2015), obtained with a special apparatus

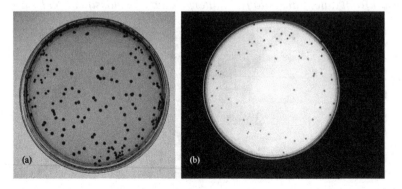

Counting evaluation can be judged according to the amount of misclassified colonies by a direct comparison between reference (ground truth) and resulted counting. The results obtained by manual counting were taken as ground truth. Colonies can be classified into four sets: well-classified colonies (true positives), incorrectly detected colonies (false positives), correctly undetected colonies (true negatives) and incorrectly undetected colonies (false negatives). True negative colonies are ignored in some evaluation measures, e.g. Precision-Recall curves.

These possible measures can be arranged in a confusion matrix as shown in Table 1. This matrix contains information about actual and detected colonies done by a counting colonies system. The diagonal elements represent correctly classified colonies while the cross-diagonal elements represent misclassified colonies.

Given two counting results, S and R, where S is the result of some method and R is the ground truth counting, *precision* is proportional to the fraction of colonies in S that matches with ground truth R, and *recall* is proportional to the fraction of colonies from R for which a suitable match was found in S. *Precision* and *recall* measures are defined as follows:

$$Precision = \frac{\text{Number of truth colonies retrieved}}{\text{Number of colonies retrieved}} = \frac{\text{True positive}}{\text{True positive} + \text{False positive}} \qquad (1)$$

$$Recall = \frac{\text{Number of truth colonies retrieved}}{\text{Number of colonies in ground truth}} = \frac{\text{True positive}}{\text{True positive} + \text{False negative}} \qquad (2)$$

In probabilistic terms, *precision* is the probability that the result is valid, and *recall* is the probability that the ground truth was detected. A low *recall* value is typically the result of under-detection and indicates failure to identify colonies. *Precision* is low when there is a significant over-detection of colonies.

Precision and *recall* have been used in the information retrieval systems for a long time. The interpretation for the *precision* and *recall* for evaluation of colony counting are a little different from evaluation of retrieval systems. In retrieval, the aim is to get a high *precision* for all values of *recall* while in colony counting, the aim is to get both high *precision* and high *recall*. The two statistics may be distilled into a single figure of merit:

$$F - measure = \frac{Precision \times Recall}{\alpha Recall + \left(1 - \alpha\right) Precision} \qquad (3)$$

Table 1. Confusion matrix used in the performance evaluation

Confusion matrix		Detected colonies	
		YES	**NO**
Ground truth	YES	*True positive*	*False negative*
	NO	*False positive*	*True negative*

where α determines the relative importance of each item. In this case α is selected as 0.5, expressing no preference for either.

The main advantage of using *precision* and *recall* for evaluation of colony counting systems is that we can compare not only the counting results obtained by different algorithms, but also the results produced by the same algorithm using different input parameters.

We also used the mean absolute percentage of error (MAPE) which is one of the most appropriate information about average percentage errors which are used to a great extent in reporting accounting results and is defined as:

$$MAPE_t = \left| \frac{A_t - F_t}{2 \times (A_t + F_t)} \right| \times 100 \tag{4}$$

where A_t is the actual value and it is represented by the manual counting obtained and F_t is the forecast value, which is the counting obtained by the automatic method.

The manual counting (ground truth) was performed by different students of Biomedical Engineer. The results were obtained by comparing each manual count with the other counts obtained from different humans. To calculate the evaluation values for the computer vision methods, each count was evaluated against each human counting and the final evaluation result is given by the mean of all comparisons.

Figure 14 shows the results of the proposed automatic method and the OpenCFU. It is possible to observe in the yellow box that both methods fail in the detection of some colonies in the rim area of the Petri dish. These failures, contribute to the high number of false negatives and thus the low *recall* value. It is also possible to see that OpenCFU detects a higher number of colonies in the rim area than the proposed automatic system. The explanations for these detection failures are the fact that some of the colonies are eliminated in the pre-processing step due to its intensity which is similar to that of the rim of the Petri dish.

Another failure that contributes to increase the false negative value of the proposed automatic system and also observed in the OpenCFU method, is the fact that the system does not identify some colonies in the central area (observed in the yellow boxes), as shown in Figure 15. By image analysis, it is possible to conclude that these problems are due to the low contrast in the central area of the Petri dish. The non-identified colonies have practically the same color as the background, which makes it difficult to segment them.

Figure 14. (a) Result from the proposed automatic method; (b) result from OpenCFU method.

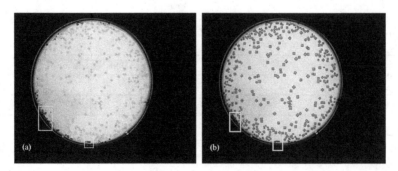

Figure 15. (a) Result from the proposed automatic method where the yellow boxes show misidentified colonies; (b) result from the OpenCFU method

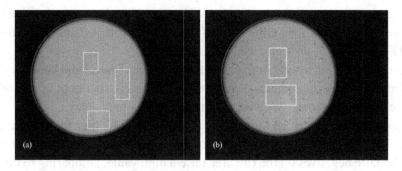

Evaluation Results

The statistical results of *precision*, *recall*, *F-measure* and mean absolute percentage error (MAPE) over the 21 images from (Chiang, et al., 2015) are shown in Table 2.

From Table 2, the values of *precision* for all the methods are really high, except for NICE, which means that the counted colonies are usually correct with a low value for false positives due to almost all the isolated colonies reach the last classification stage. The automatic method has a *precision* almost equal to 1 with only 1 false positive colony detected in the 21 images.

Concerning the *recall* values, we can see that the automatic methods have lower *recall* values than manual and interactive methods. This is due to the high number of false negative colonies, especially in the boundary of the dish. The method which has the best *recall* result is the interactive method with an average *recall* higher than 0.99. Being the *recall* the measure related with the false negatives, we can conclude that the automatic methods fail in the detection of some colonies in the Petri dish. The OpenCFU method has an acceptable result for the *recall* with an average value of 0.92.

The causes for these values include the intensity difference among colonies: the intensity values of smaller colonies are similar to that of the background of the Petri dish, leading to their elimination when the image was thresholded; clustered colonies mistaken classified as with rim: to remove the rim, components that displayed a ratio between major and minor axis length greater than 4 are eliminated. Although this method removed most of the rim from the image, clustered colonies may still have been treated as portions of the rim and removed (see Figure 8).

Table 2. Statistical results of colony enumeration with different methods

Measure	Method				
	Manual	**Automatic**	**Interactive**	**NICE**	**OpenCFU**
Precision	0.9885	0.9997	0.9831	0.9607	0.9928
Recall	0.9885	0.8725	0.9933	0.8780	0.9156
F-measure	0.9885	0.9318	0.9881	0.9055	0.9506
MAPE (%)	2.37	16.31	2.48	18.91	9.21

In contrast to the three tested automatic methods, the interactive method presents a value similar with the manual value as it was expected. The values of *precision*, *recall* and *F-measure* of the interactive proposed system are greater than the other methods. Furthermore, the mean absolute percentage error of the proposed method is 2.48% while the ones of OpenCFU, proposed automatic method and NICE are 9.21%, 16.31% and 18.91%, respectively.

Table 3 shows the evaluation results from each Petri dish area (central and boundary) compared with the whole dish. From the *precision* values, it is possible to observe that both in central area as well as in the rim area the results are similar with the results for the whole dish area.

Analyzing the *recall* values, we can see that the central area has a higher value than the rim area. It is possible to conclude that the low value of *recall* for the whole dish is due to this low value of *recall* in boundary area. The false negatives on the rim area have a high value, comparing to those of the central area. Due to this high number of false negatives, the absolute percentage of error in the rim area presents a high value (55%). As the number of colonies in the rim area is much smaller than the number of colonies in central area, the APE in central area is similar with the one of the whole dish.

To improve the results of the automatic count, the method applied to the rim area needs to be modified in order to reduce the number of false negatives.

The complexity of the image has influence in the results, as shown in Figure 16. In the first row, we have a relatively simple image with 86 colonies, with a small number of colonies in the boundary dish and a large number of isolated colonies. The automatic method identified 85 colonies, all of them classified as true positive results. In the second row, we have a complex image with 578 colonies, from which the automatic method identifies 403 true positive colonies and 175 as false negative colonies mostly positioned in the boundary area.

Time Reduction Results

As previously referred, the manual count is a time-consuming process, which can take several hours. The manual counting time depends on the experience of the researchers, the number of colonies present in the Petri dish and the number of aggregated colonies.

The average time to manual counting was about 177 seconds, while the automatic method was about 6 seconds (reduction of 96%) and the interactive method takes 37 seconds (reduction of 79%). These reductions in time counting must be compared with the F-measure of each method, 0.9885 for the manual

Table 3. Statistical results of colony enumeration with different methods

Measure	Method			
	Manual	**Automatic**		
		Petri dish	**Central area**	**Rim area**
Precision	0.9885	0.9997	0.9959	0.9615
Recall	0.9885	0.8725	0.9264	0.6360
F-measure	0.9885	0.9318	0.9599	0.7248
MAPE (%)	2.37	16.31	14.23	55.04

Figure 16. (a) Original image with 86 colonies; (b) result from automatic method with 85 true positive colonies and 1 false negative colony; (c) Original image with 578 colonies; (d) result from automatic method with 403 true positive colonies and 175 false negative colonies

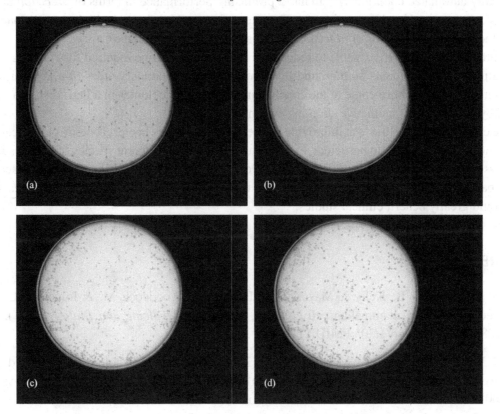

counting, 0.9318 for the automatic counting and 0.9881 for the interactive method. So, if we want only an approximated counting with a high reduction in the counting time, we could use the automatic method, however, if we pretend a high accuracy in the counting allied with time reduction, we should use the proposed interactive method.

CONCLUSION

Clinical microbiology is a wide, varied and complex field of investigation. The foreseeable diffusion of microbiology laboratory automation systems and the consequent massive image digitalization is expected to entail, on the one hand, new paradigms for clinical investigation and diagnosis and, on the other hand, new image analysis challenges and tasks.

The proposed machine vision based method is a robust yet effective method for a bacterial colonies counter. It has the ability to detect the dish regions, isolate colonies on the dish and further separate the clustered colonies for accurate counting of colonies. The first segmentation step turned out to be adequate for the extraction of material growth on Petri dishes. Of course, a more sophisticated segmentation technique could be devised for an improved colony isolation in cluttered situations, in order to attain possibly more favourable balance between segmentation and classification work.

The fully automated counting system has a promising performance in terms of *precision* and is efficient as demonstrated by the experiments. The interactive method showed a higher performance than all the others methods in terms of *precision*, *recall* and absolute percentage error.

The proposed systems are capable to reduce the manpower and time required for counting colonies while taking account colonies both around the central area and boundary areas of a Petri dish. From the current analysis, we have come to the conclusion that bacteria colonies in a Petri dish can be easily counted by the proposed interactive counting system.

More efforts need to be made at improving the performance of the bacteria colony classification and enumeration in future work. In particular, to detect and distinguish different species of bacteria not only for well-isolated colonies, but also for clustered colonies in the dish. The ultimate goal is to accurately classify bacterial colonies according to their strain types and produce the correct count for each class, which could greatly benefit clinical studies.

REFERENCES

Barber, P. R., Vojnovic, B., Kelly, J., Mayes, C. R., Boulton, P., Woodcock, M., & Joiner, M. C. (2001). Automated counting of mammalian cell colonies. *Physics in Medicine and Biology*, *46*(1), 63–76. doi:10.1088/0031-9155/46/1/305 PMID:11197679

Bewes, J. M., Suchowerska, N., & Mckenzie, D. R. (2008). Automated cell colony counting and analysis using the circular Hough image transform algorithm (CHiTA). *Physics in Medicine and Biology*, *53*(21), 5991–6008. doi:10.1088/0031-9155/53/21/007 PMID:18836215

Brugger, S. D., Baumberger, C., Jost, M., Jenni, W., Brugger, U., & Mühlemann, K. (2012). Automated counting of bacterial colony forming units on agar plates. *PLoS ONE*, *7*(3), e33695. doi:10.1371/journal.pone.0033695 PMID:22448267

Brugger, S. D., Baumberger, C., Jost, M., Jenni, W., Brugger, U., & Muhlemann, K. (2 012). Automated Counting of Bacterial Colony Forming Units on Agar Plates. *PLoS ONE*, *7*(3).

Chiang, P., Tseg, M.-J., He, Z.-S., & Li, C.-H. (2015). Automated counting of bacterial colonies by image analysis. *Journal of Microbiological Methods*, *108*, 74–82. doi:10.1016/j.mimet.2014.11.009 PMID:25451456

Chiang, P.-J., Tseng, M.-J., He, Z.-S., & Li, C.-H. (2015). Automated counting of bacterial colonies by image analysis. *Journal of Microbiological Methods*, *108*, 74–82. doi:10.1016/j.mimet.2014.11.009 PMID:25451456

Clarke, M. L., Burton, R. L., Hill, A. N., Litorja, M., Nahm, M. H., & Hwang, J. (2010). Low-cost, high-throughput, automated counting of bacterial colonies. *Cytometry. Part A*, *77*(8), 790–797. doi:10.1002/cyto.a.20864 PMID:20140968

Corkidi, G., Diaz-Uribe, R., Folch-Mallol, J. L., & Nieto-Sotelo, J. (1998). COVASIAM: An image analysis method that allows detection of confluent microbial colonies and colonies of various sizes for automated counting. *Applied and Environmental Microbiology*, *64*(4), 1400–1404. PMID:9546177

Dahle, J., Kakar, M., Steen, H. B., & Kaalhus, O. (2004). Automated counting of mammalian cell colonies by means of a flat bed scanner and image processing. *Cytometry. Part A*, *60*(2), 182–188. doi:10.1002/cyto.a.20038 PMID:15290719

EPA US. (2006). Water quality standards review and revision. Washington, DC.

Ferrari, A., & Signoroni, A. (2014). Multistage classification for bacterial colonies recognition on solid agar images. *Proceedings of theIEEE International Conference on Imaging Systems and Techniques* (pp. 101-106). Santorini, Greece: IEEE. doi:10.1109/IST.2014.6958454

Geissmann, Q. (2013). OpenCFU, a new free and open-source software to count cell colonies and other circular objects. *PLoS ONE*, *8*(2), e54072. doi:10.1371/journal.pone.0054072 PMID:23457446

Marotz, J., Lübbert, C., & Eisenbeiss, W. (2001). Effective object recognition for automated counting of colonies in petri dishes (automated colony counting). *Computer Methods and Programs in Biomedicine*, *66*(2-3), 183–198. doi:10.1016/S0169-2607(00)00128-0 PMID:11551392

Niyazi, M., Niyazi, I., & Belka, C. (2007). Counting colonies of clonogenic assays by using densitometric software. *Radiation Oncology (London, England)*, *2*(1), 1–3. doi:10.1186/1748-717X-2-4 PMID:17212832

Putman, N., Burton, M. H., & Nahm, M. H. (2005). Simplified method to automatically count bacterial colony forming unit. *Journal of Immunological Methods*, *302*(1-2), 99–102. doi:10.1016/j.jim.2005.05.003 PMID:16002082

Uppal, N., & Goyal, R. (2012). Computational approach to count bacterial colonies. *International journal of Advances in Engineering & Technology*, 4(2), 364-372.

Zhang, C., & Chen, W.-B. (2007). An Effective and Robust Method for Automatic Bacterial Colony Enumeration. *Proceedings of theInternational Conference on Semantic Computing* (pp. 581-588). Irvine, Canada: IEEE. doi:10.1109/ICSC.2007.20

KEY TERMS AND DEFINITIONS

Agar Media: A gelatinous material derived from certain marine algae. It is used as a base for bacterial culture media and as a stabilizer and thickener in many food products.

Bacterial Colony: A group of individual microorganisms clustered together originated from one mother cell and genetically identical.

Colony Forming Unit: A measure of viable cells in which a colony represents an aggregate of cells derived from a single progenitor cell.

Escherichia Coli (E. coli): A Gram-negative bacteria that normally inhabit the intestine of humans and animals. Most *E. coli* strains are harmless, but one of the main sources of *E. coli* infections is either by infection of open wounds or by food (including contaminated water) consumption.

Petri Dish: A shallow dish consisting of two round, overlapping halves that is used to grow microorganisms on solid culture medium.

Compilation of References

[alarme.wav]. (1995). *MAX SOUNDS 5000* [CD]. São Paulo: RÁDIO 89 FM, A RÁDIO ROCK.

2020 Energy. (2015). Retrieved from http://www.2020energy.eu/game

Abeykoon, A. M. H. S., & Chinthaka, M. K. C. D. (2014). Position based static friction estimation for DC motors using disturbance observer.*Proceedings of 2014 7th International Conference on Information and Automation for Sustainability (ICIAfS)* (pp. 1-6). Colombo: IEEE.

Abeykoon, A. M. H. S., & Ohnishi, K. (2006). Realization of virtual slave model of a forceps robot using bilateral control.*Proceedings of 32nd Annual Conference on IEEE Industrial Electronics* (pp. 4468-4473). IEEE. doi:10.1109/IECON.2006.348100

Abeykoon, A. M. H. S., & Ohnishi, K. (2007). Virtual tool for bilaterally controlled forceps robot-for minimally invasive surgery. *Transaction on International Journal of Medical Robotics and Computer Assisted Surgery, 3*(3), 271–280. doi:10.1002/rcs.147 PMID:17729375

Abeykoon, A. M. H. S., & Ohnishi, K. (2008). Improvement of tactile sensation of a bilateral forceps robot by a switching virtual model. *Transactions on Advanced Robotics, 8*(8), 789–806. doi:10.1163/156855308X314506

Abeykoon, A. M. H. S., & Perera, G. V. A. G. A. (2014). Review on bilateral teleoperation with force, position, power and impedance scaling.*Proceedings of 2014 7th International Conference on Information and Automation for Sustainability* (pp. 1-7). Colombo: IEEE.

Abeykoon, A. M. H. S., & Pillai, M. B. (2014, September). RTOS based embedded controller implementation of a bilateral control system. *Journal of the National Science Foundation of Sri Lanka, 3*(42), 217–228.

Abeykoon, A. M. H. S., & Senevirathne, H. R. (2012). Disturbance observer based current controller for a brushed DC motor.*Proceedings of 2012 IEEE 6th International Conference on Information and Automation for Sustainability* (pp. 47-52). IEEE. doi:10.1109/ICIAFS.2012.6419881

Abousaeidi, M., Fauzi, R., & Muhamad, R. (2011). Application of geographic information system (GIS) in routing for delivery of fresh vegetables. *Proceeding of the 2011 IEEE Colloquium on Humanities, Science and Engineering* (pp. 551–555). IEEE. http://doi.org/ doi:<ALIGNMENT.qj></ALIGNMENT>10.1109/CHUSER.2011.6163794

ACM SIGCHI. (2009). Curricula for Human-Computer Interaction. Retrieved from http://www.sigchi.org/resources/education/cdg/

ACM. (1992). *ACM code of ethic and professional conduct*. Retrieved from http://www.acm.org/about/code-of-ethics

Active8-3D (2015). 3D holographic projection displays. Retrieved from http://www.activ8-3d.co.uk/

Adikari, S., McDonald, C., & Collings, P. (2006). A design science approach to an HCI research project. *Proceedings of the OZCHI '06* (pp. 429–432). doi:10.1145/1228175.1228265

Adikari, S., McDonald, C., & Collings, P. (2009). Little Design Up-Front: A Design Science Approach to Integrating Usability into Agile Requirements Engineering.*Proceedings of the HCI International '09* (pp. 549-558). doi:10.1007/978-3-642-02574-7_62

Adis, A. A. A., & Jun, K. H. (2013). Antecedents of brand recall and brand attitude towards purchase intention in advergames. *European Journal of Business and Management*, 5(18), 58–67.

Agapito, D., Valle, P., & Mendes, J. (2014). The sensory dimension of tourist experiences: Capturing meaningful sensory-based themes in Southwest Portugal. *Tourism Management*, 42, 224–237. doi:10.1016/j.tourman.2013.11.011

Aggarwal, J., & Cai, Q. (1999). Human motion analysis: A review. *Computer Vision and Image Understanding*, 73(3), 428–440. doi:10.1006/cviu.1998.0744

Agrawal, P., & Gupta, K. (2012). Mouse Movement Through Finger by Image Grabbing using Sixth Sense Technology. *International Journal of Engineering Science and Advanced Technology*.

Agrawala, A. K. (2013, January). CMSC 818G class Information-Centric Design of Context-Aware Systems: Retrieved from http://www.cs.umd.edu/class/spring2013/cmsc818b/_professor.html

Akdogan, E., & Demir, M. H. (2012). Rehabilitation technologies: Biomechanics point of view. In A Roadmap of Biomedical Engineers and Milestone (pp. 1-36).

Akehurst, G. (2009). User generated content: The use of blogs for tourism organizations and tourism consumers. *Service Business*, 3(1), 51–61. doi:10.1007/s11628-008-0054-2

Alamri, A., Jongeun, C., & El Saddik, A. (2010). AR-REHAB: An Augmented Reality Framework for Poststroke-Patient Rehabilitation. *IEEE Transactions on Instrumentation and Measurement*, 59(10), 2554–2563. doi:10.1109/tim.2010.2057750

Alaoui, M., & Lewkowicz, M. (2013). A livingLab approach to involve elderly in the design of smart TV applications offering communication services. In Online Communities and Social Computing (pp. 325–334). Springer Berlin Heidelberg. Retrieved from http://www.aal-europe.eu/ doi:10.1007/978-3-642-39371-6_37

Albert, R., & Barabási, A. L. (2002). Statistical mechanics of complex networks. *Reviews of Modern Physics*, 74(1), 47–97. doi:10.1103/RevModPhys.74.47

Alhamid, M. F., Eid, M., & El Saddik, A. (2012, May 18-19). A multi-modal intelligent system for biofeedback interactions. *Paper presented at the 2012 IEEE International Symposium on Medical Measurements and Applications Proceedings (MeMeA)*.

Alina, G. (2013). Factors responsible for consumer's attitude towards advergames. *Annals of Faculty of Economics*, 1(1), 1733–1742.

AlKassim, Z. (2012). Virtual laser keyboards: A giant leap towards human-computer interaction. *Proceedings of the 2012 International Conference on Computer Systems and Industrial Informatics (ICCSII)* (pp. 1-5). IEEE. doi:10.1109/ICCSII.2012.6454614

AlKassim, Z., & Mohamed, N. (2014). Sixth sense technology: Comparisons and future predictions. *Proceedings of the 2014 10th International Conference on Innovations in Information Technology (INNOVATIONS)* (pp. 122-127). IEEE.

Alon, U. (2007). Network motifs: Theory and experimental approaches. *Nature Reviews. Genetics*, *8*(6), 450–461. doi:10.1038/nrg2102 PMID:17510665

Altschuler, E. L., Wisdom, S. B., Stone, L., Foster, C., Galasko, D., Llewellyn, D. M. E., & Ramachandran, V. S. (1999). Rehabilitation of hemiparesis after stroke with a mirror. *Lancet*, *353*(9169), 2035–2036. doi:10.1016/S0140-6736(99)00920-4 PMID:10376620

Alves, R., Madeira, M., Ferrer, J., Costa, S., Lopes, D., Silva, B. M., . . . Rodrigues, J. (2014). Fátima revisited: an interactive installation. *Proceedings of the SGEM2014 Conference on Arts, Performing Arts, Architecture & Design SGEM '14* (pp. 141-148).

Alves, R., Sousa, L., Negrier, A., Rodrigues, J. M. F., Cardoso, P. J. S., Monteiro, J., . . . Bica, P. (2015a). PRHOLO: Interactive holographic public relations. *Proceedings of the3rd International Conference on Advances in Computing, Communication and Information Technology* (pp. 124-128). doi:10.15224/978-1-63248-061-3-74

Alves, R., Negrier, A., Sousa, L., Rodrigues, J. M. F., Felisberto, P., Gomes, M., & Bica, P. (2015). Interactive 180° Rear Projection Public Relations. *Procedia Computer Science*, *51*, 592–601. doi:10.1016/j.procs.2015.05.327

Alves, R., Sousa, L., Negrier, A., Rodrigues, J.M.F., Monteiro, J., Cardoso, P., Felisberto, P., Gomes, M., & Bica, P. (2015c). 360° Public relations, an interactive installation. *The Visual Computer*.

Ambrosino, D., & Sciomachen, A. (2006). A food distribution network problem: A case study. *IMA Journal of Management Mathematics*, *18*(1), 33–53. doi:10.1093/imaman/dpl012

Ammenwerth, E., Iller, C., & Mahler, C. (2006). IT-adoption and the interaction of task, technology and individuals: A fit framework and a case study. *BMC Medical Informatics and Decision Making*, *6*(1), 3. doi:10.1186/1472-6947-6-3 PMID:16401336

Andersson, T. (2007). The Tourist in the Experience Economy. *Scandinavian Journal of Hospitality and Tourism*, *7*(1), 46–58. doi:10.1080/15022250701224035

Andrews, D. H., & Goodson, L. A. (1980). A comparative analysis of models of instructional design. *Journal of Instructional Development*, *3*(4), 2–16. doi:10.1007/BF02904348

Andrews, D. H., & Goodson, L. A. (2011). A comparative analysis of models of instructional design. In G. Anglin (Ed.), *Instructional technology: Past, present, and future* (pp. 205–225). Santa Barbara, CA: Libraries Unlimited.

Android Developers. (n. d.). *Android Design Principles*. Retrieved from http://developer.android.com/design/get-started/principles.html

An, S., & Kang, H. (2014). Advertising or games? Advergames on the internet gaming sites targeting children. *International Journal of Advertising*, *33*(3), 509–532. doi:10.2501/IJA-33-3-509-532

An, S., & Stern, S. (2011). Mitigating the effects of advergames on children. *Journal of Advertising*, *40*(1), 43–56. doi:10.2753/JOA0091-3367400103

Anthony, S. (2011). The New York Times' magic mirror will bring shopping to the bathroom. *Extremetech.com*. Retrieved from http://www.extremetech.com/computing/94751-the-new-york-times-magic-mirror-will-bring-shopping-to-the-bathroom

António, S., Herrera, R., & Enriquez, E. (2013). Projection's panel of models for touch screen. *International Journal of Innovative Research in Computer and Communication Engineering*, *1*(9), 2057–2064.

Archer, L. B. (1984). Systematic method for designers. In N. Cross (Ed.), *Developments in Design Methodology* (pp. 57–82). London: John Wiley.

Arif, W. O., Parasuraman, S., & Jauw, V. L. (2010). Robot-assisted stoke rehabilitation: Estimation of muscle force/joint torque from EMG using GA. *Proceedings of theIEEE EMBS Conference on Biomed. Eng. & Science* (pp. 341-347).

Arora, M. (2012). Basic Principles of Sixth Sense Technology. *VRSD International Journal Of Computer Science and Information Technology, VSRD-IJCSIT, 2*(8), 687–693.

ARToolKit community. (2015). ARToolKit - Innovation Through Community Retrieved from http://artoolkit.org/

Asaolu, O. S. (2012). International Evaluation of a Localized Geography Educational Software. *African Journal of Computing & ICT, 5*(4).

Asus. (2014). Asus Xtion pro. Retrieved from http://goo.gl/HxQcli

Atmel (2015). Atmel. Retrieved from www.atmel.com/devices/atmega328p.aspx

Attwell, G. (Ed.). (2006). Evaluating e-learning a guide to the evaluation of e-learning: Evaluate Europe Handbook Series, (2), 1-46.

aus der Wieschen, M. V. (2015). *Exploring Feedback Modalities for Robot Teleoperation* [Unpublished master's thesis]. University of Southern Denmark, Sonderborg.

aus der Wieschen, M. V., Fischer, K., & Krüger, N. (2015). Error Feedback for Robust Learning from Demonstration. *Proceedings of the Tenth Annual ACM/IEEE International Conference on Human-Robot Interaction Extended Abstracts* (pp. 225-226). ACM. doi:10.1145/2701973.2702724

Ausubel, D. P. (1960). The use of advance organizers in the learning and retention of meaningful verbal material. *Journal of Educational Psychology, 51*(5), 267–272. doi:10.1037/h0046669

AVA. (2015). AVA advanced virtual assistant. Retrieved from http://airportone.com/airportvirtualassistancesystem.htm

AVconcepts. (2015). Retrieved from http://www.avconcepts.com/

Ávila, I. M. A., & Costa, R. G. (2009). Ícones como facilitadores da interação de usuários iletrados com interfaces computacionais. *Cadernos CPqD Tecnologia, 5*(2), 15–36.

Ayed, D., Delanote, D., & Berbers, Y. (2007). MDD Approach for the Development of Context-Aware Applications. *Proceedings of the6th International and Interdisciplinary Conference (CONTEXT 2007)* (pp. 15-28). Roskilde, Denmark: Springer. doi:10.1007/978-3-540-74255-5_2

Azarkish, H., Faraha, S., Masoud, S., & Sarvari, H. (2012). Comparing the performance of the particle swarm optimization and the genetic algorithm on the geometry design of longitudinal fin. *Inter. J. Of Mech, & Aerospace Engineering, 6*(1), 262–26.

Aziz, K. A., & Siang, T. G. (2014). Virtual Reality and Augmented Reality Combination as a Holistic Application for Heritage Preservation in the UNESCO World Heritage Site of Melaka. *International Journal of Social Science and Humanity, 4*(5), 333–338. doi:10.7763/IJSSH.2014.V4.374

AZORobotics. (2013, June 11). *Applications of Robots to Clean Nuclear Power Plants*. Retrieved from http://www.azorobotics.com/Article.aspx?ArticleID=102

Azuma, R. T. (1997). A survey of augmented reality. *Presence (Cambridge, Mass.), 6*(4), 355–385. doi:10.1162/pres.1997.6.4.355

Bachmann, D., Weichert, F., & Rinkenauer, G. (2014). Evaluation of the Leap Motion Controller as a New Contact-Free Pointing Device. *Sensors (Basel, Switzerland)*, *15*(1), 214–233. doi:10.3390/s150100214 PMID:25609043

Backlund, P., & Hendrix, M. (2013, September). Educational games - Are they worth the effort? A literature survey of the effectiveness of serious games. *Proceedings of the 2013 5th International Conference on Games and Virtual Worlds for Serious Applications (VS-GAMES)*.

Badii, A., Crouch, M., & Lallah, C. (2010). A Context-Awareness Framework for Intelligent Networked Embedded Systems. *Proceedings of theThird International Conference on Advances in Human-Oriented and Personalized Mechanisms, Technologies and Services* (pp. 105-110). Reading, UK: IEEE. doi:10.1109/CENTRIC.2010.29

Badler, N., Phillips, C., & Webber, B. (1993). *Simulating Humans*. Oxford: Oxford Univ. Press.

Badler, N., & Smoliar, S. (1979). Digital representations of human movement. *ACM Computing Surveys*, *11*(1), 19–38. doi:10.1145/356757.356760

Bakker, P., & Kuniyoshi, Y. (1996). Robot see, robot do: An overview of robot imitation. *Proceedings of the AISB96 Workshop on Learning in Robots and Animals* (pp. 3-11).

Balakrishnan, R., & Kurtenbach, G. (1999). Exploring Bimanual Camera Control and Object Manipulation in 3D Graphics Interfaces.*Proceedings of the SIGCHI Conference on Human Factors in Computing Systems: The CHI Is the Limit* (pp. 56–62). doi:10.1145/302979.302991

Balasubramanian, S. K. (1994). Beyond advertising and publicity: Hybrid messages and public policy issues. *Journal of Advertising*, *23*(4), 29–46. doi:10.1080/00913367.1943.10673457

Baldwin, R. (2015). Google's Project Soli to bring gesture control to wearables. *Engadget.com*. Retrieved from http://www.engadget.com/2015/05/29/atap-project-soli/

Baptista, E. A., & Rigotti, J. I. R. (2013). *A população deficiente no estado de Minas Gerais: uma análise exploratória a partir dos censos demográficos de 2000 a 2010. CEDPLAR/UFMG – TD 487(2013)*. Belo Horizonte, MG: FACE/UFMG.

Baranauskas, M. C. C. (2009) Socially aware computing.*Proceedings of the VI International Conference on Engineering and Computer Education* (pp. 1-5).

Barber, P. R., Vojnovic, B., Kelly, J., Mayes, C. R., Boulton, P., Woodcock, M., & Joiner, M. C. (2001). Automated counting of mammalian cell colonies. *Physics in Medicine and Biology*, *46*(1), 63–76. doi:10.1088/0031-9155/46/1/305 PMID:11197679

Barker, K. C. (2005). Linking adult literacy and e-learning a national study conducted for abc Canada literacy foundation 2005. Retrieved from http://www.futured.com /ReturnonInvestmentineLearning-aGuide.pdf.pdf

Barlow, J., Wright, C., Sheasby, J., Turner, A., & Hainsworth, J. (2002). Self-management approaches for people with chronic conditions: A review. *Patient Education and Counseling*, *48*(2), 177–187. doi:10.1016/S0738-3991(02)00032-0 PMID:12401421

Barnum, C. M. (2010). *Usability testing essentials: ready, set... test!* Elsevier.

Barreda, A. A., Bilgihan, A., Nusair, K., & Okumus, F. (2015). Generating brand awareness in Online Social Networks. *Computers in Human Behavior*, *50*, 600–609. doi:10.1016/j.chb.2015.03.023

Bartlett, F. C. (1932). *Remembering: A study in experimental and social psychology London*. Cambridge University Press.

Bassett, L. (2015). *Introduction to JavaScript Object Notation: A To-the-Point Guide to JSON* (1st ed.). O'Reilly Media.

Batra, R., & Ahtola, O. T. (1991). Measuring the hedonic and utilitarian sources of consumer attitudes. *Marketing Letters*, *2*(2), 159–170. doi:10.1007/BF00436035

Baur, T., Mehlmann, G., Damian, I., Lingenfelser, F., Wagner, J., Lugrin, B., & Gebhard, P. (2015). *Context-Aware Automated Analysis and Annotation of Social Human--Agent Interactions. Transactions on Interactive Intelligent Systems, 5(2)*. ACM.

Bay, S. D., Kibler, D., Pazzani, M. J., & Smyth, P. (2000). The UCI KDD archive of large data sets for data mining research and experimentation. *ACM SIGKDD Explorations Newsletter*, *2*(2), 81–85. doi:10.1145/380995.381030

Beach, A., Gartrell, M., Xing, X., Han, R., Lv, Q., Mishra, S., & Seada, K. (2010). Fusing Mobile, Sensor, and Social Data To Fully Enable Context-Aware Computing.*Proceedings of the Eleventh Workshop on Mobile Computing Systems & Application (HotMobile '10)* (pp. 60-65). Annapolis, Maryland: ACM. doi:10.1145/1734583.1734599

Becedas, J., Payo, I., & Feliu, V. (2011). Two-flexible-fingers gripper force feedback control system for its application as end effector on a 6-DOF manipulator. *IEEE Transactions on Robotics*, *27*(3), 599–615. doi:10.1109/TRO.2011.2132850

Beilock, S. L., & Ramirez, G. (2011). 5 On the interplay of emotion and cognitive control: Implications for enhancing academic achievement. *Psychology of Learning and Motivation-Advances in Research and Theory*, *55*, 137–169. doi:10.1016/B978-0-12-387691-1.00005-3

Bellman, S., Kemp, A., Haddad, H., & Varan, D. (2014). The effectiveness of advergames compared to television commercials and interactive commercials featuring advergames. *Computers in Human Behavior*, *32*, 276–283. doi:10.1016/j.chb.2013.12.013

Beltran, V., Arabshian, K., & Schulzrinne, H. (2011). Ontology-based User-defined Rules and Context-aware Service Composition System.*Proceedings of the 8th international conference on The Semantic Web* (pp. 139-155). Heraklion, Greece: ACM.

Benjamin, S., Morris, S., McBeth, J., Macfarlane, G. J., & Silman, A. J. (2000). The association between chronic widespread pain and mental disorder: A population-based study.*Arthritis and Rheumatism*, *43*(3), 561–567. doi:10.1002/1529-0131(200003)43:3<561::AID-ANR12>3.0.CO;2-O PMID:10728749

Benselim, M. S., & Seridi-Bouchelaghem, H. (2013, February). Extending UML Class Diagram Notation for the Development of Context-aware Applications. *Journal of Emerging Technologies in Web Intelligence*, *5*(1), 35–44. doi:10.4304/jetwi.5.1.35-44

Bernsen, N. O., & Dybkjær, L. (2009). *Multimodal Usability*. London: Springer.

Besharat, A., Kumar, A., Lax, J. R., & Rydzik, E. J. (2013). Leveraging virtual attribute experience in video games to improve brand recall and learning. *Journal of Advertising*, *42*(2-3), 170–182. doi:10.1080/00913367.2013.774593

Betters, E. (2015). Virtual Reality: The VR headsets to buy in 2015, whatever your budget. Retrieved from http://www.pocket-lint.com/news/132945-virtual-reality-the-vr-headsets-to-buy-in-2015-whatever-your-budget

Bewes, J. M., Suchowerska, N., & Mckenzie, D. R. (2008). Automated cell colony counting and analysis using the circular Hough image transform algorithm (CHiTA). *Physics in Medicine and Biology*, *53*(21), 5991–6008. doi:10.1088/0031-9155/53/21/007 PMID:18836215

Beynon-Davies, P. (1993). *Information systems development. Houndsmills*. Basingstoke: The Macmillan Press Ltd.

Bhalla, M. R., & Bhalla, A. V. (2010). Comparative study of various touchscreen technologies. *International Journal of Computers and Applications*, *6*(8), 12–18. doi:10.5120/1097-1433

Bhattacharya, S., Czejdo, B., & Perez, N. (2012). Gesture classification with machine learning using Kinect sensor data. *Proceedings of the 2012 Third International Conference on Emerging Applications of Information Technology EAIT* (pp. 348-351). doi:10.1109/EAIT.2012.6407958

Bhattacharyya, S., Saravanagru, R. K., & Thangavelu, A. (2011, May). Context Aware Healthcare Application. *International Journal of Computers and Applications, 22*(3), 7–12.

Bhowmik, A. K. (Ed.), (2014). *Interactive Displays.* Chichester, UK: John Wiley & Sons, Ltd.; doi:10.1002/9781118706237

Bicker, R., Burn, K., Hu, Z., Pongaen, W., & Bashir, A. (2004). The early development of remote tele-manipulation systems. In M. Ceccarelli (Ed.), *Proceedings of the International Symposium on History of Machines and Mechanisms HMM '04* (pp. 391–404).

Bidarra, J., Figueiredo, M. J. G., & Natálio, C. (2014, November 13-14). Designing eBook Interaction for Mobile and Contextual Learning. *Proc. of 2014 International Conference on Interactive Mobile Communication Technologies and Learning,* Thessaloniki, Greece (pp. 11-19). doi:10.1109/IMCTL.2014.7011095

Bidarra, J., Figueiredo, M. J. G., Valadas, S., & Vilhena, C. (2012, November 8-9). O gamebook como modelo pedagógico: desenvolvimento de um livro interativo para a plataforma iPad. *Proc. of 6th International Conference on Digital Arts,* Faro, Portugal (pp. 373-376).

Bidarra, R., Gambon, D., Kooij, R., Nagel, D., Schutjes, M., & Tziouvara, I. (2013). Gaming at the dentist's – serious game design for pain and discomfort distraction. In B. Schouten, S. Fedtke, T. Bekker, M. Schijven, & A. Gekker (Eds.), *Games for Health* (pp. 207–215). Springer Fachmedien Wiesbaden.

Billinghurst, M. (2013). Hands and speech in space. In Proceedings of the 15th ACM on International conference on multimodal interaction - ICMI '13 (pp. 379–380). New York, New York, USA: ACM Press. http://doi.org/doi:10.1145/2522848.2532202

Billinghurst, M., Piumsomboon, T., & Huidong, B. (2014). Hands in Space- Gesture Interaction with Augmented Reality Interfaces. *IEEE Computer Graphics and Applications, 34*(1), 77–80. doi:10.1109/MCG.2014.8 PMID:24808171

Bimber, O., & Raskar, R. (2005). *Spatial Augmented Reality: Merging Real and Virtual Worlds.*

Bimber, O., Zeidler, T., Rundhoefer, A., Wetzstein, G. & Moehring, M. (2005). Interacting with augmented holograms, In SPIE, Practical Holography XIX: Materials and Applications, 41-54.

Binkhorst, E. (2007). Creativity in Tourism Experience- a closer look at sitges. In G. Richards & J. Wilson (Eds.), *Tourism, Creativity and Development* (pp. 125–145). London: Routledge.

Birkfellner, W., Figl, M., Huber, K., Watzinger, F., Wanschitz, F., Hummel, J., & Bergmann, H. et al. (2002). A head-mounted operating binocular for augmented reality visualization in medicine--design and initial evaluation.[Evaluation Studies Research Support, Non-U S Gov't]. *IEEE Transactions on Medical Imaging, 21*(8), 991–997. doi:10.1109/TMI.2002.803099 PMID:12472271

Blackman, S. (2005, February). Serious games … and less! *Computer Graphics, 39*(1), 12–16. doi:10.1145/1057792.1057802

Blattner, M. M., Sumikawa, D. A., & Greenberg, R. M. (1989). Earcon and icons: Their structure and common design principles. *Human-Computer Interaction, 4*(1), 11–44. doi:10.1207/s15327051hci0401_1

Blohm, I., & Leimeister, J. M. (2013). Gamification. *Business & Information Systems Engineering, 5*(4), 275–278. doi:10.1007/s12599-013-0273-5

Blum, T., Kleeberger, V., Bichlmeier, C., & Navab, N. (2012). mirracle: An augmented reality magic mirror system for anatomy education. *Proceedings of the 2012 Virtual Reality conference*. Retrieved from http://doi.ieeecomputersociety. org/10.1109/VR.2012.6180909Doi: 10.1109/VR.2012.6180909

Boccaletti, S., Latora, V., Moreno, Y., Chavez, M., & Hwang, D. U. (2006). Complex networks: Structure and dynamics. *Physics Reports*, *424*(4), 175–308. doi:10.1016/j.physrep.2005.10.009

Bolchini, C., Curino, C. A., Quintarelli, E., Schreiber, F. A., & Tanca, L. (2007, December). A Data-oriented Survey of Context Models. *ACM SIGMOD*, *36*(4), 19–26. doi:10.1145/1361348.1361353

Bolchini, D., Chatterji, R., & Speroni, M. (2009). Developing heuristics for the semiotics inspection of websites. *Proceedings of the SIGDOC '09* (pp. 67–72). doi:10.1145/1621995.1622009

Bolt, R. (1980). Put-that-there.*Proceedings of the 7th annual conference on Computer graphics and interactive techniques - SIGGRAPH '80* (pp. 262–270).

Borrie, W., & Roggenbuck, J. (2001). The Dynamic, Emergent, and Multi-phasic Nature of on-site Wilderness Experiences. *Journal of Leisure Research*, *33*(2), 202.

Borsook, D., & Kalso, E. (2013). Transforming pain medicine: Adapting to science and society. *European Journal of Pain (London, England)*, *17*(8), 1109–1125.

Botella, C. M., Juan, M. C., Banos, R. M., Alcaniz, M., Guillen, V., & Rey, B. (2005). Mixing realities? An application of augmented reality for the treatment of cockroach phobia.[Case Reports]. *Cyberpsychology & Behavior*, *8*(2), 162–171. doi:10.1089/cpb.2005.8.162 PMID:15938656

Botella, C., Bretón-López, J., Quero, S., Baños, R., & García-Palacios, A. (2010). Treating Cockroach Phobia with Augmented Reality. *Behavior Therapy*, *41*(3), 401–413. doi:10.1016/j.beth.2009.07.002 PMID:20569788

Boussemart, Y., Rioux, F., Rudzicz, F., Wozniewski, M., & Cooperstock, J. R. (2004). A framework for 3D visualisation and manipulation in an immersive space using an untethered bimanual gestural interface.*Proceedings of the ACM symposium on Virtual reality software and technology - VRST '04* (pp. 162–165). doi:10.1145/1077534.1077566

Bower, M., Howe, C., McCredie, N., Robinson, A., & Grover, D. (2014). Augmented Reality in education – cases, places and potentials. *Educational Media International*, *51*(1), 1–15. doi:10.1080/09523987.2014.889400

Bowker, G. C., & Star, S. L. (2000). *Sorting Things Out: Classification and Its Consequences*. MIT Press.

Bowman, D. A. (2014). 3D User Interfaces. In M. Soegaard & R. Friis Dam (Eds.), *The Encyclopedia of Human-Computer Interaction* (Ch. 32, 2nd ed.). Aarhus, Denmark: The Interaction Design Foundation. Retrieved from https://www.interaction-design.org/literature/book/the-encyclopedia-of-human-computer-interaction-2nd-ed/3d-user-interfaces

Bowman, D. A., Kruijff, E., LaViola, J. J. Jr, & Poupyrev, I. (2001). An introduction to 3-D user interface design. *Presence (Cambridge, Mass.)*, *10*(1), 96–108. doi:10.1162/105474601750182342

Bowman, D. A., Kruijff, E., Poupyrev, I., & LaViola, J. (2005). *3D User Interfaces: Theory and Practice*. Addison Wesley.

Brandt, E. (2007). How tangible mock-ups support design collaboration. *Knowledge, Technology & Policy*, *20*(3), 179–192. doi:10.1007/s12130-007-9021-9

Brasel, S. A., & Gips, J. (2011). Media multitasking behavior: Concurrent television and computer usage. *Cyberpsychology, Behavior, and Social Networking*, *14*(9), 527–534. doi:10.1089/cyber.2010.0350

Bray, D. (1998). Biofeedback. *Complementary Therapies in Nursing & Midwifery*, *4*(1), 22–24. doi:10.1016/S1353-6117(98)80009-7 PMID:9677930

Bräysy, O., & Gendreau, M. (2002). Tabu Search heuristics for the Vehicle Routing Problem with Time Windows. *Top (Madrid)*, *10*(2), 211–237. doi:10.1007/BF02579017

Breen, A., Bui, H. H., Crouch, R., Farrell, K., Faubel, F., & Gemello, R. … Mulbregt, P. (2014). Voice in the User Interface. In Interactive Displays (pp. 107–163). Chichester, UK: John Wiley & Sons, Ltd. http://doi.org/ doi:<ALIGNMENT.qj></ALIGNMENT>10.1002/9781118706237.ch3

Breivik, H., Eisenberg, E., & O'Brien, T. (2013). The individual and societal burden of chronic pain in Europe: The case for strategic prioritisation and action to improve knowledge and availability of appropriate care. *BMC Public Health*, *13*(1), 1229. doi:10.1186/1471-2458-13-1229 PMID:24365383

Brennan, I., & Babin, L. A. (2004). Brand placement recognition: The influence of presentation mode and brand familiarity. *Journal of Promotion Management*, *10*(1–2), 185–202. doi:10.1300/J057v10n01_13

Bronzino, J. D., & Peterson, D. R. (2014). *Biomedical engineering fundamental* (4th ed.). CRC Press.

Brown, E., & Cairns, P. (2004). A Grounded Investigation of Game Immersion. Proceedings of the CHI '04 Extended Abstracts on Human Factors in Computing Systems (pp. 1297–1300). New York, NY, USA: ACM.

Brown, J.S., Collins, A., & Duguid, P. (1989). Situated cognition and the culture of learning. *Educational Researcher*, *18*(1), 32–42.

Brown, J. S., Collins, A., & Duguid, P. (1989). Situated cognition and the culture. *Educational Researcher*, *18*(1), 32–42. doi:10.3102/0013189X018001032

Brown, P. J., Bovey, J. D., & Chen, X. (1997). Context-aware applications: From the laboratory to the marketplace. *IEEE Personal Communications*, *4*(5), 58–64. doi:10.1109/98.626984

Brugger, S. D., Baumberger, C., Jost, M., Jenni, W., Brugger, U., & Mühlemann, K. (2012). Automated counting of bacterial colony forming units on agar plates. *PLoS ONE*, *7*(3), e33695. doi:10.1371/journal.pone.0033695 PMID:22448267

Brugger, S. D., Baumberger, C., Jost, M., Jenni, W., Brugger, U., & Muhlemann, K. (2 012). Automated Counting of Bacterial Colony Forming Units on Agar Plates. *PLoS ONE*, *7*(3).

Brünken, R., Plass, J. L., & Leutner, D. (2003). Direct measurement of cognitive load in multimedia learning. *Educational Psychologist*, *38*(1), 53–61. doi:10.1207/S15326985EP3801_7

Buhalis, D., & Amaranggana, A. (2013). Smart tourism destinations. In Z. Xiang & L. Tussyadiah (Eds.), *Information and Communication Technologies in Tourism 2014* (pp. 553–564). Springer International Publishing. doi:10.1007/978-3-319-03973-2_40

Buhalis, D., & Law, R. (2008). Progress in information technology and tourism management. 20 years on and 10 years after the internet. The state of etourism research. *Tourism Management*, *29*(4), 609–623. doi:10.1016/j.tourman.2008.01.005

Buijzen, M., Van Reijmersdal, E. A., & Owen, L. H. (2010). Introducing the PCMC model: An investigative framework for young people's processing of commercial media content. *Communication Theory*, *20*(4), 427–450. doi:10.1111/j.1468-2885.2010.01370.x

Bulling, A., Blanke, U., & Schiele, B. (2014). *A tutorial on human activity recognition using body-worn inertial sensors. ACM Computing Surveys, 46(3)*. ACM.

Bullmore, E., & Sporns, O. (2009). Complex brain networks: Graph theoretical analysis of structural and functional systems. *Nature Reviews. Neuroscience*, *10*(3), 186–198. doi:10.1038/nrn2575 PMID:19190637

Burke, J. W., McNeill, M. D. J., Charles, D. K., Morrow, P. J., Crosbie, J. H., & McDonough, S. M. (2010, March 25-26). Augmented Reality Games for Upper-Limb Stroke Rehabilitation. *Paper presented at the 2010 Second International Conference on Games and Virtual Worlds for Serious Applications (VS-GAMES).*

Burke, J. L., Prewett, M. S., Gray, A. A., Yang, L., Stilson, F. R., & Redden, E. (2006). Comparing the effects of visual-auditory and visual-tactile feedback on user performance: a meta-analysis.*Proceedings of the 8th international conference on Multimodal interfaces* (pp. 108-117). doi:10.1145/1180995.1181017

Burke, M., & Hiltbrand, T. (2011). How gamification will change business intelligence. *Business Intelligence Journal, 16*(2), 8–16.

Burkhard, M., & Koch, M. (2012). *Evaluating Touchscreen Interfaces of Tablet Computers for Elderly People* (pp. 53–59). Mensch & Computer Workshopband.

Burr, W. E., Dodson, D. F., & Polk, W. T. (2004). *Electronic authentication guideline* (pp. 800–863). US Department of Commerce, Technology Administration, National Institute of Standards and Technology.

Business Insider. (2014). *Smart TVs are on pace to take over the entire TV market.* Retrieved from http://www.businessinsider.com/smart-tvs-are-on-pace-to-take-over-the-entire-tv-market-2014-7#ixzz3fwn3kdUm

Butler, A., Hilliges, O., Izadi, S., Hodges, S., Molyneaux, D., Kim, D., & Kong, D. (2011). Vermeer: direct interaction with a 360° viewable 3D display. *Proceedings of the24th Annual ACM Symposium on User Interface Software and Technology* (pp. 569-576). doi:10.1145/2047196.2047271

Buur, J., & Binder, T. (2006). *User Centred Product Design. MCI.* University of Southern Denmark.

Calvert, T., & Chapman, A. (1994). Analysis and synthesis of human movement. In T. Young (Ed.), *Handbook of Pattern Recognition and Image Processing: Computer Vision* (pp. 432–474). San Diego: Academic Press.

Camastra, F., & De Felice, D. (2013). LVQ-Based Hand Gesture Recognition Using a Data Glove. In *Neural Nets and Surroundings* (pp. 159–168). doi:10.1007/978-3-642-35467-0_17

Camerer, C. (2003). *Behavioral game theory: Experiments in strategic interaction.* Princeton, NJ: Princeton University Press.

Cao, Y., Klamma, R., Hou, M., & Jarke, M. (2008). Follow Me, Follow You - Spatiotemporal Community Context Modeling and Adaptation for Mobile Information Systems.*9th International Conference on Mobile Data Management* (pp. 108-115). Beijing: ACM. doi:10.1109/MDM.2008.30

Cardoso, P. J. S., Schütz, G., Mazayev, A., & Ey, E. (2015a). Solutions in Under 10 Seconds for Vehicle Routing Problems with Time Windows Using Commodity Computers. In A. Gaspar-Cunha, C. H. Antunes, & C. C. Coello (Eds.), *Evolutionary Multi-Criterion Optimization* (pp. 418–432). Springer International Publishing; doi:10.1007/978-3-319-15892-1_28

Cardoso, P. J. S., Schütz, G., Mazayev, A., Ey, E., & Corrêa, T. (2015b). A Solution for a Real-time Stochastic Capacitated Vehicle Routing Problem with Time Windows. *Procedia Computer Science, 51,* 2227–2236. doi:10.1016/j.procs.2015.05.501

Card, S. K., Moran, T. P., & Newell, A. (1980). The keystroke-level model for user performance time with interactive systems. *Communications of the ACM, 23*(7), 396–410. doi:10.1145/358886.358895

Caric, T., & Gol, H. (2008). Vehicle Routing Problem. (T. Caric & H. Gol, Eds.). InTech. http://doi.org/ doi:<ALIGNMENT.qj></ALIGNMENT>10.5772/64

Carlisle, J. H. (1976, June 07-10). Evaluating the impact of office automation on top management communication. *Proceeding of the National Computer Conference and Exposition AFIPS*, 1976 (p. 611). New York, USA: ACM Press. http://doi.org/ doi:10.1145/1499799.1499885

Carlsson, S. A. (2005). Developing Information systems design knowledge: A critical realist perspective. *The Electronic Journal of Business Research Methodology*, *3*(2), 93–102.

Carrino, F., Rizzotti, D., Gheorghe, C., Kabasu Bakajika, P., Francescotti-Paquier, F., & Mugellini, E. (2014). Augmented Reality Treatment for Phantom Limb Pain. In R. Shumaker & S. Lackey (Eds.), *Virtual, Augmented and Mixed Reality. Applications of Virtual and Augmented Reality, LNCS* (Vol. 8526, pp. 248–257). Springer International Publishing. doi:10.1007/978-3-319-07464-1_23

Carroll, J. M. (2014). Human Computer Interaction - brief intro. In M. Soegaard & R. F. Dam (Eds.), *The Encyclopedia of Human-Computer Interaction* (2nd ed.). Aarhus, Denmark: The Interaction Design Foundation.

Carter, I., Leslie, D., & Kwan, D. (2012). Applying universal instructional design to course websites by using course evaluations. *Collected Essays on Learning and Teaching*, *5*(21), 119–125.

Cary, S. (2004). The tourist moment. *Annals of Tourism Research*, *31*(1), 61–77. doi:10.1016/j.annals.2003.03.001

Casas, X., Herrera, G., Coma, I., & Fernández, M. (2012). A Kinect-based augmented reality system for individuals with autism spectrum disorders. *Paper presented at the Computer Graphics Theory and Applications*, Rome, Italy.

Cassell, J., Pelachaud, C., Badler, N., Steedman, M., Achorn, B., Becket, T., . . . Stone, M. (1994). Animated conversation: rule-based generation of facial expression, gesture & spoken intonation for multiple conversational agents. Proceedings of ACM SIGGRAPH. doi:10.1145/192161.192272

Castelli, G., & Zambonelli, F. (2009). Contextual Data Management and Retrieval: A Self-Organized Approach. *Proceedings of the IEEE/WIC/ACM International Joint Conferences on Web Intelligence and Intelligent Agent Technologies WI-IAT '09* (pp. 535-538). Milan, Italy: IEEE.

Castilla, D., Garcia-Palacios, A., Breton-Lopez, J., Miralles, I., Baños, R. M., Etchemendy, E., & Botella, C. et al. (2013). Process of design and usability evaluation of a telepsychology web and virtual reality system for the elderly: Butler. *International Journal of Human-Computer Studies*, *71*(3), 350–362. doi:10.1016/j.ijhcs.2012.10.017

Castro, A., & McDonald, K. (2012). Faces - 2012 Retrieved from http://arturocastro.net/work/faces.html

Castro-Gutierrez, J., Landa-Silva, D., & Moreno Perez, J. (2011). Nature of real-world multi-objective vehicle routing with evolutionary algorithms. *Proceeding of the 2011 IEEE International Conference on Systems, Man, and Cybernetics* (pp. 257–264). IEEE. http://doi.org/ doi:10.1109/ICSMC.2011.6083675

Cauberghe, V., & DePelsmacker, P. (2010). Advergames. *Journal of Advertising*, *39*(1), 5–18. doi:10.2753/JOA0091-3367390101

Cauberghe, V., Geuens, M., & De Pelsmacker, P. (2011). Context effects of TV programme-induced interactivity and telepresence on advertising responses. *International Journal of Advertising*, *30*(4), 641–663. doi:10.2501/IJA-30-4-641-663

Caudell, T. P., & Mizell, D. W. (1992, January 7-10). Augmented reality: an application of heads-up display technology to manual manufacturing processes. *Paper presented at the Twenty-Fifth Hawaii International Conference on System Sciences*. doi:10.1109/HICSS.1992.183317

Chai, X., Li, G., Lin, Y., Xu, Z., Tang, Y., Chen, X., & Zhou, M. (2013). Sign language recognition and translation with Kinect. *Proceedings of the IEEE Conf. on AFGR*.

Chaiamnuay, P., Darmawan, J., Muirden, K. D., & Assawatanabodee, P. (1998). Epidemiology of rheumatic disease in rural Thailand: A WHO-ILAR COPCORD study. Community Oriented Programme for the Control of Rheumatic Disease. *The Journal of Rheumatology*, 25(7), 1382–1387. PMID:9676773

Chan, B. L., Witt, R., Charrow, A. P., Magee, A., Howard, R., Pasquina, P. F., & Tsao, J. W. et al. (2007). Mirror Therapy for Phantom Limb Pain. *The New England Journal of Medicine*, 357(21), 2206–2207. doi:10.1056/NEJMc071927 PMID:18032777

Chaney, I. M., Lin, K. H., & Chaney, J. (2004). The effect of billboards within the gaming environment. *Journal of Interactive Advertising*, 5(1), 37–45. doi:10.1080/15252019.2004.10722092

Chang, K.-L., Fillingim, R., Hurley, R. W., & Schmidt, S. (2015). Chronic pain management: Nonpharmacological therapies for chronic pain. *FP Essentials*, 432, 21–26. PMID:25970869

Chaparro, A., Rogers, M., Fernandez, J., Bohan, M., Choi, S., & Stumpfhauser, L. (2000). Range of motion of the wrist: Implications for designing computer input devices for the elderly. *Disability and Rehabilitation*, 22(13-14), 633–637. doi:10.1080/09638280050138313 PMID:11052213

Charlesa, S., & Hogan, N. (2012). *Dynamics of wrist rotations. Journal of biomechanics*. Elsevier B.V.

Chen, G., & Kotz, D. (2000). A Survey of Context-Aware Mobile Computing Research. Dartmouth College, Hanover, New Hampshire. Retrieved from http://www.cs.dartmouth.edu/reports/TR2000-381.pdf

Chen, H., Finin, T., & Joshi, A. (2003). An Intelligent Broker for Context-Aware Systems (CoBrA). *Proceedings of the Fifth International Conference on Ubiquitous Computing Ubicomp '03* (pp. 183-184). Seattle: ACM.

Chen, L., & Ding, Q., Zhao & X., Han, J., (2011). Hierarchical projected regression for torque of elbow joint using EMG signals. *Proceedings of the5th International Conference on Bioinformatics and Biomedicals Eng.* (pp. 1-5). doi:10.1109/icbbe.2011.5780183

Cheng, C.-M., Chung, M.-F., Yu, M.-Y., Ouhyoung, M., Chu, H.-H., & Chuang, Y.-Y. (2008). Chromirror: a real-time interactive mirror for chromatic and color-harmonic dressing. *Paper presented at theCHI '08 Extended Abstracts on Human Factors in Computing Systems*, Florence, Italy. doi:10.1145/1358628.1358762

Cheng, H., Yang, L., & Liu, Z. (2015). A Survey on 3D Hand Gesture Recognition. *IEEE Transactions on Circuits and Systems for Video Technology*, 1. doi:10.1109/TCSVT.2015.2469551

Chen, H., Finin, T., & Joshi, A. (2003). An Ontology for Context-Aware Pervasive Computing Environments. *The Knowledge Engineering Review*, 18(3), 197–207. doi:10.1017/S0269888904000025

Chen, H.-K., Hsueh, C.-F., & Chang, M.-S. (2009). Production scheduling and vehicle routing with time windows for perishable food products. *Computers & Operations Research*, 36(7), 2311–2319. doi:10.1016/j.cor.2008.09.010

Chen, L., & Nugent, C. (2009). Ontology-based Activity Recognition in Intelligent Pervasive Environments. *International Journal of Web Information Systems*, 5(4), 410–430. doi:10.1108/17440080911006199

Chen, L., Wei, H., & Ferryman, J. (2013). A survey of human motion analysis using depth imagery. *Pattern Recognition Letters*, 34(15).

Chen, W. (2014). Historical Oslo on a handheld device–a mobile augmented reality application. *Procedia Computer Science*, 35, 979–985. doi:10.1016/j.procs.2014.08.180

Chernova, S., & Thomaz, A. (2014). *Robot Learning from Human Teachers*. Morgan & Claypool Publishers.

Chiang, I., Tsai, J. C., & Chen, S. T. (2012). Using Xbox 360 Kinect games on enhancing visual performance skills on institutionalized older adults with wheelchairs. Proceedings of the IEEE 4th International Conference on Digital Game and Intelligent Toy Enhanced Learning (DIGITEL) (pp. 263-267).

Chiang, P., Tseg, M.-J., He, Z.-S., & Li, C.-H. (2015). Automated counting of bacterial colonies by image analysis. *Journal of Microbiological Methods, 108*, 74–82. doi:10.1016/j.mimet.2014.11.009 PMID:25451456

Chiesa, A., & Serretti, A. (2009). Mindfulness-based stress reduction for stress management in healthy people: A review and meta-analysis. *Journal of Alternative and Complementary Medicine (New York, N.Y.), 15*(5), 593–600. doi:10.1089/acm.2008.0495 PMID:19432513

Chihani, B., Bertin, E., Jeanne, F., & Crespi, N. (2011). Context-aware systems: a case study. *Proceedings of theInternational Conference on Digital Information and Communication Technology and its Applications (DICTAP '11)* (pp. 718-732). Dijon, France: Springer. doi:10.1007/978-3-642-22027-2_60

Chimes, G. P., Bernstein, C. D., Cortazzo, M. H., & Huber, L. M. (2009). Poster presentation. *PM & R, 1*(9Suppl.), S220. doi:10.1016/j.pmrj.2009.08.290

Chinthaka, M. K. C. D., & Abeykoon, A. M. H. S. (2015, May). Friction compensation of DC motors for precise motion control using disturbance observer. *ECTI Transactions on Computer And Information Technology, 9*, 66–74.

Chinthaka, M. K. C. D., Punchihewa, R. U. G., & Abeykoon, A. M. H. S. (2014). Disturbance observer based friction compensator for a DC motor.*Proceedings of 2014 11th International Conference on Electrical Engineering/Electronics, Computer, Telecommunications and Information Technology (ECTI-CON)* (pp. 1-6). IEEE. doi:10.1109/ECTI-Con.2014.6839747

Chodorow, K. (2013). *MongoDB: The Definitive Guide.* O'Reilly Media.

Cholinski, A. (2012). The effectiveness of product placement: A field quasi-experiment. *International Journal of Marketing Studies, 4*(5), 14. doi:10.5539/ijms.v4n5p14

Chopra, A., & Narang, N. (2014). The Sixth Sense Technology and Its Various Security Threats. *International Journal of Information & Computation Technology, 4*(7), 663-670.

Chow, A. F., Woodford, K. C., & Maes, J. (2011). Deal or No Deal: Using games to improve student learning, retention and decision-making. *International Journal of Mathematical Education in Science and Technology, 42*(2), 259–264. doi:10.1080/0020739X.2010.519796

Christie, A. (1985). The thumbmark of St. Peter. In *Miss. Marple: The complete short stories* (pp. 72–86). New York: G. P. Putnam's Sons.

Cinto, T., Ávila, I. M. A., & de Souza, F. (2015). Inclusive Participatory Workshop: Accessible Iconography Design. *International Journal of Digital Information and Wireless Communication, 5*(3), 158–164. doi:10.17781/P001676

Cioara, T., Anghel, I., Salomie, I., & Dinsoreanu, M. (2009, June1). A generic context model enhanced with self-configuring features. *Journal of Digital Information Management, 7*(3), 159–166.

Cippitelli, E., Gasparrini, S., Gambi, E., & Spinsante, S. (2014). Depth stream compression for enhanced real time fall detection by multiple sensors. *Proceedings of the IEEE Fourth International Conference on Consumer Electronics, Berlin (ICCE-Berlin)* (pp. 29-30). doi:10.1109/ICCE-Berlin.2014.7034215

Cirtea, M. C., & Levin, M. F. (2000). Compensatory strategy for reaching stroke. *Brain, 123*(5), 940–953. doi:10.1093/brain/123.5.940 PMID:10775539

Clarke, M. L., Burton, R. L., Hill, A. N., Litorja, M., Nahm, M. H., & Hwang, J. (2010). Low-cost, high-throughput, automated counting of bacterial colonies. *Cytometry. Part A*, *77*(8), 790–797. doi:10.1002/cyto.a.20864 PMID:20140968

Clark, J. M., & Paivio, A. (1991). Dual coding theory and education. *Educational Psychology Review*, *3*(3), 149–210. doi:10.1007/BF01320076

Claydon, M. (2015). Alternative realities: from augmented reality to mobile mixed reality.

Cober, R., Au, O., & Son, J. J. (2012). Using a participatory approach to design a technology-enhanced museum tour for visitors who are blind.*Proceedings of the 2012 iConference*, New York (pp. 592-594). doi:10.1145/2132176.2132301

Cohen, E. (1979). A Phenomenology of Tourist Type. *Sociology*, *13*(2), 179–201. doi:10.1177/003803857901300203

Coleman, G. W., Gibson, L., Hanson, V. L., Bobrowicz, A., & Mckay, A. (2010, August). Engaging the disengaged: how do we design technology for digitally excluded older adults?*Proceedings of the 8th ACM Conference on Designing Interactive Systems* (pp. 175-178). ACM. doi:10.1145/1858171.1858202

Collins, K., Palmer, A., & Rathrnill, K. (1985). The Development of a European Benchmark for the Comparison of Assembly Robot Programming Systems. In R. K. (Ed.), Robot technology and Applications (pp. 187-199). Berlin: Springer. doi:10.1007/978-3-662-02440-9_18

Collins, A., Greeno, J., & Resnick, L. (1992). *Cognition and learning. B. Berliner & R. Calfee, Handbook of Educational Psychology*. New York: Simon & Shuster MacMillan.

Connolly, T. M., Stansfield, M., & Hainey, T. (2011). An alternate reality game for language learning: ARGuing for multilingual motivation. *Computers & Education*, *57*(1), 1389–1415. doi:10.1016/j.compedu.2011.01.009

Connors, M. H., & Coltheart, M. (2011). On the behaviour of senile dementia patients vis-à-vis the mirror: Ajuriaguerra, Strejilevitch and Tissot (1963). *Neuropsychologia*, *49*(7), 1679–1692. doi:10.1016/j.neuropsychologia.2011.02.041 PMID:21356221

Cooper, R. A., Dieranno, B. E., Brewer, B., LoPresti, E., Ding, D., Simpson, R., & Wang, H. et al. (2008). A perspective on intelligent devices and environments in medical rehabilitation. *Journal of Med. Eng & Physics*, *30*(10), 1387–1398. doi:10.1016/j.medengphy.2008.09.003 PMID:18993108

Corkidi, G., Diaz-Uribe, R., Folch-Mallol, J. L., & Nieto-Sotelo, J. (1998). COVASIAM: An image analysis method that allows detection of confluent microbial colonies and colonies of various sizes for automated counting. *Applied and Environmental Microbiology*, *64*(4), 1400–1404. PMID:9546177

Correa, A. G. D., Ficheman, I. K., do Nascimento, M., & De Deus Lopes, R. (2009, 15-17 July 2009). Computer Assisted Music Therapy: A Case Study of an Augmented Reality Musical System for Children with Cerebral Palsy Rehabilitation. *Paper presented at the Ninth IEEE International Conference on Advanced Learning Technologies ICALT '09.*

Costa, L. D. F., Oliveira Jr, O. N., Travieso, G., Rodrigues, F. A., Villas Boas, P. R., & Antiqueira, L. et al.. (2011). Analyzing and modeling real-world phenomena with complex networks: A survey of applications. *Advances in Physics*, *60*(3), 329–412. doi:10.1080/00018732.2011.572452

Costa, L. D. F., Rodrigues, F. A., Travieso, G., & Villas Boas, P. R. (2007). Characterization of complex networks: A survey of measurements. *Advances in Physics*, *56*(1), 167–242. doi:10.1080/00018730601170527

Crompton, J. L., & McKay, S. L. (1997). Motives of visitors attending festival events. *Annals of Tourism Research*, *24*(2), 425–439. doi:10.1016/S0160-7383(97)80010-2

Crowley, J. L., Coutaz, J., & Bérard, F. (2000). Perceptual user interfaces: Things that see. *Communications of the ACM*, *43*(3), 54–64, ff. doi:10.1145/330534.330540

Cruz, L., Lucio, D., & Velho, L. (2012). Kinect and RGDB images: Challenges and applications. *Proceedings of the Conference on Graphics, Patterns and Images Tutorials (SIBGRAPI-T)* (pp. 36-49).

Csapó, J. (2012). The role and importance of cultural tourism in modern tourism industry. In M. Kasimoglu (Ed.), *Strategies for Tourism Industry - Micro and Macro Perspectives* (pp. 201–232). Rijeka, Croatia: InTech Open Access Publisher. doi:10.5772/38693

Cui, J., & Sourin, A. (2014). Feasibility Study on Free Hand Geometric Modelling Using Leap Motion in VRML/X3D. *Proceeding of the 2014 International Conference on Cyberworlds* (pp. 389–392). IEEE. http://doi.org/ doi:10.1109/CW.2014.60

Ćukušić, M., Alfirević, N., Granić, A., & Garača, Ž. (2010). E-learning process management and the e-learning performance: Results of a European empirical study. *Computers & Education*, *55*(2), 554–565. doi:10.1016/j.compedu.2010.02.017

Cullen, K., Dolphin, C., Delaney, S., & Fitzpatrick, M. (2008). Survey of older people and ICTS in Ireland. *Age Action*, 27. Retrieved from http://www.ageaction.ie/userfiles/.../survey-of-older-people-andicts-in-ireland.pdf

Cutler, S. Q., & Carmichael, B. A. (2010). The Dimensions of the Tourist Experience, The Tourism and Leisure Experience Consumer and Managerial Perspectives. In M. Morgan, P. Lugosi, & J. R. Brant Ritchie (Eds.), *Aspects of Tourism* (pp. 3–26). Toronto: Channel View Publications.

Cycling. (2015). Cycling '74 MAX. Retrieved from https://cycling74.com/

Czaja, S. J. (2005). The impact of aging on access to technology. In: *Accessibility and computing*, SIGACCESS Newsletter, 83, 711. Retrieved from http://www.sigaccess.org/wp-content/uploads/formidable/sep05_all.pdf

D'Strict. (2014). 3D sensing holographic installation. Retrieved from http://global.dstrict.com/projects/j4.php

Dadwal, S. S., & Hassan, A. (2015). The augmented reality marketing-a merger of marketing and technology in tourism. In N. Ray (Ed.), *Emerging Innovative Marketing Strategies in the Tourism Industry* (pp. 78–96). Hershey, PA: IGI Global. doi:10.4018/978-1-4666-8699-1.ch005

Dahle, J., Kakar, M., Steen, H. B., & Kaalhus, O. (2004). Automated counting of mammalian cell colonies by means of a flat bed scanner and image processing. *Cytometry. Part A*, *60*(2), 182–188. doi:10.1002/cyto.a.20038 PMID:15290719

Dahl, S., Eagle, L., & Báez, C. (2009). Analyzing advergames: Active diversions or actually deception. An exploratory study of online advergames content. *Young Consumers*, *10*(1), 46–59. doi:10.1108/17473610910940783

Dalgarno, B., & Lee, M. J. (2010). What are the learning affordances of 3-D virtual environments? *British Journal of Educational Technology*, *41*(1), 10–32. doi:10.1111/j.1467-8535.2009.01038.x

Davies, J., & Graff, M. (2005). Performance in e-learning: Online participation and student grades. *British Journal of Educational Technology*, *36*(4), 657–663. doi:10.1111/j.1467-8535.2005.00542.x

Davis, F. D. (1989). Perceived usefulness, perceived ease of use, and user acceptance of information technology. *Management Information Systems Quarterly*, *13*(3), 319–340. doi:10.2307/249008

Davis, R., Piven, I., & Breazeale, M. (2014). Conceptualizing the brand in social media community: The five sources model. *Journal of Retailing and Consumer Services*, *21*(4), 468–481. doi:10.1016/j.jretconser.2014.03.006

De Moor, A., & Weigand, H. (2007). Formalizing the evolution of virtual communities. *Information Systems*, *32*(2), 223–247. doi:10.1016/j.is.2005.09.002

De Santis, A., Gambi, E., Montanini, L., Pelliccioni, G., Raffaeli, L., Rascioni, G., & Spinsante, S. (2015, May). Smart Homes for Independent and Active Ageing: Outcomes from the TRASPARENTE Project. *Paper presented at the 2015 Italian Forum on Ambient Assisted Living*, Lecco, Italy.

De Souze, C. S. (2005). *The Semiotic Engineering of Human-Computer Interaction*. Cambridge: MIT Press.

Demiris, J., & Hayes, G. (2002). f 3 Imitation as a Dual-Route Process Featuring Predictive and Learning Components; 4 Biologically Plausible Computational Model. In *Imitation in animals and artifacts* (p. 327).

Derboven, J., Geerts, D., & Grooff, D. D. (2013). Researching user interpretation beyond designer intentions.*Proceedings of the extended Abstracts CHI '13* (pp. 367-372). ACM Press.

Desmond, D. M., O'Neill, K., Paor, A. D., McDarby, G., & MacLachlan, M. (2006). Augmenting the Reality of Phantom Limbs: Three Case Studies Using an Augmented Mirror Box Procedure. *Journal of Prosthetics and Orthotics*, *18*(3), 74–79. doi:10.1097/00008526-200607000-00005

Deterding, S., Dixon, D., Khaled, R., & Nacke, L. (2011). From game design elements to gamefulness: defining gamification.*Proceedings of the 15th International Academic MindTrek Conference: Envisioning Future Media Environments* (pp. 9-15). New York, NY: ACM. doi:10.1145/2181037.2181040

Dey, A. K. (2001). Understanding and using context. *Personal and Ubiquitous Computing*, *5*(1), 4–7. doi:10.1007/s007790170019

Dias, P., Parracho, J., Cardoso, J., Quintino Ferreira, B., Ferreira, C., & Sousa Santos, B. (2015). Developing and evaluating two gestural-based virtual environment navigation methods for large displays. Proceedings of Human-Computer Interaction (HCI) International 2015, Chapter Distributed, Ambient, and Pervasive Interactions (LNCS) (Vol. 9189, pp. 141-151). Springer. doi:10.1007/978-3-319-20804-6_13

Dias, P., Sousa, T., Parracho, J., Cardoso, I., Monteiro, A., & Sousa Santos, B. (2014). Student Projects Involving Novel Interaction with Large Displays. *IEEE Computer Graphics and Applications*, *34*(2), 80–86. doi:10.1109/MCG.2014.35 PMID:24808202

Díaz, I., Hernantes, J., Mansa, I., Lozano, A., Borro, D., Gil, J. J., & Sánchez, E. (2006). Influence of multisensory feedback on haptic accessibility tasks. *Virtual Reality (Waltham Cross)*, *10*(10), 31–40. doi:10.1007/s10055-006-0028-4

Dick, W. (1997). A model for the systematic design of instruction. In R. Tennyson, F. Schott, N. Seel, & S. Dijkstra (Eds.), Instructional design: International perspectives (Vol. 1: Theory, research and models, pp. 361-369). Mahwah, New Jersey: Lawrence Erlbaum Associates.

Dick, J., Almeida, H., Soares, L. D., & Nunes, P. (2011) 3D Holoscopic video coding using MVC, In *IEEE International Conference on Computer as a Tool (EUROCON)*, 1-4. doi:10.1109/EUROCON.2011.5929394

Dieguez, S., Scherer, J., & Blanke, O. (2011). My face through the looking-glass: The effect of mirror reversal on reflection size estimation. *Consciousness and Cognition*, *20*(4), 1452–1459. doi:10.1016/j.concog.2011.06.003 PMID:21723147

Difei, T., Juyong, Z., Ketan, T., Lingfeng, X., & Lu, F. (2014, 14-18 July 2014). *Making 3D Eyeglasses Try-on practical*. Paper presented at the 2014 IEEE International Conference on Multimedia and Expo Workshops (ICMEW).

Dipietro, L., Sabatini, A. M., & Dario, P. (2008). A Survey of Glove-Based Systems and Their Applications. *IEEE Transactions on Systems, Man and Cybernetics. Part C, Applications and Reviews*, *38*(4), 461–482. doi:10.1109/TSMCC.2008.923862

Dix, A., Finlay, J. E., Abowd, G. D., & Beale, R. (2003). Human-Computer Interaction (3 ed.). Prentice-Hall.

Dix, A., Rodden, T., Davies, N., Trevor, J., Friday, A., & Palfreyman, K. (2000). Exploiting space and location as a design framework for interactive mobile systems. *ACM Transactions on Computer-Human Interaction*, 7(3), 285–321. doi:10.1145/355324.355325

Djedidi, A., Selliez-Vandernotte, C., & Malcolm, F. (2015, January 7). Hot cell robot. *Nuclear Engineering International*. Retrieved from http://www.neimagazine.com/features/featurehot-cell-robot-4483658/

Dohle, C., Pullen, J., Nakaten, A., Kust, J., Rietz, C., & Karbe, H. (2009). Mirror therapy promotes recovery from severe hemiparesis: A randomized controlled trial. *Neurorehabilitation and Neural Repair*, 23(3), 209–217. doi:10.1177/1545968308324786 PMID:19074686

Doi, K. (2007). Computer-Aided Diagnosis in Medical Imaging: Historical Review, Current Status and Future Potential. *Computerized medical imaging and graphics: the official journal of the Computerized Medical Imaging Society, 31*(4-5), 198-211. doi:10.1016/j.compmedimag.2007.02.002

Dollar, A. M., & Herr, H. (2008). Lower extremity exoskeletons and active orthoses: Challenges and state of art. *IEEE Transactions on Robotics*, 24(1), 144–158. doi:10.1109/TRO.2008.915453

Draganić, T., & Rajević, D. (2011). Impact of IT and other technologies to Religious Tourism. *International Journal of Economics and Law*, 1(2), 31–40.

Driscoll, M. P. (2000). *Psychology of learning for instruction*. Boston: Allyn and Bacon.

Dubey, R., Gunasekaran, A., & Chakrabarty, A. (2015). Ubiquitous manufacturing: overview, framework and further research directions. *International Journal of Computer Integrated Manufacturing*,.

Duggal, A., Misra, M., & Srinivasaraghavan, R. (2012). Categorising Context and Using Short Term Contextual Information to Obtain Long Term Context. *Proceedings of the 11th International Conference on Trust, Security and Privacy in Computing and Communications* (pp. 1771 - 1776). Liverpool, UK: IEEE. doi:10.1109/TrustCom.2012.2

Duñabeitia, J. A., Molinaro, N., & Carreiras, M. (2011). Through the looking-glass: Mirror reading. *NeuroImage*, 54(4), 3004–3009. doi:10.1016/j.neuroimage.2010.10.079 PMID:21056672

Dunleavy, M., & Dede, C. (2014). Augmented reality teaching and learning. In *Handbook of research on educational communications and technology* (pp. 735–745). New York, NY: Springer New York. doi:10.1007/978-1-4614-3185-5_59

Edwards, L. (2015). Future batteries, coming soon: charge in seconds, last months and power over the air. *Pocket Lint. com.* Retrieved from http://www.pocket-lint.com/news/130380-future-batteries-coming-soon-charge-in-seconds-last-months-and-power-over-the-air

Einsiedler, W. (1997). Research on instructional methods: An European perspective. In R. Tennyson, F. Schott, N. Seel, & S. Dijkstra (Eds.), Instructional design: International perspectives (Vol. 1: Theory, research and models, pp. 1-16). Mahwah, New Jersey: Lawrence Erlbaum Associates.

Eisert, P., Fechteler, P., & Rurainsky, J. (2008, June 23-28). 3-D Tracking of shoes for Virtual Mirror applications. *Paper presented at the IEEE Conference on Computer Vision and Pattern Recognition CVPR '08*.

Eksioglu, B., Vural, A. V., & Reisman, A. (2009). The vehicle routing problem: A taxonomic review. *Computers & Industrial Engineering*, 57(4), 1472–1483. doi:10.1016/j.cie.2009.05.009

El-laithy, R. A., Huang, J., & Yeh, M. (2012). Study on the use of Microsoft Kinect for robotics applications. *Proceedings of the 2012 IEEE/ION Position, Location and Navigation Symposium* (pp. 1280–1288). IEEE. http://doi.org/ doi:10.1109/PLANS.2012.6236985

Ellekilde, L. P., & Jorgensen, J. A. (2010, June). Robwork: A flexible toolbox for robotics research and education. *Proceedings of the 2010 41st International Symposium on and 2010 6th German Conference on Robotics (ROBOTIK)* (pp. 1-7). VDE.

Elliptic-Labs. (2015). Ultrasound Gesture Recognition. Retrieved from http://www.ellipticlabs.com/

Ellis, T. J., & Levy, Y. (2010). A guide for novice researchers: Design and development research methods. *Proceedings of Informing Science & IT Educational Conference (InSITE)*. Retrieved from http://citeseerx.ist.psu.edu/viewdoc/download?doi=10.1.1.170.2962&rep=rep1&type=pdf

Emmanouilidis, C., Koutsiamanis, R.-A., & Tasidou, A. (2013, January). Mobile guides: Taxonomy of architectures, context awareness, technologies and applications. *Journal of Network and Computer Applications*, *36*(1), 103–125. doi:10.1016/j.jnca.2012.04.007

Engelberger, J. F. (1982). Robotics in practice: Future capabilities. *Electronic Servicing & Technology magazine.*

Eonreality (2015) Eonreality. Retrieved June 30, 2015, from http://eonreality.com/

EPA US. (2006). Water quality standards review and revision. Washington, DC.

Epping-Jordan, J., Pruitt, S., Bengoa, R., & Wagner, E. (2004). Improving the quality of health care for chronic conditions. *Quality & Safety in Health Care*, *13*(4), 299–305. doi:10.1136/qshc.2004.010744 PMID:15289634

Eriksen, J., Sjøgren, P., Bruera, E., Ekholm, O., & Rasmussen, N. K. (2006). Critical issues on opioids in chronic noncancer pain: An epidemiological study. *Pain*, *125*(1-2), 172–179. doi:10.1016/j.pain.2006.06.009 PMID:16842922

Ermi, L. (2005). Fundamental Components of the Gameplay Experience: Analysing Immersion.

Erol, A., Bebis, G., Nicolescu, M., Boyle, R. D., & Twombly, X. (2007). Vision-based hand pose estimation: A review. *Computer Vision and Image Understanding*, *108*(1-2), 52–73. doi:10.1016/j.cviu.2006.10.012

Ethni, S. A., Zahawi, B., Gaouris, D., & Acarnley, P. P. (2009). Comparison of particle swarm optimization and simulated annealing algorithms for induction motor fault identification. *Proceedings of the 7th IEEE Inter. Conference on Industrial Informatics 2009* (pp. 470-474).

Evaluating the Kellogg Project. (n. d.). retrieved from http://www.trincoll.edu/orgs/planning/Kellogg/

Evaluation. (n. d.). Online Etymology Dictionary. Retrieved from http://www.etymonline.com/index.php?term=evaluation

Eveleens, J. L., & Verhoef, C. (2009). Quantifying IT forecast quality. *Science of Computer Programming*, *74*(11), 934–988. doi:10.1016/j.scico.2009.09.005

Eyeliner 3D. (2015). Dimensional studios, musion setup: How it works. Retrieved from http://www.eyeliner3d.com/musion_eyeliner_setup_video.html

EZface. (2015). The new era of virtual tester technology Retrieved from http://www.ezface.com/products/#try-it-on

Falkenberg, E. D., Hesse, W., Lindgreen, P., Nilsson, B. E., Oei, J. H., Rolland, C., . . . Voss, K. (1998, October). A framework of information systems concepts. Proceedings of IFIP WG (Vol. 8).

Favre-Brun, A., Jacquemin, C., & Caye, V. (2012). Revealing the "spirit of the place": Genius Loci, a spatial augmented reality performance based on 3D data and historical hypotheses. *Proceedings of the18th International Conference on Virtual Systems and Multimedia (VSMM)* (pp. 103-108). Milan: IEEE.

Feintuch, U., Tuchner, M., Lorber-Haddad, A., Meiner, Z., & Shiri, S. (2009, June 29-July 2). *VirHab - A virtual reality system for treatment of chronic pain and disability.* Paper presented at the Virtual Rehabilitation International Conference, 2009. doi:10.1109/ICVR.2009.5174210

Feltham, M. G., Ledebt, A., Deconinck, F. J. A., & Savelsbergh, G. J. P. (2010). Mirror visual feedback induces lower neuromuscular activity in children with spastic hemiparetic cerebral palsy. *Research in Developmental Disabilities, 31*(6), 1525–1535. doi:10.1016/j.ridd.2010.06.004 PMID:20591615

Feng, L., Apers, P. M., & Jonker, W. (2004). Towards Context-Aware Data Management for Ambient Intelligence. *Database and expert systems applications, LNCS* (Vol. 3180, pp. 422-431). Retrieved from http://link.springer.com/chapter/10.1007%2F978-3-540-30075-5_41

Ferrari, A., & Signoroni, A. (2014). Multistage classification for bacterial colonies recognition on solid agar images. *Proceedings of theIEEE International Conference on Imaging Systems and Techniques* (pp. 101-106). Santorini, Greece: IEEE. doi:10.1109/IST.2014.6958454

Ferreira, D., Kostakos, V., & Dey, A. K. (2015). AWARE: Mobile context instrumentation framework. *Frontiers in ICT, 2*(6), 1–9.

Ferris, D.P., Sawaicki, G.S., & Domingo, A., (2005). Powered lower limb orthoses for gait rehabilitation. *For Spinal Cord Injury Rehabil., 11(2)*, 34-49.

Ferris, D. P., Czerniecki, J. M., & Hannaford, B. (2005). An ankle -foot orthosis powered by artificial pneumatic muscles. *Journal of Applied Biomechanics, 21*(2), 189–197. PMID:16082019

Ferson, P. (2013). Review: Celluon Magic Cube laser keyboard. *Neowin.net.* Retrieved from http://www.neowin.net/news/review-celluon-magic-cube-laser-keyboard

Fesenmaier, D. R., Wöber, K. W., & Werthner, H. (Eds.). (2006). *Destination recommendation systems: Behavioral foundations and applications.* Cambridge: CAB International. doi:10.1079/9780851990231.0000

Fetaji, M., Loskoska, S., Fetaji, B., & Ebibi, M. (2007). Investigating Human Computer Interaction Issues in Designing Efficient Virtual Learning Environments.*Proceedings of the 3rd Balkan Conference in Informatics BCI '07*, Sofia, Bulgaria.

Figueiredo, M. J., Cardoso, P. J., Gonçalves, C. D., & Rodrigues, J. M. (2014). Augmented reality and holograms for the visualization of mechanical engineering parts. *Proceedings of theIEEE 18th International Conference on Information Visualisation* (pp. 368-373). doi:10.1109/IV.2014.17

Filgueiras, L., Martins, S., Correa, D., & Osorio, A. (2008). Personas para caracterização da experiência de uso de tecnologia pela população digitalmente excluída. *Usabilidade, Acessibilidade e Inteligibilidade Aplicadas em Interfaces para Analfabetos, Idosos e Pessoas com Deficiência*, 15-23.

Fino, E. R., Martín-Gutiérrez, J., Fernández, M. D. M., & Davara, E. A. (2013). Interactive Tourist Guide: Connecting Web 2.0, Augmented Reality and QR Codes. *Procedia Computer Science, 25*, 338–344. doi:10.1016/j.procs.2013.11.040

Fishbain, D. A., Cole, B., Lewis, J., Rosomoff, H. L., & Rosomoff, R. S. (2008). What percentage of chronic nonmalignant pain patients exposed to chronic opioid analgesic therapy develop abuse/addiction and/or aberrant drug-related behaviors? A structured evidence-based review. *Pain Medicine (Malden, Mass.), 9*(4), 444–459. doi:10.1111/j.1526-4637.2007.00370.x PMID:18489635

Fisher, S., McGreevy, M., Humphries, J., & Robinett, W. (1986). Virtual Environment Display System. *Proceedings of the 1986 workshop on Interactive 3D graphics I3D '86* (pp. 77–87). doi:10.1145/319120.319127

Fisk, A., Rogers, W. A., Charness, N., Czaja, S. J., & Sharit, J. (2009). *Designing for Older Adults: Principles and Creative Human Factors Approaches* (2nd ed.). New York: CRC Press. doi:10.1201/9781420080681

Fissaa, T., Guermah, H., Hafiddi, H., Nassar, M., & Kriouile, A. (2014). Towards an Ontology Based Architecture for Context-Aware Services Composition. *Proceedings of the 2014 International Conference on Multimedia Computing and Systems (ICMCS)* (pp. 990-995). Marrakech: IEEE. doi:10.1109/ICMCS.2014.6911303

Fitnect Interactive. (2014). Fitnect. Virtual mirror, shopping window, virtual store, and much more. Retrieved from http://www.fitnect.hu/

Flansjer, U. B., Holmback, A. M., Downham, D., Parlten, C., & Lexell, J. (2005). Realibility of gait performance test in men and women with hemiparesis after stroke. *Rehabil. Medicine*, *37*(2), 75–82. doi:10.1080/16501970410017215

Fletcher, S. (2013). Opportunities in Augmented Reality for Engineers. *Geodatapoint.com*. Retrieved from http://geodatapoint.com/articles/view/opportunities_in_augmented_reality_for_construction_operations_processes

Flyway. (2015). 3D holographic projection – the future of advertising? Retrieved from http://flyawaysimulation.com/news/3630/3d-holographic-projection-future-of-advertising/

fMRI. (2014). Magnetic Resonance, a critical peer-reviewed introduction; functional MRI. European Magnetic Resonance Forum. Retrieved from http://www.magnetic-resonance.org/ch/11-03.html

Follmer, S., Leithinger, D., Olwal, A., Hogge, A., & Ishii, H. (2013). inFORM: dynamic physical affordances and constraints through shape and object actuation. *Paper presented at the 26th annual ACM symposium on User interface software and technology*, St. Andrews, Scotland, United Kingdom. doi:10.1145/2501988.2502032

Fong, S., Zhuang, Y., Fister, I., & Fister, I. Jr. (2013). A biometric authentication model using hand gesture images. *Biomedical Engineering Online*, *12*(1), 111. doi:10.1186/1475-925X-12-111 PMID:24172288

Foresti, D., Nabavi, M., Klingauf, M., Ferrari, A., & Poulikakos, D. (2013). Acoustophoretic contactless transport and handling of matter in air. *Proceedings of the National Academy of Sciences of the United States of America*, *110*(31), 12549–12554. doi:10.1073/pnas.1301860110 PMID:23858454

Fornari, F. (2012). The future of human-computer interaction: overview of input devices.

Fothergill, S., Mentis, H., Kohli, P., & Nowozin, S. (2012). Instructing people for training gestural interactive systems. *Proceedings of the SIGCHI Conference on Human Factors in Computing Systems, CHI '12* (pp. 1737-1746). New York, NY, USA. ACM. doi:10.1145/2207676.2208303

Fotopoulou, A., Jenkinson, P. M., Tsakiris, M., Haggard, P., Rudd, A., & Kopelman, M. D. (2011). Mirror-view reverses somatoparaphrenia: Dissociation between first- and third-person perspectives on body ownership. *Neuropsychologia*, *49*(14), 3946–3955. doi:10.1016/j.neuropsychologia.2011.10.011 PMID:22023911

Fredheim, O. M. S., Kaasa, S., Fayers, P., Saltnes, T., Jordhøy, M., & Borchgrevink, P. C. (2008). Chronic non-malignant pain patients report as poor health-related quality of life as palliative cancer patients. *Acta Anaesthesiologica Scandinavica*, *52*(1), 143–148. doi:10.1111/j.1399-6576.2007.01524.x PMID:18005378

Freeman, W. T., & Weissman, C. (1995). Television control by hand gestures. *Proceedings of International Workshop on Automatic Face and Gesture Recognition* (pp. 179–183).

Friedman, J., Hastie, T., & Tibshirani, R. (2001). The elements of statistical learning. Springer, Berlin: Springer series in statistics.

Friedrich, H., Dillmann, R., & Rogalla, O. (1999). Interactive robot programming based on human demonstration and advice. In *Sensor Based Intelligent Robots* (pp. 96–119). Springer Berlin Heidelberg. doi:10.1007/10705474_6

Fuchs, H., Livingston, M., Raskar, R., Colucci, D. n., Keller, K., State, A., . . . Meyer, A. (1998). Augmented reality visualization for laparoscopic surgery. In W. Wells, A. Colchester & S. Delp (Eds.), Medical Image Computing and Computer-Assisted Interventation MICCAI'98 (Vol. 1496, pp. 934-943): Springer Berlin Heidelberg. doi:10.1007/BFb0056282

Fujinami, K., Kawsar, F., & Nakajima, T. (2005). AwareMirror: a personalized display using a mirror. *Paper presented at theProceedings of the Third international conference on Pervasive Computing*, Munich, Germany. doi:10.1007/11428572_19

Gagliardi, D., Muller, P., Glossop, E., Caliandro, C., Fritsch, M., Brtkova, G., ... & Ramlogan, R. (2012). A recovery on The horizon. *Annual report on European SMEs, 2013*.

Gagne, R. M., Briggs, L. J., & Wager, W. W. (1992). *Principles of Instructional design*. TX: Harcourt Brace Jovanovich.

Gale, S. F. (2002). Measuring the roi of e-learning. *Workforce, 81*(8), 74.

Galitz, W. O. (2002). *The essential guide to user interface design: An introduction to GUI design principles and techniques*. New York: John Wiley & Sons.

Galloway, D. L. (2005). Evaluating distance delivery and e-learning: Is kirkpatrick's model relevant? *Performance Improvement, 44*(4), 21–27. doi:10.1002/pfi.4140440407

Garau, C. (2014). From Territory to smartphone: Smart Fruition of Cultural Heritage for Dinamic Tourism Development. *Planning Practice and Research, 29*(3), 238–255. doi:10.1080/02697459.2014.929837

Garber, L. (2013). Gestural Technology: Moving Interfaces in a New Direction. *Computer, 46*(10), 22–25. doi:10.1109/MC.2013.352

García, F. B., & Jorge, A. H. (2006). Evaluating e-learning platforms through SCORM specifications. *Proceedings of theIADIS Virtual Multi Conference on Computer Science and Information Systems*.

Garrett, J. J. (2011). *The elements of user experience: user-centered design for the web and beyond*. Berkeley, CA: New Riders.

Gašević, D., Kovanović, V., Joksimović, S., & Siemens, G. (2014). Where is Research on Massive Open Online Courses Headed? A Data Analysis of the MOOC Research Initiative. *The International Review of Research in Open and Distant Learning, 15*(5).

Gasparrini, S., Cippitelli, E., Spinsante, S., & Gambi, E. (2015) Depth Cameras in AAL Environments: Technology and Realworld Applications. In L.B. Theng (Ed.), Assistive Technologies for Physical and Cognitive Disabilities (Ch. 2). Hershey, PA, USA: IGI Global. doi:10.4018/9781466673731

Gatchel, R. J., Peng, Y. B., Peters, M. L., Fuchs, P. N., & Turk, D. C. (2007). The biopsychosocial approach to chronic pain: Scientific advances and future directions. *Psychological Bulletin, 133*(4), 581–624. doi:10.1037/0033-2909.133.4.581 PMID:17592957

Gavalas, D., Konstantopoulos, C., Mastakas, K., & Pantziou, G. (2014). Mobile recommender systems in tourism. *Journal of Network and Computer Applications, 39*, 319–333. doi:10.1016/j.jnca.2013.04.006

Gavrila, D. M. (1999). The visual analysis of human movement: A survey. *Computer Vision and Image Understanding, 73*(1), 82–98. doi:10.1006/cviu.1998.0716

Gee, J. P. (2003). *What video games have to teach us about learning and literacy*. New York: Palgrave Macmillan.

Geissmann, Q. (2013). OpenCFU, a new free and open-source software to count cell colonies and other circular objects. *PLoS ONE, 8*(2), e54072. doi:10.1371/journal.pone.0054072 PMID:23457446

Gelb, A., & Clark, J. (2013). Identification for development: the biometrics revolution. *Center for Global Development Working Paper 315.*

Gellersen, H.-W., Beigl, M., & Schmidt, A. (2000). Sensor-based Context-Awareness for Situated Computing.*Proceedings of Workshop on Software Engineering for Wearable and Pervasive Computing*, (pp. 77-83). Limerick, Ireland.

Gendreau, M., & Potvin, J. (2010). Handbook of Meta-heuristics (2nd ed.). Springer + Business Media.

Georgescu, A., Kuzmanovic, B., Santos, N., Tepest, R., Bente, G., Tittgemeyer, M., & Vogeley, K. (2013). *Perceiving nonverbal behavior: Neural correlates of processing movement fluency and contingency in dyadic interactions. Human brain Mapping, 35(4).* Wiley Periodicals.

Gervautz, M., & Schmalstieg, D. (2012). Anywhere interfaces using handheld augmented reality. *Computer, 45*(7), 26–31. doi:10.1109/MC.2012.72

Ghiani, G., Guerriero, F., Laporte, G., & Musmanno, R. (2003). Real-time vehicle routing: Solution concepts, algorithms and parallel computing strategies. *European Journal of Operational Research, 151*(1), 1–11. doi:10.1016/S0377-2217(02)00915-3

Ghirvu, A. (2011). Advergames: marketing advantages and risks involved. *Marketing from Information to Decision, 4,* 174-183.

Gibbs, S. (2014, February 19). Google Glass advice: how to avoid being a glasshole. *The Guardian, Technology.*

Gimeno, J., Olanda, R., Martinez, B., & Sanchez, F. M. (2011). Multiuser augmented reality system for indoor exhibitions. *Paper presented at the Proceedings of the 13th IFIP TC 13 international conference on Human-computer interaction,* Lisbon, Portugal, 4. doi:10.1007/978-3-642-23768-3_86

Giner Martínez, F., & Portalés Ricart, C. (2005a, 3-7 October). The Augmented User: A Wearable Augmented Reality Interface. *Paper presented at theInternational Conference on Virtual Systems and Multimedia (VSMM'05),* Ghent, Belgium.

Giner Martínez, F., & Portalés Ricart, C. (2005b). El Túnel Mágico. *Paper presented at the Nuevos materiales y tecnologías para el arte,* Madrid, Spain.

Giner Martínez, F., & Portalés Ricart, C. (2007). Augmented teaching. *Paper presented at the International Technology, Education and Development Conference (INTED'07),* Valencia, Spain.

Glas, D., Kanda, T., Ishiguro, H., & Hagita, N. (2012, July). Temporal Awareness in Teleoperation of Conversational Robots. *IEEE Transactions on Systems, Man, and Cybernetics. Part A, Systems and Humans, 42*(4), 905–912. doi:10.1109/TSMCA.2011.2181162

Glass, Z. (2007). The effectiveness of product placement in video games. *Journal of Interactive Advertising, 8*(1), 23–32. doi:10.1080/15252019.2007.10722134

Globalzepp. (2015). Retrieved from http://www.globalzepp.com/

Glover, F. W., & Laguna, M. (1997). *Tabu Search.* Springer. doi:10.1007/978-1-4615-6089-0

Gnanam, S. P., Srinath, M. V., & Sivhakumaar, V. P. (2011). Emerging web instructional design model for developing web based learning resources. *European Journal of Scientific Research, 56*(4), 548–555.

Go, A. S., Mozaffarian, D., Roger, V. L., Benjamin, E. J., Berry, J. D., Borden, W. B., & Turner, M. B. et al. (2013). Heart Disease and Stroke Statistics--2013 Update: A Report From the American Heart Association. *Circulation, 127*(1), 143–152. doi:10.1161/CIR.0b013e318282ab8f

Goel, M., Whitmire, E., Mariakakis, A., Saponas, T. S., Joshi, N., Morris, D., . . . Patel, S. N. (2015). HyperCam: hyperspectral imaging for ubiquitous computing applications. *Paper presented at the 2015 ACM International Joint Conference on Pervasive and Ubiquitous Computing*, Osaka, Japan. doi:10.1145/2750858.2804282

Goh, K. Y., & Ping, J. W. (2014). Engaging Consumers with Advergames: An Experimental Evaluation of Interactivity, Fit and Expectancy. *Journal of the Association for Information Systems, 15*(7), 388–421.

Goldberg, D. E. (1989). Genetic Algorithms in Search, Optimization and Machine Learning (1st ed.). Boston, MA, USA: Addison-Wesley Longman Publishing Co. Inc. Retrieved from http://portal.acm.org/citation.cfm?id=534133

Goldfarb, M., & Celanovic, N. (2000, September). A flexure-based gripper for small-scale manipulation. *Robotica, 17*(2), 181–187.

Gold, J. I., Kant, A. J., Kim, S. H., & Rizzo, A. (2005). Virtual anesthesia: The use of virtual reality for pain distraction during acute medical interventions. *Seminars in Anesthesia, Perioperative Medicine and Pain, 24*(4), 203–210. doi:10.1053/j.sane.2005.10.005

Gomoll, A. H., O'Toole, R. V., Czarnecki, J., & Warner, J. J. (2007). Surgical experience correlates with performance on a virtual reality simulator for shoulder arthroscopy. *The American Journal of Sports Medicine, 35*(6), 883–888. doi:10.1177/0363546506296521 PMID:17261572

Gomoll, A. H., Pappas, G., Forsythe, B., & Warner, J. J. (2008). Individual Skill Progression on a Virtual Reality Simulator for Shoulder Arthroscopy A 3-Year Follow-up Study. *The American Journal of Sports Medicine, 36*(6), 1139–1142. doi:10.1177/0363546508314406 PMID:18326032

Goodwin, K. (2009). Understanding potential users and customers. In K. Goodwin (Ed.), Designing for the Digital Age: Creating Human-Centered Products and Services (pp. 112-153). John Wiley & Sons.

Google-Maps-API. (2015). Google Maps API. Retrieved from https://developers.google.com/maps/

Goslar, K., & Schill, A. (2005). Modeling Contextual Information using Active Data Structures. *Lecture Notes in Computer Science, 3268*, 325–334. doi:10.1007/978-3-540-30192-9_32

Graf, S., & List, B. (2005). An evaluation of open source e-learning platforms stressing adaptation issues. *Proceedings of 5th IEEE International Conference on Advanced Learning Technologies Computer Society*, Kaohsiung, Taiwan. (pp. 163-165). Retrieved from https://www.campussource.de/aktuelles/docs/icalt2005.pdf

Granger, C. W. (1988). Some recent development in a concept of causality. *Journal of Econometrics, 39*(1), 199–211. doi:10.1016/0304-4076(88)90045-0

Greenstein, J. S., & Arnaut, L. Y. (1988). Input Devices. In Handbook of Human-Computer Interaction (pp. 495-519). North Holland: Amsterdam.

Gregor, S. (2002). *A theory of theories in information systems. In Information Systems Foundations* (pp. 1–20). Building the Theoretical Base.

Gresse von Wangenheim, C., Thiry, M., & Kochanski, D. (2009). Empirical evaluation of an educational game on software measurement. *Empirical Software Engineering, 14*(4), 418–452. doi:10.1007/s10664-008-9092-6

Gretzel, U. (2011). Intelligent systems in tourism: A social science perspective. *Annals of Tourism Research, 38*(3), 757–779. doi:10.1016/j.annals.2011.04.014

Gretzel, U., & Jamal, T. (2009). Conceptualizing the creative tourist class: Technology, mobility, and tourism experiences. *Tourism Analysis, 14*(4), 471–481. doi:10.3727/108354209X12596287114219

Grguric, A., Mosmondor, M., Kusek, M., Stocklow, C., & Salvi, D. (2013, June). Introducing gesture interaction in the Ambient Assisted Living platform universal. *Proceedings of the 2013 12th International Conference on Telecommunications (ConTEL)* (pp. 215-222). IEEE.

Grier, R. A., Thiruvengada, H., Ellis, S. R., Havig, P., Hale, K. S., & Hollands, J. G. (2012). Augmented Reality–Implications toward Virtual Reality, Human Perception and Performance.*Proceedings of the Human Factors and Ergonomics Society Annual Meeting,*56(1), 1351-1355. SAGE Publications. doi:10.1177/1071181312561388

Grifantini, K. (2010). Sensor detects emotions through the skin. *MIT Technology Review*. Retrieved from http://www.technologyreview.com/news/421316/sensor-detects-emotions-through-the-skin/

Grigorovici, D. M., & Constantin, C. D. (2004). Experiencing interactive advertising beyond rich media: Impacts of ad type and presence on brand effectiveness in 3D gaming immersive virtual environments. *Journal of Interactive Advertising, 5*(1), 22–36. doi:10.1080/15252019.2004.10722091

Gross, M. L. (2010). Advergames and the effects of game-product congruity. *Computers in Human Behavior, 26*(6), 1259–1265. doi:10.1016/j.chb.2010.03.034

Grossman, S. (2005). "Grand Theft Oreo": The Constitutionality of Advergame Regulation. *The Yale Law Journal,* 2005, 227–236.

Grudin, J. (2012). A moving target: The evolution of HCI. In Human-computer interaction handbook: Fundamentals, evolving technologies, and emerging applications (3rd ed., pp. xxvii–lxi).

Grudin, J. (2001). Desituating Action: Digital Representation of Context. *Human-Computer Interaction, 16*(2), 269–286. doi:10.1207/S15327051HCI16234_10

Gunawardena, T., & Waiguny, M. K. (2014). So many things to do! How multitasking affects memory and attitude for product and brand placements. *Australasian Marketing Journal, 22*(4), 288–295. doi:10.1016/j.ausmj.2014.09.001

Gupta, A. K., & Shahid, M. (2011). The Sixth Sense Technology.*Proceedings of the 5th National Conference; INDIACom-2011 Computing For Nation Development* (pp. 10-11).

Gupta, G. S., Mukhopadhyay, S. C., Messom, C. H., & Demidenko, S. N. (2006). Master–slave control of a teleoperated anthropomorphic robotic arm with gripping force sensing. *IEEE Transactions on Instrumentation and Measurement, 55*(6), 2136–2145. doi:10.1109/TIM.2006.884393

Gupta, M., & Sharma, S. (2012). *Virtual Class room using six sense Technology. IOSR Journal of Computer Engineering* (Vol. 6). IOSRJCE.

Gupta, P. B., & Lord, K. R. (1998). Product placement in movies: The effect of prominence and mode on audience recall. *Journal of Current Issues and Research in Advertising, 20*(1), 47–59. doi:10.1080/10641734.1998.10505076

Gwizdka, J. (2000). What's in the context? *Proceedings of theACMSIGCHI Conference on Human Factors in Computing Systems (CHI '00)* (pp. 1-6). The Hague, Netherlands: ACM.

Hachaj, T., & Ogiela, M. (2013). Computer karate trainer in tasks of personal and homeland security defense. In A. Cuzzocrea, C. Kittl, D. Simos, E. Weippl, L. Xu (Eds.), Security Engineering and Intelligence Informatics, LNCS (Vol. 8128 pp. 430–441). Springer. doi:10.1007/978-3-642-40588-4_30

Hadalová, Z., & Samuelčík, M. Varhaníková (2014, December). Augmented Map Presentation of Cultural Heritage Sites. *Paper presented at theInternational Conference on Current Issues of Science and Research in the Global World*, Vienna, Austria (pp. 345-349).

Hafiddi, H., Baidouri, H., Nassar, M., & Kriouile, A. (2012, September). Context-Awareness for Service Oriented Systems. *International Journal of Computer Science Issues, 9*(5).

Hagen, S., & Sandnes, F. E. (2010). Toward accessible self-service kiosks through intelligent user interfaces. *Personal and Ubiquitous Computing, 14*(8), 715–721. doi:10.1007/s00779-010-0286-8

Halder, A., Mahato, M., Sinha, T., Adhikari, B., Mukherjee, S., & Bhattacharyya, N. (2012). Polymer membrane electrode based potentiometric taste sensor: A new sensor to distinguish five basic tastes. *Proceedings of the International Conference on Sensing Technology ICST* (pp. 785–789). http://doi.org/ doi:10.1109/ICSensT.2012.6461784

Hall, A. D., & Fagen, R. E. (1956). Definition of system. *General Systems, 1*(1), 18–28.

Hall, E. T. (1973). *The silent language.* Anchor Books.

Hammer, D. (1997). Discovery learning and discovery teaching. *Cognition and Instruction, 15*(4), 485–529. doi:10.1207/s1532690xci1504_2

Hamtini, T. M. (2008). Evaluating e-learning programs: An adaptation of Kirkpatrick's model to accommodate e-learning environments. *Journal of Computer Science, 4*(8), 693–698. doi:10.3844/jcssp.2008.693.698

Han, L., Jyri, S., Ma, J., & Yu, K. (2008). Research on Context-Aware Mobile Computing. *Proceedings of the22nd International Conference on Advanced Information Networking and Applications* (pp. 24-30). Okinawa: IEEE.

Han, J., Shao, L., Xu, D., & Shotton, J. (2013). Enhanced computer vision with Microsoft Kinect sensor: A review.. *IEEE Transactions on Cybernetics, 43*(5), 1318–1334. PMID:23807480

Hannafin, R., & Foshay, W. (2008). Computer-based instruction's (cbi) rediscovered role in k-12: An evaluation case study of one high school's use of CBI to improve pass rates on high-stakes tests. *Educational Technology Research and Development, 56*(2), 147–160. doi:10.1007/s11423-006-9007-4

Hansenab, H., Rezzougc, N., Gorcec, P., Ventured, G., & Isableua, B. (2015). *Sequence-dependent rotation axis changes and interaction torque use in overarm throwing. Journal of sports sciences, 34(9).* Taylor & Francis.

Harary, F., & Batell, M. F. (1981). What is a system? *Social Networks, 3*(1), 29–40. Retrieved from http://deepblue.lib.umich.edu/bitstream/handle/2027.42/24489/0000765.pdf?sequence=1 doi:10.1016/0378-8733(81)90003-4

Harvel, L., Liu, L., Abowd, G. D., Lim, Y.-X., Scheibe, C., & Chatham, C. (2004). Context Cube: Flexible and Effective Manipulation of Sensed Context Data. *Lecture Notes in Computer Science, 3001,* 51–68. doi:10.1007/978-3-540-24646-6_4

Harvey, J. (Ed.), (1998). Evaluation cook book. Retrieved from http://www.icbl.hw.ac.uk/ltdi/cookbook/cookbook.pdf

Harwin, W.S., Patton, L. & Edgerton, V.R., (2006). Challenges and opportunities for robot-mediated neurorehabilitation. *Proceedings of IEEE '06, 94(9),* 1717-1726.

Hashtrudi-Zaad, K., & Salcudean, S. E. (2002a). Bilateral parallel force/position teleoperation control. *Journal of Robotic Systems, 19*(4), 155–167. doi:10.1002/rob.10030

Hashtrudi-Zaad, K., & Salcudean, S. E. (2002b). Transparency in time-delayed systems and the effect of local force feedback for transparent teleoperation. *IEEE Transactions on Robotics and Automation, 8*(1), 108–114. doi:10.1109/70.988981

Hayashi, T., Kawamoto, H., & Sankai, Y. (2008). Control method of robot suit HAL working as operator's muscle using biological and dynamical information. *Proceedings of the IEEE Inter. on Conference Robots and Sys.* (pp. 3063-3068).

Hembrooke, H., & Gay, G. (2003). The laptop and the lecture: The effects of multitasking in learning environments. *Journal of Computing in Higher Education, 15*(1), 46–64. doi:10.1007/BF02940852

Hennicker, R., & Noch, N. (2001). Modeling the user interface of web applications with UML. In A. Evans, R. France, A. Moreira, & B. Rumpe (Eds.), Proceedings of the Practical UML-Based Rigorous Development Methods- Countering or Integrating the Extremists, Workshop of the Puml-Group Held Together with UML 2001 (Vol. P-07, pp. 158–172). Toronto, Canada. Retrieved from http://subs.emis.de/LNI/Proceedings/ Proceedings07 /ModeltheUseInterf_12.pdf

Henriques, C., Ramos, C., & Rodrigues, J. M. F. (2014). Realidade Aumentada Aplicada a Valorização do Turística do Património Religioso no Algarve. *Proceedings of Management Studies International Conference -TMS ALGARVE 2014* (p. 106). Olhão: Portugal.

Hernandez, M. D. (2011). A model of flow experience as determinant of positive attitudes toward online advergames. *Journal of Promotion Management, 17*(3), 315–326. doi:10.1080/10496491.2011.596761

Hernandez, M. D., & Chapa, S. (2010). Adolescents, advergames and snack foods: Effects of positive affect and experience on memory and choice. *Journal of Marketing Communications, 16*(1-2), 59–68. doi:10.1080/13527260903342761

Hernandez, M. D., Chapa, S., Minor, M. S., Maldonado, C., & Barranzuela, F. (2004). Hispanic attitudes toward advergames: A proposed model of their antecedents. *Journal of Interactive Advertising, 5*(1), 74–83. doi:10.1080/15252 019.2004.10722095

Hernandez, M. D., & Minor, M. S. (2011). Investigating the effect of arousal on brand memory in advergames: Comparing qualitative and quantitative approaches. *Qualitative Market Research: An International Journal, 14*(2), 207–217. doi:10.1108/13522751111120701

Hernoux, F., & Christmann, O. (2014). A seamless solution for 3D real-time interaction: Design and evaluation. *Virtual Reality (Waltham Cross), 19*(1), 1–20. doi:10.1007/s10055-014-0255-z

Herrera, G., Jordan, R., & Gimeno, J. (2006). Exploring the advantages of Augmented Reality for Intervention in Autism Spectrum Disorders. *Paper presented at theSecond World Autism Congress*, Cape Town, South Africa.

Hevner, A. R., March, S. T., Park, J., & Ram, S. (2004). Design science in information systems research. *Management Information Systems Quarterly, 28*(1), 75–105.

Hevner, A., & Chatterjee, S. (2010). Design Science Research in Information Systems. In *Design Research in Information Systems* (pp. 9–22). Springer. doi:10.1007/978-1-4419-5653-8_2

Hidler, J., Nichols, D., Pelliccio, M., & Brady, K. (2005). Advances in the understanding and treatment of stroke impairment using robotic device. *Topics in Stroke Rehabilitation, 12*(2), 22–35. doi:10.1310/RYT5-62N4-CTVX-8JTE PMID:15940582

Hilliges, O., Kim, D., Izadi, S., Weiss, M., & Wilson, A. D. (2012). HoloDesk: Direct 3D interactions with a situated see-through display. *Proceedings of theSIGCHI Annual Conference on Human factors in computing systems* (pp. 2421 – 2430). doi:10.1145/2207676.2208405

Hillman, D. C., Willis, D. J., & Gunawardena, C. N. (1994). Learner-Interface interactions in distance education: An extension of contemporary models and strategies for practitioners. *American Journal of Distance Education, 8*(2), 30–42. doi:10.1080/08923649409526853

Hilsmann, A., & Eisert, P. (2009). Tracking and Retexturing Cloth for Real-Time Virtual Clothing Applications. *Paper presented at theProceedings of the 4th International Conference on Computer Vision/Computer Graphics Collaboration Techniques*, Rocquencourt, France. doi:10.1007/978-3-642-01811-4_9

Hincapié-Ramos, J. D., Guo, X., Moghadasian, P., & Irani, P. (2014). Consumed Endurance: A metric to quantify arm fatigue of mid-air interactions.*Proceedings of the 32nd annual ACM conference on Human factors in computing systems* (pp. 1063-1072). ACM. doi:10.1145/2556288.2557130

HITLab. (2003). ARToolKit Retrieved from http://www.hitl.washington.edu/artoolkit/

Hjalager, A. M. (2010). A review of innovation research in tourism. *Tourism Management, 31*(1), 1–12. doi:10.1016/j.tourman.2009.08.012

Hofer, T., Pichler, M., Leonhartsberger, G., Altmann, J., & Werner, R. (2002). Context-Awareness on Mobile Devices – The Hydrogen Approach.*Proceedings of the 36th Annual Hawaii International Conference on System Sciences* (pp. 292-302). Hawaii: IEEE.

Hoffman, D. L., & Novak, T. P. (1996). Marketing in hypermedia computer-mediated environments: Conceptual foundations. *Journal of Marketing, 60*(3), 50–68. doi:10.2307/1251841

Hoffman, H. G., Patterson, D. R., Seibel, E., Soltani, M., Jewett-Leahy, L., & Sharar, S. R. (2008). Virtual reality pain control during burn wound debridement in the hydrotank. *The Clinical Journal of Pain, 24*(4), 299–304. doi:10.1097/AJP.0b013e318164d2cc PMID:18427228

Hoff, W. A., Gatrell, L. B., & Spofford, J. R. (1991). Machine-vision-based teleoperation aid. *Telematics and Informatics, 8*(4), 403–423. doi:10.1016/S0736-5853(05)80062-0

Hofmeister-Tóth, Á., & Nagy, P. (2011). The content analysis of advergames in Hungary. *Qualitative Market Research: An International Journal, 14*(3), 289–303. doi:10.1108/13522751111137514

Hogan, N., Krebs, H. I., Sharon, A., & Charnnarong, J. (1995, November). Interactive robot therapist. US patent 5,466,213.

Holle, H., Obermeier, C., Schmidt-Kassow, M., Friederici, A., Ward, J., & Gunter, T. (2012). Gesture Facilitates the Syntactic Analysis of Speech. *Frontiers in Psychology, 3.* doi:10.3389/fpsyg.2012.00074 PMID:22457657

Holodisplay. (2015). Retrieved from http://www.holodisplays.com/

Holomedia. (2015). 3D live interactive holographic. Retrieved from http://www.holomedia.co.uk/

Holus (2015) Holus: The interactive tabletop holographic display. Retrieved from http://www.digitaltrends.com/cooltech/holus-tabletop-hologram-kickstarter/

Holzinger, A. (2003). Finger instead of mouse: touch screens as a means of enhancing universal access. *Proceedings of User interfaces for all 7th international conference on Universal access: theoretical perspectives, practice, and experience* ERCIM '02, Berlin, Heidelberg (pp. 387–3970. Springer-Verlag. doi:10.1007/3-540-36572-9_30

Holzinger, A. (2005). Usability engineering methods for software developers. *Communications of the ACM, 48*(1), 71–74. doi:10.1145/1039539.1039541

Hong, J.-y., Suh, E.-, & Kim, S.-J. (2009). Context-aware systems: A literature review and classification. *Expert Systems with Applications, 36*(4), 8509–8522. doi:10.1016/j.eswa.2008.10.071

Hornbæk, K. (2006). Current practice in measuring usability: Challenges to usability studies and research. *International Journal of Human-Computer Studies, 64*(2), 79–102. doi:10.1016/j.ijhcs.2005.06.002

Horton, W. (2006). So how is e-learning different? In D. L. Kirkpatrick & J. D. Kirkpatrick (Eds.), *Evaluating e programs* (pp. 95–113). San Francisco: Berrett-Koehler.

Hou, J., Nam, Y., Peng, W., & Lee, K. M. (2012). Effects of screen size, viewing angle, and players' immersion tendencies on game experience. *Computers in Human Behavior, 28*(2), 617–623. doi:10.1016/j.chb.2011.11.007

Höysniemi, J., Hämäläinen, P., Turkki, L., & Rouvi, T. (2005). Children's intuitive gestures in vision-based action games. *Communications of the ACM, 48*(1), 44–50. doi:10.1145/1039539.1039568

Hsu, C.-I., Hung, S.-F., & Li, H.-C. (2007). Vehicle routing problem with time-windows for perishable food delivery. *Journal of Food Engineering, 80*(2), 465–475. doi:10.1016/j.jfoodeng.2006.05.029

Huang, C.-C., Yeh, T.-K., Li, T.-Y., & Chang, C.-Y. (2010). The idea storming cube: Evaluating the effects of using game and computer agent to support divergent thinking. *Journal of Educational Technology & Society, 13*(4), 180–191.

Huang, G., & Lee, S. (2008). PC-based PID speed control in DC motor.*Proceedings of the International Conference on Audio, Language and Image Processing* (pp. 400-407). IEEE.

Hudson, S., & Hudson, D. (2006). Branded entertainment: A new advertising technique or product placement in disguise? *Journal of Marketing Management, 22*(5-6), 489–504. doi:10.1362/026725706777978703

Huh, J., Suzuki-Lambrecht, Y., Lueck, J., & Gross, M. (2015). Presentation Matters: Comparison of Cognitive Effects of DTC Prescription Drug Advergames, Websites, and Print Ads. *Journal of Advertising.*

Huizenga, J., Admiraal, W., Akkerman, S., & ten Dam, G. (2009). Mobile game-based learning in secondary education: Engagement, motivation and learning in a mobile city game. *Journal of Computer Assisted Learning, 25*(4), 332–344. doi:10.1111/j.1365-2729.2009.00316.x

Hummen, R., & Moskowitz, R. (2014). *HIP Diet EXchange.* DEX.

Hürst, W., & Van Wezel, C. (2013). Gesture-based interaction via finger tracking for mobile augmented reality. *Multimedia Tools and Applications, 62*(1), 233–258. doi:10.1007/s11042-011-0983-y

Ibañez, R., Soria, A., Teyseyre, A., & Campo, M. (2014). Easy gesture recognition for Kinect. *Advances in Engineering Software, 76*(0), 171–180. doi:10.1016/j.advengsoft.2014.07.005

IBGE. (2010). *Censo demográfico 2010: Características gerais da população, religião e pessoas com deficiência.* Retrieved from ftp://ftp.ibge.gov.br/Censos/Censo_Demografico_2010/Caracteristicas_Gerais_Religiao_Deficiencia/caracteristicas_religiao_deficiencia.pdf

Ibis Capital. (2013). Global e-learning investment review. Retrieved from http://www.ibiscapital. co.uk/media/16158/IBIS%20Capital%20-%20e-Learning%20Flyer.pdf

IFR statistical department. (2014, February 20). *All-time-high for industrial robots in 2013.* Retrieved from worldrobotics.org: http://www.worldrobotics.org/index.php?id=home&news_id=272

IGN. (2010). THQ announces Fantastic Pets, first augmented reality title on Kinect for XBox 360. Retrieved from http://www.ign.com/articles/2010/10/21/thq-announces-fantastic-pets-first-augmented-reality-title-on-kinect-for-xbox-360

Imagine That. (2015a). 2D Fitting Room Retrieved from http://www.imaginethattechnologies.com/default.asp?mn=1.27

Imagine That. (2015b). 3D Fitting Room Retrieved from http://www.imaginethattechnologies.com/default.asp?mn=1.26

Institute of Medicine (US) Committee on Advancing Pain Research, Care, and Education. (2011). *Relieving Pain in America: A Blueprint for Transforming Prevention, Care, Education, and Research.* Washington (DC): National Academies Press (US).

Institute of Medicine (US) Committee on Advancing Pain Research. (2011). Care of People with Pain.

International Standards Organization. (1998). *ISO 9241 Part 11 – Guidance on usability.* Retrieved from https://www. iso.org/obp/ui/#iso:std:iso:9241:-11:ed-1:v1:en

Intuitive Surgical, Inc. (2015). *da Vinci Surgery: The da Vinci Surgical System.* Retrieved from http://www.davincisurgery. com/da-vinci-surgery/da-vinci-surgical-system/

InvenSense. (2015). Invensense. Retrieved from www.invensense.com

iPhone6s. (2015). Apple Inc., Retrieved from http://www.apple.com/iphone-6s/3d-touch/

Ishii, E., Katsura, S., Nishi, H., & Ohnishi, K. (2008, November). Development of multi-degree-of-freedom bilateral forceps robot system using FPGA. *Electronics and Communications in Japan, 91*(6), 23–33. doi:10.1002/ecj.10118

Ishii, T., & Katsura, S. (2010). Articulated multilateral control for haptic broadcasting system.*Proceedings of 36th Annual Conference on IEEE Industrial Electronics Society* (pp. 1872-1877). IEEE. doi:10.1109/IECON.2010.5675383

Islam, M. N. (2014). *Design and Evaluation of Web Interface Signs to Improve Web Usability: A Semiotic Framework* [PhD Thesis]. Åbo Akademi University, Finland.

Islam, M. N., & Tétard, F. (2013). Integrating Semiotics Perception in Usability Testing to Improve Usability Evaluation. In M. Garcia-Ruiz (Eds.) Cases on Usability Engineering: Design and Development of Digital Products (pp. 145-169). Hershey, PA, USA: IGI Global. doi:10.4018/978-1-4666-4046-7.ch007

Islam, M. N. (2013). A Systematic Literature Review of Semiotic Perception in User Interfaces. *Journal of Systems and Information Technology, 15*(1), 45–64. doi:10.1108/13287261311322585

Islam, M. N., & Bouwman, H. (2015a). An Assessment of a Semiotics Framework for Evaluation of User-Intuitive Web Interface Signs. *Universal Access to the Information Society Journal, 14*(4), 563–582. doi:10.1007/s10209-015-0403-6

Islam, M. N., & Bouwman, H. (2015b). Towards User-Intuitive Web User Interface sign Design and Evaluation: A Semiotic Framework. *International Journal of Human-Computer Studies, 86,* 121–137. doi:10.1016/j.ijhcs.2015.10.003

ISO IEC 19774. (2005). Specification of Humanoid animation (H-Anim). Retrieved from http://www.web3d.org/documents/specifications/19774/V1.0/index.html

Iturrate, I., Antelis, J. M., Kübler, A., & Minguez, J. (2009). A noninvasive brain-actuated wheelchair based on a P300 neurophysiological protocol and automated navigation. *IEEE Transactions on Robotics, 25*(3), 614–627.

Jackson, S. (2015). *Unity 3D UI Essentials.* Packt Publishing.

Jae Seok, J., Gi Sook, J., Tae Hwan, L., & Soon Ki, J. (2014). Two-Phase Calibration for a Mirror Metaphor Augmented Reality System. *Proceedings of the IEEE, 102*(2), 196–203. doi:10.1109/JPROC.2013.2294253

Jaimes, A., & Sebe, N. (2007). Multimodal human-computer interaction: A survey. *Computer Vision and Image Understanding, 108*(1-2), 116–134. doi:10.1016/j.cviu.2006.10.019

Jamison, R. N., Ross, E. L., Michna, E., Chen, L. Q., Holcomb, C., & Wasan, A. D. (2010). Substance misuse treatment for high-risk chronic pain patients on opioid therapy: A randomized trial. *Pain, 150*(3), 390–400. doi:10.1016/j.pain.2010.02.033 PMID:20334973

Jang, S., & Woo, W. (2006). 5W1H: Unified User-Centric Context (White Paper). *GIST U-VR Lab.*, South Korea.

Jankowski, J., & Hachet, M. (2015). Advances in Interaction with 3D Environments. *Computer Graphics Forum, 34*(1), 152–190. doi:10.1111/cgf.12466

Jarrahi, A., & Kangavari, M. R. (2012). An Architecture for Context-Aware Knowledge Flow Management Systems. *International Journal of Computer Science Issues, 9*(2), 40–51.

Jeevandam, A., & Thanusneddi, K. G. (2009). Robust design of decentrialized power system stabilizers using meta-heuristics optimization techniques for multimachine system. *Serbian J. Of Electrical Eng., 6*(1), 89–103. doi:10.2298/SJEE0901089J

Jelatis, D. G. (1975). Characteristics and evaluation of "Master-slave Manipulators". In T. B. Sheridan (Ed.), *Performance Evaluation of Programmable Robots and Manipulators* (pp. 141–146). Annapolis, Maryland: National Bureau of Standards (U.S.).

Jensen, M. P., Gertz, K. J., Kupper, A. E., Braden, A. L., Howe, J. D., Hakimian, S., & Sherlin, L. H. (2013). Steps toward developing an EEG biofeedback treatment for chronic pain. *Applied Psychophysiology and Biofeedback, 38*(2), 101–108. doi:10.1007/s10484-013-9214-9 PMID:23532434

Johansson, G. (1973) Visual perception of biological motion and a model for its analysis, *Perception Psychophys., 14*(2), 201–211.

John, B. E. (2003). Information processing and skilled behavior. In J. Carroll (Ed.), *HCI model, theories and frameworks: Towards a multidisciplinary science* (pp. 55–101). San Francisco, CA: Morgan Kaufmann. doi:10.1016/B978-155860808-5/50004-6

John, B. E., & Kieras, D. E. (1995). The GOMS family of user interface analysis techniques: Comparison and contrast. *ACM Transactions on Computer-Human Interaction, 3*(4), 320–351. doi:10.1145/235833.236054

Johnson, J. (2010). *Designing with the mind in mind: simple guide to understanding user interface design rules*. CA: Morgan Kaufmann.

Johnson, J., & Henderson, A. (2002). Conceptual models: Begin by designing what to design. *Interaction, 9*(1), 25–32. doi:10.1145/503355.503366

Johnson, M. H. (2005). How does distraction work in the management of pain? *Current Pain and Headache Reports, 9*(2), 90–95. doi:10.1007/s11916-005-0044-1 PMID:15745617

Johnson, S. (2005). *Everything bad is good for you: How today's popular culture is actually making us smarter*. New York: Riverhead Books.

Jones, A., McDowall, I., Yamada, H., Bolas, M., & Debevec, P. (2007). Rendering for an interactive 360° light field display. In ACM SIGGRAPH 2007. doi:10.1145/1275808.1276427

Jones, B., Collis, K., Watson, J., Foster, K., & Fraser, S. (1994). Images in mirrors: Recollections, alternative explanations and modes of cognitive functioning. *Research in Science Education, 24*(1), 191–200. doi:10.1007/BF02356344

Jones, M. G. (1995). Visuals for information access: A new philosophy for screen and interface design. In D. Beauchamp, R. Braden, & R. Griffen (Eds.), *Imagery and visual literacy* (pp. 264–272). International Visual Literacy Association.

Jones, M. G., & Farquhar, J. D. (1997). User interface design for web-based instruction. In B. Khan (Ed.), *Web-based instruction* (pp. 239–254). Englewood Cliffs, NJ: Educational Technology.

Jones, M. G., Farquhar, J. D., & Surry, D. W. (1995). Using metacognitive theories to design user interfaces for computer based learning. *Educational Technology, 35*(4), 12–22.

Jordan, K. (2015b). MOOC completion rates: The data. Retrieved from http://www.katyjordan.com/MOOCproject.html

Jordan, K. (2014). Initial trends in enrolment and completion of massive open online courses. *International Review of Research in Open and Distance Learning, 15*(1), 133–160.

Jordan, K. (2015a). Massive Open Online Course Completion Rates Revisited: Assessment, Length And Attrition. *International Review of Research in Open and Distance Learning, 16*(3), 341–358.

Juan, M. C., Alcaniz, M., Monserrat, C., Botella, C., Banos, R. M., & Guerrero, B. (2005). Using Augmented Reality to Treat Phobias. *IEEE Computer Graphics and Applications, 25*(6), 31–37. doi:10.1109/MCG.2005.143 PMID:16315475

Jung, T., Chung, N., & Leue, M. C. (2015). The determinants of recommendations to use augmented reality technologies: The case of a Korean theme park. *Tourism Management, 49*, 75–86. doi:10.1016/j.tourman.2015.02.013

Jun-Ren, D., Chien-Lin, H., Jin-Kun, L., Jar-Ferr, Y., & Chung-Hsien, W. (2008). Interactive multimedia mirror system design. *IEEE Transactions on Consumer Electronics, 54*(3), 972–980. doi:10.1109/tce.2008.4637575

Kablan, Z. (2010). The Effect of Using Exercise-Based Computer Games during the Process of Learning on Academic Achievement among Education Majors. *Educational Sciences: Theory and Practice, 10*(1), 351–364.

Kahneman, D. (1973). *Attention and effort* (p. 246). Englewood Cliffs, NJ: Prentice-Hall.

Kalmanek, C. (2012). The essential elements of successful innovation. *Computer Communication Review, 42*(2), 105–109. doi:10.1145/2185376.2185393

Kamali, M., Moosavian, S. A. A., & Cheraghpour, F. (2014). Improving grasp capabilities of KNTU hand using position & force sensors.*Proceedings of 22nd Iranian Conference on Electrical Engineering* (pp. 1278-1283). IEEE. doi:10.1109/IranianCEE.2014.6999731

Kamizono, T., Abe, H., Baba, K. I., Takano, S., & Murakami, K. (2014). Towards activity recognition of learners by Kinect. *Proceedings of the3rd International Conference on Advanced Applied Informatics* (pp. 177-180). doi:10.1109/IIAI-AAI.2014.45

Kang, L., Tang, X.-z., Xiang, Y.-h., & Huang, Y.-s. (2015). *Research progress and perspective of hyperspectral image projectors.* Paper presented at the Proc. SPIE 9522, Selected Papers from Conferences of the Photoelectronic Technology Committee of the Chinese Society of Astronautics 2014, Part II.

Kang, S. J., Ryu, J. C., Kim, K. H., & Mun, M. S. (2004). A real -time control of powered gait orthosis by biosignal. *Proc. Of the 11th World Congress of The Inter. Society for Prosthetics and Orthosis, Hong Kong.*

Karahanna, E., Straub, D. W., & Chervany, N. L. (1999). Information technology adoption across time: A cross-sectional comparison of pre-adoption and post-adoption beliefs. *Management Information Systems Quarterly, 23*(2), 183–213. doi:10.2307/249751

Karam, M. (2006). *A framework for research and design of gesture-based human computer interactions* [Doctoral Dissertation]. University of Southampton.

Karam, M., & Schraefel, M. C. (2005). A study on the use of semaphoric gestures to support secondary task interactions. In *CHI '05 extended abstracts on Human factors in computing systems* (pp. 1961–1964). New York, NY, USA: ACM Press. doi:10.1145/1056808.1057067

Kathawala, Y., & Wilgen, A. (2004). E-learning: Evaluation from an organization's perspective. *Training & Management Development Methods*, *18*(4), 501–513.

Katsura, S., Matsumoto, Y., & Ohnishi, K. (2007, February). Modeling of force sensing and validation of disturbance observer forforce control. *IEEE Transactions on Industrial Electronics*, *54*(1), 530–538. doi:10.1109/TIE.2006.885459

Kaufman, C. (2005). Internet key exchange (IKEv2) protocol.

Kebude, D., Morimitsu, H., Katsura, S., & Sabanovic, A. (2014). Multilateral control-based motion copying system for haptic training.*Proceedings of 2014 IEEE 23rd International Symposium on Industrial Electronics* (pp. 2250 - 2255). IEEE. doi:10.1109/ISIE.2014.6864968

Ke, F. (2008). Computer games application within alternative classroom goal structures: Cognitive, metacognitive, and affective evaluation. *Educational Technology Research and Development*, *56*(5), 539–556. doi:10.1007/s11423-008-9086-5

Ke, F., & Grabowski, B. (2007). Gameplaying for maths learning: Cooperative or not? *British Journal of Educational Technology*, *38*(2), 249–259. doi:10.1111/j.1467-8535.2006.00593.x

Kellogg (2010). W.K. Kellogg foundation evaluation handbook. Retrieved from http://www.wkkf.org/knowledge-center/resources/2010/w-k-kellogg-foundation-evaluation-handbook.aspx

Kelly, H., Howell, K., Glinert, E., Holding, L., Swain, C., Burrowbridge, A., & Roper, M. (2007). How to Build Serious Games. *Communications of the ACM*, *50*(7), 44–49. doi:10.1145/1272516.1272538

Kennedy-Clark, S., & Thompson, K. (2011). What Do Students Learn When Collaboratively Using A Computer Game in the Study of Historical Disease Epidemics, and Why? *Games and Culture*, *6*(6), 513–537. doi:10.1177/1555412011431361

Key, A., George, C. L., Beattie, D., Stammers, K., Lacey, H., & Waller, G. (2002). Body image treatment within an inpatient program for anorexia nervosa: The role of mirror exposure in the desensitization process.[Clinical Trial Controlled Clinical Trial]. *International Journal of Eating Disorders*, *31*(2), 185–190. doi:10.1002/eat.10027 PMID:11920979

Khademi, M., Mousavi Hondori, H., McKenzie, A., Dodakian, L., Lopes, C. V., & Cramer, S. C. (2014). Free-hand interaction with leap motion controller for stroke rehabilitation. *Proceedings of the extended abstracts of the 32nd annual ACM conference on Human factors in computing systems CHI EA '14* (pp. 1663–1668). New York, New York, USA: ACM Press. http://doi.org/ doi:10.1145/2559206.2581203

Khattak, A. M., Akbar, N., Aazam, M., Ali, T., Khan, A. M., Jeon, S., & Lee, S. et al. (2014). Context Representation and Fusion: Advancements and Opportunities. *Sensors (Basel, Switzerland)*, *14*(6), 9628–9668. doi:10.3390/s140609628 PMID:24887042

Kiani, S. L., Anjum, A., Knappmeyer, M., Bessis, N., & Antonopoulos, N. (2013). Federated broker system for pervasive context provisioning. *Journal of Systems and Software*, *86*(4), 1107–1123. doi:10.1016/j.jss.2012.11.050

Kifer, E. (1995). Evaluation: a general view. In G. J. Anglin (Ed.), Instructional Technology: past, present, and future (pp. 384-392). Englewood, Colarado: Libraries Unlimited.

Kim, I.-J., Lee, H. J., & Kim, H.-G. (2004). Magic mirror: a new VR platform design and its applications. *Paper presented at the2004 ACM SIGCHI International Conference on Advances in computer entertainment technology*, Singapore. doi:10.1145/1067343.1067394

Kim, K., Bolton, J., Girouard, A., Cooperstock, J., & Vertegaal, R. (2012) TeleHuman: effects of 3D perspective on gaze and pose estimation with a life-size cylindrical telepresence pod. *Proceedings of theSIGCHI Conference on Human Factors in Computing Systems (CHI '12)* (pp. 2531-2540). doi:10.1145/2207676.2208640

Kim, T., & Biocca, F. (1997). Telepresence via television: Two dimensions of telepresence may have different connections to memory and persuasion. *Journal of Computer-Mediated Communication, 3*(2).

Kim, J.-D. K., Son, J., & Baik, D.-K. (2012). CA5W1H Onto: Ontological Context-Aware Model Based on 5W1H. *International Journal of Distributed Sensor Networks, 2012*, 1–11. doi:10.1155/2012/247346

Kinard, B. R., & Hartman, K. B. (2013). Are you entertained? The impact of brand integration and brand experience in television-related advergames. *Journal of Advertising, 42*(2-3), 196–203. doi:10.1080/00913367.2013.775794

Kinect. (2015). Kinect. Retrieved from https://dev.windows.com/en-us/kinect

Kinect. (2015). The Microsoft Kinect. Retrieved from https://dev.windows.com/en-us/kinect

KinectSpec. (2015). Kinect for Windows sensor components and specifications. Retrieved from https://msdn.microsoft.com/pt-pt/library/jj131033.aspx

Kintsch, W. (1997). Introduction. In F. C. Bartlett (Ed.), *Remembering: A study in experimental and social psychology* (pp. xi–xvi). London: Cambridge University Press.

Kirkpatrick, D. L. (2006a). Preface. In D. L. Kirkpatrick & J. D. Kirkpatrick (Eds.), *Evaluating training programs: the four levels* (pp. xv–xvii). San Francisco: Berrett-Koehler.

Kirkpatrick, D. L. (2006b). The four levels: an overview. In D. L. Kirkpatrick & J. D. Kirkpatrick (Eds.), *Evaluating training programs: the four levels* (pp. xv–xvii). San Francisco: Berrett-Koehler.

Kirriemur, J., & McFarlane, A. (2004). *Literature review in games and learning. NESTA Futurelab Series*. Bristol: NESTA Futurelab.

Kirstein, F. (2014). *Comparing Control Modalities for Robot Learning from Demonstration* [Unpublished MA thesis]. Sønderborg: University of Southern Denmark.

Kistler, F., Endrass, B., Damian, I., Dang, C., & André, E. (2012). Natural interaction with culturally adaptive virtual characters. *Journal on Multimodal User Interfaces, 6*(1-2), 39–47. doi:10.1007/s12193-011-0087-z

Kleeberger, J., & Hummel, J. (2002). *Online-gaming as a marketing and sales catalyst*. Switzerland: Department of Media and Communication, University of St. Gallen.

Klein, L. R. (2003). Creating virtual product experiences: The role of telepresence. *Journal of Interactive Marketing, 17*(1), 41–55. doi:10.1002/dir.10046

Klimmt, C., & Vorderer, P. (2003). Media psychology "is not yet there": Introducing theories on media entertainment to the presence debate. *Presence (Cambridge, Mass.), 12*(4), 346–359. doi:10.1162/105474603322391596

Klopfer, E. (2008). *Augmented Learning*. Cambridge, Massachusetts: The MIT Press. doi:10.7551/mitpress/9780262113151.001.0001

Knapp, M., Hall, J., & Horgan, T. (2013). *Nonverbal communication in human interaction* (8th ed.).

Knappmeyer, M., Kiani, S. L., Reetz, E. S., Baker, N., & Tonjes, R. (2013). Survey of Context Provisioning Middleware. *IEEE Communications Surveys and Tutorials, 15*(3), 1492–1519. doi:10.1109/SURV.2013.010413.00207

Kobayashi, H., Nakamura, H., Tatsuno, J., & Iijima, S. (1993). Micro-macro tele-manipulation system. *Proceedings of 2nd IEEE International Workshop on Robot and Human Communication* (pp. 165 - 170). IEEE.

Koceska, N., & Koceski, S. (2013). Review: Robot device for gait rehabilitation. *International Journal of Computers and Applications, 62*(13), 1–8. doi:10.5120/10137-4279

Kohlbacher, F., & Herstatt, C. (Eds.). (2010). *The silver market phenomenon: Marketing and innovation in the aging society.* Springer Science & Business Media.

Koller, D., Ng, A., Do, C., & Chen, Z. (2013). Retention and intention in massive open online courses: In depth. *EDU-CAUSE Review, 48*(3), 62–63.

Kondori, F., Yousefi, S., Liu, L., & Li, H. (2014). Head operated electric wheelchair. *Proceedings of theIEEE Southwest Symposium on Image Analysis and Interpretation (SSIAI)* (pp. 53-56).

Kordaki, M. (2011). A computer card game for the learning of basic aspects of the binary system in primary education: Design and pilot evaluation. *Education and Information Technologies, 16*(4), 395–421. doi:10.1007/s10639-010-9136-6

Kreb, H. I. (2006). An overview of rehabilitation robotics technologies. *Proceedings of theAmerican Spinal Injury Association Symposium.*

Krebs, H. I., Palazzolo, J. J., Dipietro, L., Ferraro, M., Krol, J., Rannekleiv, K., & Hogan, N. et al. (2003). N. Rehabilitation robotics: Performance-based progressive robot-assisted therapy. *Autonomous Robots, 15*(1), 7–20. doi:10.1023/A:1024494031121

Krijn, M., Emmelkamp, P. M. G., Olafsson, R. P., & Biemond, R. (2004). Virtual reality exposure therapy of anxiety disorders: A review. *Clinical Psychology Review, 24*(3), 259–281. doi:10.1016/j.cpr.2004.04.001 PMID:15245832

Kristianslund, E., Krosshaug, T., & Bogert, A. J. (2012). Effect of low pass filtering on joint moments from inverse dynamics: Implications for injury prevention. *Journal of Biomechanics, 45*(4).

Krueger, M. W., Gionfriddo, T., & Hinrichsen, K. (1985). VIDEOPLACE---an artificial reality. *ACM SIGCHI Bulletin, 16*(4), 35–40. doi:10.1145/1165385.317463

Krug, S. (2014). *Don't make me think, revisited: A common sense approach to web usability.* California: Pearson Education.

Kubrick, S. (1968). 2001: A Space Odyssey. USA, UK: Metro-Goldwyn-Mayer (MGM).

Kühnel, C., Westermann, T., Hemmert, F., Kratz, S., Müller, A., & Möller, S. (2011). I'm home: Defining and evaluating a gesture set for smart-home control. *International Journal of Human-Computer Studies, 69*(11), 693–704. doi:10.1016/j.ijhcs.2011.04.005

Kukliński, K., Fischer, K., Marhenke, I., Kirstein, F., aus der Wieschen, M. V., Sølvason, D., & Savarimuthu, T. R. (2014). Teleoperation for learning by demonstration: Data glove versus object manipulation for intuitive robot control. *Proceedings of the 6th International Congress on Ultra Modern Telecommunications and Control Systems and Workshops* (pp. 346-351).

Lai, K., Konrad, J., & Ishwar, P. (2012). A gesture-driven computer interface using Kinect. *Proceedings of the IEEE Southwest Symposium on Image Analysis and Interpretation (SSIAI)* (pp. 185-188).

Lai, M., & Huang, Y. S. (2011). Can learning theoretical approaches illuminate the ways in which advertising games effect attitude, recall, and purchase intention. *International Journal of Electronic Business Management, 9*(4), 368.

Lang, A. (2000). The limited capacity model of motivated mediated message processing. *Journal of Communication, 50*(1), 46–70. doi:10.1111/j.1460-2466.2000.tb02833.x

Langhorne, P., Bernhardt, J., & Kwakkel, G. (2011). Series stroke rehabilitation. *Lancet, 377*(9778), 1695–1702. doi:10.1016/S0140-6736(11)60325-5 PMID:21571152

Lanquar, R. (2014). *Mondialisation et tourisme religieux. Vietnam Institute of Culture and Arts Studies (VICAS).* Vietnam: Novembre, Nguyen Luong Bang.

Lapointe, J., Savard, P., & Vinson, N. G. (2011). A comparative study of four input devices for desktop virtual walk-throughs. *Computers in Human Behavior*, 27(6), 2186–2191. doi:10.1016/j.chb.2011.06.014

LaViola, J., Jr. (2014). An Introduction to 3D Gestural Interfaces. Proceedings of the ACM SIGGRAPH 2014 Courses (pp. 25:1–25:42).

Lawrence, D. A. (1993, October). Stability and transparency in bilateral teleoperation. *IEEE Transactions on Robotics and Automation*, 9(5), 624–637. doi:10.1109/70.258054

Lawton, M. P. (1999). Environmental taxonomy: Generalizations from research with older adults. In S. L. Friedman & T. D. Wachs (Eds.), *Measuring environment across the life span* (pp. 91–124). Washington, DC: American Psychology Association. doi:10.1037/10317-004

Leap developer portal. (2015). Leap Developer Portal. Retrieved from https://developer.leapmotion.com/documentation/csharp/devguide/Leap_Overview.html

Leap Motion App Store. (2015). Retrieved from https://apps.leapmotion.com/

Leap Motion. (2015). Leap Motion Sensor. Retrieved from www.leapmotion.com

Leap Motion. (2015). Leap Motion. Retrieved from https://www.leapmotion.com/

Leap. (2014). Leap motion. Retrieved from https://www.leapmotion.com/

Lee, H., Choi, J. S., & Elmasri, R. (2009). A classification and modeling of the quality of contextual information in smart spaces. *Proceedings of the IEEE International Conference on Pervasive Computing and Communications* (pp. 1-5). Galveston, TX, USA: IEEE. doi:10.1109/PERCOM.2009.4912889

Lee, J., Park, H., & Wise, K. (2014). Brand interactivity and its effects on the outcomes of advergame play. *New Media & Society*, 16(8), 1268–1286. doi:10.1177/1461444813504267

Lee, M., & Faber, R. J. (2007). Effects of product placement in on-line games on brand memory: A perspective of the limited-capacity model of attention. *Journal of Advertising*, 36(4), 75–90. doi:10.2753/JOA0091-3367360406

Lee, S. Y., & Shen, F. (2009). Joint Advertising and Brand Congruity: Effects on Memory and Attitudes. *Journal of Promotion Management*, 15(4), 448–498. doi:10.1080/10496490903276874

Legon, R., & Runyon, J. (2007). Research on the impact of the quality matters course review process. *Paper presented at the 23rd Annual Conference on Distance Teaching & Learning*.

Lehne, M. (2015). Airwriting. Retrieved from http://www.informatik.kit.edu/english/309_6566.php

LEO. (2009). The Experience Pyramid. *Lapland Center of Expertise for the Experience Industry*. Retrieved from http://reiselivsnytt-utmark.sfskog.no/upload/Audny%20Chris%20%C3%98iamo-Holsen%20foredrag.pdf

Lewis, G., Novakouski, M., & Sánchez, E. (2012). A Reference Architecture for Group-Context-Aware Mobile Applications. *Proceedings of the Fourth International Conference on Mobile Computing, Applications and Services (MobiCASE 20120* (pp. 44-63). Seattle, WA: EAI.

Lewis, B., & Porter, L. (2010). In-game advertising effects: Examining player perceptions of advertising schema congruity in a massively multiplayer online role-playing game. *Journal of Interactive Advertising*, 10(2), 46–60. doi:10.1080/15252019.2010.10722169

Li, M. (2011). Ontology-based context information modeling for smart space. *Proceedings of the 10th IEEE International Conference on Cognitive Informatics & Cognitive Computing (ICCI*CC)* (pp. 278-283). Banff, AB: IEEE. doi:10.1109/COGINF.2011.6016153

Li, W. H. A., & Fu, H. (2012). Augmented reflection of reality. *Paper presented at the ACM SIGGRAPH 2012 Emerging Technologies*, Los Angeles, California, USA. doi:10.1145/2343456.2343459

Li, X., An, J., Min, J., & Hong, K.-S. (2011). Hand gesture recognition by stereo camera using the thinning method. *Proceeding of the 2011 International Conference on Multimedia Technology* (pp. 3077–3080). IEEE. http://doi.org/doi:<ALIGNMENT.qj></ALIGNMENT>10.1109/ICMT.2011.6001670

Li, Y., Fang, J., & Xiong, J. (2008). A Context-Aware Services Mash-Up System. *Proceedings of the Seventh International Conference on Grid and Cooperative Computing* (pp. 707-712). Shenzhen: IEEE. doi:10.1109/GCC.2008.62

Li, A., Montano, Z., Chen, V. J., & Gold, J. I. (2011). Virtual reality and pain management: Current trends and future directions. *Pain Management*, *1*(2), 147–157. doi:10.2217/pmt.10.15 PMID:21779307

Liang, C., Lee, Y.-Z., & Chou, W.-S. (2010). The design considerations for game-based learning. *Educational Technology*, *50*(2), 25–28.

Liao, C. C. Y., Chen, Z.-H., Cheng, H. N. H., Chen, F.-C., & Chan, T.-W. (2011). My-Mini-Pet: A handheld pet-nurturing game to engage students in arithmetic practices. *Journal of Computer Assisted Learning*, *27*(1), 76–89. doi:10.1111/j.1365-2729.2010.00367.x

Liljekrans, D. (2012). *Investigating peg-in-hole strategies through teleoperation* [MSc thesis]. University of Southern Denmark, Odense.

Lim, S., & Kim, S. (2014). Holographic projection system with 3D spatial interaction. Proceedings of the 5th International Conference on Advanced Data and Information Engineering (DaEng-2013) (pp. 409-416). doi:10.1007/978-981-4585-18-7_46

Lin, L., & Hu, J., & Shen, B. (2010). A new hybrid method of Genetic Algorithm, Tabu and Chaotic search for CVRPTW. *Proceeding of the 2010 IEEE International Conference on Intelligent Computing and Intelligent Systems* (pp. 336–340). IEEE. http://doi.org/doi:10.1109/ICICISYS.2010.5658353

Li, P., Corner, B., Carson, J., & Paquette, S. (2015). A three-dimensional shape database from a large-scale anthropometric survey. *Proceedings 19th Triennial Congress of the IEA*.

Lippmann, M. (1908). La photographie integral. *Compt. Rend. Acad. Sci.*, *146*, 446.

Litefast. (2013) Litefast MAGIC displays. Retrieved from http://www.litefast-display.com/products/litefast-products/litefast-magic/litefast-magic.html

Liu, Z., Zhang, Y., Patrick Rau, P.-L., Choe, P., & Gulrez, T. (2015). Leap-Motion Based Online Interactive System for Hand Rehabilitation. In Cross-Cultural Design Applications in Mobile Interaction, Education, Health, Transport and Cultural Heritage, LNCS (Vol. 9181, pp. 338–347). http://doi.org/doi:10.1007/978-3-319-20934-0_32

Liu, A., Tharp, G., French, L., Lai, S., & Stark, L. (1993, October). Some of what one needs to know about using head-mounted displays to improve teleoperator performance. *IEEE Transactions on Robotics and Automation*, *9*(5), 638–648. doi:10.1109/70.258055

Liu, K., & Kehtarnavaz, N. (2013). Real-time robust vision-based hand gesture recognition using stereo images. *Journal of Real-Time Image Processing*. doi:10.1007/s11554-013-0333-6

Liu, T.-Y., Tan, T.-H., & Chu, Y.-L. (2009). Outdoor natural science learning with an RFID-supported immersive ubiquitous learning environment. *Journal of Educational Technology & Society, 12*(4), 161–175.

Li, X., Ren, H., Chen, X., Liu, J., Li, Q., Li, C., & Gu, M. et al. (2015). Athermally photoreduced graphene oxides for three-dimensional holographic images. *Nature Communications, 6*. doi:10.1038/ncomms7984 PMID:25901676

Li, Y. (2000). Geographical consciousness and tourism experience. *Annals of Tourism Research, 27*(4), 863–883. doi:10.1016/S0160-7383(99)00112-7

Lo, R., Chen, A., Rampersad, V., Huang, J., Wu, H., & Mann, S. (2013). Augmediated reality system based on 3D camera selfgesture sensing. *Proceedings of the 2013 IEEE International Symposium on Technology and Society (ISTAS)* (pp. 20-31). IEEE.

Loke, S. W. (2006, April). Context-aware artifacts: Two development approaches. *IEEE Pervasive Computing / IEEE Computer Society [and] IEEE Communications Society, 5*(2), 48–53. doi:10.1109/MPRV.2006.27

L'Oréal. (2015). Makeup Genius. Introducing the first ever virtual makeup tester. Retrieved from http://www.lorealparisusa.com/en/brands/makeup/makeup-genius-virtual-makeup-tool.aspx

Lorenz, R. D., Meyer, K. M., & De Riet, D. M. V. (1990). A novel, compliant, four degree-of-freedom, robotic fingertip sensor. *IEEE Transactions on Industry Applications, 26*(4), 613–619. doi:10.1109/28.55983

Louis, S. J., Chen, Q., & Pullammanappallil, S. (1999). Seismic velocity inversion with genetic algorithm. *Proc. of the Congress on Evolutionary Computation* (p. 2).

Loureiro, R. C. V., Harwin, W. S., Nagai, K., & Johnson, M. (2011). Special review issue: Advances in upper limb stroke rehabilitation: a technology push. *Medical & Biological Engineering & Computing, 49*(10), 1103–1118. doi:10.1007/s11517-011-0797-0 PMID:21773806

Löwe, R., Mandl, P., & Weber, M. (2012). Context Directory: A context-aware service for mobile context-aware computing applications by the example of Google Android. *Proceedings of the 2012 IEEE International Conference on Pervasive Computing and Communications Workshops (PERCOM Workshops)* (pp. 76-81). Lugano: IEEE. doi:10.1109/PerComW.2012.6197616

Low, K. H. (2011, August 3-5). Robot-assisted gait rehabilitation: from exoskeleton to gait systems. *Defence Science Research Conference&Expo, Singapore* (pp. 1-10). doi:10.1109/DSR.2011.6026886

Lucas, L. (1991). Visually designing the computer-learner interface. *Educational Technology, 31*(7), 56–58.

Lü, H., & Li, Y. (2011, May 7-12). Gesture avatar: A technique for operating mobile user interfaces using gestures. In D. Tan, S. Amershi, B. Begole, W. Kellogg, & M. Tungare (Eds.), *Proceedings of the International Conference on Human Factors in Computing Systems CHI '11*, Vancouver, BC, Canada. ACM.

Lynch, C. (2012). Kinect Party review. More fun from the fun kings Retrieved from http://www.ign.com/articles/2012/12/21/kinect-party-review

Lynch, J. G. Jr, & Srull, T. K. (1982). Memory and attentional factors in consumer choice: Concepts and research methods. *The Journal of Consumer Research, 9*(1), 18–37. doi:10.1086/208893

Macedonia, M. (2009). Virtual worlds: A new reality for treating posttraumatic stress disorder. *IEEE Computer Graphics and Applications, 29*(1), 86–88. doi:10.1109/MCG.2009.18 PMID:19363961

MacKenzie, S. (2003). Motor behavior models for human-computer interaction. In J. Carroll (Ed.), *HCI model, theories and frameworks: Towards a multidisciplinary science* (pp. 27–54). San Francisco, CA: Morgan Kaufmann; doi:10.1016/B978-155860808-5/50003-4

MacKichan, F., Paterson, C., Henley, W. E., & Britten, N. (2011). Self-care in people with long term health problems: A community based survey. *BMC Family Practice*, *12*(1), 53. doi:10.1186/1471-2296-12-53 PMID:21689455

Macrae, C. N., Hewstone, M., & Griffiths, R. J. (1993). Processing load and memory for stereotype-based information. *European Journal of Social Psychology*, *23*(1), 77–87. doi:10.1002/ejsp.2420230107

Magalhães-Mendes, J. (2013). A Comparative Study of Crossover Operators for Genetic Algorithms to Solve the Job Shop Scheduling Problem. *WSEAS Transactions on Computers*, *12*, 164–173.

Magic Mirror. (2014). World market leader for interactive digital signage Retrieved from http://www.magicmirror.me/

Magnenat-Thalmann, N., & Thalmann, D. (1990). Human modeling and animation. In *Computer Animation* (pp. 129–149). Berlin, New York: Springer-Verlag. doi:10.1007/978-4-431-68105-2_10

Maguire, M. C. (1999). A review of user-interface design guidelines for public information kiosk systems. *International Journal of Human-Computer Interaction Studies*, *50*(3), 263–286.

Mahmud, U., & Javed, M. Y. (2014). Context Inference Engine (CiE): Classifying Activity of Context using Minkowski Distance and Standard Deviation-Based Ranks. In Systems and Software Development, Modeling, and Analysis: New Perspectives and Methodologies (pp. 65-112). IGI Global.

Mahmud, U., Iltaf, N., & Kamran, F. (2007). Context Congregator: Gathering Contextual Information in CAPP. Proceedings of the 5th Frontiers of Information Technology FIT '07 (pp. 134–141). Islamabad, Pakistan: COMSATS.

Mahmud, U., Iltaf, N., Rehman, A., & Kamran, F. (2007). Context-Aware Paradigm for a Pervasive Computing Environment (CAPP). Proceedings of the WWW\Internet 2007 (pp. 337–346). Portugal: Villa Real.

Mahmud, U. (2015). UML based Model of a Context Aware System.[IJAPUC]. *International Journal of Advanced Pervasive and Ubiquitous Computing*, *7*(1), 1–16. doi:10.4018/IJAPUC.2015010101

Mahmud, U., Farooq, U., Javed, M. Y., & Malik, N. A. (2012, March). Representing and Organizing Contextual Data in Context Aware Environments. *Journal of Computing*, *4*(3), 61–67.

Mahmud, U., & Javed, M. Y. (2012, July). Context Inference Engine (CiE): Inferring Context. *International Journal of Advanced Pervasive and Ubiquitous Computing*, *4*(3), 13–41. doi:10.4018/japuc.2012070102

Mahmud, U., & Malik, N. A. (2014). Flow and Threat Modelling of a Context Aware System. *International Journal of Advanced Pervasive and Ubiquitous Computing*, *6*(2), 58–70. doi:10.4018/ijapuc.2014040105

Main, S., & O'Rourke, J. (2011). New Directions for Traditional Lessons: Can Handheld Game Consoles Enhance Mental Mathematics Skills? *Australian Journal of Teacher Education*, *36*(2), 4. doi:10.14221/ajte.2011v36n2.4

Maister, L., Slater, M., Sanchez-Vives, M. V., & Tsakiris, M. (2015). Changing bodies changes minds: Owning another body affects social cognition. *Trends in Cognitive Sciences*, *19*(1), 6–12. doi:10.1016/j.tics.2014.11.001 PMID:25524273

Malik, N. A., Mahmud, U., & Javed, M. Y. (2007). Future challenges in context aware computing. Proceedings of the WWW/Internet '07 (pp. 306-310).

Malik, N. A., Mahmud, U., & Javed, M. Y. (2009, August). Estimating User Preferences by Managing Contextual History in Context Aware Systems. *Journal of Software*, *6*(4), 571–576.

Malik, S., Ranjan, A., & Balakrishnan, R. (2005). Interacting with large displays from a distance with vision-tracked multi-finger gestural input.*Proceedings of the 18th annual ACM Symposium User Interface Software and Technology - UIST '05* (pp. 43-52). doi:10.1145/1095034.1095042

Mallinckrodt, V., & Mizerski, D. (2007). The effects of playing an advergame on young children's perceptions, preferences, and requests. *Journal of Advertising, 36*(2), 87–100. doi:10.2753/JOA0091-3367360206

Malloy, K. M., & Milling, L. S. (2010). The effectiveness of virtual reality distraction for pain reduction: A systematic review. *Clinical Psychology Review, 30*(8), 1011–1018. doi:10.1016/j.cpr.2010.07.001 PMID:20691523

Mandal, S., Kar, R., Mandal, D., & Ghosal, D. (2011). Swarm Intelligence based optimal linear phase FIR high pass filter design using particle swarm optimization with constriction factor and inertia weight approach. *World Academy Of Science, Eng. & Tech., 5*(8), 1156–1162.

Mandel, T. (1997). *The elements of user interface design.* New York: John Wiley & Sons.

March, S. T., & Smith, G. F. (1995). Design and natural science research on information technology. *Decision Support Systems, 15*(4), 251–266. doi:10.1016/0167-9236(94)00041-2

March, S. T., & Storey, V. C. (2008). Design science in the information systems discipline: An introduction to the special issue on design science research. *Management Information Systems Quarterly, 32*(4), 725–730.

Marcus, A. (2002). Dare we define user-interface design? *Interaction, 9*(5), 19–24. doi:10.1145/566981.566992

Marescaux, J., Rubino, F., Arenas, M., Mutter, D., & Soler, L. (2004, November10). Augmented-reality-assisted laparoscopic adrenalectomy. *Journal of the American Medical Association, 292*(18), 2214–2215. PMID:15536106

Marhenke, I., Fischer, K., & Savarimuthu, T. R. (2014). Reasons for Singularity in Robot Teleoperation.*Proceedings of the 2014 ACM/IEEE international conference on Human-robot interaction* (pp. 242-243). ACM. doi:10.1145/2559636.2559828

Marin, G., Dominio, F., & Zanuttigh, P. (2014). Hand gesture recognition with leap motion and Kinect devices. *Proceedings of the2014 IEEE International Conference on Image Processing (ICIP)* (pp. 1565–1569). IEEE. http://doi.org/doi:10.1109/ICIP.2014.7025313

Marotz, J., Lübbert, C., & Eisenbeiss, W. (2001). Effective object recognition for automated counting of colonies in petri dishes (automated colony counting). *Computer Methods and Programs in Biomedicine, 66*(2-3), 183–198. doi:10.1016/S0169-2607(00)00128-0 PMID:11551392

Marshall, S. (2005a). Report on the e-learning maturity model evaluation of the New Zealand tertiary sector. Retrieved from http://www.utdc.vuw.ac.nz/research/emm/documents/SectorReport.pdf

Marshall, S., & Mitchell, G. (2002). An e-learning maturity model. *Paper presented at the19th Annual Conference of the Australian Society for Computers in Learning in Tertiary Education*, Auckland, New Zealand.

Marshall, S. (2005b). Determination of New Zealand tertiary institution e-learning capability: An application of an e-learning maturity model. *Journal of Distance-learning, 9*(1), 58–63.

Martínez De Pisón, M. J., Sanmartín, F., Carbonell, A., Furió, D., Cuesta, S., Rodríguez, L., . . . Piqueras, D. (2006). *Especulaciones a un tiempo.*

Martinez Plasencia, D., Berthaut, F., Karnik, A., & Subramanian, S. (2014). *Through the combining glass.* Paper presented at the Proceedings of the 27th annual ACM symposium on User interface software and technology, Honolulu, Hawaii, USA.

Martins, J. M. S., Rodrigues, J. M. F., & Martins, J. C. (2015). Low-cost natural interface based on head movements. *Proceedings of the6th International Conference on Software Development and Technologies for Enhancing*, Fraunhofer FIT, Sankt Augustin, Germany. doi:10.1016/j.procs.2015.09.275

Martí-Parreño, J., Aldás-Manzano, J., Currás-Pérez, R., & Sánchez-García, I. (2013). Factors contributing brand attitude in advergames: Entertainment and irritation. *Journal of Brand Management, 20*(5), 374–388. doi:10.1057/bm.2012.22

Masiero, S., Carraro, E., Ferraro, C., Gallina, P., Rossi, A., & Rossati, G. (2009). Special Report: Upper limb rehabilitation robotics after stroke: A perspective from the university of Padua, Italy. *Journal of Rehabilitation Medicine, 41*(12), 981–985. doi:10.2340/16501977-0404 PMID:19841828

Masoumi, D., & Lindstrom, B. (2012). Quality in e-learning: A framework for promoting and assuring quality in virtual institutions. *Journal of Computer Assisted Learning, 28*(1), 27–41. doi:10.1111/j.1365-2729.2011.00440.x

Massimino, M. J., & Sheridan, T. B. (1994, March). Teleoperator Performance with Varying Force and Visual Feedback. *Human Factors: The Journal of the Human Factors and Ergonomics Society, 36*(1), 145-157.

Mateo, J. C., Gilkey, R. H., & Cowgill, J. L. (2007, October). Effect of Variable Visual-Feedback Delay on Movement Time. *Proceedings of the Human Factors and Ergonomics Society Annual Meeting* (pp. 1373-1377).

Mayans Martorell, J. (2012a). *Augmented User Interface*. Master, Universidad Politécnica de Valencia, Valencia. Retrieved from https://riunet.upv.es/handle/10251/27578

Mayans Martorell, J. (2012b). Augmented User Interface - Artistic Essays. Retrieved from https://www.youtube.com/watch?v=aWVPZAFSidk

Mayer, R. E. (2004). Should there be a three-strikes rule against pure discovery learning? *The American Psychologist, 59*(1), 14–19. doi:10.1037/0003-066X.59.1.14 PMID:14736316

Mayer, R. E., & Moreno, R. (2003). Nine ways to reduce cognitive load in multimedia learning. *Educational Psychologist, 38*(1), 43–52. doi:10.1207/S15326985EP3801_6

Mayes, T., & De Freitas, S. (2004). JISC e-Learning Models desk study, Stage 2: Review of e-learning theories, frameworks and models Retrieved from http://www.jisc.ac.uk/uploaded_documents/Stage%202%20Learning%20Models%20(Version%201).pdf

Mayo, M. (2007). Games for Science and Engineering Education. *Communications of the ACM, 50*(7), 31–35. doi:10.1145/1272516.1272536

Mazzoleni, S., Darion, P., Carrozza, M. C., & Guglielmelli, E. (2010). Application of robotics and mechatronics systems to neurorehabilitation. Intech.

McAvoy, L. M., Chen, L., & Donnelly, M. (2012). An Ontology-based Context Management System for Smart Environments. *Proceedings of theSixth International Conference on Mobile Ubiquitous Computing, Systems, Services and Technologies, UBICOMM 2012* (pp. 18-23). Barcelona, Spain: IARIA.

McFarland, D. J., Krusienski, D. J., Sarnacki, W. A., & Wolpaw, J. R. (2008). Emulation of computer mouse control with a noninvasive brain–computer interface. *Journal of Neural Engineering, 5*(2), 101–110. doi:10.1088/1741-2560/5/2/001 PMID:18367779

McLellan, H. (2004). Virtual realities. In Handbook of research for educational communications and technology, (2nd ed., pp. 457-487).

McNeill, D. (1992). *Hand and Mind—What Gestures Reveal about Thought*. Chicago, London: The University of Chicago Press.

Mehrabian, A. (1981). *Silent messages: Implicit communication of emotions and attitudes* (2nd ed.). Wadsworth.

Meijer, M. (1989). *The contribution of general features of body movement to the attribution of emotions. Journal of Nonverbal behavior, 13(4)*.

Meinders, M., Gitter, A., & Czernieki, J. M. (1998). The role of ankle plantar flexor muscle work during walking. *Scandinavian Journal of Rehabilitation Medicine, 30*(1), 39–46. doi:10.1080/003655098444309 PMID:9526753

Melder, W. A., Truong, K. P., Uyl, M. D., Leeuwen, D. A. V., Neerincx, M. A., Loos, L. R., & Plum, B. S. (2007). Affective multimodal mirror: sensing and eliciting laughter. *Paper presented at the international workshop on Human-centered multimedia*, Augsburg, Bavaria, Germany. doi:10.1145/1290128.1290134

Melenhorst, A. S., Rogers, W. A., & Bouwhuis, D. G. (2006, March). Older adults' motivated choice for technological innovation: Evidence for benefit-driven selectivity. *Psychology and Aging, 21*(1), 190–195. doi:10.1037/0882-7974.21.1.190 PMID:16594804

Melzack, R., & Wall, P. D. (1965). Pain mechanisms: A new theory. *Science, 150*(3699), 971–979. doi:10.1126/science.150.3699.971 PMID:5320816

Memon, M., Wagner, S., Pedersen, C. F., Beevi, F. H. A., & Hansen, F. O. (2014). Ambient assisted living healthcare frameworks, platforms, standards, and quality attributes. *Sensors (Basel, Switzerland), 14*(3), 4312–4341. doi:10.3390/s140304312 PMID:24599192

Meng, Z., Pan, J., Tseng, K., & Zheng, W. (2012). Dominant points based hand finger counting for recognition under skin color extraction in hand gesture control system. *Proceedings of the 6th International Conference on Genetic and Evolutionary Computing (ICGEC '12)* (pp. 364–367). doi:10.1109/ICGEC.2012.85

Meredith, J. R., & Mantel, S. J. Jr. (2011). *Project management: a managerial approach*. John Wiley & Sons.

Merrill, M. D. (1997). Instructional transaction theory: An instructional design model based on knowledge objects. In R. Tennyson, F. Schott, N. Seel, & S. Dijkstra (Eds.), Instructional design: International perspectives (Vol. 1: Theory, research and models, pp. 381-394). Mahwah, New Jersey: Lawrence Erlbaum Associates.

Metaio (2015). Augmented Reality Museum Experience. *Metaio AR*. Retrieved from https://www.youtube.com/watch?v=RxSb4tjdTPk

Michaelson, R., Helliar, C., Power, D., & Sinclair, D. (2001). Evaluating FINESSE: A case-study in group-based CAL. *Computers & Education, 37*(1), 67–80. doi:10.1016/S0360-1315(01)00035-5

Michele, B., & Karpow, A. (2014). Watch and be watched: Compromising all smart tv generations. *Proceedings of the 2014 IEEE 11th Consumer Communications and Networking Conference (CCNC)* (pp. 351-356). IEEE. doi:10.1109/CCNC.2014.6866594

Microsoft. (2014). Kinect for Windows. Retrieved from http://goo.gl/fGZT8X

Microsoft. (2015). Kinect for windows. Retrieved from www.microsoft.com/en-us/kinectforwindows

Microsoft. (2015). Meet Kinect. Retrieved from https://www.microsoft.com/en-us/kinectforwindows/meetkinect/default.aspx

Microsoft. (2015a). Kinect Windows app Development. Retrieved from https://dev.windows.com/en-us/kinect

Microsoft. (2015b). Kinect Skeletal Tracking. Retrieved from https://msdn.microsoft.com/en-us/library/hh973074.aspx

Microsoft. (2015c). Microsoft. Kinect Namespace. Retrieved from https://msdn.microsoft.com/en-us/library/hh855419.aspx

Mihaylova, E. (Ed.). (2013). *Holography - Basic Principles and Contemporary Applications*. InTech. doi:10.5772/46111

Mikropoulos, T. A. (2006). Presence: A unique characteristic in educational virtual environments. *Virtual Reality (Waltham Cross)*, *10*(3-4), 197–206. doi:10.1007/s10055-006-0039-1

Mikropoulos, T. A., & Strouboulis, V. (2004). Factors that influence presence in educational virtual environments. *Cyberpsychology & Behavior*, *7*(5), 582–591. doi:10.1089/cpb.2004.7.582 PMID:15667053

Milano, R., Baggio, R., & Piattelli, R. (2011, January). The effects of online social media on tourism websites. In Information and Communication technologies in tourism 2011 (pp. 471-483). doi:10.1007/978-3-7091-0503-0_38

Miles, R. (2012). *Start here! Learn the Kinect API*. Pearson Education.

Miller, C. C. (2013). Google searches for style. *The New York Times. Retrieved, 5*.

Miller, J. (2015). What it's like to use the Oculus Rift and Touch you'll buy in 2016: Diving ever deeper into another world. Retrieved from http://www.cnet.com/products/oculus-rift/

Miller, G. A. (1956). The magical number seven, plus or minus two: Some limits on our capacity for processing information. *Psychological Review*, *63*(2), 81–97. doi:10.1037/h0043158 PMID:13310704

Miller, J. G. (1965). Living systems: Basic concepts. *Behavioral Science*, *10*(3), 193–237. doi:10.1002/bs.3830100302 PMID:5318173

Milo, R., Shen-Orr, S., Itzkovitz, S., Kashtan, N., Chklovskii, D., & Alon, U. (2002). Network motifs: Simple building blocks of complex networks. *Science*, *298*(5594), 824–827. doi:10.1126/science.298.5594.824 PMID:12399590

Miner, D., & Shook, A. (2012). *MapReduce Design Patterns: Building Effective Algorithms and Analytics for Hadoop and Other Systems* (1st ed.). O'Reilly Media.

Ministry of health Malaysia. (2014). Health Facts 2010. Retrieved from www.moh.gov.my

Mistry, P. (2009). SixthSense. Fluid Interfaces Group, MIT Media Lab. Retrieved from http://www.pranavmistry.com/projects/sixthsense/

Mistry, P., & Maes, P. (2009). SixthSense: a wearable gestural interface. Proceedings of the ACM SIGGRAPH ASIA 2009 Sketches (p. 11). ACM.

Mitra, S., & Acharya, T. (2007). Gesture Recognition: A Survey. *IEEE Transactions on Systems, Man and Cybernetics. Part C, Applications and Reviews*, *37*(3), 311–324. doi:10.1109/TSMCC.2007.893280

Mitra, S., & Acharya, T. (2007). Gesture recognition: A survey. *IEEE Transactions on Systems, Man, and Cybernetics, Part C: Applications and Reviews*, *37*(3), 311–324.

Mitsantisuk, C., Katsura, S., & Ohishi, K. (2010, April). Force control of human–robot interaction using twin direct-drive motor system based on modal space design. *IEEE Transactions on Industrial Electronics*, *57*(4), 1383–1392. doi:10.1109/TIE.2009.2030218

Mixed Reality Lab. (2006). Software. MXR ToolKit Retrieved from http://mixedrealitylab.org/projects/software/

Mizuochi, M., Tsuji, T., & Ohnishi, K. (2006). Improvement of disturbance suppression based on disturbance observer. *Proceedings of 9th IEEE International Workshop on Advanced Motion Control* (pp. 229-234). IEEE. doi:10.1109/AMC.2006.1631663

Mochizuki, Y., Inokuchi, S., & Omura, K. (2000). Generating artificially mastered motions for an upper limb in baseball pitching from several objective functions. *IEEE Transactions on Systems, Man, and Cybernetics*, *30*(3), 373–382. doi:10.1109/3477.846228 PMID:18252371

Mohadisdudis, H. M., & Ali, N. M. (2014, September). A study of smartphone usage and barriers among the elderly. *Proceedings of the 2014 3rd International Conference on User Science and Engineering (i-USEr)* (pp. 109-114). IEEE. doi:10.1109/IUSER.2014.7002686

Molenda, M. (1997). Historical and philosophical foundations of instructional design: A north American view. In R. Tennyson, F. Schott, N. Seel, & S. Dijkstra (Eds.), Instructional design: International perspectives (Vol. 1: Theory, research and models, pp. 41-53). Mahwah, New Jersey: Lawrence Erlbaum Associates.

Mongo, D. B. (2015). MongoDB. Retrieved from https://www.mongodb.org/

Monteiro, J., Eduardo, J., Cardoso, P. J. S., & Semião, J. (2014b). A distributed load scheduling mechanism for micro grids. *Proceedings of the 2014 IEEE International Conference on Smart Grid Communications (SmartGridComm)* (pp. 278–283). IEEE. http://doi.org/ doi:10.1109/SmartGridComm.2014.7007659

Monteiro, J., Cardoso, P. J. S., Serra, R., & Fernandes, L. (2014a). Evaluation of the Human Factor in the Scheduling of Smart Appliances in Smart Grids. In C. Stephanidis & M. Antona (Eds.), *Universal Access in Human-Computer Interaction. Aging and Assistive Environments* (pp. 537–548). Springer International Publishing; doi:10.1007/978-3-319-07446-7_52

Montgomery, D. C., & Runger, G. C. (2010). *Applied statistics and probability for engineers*. John Wiley & Sons.

Moore, E. S., & Rideout, V. J. (2007). The online marketing of food to children: Is it just fun and games? *Journal of Public Policy & Marketing*, *26*(2), 202–220. doi:10.1509/jppm.26.2.202

Moore, M. G. (1989). Editorial: Three types of interaction. *American Journal of Distance Education*, *3*(2), 1–7. doi:10.1080/08923648909526659

Mori, M. (2015). The Uncanny Valley. *IEEE*. Retrieved from http://spectrum.ieee.org/automaton/robotics/humanoids/the-uncanny-valley

Morimoto, C. H. (2001). *Interactive Digital Mirror*. Retrieved from http://doi.ieeecomputersociety.org/10.1109/SIBGRAPI.2001.963060 doi:10.1109/SIBGRAPI.2001.963060

Morris, A., Goodman, J., & Brading, H. (2007). Internet use and non-use: Views of older users. *Universal Access in the Information Society*, *6*(1), 43–57. doi:10.1007/s10209-006-0057-5

Mortara, M., Catalano, C. E., Bellotti, F., Fiucci, G., Houry-Panchetti, M., & Petridis, P. (2014). Learning cultural heritage by serious games. *Journal of Cultural Heritage*, *15*(3), 318–325. doi:10.1016/j.culher.2013.04.004

Mossberg, L. (2007). A Marketing Approach to the Tourist Experience. *Scandinavian Journal of Hospitality and Tourism*, *7*(1), 59–74. doi:10.1080/15022250701231915

Motion, L. (2015). Leap Motion. Retrieved from https://www.leapmotion.com/

Moura, A. (2008). A Multi-Objective Genetic Algorithm for the Vehicle Routing with Time Windows and Loading Problem. In *Intelligent Decision Support* (pp. 187–201). Wiesbaden: Gabler; doi:10.1007/978-3-8349-9777-7_11

Moutinho, L. (1987). Consumer behaviour in tourism. *European Journal of Marketing*, *11*(10), 5–44. doi:10.1108/EUM0000000004718

Mulder, J. D. (2006). Occlusion in Mirror-Based Co-Located Augmented Reality Systems. *Presence (Cambridge, Mass.)*, *15*(1), 93–107. doi:10.1162/pres.2006.15.1.93

Müller, H., Michoux, N., Bandon, D., & Geissbuhler, A. (2004). A review of content-based image retrieval systems in medical applications—clinical benefits and future directions. *International Journal of Medical Informatics*, *73*(1), 1–23. doi:10.1016/j.ijmedinf.2003.11.024 PMID:15036075

Muller, M. J., Haslwanter, J. H., & Dayton, T. (1997). Participatory practices in the software lifecycle. In M. Helander, T. K. Landauer, & P. Prabhu (Eds.), *Handbook of Human-Computer Interaction* (2nd ed.). New York: Elsevier Science Inc. doi:10.1016/B978-044481862-1.50077-7

Munar, A. M., & Jacobsen, J. K. S. (2013). Trust and involvement in tourism social media and web-based travel information sources. *Scandinavian Journal of Hospitality and Tourism*, *13*(1), 1–19. doi:10.1080/15022250.2013.764511

Munguba, M. C., Valdes, M. T. M., & da Silva, C. A. B. (2008). The application of an occupational therapy nutrition education programme for children who are obese. *Occupational Therapy International*, *15*(1), 56–70. doi:10.1002/oti.244 PMID:18288771

Murakami, T., Yu, F., & Ohnishi, K. (1993, April). Torque sensorless control in multidegree-of-freedom manipulator. *IEEE Transactions on Industrial Electronics*, *40*(2), 259–265. doi:10.1109/41.222648

Musion. (2015). Retrieved from http://www.musion.co.uk/

Musumba, G. W., & Nyongesa, H. O. (2013). Context awareness in mobile computing: A review. *International Journal of Machine Learning and Applications*, *2*(1), 1–10. doi:10.4102/ijmla.v2i1.5

Muxfeldt, A., Kluth, J. H., & Kubus, D. (2014).Kinesthetic Teaching in Assembly Operations – A User Study. In D. Brugali et al. (Eds.), Proceedings of the SIMPA 2014, LNAI (Vol. 8810, pp. 533-544).

Myers, B. A. (1998). A brief history of human-computer interaction technology. *interactions, 5*(2), 44-54.

Myo Armband. (2015). Retrieved from https://www.myo.com

Nacenta, M. A., Aliakseyeu, D., Subramanian, S., & Gutwin, C. (2005). A comparison of techniques for multi-display reaching.*Proceedings of the SIGCHI conference on Human factors in computing systems* (pp. 371-380). ACM. doi:10.1145/1054972.1055024

Nadiger, N., & Bhat, A. (2013). Sense, H. P. U. S. Applications (IJEBEA). Retrieved from www.iasir.net

Nagata, K., & Katsura, S. (2015). Synchronism evaluation of multi-DOF motion-copying system for motion training.*Proceedings of 2015 IEEE International Conference on Mechatronics* (pp. 500-505). IEEE. doi:10.1109/ICMECH.2015.7084027

Naka, T., & Ishida, T. (2014). Proposal of the effective method of generating characteristic gestures in nonverbal communication. *Human computer interaction, LNCS* (Vol. 8511, pp. 102-112).

Naka, T., & Ishida, T. (2015). A proposed dynamical analytic method for characteristic gestures in human communication. HCII, vol8.

Nam, Y., & Kim, J. (2010). A semiotic analysis of sounds in personal computers: Toward a semiotic model for human-computer interaction. Semiotica, 182(1/4), 269-284.

Nap, H. H., & Diaz-Orueta, U. (2014). Rehabilitation Gaming. In Gamification for Human Factors Integration (pp. 122–147). IGI Global. http://doi.org/ doi:10.4018/978-1-4666-5071-8.ch008

Nathan, E. P. (2009). Determining the roi of an online english as a second language program. *Performance Improvement*, *48*(6), 39–48. doi:10.1002/pfi.20085

Natori, K., Tsuji, T., & Ohnishi, K. (2010, March). Time-delay compensation by communication disturbance observer for bilateral teleoperation under time-varying delay. *IEEE Transactions on Industrial Electronics*, 57(3), 1050-1062.

Nedopil, C., Schauber, C., & Glende, S. (2013). *Knowledge base – AAL stakeholders and their requirements*. AAL Association.

Nef, T., Mihelj, M., Colombo, G., & Riener, R. (2006). ARMin robot for rehabilitation of the upper extremities. *Proceedings of the IEEE Inter. Conference on Robotics and Automation, Orlando* (pp. 3152–3157). doi:10.1109/ROBOT.2006.1642181

Nejad, S. K., & Salajegheh, S. (2013). A Routing optimization approach for rescue robots based on evolutionary algorithm. *Switzerland Research Park Journal*, *102*, 470–494.

Nelson, M. R., & Waiguny, M. K. (2012). Psychological Processing of In-Game Advertising and Advergaming: Branded Entertainment or Entertaining Persuasion? In *Psychology of entertainment media: Blurring the lines between Entertainment and persuasion* (pp. 93-146).

Nelson, M. R. (2002). Recall of brand placements in computer/video games. *Journal of Advertising Research*, *42*(2), 80–92. doi:10.2501/JAR-42-2-80-92

Nelson, M. R., Yaros, R. A., & Keum, H. (2006). Examining the influence of telepresence on spectator and player processing of real and fictitious brands in a computer game. *Journal of Advertising*, *35*(4), 87–99. doi:10.2753/JOA0091-3367350406

Neuhofer, B. (2013). Experiences are co-created and technology –enhanced. *eTourismLab, Bournemouth University*. Retrieved from http://blogs.bournemouth.ac.uk/etourismlab/tag/experience-economy

Neuhofer, B., & Buhalis, D. (2012, June). Understanding and managing technology-enabled enhanced tourist experiences. *Proceedings of the 2nd Conference on Advances in Hospitality and Tourism Marketing & Management*, Corfu, Greece.

Neuhofer, B., & Buhalis, D. (2013). Technology Enhanced Tourist experiences: a holistic exploration of how technology can enhanced tourist experiences. *eTourismLab, Bournemouth University*. Retrieved from http://blogs.bournemouth.ac.uk/etourismlab/tag/experience-economy

Neuhofer, B., Buhalis, D., & Ladkin, A. (2013). A Typology of Technology-Enhanced Tourism Experiences. *International Journal of Tourism Research*, *16*(4), 340–350. doi:10.1002/jtr.1958

Neuhofer, B., Buhalis, D., & Ladkin, A. (2015). Smart technologies for personalized experiences: A case study in the hospitality domain. *Electronic Markets*, *25*(3), 243–254. doi:10.1007/s12525-015-0182-1

NeuroSky. (2011). MindWave. Retrieved from http://neurosky.com/about-neurosky/

Newton-John, T. R. O., Spence, S. H., & Schotte, D. (1995). Cognitive-Behavioural Therapy versus EMG Biofeedback in the treatment of chronic low back pain. *Behaviour Research and Therapy*, *33*(6), 691–697. doi:10.1016/0005-7967(95)00008-L PMID:7654161

Ni, T. (2011). *A Framework of Freehand Gesture Interaction: Techniques, Guidelines, and Applications* [Doctoral Dissertation]. Virginia Tech. Retrieved from http://scholar.lib.vt.edu/theses/available/etd-09212011-230923/unrestricted/Ni_T_D_2011.pdf

Nielsen, J. (1995). *10 usability heuristics for user interface design.* Retrieved from http://www.nngroup.com/articles/ten-usabilityheuristics/

Nielsen, J. (2014) Memory recognition and recall in user interface. *Nielsen Norman Group Usability Report.* Retrieved from http://www.nngroup.com/articles/recognition-andrecall/

Nielsen, M., Störring, M., Moeslund, T. B., & Granum, E. (2004). A procedure for developing intuitive and ergonomic gesture interfaces for HCI. In Gesture-Based Communication in Human-Computer Interaction, (LNCS) (Vol. 2915, pp. 409–420). Springer. doi:10.1007/978-3-540-24598-8_38

Nielsen, J. (1993). *Usability engineering.* London: Academic Press.

Nie, P., Vähä-Herttua, J., Aura, T., & Gurtov, A. (2011, October). Performance analysis of HIP diet exchange for WSN security establishment.*Proceedings of the 7th ACM symposium on QoS and security for wireless and mobile networks* (pp. 51-56). ACM. doi:10.1145/2069105.2069114

Nitsch, V., & Färber, B. (2013, October-December). A Meta-Analysis of the Effects of Haptic Interfaces on Task Performance with Teleoperation Systems. *IEEE Transactions on Haptics, 6*(4), 387–398. doi:10.1109/TOH.2012.62 PMID:24808391

Niyazi, M., Niyazi, I., & Belka, C. (2007). Counting colonies of clonogenic assays by using densitometric software. *Radiation Oncology (London, England), 2*(1), 1–3. doi:10.1186/1748-717X-2-4 PMID:17212832

Noble, W. S. (2006). What is a support vector machine? *Nature Biotechnology, 24*(12), 1565–1567. doi:10.1038/nbt1206-1565 PMID:17160063

Noor, A. K., & Aras, R. (2015). Potential of multimodal and multiuser interaction with virtual holography. *Advances in Engineering Software, 81*, 1–6. doi:10.1016/j.advengsoft.2014.10.004

Nordin, N. A. M., Aziz, N. A., Alkaff, S. E., Sulong, S., & Aljunid, S. (2012). Rehabilitation for patients after stroke in a tertiary hospital: It is early and intensive enough? *International Journal of Therapy and Rehabilitation, 19*(11), 603–611. doi:10.12968/ijtr.2012.19.11.603

Norman, D. (1988). *The design of everyday things.* New York: Basic Books.

Norman, D. A., & Nielsen, J. (2010). Gestural Interfaces: A Step Backward In Usability. *Interaction*, 46–49. doi:10.1145/1836216.1836228

Novak, T. P., Hoffman, D. L., & Yung, Y. F. (2000). Measuring the customer experience in online environments: A structural modeling approach. *Marketing Science, 19*(1), 22–42. doi:10.1287/mksc.19.1.22.15184

Noy, C. (2007). The poetics of tourist experience: An autoethnography of a family trip to Elliot. *Journal of Tourism and Cultural Change, 5*(3), 141–157. doi:10.2167/jtcc085.0

Numrich, S. K. (2008). Culture, models, and games: Incorporating warfare's human dimension. *IEEE Intelligent Systems, 23*(4), 58–61. doi:10.1109/MIS.2008.63

Nunamaker, J. F. Jr, & Chen, M. (1990). Systems development in information systems research.*Proceedings of the Twenty-Third Annual Hawaii International Conference on System sciences* (Vol. 3, pp. 631–640). doi:10.1109/HICSS.1990.205401

Nykänen, O. A., & Rodriguez, A. R. (2014). Problems in Context-Aware Semantic Computing. *International Journal of Interactive Mobile Technologies, 8*(3), 32–39. doi:10.3991/ijim.v8i3.3870

Obilade, T. T. (2015). Affordances then and now: Implications for designing instruction. *Distance Learning, 12*(3), 9–16.

Obilade, T. T. (2016). *Make Me See it: Pedagogical Strategies of Visual Literacy.* Oklahoma: Tate Publishing.

Occipital (2015). OpenNI 2 Downloads and Documentation | The Structure Sensor. Retrieved from http://structure.io/openni

Occipital (2015). Structure sensor. Retrieved from www.structure.io

Ochiai, Y. (2014). Pixie Dust: Graphic generated by Levitated and Animated Objects in Computational Acoustic-Potential Field Retrieved from http://96ochiai.ws/PixieDust/

Ochiai, Y., Hoshi, T., & Rekimoto, J. (2014). Pixie dust: Graphics generated by levitated and animated objects in computational acoustic-potential field. *ACM Transactions on Graphics*, *33*(4), 1–13. doi:10.1145/2601097.2601118

Oculus, V. R. (2013). *Oculus Rift: Next-Gen Virtual Reality*. Oculus VR.

Oh, Y., Yoon, H., & Woo, W. (2006). Simulating Context-Aware Systems based on Personal Devices. *Proceedings of the4th International Symposium on Ubiquitous Virtual Reality (ISUVR 2006)*, (pp. 49-52). Daejeon, Korea.

Oh, H., Fiore, A. M., & Jeoung, M. (2007). Measuring Experience Economy Concepts: Tourism Applications. *Journal of Travel Research*, *46*(2), 119–132. doi:10.1177/0047287507304039

Ohnishi, K., Matsui, N., & Hori, Y. (1994, August). Estimation, identification, and sensorless control in motion control system. *Proceedings of the IEEE*, *82*(8), 1253–1265. doi:10.1109/5.301687

Ohnishi, K., Shibata, M., & Murakami, T. (1996, March). Motion control for advanced mechatronics. *IEEE/ASME Transactions on Mechatronics*, *1*(1), 56–67. doi:10.1109/3516.491410

Okazaki, S., & Yagüe, M. J. (2012). Responses to an advergaming campaign on a mobile social networking site: An initial research report. *Computers in Human Behavior*, *28*(1), 78–86. doi:10.1016/j.chb.2011.08.013

Okura, T., & Katsura, S. (2010). Analysis of system connection in multilateral control system considering number of subsystems.*Proceedings of 36th Annual Conference on IEEE Industrial Electronics Society* (pp. 1234-1239). IEEE. doi:10.1109/IECON.2010.5675546

Ooi, C. (2005). A theory of tourism experiences: The management of attention. In T. O'Dell & P. Billing (Eds.), *Experiencescapes: Tourism, Culture, and Economy* (pp. 51–69). Copenhagen: Copenhagen Business School Press.

OpenKinect. (2015). Retrieved from http://openkinect.org

OptiTrack. (2014). Prim. Retrieved from http://www.optitrack.com/

Orchard, B., & Clark, A. R. (2004). Optimizing algorithms for antenna design. In *The Transaction of SA Institute Elec. Engineer* (pp. 279-289).

Ortiz, M., Ayala, G., & Osorio, M. (2003). Formalizing the learner model for CSCL environments. In E. Chávez, J. Favela, M. Mejía, & A. Oliart (Eds.), *Proceedings of theFourth Mexican International Conference on Computer Science* (pp. 151-158). doi:10.1109/ENC.2003.1232889

OSRM. (2015). OSRM: Open Source Routing Machine. Retrieved from http://project-osrm.org/

Osvald, A., & Stirn, L. Z. (2008). A vehicle routing algorithm for the distribution of fresh vegetables and similar perishable food. *Journal of Food Engineering*, *85*(2), 285–295. doi:10.1016/j.jfoodeng.2007.07.008

Owston, R. (2008). Models and methods for evaluation. In Handbook of research on educational communications and technology (pp. 605-617).

Ozansoy Çadırcı, T., Sağkaya Güngör, A., & Köse, Ş. G. (2015). Segmenting the gamers to understand the effectiveness of the in game advertisement.*Proceedings of 1st Annual International Conference on Social Sciences (AICSS)* (Vol. 1, pp. 435-448), İstanbul, Turkey: Yildiz Technical University.

Paas, F., Renkl, A., & Sweller, J. (2003). Cognitive load theory and instructional design: Recent developments. *Educational Psychologist*, *38*(1), 1–4. doi:10.1207/S15326985EP3801_1

Pachoulakis, I., & Kapetanakis, K. (2012). Augmented Reality Platforms for Virtual Fitting Rooms. *The International Journal of Multimedia & Its Applications*, *4*(4), 35–46. doi:10.5121/ijma.2012.4404

Paganelli, F., Spinicci, E., & Giuli, D. (2008). ERMHAN: A Context-Aware Service Platform to Support Continuous Care Networks for Home-Based Assistance. *International Journal of Telemedicine and Applications*, *2008*, 1–13. http://www.hindawi.com/journals/ijta/2008/867639/. doi:10.1155/2008/867639 PMID:18695739

Page, C. (2014). Intel-powered Google Glass 2 set to shake up the enterprise in 2015. *The Inquirer*. Retrieved from http://www.theinquirer.net/inquirer/news/2384204/intel-powered-google-glass-2-set-to-shake-up-the-enterprise-in-2015

Paisley, V. (2013, December). Gamification of tertiary courses: An exploratory study of learning and engagement.*Proceedings of the 30th ASCILITE Conference* (pp. 671-675).

Panic, K., Cauberghe, V., & DePelsmacker, P. (2013). Comparing TV ads and advergames targeting children: The impact of persuasion knowledge on behavioral responses. *Journal of Advertising*, *42*(2-3), 264–273. doi:10.1080/00913367.2013.774605

Panoutsopoulos, H., & Sampson, D. G. (2012). A Study on Exploiting Commercial Digital Games into School Context. *Journal of Educational Technology & Society*, *15*(1), 15–27.

Pantelopoulos, A., & Bourbakis, N. G. (2010). A Survey on Wearable Sensor-Based Systems for Health Monitoring and Prognosis. *IEEE Transactions on Systems, Man and Cybernetics. Part C, Applications and Reviews*, *40*(1), 1–12. doi:10.1109/TSMCC.2009.2032660

Pantsar-Syväniem, S., Simula, K., & Ovaska, E. (2010). Context-awareness in smart spaces. *Proceedings of theIEEE Symposium on Computers and Communications (ISCC)* (pp. 1023-1028). Riccione, Italy: IEEE. doi:10.1109/ISCC.2010.5546630

Panwar, M. (2012). Hand gesture recognition based on shape parameters. *Proceedings of the International Conference on Computing. Communication and Applications (ICCCA '12)* (pp. 1–6). doi:10.1109/ICCCA.2012.6179213

Papaioannou, I., Kalatzis, N., Roussaki, I., Liampotis, N., Kosmides, P., & Anagnostou, M. (2014). Multi-user context inference based on neural networks. *Proceedings of the2014 IEEE International Conference on Pervasive Computing and Communications Workshops (PERCOM Workshops)* (pp. 466-471). Budapest: IEEE. doi:10.1109/PerComW.2014.6815251

Papastergiou, M. (2009). Digital Game-Based Learning in high school Computer Science education: Impact on educational effectiveness and student motivation. *Computers & Education*, *52*(1), 1–12. doi:10.1016/j.compedu.2008.06.004

Papo, D., Zanin, M., Pineda-Pardo, J. A., Boccaletti, S., & Buldú, J. M. (2014). Functional brain networks: Great expectations, hard times and the big leap forward. *Philosophical Transactions of the Royal Society of London. Series B, Biological Sciences*. PMID:25180303

Paradiso, J. A. (2003). Tracking Contact and Free Gesture Across Large Interactive Surfaces. *Communications of the ACM*, *46*(7), 62–69. doi:10.1145/792704.792731

Parasuraman, S., Arif, W. O., & Jauw, V. L. (2010). Robot assisted stroke rehabilitation: Joint torque/force conversion from EMG using SA Process. In H. Liu, . . . (Eds.), Proceedings of ICIRA 2010 (pp. 612–623). doi:10.1007/978-3-642-16587-0_56

Parhi, P., Karlson, A. K., & Bederson, B. B. (2006, September). Target size study for one-handed thumb use on small touchscreen devices.*Proceedings of the 8th conference on Human-computer interaction with mobile devices and services* (pp. 203-210). ACM. doi:10.1145/1152215.1152260

Park, W., Kwon, S. C., Lee, H. D., & Kim, J. (2009). Thumb-tip force estimation from sEMG and musculoskeletal for real-time trigger prosthesis. *Proceedings of the IEEE 11th Inter. Conference on Rehabil. Robotics*, Kyoto (pp. 305-310).

Park, H., & Kim, Y. K. (2014). The role of social network websites in the consumer–brand relationship. *Journal of Retailing and Consumer Services*, 21(4), 460–467. doi:10.1016/j.jretconser.2014.03.011

Park, S., & Woldstad, J. (2000). Multiple two-dimensional displays as an alternative to three-dimensional displays in telerobotic tasks. *Human Factors*, 42(4), 592–603. doi:10.1518/001872000779698060 PMID:11324852

Patton, M. Q. (1997). *Utilization –focused evaluation: the new century text*. California: Sage.

Pavlovic, V., Sharma, R., & Huang, T. (1997). Visual interpretation of hand gestures for human-computer interaction: A review. *IEEE Transactions on Pattern Analysis and Machine Intelligence*, 19(7), 677–695. doi:10.1109/34.598226

Pavone, M., Bisnik, N., Frazzoli, E., & Isler, V. (2009). A Stochastic and Dynamic Vehicle Routing Problem with Time Windows and Customer Impatience. *Mobile Networks and Applications*, 14(3), 350–364. doi:10.1007/s11036-008-0101-1

Payne, S. L. B. (2014). *The Art of Asking Questions: Studies in Public Opinion, 3* (Vol. 3). Princeton University Press.

Paysant, J., Beis, J. M., Le Chapelain, L., & André, J. M. (2004). Mirror asomatognosia in right lesions stroke victims. *Neuropsychologia*, 42(7), 920–925. doi:10.1016/j.neuropsychologia.2003.12.001 PMID:14998706

Pazuchanics, S. L. (2006, October). The Effects of Camera Perspective and Field of View on Performance in Tele-operated Navigation. *Proceedings of the Human Factors and Ergonomics Society Annual Meeting* (pp. 1528-1532). doi:10.1177/154193120605001603

Peak, D., & Berge, Z. L. (2006). Evaluation and elearning. *Turkish online journal of distance education*, 7(1), 124-131.

Peffers, K., Tuunanen, T., Rothenberger, M. A., & Chatterjee, S. (2007). A design science research methodology for information systems research. *Journal of Management Information Systems*, 24(3), 45–77. doi:10.2753/MIS0742-1222240302

Peirce, C. S. (1990). *Semiótica – Coleção estudos* (2nd ed.). Perspectiva Publisher.

Peirce, C. S. (1931-58). *Collected Writings*. In C. Hartshorne, P. Weiss, & A. Burks (Eds.). *Harvard University Press*.

Pendrana, M. (2014). Location-based services and tourism: Possible implications for destination. *Current Issues in Tourism*, 17(9), 753–762. doi:10.1080/13683500.2013.868411

Percivall, G. (2011). Increasing Market Opportunities for Augmented Reality Through Collaborative Development of Open Standards. *Position Paper for the International AR Standards Meeting*.

Père, C., & Faucher, S. (2007). Cluny: de la gestion de données à la réalité augmentée. In Actes du colloque Virtual Retrospect (pp. 61-67). Bordeaux, France: Archéovision.

Pereira, F., Silva, C., & Alves, M. (2011). Virtual Fitting Room Augmented Reality Techniques for e-Commerce. In M. Cruz-Cunha, J. Varajão, P. Powell, & R. Martinho (Eds.), *ENTERprise Information Systems* (Vol. 220, pp. 62–71). Springer Berlin Heidelberg. doi:10.1007/978-3-642-24355-4_7

Perera, C., Zaslavsky, A., Christen, P., & Georgakopoulos, D. (2014). Context Aware Computing for The Internet of Things: A Survey. *IEEE Communications Surveys and Tutorials*, 16(1), 414–454. doi:10.1109/SURV.2013.042313.00197

Perera, G. V. A. G. A., Pillai, M. B., & Abeykoon, A. M. H. S. (2014). DC motor inertia estimation for robust bilateral control. *Proceedings of 7th International Conference on Information and Automation for Sustainability* (pp. 1-7). Colombo: IEEE.

Peters, S., & Leshner, G. (2013). Get in the game: The effects of game-product congruity and product placement proximity on game players' processing of brands embedded in advergames. *Journal of Advertising*, 42(2-3), 113–130. doi:10.1080/00913367.2013.774584

Petrelli, D., Not, E., Zancanaro, M., Strapparava, C., & Stock, O. (2001). Modelling and adapting to context. *Personal and Ubiquitous Computing*, 5(1), 20–24. doi:10.1007/s007790170023

Petroman, I., Petroman, C., Buzatu, C., Marin, D., Dumitrescu, A., Statie, C., & Rus, I. (2011). A Religious and Ethnic Tourism Profile of Europe. *Scientific Papers Animal Science and Biotechnologies*, 44(2), 490–493.

Piccolo, L.S.G., Schimidt, C.P., Osório, A.F.S., Duarte, R.E., Ávila, I.M.A., Tambascia, C.A., Carvalho, R.F., Aureliano, M.G., & Rolim, L.A.G. (2010). Modelo de interação inclusivo para interface de governo eletrônico. CPqD Foundation.

Piccolo, L. S. G., Menezes, E. M., & Buccolo, B. C. (2011). Developing an accessible interaction model for touch screen mobile devices: preliminary results.*Proceedings of the 10th Brazilian Symposium on Human Factors in Computer Systems* (pp. 257-260).

Pierce, R. M., Fedalei, E. A., & Kuchenbecker, K. J. (2014). A wearable device for controlling a robot gripper with fingertip contact, pressure, vibrotactile, and grip force feedback.*Proceedings of IEEE Haptics Symposium* (pp. 19-25). doi:10.1109/HAPTICS.2014.6775428

Piirainen–Marsh, A., & Tainio, L. (2009). Collaborative Game-play as a Site for Participation and Situated Learning of a Second Language. *Scandinavian Journal of Educational Research*, 53(2), 167–183. doi:10.1080/00313830902757584

Pillac, V., Gendreau, M., Guéret, C., & Medaglia, A. L. (2013). A review of dynamic vehicle routing problems. *European Journal of Operational Research*, 225(1), 1–11. doi:10.1016/j.ejor.2012.08.015

Pillai, M. B., Perera, G. V. A. G. A., Chinthaka, M. K. C. D., & Abeykoon, A. M. H. S. (2014, July). Analysis of a DC motor based velocity controller using disturbance observer. *Indian Journal of Social Research*, 5, 1–7.

Pine, J., & Gilmore, J. (1999). *The experience economy*. Boston: Harvard Business School Press.

Pine, J., & Gilmore, J. (2011). *The Experience Economy*. Boston: Harvard Business Press.

Pires, C. G., Pinto, F. M., Teixeira, V. D., Freitas, J., & Dias, M. S. (2012). Living Home Center - A personal assistant with multimodal interaction for elderly and mobility impaired e-inclusion.*Proc. of PROPOR*. Coimbra.

Playstation. (2003). EyeToy: Play, from http://es.playstation.com/ps2/games/detail/item42149/EyeToy-Play/

Playstation. (2004). EyeToy Play 2 Retrieved from http://es.playstation.com/ps2/games/detail/item42521/EyeToy-Play-2/

Poh, M.-Z., McDuff, D., & Picard, R. (2011). A medical mirror for non-contact health monitoring. *Paper presented at theACM SIGGRAPH 2011 Emerging Technologies*, Vancouver, British Columbia, Canada. doi:10.1145/2048259.2048261

Pointgrab. (2015). Retrieved from http://www.pointgrab.com/

Poongodi, M (2012). Sixth Sense Technology. *Int. J. EnCoTe*, 102, 09 – 20.

Porambage, P., Braeken, A., Kumar, P., Gurtov, A., & Ylianttila, M. (2015, June). Proxy-based end-to-end key establishment protocol for the Internet of Things. *Proceedings of the 2015 IEEE International Conference onCommunication Workshop* (ICCW) (pp. 2677-2682). doi:10.1109/ICCW.2015.7247583

Porges, S. (2015). The Problems With Google Glass: A Eulogy. *Forbes*. Retrieved from http://www.forbes.com/sites/sethporges/2015/01/16/the-problems-with-google-glass-a-eulogy/

Portalés Ricart, C. (2007b). Live LEGO House: an interactive space to explore coexistence through gaming. *Paper presented at the International Technology,Education and Development Conference (INTED'07)*, Valencia (Spain).

Portalés Ricart, C. (2009). *Entornos multimedia de realidad aumentada en el campo del arte* [Doctoral Thesis]. Universidad Politécnica de Valencia, Valencia.

Portalés Ricart, C., Perales Cejudo, C. D., & Cheok, A. (2007). Exploring Social, Cultural and Pedagogical Issues in AR-Gaming Through The Live LEGO House. *Paper presented at theACM SIGCHI International Conference on Advances in Computer Entertainment Technology*, Salzburg, Austria. doi:10.1145/1255047.1255103

Portalés Ricart, C. (2007a). Live LEGO House: A Mixed Reality Game for the Edutainment. *Scottish Online Journal of E-Learning, 1*(1), 19–28.

Portalés, C., & Perales, C. D. (2009). Sound and Movement Visualization in the AR-Jazz Scenario. *Paper presented at theInternational Conference on Entertainment Computing (ICEC)*. doi:10.1007/978-3-642-04052-8_15

Portalés, C., Viñals, M. J., Alonso-Monasterio, P., & Morant, M. (2010). AR-Immersive Cinema at the Aula Natura Visitors Center. *IEEE MultiMedia, 17*(4), 8–15. doi:10.1109/MMUL.2010.72

Portenoy, R. K. (1996). Opioid therapy for chronic nonmalignant pain: A review of the critical issues. *Journal of Pain and Symptom Management, 11*(4), 203–217. doi:10.1016/0885-3924(95)00187-5 PMID:8869456

Portet, F., Vacher, M., Golanski, C., Roux, C., & Meillon, B. (2013). Design and evaluation of a smart home voice interface for the elderly: Acceptability and objection aspects. *Personal and Ubiquitous Computing, 17*(1), 127–144. doi:10.1007/s00779-011-0470-5

Positech Games.(2015). *Democracy 2* [Game]. Retrieved from http://positech.co.uk/democracy2/

Potter, L. E., Araullo, J., & Carter, L. (2013). The Leap Motion controller. *Proceedings of the 25th Australian Computer-Human Interaction Conference on Augmentation, Application, Innovation, Collaboration OzCHI '13* (pp. 175–178). New York, New York, USA: ACM Press. http://doi.org/ doi:10.1145/2541016.2541072

Potter, L. E., Korte, J., & Nielsen, S. (2011). Seek and sign: An early experience of the joys and challenges of software design with young deaf children.*Proceedings of the 23rd Australian Computer-Human Interaction Conference* (pp. 257-260), New York. doi:10.1145/2071536.2071577

Prensky, M. (2001). *Digital game-based learning*. New York: McGraw Hill.

President Forever. (2015). Retrieved from http://270soft.com/us-election-games/president-election-game-2016/

Prestopnik, N. (2013). *Design Science in human-computer interaction: a model and three examples* [PhD Dissertation]. Syracuse University, Syracuse, NY.

PrimeSense. (2010). PrimeSense, Retrieved from http://www2.technologyreview.com/tr50/primesense/

Prince, J. D. (2013). Gamification. *Journal of Electronic Resources in Medical Libraries, 10*(3), 162–169. doi:10.108 0/15424065.2013.820539

Probst, K., Lindlbauer, D., & Greindl, P. (2013). Rotating, tilting, bouncing: using an interactive chair to promote activity in office environments. Proceedings of the Extended Abstracts on Human Factors in Computing Systems CHI '13 (pp. 79–84). doi:10.1145/2468356.2468372

Probst, K., Lindlbauer, D., & Haller, M. (2014). A chair as ubiquitous input device: exploring semaphoric chair gestures for focused and peripheral interaction.*Proceedings of the 32nd International Conference on Human Factors in Computing SystemsCHI '14* (pp. 4097–4106). doi:10.1145/2556288.2557051

Puangmali, P., Althoefer, K., Seneviratne, L. D., Murphy, D., & Dasgupta, P. (2008, April). State of the art in force and tactile sensing for minimally invasive surgery. *IEEE Sensors Journal, 8*(4), 371–381. doi:10.1109/JSEN.2008.917481

Putman, N., Burton, M. H., & Nahm, M. H. (2005). Simplified method to automatically count bacterial colony forming unit. *Journal of Immunological Methods, 302*(1-2), 99–102. doi:10.1016/j.jim.2005.05.003 PMID:16002082

Putnam, C. (2003). Sequential motions of body segments in striking and throwing skills: descriptions and explanations. *J. Biomech.*, 26(Suppl. 1), 125-135.

Putnik, G. D., Shah, V., Castro, H., & Cunha, M. M. (2011). The Functionality of Remote Controlling in Ubiquitous Manufacturing Systems Demonstrator for I* PROMS 'efm' Showcase. *Tekhné-Revista de Estudos Politécnicos/Polytechnical Studies Review, 9*(15), 169-189.

Pyke, F. (2013). *Coaching Excellence*. Champaign, Ill: Human Kinetics.

Qin, J., Chui, Y.-P., Pang, W.-M., Choi, K.-S., & Heng, P.-A. (2010). Learning blood management in orthopedic surgery through gameplay. *IEEE Computer Graphics and Applications, 30*(2), 45–57. doi:10.1109/MCG.2009.83 PMID:20650710

Quality Matters. (2013) Higher education program. Retrieved from https://www.Quality matters.org/higher-education-program

Quan, S., & Wang, N. (2004). Towards a structural model of the tourist experience: An illustration from food experiences in tourism. *Tourism Management, 25*(3), 297–305. doi:10.1016/S0261-5177(03)00130-4

Quek, F., McNeill, D., Bryll, R., Duncan, S., Ma, X.-F., Kirbas, C., & Ansari, R. et al. (2002). Multimodal human discourse: Gesture and speech. *ACM Transactions on Computer-Human Interaction, 9*(3), 171–193. doi:10.1145/568513.568514

Rabiner, L. R. (1990). *A tutorial on hidden Markov models and selected applications in speech recognition*. In *Readings in speech recognition* (pp. 267–296). San Francisco, CA, USA: Morgan Kaufmann Publishers Inc. doi:10.1016/B978-0-08-051584-7.50027-9

Radi, M., Reiter, A., Zaidan, S., Nitsch, V., Färber, B., & Reinhart, G. (2010). Telepresence in Industrial Applications: Implementation Issues for Assembly Tasks. *Presence (Cambridge, Mass.), 19*(5), 415–429. doi:10.1162/pres_a_00009

Raghupatruni, S., Nasam, N., & Lingam, K. (2013). Sixth Sense Enabled Campus-Possibilities and Challenges. *International Journal of Computers and Applications, 75*(8).

Rahman, A. S. M. M., Tran, T. T., Hossain, S. K. A., & El Saddik, A. (2010, October 17-20). Augmented Rendering of Makeup Features in a Smart Interactive Mirror System for Decision Support in Cosmetic Products Selection. *Paper presented at the 2010 IEEE/ACM 14th International Symposium on Distributed Simulation and Real Time Applications (DS-RT).*

Rahman, M. M., Poon, B., Amin, M. A., & Yan, H. (2015). Support system using Microsoft Kinect and mobile phone for daily activity of visually impaired. In Transactions on Engineering Technologies (pp. 425-440). doi:10.1007/978-94-017-9588-3_32

Ramos, C. M. Q., Rodrigues, P. M. M., & Rodrigues, J. M. F. (2015). Opportunities, emerging features and trends in electronic distribution in tourism. *International Journal of Information Systems and Social Change, 6*(4), 17–32. doi:10.4018/IJISSC.2015100102

Raney, A. A., Arpan, L. M., Pashupati, K., & Brill, D. A. (2003). At the movies, on the web: An investigation of the effects of entertaining and interactive web content on site and brand evaluations. *Journal of Interactive Marketing, 17*(4), 38–53. doi:10.1002/dir.10064

Ranganathan, A., & Campbell, R. H. (2008). Provably Correct Pervasive Computing Environments. *Proceedings of the2008 Sixth Annual IEEE Conference on Pervasive Computing and Communications (PERCOM '08).* Washington DC, USA: IEEE Computer Society. doi:10.1109/PERCOM.2008.116

Ranganathan, A., McGrath, R. E., Campbell, R. H., & Mickunas, M. D. (2003). Use of Ontologies in a Pervasive Computing Environment. *The Knowledge Engineering Review, 18*(3), 209–220. doi:10.1017/S0269888904000037

Rao, S. (2010). Sixth sense technology. *Proceedings of the 2010 International Conference on Communication and Computational Intelligence INCOCCI* (pp. 336-339). IEEE.

Rashidi, P., & Mihailidis, A. (2013). A survey on ambient-assisted living tools for older adults. *Biomedical and Health Informatics. IEEE Journal of, 17*(3), 579–590.

Rautaray, S., & Agrawal, A. (2015). Vision based hand gesture recognition for human computer interaction: A survey. *Artificial Intelligence Review, 43*(1), 1–54. doi:10.1007/s10462-012-9356-9

Rautaray, S., Kumar, A., & Agrawal, A. S. (2012). Perception and machine intelligence human computer interaction with hand gestures in virtual environment. *Perception and machine Intelligence, LNCS* (Vol. *7143*, pp. 106–113). doi:10.1007/978-3-642-27387-2_14

Raychoudhury, V., Cao, J., Kumar, M., & Zhang, D. (2013, April). Middleware for pervasive computing: A survey. *Pervasive and Mobile Computing, 9*(2), 177–200. doi:10.1016/j.pmcj.2012.08.006

Razuri, J., Larsson, A., Rahmani, R., Sundgren, D., Bonet, I., & Moran, A. (2015). Recognition of emotions by the emotional feedback through behavioral human poses. *Journal of Computer Science Issues, 12*(1).

Rearpro. (2015). Paradigm audio visual. Retrieved from http://www.rearpro.com/

Redmond, E., & Wilson, J. R. (2012). *Seven Databases in Seven Weeks* (1st ed.). Pragmatic Bookshelf.

Redondo, I. (2012). The effectiveness of casual advergames on adolescents' brand attitudes. *European Journal of Marketing, 46*(11/12), 1671–1688. doi:10.1108/03090561211260031

Reed, M., Yiannakou, A., & Evering, R. (2014). An ant colony algorithm for the multi-compartment vehicle routing problem. *Applied Soft Computing, 15*, 169–176. doi:10.1016/j.asoc.2013.10.017

Refiana, L., Mizerski, D., & Murphy, J. (2005) Measuring the state of flow in playing online Games. In S. Purchase (Ed.), *Proceedings of ANZMAC 2005 Conference, Marketing Research and Research Methodologies (Quantitative)* (pp. 108-113). Freemantle, Australia: School of Business, University of Western Australia.

Regenbrecht, H. T., Franz, E. A., McGregor, G., Dixon, B. G., & Hoermann, S. (2011). Beyond the Looking Glass: Fooling the Brain with the Augmented Mirror Box. *Presence (Cambridge, Mass.), 20*(6), 559–576. doi:10.1162/PRES_a_00082

Rego, P., Moreira, P. M., & Reis, L. P. (2010, June). Serious games for rehabilitation: A survey and a classification towards a taxonomy. *Proceedings of the 5th Iberian Conference on Information Systems and Technologies (CISTI)* (pp. 1-6).

Ren, Z., Yuan, J., & Zhang, Z. (2011). Robust hand gesture recognition based on finger-earth mover's distance with a commodity depth camera. *Proceedings of the 19th ACM international conference on Multimedia - MM '11 (p. 1093).* New York, New York, USA: ACM Press. http://doi.org/ doi:<ALIGNMENT.qj></ALIGNMENT>10.1145/2072298.2071946

Ren, G., Li, C., O'Neill, E., & Willis, P. (2013a). 3D freehand gestural navigation for interactive public displays. *IEEE Computer Graphics and Applications, 33*(2), 47–55. doi:10.1109/MCG.2013.15 PMID:24807939

Ren, G., & O'Neill, E. (2013b). 3D selection with freehand gesture. *Computers & Graphics, 37*(3), 101–120. doi:10.1016/j.cag.2012.12.006

Rennie, J. (2014). The Tupac hologram, virtual Ebert, and digital immortality. Retrieved from http://www.smartplanet.com/blog/thesavvy-scientist/the-tupac-hologram-virtual-ebert-anddigital-immortality/454

Ren, Z., Yuan, J., Meng, J., & Zhang, Z. (2013). Robust Part-Based Hand Gesture Recognition Using Kinect Sensor. *IEEE Transactions on Multimedia*, *15*(5), 1110–1120. doi:10.1109/TMM.2013.2246148

Resmini, A., & Rosati, L. (2012). A brief history of information architecture. *Journal of Information Architecture*, *3*(2).

RFID. (2014). RFID Reader ID-12LA (125 kHz). Retrieved from https://www.sparkfun.com/products/11827

Riaz, M., Kiani, S. L., Lee, S., Han, S.-M., & Lee, Y.-K. (2005). Service Delivery in Context Aware Environments: Lookup and Access Control Issues. *Proceedings of the11th IEEE International Conference on Embeded and Real-Time Computing Systems and Applications* (pp. 455-458). IEEE. doi:10.1109/RTCSA.2005.94

Riboni, D., & Bettini, C. (2011, March). COSAR: Hybrid reasoning for context-aware activity recognition. *Personal and Ubiquitous Computing*, *15*(3), 271–289. doi:10.1007/s00779-010-0331-7

Richard, E., Billaudeau, V., Richard, P., & Gaudin, G. (2007, September 27-29). *Augmented Reality for Rehabilitation of Cognitive Disabled Children: A Preliminary Study*. Paper presented at the Virtual Rehabilitation, 2007.

Richard, P., Birebent, G., Coiffet, P., Burdea, G., Gomez, D., & Lagrana, N. (1996). Effect of frame rate and force feedback on virtual object manipulation. *Presence (Cambridge, Mass.)*, *5*(1), 95–108. doi:10.1162/pres.1996.5.1.95

Richards, G. (2005). *Cultural tourism in Europe*. Wallingford, UK: ATLAS.

Richards, G., & Wilson, J. (2006). Developing creativity in tourist experiences: A solution to the serial reproduction of culture? *Tourism Management*, *27*(6), 1408–1441. doi:10.1016/j.tourman.2005.06.002

Richey, R. (1986). Theoretical bases of instructional design: systems and communications. In R. Richey (Ed.), *The theoretical and conceptual bases of instructional design* (pp. 33–56). London: Nichols.

Ristic, B., Arulampalam, S., and Gordon, N. (2004). Beyond the Kalman filter: Particle filters for tracking applications (Vol. 685). Boston: Artech house.

Ritchie, D. C., & Hoffman, B. (1997). Incorporating instructional design principles with the world wide web. In B. Khan (Ed.), *Web-based instruction* (pp. 135–158). Englewood Cliffs, NJ: Educational Technology Publications.

Robertson, G., Caldwell, G., Hamill, J., Kamen, G., & Whittlesey, S. (2014). *Research Methods in Biomechanics* (2nd ed.).

Robina Town Center. (2012). Virtual change room. Retrieved from https://www.youtube.com/watch?v=Zmw6xMtEqro

Rochat, P., & Zahavi, D. (2011). The uncanny mirror: A re-framing of mirror self-experience. *Consciousness and Cognition*, *20*(2), 204–213. doi:10.1016/j.concog.2010.06.007 PMID:20889353

Rodriguez, C. O. (2012). MOOCs and the AI-Stanford like Courses: Two successful and distinct course formats for massive open online courses. *European Journal of Open, Distance, and E-Learning*.

Rolland, J. P., Holloway, R. L., & Fuchs, H. (1994). A comparison of optical and video see-through head-mounted displays. *Paper presented at the SPIE - Telemanipulator and Telepresence Technologies*.

Romano, J. M., Hsiao, K., Niemeyer, G., Chitta, S., & Kuchenbecker, K. J. (2011). Human-inspired robotic grasp control with tactile sensing. *IEEE Transactions on Robotics*, *27*(6), 1067–1079. doi:10.1109/TRO.2011.2162271

Rosas, R., Nussbaum, M., Cumsille, P., Marianov, V., Correa, M., Flores, P., & López, V. et al. (2003). Beyond Nintendo: Design and assessment of educational video games for first and second grade students. *Computers & Education*, *40*(1), 71–94. doi:10.1016/S0360-1315(02)00099-4

Rose, F. D., Brooks, B. M., & Rizzo, A. A. (2005). Virtual reality in brain damage rehabilitation. *Cyberpsychology & Behavior, 8*(3), 241–262. doi:10.1089/cpb.2005.8.241 PMID:15971974

Rosen, C. (2008). The myth of multitasking. *New Atlantis (Washington, D.C.)*, (Spring): 105–110.

Rosen, J., Fuchs, M. B., & Arcan, M. (1999). Performances of Hill type and neural network muscle models-toward a myosignal-based exoskeleton. *Computers and Biomedical Research, an International Journal, 32*(5), 415–439. doi:10.1006/cbmr.1999.1524 PMID:10529300

Ross, A. (2004). *Procrustes analysis (Course report)*. Department of Computer Science and Engineering, University of South Carolina.

Roto, V., Law, E., Vermeeren, A. P. O. S., & Hoonhout, J. (2011). User experience white paper. Bringing clarity to the concept of user experience. Result from Dagstuhl Seminar on Demarcating User Experience 2010.

Roussaki, I., Strimpakou, M., Pils, C., Kalatzis, N., & Liampotis, N. (2010). Optimizing context data dissemination and storage in distributed pervasive computing systems. *Journal of Pervasive and Mobile Computing, 6*(2), 218-238.

Rubin, J., & Chisnell, D. (2008). *Handbook of Usability Testing–How to Plan, Design, and Conduct Effective Tests*. Indianapolis, IN: Wiley.

Rubinstein, D. (2007). Standish group report: There's less development chaos today. *Software Development Times, 1*.

Ruhe, V., & Zumbo, B. D. (2009). *Evaluation in distance education and e-learning: The unfolding model: New York*. Guilford Press.

Russell, S., & Norvig, P. (2009). Artificial Intelligence: A Modern Approach (3rd ed.). Prentice Hall Press.

Ruwanthika, R. M. M., & Abeykoon, A. M. H. S. (2015). 3D environmental force: position impedance variation for different motion parameters. *Proceedings of Moratuwa Engineering Research Conference (MERCon)* (pp. 112-117). IEEE. doi:10.1109/MERCon.2015.7112330

Ryan, N., Pascoe, J., & Morse, D. (1997). Enhanced Reality Fieldwork: the Context Aware Archaeological Assistant. *Computer Applications in Archaeology*. Retrieved from https://www.cs.kent.ac.uk/pubs/1998/616/content.html

Ryu, M.-H., Kim, S., & Euehun Lee, E. (2009, May). Understanding the factors affecting online elderly user's participation in video UCC services. *Computers in Human Behavior, 25*(3), 619–632. doi:10.1016/j.chb.2008.08.013

Sabarigiri, B., & Suganyadevi, D. (2014). The possibilities of establishing an innovative approach with biometrics using the brain signals and iris features. *Research Journal of Recent Sciences*.

Saied, Y. B., & Olivereau, A. (2012, June). D-HIP: A distributed key exchange scheme for HIP-based Internet of Things. *Proceedings of the 2012 IEEE International Symposium on a World of Wireless, Mobile and Multimedia Networks* (WoWMoM) (pp. 1-7). IEEE. doi:10.1109/WoWMoM.2012.6263785

Saied, Y. B., Olivereau, A., Zeghlache, D., & Laurent, M. (2014). Lightweight collaborative key establishment scheme for the Internet of Things. *Computer Networks, 64*, 273–295. doi:10.1016/j.comnet.2014.02.001

Saleiro, M., Farrajota, M., Terzic, K., Krishna, S., Rodrigues, J. M. F., & du Buf, J. M. H. (2015). Biologically inspired vision for human-robot interaction. In M. Antona & C. Stephanidis (Eds.), Universal Access in Human-Computer Interaction 2015, Part II, LNCS (Vol. 9176 pp. 505–517). Doi:10.1007/978-3-319-20681-3_48

Salisbury, J. K. (1980). Active stiffness control of a manipulator in Cartesian coordinates. *Proceedings of 19th IEEE Conference on Decision and Control including the Symposium on Adaptive Processes* (pp. 95-100). IEEE. doi:10.1109/CDC.1980.272026

Salvador, S., & Chan, P. (2007). Toward accurate dynamic time warping in linear time and space. *Intelligent Data Analysis*, *11*(5), 561–580.

Salve TV. (2008). Open night lab Retrieved from http://www.salve-tv.net/web/de/webtv/webtv.php?VideoSuche=open +night+lab&RubrikSuche=0&autoplay=false&area=

Salvi, D., Ottaviano, M., Peinado, I., & Arredondo, M. T. (2009). An Architecture for Data Collection and Processing in Context-Aware Applications. *Proceedings of the3rd International Conference on Ambient Intelligence* (pp. 252-255). Salzburg, Austria: Springer.

Sambo, C. F., & Forster, B. (2011). When far is near: ERP correlates of crossmodal spatial interactions between tactile and mirror-reflected visual stimuli. *Neuroscience Letters*, *500*(1), 10–15. doi:10.1016/j.neulet.2011.05.233 PMID:21683122

Samsung Developers Forum. (2014). *Principles for Designing Applications for Samsung Smart TV*. Retrieved from http://www.samsungdforum.com/UxGuide/2014/01_principles_for_designing_applications_for_samsung_smart_tv.html

Samsung. (2015). Wearable Tech. Retrieved from http://www.samsung.com/us/mobile/wearable-tech

Sanders, B. (2014). *Mastering Leap Motion*. Packt Publishing.

Sandnes, F. E., Tan, T. B., Johansen, A., Sulic, E., Vesterhus, E., & Iversen, E. R. (2012). Making touch-based kiosks accessible to blind users through simple gestures. *Universal Access in the Information Society*, *11*(4), 421–431. doi:10.1007/s10209-011-0258-4

Sankai, Y. (2010). HAL-Hybrid Assistive limb based on Cybernetics. In *Robotic Research*. Springer.

Santos, E., Gonzalo, R., & Gisbert, F. (2007). Advergames: Overview. *International Journal Information Technologies and Knowledge*, *1*, 203–208.

Sarig-Bahat, H., Weiss, P. L. T., & Laufer, Y. (2010). Neck pain assessment in a virtual environment. *Spine*, *35*(4), E105–E112. doi:10.1097/BRS.0b013e3181b79358 PMID:20110842

Sato, H., Kitahara, I., & Ohta, Y. (2009). MR-Mirror: A Complex of Real and Virtual Mirrors. *Paper presented at the 3rd International Conference on Virtual and Mixed Reality: Held as Part of HCI International 2009*, San Diego, CA, USA. doi:10.1007/978-3-642-02771-0_54

Sato, K., Fukumori, S., Matsusaki, T., Maruo, T., Ishikawa, S., Nishie, H., & Morita, K. et al. (2010). Nonimmersive virtual reality mirror visual feedback therapy and its application for the treatment of complex regional pain syndrome: An open-label pilot study. *Pain Medicine (Malden, Mass.)*, *11*(4), 622–629. doi:10.1111/j.1526-4637.2010.00819.x PMID:20202141

Savardi, U., Bianchi, I., & Bertamini, M. (2010). Naïve predictions of motion and orientation in mirrors: From what we see to what we expect reflections to do. *Acta Psychologica*, *134*(1), 1–15. doi:10.1016/j.actpsy.2009.11.008 PMID:20015479

Savarimuthu, T. R., Liljekrans, D., Ellekilde, L.-P., Ude, A., Nemec, B., & Krüger, N. (2013). Analysis of human Peg-in-Hole Executions in a Robotic Embodiment using uncertain Grasps. *Proceedings of the9th International Workshop on Motion and Control, RoMoCo 2013*. doi:10.1109/RoMoCo.2013.6614614

Sawyer, B. (2008). From cells to cell processors: The integration of health and video games. *IEEE Computer Graphics and Applications*, *28*(6), 83–85. doi:10.1109/MCG.2008.114 PMID:19004688

Scepanovic, S., Devedžić, V., & Kraljevski, I. (2011). E-learning benchmarking: A review of approaches, models and tools in higher education. Proceedings of the ICERI '11 (pp. 3064-3073).

Scheck, A. (2014). Special report: Seeing the (google) glass as half full. *Emergency Medicine News*, *36*(2), 20–21. doi:10.1097/01.EEM.0000443910.87918.22

Schilit, B. N., & Theimer, M. M. (1994). Disseminating active map infrastructure to mobile host. *IEEE Network*, *8*(5), 22–32. doi:10.1109/65.313011

Schmidt, A. (2014). Context-Awareness, Context-Aware User Interfaces, and Implicit Interaction. In M. Soegaard & R. F. Dam (Eds.), *The Encyclopedia of Human-Computer Interaction* (2nd ed.). Aarhus, Denmark: The Interaction Design Foundation.

Schmidt, A., Beigl, M., & Gellersen, H.-W. (1999). There is more to context than location. *Computers & Graphics*, *23*(6), 893–901. doi:10.1016/S0097-8493(99)00120-X

Schneider, L. P., & Cornwell, B. T. (2002). Cashing in on crashes via brand placement in computer games: The effects of experience and flow on memory. *International Journal of Advertising*, *24*(3), 321–343.

Schneider, S. M., & Workman, M. L. (1999). Effects of virtual reality on symptom distress in children receiving chemotherapy. *Cyberpsychology & Behavior: The Impact of the Internet. Multimedia and Virtual Reality on Behavior and Society*, *2*(2), 125–134.

Schreiber, T. (2000). Measuring information transfer. *Physical Review Letters*, *85*(2), 461–464. doi:10.1103/PhysRevLett.85.461 PMID:10991308

Schrimpf, G., Schneider, J., Stamm-Wilbrandt, H., & Dueck, G. (2000). Record Breaking Optimization Results Using the Ruin and Recreate Principle. *Journal of Computational Physics*, *159*(2), 139–171. doi:10.1006/jcph.1999.6413

Schriver, K. (1997). *Dynamics in Document Design*. New York: Wiley.

Schulze, J., & Fahle, T. (1999). A parallel algorithm for the vehicle routing problem with time window constraints. *Annals of Operations Research*, *86*(0), 585–607. doi:10.1023/A:1018948011707

Scriven, M. (1974). Pros and cons about goal free evaluation. In W. J. Popham (Ed.), *Evaluation in education: current applications* (pp. 34–67). California: McCutchan.

Scriven, M. (1991). *Evaluation thesaurus*. California: Sage.

Seamon, D. (1979). *A geography of the lifeworld: Movement, rest, and encounter*. London: Croom Helm.

Sellner, B. P., Hiatt, L. M., Simmons, R., & Singh, S. (2006, March). Attaining situational awareness for sliding autonomy. *Proceedings of the 1st ACM SIGCHI/SIGART conference on Human-robot interaction HRI '06* (pp. 80-87).

Senanayake, C., & Senanayake, S. M. N. A. (2009). *Theraputic rehabilitation robotics for lower extremity: a review*. Proc. of World Academy Of Science Eng. & Tech.

Shah, V., Putnik, G. D., & Castro, H. (2012). Prototype Multiplex Communication System for Remote Control of Machine Tools. In Virtual and Networked Organizations, Emergent Technologies and Tools (pp. 241-252). Springer Berlin Heidelberg. doi:10.1007/978-3-642-31800-9_25

Shahid, S., Krahmer, E., Swerts, M., Melder, W. A., & Neerincx, M. A. (2009). Exploring social and temporal dimensions of emotion induction using an adaptive affective mirror. *Paper presented at theCHI '09 Extended Abstracts on Human Factors in Computing Systems*, Boston, MA, USA. doi:10.1145/1520340.1520562

Shahrbanian, S., Ma, X., Korner-Bitensky, N., & Simmonds, M. J. (2009). Scientific evidence for the effectiveness of virtual reality for pain reduction in adults with acute or chronic pain. *Studies in Health Technology and Informatics*, *144*, 40–43. PMID:19592727

Shakil, I., Tran, P., & Dehy, R. (2014). *U.S. Patent Application 14/167,353.*

Shattuck, K. (2007). Quality matters: Collaborative program planning at a state level. *Online Journal of Distance Learning Administration, 10*(3). Retrieved from .http://www.westga.edu/~distance/ojdla/fall103/shattuck103.htm

Shaw, C., Gromala, D., & Song, M. (n.d.). The Meditation Chamber: Towards Self-Modulation.*Proceedings of ENACTIVE/07.*

Sheng, Q. Z., Pohlenz, S., Jian, Y., Wong, H. S., Ngu, A. H., & Maamar, Z. (2009). ContextServ: A platform for rapid and flexible development of context-aware Web services. *Proceedings of the IEEE 31st International Conference on Software Engineering* (pp. 619-622). Vancouver: IEEE.

Shen, X. (2012). Empowering the smart grid with wireless technologies[Editor's Note]. *IEEE Network, 26*(3), 2–3. doi:10.1109/MNET.2012.6201208

Shi, Y., Karatzoglou, A., Baltrunas, L., Larson, M., & Hanjalic, A. (2014). CARS2: Learning Context-aware Representations for Context-aware Recommendations. *Proceedings of the 23rd ACM International Conference on Conference on Information and Knowledge Management (CIKM 14)* (pp. 291-300). Shanghai: ACM.

Shimono, T., Katsura, S., & Ohnishi, K. (2005). Improvement of operationality for bilateral control based on nominal mass design in disturbance observer.*Proceedings of 31st Annual Conference of IEEE Industrial Electronics Society* (6-10). IEEE. doi:10.1109/IECON.2005.1569217

Shimono, T., Katsura, S., & Ohnishi, K. (2007, April). Abstraction and reproduction of force sensation from real environment by bilateral control. *IEEE Transactions on Industrial Electronics, 54*(2), 907–918. doi:10.1109/TIE.2007.892744

Shiv, B., Britton, J. A. E., & Payne, J. W. (2004). Does elaboration increase or decrease the effectiveness of negatively versus positively framed messages? *The Journal of Consumer Research, 31*(1), 199–208. doi:10.1086/383435

Shiv, B., Edell, J. A., & Payne, J. W. (1997). Factors affecting the impact of negatively and positively framed ad messages. *The Journal of Consumer Research, 24*(3), 285–294. doi:10.1086/209510

Shneiderman, B. (1998). Designing the User Interface: Strategies for Effective Human-Computer Interaction (3rd ed.). Reading, MA: Addison-Wesley.

Shneiderman, B. (1998). *Designing the interface: Strategies for effective human-computer interaction.* Reading, MA: Addison-Wesley.

Shneiderman, B. (2000). Universal usability: Pushing human-computer interaction research to empower every citizen. *Communications of the ACM, 43*(5), 84–91. doi:10.1145/332833.332843

Shuhaiber, J. H. (2004). Augmented reality in surgery. *Archives of Surgery (Chicago, Ill.), 139*(2), 170–174. doi:10.1001/archsurg.139.2.170 PMID:14769575

Siebra, S. A., Salgado, A. C., Tedesco, P. A., & Brézillon, P. (2005). A Learning Interaction Memory using Contextual Information. *Proceedings of the CEUR Workshop.* Retrieved from: http://www.cin.ufpe.br/~mbjn/D1.pdf

Siegman, A., & Feldstein, S. (2014). *Nonverbal behavior and communication* (2nd ed.). Psychology Press.

Sielhorst, T., Feuerstein, M., & Navab, N. (2008). Advanced Medical Displays: A Literature Review of Augmented Reality. *Display Technology. Journalism, 4*(4), 451–467. doi:10.1109/jdt.2008.2001575

SIGA. (2012). Diverse Beliefs: Tourism of Faith Religious tourism gains ground. Strategic Initiatives & Government Advisory (SIGA) Team. New Delhi: Yes Bank-FICCI. Retrieved from http://www.ficci.com/spdocument/20207/Diverse-Beliefs-Tourism-of-Faith.pdf

Sigala, M. (2015). The application and impact of gamification funware on trip planning and experiences: The case of TripAdvisor's funware. *Electronic Markets*, *25*(3), 189–209. doi:10.1007/s12525-014-0179-1

Simon, H. A. (1996). *The Sciences of the Artificial* (3rd ed.). Cambridge, MA: MIT Press.

Simons, C., & Wirtz, G. (2007). Modeling context in mobile distributed systems with the UML. *Journal of Visual Languages and Computing*, *18*(4), 420–439. doi:10.1016/j.jvlc.2007.07.001

Sindre, G., Natvig, L., & Jahre, M. (2009). Experimental validation of the learning effect for a pedagogical game on computer fundamentals. *IEEE Transactions on Education*, *52*(1), 10–18. doi:10.1109/TE.2007.914944

Singapore, T. I. C. (2013). 3D Augmented Reality Virtual Fitting Room Retrieved from https://www.youtube.com/watch?v=gz5ynrfJSDM

Singh, K. J. (2015). Sixth Sense Technology and Its New Applications. *International Journal of Emerging Research in Management and Technology, 4*.

Singh, S. J., & Gupta, M. (2013). Comparison of particle swarm optimization & simulated annealing for weight optimization of composite leaf spring. *Inter. J. Of Computational Eng. & Management*, *16*(4), 14–24.

Singh, S., Vajirkar, P., & Lee, Y. (2003). Context-Based Data Mining Using Ontologies.Conceptual Modeling – ER 2003, LNCS (Vol. 2813, pp. 405–418).

Singlecue. (2015). eyeSight. Retrieved from http://www.singlecue.com/

Sirbirsky, D. (2001). Student perception of community learning initiative courses. Retrieved from http://www.trincoll.edu/orgs/planning/Kellogg/Reports/Student%20Perception%20of%20Community%20Learning%20Courses.pdf

Sirbirsky, D. (2002). Smart neighborhood Trinfo Café web survey 2002. Retrieved from http://www.trincoll.edu/orgs/planning/Kellogg/Reports/Smart%20Neighborhood%20Web%20Survey%20Report.pdf

Sivandam, S. N., & Deepa, S. N. (2009). A comparative study using genetic algorithm and particle swarm optimization for lower order system modeling. *Inter. J. Of The Computer. The Internet & Management*, *17*(3), 1–10.

Slater, M. (2004). How colorful was your day? Why questionnaires cannot assess presence in virtual environments. *Presence (Cambridge, Mass.)*, *13*(4), 484–493. doi:10.1162/1054746041944849

Snodgrass, J. G., & Vanderwart, M. (1980). A standardized set of 260 pictures: Norms for name agreement, image agreement, familiarity, and visual complexity. *Journal of Experimental Psychology. Human Learning and Memory*, *6*(2), 174–215. doi:10.1037/0278-7393.6.2.174 PMID:7373248

Soli. (2015). Project Soli. Retrieved from https://www.google.com/atap/project-soli/

Solomon, M. M. (1987). Algorithms for the Vehicle Routing and Scheduling Problems with Time Window Constraints. *Operations Research*, *35*(2), 254–265. doi:10.1287/opre.35.2.254

Sommerville, I. (2015). *Software Engineering* (10th ed.). USA: Pearson Education.

Song, R., & Tong, K. Y. (2005). Using recurrent artificial neural network model to estimate voluntary torque in dynamic situations. *J. of Medical & Bio. Eng. & Comput*, *43*(4), 473–480.

Song, R., Tong, K. Y., Hu, X., & Li, L. (2008). Assistive control system using continuous myoelectric signal in a robot-aided arm training for patients after stroke. *IEEE TRANS. on Neural Sys. &. Rehabil. Eng*, *16*(4), 371–379.

Sony Cooperation. (2015). SmartEyeglass. Retrieved from https://developer.sony.com/devices/mobile-accessories/smarteyeglass/

Sousa Santos, B., Dias, P., Pimentel, A., Baggerman, J. W., Ferreira, C., Silva, S., & Madeira, J. (2009). Head-mounted display versus desktop for 3D navigation in virtual reality: A user study. *Multimedia Tools and Applications*, *41*(1), 161–181. doi:10.1007/s11042-008-0223-2

Soylu, A., Causmaecker, P. D., & Desmet, P. (2009). Context and Adaptivity in Pervasive Computing Environments: Links with Software Engineering and Ontological Engineering. *Journal of Software*, *4*(9), 992–1013. doi:10.4304/jsw.4.9.992-1013

Spasojević-Brkić, V. K., & Punik, G. (2013). User evaluation of the interfaces for the remote control of manufacturing systems. *Serbian Journal of Management*, *8*(2), 201–212. doi:10.5937/sjm8-4281

Spasojević-Brkić, V., Putnik, G., Shah, V., Castro, H., & Veljković, Z. (2013). Human-computer interactions and user interfaces for remote control of manufacturing systems. *FME Transactions*, *41*(3), 250–255.

Spasojević-Brkić, V., Putnik, G., Veljković, Z., Shah, V., & Castro, H. (2014). Representational fidelity in distributed and remote lab environment. *FME Transactions*, *42*(3), 243–248. doi:10.5937/fmet1403243s

Speroni, M., Bolchini, D., & Paolini, P. (2006). Interfaces: "Do Users Understand Them?" *Proceedings of the Museums and the Web '06*. Retrieved from http://www.archimuse.com/mw2006/papers

Spiegelmock, M. (2013). *Leap Motion Development Essentials*. Packt Publishing.

Spielberg, S. (2002). Minority Report. USA: 20th Century Fox; DreamWorks Pictures.

Spinuzzi, C. (2004). The methodology of participatory design. *Technical Communication (Washington)*, *52*(2), 163–174.

Sporns, O., Tononi, G., & Kötter, R. (2005). The human connectome: A structural description of the human brain. *PLoS Computational Biology*, *1*(4), e42. doi:10.1371/journal.pcbi.0010042 PMID:16201007

Sprott, J. C. (2006). Physics demonstrations: A sourcebook for teachers of physics. Univ of Wisconsin Press.

Squire, K., & Jenkins, H. (2003). Harnessing the power of games in education. *Insight (American Society of Ophthalmic Registered Nurses)*, *3*(1), 7–33.

Staab, S., Werthner, H., Ricci, F., Zipf, A., Gretzel, U., Fesenmaier, D. R., & Knoblock, C. (2002). Intelligent systems for tourism. *IEEE Intelligent Systems*, *17*(6), 53–64. doi:10.1109/MIS.2002.1134362

Stamper, R. (1993). A semiotic theory of information and information systems/applied semiotics. In *International seminars on the teaching of computing science* (pp. 1-36). Newcastle: Newcastle University.

Starner, T. (2013). Project Glass: An Extension of the Self. In *Pervasive Computing* (pp. 1536-1268).

steepergroup. (2015). *bebionic*. Retrieved from http://bebionic.com/

Stellmach, S., & Dachselt, R. (2012). Designing gaze-based user interfaces for steering in virtual environments. *Paper Presented at the Proceedings of the Symposium on Eye Tracking Research and Applications*, Santa Barbara, California. Retrieved from http://luxator.cs.uni-magdeburg.de/uise/Forschung/Publikationen/2012-ETRA-GazeNavGUIs.pdf

Steuer, J. (1992). Defining virtual reality: Dimensions determining telepresence. *Journal of Communication*, *42*(4), 33–56. doi:10.1111/j.1460-2466.1992.tb00812.x

Stevens, J. A., & Stoykov, M. E. P. (2003). Using Motor Imagery in the Rehabilitation of Hemiparesis 1. *Archives of Physical Medicine and Rehabilitation*, *84*(7), 1090–1092. doi:10.1016/S0003-9993(03)00042-X PMID:12881842

Straka, M., Hauswiesner, S., Rüther, M., & Bischof, H. (2011). A Free-Viewpoint Virtual Mirror with Marker-Less User Interaction. In A. Heyden & F. Kahl (Eds.), *Image Analysis* (Vol. 6688, pp. 635–645). Springer Berlin Heidelberg. doi:10.1007/978-3-642-21227-7_59

Strang, T., & Linnhoff-Popien, C. (2004). A Context Modelling Survey. *Proceedings of theFirst International Workshop on Advanced Context Modelling, Reasoning and Management (Ubicomp 2004)*. Nottingham, England: ACM.

Streitz, N. A., Tandler, P., Müller-Tomfelde, C., & Konomi, S. I. (2001). Roomware: Towards the Next Generation of Human-Computer Interaction based on an Integrated Design of Real and Virtual Worlds. In Human-Computer Interaction in the New Millenium (pp. 551-576). Addison Wesley.

Streitz, N. A., Tandler, P., Müller-Tomfelde, C., & Konomi, S. I. (2001). Roomware: Towards the Next Generation of Human-Computer: Interaction based on an Integrated Design of Real and Virtual Worlds. In Human-Computer Interaction in the New Millennium (pp. 551-576). Addison Wesley.

Structure sensor. (2015). Retrieved from http://structure.io/

Structure. (2014). Structure sensor. Retrieved from http://structure.io/

Stufflebeam, D.L. (1974). Evaluation according to Daniel L. Stufflebeam. In W.J. Popham (Ed.), *Evaluation in education: current applications* (pp. 116-143). California, USA: McCutchan.

Sturman, D. J., & Zeltzer, D. (1994). A survey of glove-based input. *IEEE Computer Graphics and Applications*, *14*(1), 30–39. doi:10.1109/38.250916

Suarez, J., & Murphy, R. R. (2012). Hand gesture recognition with depth images: A review. *Proceedings of the 21st IEEE International Symposium on Robot and Human Interactive Communication IEEE RO-MAN* (pp. 411–417). IEEE. http://doi.org/ doi:10.1109/ROMAN.2012.6343787

Suganuma, T., Yamanaka, K., Tokairin, Y., Takahashi, H., & Shiratori, N. (2008). A Ubiquitous Supervisory System Based on Social Context Awareness. *Proceedings of the 22nd International Conference on Advanced Information Networking and Applications* (pp. 370-377). GinoWan, Okinawa, Japan: IEEE. doi:10.1109/AINA.2008.123

Suh, K. S., & Chang, S. (2006). User interfaces and consumer perceptions of online stores: The role of telepresence. *Behaviour & Information Technology*, *25*(2), 99–113. doi:10.1080/01449290500330398

Sukoco, B. M., & Wu, W. Y. (2011). The effects of advergames on consumer telepresence and attitudes: A comparison of products with search and experience attributes. *Expert Systems with Applications*, *38*(6), 7396–7406. doi:10.1016/j.eswa.2010.12.085

Suma, E., Lange, B., Rizzo, A., Krum, D., & Bolas, M. (2011). Faast: The flexible action and articulated skeleton toolkit. *Proceedings of theVirtual Reality Conference* (pp. 247-248). doi:10.1109/VR.2011.5759491

Sumiyoshi, Y., & Ohnishi, K. (2004). The transformation of modified 4-channel architecture.*Proceedings of the 8th IEEE International Workshop on Advanced Motion Control* (pp. 211-216). IEEE.

Sung, Y.-T., Chang, K.-E., & Lee, M.-D. (2008). Designing multimedia games for young children's taxonomic concept development. *Computers & Education*, *50*(3), 1037–1051. doi:10.1016/j.compedu.2006.07.011

Sun, M., Ren, X., & Cao, X. (2011). Effects of Multimodal Error Feedback on Human Performance in Steering Tasks. *Information and Media Technologies*, *6*(1), 193–201.

Suthar, K., Benmore, C. J., Den Hartog, P., Tamalonis, A., & Weber, R. (2014, 3-6 Sept. 2014). Levitating water droplets formed by mist particles in an acoustic field. *Paper presented at the 2014 IEEE International Ultrasonics Symposium (IUS)*.

Sutherland, I. E. (1965). The Ultimate Display. *Paper presented at theCongress of the Internation Federation of Information Processing (IFIP).*

Sutton, J. (2013). Air painting with Corel Painter Freestyle and the leap motion controller. Proceedings of the ACM SIGGRAPH 2013 Studio Talks on - SIGGRAPH '13 (p. 1). New York, New York, USA: ACM Press; doi:10.1145/2503673.2503694

Svennerberg, G. (2010). *Beginning Google Maps API 3.* Apress. doi:10.1007/978-1-4302-2803-5

Swarbrooke, J., & Horner, S. (1999). *Consumer Behaviour in Tourism.* Oxford: Butterworth-Heinemann.

Swartz, B. E. (1998). The advantages of digital over analog recording techniques. *Electroencephalography and Clinical Neurophysiology, 106*(2), 113–117. doi:10.1016/S0013-4694(97)00113-2 PMID:9741771

Sweller, J. (2011). *The Psychology of Learning and Motivation: Cognition in Education* (B. H. Ross & J. P. Mestre, Eds., Vol. 55). London, UK: Academic Press, Elsevier.

Sweller, J., Ayres, P., & Kalyuga, S. (2011). *Cognitive load theory.* New York: Springer. doi:10.1007/978-1-4419-8126-4

Takeda, H., Veerkamp, P., & Yoshikawa, H. (1990). Modeling design process. *AI Magazine, 11*(4), 37.

Takeo, K., & Kosuge, K. (1997). Implementation of the micro-macro teleoperation system without using slave-side force sensors.*Proceedings of 1997 IEEE International Conference on Robotics and Automation.* (vol. 2, pp. 1600 - 1605). IEEE. doi:10.1109/ROBOT.1997.614369

Takeya, M., & Katsura, S. (2015). Modal-space filtering by expectation value extraction for high-scaling bilateral control. *IEEJ Journal of Industry Applications, 4*(6), 681–687. doi:10.1541/ieejjia.4.681

Tang, S. L., Kwoh, C. K., Teo, M. Y., Sing, N. W., & Ling, K. V. (1998). Augmented reality systems for medical applications. *IEEE Engineering in Medicine and Biology Magazine, 17*(3), 49–58. doi:10.1109/51.677169 PMID:9604701

Tarantilis, C. D., & Kiranoudis, C. T. (2002). Distribution of fresh meat. *Journal of Food Engineering, 51*(1), 85–91. doi:10.1016/S0260-8774(01)00040-1

Tashev I. (2011). Recent Advances in Human-Machine Interfaces for Gaming and Entertainment. *Int'l J. Information Technology and Security, 3*(3), 69-76.

Taylor, R. H., & Stoianovici, D. (2003). Medical robotics in computer-integrated surgery. *IEEE Transactions on Robotics and Automation, 19*(5), 765–781. doi:10.1109/tra.2003.817058

Taylor, S., Keskin, C., Hilliges, O., Izadi, S., & Helmes, J. (2014). Type–Hover–Swipe in 96 Bytes: A Motion Sensing Mechanical Keyboard.*Proceedings of CHI 2014* (pp. 1695–1704).

Telehuman. (2013). Telehuman. Retrieved from http://www.hml.queensu.ca/telehuman

Tennyson, R. D., & Elmore, R. L. (1997). Learning theory foundations for instructional design. In R. Tennyson, F. Schott, N. Seel, & S. Dijkstra (Eds.), Instructional design: international perspectives (Vol. 1: Theory, research and models, pp. 55-78). Mahwah, New Jersey: Lawrence Erlbaum Associates.

Tennyson, R. D., & Schott, F. (1997). Instructional design theory, research, and models. In R. Tennyson, F. Schott, N. Seel, & S. Dijkstra (Eds.), Instructional design: International perspectives (Vol. 1: Theory, research and models, pp. 1-16). Mahwah, New Jersey: Lawrence Erlbaum Associates.

Terlutter, R., & Capella, M. L. (2013). The gamification of advertising: Analysis and research directions of in-game advertising, advergames, and advertising in social network games. *Journal of Advertising, 42*(2-3), 95–112. doi:10.10 80/00913367.2013.774610

The Center for Universal Design. (1997). *Universal Design*. Retrieved from http://www.ncsu.edu/ncsu/design/cud/pubs_p/docs/poster.pdf

Thieme, H., Mehrholz, J., Pohl, M., Behrens, J., & Dohle, C. (2012). Mirror therapy for improving motor function after stroke. *Cochrane Database of Systematic Reviews*, *14*(3). doi:10.1002/14651858.CD008449.pub2 PMID:22419334

Thomas, F., & Ollie, J. (1997). *The Illusion of Life: Disney Animation*. Hyperion.

Tian, X., Chen, Y. K., Girkar, M., Ge, S., Lienhart, R., & Shah, S. (2003, April). Exploring the use of hyper-threading technology for multimedia applications with Intel® OpenMP compiler. In *Proceedings of the InternationalParallel and Distributed Processing Symposium '03*. IEEE. doi:10.1109/IPDPS.2003.1213118

Tina, W., & Buckner, K. (2006). Receptiveness of gamers to embedded brand messages in advergames: Attitudes towards product placement. *Journal of Interactive Advertising*, *7*(1), 3–32. doi:10.1080/15252019.2006.10722123

Tobii. (2015). Tobii EyeX. Retrieved from http://www.tobii.com/en/eye-experience/

Tong, R. K., & Hu, X. (2008). Service Robotics: Robot- assisted training for stroke rehabilitation. InTech.

Tongrod, N., Kerdcharoen, T., Watthanawisuth, N., & Tuantranont, A. (2010). A low-cost data-glove for Human computer interaction based on ink-jet printed sensors and ZigBee networks. *Proceedings of the International Symposium on Wearable Computers ISWC '10* (pp. 1–2). IEEE. http://doi.org/ doi:10.1109/ISWC.2010.5665850

Torsi, S., Nasr, N., Wright, P. C., Mawson, S. J., & Mountain, G. A. (2009). User-centered Design for Supporting the Self-management of Chronic Illnesses: An Interdisciplinary Approach. In *Proceedings of the 2Nd International Conference on PErvasive Technologies Related to Assistive Environments* (pp. 43:1–43:4). New York, NY, USA: ACM.

Total Immersion. (2014). TryLive for eyewear. Next generation virtual try-on and fitting solutions for the eyewear and eyecare industry Retrieved from http://www.trylive.com/solutions/trylive-eyewear-virtual-mirror/overview

Trappe, W., Howard, R., & Moore, R. (2015). Low-energy security: Limits and opportunities in the internet of things. *Security Privacy, IEEE*, *13*(1), 14–21. doi:10.1109/MSP.2015.7

Trojan, J., Diers, M., Fuchs, X., Bach, F., Bekrater-Bodmann, R., Foell, J., & Flor, H. et al. (2014). An augmented reality home-training system based on the mirror training and imagery approach. *Behavior Research Methods*, *46*(3), 634–640. doi:10.3758/s13428-013-0412-4 PMID:24338625

Truong, A., Boujut, H., & Zaharia, T. (2015). Laban descriptors for gesture recognition and emotional analysis. *The Visual Computer*, *32*(1), 83-98.

Truong, H.-L., & Dustdar, S. (2009). A Survey on Context-aware Web Service Systems. *International Journal of Web Information Systems*, *5*(1), 5–31. doi:10.1108/17440080910947295

Tsang, A., Von, , Korff, M., Lee, S., Alonso, J., Karam, E., & Angermeyer, M. C. (2008). Common chronic pain conditions in developed and developing countries: Gender and age differences and comorbidity with depression-anxiety disorders. *The Journal of Pain: Official Journal of the American Pain Society*, *9*(10), 883–891. doi:10.1016/j.jpain.2008.05.005 PMID:18602869

Tschofenig, H., & Fossati, T. (2014). A TLS/DTLS 1.2 Profile for the Internet of Things.

Tuan, Y. (1993). *Passing strange and wonderful: aesthetics, nature, and culture*. Washington: Island Press.

Tubb, R., & Dixon, S. (2015). An Evaluation of Multidimensional Controllers for Sound Design Tasks. *Proceedings of the 33rd Annual ACM Conference on Human Factors in Computing Systems CHI '15* (pp. 47–56). New York, New York, USA: ACM Press. http://doi.org/ doi:10.1145/2702123.2702499

Tung, V. W. S., & Ritchie, J. R. (2011). Exploring the essence of memorable tourism experiences. *Annals of Tourism Research*, *38*(4), 1367–1386. doi:10.1016/j.annals.2011.03.009

Tunstall-Pedoe, H. (2006). Preventing Chronic Diseases. A Vital Investment: WHO Global Report.: World Health Organization Geneva.

Turaga, P., Chellappa, R., Subrahmanian, V. S., & Udrea, O. (2008). Machine recognition of human activities: A survey. *IEEE Transactions on Circuits and Systems for Video Technology*, *18*(11), 1473–1488.

Turk, D. C. (2002). Clinical effectiveness and cost-effectiveness of treatments for patients with chronic pain. *The Clinical Journal of Pain*, *18*(6), 355–365. doi:10.1097/00002508-200211000-00003 PMID:12441829

Tussyadiah, I. P., & Fesenmaier, D. R. (2009). Mediating the tourist experiences: Access to places via shared videos. *Annals of Tourism Research*, *36*(1), 24–40. doi:10.1016/j.annals.2008.10.001

Tüzün, H. (2007). Blending video games with learning: Issues and challenges with classroom implementations in the Turkish context. *British Journal of Educational Technology*, *38*(3), 465–477. doi:10.1111/j.1467-8535.2007.00710.x

Tüzün, H., Yılmaz-Soylu, M., Karakuş, T., İnal, Y., & Kızılkaya, G. (2009). The effects of computer games on primary school students' achievement and motivation in geography learning'. *Computers & Education*, *52*(1), 68–77. doi:10.1016/j.compedu.2008.06.008

Ullah, K., & Kim, J. H. (2009). A mathematical model for mapping EMG signal to joint torque for the human elbow joint using nonlinear regression. *Proc. 4th Int. Conf. On Autonomous Robots &Agents*Wellington pp.103-108.

UNESCO. (2009). *The 2009 UNESCO Framework for Cultural Statistics (FCS)*. UNESCO Institute for Statistics.

UNESCO. (2015). *Routes of Santiago de Compostela: Camino Francés and Routes of Northern Spain*. Retrieved from http://whc.unesco.org/en/list/669/

United Nations, Department of Economic and Social Affairs, Population Division. (2013). World Population Ageing 2013, ST/ESA/SER.A/348.

United Nations. (2002, April 8-12). Report of the Second World Assembly on Ageing. Madrid, 2002.

Unity 3D. (2015). Unity 3D. Retrieved September 1, 2015, from http://unity3d.com/

Unity. (2015). Unity 3D. Retrieved from https://unity3d.com

UNWTO. (2008). *International Conference on Tourism, Religions and Dialogue of Cultures Cordoba, Spain, October 2007*. Madrid, Spain: World Tourism Organization. Retrieved from http://pub.unwto.org/WebRoot/Store/Shops/Infoshop/4947/9D4A/39D1/F45C/D0A6/C0A8/0164/81C3/081216_turismo_religioso_cordoba_excerpt.pdf

UNWTO. (2011). Religious Tourism in Asia and the Pacific. Madrid, Spain: World Tourism Organization. Retrieved from http://publications.unwto.org/sites/all/files/pdf/110325_religious_tourism_excerpt.pdf

Uppal, N., & Goyal, R. (2012). Computational approach to count bacterial colonies. *International journal of Advances in Engineering & Technology*, *4*(2), 364-372.

Urey, H., Chellappan, K. V., Erden, E., & Surman, P. (2011). State of the Art in Stereoscopic and Autostereoscopic Displays. *Proceedings of the IEEE*, *99*(4), 540–555. doi:10.1109/JPROC.2010.2098351

Ushaw, G., Ziogas, E., Eyre, J., & Morgan, G. (2013). An Efficient Application of Gesture Recognition from a 2D Camera for Rehabilitation of Patients with Impaired Dexterity.*Proceedings of the International Conference on Health Informatics* (pp. 315–318). doi:10.5220/0004190103150318

Ushida, K., Tanaka, Y., Naemura, T., & Harashima, H. (2002). i-mirror: An Interaction/Information Environment Based on a Mirror Metaphor Aiming to Install into Our Life Space. *Paper presented at theInternational Conference on Artificial Reality and Telexistence (ICAT),* Tokyo Japan.

Vaishnavi, V., & Kuechler, W. (2004). Design research in information systems. Retrieved from http://www.citeulike.org/group/4795/article/6505471

Vajirkar, P., Singh, S., & Lee, Y. (2003). Context-Aware Data Mining Framework for Wireless Medical Application. *Lecture Notes in Computer Science, 2736,* 381–391. doi:10.1007/978-3-540-45227-0_38

van Bunningen, A. H., Feng, L., & Apers, P. M. (2005). Context for ubiquitous data management. *Proceedings of theInternational Workshop on Ubiquitous Data Management (UDM 2005)* (pp. 17-24). Tokyo, Japan: IEEE. doi:10.1109/UDM.2005.7

Van Krevelen, D. W. F., & Poelman, R. (2010). A survey of augmented reality technologies, applications and limitations. *International Journal of Virtual Reality, 9*(2), 1.

Van Reijmersdal, E. (2009). Brand placement prominence: Good for memory! Bad for attitudes? *Journal of Advertising Research, 49*(2), 151–153. doi:10.2501/S0021849909090199

Van Reijmersdal, E. A., Rozendaal, E., & Buijzen, M. (2012). Effects of prominence, involvement, and persuasion knowledge on children's cognitive and affective responses to advergames. *Journal of Interactive Marketing, 26*(1), 33–42. doi:10.1016/j.intmar.2011.04.005

Van Someren, M. V., Barnard, Y. F., & Sandberg, J. A. (1994). *The think aloud method: A practical guide to modelling cognitive processes.* London: Academic Press.

Venable, J. R. (2006). The Role of Theory and Theorising in Design Science Research. *Proceedings of the First International Conference on Design Science Research in Information Systems and Technology,* Claremont, California, USA (pp.1-18).

Vera, L., Gimeno, J., Coma, I., & Fernández, M. (2011). Augmented Mirror: Interactive Augmented Reality System Based on Kinect. In P. Campos, N. Graham, J. Jorge, N. Nunes, P. Palanque, & M. Winckler (Eds.), *Human-Computer Interaction – INTERACT 2011* (Vol. 6949, pp. 483–486). Springer Berlin Heidelberg. doi:10.1007/978-3-642-23768-3_63

Verge. (2015). To build a holodeck: an exclusive look at Microsoft's Edison lab. Retrieved from http://www.theverge.com/2011/12/28/2665794/microsoft-edison-lab-holodeck-tour

Verhellen, Y., Oates, C., De Pelsmacker, P., & Dens, N. (2014). Children's Responses to Traditional Versus Hybrid Advertising Formats: The Moderating Role of Persuasion Knowledge. *Journal of Consumer Policy, 37*(2), 235–255.

Vermeir, I., Kazakova, S., Tessitore, T., Cauberghe, V., & Slabbinck, H. (2014). Impact of flow on recognition of and attitudes towards in-game brand placements: Brand congruence and placement prominence as moderators. *International Journal of Advertising, 33*(4), 785–810. doi:10.2501/IJA-33-4-785-810

Vertigo. (2013). Retrieved from http://www.vertigo-systems.com/

Vichido, C., Estrad, M., & Sanchez, A. (2003). A constructivist educational tool: Software architecture for web-based video games. In E. Chávez, J. Favela, M. Mejía, & A. Oliart (Eds.), *Proceedings of theFourth Mexican International Conference on Computer Science* (pp. 144-150). doi:10.1109/ENC.2003.1232888

VICON. (2014). Bonita. Retrieved from http://www.vicon.com/products/camera-systems/bonita

Villarreal, B. L., & Gordillo, J. L. (2013). Perception Aptitude improvement of an odor sensor: Model for a biologically inspired nose, LNCS (Vol. 7914, pp. 126–135). Doi:10.1007/978-3-642-38989-4_13

Villemure, C., & Bushnell, M. C. (2002). Cognitive modulation of pain: How do attention and emotion influence pain processing? *Pain*, *95*(3), 195–199. doi:10.1016/S0304-3959(02)00007-6 PMID:11839418

Virvou, M., Katsionis, G., & Manos, K. (2005). Combining software games with education: Evaluation of its educational effectiveness'. *Journal of Educational Technology & Society*, *8*, 54–65.

Vivendo em Silêncio. (2015). Dactiologia Portuguesa. Retrieved from https://vivendoemsilencio.files.wordpress.com/2010/07/dactl-lgp.jpg

Vizoo. (2015). Vizoo, cheoptics. Retrieved from http://www.vizoo.com/flash/

Vogel, D., & Balakrishnan, R. (2005). Distant freehand pointing and clicking on very large, high resolution displays.*Proceedings of the 18th Annual ACM Symposium on User Interface Software and Technology* (pp. 33–42). doi:10.1145/1095034.1095041

Von Hardenberg, C., & Bérard, F. (2001). Bare-Hand Human-Computer Interaction. *Proceedings of the ACM Workshop on Perceptive User Interfaces* (pp. 113–120).

von Wangenheim, C. G., & Shull, F. (2009). To game or not to game? *IEEE Software*, *26*(2), 92–94. doi:10.1109/MS.2009.54

Vrasidas, C. (2011). Human-Computer interaction and usability of online learning environments. In G. Anglin (Ed.), *Instructional technology: past, present, and future* (pp. 227–235). Santa Barbara, CA: Libraries Unlimited.

W3C. (2005). Introduction to web accessibility. Retrieved from http://www.w3.org/WAI/intro/accessibility.php

Wachowski, A., & Wachowski, L. (1999). *The Matrix*. USA, Australia: Warner Bros.

Wachs, J. P. J., Kölsch, M., Stern, H., & Edan, Y. (2011). Vision-based hand-gesture applications. *Communications of the ACM*, *54*(2), 60–71. doi:10.1145/1897816.1897838 PMID:21984822

Waiguny, M. K., Nelson, M. R., & Marko, B. (2013). How advergame content influences explicit and implicit brand attitudes: When violence spills over. *Journal of Advertising*, *42*(2-3), 155–169. doi:10.1080/00913367.2013.774590

Waiguny, M. K., Nelson, M. R., & Terlutter, R. (2012). Entertainment matters! The relationship between challenge and persuasiveness of an advergame for children. *Journal of Marketing Communications*, *18*(1), 69–89. doi:10.1080/1352 7266.2011.620766

Waiguny, M. K., & Terlutter, R. (2011). Differences in children's processing of advergames and TV commercials. In *Advances in Advertising Research* (Vol. 2, pp. 35–51). Gabler. doi:10.1007/978-3-8349-6854-8_3

Waithayanon, C., & Aporntewan, C. (2011). A motion classifier for Microsoft Kinect. *Proceedings of the 2011 6th International Conference on Computer Sciences and Convergence Information Technology (ICCIT)* (pp. 727-731).

Wang, J.Y., & Lan, C.C. (2014). A constant force compliant gripper for handling objects of various sizes. *ASME Transaction of Journal of Mechanical Design, 136*(7).

Wang, D., Park, S., & Fesenmaier, D. R. (2012). The role of smartphones in mediating the touristic experience. *Journal of Travel Research*, *51*(4), 371–387. doi:10.1177/0047287511426341

Wang, L., & Buchanan, T. S. (2002). Prediction of joint moment using of neural network of muscle activation from EMG signal. *IEEE Transactions on Neural Systems and Rehabilitation Engineering*, *10*(1), 30–34. doi:10.1109/TN-SRE.2002.1021584 PMID:12173737

Wang, T.-H. (2008). Web-based quiz-game-like formative assessment: Development and evaluation. *Computers & Education*, *51*(3), 1247–1263. doi:10.1016/j.compedu.2007.11.011

Ware, C. (2003). Design as applied perception. In J. Carroll (Ed.), *HCI model, theories and frameworks: Towards a multidisciplinary science* (pp. 11–26). San Francisco, CA: Morgan Kaufmann. doi:10.1016/B978-155860808-5/50002-2

Weeks, D. L., Whitney, A. A., Tindall, A. G., & Carter, G. T. (2015). Pilot Randomized Trial Comparing Intersession Scheduling of Biofeedback Results to Individuals with Chronic Pain: Influence on Psychologic Function and Pain Intensity. *American Journal of Physical Medicine & Rehabilitation / Association of Academic Physiatrists*.

Weibel, R., Bleisch, S., Nebiker, S., Fisler, J., Grossmann, T., Niederhuber, M., & Hurni, L. et al. (2009). Achieving more sustainable elearning programs for GIScience. *Geomatica*, *63*, 109–118.

Weinland, D., Ronfard, R., & Boyer, E. (2011). A survey of vision-based methods for action representation, segmentation and recognition. *Computer Vision and Image Understanding*, *115*(2), 224–241. doi:10.1016/j.cviu.2010.10.002

Weiss, C. M., Frid, A., Malin, M., & Ladijenski, V. (2015). Generating 3D CAD art from human gestures using Kinect depth sensor. *Computer-Aided Design and Applications*, *12*(5), 608-616.

Wells, S. (2002). *The Time Machine*. USA: Warner Bros.

Westera, W., Nadolski, R. J., Hummel, H. G. K., & Wopereis, I. G. J. H. (2008). Serious Games for higher education: A framework for reducing design complexity. *Computer Assisted Learning*, *24*(5), 420–432. doi:10.1111/j.1365-2729.2008.00279.x

WHO Guidelines on the Pharmacological Treatment of Persisting Pain in Children with Medical Illnesses. (2012). Geneva: World Health Organization.

WHO. (2011). *World report on disability*. Retrieved from http://www.who.int/disabilities/world_report/2011/report.pdf

Wickens, C. D. (2008). Multiple resources and mental workload. *Human Factors*, *50*(3), 449–455. doi:10.1518/001872008X288394 PMID:18689052

Wickens, E. (2002). The sacred and the profane: A tourist typology. *Annals of Tourism Research*, *29*(3), 834–851. doi:10.1016/S0160-7383(01)00088-3

Wilkowska, W., & Ziefle, M. (2012). Privacy and data security in E-health: Requirements from the users perspective. *Health Informatics Journal*, *18*(3), 191–201. doi:10.1177/1460458212442933 PMID:23011814

Williams, K., Petrosky, A., Hernandez, E., & Page, R. (2011). Product placement effectiveness: Revisited and renewed. *Journal of Management and Marketing Research*, *7*(1), 1–24.

Wilson, A., Dehaene, S., Pinel, P., Revkin, S., Cohen, L., & Cohen, D. (2006). Principles underlying the design of "The Number Race", an adaptive computer game for remediation of dyscalculia'. *Behavioral and Brain Functions*, *2*(1), 1–14. doi:10.1186/1744-9081-2-1 PMID:16734905

Windheim, K., Veale, D., & Anson, M. (2011). Mirror gazing in body dysmorphic disorder and healthy controls: Effects of duration of gazing. *Behaviour Research and Therapy*, *49*(9), 555–564. doi:10.1016/j.brat.2011.05.003 PMID:21726855

Wise, K., Bolls, P. D., Kim, H., Venkataraman, A., & Meyer, R. (2008). Enjoyment of advergames and brand attitudes: The impact of thematic relevance. *Journal of Interactive Advertising*, *9*(1), 27–36. doi:10.1080/15252019.2008.10722145

Withana, A., Peiris, R., Samarasekara, N., & Nanayakkara, S. (2015). zSense: Enabling Shallow Depth Gesture Recognition for Greater Input Expressivity on Smart Wearables. *Proceedings of the 33rd Annual ACM Conference on Human Factors in Computing Systems CHI '15* (pp. 3661–3670). New York, New York, USA: ACM Press. Doi:10.1145/2702123.2702371

Wobbrock, J., & Aung, H. (2005). Maximizing the guessability of symbolic input. Proceedings of the Extended Abstracts on Human Factors in Computing Systems CHI'05 (pp. 1869–1872). doi:10.1145/1056808.1057043

Wobbrock, J. O., Morris, M. R., & Wilson, A. D. (2009). User-defined gestures for surface computing.*Proceedings of CHI '09* (pp. 1083-1092).

Wodehouse, A., & Sheridan, M. (2014). Exploring emotional response to gesture in product interaction using Laban's movement analysis. *Interaction Studies: Social Behaviour and Communication in Biological and Artificial Systems*, *15*(2), 321–342. doi:10.1075/is.15.2.15wod

Wongpatikaseree, K., Ikeda, M., Buranarach, M., Supnithi, T., Lim, A. O., & Tan, Y. (2012). Activity Recognition using Context-Aware Infrastructure Ontology in Smart Home Domain. *Proceedings of the2012 Seventh International Conference on Knowledge, Information and Creativity Support Systems (KICSS)* (pp. 50-57). Melbourne: IEEE. doi:10.1109/KICSS.2012.26

Wongpatikaseree, K., Kim, J., Makino, Y., Lim, A. O., & Tan, Y. (2013). Architecture for Organizing Context-Aware Data in Smart Home for Activity Recognition System. In*Distributed, Ambient, and Pervasive Interactions, LNCS* (Vol. *8028*, pp. 173–182). doi:10.1007/978-3-642-39351-8_20

Wood, B., & Hamilton, T. (2010). Narukami: The Thunder God. *University of Wisconsin Madison*. Retrieved from https://sites.google.com/site/utnarukami/home

Wood, E., Willoughby, T., Rushing, A., Bechtel, L., & Gilbert, J. (2005). Use of Computer Input Devices by Older Adults. *Journal of Applied Gerontology*, *24*(5), 419–438. doi:10.1177/0733464805278378

Woodside, A., Crouch, G., & Ritchie, J. R. (2000). *Consumer Psychology of Tourism, Hospitality and Leisure*. Wallingford, Oxon: CABI Publishing.

World Wide Web Consortium. (n. d.). Retrieved from http://www.w3.org/2002/Talks/0104-usabilityprocess/slide3-0.html

Wroblewski, L. (2011). Mobile first. New York, NY: A Book Apart.

WRTA. (2008). Religious Tourism Cultural Diversity. *World Religious Travel Association (WRTA)*. Retrieved from http://www.multifaiths.com/faith-communities/religious-tourism

Xiang, Z., & Gretzel, U. (2010). Role of social media in online travel information search. *Tourism Management*, *31*(2), 179–188. doi:10.1016/j.tourman.2009.02.016

Xiong, Y., Li, H., Kornhaber, M. L., Suen, H. K., Pursel, B., & Goins, D. D. (2015). Examining the relations among student motivation, engagement, and retention in a MOOC: A structural equation modeling approach. *Global Education Review*, *2*(3), 23–33.

Xstage. (2015). Retrieved from http://www.xstage.de/

Xtion. (2015). Asus Xtion Pro Live. Retrieved from www.asus.com/Multimedia/Xtion_PRO_LIVE

Xu, F., Weber, J., & Buhalis, D. (2013). Gamification in tourism. In *Information and Communication Technologies in Tourism 2014* (pp. 525–537). New York, NY: Springer International Publishing. doi:10.1007/978-3-319-03973-2_38

Xu, Y. (2011). *Literature review on web application gamification and analytics* (pp. 11–05). Honolulu, HI.

Yamabe, T., Takagi, A., & Nakajima, T. (2005). Citron: A Context Information Acquisition Framework for Personal Devices. *Proceedings of the11th IEEE International Conference on Embedded and Real-Time Computing Systems and Applications (RTCSA' 05)* (pp. 489-495). Hong Kong, China: IEEE. doi:10.1109/RTCSA.2005.32

Yamaguchi, M. (2015). Holographic 3D touch sensing display. In *Digital Holography and Three-Dimensional Imaging, DM3A-1*. Optical Society of America. doi:10.1364/DH.2015.DM3A.1

Yang, M. H., Roskos-Ewoldsen, D. R., Dinu, L., & Arpan, L. M. (2006). The effectiveness of 'in-game' advertising: Comparing college students' explicit and implicit memory for brand names. *Journal of Advertising*, *35*(4), 143–152. doi:10.2753/JOA0091-3367350410

Yang, M., & Roskos-Ewoldsen, D. R. (2007). The effectiveness of bran placements in the movies: Level of placements, explicit and implicit memory, and brand choice behavior. *Journal of Communication*, *57*(3), 469–489. doi:10.1111/j.1460-2466.2007.00353.x

Yang, Y.-T. C. (2012). Building virtual cities, inspiring intelligent citizens: Digital games for developing students' problem solving and learning motivation. *Computers & Education*, *59*(2), 365–377. doi:10.1016/j.compedu.2012.01.012

Yavuzer, G., Selles, R., Sezer, N., Sutbeyaz, S., Bussmann, J. B., Koseoglu, F., & Stam, H. J. et al. (2008). Mirror therapy improves hand function in subacute stroke: A randomized controlled trial.[Randomized Controlled Trial]. *Archives of Physical Medicine and Rehabilitation*, *89*(3), 393–398. doi:10.1016/j.apmr.2007.08.162 PMID:18295613

Yeh, Y.-Y., & Silverstein, L. D. (1992, October). Spatial Judgments with Monoscopic and Stereoscopic Presentation of Perspective Displays. *Human Factors: The Journal of the Human Factors and Ergonomics Society*, *34*(5), 583-600.

Yokokohji, Y., & Yoshikawa, T. (1994, October). Bilateral control of master-slave manipulators for ideal kinesthetic coupling-formulation and experiment. *IEEE Transactions on Robotics and Automation*, *10*(5), 605–620. doi:10.1109/70.326566 PMID:11539289

Yoon, S., Choi, Y. K., & Song, S. (2011). When intrusive can be likable. *Journal of Advertising*, *40*(2), 63–76. doi:10.2753/JOA0091-3367400205

Young, K. (2002). Is e-learning delivering roi? *Industrial and Commercial Training*, *34*(2), 54–61. doi:10.1108/00197850210417537

Yovcheva, Z., Buhalis, D., Gatzidis, C., & van Elzakker, C. P. (2014). Empirical Evaluation of Smartphone Augmented Reality Browsers in an Urban Tourism Destination Context. *International Journal of Mobile Human Computer Interaction*, *6*(2), 10–31. doi:10.4018/ijmhci.2014040102

Yuan, M., Khan, I. R., Farbiz, F., Niswar, A., & Huang, Z. (2011). A mixed reality system for virtual glasses try-on. *Paper presented at the 10th International Conference on Virtual Reality Continuum and Its Applications in Industry*, Hong Kong, China. doi:10.1145/2087756.2087816

Yun, Y., Changrampadi, M. H., & Gu, I. Y. H. (2014). Head pose classification by multi-class AdaBoost with fusion of RGB and depth images. *Proceedings of the 2014 International Conference on Signal Processing and Integrated Networks (SPIN)* (pp. 174–177). IEEE. http://doi.org/ doi:10.1109/SPIN.2014.6776943

Yu, Q., Cheng, H. H., Cheng, W. W., & Zhou, X. (2004). Opencv for interactive open architecture computer vision. *Advances in Engineering Software*, *35*(8-9), 527–536. doi:10.1016/j.advengsoft.2004.05.003

Yus, R., Pappachan, P., Das, P. K., Finin, T., Joshi, A., & Mena, E. (2014). Semantics for Privacy and Shared Context. *Proceedings of the International Semantic Web Conference (ISWC 2014)* (pp. 1-11). Trantino, Italy: Elsevier.

Zanin, M., & Papo, D. (2014). Characterizing Motif Dynamics of Electric Brain Activity Using Symbolic Analysis. *Entropy*, *16*(11), 5654–5667. doi:10.3390/e16115654

Zeidan, F., Gordon, N. S., Merchant, J., & Goolkasian, P. (2010). The effects of brief mindfulness meditation training on experimentally induced pain. *The Journal of Pain: Official Journal of the American Pain Society*, *11*(3), 199–209. doi:10.1016/j.jpain.2009.07.015 PMID:19853530

Zelic, G., Kim, J., & Davis, C. (2015). Articulatory constraints on spontaneous entrainment between speech and manual gesture. *Human Movement Science*, *42*, 232–245. doi:10.1016/j.humov.2015.05.009 PMID:26072361

Zhang, C., & Chen, W.-B. (2007). An Effective and Robust Method for Automatic Bacterial Colony Enumeration. *Proceedings of theInternational Conference on Semantic Computing* (pp. 581-588). Irvine, Canada: IEEE. doi:10.1109/ICSC.2007.20

Zhang, X. L., Begleiter, H., Porjesz, B., Wang, W., & Litke, A. (1995). Event related potentials during object recognition tasks. *Brain Research Bulletin*, *38*(6), 531–538. doi:10.1016/0361-9230(95)02023-5 PMID:8590074

Zhang, Z. (2012). *Microsoft Kinect sensor and its effect. Multimedia* (pp. 4–10). IEEE.

Zhu, H., Chen, E., Yu, K., Cao, H., Xiong, H., & Tian, J. (2012). Mining Personal Context-Aware Preferences for Mobile Users. *Proceedings of the 2012 IEEE 12th International Conference on Data Mining (ICDM)* (pp. 1212-1217). Brussels: IEEE.

Zichermann, G., & Cunningham, C. (2011). *Gamification by design: Implementing game mechanics in web and mobile apps*. Sebastopol, CA: O'Reilly Media, Inc.

Zimmerman, T. G., Lanier, J., Blanchard, C., Bryson, S., & Harvill, Y. (1987). A hand gesture interface device. *Proceedings of the SIGCHI/GI conference on Human factors in computing systems and graphics interface CHI '87* (pp. 189–192). New York, New York, USA: ACM Press. Doi:10.1145/29933.275628

Zugara. (2015). The Webcam Social Shopper (WSS) Retrieved from http://zugara.com/virtual-dressing-room-technology/webcam-social-shopper

Zyda, M. (2007). Creating a Science of Games: Introduction. *Communications of the ACM*, *50*(7), 26–29. doi:10.1145/1272516.1272535

About the Contributors

João Rodrigues graduated in Electrical Engineering in 1993, he got his M.Sc. in Computer Systems Engineering in 1998 and Ph.D. Electronics and Computer Engineering in 2008 from University of the Algarve, Portugal. He is Adjunct Professor at Instituto Superior de Engenharia, also in the University of the Algarve, where he lectures on Computer Science and Computer Vision since 1994. He is member of associative laboratory LARSyS (ISR-Lisbon), CIAC and the Associations APRP, IAPR and ARTECH. He has participated in 14 financed scientific projects, and he is co-author of more than 100 scientific publications. His major research interests lies on computer and human vision, assistive technologies and human-computer interaction.

Pedro Cardoso holds a PhD in the field of Operational Research from the University of Seville (Spain), a Master in Computational Mathematics from the University of Minho (Portugal) and a Degree in Mathematics - Computer Science from the University of Coimbra (Portugal). He teaches Computer Science and Mathematics at the Instituto Superior de Engenharia of the Universidade do Algarve (UAlg) and is member of LARSys/UAlg. He has high knowledge in the fields of databases, algorithms and data structures, and Operational Research. Over the past few years has been involved in 7 national and international scientific and development projects and is the co-author of about 40 scientific publications.

Jânio Monteiro graduated in Electrical and Computers Engineering in 1995 from the University of Porto, and later obtained a Master and PhD degrees respectively in 2003 and 2010, also in Electrical and Computer Engineering from Instituto Superior Técnico, Technical University of Lisbon. Since 2003, he has been a member of INESC-ID in Lisbon, where he participated in several European R&TD projects funded by the Information Society Technologies Programme (IST), of the European Commission, namely: Olympic, My-e-Director and Saracen. As part of the Algarve University, he has also participated in an international project called ENERGEIA and several national projects with regional companies. He is co-author of more than three dozen publications, including journal articles, papers in scientific conferences, several book chapters, deliverables of projects and national patents. His main areas of expertise involve communication networks, smart grids and sensor networks or Internet of Things.

Mauro Figueiredo has a PhD in computer science from the University of Salford, Manchester, since 2005. He was teacher at University of Coimbra from 1989 until 1996. Since 1996, he has been at the Algarve University where he is an adjunct professor. His research interests are in the use of information technologies for education, e-learning, b-learning, games and augmented reality. His PhD students are currently working with ebooks and augmented reality tools for e-learning. He is author of more than sixty international journal and conferences articles, book chapters and books and he collaborated and participated in different National projects. He is the international coordinator of the Erasmus+ project MILAGE: Interactive Mathematics by implementing a Blended-Learning model with Augmented Reality and Game books. He has several papers best awards and a school project in augmented reality which has been nationally recognized. He has already organized several international conferences. Most of his research is conducted at the Univ. Algarve, at CIMA (Center of Marine and Environmental Research) and CIAC (Center for the Arts and Communication Research).

***

A.M. Harsha S Abeykoon received a B.Sc. degree in Electrical Engineering from University of Moratuwa, Sri Lanka in 2002. He received his M.Sc and PhD in Robotics and Control from the Keio University, Japan in 2005 and 2008, respectively. Since 2009, he has been working in the Department of Electrical Engineering, University of Moratuwa as a Senior Lecturer. His research interests include motion control, mobile robotics and bilateral control related to biomedical engineering. Dr. Harsha is member of IEEE and IES. He has worked as the secretary of the IEEE Sri Lanka section. He has received Monbukagakusho scholarship award (from the Japanese Govt.) for 5 years and Keio Leading Lab (KLL) research grant for 3 consecutive years. Currently he is working as an assistant professor in the Asian Institute of Technology (AIT), Thailand.

Zeenat AlKassim is completing her Master's degree in Computer Engineering track under Electrical Engineering, at the United Arab Emirates University. She is fond of researching the areas related to Machine Learning and Augmented Reality, and enjoys daily readings about up-to-date technologies and inventions. Zeenat has designed a laser keyboard in the past for her graduation project at Prince Mohammad University in KSA and is keen on moving further in this interesting world of creative technologies. Zeenat believes that technological advancements has no limits.

Luis Berdun is a professor in computer engineering at the Facultad de Ciencias Exactas, Universidad Nacional del Centro de la Provincia de Buenos Aires (UNICEN), Argentina. He received his computer engineer degree from UNICEN Tandil, Argentina, in 2002, his Master's degree from the same university in 2005, and his Ph.D. degree in computer science from the same university in 2009. Since 2001, he has been a part of the ISISTAN Research Institute (CONICET - UNICEN). His research interests include: Artificial Intelligence, AI Planning, Machine Learning, object-oriented programming and frameworks.

Paulo Bica is Managing Director at SPIC – Creative Solutions. He attended Product Design Engineering at Viana do Castelo Polytechnic Institute and later Communication Design at Algarve University. At the same time, he graduated in Hotel Management from INFTUR and began his professional career in the hospitality industry, reaching the general manager position. His interests and passion for design and communication technologies led him to lead different marketing and communication projects, in addition to other personal projects and events. In 2006, he began his entrepreneurial path, creating a hotel management-consulting firm, as a marketing and communications manager and one year later, a digital creative agency, where he is currently the entire management.

José Bidarra received his PhD in Educational Communications at Universidade Aberta (the Portuguese Open University), where he is currently Assistant Professor in the Department of Science and Technology. He is head of the Informatics, Physics and Technology Section (SIFT) and has been coordinator of several master degree programs. He was co-author of the virtual pedagogical model used by Universidade Aberta. His current research interests focus mainly on the application of multimedia and digital media in distance education, including ebooks, games and simulations. Some of his master and doctorate students are developing new methodologies to engage learners in valuable experiences with digital media. Most of the research is conducted at Universidade Aberta and at CIAC (Center for the Arts and Communication Research, University of Algarve); other research includes a recent Honorary Fellowship at the Games, Learning, and Society unit, University of Wisconsin – Madison (USA), and frequent collaborations with Portuguese and European universities. Recent scientific awards: Best Paper Award of IMCL 2014 - International Conference on Interactive Mobile Communication Technologies and Learning. Winner of the sixth annual Excellence in Research Journal Awards, celebrating the best articles from the 2013 publications by IGI Global.

Vesna Spasojević Brkić is an Associate Professor in the Industrial Engineering Department, Faculty of Mechanical Engineering, University of Belgrade, Serbia. Her scientific and engineering interests are production, risk, quality management and ergonomics. She has over 100 publications, including 1 teaching book and 2 monographs, over 25 papers in journals with impact factor, over 30 papers in national journals, over 20 technical solutions and national and international projects etc. She is a member of editorial boards of five conferences and three journals.

Tuğçe Ozansoy Çadırcı has a PhD degree on marketing. She works as an assistant professor of marketing Yıldız Technical University (YTU), Turkey. Her main research areas include Consumer Behavior, Digital Consumption and Fashion Marketing. Currently, she is lecturing on the subjects of Consumption Theory, e-commerce, Digital Marketing, Consumer Behavior and Marketing Research at YTU.

Marcelo Ricardo Campo received the Ph.D degree in Computer Science from Instituto de Informática de la Universidad Federal de Rio Grande do Sul (UFRGS), Brazil, in 1997. He is currently the director of the ISISTAN Research Institute (CONICET - UNICEN). His research interests include intelligent aided software engineering, software architecture and software visualization.

João Cardoso is a graduate in Computer Engineering from the University of Aveiro, Portugal.

Sergio Casas was born in Valencia, Spain, in 1978. He received a degree in Computer Engineering in 2001, and a degree in Technical Telecommunication Engineering – Specialization in Telematics in 2007. In 2009, he received the National Award on University Studies, by the Spanish Ministry of Education for achieving the highest national average grade among all Spanish university students in his degree. He received his PhD in Computational Mathematics in 2014 for his work on vehicle simulations with motion platforms. He works as project researcher at the Institute of Robotics of the University of Valencia since 2001. His expertise is in real-time graphics, augmented reality, computer physics simulation and motion cueing generation for virtual reality systems. He is also an assistant professor in the Department of Computer Science of the University of Valencia since 2007.

Tiago Cinto received his degree of Computer Science from the Methodist University of Piracicaba - UNIMEP and Msc. in Electrical Engineering from the University of Campinas - UNICAMP in 2011 and 2014, respectively. Currently, he is a PhD student at UNICAMP and researcher at Telecommunications Research and Development Center - CPqD. His research interests are Human-Computer Interfaces, Virtual Learning Environments, Machine Learning and Data Warehousing.

Paulo Dias is an Assistant Professor in the Department of Electronics, Telecommunications and Informatics of the University of Aveiro, Portugal, and a researcher at IEETA/UA.

Irraivan Elamvazuthi obtained his PhD from the Department of Automatic Control and Systems Engineering, University of Sheffield, UK in 2002. He is an Associate Professor at the Department of Electrical and Electronic Engineering of Universiti Teknologi PETRONAS, Malaysia. He is a member of IEEE, IFAC, AEE, AAIA and BEM. His research interests include Control and Systems Engineering with focus on Robotics, Mechatronics, Power Systems and Bio-medical Applications.

Paulo Felisberto holds an electrical engineering degree and a PhD in electronic and computer engineering. He currently works as an associate professor at the University of Algarve in the electrotechnical engineering department. He is a permanent member of the Signal Processing Laboratory (SiPLAB/CINTAL/UALG) at the University of Algarve and the Institute for Systems and Robotics (LARSys/ISR/Lisbon). His main scientific interests are in the fields of signal processing in acoustics with application in localization, positioning, and acoustic environmental monitoring. He has participated in and coordinated several projects financed by national, European and Brazilian research agencies.

Beatriz Quintino Ferreira is a PhD student in Electrical and Computer Engineering.

Carlos Ferreira is an Associate Professor at the Department of Economics, Management and Industrial Engineering of the University of Aveiro, Portugal, and a researcher at IEETA/UA.

Kerstin Fischer received her PhD from Bielefeld University in 1998. After a Postdoc position at the University of Hamburg and an assistant professor position at the University of Bremen, she became associate professor in Sonderborg for the English language and linguistics in 2007 and was recently appointed as a professor (MSO) for Language and Technology Interaction. She has been working on human-computer and human-robot interaction in interdisciplinary research contexts for the past 15 years, initially regarding the improvement of speech technology (in the framework of the computer-linguistic project Verbmobil), and later broadening her work to communication and interface design, ICT and human factors research. She was the PI in the EU project iTalk and is currently leading several projects in which human-robot interaction informs linguistic research. Her teaching is devoted to communication design and technology interaction.

Ennio Gambi was born in Loreto (Ancona, Italy) in 1961. He received the Electronic Engineering graduate diploma at the Università Politecnica delle Marche in 1986 and a Microwave Engineering master degree in 1989. From 1984 to 1992, he worked with the Azienda di Stato per i Servizi Telefonici, while during 1988 he covered the role of Avionic Engineer as an Official of the Italian Military Air Force. Since 1992, he has been at the Università Politecnica delle Marche in Ancona, where he is currently an

Associate Professor. At present, on the basis of a long-time interests in the domotic system, he is working on the evolution of this technology toward the Ambient Assisted Living, with the aim to propose an integrated solution where the fusion of data provided by different sensor networks allows the desired level of home assistance for disabled or elderly people. In this research field the activity started from a theoretical approach to reach practical experiments, as the trial installation of a system for monitoring patients at a nursing home.

T. Ganesan is with the Department of Chemical Engineering Universiti Teknologi PETRONAS (UTP), Tronoh, Malaysia. He holds a bachelor's degree in Chemical Engineering (Hons.), a Master of Science in Computational Fluid Dynamics (CFD) and a doctorate in Process Optimization. His research interests include modelling, optimization and computational intelligence.

Francisco Giner Licensed in Fine Arts Degree (M.A.) in 1996, from the Polytechnic University of Valencia, Spain. Ph.D. "Cum Laude" in Fine Arts in 2002. Contemporary Art Program at the Painting Department of the Polytechnic University of Valencia. From 1999 to present, Professor in Fine Arts Degree, Design and Creative Technologies Degree and Visual and Multimedia Arts Official Master. Researcher at the Light Laboratory in the Faculty of Fine Arts of the Polytechnic University of Valencia, where he works as a meeting point, study and research of expressive aesthetic principles related to light-image. Research areas of interest: Virtual and Augmented Reality applied to artistic expression.

Diane Gromala holds the Canadian Research Chair (CRC) in Computational Technologies for Transforming Pain and is the founding director of the Chronic Pain Research Institute. Her research interests are: new tools, interaction design & interface design that address multiple facets of chronic diseases, including chronic pain; Health Informatics, BioMedia, BioTechnologies; Contemporary philosophies of experience; embodiment, interoception, neuroplasticity; Visualization: medical visualization, personal visual analytics for patients; Design of Calming Technologies & Interfaces from Immersive Virtual Reality (VR) to mobile & handheld devices; Speculative Design at the confluence of HCI, Engineering, Humanities & Interaction Design.

Ayşegül Sağkaya Güngör has a PhD degree on marketing. Her particular area of interest is new technologies in electronic mediums, particularly their impact on online consumer behavior. Specific research areas in her interest include the consumer acceptance of technology, online social networks, digital marketing methods and e-commerce. Currently, she is lecturing at various universities on the subjects of e-commerce, e-business, digital marketing and marketing management.

Cláudia H. N. Henriques received her PhD from Algarve University (Portugal) in 2002. She is a professor of Tourism Economics and Creative Economy at Algarve University (ESGHT/UALG). Main research interests: Cultural Tourism, Creative Economy, Tourism Planning and Management.

Rodrigo Ibañez received a Computer Engineer degree from the Universidad Nacional del Centro de la Provincia de Buenos Aires (UNICEN), Tandil, Argentina, in 2012, and is currently pursuing a Ph.D degree in Computer Science at the same university. Since 2013, he has been a part of the ISISTAN Research Institute, UNICEN. His research interests include machine learning algorithms, human activity recognition, and automated web services composition. Mr. Ibañez has obtained a scholarship from FONCyT to complete his doctoral studies.

Toru Ishida has been a professor at Kyoto University since 1993. Before that he was a research scientist at NTT Laboratories. His academic paths include visiting scientist/professor positions at Columbia University, Technische Universitaet Muenchen, Le Laboratoire d'Informatique de Paris 6, University of Maryland, Shanghai Jiao Tong University, Tsinghua University and Hong Kong Baptist University. He was a project leader at NTT Communication Science Laboratories from 1998 to 2004, and the National Institute of Information and Communications Technology (NICT) from 2006 to 2010. His research interest lies with autonomous agents and multiagent systems.

Muhammad Nazrul Islam, PhD, is an Associate Professor in the Department of Computer Science and Engineering at the Military Institute of Science and Technology (MIST), Bangladesh. Before joining MIST, he has worked as a visiting teaching fellow at Uppsala University and as a postdoctoral research fellow at Åbo Akademi University. He has also worked as a Lecturer and as an Assistant Professor in the Department of Computer Science and Engineering, Khulna University of Engineering & Technology (KUET), Bangladesh, for the period of 2003-2012. His research interests are focused on Human-Computer Interaction, Information Systems Usability, User Experience, and Computer Semiotics. He is the author of 40 peer-reviewed publications in journals and conferences.

Lars Christian Jensen received his MA in Business Communication & Communication Design from the University of Southern Denmark. During his studies, he part-timed as an interaction analyst for both humanistic and technical research groups and thus participated in many international interdisciplinary collaborations between designers, engineers and linguists. This work introduced him to fields such as Human-Robot Interaction, High-Tech Business Venturing and IT-Product Design. He is currently pursuing a PhD at the University of Southern Denmark in the field Human-Robot Interaction, in which he investigates how social robots can be used as a resource for teachers in foreign language learning environments.

Weina Jin is a Master's student in the School of Interactive Arts and Technology, Simon Fraser University. She holds a Doctor of Medicine (MD) degree in Neurology from Peking University, and had been a neurological resident for two years. Her research interests include health-related HCI, VR and serious games.

Jesús Gimeno received the Master degree in Computer Science from the University of Valencia (2008), with a dissertation about "Motion capture and augmented reality techniques for virtual prototyping". He is a PhD student and part-time professor at the University of Valencia (Spain). His research interests include motion capture, real-time simulation, advanced user interfaces, mobile computing and augmented reality. In the last few years, he has served as a visiting scientist for the Augmented Reality Group at Bauhaus Universitat (Weimar, Germany, 2008) and at VRAC Center at Iowa State University (Ames IO, USA, 2010).

Şirin Gizem Köse is currently a doctoral student at Yıldız Technical University where she has been working as a Research Assistant of Marketing since 2014. Her research areas include digital advertising, specifically in game advertising, advergaming and innovative technologies on digital marketing. She has national and international studies on digital marketing and corporate social responsibility.

Kamil Kukliński is a PhD student in the Mechanical Department of Bialystok University of Technology. He received his engineering and master's degrees in Automation and Robotics in 2009 and 2011, respectively, from the Bialystok University of Technology. Currently, he is developing methods to improve the controlling of robots in real-time.

Roberto Lam, born in 1960, graduated in Computer Science in 1995. In 2001, he obtained an MSc degree at the University of the Algarve in Faro, where he lectures on computer science courses at the Instituto Superior de Engenharia. Presently, he is pursuing a PhD degree in the Vision Laboratory (UAlg). He is member of the LARSyS (Lisbon) and the Portuguese Chapter of Eurographics. His major research interest is tridimensional modelling, 3D object representation, recognition and retrieval.

Robert Lanquar Doctor in "Economy and Law of Tourism" - University Aix-Marseilles III, and Ph.D. in "Recreation Resources Organizational Development" - Texas A&M University (USA). Former UNWTO civil servant, he was the expert of several international organizations like UNWTO, UNEP, the World Bank, the European Commission, the Commonwealth (for Seychelles). Coordinator for tourism of the Blue Plan, he is the tourism expert of MEDPRO, and leads various networks in relation with Mediterranean cooperation. He founded the MED-DEV - Mediterranean Sustainable Development Market (trade, tourism and environment). Author of 17 books and more than 300 reports and articles on tourism and the environment in French and Spanish, his work was translated into English, Chinese, Spanish, Turkish, Arabic, Vietnamese. During his career, he has taught at several universities in Canada, France, Belgium, Switzerland, Portugal and Spain. He is the CEO of Cordoba Horizontes (CH) which offers its know-how to enterprises and organizations in the sectors of agribusiness, trade and tourism on the Mediterranean area. CH was created with the idea of a 21st century dedicated to sustainable development: business must adapt to the new conditions produced by climate change. He is also columnist at L'Économiste, the main economic Moroccan magazine. Now, he is a professor-researcher at La Rochelle Business School where he teaches coastal tourism as well as sustainable development.

Umar Mahmud Assistant Professor Engineer Umar Mahmud is a Software Engineer with 9+ years of teaching experience in the fields of Software Engineering and Computer Science. He completed his BE (Computer Software) in 2003 and his MS (Computer Software Engineering) in 2006 from the Military College of Signals (MCS), National University of Sciences and Technology (NUST), Islamabad, Pakistan. He is currently serving as a faculty member in the Department of Software Engineering (DSE), at Foundation University Islamabad (FUI). He has published around 10+ research articles in the areas of context awareness with an i10-index of 2 and h-index of 4. His research interest include context awareness, pervasive computing, mobile networks and military history.

Nader Mohamed is an associate professor of Information Technology at The College of Information Technology, UAEU, Al-Ain, UAE. He obtained his Ph.D. in Computer Science from University of Nebraska-Lincoln, Nebraska, USA in 2004. Between 2004 to 2006, he was an assistant professor of Computer Engineering at Stevens Institute of Technology in New Jersey, USA. He worked at the University of Nebraska-Lincoln as a research assistant from 2001 to 2004 in National Science Foundation

(NSF) supported research and development projects. Dr. Mohamed received a number of recognition awards for his IT contributions and published more than 140 refereed articles in prestigious international journals and conferences. His current professional interest focuses on middleware, cloud computing, sensor networks, unmanned aerial vehicles, HCI, internet computing, and networking. He has served as a guest editor of several international journal special issues in the area of middleware, such as the Elsevier Journal of Network and Computer Applications and the Wiley Journal of Concurrency and Computation: Practice and Experience. He was co-chair of the First and Second International Symposiums on Middleware and Network Applications in 2010 and 2011 in Las Vegas, Nevada, USA. In addition, he has 8 years of industry experience in the information technology field.

Fernando C. Monteiro received his M.S. degree in computer integrated manufacturing from Minho University, Braga, Portugal, in 1998, and the Ph.D. degree in electrical engineering from the Faculty of Engineering, University of Porto, Portugal. Currently, he is an Adjunct Professor with the Department of Electrical Engineering, Polytechnic Institute of Bragança (IPB), Portugal. He is the Director of the Master Program in biomedical technology with the IPB. His current research interests include image processing and analysis, and more specifically, medical image analysis.

Laura Montanini was born in 1987 in Fermo. She obtained the High School diploma in Informatics from I.T.I.S. "Montani" in Fermo, on July 2006. She received the Bachelor's Degree in Informatics and Automation Engineering in 2010, and the Master's Degree in Electronic Engineering on July 2013, at the Università Politecnica delle Marche. Since November 2013, she has been a Ph.D. student in Telecommunications. She is working on advanced interfaces, based on computer vision techniques, for human-machine communication in Ambient Assisted Living.

Toshiya Naka received his MS in Electronic engineering from the Osaka Prefecture University in 1985, and Ph.D in Informatics from Kyoto University in 2013. In 1985, he was hired as a researcher of image processing by Fujitsu Laboratory, by 1988 he was the senior research scientist at Panasonic R&D and he concurrently serves as an Associate Professor of Kyoto University. His research interests lie with image processing, humanoid robotics and human interfaces, and he has been working on this theme for more than twenty years.

Aldric Negrier has a Master's Degree in Electronics and Telecommunications by the University of Algarve. He is an open source advocate, entrepreneur, and animal rights activist.

Titilola Obilade is a medical doctor and a senior education specialist. She earned her Ph.D. in Learning Sciences and Technologies from Virginia Polytechnic Institute and State University. She is also an alumnus of the University of Lagos, Nigeria where she earned her MBBS in Medicine and Surgery. She has authored and coauthored more than 20 refereed articles, book chapters and a textbook in areas of instructional design and technology, human computer interaction, health education and infectious diseases. Her most recent work is a textbook on visual literacy.

Ricardo Olanda He obtained his PhD in Computer Science in 2010 at Universitat de València. His Phd was aimed at processing, transmission and interactive visualization of extended terrain databases on different types of network architectures, client-server, peer-to-peer and hybrid architectures. Part of his

PhD was developed at the Future Workspaces Research Centre at Salford University (UK). He joined the ARTEC group of IRTIC in 2000, where he focused on interactive 3D graphics, virtual reality, augmented reality, virtual environments, terrain processing and multimedia transmission. He has worked on research projects related to the interactive visualization of different kinds of information over several stereoscopic display systems, like a 160° cylindrical visionarium or a 4-screem CAVE with retro-projected floor. Currently, he is a professor at the Universitat de València in the Computer Science and Networking area.

Cristina Portalés is MSc. in Geodesy and Cartography from the Universidad Politécnica de Valencia and MSc. in Surveying and Geoinformation from Technische Universität Wien (2003). Research fellow at the Mixed Reality Laboratory of the University of Nottingham (2005) and at the Interaction and Entertainment Research Centre of the Nanyang University of Singapore (2006), both in the area of computer vision. In 2008, she received a Ph.D. degree from the UPV. From 2011-2012, she worked at AIDO (Industrial Association of Optics, Colour and Imaging), where she was primarily involved in technical management of the FP7 funded project SYDDARTA. In 2012, she received the Juan de la Cierva postdoctoral grant by the Spanish Ministry to join IRTIC (Research Institute of Robotics and Information and Communication Technologies), where she continued research in accurate 3D reconstruction. Her current research interests are focused on geometric calibration, image processing, 3D reconstruction, multispectral imaging, augmented reality and human-computer-interaction.

Goran D. Putnik, Dr. Habil., DrSc., Full Professor, Department of Production and Systems Engineering. His scientific and engineering interests are distributed, agile and virtual production systems and enterprises, design and management theory, and complexity management in organizations. His publishing record comprises more than 250 publications in international and national journals and conferences, including 13 books. He serves as a member of Editorial Board for several international journals. He is an associate member of the International Academy for Production Engineering CIRP.

Laura Raffaeli received a Bachelor's Degree in Telecommunication Engineering in 2010, and a Master's Degree in Electronic Engineering on February, 2013 from the Università Politecnica delle Marche, Ancona. She was involved in a project dealing with the design of a Smart TV application, to collect medical reports from remote labs and hospitals, in cooperation with the Regione Marche ICT Department. At the Department of Information Engineering she is working on interactive apps to interface users to remote healthcare services and Ambient Assisted Living solutions.

Célia M. Q. Ramos graduated in Computer Engineering from the University of Coimbra, obtained her Master in Electrical and Computers Engineering from the Higher Technical Institute, Lisbon University, and the PhD in Econometrics in the University of the Algarve (UALG), Faculty of Economics, Portugal. She is Adjunct Professor at School for Management, Hospitality and Tourism, also in the UALG, where she lectures computer science. Areas of research and special interest include conception and development of information systems, tourism information systems, big data, etourism, econometric modeling and panel-data models. Célia Ramos has published in the fields of information systems and tourism, namely, she has authored a book, two book chapters, conference papers and journal articles. At the level of applied research, she has participated in several funded projects.

R.M. Maheshi Ruwanthika received the B.Sc .Eng. Hons degree in Electrical Engineering in 2014 and M.Sc degree in 2015 from University of Moratuwa, Sri Lanka. Presently, she is working in the Department of Electrical Engineering, University of Moratuwa, Sri Lanka as a Probationary Lecturer. Her research interests include control systems, teleoperation and haptics.

Beatriz Sousa Santos is an Associate Professor in the Department of Electronics, Telecommunications and Informatics of the Univeristy of Aveiro, Portugal, and a researcher at IEETA/UA.

Ku Nurhanim Ku Abdul Rahim received her B. Eng. Tech in Mechatronics degree from Universiti Kuala Lumpur in 2006 and her Msc. in Electrical & Electronics in 2014 from Universiti Teknologi Petronas in Malaysia and is currently pursuing a Phd at the same university. Her research interests are in robotics control and biomechanics on robotic upper and lower limb assistive devices.

João Ribeiro has a degree in Biomedical Engineering completed at Polytechnic Institute of Bragança.

Thiusius Rajeeth Savarimuthu received his Ph.D. degree in Robotics and embedded medical vision in 2011. In 2005, he received his B.Sc. degree in Computer System Engineering and the M.Sc. in Computer System Engineering in 2007 at the University of Southern Denmark. His current research interests include industrial robotics, hardware acceleration of image processing algorithms, embedded medical image processing and the design of medical robotic systems.

Vaibhav Shah received his PhD in Industrial Engineering (with Machine Learning) from the School of Engineering at University of Minho, Portugal, in 2015, where he started working as a researcher in 2007. He is a member of the research center ALGORITMI, and currently working in the Center for Computer Graphics (CCG), both located at the University of Minho. He received his MSc with Honours in Intelligent Systems from the St. Petersburg State Polytechnical University, Russia, in 2005. He worked as a Project Leader for an R&D project using Artificial Intelligence, in India, from 2005 to 2007, and has experience in software development since 1999. His research interests include Artificial Intelligence, Grammatical Inference, Human-Machine Interface and Interaction, Knowledge Engineering, Ubiquitous Manufacturing Systems, and related areas.

Bruno M. S. Mendes da Silva, graduated in Cinema and Video in 1995 from School of Arts of Oporto (ESAP), got his post-graduation in Arts Management in 1998 from Macao Institute of European Studies (IEEM) and the PhD in Literature/Comparative Literature/Literature and Cinema in 2008 from University of the Algarve (UALG), Portugal. He is an Adjunct Professor in the School of Education and Communication (ESEC), also in the UALG, where he lectures on Audiovisual Communication since 2000 and is, at present, the President of the Pedagogical Council. He is a member of the Research Centre for Arts and Communication (CIAC). He was a TV Producer and Director from 1995 to 2000 at Teledifusão de Macau (TDM) and has been invited to such International Art and Film Festivals as: Fresh (Thailand), Dokanema(Mozambique), Loop(Spain), Festival de la imagen (Colombia), and Ecologias Digitales (Colombia). He participated in six financed scientific projects and he is the author of several books, chapters of books and scientific publications. He won a scientific prize (Ceratonia) in 2008 with the project "Memory and Identity - Algarte: a study of the art in the Algarve". He currently working on his post-doctoral project in the field of Interactive Cinema.

Álvaro Soria received a Ph.D degree in Computer Science from the Universidad Nacional del Centro de la Provincia de Buenos Aires (UNICEN), Tandil, Argentina, in 2009. Since 2001, he has been part of ISISTAN Research Institute (CONICET - UNICEN). His research interests include: Software Architectures, Quality-driven Design, Gesture recognition, and Fault Localization.

Luís Sousa is a researcher at the University of Algarve and is currently finishing his master degree in Electrical and Electronic Engineering. His major interests lie in electronic systems, embedded systems and computer vision, with PoolLiveAid being one of his most recognized projects.

Susanna Spinsante was born in Osimo (Italy) in 1976. She received her Ph.D. in Electronic Engineering and Telecommunications in 2005, from the Polytechnic University of Marche (ITALY), and her Laurea (Graduate Diploma) Degree in Electronic Engineering in 2002, from the same University. Since December 2005, she has been a PostDoc in Telecommunications at the same University, where now she is Assistant Professor in Telecommunications. During her Ph.D. course, she spent a semester in the Department of Informatics of the University of Bergen (NORWAY), where she was awarded a fellowship for research activity on the iterative coding issues for asymmetric channels. Since 2007, she has been an adjunct professor at the Engineering Faculty of the Polytechnic University of Marche. At present, Susanna is studying the issues of integrating radio communication devices in networks dedicated to home automation, by investigating the problems related to data traffic management and communication reliability. She works on radio communication systems exploiting spread spectrum techniques, for indoor and outdoor communications (Wi-Fi networks, Bluetooth, CDMA systems for multiple access), and radar applications (vehicular anti-collision systems). She is IEEE Senior Member, a member of the AitAAL (Italian Association for Ambient Assisted Living) since February 2010. In December 2004, she was one of the charter members of ArieLAB, a technology start-up active in the field of Ambient Assisted Living systems and applications design, and telecommunications consultancy. She is involved in several applied research projects on AAL and home building automation, supported by regional and national funds. From 2010 to 2013, she has been the CEO of ArieLAB Srl. In September 2012 she became the co-founder of the academic spinoff DowSee Srl.

Franck Tétard, PhD, is a Senior Lecturer at Department of Informatics and Media, at Uppsala University, Sweden, and a Research Fellow in the Institute for Advanced Management Systems Research, Åbo Akademi University, Finland. He is also a Docent in Information Systems Usability at Åbo Akademi University. His research interests include mobile technology adoption, mobile usability and mobile learning. He is the author of 40 peer-reviewed publications in journals and conferences.

Alfredo Raul Teyseyre received a PhD. Degree in Computer Science, a Master's degree in Systems Engineering, and a Computer Engineering degree from the Universidad Nacional del Centro de la Provincia de Buenos Aires (UNICEN), Tandil, Argentina, in 2010, 2001, and 1997, respectively. Since 1997, he has been a part of ISISTAN Research Institute, UNICEN. Currently, he is an Adjunct Professor in the Computer Science Department of the UNICEN University at Tandil, Argentina. His research interests include software visualization, information visualization, software architecture and frameworks, and natural user interfaces.

Xin Tong received her MSc and is now pursuing her Ph.D. degree at the Pain Studies Lab, School of Interactive Arts and Technology, Simon Fraser Univeristy. She holds a Bachelor of Engineering degree from Beijing University of Posts and Telecommunications. Her research interests are designing technology for healthcare and patients, including Virtual Reality, serious games and wearables. Xin's MSc thesis is about facilitating motivation and self-reflection of physical activity data using gamification strategies.

Pandian Vasant is a senior lecturer in the Department of Fundamental and Applied Sciences, Universiti Teknologi Petronas in Malaysia. His research interests include Soft Computing, Hybrid Optimization, Holistic Optimization and Applications. He has co-authored research papers and articles in national journals, international journals, conference proceedings, conference paper presentation, and special issues as a lead guest editor, the lead guest editor for book chapter project, conference abstracts, edited books and book chapters. In 2009, P. Vasant was awarded top reviewer for the journal Applied Soft Computing (Elsevier). H-Index SCOPUS = 24, H-Index Google Scholar = 18.

Zorica A. Veljkovic is an Associate Professor of Industrial Statistics and Production management in the Faculty of Mechanical Engineering, University of Belgrade, in the Department of Industrial Engineering, Serbia. Her research interests focus on the design of experiments (DOE), Taguchi methods and methods for applied statistics for the industry. Veljkovic received a B.Sc, M.Sc, and PhD in Mechanical Engineering from Faculty of Mechanical Engineering, University of Belgrade, Serbia.

Maria Vanessa aus der Wieschen received her MA in the interdisciplinary program Business Communication & Communication Design from the University of Southern Denmark. During her studies, she focused on usability and user experience in IT product design, human-computer interaction and human-robot interaction. She is currently pursuing a PhD in early foreign language acquisition at the University of Southern Denmark and investigates how the quality and quantity of exposure to English in the primary school classroom influences young foreign language learners' rate of language learning and short-term language proficiency.

Massimiliano Zanin Principal Researcher at Innaxis, graduated in Aeronautical Management from the Universidad Autónoma de Madrid and a PhD from Universidade Nova de Lisboa. With more than 90 published peer-reviewed contributions in international conferences and journals, he has vast experience in complex systems and data mining research. He understands both theory and application and has collaborated with scientists from all over the world. His main topics of interest are Complex Networks, Data Science and its application to several real-world problems, similar to modelling and understanding the aviation system or mining complex data sets. He is a member of the editorial team of Nature Scientific Reports, the European Journal of Social Behavior, PeerJ and PeerJ Computer Science.

Index

Printed in the United States
By Bookmasters